D1742286

1 MONTH OF
FREE
READING

at

www.ForgottenBooks.com

By purchasing this book you are eligible for one month membership to ForgottenBooks.com, giving you unlimited access to our entire collection of over 1,000,000 titles via our web site and mobile apps.

To claim your free month visit:

www.forgottenbooks.com/free917189

ISBN 978-0-265-96928-1
PIBN 10917189

AMERICAN JOURNAL OF
PUBLIC HEALTH

THE JOURNAL OF THE
AMERICAN PUBLIC HEALTH ASSOCIATION

INDEX

VOLUME X

1920

JANUARY	pp.	1-104	JULY	pp.	569-632
FEBRUARY	pp.	105-200	AUGUST	pp.	633-696
MARCH	pp.	201-296	SEPTEMBER	pp.	697-760
APRIL	pp.	297-391	OCTOBER	pp.	761-824
MAY	pp.	392-488	NOVEMBER	pp.	825-920
JUNE	pp.	489-568	DECEMBER	pp.	921-1019

AMERICAN PUBLIC HEALTH ASSOCIATION
169 MASSACHUSETTS AVENUE
BOSTON, MASS.

INDEX

1220

PAGE

Accounting for Health Departments, Report of Committee on Uniform...... 172
Advertising Drug Products, Truth in. Arthur J. Cramp, M. D............. 783
Advertising of Disinfectants. Editorial..................................... 357
Administration, Economics of Health. Henry Bixby Hemenway, A. M., M. D. 105
Administration, Education and Health. Editorial........................... 734
Administration, Report of Committee on Rural Health...................... 173
Administration, Section of Public Health................................. 80
Administrative Handling of the Narcotic Addict: Its Benefits and Dangers.
　　Ernest S. Bishop, M. D., F. A. C. P................................... 1
African Aboriginal Therapy. Philip A. E. Sheppard, M. D................. 227
Aftermath of the War. Editorial... 258
Air, Bacteria of the, in an Amusement Hall. I. Forest Huddleson and Thomas
　　G. Hull 583
Air, Report of the Committee on Standard Methods for the Examination of.. 450
Albert, Henry, M. D.:
　　A Classification of Diphtheria Bacilli Based on the Toluidin Blue Iodin
　　　Method of Staining 936
　　Diphtheria Bacillus Stains with a Description of a "New" One.......... 334
American Public Health Association:
　　Committees, Reports. See Report.
　　Directors, Meeting of, at San Francisco............................... 987
　　Insignia for the. Editorial... 736
　　Meeting in San Francisco... 479
　　Present, Past and Future. W. S. Rankin, M. D......................... 297
　　Proceedings and Discussions at New Orleans, October 27-30, 1919....... 80
　　Proceedings and Discussions at San Francisco, September 13-17, 1920..... 987
　　Resolutions 987
Annual Meeting, Papers for the Next. Editorial............................ 446
Anthrax Problem in Massachusetts. Stanley H. Osborn, M. D., C. P. H....... 657
Application of Vaccines in Public Health Work. George W. McCoy, M. D... 666
Appropriations, Methods for the Defense of Public Health. Ernst C. Meyer,
　　Ph. D. 201
Armstrong, M. D., D. B., Social Uses of Medicine.......................... 921
Army Rejections, Causes of: What Health Officers Can Do to Remedy Con-
　　ditions. Frank R. Keefer, Col. M. C., U. S. A......................... 236
Arsphenamine, Supervision Over the Manufacture of. Editorial............. 536
Association News. These Items Will Be Found in the Notes Section of Each
　　Issue.
Bacilli Based on the Toluidin Blue Iodin Method of Staining—A Classification of
　　Diphtheria. Henry Albert, M. D..................................... 936
Bacilli Isolated from Immediate Contacts—A Study of the Toxicity of Diph-
　　theria. Frank W. Hachtel, M. D., and Mary Shedwick Bailey, M. D...... 42
Bacillus Stains, Diphtheria with a Description of a "New" One. Henry
　　Albert, M. D... 334
Bacillus, Studies on the Viability of the Tubercle. J. B. Rogers, M. D......... 345
Bacteria of the Air in an Amusement Hall. I. Forest Huddleson and Thomas
　　G. Hull 583
Bacteria on the Lips of Milk Bottles and Their Significance, Number of . Roy
　　S. Dearstyne and C. LeRoy Ewing.................................... 533
Bacterial Counts from Machine and Hand Washed Dishes, Comparison of the,
　　and Their Significance. Roy S. Dearstyne............................. 871
Bacteriological Examination of Soft Drinks. William Royal Stokes, M. D...... 308

Bacteriology in Food Control, Uses, Possibilities and Limitations. Professor
　E. O. Jordan. Discussion by H. W. Redfield, Ph. D...................... 142
Bailey, Mary Shedwick, M. D., and Frank W. Hachtel, M. D.—A Study of the
　Toxicity of Diphtheria Bacilli Isolated from Immediate Contacts........... 42
Baker, Henry B. In Memoriam... 448
Bass, C. C., M. D. Studies on Malaria Control............................. 216
B. Coli Tests in Fairly Safe Drinking Water, Importance of Confirmatory.
　N. Novick 305
B. Coli, Value of Brilliant Green in Eliminating Errors Due to Anaërobes in
　the Presumptive Tests for. Theodore C. Muer and Robert L. Harris....... 874
Bile, On the Solution of Pneumococci by. F. B. Kelly...................... 708
Billings, John S., M. D. Need for Standards for Recording and Classifying
　Defects and Impairments.. 410
Biology of the Pfeiffer Bacillus. Professor Edwin O. Jordan................. 648
Bishop, Ernest S., M. D., F. A. C. P. Administrative Handling of the Narcotic
　Addict: Its Benefits and Dangers....................................... 1
Bissell, William Grosvenor. In Memoriam................................. 77
Blue, Rupert; Former Surgeon General, U. S. P. H. S...................... 364
Books and Reports Reviewed.....169, 262, 359, 454, 538, 608, 679, 737, 803, 883, 984
Books Help to Health. T. S. Da Ponte 609
Botulism. Ernest C. Dickson, M. D....................................... 865
Brazil, Improved Handling of Foods in..................................... 893
Byrne, S. J., M. D. Traffic Regulation as a Means of Preventing Injury and
　Death from Street Vehicles 331
Budget; the Health Officer's First Need, A Standard. Haven Emerson, M. D. 221
Budget, A Standard: Discussion of Dr. Haven Emerson's Paper. Ernst C.
　Meyer, Ph. D... 353
Building Regulations in Venezuela.. 895
Bulletins, City Health: Their Use and Misuse, the Necessity for Additional
　Mailing Privileges. Max J. Colton..................................... 712
By-Products from Sewage Sludge. Robert Spurr Weston, Boston, Mass....... 405
California, Trip to... 611
Campaign Against Malaria in Cuba, 1918-19. F. Villuendas, M. D.......... 728
Campaign for 7,500 A. P. H. A. Members................................. 369
Campaign, Membership...................................369, 480, 682
Canners' Association, Self-Imposed Inspection of the National. H. M. Loomis.. 521
Canning Operations, Report of Committee on Problems in................... 541
Canada, Vital Statistics in. R. H. Coats................................. 224
Capillary Tubes, Improvement in Vacuum Method of Filling. Thomas A.
　Watson 445
Carter, H. R., Asst. Surg. General, U. S. P. H. S. Résumé of Methods for
　Control of Malaria; Indications; Results; Costs......................... 528
Causes of Army Rejections: What Health Officers Can Do to Remedy Con-
　ditions. Frank R. Keefer, Col. M. C., U. S. A.......................... 236
Causes of Typhoid Fever in Massachusetts. George T. O'Donnell, M. D....... 517
Center, What Is a Health? H. N. C., Editorial............................ 676
Centers, Health. Harold B. Wood, M. D., Dr. P. H....................... 474
Child Hygiene. Julius Levy, M. D.. 976
Child Hygiene, An Ideal Program for. Allan J. McLaughlin, Asst. Surgeon
　General, U. S. P. H. S... 240
Child Hygiene for the Coming Year, The Illinois Program in. Clarence W.
　East, M. D... 241
Child Hygiene, Status of State Bureaus of. Anna E. Rude, M. D........... 772
Child Welfare. Editorial... 75

PAGE

City Health Bulletins: Their Use and Misuse, the Necessity for Additional
Mailing Privileges. Max J. Colton 712

Classification of Diphtheria Bacilli Based on the Toluidin Blue Iodin Method
of Staining, A. Henry Albert, M. D................................. 936

Clinics, A Program for Organizing and Coördinating Industrial. Bernard J.
Newman 637

Coats, R. H. Vital Statistics in Canada.............................. 224

Colombia, Public Health Aspects of Cartagena. Alfredo de Zubiria, S......... 509

Colton, Max J. City Health Bulletins: Their Use and Misuse, the Necessity
for Additional Mailing Privileges.................................... 712

Communicable Diseases of Man, Further Evidence as to the Relative Importance of Milk Infection in the Transmission of Certain............ 66

Community Medicine and Public Health. Ernst Christopher Meyer, Ph. D.... 489

Comparison of the Bacterial Counts from Machine and Hand Washed Dishes
and Their Significance. Roy S. Dearstyne............................ 871

Compensation of Health Officers. John A. Ferrell, M. D., Dr. P. H......... 569

Conventions, Conferences, Meetings.196, 292, 362, 449, 539, 622, 693, 756, 808, 911, 1013

Cooledge, L. H., A. M., and R. W. Wyant, M. S. Judging the Keeping Quality
of Milk by a PH. Method... 978

Coördination of Public and Private Agencies in a State Program of Public
Health Nursing. Jessie L. Marriner, R. N.......................... 588

Coördination of State and Private Enterprises in Public Health Work. W. H.
Hattie, M. D... 961

Country Slaughterhouse; How to Build It, The. G. H. Parks.............. 731

Cretic, Quarantine of the... 802

Crum, Frederick S., Ph. D. Geographical and Seasonal Variations in Infant
Mortality in the United States, 1917-1920........................... 790

What Should Be Done in the Control of Degenerative Diseases?............ 588

Cuba, Campaign Against Malaria in, 1918-19. F. Villuendas, M. D......... 728

Culture Media, Some Important Factors in the Preparation of. Lewis Davis... 250

Cumming, Dr. Hugh Smith. Editorial................................. 261

Cumming, Surgeon General, Discusses European Health Conditions......... 363

Cumming, Lieutenant-Colonel James G., M. C., U. S. Army. Influenza-Pneumonia as Influenced by Dishwashing in 370 Public Institutions (Concluded) 576

Curtis, Francis George, M. D. Relation Between Official and Non-official Health
Agencies 956

Da Ponte, T. S. Books Help to Health................................ 609

Davis, Lewis. Some Important Factors in the Preparation of Culture Media.. 250

Davis, William H., M. D. Infant Mortality in the Registration Area for Births 338

Dearstyne, Roy S., and C. LeRoy Ewing. Number of Bacteria on the Lips
of Milk Bottles and Their Significance.............................. 533

Defects and Impairments, Need for Standards for Recording and Classifying.
John S. Billings, M. D.. 410

Development of the State Departments of Health in Relation to Health Insurance and Industrial Hygiene, The. Augustus B. Wadsworth, M. D..... 53

Diagnosis and Detection of Rodent Plague. C. L. Williams, Past Assistant
Surgeon, U. S. P. H. S.. 851

Diarrhea, Reduction of Deaths from Infantile, by Care of the Bowel Discharges
of Infants. E. C. Levy, M. D....................................... 400

Dickson, Ernest C., M. D. Botulism................................. 865

Diphtheria Bacilli Based on the Toluidin Blue Iodin Method of Staining, A
Classification of. Henry Albert, M. D............................... 936

Diphtheria Bacilli Isolated from Immediate Contacts, A Study of the Toxicity
of. Frank W. Hachtel, M. D., and Mary Shedwick Bailey, M. D......... 42

Diphtheria Bacillus Stains with a Description of a "New" One. Henry Albert, M. D... 334

INDEX

PAGE

Diphtheria Virulence Test in Public Health Work, Observations on the. E. M. Wade, M. A., and G. E. Vaughan, M. D.................................. 426
Discussion of Dr. Haven Emerson's Paper, "A Standard Budget." Ernst Christopher Meyer, Ph. D.. 353
Discussion of Relative Functions of Official and Non-official Health Agencies... 963
Diseases, Some Epidemiological Points Regarding Acute Respiratory. Frank Overton, M. D., D. P. H... 431
Diseases, What Should be Done in the Control of Degenerative? Frederick S. Crum, Ph. D.. 210
Dishes, Comparison of the Bacterial Counts from Machine and Hand Washed, and Their Significance. Roy S. Dearstyne.............................. 871
Dishwashing in 370 Public Institutions, Influenza-Pneumonia as Influenced by (Concluded). Lieutenant-Colonel James G. Cumming, M. C., U. S. A..... 576
Dishwashing: Recovery of Streptococcus Hemolyticus from Restaurant Tableware. Clarence C. Saelhof and W. J. R. Heinekamp...................... 704
Disinfectants, Advertising of. Editorial...................................... 337
Disinfection of Tuberculous Sputum, Practical. William Royal Stokes, M. D., and C. H. Douthirt, M. D... 973
Dittoe, W. H. Discussion: Treatment of Beet Sugar Plant Sewage, by Langdon Pearse and Samuel A. Greeley.................................... 320
Douthirt, C. H., M. D., and William Royal Stokes, M. D. Practical Disinfection of Tuberculous Sputum... 973
Dowling, Oscar, M. D. Sociological Aspect of Hookworm Disease........... 595
Drainage as an Anti-Malaria Measure. J. A. LePrince....................... 120
Drake, C. St. Clair, M. D. Popularizing Vital Statistics.................... 112
Drug Products, Truth in Advertising. Arthur J. Cramp, M. D................ 783
Drugs, Committee on Habit Forming.. 83
Dusts, Health Hazards of Non-Poisonous—A Resume of Some Recent Investigations. Emery R. Hayhurst, Ph. D., M. D.............................. 69
Dye Industry, Health Hazards of the. A. K. Smith, M. D................... 255
East, Clarence W., M. D. The Illinois Program in Child Hygiene for the Coming Year'... 241
Early School of Public Health at Lyons, France. Professor William T. Sedgwick 352
Economics of Health Administration. Henry Bixby Hemenway, A. M., M. D. 105
Editorials 74, 75, 76, 164, 167, 258, 259, 260, 261, 356, 357, 446, 447, 536, 537, 605, 607, 676, 677, 734, 735, 736, 800, 802, 880, 881, 980, 982
Education and Health Administration. Editorial............................ 734
Emerson, Haven, M. D.:
    Discussion of Dr. Haven Emerson's Paper, "A Standard Budget." Ernst C. Meyer, Ph. D... 353
    A Standard Budget: The Health Officer's First Need.................... 221
    Viewpoint of the Official Agency....................................... 941
Endemic Diseases vs. Acute Epidemics. Mazyck P. Ravenel, M. D........... 761
Endemic Goiter as a Public Health Problem; Additional Notes. Mayo Tolman 434
Engineering Point of View, Malaria Control from the. W. G. Stromquist...... 497
Entomology, Mosquito Work of the Bureau of. D. L. Van Dine.............. 116
Epidemic of Pneumonic Plague, An. W. H. Kellogg, M. D.................. 599
Epidemics, Endemic Diseases vs, Acute. Mazyck P. Ravenel, M. D.......... 761
Epidemiological Points Regarding Acute Respiratory Diseases. Frank Overton, M. D., D. P. H... 431
European Health Conditions, Surgeon General Cumming Discusses........... 363
Ewing, C. LeRoy, and Roy S. Dearstyne. Number of Bacteria on the Lips of Milk Bottles and Their Significance.................................... 533
Excessive Mortality from Influenzia-Pneumonia Among Bituminous Coal Miners of Ohio in 1918. E. B. Starr, M. D........................... 348
Executive Committee, Meeting of.. 171

PAGE

Exhibits at San Francisco 748
Experimental Study of the Efficacy of Gauze Face Masks, An. W. H. Kellogg,
    M. D., and Miss Grace MacMillan...................................... 34
Fair, Gordon M. An Inferential Index of Swimming Pool Purity.............. 502
Fatigue, Types of. Professor Percy G. Stiles............................. 653
Federal Meat Inspection as a Safeguard to Public Health. John R. Mohler,
    V. M. D. 421
Ferrell, John A., M. D., Dr. P. H.:
    Compensation of Health Officers..................................... 569
    Privy Symposium—II. Role of the Latrine in Control of Hookworm
    Disease 138
Fisher, L. M. What Can a Community Afford to Pay to Rid Itself of Malaria? 768
Food Control, Uses, Possibilities and Limitations of Bacteriology in. Professor
    E. O. Jordan. Discussion by H. W. Redfield, Ph. D................... 142
Foods in Brazil, Improved Handling of................................... 893
Foods, What Should be the Basis of the Control of Dehydrated?. Professor
    Samuel C. Prescott 324
France, Early School of Public Health at Lyons. Professor William T.
    Sedgwick 352
Further Evidence as to the Relative Importance of Milk Infection in the Trans-
    mission of Certain Communicable Diseases of Man..................... 66
Gebhart, John C. Relation of School and Special Feeding to Defective Nutrition 669
Geographical and Seasonal Variations in Infant Mortality in the United States,
    1917-1920. Frederick S. Crum, Ph. D................................ 790
Gillett, Lucy H. Note on the Nutrition Agencies Interested in Public Health.. 89
Goiter, Endemic, as a Public Health Problem: Additional Notes. Mayo Tolman 434
Good Health and Good Citizenship.. 478
William Crawford Gorgas. In Memoriam................................... 678
Habit-Forming Drugs., Committee on...................................... 83
Hatchel, Frank W., M. D., and Mary Shedwick Bailey, M. D. A Study of the
    Toxicity of Diphtheria Bacilli Isolated from Immediate Contacts......... 42
Hackett, A. R., M. D. Value of Plant Records in the Development of Plant
    Hygiene 525
Hanaford, Allison. Personal Hygiene..................................... 444
Harris, Robert L., and Theodore C. Muer. Value of Brilliant-Green in Elimi-
    nating Errors Due to Anaërobes in the Presumptive Tests for B. Coli..... 874
Harris, Seale, M. D. The Nation's Greatest Need: A National Department of
    Health 633
Hatfield, Charles J., M. D. Viewpoint of the Non-official Agency............ 948
Hattie, W. H., M. D. Coördination of State and Private Enterprises in Public
    Health Work 961
Hayhurst, Emery R., Ph. D., M. D.:
    Health Hazards of Non-Poisonous Dusts—A Resume of Some Recent In-
    vestigations 60
    Ideals in the Organization of an Industrial Medical Service............ 715
Health Centers. Harold B. Wood, M. D., Dr. P. H....................... 474
Health Administration, Economics of. Henry Bixby Hemenway, A. M., M. D. 105
Health Administration, Education and. Editorial.......................... 734
Health Agencies, Relation Between Official and Non-official. Francis George
    Curtis, M. D.. 956
Health Agencies, Relative Functions of Official and Non-official............. 940
Health Agencies, Team Work Among. Editorial............................ 607
Health Center, What Is a?... 474
Health Departments, Relative Functions of State and Local. Carl E. McCombs,
    M. D. 393
Health Employment Bureau....78, 171, 266, 368, 450, 539, 610, 682, 740, 806, 888, 995

PAGE

Health Hazards of the Dye Industry. A. K. Smith, M. D..................... 255
Health Hazards of Non-Poisonous Dusts—A Résumé of Some Recent Investigations. Emery R. Hayhurst, Ph. D., M. D......................... 60
Health Officer, Is There Hope for the?.................................... 447
Health Officers, Compensation of. John A. Ferrell, M. D..................... 569
Health Officers, New Specifications. for. Morris Knowles and Maurice R. Scharff 8
Health Officer's Salary, The Problem of the. Editorial..................... 164
Health Officers, Schools for: What Has Been Done at Syracuse. Frederick W. Sears, M. D.. 155
Health Officers: What H. O. Can Do to Remedy Conditions: Causes of Army Rejections. Frank R. Keefer, Col. M. C., U. S. A......................... 236
Health a Political Plank. Editorial.. 605
Health Quotations. Compiled by James A. Tobey........................... 649
Health Societies, Report of Committee on State........................... 742
Heels and Toes. Editorial... 800
Heinekamp, W. J. R., and Clarence C. Saelhof. Recovery of Streptococcus Hemolyticus from Restaurant Tableware................................... 704
Hemenway, Henry Bixby, A. M., M. D. Economics of Health Administration.. 105
Hill, Hibbert W., M. D. What Is the Matter with Public Health? Discussion. 673
Hookworm Disease, Role of the Latrine in Control of. Privy Symposium II. John A. Ferrell, M. D., Dr. P. H... 138
Hookworm Disease, Sociological Aspect of. Oscar Dowling, M. D........... 595
Hospital, San Francisco 456
Housing, Sociological Aspects of. Ira S. Wile, M. D....................... 327
Huddleson, I. Forest, and Thomas G. Hull. Bacteria of the Air in an Amusement Hall 583
Hull, Thomas G., and I. Forest Huddleson. Bacteria of the Air in an Amusement Hall 583
Hygiene, Child. Julius Levy, M. D.. 976
Hygiene, Status of State Bureaus of Child. Anna E. Rude, M. D........... 772
Ideal Program for Child Hygiene, An. Allan J. McLaughlin, Asst. Surgeon General, U. S. P. H. S... 240
Ideals in the Organization of an Industrial Medical Service. Emery R. Hayhurst, Ph. D., M. D.. 715
Illinois Program in Child Hygiene for the Coming Year, The. Clarence W. East, M. D.. 241
Importance of Confirmatory B. Coli Tests in Fairly Safe Drinking Water. N. Novick 305
Improved Handling of Foods in Brazil..................................... 893
Improvement in Vacuum Method of Filling Capillary Tubes. Thomas A. Watson 445
Industrial Clinics, A Program for Organizing and Coördinating. Bernard J. Newman 637
Industrial Health Education—A Means and an End. Jules Schevitz, B. S...... 780
Industrial Hygiene, The Development of the State Departments of Health in Relation to Health Insurance and. Augustus B. Wadsworth, M D........ 53
Industrial Hygiene, The Insurance Company in. A. D. Reilly............... 160
Industrial Hygiene and Occupational Disease. These Items Will Be Found in the Notes Section of Each Issue.
Industrial Medical Service, Ideals in the Organization of an. Emery R. Hayhurst, Ph. D., M. D.. 715
Infant Mortality in the Registration Area for Births. William H. Davis, M. D. 338
Infant Mortality in the United States, 1917-1920, Geographical and Seasonal Variations in. Frederick S. Crum, Ph. D................................ 790
Inferential Index of Swimming Pool Purity. Gordon M. Fair............... 502

PAGE

Influenza-Pneumonia Among Bituminous Coal Miners of Ohio in 1918, Excessive Mortality from. E. B. Starr, M. D............................... 348

Influenza-Pneumonia as Influenced by Dishwashing in 370 Public Institutions (Concluded). Lieutenant-Colonel James G. Cumming, M. C., U. S. Army... 576

In Memoriam:
  Henry B. Baker 448
  William Grosvenor Bissell 77
  William Crawford Gorgas 678
  Eduardo Liceaga 358

Iodin Method of Staining, A Classification of Diphtheria Bacilli Based on the Toluidin Blue. Henry Albert, M. D. 936

Insignia for the A. P. H. A. Editorial.................................... 736

Insurance Company in Industrial Hygiene. A. D. Reilly................... 160

Insurance, Health, and Industrial: The Development of the State Departments of Health in Relation to. Augustus B. Wadsworth, M. D......... 53

Is There Hope for the Health Officer? Editorial......................... 447

Jackson, Thomas W., M. D. Discussion: Venereal Disease Control: Method, Obstacles and Results, by C. C. Pierce, Asst. Surgeon General............ 136

Jones, H. O., Ph. G., M. D. Need of Standardization in School Hygiene Methods 243

Jones, W. Parker. Meat Inspection Law for Municipalities.................. 415

Jordan, Professor Edwin O.:
  Biology of Pfeiffer Bacillus................................ 648
  Uses, Possibilities and Limitations of Bacteriology in Food Control. Discussion by H. W. Redfield, Ph. D.............................. 142

Judging the Keeping Quality of Milk by a PH Method. L. H. Cooledge, A. M., and R. W. Wyant, M. S.. 978

Keefer, Frank R., Col. M. C., U. S. A. Causes of Army Rejections: What Health Officers Can Do to Remedy Conditions........................... 236

Kellogg, W. H., M. D.:
  An Epidemic of Pneumonic Plague................................ 599
  An Experimental Study of the Efficacy of Gauze Face Masks. With Miss Grace MacMillan 34
  Present Status of Plague, with Historical Review....................... 835

Kelly, F. B. On the Solution of Pneumococci by Bile...................... 708

Knowles, Morris, and Maurice R. Scharff. New Specifications for Health Officers 8

Laboratory Methods, Standardization of. Augustus B. Wadsworth, M. D...... 932

Laboratory Work, Urgent Need for the Standardization of. Arthur Lederer, M. D., C. P. H.. 876

Lansing, Mich., Pollution of Deep Wells at. Edward D. Rich, Major........ 147

Lederer, Arthur, M. D., C. P. H. Urgent Need for the Standardization of Laboratory Work 876

LePrince, J. A. Drainage as an Anti-malaria Measure...................... 120

Levy, E. C., M. D. Reduction of Deaths from Infantile Diarrhea by Care of the Bowel Discharges of Infants................................. 400

Levy, Julius, M. D. Child Hygiene.................................... 976

Eduardo Liceaga. In Memoriam.. 358

Loomis, H. M. Self-Imposed Inspection of the National Canners' Association   521

Lumsden, L. L., Surgeon, U. S. P. H. S. Privy Symposium—I. The Privy as a Public Health Problem 45

Macedonia, Public Health in Eastern. Paul Dudley White, M. D........... 14

MacMillan, Miss Grace, W. H. Kellogg, M. D., and. An Experimental Study of the Efficacy of Gauze Face Masks............................... 34

Malaria Control from the Engineering Point of View. W. G. Stromquist....... 497

Malaria Control, Studies on. C. C. Bass, M. D.......................... 216

PAGE

Malaria: Drainage as an Anti-Malaria Measure. J. A. LePrince.............. 120
Malaria in Cuba, Campaign Against, 1918-19. F. Villuendas, M. D.............. 728
Malaria, Resume of Methods for Control of: Results; Costs. H. R. Carter,
    Asst. Surgeon General, U. S. P. H. S..................................... 528
Malaria, What Can a Community Afford to Pay to Rid Itself of?. L. M. Fisher 768
Marriner, Jessie, R. N. Coördination of Public and Private Agencies in a State
    Program of Public Health Nursing....................................... 588
Marshall, Professor Charles E. Studies in the Clarification of Milk........... 152
Masks, An Experimental Study of the Efficacy of Gauze Face. W. H. Kellogg,
    M. D., and Miss Grace MacMillan.. 84
Massachusetts, Anthrax Problem in. Stanley H. Osborn, M. D., C. P. H...... 657
Massachusetts, Causes of Typhoid Fever in. George T. O'Donnell, M. D...... 317
McCombs, Carl E., M. D. Relative Functions of State and Local Health De-
    partments 393
McCoy, George W., M. D. Application of Vaccines in Public Health Work.... 666
McGee, Harold G. Mills-Reincke Phenomenon and Typhoid Control by
    Vaccine 585
McLaughlin, Allan J., Asst. Surgeon General, U. S. P. H. S. An Ideal Pro-
    gram for Child Hygiene 240
Meaning and Purpose of Socializing Medicine. Ira S. Wile, M. D.............. 969
Meat Inspection, Federal, as a Safeguard to Public Health. John R. Mohler,
    V. M. D. 421
Meat Inspection Law for Municipalities. W. Parker Jones, Attorney-at-Law.. 415
Meat Inspection, State and Municipal. John Roberts....................... 697
Medicine, Community, and Public Health. Ernst C. Meyer, Ph. D............ 489
Medicine, Meaning and Purpose of Socializing. Ira S. Wile, M. D............ 969
Medicine, Modern. (D. G.) Editorial...................................... 735
Medicine, Preventive, and War. Mazyck P. Ravenel, M. D.................... 22
Medicine, Social Uses of. D. B. Armstrong, M. D........................... 921
Members of the A. P. H. A. Elected to Various Sections.................177, 994
Members Proposed for Election to the A. P. H. A., List of..................
    ....78, 176, 266, 371, 559. 613, 683, 741, 806, 890, 993
Members, Why Not 7,500 A. P. H. A.?..................................... 267
Membership Campaign 369, 480, 682
Mental Health, Success and Failure in. Editorial........................... 677
Methods for the Defense of Public Health Appropriations. Ernst Christopher
    Meyer, Ph. D.. 201
Methods of Plague Control. Friench Simpson, Surgeon, U. S. P. H. S........ 845
Meyer, Ernst Christopher, Ph. D.:
    Community Medicine and Public Health............................... 489
    Discussion of Dr. Haven Emerson's Paper, "A Standard Budget.'"........ 353
    Methods for the Defense of Public Health Appropriations................ 201
Michigan, Pollution of Deep Wells at Lansing. Edward D. Rich, Major...... 147
Milk Bottles, Number of Bacteria on the Lips of Milk Bottles and Their Sig-
    nificance. Roy S. Dearstyne and C. LeRoy Ewing...................... 533
Milk by a PH Method, Judging the Keeping Quality of. L. H. Cooledge,
    A. M., and R. W. Wyant, M. S.. 978
Milk Infection in the Transmission of Certain Communicable Diseases of Man,
    Further Evidence as to the Relative Importance of..................... 66
Milk, Studies in the Clarification of. Professor Charles E. Marshall........... 152
Mills-Reincke Phenomenon and Typhoid Control by Vaccine. Harold G.
    McGee 585
Missouri, Water Treatment at St. Louis. Edward E. Wall.................. 437
Modern Medicine. (D. G.) Editorial...................................... 735
Mohler, John R., V. M. D. Federal Meat Inspection as a Safeguard to Public
    Health 421

PAGE

Mortality, Excessive, from Influenza-Pneumonia Among Bituminous Coal Miners of Ohio in 1918. E. B. Starr, M. D. 348

Mortality, Infant, in the Registration Area for Births. William H. Davis, M. D. 338

Mosquito Work of the Bureau of Entomology. D. L. Van Dine............... 116

Muer, Theodore C., and Robert L. Harris. Value of Brilliant-Green in Eliminating Errors Due to Anaërobes in the Presumptive Tests for B. Coli...... 874

Municipal Meat Inspection, State and. John Roberts......................... 697

Municipalities, Meat Inspection Law for. W. Parker Jones, Attorney-at-Law.. 415

Narcotic Addict: Administrative Handling of the: Its Benefits and Dangers. Ernest S. Bishop, M. D., F. A. C. P. 1

Nation's Greatest Need: A National Department of Health, The. Seale Harris, M. D. 633

National Department of Health, A: The Nation's Greatest Need. Seale Harris, M. D. 633

Need for Standards for Recording and Classifying Defects and Impairments. John S. Billings, M. D. 410

Need of Standardization in School Hygiene Methods. H. O. Jones, Ph. G., M. D. 243

Nesbitt, Charles T., M. D. What Is the Matter with Public Health............ 953

New Orleans, Proceedings and Discussions of the American Public Health Association at, October 27-30, 1919................................... 80

New Specifications for Health Officers. Morris Knowles and Maurice R. Scharff 8

Newly Elected Officers 371, 889

Newman, Bernard J. A Program for Organizing and Coördinating Industrial Clinics 637

Non-official Agency, Viewpoint of the. Charles J. Hatfield, M. D............. 948

Notes Section Reviewers, Our. Editorials.................................. 76

Novick, N. Importance of Confirmatory B. Coli Tests in Fairly Safe Drinking Water 303

Number of Bacteria on the Lips of Milk Bottles and Their Significance. Roy S. Dearstyne and C. LeRoy Ewing...................................... 533

Nursing, Coördination of Public and Private Agencies in a State Program of Public Health. Jessie L. Marriner, R. N................................ 588

Nutrition Agencies Interested in Public Health, Note on the. Lucy H. Gillett.. 89

Nutrition, Relation of School and Special Feeding to Defective. John C. Gebhart 669

Nutritional Problems, Second Report of Committee on...................... 86

Observations on the Diphtheria Virulence Test in Public Health Work. E. M. Wade, M. A., and G. E. Vaughan, M. A............................... 426

O'Donnell, George T., M. D. Causes of Typhoid Fever in Massachusetts..... 517

Officers, Newly Elected 371, 889

Official Agency, Viewpoint of the. Haven Emerson, M. D.................... 941

Official and the Non-official Health Agency, The. Editorial.................. 980

Ohio, Excessive Mortality from Influenza-Pneumonia Among Bituminous Coal Miners in 1918. E. B. Starr, M. D. 348

Ohio Public Health Association................................... 897

On the Solution of Pneumococci by Bile. F. B. Kelly...................... 708

Organization of Control of Pasteurization. Frederick O. Tonney, M. D....... 716

Osborn, Stanley H., M. D., C. P. H. Anthrax Problem in Massachusetts...... 657

Our Notes Section Reviewers. Editorial................................... 76

Overton, Frank, M. D., D. P. H. Some Epidemiological Points Regarding Acute Respiratory Diseases 431

Oysters, The Purification of O. as a Conservative Measure. William Firth Wells, M. D. 342

Papers for Next Annual Meeting. Editorial............................... 446

Parks, G. H. The Country Slaughterhouse; How to Build It................. 731

PAGE

Pasteurlzation, Organization of Control of. Frederick O. Tonney, M. D...... 716
Pearse, Langdon, and Samuel A. Greeley. Treatment of Beet Sugar Plant
    Sewage 312
    Discussion, by W. H. Dittoe 320
    Discussion, by Robert Spurr Weston 322
Percentages of Quotas Filled..612, 742
Personal Hygiene. Allison Hanaford...................................... 444
Pfeiffer Bacillus, Biology of the. Professor Edwin O. Jordan................. 648
Pierce, C. C., Asst. Surgeon General. Venereal Disease Control: Method,
    Obstacles and Results. Discussion by Thomas W. Jackson, M. D......... 132
Plague, An Epidemic of Pneumonic. W. H. Kellogg, M. D................. 599
Plague Control, Methods of. Friench Simpson, Surgeon, U. S. P. H. S........ 845
Plague, Diagnosis and Detection of Rodent. C. L. Williams, Past Assistant
    Surgeon, U. S. P. H. S.. 851
Plague, Present Status of, with Historical Review. W. H. Kellogg, M. D...... 835
Pneumococci by Bile, On the Solution of. F. B. Kelly....................... 708
Pneumonic Plague, An Epidemic of. W. H. Kellogg, M. D................... 599
Political Plank, Health a. Editorial....................................... 605
Pollution of Deep Wells at Lansing, Mich. Edward D. Rich, Major........... 147
Popularizing Vital Statistics. C. St. Clair Drake, M. D..................... 112
Practical Disinfection of Tuberculous Sputum. William Royal Stokes, M. D.,
    and C. H. Douthirt, M. D... 973
Practical Types of Sanitary Privies. C. W. Stiles, M. D..................... 48
Preliminary Returns of Membership Campaign............................. 480
Prescott, Professor Samuel C. What Should Be the Basis of the Control of
    Dehydrated Foods? 324
Prevention, Principles of. Editorial...................................... 167
Preventive Medicine and War. Mazyck P. Ravenel, M. D..................... 22
Principles of Prevention. Editorial....................................... 167
Privies, Practical Types of Sanitary. C. W. Stiles, M. D.................... 48
Privy in the Control of Typhoid Fever, Role of the Sanitary. Clarence E.
    Smith, M. D.. 140
Privy Symposium—I. The Privy as a Public Health Problem. L. L. Lumsden,
    Surgeon, U. S. P. H. S.. 45
Privy Symposium—II. Role of the Latrine in Control of Hookworm Disease.
    John A. Ferrell, M. D., D. P. H....................................... 138
Problem of the Health Officer's Salary, The. Editorial..................... 164
Problem of the Rat. Editorial.. 880
Present Status of Plague, with Historical Review. W. H. Kellogg, M. D...... 835
Presidential Address at San Francisco. W. S. Rankin, M. D................. 825
Proceedings and Discussions of the American Public Health Association:
    At New Orleans, October 27-30, 1919.................................. 80
        Section of Public Health Administration........................... 80
        Reports of Committees 83
    At San Francisco, September 13-17, 1920.............................. 987
        Board of Directors... 987
        General Sessions 963, 992
        Resolutions 987
Program for Organizing and Coördinating Industrial Clinics, A. Bernard
    J. Newman 637
Progress of Government Acquisition of the Quarantine. Editorial........... 982
Protective Value of Typhoid Vaccination as Shown by the Experience of the
    American Troops in War. George A. Soper, Ph. D..................... 301
Public Health Administration, Section of................................. 80
Public Health Appropriations, Methods for the Defense of. Ernst C. Meyer,
    Ph. D. 201

PAGE

Public Health Aspects of Cartagena, Colombia. Alfredo de Zubiria, S......... 509
Public Health Clippings. These Items Will Be Found in the Advertising Section of Each Issue.
Public Health, Community Medicine and. Ernst C. Meyer, Ph. D.............. 489
Public Health in Eastern Macedonia. Paul Dudley White, M. D.............. 14
Public Health Laboratory Notes. These Items will Be Found in the Notes Section of Each Issue.
Public Health a Live, Progressive Force. Editorial.......................... 74
Public Health Notes. These Items Will Be Found in the Notes Section of Each Issue.
Public Health Problem, The Privy as a. Privy Symposium—I. L. L. Lumsden, Surgeon, U. S. P. H. S.................................... 45
Public Health Service, United States.. 365
Public Health, A Successful School of. Editorial.......................... 260
Public Health, What Is the Matter with? Discussion. Hibbert W. Hill, M. D. 673
Public Health, What Is the Matter With? Charles T. Nesbitt, M. D.......... 953
Public Health Work, Application of Vaccines in. George W. McCoy, M. D.... 666
Public Health Work, Coördination of State and Private Enterprises in. W. H. Hattie, M. D... 961
Public Health Work, Red Cross and. Editorial............................. 356
Public Water Supply Contaminated by an Interconnected Private Water Supply. Caleb Mills Saville 724
Purification of Oysters as a Conservation Measure. William Firth Wells, M. D. 342
Quarantine of the Cretic. Editorial.. 802
Quarantine, Progress of Government Acquisition of the..................... 982
Quotas Filled, Percentage of...612, 742
Quotations, Health. Compiled by James A. Tobey......................... 649
Rankin, W. S., M. D.:
  The American Public Health Association; Present, Past and Future........ 297
  Presidential Address at San Francisco................................. 825
Ravenel, Mazyck P., M. D.:
  Endemic Diseases vs. Acute Epidemics................................. 761
  Preventive Medicine and War... 22
Recovery of Streptococcus Hemolyticus from Restaurant Tableware. Clarence C. Saelhof and W. J. R. Heinekamp.................................. 704
Red Cross and Public Health Work. Editorial............................. 356
Redfield, H. W., Ph. D. Discussion: Uses, Possibilities and Limitations of Bacteriology in Food Control, by Professor E. O. Jordan................ 145
Reduction of Deaths from Infantile Diarrhea by Care of the Bowel Discharges of Infants. E. C. Levy, M. D...400
Reilly, A. D. The Insurance Company in Industrial Hygiene................. 160
Relation of School and Special Feeding to Defective Nutrition. John C. Gebhart 669
Relative Functions of Official and Non-official Health Agencies: A Symposium. 940
Relative Functions of State and Local Health Departments. Carl E. McCombs, M. D. 393
Report of Committee on Habit-Forming Drugs............................. 83
Report of Committee on Nutritional Problems, Second...................... 86
Report of Committee on Problems in Canning Operations.................... 541
Report of Committee on Relation of the 1920 Census to Vital Statistics........ 173
Report of Committee on Rural Health Administration....................... 173
Report of Committee on Sanitation of Swimming Pools...................... 540
Report of Committee on Standard Methods for the Examination of Air......... 450
Report of Committee on State Health Societies............................. 742

PAGE

Report of Committee on Uniform Accounting for Health Departments......... 172

Respiratory Diseases, Some Epidemiological Points Regarding Acute. Frank
Overton, M. D., D. P. H... 431

Restaurant Tableware, Recovery of Streptococcus Hemolyticus from. Clarence
C. Saelhof and W. J. R. Heinekamp..................................... 704

Résumé of Methods for Control of Malaria: Indications; Results; Costs. H. R.
Carter, Asst. Surg. General, U. S. P. H. S............................. 528

Reviewers, Our Notes Section. Editorial.................................... 76

Rich, Major Edward D. Pollution of Deep Wells at Lansing, Mich........... 147

Roberts, John. State and Municipal Meat Inspection....................... 697

Rogers, J. B., M. D. Studies on the Viability of the Tubercle Bacillus......... 345

Role of the Sanitary Privy in the Control of Typhoid Fever. Clarence E.
Smith, M. D. 140

Rude, Anna E., M. D. Status of State Bureaus of Child Hygiene............ 772

Rural Communities, School Hygiene for. Grace Whitford, M. D.............. 246

Rural Health Administration, Report of Committee on..................... 173

Saelholf, Clarence C., and W. J. R. Heinekamp. Recovery of Streptococcus
Hemolyticus from Restaurant Tableware................................. 704

Safety Council, Work of the National..................................... 58

St. Louis, Mo., Water Treatment at. Edward E. Wall..................... 437

Salary, The Problem of the Health Officer's. Editorial..................... 164

San Francisco:
  A. P. H. A. Meeting in... 479
  City and County Department of Public Health......................... 455
  Exhibits at 748
  Hospital 456
  Meeting 682
  Take Your Vacation in. Editorial.................................... 537
  A Word About 268

Sanitary Privies, Practical Types of. C. W. Stiles, M. D................... 48

Sanitation in Serbia. Edward Stuart...................................... 124

Sanitation of Swimming Pools, Report of Committee on..................... 540

Saville, Caleb Mills. Public Water Supply Contaminated by an Interconnected
Private Water Supply.. 724

Scharff, Maurice R., and Morris Knowles. New Specifications for Health
Officers 8

Schevitz, Jules. Industrial Health Education—A Means and an End........... 780

School and Special Feeding to Defective Nutrition, Relation of. John C.
Gebhart 669

School Hygiene for Rural Communities. Grace Whitford, M. D.............. 246

School Hygiene Methods, Need of Standardization in. H. O. Jones, Ph. G.,
M. D. 243

School of Public Health, A Successful. Editorial........................... 260

School of Public Health at Lyons, France, Early. Professor William T.
Sedgwick ...:... 352

Schoolhouses, Why Not Sanitary? Editorial............................... 259

Schools for Health Officers: What Has Been Done at Syracuse. Frederick
W. Sears, M. D....:.. 155

Sears, Frederick W., M. D. Schools for Health Officers: What Has Been Done
at Syracuse 155

Sedgwick, Professor William T. Early School of Public Health at Lyons,
France 352

Self-Imposed Inspection of the National Canners' Association. H. M. Loomis 321

Serbia, Sanitation in. Edward Stuart..................................... 124

Sewage Sludge, By-Products from. Robert Spurr Weston................... 405

PAGE

Sewage, Treatment of Beet Sugar Plant. Langdon Pearse and Samuel A. Greeley. Discussion by W. H. Dittoe and Robert Spurr Weston......... 312
Sheppard, Philip A. E., M. D. African Aboriginal Therapy.................... 227
Simpson, Friench, Surgeon, U. S. P. H. S. Methods of Plague Control....... 845
Slaughterhouse, The Country; How to Build It. G. H. Parks................. 731
Smith, A. K., M. D. Health Hazards of the Dye Industry.................. 255
Smith, Clarence E., M. D. Role of the Sanitary Privy in the Control of Typhoid Fever 140
Social Uses of Medicine. D. B. Armstrong, M. D., M. A., M. S................ 921
Socializing Medicine, Meaning and Purpose of. Ira S. Wile, M. D........... 969
Societies, Report of Committee on State Health............................. 742
Sociological Aspect of Hookworm Disease. Oscar Dowling, M. D........... 595
Sociological Aspects of Housing. Ira S. Wile, M. D......................... 327
Some Epidemiological Points Regarding Acute Respiratory Diseases. Frank Overton, M. D., D. P. H... 431
Some Important Factors in the Preparation of Culture Media. Lewis Davis.... 250
Soper, George A., Ph. D. Protective Value of Typhoid Vaccination as Shown by the Experience of the American Troops in the War.................. 301
Standard Budget, A: The Health Officer's First Need. Haven Emerson, M. D. 221
Standard Methods for the Examination of Air, Report of the Committee on.... 450
Standardization of Laboratory Methods. Augustus B. Wadsworth, M. D...... 932
Standards, Need for, for Recording and Classifying Defects and Impairments. John S. Billings, M. D... 410
Starr, E. B., M. D. Excessive Mortality from Influenza-Pneumonia Among Bituminous Coal Miners of Ohio in 1918.............................. 348
State and Municipal Meat Inspection. John Roberts...................... 697
State and Private Enterprises in Public Health Work, Coördination of. W. H. Hattie, M. D. 961
State Health Notes. These Items Will Be Found in the Notes Section of Each Issue.
State Health Societies, Report of Committee on........................... 742
Status of State Bureaus of Child Hygiene. Anna E. Rude, M. D............. 772
Stiles, Professor Percy G. Types of Fatigue.......................... 653
Stokes, William Royal, M. D. Bacteriological Examination of Soft Drinks..... 308
Stokes, William Royal, M. D., and C. H. Douthirt, M. D. Practical Disinfection of Tuberculous Sputum................................... 973
Stromquist, W. G. Malaria Control from the Engineering Point of View...... 497
Stories from the Day's Work.......................................476, 892
Streptococcus Hemolyticus from Restaurant Tableware, Recovery of. Clarence C. Saelhof and W. J. R. Heinekamp................................ 704
Stuart, Edward. Sanitation in Serbia.................................... 124
Studies in the Clarification of Milk. Professor Charles E. Marshall.......... 152
Studies on Malaria Control. C. C. Bass, M. D............................ 216
Studies on the Viability of the Tubercle Bacillus. J. B. Rogers, M. D......... 345
Study of the Toxicity of Diphtheria Bacilli Isolated from Immediate Contacts, A. Frank W. Hatchel, M. D., and Mary Shedwick Bailey, M. D.......... 42
Success and Failure in Mental Health. Editorial......................... 677
Successful School of Public Health, A. Editorial......................... 260
Supervision Over the Manufacture of Arsphenamine. Editorial............. 536
Swimming Pool Purity, An Inferential Index of. Gordon M. Fair............ 502
Swimming Pools, Report of Committee on Sanitation of..................... 540
Syracuse, Schools for Health Officers: What Has Been Done at. Frederick W. Sears, M. D.. 155
Take Your Vacation in San Francisco. Editorial.......................... 537
Team Work Among Health Agencies. Editorial........................... 607

PAGE

Therapy, African Aboriginal. Philip A. E. Sheppard, M. D.................. 227
Tobey, James A. Health Quotations, Compiled by....................... 649
Tolman, Mayo. Endemic Goiter as a Public Health Problem: Additional
  Notes 434
Toluidin Blue Iodin Method of Staining, A Classification of Diphtheria Bacilli
  Based on the. Henry Albert, M. D.................................... 936
Tonney, Frederick O., M. D. Organization of Control of Pasteurization....... 716
Traffic Regulation as a Means of Preventing Injury and Death from Street
  Vehicles. S. J. Byrne, M. D... 331
Treatment of Beet Sugar Plant Sewage. Langdon Pearse and Samuel A.
  Greeley 312
  Dicussion by W. H. Dittoe... 320
  Discussion by Robert Spurr Weston.................................. 322
Trip to California 611
Truth in Advertising Drug Products. Arthur J. Cramp, M. D............... 783
Tubercle Bacillus, Studies on the Viability of the. J. B. Rogers, M. D....... 345
Tuberculosis Items, Little Round-Up of................................. 269
Tuberculous Sputum, Practical Disinfection of.. William Royal Stokes, M. D.,
  and C. H. Douthirt, M. D... 973
Types of Fatigue. Professor Percy G. Stiles.............................. 653
Typhoid Control by Vaccine, Mills-Reincke Phenomenon and. Harold G.
  McGee 585
Typhoid Fever, Causes of in Massachusetts. George T. O'Donnell, M. D...... 517
Typhoid Fever, Role of the Sanitary Privy in the Control of. Clarence E. Smith,
  M. D. 140
Typhoid Vaccination, Protective Value as Shown by the Experience of the
  American Troops in War. George A. Soper, Ph. D..................... 301
United States Public Health Service.................................... 365
Urgent Need for the Standardization of Laboratory Work. Arthur Lederer,
  M. D., C. P. H.. 876
Uses, Possibilities and Limitations of Bacteriology in Food Control. Professor
  E. O. Jordan 142
  Discussion by H. W. Redfield, Ph. D................................ 145
Vaccination, Protective Value of Typhoid V. as Shown by the Experience of the
  American Troops in the War. George A. Soper, Ph. D................. 301
Vaccine, Mills-Reincke Phenomenon and Typhoid Control by. Harold G.
  McGee 585
Vaccines, Application of in Public Health Work. George W. McCoy, M. D.... 666
Vacuum Method of Filling Capillary Tubes, Improvement in. Thomas A.
  Watson... 445
Value of Brilliant-Green in Eliminating Errors Due to Anaërobes in the Pre-
  sumptive Tests for B. Coli. Theodore C. Muer and Robert L. Harris.... 874
Value of Plant Records in the Development of Plant Hygiene. A. R. Hackett,
  M. D. 523
Van Dine, D. L. Mosquito Work of the Bureau of Entomology............. 116
Varieties of City Health Officers. Editorial............................. 881
Vaughan, G. E., M. A., and E. M. Wade. Observations on the Diphtheria
  Virulence Test in Public Health Work............................... 426
Venereal Disease Control: Method, Obstacles and Results. C. C. Pierce, Assist-
  ant Surgeon General.. 132
  Discussion by Thomas W. Jackson, M. D............................ 136
Venezuela, Building Regulations in.....................................895
Villuendas, F., M. D. Campaign Against Malaria in Cuba, 1918-19........... 728
Vital Statistics in Canada. R. H. Coats................................ 224
Vital Statistics, Popularizing. C. St. Clair Drake, M. D................. 112
Vital Statistics, Report of Committee on Relation of the 1920 Census to....... 173

PAGE

Wade, E. M., M. A., and G. E. Vaughan, M. A. Observations on the Diphtheria Virulence Test in Public Health Work............................. 426

Wadsworth, Augustus B., M. D.:
The Developments of the State Departments of Health in Relation to Health Insurance and Industrial Hygiene..'........................... 53
Standardization of Laboratory Methods................................. 932

Wall, Edward E. Water Treatment at St. Louis, Mo......................... 437

War, An Aftermath of the. Editorial.. 238

War, Preventive Medicine and. Mazyck P. Ravenel, M. D................... 22

War, Protective Value of Typhoid Vaccination as Shown by the Experience of the American Troops in the. George A. Soper, Ph. D................. 301

Water, Importance of Confirmatory B. Coli Tests in Fairly Safe Drinking. N. Novick 303

Water Supply Contaminated by an Interconnected Private Water Supply, Public. Cabel Mills Saville... 724

Water Treatment at St. Louis, Mo. Edward E. Wall....................... 437

Watson, Thomas A. Improvement in Vacuum Method of Filling Capillary Tubes 445

Wells, William Firth, M. D. The Purification of Oysters as a Conservation Measure 342

Weston, Robert Spurr. By-Products from Sewage Sludge.................... 403
Discussion: Treatment of Beet Sugar Plant Sewage by Langdon Pearse and Samuel A. Greeley... 322

What Can a Community Afford to Pay to Rid Itself of Malaria? L. M. Fisher 768

What is a Health Center? H. N. C. Editorial.............................. 676

What Is the Matter with Public Health? Discussion: Hibbert W. Hill, M. D... 673

What Is the Matter with Public Health? Charles T. Nesbitt. M. D.......... 953

What Should Be Done in the Control of Degenerative Diseases? Frederick S. Crum, Ph. D.. 210

What Should Be the Basis of the Control of Dehydrated Foods? Professor Samuel C. Prescott 324

White, Paul Dudley, M. D. Public Health in Eastern Macedonia.............. 14

Whitford, Grace, M. D. School Hygiene for Rural Communities............. 246

Why Not 7,500 A. P. H. A. Members?...................................... 267

Why Not Sanitary Schoolhouses? Editorial................................ 239

Wile, Ira S., M. D.:
Meaning and Purpose of Socializing Medicine........................... 969
Sociological Aspects of Housing....................................... 327

Wood, Harold B., M. D., Dr. P. H. Health Centers......................... 474

Work of the National Safety Council...................................... 58

Wyant, R. W., M. S., and L. H. Cooledge, A. M. Judging the Keeping Quality of Milk by a PH Method.. 978

Zubiria, Alfredo De, S. Public Health Aspects of Cartagena, Colombia......... 509

American Journal of Public Health

Official Monthly Publication of the American Public Health Association
169 Massachusetts Ave., Boston, Mass.

Subscription price, $4 per year.   *American Public Health Association membership, including subscription, $5 per year.*

Vol. X   JANUARY, 1920   No. 1

ADMINISTRATIVE HANDLING OF THE NARCOTIC ADDICT: ITS BENEFITS AND DANGERS.

ERNEST S. BISHOP, M. D., F. A. C. P.,

Clinical Professor of Medicine, New York Polyclinic Medical School, New York City.

Read before Food and Drugs Section, American Public Health Association, at New Orleans, La., October 27, 1919.

Dr. Bishop asserts again that narcotic drug addiction is a disease; the laws make it a crime. The appalling extent of illicit drug traffic is due largely to this mistake. Forcible control is a fundamental error. The existing laws make it hard for the physician to know where he stands in his treatment. Here is a strong plea for sensible reform.

A VERY serious question is arising from the narcotic drug situation. It constitutes an important problem for immediate consideration. This question is the extent to which the narcotic or opiate addict should be given over for handling to administrative organizations,—and with this question, its corollary, the extent to which administrative supervision, regulation and control should be exerted or exercised over the individual sufferer from narcotic drug addiction and over the therapeutic procedure and professional judgment of the practitioner of medicine in the care of the sufferer from this disease.

At the time of passage of the early anti-narcotic restrictive measures with administrative provisions for the suppression of narcotic drug use, the general conception of the nature of addiction made the problem of its eradication seem simple. Narcotic addiction, supposedly a "habit" or vice or indulgence, as it was then generally considered, seemed to require for its suppression merely forcible denial or prohibition of the means of supposed gratification.

The laws were passed and administered upon the above theories, and were followed by developments which were appalling. Among them were the practical temporary enforced abandonment of the addiction sufferer by the practitioner of medicine and the druggist, and the remarkable development and extension and organization of underworld or underground traffic with its attendant evils of smuggling, thievery, illicit manufacture and other criminality. I referred to this development in my papers before this Association last year. It is spoken of in the report of the special Federal Committee appointed by the Secretary of the Treasury which was published last June, and in which its appalling proportions are revealed.

As I have stated before, an increase seems to have followed every exacerbation of spectacular publicity emphasizing the criminal or morbid incidental phases of the addiction situation or any attitude which is unduly critical either by inference or statement of the motives and acts of the practitioner of medicine. Its increase also seems to follow unwisely drastic or impractically restrictive administrative regulations, which either surround the physician with legal and administrative technicalities beyond the bounds of reason, or which place upon the honest and innocent addict of standing and reputation such demands that he feels himself forced to seek illegitimate sources of narcotic medication to escape the potential danger and damage to his social and economic welfare and status, which he foresees as possibilities of his compliance with some of the administrative demands. He feels himself forced to break regulations and even statute law in the protection of himself and family.

The basis for many of these unduly stringent and unwisely drastic regulations is an apparent lack of appreciation in the minds of some of the administrators of the character of the addiction condition and the real needs of the situation, coupled at times possibly with a tendency towards dramatic publicity. It is unfortunate that the administration of laws must or does at times fall into the hands of those whose training and previous experience have not brought them into contact with the conditions of their administrative activities for which they are totally unprepared and unqualified.

One of the commoner arguments brought in behalf of more and more complete and drastic administrative control is the statement that the medical profession has failed to solve the narcotic situation or to bring about widespread so-called "cure" of the narcotic addict. It is pertinent to inquire as to whether or not administrative regulation and public hospital handling have done any better. From the testimony of the Whitney Legislative Investigation hearings, we are forced to conclude that on the whole no better results have followed public hospital handling of the narcotic addict than have been found in private practice. The success of hospital treatment of a disease must be measured both in contemplation and in explanation of results by the competency, diligence, humanity, and personal qualifications of its medical and nursing staff. The failure to achieve any measure of success, which was shown to exist in the case of institutional handling by public institutions or hospitals, is explained by inadequate conception of the disease treated. It is the opinion of some that the average of successful outcome will be found to be about the same in previous hospitalization as in private practice. What is really needed is scientific study and education, and doctorization. Whether the doctorization is better found in private practice or in a hospital or institution will finally depend entirely upon the personal requirements of the individual case, just as it does in any other disease, and also upon whether or not the hospital doctors have competent clinical and scientific understanding and ability. Certainly enforced hospitalization of all addicts under present conditions promises nothing more in the immediate future than hospitalization has accomplished in the past, and is, for the immediate present until better medical and nursing education is accomplished, fraught with grave dangers.

The preceding is not to be interpreted as objecting to the establishing of all possible hospital facilities for the care of the sufferer with addiction-disease. It is, however, a warning from the experience of the past, that the mere provision of hospital as a hope of aiding in the solution of the narcotic problem is foredoomed to disappointment unless those hospitals can be equipped with intelligent and humane and competent administration and medical and nursing staff which can and will treat the opiate addict with the same clinical and scientific ability and intelligence that they have been trained and educated to apply in other diseases.

We need all possible physical accommodation for the treatment of this disease. In the cry for it, however, let the fundamental requirement not be lost sight of, the greater need for clinical and addiction-disease education among those who handle narcotic addicts both within hospitals and without. Otherwise we shall simply continue the stream of those whom official investigation has shown to have entered our institutions and undergone treatment there, and have come out, deprived of their opiate and statistically "cured" but with addiction-disease as it is now scientifically conceived, still exerting its physical demands upon their bodies. A discussion of this matter with analysis of causes for both failures and successes will be found in the yearly report of the Department of Correction of the City of New York for 1915. A year's work in the narcotic wards of the Workhouse Hospital is reported and reviewed and analyzed, and the blame for failures distributed among the factors in its causation within instead of being entirely shifted to conditions existing without the administrative and medical and nursing management.

Hospitalization, however much it is requisite and indispensable for some cases, is harmful to others, and it is to be hoped that this fact will be established and analyzed before too drastic measures are adopted for its prolonged general enforcement, towards the accomplishment of which there is a tendency in some quarters.

The bill introduced in the United States Senate by Senator France, providing for the use of the available Army and Navy hospitals for the handling of addiction under the supervision of the Public Health Service in so far as they can be so utilized, is in itself an excellent move. It will not only provide hospital accommodations but will tend to awaken, in the Public Health Service, an interest in this disease and an active investigation of its clinical and other manifestations which should prove of greatest educational value in the handling of this disease, and of the situations and problems which have arisen about it, as these situations and problems, clinical and otherwise, arise or are recognized in other hospitals, in the work of the practitioner of medicine, in the life of the addict, in administration or elsewhere, as well as within the Public Health Service Hospitals provided for in the France Bill. The writer has for years expressed the hope that the facilities and equipment of the Public Health Service could be directed to the investigation of addiction-disease. In previous papers I have discussed the work which might be done.

Great as is the need for hospital facilities, however, perhaps the greatest benefit will come from the scientific and research and clinical and educational activities resulting from this move.

The narcotic drug situation is now, after years of trial of various panaceas, legislative, administrative, medical and otherwise, being rapidly appreciated in its true character and complexity. The condition lying at the bottom of it, addiction-disease, is still the subject of controversy, although of late the conception of it has been gradually and steadily spreading and crystallizing about definite and unescapable material and physical facts, in the light of which every other consideration must be interpreted and about which future progress must be grouped.

An administrative matter which is now receiving much consideration is that of the "narcotic clinics" for the supplying of opiate medication to addicts. Rightly conducted with humane and intelligent medical direction, these clinics should be of greatest benefit to the community and have great deterrent effect upon the underground or illicit traffic. They should not be associated with departments of administration only, but should be established as a part of the ordinary out-patient work of the general hospital, and should be conducted in the same spirit of medical help as other clinic or out-patient departments. There has been an unfortunate tendency to give them in effect more of an atmosphere of correctional and police activity than of public health or medical effort. There has been tendency to place too much insistence upon forcible control of drug supply and too little upon disease requirements of the individual, to over-play the side of restrictions at the expense of the more legitimate public health activity of education and medical assistance. Under such circumstances a narcotic clinic becomes in my opinion, and as I believe to be in process of demonstration, more of a menace than a benefit, and accomplishes little or nothing in the lessening of street peddling and illicit narcotic traffic.

The atmosphere and conduct must be that of a scientific and humane medical endeavor as closely as possible approximating that of a physician's office, and avoiding all spectacularity and public display of misery and suffering. There should be also attention to the general medical needs of the individual patient and advice and instruction to him and to

his as to the nature and reactions of the disease from which he suffers, and the general principles of conduct of it by which its harmful effects may be minimized, and gain in physical and economic competency secured. Every possible precaution should be taken to so conduct such a clinic that it will not tend to break down the self-respect of those forced to attend it. Where such a clinic takes on undue police and correctional aspects it drives from its doors and into the underworld many of those who are by nature law-abiding and economic assets worthy of help for themselves and for the welfare of the community. The final test of its benefit lies in the attitude of the narcotic addict towards it, whether he welcomes the help it gives him or fears and dreads associations and possible economic and other dangers to which it may subject him. The frankly criminal or degenerate or underworld type of individual cannot be helped at such a clinic and his presence there drives away more deserving sick people. It will probably be found that such of that type as go are merely adding to their illicit supply a cheaply obtained increase either for personal use or for subsequent peddling. Such types of individuals suffering from addiction-disease are possibly more correctional and custodial problems than medical or clinical, and should be handled in connection with the proper institutions.

The very great and very harmful mistake that administrators inexperienced with addiction are prone to make, lies in premature generalizing in administration and in newspaper and other statement, and in administrative regulation aimed at forcible control of those afflicted with a disease whose sufferers include the judge on the bench, the minister in the pulpit and the citizen of accomplishment and social and economic value in all walks of life, as well as the fundamentally unworthy and unfit, towards whom their attention is at first more likely to be directed, and who in one way or another evades any regulations, leaving their force to be felt by those to whom they very often should not apply.

Unfortunately often, by the time an administrator has himself become educated to the wider facts and problems of his position, and has corrected in so far as possible his earlier mistakes, he is replaced by another "new broom" and the performance has to be repeated. In this fact lies one of the gravest dangers of too extensive administrative power of control under present conditions. What is commendable and recommended towards the end of one administrator's term of service may be a matter for criminal procedure under some technical violation under his successor's interpretation. This situation is unfortunate but seems to be necessary in the development of final comprehension and rational handling.

A very interesting and instructive occupation is the review of the newspaper and other statements of almost any administrative official who tends to publicity, and to see how the positive statements of his early announcements and plans change and are replaced often by opposite views gained from failure of early endeavor and fuller appreciation by him of newly-revealed facts. Premature announcement of apparent successful results, from hospital or other effort, is one of the pitfalls of the inexperienced. Statistics often need as much cross-examination and analysis as the conditions with which they deal. The real truth of many a situation is more accurately obtained from the gossip of the "long bazaar" than from official report of inexperienced observers. Unfortunately, competent administrators and executives are largely results of training and experience and the appointment of such men who have learned conservativeness of judgment and statement is not assured under present conditions.

The theory of administrative laws is, of course, that society may be best protected in that way from the acts of the unfit or criminal in tendency. There is, however, another side to the question, which is the consideration of the extent to which the honest and deserving need protection from the administrative acts directed against the minority of dishonest. Are we assured in our administrators of any higher average of honesty, and intelligence and experience than is to be found in the average man? In the case of the narcotic problem situation, we often "strain at a gnat and swallow a camel," not consciously nor deliberately, but because the subject is still a new one and because many of the workers in it have not as yet sufficient comprehension of it as a whole to give them adequate basis for the estimation of comparative values. These remarks do not apply to administrators only, but to all classes of workers, from legislators to doctors. The situation is just coming out of past miscomprehension and chaos and is in a transition stage towards understanding. There are too many phases of it to expect any one line of effort to bring solution. There should be more open discussion and coöperation and tolerance and forbearance, and the greatest care in the promulgation of drastic regulations, and infinite care in the selection of those in whose hands the welfare of hundreds of thousands of suffering humanity is to be placed for administrative regulation.

I wish to say a word of warning as to the hasty adoption of systems of compulsory registration of narcotic addicts. If publicity had not operated in throwing about the addiction-disease sufferer such

an atmosphere of morbidity, and vicious-
ness, but had been educational in the
best sense of the word of scientific and
public health information as to disease,
there would be little objection to the
registration of all narcotic addicts on the
same plane as the reporting of tuberculosis or typhoid. As conditions are, however, compulsory registration of all addicts
carrying with it, in its technique of detailed enforcement, the suggestion of
protecting society against potential criminals or degenerates by means of pictures,
identification marks, and other data
placed upon registration cards, carries
with a suggestion of the recording of
convicted criminals which is very hu-
miliating to the honest and self-respecting citizens who constitute the majority
of addiction-disease sufferers. In the
minds of many of them it constitutes a
system of espionage parallel to the workings of the boards of parole for ex-
prisoners, and fills the minds of well-
known citizens afflicted with this disease
with fears of possible revelation of their
condition with attendant social and
economic detriment or ruin, and potentialities of possible blackmail or other
consequences. The proper and safe conduct of such an activity would call for
the extreme of confidence in those controlling it and for an appreciation of
conditions rarely found at present, and
for a preceding campaign of education
which would strip from this addiction-
disease, as a disease, the morbid and
erroneous and unjustified popular attitude towards it and conception of it
with which it has been enveloped by
unfortunate past publicity centering its
attention upon the spectacular manifestations associated with some of its incidental aspects.

I very much doubt if compulsory registration under present conditions with
photographs, employer's name, and revelation of data of a purely personal
nature manages to include more than a
minor proportion of the addiction census.
Those against whom it is originally
directed naturally tend to avoid it and
have every means and ability of so doing,
while those, in connection with whose
cases it can have no possible practical
excuse, may be influenced, through their
fears and feeling of injustice and unnecessary humiliation, to contemplate and
adopt desperate measures for its avoidance. It is more than possible that the
foregoing will be found to have been, to a
considerable extent, the actual working
out of such experiments in this direction
as are tried. There are much better
and less objectional ways of accomplishing the ends claimed for this activity in
the opinion of the writer of this paper.

The addiction problem is now fast
coming to be recognized as basically a
disease problem,—for whose basic solution we must look to clinical and laboratory and experimental medicine. It has
associated with it many problems not of
medicine, problems which are in part
incidental and in part intrinsic, and
which will call for in such cases as they
complicate the medical picture, custodial,
correctional, penal, or other handling.
No one attitude towards the situation
should overwhelmingly dominate the
others in the province of their logical
activity. Progress in some of its stages
comes through opposition and lack of coöperation, through argument and fighting.
It is to be hoped that this stage of development will soon be over, and the several
issues clarified and made manifest to all.

There are of course very many points
worthy of discussion in connection with
the subject of this paper. Space is lacking for their consideration.

In conclusion, I am copying from the
issue of the *New York Medical Journal*
of July 19, 1919, its summary of some

resolutions introduced into the Medical Society of the County of New York.

The *Journal* says:

"The resolution may be summarized as follows: "The Medical Society of the County of New York wishes to go on record as being deeply appreciative of the menace of narcotic drug addiction. It holds itself willing to coöperate with any agencies working for the betterment of conditions as long as those agencies conduct their activities 'in a competent manner' and display appreciation of the many sides of the problem. In return for this coöperation it expects from such agencies or departments 'reasonable recognition of the difficulties faced under present conditions by the practitioner of medicine.'

"The society regrets that in the various forms of publicity so much stress has been laid upon the very few medical practitioners who may be open to charges of unjustifiable conduct and that practically no attention has been called to the many honest practitioners who have been trying to the best of their ability to treat and care for the addicted sufferer. Far more harm is done by the continued existence of smuggling and street peddling and illicit traffic in narcotics than by the few medical men whose activities may be open to question.

"It has been conclusively shown that unwisely administered laws tend to drive the reputable practitioner away from the treatment of addicts and to send the addict himself to the 'underworld.'

"The society is opposed to registration and identification of narcotic addicts under conditions which will injure the innocent and worthy persons suffering from this disease, and which will subject them to the danger of blackmail and other annoyances. The society, therefore, asks that before regulations are promulgated, a public hearing be held and that they be submitted to the medical bodies in open meeting for discussion, in order that the practicability of their enforcement may be determined.

"The Department of Narcotic Drug Control is respectfully requested to investigate the matter of so-called 'underworld' traffic and to direct its activities toward this 'worst evil' as well as toward medical practitioners.

"It is also respectfully suggested that the department of health direct its energies towards the promulgation of useful information as to the disease characteristics of narcotic addiction and that it refrain from disparaging statements as to 'honest physicians' whose views of addiction may not agree.

"The addiction situation has been determined to be basically a disease problem and there is as yet no commonly accepted and standardized form of handling. The ultimate solution must be in the medical profession. Senator Whitney has expressed the opinion after long hearing of every side of this question that the remedy lies more in medical and public health education than in any forcible police or other control.

"The society demands that administrative officials recognize the facts above stated and asks of such officials 'tolerance of opinion, slowness of judgment, and coöperation with others who are working in various fields.'"

The wise administrative official will realize that the narcotic problem and situation is too great for administrative handling and control only, that while there are some aspects of it that can be handled only by administrative activity there are others which demand the help and work of many and various other forces and activities. Each should help the others, in a spirit of scientific tolerance and humanity, trying to realize the other's difficulties and problems and by coöperative effort assisting in their solution and handling for the benefit of society and humanity, and for the relief of the sick, and the education and protection for posterity against avoidable disease and misery.

◈

In the February issue of the JOURNAL look for other papers from the New Orleans Meeting,—Dr. Pierce on Veneral Disease Control with discussions, Mr. LePrince on Drainage and Malaria, Dr. Drake on Popularizing Vital Statistics, Professor Marshall on Clarification of Milk, and Drs. Ferrell and Smith continuing the Privy Symposium.

NEW SPECIFICATIONS FOR HEALTH OFFICERS.

MORRIS KNOWLES AND MAURICE R. SCHARFF,
Consulting Engineers, Pittsburgh, Pa.

Read before Sanitary Engineering Section, American Public Health Association, at New Orleans, October 29, 1919.

The new specifications include special training in sanitation for health officers, for which training the degree of M. D., although desirable, is not a satisfactory substitute. These authors advocate the incorporation of the principle in National, State and Municipal laws. A Sanitary Corps on this plan would be a desirable addition to the Army of the country. : : : : : : : : : :

ABOUT seven years ago the authors presented before the Sanitary Engineering Section of the American Public Health Association at Washington, D. C., a paper entitled "Public Health Service—Not a Medical Monopoly." This paper showed that existing state laws required 172 out of 298 members of state boards of health, and 32 out of 46 state executive health officers or commissioners of health to be physicians; and it upheld the thesis that the degree of Doctor of Medicine was not the only necessary qualification for a health executive, and that the cause of public health would be advanced if every state would remove the restriction limiting public health service to the medical or any other single profession, requiring instead that health officers should be trained and experienced in sanitary science and public health and qualified by administrative ability and judgment to perform the manifold functions of the modern health officer. Thanks to its intentionally irritating title, the paper was successful in promoting a lively and helpful discussion of the desirable qualifications of health executives.

Let us state at the beginning that our thesis was not in any sense that a medical man may not be well fitted to fill public health positions, or that a sanitary engineering course is better preparation for such work than a medical one. In fact, we would go so far as to say that a Doctor of Medicine who had had thorough training in sanitation and public health and who possessed the necessary administrative ability and judgment would probably be better qualified to fill such a position than a member of any other profession with similar education. What we did emphasize was that special training in public health, and administrative ability and experience were all more essential than the medical degree. In other words, as Prof. C.-E. A. Winslow put it in the discussion of the 1912 paper, we would consider a man with both kinds of training preferable to one with either kind alone; but would much prefer a man who knew public health and not medicine to one who knew medicine and not public health.

Since 1912 a number of developments have occurred which appear to the writers to justify the conclusion that there is a general agreement upon this "new specification for health officers." The purpose of this paper is to call attention to some of these recent developments and to suggest some lines along which it would seem that the Sanitary Engineering Section of the American Public Health Association might be helpful in applying this specification.

The developments to which reference

has been made will be considered under the headings of (1) Crystallization of Opinion; (2) Public Health Education; (3) Legislation; (4) Sanitary Corps of the Army; (5) U. S. Public Health Service.

(1) CRYSTALLIZATION OF OPINION.

Numerous expressions of opinion could be quoted from public health literature since 1912 to show the growth and development of the opinion that the ideal health officer must fulfill the new specifications. Dr. W. S. Rankin said in his paper before the American Public Health Association convention at Jacksonville, December 3, 1914:

"There is a prevalent error especially pronounced and dangerous to controvert in medical assemblages to the effect that the average physician will make, on his appointment or election to a health office, an efficient health officer. There is just as much sense in claiming that the average physician is a dermatologist, a pathologist, an ophthalmologist, a surgeon or any other specialist, as that the average physician is a health officer whenever an undiscriminating public puts him where a health officer is supposed to be. The efficient health officer is a specialist—as much a specialist as is the surgeon or the ophthalmologist."

Assistant Surgeon-General W. C. Rucker, of the U. S. Public Health Service, said in his paper on "A Program of Public Health for Cities," before the Cincinnati Convention of the American Public Health Association, October 24, 1916:

"Unfortunately, health has been considered in the past only as a medical problem, and the pendulum has been enthusiastically swung so far that health is almost regarded as an artificial state to be achieved and maintained solely through the interposition of medical safeguards. With . entire consistency, health wardenship of cities has been committed solely to physicians, those who by training have been taught to consider the pathological in human life, the symptomatology and evidences of disease rather than the great basic, underlying essential factors which enter into and are the vital part in the creation, spread and perpetuation of sickness. Expert knowledge of disease is absolutely necessary for the work of health departments, but cannot be the foundation of a broad, municipal health policy."

In the discussion of this paper, Dr. J. N. Hurty said:

"We must all agree with Dr. Rucker that in the past public health has been considered as too strictly a medical matter or a physician's problem. We have all come to recognize that efficient health wardenship requires something more than a knowledge of the diagnosis and the treatment of disease."

And in the same discussion, Dr. Henry F. Vaughan said:

"Dr. Rucker has stated that health in the past has been considered solely as a medical problem, as an artificial state to be achieved and maintained solely through the interposition of medical safeguards. It seems to me that there are undoubtedly many phases of public health administration which can be handled more effectively and more efficiently by the business man or the engineer or by others."

In his book on "American Public Health Protection," Dr. Henry B. Hemenway expressed himself as follows (page 83):

"It has long been the custom in the United States to think that any physician is competent to give sanitary advice and to head a health department, but in point of fact there is not one practitioner in five hundred who knows the rudiments of modern sanitation. The education, training, habits of thought and objects of work of a good physician are very different from those of an ideal public health executive."

Further on, on page 216, Dr. Hemenway says:

"The first question to be asked relative to the fitness of a candidate for appointment to a health department should be not 'Is he a good physician?' nor 'Does he belong to the party in power?' nor 'Is he a getter of votes?' nor 'Does he have elective influence?'; but 'Does he know the modern science of public health protection?'

"It is a very unfortunate thing that the medical profession should so frequently imagine that any competent bacteriologist is also a competent public health administrator. The contrary may be the fact. . . . It is necessary that the executive head should have a good knowledge of the methods and results of bacteriologic investigation, just as he should know the general facts of sanitary engineering, but a thorough acquaintance with the subject of administrative law is more important for the chief than either engineering or bacteriology."

Dr. M. J. Rosenau said in the *Journal of the American Medical Association* for 1915, page 351:

"It may be a surprise to the readers of the *Journal* that Hygiene is included as a major subject in the curriculum of only three medical schools in this country, namely, the University of Pennsylvania, the University of Michigan, and Harvard. . . . It is slowly becoming recognized that the training received for the M. D. degree, even in our best medical schools, does not properly fit a man to enter public health work. Sanitation and hygiene have become a separate profession."

Such quotations might be continued indefinitely, but enough have been given to show the general trend of all the recent discussions of this problem and the evidence of a definite crystallization of opinion.

(2) PUBLIC HEALTH EDUCATION.

In 1913 the School of Public Health of Harvard University and the Massachusetts Institute of Technology was instituted and since has been giving courses in Preventive Medicine, Hygiene, Sanitary Engineering, Laboratory Procedure, Public Health Practice and Administration, Vital Statistics, etc., leading to a certificate in public health and giving the training required by an efficient health officer. Other schools have followed the same line of development, and in 1918 Prof. Eugene C. Howe (*American Journal of Public Health*, Vol. 8, p. 600) reviewed the courses of twenty institutions in the United States and Canada conducting special professional courses in public health, leading to degrees, certificates or diplomas in this subject. Among those institutions might be mentioned New York University, Johns Hopkins University, Ohio State University, Tulane University, Universities of Colorado, Pennsylvania and Wisconsin,

Yale University, etc. It is no longer necessary, therefore, to employ sanitary engineers as health officers, as was formerly often the case because of the shortage of men with a reasonable degree of special training in sanitary science and public health. The supply of trained health officers and their assistants, however, is still deficient, and the facilities for training of this kind should be increased and improved.

(3) LEGISLATION.

Since 1912 at least two of the states have improved their public health legislation by incorporating into law the new specifications for health officers. Thus Ohio, which formerly had a State Board of Health of seven, of which the attorney-general was an *ex-officio* member, and a state health officer for whom no professional requirements were specified, passed a law in 1917 providing for a commissioner of health who must be "a physician skilled in sanitary science," and for a board of health to consist of the commissioner and four other members, "at least two of whom must be physicians with training and experience in sanitary science." Still more recently, in 1919, New Mexico has passed a law providing for a State Board of Health of three persons, not more than one of whom shall be a licensed physician; and a commissioner, to be appointed by the State Board of Health, who must be "a person having experience and special training in sanitary science and public health administration." It is probable that other states have similarly improved their legislation, and it would be of interest if reports of these could be received in the discussion of this paper.

It is regrettable that it is not possible to report in this connection any material improvement in the public health system of the state of Alabama, to which reference was made in the 1912 paper. In spite of·the very vigorous campaign of Dr. Thomas D. Parke of Birmingham, Ala., and other physicians, to free the public health work of the state from the control of the Alabama Medical Association, a bill has finally been passed by the Alabama legislature within a few weeks which practically confirms and establishes more firmly than ever the existing system under which the Medical Association is the State Department of Health, and its board of censors acts as the State Board of Health.

(4) SANITARY CORPS OF THE ARMY.

Some of the most interesting examples of recent recognition of the necessity of securing health executives from outside the ranks of the medical profession have been afforded by our experience in the ·Great War, and one of the best of these is found in the creation of the Sanitary Corps of the Army.

Paragraph 1386 of the Army Regulations describes the duties of the Medical Department of the Army as follows:

" The Medical Department is charged with the duty of investigating the sanitary condition of the Army and making recommendations in reference thereto, of advising with reference to the location of permanent camps and posts, the adoption of systems of water supply and purification and the disposal of waste, with the duty of caring for the sick and wounded, making physical examination of officers and enlisted men, the management and control of military hospitals, the recruitment, inspection and control of the enlisted force of the medical department and of the nurse corps, and furnishing all medical and hospital supplies except for public animals."

The qualifications required of officers commissioned in this corps are that they shall.be physicians of age 21 to 32 and graduates of a reputable medical college. The requirements for a commission in the Medical Reserve Corps are that the applicant shall be a reputable physician

(M. D.), in good standing in his community, in the active practice of his profession, licensed to practice medicine in the state where he resides, between 22 and 55 years of age, a citizen of the United States, and physically and professionally qualified.

When these qualifications are compared with the duties quoted above from the Army Regulations, it will be easy to understand why, at the beginning of the war in 1917, it was recognized that these specifications were not complete for the officers required to fulfill these functions, and the Sanitary Corps of the Army was instituted. The qualifications required by the order creating this corps were as follows:

"The officers of said corps will be provided by assigning officers of the Medical Reserve Corps thereto, or by the appointment of citizens of the United States who are found. under regulations established by the Secretary of War to possess especial skill in sanitation, in sanitary engineering, in bacteriology or other sciences related to sanitation and preventive medicine, or who possesses other knowledge of special advantage to the Medical Department."

The sanitary engineers, bacteriologists and chemists of the Sanitary Corps rendered signal service in connection with the protection of the health of our armies in camps and cantonments in America, and in France. Unfortunately, however, it is understood that provision has not been made either to continue the Sanitary Corps as a permanent part of the Army, or to provide a reserve in which the experience gained by this corps during the war may be conserved for future emergencies. The discrepancy between the functions to be performed by the Medical Corps and the Medical Reserve Corps and the qualifications required of their members is as great today as it was at the beginning of the war in 1917. It is hoped that the influence of the Sanitary Engineering Section of the American Public Health Association may be placed behind a movement to provide our Army with a permanent personnel with training in sanitary science, and with a Sanitary Reserve Corps which will be available whenever it may be necessary to put another large force in the field.

(5) U. S. PUBLIC HEALTH SERVICE.

A somewhat analogous situation exists with respect to officers commissioned in the United States Public Health Service. To obtain a commission in this organization, an applicant must be a citizen of the United States, a graduate of a reputable medical college with one year's experience in a hospital or two years' private practice of medicine. These requirements have not changed substantially since the service was known as the Marine Hospital Service. Meanwhile, the Public Health Service has extended its activities to include a wide range of sanitary work; and, since 1912, it has been specifically authorized by law to "study and investigate the diseases of man and the conditions influencing the propagation and spread thereof, including sanitation and sewage, and the pollution, either directly or indirectly, of the navigable streams and lakes of the United States." During the war, a vast extension of this sanitary work took place, covering the sanitation of extra-cantonment zones, extensive investigations of industrial hygiene and assistance and advice on many sanitary engineering problems of water supply, sewage disposal, etc. (See "War Activities of the United States Public Health Service," by Benjamin F. Warren, assistant surgeon-general, and Charles F. Bolduan, chief of the Section of Public Health Education, United States Public Health Service.)

It is, of course, true that, even prior to 1912, the service employed certain pharmacists, technical assistants, etc., and that later, but prior to the war, the new work embarked upon required the addition of sanitary engineers, chemists, bacteriologists and other non-commissioned sanitary assistants. It remained for the war, however, to bring out the inadequacy of the commissioned personnel to assume responsible charge of the sanitary work of the service in such an emergency. At the Conference of State and Territorial Health Officials, held April 30 to May 3, 1917, therefore, resolutions were adopted calling for the creation of a Public Health Reserve; and, although the resultant legislation met with many vicissitudes in Congress, it was finally passed on October 27, 1918. This measure provided for the creation of a Public Health Reserve, and that:

"The President alone shall be authorized to appoint and commission in the said reserve such citizens as, upon examination prescribed by the President, shall be found physically, mentally and morally qualified to hold such commissions."

The personnel of this reserve was assembled long prior to the enactment of the legislation authorizing commissions, and this force, supplemented by units drawn from the Sanitary Service Bureau of the American Red Cross, permitted the Public Health Service to play an invaluable part in protecting the health, both of our troops and of the civilian population, under the unusually difficult conditions created by the war.

Fortunately, the life of the Public Health Reserve was not limited to the duration of the war, as the enabling measure provided that "said commissions shall be in force for a period of five years, unless sooner terminated in the discretion of the President." And there is great promise in the existence of this trained body of sanitarians, ready for call in any national emergency—especially as the After-the-War Program of the Service (see Supplement No. 35 to the Public Health Reports) proposes to provide the members with opportunities for intensive training in public health for short periods at stated intervals, and also to order members of the reserve to active duty from time to time to participate in important field work.

The provision of this reserve, however, does not completely meet the needs of the situation. The work of the Public Health Service in the future will be in larger and larger proportion devoted to sanitation, and in less and less measure restricted to the original work of the Marine Hospital Service for which the qualifications for permanent commissions were designed. One cannot but be impressed with this fact in examining the After-the-War Program to which reference has been made above. It is proposed to carry out this program by the coöperation of Federal, state and local health authorities, and the Federal aid extension principle is recommended. Among the subjects included in the program are industrial hygiene, rural hygiene, prevention of diseases of infancy and childhood, surveys of water supplies, introduction and extension of methods of water purification, pasteurization of milk supplies, inspection of production and distribution of milk and milk products, extension of water carriage sewerage systems, establishment of standards of permissible pollution of streams, lakes and rivers used for water supplies, malaria prevention, drainage, control of venereal disease and of tuberculosis, sanitary supervision of railways, enactment of proper building ordinances and sanitary supervision of housing, promulgation of standards for sewerage and sewage disposal, standard specifications for safe water and water purification, etc.

The mere enumeration of these subjects seems to the writers to suggest the desirability of revising the requirements for commissions in the Public Health Service, and of making provision in the permanent commissioned personnel for sanitarians whose training and experience qualify them especially for the work.

CONCLUSION.

The proposals brought forward in this paper may be summarized as follows:

1. The new specifications for health officers require that such officers be qualified, trained and experienced in sanitation, public health and public health administration.

2. A medical degree is not a satisfactory substitute for the requirements of this new specification, but it is a desirable, though not a necessary supplement thereto.

3. The cause of public health would be advanced if this new specification were incorporated in national, state and municipal laws relating to the appointment or commissioning of health executives.

4. A permanent Sanitary Corps, and a Sanitary Reserve Corps, the members of which conformed to the specifications outlined above, would be a desirable addition to our Army.

5. The Public Health Reserve is a real accomplishment, to be developed and supported in every possible way. In addition, the commissioning of sanitarians in the Public Health Service itself would contribute to the important sanitary work which that service will, in future, be called upon to do.

An expression of the opinion of the Sanitary Engineering Section of the American Public Health Association on these proposals would be effective in bringing them before the public, and it is hoped that the discussion of this paper may be sufficiently complete to have that result.

PUBLIC HEALTH IN EASTERN MACEDONIA.

PAUL DUDLEY WHITE M. D.,

Lately with the American Red Cross, overseas; Boston, Mass.

In Macedonia a band of devoted, associated physicians fought the plagues of the nearer Orient, a splendid example of cosmopolitan coöperation. Here is the story as viewed by American eyes of a work which is fundamental in the removal of a very serious menace to the health of the world. : : : : : : : : : :

ON the old battle-scarred valleys and mountains of Eastern Macedonia lurk some of the most dangerous of the world's diseases. The wars, which have been waged over this territory almost constantly since 1912, have exposed to broad day the menace of this land to the world's health.

From Salonica, the chief city of Macedonia, a railroad runs north to Lake Doiran. East of this railroad and bounded on the north by Bulgaria and on the south by the Ægean Sea, lies Eastern Macedonia, one of the most picturesque countries on earth.

The chief disease centers of this land are Salonica, the Struma Valley, and the towns of Serres, Drama and Kavalla.

SALONICA.

Salonica, the Thessalonica of ancient days and the Thessaloniké of modern Greece, is a large city of some 300,000 inhabitants, once a thriving, prosperous seaport, but now a ruined, crowded and dirty metropolis. It was more than half destroyed by fire during the war in 1917. In its present state it is a likely center for the birth and spread of epidemic diseases. However, in spite of the difficulty of the situation, the Greek military and civilian authorities are doing much to prevent the onset of any serious scourge. Last year (1918) a few cases of ·cholera and plague were found, but they were quickly tracked down and no epidemics developed. Of course, during the war, much dysentery and malaria prevailed among the allied troops sick in Salonica, but these diseases were as a rule contracted on the front or near it. This year there have been some cases of exanthematic typhus both among the soldiers and among the civilian population, but by no means to the extent found in the country further east.

Salonica is the terminal of the main highway of the Balkan States to the sea and possesses a splendid harbor. Good systems of inspection and quarantine are, of course, absolutely essential to protect not only the city of Salonica and Eastern Macedonia, but the whole of the Balkans themselves from inroads of imported disease. When I visited the city last spring there were still many of the allied troops in or near it. With its natural population of Greeks and Turks and Jews and Gypsies and Albanians and Serbs, the addition of the British forces from Anzac to Scotchman and East Indian, the French forces from Parisian to African, the Italians, Jugo-Slavs, and Bulgarian prisoners, made of the city the most strikingly cosmopolitan center that one could imagine, even more so than Marseilles or Constantinople.

Many of the refugees lived in the ruins, others in huts built for them just outside

14

the city, while bazaars were everywhere. With the help of the British and French, and later of the American Red Cross, the Greek authorities have been organizing

REFUGEES LIVING IN HUTS AT SALONICA.

and equipping a number of good hospitals in and near Salonica, both military and civilian. The five most interesting hospitals from the standpoint of public health were the refugee hospital, the infectious disease hospital (with special building for exanthematic typhus), the new children's dispensary and lying-in hospital, the venereal hospital, and the new military tuberculosis hospital in the hills north of the city.

Extensive plans have been drawn up for rebuilding Salonica on excellent modern lines. With a hope of peace this vital work can be started and by so doing a very big step forward in helping remove a menace to the world's health will be taken. Salonica should some day be one of the chief cities of the world and one of the meccas for tourist travel. But we must have peace to have this dream come true.

THE STRUMA VALLEY.

Off to the northeast from Salonica 60 kilometers away in a straight line lies the Struma Valley extending from the historic Rupel Pass to the sea just west of Pangheion Mountain. Here, along this valley 80 kilometers from end to end, the

armies suffered during the war; British and Greek on the one side, Bulgars on the other. Malaria was the scourge, and one of the worst in history. There are probably few localities in the world more fatal to health than the malarial marshes of the Struma River. In the summer and fall the disease is at its height—few escape. It is apt to be of the severe æstivo-autumnal type and is often hæmorrhagic. The British tried quinine rations for their men for awhile, but without sufficient benefit to continue. Only the end of the war stopped the armies from suffering more. The villages along the valley, and particularly the town of Serres, which before the war had 40,000 inhabitants, had been swept with malaria for generations. Everywhere one sees the anæmia and chronic invalidism of this disease.

The river is a small stream coming south down through the Rupel Pass from Bulgaria, but it is flanked on both sides by marshes several kilometers wide, and wider on the left bank than on the right. Near its mouth the river swells out into a

TYPICAL GROUP OF MACEDONIAN TSIGANES.

big shallow lake, Lake Takinos, 5 kilometers wide and 35 kilometers long. In the spring the river usually overflows. This last spring there was a very high flood which carried away all the bridges and even some of the houses. From the neighboring hills one could look out over the valley and see huge sheets of water kilometers wide. Beyond the marshes is some dry land sloping slightly upwards for a few kilometers to the mountain ranges on each side of the valley. On the eastern slope is Serres. The valley from mountains to mountains is about 15 kilometers wide. It was an immobile front during the war, since neither side could advance,—marshes, malaria, river and mountains made too great a defense against attack, even had the enemy himself been weak. This front did in fact remain unbroken till the very end.

And now as to the solution. This swampy valley must be drained, and it can be, provided there be peace. We must look to the outlet of the Struma River. There we find obstruction—too narrow and shallow a mouth. An engineering feat here, a dredging of the river channel, and Eastern Macedonia and the Struma Valley will cease to be synonyms for malaria but should prove a rich tobacco land, healthful and prosperous. What a chance for the future there is here.

SERRES.

Now let me describe briefly the situation in the three towns of Serres, Drama and Kavalla. Serres I have already mentioned, a town of 40,000 before the Balkan Wars, but so devastated that now there is room for scarcely 12,000. It is beautifully located on the lower slopes of the hills on the eastern side of the Struma Valley, about half way from Rupel Pass to the Ægean Sea. It extends down to the edge of the marsh and so is infested with malaria. The single track Salonica-Constantinople railroad runs close to Serres. One can reach the town from Salonica in about 12 hours. From the picturesque old acropolis with its ruins one obtains a striking view of the whole Struma Valley from Demir-Hissar and the Belashitsa Mountains to Lake Takinos near the sea. Since the town was

on the front, one sees bordering it and actually crossing the Kaminika end of it Bulgar trenches, dugouts, and cement pill boxes. Some of the old houses, mosques, and bazaars still stand, and in the spring when I spent five weeks in Serres, the refugees were coming back and life was beginning to assume a more normal course. Greeks and Turks and Jews make up the bulk of the population

STREET SCENE. THE CENTRAL MOUND OF RUBBISH SHOWS NEED OF SANITATION.

now, the Greeks preponderating. One sees occasionally gypsies or Tsiganes living in extreme squalor, often in the ruins where they may die with hardly a soul to heed or care.

Coöperating with the Greek surgeon-general, Colonel Kanavatsoglou, and his epidemiologists, Drs. Montoussis and Kyriazides, Drs. John Hodgson, Carl Binger and I worked for several weeks in Serres combating typhus, the scourge last spring.* This work was extremely interesting and instructive, for we had the opportunity of studying the general health and sanitary conditions of the town as well as the typhus problem. It brought us into close touch with the individual inhabitants: Greek, Turk, Jew and Tsigane, and gave us a clew as to

* Our work was a part of that of the American Red Cross Commission to Greece under the general direction of Professor Edward Copps of Princeton University and Dr. Samuel J. Walker of Chicago.

how these peoples of various race and religion should be handled.

Incidentally, we found the health of Serres at the time of our visit fairly good, except for the typhus which was rapidly abating. There was some malaria and dysentery, and occasionally pneumonia, but not to any alarming degree. The decrease and final cessation of the typhus epidemic in Serres last spring as well as in

GROUPS OF ORDERLIES IN TYPHUS WORK.

all of Eastern Macedonia, and probably in every infested country, was dependent on three circumstances. One should read the following reasons remembering that exanthematic typhus is disseminated by the louse and probably only by the louse, though at one time we suspected the bedbug. The circumstances are: first, the onset of warmer weather, with changes in the habits of the people who began to wear fewer clothes, changed them more often, and lived out in the open air much more.

Second, the custom of the natives, particularly the Greeks and Jews, to have a spring-cleaning not only of their own bodies and clothes, but also of their houses. Some of them took their annual bath at about Easter time, and scrubbed and whitewashed their houses.

Third, our own efforts in coöperation with the Greek military authorities. Our program consisted of careful inspection of the entire town by districts to

discover new cases of exanthematic typhus, isolation of these cases in a special typhus hospital, quarantining the infected houses under military guard for a period of from fourteen to twenty-one days, with daily visits by medical officer, and finally delousing of all inhabitants and new comers at the special stations once a week. This program was ideal, and could not be completely carried out, but it was followed well enough to be a great help undoubtedly in stopping the epidemic.

It may be of interest if I quote a few extracts from my notebook kept at Serres. They will show better perhaps than otherwise the way we worked in the city and the problems we were up against. Malaria was beginning to crop up in May when we left, but showed itself very little except in the chronic anæmic cases earlier.

"April 14, 1919. Hodgson and I came on from Drama three days ago on a flat car, enjoying very much the four-hour ride on the single-track Macedonian railroad. The flat car was the cleanest car on the train, the wind having blown away most of the dirt. We crossed the Philippi plain in the twilight and came up the Struma Valley in the moonlight to Serres. The Red Cross Fiat Camion met us at the station and took us to the American Red Cross house in town. This house once belonged to a Turkish Bey (government official) but the Greeks had confiscated it and given it for a residence to the American Red Cross. (It was undoubtedly one of

COSMOPOLITAN GROUP OF WORKERS. NOTE THE GREEK PRIEST AT ONE END AND THE TURK AT THE OTHER, ALSO A PRIEST.

the best houses in Serres, but we could never rid it of bedbugs.) All through the town are storks with their nests on roof tops, chimneys, domes of the mosques, and trees, nearly always exposed to the elements. However, they do not come up from Egypt till March and so escape the rough winter climate. Their clacking beaks resound constantly through the town.

"Yesterday we met the Nomarch (governor of the department of Serres) and visited the orphanage where some seventy-five vigorous Greek youngsters lustily sang the Greek war-songs and finished up their performance for us by the Venizelos battle chant and native dancing. The American Red Cross has given food and clothing to this orphanage. In the afternoon we crossed the Bulgar trenches and the railroad, and walked west into the Struma marshes. After about three miles we got hopelessly blocked by the swamp in No-Man's-Land and had to return.

"This morning we spent three hours or more with Lieut.-Colonel L. inspecting the main typhus hospital and the convalescent hospital in an abandoned mosque, the main delousing station of the city at the old Hamaam (Turkish baths), the delousing stations on the Drama and Salonica roads, the refugee camp on the Salonica road, and a number of houses where there were suspected typhus cases. There are fifty-five typhus patients in the main hospital and fifteen convalescents in the mosque. Four hundred and fifty Greek refugees just returned from Bulgaria are in the camp. About three or four new cases of typhus are found daily, as compared with six or eight ten days ago. We shall begin to inspect sections of the city tomorrow ourselves, and then shall hand in to the surgeon-general our opinion and plans for improvement."

During the Easter holidays there was an increase of the epidemic in Serres due probably to the carelessness of the Greek authorities who at that time were too busy celebrating to carry out the inspections and isolations properly. The result of this and of our report was reorganization of the anti-typhus campaign.

"April 28. Much good has resulted from the 'typhus meeting' held the other day. An entirely new organization was begun by the Greek surgeon-general. Serres has been divided into six districts. Hodgson and I have each taken over control of one district. *We each have gotten hold of a team to help us,—a native civilian doctor, a Greek priest, a Turkish priest (or Hodja), two schoolmasters, two schoolmistresses, and a Greek policeman or gendarme. The section I am starting on is called Kaminika, and it in turn is divided by the Salonica road into the Anokaminika, or upper, and the

Katakaminika, or lower parts. There are about five hundred inhabited houses in the whole section, with some three thousand people. The Bulgar trenches cut the corner of it.

"The new system has done a lot of good. Each house is thoroughly inspected by a doctor every other day. Special cards have been distributed in all the houses, and these the doctors must sign at

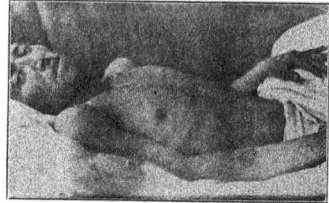

PATIENT WITH EXANTHEMATIC TYPHUS.

every visit. All the hidden cases of typhus in Serres have now been found and at the present time only about two or three new cases or suspects are entering the typhus hospital daily.

"Today we rode the 20 kilometers along the Salonica road from Serres to the Struma River and found the bridge destroyed and the country flooded for miles."

At the end of May, when we left Serres, the epidemic was practically over, rare cases being found here and there in all of Eastern Macedonia. Undoubtedly, for many years to come exanthematic typhus will be endemic in Eastern Macedonia and we shall have to label this country as a possible focus for the start of epidemics of the disease. With careful public health supervision such a danger will be reduced practically to zero, and with the draining of the swamps malaria, too, should some day be checked.

Drama and Kavalla are the other two important towns in Eastern Macedonia. Both were centers of the exanthematic typhus epidemic, and the American Red Cross coöperated again in both places with the Greek military authorities in much the same way as at Serres, though less completely. Drs. Binger, Clark, Hodgson, Walker and myself carried on with the Greek army in these towns.

KAVALLA.

We initiated the work in Kavalla where the 1919 epidemic started, and whence it spread through carelessness of the civilian authorities to the rest of Eastern Macedonia. The typhus was brought in by Greek refugees returning by

GROUP OF PHYSICIANS WHO CONDUCTED THE KEVALLA ANTI-TYPHUS CAMPAIGN. DRS. BINGER, CLARK AND HODGSON, AMERICANS, ARE IN THE GROUP.

boat from Varna in Bulgaria. They were at first incompletely quarantined, and when we reached Kavalla at the beginning of March many scores of new cases were being found, and at that time some 300 cases were collected in a large American tobacco warehouse. Soon proper measures were instituted, much like those already described at Serres. Incidentally we protected the orderlies at the hospital and at the delousing plants by having some "louse proof" gowns made for them. Though inadequate, chiefly because of the ignorance and carelessness of the Greek soldiers, they were better than nothing.

Kavalla is a picturesque sea coast town, the Neapolis of ancient days when Paul the Apostle sailed over from Troy on his way to Philippi. The old Turkish section is built on a rocky promontory jutting out into the blue Ægean Sea. Behind it lies the more modern section on the slopes of the coastal mountain range. Off to sea, southward, loom the mountains of Thasos, fifteen or twenty miles away, and far in the distance, to the southwest, rises the snow-capped peak of Mount Athos of monastery fame. On the crest of the promontory of Kavalla are the ruins of the Venetian fortress, and leading to it from the hillside opposite is the old aqueduct embellished by the Turks who governed all this country of Eastern Macedonia for centuries and until as recently as 1913. Throughout the more modern section of the town are many tobacco warehouses, largely American, belonging to familiar American tobacco companies. We were fortunate enough to live in one of the warehouses, the top floor of which had been beautifully furnished. Not the least prized article of furniture was a bath tub, a rare object in that part of the world. The best Turkish tobacco is raised on the plains over the mountains from Kavalla and is brought into town by caravans. From Kavalla it is shipped to America and Western Europe. The harbor of Kavalla needs much improvement—at present it is little more than a roadstead. With the enormously valuable tobacco trade before the war, and with the modern improvements planned for harbor and railroad to this point from the hinterland, the future of Kavalla looms up greatly. But there must be peace. Already a very important step in advance has been taken by the establishment of a good new one-hundred bed hospital at Kavalla, which has been almost completely equipped by the American Red Cross.

The population of Kavalla before the war was about 40,000; now it is 20,000 (12,000 Greeks, 6,000 Turks, and 2,000 Jews). In 1914 it was a flourishing, clean and prosperous town, but now it is barely recovering from its nightmare of Bulgar occupation, with its starvation, disease, and atrocities. It is estimated that 16,000 of the inhabitants died of starvation during the war. Back in 1916 the Bulgar troops swooped down upon it after the ignominious surrender by King Constantine of the Greek forts at Rupel Pass, and it was here that the 25,000 Greek soldiers were cornered by the Bulgars and exiled in Germany till the end of the war, first as guests and then as prisoners of war, when finally Greece formally entered the war. The typhus epidemic kept us in Kavalla about 5 weeks.

DRAMA.

Back about 35 kilometers from Kavalla in the country north of the coastal range lies Drama, a picturesque town of about 30,000 people, slightly more than half Turkish. During the war Drama was the Bulgar headquarters and as such received visits from the British airmen. Typhus never seemed to get so much a hold here in this epidemic as it did in the other two large towns. Probably this can be explained by the immunity conferred by the occurrence of a very severe epidemic of exanthematic typhus in Drama during the Bulgarian occupation. The old city physician, a Greek who had stayed on his job and had weathered the war, told me that there had been 6,000 cases of typhus in Drama in 1917, with 2,000 deaths, out of a population of about 20,000. The Bulgars had called on the Germans for help, and some well-known German physicians came down and organized the anti-typhus campaign. We found traces of their apparently efficient work in their numbers of the sections of the town on the walls of the houses. Ten days stay in Drama sufficed for our investigation and report to the surgeon-general, an average of less than one new

case of typhus being found daily. However, we did discover that the civilians sick with other diseases than typhus were being wretchedly cared for, temporarily in a dirty building, while the civilian hospital was being used for the typhus. We were of service in correcting this insanitary condition.

Finally a word as to the other parts of Eastern Macedonia. Scattered over

the country and tucked away here and there in the mountains are many small towns and villages. Rodolevos on Mt. Pangheion, and Demir-Hissar at the southern end of Rupel Pass are two of the largest of these towns. Generally the health in these places is fairly good, though life is very primitive and sanitation hardly exists. Of course, along the Struma Valley there is much malaria, and the villages there are mostly wretched little settlements, many of them merely groups of low mud huts with thatched roofs. Some of the villages are Greek, some are wholly Turkish, and in some the natives speak only Bulgarian. Midway along the bad road between Kavalla and Drama lies Philippi, once one of the great cities of Greece and of the Roman Empire, and now completely deserted, but a few stones marking the site of the ruins. Westward from the ruins of Philippi stretches the plain for miles to the Pangheion Mountain range. On the edge of this plain Brutus was defeated by Marc Antony. The western half is a swamp, where again we find malaria. Last spring an English engineer was on the scene and drawing up plans for a tunnel through the coastal mountain range. Through this tunnel is to run the all-important railroad linking the seaport Kavalla with the rich tobacco land near Drama, and also through that tunnel or a companion one will be a drain from the Philippi swamp to the sea. Draining the Philippi marsh will release many hundreds of acres of good agricultural land, as well as rid the country of a breeding place for mosquitos.

With peace, but little imagination is needed to picture the Eastern Macedonia of the future—not a perfect paradise, perhaps, but certainly far less a hell than it has been for centuries.

In conclusion, let me pay tribute to the whole-hearted work of the American nurses who served with us in Eastern Macedonia for the American Red Cross, and to the delightful spirit with which the Greek military authorities made fruitful our coöperation with them. It was a happy experience which will long remain in our memories.

Note. For reference I would recommend two small books:

"Malaria in Macedonia." By P. Armand, Delille, G. Paisseau, P. Abrami, and Henri Lemaire. Preface by Professor Laveran. Translated by J. D. Rolleston and edited with a preface by Sir Ronald Ross, Mil. Med. Manual, Univ. of London Press, 1918.

"Le Typhus Exanthematique." By M. Jean-neret-Minkine. Paris, Librairie Pagot & Cie., 1915.

Note. Dr. Carl A. L. Binger took some of the photographs shown. It is with great pleasure that I acknowledge my indebtedness to him.

❖

HEALTH POSTERS OF THE NATIONAL SAFETY COUNCIL.

PREVENTIVE MEDICINE AND WAR.

Mazÿck P. Ravenel, M. D.,

(*Lieutenant-Colonel, Medical Corps, U. S. Army, 1917–1918*), *Professor of Preventive Medicine, University of Missouri, Columbia, Mo.*

Read before the Public Health Administration Section, American Public Health Association, at New Orleans, La., October 28, 1919.

Enthusiastically received at New Orleans this paper merits careful attention. Dr. Ravenel asserts that the young man in the army was a greater health risk than the same man in civil life. The large-roomed barrack must go, and also unpreparedness, military and civil. The woful showing of draft rejections is a form of civil unpreparedness that must be amended. : : : : : : : : : :

Preventive Medicine and War.

IT has long been recognized that the microbial diseases inflict greater losses on armies than the bullets and shrapnel of the foe. In the Crimean War the French lost more than 75,000 men by disease, while only 10,240 fell in battle, and about the same number succumbed later to wounds. In our Civil War 97,000 were killed against 184,000 who died of disease. In the Spanish-American War disease proved fourteen times more fatal than battle. Such instances could be multiplied.

It is yet too early to give final figures for the Great War, but the drafting and training periods, during which preventive medicine had its golden opportunity, have passed, and the results to date bear much of interest as well as profit. The proper evaluation of many measures has been made difficult by untoward circumstances and the exigencies of military necessity. A machine should be strong enough to do the heaviest work required, —a bridge stable enough to bear the heaviest load and still have a margin of safety. It is not entirely just to compare preventive medicine to such material things in which the strength of elements used in construction as well as the loads

and stresses can be accurately measured and provided for. It is fair, however, to expect that it should be able to meet the requirements of any emergency. This paper is an attempt to review its successes and failures in the American Army, 1917–1918.

During the war the United States has raised and trained the greatest army in its history. Never before has there been such an opportunity to study the efficacy of our modern methods on such numbers of men. The drafting is now over, intensive training is past, and we can take account of what has been accomplished. Demobilization has its problems for the sanitarian which are of somewhat different character and can be considered later.

We know from past experience that the gathering together of large bodies of men means an increase in epidemic disease and also the death rate. Our own experience in the Spanish-American War is too recent for us to have forgotten. During a draft men are gathered in large numbers from every part of the country and sent to camps where they at once enter a mode of living entirely new to them. If epidemic diseases are prevalent in any of the localities from which the men are

22

drawn, carriers or cases in the incubative stage will almost certainly be brought in. The men in camps live in a closer relation to their fellows, and in more crowded quarters than most of them have ever known before. The close contact is more continuous than in any walk of civil life. The result will be affected by the extent of the area from which the men are drawn, and by their susceptibility to the diseases existing in those areas. The men exposed for perhaps the first time to diseases not prevalent in their home district will be more susceptible than others, and the death rate will probably be higher.

In the assembling and training of our Army the urgent necessity for haste brought about the neglect or over-ruling of some well considered measures, which doubtless added to our sick and death rates. It had been foreseen that the respiratory diseases would be those most to be feared, and in the designs for barracks 45 square feet of floor space and 500 cubic feet of air space had been insisted upon. However, many of the camps were occupied before completion, and in practically all of them there was overcrowding for considerable periods,— coupled with shortage of clothing and blankets. Without doubt these conditions increased the ravages of the respiratory diseases.

As an example of the overcrowding, the plans of the Quartermaster General's office called for barracks which allowed only 338 cubic feet per man. The rooms were large, and were occupied by as high as 140 men closely packed together. The newer barracks are planned to house not more than 34 men per room, and the rooms are not connected.

In the tent camps, the conditions were not much better. The War Department planned to put 12 men to a tent, the number to be decreased to 9 as more

tents became available. Most of these tents were 16 feet square, though some of the round tents were in use, and these gave even less space. Five men per tent gave approximately 50 square feet of floor space per man, and it was recommended that this number be the limit, but it was often impossible to carry this out owing to shortage of tents. The result was bad. When combined with lack of clothing and bedding, the men huddled together in the vain effort to keep warm, while ventilation was cut off as far as possible.

The physical examinations were done on a scale much larger than most of the examiners had ever seen before, and the military necessity was such that the examiners were often required to make more examinations in a given time than they could accomplish with proper care. Especially in the early days the examinations were done under extreme pressure, in unsuitable buildings or tents, and by a hastily assembled and frequently changing personnel. It goes without saying that under these conditions there were failures to detect men with diseases or defects which should have caused their rejection. While these conditions probably led to some increase in the sick rate the work of the medical officers was well done under trying circumstances, and the profession has good reason to be proud of the record it has made.

TYPHOID FEVER.

The intestinal diseases have always played a large part in the sickness and death rate of armies. Our own experience in the Spanish-American War when we had 20,738 cases of typhoid is too recent to have escaped our memory. The typhoid rate was 141 per 1,000 and the death rate 14 per 1,000. If this rate had prevailed in the present war there would have been 141,000 cases and 14,000 deaths for each million men. Between September 1, 1917, and April 18, 1919, there were in the United States 447 cases of typhoid and 45 of para-typhoid, with 50 deaths. In the American Expeditionary Force between October 18, 1917, and April 11, 1919, there were 1,410 cases of typhoid, and 270 cases of para-typhoid, with 154 deaths. Most of these cases have occurred since July 1, 1918. It appears that each heavy offensive gave a number of typhoid cases, 300 being attributed to the Argonne alone.

Vaccination against typhoid, the value of which was shown by Sir Almroth Wright, was introduced into our Army in 1909 as a voluntary measure, but made compulsory in 1911. Until recently a watery suspension of the typhoid germ alone was used, given in three injections. When our troops were sent to the Mexican Border, para-typhoids A and B were also given, at first separately, but since August, 1917, combined with the typhoid as a triple vaccine. This has now been replaced by the lipo-vaccine, in which the three are combined in oil, and given in one injection instead of the three at first required for the typhoid as well as the para-typhoid, making six in all, which were a tax alike on the time and endurance of the men.*

The practical elimination of typhoid from the Army has been considered one of the great triumphs of preventive medicine. While the figures just given are somewhat disappointing at first sight, it is evident that there is no reason for discouragement to be found in them. Among the troops in this country typhoid has fallen to an almost negligible figure. In Europe, our men have been exposed to the extremes of fatigue, and it has been

---

* Further studies on lipo-vaccines have thrown doubt on their advantages over salt suspensions, and they have fallen into disfavor. The Army Medical School has returned to the use of salt solution as a vehicle.

impossible to carry out sanitary measures to the full. All of our soldiers were supposed to have had the anti-typhoid vaccination, which has proved so wonderfully successful, but in some the immunity has been broken down by the conditions of life or massive infection, or both, and there is evidence that of the cases occurring in France up to July, 1918, many had escaped vaccination.

MEASLES.

Measles has always been the bug-bear of the sanitarian. Its prevalence is apparently uninfluenced by those sanitary measures which have proved so efficient in the control of many other diseases. The prevalent ideas of its harmlessness make preventive measures difficult to carry out in civil life. While its chief importance has usually been considered to lie in the great number of men incapacitated, and the consequent loss of time, during this war it has frequently preceded pneumonia in a number of the camps, apparently bearing the relation of cause to effect. Pneumonia following measles is very fatal, running to 45 per cent mortality. During the first year of the war, on account of the serious complications and sequelæ, it proved the most important of all diseases. The germ is unknown. It is believed to be generally spread by the secretions of the upper respiratory tract, and to be received through the same channels. In spite of a few statements to the contrary we have not yet been able to control the spread of measles to any extent. It is doubtful if any of the measures taken lessened the incidence of measles to any appreciable degree. No vaccine is possible until more is known about the causative organism. In this disease preventive medicine works without the best guides, and the best that can be said is that it has not achieved any marked success.

THE PNEUMONIAS.

Pneumonia has always exacted a large toll from armies. During the present war it has proven the preëminent medical problem, having been responsible for at least 65 per cent of all deaths in the Army in this country during 1917.

Primary lobar pneumonia of all single diseases caused the greatest number of deaths. Broncho-pneumonia was by far the most frequent complication of measles and influenza. Taking these into consideration the pneumonias have been far in the lead of all other diseases as causes of death.

The writer once heard Sir William Osler say that he doubted if we cured any more cases of pneumonia today than were cured in the days of Hippocrates. This was said about 1905. He would probably not be willing to repeat this statement today, though all must recognize the insufficiency of most of the curative measures proposed and practiced. Going no further back than our Civil War, fifty-six years ago, we find that the case mortality for 1917–1918 has been reduced from that period by about one-fourth. It must be borne in mind, however, that differentiation and diagnosis are more exact today, the term "inflammation of the lungs" covering those cases during the Civil War which are referred to now as pneumonia.

A comparison of the admission rate for the first six months of the Civil War with that of the present war, shows that for the same number of soldiers there were 1,471 more admissions for pneumonia in that war than this. Correct and entirely comparable figures cannot be obtained at this time, and at best the comparison will not be exact. It appears, however, that we have made some progress in the prevention of pneumonia along sanitary lines.

Prevention by protective inoculation has been markedly successful where tried. The pneumonias are now classified both anatomically and according to the causative organism. Type IV still baffles us, but a vaccine against Types I, II, and III is available and has been used with marked success. Lister in South Africa seems to have been the first to prove the efficacy of vaccine against pneumonia. At Camp Upton a saline vaccine of Types I, II, and III was given to 12,519 men, approximately 40 per cent of the camp strength. Among the vaccinated no case of pneumonia of Types I, II, and III were seen during ten weeks of observation, while among the unvaccinated there were 26 cases of these types. Considering pneumonia of all types, 17 cases were seen in the vaccinated against 173 in the unvaccinated.

At Camp Wheeler, 13,460 men, approximately 80 per cent of the strength, were vaccinated with lipo-vaccine. During the time the men were under observation following the vaccination, there were 32 cases of pneumonia, Types I, II, and III, among the vaccinated (80 per cent), and 42 cases among the unvaccinated (20 per cent).

Of all types of pneumonia there were 363 among the vaccinated and 327 among the unvaccinated. In other words the incidence was about the same in the two groups, but the vaccinated group represented 80 per cent and the unvaccinated only 20 per cent of the total. The most striking results are obtained in seasoned men, among whom the pneumonia incidence was almost seven times as great in the unvaccinated as in the vaccinated.

The death rate appears also to have been very favorably influenced. Of 155 cases of pneumonia (all types) in vaccinated men the death rate was 12.2 per cent, while for 327 cases in unvaccinated men it was 22.3 per cent. In primary

fresh in the memory of everyone. It will always be a notable event in medical annals, comparable to the historical plagues of the past, which we are in the habit of connecting with the dark ages of medicine. Beginning at Camp Devens, Ayer, Mass., on or about September 7, though not reported as epidemic until the 16th, it spread with explosive rapidity over the entire country, in civil communities and camps alike. From September 12 to 30 inclusive, 31 camps were invaded. The percentage of troops attacked varied largely without apparent reason, running in Camp Cody to 49.8 per cent and in 21 camps to above 20 per cent. The proportion of cases which developed pneumonia, as well as the death rate from pneumonia, varied greatly for reasons equally not apparent. The variations are too great to be accounted for by difference in diagnosis, though this possibly is a partial explanation. Several camps which reported extremely low pneumonia rates had excessively high death rates from pneumonia,—one going to 89.9 per cent. Camp Sherman, which had a very high pneumonia rate, also had an excessively high death rate from pneumonia. No rule is of general application.

From September 1, 1917, to March 28, 1919, for troops in America, and October 18, 1917, to March 28, for those in France, there were reported 1,384 deaths from influenza and 39,493 from pneumonia. In the United States between September 21, 1918, and April 25, 1919, there were reported 350,666 cases of influenza. For the same period there were 65,076 cases of pneumonia, 22,102 deaths from pneumonia, 1,184 deaths from influenza, and 145 deaths from empyema. More exact figures will not be available for several months, but it can be said positively that the great majority of these deaths were the result of influenza. They are enough

surely to demonstrate the ravages of this epidemic, and our lack of control over it.

In reviewing the epidemic we may well ask whether or not preventive measures had any influence. Some of us who were in camps which fared comparatively well like to believe that we did lessen the spread of the disease and save lives. I have been convinced that in Camp Kearny, for example, the rapidity of spread at least was controlled, obviating the necessity of any emergency measures, and insuring the best care to each case. In many camps all efforts at control seemed to be entirely without effect. A well-known epidemiologist with whom the matter was discussed said in effect, "Do not flatter yourself that what you did had any effect,—if you came out well, you played in luck,—that is all there is to it." The markedly irregular distribution of the epidemic in cities, with the apparent immunity of some areas, while the contiguous areas would be hard hit, bear out this opinion. On the other hand, the absolute exclusion of the disease from the training station on Goat Island, seems to prove the efficacy of preventive measures.

At best we must admit that no measures adopted controlled the course of the pandemic. It spread with lightning like speed, went where it listed, and ceased its ravages only when available material was exhausted. If any preventive measures prevailed they were local. We must confess that on the whole we made a dismal failure in our attempts to control the spread of influenza.

In spite of the fact that the causative organism is not positively known, many eminent men believing that it is entirely unknown, bacterial vaccines have flooded the country,—most of them built up on the shot-gun prescription plan. Inexact observations without control have convinced some men of their value. Never has the fallacy of "post hoc, ergo propter hoc" been more strikingly shown. When tried under exact conditions in which equal numbers of persons living under the same conditions and subject to the same exposures have been vaccinated, even those most exploited have failed utterly. A famous physician in discussing new and popular remedies once said: "Be sure to use them while they are still doing good." Some manufacturers will continue to exploit these vaccines, and some physicians will continue to use them, but in general they will cease to do good.

For the pneumonia which has been the chief, if not the only cause of death in influenza, the lipo-vaccine mentioned in speaking of pneumonia affords an efficacious preventive.

INSECT BORNE DISEASES.

In this country malarial fever is the only strictly insect-borne disease to which our troops have been exposed. Many of the men have come from malarial districts in which both human carriers as well as the mosquito host abounded. The Malarial Register of the Army makes it possible to keep track of patients and to insure continuous treatment,—which cannot be done in civil life. By draining, oiling, screening and other anti-malarial measures, both in the camps and in the extra-cantonment zones, the malarial fevers have been reduced to a minimum and their spread controlled.

In 1861–1865 nothing was known of the relation of the Anopheles mosquito to malarial fever. Comparing the first six months of the Civil War, July–December, 1861, with the same months of 1917, we had only one case of malarial fever for every 93 in 1861. Since there is no vaccine against malarial fever, this result is due almost entirely to sanitary measures.

Typhoid fever and the intestinal diseases, diarrhœa and dysentery, are also considered, in part at least, as insect borne. The reduction in typhoid has already been pointed out.

Dysentery and diarrhœa have also been greatly reduced. Again using the first six months of the Civil War for comparison the incidence of these diseases has been as 1 to 22. This has been brought about by good water supplies, sewer systems, the proper disposal of excreta and persistent anti-fly campaigns.

Typhus fever, and the newly worked out disease known as trench fever, both transmitted by the louse, have not been prevalent in the American armies.

Diseases borne by insects, and especially those in which a host relationship exists between the insect and the causative parasite are particularly susceptible of control, and give preventive medicine some of its most brilliant conquests.

DISCUSSION.

Even under the disadvantages of assembling in a short time a huge army, for which inadequate provisions in housing, clothing and bedding had been made, the results show a marked advance over those of the Civil and Spanish-American Wars. While the Army was being assembled the medical personnel was also in process of formation, made up of men drawn from civil life to most of whom the handling of large bodies of men was new, and whose training had been directed toward the treatment and care of the sick rather than to the great questions of prevention. The medical corps of the Regular Army was small, and with very few exceptions the officers had never been called on to deal with problems of a magnitude at all approaching those which constantly presented themselves. Most of the failures and shortcomings were due not so much to faulty principles as to the difficulty or impossibility of applying those principles in practice under existing conditions. Some of these difficulties are inherent to the assembling of large bodies of men on an emergency call,—some are capable of betterment.

Comparison of the Army morbidity and mortality rate with that of the same age period in civil life is not encouraging on the whole. Typhoid fever, diarrhœa, dysentery, smallpox and malaria have been almost banished from the Army. Some other diseases are much less common in the Army largely because of exclusion by the physical examinations on entrance,—such as tuberculosis, cancer, epilepsy, and diseases of the heart and circulation. Against these there are a number of acute contagious diseases which were much more common among soldiers, and which our present methods of assembling, travel, examinations and housing tend to increase. Among these are measles, meningitis, pneumonia,—broncho and lobar,—scarlet fever, and influenza. In other words we have not been able to control those diseases spread by the secretions of the respiratory tract, and which probably invade the body through the same channels. In this fact lies the greatest weakness of the Army defense against disease and death by disease. This group had caused more than 75 of the deaths from disease even before influenza became epidemic. When final figures are available the comparative importance of these diseases, and also our failure to control them, will be even more clearly shown.

One fact stands out,—that the young man entering the Army, although he belongs to a physically select class, is in much greater danger of illness and death than the man of the same age in civil life. The large roomed barrack must go.

It is difficult to leave this subject without a protest against the American habits of promiscuous spitting, and of using saliva as a universal moistener, and also of the general neglect to cover the mouth

and nose when coughing or sneezing. There is literally no limit to the promiscuous interchange of spit in our daily intercourse with our fellow men.

In barracks, mess halls, during religious services as well as entertainments, even those held in the open air, there is constant coughing and sneezing, a constant projection of sputum spray from which it is impossible to escape.

Habits acquired in civil life are carried into the camp, where their evil effects are given full sway by the close contact in barracks, tents, mess halls, theatres and other buildings where numbers collect together.

Two facts of interest have been brought out clearly,—first, the greater susceptibility of the rural man to the contagious diseases such as measles, mumps, scarlet fever, and the pneumonias; and second, the southern man over the northern to the acute respiratory infections.

The first may be explained by immunity established in early life through having had the so-called diseases of childhood, or by a resistance acquired through prolonged exposure to the bacteria of crowds.

The greater susceptibility of southern men may be explained partly by the fact that they are largely rural, and partly by lowering influences such as endemic malaria and hook-worm,—though the facts are not made entirely clear by these explanations.

Data based on 1,325,000 men liable to pneumonia, indicate that the susceptibility to both the lobar and bronchial forms is greatest in those born in the warm states, and encamped in warm states, and next in those born in cold states and encamped in cold states, while those moved from warm to cold or cold to warm suffered less.

The full significance of these and other observations is not entirely clear at present, though it is obvious that they should be taken into consideration in future mobilization, especially if they are confirmed by further study.

Those outstanding defects already mentioned,—insufficient clothing, bedding, barracks and tentage, with consequent overcrowding and discomfort are more or less inevitable when an emergency arises requiring a large army in a short time,—though let it be hoped that never again will this country be influenced by pacifists or be found in such a woeful state of unpreparedness as in 1917.

Some measures which were potent in spreading infections could be avoided, such as the constant movement of troops between camps,—often from those known to be infected. Men known to have been exposed were often sent to other camps,—and without proper notice to the receiving camp. At Camp Kearny, on one occasion, of a comparatively small contingent, eight men were sent direct from the train to the hospital, and four more within a few hours. A new camp had to be pitched to care for this infected lot of men. Two days later a letter arrived from the sending camp which stated that the men had been exposed to contagious disease before leaving. Many similar instances have been reported. Indeed it has been suspected that undesirables were purposely gotten rid of in this way.

Contact is the greatest factor in the spread of acute infections, and individual resistance the chief factor in restricting their ravages. Our efforts must then be directed to limiting the one and building up the other.

Among the measures which are obvious and capable of enforcement two may be mentioned: (1) better machinery available to local boards, as well as at the camps, for the detection of carriers, incipient or mild cases, and their exclusion from troop trains and camps; (2) well isolated detention camps for the reception of all recruits, and contingents from other camps where possible exposure is suspected. A third measure, which it seems could readily be enforced except perhaps in pressing emergencies, is the assembling of men in small groups not exceeding 100, in cities and towns. Here they would discard civilian clothes and receive clean uniforms, after physical examination, baths and barbering. Here also prophylactic inoculations would be administered and the first training given. Later the men could be assembled in larger groups for transportation to the training camps. The additional cost would be compensated for in lives saved.

It is too much to hope, however, that disease will be excluded from camps. Intercourse with the civil communities is necessary, and some infection will be brought in in spite of all we can do.

This opens up the tremendous question of public health in general. The draft has made it possible for the first time to ascertain the physical condition of young men throughout the country. Of 5,719,-152 men, 21 to 31 years of age examined, 1,680,175 or 29.35 per cent were found unfit for military duty on account of physical defects. A certain number of these were considered remediable, or had been remediable in their incipiency. Other countries engaged in the war have had like experiences, which they have realized much more keenly than ourselves, owing to their greater losses and more urgent need of man power. The Premier of England has recently said that but for the loss of the physically unfit one million more men could have been put in the field and the war won in shorter time. England has learned by bitter experience the value of conserving the health and virility of her young men, and the Premier puts it well in saying, "You cannot maintain an A1 Empire with a C3 population." What is true for England is equally true for America. The war did not last long enough to make serious inroads on our man power, and we have not yet fully learned our lesson. We cannot maintain an A1 country unless our population rates A1.

A study of the causes for rejection shows that some of the principal ones belong to the preventable class, or were remediable in early life. Those having the largest numbers of rejections charged to them are:

Bones and joints	12.35
Developmental defects (height, weight, chest measurements, muscles)	8.37
Eyes	10.65
Heart and blood vessels	13.07
Hernia	6.04
Mental deficiency	5.24
Nervous and mental diseases	5.07
Tuberculosis	9.55

Several points stand out clearly from this table. First is the need of better care of babies and children, as shown by the large number of developmental defects. Supervision of the health during this period of life must be intensive. Attention must be given to nutrition and proper feeding methods be taught. No breeder of fine stock would be content with the hap-hazard methods of selecting and preparing foods which prevail in the vast majority of our homes. Physical training should be begun early, not with the object of producing prize-winning athletes, but of bringing about the symmetrical development of the body, and inculcating a love of exercise and sport.

The school period requires particular attention. Medical inspection of schools will be the means of detecting and remedying many defects, including those of the eyes which were the cause of so many rejections.

Defects of the heart and blood vessels led as causes for rejection.

It is well known that syphilis exercises a predominant influence in causing disease of the blood vessels, and the large number of rejections for these defects points to the necessity of vigorous anti-venereal measures.

It is now too late to influence the percentage of mental defectives in this generation, or to lessen the number of those showing nervous and mental disorders, but if the next and succeeding generations are to be improved in these respects, preventive work must be begun at once.

Of the communicable diseases, tuberculosis stands alone as a cause for rejection, though without doubt some of the other causes given were secondary to the contagious diseases of childhood

The control of contagious diseases is a great problem. Our experience with measles and influenza shows how helpless we are before many of them, and the public must experience a change of heart before it will submit to preventive measures which involve much inconvenience, —even when death is in full view as a penalty for failure. Our greatest hope in such diseases apparently lies in the discovery of vaccines for immunization. The more general use of those already known should be constantly encouraged.

When we come to consider ways and means of accomplishing our object, education stands first. Every legitimate means should be employed, such as lectures, newspaper and magazine articles, moving picture shows, posters, exhibits, etc. The school-teachers of the country are awake and excellent work is being done by them. Already a change in the public attitude can be seen, not yet, however, reflected as it should be in the actions of our law-makers, though here also, notable advance is evident in many instances. Under the able guidance of its present chief, our Public Health Service has gained greatly in power and influence, and in funds for carrying on its good work. A notable program has been outlined, which should be supported strongly in every state.

Surely the facts demonstrate convincingly the necessity of far reaching measures for the betterment of conditions throughout the country and the education of the general public in the fundamentals of hygiene and good living. In this the medical profession must take the lead. It has required a world crisis to awaken the public, and effort must be continuous to keep it awake. Not yet has the lesson reached been taken to heart by our lawmakers. If America is to continue to hold first place, the words of Lord Beaconsfield must be our slogan: "The public health is the foundation on which reposes the happiness of the people and the power of a country. The care of the public health is the first duty of a statesman."

◈

Mental and Nervous Changes Resulting from Malnutrition.—The medical officers of the Department of Sanitation and Public Health, Civil Affairs, Advanced General Headquarters, while studying the physical changes occurring in the school children of Trier, Germany, due to malnutrition caused by war conditions, encountered so many complaints from teachers and school officials concerning the great mental deterioration of the children, that it was decided to supplement the physical examination by a psychiatric study. This study was restricted to the children of the Volksschulen, numbering about 6,500 between five and one half and fourteen years of age. The chief conclusions and findings of the study are as follows: (1) At least 40 per cent of the children in the Volksschulen of Trier, are suffering from malnutrition to such a degree as to cause a loss of nervous energy. (2) There has been no increase in the percentage of cases normally found of neuroses, psychoses, abnormal "nervousness," organic nervous diseases, tics or conduct disorders. (3) There has been an increase of the number of border line defective totaling not more than one per cent of the total school population. (4) There has been no increase in the percentage of speech defects, especially stuttering, normally found; but there has been a marked increase in poor, lisping, slurring speech due to the retardation or interference of the fine coördinations necessary for good speech, caused by malnutrition. (5) The percentage of children failing to pass their grades has increased from an average of 8 per cent in pre-war years to 15 per cent in 1917 and 1918. It is estimated about half of this 7 per cent increase in retardation has been due to malnutrition, the other half has been due to war conditions. (6) There has been a lowering of the whole standard of school work caused chiefly by malnutrition but partly by war conditions in general; half of the children who in pre-war times did superior work now do average work, and the percentage of children who do inferior work has been increased from 20 to more than 30 per cent. (7) The specific changes noted in the children caused by malnutrition are: (a) lack of nervous and physical energy; (b) inattention during school hours; (c) poor and slow comprehension for school tasks; (d) poor memory for school work; (e) general nervous restlessness while in school. (8) Children of good nervous stock of superior or good average intelligence can withstand malnutrition of even a serious degree extending over more than two years without any impairment of the intelligence or any definite emotional change; a lack of nervous energy is about all the change that occurs. Children of poor nervous stock with poor or inferior intelligence suffer a general and sometimes a permanent lowering of the whole intelligence level from even a moderate degree of malnutrition.—S. Blanton, *Mental Hygiene,* July, 1919, 343. (*D. G.*)

AN EXPERIMENTAL STUDY OF THE EFFICACY OF GAUZE FACE MASKS.

W. H. KELLOGG, M. D.,

Secretary and Executive Officer, California State Board of Health,

AND

MISS GRACE MACMILLAN,

Bacteriologist in the State Hygienic Laboratory.

Masks have not been proved efficient enough to warrant compulsory application for the checking of epidemics, according to Dr. Kellogg, who has conducted a painstaking investigation with gauzes. This investigation is scientific in character, omitting no one of the necessary factors. It ought to settle the much argued question of masks for the public. : : : : : : : : : : : : : : : :

THE recent epidemic of influenza brought forcibly to attention the use of the gauze mask as a protection against infection. The supposition that influenza is a droplet-borne infection suggested to many the idea of controlling its spread by requiring the wearing of face masks, and accordingly the measure was adopted in many towns and cities, principally in California. Unfortunately for the rational application of such a measure little was known of the requirements for the proper making of a gauze mask, although during the year 1918 four or five articles on the protective value of masks had appeared. One of these by Weaver* detailed his experiences in diminishing infections among the nursing staff at the Durand Hospital by the use of masks of two layers of gauze (quality not mentioned). The incidence of scarlet fever and of the carriage of diphtheria seemed to be markedly lessened, although the results are somewhat diminished in value by the fact that the experiment was not a controlled one; comparisons were made between two periods of time, during one of which the mask was used and during the other it was not.

Capps* at Camp Grant tried the mask to prevent infection in ambulances and among patients while temporarily outside of cubicles. He gives no information as to the quality of gauze or number of layers and no figures or specific comparisons, and his conclusions are, that after masking, no cases of scarlet fever appeared in the wards whereas there had been just before a series of six consecutive cases. Haller and Caldwell† conducted some bacteriological experiments to determine the protective value of different layers and meshes of gauze. They found that 300 strands to the inch (the sum of the warp and the woof multiplied by the number of layers) were necessary, when worn by the person coughing in the experiment, to stop the planting of colonies on agar plates, and that 220 strands were sufficient when placed over the plate instead of over the mouth of the cougher. They gave no detailed tables of their experiments, and took no account of the possible leakage around the edge of the mask, which occurs in actual practice, nor of the influence of aspiration of droplet-laden

* Weaver, The Value of the Face Mask and Other Measures. Jour. A. M. A., Jan. 12, 1918.

* Joseph A. Capps, The Face Mask in Control of Contagious Diseases. Jour. A. M. A., March 30, 1918.

† David A. Haller and Raymond C. Caldwell, The Protective Quality of Gauze Face Masks. Jour. A. M. A., Oct. 12, 1918.

air through the gauze. Doust and Lyon* also reported on some bacteriological experiments in which they used *Bacillus prodigiosus* in the mouth of the cougher. They found that colonies passed easily through ten layers of coarse and also of medium gauze, but not through three layers of butter cloth. Their results do not agree with those of Haller and Caldwell, who found that seven layers of medium gauze "gave complete protection." Masking of plates was not reported on.

If we grant that influenza is a droplet-borne infection, it would appear that the wearing of masks was a procedure based on sound reasoning and that results should be expected from their application.

Studies made in the Department of Morbidity Statistics of the California State Board of Health did not show any influence of the mask on the spread of influenza in those cities where it was compulsorily applied, and the Board was, therefore, compelled to adopt a policy of mask encouragement, but not of mask compulsion. Masks were made compulsory only under certain circumstances of known contact with the disease and it was left to individual communities to decide whether or not the masks should be universally worn.

The reason for this apparent failure of the mask was a subject for speculation among epidemiologists, for it had long been the belief of many of us that droplet-borne infections should be easily controlled in this manner. The failure of the mask was a source of disappointment, for the first experiment in San Francisco was watched with interest with the expectation that if it proved feasible to enforce the regulation the desired result would be achieved. The reverse proved true. The

masks, contrary to expectation, were worn cheerfully and universally, and also, contrary to expectation of what should follow under such circumstances, no effect on the epidemic curve was to be seen. Something was plainly wrong with our hypotheses.

We felt inclined to explain the failure of the mask by faults in its application rather than by any basic error in the theory of its use. Consequently, *Bulletin No. 31** of the Board of Health brought out the fact that where it was sought to control influenza by compulsory wearing of masks certain obstacles developed. These were:

First, the large number of improperly made masks that were used.

Second, faulty wearing of masks, which included the use of masks that were too small, the covering of only the nose or only the mouth, smoking while wearing, etc.

Third, wearing masks at improper times. When applied compulsorily masks were universally worn in public, on the streets, in automobiles, etc., where they were not needed, but where arrest would follow if not worn, and they were very generally laid aside when the wearer was no longer subject to observation by the police, such as in private offices and small gatherings of all kinds. This type of gathering with the attendant social intercourse between friends, and office associates seems to afford particular facility for the transfer of the virus. If, as seems probable, the virus is droplet-borne, this form of contact, where people are conversing with one another, would, of course, be much more dangerous than crowd association of strangers, even under the circumstances of gathering in churches and theatres. We were not satisfied, however, with this seemingly perfectly satis-

* Brewster C. Doust and Arthur Bates Lyon, Face Masks in Infection of the Respiratory Tract. Jour. A. M. A., Oct. 12, 1918.

* Influenza—A Study of Measures Adopted for the Control of the Epidemic. W. H. Kellogg, M.D.,

factory explanation. We felt it to be imperative, if the mask were not to be permanently discredited, that more definite information be obtained concerning its uses and limitations. If, as we believed, the gauze mask is useful as a protection against certain infections, it would be unfortunate if its uncontrolled application in influenza should result in prejudicing critical and scientific minds against it. That there was danger of this is evidenced by many letters received from prominent sanitarians all over the country. It was, therefore, determined to carry out a set of experiments that should demonstrate finally just what type of mask should be used against droplet-borne infections, and what measure of protection could be expected through their use.

It is the object of this paper to set forth these experiments, and it is believed that they are fairly complete, so far as it is possible by laboratory methods alone to arrive at a conclusion. It will remain for future controlled experiments in contagious disease hospitals to dispose of such questions as conjunctival entry of virus, hand infection, etc.

All previous laboratory experiments with which we are familiar have overlooked certain conditions in the practical application of masks which might have an important bearing on the true facts. It occurred to us that the mere settling by gravity of micro-organisms through layers of gauze stretched over petri plates did not simulate at all the natural conditions of forcible aspiration through the gauze that obtains during inhalation by a masked individual.

Another possible source of error which it was desired to investigate was the possibility of droplet laden air passing around the edges of a mask and then entering the nostrils without filtration. A long series of preliminary experiments

was necessary, much of which will be passed over without description as being of little interest, although of extreme importance as a foundation for the later decisive operations.

The first procedure that occurred to us, as it has to others, was the inoculation of plates, both covered with gauze and uncovered, by coughing over them at various distances. It was soon determined that an artificial enrichment of the secretions was necessary, and this was secured by spraying the mouth and throat of the cougher with a suspension of *Bacillus prodigiosus*. It was also decided, after many tests, to abandon the inoculation by coughing, as it was found that no degree of uniformity could be maintained. The counts varied enormously from one moment to another. Consequently, controls were rendered of less value and an undesirable variation was shown between individual experiments.

For the purpose of imitating, as closely as possible, natural conditions of forcible suction through the gauze, an arrangement was constructed from a glass dish $2\frac{1}{2}$ inches deep and $4\frac{3}{4}$ inches in diameter with ground edges and having for a cover a glass plate having a round groove ground on one face to fit tightly the edge

FIGURE 1.

of the dish. In use, this cover, sealed on with paraffine, served as the bottom of the apparatus, and a 1½-inch hole was bored through the bottom, now the top, of the covered dish. (See Fig. 1.) A small hole, one-half inch in diameter, was bored through the side of the dish for the attachment of a suction tube. Petri plates were placed, uncovered, inside this jar and supported on large corks, which are plainly shown in the illustration, opposite the large hole which could be masked or not, as desired.

In the earlier experiments straight and curved funnels for the attachment of gauze masks were inserted in the large opening of these jars, but later these were abandoned and the gauze placed directly over the opening in the jar. In the use of these funnels, which are shown attached to the jar in Fig. 2, it was noted that there .is a great diminution in the number of bacteria passing through them on the gentle suction current as compared to the number entering directly through the hole over the open plate. The reduction was more marked with the curved funnel than with the straight one, suggesting that possibly a tube with several bends would, if breathed through, check the passage of bacteria as well as a close gauze filter.

EXPERIMENT NO. I.

First set. No mask on cougher.

Location of plate	Colonies, 48 hours room temperature
Inside jar under straight funnel...	21
Inside jar under curved funnel....	5
Outside front...	137
Outside right side...............	98
Outside left side...............	47
Outside back.................	79

Second set. Cougher masked.	
Inside jar under straight funnel...	9
Inside jar under curved funnel....	3
Outside front..................	11
Outside right side...............	16
Outside left side...............	11
Outside back.................	19

The preceding table is an example of the results obtained with the apparatus placed four feet in front of the cougher, who was masked with six layers of 40 by 17 mesh gauze in one experiment and not masked in the other. Besides one plate under each funnel, a curved and a straight one, which were not masked, four plates were placed entirely outside in a vertical

FIGURE 2.

position, one in front of, one behind, and one on each side of the jar.

After numerous other experiments, it was decided that the coughing process was too variable and uncertain, and various types of atomizers were tried, both with compressed air with various pressures and with the ordinary rubber bulb. Example of results:

EXPERIMENT NO. II.

DeVilbiss atomizer No. 15.

Saline suspension of 48-hour culture of *Bacillus prodigiosus*.

Plates in jars.

Vacuum pump, attached to jars instead of having assistant inhale through the tube as previously done.

	Distance from atomizer		
	1 ft.	2 ft.	3 ft.
Without mask...............	5,280	31	0
Mask, 6 layers, 20 by 17......	1,380	20	..

In the following experiment a suspension of B. *prodigiosus* in light paraffine oil was used in attempting to get more uniform counts in the controls, which, with the use of saline spray, were frequently too thickly planted to be easily counted:

	Distance from atomizer		
	3 ft.	4 ft.	5 ft.
Plates outside jar..........	2,676	2,704	2,976
Plates inside jar..........	663	831	1,260

EXPERIMENT NO. III.

Mask made of gauze having 20 woof and 17 warp threads to the square inch—6 layers.
Atomizer—DeVilbiss No. 15.
Pressure—From compressed air pipe, about 40 pounds pressure.
Culture—B. *prodigiosus* 48-hour growth suspended in paraffine oil, sprayed at plates for 30 seconds allowing 4½ minutes for the droplets to settle.
Incubation—24 hours, 37° C.

	Distance from atomizer					
	3 ft.	4 ft.	5 ft.	6 ft.	7 ft.	8 ft.
No mask	12,000*	10,000*	6,756	4,548	3,372	3,120
Mask, 6 layers..	1,566	1,050	816	562	426	384
Mask, 5 layers..	1,314	1,248	624	222	282	174
Mask, 4 layers..	5,596	2,976	1,692	1,290	846	576
Mask, 3 layers..	10,560	7,360	4,248	3,504	2,472	1,378

* Number estimated.

Many details of these experiments are unrecorded in this article as being of little interest, essential facts only being presented.

As illustrating these omissions we would mention a long series of experiments to find the proper air pressure to use and the time of exposure, and those experiments leading up to the rejection of atomizers of the nebulizing type, such as DeVilbiss No. 49. As an illustration one of the final experiments for determining distances and pressure is given.

EXPERIMENT NO. IV.

Filtered oil suspension of 48-hour culture of B. *prodigiosus*.
Pressure—43 pounds.
Atomizer—DeVilbiss No. 15.
Time—just turning on and off, allowing 5 minutes for settling.
Spray comparable to a sneeze.
Suction pump attached to each jar during spray and settling time.
Rate of suction gauged to correspond as nearly as possible to normal rate of inspiration.
No gauze over opening in jar.

EXPERIMENT NO. V.

Same as Experiment No. IV, but with gauze having a mesh of 24 by 18 threads to the square inch over the inlet to the jars.
Number of layers—6.
Distance from atomizer—5 feet.

	Colonies
Control plates outside of suction jars......	4,764
Control plates inside jars, no gauze.... ...	2,468
2 layers of gauze...:...............	1,830
3 layers of gauze....................	1,280
4 layers of gauze...................	544
5 layers of gauze................ • ..	674
6 layers of gauze................•.....	369
7 layers of gauze...................	454
8 layers of gauze...................	63
9 layers of gauze...................	42

EXPERIMENT NO. VI.

Same as preceding, but allowing exposure of three minutes instead of five.

Distance from atomizer—4 feet	Colonies
Control plates outside of suction jars	2,694
Control plates inside of suction jars.......	409
2 layers of gauze.....................	358
3 layers of gauze.....................	420
4 layers of gauze.....................	344
5 layers of gauze.....................	338
6 layers of gauze.....................	294
7 layers of gauze.....................	184
8 layers of gauze.....................	167

EXPERIMENT NO. VII.

Filtered oil suspension—48-hour culture of B. *prodigiosus*.
Pressure—43 pounds.
Atomizer—DeVilbiss No. 15.
Time—Just turning cock on and off allowing 5 minutes for settling.
Suction—25 pounds on jars during spray and time for settling.
Gauze—42 by 44 threads to the square inch.

	Distance from atomizer	
	4 ft.	5½ ft.
No gauze.....................	366	421
Outside plates (no suction)......	4,400	5,280
2 layers of gauze..............	329	684
3 layers of gauze..............	391	699
4 layers of gauze..............	251	372
5 layers of gauze..............	114	264
6 layers of gauze..............	12	22
7 layers of gauze..............	4	7
8 layers of gauze..............	5	4
9 layers of gauze..............	9	12

EXPERIMENT NO. VIII.

Same as preceding, but allowing three minutes for settling instead of five.

	Distance from atomizer	
	4 ft.	5½ ft.
No gauze......................	211	127
Outside plates (no suction)......	3,594	1,836
2 layers of gauze...............	50	20
3 layers of gauze...............	29	8
4 layers of gauze...............	20	18
5 layers of gauze...............	25	13
6 layers of gauze...............	0	0
7 layers of gauze...............	0	1
8 layers of gauze...............	0	0
9 layers of gauze...............	1	0

EXPERIMENT NO. IX.

Filtered oil suspension—48-hour culture of *B. prodigiosus.*

Pressure—43 pounds.
Atomizer—DeVilbiss No. 15.
Time—Just turning cock on and off, allowing 5 minutes for settling.
Suction on jars during spray and time for settling.
Gauze—60 by 72 threads to square inch.

	Distance from atomizer	
	4 ft.	5½ ft.
No gauze......................	871	172
Outside plates (no suction)......	4,572	5,724
1 layer of gauze...............	1,771	1,110
2 layers of gauze...............	897	250
3 layers of gauze...............	133	127
4 layers of gauze...............	26	12
5 layers of gauze...............	18	14
6 layers of gauze...............	35	7
7 layers of gauze...............	21	6
8 layers of gauze...............	25	8
9 layers of gauze...............	17	4

It was noted from a study of experiments V and VI that gauze of medium texture, namely 24 by 28 threads, has no notable restraining effect up to eight layers, agreeing with Doust and Lyon's experience that ten layers of medium gauze were penetrated in their coughing experiments. Experiments VII, VIII and IX are of more importance as they deal with fine and extra fine gauze (butter cloth). Haller and Caldwell found that a total of 220 strands (warp plus woof times layers) to the inch practically stopped the passage of organisms when applied over petri plates, and Doust and Lyon concluded that three layers of butter cloth would filter *B. prodigiosus.*

They do not give the mesh of this butter cloth, but presumably it corresponded to the 42 by 44 thread gauze in our experiments Nos. VII and VIII, in which we found that with the element of aspiration introduced, as in the natural use of masks, even five layers did not give a sufficient reduction in count to make such a mask of value. Furthermore, our experiment No. IX in which the very best and finest cloth of 60 by 72 strands to the inch was used, demonstrated that under the natural conditions of aspiration of droplet-laden air through the mask, four layers, which would be extremely difficult to breathe through, are required to obtain a degree of filtration which would hold out any hope of useful result in practice.

The following series of experiments were to determine the possibility of the passage of droplet-laden air around the edges of a close mask instead of through it, and also to simulate other physical conditions attending the wearing of the mask. In these experiments artificial noses of paraffine were made for the purpose of securing the closest approach possible to the natural physical conditions of the wearing of masks by persons. Figure 3 illustrates these artificial noses which are attached to the glass jars, within which are placed the petri plates immediately behind the passages through the paraffine.

Various combinations with the models

FIGURE 3.

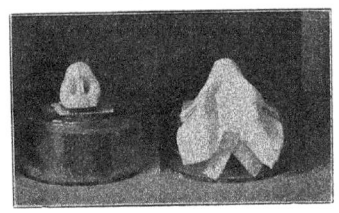

were tried. In experiment No. X a nose without nostrils was used in addition to the regular one, for the purpose of establishing the leakage around the edges of the mask. The tabulation of results shows the restraining influence of the nasal passages as the counts are larger where the air passes directly into the aspiration jar instead of by way of the nasal passage. Another outstanding fea-

EXPERIMENT NO. X.

Filtered oil suspension—48-hour culture of B. prodigiosus.
Pressure—43 pounds.
Atomizer—DeVilbiss No. 15.
Time—Just turning cock on and off allowing 3 minutes for settling.
Suction during spray and time for settling.
Gauze—60 by 72 threads to the square inch.
Large jar—two holes—one covered by wax nose with nostrils; other open with wax nose without nostrils just above hole.
Distance from atomizer—5 feet.
Jar standing vertically.

Layers of gauze	No nostrils	Nostrils
No gauze	762	150
Outside plate	2,630	
5 layers	54	15
6 layers	81	20
7 layers	35	13
8 layers	18	15
9 layers	12	9 patch
10 layers	3	8

ture of this test is that there is little difference in results obtained with different layers within the range of the number that would be acceptable from a standpoint of comfort.

Experiment No. XI (see Fig. 4 and Table I), was conducted with different types of gauze and varying numbers of layers. An inspection of the table of results in Set 1 shows that an increase of efficiency was noted with the increase of the number of layers and that the results were better in column C where the air was required to pass through the mask and no opportunity existed for passing around the edges, as was the case in column A where the mask was placed over the nose. The difference, however, was not very material showing that the

EXPERIMENT NO. XI.

Filtered oil suspension—48-hour culture of B. prodigiosus.
Pressure—43 pounds.
Atomizer—DeVilbiss No. 15.
Time—Just turning cock on and off allowing three minutes for settling.
Gauze—60 by 72 threads to the square inch in Set 1 and 24 by 28 in Set 2.
Distance from atomizer—5 feet.
Suction on all jars during spray and time for settling.
All jars standing vertically.

TABLE I·

EXPERIMENT No. XI.

	A	B		C	D		E
	Masked nose	Unmasked nose	Per cent of Efficiency	Gauze over jar—no leakage around edges	Open plate	Per cent of Efficiency	Outside of jar
Set 1—Gauze 60 x 72 threads to square inch.							
9 layers of gauze	0	10	100	0	200	100	1,000
8 layers of gauze	1	56	98	1	73	98.7	1,122
7 layers of gauze	37	160	77	64	183	70	1,265
6 layers of gauze	35	154	77	5	117	95	1,230
5 layers of gauze	127	300	57	109	407	70	1,260
Set 2—Gauze 24 x 28 threads to square inch.							
10 layers of gauze	39	654	94	34	992	96	1,776
9 layers of gauze	42	790	94	240	1,716	86	1,980
8 layers of gauze	patches						
8 layers of gauze	296	681	56	190	684	72	2,042
7 layers of gauze	450	1,980	77	189	1,440	86	Too many to count
6 layers of gauze	666	1,089	38	466	695	32	2,690

FIGURE 4.

A. Hole in top of jar covered by wax nose with nostrils and gauze mask.
B. Hole in top of jar covered by wax nose with nostrils. No mask.
C. Hole in top of jar covered by gauze mask attached by adhesive.
D. Hole in top of jar, not covered.
E. Plate outside of jar—no mask.

principal source of lack of efficiency is in the forceful aspiration of air through the mask. This table also shows that five layers of this extremely fine gauze, which would be impossible of comfortable use, gave an efficiency of only 57 per cent.

CONCLUSIONS.

1. Gauze masks exercise a certain amount of restraining influence on the number of bacteria-laden droplets possible of inhalation.

2. This influence is modified by the number of layers and fineness of mesh of the gauze.

3. When a sufficient degree of density in the mask is used to exercise a useful filtering influence, breathing is difficult and leakage takes place around the edge of the mask.

4. This leakage around the edges of the mask and the forcible aspiration of droplet laden air through the mask is sufficient to make the possible reduction in dosage of infection not more than 50 per cent effective.

5. It remains for future controlled experiments in contagious disease hospitals to determine whether the wearing of masks of such texture as to be reasonably comfortable are effective in diminishing the incidence of infection.

6. Masks have not been demonstrated to have a degree of efficiency that would warrant their compulsory application for the checking of epidemics.

◆

A STUDY OF THE TOXICITY OF DIPHTHERIA BACILLI ISOLATED FROM IMMEDIATE CONTACTS.

Frank W. Hachtel, M. D., and Mary Shedwick Bailey, M. D.,

Health Department, Baltimore, Md.

The members of the community at large are not often sources of diphtheria infection and we must look elsewhere to find the factors of greatest danger. School children do not furnish the source of infection. These investigators point to convalescents and contacts as being the probable distributors of the virulent bacilli. : : : : :

THE relation of the carrier of the diphtheria bacillus to the spread of this disease has been the object of much research, and the percentage of true diphtheria bacilli, both from the standpoint of morphology and of virulence has been determined in several distinct groups of the population.

The percentage of morphologically true diphtheria bacilli has been studied by the Massachusetts State Board of Health,[1] which found that 3 per cent of persons not known to have been exposed to infection harbored morphologically true diphtheria bacilli, while the organisms were present in from 8 to 50 per cent of those exposed to diphtheria. Park[2] found that 9.7 per cent of 330 healthy persons showed morphological diphtheria bacilli but only 2 per cent of these were virulent.

The percentage of persons in the general population harboring morphologically true diphtheria bacilli (classified according to Westbrook's types) was also studied by Goldberger, Williams and Hachtel[3] during the winter of 1913 and 1914 in Detroit. For nearly a year prior to the commencement of this investigation diphtheria had been unusually prevalent in Detroit, but the percentage of cases markedly decreased about three weeks before the collection of cultures began, so that the investigation really resolved itself into a study of the diphtheria carriers at large in a typical population shortly after a time of increased prevalence of the disease. They made cultures from a representative portion of the population, cultures from the nose and throat of 4,093 healthy persons being examined; 38, or 0.928 per cent, were found to harbor morphologically true diphtheria bacilli. Nineteen pure cultures of the diphtheria bacillus were isolated and 2 of these were found to be toxic. This would suggest that a very small percentage of the general population are carriers of virulent diphtheria bacilli; in this particular instance only about 1 in 10,000 persons were potential sources of diphtheria infection when thrown in contact with non-infected persons. This work indicates that the members of the community at large are not often sources of infection and that we must look elsewhere in order to find where the greatest danger lies.

The school children form the most natural group to select since they are of the most susceptible age and large numbers are in close contact for several hours each day. Moss[4] made a single throat culture of 1,217 public school children in Baltimore and found that 44, or 3.61 per cent, showed morphologically true diphtheria bacilli. The diphtheria bacillus was isolated pure from the cultures of 33 of these children and only 6, or 18.18 per cent, of these were found virulent. In other words approximately 0.49 per cent of these school children contained virulent diphtheria bacilli in their throats.

It would seem, therefore, we must look still further for the greatest source of danger, and our search leads us to two distinct sources, namely, the convalescent and the contact carrier. It has been proved that the diphtheria bacillus obtained from the convalescent remains virulent in a large majority of cases up to the time this organism disappears from the throat. Thus, Weaver[5] has studied the persistence of virulence in 36 patients with clinical diphtheria and has found the diphtheria bacillus toxic in all stages of the disease and well into convalescence. The cultures studied were isolated at periods ranging from the 1st to the 38th day from the onset of the disease.

This work emphasizes the danger from the patient and convalescent. Turning next to immediate contacts we might logically expect that they also would harbor virulent diphtheria bacilli in no small percentage of cases. Nuttall and Graham Smith[6] have shown that in 688 contacts 36.6 per cent contained morphologically true diphtheria bacilli. These included members of the infected families, special groups of persons attending to the sick, and relatives of the sick who may not have lived in the same house.

During the past five years our throat inspectors in Baltimore have made cultures in 7,831 instances in infected households and we have found morphologically typical diphtheria bacilli in 642 or 8.19 per cent of the cultures. In 2,775 cases during the years 1914 and 1915 the throats were not examined until the house was ready for disinfection and only one throat and no nose cultures were taken. During these years we obtained 144 or 5.18 per cent of positive results. During the years 1916, 1917 and 1918 the throat inspectors or the nurses have taken nasal and throat cultures from the entire household just after the disease is reported; thus the contacts were detected soon after the disease developed. During these years 499 or 9.86 per cent of positive results were obtained.

Over a period of several years some 100 pure cultures of morphological *B. Diphtheriæ* were isolated at the department from as many different contacts and these were all tested for toxicity. One of these was a pure culture of C[1] and the others mainly mixtures of C, A, and D and occasionally A.[1] In a trifle less than $^1/_5$ of the cases the intradermal method was used, in the rest the subcutaneous inoculation of 2 cc. of a 48-72 hour broth culture into the guinea pig. In all the experiments antitoxin controls were used; in those few instances where the control guinea pig died the experiments were repeated with smaller quantities of the culture. Of the 100 cultures 97 proved toxic.

The animals dying after subcutaneous inoculation were autopsied and showed the typical local lesion, enlargement of the regional lymph nodes, and marked congestion of the adrenals in all cases; fluid in the peritoneum and pleuræ, congestion of the lungs and fatty change in the liver and kidneys in most instances, and gastric ulcer in 2.5 per cent. Cultures were made at necropsy and the diphtheria bacillus was isolated from the local lesion in all but never from the blood or the organs.

Some 50 of these cultures were inoculated into dextrose and sucrose-broth and their action on these sugars determined by titration. All of these organisms formed acid from dextrose but only one acted upon sucrose; this, however, was found to be a toxic diphtheria bacillus.

In summary, 97 per cent of the morphological B. diphthe:iæ isolated from contacts were toxic for guinea pigs, and 100 per cent of the virulent organisms produced acid from dextrose, and only 2 per cent produced acid from sucrose.

Considering the high percentage of toxic organisms isolated from convalescents and contacts it is reasonable to believe these are the main sources of infection.

The authors express their appreciation of the aid and advice of Dr. William Royal Stokes.

LITERATURE.

[1] Rep. of Mass. Assn. Bd. of Heal., July, 1902.
[2] Park's Path. Bact. and Prot.
[3] Bull. No. 101, Hyg. Lab., Wash., Aug., 1915, p. 29.
[4] Transac. 15th Internat. Cong. on Hyg. & Dem., Vol. 4, part 1, p. 156, Sept. 23, 1912.
[5] Jour. Infect. Dis., Vol. 20, 1917, p. 125.
[6] Bact. of Diph., 1908, p. 186.

◆

Plan of Treatment of Tuberculosis.—The first essential unit is the dispensary, which must be connected in intimate working relationship with the practitioner, hospital, and sanatorium. The function of the dispensary is to serve as a centre for diagnosis, treatment, observation and dissemination of knowledge with regard to preventive treatment. The second unit of the scheme is the hospital for the treatment and segregation of acute and advanced cases of tuberculosis. The sanatorium is the next unit, and with which should be combined facilities for the industrial training of patients. The domiciliary or home treatment of tuberculosis is of great importance in relation to prevention. If a high standard of domiciliary treatment is to be attained, two conditions must be fulfilled—there must be an adequate and efficient medical and nursing service, and there must be satisfactory home conditions. Provision of open air schools is an essential unit in the scheme. An important supplementary factor is after-care. Included in the scheme of after-care there must be an employment bureau to assist patients who are able to work and who are unemployed, or unsuitably employed, to find suitable occupation.

These various component parts of the scheme of treatment will not, however, solve the problem of tuberculosis unless they are supplemented and reinforced by scientific investigation and by a scheme of prevention. From the preventive aspect there is need for immediate action in four main directions: (1) The provision of an adequate supply of food, including fats, at reasonable prices; (2) The abolition of insanitary houses and the raising of the hygienic standard in the home especially with regard to ventilation and cleanliness; (3) the segregation of advanced cases of the disease, and (4) the provision of a milk supply free from tubercle bacilli.—Thomson, H. H., Jour. of State Med., Oct., 1919, 297. (D. G.)

So important is the sanitary privy in national and local public health that the A. P. H. A. devoted almost a full session at New Orleans to a symposium by half a dozen practical men, national authorities, who contributed each one a short, pithy story. The *Journal* presents here the first group, papers by Dr. Lumsden and Dr. Stiles, with others reserved for future issues. : : : : : : : : : :

THE PRIVY AS A PUBLIC HEALTH PROBLEM.

L. L. LUMSDEN,

Surgeon, U. S. Public Health Service, Washington, D. C.

Read before Section of Public Health Administration, American Public Health Association, at New Orleans, October 27, 1919.

THE problem of excreta disposal is as old as protoplasm. No living matter can thrive for a long while under conditions exposing it to high-concentration pollution with the waste-products given off by it in the course of its physiological processes. Even the lowest forms of life—the bacteria—under such conditions soon die. To keep alive the cultures of bacteria in our laboratories we have to transplant them from time to time into a fresh, unpolluted environment.

Among the higher representatives of animal life generally, cleanliness is instinctive. Our cattle, if enabled to do so, get away from their excretions or filth. Even the hog when given a fair chance keeps clean. And the cat is a very model of sanitation. The case of what we are pleased to call the highest form of life, that of the human being, is, however, remarkably exceptional. In this representative of creation human intelligence enters as a complicating factor.

Human intelligence according to its degree uses or abuses natural opportunity. It enables us to fly through the air, to possess the surface and the deeper reaches of the land, to travel over and under the seas—and to have dominion over the earth. Human intelligence, being finite, is apt at times to become overwhelmed with its range of opportunities, lose its perspective and concentrate upon doing the less important things, or even things which are contrary to animal instinct and opposed to natural law. In frequent instances we hazard our health, our happiness and our lives to make or to save a dollar or to indulge briefly that "tired feeling" which is so common with those who are exposed to pollution with their intestinal excretions. The dollar saved or made at such risk will do but little in these days and the tendency to indulge the "tired feeling" may be eliminated for better things by a dose of thymol.

CLEANLY DISPOSAL OF HUMAN EXCRETA ESSENTIAL TO HUMAN HEALTH.

Human intelligence has determined that certain diseases—such as typhoid fever, the dysenteries and uncinariasis —which are still highly prevalent in the United States, are caused solely by our insanitary habits in the disposal of the excretions from our kidneys and intestines. The principles of cleanliness applying to the disposal of such waste-matter seem inseparable from the elementary principles of decent living. Every person fit to live and every community worthy of existence is able to do or to have done the small amount of work necessary for cleanly and safe disposal of human excreta. Therefore, the continuation of insanitary practices in this respect in our communities generally is inexcusable, indefensible and difficult to understand.

Infants and some of the hopelessly insane void their excretions into their clothing. Primitive peoples in the early stages of development of human intelligence deposit their excreta on the floors of their living compartments. Many of our people in the United States even in this day of so-called enlightenment deposit their excreta on the ground or in open privies in their yards. We house-break our pet cats and dogs. It does not seem too much to expect of human intelligence to anticipate that eventually our people generally will become "yard-broke" and discontinue the now common practice of depositing their excreta in a dangerous and disgusting manner on and in the ground within a few feet of their kitchen doors and their sources of water-supply.

NEED OF SANITARY DISPOSAL.

Partly for esthetics and comfort and in some instances partly for health protection the larger cities of the United States have made within the last half century fair progress in the application of sanitary measures for the disposal of human excreta. In our smaller cities, towns and rural districts comprising about 70 per cent of our population, however, such progress as yet has been wofully lacking. In the course of extensive surveys conducted within the last few years by the U. S. Public Health Service in coöperation with state and local health departments it was found

that at less than 2 per cent of the country homes in our average rural community is sanitary disposal of human excreta practiced adequately and consistently.

ADVANTAGES OF SANITARY DISPOSAL.

Due to the neglect of sanitary measures for the disposal of human excreta there are in our country every year thousands of deaths, tens of thousands of cases of serious illness and hundreds of thousands of instances of lowered health tone and lessened efficiency. The economic losses incident to the definite sickness and the lowered vitality resulting from insanitary disposal amount to more in dollars and cents than would be the cost of corrective measures. Therefore, sanitary disposal of human excreta is economically advantageous. In communities in which typhoid fever and hookworm disease are highly prevalent intelligent investment for sanitary disposal of human excreta will yield as a rule a larger dividend to the community than will any other possible investment. Therefore, this phase of sanitation is relatively advantageous.

Aside from the other advantages and considered only on the grounds of common decency and the looks of things, expenditures for cleanly disposal of human excreta are more than justified.

PRACTICABILITY OF SANITARY DISPOSAL.

The practicability of sanitary disposal of human excreta, under reasonably efficient management, has been demonstrated in recent years under a wide range of conditions—social, economic and climatic—in the United States. Any community now arguing that "it can't be done" argues itself incompetent to attend to its own important business. Like every other important business the business of sanitary disposal of human excreta will not run itself. For it to be made successful it must be attended to by some one or some ones competent to manage it and conscientious in the performance of vitally important duty.

SANITARY DISPOSAL MEASURES.

In densely populated centers, such as towns and cities, insanitary practices by a few persons may menace the health and offend the senses of many. Therefore, cleanly disposal of human excreta is even more important in our towns than in our sparsely settled country districts. In the incorporated town or city, under competent governmental administration, the work can be accomplished in all instances—and by concerted individual action it can be accomplished more systematically and as a rule more economically than at isolated country homes.

Wherever practicable the installation and operation of an adequate water-carriage sewerage system should be given first consideration as the means for the disposal of human excreta. Where such installation on account of cost or of lack of water, or of other conditions is not immediately practicable, serious and pressing consideration should be given at once to other means of sanitary disposal.

In the absence of conveniently accessible toilets, as in fields or woods, the Mosaic method, than which from a strictly sanitary standpoint none is better, should be practiced consistently and conscientiously. The teaching of this method has been seriously neglected. Every child over five years of age should be taught the principles and the detailed indications of the Mosaic method. It is not difficult to interest the average child with a recital about the measures administered by Moses to safeguard the Children of Israel in their march through the wilderness.

Under no conditions of human existence is insanitary disposal of human excreta necessary for any considerable period of time. The amount of work per capita to accomplish such disposal is not reasonably objectionable. The health official or advocate should insist urgently that the continued scattering about of human excreta in a dangerous and disgusting manner for a period of even twenty-four hours in any community is intolerable.

The sanitary privy can be used advantageously in the sewerable community to meet the situation while arrangements are being made for the installation and operation of a sewerage system. For a large proportion of our rural homes the sanitary privy is as far as we reasonably can expect the people at this time to go in equipment for cleanly disposal of human excreta. No type of sanitary privy yet devised is suited to all the communities in the United States. No one type is applicable to all the conditions as a rule presented by the different homes in one community. No sanitary privy is fool-proof. None is perfect. No water-closet is perfect. No machine —plow, automobile or airplane—which has been devised by human ingenuity is perfect. But because we have not attained perfection is no valid reason for our failing to use for advantageous service the best we have.

The sanitary privy is a machine which requires particular attention. For its successful operation its constructors, its users and its supervisors must have a sanitary understanding and a sanitary conscience. Without competent business-like management in the supervision and the scavenging of the privies a public sanitary privy system will fail. A reasonable degree of official supervision over privies is highly indicated to keep sanitary the privies which are constructed on sanitary principles. The scavenger engaged to clean privies should be given to understand that he is engaged in arduous and disagreeable but vitally important life-saving service as is the cultured refined woman who as nurse attends to a patient bedridden with typhoid fever. The rural dweller who does the work on his own place should be given to understand that upon the care with which he attends to the disposal system at his home depends to an important degree the health and lives of the members of his family.

All interested in the conservation of our national resources should give thought to the potential economic value of human excreta as a fertilizer of land and also seriously consider ways and means to prevent continuance of the dangerous and wide-spread soil pollution which causes annually a serious waste of our most important national resource—our human health.

CONCLUSION.

The health official should be highly intolerant about uncleanly disposal of human excreta in his community. He should insist upon the immediate adoption of measures for the correction of grossly faulty conditions. He should carry out a constructive policy for the installation and operation of the best disposal system which his community can afford. He should remember that in the two or more years often necessary for a successful campaign for a complete sewerage system a sanitary privy system, even when far from perfect, will prevent sickness and save lives and help develop public sentiment for a sewerage system. If he cannot persuade the people whom he serves to do what he thinks good he should endeavor persistently and hopefully to get them to do the best possible. In short, he should hold to his faith, use common-sense and be practical.

PRACTICAL TYPES OF SANITARY PRIVIES.

C. W. STILES,

U. S. Public Health Service, Washington, D. C.

Read before Section of Public Health Administration, American Public Health Association, at New Orleans, October 27, 1919.

YOUR program committee has placed two adjectives in the subject assigned to me, namely, "practical" and "sanitary." These words require definition.

From the standpoint of the average person involved, the word "practical" means that: (1) the original installation must cost little or nothing; (2) the privy must require no upkeep; (3) it must require no cleaning; (4) it must be without undue odor; and (5) must be "fool proof."

From the viewpoint of the health officer, a privy to be practical must be one: (1) which he can induce landlords to install; (2) which must be in keeping with the pocket-book of the poor; (3) which must not inhibit subsequent adoption of a sewer system; (4) which must be within his budget to administer; (5) which must not make too many enemies in the population; (6) which must not raise too much political antagonism; (7) which must last as long as required; and (8) for which he can obtain labor if it requires scavenging.

From the standpoint of the cautious biologist, either bacteriologist or zoölogist, a privy to be "sanitary" must be one which he is willing to recommend and for which he is willing to assume reasonable responsibility as to the spread of disease. More specifically: (1) it must protect the water supply; and (2) it must be structurally inaccessible to animals, including mammals, birds, reptiles, mollusks, and arthropods.

To harmonize all of these requirements in a single type of privy is theoretically and practically an impossibility. Accordingly, my first conclusion is that we must make up our minds to recommend certain types of privies and to admit or tolerate certain other types, according to local conditions, which are not within our control. It might, therefore, be wise to speak of "*sanitary*" *privies to be recommended*, "*improved*" *privies to be permitted*, and "*temporary*" *privies to be tolerated*.

Further, I must conclude that in selecting the types to be *recommended, permitted*, or *tolerated*, we must place the premises upon which our selections are based far back of the privy itself and we must study: (1) the mentality and characteristics of the community; (2) the permanent possibility of regular and efficient inspection; (3) the permanent availability of efficient labor for scavenging; (4) the density of the population; (5) the climate; and (6) the geological formation, with the fauna and flora.

The purpose of this preliminary study may be summarized in two statements: (1) It is unreasonable to expect a poor and ignorant negro laborer to install as good a privy as we can expect an educated white man to provide for his family; and (2) our fundamental purpose is to improve existing sanitation as rapidly as circumstances will permit, and this purpose can be realized only by an evolution, not by a revolution.

In this connection let us not inhibit results by overlooking the fact that this world is governed by three things, namely, principle, policy, and price. Any health officer who overlooks this fact will spend more of his time defending himself against attacks than he spends in constructive public health work. We must be leaders, not drivers.

The Atlanta conference, considering construction alone, classified privies as follows:

	Per Cent
(1) Water-tight construction, namely prevention of soil-pollution	25
(2) Construction, proof against Vertebrates	25
(3) Fly-proof construction	25
(4) Lack of exposure of contents, as in cleaning or moving	25

Under this plan, the following maximal ratings may be given to privies:

Types	Per Cent
B to A.....LRS system (including its many modifications)	75 to 100
B to A.....Chemical systems	75 to 100
B ....Pail system, without chemicals	75
C to B.....Vault systems, with scavenging	50 to 75
C.........Pit system	50
C........."Umbrella" pit-system, temporary	50
D.........Surface, closed in back	25
E.........Surface, open in back	10
F.........Absence of privy	0

When we consider that practically 50 per cent of all farm homes in the South have no privy at all, it is possible to form some conception of the campaign we face. When we recall that approximately one-third of the inhabitants of the South are negroes, I believe you will agree with me that we can save time if we do not aspire to attain an average of 100 per cent within the next decade; conversely, when we recall that approximately two-thirds of the population are white, I hope you will accept the thesis that we should not be content with the general adoption of the minimum standard which we can induce the average negro to install. In other words, in privy campaigns I believe in presenting various types, in urging high ideals, in encouraging the people to do the best they can, and by steady follow-up work, in helping the people to evolve from zero per cent sanitation through any necessary stages to at least 75 per cent sanitation.

By elimination, we all agree that the Type F, or zero per cent, sanitation must go, and that we cannot either recommend or permit Type E (or 10 per cent) and Type D (25 per cent) privies in towns. Practically, however, we shall have to tolerate Types E and D in backward counties for some years to come.

The "umbrella" privy of Type C (namely, a pit system without a house) is not usable in wet weather, except for "squatters," is ephemeral in character, and so far as I can see is of practical value only as a purely temporary structure for use in exceptional instances, such as in construction work in more or less out of the way localities, or among people of distinctly primitive civilization.

The pit system with a house has been the subject of much misunderstanding and controversy. Technically it is a cesspool which leaks on five surfaces. Practically, with its possible maximum rating of 50 per cent, it is a stupendous advance over the existing conditions with which many of us are personally familiar, namely, southern rural conditions with an average somewhere between 5 and 10 per cent; and, whether we like it or not, we must face the practical fact that this is the highest type of privy which we can hope to have installed on about half of the southern farms for one or two decades to come. With proper inspection and follow-up, it can be kept up to a 50 per cent basis; without inspection and follow-up, it deteriorates within a few months to five years to a surface privy open or closed in back, with a rating of 10 to 25 per cent. As a standard to be recommended, I condemn it. As a type

to be permitted, I recognize it as a practical necessity. I am, however, opposed, as uncompromisingly today as I was five years ago, to placing it before a community without giving to the people at the same time higher ideals. In presenting it as a permitted type in a community, I feel that the point should be made clear that it is only a step in an evolution, that it is more dangerous in regions of limestone formation, in swampy localities, in places recently cleared of timber, and on ground which is infested with crayfish or with June bugs, than it is in other non-wooded sand and clay regions; and I believe that the family should clearly understand that the health officer is not to be held responsible for any water pollution which may perchance result. Summarized, we know too little of underground biology to condemn the pit unconditionally, and we know too much of subterranean life to endorse the pit without reservations.

The vault and the pail systems (50 to 75 per cent) occupy a different position from that which they held five to ten years ago. The change in value is due to the fact that without efficient inspection, scavenging and disposal organization, these systems rapidly deteriorate to a surface system of 10 to 25 per cent value, and in considering this premise we are faced by the practical fact that labor is today scarcer, more expensive, and far less efficient than it was five to ten years back. The fundamental fact must be held constantly in mind that the success of these two systems depends upon efficient labor efficiently administered. If the choice lies between an inefficient can or vault system on the one hand, and a fairly efficient pit system on the other, my preference is distinctly on the side of the pit. I cannot concur in the view that the can and the vault systems are never feasible in rural districts, for this view is not in harmony with my experience; but this same experience leads me to maintain that health officers should insure proper inspection, proper scavenging, and proper disposal as the first step in introducing either the can or the vault. If these conditions are assured, I view both the water-tight can and the water-tight vault as systems which it is conservative and proper to recommend as practical systems of sanitary privies; without these assurances I hold that they are not systems which should be recommended. It will, however, be necessary to permit them during the period that they are serviceable, and then to condemn them as soon as they, like the pit, fall to a 10 per cent value. In summary: The can and the vault systems are dependent more upon proper labor and administration than upon any other factor; and, until some better method is discovered to utilize safely the contents of these privies, these two systems must be viewed as somewhat expensive when compared with the Pit or the LRS.

The best kinds of privies, to my mind, are the LRS and the chemical types with a theoretical maximum rating of 75 to 100 per cent. Each of these types has its advantages and its disadvantages, and neither is perfect. Both require regular inspection.

The best arrangement for both is a drainage for the contents, thus avoiding the necessity for scavenging.

The advantage of the LRS over the chemical lies in the lower cost as averaged over a period of five to ten years; its disadvantage is that it requires the addition of water once a week, and it occasionally produces an odor beyond the normal.

The advantage of the chemical system over the LRS is that it is seemingly better suited for use inside the house; its disadvantages are that it has a higher cost as averaged over a period of five to ten years, that when it is emptied there is sometimes a delay in recharging the vat with the proper chemical, and that occasionally (though apparently not often) burns result from splashing. The chemical used generally has caustic soda as its chief ingredient. In our experiments at Wilmington, Mr. Pfau has shown that a 3 per cent (namely, 30 grams per liter of excreta) kills the B. coli content within twenty-four hours. My tests show that the caustic kills the eggs of hookworms and of *Ascaris*, and the spores of *Endamoeba* and *Lamblia*, within a practical period of time. As our engineers (Mr. Crohurst and Mr. Hardenbergh) have, however, shown experimentally that the possibility of splashing, hence the theoretical possibility of burning, is a factor of perhaps greater importance than has been reported in actual practice, we have been searching for a substitute to take the place of caustic soda (NaOH). At Mr. Pfau's suggestion we have been experimenting with Sodium dichromate ($Na_2 Cr_2O_7$). While the results are not as yet absolutely complete, Mr. Pfau's tests on B. coli and my observations on the eggs of hookworms and *Ascaris* seem to indicate that under the conditions presented in our tests and in a strength of 4.0 grams to the liter of excreta, this is a practical disinfectant in some of the chemical closets in warm weather. It presents the great advantage of not burning in case of splash. While I do not hesitate to give you this preliminary information, I distinctly advise against the immediate adoption of Sodium dichromate until we test the chemical under certain additional conditions, notably in cold weather, in order to see what variations may be expected in its action, and its effect upon the duration of the vat.

Returning now to the title of my paper

as prescribed by your committee, with special emphasis on the adjectives "practical" and "sanitary," I wish to emphasize the point that no type of privy will be thoroughly practical and sanitary until a method is found whereby the enormous potential economic value latent in human excreta can be turned to actual economic account in order to reduce the expense of maintenance and administration. That we can render human excreta, as found in this country, absolutely safe to use as a fertilizer cannot be questioned, but our method is at present altogether too expensive for general practical purposes, and the ultimate money value of the product of our present method is not yet on a practical basis. We are now trying to reduce the expense and to increase the manureal value of the product, but this problem is exceedingly complicated and I cannot promise immediate results. All I can promise is that we are keeping at work on the subject.

In conclusion and in summary, I cannot emphasize too strongly that inspection, follow-up work, and better mechanical construction are factors of supreme importance in a sanitary privy system. No sporadic privy building campaign without persistent follow-up work can be expected to give satisfactory results, and no matter what type of privy is selected, it will be a disappointment unless it has efficient inspection and follow-up. Further, the LRS and the chemical closets are the privies which are the most sanitary; and of these the LRS is less expensive in the long run; the pail and the vault systems come next provided an efficient scavenging system is assured, but otherwise both of these systems are to be condemned; the pit system is distinctly inferior to the LRS and the chemical systems, but with efficient inspection and follow-up, it is a system which from practical considerations is a stupendous advance over present conditions, and, although it should be condemned for certain districts, as limestone and swampy localities, it must be permitted under certain circumstances in other localities whether we like it or not; the surface privy must go, and the sooner it is supplanted, even by a pit, preferably with a top soil bottom and not too deep, the better. Let us not, however, be content with a leaking cesspool like the pit, but let us give higher ideals to our people, whose health and lives we are trying to safeguard.

◆

Socialization of Preventive Medicine through the Public Health Nurse.—One of the great factors in preventing the spread of disease in recent times has been the public health nurse. At first, the visiting nurse was the result of philanthropy. Her force as a means of promoting health and preventing ill health was soon recognized, and her services were soon demanded in the home, the school, the factory, the dispensary, and the hospital. Her problems are not always medical. Often they are primarily social and economic. Not only must she aid the sick and the suffering, but she must educate the other members of the family in order to prevent the spread of disease. The public health nurse must be well-trained in home sanitation and personal hygiene. She should be able to give simple but effective demonstrations in household economics, and in the selection and preparation of proper foods. Not only must she have the welfare of the particular family at heart, but she must also appreciate the relationship of her work to the health protection of the community. Her work is primarily educational. She must teach the principles of healthy living on every occasion, and obtain the respect and confidence of her patients through devoted, unselfish service, through affectionate aid, and through a demonstration of the masterly knowledge of her profession.—S. J. Crumbine, M. D., *American Jour. of Nursing*, Sept., 1919. (*M. P. H.*)

THE DEVELOPMENT OF THE STATE DEPARTMENTS OF HEALTH IN RELATION TO HEALTH INSURANCE AND INDUSTRIAL HYGIENE.

AUGUSTUS B. WADSWORTH, M. D.,

Director, Division of Laboratories and Research, New York State Department of Health, Albany, N. Y.

Preventive medicine deserves a wider field than merely communicable disease. Some developments, like prevention of diseases of middle life are successful, others like health insurance have been less so. This has been hardly more than a sick-benefit movement. Industrial medicine is most valuable from the financial point of view as well as that of health. : : : : : : : : : :

PREVENTIVE medicine has developed so rapidly that it has greatly enlarged its scope in the conservation of the health of the community. In addition to its earlier activities based upon the discoveries in the new science of bacteriology which constitute the great achievements of modern sanitation, preventive medicine is now reaching out into every branch of the modern social organization.

At first, health departments were engaged in enforcing the regulations of quarantine and cleanliness, the removal of nuisances, and the protection of water supplies. Then they undertook the laboratory examination of samples of water and sewage in order to determine pollution and to devise methods of purification; and from these simple measures of preventive medicine, very largely through the development of laboratory facilities, they rapidly extended their practical usefulness.

Departments of health now reach out to protect the citizen by doing for him what he cannot do for himself in the present circumstances of life. His food and drink are safeguarded; his waste and that of his neighbor are safely disposed of. If occasion demands it, the essentials of personal hygiene and cleanliness for himself and his family are brought to his attention; public nuisances are abated for him; finally, if he lives in close contact with his neighbor, precautions are taken for him and for every member of his family as well, against the spread of diseases which are communicable. All of these things are done; and in order to do them, departments of health have developed into complex organizations with various branches which operate centrally in an administrative capacity through a field force in touch locally with the citizen and his needs.

Despite this wonderful development, preventive medicine has nevertheless progressed in a comparatively narrow field—the control of the infectious diseases. Yet these diseases usually develop as a result of predisposing conditions, the prevention of which falls within the province of public health work. The infectious diseases are but a part and, from the economic point of view, a comparatively small part of preventable human sickness and disease. The diseases of adult life, constitutional diseases resulting from cardiac, renal and digestive disorder, cancers of all kinds, the occupational diseases, both chronic and acute disturbances of function, psychic and nervous derangements, even structural deformities, and a great variety of minor illnesses, are all to an extent preventable. All these facts are now fully recognized, not only by public health officials and the medical profession, but also by every one who, whether in public or in private life, carries any responsibility. We see everywhere in the civilized world attempts to improve the conditions that vitally affect health and happiness. Dissatisfaction with the present order of things and the demand for new adjustments in the social organization are pressing for governmental action. The rights of labor and the responsibilities of capital are being developed with a rapidity that is on the one hand encouraging and on the other alarming lest gross errors be made, serious injustice be done or our resources dissipated.

The three major functions of all public health work are regulation, education, and personal or community service. Chief of these is the personal or community service which is rendered; but if this is to be made effective all three functions must be fully developed and carefully coördinated. Regulation is essential and education necessary in order to secure coöperation. Sanitary regulations must be very carefully and discreetly adapted to the situation in order to gain the confidence and coöperation of the people they are designed to serve. It is extremely difficult if not impossible to enforce regulations which the people do not fully understand; and the enforcement of these regulations is an essential part of the work of all health departments. Hence, educational work is indispensable in order to prepare the people for the necessary regulation, and thus health departments have been encouraged and even forced to make the educational phase of their work an important one.

Such educational work brings to the physicians and to the people a reliable presentation of the practical value of all the new methods that are from time to time being developed and applied. It also brings to the physician and every citizen a knowledge of what the department of health is doing, or will do, or hopes to do for him through the established agencies of preventive medicine which it has developed. The establishment of the School of Hygiene at the Johns Hopkins University and of the School of Industrial Hygiene at Harvard University are striking examples of professional interest, and the agitation for health insurance and for various sorts of social welfare work is evidence of the awakening of the public conscience.

In regard to Health Insurance:* As it has been tried in different countries it is generally recognized as a failure. It provides an unsatisfactory service for its beneficiaries, and is subject to abuses. Moreover, so far as it has been developed in other countries, notably Germany and England, it does not tend to increase the efficiency of the medical service which is rendered to its beneficiaries. Whether the physicians are selected and maintained by salary or chosen on a panel, from which the beneficiaries may in turn choose their

---

* The term "health insurance" has been used without any very critical appreciation of its precise meaning—in the sense that one may insure against loss from sickness as one insures against loss from fire. Compensation for disability and sickness, for funeral expenses in case of death, sick benefits, poor relief, and the like, all may possibly be considered to be a form of health insurance. All of these compensations might conceivably indirectly tend to conserve the public health to a limited extent, if they are advantageously administered. Certainly such compensations are wise and just and necessary if the privileges are not abused. But they have nothing to do with a larger and truer conception of health insurance that marshals all the agencies of preventive medicine to assure the public health—the health insurance the chief aim of which is to prevent disease, disability, and human suffering. Comparatively few authors make these distinctions, doubtless owing to the fact that they are not in sufficiently close touch with public health work to appreciate the significance of preventive medicine. A notable exception, however, is the discussion of the subject by Brend in his book "Health and the State." (Constable & Company, Ltd., London, 1917.)

physicians, or whether the beneficiaries are left free to choose their own physicians, health insurance does not provide for securing the more competent physicians of the community for this work. On the contrary, except in special instances, the leading men connected with hospitals and communities have not undertaken the work. In fact the health insurance has followed, to some extent, "lodge" practice and is said to perpetuate the odious features of it.

But quite apart from all these objections, health insurance is not what the term connotes. This is clearly demonstrated by the experience with it in other countries, notably England, where the laws were formulated by Lloyd George and his political adherents, and no advantage was taken of the advice or counsel of experts in public health work. Health insurance is not health insurance. It is not in any sense preventive medicine. On the contrary, it is a series of sick benefits or poor-relief, utterly inadequate and usually badly administered. And thus it has been a complete failure in England and Germany, where it has been extensively tested. It has not affected the incidence of disease, the mortality or morbidity rates, save possibly to increase the statistics of them through the abuses to which this so-called health insurance is subject. It is a fetish which has appealed to the awakened but misinformed public conscience. Legislators whose duty and responsibility it is to formulate and pass laws to meet the pressing needs of the situation will do well to heed the lessons that are to be learned from all the practical experience with health insurance; they will do well to take expert advice and counsel in deciding these difficult questions which appear plausible but which are' so beset with dangerous pitfalls; but above all will they do well if, taking a safe conservative stand, they

devote all their efforts to developing the departments of state service which are already organized and have already had practical experience in preventive medicine.

In industrial medicine, however, conditions are quite different. The large industrial organizations employ physicians who are responsible for their work and well trained in it. Hospitals, clinics, lectures, demonstrations and a factory and house nursing service are all established as occasion demands and practical results secured. The labor organizations have also caught the spirit of the times and many of them have their own corps of experts who are entering this field of preventive medicine. This is a most significant sign and confirms more forcibly than anything else the practical value of a proper organization of the work. The scope of the service of such organization in preventive medicine might very easily be greatly extended with the coöperation of the State departments of health. The medical service is thus expanded and developed to meet the needs of conditions as they arise. Efficiency is increased as the organization develops. While there has been considerable opposition to and criticism of health insurance, industrial medicine has received unqualified support from every quarter. The results that have already been obtained have so fully justified the expenditure of time and money that the capitalists of the corporation have profited financially, and the laboring man has gained substantially in health. The economic value of such work has been fully established. But this plan of industrial medicine fails to provide for the greater number of all employees who work in smaller places, and are not beneficiaries of the medical organization of the large corporations. Obviously all the people must be taken care of, and there is no provision for this at present; nor is there any immediate prospect of securing such a well-organized medical service for all of the people, save through the agency and the development of the state organizations that already exist; mainly the departments of health.

New York State has not done anything as yet which deserves special recognition in the way of industrial medicine. It has never taken the lead in this phase of public health work. One of the first attempts of the state commissioner of health to establish new methods and to develop practical service to the medical profession and the public along these lines met with discouragement from the medical profession. The purpose of it was misunderstood. Dr. Biggs proposed to establish, at different points in the state, centres from which public health activities could radiate to the surrounding community. Through these centres laboratory facilities, and counsel and advice of qualified experts would be at the service of the physicians of the district, to bring them into touch with these broader aspects of preventive medicine, and to supplement their knowledge and experience. Physicians thought that they were to be supplanted by state medicine and so opposed it, little realizing that it would have greatly strengthened their position, increased their efficiency, and safeguarded their future. Without some such aid many communities will soon be without physicians.

The New York State Department of Health is already partially organized, and could be completely organized to meet this situation. In the first instance, the State Department of Health provides a central nucleus from which educational and other necessary work can be organized and operated in the state through branch or local centres. There are now thirty or more municipal and county laboratories established in the state outside New York City. These laboratories coöperate with the central laboratory in Albany. Standard methods of making the diagnostic examinations of specimens from many of the infectious diseases have been formulated and are now very generally adopted. They are subject to inspection and control. They turn to the central laboratory of the State Department of Health in Albany whenever their problems require aid. Extension of this laboratory service to meet the developing needs of preventive medicine in a much larger field than has hitherto been attempted would not be a difficult problem. Laboratories form excellent centres from which to reach and serve physicians of a district. In any event, these local branch centres could coöperate with the physicians generally, so that a physician would always have near at hand a reliable source of counsel and advice and all the laboratory aids necessary in his work. By similarly coöperating with the institutions and hospitals of the district and also with all of the physicians engaged in industrial medicine in the district, such a centre would tend to organize the work and standardize it and increase not only their own efficiency through broader and larger experience but the efficiency of every physician in the district also. Such an organization of the health department would not in any way interfere with the practice of physicians, but it would tend to establish them in their work and to promote and increase their efficiency.

In order to accomplish the best results, however, competent experts must be induced to enter the state service. The recognition of the scope and importance of state service has been greatly extended by the experience of medical men in the Army during the war. One meets continually men of the highest education and experience returning from service in the war who have acquired a keen interest in the broader problems of public health work and preventive medicine. If adequate salaries were appropriated, the the state could easily secure the best talent; but it requires considerable additional experience in state work to appreciate the problems; and such men must specialize in the state service. Health departments, if they are to discharge properly their duties to the citizens, must maintain their work on the highest planes. They must have experts in every branch who are unquestionably competent. This means quite a different order of things than now exists. It is only in the larger universities and medical schools and hospitals that trained experts in medicine are to be found in any of the branches of practice. In these university and medical school centres the men focus their attention on the investigation of very limited fields of medicine. The full development of preventive medicine, if it is to be a part of public health work, must follow these lines of investigation, and research with a corps of trained experts in each branch of medicine in order that all educational publications may be of the highest standard and critical balance and the personal or community service that is extended to the physician may be maintained at a high standard.

Although seriously handicapped by disorganization of the staff during the war, the commissioner is deeply interested in all these problems and is fully prepared at the first opportunity to develop preventive medicine along these lines for the state of New York.

The literature upon industrial hygiene and internal medicine in their relation to public health work is scanty and fragment-
and all of it is comparatively recent.
ng the last few years, besides infor-
on on health insurance, reports have

been published upon the work that industrial and commercial establishments have organized in the way of medical care and inspection for the employees. These have usually appeared in the more popular engineering and technical journals here and abroad. But now this so-called welfare work has broadened, and the subjects of industrial hygiene, preventive medicine, and the question of a unified public health service are of paramount and present interest. The medical journals generally are beginning to devote space to editorials and notes upon industrial hygiene, and a new journal upon industrial hygiene is being published under the auspices of the Harvard Medical School which will be devoted entirely to the subject in its various aspects. Suggestive material may be found especially in the recent numbers of the United States Health Reports and the AMERICAN JOURNAL OF PUBLIC HEALTH—periodicals accessible to all—and scattered editorials and notes in the English and Canadian as well as in journals of this country. A short list of references on these subjects is appended herewith.

These are stirring times; nearly everyone is feverishly alert and in a degree apprehensively so for any eventuality. It devolves upon the medical profession everywhere, and especially upon the members of it who are engaged in preventive work, to consider carefully all public measures in whatever guise they may appear, in order to determine their true relation to the public health and to preventive medicine, and to direct all this energy into the proper channels; and especially is this the duty of all those who are actively engaged in public serving—politicians, legislators, social welfare workers, labor leaders or public health officials —who as experts in their fields mold public opinion.

REFERENCES.

American Association of Industrial Physicians and Surgeons. Annual Meeting, 1917. Reports.

Brend, Health and the State—Lond. 1918.

Blue, Rupert. Urgent public health of the nation. Am. Jour. Pub. Health. 1919, *9:* 99.

Boyce, P. H. The Medical profession as a public service for health. Pub. Health Jour. 1919, *10:* 112.

Clark, W. I. Medical supervision of factory employees. Bost. Med. and Surg. Jour. 1917, *176:* 239; Jour. Am. Med. Assn. 1917, *68: 5.*

Curram, J. F. Relation of the industrial surgeon to industry and to society. Bost. Med. and Surg. Jour. 1918, *178:* 215.

Harris, L. I. Relation of industrial hygiene to general practice. New York Med. Jour. 1918, *107:* 928.

Hoffman, F. L. Plan for the more effective federal and state health organization. Am. Jour. Pub. Health. 1919, *9:* 161, 275.

Metropolitan Life Insurance Company. Welfare work. Report for 1917.

Mock, H. E. Industrial medicine and surgery, the new specialty. Jour. Am. Med. Assn. 1917, *68:*1.

Selby, C. D. The Relation of industry to the health department. Ohio Pub. Health Jour. 1917, *8:* 66.

Stapleford, F. N. Physician as a factor in social efficiency. Pub. Health Jour. (Canada) 1918, *9:* 128.

Warren, B. S. A Unified health service. U. S. Pub. Health Reports. 1919, *34:* 377.

❖

WORK OF THE NATIONAL SAFETY COUNCIL.

The activities of the Health Service Section of the National Safety Council are chiefly educational, and include bulletins, lectures to executives, an annual meeting, and occasional special investigations.

The members of the National Safety Council employ nearly seven million workmen and women and these are reached every week by the bulletins on accident prevention and allied subjects, sent out by the Council. Every two weeks, a health bulletin is included—like those shown herewith. These are written in simple, non-technical language and illustrated wherever possible. The one on influenza was sent out at the beginning of the epidemic in 1918 and in addition to the regular distribution of 18,000 copies, more than 7,500 additional copies have been circulated. Some companies are using this same bulletin again this year. Suggestions for health bulletins have been received, and are welcomed, from the National Tuberculosis Association, The Committee for the Prevention of Blindness and other organizations.

In addition to bulletins dealing with preventive health measures, the Council issues occasional bulletins dealing with the avoidance and treatment of infection or blood poisoning which so frequently results from the neglect of slight injuries. Those bulletins are intended chiefly to impress on the minds of the workmen the serious consequences which may follow failure to report slight injuries and have them dressed at the plant hospital or first aid room.

The local chapters or local councils of the National Safety Council, in the larger cities, hold occasional meetings, and in some cases regular lecture courses, for industrial executives, safety engineers and

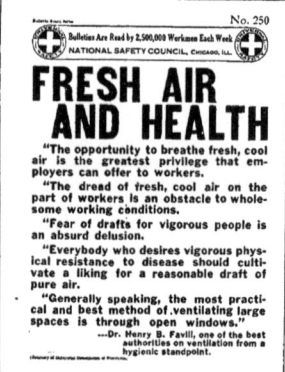

supervisors, and foremen. The regular courses given for safety supervisors and for foremen include lectures on plant sanitation and on first aid; these are generally given by a local physician, preferably a physician in touch with industry. The meetings for the higher executives frequently include address on the importance of health work in industries, by speakers such as Doctor Thad Darlington.

Probably the outstanding activity of the Health Service Section of the National Safety Council is its annual meeting, which forms a part of the Annual Safety Congress held by the Council. At the recent Congress in Cleveland, the Health Service Section conducted three half-day sessions; one of these was of a general or popular nature and was one of the general sessions of the Congress. The other two were sectional meetings attended principally by industrial physicians. The papers and discussions at these meetings, and at previous Congresses, have formed an important contribution to the literature on industrial health, medical, and surgical topics.

One of the discussions at the recent Congress

resulted in the appointment, by the section, of a special committee on industrial dermatoses consisting of: Dr. C. P. McCord of the University of Cincinnati, Dr. C. A. Lauffer of East Pittsburgh, Pa., and Dr. C. P. Schram of Beloit, Wis.

This committee is now gathering information on the extent of skin diseases or dermatoses caused by or aggravated by industrial conditions, and the nature and success of the various remedies which have been tried. The information secured will be presented in the form of a report to the section and to the members of the National Safety Council.

The general policy of the Health Service Section

of the National Safety Council is not to duplicate any of the work which is already being done by other health agencies, but simply to give to its industrial members such information and assistance as it can, in connection with their health and medical problems, making use of its favorable position of close contact with most of the largest industries of the country.

HEALTH HAZARDS OF NON-POISONOUS DUSTS—A RÉSUMÉ OF SOME RECENT INVESTIGATIONS.

EMERY R. HAYHURST, PH. D., M. D.,

Assistant Professor of Hygiene, Ohio State University; Consultant, Division of Industrial Hygiene, Ohio State Department of Health, Columbus, O.

Read before Section on Industrial Hygiene, American Public Health Association, at New Orleans, October 29, 1919.

Five million workers are subject to industrial dust hazards in this country. The risk to them may be decreased if what is becoming known is utilized. A scientific basis for estimating maximum amounts permissible is near at hand, while the body defenses are becoming better understood.

HISTORICAL.

HOFFMAN says: "The importance of dust as a factor in occupational mortality has attracted the attention of every authority on occupational diseases from Rammazini to Sir Thomas Oliver." Rice, however, in his "Historical Review of Silicosis," points out that Hippocrates, Pliny the Elder, and other ancient writers made similar observations. Renewed interest centers around several recent advances: the greater perfection of dust estimation methods; field studies in certain dusty industries; X-ray refinements; immunity studies; new estimates of personal hygiene; and the reports of much closer statistical analyses of morbidity and mortality rates.

IMPORTANCE OF THE SUBJECT.

It is probably safe to say that today over 4,000,000 males and 1,000,000 females are exposed to the industrial dust hazard in the United States. Hoffman's figures based on the 1910 census were only slightly under these estimates. These figures represent over 10 per cent of all workers.

CLASSIFICATION OF DUSTS.

From the point of view of harmfulness as generally accepted the non-poisonous dusts may be classified as follows:

(1) *Hardness.*

  (a) Flour, soot, soft wood, coal, shale, soapstone, bone, horn, shell, ivory, amorphous silica.

  (b) Iron, zinc, brass, copper, cement, chalk, lime, limestone, slag, plaster of paris.

  (c) Organic dusts, such as hard woods, vegetable fibers, hair, etc. (These usually contain admixture of inorganic materials.) Landis, in particular, questions the harmfulness of organic dusts *per se.*

  (d) Sand, granite, marble, slate, glass, ganister, flue dust, flint, chert, quartz, emery, gold, diamond, corundum and carborundum.

(2) *Density or Specific Gravity.*

It seems to be generally agreed to that the heavier particles of dust are the least harmful, probably because they settle more quickly. This should be qualified, however, in respect to fine particles which, although of high specific gravity, are capable of being air-borne for some time and distance.

(3) *Shape.*

  (a) Amorphous. Dusts of this group are probably quite innocuous.

  (b) Crystalline (angular, acicular, jagged, spined, etc.). These shapes are regarded as harmful largely on the basis of lacerating properties.

(4) *Size.*

Particles larger than ten microns in diameter, though constituting the chief reason for easy visibility, are least harmful since they are rarely found far within the respiratory passageways. When dust particles are under two microns they appear to be capable of the greatest accumulation in the lungs.

(5) *Infectious Character.*

Dusts may contain spores of disease-producing germs, and the more resisting forms of germs themselves, such as anthrax, streptococcus, diphtheria, tuberculosis. As far back as 1891 Prudden championed the causal relationship between dust in the breathing atmosphere and the spread of tuberculosis, in a tuberculous environment, and his views appear to be receiving renewed emphasis today. The worker with an open case of tuberculosis must be kept from infecting a dusty atmosphere.

(6) *Hydroscopy.*

There is no doubt that dry dust, or dust in excessively dry atmospheres, is more irritating, because of its demand for moisture in impingement upon the mucous membranes. Lowered humidity increases the number of particles while at the same time decreasing their size. Some dusts are so hydroscopic apparently as to be caustic or escharotic in action.

(7) *Chemical Composition.*

It is assumed that practically all poisonous dusts are soluble in the mucous secretions. On the other hand the non-poisonous dusts are either soluble or insoluble, the emphasis for hazard being naturally placed upon the insoluble forms.

(8) *Protein Sensitizers.*

Anaphylactic phenonema follow upon the breathing of some dusts by some individuals. Recent writers lay stress upon this point in connection with cer-tain dusts, particularly pollens but also any dusty protein matters. To these forms of dusts an immunity is frequently established in a few days and maintained thereafter throughout the period of exposure. This is probably the explanation to the immunity obtained in zinc ague—a complex due to the resorption of killed protoplasm. Landis emphasizes this explanation in the various afflictions known as "shoddy fever," "grain fever," "threshers' fever," "mill fever," etc.

(9) *Reduction of Illumination Resulting in Eye Strain, Distraction and Accidents (Albaugh).*

The above is believed to be a practical and working classification for industrial dusts. It will be observed that little attempt is made to distinguish the inorganic from the organic dusts. Practically all authorities are agreed that inorganic dusts constitute the chief hazardous group to which Mavor-gordato lays stress on the crystalline character. He found that even siliceous dusts are harmless if amorphous. As stated, it is a disputed point as to whether organic dusts are in themselves harmful, irrespective of the apparently sharp edges and contours of vegetable fiber dust, hair scales and the like.

Some other factors enter essentially into the question of the harmfulness of any dust: (1) The duration of exposure; (2) the amount of the dust inhaled per each tidal respiration; (3) the respiratory physiology of the individual, particularly as to whether the person is a nose-breather or a mouth-breather, a deep breather or a shallow breather, etc. An important association is the matter of eyesight,—near-sighted individuals getting closer to their work. Furthermore, the careless habits of the individual are important in the matter of creating an unnecessary amount of dust or of habitually placing himself in its thickest clouds. Under this head, idiosyncrasies must also be recognized,—some persons seem peculiarly susceptible to respiratory damages, some to skin or scalp afflictions, etc. It is a matter of common observation that among those exposed to the most harmful types of dust are to be found certain individuals who are singularly little affected. After all it would appear that perhaps correct personal hygiene is as big a factor in the question of immunity as any other single item, and, particularly if we include a normal atomical state of being, that is, a normal nasal construction and a normal bronchial tree. (4) Season and climate, —the general rule being that for the skin, at least, the warmer the season the greater the irritant effects. Perhaps an increase in the amount and, particularly, in the acidity of the perspiration is a factor.

STATISTICS.

"These are the bold, relentless records of death," wrote Prudden nearly thirty years ago. Nowhere do statisticians find that the inhalation of dust of any type is virtuous. The earthy dusts, such as clay, loam, lime, chalk, cement and coal, appear the least harmful, yet for cement workers, for instance, Kober points out that diseases of the respiratory organs decreased from 9.3 per cent to 3.3 per cent after installing dust prevention apparatus in certain German cement works. In a like manner many statistics have been compiled showing the decrease in the mortality rates following a decrease in the amount of dust exposure.

The tuberculosis death rates in workers in *organic* dusts, whether such dusts are in themselves harmful or not, are about the same (5.64 per thousand) as those who work in metallic dusts (5.84 per thousand), while both are excessive as compared to the normal tuberculosis death rate (2.98

per thousand) according to Sommerfeld. Lanza estimates that 30 per cent of the Joplin zinc miners have "consumption," which is not necessarily tuberculous, but for practical purposes both are the same. The reputation which soft-coal miners have had of being practically immune to tuberculosis certainly is not in accord with the evidence which my own investigations developed in a field study of coal miners in Ohio and Illinois in 1918. Several circumstances favored rather a high degree of accuracy in dealing with these coal miners' statistics. All of the coal miners, approximately 50,000 in Ohio and 90,000 in Illinois, are unionized and, in Illinois, a state-wide death insurance scheme, inaugurated in 1908, resulted in a careful inquiry by the union into the cause of each miner's death. Evidences of death in practically every one of 5,428 recorded deaths which occurred between February 1, 1912, and July 21, 1918, consist of (1) a copy of the official death certificate, (2) a written opinion rendered by the physician in attendance, and (3) a report by the secretary of the local to which the deceased miner belonged. Furthermore, the man who is once a coal miner in Illinois is, almost without exception, kept in good standing with his local because of the insurance fund until his death, irrespective of change of residence, occupation, etc. Change of occupation among coal miners is also rare. In this study, the field work at first appeared to develop the prevalent idea that the coal miner is relatively immune to tuberculosis. However, some mining physicians were found who were doubtful and others emphasized respiratory diseases in general. The actual recorded deaths of the 5,428 miners showed a rate of 99.4 per 100,000 employed, for tuberculosis, in spite of a violence rate of 398.2. They also showed a percentage rate of 14.6 as against 16.6 for occupied males in the registration area (Census, 1909) when deaths due to violence (36.8 per cent among miners) and (10.6 per cent for occupied males) were excluded from both sets of figures.

Miller and Smyth have estimated that a man may inhale from 5 to 106 grams of dust per year into his lungs depending upon its character (pottery dust, flint, steel, carpet or cement dust) and that at this rate a pound of cement dust, for instance, could reach the lungs in from five to ten years.

Infants' lungs contain no silica. Hence probably all of the silica found in lung tissues comes from the exterior. The same holds true of carbon as it darkens solutions resulting from anti-formin digestion of lung tissues. McCrae found that the native adult Zulu had 0.73 per cent of silica in dry lung tissue, whereas a worker exposed to the rock dust of the mines of South Africa accumulated as much as 4.57 per cent. Hirsch found from 0.24 per cent to 3.40 per cent of carbon by dry weight in the lungs of Chicago dwellers.

Winslow believes that he has discovered the greatest amount of dust yet reported, in the abrasive manufacturing industry, where test showed from 15 to 222 million one-fourth-standard particles per cubic foot. These figures exceed the estimates of Lanza for the dusts of the Joplin mines. It is probable, however, that the flint-mills, located in some pottery centers would show as high dust counts as any.

COMMON SOURCES OF HARMFUL DUSTS.

The common sources of harmful dusts in industry may be summarized as follows:

(1) Dry sweeping, dusting and cleaning methods.

(2) Dirt, pulverized,—brought in on materials used.

(3) Dirt floors, or dust kicked up from dirty floors.

(4) Street dirt and smoke wafted in through windows.

(5) Personal carelessness in handling dusts or performing dusty operations.

(6) Dust from the drying out of pulverized wet materials.

(7) The manufacture or mining of dusty products or substances.

(8) Cleansing and finishing operations, including polishing, grinding, and sand-blasting.

(9) False sense of security when dusts cannot be easily seen or where supposedly protective devices do not protect (Winslow et al).

BODY DEFENSES AGAINST DUST.

(1) The narrows of the air passages (nose, pharynx, glottis, bronchi, etc.). Lehmann found that from 35 to 42 per cent of fine dust, like white lead, reached the lungs in nose breathing, and as much as 80 per cent in mouth breathing.

Rivers finds that horses in coal and ganister mines has no pneumokoniosis, which he considers is due to exclusive nasal breathing. These horses also never have tuberculosis, yet the horse is very susceptible to tuberculous lung invasion, experimentally. He notes also that many human cases of pneumokoniosis and miners' phthisis are frequently associated with wide, atrophic nose conditions (useless as a filter).

(2) Impingement in mucus, by which dust is removed in spitting, coughing, sneezing, etc., the whole greatly assisted by the action of the ciliated epithelium.

(3) The toughness or resistance of the mucous and submucous tissues.

(4) The activity of phagocytes composed of leucocytes, endothelial cells, alveolar cells and plasma cells.

(5) Pigmentations. Even colorless dusts become pigmented in the lung tissues and perhaps this pigmentation is a

defensive mechanism, as pigmented dusts are more readily eliminated (Mavrogardato).

(6) The lymph spaces with their valvular arrangements and filtering lymphnodes, draining eventually through the bronchial walls and discharging the particles loose into the bronchial secretions to be expectorated.

(7) Anti-bodies for certain germs. For the B. Tuberculosis there appears to be a positive reaction stimulating cell growth and tending to encapsulation. Under this heading, also, the anti-bodies bringing about immunity toward foreign proteins to which some persons seem especially susceptible.

(8) Tissue cell proliferations, fibrosis (Beattie) and perhaps calcification, including fixation of the diaphragm and adherent pleurisy in advance cases (Landis).

(9) Shortness of breath, because the shallower breathing, brought about as the result of dust pathology, limits the respiratory excursion.

DUST ACCUMULATION.

Thompson emphasizes the point that "colds" are often only the reactions brought about by breathing dust.

A most important advance in dust pathology of the lungs has been made by Mavrogordato who points out that accumulation of dust in the lung tissues is the main point after all, and not the amount of dust in the breathing atmosphere, nor, indeed, the amount inhaled. Some dusts are eliminated much more readily and completely than others, hence produce less damage in the long run. In general, dusts producing an immediate catarrhal reaction (coal, soot and shale) are well eliminated, whereas, those, the inhalation of which produces little initial reaction, tend to get in farther, go deeper, or in other words to accumulate and bring about the deeper seated tissue changes. However, the rate of dust invasion should be kept below the rate of elimination. Hence the advisability of limiting all dust clouds in the breathing atmosphere.

Mixed dusts are less harmful than pure metallic or crystalline dusts, and the admixture of organic dusts to the same appears to be beneficial in helping elimination.

SUMMARY

(1) The health hazards of non-poisonous dusts have been recognized since time immemorial.

(2) Some 5,000,000 persons, or 10 per cent of all workers, are subject to these hazards in the United States.

(3) As a working basis dusts can be classified as to degrees of hardness, density, shape, size, infectiousness, hydroscopy, chemical make-up, protein sensitiveness, and illumination determent, with emphasis on crystalline, insoluble, inorganic character.

(4) With any type of dust, duration of exposure, amount actually inhaled, non-protective physiology and anatomy of the individual with stress on lack of personal hygiene are all-important points.

(5) Practically never do vital statisticians commend any dust as beneficial. The relationship to consumption, if not to actual tuberculosis, is always ominous. Recent investigations by the author throw much doubt on the alleged immunity of soft coal miners to consumption.

(6) Improvements in estimating the amounts of dust in the breathing atmosphere and the amounts and character of foreign matter in the lungs have thrown much light on the dangerous nature of inhaled dusts.

(7) The more usual sources of industrial dusts which are inhaled are becoming subject to classification and thereby successful prophylaxis.

(8) The body defenses against dust,

while intricate and subject to wide varia-tions, are becoming better understood and appreciated, and are wonderfully efficient if coupled with a reasonable amount of practical hygiene.

(9) The amount of dust accumulation in the lungs seems controllable by keeping the rates of invasion below the rates of elimination and, with these things known or ascertainable, it begins to appear as though a scientific basis is near at hand for estimating the maximum amounts of dusts permissible in the breathing at-mosphere, and the proper modifications or admixtures of otherwise uncontrollable dusts that will render them compara-tively harmless.

BIBLIOGRAPHY

Albaugh, R. P.: Wood Dust, Its Effects on Health. *Ohio Pub. Hlth. Jour.*, Jan., 1919, pp. 14–17.

Baker, Valentine C.: Dusty Occupations. *Jour. A. M. A.*; May, 1919, pp. 1453–1456.

Beattie, J. M.: Dust Diseases. *Jour. State Med.*, Feb., 1916, pp. 33–39.

Great Britain. Home Office: Effects of Dust Inhalation Upon Workers in the Manufacture of Silica Bricks. London, 1917, 16 pp.

Hanson, William C.: Dangers to Workers from Dust and Fumes and Methods of Protection. *Bull. 231, U. S. Bur. of Lab. Stat.*, June, 1918.

Hayhurst, E. R.: Health of Illinois Coal Miners. *Report of Health Insurance Commission*, Illi-nois, May 1, 1919, pp. 376–402.

Hoffman, Frederick L.: Mortality from Respira-tory Diseases in Dusty Trades. *Bull. 231, U. S. Bur. of Lab. Stat.*, June, 1918.

Higgins, Edwin; Lanza, A. J.; Laney F. B., and Rice, G. S.: Siliceous Dust in Relation to Pulmonary Disease among Miners in the Joplin District, Missouri. *Bull. 132, U. S. Bur. of Mines,* 1917.

Hirsch, Edwin F.: The Inorganic Matter and Carbon in Chicago Lungs. *Trans. Chicago Path. Soc.*, April 1, 1916, pp. 65–69.

Kober, George M.: Dust and Tuberculosis. *U. S. Pub. Health Reports*, Oct. 29, 1915.

Landis, H. R. M.: Pathological and Clinical Mani-festations Following the Inhalation of Dust. *Jour. Ind. Hyg.*, July, 1919, pp. 117–139.

Lehmann, K. B.; Saito, Y., and Gfrörer, W.: Uber die quantitative Absorption von Staub aus der Luft den Menchen. *Arch. für Hygiene,* 1911, No. 75, part 3, pp. 152–160.

Mavrogordato, A.: Experiments on the Effects of Dust Inhalations. *Jour. Hyg.*, Oct., 1918, pp. 439–459.

McCrae, J.: The Ash of Silicotic Lungs. *So. Afr. Inst. Med. Research*, 1911.

Miller, T. Grier and Smyth, J. F.: The Dust Hazard in Certain Industries. *Jour. A. M. A.*, March, 1918, pp. 599–604.

Pancoast, H. K.; Miller, T. G., and Landis, J. R. M.: A Roentgenologic Study of the Effects of Dust Inhalation Upon the Lungs. *Amer. Jour. Roent.*, March, 1918, pp. 129–138.

Prudden, T. Mitchell: Dust and Its Dangers. G. P. Putnam's Sons, N. Y., 1891, 111 pp.

Rice, George S.: Historical Review of Silicosis. *Bull. 132, U. S. Bur. of Mines*, 1917, pp. 81–98.

Rivers, W. C.: Pneumokoniosis in Man and Horse. *The Lancet*, July 12, 1919, pp. 55–56.

Thompson, W. Gilman: The Menace of the Dusty Trades. *Am. J. P. Health,* Sept., 1917, pp. 737–741.

Winslow, C.-E. A.: Greenberg, L., and Greenberg, D.: The Dust Hazard in the Abrasive Indus-try. *Reprint No. 531, U. S. Pub. Hlth. Reports,* May 30, 1919, pp. 1171–1187.

◆

Unit Hospital for Industrial Plants.—A plan is shown for the type of hospital necessary to care for 3,500 employees. The unit hospital to be really efficient must return men to work or pass them to the surgeon in the least possible time. If the waiting period can be reduced even three minutes it will amount to hundreds of dollars in a year's time.—W. T. Corbusier, Long Beach Ship Building Co., Cal., *Hospital Management*, August, 1919, pp. 60–62.

Standard Methods for Plant Sanitation.—Standards for drinking water, wash and locker rooms and toilet facilities have been set. A special committee in "safe practices" reports methods of distribution, cooling, drinking-cups and fountains, drinking-water buckets, wash and locker rooms with their lighting, heating, ventilation and clean-ing, types of lockers and locker rooms. The report contains illustrations and diagrams.—*National Safety Council*, 16 pp., price 25 cents. (*E. R. H.*)

FURTHER EVIDENCE AS TO THE RELATIVE IMPORTANCE OF MILK INFECTION IN THE TRANSMISSION OF CERTAIN COMMUNICABLE DISEASES OF MAN.

Eugene R. Kelley, M. D.,

State Commissioner of Health, Massachusetts,

AND

Stanley H. Osborn, M. D.,

Epidemiologist, State Department of Health, Boston, Mass.

Read before Section on Food and Drugs, American Public Health Association, at New Orleans, October 28, 1919.

THESE studies are based on investigations by the district health officers of the Massachusetts State Department of Health from 1915 to 1918, inclusive. The records of the department for 1915 to 1918, inclusive, were examined and tabulated as were the similar figures from 1910 to 1914, inclusive, which appear on pages 141 and 142 of the report of the special milk board of the Massachusetts State Department of Health, submitted to the Commissioner of Health and Public Health Council December 29, 1915.

As in the report of 1915, diphtheria, septic sore throat, scarlet fever and typhoid fever. were studied. Except in typhoid fever a considerably larger number of investigations were made during this four-year period than in the previous five-year period of the report. This study has to do with the relation of milk to the spread of communicable diseases, no other phase of the milk question being considered.

It was found as in all earlier epidemiological studies of epidemics due to milk that cases are sure to follow once the milk is infected, because milk is an ideal medium for the transmission of pathogenic organisms. Raw milk is usually the cause of outbreaks of disease due to milk but pasteurized milk has also been the source of outbreaks, due to infection of the milk after pasteurization, for pathogenic organisms grow in pasteurized milk as in raw milk.

On March 1, 1914, regulations of the State Department of Health became effective making the reporting of all cases of typhoid fever, diphtheria and scarlet fever mandatory, when occurring on premises where milk is handled or produced, the report being sent direct to the State Department of Health as well as to the local board of health. This regulation markedly increased the number of investigations of disease on milk dealers' premises. Thus a single case of one of these diseases in the family of a milk dealer or on a milk farm would call for immediate investigation by the State District Health Officer.

The first fact that was apparent early in this study was the small number of cases found to be due to milk in proportion to the total cases reported in all the diseases studied, with the exception of septic sore throat.

For the four-year period covered, out of a total of 382 investigations of disease, of which 102 were on milk premises, there were but 28 outbreaks in which milk was proved to be the cause or in which evidence pointed to it as the only probable factor producing the cases of disease. In other words 7.3 per cent of the outbreaks of disease studied were found to be due to infected milk.

TOTAL OUTBREAKS STUDIED.

Disease	Outbreaks due to milk	Total outbreaks studied
Scarlet fever.......	4	117
Septic sore throat...	7	10
Diphtheria.........	1	171
Typhoid fever......	16	84
Totals........	28	382

It will be noted that of the outbreaks due to milk, over one-half were outbreaks of typhoid fever. A surprisingly small number of scarlet fever and diphtheria outbreaks due to milk infection have been listed. The septic sore throat outbreaks were seven in number, but due to the rapidity of infection when they do occur, the outbreaks usually are relatively large. In this instance seven outbreaks produced 867 cases and there is no doubt that there were an equal number of cases that were not found.

INVESTIGATION OF DISEASE ON MILK PREMISES.

During 1915-1918, inclusive, an attempt was made to investigate each case of communicable disease on the premises of a milk farm or milk dealer. This was probably carried out in nearly every instance but undoubtedly a stray mild case here and there escaped the vigilance of local health authorities because of the non-reporting of the case or the fact that a physician was not called by the householder. The result of this study shows that milk in Massachusetts is very well protected from infection by clinical cases of disease that may occur at the place where milk is handled or produced.

There were found 496 cases of typhoid fever due to infected milk for the four-year period, but of this number only 22 cases, all occurring in one outbreak, were proved to be due to infection by an active typhoid fever case. In the case of septic sore throat, this disease has a short incu-

bation period and is often of such a mild type that cases are liable to occur among employees and the milk infected before the case is discovered. Thus, in every outbreak of septic sore throat it has been found that some employee or person associated with the owner of a farm or milk depot has had the hemolytic streptococcus of the disease in the throat. Then again, in every outbreak of this disease there occur carriers who give no visible symptoms and the only way to combat them is to take cultures from all employees and isolate those who give a positive result. There were four outbreaks of scarlet fever and one outbreak of diphtheria also found in this period which had their origin from active clinical cases of these diseases on the premises of the milk dealers.

CASES OF CERTAIN COMMUNICABLE DISEASES CAUSED BY INFECTED MILK.

Diseases	1909–14 Cases due to milk	1909–14 Total cases reported	1915–18 Cases due to milk	1915–18 Total cases reported
Diphtheria.......	6	42,344	30	33,807
Scarlet fever......	845	46,031	140	25,328
Septic sore throat..	1,000	*	867	1,401
Typhoid fever.....	365	15,252	496	6,331
Totals........	2,216	103,627	1,533	66,867

* Septic sore throat made reportable September, 1914.

This table shows that 2.1 per cent of the cases of disease were milk borne during 1915–1918.

The periods given in this table are roughly though not exactly comparable, for one is a six-year period and the other a four-year period. It will be seen that scarlet fever and septic sore throat cases due to milk have decreased in recent years. On the other hand, the number of typhoid fever cases determined to be due to infected milk has somewhat increased, and diphtheria also shows a slight increase, though only one diphtheria outbreak is covered where two, of three cases each, were included in the earlier period.

The increase in typhoid fever cases is principally because of the fact that there were two large outbreaks due to milk in the 1915–1918 period, one causing 114, and the other 80 cases. It is rather surprising that outbreaks of septic sore throat should assume such proportions while outbreaks of diphtheria, and scarlet fever, diseases that are spread in a similar way as septic sore throat,—that is, by nasal and oral secretions,—should produce such a small number of outbreaks and so few cases per outbreak.

The percentage of typhoid cases due to milk has been variously stated. Some authors place it as high as 25 per cent of the cases reported. The study of the outbreaks in the state since 1910 is given below. The cases of typhoid used in this table are those cases in which milk was definitely proven to be the source of infection or in which epidemiological evidence was considered sufficient to classify the case as one due to milk.

TYPHOID FEVER CASES DUE TO MILK.

Year	Total cases	Due to milk	Percentage milk borne
1910............	3,452	537	15.5
1911............	2,238	64	2.9
1912............	2,088	17	0.8
1913............	2,398	214	8.9
1914............	2,333	223	9.6
1915............	2,204	153	6.9
1916............	1,515	166	10.8
1917............	1,547	85	5.5
1918*...........	1,065	92	8.6
1919*...........	654	20	3.1
Totals.......	19,494	1,571	8.1 (average)

*9 months.

Thus in this state 8.1 per cent of the typhoid cases are known to have been milk borne.

Typhoid Bacilli Carriers.—Efforts have been made to find typhoid bacilli carriers in all typhoid cases of unknown origin. A résumé of the past nine years and nine months of this year gives the following result:

TYPHOID BACILLI CARRIERS IN MASSACHUSETTS.

Year	Total carriers found	B. Typhosus isolated in	No. of carriers who infected milk	Cases due to milk infected by carrier
1910.....	2	Feces 2	1	55
1911.....	0	None	None	None
1912.....	1	Feces 1	"	"
1913.....	2	" 2	2	70
1914.....	0	None	None	None
1915.....	5	Feces 5	1	66
1916.....	8	" 7	3	19
1916.....		Urine 1		
1917.....	10	Feces 9	None	89
1917.....		Urine 1	2	None
1918.....	7	Feces 6	5	57
1918.....		Urine 1	1	2
1919*....	6	Feces 5	3 }	16
1919.....		Urine 1	None }	
Totals..	41	41	18	374

* 9 months.

By this summary we see that three carriers who handled milk were found to have caused 125 cases of typhoid fever in the period 1910–1914, while 15 carriers causing 249 cases were found for the period 1915–1919. This increase in carriers is probably due entirely to the increased facilities for seeking the source of infection of cases in outbreaks of typhoid fever in the state, together with the intensive work carried out in the search for carriers by local boards of health working in conjunction with the State Department of Health.

It is interesting to note that of the 861 cases of typhoid due to milk for the period 1909–1918, there were 358 cases due to typhoid-bacilli carrier-infected milk.

MILK BORNE TYPHOID DUE TO CARRIER.

Years	Milk borne	Cases due to typhoid bacilli carrier infecting milk	Per cent due to carriers
1909–14.......	365 cases	125 cases	34.2
1915–18.......	496 "	233 "	46.9
	861 "	358 "	41.6

Some outbreaks occurred, where carriers were suspected, but not proven.

For instance, in 1916, 114 cases occurred on a single milk route, and no clinical case or carrier was found. There is a total of 241 such cases for the period 1915–1918.

The total cases due to milk, infected by clinical cases, is very small, only one epidemic of 22 cases during 1915–1918 was proven to be due to this cause. Forty-nine other cases are epidemiologically attributable to active cases but complete laboratory confirmation was not possible.

Pasteurization.—This undoubtedly has been a large factor in the reduction of communicable disease spread by milk, this being especially true, probably, in respiratory diseases such as scarlet fever, septic sore throat and diphtheria. These organisms are easily killed by exposure to the elements and by pasteurization. In many instances outbreaks of disease have furnished the necessary incentive for the installation of pasteurization plants in dairies and milk farms. The highest class of raw milk produced in the state has been a source of septic sore throat infection more than once. At the time of the outbreak, pasteurization was resorted to, then, later, raw milk was again produced with the result that another outbreak occurred. Conditions such as this have resulted in the number of pasteurized plants being doubled and trebled in many towns and cities of the state.

This year an attempt was made to collect accurate data on the consumption of raw and pasteurized milk in the state. Accordingly a circular letter was sent to each city and town in the state and data was returned from communities covering 61 per cent of the population. This data showed that the annual consumption of milk was 203 quarts per capita for the population where the data was furnished, or at the same rate there would be a total of 810 million quarts consumed per year in the entire state.

DATA OBTAINED FROM 61 PER CENT OF POPULATION OF MASSACHUSETTS.

Population on which data was obtained......	2,425,950
Population of state (Est. as of July 1, '19).....	3,991,969
Raw milk used.............	325,378,464 quarts annually
Pasteurized milk used........	168,048,437 " "
Total.................	493,426,901 " "

On the same basis for the entire state, this indicates that at the present time 34 per cent of the milk used in the state is pasteurized. Unfortunately no reliable records are at hand to show the increase in pasteurized milk in comparison with previous years.

SUMMARY OF EPIDEMIOLOGICAL INVESTIGATIONS BY THE DISTRICT HEALTH OFFICERS OF MASSACHUSETTS FOR THE FOUR-YEAR PERIOD 1915–1918, INCLUSIVE, WITH REFERENCE TO THE FREQUENCY OF MILK TRANSMISSION.

DIPHTHERIA.

Year	No. of investigations	Per cent of investigations on milk premises	No. due to milk	No. due to other causes	Per cent milk borne
1915.....	33	18.2	2	31	6.0
1916.....	24	12.5	0	24	..
1917.....	102	19.6	0	102	..
1918.....	12	9.6	0	12	..
Totals..	171	27.1	2	169	1.2

SCARLET FEVER.

1915.....	26	23	0	26	..
1916.....	30	23.2	1	29	3.3
1917.....	48	35.4	1	47	2.1
1918.....	13	15.4	0	13	..
Totals..	117	27.3	2	115	1.7

SEPTIC SORE THROAT.

1915.....	1	100	1	0	100
1916.....	2	100	1	1	50
1917.....	6	83.5	5	1	83.5
1918.....	1	100	0	1	..
Totals..	10	90	7	3	70

TYPHOID FEVER.

1915.....	23	25	8	15	34.7
1916.....	14	43	4	10	28.5
1917.....	32	31.3	2	30	6.2
1918.....	15	68.7	7	8	46.6
Totals..	84	39	21	63	25.0

COMPOSITE OF FOUR PRECEDING TABLES.

1915.....	83	22.5	11	72	13.3
1916.....	70	24.6	6	64	8.6
1917.....	188	35.7	8	180	4.2
1918.....	41	23.5	7	34	17.1
Totals..	382	27.1	32	350	8.4

Conclusions.—Many of the conclusions tentatively formulated in a study by one of us (Kelley)* three years ago are strengthened by this study based on more complete epidemiological data. It is believed to be practically impossible for an outbreak of any size to have occurred in Massachusetts in recent years where the evidence for possible milk origin has not been critically and impartially studied.

Nevertheless, the results are not materially different than in earlier studies where our epidemiological data was not considered as trustworthy, and where the possibilities of "missed" milk origin, especially in small outbreaks was admitted.

(1) When the total aggregate of cases

* *Journal of the American Medical Association,* December 30, 1916.

reported is considered, milk, while a dangerous factor and one of potential significance, does not assume any great quantitative factor as a channel of infection, provided prompt investigations are instituted as a routine procedure of all cases occurring on milk producing and milk handling premises.

(2) Milk as a source of diphtheria is practically negligible.

(3) Scarlet fever though much more frequently transmitted by milk than is diphtheria in our state, is milk borne in only a very small percentage of instances, as compared with other sources of infection.

(4) Milk borne typhoid is a more serious epidemiologic problem, 496 cases out of a total of 6,331 typhoid cases reported being attributed to this cause, or 7.7 per cent. This is a considerably higher percentage than in our earlier studies (5.0 per cent) due to the relatively larger milk borne outbreaks.

(5) Increased pasteurization ought to greatly decrease the per cent of frequency of milk borne cases. Curiously although pasteurization plants have greatly increased in Massachusetts during the past four years, the relative proportion of total cases traced to milk, compared to the total cases reported, has remained about the same.

TABLES.

DIPHTHERIA.

Year	Locality	Date	No. of cases	History	Method of milk infection
1915	Holbrook Brockton	September	27	Five carriers found on milk farm.	Carriers on farm.
1915	Wellesley	October	3	One case found on premises of milk dealer.	Active case on milk dealer's premises.
1916	None were found due to milk.				
1917	None were found due to milk.				
1918	None were found due to milk.				

SEPTIC SORE THROAT.

Year	Locality	Date	No. of cases	History	Method of milk infection
1915	Milton	March April	227	All on route of one distributor who did not pasteurize his milk. Four possible sources found on different supply farms.	1. Boy with sore throat then desquamating. 2. Cows with garget. 3. Cows whose milk contained pus. 4. Members of distributor's family with sore throats.
1916	Watertown	May	· 46	Man found on dairy with no constitutional symptoms. Culture from his throat showed hemolytic streptococcus of the disease. Pus with organism also found in quarter of cow. Milk not pasteurized.	1. Carrier on farm. 2. Cow with organism in milk.
1917	Needham Newton	January March	50 (estimated)	None officially reported. Two milk handlers found with hemolytic streptococci in their throats. Streptococci also found in quarter of cow.	1. Two milk handlers. 2. Cow with organism in milk.
1917	Somerville Medford	April	150 (estimated)	42 cases reported. Three employees were sick, one showed hemolytic streptococci in his throat.	A milk handler.
1917	Dedham Brookline	February	125	None officially reported. Three employees on dairy with sore throat.	Not proven.
1917	Gloucester	April May	150	All on route of one dealer, supplied by five farms. At one farm, housewife had hemolytic streptococci in her throat.	Case on farm.
1917	Wellesley, Natick Dover	July August	119	42 cases reported, others found; two employees on dairy farm found with hemolytic streptococci.	Two milk handlers.
1918	None were due to milk				

SCARLET FEVER.

Year	Locality	Date	No. of cases	History	Method of milk infection
1915	None were found due to milk				
1916	Clinton Lancaster	May	7	Four cases appeared on the route of a dairy prior to a case in the family of the dairyman. The severe cases following used milk from the dairy.	Active case on farm.
1917	Malden	January February	3	Three cases appeared on a small route of a milkman who had two cases of scarlet fever in his own house.	Two cases on farm.
1917	Arlington	May	5	The milk dealer had two cases in his family and five cases occurred on his route. There were 12 cases reported as septic sore throat.	Two cases in a milk dealer's family.
1918	Holliston	April	125	All cases were on one route; 27 cases were reported. Son of milkman and a milker had scarlet fever.	Two cases on farm.

TYPHOID FEVER.

Year	Locality	Date	No. of cases	History	Method of infection
1915	Lynn	March	23	All cases were customers of a single milk producer.	Infecting agent was not found.
1915	Gardner	July	4	Four cases were reported on the route of one milk man. Typhoid bacilli were isolated from feces of a milker.	Carrier on farm.
1915	Northbridge	October	22	Cases were on the route of a single dealer.	Active case on farm.
1915	Quincy	November	7	All cases were on the route of a small dealer.	Not found.
1915	Grafton	May	22	All cases were in Grafton Insane Colony. All cases used the same milk. Positive Widal tests were obtained from a milker on the farm and two of the kitchen helpers.	A probable carrier.
1915	Newburyport	July	11	Seven of the cases used milk supplied by a man who was sick with probable typhoid. Thorough tests were not permitted.	Producer probably an active case.
1915	Rochdale	October	18	All cases supplied by milk from a farm where the son of the producer, who milked and peddled, had a positive Widal test.	A probable carrier.
1915	Mansfield	March April May September October	46	Cases occurred while a temporary helper, who had typhoid 45 years previous, worked on the farm. Typhoid bacilli were isolated from the feces of this helper.	Carrier on the farm.
1916	Fall River	January	38	The cases occurred on a single route.	Investigation showed milk bottles were collected from houses where cases of typhoid existed.
1916	Whitman and Bridgewater	June	5	Cases occurred on route of a single farm. Typhoid bacilli were isolated from feces of a milker.	Carrier on farm.
1916	Nantucket	August	9	Cases bought milk from a single farm. Typhoid bacilli were isolated from the feces of a milker.	Carrier on farm.
1916	Lynn	August	114	All the cases used milk of a single dealer.	Not found.
1917	Gardner	April May August September	80	All the cases used milk of a single dealer. Typhoid bacilli were isolated from the feces of a milker.	Carrier on farm.
1917	Marshfield	June	5	Cases used milk from the same farm. Typhoid bacilli were isolated from the feces of a milker.	Carrier on farm.
1918	Westminster	February	2	Both cases used milk bought from a nearby farm. Typhoid bacilli were isolated from feces of milker.	Carrier on farm.

TYPHOID FEVER.—*Continued.*

Year	Locality	Date	No. of cases	History	Method of infection
1918	Woburn	April May	6	All of the cases were on a small milk route of a single farm. Infection caused by manner in which returned bottles were used as a measure for dispensing milk. Typhoid bacilli isolated from feces of the carrier.	One of the customers was found to be a carrier.
1918	Marlboro	August	30	All of the cases used milk from the same dealer. Typhoid bacilli were isolated from feces of the carrier on the farm.	Carrier on farm.
1918	Wilmington	August November	10	All the cases were on the route of the same dealer of milk. Source of infection was not definitely located. Two milkers gave atypical Widal tests but typhoid bacilli were not found in the discharges.	A probable carrier.
1918	Athol	September	8	All of the cases were on the route of a single dealer. One of the milkers gave a positive Widal and a history of never having typhoid, but typhoid bacilli were not isolated.	A probable carrier.
1918	Gloucester	October	6	All of the cases used milk from the same source. Typhoid bacilli were isolated from feces of carrier on farm.	Carrier on farm.
1918	Beverly	October	30	All the cases were on the route of a single milk dealer. A suspected carrier was found on the farm.	A probable carrier.

Experiments on Tuberculosis.—The fact is recognized that neither sickness benefit nor sanatorium treatment has hitherto stopped the spread of tuberculosis; but experience with the sanatorium method has paved the way for a new line of practice, which bids fair to yield better results for both the community and the individual patient. The establishment of farm colonies where consumptive persons can be treated along approved hygienic lines and can also be enabled to earn sufficient wages to maintain themselves and their families, as soon as their health is sufficiently restored to permit of suitable work, has now been proved to be possible. Many tuberculous patients, even with advanced disease, are capable of undertaking light work under truly hygienic conditions, and not in crowded and perhaps ill-ventilated factories. It might be possible to carry out on a large scale such a system as has worked well at Papworth in Cambridgeshire, where provision is made for patients in all stages of the disease. Advanced cases are segregated, but permitted some occupation whenever possible, and many of them are soon able to be classified as medium cases, and become able to undertake work for which they earn wages. With the establishment of village colonies, they will be able to start home life again. The early cases may be so completely arrested as to be able to return to their former life. The problem is many sided and has to be examined from the social, economic and psychological aspects as well as from the medical side, but by slow progress on the lines already indicated, and by taking advantage of the experience acquired, there is reasonable prospect that in time the disease may be materially decreased, if not suppressed.—Editorial, *British Med. Jour.*, 1919, 385. (*D. G.*)

EDITORIAL SECTION

AMERICAN JOURNAL OF PUBLIC HEALTH

EDITORIAL OFFICE: 169 MASSACHUSETTS AVE., BOSTON, MASS.

A. W. HEDRICH, C. P. H., Editor   J. RITCHIE, Jr., Associate Editor.

Editorial Assistants

E. R. HAYHURST, M.D.   DAVID GREENBERG   JAMES A. TOBEY
R. P. ALBAUGH, M.D.   M. P. HORWOOD, M.S.   FRANCIS H. SLACK, M.D.
E. B. STARR, M.D.   P. M. HOLMES, M.D.   JAMES M. STRANG

Board of Advisory Editors

PETER H. BRYCE, M.D., Ottawa, Canada   PROF. M. J. ROSENAU, Boston, Mass.
CHARLES V. CHAPIN, M.D., Providence, R. I.   PROF. W. T. SEDGWICK, Cambridge, Mass.
EUGENE R. KELLEY, M.D., Boston, Mass.   PROF. GEORGE C. WHIPPLE, Cambridge, Mass.
W. A. EVANS, M.D., Chicago, Ill.   PROF. S. M. GUNN, Paris, France.

All expressions of opinion and all statements of supposed facts are published on authority of the writer under whose name they appear, and are not to be regarded as expressing the views of the American Public Health Association, unless such statements or opinions have been adopted by vote of the Association.

NOTICE TO SUBSCRIBERS: Subscription Price, payable in advance, $4.00 per year for United States and possessions; $4.50 for Canada and other foreign countries. Single copies, 50 cents postpaid. **Membership** in the American Public Health Association, including subscription to JOURNAL $5.00 per year. **Expiration Months** are stamped upon the wrapper surrounding the JOURNAL. Prompt renewals are requested to prevent discontinuance. **In Change of Address** please give both old and new address, and mail before the first of the month to take effect with the current issue. **Mailing Date** 5th of each month. **Advertisements** accepted only when commendable, and worth while both to reader and advertiser. **News Items**, interesting clippings and illustrations are gladly received, together with name of sender. **Copyright, 1919, by A. W. Hedrich.**

PUBLIC HEALTH: A LIVE, PROGESSIVE FORCE.

It is interesting at the close of the year to pass in review some of the more important events which have taken place during the year in the various fields of human activity; but possibly no one has been more fruitful in events than the field of public health during the year 1919.

The outbreak of influenza of the last quarter of 1918 was still present in the early months of 1919 in some parts of this continent, and not until the warm weather had come did its frightful ravages cease. Partly due to the epidemic, but largely to the remarkable advances of sanitation and preventive medicine during the year and to the notable advancement in common knowledge amongst the people concerning the physical defects in a large part of the population, as shown by examination of recruits during the War, legislative bodies everywhere have found it easy to set aside appropriations for preventive work even in these days of high prices.

Not only have such appropriations been made for specific purposes, but in several countries, notably in England and Canada, much progress has also been made in the work of consolidating public health activities. In both these countries Departments of Health have been created with a separate Cabinet Minister in charge. The object of this has been especially to develop existing public health activities and to further concentrate practical work upon definite problems, especially demanding executive action. In fact everywhere it would seem as if the principle that the welfare of any State demands universal provision by the State of an adequate education of its people is now being supplemented by a further postulate that the State must logically provide equally for the health of its people, whereby the benefits derived from education may become effective.

The enormous increase in population generally in the great centers on this continent during the past century, and especially in cities during the last quarter of it, has shown the need of coöperation in matters of public health in providing pure public water, disposal of wastes and for the care of persons suffering from contagious diseases. Obviously in every age, each country and each district has had its special problems and fortunately human progress is constantly supplying the means for their solution.

Today in many of our cities public health organization had advanced far towards supplying the needs. Not only have Federal Departments been established but State Health departments have also long been enlarging their functions and extending their operations to effect reforms in every city and even in the small municipalities. Not only has this work of organization gone on with ever increasing momentum in recent years, but it has become relatively easy because of the scientific knowledge which serves as the basis of its operations. In 1918 Sir Bertrand Dawson published two lectures on what he has called "The Nation's Welfare," in which he lays down two principles: 1st, that much disease is preventable, and therefore should be prevented, and 2nd, that the welfare of the State demands that every citizen when sick shall receive every care which modern medical science can give. He then proceeds to show how physicians can be united in closer coöperation to do effective work through hospitals and other institutions.

But more than this, the advance of scientific medicine in its most exact phases has been so great as to cause Sir Clifford Allbutt, M. D., to adopt for his paper before the British Medical Association meeting of April last, the title "The New Birth of Medicine." In this paper we are carried into fields as yet quite beyond the comprehension of the ordinary reader in so far as the study and analysis of the chemical and physico-biological principles underlying physiological action are concerned. Investigation and experiment are constantly showing some new relationship between the inorganic, the organic and its environment and the persistency and potency of germ plasm to the point of helping us to realize how delicate are the actions, re-actions, and inter-actions, which govern the most vital functions, whether in plants, in animals or in man.

Obviously the practical application of new facts of this sort by executive health officers and practitioners of medicine in the promotion of public health must always be behind those theories, which at first sight seem to be purely academic. No one, however, who realizes how the Great War was won can fail to see at once that had we not known the laws of gases, had electricity been still a plaything, had internal combustion engines not been invented and had the germ theory of disease not been established; a great mass of humanity in 1914–1918, with more than twenty million men in the field, would practically have disappeared as fighting forces and the plains of Europe would have become scenes of devastation through epidemics, which would have made them as barren of life as if a glacial catastrophe had overwhelmed them or a Martinque volcano had launched its suffocating vapors.

Obviously, if the intense modern aggregations of humanity are producing new problems of increasing complexity, the means for accomplishing their solution are increasing with them; and the people within the countries represented in the great American Public Health Association can move forward into the new year with ever increasing confidence and hope, knowing that science in the hands of its faithful interpreters will prove yet more and more efficient in providing for their wellbeing; while therewith will be evolved an ever increasing ethical sense of responsibility in each member of society to perform the special duties which fall upon him.

P. H. B.

CHILD WELFARE.

Child welfare is a subject that looms large in the immediate future of the public health administrator. The attention that has been focused on the matter and the movements that have been initiated in different quarters of the country and the world, testify to the attention that is being paid to this subject, which is truly a philosophical one to attack. As has been said, it is of the greatest importance, if the health of the adult member of the community is to be guarded, to begin by giving him a good foundation of health while he is a baby and a child.

The movement is beginning, as many such movements have begun before, in individual definition of the problems and their solution by different communities, each working with whatever light of experience or reasoning may be at its command. The country is, however, learning a better method; namely, that of coöperation and coördination. In coöperation the communities have the benefit of the thought and experiences of each of the others; in coördination, the elements that are best fitted to work can work each in the field that best suits it, but focused, all of them, on the same end.

Massachusetts, which has ever been a leader in the sanitary thought of the country, is through its State Health Department, at present carrying forward a definite State program in child hygiene, and the benefit of its thought and experience may be helpful to other states that are at work on the same questions.

In Massachusetts four points of attack upon the problems have been laid down. The first includes a plan of coöperation with the American Red Cross towards the development of an adequate system of public health nursing. The second feature considered, is that of nutrition; the third is mouth hygiene, and the fourth, the establishment of health centers.

In coöperation with the American Red Cross a whole-time worker has even added to the department force who will be able to aid in coördinating public health nursing throughout the state, and avoiding overlap, conflict and lost motion. In the nutrition work, emphasis will of course be laid upon breast feeding; but besides this, there is a field for useful effort in the coördination of nutrition methods, and stress will be placed upon the education of the people. This is being done through the various familiar ways of literature and exhibits; coöperation with those engaged in nutrition work and, it is to be hoped, through health centers.

In oral hygiene the same ideas in public education are to be carried out, while every effort will be made to induce communities to establish dental clinics. At the present moment, there are about fifty such clinics in the State of Massachusetts in about forty places, the cities in some cases having more than one clinic. It is true today, that there is no standard for equipment, each place furnishing its own, according to the wishes of its local practitioner who looks after the work. It is hoped to change all this uncertainty, and to furnish specifications of what their equipment should be to communities which have the public spirit to establish clinics.

With reference to health centers, the idea is so new and the interpretation of what the term means is so different in different places that what the State Health Department of Massachusetts is to do, will be likewise in the line of standardization. It should be understood that there are two broad divisions into which the centers may be divided; those which are established within some large town or city, and which may be deemed to be local; and again, those which are to care for more sparsely settled districts and which will be community centers. It will be the purpose of the kind last named to coördinate all the local health activities, and in this they will have the assistance of the State.

It will thus be seen that in the organization in a up-to-date State of one of the newest of health movements—child hygiene,—the policy may be expressed in all of the divisions of the subject to be; coördinate with a view to the conservation of energy the existing agencies, standardize the modes of procedure, and devote no small portion of the time and energy to the health education of the people. The item last named is absolutely essential, for it is unquestionably true that the health officer and his assistant, the voluntary health worker, can take not a single step forward without the support of the people.

OUR NOTES SECTION REVIEWERS.

Readers of the JOURNAL who make use of the various portions of the Public Health Notes section, will find with the beginning of the year a number of changes in the personnel of the reviewers. Dr. Arthur Lederer, whose abstracts through so many months have been of that quality that "needs no bush," finds that his responsibilities in his new work in Chicago make such demands on his time, that a continuance of this work of keeping the members of the A. P. H. A. in touch with the new things in laboratory work is out of the question. The JOURNAL regrets that this should be the case. His mantle falls on willing and competent shoulders, however, for Dr. F. H. Slack of the Sias Laboratories of Brookline, Mass., and Mr. James M. Strang, Instructor at the Massachusetts Institute of Technology in the Department of Biology and Public Health, have undertaken the work. To the reviewers in Industrial Hygiene and Occupational Disease, the name of Dr. E. B. Starr has been added, another of the strong group of industrial health experts of which Ohio can boast.

There is due to Dr. Lederer the thanks of every member of the Association for his intelligent, accurate and painstaking work.

In Memoriam.

WILLIAM GROSVENOR BISSELL.

William Grosvenor Bissell passed away at his home in Buffalo, N. Y., on November 14, 1919, at the early age of 49.

Dr. Bissell spent his life in Buffalo, occupying primarily the responsible position of Director of Laboratories, in the Department of Health. His local activities were varied and extensive. In addition he was widely known throughout the country as a sanitary expert.

He was born in Lockport, N. Y., January 30, 1870, received his early education in his home town, and graduated from the University of Buffalo in 1892, receiving the degree of M. D. For the next few years he occupied himself with hospital work in Rochester. During this time he laid the foundation for his subsequent work in bacteriology. It was during this period that he accomplished many original investigations, notable among them, that on the preparation of sterile surgical ligatures.

In 1894, after a stringent competitive examination, he was appointed City Bacteriologist of Buffalo, the title of this position subsequently becoming Director of Laboratories. Dr. Bissell occupied this position up to the time of his death, and by his efforts, succeeded in developing an extensive laboratory, a fitting monument to his twenty-five years of labor. He was an indefatigable student, and painstaking in all his work. It is not surprising that he occupied many public positions, and received many honorary degrees. Among these was that of LL. D., from Canisius College, and D. P. H. from New York University.

Dr. Bissell was health officer for the Chautauqua Institution, and at the time of his death, was vice chairman of the Laboratory Section, of the American Public Health Association.

He was actively interested during the greater part of his life in military affairs, and for more than twenty years was surgeon of the 74th Regiment, N. G. N. Y. At the time of his death, he was major, in the Medical Corps, New York State Guard, assigned to the 65th Field Artillery. He was lecturer in Preventive Medicine at Long Island College Medical School; examiner in Preventive Medicine and Hygiene for the New York State Board of Medical Examiners, of which board he was also president; he was a member of the American Congress of Hygiene, the American Public Health Association, Military Surgeons, New York State Medical Society, Erie County Medical Society, president of the New York State Sanitary Officers Association, and a member of many other organizations, both scientific and social.

All those who were associated with Dr. Bissell, either in his capacity as a sanitarian, or socially as a friend, will feel his loss keenly.

ASSOCIATION NEWS

HEALTH EMPLOYMENT BUREAU.

Help-wanted announcements will be carried free in this column until further notice. Copy goes to the printer on the fifteenth of each month. In answering keyed advertisements, please mail replies separately.

The Health Employment Bureau also sends lists of applicants to prospective employers without charge.

Woman technician for laboratory of City Health Department. Must be capable of doing water and milk analyses, routine bacteriology, some food analysis. Salary to start $100.00 per month. Apply with full particulars to Dr. R. L. Carlton, City Health Officer, Winston-Salem, N. C.

Good serologist, or person for Wassermann and tissue work; non-medical; man or woman. Drs. Ellis and Butler, Shreveport Laboratories, Box 201, Shreveport, La.

Competent sanitary engineer for position of second assistant sanitary engineer of State Board of Health. Usual duties, particularly inspection of operation of water works, water purification and sewage disposal plants. $1800, with two weeks' vacation. Address H. A. C., 312, care of this Journal.

Epidemiologist with or without experience. Apply giving full information and references. Address H. E. B., 314.

LIST OF NEW MEMBERS

PROPOSED FOR ELECTION TO THE

A. P. H. A.

FROM NOVEMBER 22, TO DECEMBER 20, 1919.

Sponsors	—and—	The New Members
	(States arranged in alphabetical order)	Whom They Introduced

MISS FLORENCE BODDY, R. N., Pasadena, Cal. — HELEN S. BLOODGOOD, R. N., Health Department, Pasadena, Cal.

C. F. BROMAN, M. D., Greeley, Colo. — FLORENCE FEZER, M. D., City Physician, Greeley, Colo.

T. E. REEKS, M. D., Hartford, Conn. — CHAS. W. JACKSON, M. D., Health Officer, Watertown, Conn.

A. C. HUNTER, M. D., Washington, D. C. — ERNEST D. CLARK, Ph. D., Seattle, Wash.

MR. JAMES A. TOBEY, Washington, D. C — E. A. PETERSON, M. D., Director Am. Red Cross, Washington, D. C.

F. A. BRINK, M. D., Pensacola, Fla. — MISS MARGARET L. IRWIN, Bacteriologist, Jacksonville, Fla.

ROY S. DEARSTYNE, Takoma Park, Md. — MR. GEORGE BURNHAM, Jr., Philadelphia, Pa.
LOUIS E. FOULKS, M. D., Health Officer, Alexandria, Va.

MR. JOHN Le FEBER, Milwaukee, Wis. — MR. JOHN BINGHAM, Ottawa, Can.

MR. CHARLES H. HOOD, Boston, Mass. — RIECK-McJUNKIN DAIRY COMPANY, Pittsburgh, Pa.

VICTOR SAFFORD, M. D., Boston, Mass. — MR. STEPHEN LAWRENCE MALONEY, Secretary, Boston Health Department, Boston, Mass.

WILLARD E. WARD, M. D., Brookline, Mass. — MR. CHARLES F. WHITING, Boston, Mass.

WARREN E. FORSYTHE, M. D., Ann Arbor, Mich. — MISS MARJORIE DELAVEN, A. B., State Dept. of Health, Lansing, Mich.

MISS LAURA L. GILMAN, St. Paul, Minn. — MISS WINIFRED KELLY, B. A., Laboratory Technician, Minneapolis, Minn.

MISS LAURA FRANKLIN, A. B., R. N., Columbia, Mo. — MRS. ANNA PAGE SMITH, R. N., Boston, Mass.

MR. WILLIAM B. PALMER, Orange, N. J. — MR. EUGENE H. SULLIVAN, Health Officer, Nutley, N. J.

HAROLD F. GRAY, M. D., Santa Fe., N. M. — DUDLEY B. WILLIAMS, A. B., M. D., City Health Officer, Portales, N. M.

MR. CURTIS E. LAKEMAN, New York City. — MR. JOHN MELPOLDER, Dir. Hlth. Serv. Dept., Red Cross, New Orleans, La.

E. DeM. LYON, M. D., Peekskill, N. Y. — CHARLES RICH, M. D., Health Officer, Yorktown Heights, N. Y.

VICTOR G. HEISER, M. D., Broadway, New York City. — J. HERBERT WAITE, M. D., Flemington, Pa.

MR. JOHN W. RITCHIE, Yonkers, N. Y. — MISS BERNICE JENKINS, New York, N. Y.

E. E. ECKER, Ph. D., Cleveland, Ohio.

G. E. HARMON, M. D., Cleveland, Ohio.

MR. H. C. KNOPF, A. B., Cleveland, Ohio.

MR. J. ATLEE DEAN, Philadelphia, Pa.

V. JESUS, M. D., Philippine Islands.

MR. JOHN Le FEBER, Milwaukee, Wis.

CHAS. F. DALTON, M. D., Burlington, Vt.

MR. ERNEST H. STRONG, Milwaukee, Wis.

JORGE Le-ROY, M. D., Havana, Cuba.

F. L. HOFFMAN, LL. D., London, Eng.

JAMES R. DAVIS, M. D., Pathologist, Cleveland, Ohio.

H. J. KNAPP, M. D., Diagnostician, Cleveland Board of Health, Berea, Ohio.

G. W. MOOREHOWSE, M. D., Cleveland, Ohio.

H. O. RUH, M. D., Cleveland, Ohio.

MR. CHAS. ROBT. STEWARD, Student, Philadelphia, Pa.

PEDRO BUENASEDA, M. D., Philippine Health Service, Malolos, Bulacan, P. I.

MR. C. THOMPSON, Washington, D. C.

IOWA DAIRY COMPANY, Dubuque, Iowa.

C. S. LEACH, M. D., District Health Officer, Brattleboro, Vt.

MR. HARRY T. CAMPION, Ironton, Ohio.

MR. H. De WITT VALENTINE, M. S., Chemical Engineer, Milwaukee, Wis.

FERNANDO MARTINEZ LAMO, M. D., Laboratory Technician, Camaguey, Cuba.

MRS. WORTHAM JAMES, New York City.

Names of Proposed Members Whose Sponsors Are Not Known

R. B. DURFEE, M. D., Bacteriologist, Board of Health, Bisbee, Ariz.

CRESCENT CREAMERY CO., Los Angeles, Cal.

W. E. BUCK, M. D., Health Officer, Pueblo, Colo.

CONNECTICUT PUBLIC HEALTH ASSN., Hartford, Conn.

MRS. E. A. INGHAM, Larned, Kan.

MR. C. OSCAR EWING, Louisville, Ky.

IRVIN LINDENBERGER, M. D., Louisville, Ky.

MR. W. H. FROST, Johns Hopkins University, Baltimore, Md.

W. F. WILD, M. D., Boston, Mass.

MISS DAISY L. DODGE, R. N., Mansfield, Mass.

A. L. STONE, M. D., Health Officer, Pittsfield, Mass.

SALEM BOARD OF HEALTH, Salem, Mass.

BRIDGEMAN-RUSSELL CO., Duluth, Minn.

CHAUNCEY F. CHAPMAN, M. D., Supt. of Health, Lincoln, Neb.

NEB. STATE BOARD OF HEALTH, State House, Lincoln, Neb.

L. H. PATE, M. D., Carlsbad, N. M.

W. C. McMURTRY, M. D., Wolford, N. D.

MR. MURRAY A. AUERBACH, Atlanta. Ga,

 HOWARD E. FELTON, M. D., Cartersville, Ga.

POCATELLO PUBLIC SCHOOLS, Pocatello, Idaho.

PEORIA LIFE INSURANCE CO., Peoria, Ill.

E. M. VANBUSKIRK, M. D., Fort Wayne, Ind.

FLYNN DAIRY COMPANY, Des Moines, Iowa.

MOORES & ROSS, Columbus, Ohio.

L. G. KLEPINGER, M. D., Dayton, Ohio.

G. W. TAYLOR, M. D., El Reno, Okla.

MR. J. B. McCUNE, Health Officer, Donora, Pa.

MR. C. R. LINDBACK, Philadelphia, Pa.

V. JESUS, M. D., Acting Director of Health, Government of the P. I., Manila, P. I.

GUILLERMO ZANDUETA, M. D., District Health Officer, San Fernando, La Union, P. I.

DOMINGO R. FABLAN, M. D., District Health Officer, Philippine Health Service, Manila, P. I.

A. KRISTOFERSON, INC., Seattle, Wash.

GRACE PEARL JENNINGS, M. D., Seattle, Wash.

MR. H. H. HAGERMAN, Fredericton, N. B., Can.

THE UNION AGENCY, Bombay, India.

◆

CONVENTIONS, CONFERENCES, MEETINGS

January 13-14, Washington, D. C., National Public Work Department Association.

January 25-27, Birmingham, Ala., Alabama Sociological Congress.

January 27, Birmingham, Ala., Alabama Anti-Tuberculosis Association.

January 27-30, Montreal, Engineering Institute of Canada.

February —, Austin, Texas, Texas Public Health Association.

February —, Canadian Red Cross Society.

February —, Boston, Mass., Tuberculosis League.

February 6, Cheyenne, Wyo., Wyoming Public Health Association.

March —, Chicago, American Conference on Hospital Service.

March 5, Providence, R. I., Rhode Island Medical Society.

March 22-23, New York City, New York State Medical Society.

April 12-17, Atlanta, Ga., National Organization for Public Health Nursing.

April 14-21, New Orleans, La., National Conference of Social Workers.

April 14-21, New Orleans, La., American Association of Hospital Workers.

April 20-22, Charlotte, N. C., Medical Society of North Carolina.

April 26-30, New Orleans, La., American Medical Association.

May 11, —, American Association of Eugenics.

May 25-27, Columbus, O., Ohio Hospital Association.

PROCEEDINGS AND DISCUSSIONS OF THE AMERICAN PUBLIC HEALTH ASSOCIATION AT NEW ORLEANS, LA., OCTOBER 27-30, 1919.

SECTION OF PUBLIC HEALTH ADMINISTRATION.

THE Section of Public Health Administration had six sessions, one of them a round-table luncheon on Wednesday, October 29, at noon, when the topic for discussion was "Appropriations for Public Health Work," while two others, those of Wednesday morning and Thursday morning were joint sessions, the one first, named being with the Laboratory and the Food and Drugs sections, and the one last named, with the Section on Vital Statistics.

The section was called to order on Monday afternoon, October 27, 1919, by the chairman, Dr. C. H. Wells of Wilmington, Del., who announced the Committee on Nominations to comprise Dr. Oscar Dowling of New Orleans, Dr. Ernest C. Levy of Richmond, Va., and Dr. Charles J. Hastings of Toronto, Ont.

The chairman then called upon the six gentlemen whose papers formed the symposium on the Privy, Drs. Lumsden, Smith, Ferrell, Levy, Cogswell and Stiles, and these papers followed one another without much interlude. Those of Dr. L. L. Lumsden on "The Privy as a Public Health Menace," and Dr. C. W. Stiles on "Practical Types of Sanitary Privies," find place in this issue of the Journal, on pages 45 to 48 and 48 to 52, respectively. Others of the series will follow in later numbers of the Journal.

In the discussion which followed, the remarks of Dr. James A. Hayne of Columbia, S. C., and Dr. J. W. S. McCullough of Toronto, Ont., were especially with reference to the statistics quoted by Dr. Levy. Dr. Charles E. Low of Wilmington, N. C., supported the opinion of Dr. Stiles that to maintain an efficient privy it is necessary to have "privy sense." He stated that out of his experience he was forced to the belief that there does not exist today a fly-proof privy. "It is an ideal," he said, "towards which we are striving but which I think none of us has reached. So I am very strongly inclined to the use of either the L. R. S. type or the chemical closet." Dr. Low spoke of the value of inspection and follow-up work.

Dr. B. S. Beach, health officer of the Illinois Central Railroad, spoke of the difficulties that the railway companies have in maintaining clean privies. He has constant travel through nine states and meets the men who have these matters in hand. The Illinois Central makes every effort to keep the privies clean. It hires men who work regularly and continuously, but even then the burden is on the public and until the individual has learned "privy sense," the railways cannot get away from the contaminated privy.

In the conclusion of the discussion by the readers of the original communications on the subject, Dr. Stiles noted that there is such a thing as fly-proof construction, but men of experience will agree that there is no such thing as fly-proof maintenance. He suggested that it might be possible to turn a liability into a benefit by making the privy a fly trap, and experiments along this line suggest ultimate success. With reference to the railways, their position should arouse sympathy. The condition of a Pullman toilet after a run of thirty-six hours is to be decried, and yet it is not the poorest members of the community who have made use of it; while the condition of a day coach after twenty-four hours of use rivals that of privies on the farm. The railroad sanitarians are giving health administrators their utmost coöperation. In conclusion Dr. Stiles said: "I do not see how we can put the screws any tighter on the railroads along the right of way until we make the farmers along the railroads come up to the standards the railroads have already met."

In conclusion Dr. Lumsden noted the progress that had been made in the past ten years in the matter under discussion; he touched on the figures presented by Dr. Levy and deemed his conclusions reasonable and called attention to the importance of the fundamental problem of disposing of human excreta, suggesting that there may be means devised to make practicable the use of chemicals and a possibility of conserving these wastes and using them sanely and safely for fertilizer.

The Committee on Rural Health Administration presented its report, which was adopted and the recommendations endorsed. It will find place in the Journal for February. The session closed with the reading by Dr. B. L. Arms of Jacksonville, Fla., of his paper, "Hookworm Infection in Florida."

The second session of the Public Health Administration Section was called to order on Tuesday, October 28, in the morning by Chairman Wells. The first paper of the session was that of Dr. D. B. Armstrong of Framingham, Mass., "The State, the Municipality and the Private Tuberculosis Association in the Control of Tuberculosis." In the discussion Allan J. Hruby of Chicago, Ill.,

80

was the first speaker, outlining the anti-tuberculosis program of the city of Chicago. Here the work is in the hands of the municipal government. Eight dispensaries handle about 30,000 patients and at the sanatarium there are 1,000. He expressed the opinion that the municipality should control the business program in the municipality. He was in accord with Dr. Armstrong in that private agencies are well fitted to initiate and demonstrate, and pave the way for legislation.

DR. JOHN DILL ROBERTSON of Chicago emphasized his belief that it is necessary to "educate with the law." "That is the strongest weapon we have," he continued, "tuberculosis is a contagious disease and we are enforcing the law. When you put it in the same category as infantile paralysis, smallpox, scarlet fever, diphtheria and venereal disease, then you get somewhere."

Next in order came the report of the Committee on Venereal Disease, presented by COL. W. F. SNOW of Washington, D. C., which was placed on file and the committee continued. An abstract of this report is listed for presentation in the February JOURNAL. The report of the Committee on Standard Regulations for the Control of Communicable Disease was presented by DR. HAVEN EMERSON of New York City. It was accepted and the committee continued with instructions to carry out the recommendations made in it. This report is listed for the February JOURNAL.

Next in order was the presentation of a communication, "Causes of Typhoid in Massachusetts," by DR. GEORGE T. O'DONNELL of Boston, Mass. Discussion followed in which DR. HERMAN BUNDESEN, DR. JOHN DILL ROBERTSON, DR. PERCY G. STILES, and DR. H. W. HILL took part with closing arguments by DR. O'DONNELL. The original paper will appear in a future issue of the JOURNAL, and in connection with it these various discussions will be presented in abstract.

"The Health Officers' Care of Lepers," by MR. JOHN A. VOGELSON of Philadelphia, Pa., was the next paper, with discussion by DR. ARCHIBALD L. HOYNE of Chicago, Ill., DR. H. H. CARTER and DR. G. W. MCCOY of Washington, with concluding remarks by the author of the paper.

Next in order came the paper by DR. MAZYRK P. RAVENEL of Columbia, Mo., entitled, "Preventive Medicine in War," presented in this issue of the JOURNAL, pages 22 to 33. The discussion was opened by DR. A. T. MCCORMACK of Louisville, Ky., who called attention to the notable need of the times, the recognition that there is a difference between the training of the physician to treat those already sick and that of the sanitary physician, to prevent those not sick from becoming so. "When

we recognize," continued the speaker, "and when the people recognize, that between one tenth and one fifth of the population of the United States are totally disabled, not only for soldiers but for efficient citizenship, because of diseases that we know how to prevent—not to cure—and have failed to prevent because we have not had the trained personnel to do the prevention—the local organization—when we and they realize that, the plans suggested by Dr. Ravenel will be put into operation immediately." Dr. McCormack went on to say that the care of infants outside the cities is practically negligible. The time to impress these lessons upon the people is while they are children, and we must go into our schools and teach the children the things that we know. A farmer who will not build a sanitary privy is an undesirable citizen and the man who lives in a city that will not provide itself with a sewage system is not the type of citizen that this country needs. "We have had one hundred years of conversation on this subject in the United States," said Dr. McCormack in concluding, "and you can build a sanitary privy in twenty-four hours. Until every doctor in this country has his own house with a screen about his kitchen and dining room and a sanitary system of sewage disposal, and knows his own family is supplied with pure water, we cannot get action from our law-makers."

DR. FRANCIS E. FRONCZAK of Buffalo, N. Y., came next with a statement about conditions in the army of Poland and a plea for the United States to extend assistance in the way of preventive medicine to this country and these men. DR. CHARLES J. HASTINGS of Toronto, Ont., and DR. A. L. HOYNE of Chicago joined in the discussion, the latter speaking particularly of the need of men educated to carry out the proper precautions. DR. RAVENAL closed the debate.

The paper entitled, "Venereal Disease Control," by DR. C. O. PIERCE of Washington, D. C., came next in order (to be presented in the February issue of the JOURNAL), at which time the discussions by DR. ALLEN W. FREEMAN of Columbus, Ohio, DR. J. D. ROBERTSON of Chicago, Ill., DR. JOHN D. McLEAN of Harrisburg, Pa., representing the state health commissioner of Pennsylvania, and COL. W. F. SNOW of Washington, with the original speaker, DR. PIERCE, in conclusion.

First on the program of the third session of the Section on Public Health Administration was the report of the Committee on Uniform Accounting for Health Departments, presented by ERNST C. MEYER, PH.D., of New York City. It was voted that the report be accepted, the recommendations carried out, and the committee thanked for its excellent work. In reporting for the Committee on a National Program of Prenatal and Maternal Care Dr. Haven Emerson of New York City added the suggestion that it would be well to hand this subject to the Child Hygiene Section, which was voted.

Col. Frank R. Keefer of Carlisle, Pa., next presented his paper entitled "Causes of Army Rejections and What the Health Officer Can do to Remedy Conditions," following which came the discussion on "Methods for the Defense of Health Appropriations." In this Dr. E. C. Meyer was the first speaker, presenting a paper scheduled for publication in the Journal in the spring. There was much discussion by Dr. Carl E. McCombs of New York City, Dr. Charles J. Hastings of Toronto, and Dr. Haven Emerson of New York City. These discussions had best be presented in the issue containing the original paper. Dr. McCombs then followed with his paper on the "Relative Functions of State and Local Health Departments," with discussions by Paul B. Brooks of Albany, Dr. A. T. McCormack of Louisville, Ky., Dr. A. W. Freeman of Columbus, Ohio, Dr. W. S. Rankin of Raleigh, N. C., Dr. W. H. Brown of Bridgeport, Conn., and Dr. J. A. Kappelman of Canton, Ohio, with Dr. McCombs in conclusion. Incidental to the discussion it was voted that a committee be appointed by the Chair on which there shall be represented both local and state health officers, to make a report to the section on the proper relations which should exist between state and local health officers.

The concluding paper of the session was that of F. S. Crum, Ph. D., of Newark, N. J., entitled, "What Should Be Done in the Control of Degenerative Diseases?" with a discussion by Dr. Eugene A. Fisk of New York City. The paper is listed for the March issue of the Journal.

On Wednesday, October 29, at noon a round-table luncheon was the regular order of exercises, at which the subject of appropriations was discussed extemporaneously by various speakers. The first of these was Dr. Henry F. Vaughan of Detroit, Mich., who stated that his city had been fortunate in getting decent appropriations for health work. On an estimated population of one million, the city spends annually one dollar a head. "Every man in his own community," said Dr. Vaughan, "has to a certain extent to work out his own problems." In Detroit the effort is made to put the method of obtaining money on a sound basis and political "pull" is not in its plan. Posters and bulletins, notices in theatres, street cars and other public places and newspapers are among the useful methods. The speaker attributed a million dollars for a tuberculosis hospital entirely to the press.

In the technique of application, Dr. Vaughan advised his hearers to begin at the beginning of the year. It is unfortunate to wait until a couple of weeks before the appropriating body sits and then over night explain what is to be done. Take out the mayor or the governor and let him see what is being done. Divide the budget so that what is spent on the different items is clear, and make the figures in cents per capita. The speaker outlined in some detail the Detroit methods, which seek to present to the authorities a picture of what is actually accomplished. For example the mayor will have on his desk this year a tabulated card from each of the 600 employees of the Health Department, individually signed and countersigned by the commissioner, showing just what he is doing. District maps are very useful in conveying information to the authorities.

Dr. E. C. Levy of Richmond, Va., was the next speaker and he classed himself as a man who cannot get appropriations. He has used the same methods, but without the same success. While he believes them to be good, it is often necessary to go to work in other ways, and work with individuals by conveying special arguments. He detailed one successful effort of this kind. The greatest appropriation has been thirty-five cents per head of population. He advocated the personal method as being with him the most effective.

Dr. Allen W. Freeman of Columbus, Ohio, said that in his state they were taking a lesson from the plumbers. The plumbers get one dollar an hour and the reason that they can get it is because they have, through a long campaign of education, convinced the people that plumbing has very vital relationships to the public health. In the older days all that was necessary was for the health officer to get appointed. But in order to have adequately paid officers it is necessary to do just what the plumbers have done, create a public opinion. Build up in the minds of the people the idea that health administration is a business that requires special training and experience. If these positions are open to any physician who cannot make a living at his profession, the rating will be low and the salary the minimum. Ohio has realized that the success of the public health system is dependent on the man who administers it. The system is going to depend on merit appointments and the scale of salaries will make it possible for good men to go into the business with proper prospects of advancement. In outlining the system Dr. Freeman noted that the state is going to start under the new law with forty men who know something about health. "We want every good health officer in the United States to take our examination," he said, "and I confidently expect, on the first of January, to have a good proportion of them working in the state. We are trying to build up in Ohio a system of professional sanitarians."

DR. OSCAR DOWLING of New Orleans, La., spoke of the inertia of the people and the difficulty that exists in getting them interested in health work. He spoke of compensation, and noted that on one occasion, talking with a health official who is paid $300 a year, he asked him to show anything that he had done to justify even this salary, and the official was dumb. Interest is improving, but it is not what it should be. Dr. Dowling's talk was illustrated by several bright stories.

DR. CHARLES J. HASTINGS of Toronto, Ont., outlined the qualifications of a health officer stating that all the scientific knowledge on the earth is not worth the snap of the finger if it is not seasoned with good common sense. What is required in health administration is men with vision and determination of purpose. Such things are the the first requisite, and then comes scientific knowledge. Such men would be competent to educate the community, and when this is done the most important step has been taken towards securing appropriations. In his city DR. HASTINGS had addressed the board of trade, women's clubs, and other organizations, and these addresses have never failed to elicit resolutions endorsing appropriations for the Health Department. He illustrated his point by noting that on the occasion of a recent proposal to cut the budget, spokesmen representing the organizations and the press united in requesting the full appropriation. In 1909 the appropriation was $79,000 and in 1919 it is $540,000. The general death rate in Toronto in 1909 was 14.9 per thousand inhabitants; in 1917 it was 11.05; in 1909 the infant mortality was 157 per thousand births; in 1917 it was 81.

DR. CHARLES V. CRASTER of Newark, N. J., asserted that health appropriations depend largely on the locality and on the type of persons who are charged with naming the appropriations. His experience showed it to be true that under a commission form of government there is a better chance of getting an adequate appropriation, provided the right man is in charge of the health administration. The present mayor of Newark "is from Missouri" in his mental attributes, and questions very closely when you ask for anything. In undertaking the education of the people in health matters, it is necessary to make the subject very attractive.

DR. J. M. FURSTMAN of Bloomington, Ill., was the last speaker at the luncheon, and discussed "the hard row to hoe" of the officials in a small community. With 30,000 population in Bloomington, $6,000 for health purposes seems a very large sum for "what seems little more than a fad." "We wanted to enlarge the activities," the speaker continued, "and started in to get $3,000 additional." The campaign included information about infant mortality,—in 1915 it was the lowest among cities under 50,000 population—the value of school nurses and the reduction in the death rate. One member of the Finance Committee on seeing the figures said, "If that is the case, we don't need a health officer." The effect of the educational effort may be judged, however, by the statement of the chairman of the Finance Committee who, in his address to his committee, said: "You must realize that health department work is preventive work. You cannot show in dollars and cents what you are accomplishing. If we can pay $1.02 for the Police Department, and $2.00 for every thousand for the Fire Department, we certainly should be able to pay 28 cents for the Health Department."

REPORTS OF COMMITTEES.

REPORT OF COMMITTEE ON HABIT FORMING DRUGS*

In the following report, your Committee has confined itself to the consideration of certain so-called "habit-forming" drugs only, for the reason that these drugs present a peculiar problem of the utmost importance and one quite distinct from that of other drugs commonly classed as "habit-forming." The drugs selected are the true narcotic or opiate drugs, i. e., opium and its derivatives, to the exclusion of cocaine, alcohol and the

various coal-tar drugs which are commonly habitually used, but which clinical study and laboratory experimentation fail to show possess sufficient physical or other similarity in their fundamental characteristics to warrant their further grouping with the opiates as of one class under "habit-forming" drugs.

It is necessary that the matter of terms and definitions should be cleared up and established on a basis of physical and scientific fact, if those who frame and administer restrictive laws and those who make judicial decisions shall act with intelligent understanding.

Thus the term "narcotic addict" has never yet been given an authoritative definition upon the

*Presented to the Section of Food and Drugs, American Public Health Association, at New Orleans, La., October 27-30, 1919.

basis of the known facts of his condition and the "practice of medicine" upon those afflicted with narcotic addiction-disease, as the condition must now unquestionably be called, has never been so defined as to determine its legitimate procedure upon disease facts.

Your Committee, therefore, would offer for your consideration the following basic definition to apply to those who suffer from narcotic, i. e., opium addiction.

Narcotic drug addiction is a physical condition in which continued administration of narcotic drugs—from whatever cause or origin and in whatever type or class of individuals—has set up within the body a mechanism of protection against the toxic action of narcotic drugs. This mechanism of protection constitutes the mechanism of addiction-disease. A narcotic drug addict is an individual in whose body the continued administration of opiate drugs has established a physical reaction, or condition, or mechanism, or process which manifests itself in the production of definite and constant symptoms and signs and peculiar and characteristic phenomena, appearing inevitably upon the deprivation or material lessening in amount of the narcotic drug, and capable of immediate and complete control only by further administration of the drug of the patient's addiction. In general the symptoms, signs and phenomena consist of a sense of restlessness and depression followed by yawning, sneezing, excessive mucus secretion, sweating, nausea, uncontrolled vomiting and purging, twitching and jerking, intense cramps and pains, abdominal distress, marked circulatory and cardiac insufficiency and irregularity, pulse going from extremes of slowness to extremes of rapidity, with loss of tone, faces drawn and haggard, pallor deepening to greyness, exhaustion, collapse and, in some cases, death. A definition along no other lines will include all who suffer from narcotic drug addiction. This symptomatology and the mechanism or process which produces it are the only common and characteristic attributes and possession of all narcotic addicts.

We would emphasize the fact that cocaine, alcohol and other drugs of indulgence do not fall into this definition, and they and their problems of handling, treatment and control, are quite different and distinct from the matter of opiate addiction-disease.

The matter of "legitimate professional practice," as applied to medical procedures directed at those suffering with narcotic addiction-disease, has never been satisfactorily outlined. The reason for this is doubtless because the facts of this disease and the clinical reactions of narcotic addiction are not sufficiently known in the courts and elsewhere, to give a basis for the determination of legitimacy of practice on the same intelligent lines of application of medical and scientific knowledge, as are applied to the question of legitimate practice in the cases of other diseases.

We feel that this should be determined upon the basis of honesty of application of clinical and scientific facts, along with a reasonable familiarity with the disease rather than upon various ideas originating in the minds of lawyers, police officials, reformers, promoters of cures or others interested in technicalities of profit rather than in scientific medicine and public health.

It is necessary to clear up and establish medical facts and from them to reasonably interpret the law, both for the protection of the honest and innocent and for the more efficient punishment of the dishonest and criminal.

Measures to restrict or control the use of narcotic drugs by purely forcible means have, in every instance, so far as your Committee can ascertain, failed of their purpose, and furthermore, where restrictive measures have been drastic or rigidly enforced, the illegitimate traffic in narcotics has for obvious reasons increased. Thus in spite of the enforcement during the past four years of the Harrison Act, the Committee appointed by the Secretary of the Treasury to investigate the extent of traffic in these drugs, reports that the underground supply equals that coming through legitimate channels.

Reasons for this universal failure are found in the neglect of the clinical and other scientific aspects of the subject, with failure to disseminate authoritative and useful information, and also the tendency to emphasize in a spectacular manner in the daily press, periodicals, and elsewhere, the old theories to the effect that the continued use of narcotic drugs is a vicious habit or an evidence of a neurosis or degeneracy, thus perpetuating the almost universal condemnation that has attended the addict. The same over-publicity has been accorded the occasional medical offender and has led to neglect to recognize and encourage the efforts of the conscientious majority of physicians.

The administration of laws and regulations of a too restrictive character, as applied to physicians and druggists as a whole, has apparently resulted in the neglect of this disease by the medical profession and the consequent retarding of the solution of the problem, just as they would if thrown around the treatment of any other disease. The demands of various minor technicalities and the possibilities of unintentional violations render so hazardous the practice of medicine as applied to these cases as to drive away from help to the addict the average honest practitioner of medicine, while they encourage the shyster and charlatan as they do underworld commerce.

Compulsory registration of all narcotic drug addicts with photographs and other identification data as heretofore tried and in present execution, has failed as yet to demonstrate its usefulness. It has likewise failed to accomplish the registration of a great majority of those afflicted with this disease, who apparently prefer the chances of illegitimate narcotic supply to possible revelation of their condition with its social, personal and economic menace.

It seems to be the fact that such addicts as may be said to be a menace to society find their supply in the underworld and hence do not register while those whose lives are an economic asset to the community do not dare to register through possible jeopardy to themselves and reputations. Compulsory registration in its present status as described above and as resulting from past and present experiment and experience, appears to your Committee to serve no practical purpose either from the point of view of the sufferer or of the public.

It would further appear that regulatory and restrictive administrative measures should be framed and executed only upon the advice of practitioners of medicine conversant with the subject and, so administered as not to interfere with the honest practice of medicine and the welfare of the honest narcotic addict.

Your Committee would also condemn enforced hospitalization for all addicts as an unsuccessful procedure at the present time, due, apparently, to lack of intelligent medical and nursing handling of these patients. Ample testimony before the Whitney Committee of the New York Legislature justifies this conclusion. The Report of the abovementioned Committee states:

"Evidence offered by physicians shows that many addicts have died under the methods of treatment existing today and that a large percentage of those discharged from institutions as 'cured' are driven back to the use of narcotics through unbearable physical torture induced by improper withdrawal of their drug." Evidence of this nature was adduced as applying to both public and private institutions in New York State.

Success in hospitalization is to be expected only under the same conditions as attend success in private practice, namely, medical and nursing competency and skill.

Your Committee believes there is no more reason to require narcotic drug-disease sufferers to undergo unusual and potentially harmful procedures in the name of "treatment" and "cure" of their condition than there is those who suffer from other diseases. The innocent contractor of addiction-disease should

have the same rights of selection of treatment and of personal choice and the same protections from ignorance and other medical and institutional shortcomings as have other patients.

Vicious, degenerate and criminal types of addicts should be handled on a basis of vice, degeneracy or criminality and treated for their addiction-disease in places suitable to their personal and class characteristics.

Your Committee believes that one of the greatest present needs is for experimental and clinical research and the education of the profession and laity through all possible channels. Such activity will, your Committee feels, prove the most important factor in the solution of the situation which should be through medical and public health channels rather than through police measures.

Such is the present trend of development now rapidly coming to pass and this Section and the American Public Health Association as a whole should take a prominent part in the movement and through its influence and publications assist in all appropriate ways.

In this connection your Committee would emphasize the fact that there is no specific or routine treatment for narcotic addiction-disease and both the public and profession should be warned to regard with suspicion any promulgation of so-called "cures" and of special routine treatments. The tendency to exclude these patients from hospitals other than custodial and correctional constitutes a serious loss of clinical material for study and teaching to physicians and nurses and should be combatted.

The Committee also feels that in proportion as the medical and nursing professions become more familiar with this disease in its modern conception and clinical manifestations, the need for enforced restraint in special institutions or elsewhere will become less and finally will only be required for such cases of addiction-disease as are fundamentally in need of restraint because of inherent defect in their mental or moral make-up.

That improvement is needed in the methods of instructing medical men in the care and treatment of narcotic addiction-disease is evidenced by the replies received to a questionnaire relating to the subject, recently sent to the medical schools of the country, by a member of your Committee. Of the 85 institutions queried, 37 or 43 per cent replied. Among these replies, were included the leading schools of this country. A brief review of the data so obtained indicates that the time devoted to the physiological, clinical and therapeutic consideration of opiate drug addiction averaged about two hours, and that in several institutions the subject was not considered at all. In 25 of these schools, the subject was taken up only under materia medica or therapeutics in the second year's course and, in nine schools, under the consideration of nervous and mental diseases. Clinical material was woefully lacking, none at all being available in 13 of these schools, while in the others the replies stated that opportunities to observe cases were "rare," "infrequent," or limited to an occasional case seen in the insane asylums or jails.

The textbooks used were, with but one exception, those which teach the old "habit" and "vice" theories, and in which treatment is confined to routine procedures and "specific" formulas. None of the more recent experimental or clinical work was mentioned.

While realizing fully the possible social dangers of narcotic addiction-disease, your Committee distinctly deprecates the sensational manner in which the statistics of this disease have been handled by the lay press and uninformed or notoriety-seeking officials in the emphasis which is laid on the number of addicts said to exist in the United States. By reliable method of computing the number of addicts existing, these numbers have been determined, by some civilian investigators, as being a mere fraction of the numbers alleged by the extreme sensationalists; and it is very significant that the estimates of civilian observers have been strikingly borne out by the experience of the Division of Neurology and Psychiatry of the Office of the Surgeon General of the Army during the late war. It is obvious that such exaggerations inflame the public imagination and tend to produce that atmosphere of fear and apprehension which is so potent a deterrent of intelligent and scientific consideration and action.

Your Committee would not be understood as opposing the restriction of the use of narcotic drugs, but it feels that the principal effort of such restrictions should be directed at traffickers, the underworld, and criminal commerce, medical charlatans and incompetents and in general such as have to do with the needless dissemination of this disease, while greater consideration should be accorded the true disease nature of narcotic drug addiction, together with encouragement and cooperation for the honest practitioner and the honest addict with the protection of the latter's physical, social and economic welfare and rights.

A partial bibliography covering some of the more useful contributions to the subject is attached to this report, and it is suggested that the frequent publication in the Association's Journal, of short articles, abstracts or reviews, such as might be prepared by some suitable board or committee, would assist materially in stimulating in proper quarters interest in the more modern views and teachings on this important subject.

Respectfully submitted,

C. E. TERRY, M. D., *Chairman*,
OSCAR DOWLING, M. D.,
LUCIUS P. BROWN,
ERNEST S. BISHOP, M. D.

HERMANN C. LYTHGOE, M. D., dissents from most of the opinions expressed in this report:

SECOND REPORT OF COMMITTEE ON NUTRITIONAL PROBLEMS.

The first report of this Committee, presented at the Chicago meeting last year, dealt chiefly with the quantitative requirements of nutrition which must constitute the scientific basis for any sound teaching of nutritional needs or of the relation of adequate diet to health. Proceeding from this, your committee would, at this and subsequent meetings, direct attention to, and invite discussion of, the probabilities of occurrence of certain specific dietary deficiencies under present conditions of food supply and with existing food habits in America, and consider the problem of presenting our present conception of adequate diet in every-day terms and with practical illustrations of diets which shall be economically within the reach of all. The present report refers specifically to the problem of the relation of the food supply to pellagra, which is of such peculiar importance in the section where our meeting is held this year.

Fully recognizing the importance of specific deficiencies in the diet of the type particularly referred to in this report, and elementary and old-fashioned as the suggestion may seem to some of our members, we must still insist upon the great need of disseminating knowledge as to which foods furnish the most calories in proportion to their cost. The importance of the fundamental nutritional requirement of adequate calories should not be lost sight of while we are evaluating the more complex phases of the diet. Abundant as our food production is and notwithstanding that the corn crop alone supplies calories sufficient for a population of three hundred millions of people, there is reason to believe that deficiency in calories characterizes the dietary of large groups in our population. This condition is due both to high cost of food and to lack of full appreciation of the high food requirements of children. There is danger of misunderstanding any attempt to formulate a fixed standard as to the energy requirements of the average citizen.

Recent observations of the metabolism of the child and adolescent show higher energy requirements than formerly supposed, and it is in this group that widespread deficiency as to calories exists.

The general propostion may be laid down that among adults the adjustment of the calories to maintain a vigorous, active state free from excess adipose, is desirable, the reading of the scales and general well being of the individual being the criterion, rather than any fixed standard as to calories. In children and especially adolescents, the risk of over-nutrition should be taken and a special standard as to energy requirement established without any mathematical relation to that of the adult. The following table based on that of Professor Lusk presents a fair picture of the energy requirement of a family group, from which the needs of the general population can be roughly gauged:

	Calories per day.
Father	3,000
Mother	2,500
Boy of 13	3,000
Boy or girl of 11	2,500
Boy or girl of 7	2,000
Family Requirement	13,000

This represents the requirement of about four men.

(In estimating the calorie requirement of a nation, about 10 per cent is added to cover unavoidable wastes in handling, storage and distribution of the food supply.)

The number of under-nourished children at present in the United States has been variously estimated as from three to six millions, based on Government reports. There can be no question as to the need for thorough education of the public in the food needs of the child and the adolescent, and in the relations of food values to costs. The figures for certain typical foods cited in the table following showing the number of calories obtained for each cent have recently been prepared by the Department of Public Health of the American Museum of Natural History on the basis of retail prices in New York. The comments are added by this Committee.

Turning from calories to protein we meet less occasion for anxiety. We know of no locality or group of people in this country which presents any real danger of an inadequate intake of protein in general. Indeed, it is probable that many persons whose food budget is not closely limited by economic considerations, suffer from the opposite extreme of high protein feeding. Especially is there such danger among those who are liberal meat eaters and at the same time inclined to sedentary habits. An excess of protein, and particularly of meat protein,

RELATIVE ECONOMY OF TYPICAL FOODS AT NEW YORK CITY PRICES.

Kind of Food	Calories for 1 cent	Comments
Lean Meats, cheaper cuts ..	20	Rich source of protein but poor source of mineral elements and vitamines.
Eggs	19	Much superior to meat as source of calcium and vitamines.
Milk	47	Much more economical source of calories and protein than meat, and the best of all sources of calcium and vitamines.
Sugar	180	Furnishes nothing except calories.
Bread	117	Very economical source of energy and also of fairly efficient protein.
Potatoes	68	Valuable also for mineral elements and vitamines.
Canned tomatoes	10	Exceedingly efficient as anti-scorbutic.
Prunes	48	Valuable for mineral elements also.
Apples	24	Not so cheap a fruit as prunes, but a better anti-scorbutic.
Peanut butter	98	Good source of protein and mineral elements as well as a cheap fuel.

in the diet may be unfavorable from several different standpoints. It may promote an excessively high rate of oxidation due to the much discussed "specific dynamic" or heat-producing power of protein in the body tissues; it necessarily increases the amounts of urea, uric acid and other end products of protein metabolism which must circulate in, and be excreted from, the body; at the same time it tends through an excess of acid decomposition products to diminish the alkaline reserve of the blood and its capacity, and that of the urine, for carrying away and excreting the uric acid formed; and a large proportion of protein in the diet tends to favor the development of putrefactive bacteria in the intestines with the possibility of resulting autointoxication.

The experiments made some years ago by Kendall show that a high protein diet administered to monkeys produces a characteristic condition of general malaise with the preponderance of putrefactive bacteria in the stools; the substitution of carbohydrate diet quickly relieves the symptoms and causes the replacement of putrefactive by fermentative bacteria, while the stools lose their highly offensive odor.

Yet while as regards protein in general, American dietaries are more often open to criticism because of excess than of deficiency, yet individual amino acids may not infrequently be present in the dietary in less than optimum amounts, particularly when the exacting requirements of growth or of reproduction are being met by a dietary consisting too largely of the products of seeds (e. g., breadstuffs and other cereal products) more or less extensively supplemented by sugars and fats which contribute nothing to the amino acid supply. Recently, however, it has been convincingly shown that when a dietary contains enough milk to furnish one-fourth to one-third of the amount of protein required the remainder may be drawn from any·of our staple breadstuffs or cereal foods without danger of inducing a deficiency of any essential amino acid.

Among the mineral elements, calcium is the one in which American dietaries are most often deficient. The best safeguard against such deficiency is a liberal use of milk in the dietary, which, as we have pointed out, is so desirable on other grounds as well.

Three "vitamines" are now generally recognized as essential to an adequate diet: "Fat Soluble A," best known for its growth-promoting property; "Water Soluble B," the antineuritic vitamine; and "Water Soluble C," the antiscorbutic factor. The products of cereal grains, so economical as sources of energy and of proteins fairly efficient for maintenance but less well suited to supply certain amino acids needed in abundance for normal growth and reproduction, are relatively poor sources of "Fat Soluble A" and "Water Soluble C," and if too highly milled may be seriously lacking in "Water Soluble B" as well. The calcium content of the cereal grains, as of seeds generally, is also too low to permit them to serve as adequate food for growth or reproduction unless some suitable supplement be added in sufficient amounts. Meat supplements the amino acid deficiency, but neither the calcium nor the Vitamine deficiency of the seed; leaves supplement seeds much better, and milk best of all. In view of the experimental evidence of Chittenden and Underhill referred to.in our last report, and that of McCollum, Simmonds and Parsons, summarized and extended in their recent paper in the *Journal of Biological Chemistry* (May, 1919), your committee urges the closest study, especially upon the part of the Southern members of the Association, of the accumulated evidence that susceptibility to pellagra is largely, if not chiefly, the result of dietaries which in chemical terms are low in calcium and fat soluble vitamine (perhaps also in one or both of the water soluble vitamines and certain individual amino acids), or in terms of the articles of food chiefly concerned, are made up too largely of breadstuffs and other products of seeds, with varying amounts of meats, fats and sweets, but which contain too little of milk, eggs, green vegetables, and fruit. As eggs and fruit are often too expensive, and green vegetables too bulky, to make up an important part of the diet, *an increased production and consumption of milk would seem to be the most important single measure for the eradication of pellagra from the Southern states.*

To illustrate adequate proportions of milk and other foods in a well-balanced, low-cost dietary, we append the following data (American Museum of Natural History, New York City).

FOOD SUPPLY FOR A FAMILY OF FIVE FOR A WEEK.

Kind of Food	Amount lbs.	Cost		Percentage of Total Cost of Food	
		Dec. 1918	Aug. 1919	Dec. 1918	Aug. 1919
Meats and Fish .	6¼	$1.49	$1.31	12.1	10.9
Eggs (¾ doz.)....	(15 oz.)	0.40	0.30	3.2	2.5
Milk (21 qts.)....	46	3.36	3.08	27.4	25.7
Cheese..........	1	0.40	0.43	3.2	3.5
Fats...........	3¼	1.26	1.26	10.2	10.5
Sugar..........	4	0.40	0.44	3.2	3.3
Grain products (bread, cereals, etc.)....	20	1.88	1.85	15.3	15.4
Vegetables.......	23	1.50	1.65	12.2	13.8
Fruit...........	8¼	1.30	1.45	10.2	12.1
Nuts (Peanut butter)	½	0.17	0.14	1.3	1.2
Coffee..........	¼	0.08	0.08	0.7	0.7
Total Cost...		$12.24	$11.99		

It is hoped that this may serve as a basis for discussion, by members of the Section and others, of the proper prominence to give to the different types of food in the family dietary; and that it may perhaps be of practical assistance in the educational work of the health officer in regard to dietary values.

For a sound and thorough, yet very readable and highly practical, discussion of the problem of food and nutrition from the standpoints of the consumer and the home-maker, the health official engaged in such educational work will find the book entitled, "Feeding the Family" by Professor Mary S. Rose of the greatest value.

HENRY C. SHERMAN, *Chairman,*
C. E. A. WINSLOW
H. S. GRINDLEY
A. G. WOODMAN
E. L. FISK
Committee on Nutritional Problems.

NOTE ON THE NUTRITION AGENCIES INTERESTED IN PUBLIC HEALTH.*

LUCY H. GILLETT, BOSTON.

In reporting progress in nutrition, it seems appropriate to mention one of the recent developments in the dissemination of such knowledge which will improve the health of a group of people, that would not be reached in any other way, a group however that plays considerable part in public health.

In families of limited means there are large numbers of children who should be able to take their place in the community with plenty of strength and vigor, but whose health is in danger because their parents are indifferent, ignorant, or foreign-speaking people who are not reached by material sent out through folders, newspapers, or by lectures. They either do not appreciate such information or are unable to apply to their own problems what they do understand. It would take several generations for the schools to function in these districts through the children.` These people must be reached individually, and in each case the interrelation of cause and effect studied as a separate problem.

Those coming in closest contact with these families, and those having most influence with them, are a group of people especially interested in public health and public welfare. They are the nurses and social workers of either public or private agencies. There seems to be a general awakening of interest in this group as to the part proper nutrition should play in health and efficiency. Aroused to the need, they are seeking information as to the proper feeding of children from those trained in the subject of nutrition. In connection with these families, there are more problems than the teaching of proper feeding habits. There is reconstruction of habits already formed, the overcoming of abnormal conditions brought about because of irrational habits, and in the majority of cases there is also the question of economy. The problem is therefore one needing more than general information concerning the feeding of a family.

While a person well-trained in foods, nutrition and economy is needed, one nutrition specialist may act as adviser to a large group of social workers. This plan is being tried in various organizations in many of our large cities with much success. Some of the hospitals in New York, Philadelphia, Chicago, Boston, and other cities are putting nutrition specialists in their clinics. In Brookline, Mass., a nutrition worker, who has been placed upon the Board of Health staff, has the hearty support of the Medical Association of that town because of her influence in arousing interest in proper nutrition. In Boston, a group of social agencies has been instrumental in having established a central bureau to help the workers of any agency in that city with the food problems in the homes of the families with which they come in contact. In connection with the bureau, centres are being established in some of the most congested districts so that the workers may come in closer contact with both mothers and children, and interest them in the fundamentals of proper nutrition.

In addition to the direct assistance given in individual cases, the point of view of both mothers and workers is changing so that what they previously looked upon as "inevitable," they now consider preventable. They are more and more seeking a means for prevention of the conditions leading to mal-nutrition because they have seen by a concrete and practical method, what may be accomplished through diet suited to the needs of the individual both physiologically and economically.

This group of nutrition specialists working in the interest of public health is the medium for reaching a very vital part of the community, a part that has perhaps been a detrimental factor in progress because it is so hard to reach. The nutrition adviser promises to be a very essential part of any community.

Public Health Activities of the Rockefeller Foundation in 1918.

In a recent, special report, published by the Rockefeller Foundation, Dr. George E. Vincent, its President, gives a brief résumé of the activities conducted in 1918. The following is a list of the more important ones. The campaign against tuberculosis in France was extended; demonstrations on how to control malaria were conducted in Arkansas and Mississippi; assistance was given in checking an epidemic of yellow fever in Guatemala; yellow fever surveys were made in Ecuador; the campaign against hookworm was continued or begun in 21 foreign states, and 12 states of the Union; extensive aid was given to reorganize public health work in Brazil and Australia; a school of public health at the Johns Hopkins University was supported; aid in establishing medical schools and hospitals in China was continued; studies in mental hygiene were supported; further work on the aftercare of cases suffering from poliomyelitis was also supported; and additional gifts were made to the Rockefeller Institute for Medical Research. (*M. P. H.*)

* A statement made to the Committee on Nutritional Problems.

PUBLIC HEALTH NOTES

Abstracts by D. Greenberg, M. P. Horwood and Mayo Tolman.

Heating and Ventilation.—In the course of an address on "Heating and Ventilation in Relation to the Housing Problem," Professor Leonard Hill said: Close air affects us through lack of adequate cooling and evaporating powers and by the spread of infection from carriers of the germs of disease, while cool moving air is the natural stimulus to activity and appetite, to deep breathing and good digestion. The evils of crowding can be overcome by adequate ventilation, and ventilation inside a building should be induced naturally by virtue of differences in temperature. Cold outer air should be drawn to the warm zone inside by fans at an 8 ft. level round the walls and this current should be kept moving and not allowed to grow stagnant, the air being extracted through a number of vents in the ceiling by means of an extract fan. Windows should be pivoted vertically, so that they may be fixed open as wind screens, and be rotated inwards for cleaning, while in the hot weather the extract fans can be reversed and made to blow inwards with all the windows open.

As to the question of heating, the ideal conditions are afforded by radiant heat and abundant cool moving air, but it is necessary to secure these ideal conditions and at the same time to save coal. In a large hall or workroom multiple units of radiating surface with separate control are required—multiple so that no one person shall be unduly heated by proximity to a unit.—*Medical Officer*, Nov. 15, 1919, 180. (*D. G.*)

✤

Lessons Taught by War in Disease Control.—The war has taught that it is persons and not things that are to be feared, that danger lies in short, direct and often obvious channels of infection rather than in long, roundabout and mysterious ones. The war has demonstrated the need of searching out the sources of infection rather than waiting for them to come to light later on. The value of isolation was abundantly proved. This is the basis of a great variety of practical procedures, such as quarantine. The use of masks and cubicles afford applications of the same principle.

Great emphasis has been placed on indirect measures of prevention. Such simple and well tried measures as ventilation and cleanliness were among the most valuable steps taken to prevent disease in the American Army. The war has demonstrated the great value that attaches to focused attacks on disease. This was illustrated in two entirely different groups of infections, the typhoid group and the venereal group.

It is interesting to note the failures which the war has brought out. It has shown the hopelessness of the efforts conducted along ordinary lines in the fight against respiratory infections. Little was done successfully in handling this group of diseases in the camps. It has taught that the time to study the management of infections is before the pressing necessity for this knowledge occurs; that disease must be looked for and not waited for.

There is a great field quite uncultivated as yet for the competent instruction of the public in measures for the prevention of disease. How to live and work and enjoy the greatest share of health should be taken out of the realm of uninformed guesswork where it now exists and set before the public on a substantial basis of scientific fact and authoritative opinion.—G. A. Soper, *Jour. A. M. A.* November 8, 1919, 1405. (*D. G.*)

✤

Child Labor and National Health.—"The health of the child is the wealth of the nation." The termination of children's year has not ended but has rather emphasized the need for continuing the work of child protection in this country. The child labor movement assumes a new and broader significance in the peace-time program of the nation. It becomes, in a very real sense, a movement for the conservation of children—for development of the normal, healthy child life which we have come to recognize not only as the heritage of every child, but as a necessity to the welfare of the nation. For among the serious lessons which the war brought home to us is the realization that the nation's health is dependent, in large measure, upon the health of its children.

In the first selective draft 29 per cent of the men between the ages of 21 and 31 were rejected as physically unfit. In the state of Pennsylvania, where for many years child labor laws were inadequate, the percentage of rejections for physical disability was 55. The men rejected, according to Dr. Willard S. Small, were nearly all "physical illiterates"—uneducated in the first principles of health and physical fitness. Among our school children, too, investigations have shown that more than 20 per cent of the money expended yearly in the United States for educational purposes is wasted because of physical deficiencies in children which impede normal development. The economic loss to the nation through adult illiteracy has been computed by Secretary Lane at $825,000,000. The economic cost of this physical illiteracy cannot be computed.

The movement to eliminate children from industry has come to be a positive movement for health—mental and spiritual, as well as physical. It aims beyond the protection of children from the actual physical effects of premature labor, to the provision of opportunity for.play, for education, and for all that contributes to the normal, healthy development of all children. The National Child Labor Committee is asking churches, schools and clubs to coöperate in the national observance of Child Labor Day on January 24, 25, and 26, and material and suggestions for programs may be obtained from the Committee's offices, 105 East 22nd Street, New York City.—Special Note for the JOURNAL by Josette Frank.

✼

Incubation of Influenza.—The following original notes are illustrative of influenza as a specific disease with a definite incubation of 36 to 48 hours, and of how independently of other contributory factors it is spread through contact infection in the confined air of the bunk house in a lumber camp.

Dr. Henderson L. Bryce, B. A., was medical officer to an aëroplane Spruce Lumber Co., on Queen Charlotte Islands on Massett Harbour Inlet, eight hours steaming from Prince Rupert, British Columbia, whence a supply steamer reached the islands once every ten days. There were twelve camps under the company scattered over the shores of an inland bay of the ocean, some five miles apart. No other inhabitants were in that part of the island. The notes state, "The Prince Albert S. S. came to Buckley Monday noon with the captain, purser and steward ill at the time. Two men who had been sick in Prince Rupert came over on her and in the afternoon left for Camp V, of course without my knowledge. Two days after this several there were taken sick in their bunk house. So reckoning from the time they came in contact first with the carriers, it took between 36 and 48 hours for incubation. That camp developed 50 per cent of strength laid out. At Buckley Bay at least 75 per cent came down with the disease with only one death. No cases broke out in any of the other camps of the company. All the earlier cases were of the mild type except the Munition Board Inspector at Port Clements. He developed the cyanotic type with sanious expectoration and high temperature from the beginning and eventually died at Prince Rupert. It hit the Indians very hard at Massett Village, 25 or 30 dying in 300."

It may be noted that the official report of the Epidemic Commission in South Africa states that sailors on the vessels going both north and south touching at Sierra Leone, where the disease was raging, though but a few hours in port developed the disease within forty-eight hours though before in all cases they had been free from the disease. Due to whatever cause, it is worth noting that while but one death occurred in two aëroplane camps of 200 persons, 68 and 38 deaths respectively occurred in the "Tahiti" and "Chepstow Castle" between Sierra Leone and Plymouth. (P. H. B.)

✼

Industrial Nursing.—There has been a definite expression of opinion recently among industrial nurses generally that there is need for uniform standards of service and for better preparation for their work. Employers are seeing similar needs. Industrial nursing is still a field for the pioneer nurse who often takes up her work without thought of preparation other than a hospital training. She finds immediate need for a broader knowledge, which is often fairly easy to obtain if the way is pointed out.

The industrial nurses of the National Organization for Public Health Nursing plan to form an Industrial Nursing Section in the National Organization at the meeting in Atlanta next April. The object of this section will be the formulation and maintenance of high standards for service in industry. It is planned to make known to nurses throughout the country the opportunities for education for industrial nurses. Opportunities exist or may be developed in many large centers.

✼

Shall Schools Be Closed During Epidemics?—It is the opinion of a committee of experts consisting of Dr. W. S. Small, Dr. W. C. Woodward, Dr. F. G. Curtis, Dr. Bernard Kahn and Dr. Taliaferro Clark, that the schools should not be closed during epidemics of children's diseases. The successful control of epidemic diseases among school children requires that the schools be kept open, except perhaps in the sparsely settled rural districts where medical inspection is absent. During the epidemic, the children should be carefully inspected every day and provision should be made to exclude all cases of the disease and all contacts. The contacts should be excluded until the clinical data warrant their return to the classroom. This method is preferable to a fixed period of exclusion. Children who are ill should be visited regularly by the school nurse. The disinfection of the school room and the sick room should be accomplished through natural and physical cleansing, rather than chemical disinfectants.—Public Health Reports, November 21, 1919. (M. P. H.)

✼

Cho Cho, the Health Clown.—Cho Cho bounced into being but yesterday, coming from the mystic land of Nowhere, which has produced other distinguished personages, such as Mr. Santa Claus.

He did not become a national figure until one day last spring when he was roped, thrown, and broken by a scientific expedition sent out by Director Sally Lucas Jean of the Child Health Organization of New York, which is headed by Dr. L. Emmett Holt, Dr. Thomas B. Wood, who is chief of the department of physical education of Columbia University, and many other noted scientists.

Cho Cho is spectacular. He visits schools and ricochets down the aisle to the stage. Thereafter, for an hour or more, indoors becomes a prolonged shriek of purest joy, but punctuated with moments of comparative stillness as Cho Cho again and again and again rhythmically retards the waves of delirium long enough to make himself heard while pronouncing and elaborating upon the eight commandments of child health that Dr. Holt says, guarantees, can remake the human race. Not only the children are being taught as Cho Cho talks and capers, he also is teaching the assembled teachers.

Cho Cho's very motto is "Health, Strength, Joy!" —these three, and the greatest of these is Joy. Cho Cho early makes it known that there can be no joy without health and strength. But never is he an obviously didactic Cho Cho. Cho Cho's show is— a show. Perhaps somewhere between his capers the fact does leak out that five little prunes have more value as food than thirty big tomatoes, or that tableroom given to radishes should be occupied by carrots or spinach, but if the little enthusiasts watching and listening to Cho Cho learn these things, they swallow the knowledge without recognizing the taste.

It is the greatest game of child life. To millions of American children the goal of the game is the gift of life itself. And the goal of the game is reached and won only when every child, healthy or subnormal, is conscious of the desirability of health and obtains and retains it.—*Red Cross Magazine*, November, 1919. (*J. A. T.*)

✢

Rural Sanitation.—According to the 1910 census 53.7 per cent of the population of the United States lived in communities having less than 2,500 people. It has always been known that sanitary conditions in the rural parts of the country were much inferior to those that prevail, as a rule, under urban conditions, but the degree of backwardness was not known. In order to get exact information on the sanitation of rural districts, and in order to improve the sanitary conditions in the country, the U. S. Public Health Service undertook some studies in rural sanitation and placed the investigation in charge of Surgeon L. L. Lumsden. That it is exceedingly important to protect the health of the rural population is evidenced not only by their numbers, but by the fact, that in spite of the absence of overcrowding and the abundance of fresh air and sunshine which city dwellers as a rule do not have, the annual rural death rate is only about 2 per 1,000 less than the urban death rate. There are numerous difficulties which make the organization for rural health work very trying. First, there is the great area to be covered; second, is the lack of adequate funds; and third, is the absence of a concentrated local government. Usually, the county forms the unit of local government, but the farmer's home really represents the unit of local government in all its phases. He and his family are a community unto themselves.

In the investigation, attention was concentrated on the proper disposal of excreta, the safeguarding of water supplies, and conditions that favor the spread of hookworm and insect borne diseases like malaria and typhoid fever. Fifteen counties in different parts of the country were surveyed. The survey consisted in making a complete sanitary inspection of each home, and obtaining certain general information. Defects were pointed out as a rule, and directions for remedying unsatisfactory conditions, were given. In one county, the P. H. Service furnished labor and materials at cost to the farmers, in order to improve the methods in use for the disposal of excreta. It is remarkable how many people availed themselves of the opportunity to improve the existing systems of sewage disposal. The surveys thus took the form of a great and intensive educational movement, with much good.

Of 51,544 farm houses that were surveyed only 1.22 per cent were equipped with proper methods for the sanitary disposal of excreta. Sixty-eight per cent of the water supplies used for drinking purposes were exposed to dangerous pollution. Only 32.88 per cent of the homes were effectively screened against flies and other insects during the summer. The amount of ignorance regarding elementary principles of hygiene and sanitation was astounding.—*Public Health Bulletin No. 94*. (*M. P. H.*)

✢

The Nursing Mother and Industrial Employment.—Dr. Helen Y. Campbell, chief medical officer of the Bradford municipal infants' department maintains that the care of the health of our potential mothers (during earlier and industrial life) and of the mothers during the period of expectancy and afterwards is one of the essential requirements of provision for child health and welfare. Apart from those cases of chronic ill health, often serious, and sometimes dating from childhood, young Bradford millhands, bring up their first babies, who are anæmic and lacking in vigor, often give themselves a history of anæmia, tiredness, and generally indifferent health for some years before marriage. Dr. Campḷell urges that the correction of long hours and too early start in industrial life, of bad feeding, inadequate health supervision and other factors such as unsuitable clothing, which those responsible for adolescence and industrial health will take cognizance of in the future should send these young mothers forward in a state of higher fitness for the functions of maternity.

Provision for the skilled supervision, all necessary treatment and the hygienic instruction of the expectant mother, detecting causes of chronic ill health, and securing her better preparation for suckling and motherhood generally, would undoubtedly secure more breast feeding. The skilled care of lactation by well-trained midwives, and the provision of all medical attendance necessary to secure an easier confinement and more relief for the mother than she now experiences in many cases of labor, and to ensure normal recovery from confinement definitely diminish the number of cases in which the milk now fails so early.

Further, the early and continued supervision of the infant at a health center securing not only the expert oversight of lactation, but the early detection and treatment of disease and causes of incessant restlessness and crying, would because of their tendency to prevent unnecessary weaning and the reaction of these conditions in the infant upon the mother's nervous health and breast milk secretion, preserve the milk for some babies.—*Medical Officer*, Oct. 18, 1919, 143. (*D. G.*)

✱

Teaching Public Health by Demonstration.—It is time that public health progress is swifter and more lasting, once the demand for efficient public health protection is made by the people. To convince the people that public health protection pays, there is nothing better than effective public health demonstrations. A few years ago the International Health Board instituted some work in the Southern states, aiming at the relief and control of hookworm. At first there was much popular opposition. Nevertheless several small dispensaries were started, and patients who volunteered for treatment were soon cured. It was not surprising, therefore, that thousands of people, who learned of the cures that had been effected, flocked to the dispensaries for treatment. This great practical public health demonstration led to a more vigorous attack on other diseases and in particular, on typhoid fever. The appropriations for Southern state boards of health had been only $250,000 per annum before the hookworm campaign began. In 1918, they had been increased to $1,500,000 per annum, and some

states were attempting to place a health officer in every country. Similarly, demonstrations have been conducted aiming to control malaria. It has been shown that small towns in Arkansas can control malaria and that the effective work can be maintained after the first year at about 50 cents per capita per annum. An engineer of the U. S. P. H. Service has been able to maintain the agencies controlling malaria at 16 cents per capita per annum. By such effective, practical demonstrations, it is comparatively easy to arouse a popular demand for efficient public health protection.—Victor Heiser, M. D. *N. Y. Health News*, Sept., 1919. (*M. P. H.*)

✱

Save The Youngest.—The Children's Bureau of the U. S. Department of Labor has recently issued *Bureau Publication No. 61*, which consists of seven charts on maternal and infant mortality with explanatory comments in each case. It is estimated that 16,000 mothers lose their lives in this country every year in childbirth. About 7,500 of these die from childbed fever. This and the other diseases which cause maternal deaths are mostly preventable or curable. Although the infant mortality is only 94 in this country, the rate is higher than in 10 other countries. Maternal and infant deaths can be greatly diminished through the following agencies: Public health nurses; prenatal centers; dental and venereal disease clinics; maternity hospitals or wards in general hospitals; training, registration and supervision of midwives and household attendants; prompt and accurate birth registration; nutrition clinics; children's hospitals or beds in general hospitals; state registration and supervision of all child-care institutions; general educational work, including the teaching of child hygiene in the public schools; physical examination of the mother by a physician as early in pregnancy as possible; internal examination and pelvic measurements before the seventh month in primipara; examination of urine every four weeks during the early months, and at least every two weeks after the sixth month, and more frequently, if necessary; confinement at home by a physician or a properly trained and qualified attendant, or in a hospital; nursing service at home at the time of confinement and during the lying-in period, or hospital care; at least ten days rest in bed after a normal delivery, with sufficient household service to allow the mother to recuperate; examination by a physician before discharging the patient not later than six weeks after delivery; breast feeding during the first six months of infant life; a clean and safe milk supply; absence of hard work during pregnancy; and a living wage for the bread winner of the family. (*M. P. H.*)

An Artist's View of
How Babies Should Be Registered

Is Your Baby's Birth Recorded?

It is very important that it should be:---

To prove his age and citizenship,
To prove his right to go to school,
To prove his right to work,
To prove his right to an inheritance,
To prove his right to marry,
To prove his right to secure passports for foreign travel,
To prove his mother's right to a widow's pension.

*HAVE YOUR BABY'S BIRTH REGISTERED
AT YOUR LOCAL REGISTRAR'S OFFICE*

Oklahoma Pow Wow. (*M. P. H.*)

STATE HEALTH NOTES—LEGISLATION

National.—A bill for the public protection of maternity and infancy—S. 3162—was introduced into the Senate on October 3, 1919, by Senator Sheppard of Texas, and into the House on December 5 by Judge Towner of Iowa. It has been referred in the former body to the Committee on Public Health and Quarantine and in the House to the Committee on Interstate and Foreign Commerce.

This bill provides for a Federal appropriation for the use of the states accepting the provisions of the act and undertaking public measures for the protection of mothers and children. The amount of appropriation is to be $2,000,000 for the first year, the sum to be gradually increased until it reaches $4,000,000 annually. It will be appropriated among the states in the proportion which their population bears to the total population of the United States, provided that each state appropriates a like sum. In addition to this sum, the bill provides for an annual appropriation of $480,000 to be divided equally among the states without guarantee of a like sum.

The act is to be administered by a Federal board composed of heads of departments or divisions and for the states there are to be specially created administrative boards working with committees, half the membership of the latter to be women.

The work done under the act must include instruction in the hygiene of maternity and infancy through public health nurses, consultation centers and other suitable methods and the provision of medical and nursing care for mothers and infants at home or at a hospital when necessary, especially in remote regions. The act provides for the coöperation of the state board with the state universities or land grant colleges in furnishing popular, untechnical instruction in the hygiene of maternity and infancy and kindred subjects.

✚

Alaska.—Legislation of the past summer in this Territory creates the office of commissioner of health and prescribes the powers, duties and fixes the salary of such officers. It makes an appropriation for the suppression and control of epidemics in the Territory and for the registration and restriction of communicable disease. The commissioner is to be appointed by the governor of Alaska and is to hold office for two years, preference to be given to an officer of the U. S. P. H. Service. This commissioner must be a physician and licensed to practice in Alaska, and is to receive a salary of $1,800 a year. The governor is empowered to appoint also one physician, also licensed to practice medicine in the Territory, for each judicial division where the commissioner does not reside, these assistant commissioners of health to receive an annual salary of $400 each, with a term of two years.

The commissioner of health is empowered specially to establish quarantine, effect isolation, and promulgate regulations against communicable disease, to remove decaying bodies, garbage, etc., to disinfect houses, rooms, property, places or localities, persons and other things, with the power to destroy material or buildings. He has the right to establish regulations with reference to food-handling industries and is to prepare forms for proper returns. In these matters the assistant commissioners have authority within their respective districts, under his approval. Every school district outside of incorporated towns, shall constitute a health district, and in every such district there shall be established a board of health. These boards shall be subordinate to the assistant commissioners. A number of sections prescribe the conditions under which persons shall be subject to isolation or quarantine, the duties of persons or householders knowing of cases of infectious disease, the technique of administration, together with penalties. The act repeals various previously existing laws.

✚

New Mexico.—State regulations governing the disposal of the dead and the reporting of births and deaths are now in effect. These follow the model law and the standard certificates are now in use. Regulations with reference to reporting and control of communicable diseases are now in effect together with other regulations concerning water supplies and sewage disposal, milk supplies and the sanitation of food-handling establishments.

✚

North Carolina.—The State Board of Health has won its first case in the courts for violation of the state-wide privy law. In this case the judge remitted the fine because it was the first case, and in view of the circumstances and to avoid future misunderstandings he passed specifically on certain items in the law. Suspension of the fine was not because anything is lacking in the law, or because the defendant was not guilty. The state has the right to bring actions into court under this law. The tax levied by the state under this law is affirmed as well as the manner of its collection, which is prescribed to be to the inspector at the time of his visit.

An interesting State Health Note is that the American Public Health Association will meet this fall in the State of California.

STATE HEALTH NOTES, GENERAL.

Nova Scotia.—Halifax has had a baby week. This was in November, but the accounts of it were too late for the December JOURNAL. There were 17 sessions and 10 motion picture exhibitions, 8 of the latter to school children. Among the presiding officers were the governor of the province, the mayor of the city, the chairman of the Massachusetts-Halifax Committee, the president of the Halifax Medical Society, and a rare group of educators, public health administrators and public spirited men and women. The local Council of Women shouldered the responsibility of undertaking the conference. The Montreal Baby Welfare Bureau loaned an exhibit and sent a lecturer and a dozen other activities sent exhibits or demonstrators. There were three booths in the exhibition hall devoted to the measurements of babies. All the health agencies of the city were enlisted in the conference. The social side was upheld by half a dozen luncheons with at least one speaker at each. There were about twenty-five addresses to bodies outside the regular sessions, and these included gatherings like Commercial Club, a meeting in the Council Chamber, at which the principal subject discussed was "Milk," a clinic at Dalhousie, an Anti-Tuberculosis League talk, and Y. M. C. A. and W. C. T. U. meetings at which the subject was the "Salvaging of Babies." The Halifax work, of which B. Franklin Royer, M. D., executive officer of the Massachusetts-Halifax Commission, is to a very large extent the center, is moving forward in splendid fashion. On every hand during the conference were heard the praises of the Victorian Order Nurses.

✢

United States Government.—The U. S. Public Health Service is issuing useful "fillers," which from their brevity and aptness will carry health maxims through the press into every quarter of the land. Some of these little items follow:

All colds are "catching" and may lead to dangerous diseases in others, especially children.

Thousands of children are killed every year because parents say, "They will have it anyway," and permit the little ones to expose themselves to whooping cough, measles and scarlet fever.

Germ diseases kill off more people than the deadliest wars. In 1917 pneumonia and tuberculosis killed 223,000 Americans, more than seven times the number killed in action in France.

Heart diseases caused more deaths in 1917 than any other ailment (115,337). Right living would materially reduce this. Don't wait for the disease to develop before you see your physician.

Carelessness with the hands and teeth causes more deaths in America every year than carelessness with motor vehicles. Keep the hands clean, free from germs, away from the mouth and visit the dentist regularly.

Properly fitting shoes of correct shape with a straight inner edge are the most effective preventive of weakfoot, bunions, corns, calloses and painful joints, according to the United States Public Health Service. Except for paralysis, clubfoot and deformities resulting from injuries, most foot trouble is caused by improper shoes.

The U. S. P. H. Service has issued a note on the destruction of rats that should be of great value. It tells the kind of bait, meat or animal substance, fresh fruit or vegetable foods or cooked foods, and outlines the most effective way in which to mix the poison, barium chloride, with this. General instructions follow. The Service will be glad to send to any applicant the notice in question.

✢

"Is your child getting a square deal?" is the question that the Children's Bureau pertinently asks. To help parents in this one of its recent publications presents in simple and concise language the essential requirements for the normal growth and development of the child which are listed under the headings, shelter, food, clothing, health and personal habits, play, education and work, religion and moral training.

These simple standards include nothing that is not fundamental. It would be easy for the parent to check each item and discover in what respects, if any, his child is not getting what is absolutely necessary for his proper development.

The Bureau is supporting in whole-hearted fashion the Back-to-School and Stay-in-School campaigns which have shown that in many places school attendance and child labor laws are not enforced. Many children were found to be working in violation of the statutes of their states, and many children of school age were in factories because there was not a sufficient number of attendance officers and factory inspectors to keep them in school and out of industry. In one state it was found that 10,895 children did not go to school at all last year. In a single district an inspector reported 1,700 children as not having had a day of schooling. In many rural districts the children attend school only about half the time, and the hours are short.

It is conditions such as these, the bulletin points out, that make the United States eighth instead of first on the list of civilized countries with regard to the proportion of literacy among its citizens, and education must be the foundation of good public health.

Florida.—The personnel of the State Board of Health is the following: Ralph N. Greene, M. D., state health officer; William J. Buck, M. D., assistant health officer. Heads of Departments: B. L. Arms, M. D., chief of bureau of diagnostic laboratories; Geo. W. Simons, Jr., chief sanitary engineer; S. T. Thompson, chief of bureau of vital statistics; L. A. Greene, M. D., director of bureau of venereal diseases; W. B. Keating, M. D., director of bureau of child welfare. District Health Officers: F. L. Tatom, M. D.; John Keely, M. D.; A. C. Hamblin, M. D.; Geo. A. Dame, M. D. Specialists: William B. Keating, M. D., child welfare work; L. A. Greene, M. D., and D. C. Campbell, urologists.

Under the plans of reorganization the State Health Officer as the executive officer of the State Board of Health has adopted a policy of strict central administration with decentralization of routine. There has been established a central supply depot which abolishes the former practice of indiscriminate buying. The departments of the Board of Health are as follows: Bureau of Venereal Diseases, Bureau of Child Welfare, Bureau of Sanitary Engineering, Bureau of Vital Statistics, Bureau of Diagnostic Laboratories, Bureau of Publicity, and Orthopaedic Service. Politics has been eliminated from the activities of the State Board of Health and the activity in politics by employees of the Board of Health either in person or on State Board of Health stationery or time is a dischargeable offense. It is the policy of the Board of Health to coöperate to the fullest extent with the United States Public Health Service.

The State has recently concluded intensive course of instructions for sanitary inspectors, and all district health officers are to receive training under supervision of the International Health Board.

✢

Illinois.—On account of obvious incompleteness of reports of births from several sections of the state, the Division of Vital Statistics of the State Department of Public Health is now checking up delinquencies through special agents and extended correspondence. In many instances it has been necessary to send final notices to negligent physicians and midwives notifying them that further failure to report births will cause all cases to be referred to the attorney general for legal enforcement of the provisions of the statutes.

During the past few months six cases of epidemic meningitis have been reported in Clinton County. Bacteriologists from the Division of Diagnostic Laboratories have been sent to assist the local authorities.

Fifty cases of typhoid fever have been reported in the city of Joliet and Joliet Township.

In a number of the state institutions, the inmates are being vaccinated for protection from influenza and pneumonia and to determine the efficacy of the vaccine approved by the Commission on Respiratory Diseases made up of Prof. Milton J. Rosenau, of Harvard University Medical School; Dr. William H. Park, director of laboratories, New York City, and Prof. E. O. Jordan, Director of the Department of Bacteriology of the University of Chicago. The use of this vaccine is not compulsory upon the inmates.

Representatives of the McLean County Sanatorium and of the LaSalle County Sanatorium, the first two counties to open their institutions under the Glackin Law, reported that these institutions were filled to capacity from the time of opening and that both had been required to erect additional buildings.

Four training schools for nurses, including the Mt. Sinai Hospital, a Jewish institution in Chicago, have been added to the accredited list of the state. There are now 84 such institutions in the state of Illinois.

The first of a series of conferences between the State Department of Health and the officers and trustees of the public Tuberculosis Sanatoria of the state was held at Springfield on November 18, and was attended by the officers of practically all of the forty county institutions for which provision has been made within the past three years. Dr. C. St. Clair Drake, director of public health, presided.

The principal speakers were Dr. George Thomas Palmer, president of the Illinois Tuberculosis Association, and chief of the Division of Tuberculosis of the State Department of Public Health; Paul Hansen, chief of the Division of Sanitation. Miss Ann L. Tillinghast, former superintendent of the Edward Sanatorium and of the Springfield Open Air Colony, and Dr. J. W. Pettit of Ottawa.

The Division of Sanitation of the State Department of Public Health is devoting considerable attention to the polluted water supplies and the sewage disposal system of a number of Illinois communities in which large sums of money have been expended for adequate public utilities. In a great many instances, filtration plants for water supplies and treatment plants for sewage disposal have been installed but have become relatively useless on account of the neglect to which they have been subjected or to the incompetent manner in which they have been operated.

The installation of water filtration plants has a tendency to give a false sense of security to the citizen, but the frequency with which such plants become ineffective through neglect, has caused the Division of Sanitation in making recommendations to committees to advise the installation of filtration

8

plants, but in addition to recommend the obtaining of full control of the water sheds which should be adequately policed to prevent original contamination.

❋

Massachusetts.—The third Convocation of Public Health arranged by the Committee on Public Health of the Massachusetts Medical Society was held in Springfield, Mass., November 21 and 22, 1919. The speakers included Enos H. Bigelow, M. D., chairman of the committee; Alfred Worcester, M. D., president of the Massachusetts Medical Society; His Honor, Arthur A. Adams, mayor of Springfield; Hon. Calvin Coolidge, governor of Massachusetts; Eugene R. Kelley, M. D., state commissioner of health of Massachusetts and Victor G. Heiser, M. D., of the International Health Board. There were three sessions on November 22 with ten speakers and the attendance was gratifying, testifying to the interest and enthusiasm of the public health workers and medical profession of the Connecticut Valley. The members of the committee were, Enos H. Bigelow, M. D., of Framingham Center, Roger I. Lee of Cambridge, E. F. Cody of New Bedford, Victor Saford, M. D., of Jamaica Plain and Annie Lee Hamilton of Boston.

Under the general scheme of reorganization of state departments in Massachusetts the Health Department organization was left untouched. The State Tuberculosis Sanatoria, formerly under the trustees of hospitals for consumptives, were transferred to the Department of Health, as was the Penikese Institution for Lepers, formerly under the supervision of the State Board of Charity. A new division of sanatoria was created by law in the Department of Health. The new title of the department is Department of Public Health.

A conference of the tuberculosis nurses of the eastern section of the state was held by the State Department of Health Wednesday, December 10, in the auditorium in the State House. Various papers were read in the morning by different nurses, while the afternoon session was devoted to a talk on "How to Find Tuberculosis" by Dr. P. Challis Bartlett of Framingham.

❋

Montana.—The State Board of Health, the Montana State Tuberculosis Association and the Nursing Department of the Northern Division of the American Red Cross have completed an agreement of coöperation in the stimulation and supervision of all public health nursing activities. The three agencies will jointly share the expense of a State Supervisor of Nursing, as an especial feature of the Division of Child Welfare of the State Board of Health.

The State Teachers of Montana met in annual conference on November 24, 25, and 26 at Helena. As a departure from the regular program, one full general session was devoted entirely to a health program. On adjournment the teachers passed resolutions endorsing the program of the State Board of Health and of the Montana State Tuberculosis Association for the improvement and protection of the health of school children.

Dr. W. A. Russell, county health officer of Big Horn County, at Hardin, has recently completed a physical examination of 1,200 school children in his jurisdiction. With only one exception every school board in the county employed Doctor Russell's services.

On report of Miss M. A. Zogarts, industrial nurse employed by the American Smelting and Refining Company at East Helena, that many school children in that city were below normal weight, many of them decidedly under nourished, the Board of Education has taken steps to supplement the meals of all school children with one pint of milk given at recess periods at school.

❋

New York.—The Board of Regents of the State of New York has under consideration the establishment of a Department of Health Education in each of the State Normal Schools. It has already such a department in operation at the Oswego State Normal School, and a similar department in effect at the State College for Teachers at Albany. In five of the State Normal Schools there are health teachers devoting full time to health activities among the teachers and the pupils of the grades.

Over 4,000 cases of smallpox have recently occurred in the province of Ontario, and four cases have been found in Buffalo, according to New York State Department of Health officials, who have investigated conditions at the border. Health officials of cities here have been notified in regard to the conditions to be imposed, and railroad ticket offices in the Canadian district where the disease exists have been requested not to issue tickets to points in the United States except on the presentation of a certificate of vaccination from U. S. Public Health Service representatives.

At a meeting of the directors of public health laboratories of New York state, held at the new state laboratory on November 12, it was voted to form a permanent organization, the New York State Association of Public Health Laboratories. The following officers were elected: Dr. Warren B. Stone, Schenectady, president; Miss M. B. Kirkbride, State Laboratories, Albany, secretary-treasurer; Dr. Jos. S. Lawrence, Albany, vice-president.

The officers with the following two elected members constitute the council: (For two years) Dr. Wm. A. Bing, Ontario County Laboratory, Canandaigua; (for one year) Miss Margaret K. Preston, Utica City Laboratory.

Disturbed at the high infant death rate recorded for Troy, the Women's Civic League of that city launched a child welfare campaign in June and engaged a child welfare nurse who made house to house visits in those sections of the city where the infant death rate had been highest. Clinics also were established. Five hundred and seventy-six house visits were made and 200 babies were brought to the clinic. Of these but two died. The expenses of the campaign have now been assumed by the Chamber of Commerce. An effort is being made to have the city continue the work during the coming year.

As a result of the educational work among the Jewish boarding house keepers of Ulster and Sullivan counties by the Department of Sanitation of the Jewish Agricultural and Industrial Aid Society, a distinct improvement in sanitation has been reported. A total of 372 farms were visited and sanitary instruction given both to the proprietor and the boarders by means of actual demonstrations, lectures, lantern slides, posters and literature. Many polluted wells had been abandoned and new wells dug. The work is carried on under some difficulties since about 40 per cent of farms in this region change hands yearly.

Five hundred and seventy-five more cases of diphtheria were reported during October in New York state, exclusive of New York City, than were reported for September, and 945 more cases than for October, 1918. One-third of the new cases were reported from the city of Buffalo.

*

Ohio.—The state health authorities are advising vaccination against smallpox, and especially those living in Darke, Miami, Mahoning, Jefferson or Richland counties. A number of other counties have reported the disease prevalent. The usual winter increase is on, according to the health authorities, and with the disease so widely scattered as it now is, any resident is in danger of exposure. Vaccination is a practically certain protection.

School health surveys will be carried out in many Ohio counties this winter by local women's child welfare committees.

The State Department of Health has prepared blanks to be filled out in grading schools according to health supervision and sanitary conditions. These standard blanks will be used in all counties engaging in the survey and will provide a means of accurate comparisons between different schools and different localities. Facts disclosed by the survey

will be published in statistical form by the health department.

High diphtheria prevalence throughout the state demands careful attention of school and health officials. November reports, still incomplete, promise to go beyond the high mark of 1,232 cases set in October. Communities where diphtheria was present in November included: Cincinnati, Miamisburg, Dayton, Columbus Grove, Crestline, Delaware, Chillicothe, Lancaster, Portsmouth, Cleveland, Youngstown, Steubenville, Cadiz and Canton.

Ohio has more public health nurses in proportion to population than has any other state in the Mississippi Valley; the state has 98 nurses per million inhabitants at the time of a recent survey. Illinois was second with 88 per million, and had the largest actual total—531. Ohio had the second largest total—490. Two hundred and forty communities in the states covered by the Mississippi Valley Tuberculosis Conference, with an aggregate population of 12,840,525, had 1,499 nurses engaged in tuberculosis work.

*

Texas.—The State Board of Health has instituted at the request of the governor of Texas a sanitary survey of the eleemosynary institutions of the state. This survey is for the purpose of presenting data to the Legislature concerning the conditions existing in these institutions and will serve to standardize the sewage plants, and water supplies of the institutions. There will be twenty-four institutions included in this survey, the work being already under way and soon to be completed.

Acting upon the request of the State Board of Health and of Mrs. Ethel Parsons, director of Public Health Nursing of the American Red Cross in Texas, the University of Texas will in January inaugurate a three months' course in public health nursing. This work will be under the direction of Miss Jane Duffy, formerly of New York, and will deal with the theoretical side of public health nursing. The course in theory will be followed by a two months' course in field work, to be given in Houston, under the supervision of Miss Sabina Fritsch, formerly of New Orleans, and who has had wide experience in this work. This school will aid the State Board of Health in securing competent public health nurses to take charge of the county work that is being inaugurated in the different counties of the state.

Under an appropriation recently made available by the state Legislature, the Texas State Board of Health is now instituting in several counties of Texas a county health department, which will be a continuation of the work of the State Board, and will bring that board closer to the people through the work of the county health officer. The appropriation makes a fund of $10,000 available for the work in each county, the county commissioners being asked to appropriate one half of this amount to be devoted to the purpose paying the salary of the full-time health officer, and the expenses of the administration of that office. This work will by the first of the year have been installed in five counties of the state.

The Bureau of Sanitary Engineering of the State Board of Health has recently added to its equipment a portable laboratory secured especially for work in epidemic centers for the purpose of analysing any liquid that may be suspected as a source of infection. The laboratory equipment consists of sterilizers and incubators, there being a unit that is equipped for electrical operation, and a unit furnished with oil heaters for the cities or villages that may not be supplied with electrical power. With this equipment the engineers may work in the midst of an epidemic center.

Virginia.—The Danville Health Department opened on November 1 a dental clinic which is meeting a real need.

Nutrition classes composed of the school children who are found, during the medical inspection, to be 5 pounds or more under weight, are being formed. The nutrition classes receive special instruction regarding proper diet and the mothers, whenever possible, are visited by a public health nurse. The monthly weights of all under weight children are to be reported to parents and information furnished regarding proper feeding.

The Venereal Disease Clinic in Danville has had, for the past three months, an average daily attendance of 14.5.

The work of the Danville Health Department Tuberculosis Nurse shows 1,160 visits made during the six months ending November 15. Twelve patients were sent to local sanatoriums, three colored patients sent to the State Sanatorium at Burkeville, and ten sleeping porches constructed.

◆

Vital Statistics of the Principal American Cities in 1918.—As a result of a questionnaire sent out by Dr. W. H. Guilfoy it has been possible to compile the following table. It is of particular interest in view of the great pandemic of influenzal pneumonia which occurred in 1918, and also because of the extra

deaths resulting from the war. Although it is usually unfair to compare the crude death rates of cities without at least considering the age, race and sex distribution of the population, the variations in these larger cities are not so great, so that the comparison does have unusual interest.

	Death Rate per 1,000 Population	Birth Rate per 1,000 Population	Still-Births per 1,000 Population	Death Rate per 100,000 Population														Death Rate under One Year per 1,000 Births
				Typhoid Fever	Measles	Scarlet Fever	Whooping Cough	Diphtheria	Influenza	Lobar-Pneumonia	Broncho-Pneumonia	Cerebro-Spinal Meningitis	Pulmonary Tuberculosis	Other Forms of Tuberculosis	Cancer and Sarcoma	Diarrhœal Diseases under Two Years per 100,000 Population, All Ages	
New York City, N. Y.	16.71	23.51	1.16	3	13	3	11	21	214	232	119	4	150	22	84	41	92
Chicago, Ill.	17.18	24.50	1.03	1	2	2	7	28	268	176	92	3	126	21	93	114	104
Philadelphia, Pa.	25.68	28.48	1.34	5	7	3	20	23	502	339	177	6	200	22	106	83	126
Detroit, Mich.	14.35	30.00	1.53	7	14	5	16	30	154	196	75	4	105	19	61	75	101
St. Louis, Mo.	16.76	17.84	1.01	7	2	2	21	14	251	166	109	5	147	18	91	37	94
Cleveland, Ohio	16.12	26.48	.49	5	2	1	8	13	348	148	62	4	126	21	75	80	94
Boston, Mass.	22.24	25.43	1.06	3	14	3	23	28	512	196	107	11	151	23	126	54	115
Los Angeles, Cal.	15.68	14.75	.43	3	2	1	2	9	334	67	62	3	174	17	108	25	77
Pittsburgh, Pa.	25.65	26.07	1.47	10	15	1	20	19	87	470	234	5	116	21	*	98	129
San Francisco, Cal.	20.08	16.93	.65	4	2	2	8	8	479	133	72	3	150	22	138	9	57
Buffalo, N. Y.	20.88	29.37	1.12	8	9	4	13	23	394	173	122	3	150	22	102	128	121
Newark, N. J.	19.73	26.98	1.24	3	28	3	13	19	322	230	109	10	159	27	77	71	105
Washington, D. C.	22.95	19.69	1.23	11	11	4	10	10	486	194	117	7	155	22	100	49	111
New Orleans, La.	25.47	19.95	1.36	20	6	.	19	5	415	268	67	8	277	32	98	62	123
Minneapolis, Minn.	14.13	22.65	.82	8	7	9	21	23	258	89	40	2	108	16	92	17	72
Jersey City, N. J.	18.99	23.32	1.18	4	6	3	11	16	258	329	141	9	119	10	68	72	119
Denver, Colo.	19.37	14.23	.70	9	1	3	11	10	60	283	282	.	272	26	105	19	107
Rochester, N. Y.	17.34	25.64	1.00	2	10	3	21	14	358	117	74	3	91	14	116	55	91
Providence, R. I.	19.78		1.03	5	20	7	28	21	356	242	65	10	121	40	94	52	.
Louisville, Ky.	20.64	14.91	1.06	11	2	.	.	10	65	167	103	8	165	19	65	27	123
Columbus, Ohio	18.92	30.04	.95	9	4	2	17	3	199	189	71	2	138	40	101	30	99
New Haven, Conn.	20.28	30.12	.75	5	2	2	21	13	482	*	*	7	106	27	93	39	89
Portland, Me.	21.11	22.15	1.04	6	10	.	10	7	537	146	87	.	102	38	134	30	103

* No report received from city.

[From *Monthly Bulletin*, N. Y. C. Health Department (M. P. H.)]

INDUSTRIAL HYGIENE AND
OCCUPATIONAL DISEASE

Abstracted by DRS. E. R. HAYHURST, R. P. ALBAUGH, P. M. HOLMES, and E. B. STARR.

Studies of Medical and Surgical Care of Industrial Workers.—A recent bulletin (No. 99) of the U. S. Public Health Service presents many interesting observations relative to the present status of industrial medicine. The bulletin was prepared by C. D. Selby, consulting hygienist, U. S. P. H. S., and represents his report to the surgeon general based upon a study of 170 industrial establishments in the Eastern and Middle states, the observations covering a period of six months. Careful studies were made of the personnel, activities, equipment, methods and records of medical departments, and of the attitude of the employer and employee toward Industrial Medical Service. Fifteen of the industries studied were of the large type, with elaborate medical departments. The place of the medical department in the industrial organization varied greatly. In 42 per cent of the cases, the medical department operated under the supervision of production officials; in 21 per cent, it was responsible to the chief administrative office; and in 15 per cent, responsible to the department of industrial relations. It was found that the medical department functions best when operating under the direction of the chief official rather than when it looks for authority to department heads. Of seventeen establishments having 500 or less employees, two had full-time physicians in charge of medical work, and six had part-time physicians. Of twenty-seven plants with 500 to 1,000 employees, five had whole-time physicians; eight, part-time men; two of them also employing dentists, and twenty-one having dispensaries. Of nineteen establishments employing from 1,000 to 1,500 employees, seven had full-time physicians and eight, part-time physicians. Seventeen out of the nineteen in this group had dispensaries. In twenty-one establishments employing from 1,500 to 2,000 employees, seven had full-time physicians and fifteen of them, trained nurses. The trained female nurse was found to predominate in the personnel of all medical departments. The large plants employing over 4,000 nearly all had, in addition to the whole-time physicians and nurses, various expert medical consultants subject to call. Only eighteen out of the 155 plants which lend themselves to analysis were without dispensaries. In sixty-nine of the establishments, and in many they were used to determine fitness for special work. In only a few places was communicable disease the only cause for rejection. In 16 per cent of the establishments,

health bulletins were issued and in 12 per cent health talks were given. In the bulletin, 103 different forms are exhibited which have been found convenient in transferring patients to and from the medical departments for diagnosis, dressing, dental and surgical care, etc. There are also shown a number of case, laboratory and nurse's record forms. The author discusses at some length the equipment and operation of dispensaries, examining and operating rooms. The value and popularity of good dental service is well shown by the experience of one firm in which, during the second year of operation, there was an increase of 9,623 in the number of dental examinations; 3,306 in the number of treatments; 203 in the number of cases. receiving prophylactic treatments; and an increase of 507 in the number using tooth brushes. In its practical application to industry, Dr. Selby conceives industrial medicine to be measured by its ability to increase production. Its value to the employee is measured by its ability to recognize disease and conditions which impair bodily health. The point is made that safety men are in no sense qualified to accept responsibility for the physical welfare of the workers. Emphasis is laid on the menace to health of certain monotonous, concentrating operation, and the importance of the physician in selecting persons temperamentally suited to such work. The industrial physician also has an opportunity to help in clearing up differences between employer and employee by interpreting the one to the other. The author divides industrial physicians into four classes:

(a) Those who have drifted into industrial work but not lived up to opportunities for service of the highest order;

(b) Those to whom industrial service is a job;

(c) Those who use their industrial connections to establish themselves in surgery; and

(d) Those who are qualified and are making industrial medicine their life work with the ultimate object of applying the principles of preventive medicine.

The disadvantages of detached medical service are summarized as:

(a) The untreated or poorly treated trivial injury;

(b) Danger of delayed treatment;

(c) Time loss to employer and employees; and

(d) The physician has no incentive for prophylactic work.

Too many industrial physicians allowed the press of surgical dressings to interfere with the prophylactic work in the plants. Regret is expressed over the tendency among industrial physicians to neglect the reporting of communicable and occupational diseases to public health authorities, and attention is directed to advantage to close coöperation with public health officials. Stress is laid on the fundamental importance to both employees and employer of physical examinations. The need is expressed for some standards for recording and reporting morbidity statistics, and that courses of instruction in industrial medicine be provided by medical colleges.

Wholesome advice is given to employers who may contemplate the selection of industrial physicians. The bulletin should prove a valuable aid to any one interested in industrial medicine.—C. D. Selby, *Bull., No. 99, U. S. P. H. Service*, 1919. (*E. B. S.*)

Rehabilitation of Tuberculous Soldiers.—Occupational therapy is divided into (a) diversional therapy, (b) occupational therapy, and (c) prevocational training. The Federal Board has introduced the last two forms in sanatoria of North Carolina, El Paso, and Rutland. "The more useful the work, the more its therapeutic results." Work must stop short of mental and physical exhaustion. The principle of exercise with a purpose should be adopted in our civilian institutions. Cardiac and gas, as well as tuberculous cases, need supervised work after discharge from treatment. The "light outdoor job" which a man thinks he must have is seldom to be found. Part-time work is still more difficult to obtain. Prejudice against tuberculous workers still obtains. Normal industry will, however, absorb some. Colonization schemes including the purchase of small farms are advocated.—H. A. Pattison, *Vocational Summary*, Vol. II, No. 4 (*Federal Board for Vocational Education*, Washington), August, 1919, pp. 65–66.

British Studies on Atmospheric Pollution.—An extensive report on the methods and findings of atmospheric pollution is included. One especially interesting discussion is the invention of precision apparatus for carrying out some of the determinations. This report, which is the fourth, shows that on the whole there is an unusual amount of industrial air pollution which is improved during the winter months.—Meteorological Office, *Lancet*, London, June 14, 1919, 23 page supplement.

The New Science of Industrial Physiology.—This science has two objects: (a) How the worker works and what are the conditions under which he can work most efficiently, and (b) the establishment in factories of those conditions which conduce to maximum output coupled with maximum power of the worker. The methods of industrial physiology are observation and experiment. The topics that have been, or are being, investigated are the practicability of certain personal tests, the output of successive hours of the day, the optimum day's work, the influence of rest periods, overtime, the detriment of hot days, the loss in efficiency with night work, the recognition that women are capable of much greater variety of work, the association of accidents with fatigue (especially inexperience, speed, lighting, temperature, etc.), the inter-relation between food and efficiency, the loss due to labor turnover, the elimination of some unnecessary motions through study by the cinematograph and other methods, and the demonstration that ultimate limitation of work on the part of workers is common. Mention is made of the work and personnel of the British Industrial Fatigue Research Board.—Frederic S. Lee, *U. S. P. H. Report, No. 513*, April 11, 1919, 7 pp.

Elimination of Industrial Poisoning in Felt Hat Making.—The process for eliminating the evils of "hatter's shakes" and "hatter's asthma" and other effects of mercury poisoning is made possible through a new method in which mercury is done away with entirely. The method was discovered by one William Braun, a brushmaker by trade, who found that the reason for treating hides with nitrate of mercury was for the purpose of roughing the surface of the hair, this causing it to mat more easily. Braun found this could be done by shaving the hair from the pelt, immersing it in a hot solution of sodium carbonate for 18 to 25 minutes when it is ready for immediate use. By this process a hat may be completed and made ready for sale the same day the hair is removed from the raw pelt. Aside from the tremendous health gain for the workers the saving in the cost of production is enormous. By the nitrate of mercury method the cost was $5 for treating 35 pounds of fur, whereas the new method costs but two cents a pound. Under the old method hats which wholesaled for $21 a dozen can now be sold for $9.50. The method has been subjected to the most exacting tests.—Christine Kefauver, *Monthly Bull. Dept. of Health, N. Y. C.* (*E. R. H.*)

Oil Acne.—Illustrating with cases of dermatitis observed in workers in factories using lubricating oils cutting compounds, Blum concludes that oils and oil-mixed metals or even cotton dusts obstruct the follicles in the skin producing occupational folliculites or "oil pimples."—P. Blum, *Paris Medical Journal*, June 7, 1919, pp. 445.

Compensation for Occupational Diseases.—In this country only five states and the Federal government compensate for occupational diseases. The states are California, Connecticut, Massachusetts, Wisconsin and Hawaii. For Massachusetts and the Federal government occupational diseases were included through rulings of the court and commission; in the others by statutory enactment. The Wisconsin law specifies twenty vocational diseases that are compensable. The Connecticut act includes diseases due to "causes peculiar to the occupation and which are not of a contagious, communicable or mental nature." The other laws providing compensation do not name specific diseases arising out of and in the course of employment. In the other thirty-eight states compensation jurisdictions for occupational diseases are excluded. To determine whether a disease is occupational or not is often impossible especially such a one as tuberculosis; Hookstadt classifies industrial diseases according to cause and nature as follows:

1. Diseases due to gradual absorption of poisons (lead poisoning).
2. Diseases due to poisons or germs which enter through breaks in the skin (anthrax).
3. Skin affections from acids or other irritants (eczema—dermatitis).
4. Dust, fume and gas diseases through the respiratory tract (tbc., gas poisoning).
5. Diseases due to vibrations or constant use of certain members (house-maids knee, neuritis, telegrapher's cramp).
6. Miscellaneous diseases (caisson disease, miner's nystagmus).

The author mentions two additional classes of diseases usually compensated:

1. Diseases such as typhoid fever, sun-stroke, ivy poisoning, erysipelas, pneumonia when there is a clear connection between the employment and the sickness.
2. Those diseases that either result from an accident or are aggravated, accelerated or developed by an accident.

Occupational diseases are generally compensated for if one or more of these conditions are present:

1. If the disease results from violence to the physical structure of the body.
2. If the injury occurs unexpectedly or not in the usual course of events.
3. If the injury can be traced to a definite time and place in the employment.
4. If the injury is not due to a known and inherent risk of the occupation, or even though known and inherent, if the employment has not provided reasonable safeguards such as would have prevented the injury.

According to the English and Massachusetts' experiences from 2 to 5 per cent of accident compensation is for occupational diseases.—Carl Hookstadt, *Modern Medicine*, Aug., 1919, pp. 311. (*P. M. H.*)

✣

Industrial Medical Service.—The two most important duties of a real factory physician are: (1) Close familiarity with actual working conditions and (2) the investigation of all cases of injury. To get these, the doctor should practically live and work amongst his workers. His "tentacles" are the foreman, works-managers, etc., who work with him to the common end of good output, health, and contentment of the workers. The industrial medical expert should handle absenteeism, causes of wastage, the administration of the Workmen's Compensation Act, canteen supervision, and grievances. He should be a full-time medical officer for the occasional inspection method is inadequate. His function is preventive rather than curative so far as the individual is concerned. The afflicted worker has the legal right to free choice of a doctor. The enlightened manager is convinced of the value of a full time doctor, trained in factory medicine and law. To get trained factory doctors, we should address managers in terms of output, workers in those of wages, and the general public in those of industrial peace and health. The type of man to train as a factory doctor is the enthusiast with the doggedness of the "importunate widow." He should know something of mass-psychology.—George P. Castellain, *Lancet*, London, July 19, 1919, p. 128.

✣

Making Use of Physical Examination Data.—Curry states that at the beginning they endeavored to establish a standard set of qualifications for an employee in each operation that would as nearly as possible represent the ideal individual for that position, from both the viewpoint of the foreman and the physician. These standards were grouped under the following seven heads: age, height, weight, sight, hearing, dexterity, mentality, temperament, and lifting. The system has been in use two years and has proved satisfactory. Instead of a physical examination card, he terms his form a personnel card.—B. J. Curry, American Thread Co., Holyoke, Mass., *Hospital Management*, August, 1919, pp. 58–59.

PUBLIC HEALTH
LABORATORY NOTES

Abstracted by Francis H. Slack, M. D., and Mr. James M. Strang.

Complement Fixation Tests for Streptococcus Infections.—In an article entitled "Oral Infections and Mental Diseases," this test is highly spoken of. Because of the many races of *Streptococcus viridins*, it is necessary to use at least 50 strains in the antigen. Like the Wassermann test, the reaction is not infallible, and will be negative in some cases in which the infection is present. It could be used with advantage by the dentist to determine the necessity for extracting suspicious teeth where there were no apparent constitutional symptoms.— Henry A. Cotton, *Jour. Dental Research*, Sept., 1919.

✣

Occurrence of B. Influenzae in the Normal Throat. —Whatever may be the etiologic relationship of *B. influenzæ* to epidemic influenza, there is little doubt of the significance of this organism as a secondary invader in this type of respiratory infection. Pickett and Stillman found *B. influenzæ* present in 42 per cent of 177 healthy persons from whom no history of respiratory infection was obtainable. Lord, Scott and Nye demonstrated the bacilli in 76 per cent of 34 healthy men at the Harvard Student Army Training Corps. Opie and his collaborators found *B. influenzæ* in the mouths of 35.1 per cent of all healthy men examined at Camp Funston. The group studied by Pritchett and Stillman comprised for the most part the personnel of the Rockefeller Institute, and repeated cultural study of the same group by the authors of this paper indicates the occurrence of *B. influenzæ* in the throats of normal individuals to be as great in the period subsequent to the epidemic as during it, and that the organisms may persist in the throats of healthy carriers for a long period of time.—Agnes I. Winchell and Ernest G. Stillman, *Jour. of Expt. Med.*, Nov., 1919.

✣

Detection of Diphtheria Bacilli from Swabs.—In a series of 250 specimens, the author found 21 per cent positive by the usual method of streaking an Loeffler's serum agar, and 27 per cent by the use of a fluid medium. This medium consists of fresh ox serum which has been somewhat concentrated and carefully sterilized at 56° for 3 hours. The swab itself is placed in the medium overnight, and the examination is made from a swab smear. In addition to the more rapid growth on the medium, the bacilli show more clearly the normal growth characteristics. Another feature is the production of acid in the medium.—Wang, *Jour. of Path. and Bact.*, 1919, 22, 239.

✣

Simple Method for Determining the Reaction of Feces.—The author calls attention to the difficulty of obtaining the reaction of feces correctly either with litmus paper or phenolphthalein and advises the following method as satisfactory: Prepare a 1 per cent aqueous solution of alizarin. Place 2 drops of this indicator about one and a half inches apart on a glass slide. Dip a glass stirring rod into the liquid part of the specimen (or if the feces is formed, merely puncture the mass). By this means, a sufficient amount of feces will be obtained for the test. Mix thoroughly in one of the drops using the other drop as a control. An alkaline reaction is indicated by a reddish violet to a violet color, neutral no change, and acid a light yellow color. The density of these colors will depend on the amount of acid or alkali present. By placing the slide on a piece of white paper, the depth of color can be more easily determined, or the test may be more easily made on a piece of white porcelain.— W. J. Bruce, *Jour. Lab. and Clin. Med.*, Oct., 1919.

✣

Presentation of Wassermann Reagents.—The author advises the use of chloroform for the preservation of amboceptor and of the suspected sera and control sera. He adds 5 or 6 drops of chloroform to 10 cc. of amboceptor and finds such amboceptor uninjured in its combining properties, and not subject to bacterial contaminations. Amboceptor so treated may be kept at room temperature for weeks without appreciable change. From time to time, when the chloroform has evaporated, as evidenced by the odor, more is added.—Clarence Emerson, *Jour. of Lab. and Clin. Med.*, Oct., 1919.

✣

Superiority of Method of Ice-Box Fixation in the Wassermann Test.—Ice-box fixation from 18 to 20 hours at 0° and 2°C. increases the number of positive reactions with serum of known syphilitic patients. There is no evidence to show that it tends to cause false positive reactions. The antigen used was a simple alcoholic extract of a syphilitic organ.— O. Berghausen, *Jour. A. M. A.*, 72, 996 (1919).

American Journal of Public Health

Official Monthly Publication of the American Public Health Association

Publication office: No. 124 W. Polk Street, Chicago, Ill.

Editorial office: 169 Massachusetts Ave., Boston, Mass.

Subscription price, $4 per year.   American Public Health Association membership, including subscription, $5 per year.
Subscriptions and memberships may be sent to the A. P. H. A., 169 Massachusetts Ave., Boston, Mass.

Vol. X   FEBRUARY, 1920   No. 2

ECONOMICS OF HEALTH ADMINISTRATION

HENRY BIXBY HEMENWAY, A. M., M. D.,
District Health Officer, Springfield, Ill.

Read before Section on Vital Statistics, American Public Health Association, at New Orleans, La.,
October 28, 1919.

Health administration lies at the foundation of economic prosperity. It is a business and like other business is subject to commercial laws. Quality, whether of brain or brawn may be appraised by the wages paid. Loss from disease, does vary with the money spent. Compared with fire fighting health appropriations are grossly inadequate, whether the health risk is considered or the actual loss.

FERTILITY of soil, richness of mines, and abundance of resources for manufacture are only available in proportion as the people are strong and active. It is the special function of the health department to prevent sickness and untimely death, and particularly to wage war against those communicable diseases which attack large numbers, and against whom individual effort is inefficient. Health administration is, therefore, at the foundation of economic prosperity.

Public health administration is a business. As such it is subject to ordinary commercial laws, may be judged by commercial standards, and compared with other lines of economic activity. In the business world a concern is considered successful when it so applies scientific knowledge that it produces the greatest output with the least expenditure of money, labor, and material.

The one measure which is used as the gauge in commercial life is money. Material is valued according to its cost. Labor, whether of brain or brawn, may be appraised by wages paid. The product likewise is estimated according to the amount of money which it brings in exchange.

Put in the form of an equation:

$$R = E + P$$

where R represents receipts for product, E indicates expenditures, and P means profits. If R is smaller than E, P becomes a minus quantity, and the business must sooner or later die through exhaustion of capital. A business is successful in proportion as P is large as compared with E.

In the commercial world this last statement is a guiding principle. Though profit may be increased by increasing the outlay, if it be not increased in ratio equal to or greater than the outlay the manager will hesitate and look for other use for his excess of capital. Amount of investment is largely governed by this general commercial law. Applied, this means that economic rules should guide in determining the amount of appropriation for health departments.

There is an old saw: "A penny saved is a penny earned." In other words, the product may be as truly profit when it represents the saving of loss as when it means excess in receipts. The fences on a farm, preventing the roaming of stock and destruction of crops, are as truly profitable as the sowing of seed and the harvesting of grain. The value of the crops thus saved, and of stock not lost, would be the measure of the value of the fence.

Cities, counties, states and nations do not have unlimited funds for their various activities. Judged according to commercial standards the funds at their disposal should be applied where and in proportion as they will produce the greatest returns, including savings as well as receipts.

The profits of public health administration must be measured by the value of lives saved and the losses which would have resulted from sickness prevented. Unfortunately it is not possible to make exact measurements of the products ot a health department. We must depend upon estimates, with a large possibility of error. We must estimate populations, value of lives, cost and losses through sickness, and even the amount of disease and death. Fortunately for our present purposes the margin is so very large that the greatest possible allowance for error is relatively unimportant.

A year ago an effort was made in Illinois to estimate the loss to each county in the state resulting from the prevalence of certain communicable diseases during the fiscal year ending June 30, 1918. So far as we are aware this was the most extensive computation of the kind which had ever been attempted up to that time, but it was far from satisfactory. Inasmuch as other states have since made computations upon these data, and since

they are the basis of our own further studies, it is proper to devote a little attention to the methods used.

Realizing that cases of communicable disease are very imperfectly reported, we first based our estimates solely upon deaths recorded. While this may be satisfactory for a very large area we soon found that a county which had reported over 400 cases of smallpox had no charge for that disease because there were no deaths.

Discovered cases of smallpox are generally reported, but few cases of pneumonia are reported, and the fullness of reports of the incidence of diphtheria, measles, scarletina, and whooping-cough vary according to locality. We took the reported cases of smallpox as the correct number. For most other diseases we estimated the number of cases per death, and if in any county the number of reported cases for a given disease was markedly less than such estimate, we "equalized" by multiplying the number of deaths by the estimated proportion. That is the number of deaths from diphtheria multiplied by ten gave us the estimated number of cases; and pneumonia deaths multiplied by four we took as the number of cases of pneumonia.

Malaria is not likely to arise in some sections of the state. A death reported from that disease in such counties was presumed to have been an imported case or an error in diagnosis, and no addition was made for nonfatal cases. In southern counties a death was taken to indicate 200 cases. Other counties were estimated between these extremes according to location and character of surroundings.

Diseases affecting chiefly children were considered as only of children; and those affecting chiefly adults were considered as all adults. Under normal conditions meningitis should be considered as a children's disease. The year taken for our computation was one in which there were a great many deaths from the disease in army and navy stations and camps. We, therefore, counted this disease as half adults and half children. The point should be remembered in using our table.

These computations showed a loss in one year from certain communicable diseases in the state approximating $155,000,000, a sum equaling 6.01 per cent of the entire assessed valuation of property, and representing a per capita loss of $24.67. In Kendall county the per capita loss was $124.16, and in Pulaski county the loss was equal to 37.61 per cent of the assessed valuation of property.

These figures show one reason why some communities are poor. "The man with the chill can't work and his farm runs to weeds. The county which needlessly throws away an amount equivalent to from 10 to 35 per cent of its capital must be lacking in funds for ordinary transaction of business.

This same basis of computation was next applied to various cities of the state, adding other elements (Table I). Out of about forty-five cities studied, with the exception of Chicago, Evanston paid the most per capita for health administration, and its loss from communicable disease was the least. It paid 31 cents per capita, and its loss was $12.82 per capita, or 2.71 per cent of its assessed valuation.

Waukegan and North Chicago are contiguous. Waukegan paid 8 cents per capita, for health protection. The losses were:

	Per capita.	Per cent of assesed valuation.
Waukegan	$17.45	9.97
North Chicago	41.40	19.15

These three cities are all located on Lake Michigan, not far apart, and may well be compared. The comparison tends to show, as more extended studies indicate, that losses from communicable disease vary inversely with the amount spent.

TABLE I.

Economic Losses in Illinois Cities Due to Communicable Diseases, Fiscal Year July 1, 1917, to June 30, 1918.

(Data as to amount of appropriations for health departments were not obtained from most of these cities.)

City	Population	Loss due to Communicable Diseases		Per cent of ass'd val.
		Aggregate	Per capita	
Quincy........	36,849	$844,955	$22.93	7.28
Kankakee.....	14,289	1,308,435	92.56	29.61
Galesburg.....	24,805	422,945	17.05	5.46
Waukegan.....	21,253	370,700	17.45	9.97
No. Chicago...	4,989	206,580	41.40	19.15
Evanston......	29,596	379,560	12.82	2.71
Decatur.......	42,409	741,200	17.48	7.43
Bloomington...	27,520	649,670	23.60	7.94
Jacksonville...	15,519	1,125,780	72.54	27.82
Peoria........	72,184	1,542,720	21.37	6.04
Moline........	27,976	765,500	27.36	10.41
Rock Island...	30,489	859,945	28.21	10.88
E. St. Louis...	77,613	2,176,750	28.05	14.53
Cairo....?....	16,096	991,720	61.60	25.56
Champaign...	15,323	283,355	18.40	6.14
Urbana.......	10,306	250,745	24.33	9.12
Mattoon......	12,842	298,065	23.26	13.60
Chicago.......	2,571,941	67,435,510	26.21	6.13
Chicago Hgts..	24,070	755,545	31.39	33.24
Cicero........	21,282	674,455	31.69	10.62
Maywood.....	11,238	162,730	14.48	8.15
Oak Park.....	28,398	426,890	15.03	4.54
Blue Island....	9,548	216,595	22.68	15.19
DeKalb.......	9,816	138,350	14.09	6.61
Canton.......	14,062	209,360	14.89	7.07
Kewanee.....	15,466	286,205	18.50	10.13
Mt. Vernon....	10,164	402,610	39.54	22.21
Aurora........	35,091	906,655	25.84	9.23
Elgin.........	28,742	899,075	29.19	9.19
LaSalle.......	12,387	372,500	30.01	11.60
Ottawa.......	9,535	439,160	46.06	17.15
Streator......	14,313	285,450	19.94	10.26
Lincoln.......	11,991	1,352,365	112.78	55.61
Alton........	25,868	993,565	38.41	19.87
Granite City...	16,752	304,035	18.15	11.63
Centralia.....	11,987	303,505	25.30	14.13
Springfield....	63,375	1,541,390	24.32	9.61
Belleville......	21,157	567,600	26.83	11.20
Freeport......	19,844	453,800	22.87	8.09
Pekin........	11,361	260,025	22.89	9.31
Danville......	32,969	881,420	26.37	9.07
Monmouth....	10,431	185,920	17.82	6.44
Joliet.........	38,817	1,240,980	31.97	13.11
Rockford.....	57,897	1,316,595	22.74	5.24

Exact comparisons are difficult for many reasons. Methods of bookkeeping vary. In one city collection of garbage and ashes is a duty of the health department; while in another this expense is against the street fund. In some cities the presence of large state establishments such as insane asylums, epileptic colonies and penal institutions, may cause the figures to show unfairly against such municipalities.

Waukegan invested 5 cents more per capita in the business of health protection than did North Chicago, and its loss was $23.95 less, or a profit of 47,900 per cent on its investment. Evanston invested 23 cents more per capita in the business than did Waukegan and its loss was $4.63 less, or a profit of 2,013 per cent. If these figures are indicative of anything they show that health protection is a most paying form of municipal investment.

If it be granted that these figures are any guide, they suggest that there is a point beyond which additional appropriations would not be financially profitable. They also indicate that there will be a residual loss which cannot be overcome by present methods. Both of these suggestions seem to be in harmony with municipal experience in fighting fire. Just where the line between financial profit and loss comes in health appropriations present data are insufficient to demonstrate.

The work of a health department may very properly be compared with that of a fire department. Both are municipal functions. The object of each is to prevent unnecessary loss.

There are also differences to be remembered. In some cities fire losses are recorded in two columns; one for "primary loss," that is buildings in which fire originates with their contents, and the other for "contact loss," that is buildings and contents to which fire has extended from without. Communicable disease loss is all contact loss.

A fire in San Francisco or New York does not endanger property in Chicago or New Orleans; but a communicable disease may be contracted in New York, and its presence in New Orleans or Chicago may not be suspected until after it has spread to other victims.

As in the case of fire, every case of communicable disease serves as a new focus from which infection may spread.

Fire insurance premiums are small where the fire department is efficient, but they are large where the fire equipment is small and poorly managed. The amount spent on the fire department is, therefore, a form of fire insurance. The

money spent wisely for the support of a health department is just as truly a form of life and health insurance.

The wise man places his larger policy where the risk is greatest. He more fully insures property which cannot be replaced. Buildings and stock destroyed may be reconstructed, but life once lost cannot be restored, and health shattered may be beyond repair.

Appropriations should bear a direct relationship to the risk. The risk means money value and conditions. The appropriations for a fire department should be greater where buildings are of wood construction, than where most of them are of brick or stone, though the money value may be the same. So local conditions may demand a larger appropriation for health protection in one city than in another having the same number of inhabitants. These special conditions include character of soil and surroundings, water and sewerage arrangements, density of population, and the intelligence and manner of life of the inhabitants.

The twelve cities from which were taken the data for certain special studies are considered as fairly representative. They were selected largely by chance. Chicago was included as the largest city of the state. Joliet, Jacksonville, Kankakee, Lincoln and other cities were omitted, because it was felt that the presence of state institutions modified too greatly the apparent results.

If the life of an adult is valued at $3,000, and that of a child at $500, on the basis of the 1910 census for Illinois the average human life in the state is worth slightly over $2,000. Ignoring the fractional excess, the value of the life risk was, therefore, found by multiplying $2,000 by the number of population for each city.

In these twelve cities the appropriation for health departments in 1918 varied from .0007 to .0227 per cent of the risk, while the loss from communicable disease ranged from .6 to 2.8 per cent

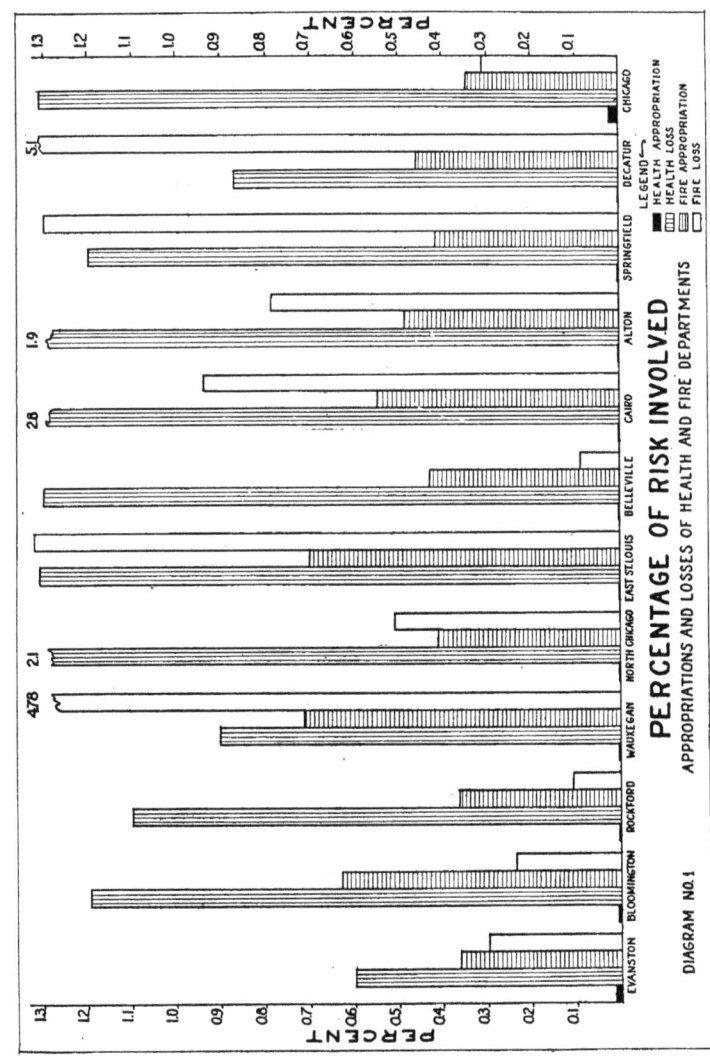

PERCENTAGE OF RISK INVOLVED

APPROPRIATIONS AND LOSSES OF HEALTH AND FIRE DEPARTMENTS

DIAGRAM NO. 1

of the risk. See Diagram I, and Table II, columns 3 and 4.

It was practically impossible to get an accurate estimate of the actual value of the fire risk. Instead we satisfied ourselves by taking the assessed valuation of property, realizing that much of this valuation represented land which is not destructable. This assessed valuation is, therefore, greater than the real fire risk, but we found that the fire department appropriation ranged from .346 to 7.01 per cent of the risk, while the loss was from .09 to 5.11 per cent of the risk. Diagram I, Table II, columns 7 and 8. In a general way we may roughly say

If a column a fifth of an inch high represented the fire loss, it would take one almost 158 feet high to show the loss due to communicable disease. In only one city was the fire loss ten times as much as the appropriation for fire protection, while the best showing for health loss was forty-one times the amount of appropriation.

A study of the tables and diagrams very clearly indicates that as compared with fire protection far too little is appropriated for health departments. This is the conclusion whether we consider the value of the risk involved, or the losses experienced. In other words, in making

TABLE II

	Comparison of appropriations and losses, fire and health										Per capita assessed valuation of property
City	Health				Fire				Ratio of loss appropriation		
	Per capita		Per cent of risk		Per capita		Per cent of risk				
(Column)	A 1	L 2	A 3	L 4	A 5	L 6	A 7	L 8	Health 9	Fire 10	11
Evanston............	$0.31	$12.82	.015	0.6	$1.72	$1.40	.365	.295	41.	.80	$473.416
Bloomington.........	.13	23.60	.006	1.2	2.09	.77	.627	.233	182.	.36	332.674
Rockford............	.08	22.74	.004	1.1	1.60	.47	.365	.109	284.	.29	433.588
Waukegan...........	.08	17.45	.004	0.9	1.29	8 31	.716	4.780	271.	6.44	174.894
North Chicago.......	.03	41.40	.0015	2.1	.90	1.12	.417	.510	1360.	.82	216.158
East St. Louis........	.13	28.05	.0064	1.4	1.35	2.76	.701	1.431	217.	2.04	192 960
Belleville...........	.014	26.83	.0007	1.3	1.02	.21	.426	.090	1829.	.21	239 419
Alton...............	.08	38.41	.0038	1.9	.93	1.55	.479	.778	446.	1.79	193.330
Springfield..........	.14	24.32	.0073	1.2	1.04	3.46	.415	1.378	165.6	3.32	251 394
Decatur.............	.177	17.48	.0088	0.87	1.09	11.99	.466	5.106	98.8	10.93	234.851
Chicago.............	.454	26.21	.0227	1.31	1.46	1.35	.346	.310	57.8	.92	421 000

A—Appropriation.　L—Loss.

that though the life risk was ten times greater than the fire risk the per capita appropriation was ten times greater for fire protection than for health. Diagram II, Table II, columns 1 and 5.

Table II, columns 9 and 10, showing the ratio of loss from disease and fire to the respective appropriations is particularly striking, though it is practically impossible for this comparison to be made in diagram: In Belleville the fire loss, which happens to be all primary loss, by the bye, was only .21 per cent of the appropriation, but the disease loss was 1,892 times the health appropriation.

the appropriations city governments have shown an unwarranted disregard of ordinary business principles.

Carrying these reasonings a little further, in so far as its different lines of activity can be measured, appropriations for a health department should be expended proportionally. In the control of communicable disease the health department has a practical monopoly. In the treatment of the sick, and in conducting clinics, the department is in competition with private practitioners of medicine. In treatment the department is dealing with units. In its preventive

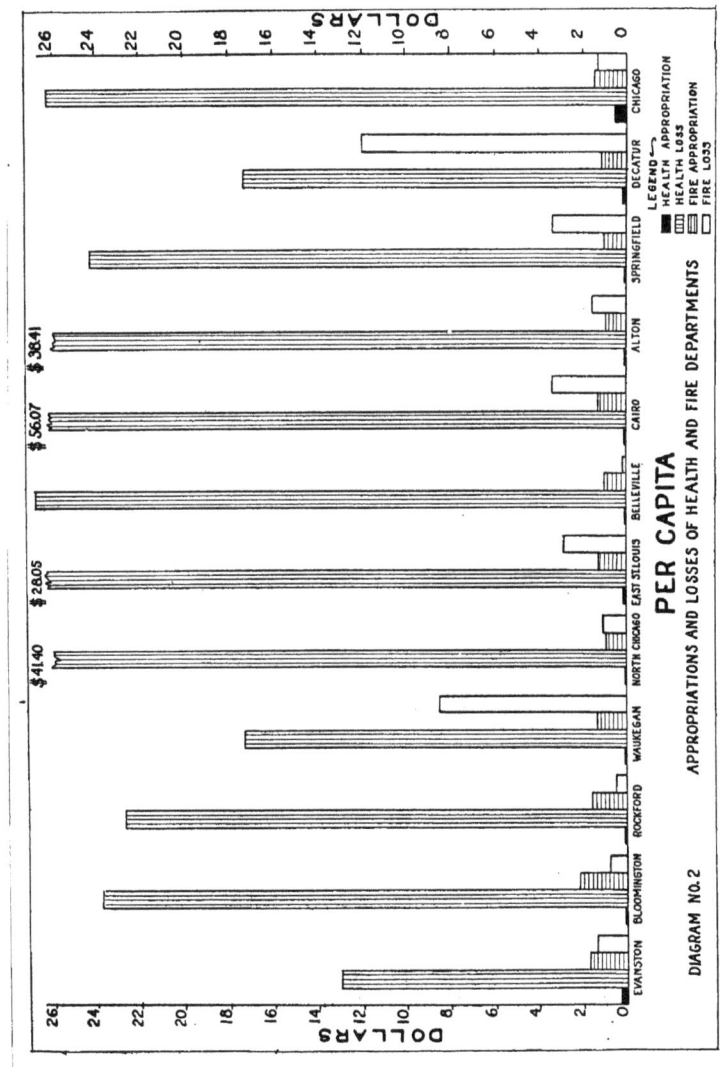

DIAGRAM NO. 2   APPROPRIATIONS AND LOSSES OF HEALTH AND FIRE DEPARTMENTS

PER CAPITA

work it is dealing with scores, hundreds, or even with thousands. Whether we consider the value of the risk involved or the losses that might result, treatment is like the retail business, and prevention is on a wholesale scale. It may, therefore, be questionable whether a depart-

ment is justified in entering the competition in treatment of cases, except only so far as it may be necessary in order to prevent the spread of disease, especially so long as the governmental work of restriction of communicable disease is so imperfectly managed as at present.

□

POPULARIZING VITAL STATISTICS

C. St. Clair Drake, M. D.;

Director, Illinois State Department of Public Health, Springfield, Illinois.

Read before Section on Vital Statistics, American Public Health Association, at New Orleans, La., October 29, 1919.

Fitting dry-as-dust vital statistics to the psychology of the people is one of the most important problems in modern popular health education. For the benefit of brother health officers Dr. Drake gives a few leaves out of his own experience in impressing fundamental statistical truths on a public that demands interesting presentation together with pictures and variety and novelty.

Vital statistics constitute our one means of accurately proving the necessity for and the success of our public health activities and of demonstrating the value of such activities to the public with mathematical precision. For the first purpose —for the guidance of health officers and technical workers — vital statistics, in their usual prosaic, tabular form may prove entirely satisfactory; but for the information of the people and for public demonstration the material contained in statistical reports must be redressed, interpreted into a new language and made readily intelligible. To transform the contents of statistical tables into interesting reading in a day when the public mind is over-occupied by varied activities and stirring events, requires a high degree of originality and ingenuity and yet, unless we can present our morbidity and mortality data in a form which will attract attention and carry conviction, we shall fall far short of our ideals and pos-

sibilities of accomplishment in public health work.

The two fundamental aims of the health official are the saving of human life and the prevention of unnecessary human illness. To accomplish these ends it is essential that there be provided reasonable financial appropriations, and it is necessary that there be created a very general popular interest in the maintenance of health.

In this age of specialization, when individual phases of health work are subject to enthusiastic over-accentuation, and in this day of almost hourly sensations and thrills, legislators are not influenced or impressed and the people are not aroused by glittering generalities. They demand something definite and tangible. They insist upon evidence rather than what they may regard as biased or prejudiced opinion. Language has been combed during the past few years for superlatives and extreme expressions and these have been so constantly employed that they have lost their original force. Lawmakers and the public alike must be actually shown and it is the job of the successful health official to visualize convincingly and attractively the evidence which comes to him in a form which is dry and unappealing.

It has long been recognized that the average citizen, rich or poor, can appreciate the value of dollars and cents more clearly than that of human life or human efficiency and, on this account, a common method of popularization of vital statistics has come to be the expression of human wastage in terms of money. This is naturally capable of innumerable variations and applications.

The legislator who has been elected to office on the popular platform of public economy can be impressed by statistical information expressed in cash terms and showing big cash dividends accruing to the people of the state through the investment of public funds in certain definite phases of public health work. The average householder finds something of personal interest in a showing of the financial loss suffered by his own community through the maintenance or tolerance of definite insanitary conditions. An attractive display of the comparative cost of a funeral with the cost of typhoid vaccine may cause the busy citizen to give his first thought to this and other preventive agents.

But even when we have translated our deaths and births and illnesses into terms of money, we must seek some means of bringing the facts to the attention of the people—of visualizing them so that "he who runs may read." Some years ago, when it seemed particularly desirable to impress upon the people of Chicago the unnecessary wastage due to communicable diseases and when mere words, however expressive, seemed to arouse little attention, we employed the plan of measuring the cost of these diseases to the several city wards in silver dollars and

illustrated the cost by pictures showing these piles of dollars as compared in height with the Masonic Temple, then the highest and best known building in the city. When it was shown that diphtheria, scarlet fever and measles, for a period of six months, had cost one city ward a stack of silver dollars over nine times as high as the twenty-story Masonic Temple, there was general surprise and very extensive discussion, while the comparative showing of the various wards created considerable comment and even some resentment on the part of the political and civic leaders in those wards which made the more unsatisfactory showing. Whatever the reaction, agreeable or disagreeable, commendatory, critical or resentful, the important thing was that a much larger percentage of the Chicago population was thinking of the value of health more definitely than it had been formerly.

Incidentally, the comparison of morbidity and mortality statistics, expressed either in numbers or in terms of money of several neighboring and competitive communities, has proven an excellent means of bringing public health to the attention of the people. While the citizens of Smithville may be quite indifferent to the fact that the city has an abnormally high death rate, they do not wish it pointed out that Jonesborough, its bitterest competitor for commercial and civic honors, makes claim to a much lower rate and, in virtue of this fact, is declared to be a better and safer place to live in.

After impressing upon the people with stacks of silver dollars the cost of communicable diseases and thereby arousing popular interest if not genuine concern, graphic charts were prepared showing the cost to the community of losses by fire and losses through lawlessness, proving definitely that community wastage through preventable disease is far greater than either. And then the stacks of silver dollars were brought into play to indicate to the people the relative public expenditures for fire department, police department and health department. It is, of course, exceedingly difficult to measure the exact results of any form of publicity; but it has been demonstrated over and over that, if the essential facts of community vital statistics can be gotten to the people, more liberal appropriations for public health work almost invariably follow. If the people as a whole can be made to realize, even in a general way, that they have a definite interest in community health, the politician may be quickly made to see that the promotion of public health is a matter of good politics.

The public health official, who is compelled to go from time to time before finance or appropriation committees, is soon impressed that his case is tremendously strengthened if he can support his pleas with reliable statistical data; but he is also often impressed that two or three forceful charts or pictures hung on the committee room wall are more effective than the most elaborate verbal addresses or type-written arguments.

Even after obtaining liberal appropriations, the results of health activities will not be satisfactory unless it is possible to arouse popular interest and to convince the people as a whole of their own interest in health conservation. For this purpose, if judiciously handled, vital statistics are of inestimable value. For public consumption, however, statistical information must be administered in small doses and, if possible, must be given local application. The morbidity and mortality figures of a man's own home town will attract his attention when he would ignore the data of other communities or of the state as a whole and, as a rule, it is better to let the individual community meditate on its scarlet fever problem this week, its tuberculosis problem next week and its child welfare problem the week after, than to fire the whole shot at one time, to produce a ripple and then be forgotten. A relatively apathetic and un-interested people will not absorb large doses of public health instruction at one sitting, while constant repetition of the same essential facts delivered from different angles has been found effective in all lines of commercial advertising.

But the public requires variation and novelty. It must in some way have its curiosity aroused and must be attracted by the element of surprise. The lessons of vital statistics must at times be taught by devices that arrest the attention first and then impress the brief lesson upon the arrested attention. In visiting a county fair, the sightseer is attracted by the sounding of a gong which rings out with endless, monotonous repetition. His curiosity is excited and he asks what it means and is told that every time the gong sounds someone has died from tuberculosis in his state or in the nation. He is apt to question the accuracy of the statement. He may get the figures and try to disprove it. At any rate, he is thinking public health as he never would have thought it had not the incontestable evidence of vital statistics been beaten into his unwilling ears by the sounding of the gong.

That babies die and that a considerable number of them die is accepted as a matter of course by the average citizen. It has always been so and he gives the matter little thought. A mechanical device showing the figure of death hovering over a moving group of babies and cutting down every fourth child with a scythe, arrests his attention as he wanders from the stock pens to the race track at a state fair. He stops and watches it, his chief interest, perhaps, being in how the "contraption" works. Whatever the point of attraction, he is likely to move on thinking for the first time in his life of what unnecessary infant mortality actually means to his community.

It is obviously impossible at this time to refer even to the many ways in which the facts elicited from vital statistics are being brought to the people through the ingenuity and originality of health officials; but however extensively this popularization 'of statistics has been developed in certain states or communities, it is safe to say that the possibilities of development have but been touched. Public health has ceased to be above the heads of the general public. If properly conveyed, the people are receptive of instruction; but they want proof rather than theory. Our best and most reliable source of evidence lies in our vital statistics and the health official who can master the art of actually popularizing his statistics will go far in the attainment of the greatest good.

□

THE MEETING IN SAN FRANCISCO.

The time for the Forty-eighth Annual Meeting of the American Public Health Association has been set at August 30 till September 3, 1920, and the place, San Francisco, Cal. To show to some extent the character of the city in which this great gathering of health officers and executives is to be held, this view of the City Hall is presented. It is the rallying point of a group of buildings forming a civic center, of which any American might feel proud, suggestive of municipal spirit of highest quality. The ornamented square in the foreground is surrounded by public structures of the same character as the City Hall, including the Public Library, and the Municipal Auditorium, in which the meetings will be held, with the plannings still calling for other structures. The meetings of the A. P. H. A. never have had more auspicious environment.

MOSQUITO WORK OF THE BUREAU OF ENTOMOLOGY

D. L. Van Dine,

Entomologist, Bureau of Entomology, United States Department of Agriculture, Mound, La.

Read before General Sessions, American Public Health Association, at New Orleans, La., October 29, 1919.

The early work of the Bureau of Entomology on mosquitoes was summarized in a publication of the Department in the summer of 1896.[1] The important features of this work were the demonstration of the practical use of kerosene oil in the destruction of mosquito larvae by Dr. Howard in 1894, and the complete life-history, with figures, of the common mosquito, *Culex pipiens*, based upon the original studies of Dr. Howard in the summer of 1895. The work of the Bureau up to this date dealt with the mosquitoes from the standpoint of the annoyance and the discomfort they cause. The theory that mosquitoes were possibly concerned in the transmission of malaria, presented forcibly by Dr. A. F. A. King in 1882,[2] did not serve to justify more extended considerations. Dr. Howard in commenting at that time upon the views held by Dr. King, said "they may go so far as to initiate and encourage experiments and observations by which the truth or fallacy of the views held may be demonstrated."

The demonstration by Ross in 1897, which was inspired by the discovery of Laveran (1880) and the ideas of Manson (1894), gave to the subject of mosquitoes and their repression a vital interest and fastened the attention of the medical world upon this group of insects. It became necessary to have full details concerning those which had been incriminated in carrying the disease and information that would enable the sanitarian to distinguish the disease-conveying species from those that are harmless in this respect. In 1900 Dr. Howard published an account of the life-history of *Anopheles quadrimaculatus* which permitted recognition of the mosquito in all stages of its development, a point he recognized as important in any control effort.[3] The biology of this malaria mosquito was given in comparison to that of the common domestic mosquito, *Culex pipiens*. This publication was followed by an official bulletin,[4] published the same year, which gave a general account of the mosquitoes of the United States and the known facts of their biology, special attention being devoted to the American species of Anopheles and their geographical distribution. The following year the same author published a volume on mosquitoes,[5] which also attracted wide attention. This little book at once became the "bible" of all interested in mosquito warfare. The writer speaks from experience as during that year he began his first mosquito work in the Hawaiian Islands. The universal interest and value of these early publications can hardly be appreciated at this late day when the details of mosquito development are so well known. But it is not out of place to discuss them thus briefly when we consider that they constituted the basis of mosquito control effort in this country.

Up to 1901 some 25 species of mosquitoes only were recognized among those occurring in the United States. It became apparent to Dr. Howard that all species must be studied carefully as to distribution, biology and sanitary significance in, particularly, the regions included in North and Central America and the West Indies. This work was undertaken in the early part of 1903 and was made possible by a grant from the Carnegie Institution of Washington. The grant covered a period of three years, but at the expiration of this period the project was far from complete and many regions remained unexplored. The work was continued during 1906, 1907 and 1908 partly by funds appropriated by Congress for the study of insects affecting the health of man and domestic animals, partly by the help of the Isthmian Canal Commission, partly by the help of volunteer observers in the West Indies and Central America and partly at the expense of the men associated with Dr. Howard in the work—Dr. H. G. Dyar and Mr. F. Knab. The result of this work has been published in four volumes,[6] the first volume appearing in 1912 and the last in 1917. How well the authors succeeded in their undertaking can be judged by this publication, which stands as a monument to their fifteen years of endeavor.

Subsequent to the early work of the Bureau on mosquitoes and prior to the appearance of the monograph above mentioned, results of economic significance were published, a review of which is not permitted by the time limit of this paper or indicated by the purposes of this meeting.[7]

In the summer of 1913 a project was undertaken by the Bureau to deal especially with the mosquitoes concerned in the transmission of malaria in this country. A laboratory for the purposes of this investigation was established in the delta region of the Mississippi valley at Mound, Louisiana, where the Anopheles mosquitoes and malaria, are prevalent.

One result of this project has been given in the conclusions on the loss in crop returns from malaria.[8] The loss occurs in the time and the reduced efficiency of the plantation labor during the crop seasons. As the negro tenant performs the greater part of the agricultural labor in the delta region, the important point in the prevention of malaria in this region is the control of the disease among the tenant class.

It was determined that the amount lost in crop returns is equivalent to a direct annual tax of $3.88 per acre upon the land under cultivation. It is estimated that the average cost of primary drainage of swamp lands, which are permanently wet and never fit for cultivation even during most favorable years, is $4 per acre in any project that involves a large territory; for secondary drains, to place the land in productive condition, an additional amount of $8 is required; and for bringing the land into cultivation a further expenditure of $5 an acre is necessary. This is a total average cost of $17 per acre to bring permanent swamp land into cultivation.[9] The tax of malaria on the land under cultivation is sufficient to pay in less than five years the cost of bringing an equal number of acres of permanent swamp land into cultivation.

Four species of Anopheles have been encountered in the work in progress in the delta. These are *A. quadrimaculatus*, *A. punctipennis*, *A. crucians* and *A. pseudopunctipennis*. One of these species, *A. punctipennis*, heretofore considered a mosquito which did not convey malaria, was incriminated as an efficient host by Dr. W. V. King of this Bureau.[10] The rearing of the mosquito material for this and subsequent demonstrations of Dr. King[11] was done at the Mound laboratory and the experimental work with the same accomplished by him in the laboratories of Clinical Medicine of the School of Medicine of Tulane University together with Dr. C. C. Bass and Dr. F. M. Johns.

The ability of a species of Anopheles to act as the agent in the transmission of malaria depends not only upon its efficiency as a host of the malaria parasites, but also upon its numbers in any region, its seasonal appearance, and the extent to which it enters dwellings to feed or is successful in finding human blood elsewhere where malaria occurs. To determine the species of Anopheles concerned in the transmission of malaria in any region, their numbers, their sources, their habits and the environmental conditions in that particular region must be studied. An important carrier of the disease in one region may be of comparative little importance or of no concern in another region under varying factors of season, breeding places, shelters and class of people concerned.

The species of Anopheles that occur in the delta have been associated with the types of the malaria parasites found in that locality. The important carrier of malaria in the delta region is *A. quadrimaculatus*. The species is thoroughly adapted to the environment of the swamp country. It is by far the more common Anopheles and the one encountered in numbers throughout the season in and about habitations. The prevailing type of malaria parasite is estivo-autumnal.

It has been determined that the capacity of certain classes of artificial collections of water is very limited in the production of Anopheles. These domestic breeding places do not contribute sufficient Anopheles for the purposes of malaria transmission. This point of source of Anopheles is of special interest to the sanitarian engaged in malaria mosquito control. The larvae of Anopheles are found in water barrels, in troughs used for stock, in disused cisterns, and in other artificial collections of water about habitations. Careful observations with adult emergence tests from these sources have been made. At most the emergence was very small and in some instances negative from containers that had been stocked with larvæ in some numbers. The typical sources were found to be the margins of bayous, swamps and shallow lakes; woodland pools; water shallow enough to support aquatic vegetation other than at margin; and open water with logs, stumps or brush, or with the surface covered with trash, debris or floating vegetation.

The idea prevails that Anopheles mosquitoes do not bite in the daytime, that malaria infection is obtained only after nightfall. If this were true it would be difficult to explain many infections that are contracted. It has been found that while these mosquitoes are more active just at dusk and afterwards, they will bite any time of the day a blood meal is required and the opportunity to obtain same is offered. This is particularly true of those in dwellings where the occupants are sheltered during the night by mosquito-bars and in offices or other places of business that are vacated during the night. These mosquitoes when trapped within a screened house become very persistent in seeking a blood meal day or night.

The screening of dwellings has been an important factor in the reduction of malaria when the screening work has been done thoroughly and proper use has been made of the protection afforded. Imperfect screening will defeat its own ends by the trapping of the mosquitoes within the dwelling and the improper use of a perfectly screened dwelling will give the same result. Dr. Howard estimates that the people of the United States spend $10,000,000 every year for screening against flies and mosquitoes and concludes that if this enormous expense is at all necessary, it should be done thoroughly.[12] There is a distinction between screening to obtain comfort and screening for protection against disease transmission. After the screening has been thoroughly done, the proper use of the screened dwelling implies care that the doors do not offer entrance to mosquitoes through carelessness in leaving them open, or in entering and leaving the house, in replacing or repairing screening where it has been damaged or is worn out, in not leaving unsuspected openings unprotected, in making certain that the construction of the building is mosquito tight, and in searching for and destroying all the mosquitoes that do find entrance despite all possible precautions. Constant care and watchfulness on the part of all members of the household are required. Without any doubt screening is an efficient protection against malaria infection among an intelligent class of people. The question of how much dependence can be placed upon screening among the negro tenant class on a plantation is one open for discussion. In the first place the usual construction of the tenant houses does not lend itself to effective screening. The open construction of the floors and walls, the irregular construction of the door and window casings, the absence of a ceiling in some instances, and the use of the fireplace for cooking during the summer months (preventing the covering of the chimney flues) would demand the reconstruction of the tenant houses on the average plantation in the delta and the substitution of cooking stoves for fireplaces. Ventilation must be considered in such a change among the tenants. The open construction offers an amount of ventilation that would otherwise be denied because of their aversion to the night air. Admitting that the reconstruction is practical, it is open to question whether or not the tenant class would properly use the protection offered and, even if the screening remained intact, the extent to which this class would remain at home after nightfall to take advantage of the protection. We can reconstruct houses, but how far can we go in reconstruction of habits and impulses that are characteristics of the class under consideration?

The individual use of the mosquito bar over beds is a more promising protection against malaria infection than screening the house among the tenants. One careless member in a household will offset the care taken by all other members in a screened house, but the mosquito bar protects the individual. The mosquito bar also implies no reconstruction of buildings, and places no restrictions upon the movement of individuals from point to point.

As applied to a plantation the methods to be employed in the prevention of malaria cannot count to any great extent upon the control of the tenant class under present conditions. Lacking control of the human host, with the difficulties that confront screening, with large tracts of permanent swamp having no outlet, and with expenditures for protection limited by the profits on the crops grown, the prevention of malaria on the plantations in the delta offers a problem in the solution of which the usual suggestions do not apply. The investigation of the Bureau aims to assist in solving the problem in so far as the measures directed against the mosquitoes are involved.

REFERENCES

1. L. O. Howard, Chapter I, Principal Household Insects of the United States. Bulletin No. 4, new series, 1896.
2. Popular Science Monthly, September, 1883, Vol. 23, pp. 644-658.
3. Scientific American, July 7, 1900.
4. L. O. Howard. The Mosquitoes of the United States. Bulletin No. 25, new series, Bureau of Entomology. 1900. 22 figs. 70 pp.
5. Mosquitoes: How they live, how they carry disease, how they are classified, how they may be destroyed. New York, 1901. 241 pp.
6. The Mosquitoes of North and Central America and the West Indies. L. O. Howard, H. G. Dyar, and F. Knab. Vol. I—A general consideration of mosquitoes. their habits. and their relations to the human species, 1912; Vol. II, plates, 1912; Vol. III, systematic description, Part 1, 1915; Vol. IV, systematic description, Part 2, 1917. Washington. 1064 pp. 150 plates.
7. The more important publications to which reference is made are:
D. W. Coquillett. A Classification of the Mosquitoes of North and Middle America. Tech. Bul. No. 11, 1906.
H. G. Dyar. Key to the Known Larvae of the Mosquitoes of the United States. Circular No. 72, 1906.
L. O. Howard. How Insects Affect Health in Rural Districts. Farmers' Bulletin No. 155, 1908.
L. O. Howard. Economic Loss to the People of the United States Through Insects That Carry Disease. Bulletin No. 78. 1909.
L. O. Howard. Preventive and Remedial Work Against Mosquitoes. Bulletin No. 88. 1910.
L. O. Howard. Some Facts About Malaria. Farmers' Bulletin No. 450, 1911.
L. O. Howard. The Yellow-Fever Mosquito. Farmers' Bulletin No. 547, 1913.
8. D. L. Van Dine. The Relation of Malaria to Crop Production. The Scientific Monthly, November, 1916.
9. C. G. Elliott. Swamp Lands of the United States. Senate Doc. No. 443, 60th Congress, 1st Session. 1908.
10. The rôle of Anopheles punctipennis Say in the Transmission of Malaria. Science. 1915. Vol. 42, pp. 873-874.
11. Anopheles punctipennis, a Host of Tertian Malaria. Am. Jl. Trop. Diseases and Preventive Med., Vol. III, No. 8, February, 1916 pp. 426-432.
Experiments on the Development of Malaria Parasites in Three American Species of Anopheles. Jl. of Expt. Meu., June 1, 1916, Vol. 23, No. 6, pp. 703-716.
The Effect of Cold Upon Malaria Parasites in the Mosquito Host. Jl. Expt. Med., March 1, 1917, Vol. 25, No. 3, pp. 495-498.
12. Prevention and Remedial Work Against Mosquitoes. Bul. 88, Bureau of Entomology, U. S. Department of Agriculture, 1910, p. 14.

DRAINAGE AS AN ANTI-MALARIA MEASURE

J. A. LePrince,

*Senior Sanitary Engineer, United States Public Health Service,
Memphis, Tenn.*

Read before General Sessions, American Public Health Association, at New Orleans, La.,
October 29. 1919

This author argues the necessity of liberal interpretation of laws.
The Health Officer can then be able to use prevention at malarial
sources beyond his borders. He urges co-operation of the health
officer in drainage plannings and suggests value of permanent
improvements, following, of course, study of local conditions.

MANY states have drainage laws which enable large tracts of land to be so drained as to fit them for agricultural development. Such drainage laws are effective in many states in the so-called "malaria belt." When these laws were written, little was known of the difference between land or farm drainage and what is now called "Anopheles drainage." The laws as written plan for the partial removal of present standing water or more rapid removal of storm water, and to some extent the lowering of the sub-surface water level in the areas involved. Up to the present time the state health officers have not even been consulted in connection with country drainage projects, and consequently malaria prevails in areas which are said to be properly drained.

Every drainage project of county or township should be required by law to have the written approval of the state health officer. Also, the laws should be so amended as to include and require the installation of such auxiliary or lateral drains as the state health officer finds essential—and a certain sum or percentage of the cost of the project should be set aside by law for the installation of such minor drainage as is essential for prevention of malaria and also for maintaining the ditches of the general drainage scheme in such condition that they will not become a real menace to health. At the present time in many instances the main drains are neglected until they are silted up, overgrown and obstructed so that the loss in value to the adjacent lands is far greater than the cost of proper and efficient maintenance. In addition, such conditions are too frequently accompanied by lowered vitality among the rural population and a subnormal property value.

The main lines of the drainage systems, and many of the larger branch lines, frequently become matted with vegetation, and those species of fish which prefer mosquito larvæ to other food are prevented from destroying the Anopheles wiggle-tails. This condition can frequently be remedied by having a channel of smaller cross-section within the bed of the ditch to give a greater depth of water, and clean-cut edges, free from vegetation at the water surface during periods of minimum flow, which often corresponds to the season of maximum production of malaria-bearing mosquitoes.

The recent advance in cost of farm lands will undoubtedly result in increasing reclamation projects of swamp lands. Companies attempting to colonize such areas must remember that the drainage of a dike enclosed or other area will not keep the people living within a quarter of a mile to a mile from the boundary line free from malaria nor the mosquito pest. Mosquitoes produced on adjacent lands will probably travel toward the drained farm colony. A zone of drainage protection around habitations is essential.

In planning Anopheles drainage schemes for towns, we must remember that frequently in small towns and also in the suburbs of large ones we have the highest malaria rate and maximum Anopheles production. It is necessary, therefore, that state health officers in revising sanitary procedure arrange for the authority and jurisdiction of the town health officer to extend a safe limit beyond the so-called town lines, and the city health officer should be given authority to spend city funds in such a manner as will produce a maximum of good health among town people for a minimum of expense. If a city or town health officer can keep more town people well per dollar expended by doing sanitary drainage work one inch or one-quarter of a mile beyond the town limit than he could by spending two dollars on less important work within the town limits, there is no sane reason why he should not be authorized to do it. The mere fact that it has not been done before merely indicates that the public has not been properly informed that the taxes are, relatively speaking, being wasted.

FARM DRAINAGE VERSUS ANOPHELES DRAINAGE

The farmer in draining his land has two objects in view: to lower the subsurface water table sufficiently to allow crops to grow to best advantage and to carry off storm water. On some farms part of the land is in pasture and little attention is given to wet areas on pasture lands. The latter frequently cost the farmer a heavy annual malaria tax.

It is frequently stated that it is out of the question to consider the drainage of rural areas for malaria-control purposes, as the cost would be prohibitive. In some areas this statement may be true, but the writer refuses to accept the statement as generally true. He is convinced that there are highly malarial areas containing hundreds of square miles that it will be more economical to drain than to leave in their present condition. Before the recent war, when farm wages were normal, a thorough investigation, under the direction of Capt. D. L. VanDine, of a large, well-managed plantation in Louisiana showed that the cost of malaria (malaria tax) per acre per year was approximately three dollars and eighty cents ($3.80) per acre. During the war, and in connection with the protection of the army and naval forces and industries concerned with war supplies, 1,300 square miles were drained and kept practically free of Anopheles at a cost of $1.61 per acre for a year. Figures will soon be available to show the cost of maintenance work in those communities which have continued practically free from malaria. During the war period, near war industries and cantonments, laborers' wages were higher than in any previous period in history, and yet we find a cost of $1.61 to be free of malaria, as against $3.80 to pay for the privilege of having malaria.

Recent inquiries in another state in a highly malarious agricultural district indicate a direct loss from malaria to the farm tenants and owners of more than $10 per acre during 1918.

The farmer arranges his drains, as stated, to carry off storm water, and cares little as to their condition after the storm water has gone by. It is then, from the sanitarian's viewpoint, that the ditch is most dangerous and most important. As a rule, the cross-section of the bottom portion of the farm drainage ditch, storm water ditch, or stream, is unsatisfactory for "Anopheles drainage" because it is such that it does not become dry or produce a maximum velocity at times of normal or at times of minimum flow, and because its ragged edges produce places where the water has no velocity and where the mosquito larvæ can find protection from their natural enemies.

SUBSURFACE DRAINS OR TILE DRAINAGE

Although tile drainage has been used for many years in improving farm soils and increasing productivity of farm lands, health officers have given but little thought to this subject and have failed to co-operate with the state and Federal agricultural agents in their efforts to make tile drainage more popular. The particular advantages of tile drainage are that it often enables us to permanently eliminate malaria mosquito production areas and improve the agricultural value of farm lands in one operation at a reasonable cost. It is safe to state that the agricultural value of farm lands so treated will increase, and frequently the increased productivity will represent a much larger dividend than could be obtained by investing a similar amount of capital in safe mortgages.

It should be stated that tile drainage schemes should be properly planned and installed by experienced persons, and that tile drainage systems can be and have been incorrectly located, and consequently have failed to accomplish expected results.

PRESENT METHODS OF ANOPHELES DRAINAGE AND ANOPHELES CONTROL

Rapid strides are being made in sanitation today, and it is to be hoped that within a few years communities desirous of freedom from malaria and the mosquito pest will issue bonds that will furnish sufficient capital to install adequate permanent drainage systems, to maintain which will cost but a very small fraction of the original cost. Some towns and counties have already taken such action.

Where conditions are favorable, the writer believes in so planning the drainage system as to eliminate the necessity of supplementary measures, such as oiling and maintenance of open ditches. He carried out experimental investigations along this line on the Isthmus of Panama and thereby largely reduced the cost of malaria control.

Until such time as the public is sufficiently interested in malaria control to take the steps above mentioned, it is advisable to carry out the present system of procedure. This consists of draining useless ponds, swamps, and wet lands with open ditches, and where necessary, intercepting ditches. As a rule, engineers, as well as other people, make the bottoms of ditches unnecessarily wide, and this fault increases mosquito-producing capacity of the ditch because it decreases the velocity of flow of water, decreases depth of water in the ditch, and favors clogging of the ditch with vegetable growth. The latter furnishes a secure hiding place for mosquito larvæ and also protects them from those species of fish that destroy all mosquito larvæ if given half a chance.

Open ditches installed for mosquito control purposes should, so far as possible, have clean-cut sloping edges, narrow bottoms and courses as straight as practicable.

Streams should, where practicable, have steep banks from directly above the normal flow line to below the dry season low water line, and be freed from vegetation, sticks, stones, and obstructions that interfere with the current. It is not necessary to remove all brush from both banks of a stream, and is generally advisable to clear one bank and only as much of the vegetation from the other as does, or will, hang into the water.

The objectionable feature of the present method of procedure is the question and expense of maintenance and oiling. Where the annual cost of this maintenance work is greater than the interest on the cost of light reinforced concrete lining of the ditches with intercepting key walls or greater than tile drainage, then unquestionably one of the latter should be used. The problem is one for the health officer to consider. If his town will consent only to temporary measures, of smaller initial outlay, he is forced to follow that procedure. However, in many cases, with sufficient expenditure of effort, he can probably get a small appropriation for the installation of a sample (say 100 yards) of some permanent ditch-lining work and locate same at a point of maximum traffic where it will be seen by everybody and thus induce the town people to see the wisdom and economy of carrying out the extension of the permanent system. Undoubtedly years ago the people were against the installation of sewers much more than they would now object to being taxed for permanent malarial control measures, and yet the sanitarians that preceded us changed the public viewpoint just as it is now our privilege and duty to do so, so far as malaria control in growing towns and suburbs of cities is concerned. If the health officer is at first not successful in his efforts of persuasion, he can, if he wishes, have a sample section of ditch lined by obtaining funds by subscription and then keeping record of cost of maintenance and oiling in open earth ditches per mile per year as compared with cost of maintenance of permanent ditching.

While sanitary improvements cost money, it is always well to make a study of the local problem and determine whether or not the lack of sanitary improvements is not far more expensive. Dr. L. O. Howard, the father of the mosquito extermination campaigns in this country, estimated some time ago that the malaria mosquito alone cost citizens of America $100,000,000 per year. Since that time many new towns and villages have been built and tons and tons of mosquito wire have been purchased and have been ineffectively installed and decayed.

If a portion of the money expended had been used for permanent drainage construction, many of our malarial suburbs of towns would be practically mosquito-free and hundreds of persons who died as a result of malaria fever would be alive today.

The writer knows that in many localities effective screening of houses is the best preliminary procedure for malaria control, but has visited numerous villages and towns where thousands of dollars are being spent each year for expensive screening, most of which is ineffectively installed, and where it would have been more economical and satisfactory to have installed permanent drainage systems and obtained permanent benefits at a reasonable cost.

San Francisco, August 30-September 3, 1920.
For the Forty-eighth Annual Meeting of the A. P. H. A.
Today Is Not Too Early to Be Making Your Plans.

SANITATION IN SERBIA

EDWARD STUART,

Major, Sanitary Corps, U. S. Army.

Formerly Director American Red Cross Sanitary Commission,
Paris, France

We must maintain health programs in Serbia according to Major Stuart, who tells plainly of conditions as his party found them. Serbia, with other Balkan countries, is a menace to the health of the Western world. Typhus and malaria are endemic, while tuberculosis and other communicable diseases enfeeble the people.

The Great War now being over, it may be well, at this time, to record something of the history of disease in the Balkans during the past five years. The enormous amount of suffering throughout Europe has been so extensive that one focus of epidemics sinks into relative insignificance; but the intensity of sickness and misery which has existed in that region has made the Balkans almost a synonym of death, starvation, and disease.

There have always been epidemics in the Balkans. The history of their wars runs hand in hand with the history of their epidemics, and the latter are bound to continue unless radical changes can be made. Sanitation, health organizations, and the hygiene of the person are so bad that nearly all the diseases considered by us as preventable, stalk about unhindered, uncontrolled; and even diseases ordinarily found only in the tropics occur, such as pappataci fever, dhobie itch, and a malaria which is tropical in its perniciousness.

The abdominal infections, typhoid, cholera, and dysentery have been very common, and outbreaks of these have followed one another in sudden and terrific attacks which have taken their toll in thousands of lives in many towns, sometimes a third of the population of the community at one time, and among

the armies which have waged so many wars against one another. Such mortality seems exaggerated from our point of view in the United States, but when one realizes the condition of the water supplies, taking an example, it is not surprising. The writer has seen towns in which all the night soil of the household is collected in buckets and thrown out upon the surface of the cobbled street in front of the house, to be washed by the first rain to the next corner, where there may be a collecting basin for the water supply of the neighborhood. The collecting basin, protected by a few loose pieces of sheet iron, receives a large portion of the surface drainage, which then passes through small pipes directly to the fountains from which the population take all their water.

A few of the cities in northern Serbia, situated in the valleys of the Save and the Danube, have artesian supplies, but nine tenths of all the supplies are exceedingly dangerous to drink. The city of Belgrade has the only sewer in all Serbia; all other towns, institutions, barracks, and hospitals accumulate their wastes in large putrescent pools, or permit the wastes to shift for themselves.

The insect-borne diseases are the best-known scourges, of which typhus fever is pre-eminent. It is endemic throughout the Balkans, parts of Hungary, and, extending up through Galicia, reaches Poland and the Baltic Provinces. Malaria, very serious in southern Serbia, is endemic in Macedonia and parts of Albania. In·fact, it is so serious in these regions that the whole population has deteriorated to a very low state of efficiency. Hundreds of square miles of marshland along the valley of the Vardar, north of Saloniki and along the Adriatic coast, near Durazzo, breed the mosquitoes which spread the disease. The European type of relapsing fever is extremely common throughout the Balkans, and occurs during both hot and cold seasons, in this respect unlike the typhus, which usually dies out during the summer. Pappataci fever has already been mentioned, and it occurs along the stretches of the rivers haunted by the moth midge, *Phlebotomus papatassii,* which can pass through the finest mosquito nets.

Of other diseases, the most common are tuberculosis, its prevalence being largely due to the low standard of living, the venereal diseases, pneumonia, and skin and eye diseases everywhere.

The War

When Austria declared war on Serbia in the summer of 1914, her armies seized a certain portion of the Serbian territory. The Serb army promptly drove them out. Later, in December of that year, Austria, with an army of 600,000, again invaded the country, descending about a hundred miles into Serbia; and was again forced back by a Serb army, half the size of the other, to her territory north of the Danube and Save rivers; the Serbs capturing 60,000 prisoners, among whom were some already infected with typhus. These prisoners crowded into rough barracks and camps with no facilities for any sort of cleanliness, sleeping on the floors, huddled together for mutual warmth, soon became victims of the disease which spread rapidly as the vermin increased, until ulti-

mately practically every prisoner became infected. Moreover, as the prisoners were continually being broken up into smaller groups and shifted about from one part of the country to another in close proximity to the Serbian soldiers themselves, the infection soon spread into the Serbian army and into the military hospitals where the sick prisoners had been brought, no adequate isolation having been attempted.

From the army the disease traveled to the civilian population, until the whole country was in a conflagration of typhus. Vital statistics being non-existant, it is impossible to know how many were stricken, but it can be stated with reasonable certainty that approximately one quarter of a million people became ill with typhus in Serbia between December, 1914, and July, 1915. It was a very virulent type, with a high mortality, fatal to 50 per cent of the Austro-Hungarian prisoners, it is known. The mortality among the Serbians is unknown and the estimates are very varied; but, personally, I am inclined to believe that a conservative estimate would place the number at about 85,000, including the 30,000 prisoners who died. With a total population in Serbia of 4,000,000, this makes a mortality of 2,125 per 100,000 in six months! Such a mortality among a population as large as that of the United States would mean over two million deaths.

The conditions in the country at that time beggar description. At war against a great enemy, a primitive civilization (half the country had been freed from the Turks only two years before; the other half, excluding a small section, only 40 years before), inadequate hospitals, supplies, medicines, and but 300 doctors in all, of whom 125 perished in the epidemic; it is difficult to conceive of more misery. But it was the fate of this country to learn more horror later.

At the call of diplomatic and consular representatives, many Allied and neutral missions were sent to aid in combatting the epidemic. The Russian Government sent the personnel and supplies for several complete typhus hospitals; France, one hundred military doctors; England, a military commission under Colonel Hunter, R. A. M. C., and a large number of field and base hospital units; America, several Red Cross hospital units and a sanitary commission supported by the American Red Cross and Rockefeller Foundation jointly, under the direction of Dr. Richard P. Strong of Harvard; and even small nations such as Belgium and Holland furnished doctors and nurses. An international committee was formed of the heads of the larger missions, together with the representatives of the Serbian army and civil sanitary administration, the country divided into sanitary zones, and the latter assigned to various missions in accordance with their kind of personnel and equipment.

Concentrated efforts were applied at those points where the epidemic was most severe. It was considered that the most practicable method of killing lice in clothing and blankets was with steam. For this large refrigerator cars of the railroad were transformed into improvised sterilizers, in which, although the pressure was nil, the vermin were killed by the heat, the clothing having been hung up very loosely to allow easy access by the steam. Many large portable autoclaves were employed; and where these were not available the simple "Serbian barrel" (a device in which the clothing is supported over a vat of boiling water), was erected in large quantities. Haircutting, bathing, kerosene baths, and the fumigation of barracks and other buildings with large quantities

THE BREAD LINE IN BELGRADE (1916) -
It was among these unfortunates that the mortality from tuberculosis assumed enormous proportions.

accord-
unel and

plied at
zic was
that the
ig lice in
n steam.
s of the
impro-
ough the
re billed
ing been
easy ac-
portable
d where
simple
which the
t of boil-
e quanti-
kerosene
barracks
quantities

of sulphur were, principally, a matter of organization; but to efficiently organize such work for groups of troops continually being shifted from one part of the country to another, and where it is necessary to require various authorities to properly exercise their functions when they personally happen to see no necessity for it, and where the above mentioned processes must be carried out in the right sequence, it is difficult and, very often, impossible.

Delousing of cloth-stuffs by dry heat was found to be very impracticable on account of the damage caused by the ensuing destruction of the strength of the fibres. In the fumigation of buildings which had been badly constructed and therefore porous, sometimes as much as ten pounds of sulphur per 1,000 cubic feet were used with fairly good success. One problem remains unsolved, that is, the delousing of large fur coats. Many a fur coat was accidentally put into the autoclaves, and brought out about a square foot in size. Shoes can be successfully dipped into kerosene.

It may be well here to make a slight digression by mentioning a few precautions which experience has shown should be taken by small parties and individuals traveling in the Balkans during outbreaks of typhus. It is highly advisable to have the hair of the head clipped as short as possible. I have not found it necessary to cut the hair of the body and the pubes, because the louse which has made its way as far as the body will bite anyway and then find its home in the clothing; moreover, one is not apt to become infected on toilet seats because the "Turkish closet," where one squats over a hole, is almost universal. It is also a great personal discomfort. It is necessary to bathe, and change and wash the underclothing very frequently; to carry at all times one's own bedding-roll and folding cot and use them exclusively of all other beds; to avoid touching peo-

ple as much as possible; to carry a rubber bath tub in the bedding roll; and if once infested with lice to find the nearest steam disinfector, which probably can be found at the nearest hospital. We have not found the use of powders or

Fumigating barracks with sulphur. 350 men
slept in this room on the floor.

insecticides of any great value, but I would not go so far as to say they are of no use, as they can be used with good effect particularly against bedbugs. In regard to lice I can see no value in the use of silk underclothing.

The epidemic of 1915 was so widespread, and the sanitarians so few, comparatively, in numbers, that the good results of the work would have been limited to only a few large towns, had it not been for the advent of the warm weather, which is the greatest enemy of the louse, for the people wear less, bathe more, and do not group together in small rooms. Typhus can be easily checked by proper organization when it is limited to a few definite foci; but when widespread over an entire country, with a more or less ignorant and primitive civilization, only a personnel which has the proportions of an army, and with unlimited supplies, can check alone a pandemic of this disease.

In July, 1915, the epidemic was officially declared over, and the country settled into a condition of rest and recuperation, as fortunately the front along the Save and Danube rivers was inactive through the winter, spring and summer of 1915. Other diseases had appeared among the troops, such as typhoid, cholera, and relapsing fever. Dr. Aldo Castellani, the eminent specialist in tropical medicine, attached to the American Red Cross Sanitary Commission at that time, prepared a "tetravaccine" against the two former diseases and the two paratyphoids with which the whole Serbian army and all the remaining prisoners of war were vaccinated with success.

In October of that year the great combined offensive of the Germans, Austro-Hungarians and Bulgars was launched, and the whole country plunged into another turmoil. After a few weeks of fighting and continual retreating, practically the whole Serbian army and several hundred thousand civilians (refugees) were concentrated in one valley, where Albania, Montenegro and Serbia join. The food supply gave out, all automobiles and other vehicles obliged to be destroyed because the roads ended at this point and it was not desirable to have them fall into the hands of the enemy; and the army, twenty thousand prisoners of war, many thousands of young recruits in an unorganized mass, and a few thousand of the hardier refugees began their slow agonizing progress through the snow-covered, roadless mountains of Albania towards the Adriatic. The horrors of that terrible journey in which many thousands succumbed to cold, hunger and fatigue has been described many times by able pens.

As the survivors of the retreat straggled into the ports on the Adriatic, they were conveyed in small groups to the island of Corfu, where after a period of rest and inactivity the reorganization of the army was begun. The men were, however, in a very weak and debilitated condition and recovered their health but slowly, their recovery being retarded by an epidemic of cholera, which still further thinned their ranks. Six months later, this army was transported to Salo-

niki where it was made part of the Allied army under General Sarrail (later under General Franchet d'Esperey), and given a sector of that front near Monastir, where it remained for over two years until September, 1918, when there was started the victorious offensive against the Bulgarian army.

Serbian soldiers about to be sprayed with kerosene. Note the physique of these men. The palatial railway car has space for 6 horses or 40 men.

On the whole, that is to say, for all the diseases with the exception of malaria, the health of the army remained in fair condition, and the same may be said of the armies of the other Allies on that front, largely because sanitary facilities such as hospitals, disinfectors, and well-drilling apparatus were available from England and France. Malaria is endemic in the valleys of the rivers of southern Macedonia, and the uninfected blood of the allied armies proved to be fertile soil for the disease. They found it as great a foe to combat as the enemy himself, whereas the enemy had the advantage of holding superior positions among the hills where there was much less breeding ground for the mosquitoes. English, French, Italians, Russians, Greeks, and Serbs suffered alike; hundreds of men stricken down in every battalion; and in a number of cases one or two officers and a few men only being left of a full battalion. One British battalion was reduced to one officer and 19 men. Hospital admissions for malaria totaled as high as 75,000 in 1916, and approximately 200,000 in 1917 and 1918 for all the Allies on that front, out of a total force which varied between 600,-000 and 900,000 in number. The British hospital admissions alone were 30,000, 63,000, and 67,000 for those three years.

Traveling autoclave for steaming infested blankets.

Preventive measures of all kinds were taken; quinine, ditching, draining, oiling, cutting and burning brushwood, and personal protection by mosquito-proof huts, nets, gloves, and ointments; but the war required many of the above precautions to be discarded for the more pressing business of fighting, so that malaria proved to be very difficult if not impossible to stop. Moreover, the marshy region covers such a large area that drainage operations on a much larger scale than any attempted would have to be initiated.

The many thousands who had to be invalided home on account of malaria proved a very serious blow to the allied cause; but even now, with practically nothing of the army left, the problem remains with the inhabitants of the region keeping them in both a very low state of health and, indirectly, mentality. It is also a menace to travelers passing through Saloniki on their way to the north.

In the meantime, from the autumn of 1915 until the armistice, the Austro-Hungarian army was in control of northern Serbia as far south as Mitrovitsa, and the Bulgars were in possession of southern Serbia; and their respective sanitary organizations, corresponding to our medical corps, took charge of all hospitals, dispensaries, and preventive measures. The Bulgarian military doctors, practically all educated in Paris, Berlin or Vienna, were fairly numerous, for a Balkan state, but were in great fear of another large epidemic of typhus. They, therefore, secured the assistance of a number of German and Austrian doctors to organize against the disease, and Drs. Baehr and Plotz of New York, who had remained in the Lady Paget hospital at Uskub when that hospital was captured by the Bulgars, were given the opportunity of testing out the vaccine which they had prepared from the Plotz bacillus by vaccinating a large portion of the Bulgarian army. Although there were a good many cases of the disease scattered over Macedonia, there was no serious epidemic, as nearly as one may judge from the verbal reports which came from that region. All Bulgarian records of the period have so far been unavailable; but we realize that disease conditions must have been very bad indeed, in a country where the normal condition is serious, and where during the occupation the civil population suffered so many privations inflicted upon them by the army of occupation and were obliged to get along with practically no medical attention whatsoever.

In northern Serbia, however, the Sanitary Department had a numerous personnel and was well equipped. Military and civil hospitals were organized at the important centers; delousing stations were set up both for troops and civilians; laboratories installed; and sanitary regulations issued and enforced. The Serbian doctors who had been captured by the Austrians during the advance, were employed in the civilian hospitals and dispensaries, and all municipal authorities were obliged to keep the cities and towns clean.

During the winter of 1915-16, several small epidemics of typhus broke out in Mitrovitsa, Tchatchak and Uzice, the first totaling only 160 cases; but adequate measures to prevent further numbers were promptly taken, and these epidemics died out, as was also the case in many other towns where the disease appeared. The following winter, so strict were the regulations and the control of traffic between the districts into which the country was divided, that there were only sporadic cases here and there. As an example of the typhus-prevention methods, it was interesting to see the transportation of 200,000 Turkish soldiers in 1916 from Turkey to Galicia, every one of whom was obliged to be thoroughly bathed and de'oused before crossing the Danube into Hungary. All suspected cases of typhus were held in quarantine, and thus a number of cases sent back to Constantinople.

The Austrians had their greatest success against typhus. Measures were taken against the intestinal diseases and the numbers of cases were kept within reasonable limits so that there were no epidemics; but no striking reduction as in the case of typhus. Smallpox was reduced from 150 cases the first year to 60 cases the second year; malaria increased to some extent, and scarlet fever

and diphtheria were reduced. A great deal of attention was paid to the venereal diseases by the supervision and regular examination of prostitutes, the control and licensing of houses of prostitution, and medical prophylaxis; supplemented by venereal clinics and hospitals for venereal diseases only. But the statistics of the Austrians show an increase in these diseases during the occupation, which is another point of evidence against the methods of venereal disease control which we have rejected in the United States.

A battery of bath-tubs. Austrian prisoners enjoying the first bath in many months.

Efficient as the sanitary organization may have been, it could not prevent the Austro-Hungarian Government's policy of exporting large quantities of food out of Serbia throughout the period of occupation, thereby reducing the people to various conditions of starvation, which was especially acute in Belgrade and some of the other cities. Many were reduced to absolutely nothing and died of veritable starvation, but the majority were able to obtain something, although entirely insufficient, and as a result the tuberculosis mortality began to assume large proportions. There has always been a high mortality in Serbia due to the unhygienic conditions and the low standard of living, and one of the Austrian military doctors gives a pre-war list of tuberculosis mortality in a number of cities as follows:

Mortality due to tuberculosis.
Deaths per 100,000 population.

Belgrade 720*
Athens 393.3
Vienna 289.4
Berlin 186.3
Dresden 184.1
Hamburg 154.9

*Pre-war population of 77,500.

But the figure of 720 is lost sight of when one considers the official Austrian record of deaths from tuberculosis recorded for the year 1917, in the city of Belgrade which totaled 654. This in a population of 45,000 in 1917, gives a tuberculosis mortality of about 1,430 per hundred thousand!

The fall of 1918 saw the collapse of the Central Powers; and the remnants of the Serbian army returned to their homes to find them sadly depleted, with the task of reconstruction looming before them, as well as the great necessity of initiating steps to protect the health of their people in order to conserve their race. Their first winter at home saw a serious outbreak of typhus with an inadequate organization to combat it, and the whole country rife with disease. There are only a little more than 100 doctors in Serbia at the present time. The American Red Cross and the Serbian Relief Committee of America have inaugurated public health programs in the country, but unless they continue or without some form of continual outside aid, the few doctors have a task ahead of them which is difficult indeed.

□

Causes and Remedy of Malnutrition.— It is estimated that from three to six million American children are not getting enough to eat. These children are usually delicate and readily susceptible to disease. They are frequently those children who are considered lazy and backward. The causes of malnutrition are primarily poverty and ignorance. Many children go hungry because their parents cannot afford to buy enough suitable, nourishing food. In other cases the mothers do not know how to buy foods sanely and wisely. They know very little concerning a proper and adequate diet. In other cases the mothers do not have sufficient control over their children to induce them to eat proper foods and to make them take the sleep and rest necessary for their development. The best way to overcome malnutrition is by the establishment of malnutrition clinics and classes, where children may be instructed concerning proper diets and good health. Mothers should be invited to attend these classes, and later the education may be carried into the homes through visiting instructors. Malnutrition classes have been formed in Boston, Chicago and New York with success. Other means of combating malnutrition are by establishing school lunches and by instituting medical supervision over school children. Defects that are observed should be corrected.—*Children's Bureau Bulletin*, Aug. 4, 1919. (*M. P. H.*)

✛

Outbreak of Dysentery.—The Medical Officer of Health for Aberdeen, England, records an outbreak of dysentery in that city which has many interesting features. Attention was directed to a small group of cases with febrile and diarrhoeal symptoms which were regarded at first as possible cases of influenza of a gastro-enteric type. Inquiry revealed the fact that all the cases were being supplied with milk from one dairy. All the farmers supplying this dairy were communicated with and it was found that on one of the farms certain cases of severe diarrhoeal symptoms had occurred in the family of the farmer a few days before the outbreak in the city. Further investigation of the cases at the farm made it clear that they were of the same type as those in the city and that they had been the source of infection. A bacteriological study of the outbreak revealed the fact that the cases were bacterial dysentery, the bacillus being of the Flexner type.—*Medical Officer*, Aug. 2, 1919, 41. (*D. G.*)

VENEREAL DISEASE CONTROL: METHODS, OBSTACLES AND RESULTS

C. C. Pierce,

Assistant Surgeon General, U. S. Public Health Service,
Washington, D. C.

Read before Section of Public Health Administration, American Public Health Association,
at New Orleans, La., October 27, 1919.

This is really a report of progress. Co-operation of the Government with state health departments has produced such results that the backward step of discontinuance can never be taken. The problem of preventing venereal disease has become one of the principal phases of preventive medicine and physicians and health officers can not possibly longer remain indifferent.

One object in discussing the methods, obstacles and results of the venereal disease control program is to bring forth constructive criticism which will enable the state boards of health and the Public Health Service to improve the methods, remove the obstacles and thereby secure more satisfactory results. The desired objective can be accomplished when the cause and serious nature of these diseases are generally understood; the necessity for treatment of infected persons is appreciated; a sympathy and understanding of the general problem is developed; and when each local community has accepted responsibility for enforcing measures that will make the spread of venereal diseases more difficult.

METHODS.

The foundation for the plan to be used in combatting venereal diseases in the United States was expressed in the Act of Congress creating the Division of Venereal Diseases in the Public Health Service. The method was stated as one of the duties of the Public Health Service—"to co-operate with state boards or departments of health for the prevention and control of such diseases within the states." The entire program has been created upon this principle—one of co-operation between the Public Health Service and the various state boards of health. It should be remembered that at the time this responsibility was placed upon the Public Health Service, the country was involved in war, and there was necessity for immediate action. The fighting forces, actual and potential, urgently required protection. It was, therefore, necessary to launch at once a campaign for the prevention and control of a group of dangerous, communicable diseases which differed from all other communicable diseases for the reason that social, moral, economic, ethical and psychological problems had to be considered in addition to the medical measures. To add to these complications, it was necessary to plan a comprehensive and uniform system for the control of venereal diseases which would be applicable to the entire United States, which could be operated by a practically untrained personnel and which, furthermore, would fit in as a part of the other activities of the state boards of health. It is evident, therefore, that no easy task confronted the Public Health Service and the various state boards of health. The difficult conditions were met, however, by concerted action on the part of the state boards of health until at the present time a practically uniform method for the control of venereal diseases is actually in operation in the United States. The de-

132

tails of the plan have been discussed in numerous articles appearing in the Public Health Reports during the past two years and as these details are familiar to health officers and other sanitarians it is unnecessary to discuss them here.

It has been customary in discussing the plan to group the various activities as medical, educational, legislative and social measures. However, no arbitrary grouping of these measures is possible. Medical effort is in the best sense educational. Education in this field includes medical and legislative information, and both are vitally social in addition to the activities of a distinctly sociological nature on which the permanent control of syphilis and gonorrhea, as of other communicable diseases, depends.

OBSTACLES.

Without devoting time to the discussion of the methods used, since they are a matter of record and can be studied by anyone interested, it would be of interest to refer briefly to some of the obstacles encountered so that in further development of methods these obstacles may be more easily overcome.

One of the greatest obstacles encountered has been, in my opinion, the reluctance of a certain percentage of practicing physicians to participate wholeheartedly in the program for venereal disease control and report their venereal infections to their state board of health. This attitude on the part of certain doctors was expected and is being gradually overcome. The same reaction occurred when tuberculosis was made reportable many years ago, the argument being advanced then that a stigma would be placed upon the family by the physician reporting cases of tuberculosis, a stigma which would prevent the social and economic advancement of the tuberculous family. This view has of course long since been proven erroneous and now the general population of the country is more or less educated as to the value of re-

porting communicable diseases with the exception of gonorrhea and syphilis. The co-operation of physicians in reporting venereal diseases is, however, developing rapidly and each month shows progress. Reporting by serial number only, except under certain conditions, the plan adopted by forty states, certainly removes the objection that professional confidences are violated by reporting gonorrhea and syphilis to the state board of health. The conditions under which the name and address of an infected person are to be reported being the failure of the infected person to observe precautions to prevent the spread of the disease to others or failure to continue treatment; are such as to legally forfeit any personal rights the patient may have possessed. It is a well established principle of constitutional law that no individual right or privilege can be claimed which reacts to the detriment of the rest of the community or the general public.

The reason that reporting by serial number was endorsed by the Public Health Service, rather than by name on the first report as with other communicable diseases, was because reporting by serial number furnishes data regarding the prevalence of these diseases and, further, because it was believed to be impossible to quickly get forty states to include syphilis and gonorrhea among the diseases to be reported by name until the program for control of these diseases was better understood and its value more appreciated. The time will come when reliable data regarding syphilis and gonorrhea will be on file in the various state departments of health to show the exact progress that is being made in limiting the spread of these dangerous, communicable diseases.

Another obstacle to the progress of the work has been the lack of information on the part of the general public regarding the serious consequences of the venereal diseases. This lack of information has been due partly to the indifference of many physicians towards persons infected with venereal diseases. The method of treatment of individual cases and the advice given for preventing the spread of the infection, has been such as to lead infected persons to regard their condition lightly. False modesty and prudery has prevented the discussion of these diseases by intelligent laymen and therefore but little authentic information was available until very recently.

This ignorance of the general public has been not only of uneducated persons, but of the business men and leaders of the community. Contrast the opinion of the ordinary substantial citizen of your community with the opinion of Sir William Osler, who said, "From the standpoint of race conservation, gonorrhea is a disease of the very first rank. It costs the country, annually, thousands of lives. With 30 or 40 per cent of all congenital blindness, with chronic pelvic mischief in women and with the unhappiness of sterile marriages—with these and many other minor ailments scored up against them, we may say that while not a killer, as a misery producer Neisser's coccus is king among germs." Contrast also the view of the business man in regard to syphilis with the actual facts in regard to this infection. Comparatively few people realize that syphilis is one of the greatest killing diseases; that all of the deaths now accredited to locomotor ataxia and general paralysis of the insane are due to syphilis; that many deaths now attributed to organic diseases of the heart, diseases of the arteries, aneurism, cerebral hemorrhage, apoplexy, Bright's disease and encephalitis, are really due to syphilis. Nor is it realized that a tremendous burden of taxation is placed upon every community as a result of the sequelae of improperly treated cases of syphilis and gonorrhea. This ignorance regarding venereal diseases is rapidly being overcome by the educational campaign carried on by the various state boards of health. In the educational campaign the previous reticence of newspapers and other publicity agencies in informing the public regarding sex problems and venereal diseases, is being rapidly changed. In addition to developing proper publicity leading to the discussion of these diseases, it is necessary to restrict the misleading publicity given to remedies advertised for the self-treatment of venereal infections and the false statements of unscrupulous persons promising impossible cures.

Another obstacle to the successful prosecution of the program for venereal disease control has been the mistaken opinion held by many honest persons that regulated prostitution is necessary and cannot be eliminated. The result of following this opinion has been responsible in many communities for hindering the venereal disease control program of state boards of health.

The advocates of segregation claim that this measure concentrates prostitution, thus facilitating the control and reduction in the number of prostitutes. The truth is that segregation increases prostitution, making it familiar by continual advertising. A segregated district offers a place of commerce to the least competent of prostitutes, mentally and physically.

The advocates of segregation also claim that such a procedure prevents crimes against women. The actual facts are that the existence of houses of prostitution incite to crimes against women by fostering sexual promiscuity and providing a source of sexual brutalization and degeneracy.

It has also been claimed that segregation protects a community from offensive and detrimental proximity of prostitutes, whereas the truth is, that it exposes the community to this condition. By advertising prostitution as a community necessity and by making prostitutes easily accessible and tolerated, a condition is established conducive to the spread of venereal diseases within the community.

Another obstacle in the progress of the campaign has been the hesitancy of health officers to assume any function which would tend to indicate that they were departing from the usual methods of controlling communicab'e diseases. For instance, some health officers believe that it is not a function of the health authorities to be interested in the operation of laws having for their purpose the abolition of prostitution, this being regarded as strictly a police function. As a matter of fact, all of the power of boards of health are po'ice powers and the laws enacted for the elimination of prostitution are, so far as health departments are concerned, laws to prevent or at least make difficult, contact between healthy persons and persons infected with dangerous, communicable diseases. When health officers accept this viewpoint, considerable progress will be made in controlling venereal infections.

RESULTS.

The results to date of the co-operative work of the Public Health Service and the state boards of health for the control of venereal diseases cannot adequately be summed up with statistical data, but some of the outstanding facts may be briefly mentioned. The requirement that venereal disease be reported to state boards of health is gradually being met by the practicing physicians of the country. In response to a circular letter sent to physicians, 60,666 have signed a written statement to the effect that they intend to co-operate with their state board of health by reporting cases of venereal diseases. The records for the fiscal year ending June 30, 1919, showed that in forty-two states, 239,502 cases of venereal disease have been reported. Of these, 131,193 were gonorrhea, 100,466 were syphilis and 7,843 were chancroid.

These figures show plainly how syphilis and gonorrhea are regarded by both the laity and physicians. It is generally accepted as a fact that there are at least five times as many cases of gonorrhea as syphilis, but during the past year the number of cases of gonorrhea reported exceeded the number of cases of syphilis only about 30 per cent. This, in my opinion, shows that gonorrhea is still regarded as a relatively unimportant disease. The total number of cases reported is not great, but it should be remembered that many of the states did not have laws or state board of health regulations requiring these diseases to be reported until late in the year.

Another evidence of progress is the increased number of free clinics where cases of venereal disease may receive proper treatment. On June 30, 1919, the various state boards of health reported that there were approximately 260 free venereal clinics being operated under their direction. Many of these clinics are not yet making monthly reports to the Public Health Service, but 162 clinics that did report during the fiscal year ending June 30, 1919, treated 64,164 persons. These figures may also be criticised as insignificant, but when it is remembered that during the previous year no reports were available and that during the year in question only about one-half of the clinics made reports, it is felt that very substantial progress is being made towards securing prompt and efficient treatment for persons infected with venereal diseases. This progress is at an increasing rate, this being definitely shown by the reports for the month of July, 1919, when 5,642 new patients were admitted for treatment to 131 clinics whose reports were available at the time this paper was prepared.

The results of educational and publicity measures cannot be adequately expressed in figures. It is known that the various state boards of health and the Public Health Service have prepared and distributed more than fourteen million separate pieces of literature, mostly leaflets, on the question of venereal disease. The real effect of this widespread publicity can never be definitely known, but all those in touch with the problem know that one effect has been to greatly stimulate interest on the part of the general public in this phase of public health work. It is also known that the general public are appreciating more and more the necessity for prompt and efficient treatment of these infections. This is shown by the reports to the effect that the practice of all specialists in genito-urinary and venereal diseases has greatly increased during the past year. Seventy-seven thousand two hundred and ninety-eight individual letters have been received by the Public Health Service asking for literature in regard to the venereal diseases, and 1,339 letters have been received in which the writer frankly stated that he had gonorrhea or syphilis, and asked for advice.

The problem of preventing venereal diseases has been removed from the list of neglected opportunities and made one of the principal phases of preventive medicine toward which it is no longer possible for the individual physician or health officer to maintain an isolated or indifferent attitude.

CONCLUSION.

To sum up briefly the methods, obstacles and results of the program for venereal disease control, I am of the opinion that the following is a fair statement of the present status of this work:

The method was definitely determined by Congress and is in actual operation—that is, co-operation between the various state boards of health and the Public Health Service for the prevention and control of venereal diseases.

All obstacles could be entirely removed if sufficient funds were provided to employ trained and enthusiastic personnel to actively stimulate the various phases of the program and secure the interest of business and professional men.

The result of the work up to the present time has been to put into action an increasingly great organization of business and social agencies interested in co-operating with health authorities for the elimination of these dangerous communicable diseases. The work has acquired such a status that it is absolutely out of the question that it should ever be discontinued or even be seriously interfered with. Therefore, we may confidently look forward to the future with the assurance that every official health agency of the United States will gradually increase its facilities for meeting today's world problem in disease prevention.

□

DISCUSSION

In the discussion of Major Pierce's paper, *Thomas W. Jackson, M.D.,* Assistant Commissioner of Health of Pennsylvania, spoke in place of the Commissioner, Edward Martin, who was regretfully absent from the meeting. The discussion outlines the program and principles underlying the attack on the problem of venereal disease control in that Commonwealth.

"In Pennsylvania we have a major campaign," said Dr. Jackson, "and a minor campaign. Most of our time, effort and money are spent in the major campaign but the minor one is not neglected although it is recognized as minor."

Our Major Campaign embraces the following objects and measures:

I. The elimination of the prostitute.

The feebleminded of this class are to be institutionalized; the subnormal and normal are to be put at self-supporting work. All are to be rendered non-contagious.

Our means of accomplishing these ends are (a) the application of existing, adequate laws, enforced through and by local health committees of able and determined women, who form an integral part of the State Health Department in all counties and communities. In our state the *County* is the administrative unit.

(b) The utilization of hospitals, reformatories, county infirmaries, asylums and the resources of certain organizations devoted to civic betterment. (c) This is all to be done quickly, systematically and persistently. (d) It is the opinion that raids are corrupting, brutal and futile.

II. Controlling and curing the infected through (a) the state clinics and (b) venereal clinics established in practically all hospitals of the state. The clinics are to conduct an active campaign against carriers, to control these diseases in the regions which they serve; the personnel of these clinics to be responsible for this control. They have police powers and quarantine powers. The following regulation, with the force of law, was recently passed by the Advisory Board and was approved by the Commissioner of Health August 6, 1919.

"From and after the passage and promulgation of this regulation, gonorrhea and syphilis in its primary and secondary stages, and chancroid are declared transmissible diseases subject to quarantine when in the opinion of the attending physician or the county medical representative of the State Department of Health, the character, occupation, habits or neglect of treatment and methods to protect others, make those infected menaces to public health."

III. Efficient immediated treatment through packages and wide knowledge of their usefulness and where they may be found. Most of the drug stores in Pennsylvania now sell a simple and efficient package. Approved after careful laboratory tests by the Department of Health and sold for twenty-five cents. The state newspapers have announced that such packages are to be secured.

IV. The suppression of quack medicine advertisements, which is made possible by Pennsylvania laws.

V. In seaports enforced protection against the large influx of fresh venereal cases.

VI. The elimination of the pimp, cadet or panderer by means of the strong arm of the law.

Turning to what we style our Minor Campaign, the first measure to be mentioned is (I) Education. (a) In every school in the State, as a part of a systematized and graded course in health, sexual function and venereal infection will be taught judiciously. (b) Group talks to adults and adolescents are to be given but unless followed by the teacher meeting the class individually they are of little value. People who like to do this teaching are usually unfitted for it. It calls for a special and rare ability. There will be coöperation with the State Department of Education in this matter. (c) Newspapers, pamphlets and leaflets: We deem them moderately useful. (d) Placards: We deem them useful as indicating the location of state clinics and the value of the immediate treatment package. (e) Motion Pictures: We fear that they are usually more hurtful then helpful. Those dealing with anatomy and pathology are the only ones we view as particularly valuable. None should be shown commercially.

II. Other agencies are recreation, amusements and occupational night schools, constituting a group of great value.

Finally, there is another combination of favoring agencies entirely too potent to be described as minor measures. These agencies are equally vital and equally helpful in nearly every public health problem when provided. They are improved housing and bettered living conditions. They have a bearing upon venereal-disease-control methods so obvious that they need not be specially dealt with in this enumeration.

Dr. Harris characterized the movement as a "going campaign." He referred to the fact that in the public prints the State of Pennsylvania has been termed as inactive in attacking the venereal problems. "This is not true," he said, "and has never been true." He brought the program and campaigns to bear as evidence against the statement, and asserted that Pennsylvania spends liberally for health purposes and offers its coöperation to every other state in the Union. "We are striving to control an infectious, communicable disease sanely," said the speaker in conclusion, "and at present time do not feel the need for additional laws. In the coördinated, statewide social service, emphasis is placed to the utmost on moral teaching."

The A. P. H. A. Goal for 1920 Is 7,500 Members.
The More Members the Greater Its Influence and the More It Can Do. Will You Help?

Passing from construction to disease relations, two maladies are here considered in connection with the privy. Dr. Ferrell discusses hookworm and gives a few rules that can eliminate the link of soil pollution. Dr. Smith presents results in typhoid and asserts that the sanitary privy, properly maintained can be an important factor in its control.

ROLE OF THE LATRINE IN CONTROL OF HOOKWORM DISEASE

JOHN A. FERRELL, M. D., D. P. H.,
Director for U. S., International Health Board, New York City.

Presented Before the Public Health Administration Section, American Public Health Association, at New Orleans, La., October 27, 1919.

The spread of hookworm disease is attributable to the improper disposal of human excreta. To the end that the work of hookworm control and prevention may be advanced, a series of surveys of individual homes has been made with reference to hookworm infection, and to the method employed in disposing of human excreta. The 1918 study included 95,706 homes in 236 rural areas in this and in other countries. It showed that only 9.8 per cent of the homes had adequate latrine accommodations, and that 53 per cent were without latrines of any description. Considerable reduction in the prevalence of hookworm disease has been obtained by curing those who showed infection, but in the absence of soil sanitation the re-infection rate, especially in tropical countries, runs quite high even within one year after the time of original cure. This has been pointed out in the 1918 Annual Report of the International Health Board.

The crux of the hookworm problem then is twofold:

(1) To prevent the soil from becoming infected, i. e., to prevent the deposit of ova-impregnated feces upon the surface of the ground; and

(2) To prevent infected soil from coming in contact with human beings.

This means both that the skin of the feet or hands, for example, should not come in contact with the infected soil, and that no one should eat foods which have been exposed to infected soil.

It is the role of the latrine, in the absence of sewage disposal plants, to give general and permanent protection against hookworm disease. The problem, which is essentially rural, can be solved if the following procedure is carried out:

1—Construct at every home an adequate latrine to serve as a receptacle for human discharges.

2—Educate every man, woman, and child to use the latrines.

3—Educate all persons to care for and maintain the latrines properly.

4—Employ, by way of public health protection, a sufficient number of inspectors to carry on the educational work and, when necessary, to use legal measures for the enforcement of sanitary practices.

Theoretically, the carrying out of this program is quite simple. Practically, it is a most formidable task. As suggested by the figures given above, it involves inducing a majority of the people in rural districts (1) to abandon habits ingrained by centuries of custom; (2) to purchase material for structures hitherto regarded as unnecessary; and (3) to devote a considerable amount of time and labor to the building and maintenance of the latrines. The undertaking has been complicated by a lack of scientific information regarding many aspects of the problem. The health officers were therefore unable to specify minimum latrine requirements for any particular locality. Fortunately, a number of scientists are now seriously at work seeking the necessary information. Among health officers, moreover, fairly uniform ideas are gradually developing as to types of latrines, and plans and specifications of one or more types that will be acceptable have been widely distributed.

During recent years measures have been taken in many countries for the control of hookworm disease, and progress in curative measures has been relatively rapid. The people have been urged to install, use, and maintain sanitary latrines. Progress in soil sanitation, however, as might have been expected, was comparatively slow at first. An intensive house-to-house campaign has been found necessary to obtain the best results. During the more recent years considerable progress in this phase of the work has been made and the movement has now acquired considerable momentum. In this country there are now three southern counties each of which has reported that a latrine which meets the minimum requirements of the State Board of Health has been installed at every one of its rural homes. These counties are Harrison, Stone and Jackson, in Mississippi. The task was first completed in Harrison county. In accomplishing it the county health department had the co-operation of both the Mississippi State Board of Health and the United States Public Health Service. In various other southern counties the record of latrine construction for rural homes ranges between 50 and 100 per cent. Ten southern state boards of health reported that during 1918 an aggregate of 4,586 new latrines were erected and 15,568 old latrines improved.

This is a striking increase over the results of previous years.

North Carolina has enacted a state-wide law which requires that all latrines situated within 300 yards of a home shall be constructed and maintained in a manner satisfactory to the State Board of Health. The law applies to approximately 85,000 latrines in the State and places an annual inspection tax of forty cents on each. The proceeds will be used to pay a staff of sanitary inspectors who will educate the people along health improvement lines, and who will enforce the provisions of the law.

Hookworm disease is not commonly a reportable disease. Consequently there are few morbidity and mortality statis- tics to aid in ascertaining its prevalence at any particular date. A series of infection surveys will be necessary to give a reliable index of the degree to which the disease may be reduced by the use of sanitary latrines. Considerable data are available showing the reduction obtained by curative measures, the extent to which re-infections occur, and, to a limited extent, the degree of control effected by the prevention or reduction of soil pollution.

In St. Vincent, 1,525 persons who two years previously had been reported as cured were re-examined in 1918, and it was found that 60.5 per cent of them were infected. The re-infection rate was 46.9 per cent in the Belair district, 64.8 per cent in Calliaqua, and 68.2 per cent in Sion Hill. It was lowest in Belair, where the greatest amount of sanitary work was done. In Trinidad, the amount of re-infection was found to vary with the sanitary condition of the districts. Areas with very poor sanitation invariably had more than 60 per cent re-infection, and even districts in which the sanitary conditions were good had relatively high rates of infection if poorly sanitated districts surrounded them. Both of these islands, it should be remembered, are in the tropics, where climatic conditions render control·measures more difficult than in temperate zones. As the sanitary work progresses, a number of infection surveys will be made from year to year in average areas, and in time the role of the latrine in the control of hook-worm disease can be shown by indisputable figures. However, even the limited data now available offer encouragement.

Typhoid fever is a reportable disease. Its prevention has so much in common with hookworm disease that its reduction through the use of adequate latrines should be very suggestive. A few striking examples of typhoid reduction which have appeared in reports by state boards of health are therefore presented. In Wicomico county, Maryland, for the period from January 1 to October 1, 1916, there were 78 cases of typhoid fever; in 1917, for the same period there were 76 cases. In 1918 a campaign to encourage health education and the building of sanitary latrines was conducted, with the result that several hundred new latrines were built and many old ones remodeled.

In 1918—during a 6-month period, as in 1916 and 1917—there were only 26 cases of typhoid fever, this figure being 66.2 per cent lower than the average rate for the two previous years. In North Carolina, nine counties having an aggregate population of 305,016, for the four-year period of 1914 to 1917, had 478 deaths from typhoid fever—a yearly average of 119.5 deaths, or 39.2 deaths annually per hundred thousand. During 1918, 6,480 improved latrines were installed in these counties, with the result that the annual typhoid death rate was reduced to 24 deaths, or 7.9 deaths per hundred thousand. The typhoid reduction in Virginia during the past ten years is particularly striking. Several charts just issued by the Mississippi State Board of Health also give in a graphic manner concrete examples of typhoid reduction following the installation of sanitary latrines. The Doubtless the Mississippi State Board of. Health will be pleased to furnish copies of these graphs to interested persons. These examples may be regarded as typical of the very important role of the latrine in rural sanitation.

ROLE OF THE SANITARY PRIVY IN THE CONTROL OF TYPHOID FEVER

Clarence E. Smith, M. D.,
Health Officer, Columbia, S. C.

Read before Section of Public Health Administration, American Public Health Association, at New Orleans, La., October 27, 1919

There is no one factor more responsible for the spread or control of typhoid fever than the privy. Properly handled, the sanitary privy eliminates the spread of typhoid to a very great extent. Typhoid fever is an intestinal disease of human beings only, and is, therefore, spread through the careless handling of the discharges of the intestines and kidneys. The sanitary privy offers a safe method of disposal of these discharges, often more so than a sewerage system. The properly operated sanitary privy eliminates soil pollution and if properly constructed it eliminates fly-borne typhoid insofar as the privy is concerned.

It is not my intention to burden you with a long paper concerning the control of typhoid fever by means of the sanitary privy, but instead I am going to give you my personal experience, while health officer of the city of Greenville, S. C., with the hope that it will stimulate a discussion which will bring out points of importance and interest.

We installed the sanitary privy system in Greenville on January 1st, 1915. (The ordinance was passed in 1914 to take effect January 1st next succeeding.) Previous to this time the number of cases of typhoid fever ran from 35 to 45 per year. ·During the first six months of 1915 we had 3 cases reported, all of which were of doubtful origin, but from the middle of 1915 to September 1st, 1918, there was not a case of typhoid fever reported in Greenville that could not be traced directly to outside infection. For more than three years there was not a single case of typhoid fever in the city of Greenville of local origin, and this city had over 1200 shallow wells that were used for supplying water for drinking purposes. The Health Department declared war on typhoid fever and the sanitary privy was chosen as the means of defense. The property owners were compelled to install sanitary privies equipped with cans. The city supplied the scavanger service, which, of course, was not operated for profit. The contents of the cans were not allowed to be transferred on the premises. The scavenger wagon would start out in the morning with a load of clean cans fitted with tight-fitting friction covers. These clean cans were exchanged for the cans found in the privies. When the wagon had accumulated a load of full cans they were driven to the place of disposal, which consisted of a concrete basin 10 ft. by 10 ft. and 4 ft. deep. This basin was connected with the city sanitary sewer. The contents of the cans were emptied into the basin and flushed into the sewer. The outlet of the basin was provided with a heavy iron grating which prevented sticks, rags and other articles from passing into the sewer main. Everything that would not pass through the openings in the gratings was cleaned out and disposed of by cremation, after which the basin was thoroughly washed. The cans were then stacked on their sides in the basin and washed with a one-half-inch stream of water under 70 pounds pressure. The cans were then rinsed in a 2 per cent solution of one of the coal tar disinfectants, when they were ready for another trip.

The privy box should be absolutely fly-tight and the openings should be provided with tight-fitting covers. The vent flue should be screened at the top.

By using metal cans for receptacles for the night-soil and emptying the can only at the place of disposal, soil pollution is prohibited. By screening the vent flue at the top the flue is made to serve the purpose of a fly trap, as any flies that happen to find their way into the privy box will eventually work their way up the flue where they will remain until they die.

I am thoroughly convinced that the sanitary privy, when properly constructed, maintained and operated, plays a very important role in the control of typhoid fever. I can, however, see where an improperly constructed, maintained or operated privy would be little, if any, better than the old familiar open back E type privy, since the users might possibly think that they were getting a protection that did not exist and in consequence be more careless than they would with the old type.

The A. P. H. A. Does Not Often Get to the West Coast.
Do Not Miss This Opportunity!
San Francisco, August 30-September 3, 1920.

USES, POSSIBILITIES AND LIMITATIONS OF BACTERIOLOGY IN FOOD CONTROL

PROFESSOR EDWIN O. JORDAN,

Department of Hygiene and Bacteriology, University of Chicago, Chicago, Illinois.

Read at joint session of Sections on Public Health Administration, Laboratory and Food and Drugs, American Public Health Association, at New Orleans, La., October 29, 1919.

The question presented to me for consideration is the uses, possibilities and limitations of bacteriology in food control. I have elsewhere[1] discussed some of the limitations of bacteriology in food control and there seems no need to repeat this task. At the present time it may be more useful to review some of the opportunities for extending the applications of bacteriology in food examination.

As regards the bacteriology of the milk industry it is certainly true that the large amount of work done by American investigators has thrown much light on the sources of milk contamination and has enabled us to evaluate fairly well the relative share of the cow and the milker, the barn surroundings, utensils and methods of transportation as they affect the number of bacteria in the milk delivered to the consumer. No one can doubt that the information thus obtained has been of great value in improving the quality of city milk supplies in this country. This has come about largely through insistence on the correlation between the bacterial findings and the various physical conditions surrounding the collection and transportation of this highly perishable food substance. It is chiefly through the interpretation of colony counts in the light of practical farm and dairy inspection that the excellent practice of milk-grading has become possible. It is evident, however, that there remain numerous questions about which opinion is at variance, an indication in itself that the available evidence is insufficient and that more investigation is needed. Our knowledge of the bacterial products ordinarily present in dirty or stale milk and of their influence on health is quite meager. Different answers will doubtless still be given to questions about the permissible bacterial limit for milk that is to be submitted to the pasteurizing process and the degree to which this limit should be correlated with the temperature at which the milk has been kept and the initial seeding that the milk has received. Can a certified milk kept under cleanly conditions, but in which bacteria have multiplied to a relatively high point be used with safety after pasteurization? Should a milk that has received considerable bacterial contamination shortly before pasteurization be pronounced injurious to health? One has only to ask these questions to feel again the necessity for knowing more about the nature and physiological action of the bacterial products formed in milk. To quote from an earlier paper[1]: "We simply do not know at what point the products of bacterial growth become hurtful, or even what effect is caused by the growth of specific kinds of bacteria. Are most of the products of bacterial growth in foods physiologically indifferent in the quantities in which they are ordinarily consumed, and when injurious products are present, are they due to rare accidental contamination, or do all bacteria growing in milk, meat or eggs generate noxious substances which

1. The Bacteriology of Foods: Jour. Amer. Med. Assoc. 1917, 68, p. 1080.

1. J. A. M. A. 1917, 68, pp. 1080-1084.

can inflict damage on the human organism, albeit such danger is not immediately recognized? Such questions cannot be satisfactorily answered at the present time, and need but to be asked to make clear the limitations of our present knowledge and the necessity of further investigation."

As respects the significance of special groups of bacteria in milk important studies have been made by Ayres and his associates in the Bureau of Animal Industry. The alkali-forming bacteria in milk, meaning by this term those bacteria that produce an alkaline reaction in milk without visible signs of peptonization, appear to be principally soil bacteria introduced into milk from dust, unsterilized utensils or through the dirty hands of milkers.[1] The much discussed question of the significance of the enumeration of colon bacilli in raw milk seems to be approaching solution. Ayres and Clemmens[2] point out that the colon count as determined at the present time includes both the B. coli and the B. aërogenes types of organism and that since the B. coli type is chiefly of fecal and the B. aërogenes type of nonfecal origin, the colon count at best cannot be a direct measure of manurial contamination. They add that "In milk of unknown history no significance can be attached to the colon count other than that high counts usually indicate that it has been held above 50° F. (10° C.), or rarely, that it was produced under very abnormal conditions." From the results of these investigators it does not appear that the differentiation of the B. coli and B. aërogenes types assists materially in tracing the conditions under which milk is produced, but as they themselves admit, examination of a larger number of samples may show that it possesses some value.

Little is yet known about the significance to the public health of the presence of B. abortus in milk. This organism which is the cause of enormous loss to the dairy industry—even greater than that caused by bovine tuberculosis—is wide-spread and has been found in certified milk. It seems probable that it is not pathogenic for man, but we should have more definite information. In guinea pigs the inoculation of B. abortus has been shown to produce lesions of the lymph-nodes, spleen, liver, kidney, testicle, lung and bones.[1] A considerable proportion of children show the presence in their blood of antibodies for this organism. It is not known how far this is due to passive and how far to active immunization.[2] The significance to human pathology and public health of another organism of bovine abortion recently discovered by Theobald Smith,[3] Vibrio fetus, is quite unknown.

An important set of problems has been opened up by the discovery of the relative frequency of botulism in this country. It seems to be true that different varieties of B. botulinus exist possessed of very different degrees of heat resistance, and that some strains found in the United States are much more resistant to high temperatures than was the organism originally described by van Ermengem under this name. Practically nothing is known, however, about the normal habitat and distribution of this dangerous pathogen. It has never been reported in Great Britain, and the majority of the instances of botulism in the United States have occurred west of the Rockies. Fortunately in most, perhaps in all, cases where significant growth of this organism has occurred physical signs of

1. Ayers. Rupp and Johnson: Bull. No. 782, Bureau of Animal Industry. June 17, 1919.
2. Ayers and Clemmens: Bull. No. 739, Bureau of Animal Industry, Dec. 30, 1918.

1. Larson and Sedgwick: Am. Jour. Dis. of Children, 1913 6, p. 326.
2. Sedgwick, Larson and Ramsey: Am. Jour. Dis. of Children, 1915, 10, p. 197; Coolidge; J. Med. Res. 1916, 29, p. 459.
3. J. Exp. Med., 1919, 30, pp. 299-359.

decomposition are present and should
serve as a signal of warning.[1] Articles
of food heated by the method of household canning have been implicated with
especial frequency in botulism poisoning.

Discussion of the relation of bacteriology to the great canning industries may
well be deferred until the results of the
extensive investigations by Rosenau and
his associates at the Harvard Medical
School become available. As far as this
work has advanced it appears to Rosenau
to warrant the statement that "it is becoming increasingly evident that canned
goods are the safest foods that come to
our table."[2] It is interesting to note that
increasing stress is being laid by the
canners on systematic inspection and that
detailed regulations for inspection have
recently been drawn up by the National
Canners Association.[3] These regulations
deal with such matters as factory location, lightness of rooms, cleanliness of
rooms and utensils, wash rooms, toilet
rooms, cleanliness and health of employ-
ces. It is the writer's belief that bacteriological methods may be used to supplement physical inspection at many points
and will serve to reveal weaknesses in procedure that might not otherwise be detected. It seems likely that the condition
of certain finished food products may be
determined at least as definitely by physical signs as by bacterial examination.

Food-borne infection with members of
the paratyphoid-enteritidis group is by
far the most important of the typical
forms of food poisoning that have been
traced to their source. It is, however,
to judge from the recorded instances,
much less common in this country than
in Germany, France or England. The
whole subject of paratyphoid-enteritidis

infection bristles with unsolved problems. We do not know whether bacilli
of the B. suipestifer type are pathogenic
for man, we do not know the significance
of the occasional occurrence of bacilli of
the B. paratyphosus B type along with B.
suipestifer in the bodies of diseased hogs,
we do not know the relative share of human carriers and diseased food animals
in causing infection or poisoning through
food products. Despite numerous careful investigations the nature of the toxic
agent produced by these organisms remains obscure. Ecker,[1] however, has
shown that some strains produce soluble
toxic substances which apparently stimulate the formation of specific antibodies
when injected subcutaneously. Greenwald,[2] working more recently with a
series of selected strains, has failed to
demonstrate the presence of a heat stable toxin, and in general the results of
animal feeding with the products of this
group of organism have not given constant and unambiguous results.

In summing up the future outlook for
the application of bacteriology in food
control it seems probable that increasing
emphasis will be laid on bacterial methods as an aid to the interpretation of the
sanitary inspection of foodstuffs and as
a guide to satisfactory sanitary procedure. Continued laboratory investigation of the two best-known instances of
so-called "food poisoning" traceable to
primary bacterial food contamination,
botulism and paratyphoid meat-poison-
ing, seems urgently called for since both
are intimately connected with the vital
problems of food conservation. Finally
the nature and sanitary significance of
the products generated by bacteria, particularly the so-called saprophytic bacteria, in foodstuffs affords a practically
untouched field for investigation.

1. Signs of spoiling are, however, sometimes disregarded and the obviously spoiled food eaten. An
example has been recorded by Thom and his co-
workers—J. A. M. A. 1919, 73, p. 907.
2. Amer. Food Jour., June, 1919, p. 40.
3. Amer. Food Jour., Apr., 1919, p. 82.

1. Jour. Inf. Dis. 1917, 21, p. 541.
2. Amer. Jour. Pub. Health, 1919, 9, p. 595.

DISCUSSION

Discussion of Professor E. O. Jordan's paper by *H. W. Redfield, Ph.D.*, U. S. Department of Agriculture, Bureau of Chemistry, Washington, D. C.

It seems to me that we must consider this subject from two points of view. First, from that of the investigator who has ample time and opportunity to study minutely the floras of food stuffs in order to identify definitely the causes of poisoning, of spoilage, etc., and second, from that of the bacteriologist who is charged with protecting the public from inferior or harmful foods, and who must in that capacity examine such a large number of samples in a short period of time that it is impossible for him to study very closely the floras of the samples with which he must deal.

To the investigator Prof. Jordan has pointed out a great number of problems concerning which our knowledge is at present inadequate and which urgently demand immediate study. He has not, however, touched more than casually upon the uses which can be made of bacteriology by the very busy food bacteriologist employed in control work in deciding the fitness or unfitness of these food products with justice alike to producer and consumer. Such a bacteriologist not only has a great responsibility, but he has a very real problem, and I should like to discuss this problem briefly.

I believe that the large majority of those here will agree with me in the statement that the control bacteriologist in examining bottled table water cannot be expected to make examinations for *B. typhosus*, for *Sp. cholerae*, for *B. paratyphosus A*, for *B. paratyphosus B*, for *B. enteritidis*, etc., etc., etc. If he is examing milk he cannot be expected to test for all of these and for alkali forming bacteria, peptonizing bacteria, *B. abortus*, *Vibrio fetus*, etc. Neither if he is examining frozen eggs can he be expected, in the time at his command, to analyze the flora which he will find. Without mentioning them in detail, the same is true in principle of all of the foodstuffs with which he may have to deal. I grant you that it would be most desirable if the bacteriologist doing routine work could in the case of each sample submitted to him make examinations for all of the organisms which might have any significance in that particular foodstuff, but this he cannot do—he cannot make a public health interpretation

of every bacterial count. It would make the cost of inspection prohibitive, it would cut down to unwarrantable limits the number of samples possible to examine, and it is not an indispensable necessity.

What then can the food control bacteriologist do? He can begin by dividing foodstuffs into stable and perishable. Stable foodstuffs may be dirty, may be contaminated, may carry a great variety of micro-organisms, harmless or harmful; but these stable foodstuffs can be disregarded for the most part by the bacteriologist, since they are, as a rule, washed and cooked, under circumstances which relieve the food control officer of much of the responsibility which he would otherwise bear. In this connection I am not forgetting the very excellent work which was done in Prof. Jordan's laboratory with reference to the difficulty of freeing contaminated lettuce and radishes from typhoid organisms by washing. The probability, however, of such contamination is so remote in the average run of stable samples that it would hardly pay a bacteriologist to examine for *B. typhosus* or *B. coli* as a routine matter.

But in dealing with perishable foodstuffs, the responsibility of the bacteriologist becomes acute, and since it is impossible for him to determine in detail what all of the significant organisms may be, adherence to the following principles is in my judgment the only solution of the problem. He needs first to know to what extent initial contamination of a product must be frankly admitted as unavoidable. He must also know the sources and general nature of possible contamination and he must know what amount of unavoidable contamination and what amount of bacterial increase through multiplication takes place in properly conducted channels of trade, and he must use this knowledge in interpreting his results. In other words, the responsibility of the control bacteriologist is to determine the bacteriological condition which may be shown by sound experiment to represent the proper handling of a product and to exact from the trade in handling human foods in as nearly such a condition as it is possible to obtain. Pasteurization, secondary cooking and other treatments must all be taken into account. But fundamentally, in all foods other than those intentionally fermented under controlled conditions in order to arrive at a preconceived and desired product, bacteria must be recognized as contamination along with dirt, unavoidable perhaps, but to be reduced to an absolute minimum. When that absolute minimum still carries with it an element of danger, the bacteriologist must insist upon the practical destruction of even this absolute minimum. It is on this basis that the maximum allowable counts in different grades of milk as adapted by the New York Milk Commission was fixed, and it is upon the same basis that the maximum allowable bacterial counts have been worked out for other food substances, among which are notably water, egg products, processed meats, such as sausages or hamburger, oysters, various types of canned goods, and butter. From this list it is seen that the application of bacteriological methods, according to the conception which I have just given you has only been begun.

In addition to the quantitative determination of the number of bacteria allowable in various food products handled properly in trade channels in accordance with the principles of decency, it is possible for the control bacteriologist, even with the rush of work which is ordinarily imposed upon him, to make a few qualitative tests for bacteria which have been shown by the investigators to be of vital significance. In this connection, he may rely upon examinations for organisms which are found regularly as a part of filthy or polluted or decomposed substances, and may use the fact of their presence as presumptive evidence of such contamination or decomposition. And he may also rely upon the detection of organisms which, while themselves harmless, may point to sources of infection which carry the menace of disease germs. To illustrate, in the routine examination of oysters the bacteriologist need not search for *B. typhosus* or other sewage organism capable of producing disease, since the detection of *B. coli* is sufficient to show the product to be sewage polluted and a possible menace to health.

To summarize briefly what I have said, my conception is that the food control bacteriologist who must examine many samples a day of various products must rely upon the bacterial counts which have been found by careful experimentation to be the maximum allowable for any food material handled properly in the channels of trade, and should supplement this by the few qualitative tests which he can make of the most significant organisms which may be present.

□

NORTH CAROLINA SCHOOLHOUSE IMPROVEMENTS

If it were one of the old-fashioned patent medicine advertisers who presented these little pictures, they would be labelled, "Before and After Taking." They show the old

In its present disrepair, with broken windows and leaky roof, it could have only a dispiriting influence on the pupils. Contrast it with the spruce, new building, with its high win-

Thompson schoolhouse in Rowan Co., N. C., and the new one. The old, ramshackle structure, built of logs hewn square and chinked, was good in its day, but that was long ago.

dows and air of cleanliness, and you will realize how North Carolina is beginning with the children in some of its steps forward.

POLLUTION OF DEEP WELLS AT LANSING, MICHIGAN

MAJOR EDWARD D. RICH,

State Sanitary Engineer, Lansing, Mich.

Read before Sanitary Engineering Section, American Public Health Association, at New Orleans, La., October 29, 1919

This story is out of the book of bitter experience. Sanitary engineers will be especially interested in the way in which germs found a passage the moment man relaxed his vigilance. The special lesson to be learned is that deep wells require the same watchful care as shallow ones.

LANSING, the capital city of Michigan, is situated about 50 miles south of the center of the southern peninsula. Its population is estimated at about 60,000, and its area is about 16 square miles, only about two-thirds of which is fully built up. The city has always been supplied with water taken from deep wells. There are 32 such wells in use at present, which vary from 350 to 400 feet in depth and take their supply from what is known as the "Coal Measure" sandstone. The rock formation is covered with from 20 to 100 feet of sand, gravel and mixed clay. Various strata are encountered between the bottom of the overlying earth and the water-bearing horizon. The wells are cased with iron pipe driven a short distance into the upper rock layers, but it is doubtful if these casings fit tight enough against the rock walls to exclude any seepage that might follow down along the casing. On account of the age of some of the wells it is possible that some of these casings have deteriorated enough to permit some leakage through the pipe itself. The casings vary in diameter from 8 to 20 inches and the present water consumption is about 8,000,-000 gallons per 24 hours.

There are five separate stations pumping directly into the distribution mains. Central station is situated just east of the center of the city, Pennsylvania Ave. station is about a mile south of Central station, Seymour street station is about a mile and a quarter northwest of the Central station, Townsend street station is in the southwest part of the city, at the corner of Isaac and Townsend Sts., and Logan street station, the last constructed, is about a mile west and a little north of Central station. Originally, many of the wells flowed to a slight extent, but there was not sufficient head to furnish any great quantity of water, and pumps were installed. As the demands of the city grew and the pumping increased in volume, the ground water level receded to some extent and it became necessary to install deep well pumps at Central station to increase the yield. Logan street station being on higher ground than the rest was equipped with a triple stage deep well pump, electrically driven, when it was constructed. Pennsylvania avenue, Townsend street, and Seymour street stations are all pumped through horizontal suction mains connected to each of the wells. The length of the suction main at Pennsylvania avenue is about 3,500 feet, and at Townsend street about 1,000 feet, while the Seymour street line is considerably shorter. At each well a drop suction pipe extends down into the casing for about 20 feet, leaving an annular space of about half an inch between the pipe and the casing. The drop pipe is connected with the horizontal suction line by means of a "T" just above the top of the casing. The top of this "T" is tightly capped. Between the "T" and

147

the horizontal suction line there is a gate valve and a check valve.

The growth of Lansing during the past five or ten years .has been very rapid and it has been difficult to obtain enough water from the city wells to supply the rapidly increasing demands. Consequently, it has been necessary, on account of increased pumping, to maintain a heavy suction vacuum, particularly at Pennsylvania avenue and Townsend street. On account of the depth of the wells, they have always been considered pollution proof. For this reason, and also because in the early days the nature of the transmission of waterborne diseases was not clearly understood by waterworks officials, insufficient precautions were taken to make the joints at the top of the wells absolutely tight. In later years apprehension of the possible entrance of pollution has led to the use of more efficient pipe connections. This has been accomplished by means of flanges on both the drop pipe and the casing, with a rubber gasket securely bolted between them. This, of course, insures a water-tight joint if reasonably good workmanship is available. When some of the older wells were constructed it was attempted to obtain a water-tight joint by placing concrete arond the opening between the drop pipe and casing and extending it up a few inches to form the bottom of the valve chamber or manhole built over the well to give access to the valve. These valve chambers are not water-tight and particularly at the Pennsylvania station they have been regarded as a source of possible contamination, inasmuch as they are subject to flooding at times of high water from the Red Cedar River, which carries a considerable sewage flow from the eastern part of the city and from the city of East Lansing. It is believed, however, that most of the wells at the Pennsylvania station were constructed with flange and gasket joints. It has been customary to collect samples at this station whenever

high water indicated the possibility of contamination, but only once or twice has anything suspicious been discovered.

The clearness of the water, the depth of the wells, and the absence of epidemics or serious illness all tended to create a false sense of security and led to a lack of that watchfulness which should always be maintained over every water supply. The upper layers of the rock are coarse, poorly cemented, and very liable to develop fissures capable of transferring laterally any pollution which might reach these openings through abandoned wells or other excavations deep enough to communicate with them.

Townsend street station is on Townsend street at the foot of Isaac street and only about 200 feet from the Grand River. Townsend street runs approximately parallel to the course of the river. In Townsend street and in Ann street, which is practically a continuation of Townsend street, there are five 6-inch wells connected to a single horizontal suction line about a thousand feet in length. Two other wells, one 10-inch, directly behind the station, and another 6-inch about 200 feet west of the station on Isaac street, complete the series of wells.

A sewer which serves quite a large portion of the southwestern part of the city extends along Townsend street and Ann street and lies only 10 or 15 feet from some of the wells. This sewer discharges directly into Grand River above the pumping station. During normal stages of the river this sewer has a free outlet and no excessive pressures are maintained in the pipe. At times of high water, however, the river rises to such height as to set back the sewage to a height above the tops of most of the wells connected with the Townsend street station. Under such circumstances, of course, this sewer is under hydraulic pressure, and the joints being far from tight, offer a ready means for sewage to percolate through the sandy soil into the valve chambers. This pumping station has for a number of years been looked upon with a certain degree of suspicion and it has been customary to shut it off during high water stages. When this is done, the ground water rises nearly to the top of the casings, thus preventing an extensive amount of pollution from settling into the wells and reaching the lower level. But when the station is running and drawing heavily upon the wells there is a strong tendency to draw in polluted ground water through any leaks that might be present in the suction lines. Heavy rains caused the Grand River to rise 8 feet on March 15, 1919, reaching a river stage of 12 feet. This placed a static head of 2½ feet on the sewer at the wells forcing concentrated sewage into the sandy soil around them. Through an oversight, the station was not shut down at that time and the vacuum of 22 inches normally maintained pulled in such a quantity of highly polluted ground water that dysentery was epidemic by the 18th. The first complaint reached the State Department of Health from the Olds Motor Works, a large factory located about a quarter of a mile west of the Townsend street station, that a large number of their men were sick from bowel trouble. The department collected a sample of water and took action by ordering the station shut off at once. On the 20th a notice was published to boil all city water used for domestic purposes and the water department was directed to make the arrangements necessary for chlorinating the supply by means of the emergency machines furnished by the Department of Health. Systematic sampling of the supply at all the pumping stations and at various points on the distribution system was begun at once. Seymour street station alone showed safe results and has since continued to do so with one or two minor exceptions, all others being reported as unsafe or suspicious. On March 25th arrangements had been completed for chlorinating at the rate of 1.5 p. p. m. at Central and Pennsylvania stations. Continued flushing of dead ends was ordered and this, together with the chlorination,

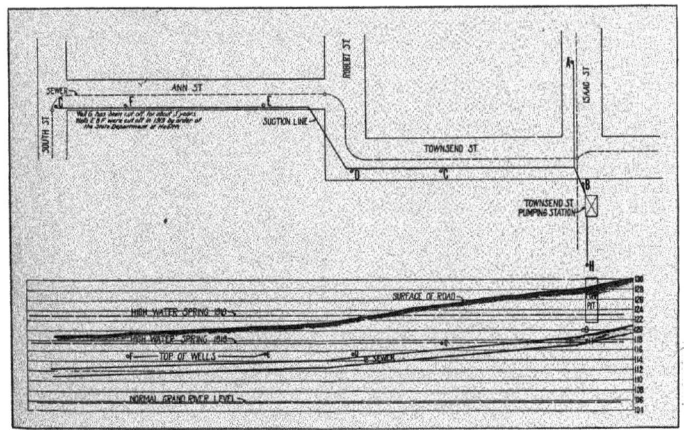

resulted in sterilizing the water in the mains by the 29th. Chlorination has been maintained ever since.

On the 22nd the Townsend street wells were carefully inspected and a plainly audible leak was found at the top of well "C." There was also a poorly made and leaky shred-lead joint at well "D." A defective flange at the top of the casing of well "H" was also admitting surface water which, although some distance from the sewer, was probably polluted to some extent. All the other wells appeared to be tight. The old manholes were torn out and all the wells ordered repaired. This was done with standard flange couplings wherever possible. In some instances it was found impossible to lift the drop suction pipes for the purpose of fitting the flanges. In these cases the casings were cut off a few inches below the "T" and a poured lead joint about 6 inches deep was put into the annular space and thoroughly calked. There is no doubt that such a joint is fully as impervious as a flange coupling. Concrete manholes were ordered built at each of these wells.

After these repairs were completed samples taken from the Townsend street station, which had previously been connected so as to pump to waste for sampling purposes, showed continued gross pollution. It was attempted to obtain samples from the individual wells by shutting off all but one and pumping that in the usual way. This proved unsuccessful, however, due either to inability to shut the valves at the various wells absolutely tight or to the fact that the suction line and pump had become so seriously polluted as to communicate contamination to pure water, which might be drawn to the well being pumped. In order to study the individual behavior of each well sampling devices were installed at the top of each well between the "T" and the horizontal suction line. This made it possible to pump all the wells at the same time and

to obtain samples from each before its output came in contact with that of the others.

After a series of about 75 samples had been collected from the individual wells the State Department of Health ordered on June 14th wells "E" and "F" permanently disconnected and plugged. Marked improvement in the quality of the water delivered by the Townsend street pump followed immediately and subsequent samples have indicated that the other wells have slowly returned to their normal state of purity.

The number of cases of dysentery which occurred during March and April is conservatively estimated at 3,000. The fact that dysentery is not a reportable disease in Michigan makes it impossible to obtain complete statistics of the number of cases. Dysentery was followed by an epidemic of about 82 cases of typhoid fever, with 11 deaths.

It is, of course, impossible to estimate the economic loss directly due to the pollution of the Lansing water supply, but some idea of its magnitude may be obtained from the following table showing the effect of the epidemic on the employees of the Olds Motor Works.

EFFECT OF THE DYSENTERY EPIDEMIC ON OLDS MOTOR WORKS.

Date	Men Absent	Output Cars
March 19	171	138
20	418	88
21	1,703	19
22	2,100 (shut down)	0
23	Sunday	0
24	486	104
25	413	137
26	395	123

Normal production, 150 cars per day.
Loss of wages, $30,000.

The officials of the Reo Motor Car Co. report the average number of men absent from the factory March 20th to April 10th as 150. Loss of wages $15,000. Estimated loss to the company $40,000. This factory employs about the same number of men as the Olds Motor Works.

Chlorination has rendered the Lansing

city water supply safe for domestic purposes since April 1st. Systematic sampling several times each week was carried on until about August 1st, after which the interval between the collection of samples was considerably increased because no serious results had been found. The city has provided itself with chlorine machines and installed them at all stations except Seymour street, where the results of continued sampling justify its use without treatment. More than 800 samples of water were collected and analyzed during the course of the investigation. A chart has been prepared on the basis of these analyses showing the progress of the typhoid epidemic and the results of the tests, together with the stage of the river and record of rainfall for the entire period covered by the investigation.

The principal lesson we should learn from this epidemic is that deep wells situated in the midst of urban development require the same watchful care that would be accorded to a shallow well supply or to a surface supply known to be subject to periodical contamination, even though their depth and manner of construction would seem to preclude the necessity for such care. Assuming that such wells are constructed in the best manner possible, there are still three avenues by which dangerous pollution may suddenly gain access: 1. Deterioration in joints and piping. 2. Pumping in excess of the normal capacity of the wells tends to open the texture of the rock in the case of sandstone and to enlarge any fissures that may be present, and thus make the entrance of surface water seepage easier. 3. The careless

abandonment of old wells penetrating the same water-bearing stratum, whether drilled for water, oil or salt, without plugging them tightly enough to exclude surface water.

It has been suggested that the state of Michigan pass a law requiring all such wells to be plugged. It is doubtful if such a law would be feasible. It might look effective on paper, but it would seem that its enforcement would be attended with many difficulties.

In the construction of deep wells there is certainly needed a better class of workmanship than is often obtained and a thorough inspection of all that is going on during the course of the drilling, for the purpose of ascertaining the exact amount of casing driven into the ground, and of collecting samples of all the materials passed through during the operation. It is quite likely that in many instances double casings should be used, the first reaching down as far as it is possible to drive it into the upper layers of the rock, and the second placed inside and extending to a depth sufficient to cut off all ground water likely to be subject to pollution. A water-tight packing should be placed between the bottom of the inner casing and the rock wall to accomplish this result.

The bitter experience of Lansing indicates that no matter how perfectly deep wells may be constructed and how remote their possibility of contamination may seem to be, it is a matter of the greatest importance that systematic sampling be carried on with sufficient frequency to detect any possible dangerous symptoms before they reach epidemic proportions.

STUDIES IN THE CLARIFICATION OF MILK

CHARLES E. MARSHALL,*

Professor of Microbiology, Massachusetts Agricultural College, Amherst, Mass.

Read before Joint Session of Sections on Public Health Administration, Laboratory and Food and Drugs, American Public Health Association, at New Orleans, La., October 29, 1919.

These studies were started during the summer of 1914 and have been continued in varying degrees since that time. They were made possible by the De Laval Separator Company of New York City, which established a fund placed in the hands of the Treasurer of the College to meet the expenses incurred.

The firm was desirous of knowing the truth about clarification, so far as it can be determined; accordingly, the work was placed on the usual basis of Experiment Station investigational undertakings with the enjoyment of complete independence. The firm has been a constant source of helpfulness and at no time has it attempted or interfered to influence results or the free publication of the findings.

I make this statement as a due appreciation of the helpfulness, generosity and sympathetic attitude of a commercial firm. If any commercial motive exists, it can be only a desire to have facts and truth as a basis for their procedure and progress in manufacture.

THE clarifier, as you know, is a centrifugal machine and is the result of an effort to establish a more effective device to accomplish that for which the separator has been used in a secondary capacity. The separation of cream by the separator, its primary function, could not be sacrificed to improve the "clarifier" or secondary function. The purpose of the clarifier is one of helpfulness in the purification of milk. As a machine, its efficiency is restricted only by the limitations of centrifugation as applied to milk.

Does it assist in the purification of milk? This question is the gist of what is involved in these investigations. If this machine does render the milk better, then we want to know how it does it and to what extent. Since it is a limited centrifugal mechanical device, all elements which may not be influenced by its centrifugation are eliminated from these studies.

Only conspicuous matters pertaining to clarification which may be of particular interest will be considered summarily. Other aspects will be published in the comparatively near future if not already published. Time and circumstances preclude exhaustive treatment at this moment.

1. *The clarifier strains the insoluble dirt out of milk much more effectively than any strainer now employed.*[1]

It is possible for dirt that is lighter than milk to pass through, but this has been noted only twice in our prolonged experience. Even when present in large amounts, only traces of such dirt can be detected. Of course, the clarifier, like the centrifuge, does not remove soluble dirt. Since the solubility of stable dirt from different sources varies from 10 to 30 per cent, the amount removed would vary from 70 to 90 per cent.

This, you will admit, has considerable material value and also great aesthetic value.

2. *The clarifier removes cellular elements or masses of cellular elements in a large degree.*[1]

The so-called leucocytes are removed in very large numbers, colostral cells almost completely, massed cells or garge completely, and any other cells incidenta in milk in varying degrees.

*This is a summary of the laboratory work of E. G. Hood, S. G. Mutkekar, John Yesair and Max Marshall.

Anyone familiar with milk production realizes that a herd of twenty cows furnishes particles of garget in practically every milking, sometimes more and sometimes less. Garget suggests at once an udder disturbance somewhere in the herd which is not easily located. Whether or not garget or any massing of cells should lead to the isolation of cow or herd, we need not answer, for it is impracticable, perhaps impossible. The removal of all traces of garget is regarded as a real necessity. Colostral milk is much altered and can be improved and detected when desired. The excessive accumulations in the form of slime upon the bowl of the clarifier indicate at once abnormal conditions in the cow or herd.

The clarifier, therefore, removes clots or garget or any massing of cells; it modifies colostral milk and can be used to detect colostrum; it tends to eliminate all cellular elements. This is demanded by the public for aesthetic reasons and it may be that the removal of such substances does contribute to the real purity of milk. No one has furnished proof for this assumption, but we all admit that such eliminations are in the direction of improvement.

3. The clarifier removes micro-organisms in varying amounts, the larger more readily than the smaller.[1]

Too much has been made of the apparent increases of micro-organisms in market milk after passing through the clarifier. Those who know little about micro-organisms have taken the counts of bacteriologists, who have furnished them, and claimed that the clarifier actually increased the numbers. Such interpreters seem to have no conception of microbial development in milk and no knowledge of the crudities of plating. The milk passes the clarifier instantly. With certified fresh milk, where few colonies have developed, results diametrically opposed to market milk are obtained. It can be actually shown that the

number of micro-organisms is reduced very materially even in market milk. The very evident facts that large numbers are found in slime, that 50 per cent and over can be demonstrated to be eliminated and that the increase cannot possibly take place while the milk is passing should be conclusive proof of the casting out of micro-organisms in large numbers. Again, if micro-organisms are in a very marked manner broken up when in colonies or clumps and if the numbers are not seriously increased, in fact, in certified milk are greatly reduced, then also we may conclude that very large numbers are thrown out. It appears, too, that when counts are made over a period of 72 hours at 2-hour intervals, the curves resulting from plate counts are practically identical even after the breaking up of clumps and colonies. We have charted these determinations to illustrate the real nature of clarification upon counts so much employed for interpretation. It is not justifiable to stop with a single count determination as is usually done.

While it is possible to say that there is no great difference in the time of alteration of clarified as against unclarified milk, it may be correctly asserted that the character of alteration is usually different and is in favor of clarified milk. This can be easily observed by comparison at suitable temperatures.

The releasing of individual organisms from their colony-involvement, which accounts for the apparent increase of numbers after clarification, seems to indicate that their individual physiological efficiency has been stimulated. Although increased, this efficiency serves as a directive force or produces the effect of a lactic starter in controlling the kind of fermentation, but does not hasten the time of action because of the reduction in numbers. This is readily demonstrated in a study of the clarifier when acting upon known organisms. Of three tests, the average of *Oidium lactis* removed by the clarifier from milk was 99+%, of *Sacch. cerevisiæ* was 99+%, of *B. tumescens* was 63%, of *Strept. lacticus* 24%, of *B. prodigiosus* 23%. The smaller percentage of lactic organisms removed as against the larger percentage of *Øidium lactis, Sacch. cerevisiæ,* and B *tumescens* accounts for the ascendency of the lactic organisms and the lactic starter effect.

4. *If micro-organisms are removed and if milk still changes after clarification nearly as quickly as before clarification, it is necessary to justify the process of clarification from the standpoint of micro-organisms.*

This can be accomplished succinctly in the time available by simply indicating the evidence at hand.

a. When the two samples of milk, unclarified and clarified, are allowed to ferment side by side at a suitable temperature there is a noticeable difference in favor of clarified milk. The clarified milk trends more closely toward typical lactic acid fermentation while the unclarified milk will manifest obnoxious signs.

b. The curds removed by filtration undergo different changes: The unclarified will develop molds in abundance and putrid decomposition while the clarified will commonly have a more limited molding and non-odorous change or may even dry up without decomposition.

c. There is a difference in gas formation. Carbon dioxide develops in greater abundance in the clarified. The exact amount of total gas has not yet been measured. It has seemed to the workers that there is a greater amount of gas produced in the unclarified. This must be held in abeyance for proof with actual determinations of the total amount of gas.

d. Obnoxious odors were detected in the unclarified milk usually as against clarified. The flavor of the milk is usually improved by clarifying.

e. If allowed to stand for a time, *Øidium lactis* grows in abundance on the unclarified as against a few scattering colonies on the surface of the clarified.

f. Proteolysis is more marked in the unclarified as against the clarified.

g. Methylene blue is usually reduced more slowly by the clarified as against the unclarified milk.

h. The acidity is slightly increased by the clarified over the unclarified.

i. In the making of cheese the results seem to indicate that the flavor has been improved by clarification.

5. *If these observations are correct, an explanation is demanded. Why does clarification accomplish such results?*

My answer will not be complete for I suspect other reasons or elements beyond those I now give but which I cannot demonstrate positively at present or furnish satisfactory proof.

I align these reasons or factors entering into clarification in this manner:

a. Elimination. This has been discussed in connection with cellular elements, micro-organisms and dirt.

b. Selection. I have already shown how *O. lactis., Sacch. cerevisæ, B. tumescens,* are eliminated from milk by clarification in much larger percentage than *Strept. lacticus* and have suggested the result.

c. Association. This act of selection of heavier organisms over light disturbs the germ-equilibrium of the milk and directs or favors approved lactic fermentation through the changed association.

d. Distribution. The breaking up of colonies and the distribution of individual organisms throughout the milk acts like the shaking of a young culture of *Strept. lacticus* by stimulating activity, favoring lactic development along with the factors of selection and association.

e. Æration. This factor is present in the machine used by us and undoubtedly performs the same function as when employed with cultures.

From the investigations thus far completed and from the results indicated there appear to be tangible values o practical significance in clarification These values may possibly be increased Our knowledge in the use of centrif ugal force upon micro-organisms i milk is too youthful and too restrict to predict at this time its possibilities.

1. Bulletin No. 187, Massachusetts Agricultur Experimental Station.

SCHOOLS FOR HEALTH OFFICERS:
WHAT HAS BEEN DONE AT SYRACUSE

FREDERICK W. SEARS, M. D.,

State Sanitary Inspector; Director of the Course,
Syracuse, N. Y.

A RADICAL change has been effected in the administration of public health in New York state under the present Health Commissioner, Dr. Hermann M. Biggs, who has been able to put into effect the laws enacted by the State Legislature in 1913.

To appreciate what these changes have been, one must be familiar with the general conditions which prevailed under previous regulations. It is evident to all that the general health of the state depends principally upon the conditions existing in the health units, as represented by the various health districts, in the cities, towns and villages which make up the state.

When these new laws went into effect there were in the State of New York approximately 1,500 such units and there was no tangible connecting link between these units and the administrative body at Albany.

Each of these units had a health officer who was, to a certain extent, responsible for the health of his community, and the only contact which he had (with rare exceptions) with the State Department of Health was at the Annual Convention of Health Officers.

I was told by one health officer, when I questioned him as to his activities that he received practically no compensation for his services and there was little service required. The only reason he consented to serve was for the good time he had at these conventions.

The health officers in the various townships were usually appointed for their political activity or at the solicitation of some influential friend without regard to their qualifications for the position. His remuneration was in the hands of a board of health, which board was usually selected for complying with the law, with the least possible expense to the taxpayer —rather than from any knowledge which the members of the board may have had of constructive health work.

The health officer rarely, if ever, came in contact with his board. One of the health officers in my district had held the office of health officer for 30 years and had never met with his board of health.

The attitude of the board of health toward the health officer in the majority of the districts was that he should not receive compensation except when communicable disease was present during the year, and his compensation was in proportion to the amount of communicable disease, and the number of placards which he had posted.

The prevention of disease was too indefinite and intangible to receive consideration. Insofar as the board was concerned the health officer was most satisfactory who was willing to receive the criticism of the public and attend to his other duties with the least possible expense to the community.

He was regarded by the heads of families, many of whom were his private patients, as grossly incompetent if he did not keep a strict quarantine upon his neighbor's house when one of its inmates was afflicted with a communicable disease, and as an over-zealous official when he restricted their own liberties, under similar circumstances. It was, therefore, a great temptation to pursue the easier way of retaining the good will of the patients at the sacrifice of his duties as a health officer. As a result, a premium was placed upon inefficiency and a penalty for doing his duty properly.

Were it not for the high sense of duty which is possessed by most of the members of our profession, conditions would have been much worse than what we found them.

An intimate association with rural health officers has (with few exceptions) given me a high appreciation of their sturdiness of character and conscientious work, under most trying conditions.

As an instructor and co-worker, I have never known men, taken, as a whole, who were more eager to improve their knowledge or more appreciative of efforts made in behalf of their municipalities; and their inspiration under the present administration has not come so much from the increased remuneration which the law has determined by fixing a minimum per capita salary, as from the moral support and encouragement which they have received through the state sanitary supervisors and the heads of the various divisions of the State Health Department, as now constituted.

No matter how conscientious a public health worker may be, his enthusiasm soon wanes when he becomes conscious that his work is not appreciated by his community. Indifference of his associates is a great handicap to good work.

To a health officer who is not interested in his work, the salary is the chief consideration—but a health worker who regulates his efficiency from the standpoint of salary and his attention is fixed upon the clock rather than his results, will never be of any great value to his community in public health work.

The above were in general the conditions which the sanitary supervisor found in New York state when he entered upon his duties early in the year 1914. The proposition which confronted the health commissioner was how can they be remedied?

The State Health Department first secured through the legislature the enactment of a law which fixed a minimum per capita salary for all districts with a population of 8,000 or less.

On July 6, 1915, the New York State Public Health Council passed a resolution requiring certain qualifications as necessary to the appointment of a health officer, by the local boards of health throughout the state. These regulations took effect on June 1, 1916.

Two courses were prescribed for the purpose of fitting them for these requirements. One course was a residence course of six weeks in connection with a recognized university. The alternative was a reading course extending over a period of one year with one week's residence, in connection with a recognized university.

From my knowledge of the conditions in the district over which I had jurisdiction, I felt that I would have difficulty in bringing my health officers to the required standard of efficiency by either of these courses.

My principal reason was that these health officers needed to be brought into more intimate association with their sanitary supervisor in order to secure the enthusiasm necessary for the work.

Under the old environment, the men had become self-satisfied and discouraged. They needed to be lifted out of themselves and to be thrown more frequently into contact with those with similar occupations and purposes.

The opportunities for social intercourse and contact are not numerous in the smaller rural communities, and excellent men have gradually lost faith in themselves and their incentive for work has waned through the lack of opportunity to associate with those of similar environment. I consider that one of the great advantages which the Health Officers' Course at Syracuse offers is that it brings these men from various communities together each week to exchange their ideas and for social contact.

With these principles in mind, I asked and was granted the privilege by the Public Health Council of substituting in connection with Syracuse University the course which I will briefly outline.

This course consists of intimately combining reading and residence work over a period of 12 weeks. A tentative program is sent to the men who enter the class about 6 weeks before the course opens. When the course is under way a program is furnished every week to each member of the class, designating the work to be taken up for that week, to enable him to do some reading in advance. The class convenes in Syracuse every Friday and Saturday of each week for the entire period of the course, and the program, as outlined, is put into effect by means of lectures, demonstrations, clinics and actual participation in the work.

This work is made as practical as is possible and covers the subjects that the men must meet most frequently in their own communities. For this purpose teachers are drawn from the Faculty of the University, the municipal officers whose work touches upon Health Problems, the various local laboratories, dispensaries, the hospitals, including the County Hospital for Tuberculosis, City Hospital for Communicable Diseases,

State Institution for Feeble Minded, industrial institutions, public schools, water and public works departments, milk pasteurizing plants, child welfare stations and, in fact, all facilities which bear upon public health directly or indirectly.

The object is not to fit men to specialize in any one branch of public health work, but to give them a broad idea of the significance of public health activity in its various branches.

Sir Arthur Newsholme expresses his ideas of the purpose of public health work in the following sentence: "It is to secure the maximum attainable health for every member of the community."

Our object is to give the health officer a knowledge of this work that will inspire confidence in himself and in those about him. The health officer should be regarded by his community as a specialist in public health and hygiene. In order to meet the dignity of his position his knowledge of public health subjects should be broad and comprehensive. His selection to office should be made solely in regard to his fitness for the position. His duties should not be the perfunctory

Health Officers' Class at Syracuse University.

one of a sanitary policeman who is often regarded by the public as worse than the diseases he quarantines.

The health officer should be entrusted with the giving of instructions as to the methods to be adopted in preventing the spreading of disease, a function which the family physician too frequently assumes. The attending physician should seek the health officer's advice in matters pertaining to health regulations in the same spirit which he would that of the consulting surgeon or internist.

Through a better knowledge of his specialty the work of the health officer should impress itself upon the municipality in a manner sufficient to command coöperation and assistance from all societies and organizations in his community. His visits to the afflicted home should be looked upon as that of a wise counsellor and friend and not of a heartless official to be dreaded. This will ensure more prompt reporting of disease.

To secure such a recognition the health officer must possess certain qualifications of character and education which will command the respect of the entire community. He should be prepared to answer promptly and intelligently all questions relating to the fundamental principles underlying public health work, when such questions are asked by the local physicians. His knowledge of epidemiology should be sufficient to enable him to meet effectually all outbreaks of disease and as far as possible to trace them to their sources.

The question naturally arises, "How can the health officer secure such qualifications without too great a sacrifice of time and money?" When we consider the meagerness of his salary in proportion to the income from private practice, we are but little surprised at the common query by him "How can I afford to do it?"

We must furnish him a course which will afford him these opportunities with the least possible loss of time from his regular practice. It must be of such a character that its teachings will be of the highest value to him as a practitioner in medical lines which are so closely allied to public health work. Our aim should be to open up to him the broader fields which he can cultivate and supplement by future reading.

It would require years of training to qualify him as a specialist in bacteriology, but he can be taught the fundamental principles of laboratory work and laboratory methods, which will enable him to appreciate their limitations and the wonderful assistance to be obtained from them when properly understood. He should, in a general way, know the principles which govern the growth and propagation of bacteria, something of their morphology, selective staining, and the difficulties encountered by the bacteriologists when specimens are improperly collected, tabulated and dispatched to his laboratory.

He should have some knowledge of the methods used in isolating pure cultures and for what purposes they are isolated. He should know what is meant by "dark field illumination" in the diagnosis of certain diseases; the principles underlying agglutination tests and complement fixation and the methods of ascertaining the various types of pneumonia for the purpose of serum treatment. He should understand some of the underlying principles of immunity, both active and passive, and the great value of immune sera when administered properly. He should understand in a general way the phenomena of anaphylaxis and the dangers of administering large amounts of foreign proteins without suitable precautions.

He should have some knowledge of vaccine therapy and its limitations. He should understand the difference between vaccines and immune sera. He should have a general knowledge of the production of diphtheria anti-toxin, its standardization, dosage, and administration.

under varying conditions; should know how Vincent's angina can be distinguished from diphtheria; what is meant by the "Schick test" and see its application; should have a general idea of the toxin-anti-toxin method of immunization against diphtheria. He should be shown how to secure blood for the Wassermann test, and other similar reactions, and have a knowledge of spinal puncture and its importance as a diagnostic and therapeutic measure in certain meningeal affections. To my mind, this knowledge of these various phenomena cannot be obtained without practical demonstrations and an intimate association with his teachers.

To teach this work effectually the class must be limited in numbers and must have teachers who have the enthusiasm and personality which will bring out the difficult points through questioning, explanations and clear demonstrations.

The same practical methods should be used in other phases of the work. Practical demonstrations should be given in the early diagnosis of tuberculosis by the best specialists obtainable in this line of work. He should be shown that sanitarium treatment for this disease should be both educational and for the arrest of the progress of the disease.

He should be familiar with the treatment of venereal diseases and have practical demonstrations in the administration of remedies, and so far as possible be taught the technique of intravenous therapy, by actual demonstration. The same practical methods should be used in demonstrating school examinations, school inspection and the problems underlying its various branches.

He should be shown open air schools in operation. Should be taught the value of substituting industrial teaching for atypical and backward pupils. He should be taught industrial hygiene particularly as applied to foods; should visit certified dairies, pasteurization plants, ice cream factories, and should be shown the methods used in scoring dairies by men of experience. He should visit hospitals for communicable diseases and observe these diseases in their various manifestations throughout their course. He should be taught the rôle of the carrier in the spread of disease and how best to protect the public from them with the least amount of hardship to the afflicted family. He should be taught the various methods of the purification of water for municipal purposes, including chlorination, mechanical and slow sand filtration, should visit sewage disposal plants in operation and the various other municipal health activities, and should be given practical demonstration in prenatal care and infant welfare work. He must realize the value of vital statistics and the general laws governing his activities and should be well drilled in the requirements of the sanitary code.

The question naturally arises in one's mind "Is all this possible in so short a course?" Without enthusiasm, coöperation and a determination to succeed would be impossible.

If you can secure a corps of instructors with enthusiasm for the work and who can inspire their men with the highest ideals, it is possible.

A spirit of coöperation has been stimulated to a high degree and the men so trained are having their field of work gradually extended through the consolidation of districts and the demonstration of their superior fitness for the work. Other schools in New York state have been recently developed along these lines.

We fully realize that the ideal toward which we are working can only be accomplished by the securing of well-paid full-time health officers. But until we can create public sentiment and an appreciation by physicians of the great importance of preventive medicine, we must use the material at hand, not only in order to meet our present health situation, but to stimulate the public to a higher appreciation of this work.

THE INSURANCE COMPANY IN INDUSTRIAL HYGIENE

A. D. REILEY,

Assistant Inspector of Risks, Mutual Life Insurance Co., New York City.

Read before Section on Industrial Hygiene, American Public Health Association, at New Orleans, La., October 30, 1919.

We are all cognizant of the work that has been performed by the insurance companies of this country in starting, fostering and giving impetus to the safety movement. I think it not too much to say that the institution of insurance is entitled to more credit than any other force operating toward the ultimate success of that great movement.

This work was carried on almost wholly by the accident companies and those doing employers' liability and workmen's compensation insurance. The systems inaugurated by them and giving a specified rebate on the premium for each safety device and guarded machine; the willing assistance rendered by their engineers to all plants which wished to advance the safety-first movement; the industrial work of their rating boards and the yeoman service rendered in their backing of the great safety organizations, such as the National Safety Council and the American Museum of Safety, cannot be too highly commended. It is perfectly true that the lessening of industrial accidents meant thousands of dollars saving to them; but it is also true that good working conditions undoubtedly return a profit to the plant possessing them and I have never heard the mead of praise denied to the plant on that account.

During the war the insurance companies were one of the government's most efficient aids in working out the protection of the great munition producing plants, both from the standpoint of physical protection of the property and the lives of the workers. They supplied a great part of the trained personnel necessary to this work and did a great part of it direct from their offices.

Thus far the companies have not done nearly the amount of work in industrial hygiene that they have in safety. Some things they have done it is true. In certain cases they have acted in the capacity of expert adviser on industrial conditions to the plant management and have rendered excellent service, but their work in this line has been in the main incidental and has not left its impress on industry with any particular force.

It must be admitted that, in the main, the great life insurance companies have not contributed to the betterment of working conditions in industry to any very great extent. It is true that many valuable studies of industrial mortality have been contributed, mostly by the industrial companies, but life insurance has done almost no direct work of consequence in this field.

It is of comparatively recent date that the old line companies have waked up to the value of a scientific industrial selection. Twenty years ago industrial selection in life insurance was a rather perfunctory affair. There were various occupations known to be dangerous which were on prohibited lists, and men engaged in these occupations could not procure insurance at any price. These were, for the most part, occupations of accident hazard and, in life insurance circles in general, very little was known of the great trade poisons.

During the past ten years an increasing feeling that it is the duty of a life insurance company to cover by its protection as many lives as possible has induced the wiping out of many of the occupational restrictions; the opening of many industries to insurance which had hitherto been closed, and the search on the part of the companies for material and data on which to base the rates charged for dangerous and unhealthy employment. This growth of a broader idea in insurance; the spread of an insurance propaganda to the effect that every man engaged in a useful occupation who wishes to buy straight insurance protection should find a market where he can purchase at a rate commensurate with the actual cost, has forced life insurance companies to investigate industrial hazards with a steadily increasing interest. As yet this movement is in its infancy; but we in the business can see it gathering momentum from year to year and showing itself largely in the studies of industrial mortality which life insurance men are publishing with increasing frequency.

There are forces operating now in the insurance and industrial worlds which will in the end compel both the accident and workmen's compensation group of companies and the industrial and old line life group to do more and more work in industrial hygiene. Both groups have a capacity for usefulness in this field which we cannot overestimate and which will be a tremendous power for improvement when in active operation.

industrial movement, with which we are all familiar, toward better general working conditions. I think we can say that the Great War or possibly the curtailing of the world's labor supply, owing to the losses sustained in the war, have united the safety-first idea and the work for improvement in industrial hygiene into one great movement which can be called "the conservation of industrial man power." The U. S. Government felt the necessity for this work keenly during the war and gave the movement its hearty support, and to those of us who have been intimately connected with it, it is one of the most important problems of the day. Insurance as an institution is woven so deeply into the fabric of trade that companies must look beyond the mere question of dollars and cents and proceed on the basis that, with an institution so necessary to the public good, whatever

benefits the public will benefit it. I know that no life insurance underwriter can deal with the problems of industrial selection without feeling keenly the opportunity and an intense desire to co-operate in this really great work.

The payment of compensation for industrial diseases talked of in a number of states, and attempted in a timid, faltering manner in one, will be an accomplished fact of the industrial future. When that comes, if not before, the companies dealing in that type of insurance will meet the situation as they have met the accident situation, with skill and efficiency, and a tremendous aid in the final solution of the problem will have been enlisted.

I do not, however, feel competent to speak of the part taken, and to be taken, by this group of companies. It is of the life insurance companies and their work to which, as a life insurance man, I must confine myself.

There are, speaking generally, two methods of selecting a life insurance risk from the industrial standpoint. These are the individual method and the class method. In the latter, the mortality experience of the industry is procured as nearly as possible from the whole country, and a general rate imposed on the hazardous jobs which is the same for all similar operatives in all similar factories. By the individual method, some means is used for charging a different rate for selected risks. By a selected risk is meant one which is employed in a plant which takes care of its problems of safety and health in a skillful and painstaking way.

As a concrete instance, take a plant handling a trade poison. The company insuring an operative in that plant, if it proceeds on the individual method, may have three rates which it can charge the operative; say $5, $7.50 or $10 per $1,000 of insurance in addition to the usual premium. If the plant is well equipped with mechanical devices for dust and fume removal; has its dangerous processes properly isolated; furnishes ample means for personal sanitation; provides clean and healthful rooms in which meals may be eaten; in short, conducts its operations in a manner which shows it is keenly alive to the dangers of its work, and the operative himself has an intelligent comprehension of the hazards of his trade and a desire to guard himself against them, the low rate can be charged with confidence even though it be lower than demanded by the general mortality in the class. It may be charged against this plan that on account of the floating character of labor we have no guarantee that an operative will not leave a plant in which he obtains a policy with a low extra and go to work in one where conditions are such that a much higher rate should be charged. This is, of course, true, but all those who have studied industrial conditions have often commented on the fact that there is a direct relation between working conditions and labor turnover, and the plant which has the worst conditions will invariably have the highest turnover. Consequently what self selection there is, is generally in favor of the company, more risks proceeding from unfavorable to favorable factories than the reverse. This method forces the company employing it to make a careful study of all industries whose operatives they wish to insure; to watch the trend of conditions in an industry and to make careful investigations of all hazards involved. I have known manufacturers frequently to evince a great interest in the rate at which their employees could buy insurance and ask if certain changes would enable them to procure insurance at a lower rate. The educational advantage to the workman himself is also great as, if he sees himself able to procure insurance at a lower rate because of the excellent condition of the plant in which he works, the importance of good working conditions is emphasized as it could be in no other way.

During the last few years it has been the universal practice of life insurance companies to place upon policies issued to selected lives certain special benefit clauses. These clauses usually take three forms; the double indemnity, the disability benefits and the waiver of premium. The first of these need not be discussed at length. It provides for the payment of double the face of the policy in the event of accidental death. As the selection of lives to receive this benefit deals only with the chance of traumatism we may dismiss it. The disability benefits clause provides that in the event of the insured becoming totally and permanently disabled by reason of disease or bodily injury the company will waive all subsequent premiums and pay the insured a sum equal to 10 per cent of the face of the policy until his death, recovery, or the earlier maturity of the policy, as in the endowment form. Up to the present time most of the adverse experience from this feature of the policy has been due to three causes, syphilis, tuberculosis and insanity. Whether the unhealthy trades will contribute their quota to this we do not know, as men engaged in such pursuits have not generally been given the clause. But with the necessary extension of all features of life insurance to all classes it will be necessary to make intensive studies of all unhealthful industries before extending the protection of the clause to their operatives.

Presumably the great hazard will come in the dusty trades through their predisposition toward tuberculosis; and the difficulty of ascertaining the experience in such trades because of the drifting character of labor has often been pointed out. This is, of course, dipping into the realm of accident and health insurance, but this overlapping tendency is going on through all lines of insurance. At least one life insurance company is, at the present time, issuing what it terms a complete protection policy. This insures life, accident and health all under one cover. It is very doubtful whether that tendency will spread very far among the old line companies, but it is undoubted that they will be under the necessity of proceeding further in industrial health research under the present policies issued than under the old.

While all these various movements and changes in the life insurance business have this drift toward a more scientific industrial selection, it is undoubtedly the group insurance plan which will produce the most work and the greatest direct benefit to industry from the standpoint of industrial hygiene of all life insurance efforts. You are all probably familiar with this form of insurance, but for the sake of continuity I will outline it briefly. Group insurance provides for the insurance, by a plant, of all its operatives without medical examination. The plan, originally designed to protect against death only, now has been broadened to include health also and certain companies are issuing group life and group health insurance in large volume.

It will be immediately seen that the opportunity for constructive work in studying and improving industrial conditions offered to a company doing this type of insurance is enormous. It can probably be best illustrated by stating briefly how one great company tackled the problem. My description of their method must be very general as it is not my company and the details of their system are not at my fingers' ends.

This company has established a bureau composed of skilled industrial men, whose duty it is to study each problem presented on the ground, and not only to give their opinion as to conditions and recommend the rate to be charged, but to work actively with the plant management in instituting improvements in safety and sanitation. They will go to the extent, if it is desired, of organizing completely the employment management department in the plant; recognizing that, after all, the key to the situation lies in scientific employment management. Of course, as a business proposition this method speaks for itself and practically all companies who do group insurance will be compelled by the stern spur of competition to follow it, even though they might not have done so if left to themselves. If all life insurance companies did group insurance I think there is no doubt that the work done in industrial hygiene by the life companies would be the most important in the field. The number of companies that are operating is constantly increasing and excellent results have already been obtained in many instances.

I have been endeavoring to show in the brief space alloted to me that although life insurance companies on the whole have not realized their opportunities in the work for improvement of industrial conditions, the drift is ever in the direction of increasing interest.

It is also being made gradually more apparent that the importance of environmental and industrial selection has not in the history of life insurance been fully recognized. According to the ancient and time-honored methods, a risk was practically selected on the medical examination only and its value was practically determined by its physical condition. Modern opinion and knowledge have determined conclusively that the value of a life insurance examination has wholly evaporated at the end of about a five-year period or slightly longer, and from then on the lives are on a community basis. Selection from the industrial and environmental standpoint lasts generally through the entire lifetime of the policy and thus has a continuing value as long as the risk remains on the books.

We who are working constantly on this phase of the insurance business are anxious for the day to dawn when the mighty institution of insurance places its whole weight to the wheel in the solution of this mighty problem.

EDITORIAL SECTION

AMERICAN JOURNAL OF PUBLIC HEALTH

EDITORIAL OFFICE: 169 MASSACHUSETTS AVE., BOSTON, MASS.

A. W. HEDRICH, C. P. H., Editor   J. RITCHIE, Jr., Associate Editor

Editorial Assistants

E. R. HAYHURST, M.D.   DAVID GREENBERG   JAMES A. TOBEY
R. P. ALBAUGH, M.D.   M. P. HORWOOD, M.S.   FRANCIS H. SLACK, M.D.
E. B. STARR, M.D.   P. M. HOLMES, M.D.   JAMES M. STRANG

Board of Advisory Editors

PETER H. BRYCE, M.D., Ottawa, Canada   PROF. M. J. ROSENAU, Boston, Mass.
CHARLES V. CHAPIN, M.D., Providence, R. I.   PROF. W. T. SEDGWICK, Cambridge. Mass.
EUGENE R. KELLEY, M.D., Boston, Mass.   PROF. GEORGE C. WHIPPLE, Cambridge, Mass.
W. A. EVANS, M.D., Chicago, Ill.   PROF. S. M. GUNN, Paris, France.

All expressions of opinion and all statements of supposed facts are published on authority of the writer under whose name they appear, and are not to be regarded as expressing the views of the American Public Health Association, unless such statements or opinions have been adopted by vote of the Association.

NOTICE TO SUBSCRIBERS: Subscription Price, payable in advance, $4.00 per year for United States and possessions; $4.50 for Canada and other foreign countries. Single copies, 50 cents postpaid. Membership in the American Public Health Association, including subscription to Journal, $5.00 per year. In Change of Address please give both old and new address, and mail before the tenth of the month to take effect with the current issue. Mailing Date, 5th of each month. Advertisements accepted only when commendable, and worth while to reader and advertiser. News Items, interesting clippings and illustrations are gladly received, together with name of sender. Copyright, 1919, by A. W. Hedrich.

THE PROBLEM OF THE HEALTH OFFICER'S SALARY.

The Medical Officer for Dec. 6, 1919, contains a memorandum submitted by a special committee of the Society of Medical Officers of Health of Great Britain, formally adopted by the Council of the Society November 21, 1919, which is of great interest to public health workers in this country as well as in England. Its subject is the remuneration of public health officials and the argument which it presents in favor of a standardization of salaries, and of material increase in salaries, is of world-wide application.

The memorandum points out two principal reasons for an increase in the scale of remuneration for health officials. The first is the rise in the price level which as we are all aware in this country has made the purchasing power of the dollar about one-half of what it was five years ago. This argument, of course. applies to all salaried employees. There is another special argument for the increase of the salaries of health officers which depends on the vastly increased responsibilities which are being placed upon such officers year by year. The memorandum in question speaks of the fact that a minimum commencing salary of 500£ for a whole-time medical officer of health was fixed by the Medical Officer in 1912. "It is since that date," the memorandum continues, "that the responsibilities of a medical officer of health have enormously increased and the character and scope of the work materially altered. The work of a medical officer of health becomes more and more medical in character and is now concerned with the individual at least as much as with the environment of the individual. The old and artificial boundary between preventive and curative medicine is rapidly disappearing, and every session of Parliament throws new work upon the medical officer of health, requiring of him a wide knowledge of medicine and its latest ramifications, administrative ability of a high order, and the exercise of first class powers of conception and initiation in the development of the health work of local authorities.

Since 1912 the majority of schemes for the treatment of school children, including the establishment of clinics and dispensaries, have been instituted, and propaganda campaigns inaugurated in connection with various health subjects of national interest and importance."

As a result of these considerations the Society of the Medical Officers of Health recommended the salary scale indicated below, and voted to forward it with its approval to the British Medical Association, and to ask that a joint standing committee of the British Medical Association and the Society of the Medical Officers of Health in equal numbers be formed to take charge of the case for improvement in the salaries of medical officers; and that the Ministry of Health be approached with a view to giving effect to the scale of salaries in question.

RECOMMENDATIONS.

I. WHOLE-TIME MEDICAL OFFICERS.

1. That the tabulated scales of minimum salaries below be approved.

2. That the following scales of minimum salaries be subject to bonus according to the Civil Service award in force for the time being.

3. That the following scales of minimum salaries represent inclusive salaries and the value of the whole-time service of medical officers in the various classes indicated.

Minimum Salaries of Whole-Time Resident Medical Officers, Medical Officers, Medical Officers in Charge and Assistant Medical Officers of Health.

	Minimum Salaries	
Resident medical officers in hospitals and sanatoria	350 £ ($1750*) (including board, lodging and washing.	
Medical officers *employed in* School medical departments Tuberculosis departments Mental deficiency departments Maternity and child welfare departments Venereal disease departments or any other similar department or combination of departments.	500£ rising to 750£ per annum within a period of not more than 10 years ($2500 to $3750).	With in addition bonus according to the Civil Service award in force for the time being.
Medical officers *in charge of* School medical departments Tuberculosis departments Mental deficiency departments Maternity and child welfare departments Venereal disease departments Hospitals Sanatoria or any other similar department or combination of departments. Assistant medical officers of health employed in the administrative *work of a medical officer of health.*	700£ rising to 900£ per annum within a period of not more than 8 years. ($3500 to $4500).	

*Figured approximately at normal pre-war rates of exchange.

Minimum Salaries of Whole-Time Medical Officers of Health.

Population of area	Minimum salaries
Up to 50,000	800£, rising to 1,000 ($4000 to $5000) pounds within a period of not more than 5 years.
50,001 to 100,000	1,000£, rising to 1,200 ($5000 to $6000) pounds within a period of not more than 5 years.
100,001 to 200,000	1,200£, rising to 1,500 ($6000 to $7500) pounds within a period of not more than 5 years.
200,001 to 300,000	1,500£, rising to 1,800 ($7500 to $9000) pounds within a period of not more than 5 years.
Over 500,000	1,800£ ($9000) with in addition bonus according to the Civil Service award in force for the time being.

II. PART-TIME MEDICAL OFFICERS.

4. That part-time medical officers of health be paid at the rate of 4£ 4 s. ($21.) per day according to the time devoted to their duties, subject to a minimum payment of 100£ ($500) per annum.

5. That part-time specialist officers be paid at the rate of 1£ 11 s. 6d. ($7.87) per hour subject to a minimum payment of 2 pounds 2 s. ($10.50) for any session.

It is interesting to note in this connection that the Engineering Council, in this country has appointed several committees on the classification and compensation of engineers, and that a recent report issued under date of November 11 from the office of the Council, 29 West 39th St., New York City, has presented with admirable clearness the need for better classification and more adequate compensation of the engineers in the service of the Federal Government. The following recommendations made by the committee are as applicable to public health as to engineering:

1. Positions should be classified in accordance with the character of the duties to be performed and with the training and experience necessary for their performance, as indicated by a system of grading.

2. Within the salary limits fixed for each grade, there should be a system of advancement through the grade based upon experience gained in the position and upon proof of increase in the proficiency of the employee in performing the duties of the grade.

3. Promotions from grade to grade should depend upon the existence of a vacancy in the higher grade and proof that the employee is qualified to fill the vacancy.

4. The determination of adequate salary schedules should take into account and properly weigh the following considerations:

(a) The capital invested, both in money and in time, in obtaining the requisite fundamental training.

(b) The amount and character of experience and the degree of personal ability required.

(c) The relative value of the classes of work to be performed.

(d) The amount paid for similar work in private employment.

(e) The amount necessary to enable the employee to maintain a standard of living commensurate with the general standards of the community for positions of similar dignity and responsibility.

(f) The amount necessary to procure for and retain in the Government service a class of employees capable of conducting the business of the

Government with an efficiency and a spirit of initiative equal to that of private business.

5. In the interest of an adequate social policy, no position likely to be occupied by individuals of an age to assume family responsibilities should fail to pay an amount sufficient to permit the maintenance of the average family in reasonable decency and comfort.

6. In the interest of the employees as a whole and of the proper conduct of the work of the Government, a system should be established by which employees who fail to maintain satisfactory standards of service should be removed, transferred, demoted, or retired as may be equitable in the circumstances.

The definite scale of salaries suggested by the Engineering Council for Federal engineering employees ranges from a minimum to $1,620 for a junior assistant engineer to a minimum salary of $8,100 for a chief engineer, the time taken in passing from the first to the last grade being assumed to be 14 years. Since the training adequate for a competent public health official is longer and more arduous than that of the engineer it would be proper to fix a higher minimum rate for junior positions than that specified above. The report of the Engineering Council and the action of the British Society of Medical Officers of Health should serve as an inspiration to public health workers in this country, and particularly to the American Public Health Association, to take this matter up in a definite way and to make a serious effort to standardize the salaries of public health workers and to raise them to a level sufficient to insure the type of service which the community demands and deserves.

Governor Alfred E. Smith of New York state, in his inaugural address, delivered June 7, has well said:

"The state can make no more profitable expenditure than that wisely made in public health education and in advancing public health administration. It is essential for future progress that the careers open to physicians in the public health service should be made attractive and that the compensation of health officials of all kinds should be more nearly adequate to the service which they should be required to render to the public. In this way only can the best qualified men be attracted to the service and the best results for the state be attained."

C.-E. A. WINSLOW.

PRINCIPLES OF PREVENTION.

The experiment made jointly by the U. S. Public Health Service and the Bureau of Medicine and Surgery, Navy Department, during the pandemic of influenza, in an effort to determine the method of spread of that disease, gave results which furnish much food for thought. Acting upon the hypothesis that influenza is communicated from the sick to the well through transference of discharges from the throat and nose, the noses and throats of a large number of healthy, presumably non-immune, enlisted men of the Navy, were sprayed with fresh moist material from the throats and noses of influenza patients in all stages of the disease. The material was also swallowed and inoculated subcutaneously. Not one of the volunteers experimented upon developed influenza.

So far as we know this is the only instance where experiments on a large scale have been carried on in a disease of the respiratory type, using man as the subject of experimentation. Positive results were expected. That they were negative was disconcerting, but the theory that mouth and nose discharges carry dangerous and infective material was not disproved. On the contrary, negative results only brought us to a realization that there are many other, but little understood, epidemiological factors to be taken into consideration, apart from the mere transfer of infective discharges, which determine the occurrence either of a single case or many cases of a given disease. Certain physico-chemical phenomena are involved and these include the state of individual immunity, which varies from time to time; the varying aggressive power of the microorganism; symbiotic condition, etc. Be that as it may, the transfer of infectious material is necessary before disease can develop even in those who are otherwise ripe for infection.

The transfer of discharges from the mouth and nose may take place in many and devious ways; the material is often given off in minute particles which are invisible, and it is discharged frequently, unexpectedly, unknowingly and promiscuously, making it impossible for a health officer to erect effective barriers. In practice it would seem that in spite of efforts on the part of health authorities, diseases like measles, scarlet fever, tuberculosis and kindred affections, go onward through their endemic and epidemic cycles governed only by the laws of nature which man so far has been unable to determine. Certainly isolation, quarantine and disinfection applied to a community do not seem to have had much effect. Success in prevention must lie with the individual and it is, therefore, one of the most important duties of a health department to educate the public so that every person may be able to do all in his power to protect himself and his neighbor. Education must commence in the schools and results may be hoped for along these lines from the coming generation.

There are, however, some diseases in which epidemiological studies have pointed out methods of prevention that are certain in their results. Such barriers to the spread of disease may be immunologic barriers, Nature's method, or they may be artificial, devised by man. Where immunity is induced as in smallpox and vaccination, Nature's method of prevention is utilized; in diseases which are carried by insects and those spread through intestinal discharges, purely artificial methods are especially useful. With regard to the former it may be said that "No Anopheles mosquitoes—no malaria" and "No Stegomyia mosquitoes—no yellow fever" are slogans which have been proved repeatedly. Of diseases of the intestinal type, it may be said that well recognized preventive measures, logically applied, will reduce the amount of typhoid fever and other maladies of the group to a negligible quantity. In these so-called "filth" borne diseases, the ways in which infectious material is disseminated, are not so numerous or varied as in diseases of the respiratory type. Defecation is an act which is definitely limited as to time and place; the discharge is gross and visible. The health officer himself can establish the conditions under which it is to take place, thereby reducing to a minimum the danger of disseminating infection.

To sum up, it would seem from the standpoint of health department activities and expenditures, that the communicable diseases might be placed in two great groups; those the control of which depends mainly upon education and individual effort and those in which preventive measures depend mainly upon education and community effort. In either case education is the foundation upon which all preventive measures must be built.

BOOKS AND REPORTS
REVIEWED

Hygiene and Sanitation. *Seneca Egbert, A.M., M.D., Professor of Hygiene, University of Pennsylvania. Philadelphia and New York: Lea and Febiger. 1919. Pp. 554. Price $3.00.*

This is the seventh edition of an old standby. The last edition has been revised and much new material added, especially on sewage disposal, industrial hygiene, and military hygiene. It is difficult in these days of rapid progress, however, to revise a book on this subject without practically rewriting it. In this one there are many obvious and abrupt transitions from old ideas to new and the book is tinged throughout with obsolete theories. A section entitled "Diseases caused by impure air" seems out of place in a modern text book. Houseplumbing and disinfection are given more space than they are worth. There is no description of purification of water by liquid chlorine, nor of standard methods of analysis. The illustrations are occasionally antiquated and the references are absolutely not up to date. For instance, though many references are cited in the chapter on Sewage Disposal, no mention is made of Metcalf and Eddy's books, nor of Fuller's, and in the chapter on Industrial Hygiene, Price and Thompson are ignored. As a manual of general fundamental principles, this book is valuable, but for the person who desires information of an advanced character, it would seem to be too conservative.

JAMES A. TOBEY.

✠

The Health of the Teacher. *William Estabrook Chancellor, Chicago: Forbes & Company. Pp. 307. Price $1.25.*

In modern plannings by public health officers the health of the children stands as one of the most important features. Further than this, health education in which the children to a very considerable degree are to be the instructors of their parents is an important consideration in the public schools. The plan is a philosophical one to teach children the fundamental facts in health and hygiene in the same institutions and by the same methods whereby they are taught reading, writing,

grammar and geography. The value of such teaching is patent to every one who will bestow a moment's thought on the problems of the health administration of today. There has been lacking here, however, the preliminary training on the part of the teacher to fit her for her part in such a program.

Dr. Chancellor's volume comes in here to fill the gap, to teach the teacher, and to make it easy for her to instruct her scholars in the rudiments of health. The foundation principle is, of course, that the teacher of health should herself be healthy. This little book makes that practicable for her, for it tells how to keep in perfect health and at the highest point of efficiency. From cover to cover it is filled with cogent statements, and what it has to say is phrased in plain, unmistakable terms. "The body is a chemical laboratory whose output is life-and-death, force-and-pain, strength-and-weakness. It has come to pass that 98.5° registers the correct point for these chemical processes." "Human life is a flame as of gasses that burn into 'mind' at a temperature within one or two degrees of 98.5°; varying much from which the flame dies."

Hundreds of topics of interest are brought out for brief consideration, all of them of consequence in health education, among them the effect of race components, the difference in temperaments, the age factor, the two sexes, and in connection with these there is discussed a wide range of conditions and circumstances of greatest educational value.

Many excellent suggestions are made, some of which run counter to popular belief or fads. "Exercise is not the key to health," Dr. Chancellor writes. "It is not the most important of all hygienic prescriptions; it is far from a cure-all." He further asserts that there is no proper and adequate diet for all persons even if of one type. There are too many with a fixed dietetic idea bound to convert the world to it. Nine hours sleep for the woman teacher is an excellent prescription which could lessen the evils of our rushing, strenuous age. Sleep is not a uniform phenomenon and follows interesting laws of its own. All light should be screened from the room, even starlight, and plenty of fresh, outdoor air should be moving in it. Diet is made to include fresh air as well as drink and food.

Many facts are very neatly expressed. What do we know of chocolate? Here is Dr. Chancellor's reply: "The little borrower, mild chocolate comes with a gift of his own fat for the nerves, but he takes a loan of the future all the same and a side loan from the tissues, the so-called vital reserve." "Take three hundred baths a year," is a suggestion of consequence. "What is the problem of dress?" questions Dr. Chancellor, and he answers it by noting that since it is not possible to change the garments from hour to hour, it is well to wear light or medium underwear, medium weight outer clothing, with then a choice of four outer garments.

In shoes this author conforms to the best modern opinion, namely that the very high heel is an outrage, but on the other hand that the low, flat heel of the "conventional ladies' magazine article" is only for the few women whose feet have low arches. Care of the eyes, care of the ears, care of the voice and throat are other captions in the long list of plain and authoritative discussions that the volume has brought together. It is a book of sense and utility deserving of careful consideration.

R.

✦

Chlorination of Water. *Joseph Race, F.I.C., City Bacteriologist and Chemist, Ottawa, Canada, New York, 1918: John Wiley & Sons, Inc. Pp. 155 illustrated. $1.50 net.*

This small book gives an historical account of the use of chlorine for the disinfection of water, a practice which, during the last twenty years, has advanced from an academic to a practical stage, due largely to the efforts of Dr. A. C. Houston in England, and Mr. G. A. Johnson, Dr. Leal and the author in America.

The book discusses the chemistry of chlorine and those of its compounds which are used for treating water, and also the methods of application used in practice, an well as the sizes of doses required and their effects upon the various water bacteria.

Particularly important is the chapter on complaints which discusses the methods of overcoming the objectionable tastes and odors which are due to the improper application of the chemical. The chapter also discusses the effect of chlorine upon animal and plant life, and upon iron, lead and other pipes used to convey solutions of it or its compounds.

Separate chapters are devoted to bleach treatment, liquid chlorine, electrolytic chlorine, hypochlorites and chloramine, respectively. These chapters are comprehensive and very little of importance to the sanitarian and the water analyst has been omitted from them. All the devices for the application of bleach are described in sufficient detail for beginners, and the chapters contain many practical notes regarding the use of the various forms of the disinfectant. The author has had the wisdom not to discuss at length devices which have become obsolete, or which are subject to serious defects. In fact the whole book is written in a spirit of fair criticism.

Particularly important is the chapter on chloramine, a process first noticed by Rideal, but developed largely by the author who, in 1915, during a series of experiments on the relative germicidal action of hypochlorites, discovered that ammonium hypochlorite not only had ten times the germicidal velocity of other hypochlorites, but that it was very unstable and decomposed into chloramine. This latter compound was found to have a higher germicidal velocity than the equivalent amount of chlorine in the form of calcium hypochlorite. The author then discovered that the chlorine in chloramine was far more efficient than the same element in the form of calcium hypochlorite, or liquid chlorine. The chapter gives an account of the author's studies and experiences at Ottawa, and it may be stated in passing that equally good results have been obtained at Denver, Colorado and on Essopus Creek on the New York Water Supply. Much of the material in the book has appeared elsewhere, but the author has performed a useful service, not only in again recounting some of his own published experiences, but in bringing together in one volume valuable data scattered through technical and scientific publications, to which abundant references are given. A bibliography follows each chapter.

The tables and illustrations in the book are very valuable, and the appendix contains useful data for the convenience of the chemist in charge of chlorination plants. A few unimportant typographical errors have been noted by the reviewer.

The book is honest and thorough and should be in the library of every sanitarian, chemist and engineer who has to do with chlorinated water, which is now being supplied to between 40 and 50 millions of people in North America alone.

R. S. WESTON.

ASSOCIATION NEWS

HEALTH EMPLOYMENT BUREAU.

Help-wanted announcements will be carried free in this column until further notice. Copy goes to the printer on the fifteenth of each month. In answering keyed advertisements, please mail replies separately.

The Health Employment Bureau also sends lists of applicants to prospective employers without charge.

For a city in New England of 67,000 a health officer. Must be a medical man. Salary to the right man $3,500 to $4,500 to begin. Address R. E. T. 323, care of this JOURNAL.

Director for new Tuberculosis Division of Indiana State Board of Health. Salary $2,000, may be increased to $2,400 if efficiency is shown. Address N. H. J. 325, care of this JOURNAL.

Assistant Diagnostician for examination of diphtheria, sputum, Neisser, Widol, etc. City laboratory. Salary $1,500. Address H. E. B. 327, care of this JOURNAL.

Full-time health officer for small city in Connecticut. Salary $3,500 per annum. Applicant must be experienced and a hustler. Address State Department of Health, Hartford, Conn.

MEETING OF EXECUTIVE COMMITTEE

The Executive Committee, A. P. H. A., met in New York City on Thursday, December 4, 1919.

Dr. L. L. Lumsden reported as the chairman of a committee appointed to consider a plan for saving 250,000 lives during the next 5 years, the committee consisting of the chairman, Dr. Haven Emerson, Dr. W. A. Evans, Dr. Lee K. Frankel and Dr. M. P. Ravenel. The report outlined the advantages and possibilities of such a campaign and recommended that the work be undertaken. After discussion it was Voted: That the report of the committee be adopted and that the present temporary committee be continued for the purpose of conferring with other organizations. The committee is to select its own chairman and to report back to the Executive Committee of the Association.

With reference to changing the printer of the JOURNAL, is was Voted: That the matter of printing the JOURNAL be referred to the President and Secretary, with power to act.

President Rankin outlined a plan for a membership campaign to be conducted with the co-operation of state health officers, each state to be a unit with a quota of new members to fill. State officers in turn were to organize their local committees for the drive.

President Rankin announced the appointment of a committee to work with com-

mittees from the American Medical Association, and the Conference of State and Provincial Health Authorities, for the purpose of promoting the movement to co-ordinate and enlarge Federal health activities. The action of the President was approved by the Executive Committee.

It was voted: That Dr. Frankel, Dr. Rankin and Dr. Evans be appointed a committee to visit the American Red Cross and the National Tuberculosis Association with a view to arriving at a plan of co-operation with those agencies in connection with the organization of state health societies. This committee has the power to appoint an organizer of state societies.

Voted: That the Executive Committee approve of the principle of establishing health nursing branches in state and municipal health organizations.

Voted: That the President appoint a standing committee on constitution and by-laws.

Voted: That the President appoint a committee to take up with other child hygiene organizations the question of organizing a Child Hygiene Section in the A. P. H. A.

Voted: That the A. P. H. A. become a member of the National Information Bureau with the understanding that such membership involves no financial obligation.

The question of improving and standardizing programs was discussed. The Secretary was requested to prepare a program policy for consideration by the Committee.

REPORTS OF COMMITTEES

REPORT OF THE COMMITTEE ON UNIFORM ACCOUNTING FOR HEALTH DEPARTMENTS.

In reporting for this Committee, Ernst C. Meyer, Ph.D., made note of the fact that, owing to the absence of Haven Emerson, M.D., in Europe in 1918, he had been asked to succeed Dr. Emerson as Chairman. Two new members were appointed, Allen W. Freeman, M.D., State Health Officer of Ohio, and Walter H. Brown, M.D., Health Officer of Bridgeport, Conn.

After a statement with reference to the previous report, Dr. Meyer emphasized the importance of uniform accounting as the foundation of permanent success in public health work. The text of the report follows:

It is important to emphasize that uniform accounting alone can accomplish little unless it is accompanied by, and is an integral part of a complete scheme of uniform business procedure comprising the following fundamental steps.

1. General adoption of a standardized budget.

2. Embodiment in the appropriation act of the essential plan, lacking only the details of the standardized budget.

3. Keeping accounts in accordance with the standardized appropriation act and embodying in the accounts such additional detail of the standardized budget as may seem advisable.

4. Keeping of standardized records of work done.

5. Publication of appropriate data produced by the uniform system of accounts, and the uniform records of work done in standardized report form.

The last requirement is the most important. Without a uniform method of reporting much of the value of standardized budgets, appropriation accounts and records is lost. The possibilities of usefulness of a uniform and standardized system of business records are almost unlimited. Not only will such procedure greatly facilitate the defense of health appropriations and pave the way for larger appropriations, but it will also mean larger freedom of administrative action for the health officer. The legislative appropriating authority will be far more ready to grant funds on general terms than, as is customary at present, in minute detail, because the uniformity and completeness of the business methods sketched above provides the means for accurate control over all expenditures. That such greater freedom of action tends to accompany the improvement in business methods advocated is amply shown by the experiences of states and cities in which some form of locally standardized procedure has been put into operation.

As concrete steps looking towards the attainment of the goal set, your Committee submits the following recommendations for your approval:

1. That accounts covering payments for capital outlays as for building construction, equipment of all kinds, furniture, and other

22A—Am jr pub health 2123   1-21   BEA

more or less permanent properties, be kept distinct and separate from accounts covering payments for current expenses of operation and of maintenance.

2. That in publishing expenditures for lines of health work which also produce receipts through sales of products, as for example vaccines, serums, or issuance of licenses, etc., the grand total expenditures be published without previous deduction of the off-setting receipts. However, all such receipts should be so published as to indicate clearly what accounts they offset.

3. That accounts be so kept as to show clearly and separately the total expenditures for those activities which are considered by the best modern standards to be health work, and the total expenditures for activities which only indirectly or not at all affect public health, as, for example, collection of ashes, rubbish, garbage, inspection of weights and measures, of foods other than milk, of abatement of nuisances.

4. That there be published in the reports of public health officers statements of expenditures for public health done by other Government agencies, as, for example, school medical inspection and general school hygiene by educational authorities, food and drug inspection by agricultural and related bodies, industrial hygiene by industrial commissions.

5. That an advisory committee of twelve be appointed to finally formulate pronouncements upon the following fundamental matters:

1. Formulate a classification of functions for inclusion in a standard budget for health departments together with a definition of what each function includes.

2. Formulate a classification of objects of expenditures for inclusion in a standard budget for health departments.

3. Formulate a classification of activities of health departments in two classes: health work proper, and non- or near-health work.

4. Formulate a plan for the reporting on a uniform basis of physical statistics of work done.

6. That copies of the various classifications just referred to when finally adopted by the advisory committee of twelve be sent to health offices for incorporation in the business practice of their office, including budget making, drafting of appropriation acts, accounting, recording of physical statistics, and reporting.

7. That sample forms of loose leaf accounting sheets be printed and distributed to health officers who evince interest in them.

8. That the present committee, though not necessarily of course its present personnel, be continued under the broader name as a "Committee on Business Procedure" and under that title be charged with consideration of budget making, appropriating, accounting, record keeping, and reporting.

The report was presented to the Section of Public Health Administration and the section voted to approve it.

REPORT OF COMMITTEE ON RURAL HEALTH ADMINISTRATION.

Your committee wishes to make the following report and recommendations:

1. That the County be recognized as the logical unit for the development of local health departments for rural communities. We must strive to get a full-time county health officer in every county just as soon as possible, but we must recognize the necessity of making a beginning with a part-time man in certain counties. The department will gradually be developed by adding pubic health nurses and medical and sanitary inspectors, etc., as funds and public sentiment permit.

2. We recognize that it will be more desirable and easier in some states to develop the district health officer plan instead of the county plan. In the logical development of the district plan, however, we must aim to gradually reduce the size of the district until each district corresponds in area to one county. The final development of the district plan therefore leads to the county plan. With the full development of the county health departments, whether we start with the large district plan or with the county plan, it will become

necessary to have district health supervisors over a given number of counties which are placed in a district. The district supervisors are connected directly with the state department of health.

3. The state department of health shall have the right to determine the competency of candidates for the positions of full-time county health officers. The actual appointments of county health officers shall be made by the county commissioners or by some other proper county authority. The state health department shall be given the right of removal from office of any local health officer who refuses or neglects to perform his duties as prescribed by either state or local laws and regulations.

4. Within the limits of authority delegated by law to the state department of health, it shall have the right of approval, modification or rejection of the plan of the scope and character of the health work contemplated by the county health department before such plan is put in operation.

5. We endorse the application of the Federal aid principles to the development of local health departments.

G. F. RUEDIGER, Chairman.
W. S. RANKIN,
W. A. EVANS,
W. R. BELL,
F. W. SEARS.

This report was presented to the Section of Public Health Administration and the section voted to approve it.

REPORT OF THE COMMITTEE ON RELATION OF THE 1920 CENSUS TO VITAL STATISTICS*

The work of the Committee during the year has been in correspondence with various vital statisticians and with officials of the Federal statistical departments on matters coming within the purview of the Committee's work.

On April 11, 1919, a letter was sent to the Director of the Census outlining the ideas of the Committee and of its correspondents on topics or heads of information to be included on the schedule for the enumeration of the population. (It will be recalled that on March 18, 1918, the Committee wrote to the Director of the Census with regard to the inclusion of

*Presented to Section on Vital Statistics, American Public Health Association, at New Orleans, La., October 27-30, 1919.

certain items in Section 8 of the Bill enabling the 1920 census). In this most recent letter we asked what would be done in 1920 to determine (1) the number of natural families and the number of children born to and surviving in such families; (2) to enumerate the survivors of the war with Germany; (3) to improve the enumeration of children at the single ages under five years (4) to provide for interdecennial censuses. Suggestions to the Director of the Census were also made as to (5) that statistics of the population in "sanitary areas" of a selected number of cities, according to nativity, parentage, color, sex and broad age groups be provided; (6) that for certain States and cities, parent-nativity, country of origin, sex and age tables be shown; (7) that nativity, color, sex and age be shown in tabulations of the statistics of the institutional population (prisons, hospitals, homes for the aged, dependent and infirm, etc.); (8) that the classification of occupations used in compiling such statistics in 1910 be revised to meet the severe criticisms leveled against it by health workers, statisticians and others; (9) that statistics of "urban" and "rural" population as defined for mortality statistics purposes be tabulated to show nativity, color, sex and age and that the mortality and birth data be published to correspond with these population figures; (10) that tabulations for at least three consecutive calendar years, preferably 1919 to 1921, be made for:

10-(a) Births, in certain registration units, by nativity, color and age of the mother, and, if the data are in the opinion of the Census Bureau fairly reliable, according to the order of birth. It was also suggested that births be tabulated by age of the father in relation to age of the mother.

10-(b) Deaths, in certain registration units, for the Abridged International List titles, by color, sex and age.

10-(c) Infant mortality; that more subdivision of the age classes under one year of age be made.

Point (10) was: That 1900, 1910 and 1920 midyear estimates for nativity, color, sex and age be shown for the population of the Registration States as constituted in 1900, for 1910 and 1920 as constituted in 1910, and in 1920 for the Registration States of that year.

(11) That monographic reviews of the decade 1900-1919 be prepared for mortality from tuberculosis, cancer, malaria, typhoid fever,

pellagra, influenza and pneumonia, accidents, suicides and homicides. It was suggested that this be done by private students on invitation of the Bureau of the Census.

(12) That the International List of the Causes of Death be revised, and in such revision some place be made for the classification of accidental causes of death according to the nature of hazard obviously involved as (a) industrial hazard, (b) domestic hazard, (c) public liability hazard and (d) unknown hazard.

(13) That the life table series, with commutation columns, be continued for the decade 1910-1919 and for 1919-1921.

(14) That statistics of marriages for the leading States be collected to show marriages and remarriages according to previous conjugal condition, age and sex, perhaps color and nativity, of the contracting parties.

(15) That the Census Bureau initiate higher analysis of published population and vital statistical data after the manner of the work shown in Vol. I of the Census of Australia, 1911.

The reply of the Director of the Census to the several proposals was:

(1) *On statistics of natural families in 1920.*

"It does not seem practicable to include these inquiries in the population schedule for the fourth time, without some provision beforehand for the tabulation of the data immediately following the completion of the decennial census work. This would undoubtedly need Congressional action, and this could not be obtained now without seriously delaying the decennial census preparations. At a later date it may be possible, however, to secure authority for the tabulation and publication of the 1910 data as a part of the Bureau's regular work after the decennial census is out of the way, and in the event that an interdecennial census of population in 1925 should be authorized by Congress, the inquiries as to the natural family could be easily included in the schedule for population without seriously burdening the work of the enumerators."

(2) *Enumeration of survivors of the war with Germany*

"There is no provision of law for such an enumeration in 1920. Section 8 of the census bill was amended in the Senate to include an inquiry as to "whether or not a survivor of any war in which the United States has been engaged, and, if so, of what war" but this amendment was stricken out by the House and Senate conferees."

(3) *Increasing accuracy of the enumeration of children under five years of age*

"The instructions to enumerators in 1910 called for the age in completed years at last birthday and the question as to age, like other questions on the schedule, related to April 15, 1910, the census day. In the case of children not 2 years old, the enumerators were also instructed to give the age in completed months, expressed in twelfths, as 3/12, 7/12, 13/12, etc. This instruction was quite generally observed by the enumerators, although not in all cases, and it may be practicable to require in 1920 a similar return of age for all children under 5 years of age."

(4) *Censuses of the population at five calendar year intervals*

"The desirability of having a more frequent enumeration of population is recognized by the Census Bureau, and it is hoped, after the completion of the decennial census work, to secure the necessary legislation for a limited census of population in 1925, to be taken in conjunction with the census of agriculture provided for in Section 31 of the Fourteenth Census Act."

(5) *Population of "sanitary areas" in selected cities*

"At the census of 1910 eight of the largest cities of the country were divided with respect to wards according to 40- and 80-acre tracts and tabulations of their population according to sex, color, general nativity, parentage and age were made for each of these tracts, but the results were not published. In the work of the census of 1920, it is the purpose to adhere to the boundaries of these tracts, even though some of them may be further subdivided, and to make similar tabulations." These eight cities and the number of tracts in each case, are as follows:

City	Wards	1 Tracts
New York	64	708
Chicago	35	431
Philadelphia	47	272
St. Louis	28	178
Boston	25	126
Cleveland	26	131
Baltimore	24	142
Pittsburgh	27	160

1 Assembly districts

(7) *Enumeration of the institutional population*

"The provision in Section 8 of the Thirteenth Census Act (1910) for the enumeration of institutional population at the time of the decennial census was omitted from the Fourteenth Census Act (1920) and this work deferred until 1922. It can then be carried on under the terms of the permanent census act, in which there is provision in Section 7, as amended by the act of June 7, 1906, for the collection decennially of statistics relating to the defective, dependent, and delinquent classes."

(8) *Revision of classification of occupations*

The Director of the Census invited statisticians to submit their views on the changes thought necessary in the classification of occupation proposed for the 1920 census. He sent a copy of the outline of the classification to the Secretary of this Committee.

(9) *"Urban" and "rural" population of the United States*

Additional statistics on these subjects are planned for 1920.

(10a) *Birth statistics*

Data mentioned in the Committee's letter was already in preparation for 1917 when the letter was received.

(10b) *Deaths by color, sex and age for titles of Abridged International List*

Data are now available in manuscript form.

(11) *Monographic reviews of mortality from principal diseases during decade, 1910-1919*

Monographs would be prepared, it was hoped, as opportunity offered.

(13) *Life tables*

Additional life tables are in preparation.

(14) *Marriage and divorce statistics*

There is now no provision of law by which statistics of marriage and divorce can be collected.

Your Committee has felt that there is not sufficient interest shown by practical health workers in population and vital statistics, *before* such statistics are collected. Usually, too much is said *after* the census publications come out, and then to no good purpose. The health worker should be constantly alert to secure a hearing for plans covering the data he needs in the practical conduct of the affairs of the health department he represents. At present, health workers ought to urge that plans be made now for an inter-decennial enumeration of the population in 1925, and in the subjects then to be included on the schedule. They should stimulate private students to review the achievements of preventive medicine during the period included between the 1910 and 1920 censuses; they should see that local and State registrars tabulate their statistics with a wealth of detail which cannot be given in Federal reports. What, for instance, have health officials done to secure an enumeration of the natural family? There is entirely too much indifference on the part of health workers to the important subject of the decennial annual inventory of human resources.

JOHN EMERSON MONGER, M.D.,
Chairman.
WILLIAM H. GUILFOY, M.D.,
JAMES W. GLOVER,
WALTER F. WILLCOX,
WADE H. FROST, M.D.,
JOHN S. FULTON, M.D.,
WILLIAM H. DAVIS, M.D.,
EDWIN W. KOPF,
Corresponding Secretary.
CRESSY L. WILBUR, M.D.,
Honorary Member.

□

LIST OF NEW MEMBERS
PROPOSED FOR ELECTION TO THE
A. P. H. A.
FROM DECEMBER 21, 1919, TO JANUARY 12, 1920.

SPONSORS
and
THE NEW MEMBERS
Whom They Introduced
(States arranged in alphabetical order)

B. L. ARMS, M. D.............Jacksonville, Fla.
  W. T. LANIER, M. D.,
  City Health Officer,
  Miami, Fla.
M. F. HAYGOOD, M. D..............Atlanta, Ga.
  EDD R. ANTHONY, JR., M. D.,
  Commissioner of Health,
  Marietta, Ga.
MR. H. NORMAN OLD.............Camilla, Ga.
  MR. CHARLES O. STRUSE,
  Housing and Sanitation Officer,
  Philadelphia, Pa.
S. J. CRUMBINE, M. D. ....Topeka, Kan.
  MISS EDNA FLANAGAN,
  Public Health Nurse,
  Abilene, Kan.
MR. JOHN H. GREGORY........Baltimore, Md.
  MR. CLARENCE E. KEEFER,
  Baltimore, Md.
MR. A. W. HEDRICH.............Boston, Mass.
  MR. B. C. ROLOFF,
  Exec. Sec'y Ill. Social Hygiene League,
  Chicago, Ill.
PROF. W. T. SEDGWICK.....Cambridge, Mass.
  JOHN B. NELSON, B. S.,
  Assistant Bacteriologist, Public Service
  Laboratories,
  Lexington, Ky.
J. F. WINCHESTER, M. D.......Lawrence, Mass.
  E. C. SCHROEDER, M. D. V.,
  U. S. Exp. Station,
  Bethesda, Md.
B. E. ROBERTS, M. D. ....Springfield, Mass.
  ALAN GREGG, A. B., M. D.,
  Caixa Postal 49,
  Rio de Janeiro, Brazil.
MATTHIAS NICOLL, M. D. ....Albany, N. Y.
  JAMES S. WALTON, M. D.,
  Sanitary Supervisor,
  Amsterdam, N. Y.
V. A. MOORE, B. S., D. V. M., M. D.,.Ithaca, N. Y.
  J. G. WILLIS, B. S. A., D. V. M.,
  Albany, N. Y.

LEE K. FRANKEL, Ph.D. ....New York City.
  T. B. YANCEY, M. D.,
  Health Officer,
  Kinksport, Tenn.
VICTOR G. HEISER, M. D. ......New York City.
  EDWIN W. SCHULTZ, M. D.,
  Stanford Univ., Cal.
H. B. LARNER, S. B. ....Goldsboro, N. C.
  R. W. SPICER, M. D.,
  Goldsboro, N. C.
MR. H. W. STREEKER ....Cincinnati, Ohio.
  KATHRYN D. MILLER, A. B.,
  Markesan, Wis.
MISS WANDA PRZYLUSKA......Columbus, Ohio.
  LOLA G. YERKES, R. N., B. S.,
  State University of Ohio,
  Columbus, Ohio.
THOS. BUTLER, M. D. ....Bethlehem, Pa.
  EMILY M. DINAN, R. N.,
  Visiting Nurse for Red Cross,
  Bethlehem, Pa.
JOHN W. WRIGHT, M. D. ....Erie, Pa.
  A. G. CRANCH, M. D.,
  Lawrence Park, Erie, Pa.
P. A. VAN DER MEULEN, M. D., Philadelphia, Pa.
  J. BENNETT HILL, B. S., Ph.D.,
  Frankford, Philadelphia, Pa.
LAWRENCE P. GEER, B. S......Columbia, S. C.
  MR. JAMES HEALD,
  Health Department,
  Winston-Salem, N. C.
MR. T. J. ROBINSON.............Lexington, Va.
  MR. MARVIN E. GORE,
  Warm Springs, Va.
JOHN WEINZIRL, M. D. ....Seattle, Wash.
  HERMAN A. FELDER, M. S.,
  Laboratorian,
  South Bend, Ind.
MR. JOHN LE FEBER ....Milwaukee, Wis.
  PORTLAND-DAMASCUS MILK CO.,
  Portland, Ore.

OTHER APPLICATIONS RECEIVED.

THE KOLYNOS CO. ....New Haven, Conn
R. C. EATON, M. D. ....Chicago, Ill
WILLIAM E. BURNS, A. B., M. S., Johnson
  Hospital Laboratory ....Chanaute, Kan
L. B. GLOYNE, M. D., Health Officer,........
  ....Kansas City, Kan

C. G. Gillespie, Director, Bureau of Sanitary Engineering, Berkeley, Calif.

Isidor Greenwald, Chemist, New York City.

Miss Reba C. Haner, Instructor in Agr. Bacteriology, University of Wis. Home address, Sun Prairie, Wis.

Samuel R. Haythorn, Director William H. Singer Research Laboratory. Pittsburgh, Pa.

Jack J. Hinman, Jr., Bacteriologist and Chemist, Iowa State Board of Health, Iowa City, Iowa.

Gustave Horstman, M.D., City Pathologist, Mt. Vernon, N. Y.

Miss Ruth Frances Horel, Oklahoma Tuberculosis Association, Oklahoma City, Okla.

Albert C. Hunter, Bacteriologist, Bureau of Chemistry, Washington, D. C.

Charles A. Hunter, Bacteriologist, Pennsylvania State College, State College, Pa.

Walter Hilton Junkins, Board of Health, Westfield, Mass.

James Wieford Kellogg, Bacteriologist, State Laboratory of Hygiene, Raleigh, N. C.

Sarah R. Kelman, A.B., M.D., University Hospital, University City, Iowa. Address, Keokuk, Iowa.

Miss Sophie Johanna Dorothea Klein, M.D., A.B., New York, N. Y.

Simon Robert Klein, M.D., Ph.D., New York, N. Y.

Martin M. Klosen, Chemist for Board of Health, Shreveport, La.

Francis H. Lally, M.D., Milford, Mass.

Miss Mae E. Larkin, Bacteriologist, State Board of Health, Seattle, Wash.

Herbert B. Larner, Health Officer, Goldsboro, N. C.

Henry William Lehmkuhl, Technician, Rochester, N. Y.

Mrs. Florence M. Lytle, Laboratory Technician, U. S. Army Base Hospital, Fort Riley, Kan.

Miss Lois V. Lyon, Bacteriologist, State Public Health Laboratory, University, N. D.

Miss Orianna McDaniel, M.D., Bacteriologist, State Board of Health, Minneapolis, Minn.

Frank A. Mantel, City Chemist and Bacteriologist, Memphis, Tenn.

Leon S. Medalia, M.D., Research Bacteriologist, Boston, Mass.

Isador W. Mendelsohn, Chemist and Sanitary Engineer, North Dakota Public Health Laboratory, Grand Forks, N. D.

H. Lionel Meredith, Bacteriologist, Hagerstown, Md.

Abraham Louis Metz, M.D., City Chemist, New Orleans, La.

Paul, S. Nice, B.Sc., M.Sc., Chemist, Denver, Colo.

Miss Annetta Joanna Nicoll, City Bacteriologist, Topeka, Kan.

Howard Wilbert Norwell, Bacteriologist, Massachusetts Homeopathic Hospital, Boston, Mass.

Jay Bergen Ogden, M.D., Physician and Medical Chemist, Metropolitan Life Insurance Co., New York, N. Y.

George W. O'Grady, Director of Laboratories, Youngstown Hospital, Youngstown, Ohio.

Edward Blake Oliver, Fort William Outwork, Fort William, Ontario, Can.

Paul F. Orr, Research Bacteriologist, Harvard Medical School, Boston, Mass.

Francis LeJau Parker, Professor of Chemistry and Sanitation, College of the State of South Carolina, Charleston, S. C.

Miss Ruth Ogden Pierson, Director of Red Cross Laboratory, Chillicothe, Ohio.

C. R. Potteiger, Chemist and Bacteriologist, Camp Meade, Md.

S. T. Powell, Bacteriologist, Baltimore, Md.

J. Walter Ramsdell, Bacteriological Director, Detroit, Mich.

Hiram H. Roehm, Bacteriologist, Calumet, Mich.

Kakukaro T. Sasano, B.A., Serologist, Division of Health of the City of Cleveland, Lakewood, Ohio.

Charles William Schery, M.D., City Pathologist and Bacteriologist, St. Louis, Mo.

Warren Sylvester Shields, M. D., Bacteriologist, Boston, Mass.

Milton F. Stein, Sanitary Engineer, Chicago, Ill.

E. G. Stillman, M.D., Assistant in Rockefeller Institute Hospital, New York City.

Ernest H. Strong, Bacteriologist, Milwaukee, Wis.

H. A. Tarbell, M.D., Assistant Bacteriologist, Department of Health, Newark, N. J.

George Teasdale-Buckell, A.M., Bacteriologist, State Board of Health, Houghton, Mich.

William A. Walker, State Chemist and Director of State Board of Health Laboratories, Oklahoma City, Okla.

Herbert James Watson, Ph.D., State Bacteriologist of Delaware, Wilmington, Del.

Charles Weisman, Sanitary Chemist, U. S. Public Health Service, Pittsburgh, Pa.

Oscar C. West, Sanitary Inspector U. S. Army, Camp Stanley, Texas.

Miss Ruth West, Laboratory Assistant, H. R. Mulford Co., Glenolden, Pa.

Wilbur S. White, Chief Chemist, Health Department, Cleveland, Ohio.

Alpheus Grant Woodman, Food Expert, Mass. Inst. of Technology, Cambridge, Mass.

Zelma Zentmire, Chemist and Bacteriologist, State Board of Health Laboratories, Iowa City, Iowa.

Ernest Zueblin, M.D., Professor of Experimental Clinical Medicine, University of Maryland, Baltimore, Md.

VITAL STATISTICS SECTION.

J. W. Armstrong, Municipal Commissioner of Manitoba, Winnipeg, Manitoba, Can.

Gladden W. Baker, Statistician, New York State Department of Health, Albany, N. Y.

James P. Balfe, Director, Bureau of Vital Statistics, State Department of Health, Hartford, Conn.

Pansy V. Besom, 16 Moore St., Winthrop, Mass.

J. T. Biggerstaff, M.D., Wabash, Ind.

Arthur B. Bisbee, M.D., Medical Director, National Life Insurance Co., Montpelier, Vt.

John T. Black M.D., State Commissioner of Health, Hartford, Conn.

D. E. Breed, Executive Secretary, Texas Public Health Association, Austin, Texas.

Leverett Dale Bristol, M.D., State Health Commissioner, Augusta, Me.

R. H. Coats, Dominion Statistician, Ottawa, Ontario, Can.

Frank S. Drown, State Registrar of Vital Statistics, Boston, Mass.

Mrs. K. R. J. Edholm, Omaha, Neb.

R. W. Hall, M.D., Statistician, Mississippi State Board of Health, Jackson, Miss.

Robert R. Harkness, Epidemiologist and Statistician, American Social Hygiene Association, New York City.

Henry B. Hemenway, M.D., Chief, Division of Public Health Instruction, Illinois State Department of Public Health, Springfield, Ill.

Sheldon L. Howard, State Registrar of Vital Statistics, Springfield, Ill.

Frank L. B. Jenney, M.D., Medical Director, Federal Life Insurance Co., 168 North Michigan Ave., Springfield, Ill.

Ray Eckerson, Minister, Humeston, Iowa.

Mrs. Grace Engblad, Director, Public Health Nursing, Gulf Division, A.R.C., New Orleans, La.

Executive Secretary, Massachusetts Tuberculosis League, Little Bldg., Boston, Mass.

James P. Faulkner, Division of Tuberculosis, Georgia State Board of Health, Atlanta, Ga.

Charles Lee Ferguson, M.D., Cincinnati, Ohio.

Genevieve Fisher, Federal Agent for Vocational Education, Washington, D. C.

Miss Elizabeth G. Fox, Acting Director, Bureau Public Health Nursing, American Red Cross, Washington, D. C.

Harry N. Freilich, M.D., Chicago, Ill.

Anton P. Freund, M.D., Medical Inspector, Chicago, Ill.

Miss Vera Grannis, Wolcottville, Ind.

J. Victor Greenbaum, M.D., Cincinnati, Ohio.

Robert R. Harkness, Epidimiologist and Statistician, American Social Hygiene Association, New York City.

Joseph Herzstein, M.S., Executive Secretary, Rennselaer County Tubercular Association, Troy, N. Y.

Maurice B. Hexter, Sociological and Industrial Hygiene Work, Cincinnati, Ohio.

Percy Kendall Holmes, Director, Department of Hygiene and Physical Education, Delaware, Ohio.

Ruth Frances Horel, Oklahoma City, Okla.

L. F. Huffman, M.D., Acting Assistant Surgeon, U. S. P. H. Service, Lakewood, Ohio.

Miss Margaret Hughes, Director, Child Welfare Division, State Board of Health, Helena, Mont.

William S. Keller, M.D., Cincinnati, Ohio.

Sarah R. Kelman, A.B., M.D., Director of Keokuk Diagnosic Laboratory and Branch of State Board of Health, Iowa City, Iowa.

Philip G. Kitcher, Sociological work, Upper Darly, Pa.

Sophie Johanna Dorothea Klein, M.D., New York City.

Margaret P. Kuyk, M.D., Professor of Department of Physiology and Hygiene, Richmond College, Richmond, Va.

Cecelia A. Lemmer, Nursing Assistant, State Health Department, Hingham, Mass.

Julius Levy, M.D., Director, Ch. Hygiene, Newark Department of Health, Chief, State Bureau Child Hygiene New Jersey, Newark, N. J.

W. H. Lipman, M.D., Medical Director, Swift & Company, Chicago, Ill.

Rosa Lowe, Executive Secretary, Atlanta Anti-Tuberculosis Association, Atlanta, Ga.

Florence M. Lytle, Laboratory Technician, U. S. Army Base Hospital, Fort, Riley, Kan.

Mary E. Marshall, R.N., Associate Superintendent, Visiting Nurse Association, New Haven, Conn.

J. A. McGarvah, M.D., Industrial Physician and Surgeon, Lincoln Motor Company, Detroit, Mich.

S. Abraham Louis Metz, Vice-President, National Institute of Social Science, New Orleans, La.

A. L. Miller, M.D., City Health Officer, Marysville, Cal.

Harry H. Moore, Director of Education, Division of Venereal Diseases, U. S. P. H. S. Washington, D. C.

J. H. Morrison, A.M., M.D., Health Commissioner, Bartholomew County, Ind., Hope, Ind.

Gayle Graham Moseley, M.D., Medical Director, Workman's Compensation Department, Aetna Life Insurance Co., San Francisco, Calif.

Saidie Orr-Dunbar, Executive Secretary of Oregon Tuberculosis Association, Portland, Ore.

Claude L. Peake, Industrial Secretary, Y. M. C. A., Niagara Falls, N. Y.

Lawson Purdy, LL.D., New York City.

Alice Ravenhill, Professor of Home Economics, Utah Agricultural Collge, Logan, Utah.

Ben L. Reitman, M.D., Health Officer, Chicago, Ill.

Stanley M. Rinehart, M.D., Pittsburgh, Pa.

Abbie Roberts, Instructor Public Health Nursing, University of Cincinnati, Cincinnati, Ohio.

Elmo A. Robinson, Minister, Universalist Church, Plain City, Ohio.

Leopold M. Rohr, M.D., Medical Inspector, N. Y. City Departmentof Health, Jamaica, N. Y.

George Chevrus Ruhland, M.D., Commissioner of Health, Milwaukee, Wis.

Kakubaro T. Sasano, B.A., Serologist, Division of Health, Cleveland, Ohio.

Charles C. Sellers, Memphis, Tenn.

C. T. Sharpe, Medical Supervisor, Life Extension Institute, New York City.

George H. Shaw, Chief, Division of Housing and Sanitation, Philadelphia, Pa.

Louise Sistenstock, Assistant Director and Instructor, University Public Health Nursing District, Cleveland, Ohio.

James Franklin Smith, M.D., Member of Executive Commission of League for Conservation of Public Health, San Francisco, Calif.

Edith L. Soule, Supervisor, Public Health Nursing Association, Hyannis, Mass.

Ernest G. Stillman, M.D., Secretary, Hospital Social Service Association, New York City.

Seymour H. Stone, Secretary, Boston Association for Relief and Control of Tuberculosis, West Roxbury, Mass.

Simon Tannenbaum, M.D., Superintendent of Jewish Hospital, Philadelphia, Pa.

Sidney A. Teller, Pres. Director, Irene Kaufmann Settlement Health Center, Pittsburgh, Pa.

John Tombs, Executive Secretary, New Mexico Public Health Association, Albuquerque, N. M.

Mrs. E. P. Wanzer, Chairman Red Cross Seal Commission of South Dakota, Armour, S. D.

Miss Ruth West, Laboratory Assistant, H. R. Mulford Co., Glenolden, Pa.

Henry E. Whitford, M.D., Ozona, Fla.

Ralph Chester Williams, Medical Officer, U. S. Public Health Service, Chicago, Ill.

Miss P. Pauline Wisotski, Social Service Nurse, Department Store, Baltimore, Md

Ruth I. Workum, Executive secretary, Ohio Humane Society, Cincinnati, Ohio.

SANITARY ENGINEERING SECTION.

T. A. Boirradaile, City Chemist, Departmen of Health, Charleston, W. Va.

Alfred J. Bolus, Sanitary Inspector to th City of Weyburn, Saskatchewan, Can.

Eugene Thompson Cranch, City Sanitary Er gineer, Port Arthur, Texas.

John C. Diggs, Director, Water and Sewag Department, Indiana State Board o Health, Indianapolis, Ind.

V. M. Ehlers, State Sanitary Engineer, Austin, Texas.

O. L. Eltinge, Chicago, Ill.

Ellsworth L. Filby, State Sanitary Engineer, Columbia, S. C.

J. Warren Fortenbaugh, Assistant Engineer, State Department of Health, Harrisburg, Pa.

Wilfred D. Gerber, Sanitary Engineer, Chicago, Ill.

C. G. Gillespie, Sanitary Engineer, California State Department of Health, Sacramento, Calif.

M. S. Hasbrouck, Sanitary Engineer, New York City.

George R. Hazelhurst, State Sanitary Engineer, State Board of Health, Montgomery, Ala.

Jack J. Hinmon, Jr., Bacteriologist, State Board of Health, Iowa City, Iowa.

C. R. Hervey, Sanitary Supervisor, New York State Department of Health, New York City.

William C. Hirn, Assistant State Sanitary Engineer, Lansing, Mich.

Everett Judson, Civil Engineer, University of Chicago, Chicago, Ill.

Herbert B. Larner, Scientific Assistant, U. S. Public Health Service, Washington, D. C.

J. A. Le Prince, Senior Sanitary Engineer, U. S. Public Health Service, Memphis, Tenn.

E. H. Magoon, Sanitary Engineer, Atlwood, Ill.

Herbert P. Matte, Chief Sanitary Engineer, Illinois State Department of Health, Springfield, Ill.

Isador M. Mendelsohn, Chemist and Sanitary Engineer, North Dakota Public Health Laboratory, Grand Forks, N. D.

A. E. Miller, State Board of Health, Raleigh, N. C.

George T. Palmer, Epidemiologist, Dept. of Health, Detroit, Mich.

Lieut. C. R. Potteiger, Camp Meade, Md.

L. H. Salter, Dept. of. Health, Jefferson County, Ala., Birmingham, Ala.

Milton F. Stein, Sanitary Engineer, Chicago, Ill.

V. G. Stromquist, Sanitary Engineer, U. S. Public Health Service, Memphis, Tenn.

Nelson E. Young, Sanitary Hospital, Williamsport, Pa.

INDUSTRIAL HYGIENE SECTION.

Mrs. Isabelle W. Baker, R.N., Supervisor Dept. of Education, Hampden County Chapter, A. R. C., Springfield, Mass.

J. P. Bill, M.D., Instructor, Dept. Prev. Med., Harvard Medical School, Boston, Mass.

Arthur B. Bisbee, Medical Director, National Life Ins. Co., Montpelier, Vermont.

Miss Estella M. Bogardus, Exec. Secretary to the Yonker Committee Prevention of Tuberculosis, Yonkers, N. Y.

Alfred J. Bolus, Sanitary Inspector to the City of Weyburn, Saskatchewan, Can.

Miss Marguerite Bond, Bacteriologist and Chemist, Adams, Mass.

Emanuel S. Brodsky, M. D., Health Officer, Westport, Conn.

Arthur H. Burnett, Executive Secretary, Public Health Federation, Cincinnati, O.

Daniel Crosby, M.D., Health Officer, Oakland, Cal.

William J. Curry, M. D., Industrial Physician, Holyoke, Mass.

P. E. Davy, M.D., Rockefeller Foundation, Commission for the Prevention of Tuberculosis in France; 12 Rue Boissy d'Anglas, Paris, France.

Olive Z. De Lany, R.N., Dist. Supt. Victorian Order of Nurses for Canada, Montreal, Que.

J. H. Dunkley, Medical Director, Roanoke, Va.

Lyman M. Ellis, M.D., Supervising Surgeon, Kensington, Ill.

James P. Faulkner, Div. of Tuberculosis, Georgia State Board of Health, Atlanta, Ga.

Charles L. Ferguson, M.D., Industrial Physician and Surgeon, Cincinnati, O.

Harry N. Freilich, M.D., Chicago, Ill.

William Fugate, Secretary Board of Health, New Castle, Ind.

Miss Vera Grannis, Wolcottville, Ind.

Andrew R. Hackett, Surgeon, Detroit, Mich.

Raleigh P. Hall, County Health Commission, Chicago, Ill.

L. A. Hansen, Editor, "Life and Health," Takoma Park, D. C.

Virginia Hawkins, Health Director Duplan Silk Corporation, Hazleton, Pa.

Samuel R. Haythorn, M.D., Director of W. H. Senger Memorial Research Laboratory, Pittsburgh, Pa.

C. R. Hervey, Sanitary Supervisor, N. Y. State Dept. of Health, Oswego, N. Y.

Percy Kendall Holmes, M.D., Director Dept. Hygiene and Phys. Education, Ohio Wesleyan University, Delaware, Ohio.

Miss Margaret Hughes, Director Child Welfare Division, State Board of Health, Helena, Mont.

L. M. Jayne, M.D., La Salle, N. Y.

William D. Keller, M.D., Pres. Cincinnati Hygiene Society, Cincinnati, Ohio.

Sarah R. Kelman, M.D., State Board of Health, Keokuk, Iowa.

Philip G. Kitchin, Industrial Hygiene, Upper Dorly, Pa.

Sophie Johanna Dorothea Klein, M.D., New York City.

Margaret Kurjk, M.D., Professor of Departments of Physiology and Hygiene, Richmond College, Richmond, Va.

Cecelia A. Lemner, Nursing Asst. State Health Dept., Hingham, Mass.

Philip Leiboff, Industrial Hygiene, New York City.

Rosa Lowe, Exec. Secy. Atlanta Anti-Tuberculosis Assn., Atlanta, Ga.

Amy Grace Maher, Pres. Toledo Consumers' League, Toledo, Ohio.

Julius Irving Mandel, M.D., Plant Physician, Int. Lead Refining Co., East Chicago, Ind.

Mary E. Marshall, R.N. Associate Supt., Visiting Nurse Assn., New Haven, Conn.

Leon S. Medalia, M.D. Visiting Pathologist, Beth Israel, Boston, Mass.

Abraham Louis Metz., Vice-President National Institute of Social Science, New Orleans, La.

Carey P. McCord, Director of the Dept. of Industrial Medicine and Public Health, University of Cincinnati, Cincinnati, Ohio.

Emma McKay-Appèl, M.D., Medical Examiner, Board of Education, Chicago, Ill.

Gayle Graham Moseley, M.D., Medical Director, Workman's Compensation Department, Aetna Life Insurance Co., San Francisco, Cal.

Mozart Monae-Lesser, M.D., New York City.

Augustus S. Newmark, Industrial First Aid, New York City.

J. Anna Morris, M.D., Director of Dept. of Physical Education for Women, University of Minnesota, Minneapolis, Minn.

Saidie Orr-Dunbar, Exec. Secy. of Oregon Tuberculosis Assn., Portland, Ore.

Thomas Parran, Jr., Asst. Surgeon, U. S. Public Health Service, Washington, D. C.

Claude L. Peake, Industrial Secretary, Y. M. C. A., Niagara Falls, N. Y.

W. E. Rice, M.D., City Health Officer, Tuscola, Ill.

Rev. Elmo A. Robinson, Plain City, Ohio.

Emil C. Robitshek, Minneapolis, Minn.

Hiram H. Roehm, Bacteriologist, Calumet, Mich.

A. L. Rose, Akron, Ohio.

Charles C. Sellers, Memphis, Tenn.

C. T. Sharpe, Medical Supervisor, Industrial Department, Life Extension Institute, New York City.

Marvin D. Shie, M.D., Asst. Surgeon, U. S. P. H. S. (Reserve), Cleveland, Ohio.

Samuel A. Shoemaker, M.D., Blufftown, Ind.

Loyal A. Shoudy, M.D., Bethlehem, Pa.

James Fant Slaughter, M.D., Midnight, Miss.

Henry Field Smyth, M.D., Acting Director, Laboratory of Hygiene, Univ. of Pa., Pittsburgh, Pa.

Miss Edith L. Soule, Supervisor Public Health Nursing Association, Hyannis, Mass.

Frank E. Stewart, Sanitary Engineer, New York, N. Y.

Simon Tannebaum, M.D., Supt. of Jewish Hospital, Philadelphia, Pa.

Geo. H. Tefft, Secy. and Gen'l. Manager, Clay Products Assn., 913 Chamber of Commerce Bldg.

John Bain Thom, M.D., Trail, B. C., Can.

Peter W. Tomlinson, Wilmington, Del.

Roxana H. Vivian, Dept. of Hygiene, Wellesley College, Wellesley, Mass.

Mrs. E. P. Wanzer, Chairman Red Cross Sea Commission, Armour, S. D.

James S. Ward, Medical Director of th Life and Casualty Insurance Company o Tennessee, Nashville, Tenn.

Miss Ruth West, Laboratory Assistant, H. F Mulford Co., Glenolden, Pa.

Grover C. Weil, M.D., Surgeon, Mercy Ho: pital, Pittsburgh, Pa.

P. B. Williamson, M.D., Poplarville, Miss.

Nelson E. Young, Health Officer, William port, Pa.

FOOD AND DRUGS SECTION.

E. F. Benson, Commissioner of Agriculture, Olympia, Wash.

Ernest S. Bishop, M.D., New York City.

E. S. Bolton, Medical Health Officer, Brondon, Manitoba.

T. A. Borradaile, City Chemist, Health Department, Charleston, W. Va.

C. G. Craig, M.D., Rock Island, Ill.

George G. DeBord, Instructor in Chemistry at Lehigh Univ., Bethlehem, Pa.

Floyd O. Foster, Manager Detroit Branch, Walker-Gordon Laboratories, Detroit, Mich.

Isidor Greenwald, Physiologist and Chemist, New York City.

Dr. Gustave Horstman, Professor of Chemistry, Fordham University, Mount Vernon, N. Y.

Frederick W. Howe, Framingham, Mass.

Albert C. Hunter, Bacteriologist, Bureau of Chemistry, Washington, D. C.

Charles Axtell Hunter, Bacteriologist, Experiment Station, State College, Pa.

Thomas P. B. Jones, 1st Lt. San. Corps, Div. Food and Drugs, Langley Field, Va.

John A. Kappelman, M.D., Health Commissioner, Canton, Ohio.

Simon Robert Klein, M.D., Ph.D., Pathologist and Chemist, New York City.

Sophie Johanna Dorothea Klein, M.D., A.B., Chemist and Bacteriologist, The H. & J. Laboratories, New York City.

Harold C. Knopf, City Chemist, Cleveland, O.

Herbert B. Larner, S.B., Health Officer, Goldsboro, N. C.

Major Henry W. Lehmkuhl, The Normandie Courts, Rochester, N. Y.

Florence M. Lytle, Laboratory Technican, U. S. Army Base Hospital, Fort Riley, Kans.

Frank A. Mantel, City Chemist and Bacteriologist, Memphis, Tenn.

S. Abraham Metz, City Chemist, New Orleans, La.

J. H. Morrison, A.M., M.D., Health Com. of Bartholomew County, Hope, Ind.

John R. Murlin, Director Dept. of Vital Economics, Univ. of Rochester, Rochester, N. Y.

Jay Berger Ogden, M.D., Chemist, New York City.

Paul F. Orr, Bacteriologist, Dept. of Preventive Medicine, Harvard Medical School, Boston, Mass.

Dr. C. R. Potteiger, Capt. Q.M.C., Officer in charge of water and sewers, Camp Meade, Md.

Hiram H. Roehm, Dairy Bacteriologist, Calumet, Mich.

Edith L. Soule, Supervisor Public Health Nursing Association, Hyannis, Mass.

Louise Sitsenstock, Asst. Director and Instructor, Western Reserve University, Cleveland, Ohio.

William A. Turner, Asst. Professor of Chemistry, Wesleyan University, Middletown, Conn. Address, Housatonic, Mass.

Halpdan S. Tvedt, Sanitary Engineer, Pittsburgh, Pa.

William A. Walker, State Chemist and Director, State Board of Health, Oklahoma City, Okla.

P. B. Williamson, M.D., Poplarville, Miss.

John F. Winchester, B. Sc., Inspector of Slaughtering, Lawrence, Mass.

Ernest Zueblin, M.D., Cincinnati Tuberculosis Sanitarium, Pine Hill, Cincinnati, Ohio.

□

A. P. H. A.

The attention of members is called to the fact that election to the sections takes place only at annual meetings. Applications should be made well in advance of the meeting to the Section Chairman.

PUBLIC HEALTH NOTES

Signing up for Health.—The American Red Cross classes in home hygiene and care of the sick attack the problem of the health of the people from a psychological and popular angle. There are traveling nurses in different sections of the country engaged in the work of organizing such classes. The women in rural places have particular interest in the movement and continual calls are made upon the nurses by the dwellers in communities who have learned of the good work in other towns or villages in the neighborhood. The general plan is to send a nurse, free of charge, to a town, who teaches those who desire her instruction in the elements of cooking for the sick and for growing children; nursing in the home, so that the lack of a skilled attendant may be felt less keenly; to which are added classes in sanitary living, public nursing, first aid and the like. It is not infrequently that a community will be in search of a public health nurse and the A. R. C. is placing such women on demand. Where there is already established some social organization competent to care for the work, the Red Cross comes in to co-operate with it, to afford it any kind of help that is needed, but many places have not yet established such agencies, and here the Red Cross undertakes the whole burden of finding some trained woman and placing her at their disposal. Such a public nurse has her work standardized and systematized so that she may make a daily visit to each home where her services may be asked for, examine school children, give good advice with reference to subnormal children, consult with expectant mothers, teach young mothers how to care for their infants, and thus take a prominent part in the life of the community. Such service is most valuable, aside from its emergency phases in its ability to undertake and accomplish the very necessary education of the public that must underlie all effective work towards the improvement of the health of the people.

✦

Some Pressing Public Health Problems. —At a meeting of the Society of Medical Officers of Health held in London on October 17, Dr. George Reid outlined some pressing public health problems. Besides the solution of the housing problem which is so urgent, it is important to substitute water carriage sewerage systems in all urban areas for privies and pail closets. He also urges the immediate palliation of overcrowding in houses while building schemes are in progress; also the need for more adequate control of the "dirty tenant"; the proper care of the tubercular soldier and the provision of residential institutional treatment; a more adequate control of the milk supply and the control of tuberculosis among cows.—Public Health, Nov. 1919. (*M. P. H.*).

✦

The Tuberculosis Problem.—In a stirring address delivered before the New England Tuberculosis Conference, Dr. Allen K. Krause, Editor of the *American Review of Tuberculosis,* speaks of the method of attacking the tuberculosis problem. "I believe that the modus operandi of any progressive movement against tuberculosis must follow this line. We must get to the people, to all the individuals who constitute society. In the language of the street, 'We must put what we know about tuberculosis across.' For all but a negligible proportion of tuberculous infections, we know to a certainty the original vehicles of infection. These are human sputum and cow's milk. There is not the least doubt concerning the method of infection by cow's milk; it is by ingestion. The method of infection by human sputum may be debatable. It seems to me that to explain the bulk of early infection we must look somewhere else than in the home. Our highways are still besmeared with the offal of the throats and lungs of myriads. And I am equally certain that every child at play in these highways, day in and day out, is putting into its mouth the sputum of others, sputum that can and does contain every variety of pathogenic micro-organism to be found in the sputum of walking men And then we walk through all this sputum and bring it to our homes; and in the handling of our shoes even you and I have ample opportunity of acquiring others' sputum to our selves.

Behind and ahead and on all sides of spe

cific measures let us always project the larger vision—manifestly tuberculosis is due to anything and everything that adversely influences health.—(D. G.).

✛

Appeal for Health and Statistical Books. —A very serious loss to the scientific world was incurred through the recent destruction by fire of McCoy Hall at Johns Hopkins University, whereby the equipment and library of an important department of the School of Hygiene was lost. Just before the fire, Dr. Raymond Pearl had moved his department, that of Biometry and Vital Statistics, into the building, and with the departmental library, his own private library. These collections were almost unrivalled in their special fields. Dr. Pearl is therefore asking of his fellow scientists contributions from their stores of books and pamphlets to form the nucleus of the new collection of material on these subjects. What he is most in need of at present is in the line of vital statistics, population statistics, and statistical theory. State or federal census or health department reports will be especially welcomed, while aid in any of the allied departments will be greatly appreciated. Address Dr. Pearl at Johns Hopkins University, Baltimore, Md.—Special Notice, Public Affairs Information Service.

✛

Tuberculosis in New York City During 1918.—Although the campaign waged against tuberculosis has been a constant and aggressive one, and has resulted during the past twenty years in a reduction of the death rate from pulmonary tuberculosis from 239 per 100,000 population to 150, its importance as a major disease has not diminished. During 1918, out of 98,119 deaths that were reported, 10,097, or over 10 per cent, were due to tuberculosis. While only 3,332 deaths occurred from typhoid fever, measles, scarlet fever, diphtheria, whooping cough and cerebro spinal meningitis combined, there were 8,779 deaths from pulmonary tuberculosis alone. The actual number of cases of tuberculosis on record was less at the end of 1918, than at the beginning of 1917. This unusual phenomenon is supposed to be due to the drafting of 171,422 men into the service who belonged to the most susceptible age group, to the cessation of immigration due to the war, and to the migration of thousands of men and women to other communities where war industries had their allur-

ing attractions. It is interesting to note that only 25 percent of the cases on record left their homes to receive institutional treatment. The rest remained in the family circle and doubtless constituted a source of infection. It is urged that where patients receive treatment in hospitals and sanatoria, they should not be required to overwork or overexercise. The number of homeless and lost cases of tuberculosis was quite large, numbering 8,472. This problem is created primarily by the lodging house population.

At the beginning of 1918 there were 12,218 patients under the supervision of the nurses of the Board. These nurses not only gave the usual care, but they served as connecting links between the patients and all outside agencies, to help solve financial, social and other problems affecting the welfare of patients and their families. The clinics again proved to be exceptionally efficient forces in the actual treatment and care of tuberculous patients, and represent the main line of defense in the prevention and control of the disease in the community. Day camps for children which served as prevention were also continued. Here the children were fed and given proper medical and nursing care. The mothers were instructed in proper hygiene and sanitation of the home and also in matters pertaining to diet, foods, and feeding of children. It is believed that these day camps serve a very useful purpose. Louis I. Harris, M. D. Health Department. Monthly Bulletin, N. Y. C., October, 1919—(M. P. H.)

✛

Saccharin Not a Proper Substitute for Sugar.—During the shortage of sugar which exists at the present time, attempts are being made to educate the public to the use of saccharin. The *Weekly Bulletin* of the New York City Health Department for November 22, 1919, points out that saccharin is a coal tar product, and not a food; that saccharin has no food value, and if substituted in whole or in part for sugar in a food product, it reduces, lowers, and injuriously affects the quality and strength of such food product; and that saccharin is inferior to and cheaper than sugar. It is much more desirable to substitute molasses, syrups, or other sweetening food products, having distinct food value, during the temporary shortage of sugar, than to use a substitute which is not a food, and which has no food value. (M. P. H.)

Army Venereal Record.—The official records indicate a lower rate of incidence of venereal disease in the American Army in France than that in the United States. An effort was made, therefore, to obtain information that would account for the low rate reported, and answer certain questions that arise, such as the percentage of chaste men among soldiers, the average number of nonprotected venereal contacts to each venereal case, and what proportion of men have been exposed without prophylactic protection. Direct inquiries to the men were more or less completely answered by 13,648 soldiers in base sections, principally at Bordeaux, St. Nazaire, Brest and Tours. From the direct answers and compilations received by Ashburn in reply he concludes that antivenereal measures are effective in the following order: 1. Those that keep men chaste. 2. Those that diminish opportunity for sexual contact. 3. Those that diminish the dangers of contact, especially venereal prophylaxis. 4. Those that exact punishment. Thirty-four per cent of the 13,648 white men, taken at random in the Service of Supply, abstained from sexual intercourse while in France, and the most important factors in this were inherent in the men rather than in the antivenereal campaign —factors such as character, religion, love, loyalty and self-respect. Another third indulged so infrequently as to render their chances of disease quite small. The stand of the commanding officer in regard to this question, and his following by his subordinates, from generals down, almost deserves the name of public opinion in its effects on the conduct of the men. The influence of work, play and amusement supplied by the Red Cross, Y. M. C. A., Knights of Columbus, etc., was also a valuable factor.—P. M. Ashburn, Jour. A. M. A., Dec. 13, 1919, 1824. (D. G.)

✚

Typhoid Fever in the Army.—The author in a statistical discussion describes the conditions as to typhoid occurrence in the U. S. Army in the great war. The tables show a larger proportion of cases among the National Guard, due to the fact that they were mobilized in their own states and did not come directly under federal control. In 1917, the ratio in the entire army was 0.03 per thousand. In 1918 it was a little higher (0.05) owing to cases which developed in France.

The mortality was eight and seven-eighths times as high, and the morbidity four and one-eighth as high among the unvaccinated as among the vaccinated. It is evident from the tables that anti-typhoid vaccination, even when performed by an untrained personnel, gave a high degree of protection under conditions of hurried mobilization and warfare and reduced the rate not only below that of previous wars, but also below that found in civil life in some of the older states where sanitation is best carried out.—F. F. Russell, Jour. A. M. A., Dec. 20, 1919, 1863. (D. G.)

✚

Etiologic Studies in Tuberculosis.—In this experimental study an attempt was made to discover whether infection in guinea pigs at least followed exposure to what many have by inference referred to as sufficient exposure for infection of men. These experiments were carried on at Trudeau, N. Y., a health resort. The results obtained indicate that the danger of the dust in rooms in a health resort from telephone receivers, the danger from fairly well cleansed eating utensils, the danger from infected hands through hand-shaking or from knobs of doors and the danger of transmission by infected flies (at least in guinea pigs) have not yet been conclusively proved. On the other hand the danger of transmission of tubercle bacilli by kissing or through eating utensils to a second person has been borne out. —L. Brown, S. A. Petroff, G. Pasquera, Jour. A. M. A., Nov. 22, 1919, 1576. (D. G.)

✚

The Larger Field in Tuberculosis.—Once in a great while I think I have learned a new fact; and then with full force there surges the query, What is its place in the larger field, in the conquest of consumption? The conquest of consumption—a subject that engages much of my thoughts. And whenever I brood over it, after all the fringes have been cut away, as the matter seems to take shape and stand out in the fog, I always find myself thinking in terms like these: If I had my way, if I could so order it, I should call to me my best and most sympathetic students. And I should say, Here are the facts, the premises. We have found them out here; but, confined here, they are useless. Go now out into the world and lay them before the people. Go not as Republicans or Democrats, not as individualists or communists, not as scientists or physicians. Go as men with a theme to teach and preach. Go with only one idea, and let this idea be the persuasion. Point out the things that man must do to achieve freedom from disease; and in this demonstration let nothing deter or divert you. Follow the trail wherever it may lead; and be not fearful of the consequences. You have only one responsibility, and this is the achievement of better health for man, and in this, the holiest, most unselfish and most blessed cause that a human being can enlist in, you need suffer no misgiving concerning anything else that may occur in or because of the process of achievement.—A. K. Krause, *Amer. Rev. of Tuber.*, Nov. 1919, 513. (*D. G.*)

Ventilation of Motion Picture Theatres.— As the result of an investigation of the ventilation of motion picture theatres in Birmingham, England, the author has reached conclusions and has made some definite recommendations which are worthy of careful consideration:

(1) The existing means of ventilation in a considerable number of cinematograph exhibitions is insufficient and it is impossible adequately to ventilate buildings of this type by ducts in the roof unprovided with fans. It is only by the employment of fans that anything approaching adequate ventilation can be secured.

(2) Better ventilation could be secured in the majority of cinematograph exhibitions with the existing plant working regularly and efficiently. Interference with the fresh air inlets and failure to keep the ducts and fans clean contribute to the unsatisfactory results obtained.

(3) The area of the fresh air inlets is inadequate in many cases, and there is a tendency to close these openings.

(4) More satisfactory arrangements could be made for heating of fresh air supplied and prevention of draughts arising from the fresh air inlets by placing the radiators in front or under these openings.

(5) As regards lighting, there does not appear to be any objection to the provision of windows, provided they are properly screened.

Recommendations.

(1) That such a standard of ventilation be prescribed for the cinematograph exhibitons in the city that the ratio of carbonic acid in the air at about the breathing level should not rise beyond 20 volumes per 10,000 of air

(2) That the space allowed per person should be fixed at a minimum of 120 cubic feet.

(3) That efficient exhaust fans should be kept continuously at work during the programme.

(4) That any defects in the fans or other means of ventilation should be reported immediately to the managers, and a book provided in which a record is kept, stating the nature of the defect when it was discovered, and steps taken to have the necessary repairs effected. This record to be available for inspection by the licensing authority on application for the renewal of the license.

(5) That all fans be tested either before or immediately after being placed in position, in order to ascertain their efficiency for the work they are required to do.

(6) That an automatic indicator, such as a colored light, be fixed in a prominent position in the building indicating where the fans are working.

(7) That adequate inlet openings be provided and kept freely open in such situations as will permit of uniform distribution of fresh air, and that all means of regulating the size of these openings or of closing them be removed.

(8) That in cold weather the incoming air should be heated, otherwise unbearable draughts will be experienced.

(9) That the provision of windows and the position of entrance and exit doors be considered in relation to the flushing of the building with fresh air during intervals in the performance and during cleaning operations. —W. H. Davison, *Medical Officer*, Aug. 2, 1919, p. 39. (*D. G.*)

✦

Causes of Blindness.—The National Committee for the Prevention of Blindness has tabulated the statistics of schools and day classes for the blind in its *News Letter* for October, 1919. Among these out of a total of 3,847, 879 or 22.8 per cent were caused by ophthalmia neonatorum. Some of the other causes of blindness in the above total are: Blind from accident, 304; progressive nearsightedness, 80; trachoma, 53; interstitial keratitis, 178; optic nerve atrophy, 394; congenital cataract, 411, and other congenital causes, 556. (*D. G.*)

Typhoid Fever in Baltimore.—This subject has been considered by William T. Howard, Assistant Commissioner of Health of Baltimore, who presents in the *Municipal Journal* of Baltimore an article which is useful in showing how morbidity and mortality reports may indicate the health needs of the community.

There are many problems concerned in the study of the spread of typhoid fever. The problem of rural and urban typhoid present a number of difficulties. For a while sanitarians assumed that by instituting pure water supplies, guarding milk supplies, establishing efficient sewage disposal systems, and controlling the breeding of flies, that urban typhoid would be easily controlled. But rarely, if ever, has a city become completely typhoid-less in consequence of these sanitary measures. "Residual" typhoid usually occurs, accounted for partly by typhoid carriers. A considerable number of cases is due to direct contact and a variable number is imported, especially into seaport towns and medical centres. The amount of typhoid in the extra-urban zone into which numbers of the city population go, will, of course, influence the typhoid rate of that city. In considering these statistics the number of cases infected within the city should be the standard rather than the number of cases treated and dying there.

For many years and until 1912, when the modern sanitary imrovements were first utilized there, Baltimore had a very high mortality rate. Between 1871 and 1912 the curve of the typhoid death rate was a declining one, falling from 99 to 23.87 per hundred thousand inhabitants. During the latter part of this period there was also a considerable drop in the rate in the community of rural Maryland, frequented by Baltimoreans. Since 1914 the drop in the morbidity rate and in the mortality from typhoid fever in Baltimore has been sharp and continual, until in 1918 the mortality reached the low figure of 12.2 per hundred thousand. The goal will not be reached, however, until a further large decrease has been achieved. The fall in the last six years is to be attributed largely to improvements in the water and milk supplies, elimination of privies and well contamination from this source, and the curbing of the breeding of flies. For a number of years, at least,

typhoid fever in Baltimore has been pre-eminently a summer and autumn malady.

In 1916, Dr. Howard started to investigate the cases of typhoid fever in the city. The results of his investigations for the years 1917 and 18 are of interest:

Total number of cases, 846; infected outside the city, 195 or 23.5 per cent; infected from recent cases, 60 or 7.2 per cent; infected from old cases, 39 or 4.33 per cent; from milk, 43 or 5.8 per cent; secondary cases in the same person, 8 or 0.93 per cent; laboratory infection, 1 or .0.12 per cent. In this way the analysis of the source of infection was determined in 346 or 41 per cent of the total number of cases, leaving somewhat less than 60 per cent to be explained by other infections, such as water, flies, etc.

Up to July 1, 1919, there were reported 101 cases against 81 for the first six months of 1918. The data of these two periods, however, cannot be fairly compared, without separating the cases of 1919 into classes, those occurring in the old city, and those in the territory annexed, January 1, 1919. When this is done it is found that in the old twenty-four wards there were only 66 cases for 1919 against 81 for 1918, an actual reduction of 19 per cent. The morbidity for the same period for the old city was 21.49 per annum for 1919 against 27.01 for 1918, while for the annex during the first six months of 1919 the morbidity was at the rate of 102.5, more than five times greater than in the original twenty-four wards. The mortalities show the same diversity, 4.95 in 1919 against 6.33 in 1918 in the old city while the mortality in the annex for the first six months of 1919 was at the rate of 22.77 per annum. On account of the very high incidence in the annex the figures for the whole city for the first six months of 1919 show a higher rate than for the city in 1918.

The Baltimore authorities propose to bring the new territory up to the standard of the old city, furnishing it a supply of pure water and abandoning as soon as possible the use of wells. The proper treatment of household wastes is the second problem, while for a fundamental principle it is clearly indicated that the health department must push in all practical ways the education of the physicians and people in typhoid prophylaxis while at home and abroad.

STATE HEALTH NOTES—GENERAL

United States.—In its note of thanks to publishers, the U. S. Public Health Service through Rupert Blue, Surgeon General, the statement is made that during the last twenty years it has been possible to reduce the general death rate in the United States from 17.6 to 14.2 This represents a truly enormous saving of life. Had the condition of twenty years ago prevailed during the year just passed some 350,000 more persons would have died than actually did die. By dissemination of health educational matter the newspapers must be given credit for very material aid in this substantial achievement.

The U. S. Public Health Service has taken hold in earnest of the question of cancer, a field in which the American Society for the Control of Cancer has been at work for some years. The Service is now in active co-operation with the Society and for the "Keep Well Series, No. 6," has issued a booklet, "Cancer: Facts Which Every Adult Should Know." This is probably the first instance in which a national governmental department has entered into educational work in this line. The little pamphlet, which is to be had free on application to the U. S. P. H. S., Washington, D. C., goes into the subject in common sense fashion. The importance of very early treatment is emphasized and simple suggestions are made with reference to some of the danger signals. "Three kinds of worry" are disposed of by statements that cancer is not contagious, so far as is known, that it is practically not inherited and that it is not a blood disease. A chapter warns the reader that there is no medicine known that will cure cancer, so that advertised "cancer cures" should be avoided, since they must be "fakes." Examination by a competent doctor whenever one of two or three kinds of symptoms persist, is the safe rule, while the doctor must on his part make a thorough examination when these suspicious symptoms appear.

The Children's Bureau of the U. S. Department of Labor has appointed a permanent committee to formulate physical standards for the use of physicians who are to examine working children. The committee is the result of child welfare conferences held in Washington and other cities a few months ago. These conferences agreed upon certain minimum standards for children in employ-ment, which are in effect, that a child shall not be allowed to go to work until he has had a physical examination by a school physician or other medical officer especially appointed for the purpose by the agency charged with the enforcement of the law, and has been found to be of normal development for a child of his age and physically fit for the work at which he is to be employed. Periodical physical examinations for all working children were also recommended. The committee that has just been appointed will determine the standards of normal development, physical fitness and health for boys and girls of specified ages:

The committee is composed of :

Emma M. Appel, M.D., Employment Certificate Department, Chicago Board of Education.

S. Josephine Baker, M.D., Chief, Bureau of Child Hygiene, Department of Health, New York City.

George P. Barth, M.D., Director of Hygiene, City Health Department, Milwaukee, Wis.

C. Ward Crampton, M.D., Dean, Normal School of Physical Education, Battle Creek, Mich.

D. L. Edsall, M.D., Dean, Harvard Medical School, Boston, Mass.

George W. Goler, M.D., Health Officer, Rochester, N. Y.

Harry Linenthal, M.D., Director of Industrial Clinic, Massachusetts General Hospital, Boston, Mass.

Anna E. Rude, M.D., Director, Division of Hygiene, U. S. Children's Bureau.

Thomas D. Wood, M.D., Chairman on Health Problems and Education, Columbia University, New York City.

✛

California.—Under the caption "Invest in Health," Alameda County, Calif., describes its recently established health center. The present arrangements are acknowledged to be but temporary, but it has an option on a site that is accessible to all parts of the country, plans for the building and a campaign for funds. Towards its maintenance the Board of Supervisors of Alameda County has appropriated $23,000 for the clinics of the year.

In the organization a large number of factors are interested and its Board of Governors is composed of representatives from 4 health departments, 10 hospitals and dispensaries, 10 relief organizations, 2 educational institutions, 4 public school systems, 3 chambers of commerce, 6 public welfare organizations, 2 probation boards, 2 labor organizations, 1 bureau of occupations and the 4 county associations, medical, dental, nurses' and psychopathic; truly a body representative of many phases of the county public work.

Two excellent groups of statements have been set forth by the local committee, which define the health center and tell the reasons why it should be supported by the community. They are here presented for the benefit of other communities that may have similar organizations in prospect.

The definition of a Health Center is this:

It is an institution which co-ordinates the Public Health work of the community in a centrally-located building, available to every man, woman and child.

It conducts clinics—surgical, medical and dental—with the aim of making hospital care unnecessary.

It provides health instruction in personal hygiene to both school children and adults by means of popular lectures, lantern slides and distribution of literature.

It offers instruction in maternity and child-welfare, thus reducing the infant mortality.

It serves as a clearing house for all Public Health information, thus affecting a closer co-operation among hospitals.

It divides the community into health districts, each with a definite health organization which can instantly be mobilized in case of a threatened epidemic.

It prevents overlapping, duplication and waste because it co-ordinates all health and relief organizations.

The ten reasons why every community should establish and support a health center are:

1. It promotes community health. Your own safety depends upon healthful surroundings.

2. It reduces loss of income caused by sickness. Earning power rests upon health.

3. It decreases infant mortality.

4. It fosters health education. One school child out of two is defective; three out of four have defective teeth.

5. It reduces labor turn-over—makes fewer hands to train.

6. It mobilizes the forces of public health and welfare.

7. It increases wealth. A healthy community is a good banking community.

8. It prevents epidemics.

9. It protects the home. A healthy home produces a more efficient worker, a more contented citizen.

10. Public health is purchasable. A community to a large extent can determine its own death rate.

This Public Health Center is under the directorship of Richard A. Bolt, M.D.; it is caring for a couple of thousand cases a month at its Health Center, No. 1; it has been made the out-patient department of the new County Hospital and it acts through its Division of Tuberculosis as the clearing house for the Arroyo Sanatorium.

✠

Colorado.—The Denver Anti-Tuberculosis Society has issued in a letter to the New York Department of Health a warning to those afflicted with tuberculosis that should have the widest circulation, especially among those of slender means who think of seeking the state of Colorado on account of its climate. The Society states that each year several hundred tuberculous persons without funds come to Denver, hoping to improve their health. Since Colorado has no state hospital for this class of patients and the city of Denver has merely 35 beds at the county hospital for tuberculous residents, the accommodations for those who came from outside are limited to a few free private sanatoria, and these are always so overtaxed that admittance is a long and difficult matter.

Thus it is that the tuberculous poor who migrate to Denver find no place where they can be cared for, and they are forced to look for light work in order to maintain themselves; but the demand for such work is far in excess of the supply. Driven to any work they can get, they rapidly grow worse and usually soon die. They die for the lack of proper rest, food, fresh air and medical attention:—the essentials of treatment which many of them could have had at home.

A communication such as this makes clear the necessity of pushing various state and county tuberculosis programs with greater rapidity, for if care were available to all, its is not likely that many would attempt the long trip away from their home, family and friends.

Florida.—There are about 6,500 school teachers in the state and to them the State Board of Health has given a series of six lessons in health. These are to be passed on in turn to the school children, of whom there are about 325,000. Thus the authorities hope to establish the foundation for wide-spread public health education. A campaign is under way for county health boards and for eradication of malaria. Another campaign is among the citizens, to persuade them to see that all members of the family subject themselves to a thorough medical examination at least once in two years.

The work of the ambulatory clinic in Florida has been extended and is important. It has just completed a round in one of the most remote rural districts of the state. Among sawmills and turpentine camps more than 200 active syphilitics were treated and restored to a salary-drawing status. About 50 negroes, who were absolute objects of charity, are now doing their daily work and drawing pay. The next matter laid out for the clinic is at the State Penitentiary at Raiford, where it is said that 90 per cent of the convicts show positive Wassermanns. These men will be turned over to the State Road Department for labor, and it is proposed to have them put into good shape.

✛

Illinois.—The prophesy that the influenza epidemic would be responsible for an increase in deaths from all causes seems to be borne out by the statement in the November 8th Bulletin of the Chicago School of Sanitary Instruction, which states:

"Comparing totals of both cases and deaths from all causes with those for October of last year, there is every reason for satisfaction and thankfulness as to general health conditions. This applies, as stated, only to the general totals. The detailed figures for the month outside of two diseases, influenza and pneumonia, show increases rather than decreases over those of the corresponding month of last year. This means, of course, that eliminating the epidemic conditions for the month of October of last year, October of this year has been rather above the normal as to both the morbidity and mortality status." —(*M. T.*)

✛

Indiana.—The Tuberculosis Division of the Indiana State Board of Health was in action the first week in January. The efforts of this division will for the first year be entirely upon one point of the many which are to be attacked in order to prevent the white plague. The Division will be supplied with an extensive special exhibit and with a motor truck having a panel body and with an enclosed front for winter use. This will carry the exhibit and the personnel of the force—four in number—about the country. This outfit will conduct an intensive campaign based on the fact that 80 per cent of tuberculosis is acquired in childhood.

✛

Kansas.—The Kansas Tuberculosis Association during 1920 will organize local associations in every county where it meets any response whatever from local enthusiasts. Dr. Seth L. Cox is the medical director or field organizer in charge of this work. During the year 1919 the association employed eight district nurses, who have done a great variety of work including school nursing, district nursing, making addresses to clubs and other organizations, and promoting the work of the Modern Health Crusade.

✛

Maine.—Five free clinics for persons who are unable to pay for treatment but are suffering from venereal disease are already established in Maine. Two more are nearly ready to be opened and several more are in prospect, according to Dr. H. E. Hitchcock, director of the Division of Venereal Diseases of the State Department of Health. The clinics which are already opened are the Augusta Health Center, Dr. G. A. Coombs; Mason Dispensary, Portland, Dr. G. A. Pudor; Eastern Maine General Hospital, Bangor, Dr. H. J. Hunt; Bath Health Center, Dr. L. T. Snipe; Dr. Miner's Hospital, Calais, Dr. W. T. Miner. Rockland and Waterville are two cities where a clinic of this type will soon be in operation.

Physicians are very generally awaking to the value of the police powers of the Health Department in suppressing the use of the so called patent or proprietary remedies. Also in some communities, splendid success is being attained where police and health board work is combined and free treatment offered.

One of the difficulties that have been encountered by the State Health Commissioner, L. D. Bristol, M.D., in the work of the registration of babies lies in the fact that parents delay for weeks sometimes to choose a name for the baby. After reasonable delay, the report is sent in and often reaches Augusta without the name which renders the record useless. Then of course it must be sent back to the clerk or doctor from whom it came. Parents are urged to facilitate in every way the efforts of the Division of Vital Statistics to preserve such valuable records concerning their children.

To show the importance of registration the Maine State Board of Health gives the following advantages which result from registration:

It will enable the baby later to prove:
His age for school purposes.
His age for employment purposes.
His right to marry.
His right to vote.
His right to hold public office.
His right to inherit property.

✛

Massachusetts—In his inaugural address Governor Calvin Coolidge set forth some plain principles of public health, emphasizing the fact that unsound moral, social and economic doctrines have no place in the healthy body. Here are some of his ideas on the conservation of Public Health.

"Along with economy of resources should go conservation of the public health. The physical well-being of a people is the foundation for all advancement. Lack of bodily vigor is the beginning of a state's decadence in all things. With a people in a sound physical condition all things are possible. Great progress has been made in medical science and skill, and relief has been found from many of the terrors of disease. But too little attention has been given to full bodily development, which after all is not a matter of accident, of heredity or environment, but of intelligent training. This work should be attacked with great vigor in all our schools. We cannot breed a race of weaklings and hope to survive in any of the world competitions.

"It has, besides, a moral aspect. The unsound social and economic theories which deluge the earth from time to time are not the progeny of stalwart men and women. Sound bodies do not breed that kind of unsound doctrines. Along with a vigorous

training for physical development should go a teaching to think healthful thoughts. For after all it must be remembered that 'as a man thinketh in his heart so is he.'

"For some years Massachusetts has been committed to the policy of aiding children by assisting the mother to care for them. This has proved to be a wise and beneficial policy. Institutional and family care have much to commend them, but no mother should be parted from her children on account of poverty alone. This policy may well be extended in its scope to the giving of aid, nursing and medical care to needy expectatnt mothers. Motherhood should be honored, childhood protected. I earnestly recommend the extension of this relief through the same or like agencies as now administer mothers' aid. In our desire to assist those who come from other shores we must not neglect the native born. Coming into the royal estate of every American, he should have a royal welcome. It was the wise men who bore gifts. A wise commonwealth will not be neglectful of the days of nativity."

✛

Minnesota.—In this state the State Teachers' Association has taken an important action with reference to public health in the adoption of a formal resolution, the text of which follows:

"We recommend that each town and city school system organize a department of hygiene that the health and strength of the children of the State may be developed and conserved. Moreover, we desire that such Health Instructions given by the teacher shall be motivated in such a way as to function in the formation of fundamental health habits; and that the children of the State may the better protect themselves against infectious diseases. We further recommend that rural schools organize committees of hygiene as soon as possible in co-operation with Physicians of the vicinity."

The Association recognizes and commends the work of the Junior Red Cross and that of the Missouri Tuberculosis Association and requests the co-operation of all teachers with the latter organization in the Modern Health Crusade.

✛

New Mexico.—Reports of an alleged epidemic of chickenpox in Sierra County were investigated by Dr. G. S. Luckett, Chief of the Division of Preventable Diseases, and it was found that mild smallpox has been prevalent for several months without being recognized. Quarantine and vaccination are giving the health officer the upper hand over the outbreak.

The State law requires the vaccination of every child of school age against smallpox. In spite of many handicaps this work is being well carried out in general. Some county health officers have had to travel a hundred miles in their own counties to reach outlying schools.

An amendment to the health law is to be introduced at the coming special session of the Legislature which will permit every county and city to levy sufficient funds to support adequate local health administration. This will permit full-time county units in many parts of the State. In fact, several counties are considering such organizations already.

On January 5 the first free venereal disease clinic for the State was opened at Santa Fè. Three local physicians, Drs. J. A. Massie, R. O. Brown and E. W. Fiske, are giving their services free. Rooms have been furnished by the City Council in the City Hall. The city health officer of Deming, Dr. S. D. Swope, reports that the County Medical Society has agreed to support a free venereal disease clinic for that town. Operations will begin in the near future.

Miss A. Metzger of Santa Fé has been assigned to the local Red Cross Chapter for duty under the city and county health department as public health nurse. Miss Metzger has just completed a course of training for her new duties, after spending a year of war service in the embarkation hospital at Liverpool.

✛

New York City.—The anti-tuberculosis work in the city, which, for seventeen years, has been thoroughly and energetically carried on by the Committee on the Prevention of Tuberculosis of the Charity Organization Society, has been taken over by a new and larger corporation, the New York Tuberculosis Association, Inc. All the members of the old committee, including such prominent workers in the tuberculosis field as Dr. Hermann M. Biggs, State Commissioner of Health; Dr. Royal S. Copeland, Health Commissioner of New York City; Mr. Lee K. Frankel, Dr. S. S. Goldwater, Mr. Thomas W. Lamont, Dr. S. A. Knopf, and others, are members of the Board of Directors of the new Association.

The objects of the Association are: The study of tuberculosis and of the means of preventing it; the dissemination of knowledge as to the nature of the disease, its causes and the methods of its prevention and its treatment; the promotion of adequate facilities for the prevention of tuberculosis and for the care, treatment and economic rehabilitation of persons afflicted therewith, and the co-ordination of the work of public and private agencies engaged in any of the foregoing activities.

A broad program of education, publicity, preventive work among children, of home treatment and after-care, co-ordination of existing clinics and of relief agencies, will be developed by experienced secretaries. A novel addition, in co-operation with the Federal Vocation Board, will be the opening of a workshop where, under the best sanitary conditions and medical supervision, arrested cases of tuberculosis will be restored to productive capacity under healthful surroundings.

Through its Bureau of Preventable Diseases the New York City Health Department has recently conducted a series of demonstrations of the technique of the Schick test and its interpretation, for the benefit of all private physicians who desire to become acquainted with the application of this test. These demonstrations were conducted at some twenty health centers throughout the city. It is hoped that as a result of these demonstrations the physicians will become better acquainted with the Schick test and use it quite largely in their practice. The test when combined with active immunization by toxin-antitoxin, is bound to become a measure of great importance in the prevention of diphtheria.

The Municipal Health Department is again appealing to the physicians of the community to persuade their patients to have all members of their families successfully vaccinated against smallpox, and to urge upon all the value and desirability of at least one vaccination after puberty. The absence of smallpox causes a diminution in the practice of vaccination and with this diminution comes a greater opportunity for the reappearance of this disease. An increase in vaccination gradually banishes smallpox.

A recent census shows that there are approximately 8,500 crippled children in the Borough of Brooklyn alone. Every one of these needs special attention. Some need special treatment, others special training or instruction to fit them for whatever positions their handicaps allow. As yet the facilities for the care of such cases are totally inadequate, and the crippled child is not receiving the attention due it.—(M. T.)

✤

New York.—This state is going seriously into the matter of establishing health districts in which a number of adjoining towns cooperate in maintaining one health board and full-time health officer for the group. The recent consolidations of the kind are: Village of Corfu and town of Pembroke; towns of German, McDonough, Pharsalia and Preston; town of Ogden and village of Spencerport; towns of Clarksville, Cuba and New Hudson; and the village of Oneida Castle joins with Vernon Consolidated Districts.

Miss Ruth Gilbert, Bacteriologist in charge of the diagnostic branch of the State Laboratory Service, recently began a series of visits to the local laboratories of the State. It was planned to have each laboratory engaged in public health work inspected before January first, when annual certificates of approval were issued. Under the Public Health Law and Sanitary Code it is necessary for all such local laboratories in the State outside of New York City to be approved by the State Commissioner of Health in order to have their reports accepted as official.

At a special meeting of the Plattsburg Chapter of the American Red Cross, it was voted to employ a County Community Nurse for general public health work. Contributions were received from West Chazy, Lyon Mountain and Ellenburg branches, to be used for this purpose.

The 1920 budget of the city of Amsterdam will contain an appropriation for the full time employment of a public health nurse. During 1919, only enough money was appropriated to pay for the employment of a nurse during the summer months.

It is proposed to establish a county laboratory at Amsterdam. The Visiting Nurses' Association of Watertown, which has been conducting a child welfare clinic and instructing young women in the care of children, has added to its public spirited work by opening a pre-school clinic. A recent survey in Schenectady County proved that of 120 cases examined 14 per cent were positive and 29 per cent suspected.

At the Executive Committee meeting of the Cobleskill Chapter of the American Red Cross, it was voted to secure the services of a public health nurse for Cobleskill and vicinity. Two thousand dollars was appropriated for the salary of a nurse for the coming year.

Samples of home-canned corn supposed to have caused the death of five persons—a mother and four children at Fine, N. Y., recently, have been submitted to the laboratory for examination.

✤

North Carolina.—The city of Goldsboro has entered into an agreement with a private corporation with reference to the establishment of an abattoir and packing house within the city limits. Regulations for the conduct of this new establishment include the following:

1. That all meat not Government inspected shall be inspected at this abattoir.

2. That the city shall regulate the fees charged for the slaughtering of cattle, hogs, etc.

3. That all slaughtering shall be done under Government regulations, under supervision of the city and at hours set by the city.

4. That should the city at any later date decide to erect a municipal slaughter house that this private corporation shall pay to the city inspection fees, the amounts to be determined later.

At a special meeting of the Board of Aldermen, this year, $6,600 was appropriated for the purpose of carrying on anti-malarial work during 1920. This amount represents half of the money required, the remaining half to be furnished by the State Board of Health and the International Health Board. The U. S. Public Health Service, as its share, will contribute the services of a sanitary engineer who will supervise the work. Should the demonstration prove satisfactory it was further agreed that the city should appropriate annually during 1921, 1922 and 1923 the sum of $4,000, the sum estimated as being necessary to maintain the yearly work.

✛

North Dakota.—In a recent Bulletin of the State Board of Health it is stated that "Letters are going to be sent to many of the cities and towns in close proximity to the several laboratories, inviting them to let us make weekly bacteriological examinations of their water supplies."

In commenting on this notice a prominent Eastern sanitary engineer said, "It seems a great pity that in these times, when the public health should be so carefully protected, that it should be deemed necessary to ask permission of any municipality to make bacteriological examinations of its water supplies. These supplies should be under a constant supervision of the State, either with or without the consent of the municipality."

✛

Ohio.—The situation in Ohio is interesting for the reason that the Griswold Act, which amended the Hughes Act with reference to the new districting of the State, caused village and town boards of health to go out of existence automatically on January first. It was enacted so late in the session that preliminary organization in the townships could not get under way in time for the new officials to take up the work where the older boards dropped it.

Emphasizing the need for haste in reorganization, the State Department of Health has called attention to high prevalence of diphtheria, measles, whooping cough and scarlet fever in December. It is feared that much unnecessary loss of life may result if adequate control measures are not carried out promptly by district boards of health.

To get the new health organization into operation in a county, the district advisory council must fill vacancies on the board of health (except in 38 counties whose original Hughes Act boards hold over in their entirety), the board of health must adopt a new budget, the advisory council must approve this budget and the board of health must select a health commissioner and any other necessary employees.

The State Department of Health has communicated with all members of district boards of health, mayors, township chairmen, county auditors and county prosecutors, explaining their duties under the amended law and strongly advising against delay.

More than 3,000 cases of measles were reported in December, twice as many as in November and more than in any December of the previous five years. Measles prevalence in 1920 is expected to rival that of 1916, when there were 56,000 reported cases and 782 deaths. Strict quarantine will reduce the danger.

Diphtheria, whooping cough and scarlet fever show high prevalence this winter. Several of the most severe local outbreaks are in villages and rural districts which are at present unprotected.

Under a law passed by the recent Legislature the Ohio State Sanatorium is expected to be nearer self-support than ever before. The following schedule is in effect: Pay patients, not less than the minimum ($5 per week), nor more than the maximum ($25 per week) ; patients admitted upon request of industrial concerns, one-half of full per capita cost ; patients admitted upon request of county commissioners, one-half per capita cost ; patients admitted upon request of bureau of war risk insurance, full per capita cost ; patients, admitted upon request of charitable, philanthropic, benevolent and anti-tuberculosis societies, minimum to one-half per capita cost.

✛

Oklahoma.—Dr. D. Long of Duncan, Okla., has just been appointed by Arthur R. Lewis, State Health Commissioner of Oklahoma, as Director of the Tuberculosis Bureau of the Health Department. One of Dr. Long's first duties will be to tabulate and classify each and every case of tuberculosis within the state. He will also have supervision of the construction of the three tuberculosis sanatoria, two of which will be built during 1920.

Mr. John Harrison, Oklahoma City, assumed the duties of State Health Inspector on January 1.

✛

Utah.—The Department of Public Instruction, Division of Health Education of the State has pointed out to the citizens the dangers of under weight among children. Seven per cent below the normal in the weight of the child is considered evidence of malnutrition. The schools are urged to weigh the children and to bring to the supervision of the medical inspectors the cases of under weight. Such cases, it is suggested, should be subject to a thorough examination by the health supervisor in conjunction with the family physician and the mother. The Division is making use of the Alphabet of the Child Research Organization, while the pamphlet by the same association on the "Standards of Growth and Nutrition,' is to be in the hands of every supervisor.

The University of Utah proposes to extend its benefits to the people of the state who are unable to attend its regular courses, by teaching hygiene, sanitation and the prevention of diseases, through extension courses.

It will also emphasize methods of preventing physical defects and the correction of such defects as are corrigible, so as to make for the highest physical efficiency.

The methods to be adopted will be popular health lectures or courses of lectures, exhibits, educational motion picture entertainments and the distribution of health literature. These activities are to be conducted in schools, churches, amusement halls, clubs, etc., with the support and under the auspices of any and all organizations interested in the work.

No less than twenty such courses will be given together with motion pictures and lectures with the lantern. The University pro-

poses further to make sanitary surveys covering milk supply, water supply, sewage disposal and kindred subjects. Traveling exhibits will be a part of the program, which will be the motif for a Health Week. Villages and towns will be encouraged to institute a program in hygiene and sanitation, with a view of approaching as nearly as possible the ideal. Civic pride in these matters will be developed.

The University has organized a Mothers' Club for the benefit of the mother or the expectant mother. Twenty-four bulletins have been issued; one for each month during the period of gestation and the remainder of the twenty-four bulletins cover the care of the child until the end of its second year. An enrollment fee of $1.00 is charged those who join the Mothers' Club, in order to cover the expense of postage and mailing of these bulletins.

✛

Wisconsin.—The city of Oshkosh has opened a health center with Bertha V. Thomson, M.D., Health Commissioner of the city, at its head. It has a great variety of clinics including medical, nervous diseases, tuberculosis, stomach, heart, genito-urinary, children, eye, ear, nose and throat, skin diseases and those of women. Each has special hours assigned for it with a group of physicians and a staff of nurses.

CONVENTIONS, CONFERENCES, MEETINGS

February 27-28, Trenton, N. J., New Jersey State Health Officers' Association.

March —, Chicago, American Conference on Hospital Service.

March —, Wilmington, Del., Delaware State Health Association.

March 1, Salt Lake City, Utah, Utah Nurses' Association.

March 5, Providence, R. I., Rhode Island Medical Society.

March 8-13, Dallas, Texas, State Dental Association.

March 17-19, Burlington, Vt., State Dental Society.

March 22-23, New York City, New York State Medical Society.

April 6, Newark, N. J., State Nurses' Association.

April 12-17, Atlanta, Ga., National Organization for Public Health Nursing.

April 14-21, New Orleans, La., National Conference of Social Workers.

April 14-21, New Orleans, La., American Association of Hospital Workers.

April 19, Charlotte, N. C., North Carolina State Health Association.

April 20-22, Charlotte, N. C., Medical Society of North Carolina.

April 20-22, Anniston, Ala., Medical Association of the State of Alabama.

April 22-24, St. Louis, Mo., National Tuberculosis Association.

April 26-30, New Orleans, La., American Medical Association.

April 27, Huntington, W. Va., West Virginia State Health Association.

April 29-30, Bismarck, N. D., State Nurses' Association.

May 11, American Association of Eugenics.

May 11-12, Indianapolis, Ind., Indiana State Health Association.

May 20-24, Brussels, Belgium, Congress of the Royal Institute of Public Health (English).

INDUSTRIAL HYGIENE AND OCCUPATIONAL DISEASE

Abstracted by Drs. E. R. Hayburst, R. P. Albaugh, P. M. Holmes, and E. B. Starr.

Industrial Health and Efficiency.—This final report of the British Health of Munition Workers' Committee comprises a bulletin of 374 pages as prepared by the U. S. Bureau of Labor Statistics. The chief subjects discussed are relation of fatigue and ill health to industrial efficiency, employment of women, hours, rest spells, incentive, canteens, sickness and ill health, injuries and accidents, industrial diseases, industrial health hazards and welfare supervision both within and outside the factory. An appendix of over one hundred pages copies the memoranda of various special investigators.—Bulletin 249, *U. S. Bureau of Labor Statistics*, Washington, D. C.

✢

Physical Defects Among 10,000 British Recruits.—This article is a summary in relation to age, types and location of defects. The conclusions are: (1) Physical defects worthy of note are present in four-fifths of the adult male population; (2) many of these develop after the age of 18 years (three men out of four are fit for general military service at age 18, but only two out of four by age 23); (3) many of the defects are preventable or curable, *e.g.*, defective teeth in 20 per cent of men, varicose veins in 5 per cent, hernia in over 3 per cent, deformities of limbs in 7 per cent, skin diseases in 3 per cent.; (4) "There appears to be great scope for improvement of the general physique of the nation by medical examination of and attention to, children and adolescents as regards tooth, eye and ear defects, deformities, and early diagnosis of chest diseases and of congenital defects."—John D. Comrie, *The Lancet*, November 29, 1919, pp. 957-960.

✢

Safeguarding Workers in the Tanning Industry.—This special Bulletin of 121 pages, illustrated, points out that there are about 250,000 engaged in the leather industry in the United States, some 55,936 of whom are in the tanning and leather trades, the remainder being principally shoemakers and harnessmakers, and the neglect of safety work is conspicuous in the industry. The purpose of the pamphlet is to outline steps which should materially reduce the hazards involved in tanning and leather production. The information is based on personal visits to tanneries, on correspondence and on a wide study of publications. A number of large industries coöperated to the fullest extent in preparing the Bulletin.—*Working Conditions Service*, U. S. Department of Labor, Grant Hamilton, Director General, Washington, D. C.

✢

Munitions Intoxicants in France.—This is a technical article prepared with great care by Dr. Perkins under the auspices of the (U. S.) National Research Council. Study of the effects of various chemical combinations and radicals, portals of entry into the human system, factors of susceptibility, clinical histories, findings of experimental work, and a series of appendices comprise the report.—Roger G. Perkins, *U. S. Public Health Reports*, October 24, 1919, Vol. 34, No. 43, pp. 2335-2374.

✢

Arsenid Poisoning in Submarines.—The correspondent summarizes the reports of hydrogen arsenid in submarines, the severity of which compelled one boat to return to its base at the end of four days. The source of the harmful arsenious gas was at first believed to be in the sulphuric acid used in the batteries but was ultimately traced to an alloy in the battery grids. The gas increased as the batteries got old. The two symptoms most complained of were vomiting and dyspnea, the color of the urine varied from brown to blood red. Jaundice was a constant sign. The nervous symptoms were slow in appearance but took from two to three weeks to pass off. Arsenic was found in the urine, hair and nails. —London Letter, *Jour. A. M. A.*, October 11, 1919, pp. 1148.

✢

Velocity of Carbon Monoxid Poisoning.— "Gertz' calculations show that the toxic action of carbon monoxid develops comparatively slowly at first. With twenty normal respirations—about one minute's time—there is no risk of asphyxia or of loss of consciousness unless the air contains very large amounts of carbon monoxid."—H. Gertz, (Stockholm), *Jour. A. M. A.*, October 11, 1919, pp. 1172.

✦

Ford Motor and Ship Plants Reduce Accidents 75 to 83.5 Percent.—While markedly reducing accidents, production was also increased by installing iron-dust suction systems. The finishing operation of Ford pistons created iron dust which resulted in a request to be transferred to other work, from 25% of the entire membership of this department. After installing a dust suction system such transfers dropped to 3% a month or the average throughout the plant. "Of course the health of the men was greatly improved and the inception of many tuberculosis cases stopped."—*Safety News, National Safety Council*, Dec. 1, 1919, No. 312, p. 2.

✦

The Heart Disease Defective.—There is a class of young men of usually healthy appearance who nevertheless suffer from a group of symptoms following mild exercise, characteristic of impaired heart conditions, who might not ever have been discovered except from the Army Draft which caused young men to be examined physically. These men have no complaints, as a rule, which leads them to seek medical advice. They tend to drift into the lighter occupations and the majority are surprised when told that there is something really the matter with them. They are a class of constitutional inferiors rather than that there is any common cause for their impaired hearts. These types of cases are distinct from those who have had past disease recognized as likely to result in heart trouble.—Louis M. Warfield, *Amer. Jour. Med. Sc.*, August, 1919, pp. 165-178.

✦

Review of Methods for the Study of Dust Content of Air.—No single method of air sampling for dust content, as yet devised, is ideal. For complete studies and for fixing of permissible limits of dustiness, tests must permit of estimating weights and counts and determinations of the physical and chemical nature and size of dust particles. These tests are at present best and most easily made on samples collected with the Palmer apparatus, though the sugar filter samples treated according to Muir and Johnson's technic give

as much information. Some other tests have distinct values for certain purposes. The article has a full bibliography.—Henry F. Smyth, *Jour. of Indus. Hyg.*, July, 1919, pp. 140-148.

✦

Effects of the Inhalation of Dust.—This comprehensive article should be read in the original to appreciate its contents and significance. Among other important deductions the author questions whether organic dusts of any type are injurious from a mechanical standpoint. Diseases produced by organic dusts are probably due to inorganic material mixed with such dusts, direct poisonous properties excluded. The higher incidence of tuberculosis among those exposed to inorganic dusts is due to the fact that the dust acts as a convenient carrier of tubercle bacilli. But dust is only incidental and the universal tendency is to emphasize the danger of dust and to forget the tubercle bacillus. The dust might be eliminated and yet the persons exposed to the danger of tuberculosis when active cases expectorate freely about the working place. The author believes tobacco dust to be free from that industry because of economic reasons. The efficiency of the respiratory tract as a filter for bacteria was shown by Strauss, who found that exhaled air contained only 40 bacteria when inhaled air held over 20,000. The mouth breather is at a great disadvantage. The symptoms and physical signs, X-ray findings and pathology are detailed.—H. R. M. Landis, *Jour of Ind. Hyg.*, July, 1919, pp. 117-139.

✦

Back Strain—An Accident or a Disease?—The author indicates the lines along which the analysis of any given case of "back strain" must proceed, and demonstrates through excellent X-ray reproductions, factors which contribute to solution. A previous faulty structure or defect up to the time of a given accident has usually been unsuspected and unfelt. Static conditions, birth defects, accidents and disease constitute the primary causes. Each of these is concisely discussed.—Robert B. Osgood, *Jour. of Ind. Hyg.*, July, 1919, pp. 117-139.

✦

Hours of Work as Related to Output and Health of Workers.—This study was made in connection with typical metal manufacturing industries principally by questionnaires sent out, from which replies were received from

1,252 establishments employing 753,561 workers. Out of these, 413 establishments employing 358,336 workers had reduced hours and furnished data as to the effects of such reduction. Conclusions are not complete for the reason that the time study was too brief. However, the death rate from tuberculosis in certain branches of the industry is high. The death-rate from occupational and chronic poisoning is almost insignificant according to the U. S. Census figures. Tuberculosis among gas workers, tinplate and tinware workers is especially high. Statistics show an unusually high death-rate from pneumonia as well as tuberculosis in the moulder's trade. These branches, however, employ a relatively small proportion of the workers in the industry but it is obviously incumbent upon industrial managers to look closely into these matters. There is considerable evidence to indicate that there is a definite connection between the prevalence of tuberculosis and inadequate nourishment and poor housing conditions.—*Research Report No. 18, Nat. Industrial Conference Board,* 10 Beacon St., Boston.

✦

New Hazards in Electric Arc Welding.— While the effect of the electric arc upon the eyes has been adequately provided for, the harmful effect of the light rays upon the tissues of the human body has had little attention. The invisible rays (ultra-violet and infra-red) are those which are harmful. The painful body burns, it has been found, are not due to the infra-red rays which are only irritating, and rather uncomfortable and fatiguing, but not especially dangerous. Whether the harmful rays are the ultra-violet *per se* or the rays in that part of the spectrum where the X-ray is found has not been determined. Ordinarily where work is done in the open, in shops, or in places where special screens are erected the hazards are not great. But on board ship, in close quarters where surroundings are often covered with red lead, the dangers of the light rays appear to be greatly increased. Complaints of burns on the neck and chest occur within a few hours. Those on the back of the neck appear to be caused by reflected rays from the red lead painted surfaces. A worker who was supplied with a bandage lined with lead foil had no further burns, whence it was decided that the ultra-violet rays were the cause of the trouble.

Burns were not nearly so noticeable in compartments which had not been red-leaded. Cancer may be the ultimate results of such burns. As a further precaution, all welding should be done before surfaces are red-leaded.—Alfred W. Jansen, abstracted from "Safety" by *Monthly Labor Review,* May, 1919.

✦

Medical Features of Industrial Relations. —A practical plan for including the medical features of industrial relations in a typical American plant (Richmond, Indiana), which has had some experience, is described by George Hodge, on pp. 64-66 of *Hospital Management* for September, 1919. In addition to the medical phase, betterment, accidents and insurance are discussed. "The fundamental principle of our Industrial Relations Department is based on the golden rule."

✦

Instruments for Showing the Presence and Amount of Combustible Gas in the Air. —New forms of instruments have been devised by Weaver and Weibel of the *U. S. Bureau of Standards* (Scientific Paper, No. 334, 90 pp.) for determining the presence and amount of such gases as hydrogen, carbon monoxide, illuminating gas, methane and others. The apparatus devised operates an alarm for any desired percentage of combustible gas. The initial cost of construction of the apparatus is not great; it is portable and the indicating instrument may be located at a distance as well as the alarm. The apparatus, when once properly calibrated, will indicate changes of concentration of hydrogen smaller than can be detected by the methods of gas analysis commonly used in commercial practice.

✦

Rubber Gloves Urged for Ice Cream Workers.—Because of the effect of ice and salt upon the human skin Wm. A. Hays advises the wearing of rubber gloves for ice cream workers. "Salt extracts water from the tissues and also causes a deposit of moisture from the air on these tissues; it is impossible to dry any substance impregnated with salt. Salt and ice combined produce a rapid freezing agent, which has a deleterious effect on the skin, acting in the same manner as a burning agent."—Bulletin, *New York State Industrial Commission,* Vol. 4, No. 9, June, 1919, p. 175.

PUBLIC HEALTH
LABORATORY NOTES

Abstracted by Francis H. Slack, M. D., and Mr. James M. Strang.

Isolation of Typhoid and Paratyphoid Organisms in Water Supplies.—In this note the authors give an account of their method based on the employment of malachite-green broth for the isolation of such organisms in water supplies, the method having been employed daily for some time in the routine testing of the water supply of Paris. Several litres of the water to be tested are filtered through a collodion filter to concentrate the germs, and a suspension of the deposit on the surface of the filter is made in 50 cc. of sterile saline. A 6 per cent peptone water, to which has been added 3 cc., of sterile bile and 2.5 cc. of a 0.5 per cent solution of malachite-green, is then inoculated with the suspension, and the mixture incubated at 37° C. for twenty-four to forty-eight hours. Five tubes, each containing 25 cc. of nutrient agar to which 0.5 cc. of a 10 per cent solution of subacetate of lead has been added for every 10 cc. of agar, are melted in a water-bath at 46° C. and each inoculated in succession, without recharging the needle, with a loopful of the malachite-green culture. The tubes, after shaking to distribute the microbes, are poured on Petri plates. When the latter have set, to each is added the contents of a tube of 40 cc. of ordinary nutrient agar at 46° C. with the object of permitting anaerobic culture of bacilli in the lead agar. When set anew, the plates are incubated at 37° C. and the development of colonies followed. B. typhosus and B. paratyphosus B grow as brown colonies surrounded by a pale halo, whilst B. coli grows as a colony hardly at all brown and without halo. B. pyocyaneus also develops as colonies having the same appearance as B. paratyphosus B. The brown colonies with halos are isolated and differentiated by sub-culturing in peptone water (indol and agglutination), on an agar slope (Gram staining), on neutral-red glucose agar, on litmus lactose agar, and in litmus milk.

The authors assert that their method permits B. Typhosus and B. paratyphosus B to be determined with certainty in 50 cc. of Seine river water taken at Paris. If, instead of lead agar, litmus lactose agar is employed, the results are not so good, in the proportion of 347 colonies having to be isolated from the latter medium, as against 64 colonies from the former, in order to demonstrate the presence of 10 typhoid or paratyphoid bacilli.—Dienert F., Guillerd A., Leguex A., Comptes Rendus, CLXVI, 84 (D. G.).

Colloidal Gold Test in Public Health Work.—Throughout the studies of the past two years, careful attention has been given to the comparative value of the colloidal gold and other spinal fluid reactions. Lee and Hinton are of the opinion that the gold test is much more delicate than the spinal fluid Wassermann reaction and for the same reason some have expressed their belief that reactions typical in the "Luetic Zone" confirm the clinical suspicions of central nervous system lues, even though the Wassermann is repeatedly negative; moreover, such reactions may foreshadow the outbreak of a latent lues and may prove quite as valuable as the "Provocative salvarsan reaction." Whenever the colloidal gold reaction is absolutely negative, all other reactions are also negative in the vast majority of cases. There is, however, a close relationship between an increased globulin content and positive colloidal gold reactions. No strong color changes in colloidal gold occur with fluids that give a negative globulin test. On the other hand, positive globulin tests are rarely observed in spinal fluids that give negative or weak gold curves.

Detailed directions are given for the preparation of colloidal gold solutions.—W. E. Zielinski, N. Y. State Jour. Med., 1919, 195. (D. G.)

✛

A New Double-Way Syringe for Use in Intravenous Medication, Transfusion and Aspiration.—The barrel of this syringe is the same as in all glass syringes, but the plunger has a bore running throughout its entire length with the upper end drawn out so that a rubber tubing may be securely attached. The needle is also attached with rubber tubing. By compression of the tubing at either end, according to the purpose desired, the syringe may be repeatedly filled or emptied in either direction. H. O. Ruh, Jour. of Lab. & Clin. Med., Nov., 1919, p. 123.

(Continued on Page XX, Advertising Section)

American Journal of Public Health

Official Monthly Publication of the American Public Health Association
Publication office: No. 124 W. Polk Street, Chicago, Ill.
Editorial office: 169 Massachusetts Ave., Boston, Mass

Subscription price, $4 per year. American Public Health Association membership, including subscription, $5 per year.
Subscriptions and memberships may be sent to the A. P. H. A., 169 Massachusetts Ave., Boston, Mass.

| Vol. X | MARCH, 1920 | No. 3 |

METHODS FOR THE DEFENSE OF PUBLIC HEALTH APPROPRIATIONS

ERNST CHRISTOPHER MEYER, PH. D.,

Director of Surveys and Exhibits, International Board of the Rockefeller Foundation.

Read before the Section of Public Health Administration, American Public Health Association, at New Orleans, La., October 29, 1919.

This paper will be especially helpful to the health officer because it tells him things he needs to know; for example, the place for arguments based on comparisons, on expenditures, on efficiency and on results attained, that will carry weight with intelligent public bodies. Statistics are given their place, as an index of the real value of health work, with a warning against crude statistics.

This paper is addressed more particularly to public health officers in the smaller communities to whom the literature of public health administration is seldom readily accessible and who, no matter how ambitious they may be to render the best possible service, are greatly handicapped by inability to keep in touch with progress in the public health field. Unfortunately, I can not speak as a practical administrator of public health, but appear before you rather as a student of public health administration, or if you please, as a student of government administration in general.

In late years expenditures for health purposes have been mounting rapidly by millions of dollars. A series of careful compilations and estimates, based on the best sources available, permit of the statement that, exclusive of the federal government, we are today spending about $33,700,000 per year for health conservation. Of this huge sum $11,250,000 were spent, in 1917, by State Boards of Health and other state agencies alone. Cities of over 30,000 population spent no less than $15,950,000 in the same year. Smaller cities spent about $3,000,-000, and counties about $3,500,000. Only fifteen years back, in 1902, the total expenditures for health purposes by these same administrative authorities were but about $9,500,000. There was hence an increase of about 355 per cent. in the expenditures for health purposes within fifteen years.

As public attention centers more and more on public health work, it becomes increasingly important that the health officer develop his case before the appropriating body along thorough, scientific, and convincing lines, and that in doing so he has in mind also the educational value of a properly prepared argument.

It is hoped that the things here put forth will prove of assistance in meeting this growing obligation.

In refreshing your memories on certain useful reservoirs of information and planning a line of argumentation, it is proposed to consider the material under several general headings.

1. Arguments dealing with expenditures for public health purposes.

2. Arguments dealing with scope or quality of work done.

3. Arguments dealing with the efficiency of administrative organization and with the results obtained.

In the brief compass of a fifteen minute paper it is not possible to do more than skip over the general ground here outlined.

THE ARGUMENT OF EXPENDITURES.

Great difficulties surround all attempts at comparisons of expenditures. Things which in fact are unlike may not safely be compared without appreciation of their differences. The objects of expenditures for health purposes in one city are apt to vary considerably from the objects of expenditure for health purposes in some other city. So-called health activities differ widely. The inclusion of irrelevant non-health work is not only a great handicap to health departments financially burdened in this manner, but thoroughly removes the possibility of fair comparison.

Furthermore, in only rare instances do the statements published by health officers distinguish between outlays in the form of capital expenditures for hospitals and other buildings and for expensive equipment and furniture, and the current expenses of operation of the health department. Where this is not done it is obviously impossible to compare the expenditures of one city with those of another city on the basis of the cost of the work. In 1917 cities of over 30,000 population spent $15,945,361 for current expenses of health conservation and no less than $2,208,951 for capital outlays, or 14% of the total spent on health work.

It is true also that health work is not always concentrated in the health department. School medical inspection may rest with the bureau of education or with the health department. Industrial hygiene may be the function of some special industrial commission, rather than of the health department. The total expenditures for health purposes as given out by health departments in such cases do not express the actual sums of money devoted to public health work.

However, the expenditure argument has its uses. The example of others has its force. There are various ways in which comparisons of expenditures may be made. Nor are the statistics of expenditures for health purposes, unlike other statistics in that you can, by proper manipulation, make them tell most any sort of story. Among the different comparisons, which may readily be made are:

1. Comparison of per capita expenditures for health conservation. If you are health officer at Morristown, New Jersey, you may, if you wish, point with sorrow to the fact that this city of 13,410 population in 1917 spent only $.07 per capita for health conservation, whereas Brookline, Mass., with a population of 33,526 spent no less than $1.58. On the other hand, if you are health officer of Brookline you would not be able to use the comparison of per capita expenditure for health as an argument for increased appropriations. You will find that on that basis you are evidently already spending more than you ought to.

Various guesses have been made. as to how much per capita should be devoted to public health purposes. These vary from $.50 to $1.00 and more. It is of interest to note that many cities have already exceeded this per capita expenditure. This suggests discretion in commitment to a standard of this sort as it might prove a boomerang. What may seem to be a very large expenditure at the present time may be quite insignificant at some future date. The tremendous increase in health appropriations tends to confirm this point of view.

2. A comparison of expenditures for various years within the same city has distinct value on the theory that the amount of public funds used for health purposes should at least keep pace with the growth of the city and the consequent expansion of the public health problem.

3. Another way of doing is to compare the expenditures for health conservation with those of other activities of the city government, as for example, the fire department, police department, education, charities, etc. The per cent distribution of the expenses of city governments in this manner likewise varies tremendously. Taking all cities of over 30,000 population as a whole with a total population of over 33 million, and total expenditures in 1917 for all purposes of municipal government of $634,-345,219, we find that conservation of health represented but 2.5 per cent of the total expenditures of these cities. Schools alone took up 31 per cent, police departments 10.9 per cent, highways 10.6 per cent, fire departments 8.6 per cent, and sanitation, or the promotion of cleanliness 7.6 per cent.

Health officers in search of financial data will find a considerable body of information on this subject available in the publications of the Division of Statistics of States and Cities of the U. S. Census Bureau. The Statistics of Cities have appeared since 1902, those of States since 1915. The Statistics of Cities, published annually, cover all cities of 30,000 and over. In addition to these annual volumes, Statististics of Cities of 8,000 to 25,000 appeared in the report on

"Wealth, Debt and Taxation" of 1902, and in a special report for cities for 1903. In 1903 and 1913, Statistics of Cities of 2,500 and over were published in "Wealth, Debt, and Taxation," and in 1913 also in the report on "Municipal Revenues, Expenditures, and Public Properties."

The annual reports on Statistics of Cities cover expenditures of all cities of over 30,000 population. The volume of 1917, by way of illustration, contains -373 quarto pages. We find here a classification of the expenditures of city governments for all purposes in minute detail. Those concerning health conservation are given under the following heading:

I. Health Department Administration.
II. Vital Statistics.
III. Prevention and Treatment of Communicable diseases.
    1. Tuberculosis.
    2. Other communicable diseases in hospitals.
    3. Other treatment of communicable diseases.
IV. Conservation of Child Life.
    1. Medical work for school children.
    2. Other conservation of child life.
V. Food Regulation and Inspection.
    1. Milk and dairy control.
    2. Other food regulation.

In addition to some general tables there are tables, from which I have already quoted, which indicate the amount spent per capita by different city departments. There is a wealth of diagrammatic material dealing with interesting summaries and comparisons. Each volume is in itself a liberal treatise on government accounting and bookkeeping.

The annual publication of Statistics of States covers the same ground and is gotten out in a uniform manner with that covering cities.

The usefulness of these statistical data to health officers who wish to fortify themselves before appropriating bodies by calling forth comparisons with what other cities are doing may well be emphasized. I have observed very erroneous impressions as to the accuracy of these statistics based on wrong ideas as to how they are compiled. It may not be clear to you why the Bureau of the Census should be able to produce statistics of a higher degree of comparability than are compiled or can be compiled by the health officers of the various municipalities themselves.

The explanation is simple and illuminating. The Bureau of the Census employs trained accountants who are given highly technical office instruction before being sent out. They are armed with an elaborate book of instructions covering almost every conceivable question that might be raised in the performance of their duties. They spend from a few weeks to a number of months in the various cities gathering up from the public records the statistics on expenditures for the various purposes of government. If necessary, they go back to the original vouchers, or to the detailed accounts, to reclassify the information so that it may conform to the uniform plan that has been adopted. The result is that the statistics given out by the Census Bureau are, with few exceptions, the only statistics published which present expenditures for health conservation on a reasonably comparable basis.

It may not be amiss here to emphasize the unfortunate lack of comparability of the financial statistics of our governments and the lack of uniformity in accounting systems, method of budgeting, and reporting. The fact that capable and trained accountants must at times spend months in middle sized cities to juggle statistics of governmental expenditures into the forms of a standardized plan is striking comment on the conditions which at present prevail. Nor can we look forward to any remedy of this condition of affairs until the municipal and state governments of this country come to recognize more clearly the importance of adopting not merely budgets but standardized budgets and uniform systems of accounting and reporting. The subject of budgets will receive atten-

tion in a paper in this section by Dr. Haven Emerson.* Uniform accounting has been under consideration by the committee on uniform accounting for health departments.

Such progress as is being made at this time is difficult and slow owing largely to lack of interest and understanding on the part of public health officers of the significance and fundamental importance of statistical data to their own work.

Aside from the comparable statistics published by the Bureau of the Census, reference may be made to statistics published by various state statistical bureaus, as for example, the Municipal Division of Statistics of the State of Massachusetts, the work of which has received national recognition through the efficient guidance of Dr. Charles F. Gettemy; various investigations of the U. S. Public Health Service, notably the reports of Dr. Carroll C. Fox, Dr. Taliaferro Clark, Dr. Paul Prebble and Dr. S. B. Grubbs have also provided health officers with much useful information.

Such private institutions as the Bureau of Municipal Research of New York City, the public health work of which is in the hands of Dr. Carl McCombs, the Detroit Bureau of Government Research, and of similar institutions in some of the other large cities, have much useful data in their libraries for the assistance of health officers. Legislative reference departments which have been organized in many states, and municipal reference divisions which have been organized in connection with some of our largest universities are also in a position to assist the health officer who thirsts for information. These agencies were all created to serve the public. They welcome letters of inquiry.

THE ARGUMENT OF WORK DONE.

Where the appropriation authorities are interested in something more than whether the funds asked for are as great

---

*See this issue of the JOURNAL, page 221, for this paper.

or greater than those called for in preceding years, or whether they compare favorably or unfavorably with similar expenditures by other cities, or whether they represent a proper proportion of the total expenditures of the city or state, the health officer may be called upon to justify the necessity of carrying on certain lines of health work and to establish their intrinsic practical public health value.

Back in 1915, one of the leading health officers of the country wrote:

There is probably not a single large municipal health department in the country which is operated along strictly logical lines. They are mostly ill-balanced. Much is done that counts little for health and much is left undone which would save many lives.

This may not be as true in 1919 as it was when uttered by Dr. Chapin in 1915. There is much reason to believe that health officers are willing to admit that there is a great deal more of truth to it even today than there should be.

Health officers, of course, cannot always determine for themselves what work shall be done or shall not be done. On this, if I may once more quote Dr. Chapin, we are told:

Much of the mischief comes from without. The health officer is not allowed to map out his work. It is mapped out for him. The ambitious councilman and the enthusiastic reformer are often neither well balanced nor logical. They see only one thing. They think that their pet project is more important than all other health work put together. They have push, and sometimes pull, and burden the health department with new expenses when no money can be obtained for old and tried lines of work. The average man, or quite as often it is a woman, gets his or her scientific knowledge from the Sunday edition of the yellow press or from some ten-cent magazine. When the reformers' fire is kindled in this way no one can tell what the result will be, but it certainly will not be a well-balanced health department.

It is possible that not all of you can make readily accessible for your use what current literature there is on the important subject of relative values in public health work. The importance of constant attention to this by men who are charged with the expenditure of over $33,000,000 of public funds is obvious.

Little has thus far been published specifically on this point, but most of what has been given out is suggestive and exceedingly helpful. It is interesting, too, that the few writers who have tackled this difficult subject in a concrete and definite manner show a constant evolutionary progress in the development of the general thesis. Back in 1912, Professor George C. Whipple in the American City published a paper under the title "How to Determine Relative Values in Sanitation." In 1913, there appeared Dr. Chapin's "How Shall We Spend the Health Appropriation." In 1914, Dr. D. D. Armstrong discoursed on "Public Health Values—a Few Modern Fallacies." In 1915 appeared Dr. Chapin's "Effective Lines of Health Work"; and in 1916, we were favored with what seems to be the latest and, in spite of the many doubts it leaves unsettled, most scholarly presentation of this subject, Franz Schneider, Jr.'s "Relative Values in Public Health Work." Quite obviously in considering this material one must bear in mind the fact that the values set down by these men of necessity have a different rating in different parts of the country and in rural regions as against urban conditions of life, and that at best they are frankly pioneer effort.

The following table shows the relative values attached to the various lines of health work by Mr. Franz Schneider, Jr.:

Tuberculosis	12.1
Venereal Diseases	6.6
All other communicable diseases	25.3
Infant Hygiene	20.3
Privy and well sanitation	3.5
Milk Control	2.7
Fly and Mosquito suppression	2.4
Food sanitation	0.1
Inspection of school children	7.0
Vital statistics	5.0
Education	5.0
Dispensary and clinics	5.0
Laboratory	5.0
Total	100.0

One of the most interesting though not wholly novel methods of defense of health appropriations, on the ground of effective lines of work followed, was employed by Dr. W. S. Rankin, the efficient health officer of the State of North Carolina. The details were published in the Health Bulletin of that state in February, 1919, under the title "Dividends on Investments in Public Health." In exceedingly concrete fashion, we have here set forth item by item the estimated value in dollars and cents which the people of the state have received in return for their appropriation for public health purposes. By way of illustration I will quote a few items. The paper in question enumerates exactly twenty items.

Item 4. The State Laboratory of Hygiene has distributed annually for the last two years 248,876 doses of typhoid vaccine, 7,896 doses of whooping cough vaccine, and 29,580 doses of smallpox vaccine, which vaccines, if purchased at the ordinary retail price, would have cost a minimum of $100,000. This $100,000 is, then, a fourth dividend paid on the State's investment of $86,991.13 in the health of her people.

Item 5. The State Laboratory of Hygiene has distributed annually for the last two years 2,412 doses, or 12,060,000 units, of diphtheria antitoxin. The antitoxin, distributed free of cost to the people in 1918, at the old retail price would have cost $12,060. The antitoxin distributed in 1917, at about one-fourth the previous retail price of antitoxin, saved our people an additional $9,000, making a total saving on diphtheria antitoxin of $21,000 for the last two years, or an annual saving of at least $10,000. But this by no means represents the total amount saved under this item to the citizens of North Carolina. Commercial manufacturers of antitoxin, in order to sell their product at all in North Carolina in competition with the State's free antitoxin, have had to cut their original price to one-third of what it was. The people are now paying only one-third of what they otherwise would have to pay for the antitoxin of private manufacturers. The arrangement of the State Board of Health for supplying antitoxin to the people of North Carolina saves our State not less than $20,000 a year. This $20,-000 is, then, a fifth dividend paid on the State's investment of $86,991.13 in public health.

Even after due allowance is made for the element of inaccuracy or of estimate, the definite figures given by Dr. Rankin in themselves tend to raise in the minds of those who hear them, the presumption of value received.

THE ARGUMENT OF EFFICIENCY IN ORGANIZATION.

Successful defense of appropriations may depend in part upon ability to establish the efficiency of organization. And again where inefficiency in organization exists, the health officer may be enabled to establish an alibi by demonstrating that this lack of efficiency is due to shortcomings largely outside of his department,—possibly to inadequate legislation and imperfect health regulations.

The efficiency in organization may have to do with one or more of five different things, to each and all of which the health officer will need to give close attention if the machinery of his office is to run smoothly and effectively. These are:

1. The form of the machinery of administration, including the organization of the legislative machinery,—the Board of Health, the administrative machinery,—the executive health officer, the bureau and district organization, the distribution of governmental power within the central administration, and between central and local authorities.

2. The personnel, including such matters as method of appointment, promotion, discipline and removal of employes, training and qualifications for office, term of office and compensation.

3. The physical plant, equipment and supplies, including the method of providing the plant, the acquisition of equipment and supplies, storage and inventory, character and effectiveness of the materials to serve the purpose for which acquired.

4. The financing of the health administration, including the provision of adequate funds and development of effective sources of revenue and the proper planning of budgets and financial statements.

5. The business practice and procedure, including the keeping of proper financial accounts, of current administrative records of work done, of property owned, handling and filing of documents, rendition of reports.

THE ARGUMENT OF RESULTS ATTAINED.

1. The crude death rate as an expression of results attained.

The number of people who die each year per one thousand population has long been the accepted measure of mortality. We speak of this measure as the death rate. The reduction of the general death rate is obviously the large objective of public health work. It is but natural, therefore, that this rate should be utilized by health officers to estimate the influence of their work and to defend their expenditures before appropriating authorities. Such rates must, however, as you will agree, be used with · great circumspection. They are double edged swords. They may harm as well as help. The crude death rate of a given city through a series of years may be a fairly accurate index of the fluctuation in the health of the community and may indicate correctly the relative mortality of different years, but when it is used for comparison with other cities blunders can readily be made. For comparative purposes, as we know, conditions must be similar. The populations for which death rates are compared must be in a broad way similar in age and sex distribution and in race, nationality, and occupation. If they are strikingly dissimilar proper corrections must be made. It may not always be possible to go into all refinements of correction, but attention to them is essential if the comparisons which are made are to be convincing. While this seems quite obvious it is of interest to note that corrections of the general death rate, in so far as the evidence is contained in published reports, are very rarely attempted by public health officers.

At best, however, and after all possible corrections have been scrupulously made, the general death rate represents but a poor substitute for a proper means of measurement of the efficiency of health work as a whole. Being a general death rate it represents deaths from all causes and, as is well known, preventable deaths represent only about 33 per cent., or one out of every three, of the deaths which occur in a given community. The use of the crude death rate hence greatly encumbers the comparison and clouds the real issues involved.

On this point Dr. Wilmer R. Batt. Registrar of the Pennsylvania State Board of Health, in his admirable paper "The Sanitary Index" says:

The general or crude death rate, including deaths from all types of diseases, from old age as well as from all forms of violence, accidental or otherwise, certainly does not form such a standard of measurement of efficiency of health administration, although it is the most frequently employed method of expression in public discussions of the value of public health work. It represents the simplest form of mortality accounting and without appreciation of its insignificance it has been most thoroughly misapplied.

The manner in which this difficulty may be overcome will be presently described. Excellent help in the use of death rates is given in a recently published book "Vital Statistics" by Professor George C. Whipple, of Harvard University. This volume is to be highly commended to health officers for sundry other reasons as well.

2. Death Rates of Individual Diseases as an Expression of Results Attained.

Realization of the shortcomings of crude death rates has caused health officers to resort also to the use of death rates of individual communicable diseases, not only in comparing conditions in a particular city from year to year, but in comparing conditions with other cities. This practice has its distinct value but calls for a good deal of care and exhaustive study if the comparisons are to be worth while. Various corrections for differences in conditions which influence this or that communicable disease will need to be made; and unless the health officer has thoroughly posted himself in advance, the use of individual disease death rates may prove a serious stumbling block when he is subjected to inquisition by a wide awake member of an appropriating board.

3. The Sanitary Index as an Expression of Results Attained.

The sanitary index is constructed by adding the death rates of the acute communicable diseases and tuberculosis, and the death rates of either infants under one or under two years of age, or where these are not accessible, all deaths from diarrhea and enteritis under two years of age as given by the federal census bureau.* In short, the sanitary index is intended to be a summary expression of the death rates of those diseases which are particularly amenable to control through public health administration or which, at any rate, are the particular object of sanitary effort. No standard, so far as is known, has, as yet, been developed for the construction of a sanitary index.

Beyond the group of diseases included in the sanitary index there exists, as Dr. Batt states, a rather extensive variety of diseases the occurrence of many of which may be influenced by general educational effort to promote personal hygiene. The group first described, however, absorbs the maximum of effort and resources of a public health department. The reduction in deaths for this group may hence be recorded as a fair index of efficiency in conserving life and health through public health agencies.

The death rate which represents all deaths, exclusive of those included in the sanitary index, has been described by Dr. Batt as the "residual death rate." The sanitary index, plus the residual death rate, hence equals the general or crude death rate.

The effective manner in which the sanitary index may be used to express the efficiency of public health work is indicated by the statistics for the State of Pennsylvania covering the ten year period, 1906 to 1915 inclusive. The general death rate during this period declined from 16 per thousand population to 13.8, a reduction of 13.8 per cent. During the same period the sanitary index declined from 6.5 to 4.5, a reduction of

30.8 per cent, while the residual death rate declined from 9.5 to 9.3, a reduction of only 2.1 per cent. Demonstration of a reduction of 13.8 per cent in the crude death rate is not nearly as effective as proof that the death rate from preventable diseases dropped 30.8 per cent.

It is evident, too, from the figures just quoted "that almost the entire reduction that has taken place in the general death rate (in the case of Pennsylvania before us) has been due to the decline in the deaths from those diseases that are the objects of sanitary attack, and when we employ only the general death rate as an expression of progress in public health work, we fail utterly properly to measure the returns accruing from sustained and intelligent expenditures of both knowledge and money in this direction."

The use of morbidity statistics to demonstrate the efficiency of public health work is very important. Although mortality statistics obviously must remain our main reliance to express the results of public health work, the opportunity offered by a careful use of morbidity statistics may not be safely neglected. The case rate provides illuminating information concerning prevalence of preventable sickness in the same manner in which the death rate tells the story of mortality. The case fatality rate in another fashion is exceedingly useful in judging the efficiency of that part of the mechanism of health administration through which sickness in the field of preventable diseases comes to the attention of public health officers. A vast amount of information on the prevalence of preventable diseases is published periodically in the United States Public Health Reports. These statistics show the prevalence of notifiable diseases by individual cities and in population groups from 10,000 up for the entire country. They unfortunately are not as complete as they appear to be.

Health officers who are interested in

*In constructing a sanitary index on the basis of mortality statistics published by the U. S. Census Bureau, it is suggested that the following diseases may consistently be included: Typhoid fever, typhus fever, malaria, smallpox, measles, scarlet fever, whooping cough, diphtheria and croup, Asiatic cholera, cholera nostras, other epidemic diseases tuberculosis of the lungs, tuberculosis meningitis, other forms of tuberculosis, diarrhea and enteritis.

securing general information on morbidity conditions are referred to a number of sickness censuses, which were conducted during the last few years. Notable among these are the series of sickness surveys by the Metropolitan Life Insurance Company made in 1915 to 1917 under the direction of Drs. Lee K. Frankel and Louis I. Dublin; the three illness censuses of New York City conducted from 1915 to 1918 by Drs. W. H. Guilfoy and S. W. Wynne; the sickness census of the Framingham community health and tuberculosis demonstration conducted by Dr. Donald B. Armstrong in 1918; the sickness survey of the State Charities Aid Association made by Mr. J. J. Weber in 1915; the report on "Disabling Sickness among the Population of Seven Cotton Mill Villages of South Carolina in Relation to Family Income" by Drs. Edgar Sydenstricker, G. A. Wheeler and Joseph

Goldberger, of the U. S. Public Health Service; the report on disability by age and occupation by Dr. Boris Emmet in "Modern Medicine" September 1919.*

These then are among the various lines of argumentation open to the health officer and some of the sources from which helpful facts may be drawn. At all points the local conditions must, of course, be illumined. The best time to begin preparation for defense of appropriations is the first day of the year. The best time to complete the preparation is the last day of the year. And it is certain, too, that the public, which at present is providing over 33 million dollars per year for health purposes, will, in increasing measure, want to be convinced why the amount now being supplied is needed or why even greater sums should be provided.

*This report is being issued officially by the United States Bureau of Labor Statistics.

□

Conjugal Tuberculosis.—An interesting contribution to the question as to whether tuberculous infection occurs more frequently in the other of a married couple when the one is already infected, than would be the case if the parties were not so related, is made by Dr. E. Ward, the tuberculous officer for South Devon, England.

Having on hand a list of some 4,000 cases and contacts, he finds that in the 156 instances where the mate of a tuberculous husband or wife was examined, 16 suspect and 49 negative, or, expressed in percentages, 58, 10, 32 per cent respectively. In applying a similar analysis to the two classes distinguished accordingly as the husband or the wife was first notified, the divergence in the percentage figures of the groups was not great and was distinctly of the same order. The figures are (a) husband first notified, wife definitely tuberculous 55 per cent, suspected 10 per cent, negative 35 per cent, total cases 120; (b) wife first notified, husband found to be tuberculous on examination 69 per cent, suspected 11 per cent, negative 20 per cent, total cases 36.

Comparing now the results of examining contacts other than husband and wife, out of 1,057 examined, 219 were tuberculous, 284 suspect, and 564 negative; or, roughly, 20 per cent, 27 per cent and 53 per cent. Taking as a further control the contacts of cases seen for an opinion and diagnosed non-tuberculous, either at the time of the first visit or later, out of 81 examined, 4 are found to be tuberculous, 7 suspect and 70 negative; or, in percentages, 5 per cent, 8 per cent and 87 per cent. Cases of definite surgical tuberculosis and their contacts are included but the number of such cases was relatively small.

Ward takes the view that the great majority of the mates of tuberculous husbands or wives do sooner or later show signs or develop symptoms of tuberculosis; but that the great majority of those infected recover, and make a speedier recovery than most tuberculous patients. This may reasonably be attributed to an enhanced immunity conferred by the graduated doses of bacilli which they usually receive.—E. Ward, *Lancet*, Oct. 4, 1919, 606, Medical Officer, Oct. 25, 1919, 153. (*D. G.*)

WHAT SHOULD BE DONE IN THE CONTROL OF DEGENERATIVE DISEASES?

FREDERICK S. CRUM, PH.D.,

Assistant Statistician, The Prudential Insurance Company of America, Newark, N. J.

Read before Section of Public Health Administration, American Public Health Association, at New Orleans, La., October, 28, 1919.

Dr. Crum's six lines of attack are: bettered scientific methods in infant and pre-school care; extension of school hygiene, medical inspection and physical training, more intensive health education of the people and the extension of industrial sanitation and industrial hygiene.

AS a preliminary to the discussion of this problem, it is desirable that a brief statement be made as to the philosophy of disease origin and causation. The life of a complex organism has been defined as the sum of all those interactions which take place between the various cells constituting the organism and their several environments. All disease is ultimately an improper interaction of cells and their environment. Cell environment may be morbidly modified or affected in various ways and Dr. Campbell* enumerates these under nine headings, as follows:

1. By insufficient, excessive or improper ingesta.
2. By disease of the blood-plasma-forming tissues.
3. By inhalation of insufficient oxygen or nocuous matters; mechanical, germinal or gaseous; also imperfect exhalation of lung excreta. Temperature and dampness of atmosphere also may exert ill effects on the body.
4. By disease of the blood-cell-forming organs.
5. By disease of the respiratory organs.
6. By disease of the vascular system; heart, blood-vessels and their nervous regulating systems.

7. By disease of the excretory organs.
8. By direct nervous influence upon cells.
9. By injurious influence upon the exterior of the body, e. g., violence, extremes of temperature, filth, parasites.

Dr. Campbell also well defines disease as "an abnormal mode of life."

In very recent times emphasis has properly been placed upon the fact that all of the various parts of the body are so closely connected and interrelated that it is almost impossible for one part, organ or function to get out of order without throwing the whole machinery out of gear. To illustrate, a decayed tooth may cause neuralgia, dyspepsia, acute rheumatism or other serious disease or disorder.

In considering the origin of disease, therefore, it is necessary to keep in mind that attacks of sickness or injuries received in early life may often result in future disease. It is not rare that the seed of disease is planted by some attack in infancy or childhood and, after lying dormant for years, develops in middle life or old age.

It is important also to keep in mind that many diseases which formerly were considered as confined to one organ are seldom so limited, for numerous autop-

*The Causation of Disease, p. 20, by Harry Campbell. M.D., B.S. (Lond.), London, 1889.

210

sies have demonstrated beyond doubt that there are lesions of other organs that are just as definite as those of the part which once was quite generally considered to be the sole seat of origin. At the same time many of the lesions are of such a nature as to render it certain that they existed long before the onset of the fatal attack.

In considering therefore, the sum of those material conditions from which disease or diseases necessarily follow, our search must be directed to the material conditions out of which the disease or diseases may have arisen.

DISEASE CLASSIFICATION.

Dr. Meigs, Physician to the Pennsylvania Hospital,* has very clearly set forth the fact that many of the present disease classifications are faulty in that they do not follow any consistent principle. He also quite properly, I think, classifies all diseases as falling into one of two groups, those of extrinsic origin and those of intrinsic origin. He also brings out very clearly the fact that the diseases of extrinsic origin are generally those common to early life and are quite rare in old age. The diseases of extrinsic origin are smallpox, measles, whooping cough, diphtheria, etc. The diseases of intrinsic origin, on the other hand, are quite rare in early life and very common to old age. An illustration of this is cysts in the kidneys. There are, of course, a number of diseases which at the present time cannot be definitely assigned as being of extrinsic or intrinsic origin largely because such diseases are not at present thoroughly enough understood. It is also possible that some diseases may be of dual origin, that is, in part extrinsic and in part intrinsic. Cancer is probably such a disease.

Dr. Meigs has pointed out that if the subject of disease origin and causation is considered from the standpoint of pathology and the conditions of the tissues examined, the meaning of the assertion that youth and age may be mingled will be understood and it will be perceived that disease can so far change a person young in years as to produce all the conditions which under natural circumstances are found only in the old.

Recent advances in medical science and practice have developed a wider knowledge of the fact that persons affected with chronic diseases, such as certain chronic lung diseases, nephritis, etc., may have their lives prolonged for several years by proper curative treatment and personal care. The same truth is even more susceptible of demonstration in instances of chronic heart diseases. This fact has been brought out very clearly by Dr. Oliver T. Osborne in his little book entitled "Disturbances of the Heart; Discussion of the Treatment of the Heart in Its Various Disorders."†

With these preliminary statements we may ask the question, have the degenerative diseases increased? For the purposes of this discussion I am limiting the term degenerative diseases to include chronic valvular diseases of the heart, fatty degeneration of the heart, chronic myocarditis, chronic dilation of the heart, heart disease of rheumatic origin, certain types of nervous diseases such as apoplexy and chronic nephritis, or Bright's disease. For the purposes of this discussion it is not of prime importance to determine positively whether or not there has been an increase in the degenerative diseases, so-called. There are good reasons to believe that there have been exaggerated statements made as to the increase in this class or group of diseases and there are good reasons to believe from a very extended insurance mortality experience based upon millions of lives and hundreds of thousands of deaths that there has been no very considerable increase in the mor-

---

*The Origin of Disease, p. 2, by Arthur V. Meigs, M.D., Philadelphia, 1897.

†The American Medical Association, 1913.

tality from this group of diseases in recent years in this country.* Entirely aside, however, from that question there are numerous facts in mortality experience both general and special, in proof that there is at the present time a very large and probably preventable mortality at premature ages in this group of diseases. There are many difficulties in the way of determining whether or not there has been an increase in the mortality from these diseases, not the least of which is our imperfect nosology and the resulting imperfect and changing classification of diseases or causes of deaths as reported by the United States Census Bureau, State health authorities, etc. One illustration will suffice to bring out this fact. In the four States of Connecticut, Massachusetts, New Hampshire and Rhode Island, combined, in the period 1889 to 1891 and at ages 60-69, 2.6 per cent of the total mortality was assigned to the indefinite term "old age." In the period 1909-1911, same age group, the percentage was only 0.6. The similar comparison, ages 70 to 79. was 11 per cent for the earlier period as against 3.2 per cent for the later period. Again, the similar comparison for ages 80 and over gives 38 per cent for the earlier period as against 17.6 per cent for the later period. These facts illustrate the danger of drawing conclusions as to the increase of degenerative diseases on the basis of mortality returns of the registration area of the United States, much, if not all of which apparent increase is due to the change in titles and reassignments of causes, particularly in the comparatively recent period during which there has been anything like accurate or complete registration of deaths even in the registration area of the United States. After a very extended and careful investigation of the subject I cannot but conclude, as many other investigators have, that although there may have been an increase in the mortality from degenerative diseases in

*See Appendix A.

recent years, such increase has not been relatively important and, indeed, if the classification could be made with absolute accuracy, there is a strong probability that the increase has been very small and possibly *nil*.

For the present we can probably dismiss as of no practical value the much heralded, alleged discovery by Dr. Serge Voronoff. Judging from analogy and the consensus of opinion of the most able and experienced medical and surgical experts, there is no very strong probability that the fountain of youth will be found in an "interstitial" or any other gland or part of the human body. As "The Cincinnati Post" in an editorial of October 23, 1919, states: "While positive as to the restoration of vim, vigor, etc., Dr. Voronoff is careful to state that gray hair does not return to black, new teeth don't sprout and weak eyes do not become strong. White-headed, toothless and wrinkled, the old man is just filled chock full of youthful gaiety—everything in the way of youth except the looks." Apropos, it is interesting to note that Dr. W. J. Mayo is reported to have recently stated before the American College of Surgeons that some fifteen years have been added to the span of human life since the Civil War and he has predicted, according to report, that within a short period, or within twenty years, there are likely to be from ten to fifteen more years added to the span of human life in the United States. This addition to our years, however, according to Dr. Mayo, will be by the well-known methods of life conservation rather than by any such remarkable, alleged discoveries as that claimed by Dr. Voronoff.

Principal Causes of Premature Death from Degenerative Diseases. On the basis of the philosophical theories of Drs. Campbell, Meigs and others, which theories are at least partially confirmed by an enormous body of reliable experience, we may briefly enumerate some of the principal causes of these premature deaths as follows: Focal infections, in cluding mouth infection; faulty habits, such as over-indulgence in alcohol, tobacco, sexual excesses, etc.; lack of exercise leading to constipation and other serious contributory causes of chronic affections; dietetic excesses, such as over-indulgence in food, undernourishment, malnutrition, unbalanced rations, etc.; overweight, physical and mental strain, etc.

It would be impossible to dwell at length upon any one or all of these and other causes in this brief paper; I will, therefore, confine myself to the one item, focal infections. Dr. W. J. Mayo is reported to have said before the recent Congress of the American College of Surgeons that, "Better care of focal infections in the earlier decades will prevent many deaths in later life." Of course, I assume that Dr. Mayo meant postpone instead of "prevent." It is a well known fact, which has recently received considerable emphasis, that good dentistry will prevent many serious diseases, some of which are likely to become chronic. In fact, Dr. W. J. Mayo in this same address is reported to have said that good dentistry has eliminated a percentage of cancers of the jaw due to the irritation of defective teeth. In this connection I may also mention the recently published industrial mortality experience of the Metropolitan Life* Insurance Company in which it appears that there was a quite significant increase in organic heart disease, pulmonary tuberculosis and puerperal diseases during the recent epidemic period of influenza when the mortality experience of that company for the period October to December, 1918, is compared with the similar period for the year 1917.*

STATISTICS.

We need much more full and complete statistical information as to the effect

of previous diseases and injuries on mortality. There is every prospect that such statistics will be available in large numbers in the near future. Industrial insurance companies, hospitals, employees benefit associations, experiments like the Framingham Health and Tuberculosis Demonstration and the Cincinnati Unit Plan, the statistics of school medical inspection and the statistical data which are being collected by the Life Extension Institute are instances, among others, of the possibilities and probabilities in this direction.

METHODS OF CONTROL OF DEGENERATIVE DISEASES.

I have nothing new to propose in the way of methods of controlling degenerative diseases. I believe that the methods which must be followed are practically all in use somewhere and to some extent at the present time. It is only a matter therefore, of coordinating and extending these methods on a more wide and practically universal scale, and if this is done, unquestionably a large proportion of the premature deaths from the so-called degenerative diseases will be postponed in many cases for several years. In fact I believe that the considerable reduction in industrial accidents which has already taken place; the reduction in infant mortality and in certain diseases of early childhood, particularly diphtheria; and the reduction of the mortality and morbidity from certain diseases of middle life, such as typhoid fever and pulmonary tuberculosis, are certain to reflect favorably upon the so-called degenerative diseases in the near future if such has not already been the case.

In conclusion, let me enumerate very briefly some of the principal methods which, in my opinion, will go a long way towards controlling the premature mortality from degenerative diseases if they are extended and correlated under some well-devised system of Federal and State Health Administration such as has recently been put into effect in Great

---

*Influenza Mortality Among Wage-Earners and Their Families, by Frankel and Dublin, Amer. Jour. Pub. H., October, 1919.

Britain and Canada, through the establishment of Ministries of Health:

1. An extension of the most scientific methods of infant care and medical supervision.

2. An extension of the most scientific methods of care and supervision of children of pre-school age.

3. An extension of school hygiene, in which shall be included medical inspection and physical training of children in the grade schools, high schools and institutions of higher learning. This also includes provision for school lunches wherever there is need for the same.

4. A continued and even more intensive and wide-spread scientific educational propaganda in the principles of good personal habits, including cleanliness, diet, exercise, proper recreation, etc. This education should also include instruction in the principles of personal safety and of industrial, public, and home accident prevention. The need for periodical dental and other physical examination should be a part of such propaganda.

5. An extension of the work, now so well done in many large industrial plants, of industrial sanitation. This should include factory good housekeeping, which in turn includes cleanliness, good lighting, good ventilation, the elimination so far as possible of dusts, fumes, gases, industrial poisons, etc.

6. Industrial hygiene. A very considerable emphasis has been placed upon this factor in recent years. The principles have already been worked out quite satisfactorily in some countries and in many plants and establishments in this country. The factors in industrial hygiene are numerous. Undue fatigue should be avoided; there should be provision for physical examinations of employees and for industrial clinics; recreational facilities should be made available to employees wherever possible and industrial cafeterias have been found of inestimable value in certain plants where good eating facilities are otherwise difficult to obtain.

I have not attempted to cover this subject with any completeness; that, would be utterly impossible in so brief a paper. I have only attempted to open the subject and trust that it will receive amplification from the discussions that may follow.

There are added to the paper a few illustrative statistics and a brief bibliography of some of the more important recent books and pamphlets dealing with this large problem.

APPENDIX A

Mortality from Degenerative Diseases*
Ages 40 and Above
Industrial Mortality Experience
The Prudential Insurance Company of America
1911-1918

Years	Approximate Number Persons Exposed to Risk, Ages 40 and Over	Number of Deaths	Death Rate Per 10,000 Persons
1911	1,690,902	16,377	96.85
1912	1,807,395	17,079	94.50
1913	1,944,160	18,103	93.11
1914	2,046,162	18,793	91.85
1915	2,182,878	21,878	100.23
1916	2,336,044	23,966	102.56
1917	2,484,131	25,349	102.04
1918	2,712,165	25,058	92.39

The statistics of the Metropolitan Life Insurance Company's experience may be found in "Mortality Statistics of Insured Wage-Earners and Their Families." The data, however, are not given by age in such manner as to make possible a comparison of 1911 with 1917. The death rates from Organic Heart Diseases, Apoplexy and Cerebral Hemorrhage, Diabetes and Bright's Disease combined, all ages and both sexes, were as follows:

Death Rate Per 10,000 Persons Insured
All Ages
Degenerative Diseases
Metropolitan's Industrial Experience

1911	31.43	1915	31.60
1912	32.72	1916	32.38
1913	31.77	1917	31.98
1914	31.69		

In these two mortality experiences, which represent several millions of lives exposed to risk, there is no conclusive evidence that the so-called degenerative diseases have increased in prevalence or fatality in recent years in the United States.

---

*Including Organic Heart Disease. Apoplexy and Cerebral Hemorrhage, Diabetes and Bright's Disease

APPENDIX B

A Partial Bibliography

The Causation of Disease. Harry Campbell, M.D., B.S., (Lond.), London, 1889.

The Origin of Disease. Arthur V. Meigs, M.D. Philadelphia, 1897.

American Life-Waste, Where and How It Is Increasing. E. E. Rittenhouse, President, Provident Savings Life Assurance Society. New York, 1910.

Circulatory Disease: Its Prevalence in New England, Massachussets and Boston. Edwin Welles Dwight, M.D. Boston, Mass., June 13, 1911.

The Upward Trend of Mortality in Middle Life and Old Age. E. E. Rittenhouse. American Association for the Advancement of Science, January 3, 1913.

The Increase in the National Death Rate from Heart Disease, Bright's Disease and Apoplexy. George H. Cunningham. February, 1913.

The Increasing Mortality from Degenerate Maladies. E. E. Rittenhouse. The Popular Science Monthly, April, 1913.

Possibilities of Reducing Mortality at the Higher Age Groups. Louis I. Dublin, Ph.D., September, 1913. Metropolitan Life Insurance Company, New York, 1913.

Disturbances of the Heart. Oliver T. Osborne, M.D., Chicago, Ill., 1913.

What Heart Patients Should Know and Do. James Henry Honan, M.D. New York, 1913.

The Significance of a Declining Death Rate. Frederick L. Hoffman, LL.D. Prudential Press, Newark, N. J., 1914.

Periodic Examination of Supposedly Well Persons. Eugene Lyman Fisk, M.D. Life Extension Institute, New York, 1915.

Health Conservation After Forty. John L. Davis, M.D. Texas State Journal of Medicine, January, 1916.

Increasing Mortality in the United States from Diseases of the Heart, Blood-vessels, and Kidneys. Eugene Lyman Fisk, M.D. New York Medical Journal, January 15, 1916.

Geriatrics: The Diseases of Old Age and Their Treatment. I. L. Nascher, M. D. Philadelphia, Pa., 1916.

Chronic Diseases of the Heart, Kidneys and Arteries from the Standpoint of Etiology, Prevalence, Mortality and Prevention. Charles F. Bolduan, M.D. New York, 1916.

Risks of Middle Age. Report of Committee Concerning Causes of Death and Invalidity in the Commonwealth of Australia. Melbourne, 1916.

The Classification and Relations of Cardio-Vascular-Renal Disease. Lewellys F. Barker, M.D. Southern Medical Journal, January, 1917.

Disturbances of the Kidneys. Oliver T. Osborne, M.D. Chicago, Ill., 1917.

The Road to a Healthy Old Age. T. Bodley Scott, M.D. London, 1917.

The Increasing Mortality After Age Forty-Five — Some Causes and Explanations.

Louis I. Dublin, Ph.D. Quarterly Publications of American Statistical Association, Boston, Mass., March, 1917.

Civilization and the Diseases of Adult Life. Edward O. Otis, M.D. Medical Record, July 28, 1917.

The Causes of Disease. Ernest S. Reynolds, M.D. (Lond.), F.R.C.P. The Lancet, November 10, 1917.

Evidences of Full Maturity and Early Decline. J. Madison Taylor, M.D. The Scientific Monthly, February, 1918.

Diseases of the Cardio-Vascular System. Eugene Lyman Fisk, M.D. Texas Medical Journal, February, 1918.

Physical Training in Public Schools as an Aid and Remedy for the Physical Defects Found Through the Draft. Thomas A. Storey. M.D. February 19, 1918. The Military Training Commission, Albany, N. Y., 1918.

The Mortality from Degenerative Diseases. Frederick L. Hoffman, LL.D. Journal of the American Institute of Homeopathy, March, 1918.

State Legislation for Physical Training. Thomas A. Storey, M.D., June, 1918. The Military Training Commission, Albany, N. Y., 1919.

Is It Worth While for the Man of Fifty to Get into Physical Condition? Conservation of Man Power at or Beyond Full Maturity. J. Madison Taylor, M.D. Boston Medical and Surgical Journal, September 5, 1918.

The Relation of Habits to Life Expectancy. J. H. Kellogg, M.D. Good Health, Battle Creek, Mich., December, 1918.

The Evolution of Disease. Sir W. Arbuthnot Lane, Bart., M.S., F.R.C.S. The Lancet, December 20, 1919.

Physical Training an Essential to the Better Health Defense of Society. Thomas A. Storey, M.D. The Military Training Commission, Albany, N. Y., 1919.

The Growing Movement to Prolong Human Life. Life Extension Institute, New York, 1919.

Prolonging Life as a Function of Life Insurance. Life Extension Institute, New York, 1919.

How to Live. Irving Fisher and Eugene Lyman Fisk, M.D. New York and London. 1919.

Mortality Statistics of Insured Wage-Earners and Their Families. Louis I. Dublin, Ph.D., E. W. Kopf, and G. H. Van Buren. Metropolitan Life Insurance Company, New York, 1919.

Geriatrics: A Treatise on Senile Conditions, Diseases of Advanced Life, and Care of the Aged. Malford W. Thewlis, M.D. St. Louis, Mo., 1919.

A Plan for a More Effective Federal and State Health Administration. Frederick L. Hoffman, LL.D. Prudential Press, Newark, N. J., 1919.

Physical Examination of the First Million Draft Recruits; Methods and Results. Compiled under direction of the Surgeon General, M. W. Ireland, Maj.-General, M.C., U.S.A. Love and Davenport. Government Printing Office, Washington, D. C., 1919.

STUDIES ON MALARIA CONTROL

X. Cure of Infected Persons as a Factor in Malarial Control*

C. C. BASS, M.D.,

*Department of Experimental Medicine, Tulane Medical College,
New Orleans, La.*

Read at General Sessions, American Public Health Association, at New Orleans, La., October 29, 1919.

Nine-tenths of the malaria would be gone in ten years if the
doctors could only cure all the cases they treat. Intensive survey
and follow-up can effect like results. This is no idle story, for in
Sunflower County, Miss., in 1918, malaria was reduced ninety
percent.

THE only source of malaria to man
is infected anopheline mosquitoes.
The only source of malaria to
mosquitos is infected man. The greater
the number of infected mosquitoes in
a given region, the greater the probability of people who live in the region
becoming infected. Likewise, the greater
the number of infected people living in
a given region, the greater the probability of mosquitoes in the region becoming infected.

The number of infected mosquitoes in
a given region may be reduced either
by reducing the total number of mosquitoes susceptible or exposed to infection or by reducing the number of
infected persons — potential sources of
infection—who are exposed to the bites
of mosquitoes.

The number of mosquitoes in a given
region may be reduced by various
methods of mosquito control, all depending, however, chiefly or entirely upon
elimination, reduction or treatment of
breeding places. It is possible to do
this thoroughly enough to entirely prevent the transmission of malaria. This
is possible because, fortunately, the
length of life of anophelines during the
warm season, during which malaria is
transmitted chiefly, is quite short.

Use of screens and other means of
protecting the people from the bites of
mosquitoes also reduces the number of
infected mosquitoes in a region by reducing the chances of mosquitoes biting
infected individuals and getting infected.
They also reduce the chances of transmission by infected mosquitoes by protecting uninfected persons from their
bites.

Disinfecting or curing infected persons also reduces the number of infected
persons—the only source of infection
of mosquitoes—in a given region to
whatever extent it is carried out. Theoretically, it would be possible to prevent
completely the transmission of malaria
and to eliminate it from a given region
by curing or disinfecting all infected
persons in the region. This would result, regardless of the abundance of

*This is one of a series of papers to be published,
based largely or entirely upon malaria control work
conducted jointly by the International Health Board
and the Mississippi State Board of Health. The
author, however, is alone responsible for the views
expressed.
I. Appeared in the Southern Medical Journal,
Vol. XII, No. 8, p. 456.
II. Journal A.M.A., Vol. 72, No. 17, p. 1218.
III. Southern Medical Journal, Vol. XII, No. 4,
p. 190.
IV. Will appear shortly in the Osler Memorial
Volume, Paul B. Hoeber, New York,
publisher.
V. Southern Medical Journal, Vol. XII, No. 6,
p. 306.
VI. Southern Medical Journal, Vol. XII, No. 8,
p. 460.
VII. Southern Medical Journal, Vol. XII, No. 8,
p. 462.
VIII. Southern Medical Journal, Vol. XII, No. 8,
p. 465.
IX. Journal A.M.A., Vol. 78, No. 1, p. 81.

mosquitoes, provided all infected persons could be treated and disinfected. The reduction both in prevalence and transmission will be in proportion to the proportion of the infected persons disinfected. This statement applies alike to small areas, larger areas or the entire malarial section of the country. Malaria could be eliminated from the entire United States by disinfecting all infected persons in the country.

It will be convenient to discuss this phase of the subject under three heads:

I. CURE OF CASES TREATED BY PHYSICIANS.

The proportion of the total number of persons who have malaria, who are treated by physicians, varies no doubt considerably in different localities. We have no extensive data indicating what proportion of the total amount of malaria is treated by physicians. By taking the number of cases of malaria reported to the State Board of Health by the physicians of Bolivar and Sunflower Counties, Miss., which are supposed to be representative of the malarial region of the Mississippi Delta, and data obtained by intensive malaria surveys of some 40,000 persons during 1916, 1917 and 1918 in these counties, we have been able to arrive at fairly definite conclusions as to the proportion of the total amount of malaria, that is treated by the physicians in this particular region. These data indicate that approximately 20 to 25 per cent of the total number of persons infected with malaria are treated by physicians. Having this information, we may calculate the rate of reduction in the prevalence and transmission of malaria that would occur if all physicians disinfected all of their cases.

It is perhaps not generally appreciated but it is nevertheless a fact that only a small percent of the cases of malaria treated by physicians are actually disinfected. It is true that most of them are relieved of their clinical symptoms temporarily, but proper treatment is not continued for sufficient length of time to disinfect them. They relapse from time to time. Many individuals carry their infection for an entire year or even longer, during all of which time they are potential sources of infection. A recent analysis* of data obtained in a study of malaria in Sunflower County indicates that between 50.77 per cent and 68.86 per cent of all persons who have attacks of malaria during a given year have relapses and not new infections. This serves to emphasize the great frequency of relapse resulting from insufficient treatment.

Generally, when a physician is called to treat a case of malaria, if proper diagnosis is made the patient is put on treatment with the specific remedy, quinin in some form or other, and the clinical symptoms are relieved in comparatively short time. Soon afterward the patient feels well, and no practical method of examination will determine whether he has been disinfected or not. As a rule, he has not, and if treatment is discontinued, sooner or later relapse occurs. During much of the time in the interval between attacks he has malaria parasites in his blood and may infect mosquitoes and thereby be a source of transmission to others.

Following the relief of clinical symptoms, the practice among many physicians is to prescribe some tonic containing more or less quinin but seldom sufficient to disinfect the patient. In some instances sufficiently large doses may be advised to actually disinfect and the advice to keep it up long enough to do so is given. However, it is usually done in such a way as not to impress the patient with the importance of carrying it out. As a result, he neglects or stops treatment long before he is disinfected.

In other instances, the treatment advised to follow the acute attack is so unpleasant, produces so much discom-

*C. C. Bass. The Frequency of Malaria Relapse in an Area of Great Prevalence in the Mississippi Delta. Osler Anniversary Volume, Paul B. Hoeber, New York, publisher.

fort or causes so much inconvenience that the patient does not carry it out, resulting in failure to disinfect.

One of the reasons for the failure to disinfect patients treated by physicians is the lack of a standard, effective method of treatment. Different authorities advocate different methods of treatment, many of them impractical, to say the least. The physician who is actually anxious to find and employ the best treatment is unable to know which is best because of the great variety of methods advocated by different authorities. The more spectacular methods are more likely to be employed and they are much less likely to be practical or effective. In fact, most of them are very impractical from the standpoint of disinfecting infected persons. These facts serve to emphasize the very great need of some standard, practical method of treating and disinfecting persons who have malaria. The standard treatment adopted in the Bolivar and Sunflower Counties work* consists of a proper dose of quinin every night before retiring for a period of eight weeks. The proper dose for different ages is: under one year, ½ grain; one year, 1 grain; two years, 2 grains, three and four years, 3 grains; five, six and seven years, 4 grains; eight, nine and ten years, 6 grains; eleven, twelve, thirteen and fourteen years, 8 grains; fifteen years and older, 10 grains. This treatment appears to disinfect more than 90 per cent of cases and the writer's opinion is that it is the most practical method for this purpose.

If we assume that 20 per cent of the malaria that occurs each year in a given region is treated by physicians, we can estimate the rate of reduction in the prevalence of malaria that would result if all physicians disinfected all the cases they treat, a thing that is quite practical

*C. C. Bass. The Treatment of Malaria, with the Special Object of Disinfecting Infected Persons. Adopted After Wide Experience in Malaria Control by Treating Malaria Carriers in the Mississippi Delta. Journal A.M.A., Vol. 72, No. 17, p. 1218.

and that should be done. (Chart 1.) There would be a reduction of 20 per cent during the first year and 20 per cent of the remainder during the second year, etc., until finally by the end of a period of ten years there would be a reduction of approximately 90 per cent

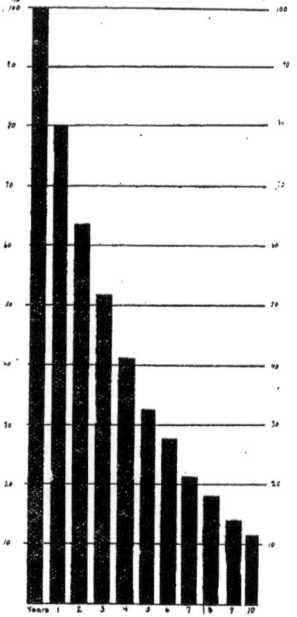

Chart 1.—Reduction of the amount of malaria that would result from disinfection of all cases treated by physicians.

in the prevalence of the disease over what existed at first.

These figures represent the contribution the medical profession could make to the control of malaria if they would do so. This is perhaps the avenue of approach of the great problem of malaria control through which results can be accomplished with less expenditure of money and effort than any other. If we can settle upon some standard method of treatment and in some way bring it impressively to the attention of the medical profession, it will be adopted to a considerable extent, at least, and to whatever extent this is done, to that same extent malaria will be controlled throughout the entire country. It may be of interest to state that the State Boards of Health of Mississippi and Louisiana have taken some steps in this direction. They have called to the attention of the medical profession of their respective states the method of treatment which has been adopted as standard as a result of the malaria control work in Bolivar and Sunflower Counties in Mississippi. It is impossible to say to what extent this method of treatment is being employed by the medical profession of these states, but there is information that it is being done to considerable extent, at least.

II. Cure of Persons Who Treat Themselves.

In an analysis of the data obtained by an intensive survey of 31,459 persons in Bolivar County, Miss., during 1916 and 1917,* it was found that of the total number of persons in whose blood malaria parasites were found present, only 55.09 per cent gave a history of having had one or more attacks of malaria during the previous twelve months and that 44.91 per cent had not had attacks that were recognized either by physicians or by themselves as being due to malaria. This indicates, therefore, that approximately 55 per cent of the total number of persons infected with malaria, in this locality at least, know that they have malaria and are treated either by physicians or by themselves. If all persons who know they have malaria and treat themselves should employ a method of treatment which disinfects them—and if those who are treated by physicians are treated so as to disinfect them, we would

*C. C. Bass. The Frequency of Malaria Infection Without Recognized Attacks, in an Area of Great Prevalence. Southern Medical Journal, Vol. XII. No. 8, p. 466.

have, therefore, theoretically 55 per cent of reduction in the prevalence of malaria each year. There would be at the end of the first year only 45 per cent as much malaria as otherwise. At the end of the second year there would be 20.25 per cent and at the end of the third year 9.11 per cent. (Chart 2.)

Chart 2. Reduction in the prevalence of malaria that would result from the cure of all recognized cases, both those who are treated by physicians and those who treat themselves.

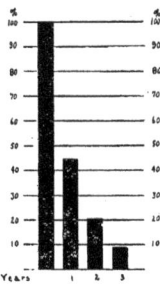

The layman who undertakes to treat himself for malaria buys either quinin in some form or other or perhaps more likely some one of the many chill tonics and patent medicines containing quinin. He is usually relieved in a short time and so far as he knows there is no necessity to continue treatment. The treatment is discontinued and in due course of time, perhaps a few days, weeks, months or even a year afterwards he relapses, carrying the infection all the time. During part of the time at least he has enough malaria parasites in his circulating blood to infect mosquitoes. He has not been informed and does not realize the importance of disinfection and even if he did he is unable to select a suitable method of treatment from those available to him.

Public health agencies can contribute very largely to malaria control by bringing the proper treatment and the importance of disinfection to the attention of the public who treat themselves for malaria, by publicity, by advocating a suitable standard treatment and by making such standard treatment available at reasonable cost to those who have malaria. Proper standard treatment for malaria should be sold at all stores of the country where medicine is sold. It should be just as available to people who have malaria as are the much less effective chill tonics, etc. This very thing is being done in Sunflower County, Mississippi, during the present year (1919) under the direction of the State Board of Health.

III. CURE OF PERSONS WHO ARE INFECTED BUT HAVE NO RECOGNIZED CLINICAL SYMPTOMS.

The data referred to above indicate that 44.91 per cent, or approximately 45 per cent of the total number of persons infected with malaria have no clinical symptoms that are recognized as due to malaria. Neither they nor the physicians who treat them know that they are infected. Some of them, no doubt, later on develop clinical symptoms of the disease and are then recognized, but many finally lose their infection without ever having recognized clinical symptoms of malaria. The only way that they may be found is by microscopic examination of the blood and even that does not find all of them. At times there are very few parasites in the blood, but at other times there are sufficient to infect mosquitoes and thereby to be a source of infection to others. Such persons are potential sources of infection at all times. The only way by which all persons who have malaria in a given locality can be found is by intensive malaria surveys. The history of previous attacks must be taken and those who give histories of having had one or more attacks during the previous twelve months should be considered probably still infected and therefore should take the necessary treatment to disinfect them. A proper blood examination should be made of those who give negative histories and those who are found to have parasites should also be disinfected. Theoretically, it would be possible to eradicate malaria entirely from a given region in this way. Unfortunately, it is not possible to find 100 per cent of infected persons by present methods and treatment necessary to disinfect 100 per cent is not very practical. It is possible, however, to disinfect a very high per cent, considerably more than 90 per cent, with treatment that is not impractical.

During 1916 and 1917 experiments in malaria control were conducted in Bolivar County, Miss., under the auspices of the Mississippi State Board of Health, as a result of which, a suitable method of treatment and methods of carrying out this more or less intensive method of malaria control were developed. During 1918, the most promising method of control by disinfecting infected persons was carried out in an area of 100 square miles, containing a population of approximately 9,000, in Sunflower County. The reduction in the prevalence of the disease in this area indicated by the cases treated

CONTROL OF MALARIA IN SUNFLOWER COUNTY, MISSISSIPPI
BY CURING INFECTED PERSONS.

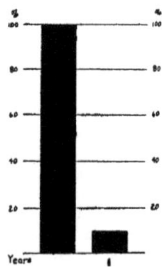

Chart 3. Reduction in prevalence of malaria in a 100 square mile area in Sunflower County, Mississippi, 89.9%, following intensive malaria control work in 1918. (The tall column represents the total number of persons who had attacks of malaria during the 12 months previous to the first survey and the short column the total number who had attacks during the 12 months following.)

by the physicians was 88.82 per cent. The reduction indicated by a resurvey of a large part of the area just one year from the first survey was 89.9 per cent. (Chart 3.) In other words, during the 12 months following the survey and treatment of all infected persons, there occurred only 10.1 per cent as much malaria as occurred during the 12 months previous to the survey and treatment.

SUMMARY.

1. Cure of infected persons is an important factor in control of malaria. Its usefulness depends upon the extent to which it is carried out.

2. If the physicians of the country would cure all the cases of malaria they treat, this alone would result in a reduction of approximately 90 per cent in the prevalence of the disease in a period of ten years.

3. If all persons who treat themselves for malaria, as well as those who are treated by physicians, took proper treatment and were disinfected, this would result in a reduction of 90.89 per cent in the prevalence of the disease in three years.

4. By proper intensive survey and treatment it is theoretically possible to eradicate malaria entirely from any given region. A reduction of 89.9 per cent followed carrying out this method in an area of 100 square miles in Sunflower County, in 1918.

□

A STANDARD BUDGET;
THE HEALTH OFFICER'S FIRST NEED

HAVEN EMERSON, M.D.,

Medical Adviser, Charity Organization Society,
New York City.

Read before Section of Public Health Administration, American Public Health Association, at New Orleans, La., October, 28, 1919.

"Budget hearings are a public forum," writes Dr. Emerson, "and preparation of the budget commits the health officer to measure his own with his neighbors' work." These are wise words from a health officer of experience in a great city, who writes for the benefit of brother officers.

WHAT is a budget and what is the Health Officer's first need? Then let us see if the title of the paper can be justified. A budget is a necessary instrument of administration. A budget is a report, an estimate and a proposal. It is a document of information. It is not a budgetary system but is indispensable for such a system. The health officer's greatest need is public knowledge of the service he can render, and public interest in supporting his request for appropriations.

If a budget is intelligible, logical, giving as a background an accurate history of service, and costs, and offering comparison on equivalent basis in the same terms with service and costs in other similar communities, the support of business, labor, social and general citizen groups can be readily enlisted.

A budget is in its perfection a triple

annual report giving on parallel sheets certain data for the last completed year, for the current year up to date of report and proposals for the next full fiscal year.

Briefly a budgetary system requires submission of a report of past work, expenses and income, and a program and plan for work and expenses, for consideration by the chief executive who then calls upon the legislative or appropriating body for an act of appropriation which amounts to an order or authorization to carry out the program approved.

For the health officer this means submitting to the Governor or Mayor or some reviewing body his document of information, which commits him to a program and an organization to perform the functions for which his department or bureau was created. In making such a statement he assumes responsibility as he should for the wisdom of the entire plan and organization.

In justifying his plan of work, in argument for his organization, and in pleading for the funds he requires, he will be chiefly helped by comparable statements in previous budgets for his own area and by reference to budgets of other health officers, administering similar areas.

The health officer's first need is to have his own statements comparable for a series of years, and the next need is to have his fellow officers agree in following identical methods of report.

The agreement need not be 100 per cent or take place all at once, but a beginning can be made in this as in standard methods for water, milk or air analysis.

If there is nothing more than an agreement to report work, plan, organization and costs according to a few relatively simple functions, such as registration of births, morbidity and deaths, control of communicable diseases, infant hygiene, school medical inspection, sanitation, food control, a gain would be

apparent, for this would result in the keeping of accounts by functions or objects of work, the auditing of accounts on the same lines, and the description of organization with direct relation to function.

The health officer being responsible for but one of the administrative divisions of civil government the chief executive or his representatives must judge and balance the needs of the public for the increase of services which the health officer clamors for, against the tax or other incomes he can count upon and the requests of other departments. Health development and protection depend on so many services that often the appropriation for parks, sewers, tenement houses and hospitals provided for in other budgets will permit of reduction in the health officer's requests.

The helpful tax payer must have it made easy for him to support his best friend the health officer by having costs and results reported by function, service or organization unit. In this way each interested group or individual can see what share of his tax dollar goes to fill the need he particularly feels.

Costs of functions or organization units must be reported according to the three main usual business subdivisions, Capital Outlay, Fixed Charges, Current Expenses as well as having services, transportation, materials and other objects of expense listed under each function.

Analysis of relative values stares one in the face when such logical elements for study are presented.

In order to present the problem and support the claims for public funds a health officer must show the object or thing purchased, the character of expenditure, the function served, the organization responsible for the function and the fund chargeable. Organization represents in the main the functions served.

Thus the budget and appropriation act should reveal the complete organization.

Whatever aids or encourages an interest in people in the character, quality and costs of the functions of government will contribute to practical democracy, and few opportunities occur so favorable to this kind of education as the public hearings on budgetary requests by department heads where a budgetary system is in effect. Such opportunities are a great satisfaction to the health officer and to the citizen.

Unless the health officer and other administrative heads take the lead and establish the practice of itemized budgetary reports, the present tendency of legislatures to assume executive functions will be accentuated to the detriment of orderly public service.

Preparation of a budget commits the health officer to study the history of his department, to think ahead and measure his own with his neighbors' work. None of this can he do with profit until there is agreement as to certain elementary forms and contents of reports.

Budgetary hearings are a public forum. Here the health officer can show the superior claim of the kind of insurance he has to sell as compared with the insurance against property loss which most of the rest of public funds are spent for.

Appeals of Health Officers direct to legislatures are not free from political entanglements. The health officer should present his budgetary report to his chief executive whose function it is to call for legislation to supply funds.

More than two thirds of the states have passed or are preparing enabling legislation to permit of the introduction of budgetary systems and a call for annual departmental budgets.

In Wisconsin there is an admirable system in effect but unfortunately the budget sheets called for from the State Health Officer do not provide for data by functions or by organization, and the facts of past service and proposals for future activities can not readily be extracted for comparison.

Budgetary systems are coming. Uniformity is indispensable. Health officers should specify their own needs and express themselves as a body. Without a budget the health officer's requests are likely to lack responsible revision and approval by the executive. Without a budget the health officer is likely to see legislative bodies controlling administrative organization for performing technical health functions. Without a budgetary report the health officer is without any formal public opportunity to defend his requests and explain his plans so that those whom he serves may know, understand and support him.

One of the important services which this section could do for Health Administration on this continent would be to encourage, by the example of its members, the introduction of budgetary systems and standard budget reports.

□

Investigations on Influenza.—Through the aid of a grant provided by the Metropolitan Life Insurance Company, a commission has been appointed to conduct studies on influenza. The Commission consists of Dr. G. W. McCoy, Dr. W. H. Park, Dr. Lee K. Frankel, Dr. A. S. Knight, Dr. M. J. Rosenau, Dr. E. O. Jordan and Dr. W. H. Frost. The work will be conducted in Washington, New York, Boston and Chicago. The purpose of the investigation is to study the cause, mode of spread and treatment of influenza and its complications. Studies are being made on the prophylactic value of vaccines against influenza, common colds and pneumonia. Work is also being done aiming to determine the cause of these infections and a special study is being made of the bacterial flora of the upper respiratory tract in health and disease. Special attention is given to the possibility of a filterable virus being the cause of these infections. Science, December 5, 1919.—(M. P. H.)

VITAL STATISTICS IN CANADA

R. H. Coats,

Dominion Statistician,
Ottawa, Ont.

Read before Section on Vital Statistics, American Public Health Association, at New Orleans, La., October 28, 1919.

Canada for the first time has undertaken a comprehensive survey in vital statistics, and this paper is a report of progress. It is proposed to make monthly compilations, prepare annual reports, collate statistics of immigration and emigration and supply standard forms for collection and record.

IN this short paper and before the present audience, it is unnecessary to point the need in every country of a comprehensive scheme of vital statistics, so framed that results may be collated and compared not only as between place and place but with those of similar geographical entities in other countries. In Canada we are now for the first time, thanks to the excellent co-operation of Provincial registrars-general and public health officials, in a fair way to meet this necessity, and a brief report of progress may be of general interest.

Legislative authority in Canada, it will be remembered, is delimited as between the Dominion and the Provinces by the British North America Act, 1867. Under this instrument, "property and civil rights" fall within the jurisdiction of the provinces. As vital statistics are widely used in the transfer of property and in the establishment of civil rights in general, they have been held to lie under provincial control, and in point of fact each of the nine provinces has for some time had legislation on the subject.

Concurrently, however, the Dominion government was assigned the duty of taking the census, and was given charge of statistics in general. Now the census, as the great stock-taking of the population, has a well-defined part to play in vital statistics. The Canadian census office was, however, given more even than the usual stock-taking role: in the original census act the office was instructed to collect also a record of all persons deceased within the census year, aside and apart from the enumeration of the living. Furthermore, in a general statistical clause, the Dominion government took express power to co-ordinate the vital statistics collected annually by provincial or other agencies. In outlining the past history of vital statistics in Canada, we may first glance at the activities of the Dominion under these provisions.

With regard to the collection of data concerning deaths in the census year, an attempt to comply with this instruction has been made in every census since confederation. The results, however, have not been happy. It is a fundamental rule of census-taking not to ask questions involving the extensive use of memory or of scientific knowledge. In experience, it was found that 20 per cent of the deaths were missed as the result of migration of population, lapse of memory or lack of knowledge in the person supplying the information, or through imperfect qualifications in the enumerator. Moreover, the information actually obtained was unsatisfactory, especially in the all-important matter of the cause of death. Even had the results been otherwise, mortality statistics at ten-year intervals are of little value.

Again, birth rates and marriage rates are needed only less insistently than death rates. The Dominion government last year revised its entire statistical system, greatly amplifying its range and centralizing the work in the Dominion Bureau of Statistics. In revising legislation to this end, it was resolved to discontinue altogether the provision for the decennial mortuary census, in which respect we were but following the lead of the United States, France, Germany and other countries, fortified by our own experience.

Coming to the second duty enjoined upon the census, that of co-ordinating the vital statistics annually available through provincial or municipal records, the Dominion has found it equally impossible hitherto to achieve satisfactory results. The reason lies in the provincial situation. One province has no vital statistics at all. In the others, legislation and methods have differed in the widest way. For example, the statistical year was not uniform, the International Classification of Causes of Death was not universally followed, and each province had its own formulæ for the compilation and presentation of the statistics. Taking the highly important matter of the form of death certificate as an example: of the 24 items which such a certificate usually covers, two of the provinces omitted 16, another 15 and another 13, whilst the least number of omissions was 3. Moreover, standards of administration have differed as between province and province and from time to time in the same province. Accordingly, though the Dominion has made an annual practice of bringing together for publication the more recent provincial vital statistics, we have always prefaced the figures with a note that they must not be made the basis of any calculation of mean birth or death-rate.

It may be interjected here that more than a quarter of a century ago, during the years 1883 to 1891, the Dominion government operated a scheme of annual mortuary statistics for cities of 25,000 and over by direct arrangement with the municipalities. This work, however, was abandoned when the provincial bureaus of vital statistics came into being. Its passing was marked by a significant incident, namely, a conference of Dominion and Provincial officials, held in 1893, which passed a resolution calling on the provincial and federal authorities to co-operate in the work of collecting, compiling and publishing the vital statistics of the Dominion.

It is on the principle laid down in this resolution that we have now at last attacked the problem of nation-wide vital statistics for Canada. The creation of the Dominion Bureau of Statistics above adverted to and the general statistical reorganization which was planned as a result may be said to have provided the primary motive-power. Though the initial step was taken by the Dominion bureau, the scheme, as already remarked, has owed its success throughout to the cordial good will and active practical assistance of the provincial authorities on whom devolves the crucial parts of its execution.

Briefly, the plan suggested was that each province bring its legislation and administration to a standard to be agreed upon, the bureau to act as intermediary for the maintenance of the standard and to furnish machinery for the compilation on a uniform basis of the resulting statistics. The bureau also undertook to secure all necessary supplementary data through the decennial census and to co-ordinate the statistics of migration with the scheme. It was not intended, of course, by the above that any province must cast its system in an iron mold or surrender individuality; the standard is a minimum standard, pure and simple.

In laying this proposal before the provinces, a memorandum was in the first instance drawn up for private discussion, including a model provincial bill, model forms of registration and model regulations for procedure in detail, the whole based on thorough examination of vital statistical legislation and administration both in the provinces and in other countries. By June, 1918, sufficient progress had been made to warrant the calling of a formal conference. In addition to the provincial officials who, with the representatives of the Dominion bureau, constituted the principals in the negotiations, there were also invited representatives of such bodies as the Department of Insurance, the Dominion Pensions Board, the Commission of Conservation and the Canadian Medical Association. The American Society of Actuaries kindly consented to send a committee, and the Union of Canadian Municipalities and the Municipal Improvement League of Canada furnished delegates. Finally, we were fortunate enough to obtain the attendance of Dr. W. H. Davis, the chief of the vital statistical division of the United States Bureau of the Census. The main business of the conference consisted of a detailed examination of the proposed model bill and of the forms appertaining thereto. Resolutions were passed approving the policy of co-operation and centralization suggested and generally defining its scope. The model bill was sent on to a committee which duly met and completed its revision. If any one is interested in the details of the conference, I may say that an official report containing the agenda, resolutions, model bill and schedules was published and may be had from the Dominion Bureau of Statistics, Ottawa.

Machinery of this character is necessarily somewhat slow in setting up. During the year that has elapsed five of the provinces have passed the required legislation and have adopted the reforms, and three others will take action this year. Simultaneously the Dominion has defined its obligations by formal order. Briefly, these are as follows: (1) To furnish free of charge all forms required in the collecting of vital statistics; (2) to effect all compilations monthly according to a plan agreed upon; (3) to pay the cost of transcribing the forms required for compilation; (4) to make annual publication of the vital statistics of the whole of Canada, according to a plan to be agreed upon; (5) to meet the expenses of periodical conferences of provincial officials for the discussion of working methods; (6) after each decennial revision of the International Classification of Diseases and Causes of Death, to have prepared a Manual of the International list and if necessary to have the same approved by the Canadian Medical Council; (7) to prepare and supply free of charge to provincial registrars for distribution to physicians a pocket reference book to the international list of the causes of death; and (8) to collate the statistics of immigration and emigration with vital statistics, and to take the decennial and quinquennial censuses after approved methods, so that Canada will possess a complete, co-ordinated scheme of demographic statistics, including the day-to-day records of change and periodical stocktaking. The foregoing, of course, applies only to the provinces which furnish satisfactory evidence that they receive returns of at least 90 per cent of all births, marriages and deaths occurring in the calendar year.

It is hoped that with the beginning of 1920 these plans will go into operation, though another year may be required to bring everyone into the scheme, and though results for a time may leave something to be desired in the way of comprehensiveness. It may be added that a divorce bill recently before the Canadian Parliament opens the way to including the statistics of divorce within the scheme. We hope that throughout our policy we have kept the best traditions of vital statistics elsewhere in view, so that when we attain to final running order, and when some eighteen months hence we publish the first Canadian report relating to births, marriages and deaths, our work will be found not merely Canadian but general in interest.

AFRICAN ABORIGINAL THERAPY

PHILIP A. E. SHEPPARD, M.D.,

Boston.

No other man in America has so complete a knowledge of the aborigines of South Africa as Dr. Sheppard. For twenty-one years he spent his vacations in their kraals. He is a blood-brother in two tribes, and a chief, and sits on his own mat at tribal councils. His picture of their aboriginal therapy is unique.

AT the very outset we may say that apart from a few safe and sane measures practiced by the native tribes of southern Africa, everything is in the hands of the unconstitutional "Medicine Man" or "Witch Doctor," of whom there are legion. Our readers must know the aborginal doctors of Africa are not mere "general practitioners," they are "specialists" of no mean merit. Their characters and functions are those of "diviners" or "spirit doctors." Various names are given to these specialists, depending on their particular jobs. One is "Izinyanga Zokubula" (the doctors of "smiting"), simply and for no other reason than that a tremendous use is made of canes for the purpose of smiting the ground by any of those who call upon them by appointment for a consultation. Then there are the "Izanusi" or the "Smellers out," a rather high-toned medico-legal affair for running down criminals (alleged), consulted in extreme cases for the purpose of discovering those possessed with witchcraft. These are believed to be in communication with the spirits of the great and glorious "Amatonga," or spirits of the departed, and reverenced among the tribes. These crafty semi-lunatics receive nothing short of an ox in compensation for their services and often a he-goat thrown in for good measure. The spirit doctors are the health inspectors of their respective communities, through the discharge of their sacerdotal functions, and in their prayers and invocations of the spirits own their poverty, weakness and dependence, and ask, inter alia, for health, strength, etc. To the Zulu's mind the whole of southern Africa is peopled with wizards, with most dangerous dispositions, depositing poisons along the trails and in their kraals.

An important functionary, and one who stands on a par with the laboratory research man in the therapeutic medicine of our lands, is the "Lightning Doctor." Because of the great fear engendered in the mind of the native for lightning, and the supposed powers possessed by these lightning doctors of diverting the electric currents in any direction they may choose, these experts are largely consulted during thunderstorms by those who stand in awe of them. They use a charm consisting of a little bundle of sticks which are supposed to have been medicated by the lightning doctor so that no harm may occur to the huts or kraals which bear them. The medication, they are told, consists of the fat of the "thunder storm bird," which these specialists avow they go out and find in the thunder storms.

Then there are the Rain Doctors, the Drought Doctors, the Sunshine Doctors, the Doctors of men, the Doctors of women, the Doctors of children and babies, and a thousand and one other doctors—all quacks, with their quantities of fetich medicines and enchantments. The specialization of modern medicine even

227

might take a few hints from the great subdivision of the Zulu doctors For the hunter they have one kind, and for the warrior another; and so on, down the line of their clientele. In their divining baskets, or what would tally with the modern civilized medicine-man's medicine cabinet or instrument cases, may be found a weird and woozy collection of human finger bones, teeth,—human, animal and reptile; claws of wild birds and monkey paws, seeds of all descriptions, stones of grotesque shapes (which are rattled together by the diviner until the spirit comes and speaks to him). There is not so very much difference between them and ourselves—the spoiled pets of civilization, from this angle of "medical" incidence.

There are two of these idols to the tribe. The wooden one is for men and children, and the ivory one for women. They hold the tribesmen in abject submission.

When you remember Voltaire's cutting observations about the class of people who pour "drugs of which we know little into bodies of which we know less," you cannot then blame these ebony sons of Africa when they order some relation or friend to swallow the nasty, sometimes death-dealing dose, preferring to be cured by proxy, if cure it may be called. I feel that for their age and generation they know considerably more than we are prepared to credit them! During my travels in the "dark continent," which extended over a period of twenty-one years, I have known of many unfortunates sent to an early and painful death at the hands of the "medicine-man."

A baby is ill, and the anxious heathen mother rushes out for the medicine-man, her soul filled with superstition and fear. She arrives at the kraal of this autocrat of the African jungles, does obeisance to this most cunning of all rogues in the world, tells her sad story, and rushes home for her child. Upon her return, lo! the medicine man has arranged his "lay-out," topped off by one of the healing idols of the tribe and put on his mask to make him look wise. There are two of these idols to the tribe, the wooden one for men and children

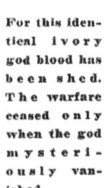

For this identical ivory god blood has been shed. The warfare ceased only when the god mysteriously vanished.

and the ivory one for gynecological difficulties. These idols hold the tribesmen in abject submission, they are among the highest prized possessions and for them tribes will go to war. Blood has been shed over the ivory god here pictured and the strife ceased only when the idol mysteriously vanished.

Upon her return the Witch Doctor has arranged his paraphernalia, topped with one of the idols, put on his mask to make him look wise, and armed himself with his medicine wand.

The medicine-man then produces his medicine stick, in which is bound all manner of venoms (including human heart flesh), with which he produces an infusion by dipping it seven times in warm water, and then pulling out a lion's mane hair from the head of his mask, places it in the concoction, and gives it to the child to drink. I have often wondered if the poisons are a savage version of the more modern "Similia similibus curantur," another of which is, "a hair of the dog that bit you," in order to reach directly the heart of the distress. It may happen that the child vomits violently and is sometimes purged, and perhaps gets well—so the medicine man gets the credit, and is largely advertised thereby.

Should the child die from pathological conditions, or from the poisoning of the medicine-man, then it is avowed that the evil spirits killed the child in spite of all that the regular practitioners could do to save it.

Among the Zulus I have observed that they resort to herbs more or less, using as many as several hundred of them. For example, they have found a plant the leaf of which is used in hemorrhoids with good results in some cases, through local application of leaf. They use another plant known commonly as the "sour fig"—a sort of running succulent vine, found in sandy soil and along the beaches of lakes. The fig is gathered and dried and may be eaten as a food, or used in syrup form for coughs; the leaves are crushed by the natives and an infusion freshly made and used in cases of sore eyes. (Modern Americans make use of a syrup of figs) Fresh cow manure is universally used among the tribes for poultices, in much the same way that bread or flax seed are used by

Here is Banzi N'Tuli, son of a chief and now a chief himself. He is an example of the splendid Zulu, active, muscular, with every muscle under control. He can throw his assegai fifty yards and put it through a corn stalk. His name signifies John of the Water, having been born by a river.

us. This measure, however, they employ as a general household remedy, and without consulting the medicine-man.

Among certain of the tribes is a rather interesting practice of an awkward and somewhat crude form of spinal vertebral adjustment. The men and women of the kraal, after returning from the long trail, or the hunt or the war-path, throw themselves on the ground on their ventral surfaces, which is taken as the sign by the youngsters to walk barefooted or crawl on their knees up and down their spines. The person so treated then rolls over and basks in the sunshine thoroughly relaxed. Incidentally, it may be mentioned that our Indians practice this health measure, and I have learned recently from an old Armenian woman patient that when she was a child she remembers crawling on her bare knees up and down her old mother's back whenever she was tired. The object aimed at is that any strained, twisted or subluxated vertebrae may by this primeval concussion be adjusted so that pressure may be taken off any impinged nerves. They certainly have a crude idea of the underlying principles of modern Chiropractic, which has come to them through centuries of experience.

In a general way, the native of Africa attends to his personal hygiene pretty much after this fashion: He indulges in the bath as often as he gets near running water, provided it is not infested with man-eating animals. In case it is, he stands on the brink and keeps a sharp lookout for any monster, such as a crocodile, hippopotamus, or rhinoceros, or for reptiles. He then plasters his feet with sand, wets them and rubs off the dirt and calluses on the smooth surfaces of stones of the river; he then scoops up water with a dipper formed out of his hand and rinses his mouth. He cleans his teeth with his index fingers—the only tooth brush known to the aboriginal. Nasal douching is practiced by sniffing water from his hands at running rivers —this is in the warm weather. After these ablutions, he moves further up the river and quaffs his thirst by lying on his belly and drinking. During the winter months, however, he anoints his body with oils and any kind of old, rancid fat he can secure to keep out the cold, and then adds colored clays till the final result is a grotesque picture. All this coating is removed, as indicated above, in the summer time, usually with the assistance of the inside fiber of an alkaline gourd, thus breaking up the fats, etc., and our dusky warrior emerges as from a cocoon to wing his way through the spring and summer months.

Circumcision is practiced. With reference to their women; they are kept from immorality, first by careful kraaling and a constant watch over them. They are classed with cattle as property. Adultery is swiftly and surely punished. The man suffers death, while the woman is marked by the cutting off of her right ear. She is turned out of her master's kraal and is practically branded as an outcast. Venereal disease is practically non-existent, and bears among the natives the name the "white man's sickness." Widows are expected to marry their husband's brothers, and raise up children to their deceased husband's name.

Dentistry is no part of the native methods. I have occasionally extracted teeth from members of the tribes. It has always been an occasion of festivities, with the immediate members of the kraal and their dogs admitted. All joined in chanting and singing and clapping of hands, while the dogs contributed their share in the concert most lustily—the underlying idea of all this being that the patient would not feel pain. At all events, even if he did, they have made sufficient noise to satisfy or frighten the spirits, and evil after effects have been warded off. This relationship of noise to the disturbing of evil spirits is fairly common in primitive folk lore, and in America is exemplified by the increasing

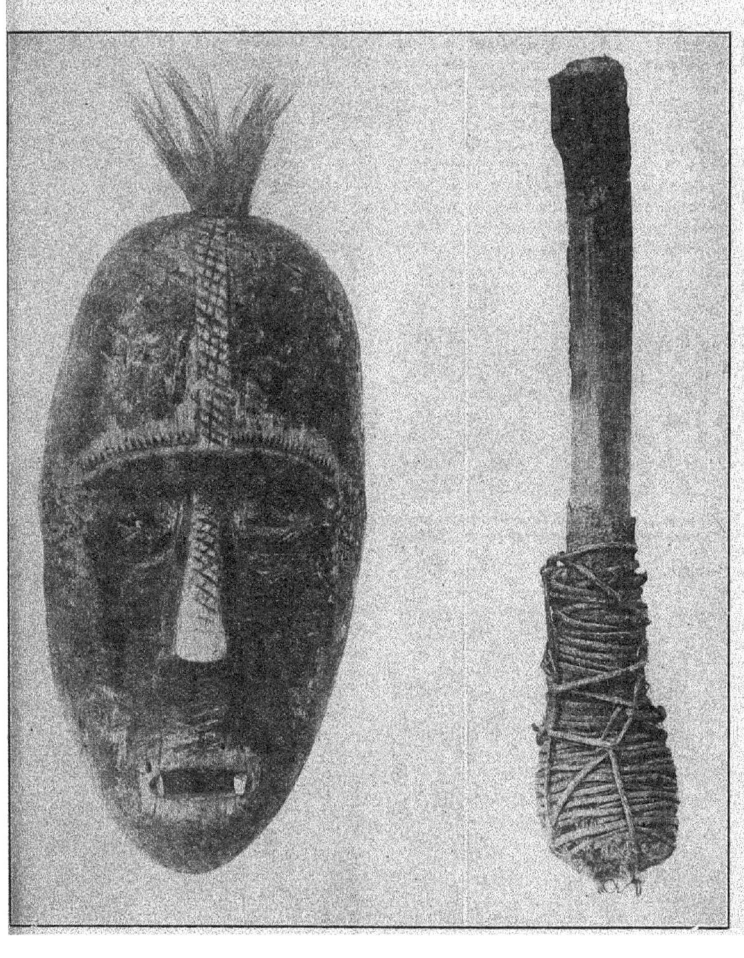

custom of celebrating New Year's day with gunfire and noise.

Among these people there is no science of sanitation, but a few customs that they practice probably in the light of experience. There is no system in the caring for household wastes, the grounds about the kraal always being littered with them. When, however, the place becomes too unutterably dirty for them to remain in any longer, they simply move to some other spot. Their huts are light wattle construction, thatched with grass and easy to build, while the household impedimenta are not

The place sometimes becomes too unutterably filthy for even savage people to endure.

difficult to transport. One of the pictures which I was fortunate enough to catch is that of a kraal which the inhabitants are on the point of forsaking for a cleaner abode. With reference to location, as a general rule, the natives of southern Africa have found out that the highlands are more healthful than the lowlands; islands preferable to the mainland, and dry localities better than swamps and humid areas.

For bedding, the savages use mats, easily made and easily disposed of when worn, and they have the wooden affair that is common through the Orient, which is truly a vermin-proof, hygienic pillow.

While the South African tribesman has, of course, no very accurate notion of anatomy, there are occasionally inci-

dents which show the result of experience, probably acquired in the time-honored method of being handed down from father to son. The following incident was my own observation, the very converse by the way, of their system of recuperation after strenuous times of exercise, in which a subluxation is caused with a definite object in view. On inspecting the possessions, including the cattle, of a worthy young chief of the Zulu tribe, the following remarkable feat was performed: milking a savage cow, that kicked over Kaffir after Kaffir in succession the moment they attempted to milk her. The young chief, however, walked boldly up and seizing the cow's hind foot with both hands, dragged it out behind her, holding it firmly in spite of her struggles, until he succeeded in resting her hoof on his shoulder, when the frantic cow became quiet, and stood still to be milked by him, giving no further trouble. What really happened was, in my judgment, a subluxation either in lumbo-sacral, or sarco-illiac region, or both, and an impingement of nerves of sufficient pressure to prevent pain or induce numbness of temporary duration resulted, so that the animal either did not feel the milking or the unpleasantness caused by milking was removed. In any case the young chief knew something of practical anatomy, which was the point to be considered.

In some places the housing problem is under solution, for the missionaries with good advice, and with examples of

They merely flit to some other locality and set up their kraal anew.

their own handicraft, are showing the natives how to construct little frame buildings, using the materials of the country, the regular thatch, etc., but making houses rather than huts. These two or three room cottages are thus gradually replacing the old filthy huts.

The missionaries are attacking the housing problem in South Africa, and with examples of their own handicraft are teaching the natives how to construct two or three room cottages.

In the matter of diet—the material provided for the meals and the manner of partaking of them are both curious and interesting. For the fundamental principle in communal supplies, or as a guest, or as a member of a family, is the measure of food. The measure of meal then to be taken is two handsful. The hand is dipped into the supply of meal and what can be brought up in the successive dippings of right hand and left is the ration. The reason for this custom is because their gods gave them two hands and one stomach, and they are entitled to fill both hands to fill the stomach. It is by no means a bad measure. Occasionally, among these people, as among their civilized brethren, there are means of securing a larger share, as when one can get some reason for employing a larger hand than his own in the apportionment of the meal. Their dietary is varied and curious to a white man. Monkey flesh is rather choice when soaked in banana vinegar; field rats may

be used to strengthen your dish of baked beans; snails are eaten (certainly of high caloric value), while snakes may be worshipped when alive or boiled and eaten after they are killed. New milk is a staple article of food and also a mixture of sour milk and kaffir beer (Amarsa), making a "bonny clabber." Locusts and white ants are roasted by themselves, or boiled together with green seeded grass reduced to a gelatinous mass —a good food under conditions of famine; coarse meal boiled or sodden is a staple. Almost any kind of game is eaten, but be it remembered all meats are prepared intact, and, after the native custom, insides and outsides in toto, otherwise the good flavor is lost—and as with our epicures they should be kept until quite gamey and are then most delectable.

To live among these people, you must eat "a l' African," and you do, if you eat anything from their kitchens. Their diet in certain localities has a tendency to be rather monotonous, for the reason that should you die they can more readily ascertain which food killed you. As a general thing, honey, both wild and sweet, figures largely as a part of the diet among the tribes in the highlands, while wild fowl figures largely in the menu of the lowlanders—fish, of course, being the staple food along the lake districts. On the Zambese watershed the Somali tribes both eat and worship snakes of all kinds, while the Zulus use various parts of their bodies for medicinal purposes only. Caterpillars (furry ones) are said to be dainty morsels among the Bangala, Bafioti and the Massai tribes along the tributaries of the Congo, and one can just imagine what a delightfully velvety feeling they must cause on deglutition. In these latter days, dogs are petted and pampered, pretty much as "fatted calves" reserved for special feast days, when they are gluttonously devoured. Even human flesh is indulged in among some of the tribes and considered a noble delicacy.

Of course, cattle are eaten betimes, but are more often used in trading for wives and other merchandise. When other delicacies fail, there are the staple kidney beans, bananas and meal. Swine flesh is rejected as a thing unclean.

Beer, of native brew, is the national drink—I may say beer drinking is their national sport. Never attend a Zulu beer drinking party unless you are well covered and have your umbrella with you, for they worship their respective family spirits by drinking and spitting or spouting the beer into the air and at each other.

There is a very rude and primitive pharmacology practiced by these natives. Native mothers have been known to administer powerful emetics to their children who have dared to profess Christianity in order that they give up the new religion. For snake bites the natives use the root of the yellow daphne. This they learned from the toads, as, according to their tradition, these intelligent creatures had been seen to hop to this herb after having been bitten by serpents. In general, however, the use of home medicines is very limited and rudimentary and the main dependence is placed on charms which are worn as prophylactics. There are some common charms, such as the cure of mumps by a visit to the hole of the antbear. Here the afflicted one shouts "Uzagiga! Uzagiga!" (the mumps, the mumps), and returns to his home without looking backward. This idea of not looking back, or of not ceasing to look, is of importance in certain ceremonies. For example, during the funeral observances attending the death of a chief (one of which is the slow smoking of his body for a number of months), his wives must lie in the kraal in which the preservation process is under way, and never turn their faces from his body. The same idea of looking is common in the superstitions of other peoples, as, for example, the omen bird of Borneo; while the looking backward idea persists in the Halloween divination games of civilized peoples in Europe and America.

In the use of charms these African natives have but their own version of the world-wide superstitions, and if I am not mistaken, they are not so very far removed from ideas prevalent not so many centuries ago in lands considered then to be civilized. Somewhere I have read of this interesting prescription:

Tooth of fox and weasel's bone,
Eye of cat and skull of cat,
And the hooked wing of the bat;
Mandrake root and murderer's gore,
Henbane, hemlock, hellebore,
Lithium, storax, bdellium, borax,
Ink of cuttlefish and feather
Of screech owl, smoke together.

and it is a prescription something like this used by the natives in the purification known as "Icima mlilo" (fire quencher). It is usually necessary to bathe in the river after taking such a medicine.

Good health is indicated by the power to sneeze. Sneezing thanks are offered to the spirits of ancestors upon occasion. Lucky is the time spent in sneezing and on occasions the natives will suspend all operations for a time for a sneezing festival. To induce the pleasurable explosions, a kind of snuff is used. It is the custom for the witch doctors to sneeze quite a bit during their divinations and this indicates that the spirits are present and propitious.

There are among these people quite a number of health factors which should not be left unconsidered, even in so general an outline as this. They live entirely in the open with all the advantages that fresh air can afford. Their garments are few and loose—usually a kaross or moochie, which is the suggestion of a girdle, a bull's hide shield and a bunch of assegais or arrow spears. There are no constrictions—having no corsage there are no wrong lines induced with their consequences, and it may be said in this freedom, their feet being shoeless, these are about as intelligent as their hands.

Cheerfulness and contentment are

likewise powerful factors for good among these people. They have these conditions in almost perfection, and are saved from those results that attend gloomy and depressed dispositions.

Innumerable objects of interest pass under their observation; there is the prospect of constant change of scene when on the trail, the hunt or the war-path. If the outlook is not pleasing, the native simply moves his whole kraal, family or tribe, to pleasanter scenes. His

They live entirely in the open, with all the advantages that fresh air affords.

one hope is that of success. The African savage is a thinking man—an innate. philosopher. He is rarely, if ever, morose; he eats well and sleeps well, and he engages in healthful recreation. He sings, dances and tells stories to pass the time, smokes and snuffs in moderation—these two latter items being somewhat of a quasi-religious observance. He avoids as much as possible the rays of the sun and does not work or travel during the hottest parts of the day, but indulges in a quiet siesta in the shady parts of the jungles or under cover of his kraals.

In conclusion, it is simply to be said that the health administration of the South African tribes leaves much to be

desired. Some practices have grown up like that of the measuring of proper ration by the two filled hands, that seem to be original and sensible; but, on the other hand, some rules, such as the omission of pork from their menu, suggest Hebrew or other influences in the distant past. Their care of their women results in a scarcity of venereal disease from which condition the civilized nations of the earth may well take pattern. The climate is essentially one conducive to living in the open air, which is an important factor in health. Their seasons are two, either luxuriously wet or hopelessly dry. Their day shifts into night or night to day without the intervening twilight, a condition set forth by Kipling in those lines that puzzle so much the dwellers in temperate latitudes:

"And the dawn comes up like thunder
From old China, 'cross the bay."

Permeated with superstition, sustained by the coincidences that seem to support the practices of the witch doctor, their religion and their therapy need the help of the civilized nations, for both of them linger in aboriginal shadows. The Zulu is happy in his free life and contented with his quiet fortunes, but in this country there is ample room for the gentle influences of a twentieth century helping hand, now being extended to other nations hitherto on the outskirts of the earth.

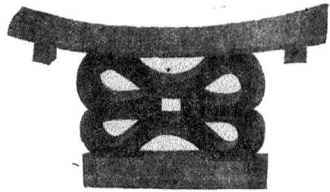

Zulu wooden pillow.

CAUSES OF ARMY REJECTIONS: WHAT HEALTH OFFICERS CAN DO TO REMEDY CONDITIONS

FRANK R. KEEFER,

Colonel Medical Corps, U. S. A.,
Carlisle, Pa.

Read before Section of Public Health Administration, American Public Health Association, at New Orleans, October 28, 1919.

Colonel Keefer, who advises that every health officer become a member of the A. P. H. A., outlines the story of army rejections and analyzes the causes. Health officers hold the strategic position. They should invoke prevention, get statistics, establish machinery for corrective work and foster and direct public opinion through education.

I. CAUSES OF ARMY REJECTIONS,

The examination of millions of our young men, incident to the selection of those who composed the great army which served under our flag in the world war, afforded a unique opportunity to make a physical census on an unprecedented scale. The opportunity was not neglected, and the immediately available records have just been fully compiled. They include 2,000,000 men sent to camps and 550,000 rejected by local boards. The studies so far published are contained in the first and second reports of the Provost Marshal General of the Army, a bulletin from the office of the Surgeon General entitled "Physical Examination of the First Million Draft Recruits," and a Senate committee report on "Defects Found in Drafted Men."

Of more than 24,000,000 selective service registrants who were enrolled, 5,719,152 were subjected to physical examination, and their records turned in to the Adjutant General of the Army. These figures do not include the hundreds of thousands of volunteers for the army, navy and marine corps, the records of whose physical condition may also presently be available for complete study.

The data used for the purposes of this discussion are based on the second report of the Provost Marshal General, and include nearly half a million individuals rejected for physical defects. During the period covered by this report, 3,208,446 registrants were physically examined. Three sets of figures are employed: these comprise 255,312 rejected by local boards; 172,000 refused by camp surgeons after acceptance by local boards; 40,382 discharged from the army after acceptance by local boards and by camp surgeons. These figures represent the broadest basis ever available for such an inquiry. They were prepared under circumstances of fair uniformity as to area, time, physical standards, and working conditions hitherto unequaled.

Of those listed under the first head (local board rejects), 29.59 per cent of men examined were found to be physically disqualified; 8.1 per cent of those who reported at army camps were rejected on re-examination. Thus, considerably more than one-third of our drafted youths were found to be unavailable for military purposes by reason of physical defects. In addition, a considerable percentage of accepted men required discharge shortly after enlistment for similar reasons.

Furthermore, the figures and percentages given are more favorable than are fully warranted, since the physical standards required in peace times were markedly lowered. As a result of these lowered standards, the commander of each mobilization camp was obliged to segregate, in so-called "Development Battalions," several thousands of incompetents having defects which unfitted them for immediate military training. The number of cases of venereal disease, bad teeth, hernia, flat feet, toxic thyroid, middle ear disease, underdevelopment, and other correctible physical defects was very large. The presence of these individuals constituted a serious drag in the training of each division. Later, many such substandard individuals were utilized for positions (clerical, etc.) in the military service which did not require robustness and mobility. To illustrate by a single example, at Camp Funston, Kansas, within two months, more than 5,000 venereal cases were found among drafted men. During the same period only 28 new cases of this character developed among the men already in service at Camp Funston, which fact demonstrates the efficiency of the preventive measures adopted by the Army and the Public Health Service.

The causes for rejection of the cases studied are listed under general headings which, with the figures and percentages for each, are shown in the table below:

An analysis of the figures given in the foregoing table shows that more than 88 per cent of the rejects could be classified under a few heads, as follows:

Per
cent.
Conditions which prevented free mobility . 26
Defects of special senses 15
Cardiovascular cases 13
Nervous and mental abnormalities 10
Tuberculosis 9½
Defective physical development 8
Hernia 6

In the general study of the available data, several striking facts are promptly apparent. One of these is that certain physical defects show a wide variation in regional distribution. Another is that a considerable physical advantage accrues to the boy reared in the country. A third is that a comparison between alien and native-born registrants is decidedly fa-

VARIETIES OF PHYSICAL DEFECTS DISQUALIFYING FOR MILITARY SERVICE.

Causes for Rejection.	Total rejections by local boards and camp surgeons.		Rejected by local boards.		Accepted by local boards but rejected by camps surgeons.		Discharged from Army after accept ance by local boards and camp surgeons.	
	Number.	Percent.	Number.	Percent.	Number.	Percent.	Number.	Percent.
1. Total for all causes	467,694	100.00	255,312	100.00	172,000	100.00	40,328	100.00
2. Alcohol and drugs	2,007	.43	231	.09	1,238	.72	538	1.33
3. Bones and joints	57,744	12.35	33,283	13.04	19,623	11.41	4,838	11.98
4. Developmental defects (height, weight, chest measurements, muscles)	39,166	8.37	27,293	10.69	11,538	6.71	335	.83
5. Digestive system	2,476	.53	1,586	.62	448	.26	442	1.09
6. Ears	20,465	4.38	12,100	4.74	6,445	3.75	1,910	4.73
7. Eyes	49,801	10.65	32,775	12.83	15,367	8.93	1,659	4.11
8. Flatfoot (pathological)	18,087	3.87	3,342	1.31	13,234	7.69	1,511	3.74
9. Genito-urinary (venereal)	6,235	1.33	2,042	.81	2,744	1.60	1,449	3.59
10. Genito-urinary (non-venereal)	6,309	1.35	3,054	1.21	2,226	1.30	1,029	2.55
11. Heart and Blood vessels	61,142	13.07	36,470	14.28	19,268	11.20	5,404	13.38
12. Hernia	28,268	6.04	8,473	3.32	18,353	10.67	1,442	3.57
13. Mental deficiency	24,514	5.24	14,417	5.65	6,293	3.66	3,804	9.42
14. Nervous and mental disorders . .	23,728	5.07	10,945	4.29	7,319	4.26	5,464	13.53
15. Respiratory (tuberculous)	40,533	8.67	27,559	10.77	10,792	6.27	2,182	5.40
16. Respiratory (non-tuberculous) . .	7,823	1.67	3,081	1.21	3,483	2.02	1,259	3.12
17. Skin	12,519	2.68	12,207	4.78	213	.12	99	.25
18. Teeth	14,793	3.16	4,314	1.69	9,952	5.79	527	1.31
19. Thyroid	8,215	1.76	3,151	1.23	3,697	2.15	1,367	3.38
20. Tuberculosis of parts other than respiratory	4,136	.88	3,853	1.51	159	.09	124	.31
21. All other defects	14,314	3.06	12,671	4.96	1,373	.80	270	.67
22. Causes not given	25,419	5.44	2,465	.97	18,225	10.60	4,729	11.71

vorable to the latter; thus, in every 100,-000 men, the native Americans would yield 3,500 more, a number which would fill the ranks of an additional regiment of infantry, at war strength. Fourth, that more than 50 per cent of rejections at camps were on account of defects that were so obvious that they should have been readily recognized by any competent examiner.

II. WHAT THE HEALTH OFFICER CAN DO TO REMEDY CONDITIONS.

If such fact were not already a matter of common knowledge, the data just cited clearly indicate that an immense amount of preventable and correctible physical disability exists among our population.

More than any special group, even in the medical profession, health officers occupy a position of strategic opportunity with reference to the matters under discussion. They are first to apprehend conditions threatening community health and to take measures for their prevention; they have a fine organization—the American Public Health Association—and they are charged with the duties of shaping public opinion and of influencing legislation. The routine duties of health officers are all in the direction of remedial action of this kind. And, by an extension along the lines urged by advanced sanitarians and already largely practiced by many, the desired ends can be accomplished.

It is not necessary here to enter into an extended discussion of well known courses of action, and I shall merely indicate the lines along which, it is thought, the health officer may and should proceed in his efforts to improve the physical conditions of young men; and, incidentally, of all others, in so far as circumstances may apply.

First: The prevention and control of transmissible diseases. This, as a matter of course, includes the teaching and enforcement of hygiene, personal, juven-ile, school, industrial, and social, as well as the practice of useful measures of sanitation.

Second: A census of the population with special reference to remediable physical defects. This might be arranged for as a part of the next general census. So far as young men are concerned, the physical examinations incident to universal military training, if such is instituted, will provide the necessary information. Thereafter, regular examinations should be held.

Third: The development of effective machinery for the correction of remediable defects found in individuals. Thus, classes may be organized for exercises to strengthen weak muscles and to correct certain foot deformities or developmental defects. Operations may be performed for the cure of hernias, of bone and joint abnormalities, and of other surgically remediable imperfections. Defective vision may be aided by appropriate lenses. Diseased teeth and gums may be restored to a healthy state.

When individuals cannot afford the necessary hospital and other expenses, arrangements might be made with members of the medical and dental professions, with hospitals, and with municipal and state authorities, to render such aid as the circumstances warrant. This action was successfully taken in certain states during the war, under the direction of the Medical Aide to the Governor in association with the draft. A number of individuals disqualified by reason of remediable defects were then made available for service. Reconstruction work for cripples, as now practiced by the Army Medical Department, has had excellent results and points the way for an extension to the general public.

Fourth: The creation and fostering of public sentiment; the shaping of legislation looking to the improvement of health conditions, general and local; the correction of defects and deficiencies within the municipal, state and Federal health organizations.

Many communities have no health officers, or only such as are untrained, indifferent, or under the control of politics. Health laws are largely deficient or non-enforceable. Funds are everywhere lacking or inadequate.

Enthusiasm—not merely time serving—is the greatest asset. Health officials should be chosen on the basis of their special knowledge of the subject, or because of known executive ability. Public health study might well be made a requirement for graduation in certain medical and engineering schools. More post-graduate medical schools should give courses in this subject and should confer the degree, Doctor of Public Health.

To my mind, the greatest need is the education of the public as to the importance and practicability of the measures necessary to safeguard the public health and to correct existing defects. The time is ripe; as a result of experiences gained during the war there has been a notable awakening, general as well as medical, in the matter of public health. Thousands of our physicians, millions of our young men, have acquired some knowledge of the importance of disease prevention, and of the principles and methods involved.

In the improvement of the conditions under discussion, the health officer can join forces wholeheartedly with the military medical officer. The one is solicitous for better health conditions within his sphere of influence. The other is desirous to make available for the military needs of the nation, the full power of youthful manhood. Both are anxious to elevate physical conditions among the American people.

It is quite conceivable that if we determine to "get together" and to develop efficient team work among the intelligent elements of our citizenship, it may be readily possible to bring about the establishment of a Federal Department of Health, with a presidential cabinet member as its head. Federal, state and allied health organizations, doctors, lawyers, engineers, educators, nurses, religious bodies, city officials, chambers of commerce, rotary and civic clube, labor employers and labor federations, granges, welfare societies and the press, should all be enlisted. And the first step in the campaign should be to induce every official associated with public health work to join the American Public Health Association.

□

Are Postage Stamps Dangerous?—This question has doubtless occurred to many sanitarians, and the answer has not always been forthcoming. Recently postage stamps were collected from 50 different sources. The bacteria on them were shaken off into sterile salt solution, and 1 cc. portions were plated out on agar, and incubated at 37° C. for 48 hours. Twenty specimens contained colonies too numerous to count. No stamp was free from germs. Some of the organisms identified were B. coli, staphylococci, streptococci, pneumococci, and diphtheroid bacilli. No virulence tests were made. Since most of the organisms are normal to the mouth, the results are not particularly significant. It should be remembered that if stamps were a grave source of infection, a large percentage of the population would be suffering from some disease common to all, as almost everybody licks the postage stamp. Since the gum of the stamp is a favorable medium for bacterial growth, it is important not to infect the stamps before they are used. Since the opportunties for mouth infection from other sources are so numerous, it is concluded that the danger from postage stamps is comparatively small.—*Am. Medicine*, October, 1919. (*M. P. H.*)

AN IDEAL PROGRAM FOR CHILD HYGIENE

ALLAN J. MCLAUGHLIN,

*Assistant Surgeon General, U. S. Public Health Service,
Washington, D. C.*

Read before Special Sessions on Child Hygiene, American Public Health Association, at New Orleans,
La., October 30, 1919.

A nation-wide program is here recommended to include Federal
assistance to the states not to exceed fifty percent of the cost,
with the states effecting an immediate stock-taking of baby
saving machinery, together with the pooling of resources.

The scope of this paper will not permit treatment of the subject in its ultimate details, but the general lines of organization should be as given below:

The ideal program for Child Hygiene must be nation wide in scope in order to secure the maximum results.

To secure a synchronous attack upon infant mortality and the many other problems involved, it is necessary to have a coördination of all state activities according to minimum standards established in a federal program. Similarly to make the ideal state program effective there must be a uniform state plan applied by every health unit within the state.

The state program should provide for an immediate survey of every health unit in the state to show what each community now possesses in baby saving and child hygiene machinery and to show also exactly what each community lacks in this regard. The survey report with accurate statement of needs and specific recommendation for supplying those needs should be placed in the hands of the local authorities to be carried out with such amplification as the local committee might deem advisable.

The local plan should be outlined by the state and carried out by the local authorities with such additions or modification as may be necessary to suit local conditions.

The secret of success for any program, federal, state or local, will be found to be a pooling of the resources and activities of all the official and unofficial agencies operating within the given jurisdiction.

It must be borne in mind that unofficial agencies have initiated most of the work which has been done in infant mortality and other problems of child hygiene. There is just one way to coördinate properly and utilize to the fullest extent, without duplication and conflict, the splendid activities of the unofficial agencies with the Public Health authorities, and that is by means of a consulting and advisory board to the official body having jurisdiction. The board or committee must exist in all three types of organization, federal, state and local, and should be composed of experts in every phase of child hygiene and representatives of all unofficial agencies whose work comes within the scope of child hygiene.

The federal program should provide for assistance to the states on a basis of not to exceed 50% of the preliminary expense of making the necessary surveys and demonstrations. This will require legislation analagous to that enacted for good roads, vocational education, and farm demonstration work.

The Federal Government by means of its advisory board would have the support for the official agency of every national organization represented thereon, and from its consulting experts receive invaluable advice in framing its policies and putting them into effect.

The State Government would find the same valuable expert advice in its advisory board and the same support from the unofficial bodies represented. The state program would thus appeal to both official and unofficial agencies in the local health units, and insure through the local advisory committee the united effort of both the local health authorities and the unofficial agencies upon a common program.

THE ILLINOIS PROGRAM IN CHILD HYGIENE FOR THE COMING YEAR

CLARENCE W. EAST, M.D.,

Chief of Division of Child Hygiene, Illinois State Department of Health, Springfield, Ill.

Read before Special Sessions on Child Hygiene, American Public Health Association, at New Orleans, La., October 30, 1919

In its child hygiene work Illinois will use its health centers for a foundation and pursue salesmanship methods for follow-up. Rural public health centers, child hygiene stations and public school nurse units are to be established and all these agencies worked in coördination.

THE Illinois Program in Child Hygiene for the coming year consists of what we shall do and what we shall attempt.

I. What We Shall Do:

(1) We shall build upon the foundation of the twenty centers which we now have for reconstruction work among crippled children.

Beginning with the summer of 1916 Illinois has had recurring outbreaks of infantile paralysis. Each year has furnished reports of from 300 to 1000 cases. In an endeavor to remedy the sad results we have been conducting 20 field clinics throughout the State which we visit from once weekly to once every two months, and examine and treat from 15 to 60 children in each clinic. An important result has been a general stimulation of interest in child welfare and public health. We have been able to broaden our work in every center and to reach communities tributary to our clinic centers not only for educational effort, but for the establishment of child welfare stations, school nursing and other public health activities.

Were it within the province of this paper we would strongly recommend some definite form of obvious service, such as work for crippled children, as a most efficient method of propaganda.

(2) We shall follow up a large number of "prospects" as a salesman does.

These prospects come to us out of the rising general interest in child welfare, out of the various public health nursing services so rapidly being established by various agencies, out of the interest created by our State Department of Public Health Baby Contest which is a big feature annually of the Illinois State Fair, and out of the propaganda work done in season and out of season by our workers. In following our prospects our first objective is the establishment of public school nursing and then child welfare stations. We have enough of these prospects to keep one field nurse busy all of the time with not infrequent assistance afforded by the Chief of the Division and the Supervising Nurse.

II. What We Shall Attempt:

(1) What we shall attempt this year is founded upon the axiom that public health nursing is fundamental to all child hygiene activities.

We shall attempt to coördinate all nursing activities in every field where several agencies are at work. This will be the entire program of our State Supervising Nurse. At the end of the year we expect to have no overlapping of public health nursing services anywhere in Illinois. We shall expect to develop each service to its very highest efficiency.

(2) We shall attempt the following definite items of work:

(a) The engrafting upon every nursing service whatsoever of a comprehensive program in child hygiene.

(b) The establishment of public school nursing in every place where there is a nursing service of any kind.

(c) The establishment of public health nursing in rural communities. After adequate survey we shall seek to join the efforts of rural school districts, township governments and whatsoever agencies we may enlist in a given field in support of public health nursing service.

Child hygiene will be the keynote of all such services established.

TO SUMMARIZE.

(1) To render service of a striking type such as reconstructive work for crippled children.

(2) To coördinate nursing agencies.

(3) To establish child welfare stations in every place where public health nursing is done.

(4) To establish public school nursing.

(5) To establish rural public health nursing centering usually in the school houses.

□

Medical Supervision in the Framingham Schools.—It is recognized that Framingham has one of the best systems of medical inspection of school children which can be found in this country today. The personnel employed to safeguard the health of the children consists of a full-time school physician, a nurse, a dental hygienist, a teacher of posture training, a physical training director, and a part-time dentist for approximately 2,500 grade children. The following results were found from a very careful survey of approximately the whole number. The tests to determine the condition of nutrition showed that 6.8 per cent were excellent; 43 per cent good, 41.9 per cent fair, 8.2 per cent poor, and 16 per cent anaemic. The tests for defective teeth, enlarged tonsils and glands showed that 60 per cent had defective teeth, 45.2 per cent enlarged glands, 20 per cent slightly enlarged tonsils, 10.9 per cent tonsils of considerable size, 7.7 per cent tonsils, markedly enlarged; and 12 per cent suffered from nasal obstruction. Other tests showed that 6.5 per cent had defective vision, 2.3 per cent had other eye diseases, 2.2 per cent had defective hearing, 2.5 per cent had discharging ears, 3.5 per cent had skin diseases, 12 per cent had postural defects, 3.6 per cent had initial murmurs, 1.3 per cent had aortic murmurs, 0.9 per cent had pulmonic murmurs, 1.5 per cent had functional irregularities of rhythm, 1.0 per cent had organic diseases, 7 per cent had bronchitis, 0.45 per cent had pulmonary tuberculosis, 0.24 per cent had pleurisy. 0.9 per cent had nervous diseases, 0.48 per cent had speech defects and 0.9 per cent had mental defects.—W. B. Howes, M. D., *Boston Medical & Surgical Journal*, Oct. 2, 1919. (*M.P.H.*).

Get Ready for April A. P. H. A. Campaign.

Objective—Membership of 7,500.

NEED OF STANDARDIZATION IN SCHOOL HYGIENE METHODS

H. O. JONES, PH.G., M.D.,

Asst. Bureau Chief; in Charge of Division of Child Hygiene, Department of Health, Chicago, Ill.

Read in the Program on Child Hygiene, American Public Health Association, New Orleans, La. October 28, 1919.

The time is ripe for a national campaign in educating communities about safeguards for healthy development of school children. There is urgent need for this. Standards do not exist, nor are there means of enforcing any. School hygiene is truly formless with conflicting information and advice.

THE consensus of opinion is that the necessity for school hygiene activities has long passed the questionable and experimental period.

The vast supply of information and statistics that have been gathered and compiled by those who have done pioneer work in school hygiene for the past twenty-five years, leaves no doubt in our minds as to the necessity of extending this work to all communities where it has not been established. Every school child is entitled to have every possible help and safeguard operating to his benefit during his school life.

Authorities under the compulsory education law, force the child to attend school a certain number of hours each day during a given period each year for a certain portion of his life. This is sound policy and leads to better education; but hand in hand with this wise provision for enforced education of the child, communities should also secure and enforce laws that will enable the authorities to supply suitable buildings, adequate light, satisfactory heat, proper and efficient medical protection and physical control for the children, so that finally we will have physically well developed bodies as well as educated minds.

The time is ripe for a national campaign that will have for its purpose the educating of all communities that now lack in part or whole, safeguards for the healthy development of their school children. A public health movement of this sort would have the support of the five millions of our young men who have just returned from army service. These men know the splendid results to their health acquired through the safeguards furnished them in the army.

The practical absence of epidemics, excepting influenza; the marked physical improvement in all the soldiers during this period of service speaks more than words of what can be accomplished by use of standard public health measures as worked out, adopted and enforced in the army. What has been done for the soldier army, can be and must be done for the army of school children.

As the Federal Government realized the need and provided this service for the army, so must every community be made to feel its responsibility for measures of this kind for their school children. The successful results in the army were due to two factors:

1st. Adoption of standard Methods.

2nd. The enforcement of these standards.

In our work we should utilize these same successful factors to achieve like results.

Is it not the function of this group of the American Public Health Association to formulate and adopt the best standards of school hygiene for the school children of this country, and advise the necessary legislation to provide and enforce such methods?

A questionnaire sent out by the Department of Health of Chicago brought the following information from sixteen of the largest cities in the United States:

I. ADMINISTRATION AND APPROPRIATION.

Nine cities report school hygiene entirely under the supervision of the Department of Health and eight financed by the Department of Health; five cities under the supervision of the Board of Education and six financed by the Board of Education. Two cities report school hygiene activities jointly under the Board of Health and the Board of Education, and in these cities financed by both the Department of Health and the Board of Education.

II. DISTRIBUTION OF SCHOOL HYGIENE SERVICE.

(a) When under supervision of Department of Health: In three cities all schools, public, parochial and private, were provided medical inspection; in five cities the public and parochial schools only; in one city public schools only; in two cities parochial schools only.

(b) When under the supervision of Board of Education: In no city were all the schools inspected. In one city both public and parochial schools are inspected, but the parochial schools only occasionally. In seven cities public schools only were inspected. In no cities parochial schools only were inspected.

3. The per capita appropriation based on reported appropriation and number of school children varied from a minimum of 10.7c to a maximum of 74c for each school child.

4. The number of school children for

each school health officer provided: minimum, 2,000 children; maximum, 22,000 children.

5. The number of school children for each nurse provided: minimum, 1,161; maximum, 35,109.

6. The number of children to total corrective agencies available (dispensaries, hospitals) in any city: minimum, 2,194; maximum, 11,700.

7. Percentages of corrections of physical defects found: minimum, 15 per cent; maximum, 54 per cent.

8. Percentage of total children who received physical examinations: minimum, none; maximum, 200 per cent.

This demonstrates the evident lack of standards.

Requests for information relative to the following are frequent:

1. What do you consider desirable legislation?

2. What are the details of your methods and examinations for:

(a) Control of contagious diseases in schools.

(b) Physical examinations.

(c) Mental tests.

3. What forms do you use in school hygiene work?

4. What are your recommendations as to sanitary plans for school buildings with reference to heating, ventilating, plumbing, lighting, etc.?

5. What do you consider desirable equipment for school hygiene activities in school buildings?

6. What are the duties of your school health officer, nurse, dentist, etc.?

7. What educational propaganda do you conduct?

8. What salaries are paid to health officers, nurses, and dentists?

9. Information as to malnutrition and results of surveys of school children.

The Children's Bureau at Washington is now working on minimum standards for children, taking into consideration hours of work, character of work, educational requirements; consideration of sex and work; prenatal and infant welfare work.

May I suggest to the American Public Health Association that it take some action for the preparation and adoption of standards for school hygiene? The adoption of standards would result in a more uniform progress. It would do away with or minimize the conflicting advice and information now so prevalent. It would result in saving of time and money by eliminating experiments. A better impression would be made on the public if the requirements and the service were universally the same; it would stimulate local health officers and raise the character of their work. It would result in causing a demand from the public on officers of the local governments to provide school hygiene service where none is rendered. It would result in uniformity of information for statistical purposes, and help gain for the school children medical service to which they are entitled.

I would suggest that this section of the American Public Health Association consider the desirability of appointing a special committee for each of the following subjects:

1. Committee on Standardization of Legislation.

(a) To consider desirable laws to provide for the establishment and enforcement of school hygiene.

(b) Standard requirements for admission of children to schools.

(c) To provide funds.

(d) To insure co-operation.

It might be desirable for this committee to work with representatives from the section on Public Health Administration.

2. Committee on Standards for Examinations and Procedures.

(a) For contagious diseases.

(b) For physical defects.

(c) For mentality.

(d) Number of children per health officer; nurse; dentist; corrective agencies, etc.

3. Committee on Standards of Equipment, Records and Nomenclature.

(a) Combined scholastic and health records.

(b) System of forwarding records with child.

(c) Co-operation of educational representatives and health officers.

(d) Provisions for this work in schools.

4. Standards of Qualifications and Duties.

(a) Of school health officers.

(b) Of school nurse.

(c) Of school dentist, etc.

5. Standards of Corrective Agencies.

(a) Eligibility to charities.

(b) Number necessary.

(c) Assignment of nurses, etc.

6. Standards for Prophylactic Work.

(a) Smallpox.

(b) Typhoid.

(c) Diphtheria.

(d) Tuberculosis, etc.

7. Committee on Standards for Educational Propaganda.

(a) Courses in Normal Schools for preparations of teachers.

(b) Courses in regular school curriculum for children.

(c) Text-books for teachers and children.

8. Committee on Engineering Standards from the Engineering Section.

These committees should consider the standards from the standpoint of the needs of urban and rural communities. The executive committee of the American Public Health Association could keep in touch with the progress of the various special committees and render such aid as possible and be responsible for presenting this subject as committee reports, with information accumulated and recommendations for the consideration at an annual meeting, at which time a committee can be appointed to mould and formulate the various committee reports in shape to present as completed standards to the section on Child Hygiene; to be referred to the association for approval and adoption.

SCHOOL HYGIENE FOR RURAL COMMUNITIES

GRACE WHITFORD, M.D.,

*Former Director, Bureau Child Welfare, Florida State Board of Health,
Ozona, Fla.*

Read before Special Meetings on Child Hygiene, American Public Health Association, at New Orleans.
La., October 28, 1919.

An opportunity for the rural school child equal to that of his
city brother is the text of this article. Interest the parents by
making the schoolhouse the community center. They will then
realize what it stands for. Rest rooms are needed and playgrounds and the general development of the spirit of play, together with medical inspection and regular physical exercise.

THE problem of hygiene for rural schools naturally divides itself into a consideration of the school building, its construction, situation, sanitation, proper room space, illumination, ventilation, heating, general attractiveness; the surroundings of the school; its equipment; possibilities of giving proper care to the children during school hours; a program for physical inspection and supervision of the children by trained workers, and educational work in personal and general hygiene which will radiate from the school into the home.

We will assume that the school is the one common center for the rural community; if not, it should be made to become such a center. It should become the true community home, especially in neighborhoods of scattered population. To achieve any constructive health program for the school and its children, the people themselves must feel this. It must be their school with the knowledge that all that goes into it and comes to their homes from it is theirs, put there by them. They must be made active participants, real principals, in any hygiene work introduced.

Country school housing conditions have improved markedly in the last decade. Whole countries, North, East, South, West have built schools for every district. However, though the buildings may be new and even presentable in appearance, many of them retain the faults of construction of the "little red school house." They are often placed in a bad situation, demanding impossible sewerage and water supply systems; lighting has not been studied and is apt to be as glaring in arrangement as that of the former was, dim; ventilation too often consists of drafts, and heating systems are frequently utterly inadequate, if, indeed, they have been installed at all, for many a school builder who serves as his own architect puts the heating plant in as an afterthought when the structure itself is complete. The site selected is too frequently that cramped space donated by a trustee who is more concerned over enhancing the value of his adjoining property than over the welfare of his children.

In building, it is well to impress upon the community that the school is the only attractive place some of the children know, and that it is as cheap to build what is pleasing to the eye as the ugly.

As yet, in many rural schools, even those soundly built, one finds the inadjustable desk and seats made to stretch the legs of the short and cramp those of the long, to make the child conform to the furniture, since he is of more plastic material than wood or metal. They still have the glaring surfaced "blackboards," powdering chalk, old type erasers, unshaded or incorrectly shaded windows.

Since definite standards for school building and furnishing have been maintained for years, it seems strange that old mistakes continue to be repeated. The neghborhood points proudly to a more sightly new structure that is basically as poor as the old. There should be some definite plan for issuing permits for rural school buildings, making obligatory established standards. The cost would probably be less than for those not so planned. Buildings should provide for the inevitable increase in school population; with the whip of compulsory education, particularly in the South, the overcrowding of the children is appalling. The consolidated school, most noticeably in the South, where severe winters are not to be reckoned with, has solved many a problem in school hygiene for the community. Not only does it afford better educational advantages, but better sanitary conditions, since it is large enough to warrant, in the eyes of the local school board, some sort of sewerage and water system. However, it brings problems of its own: it makes long hours for the children, especially the little ones, for a rest room is seldom provided for them. If a child becomes ill, there is no place for him to lie down, nor, unless he is ill enough to warrant sending for a conveyance, can he go home until the entire school is dismissed at the end of the day. The vehicle which gathers up the children, some from considerable distances, is apt to be an overcrowded makeshift, with scant means for protecting the children from wind and weather. Many a child sits in school all day wet from his morning's ride in the school 'bus. Some boards, of course, provide suitable motor 'busses with easily adjustable windows. Practically all of them, however, are overcrowded and this close contact must be a frequent source of contagion.

Not only should there be a place in the school outside of the regular classrooms for the care of the child, but outside of the building there must be the place for the child's time of recess and relaxation. When air and sunlight are two of the few inexpensive things to be obtained nowadays, is it not strange that rural children are given so little along with their school life? Ground space, too, is not yet sold by the inch in the country, nor in the average town of a population of ten thousand or less inhabitants. Yet, in small towns, the school with adequate playground space is the exception, even in the country, the school-house surrounded by enough cleared and cared for space sufficient for all of the children to play games in at the same time, is the exception of only rarer frequency. Perhaps it is not so apparent to the casual onlooker because so few of the children do play games together. The small number of active ones are the participants, the larger number the "watchers" in almost every school yard. It is not only because the average country child does not know how to play, but because in addition he is too inert to want to; undoubtedly a symptom of the high percentage of malnutrition found among our children, or, in the South, of hookworm disease. The school built on the Spanish bungalow type (one-room units enclosing a patio) gives an ideal playground for small towns and country districts where teaching force is small and there cannot be a trained playground supervisor, and the grade teachers themselves must supervise recess periods. Given recreation space, the next consideration is to secure for the children, not special coaching for the few, but physical training for all. Many counties have solved the problem by employing a graduate of an established school for physical education to supervise the work of the entire county, the teachers themselves doing the daily work. Such a supervisor can do a great deal in the physical inspection of the children as well. Because of the lack of funds and the scarcity of such teachers, many schools are without physical training for the children. The fortunate school is the one with the grade teachers trained properly along this line as part of their education for their profession. Such schools in the country are, alas, few. There are many college girls who have been well trained athletically who come back home without definite work to do who could be engaged for part time and who could do volunteer service as part of their share in the health program of their counties. Everyone who has learned to do a definite, useful thing should be made to pay for such training by giving some of the fruits of it back to the community. This is a definite piece of work that can be given to a young woman or a group of young women of the county. We must not allow our trained girls to rust for want of presenting them with a concrete "job." Most of them welcome the opportunity for service. Simple playground equipment can be put in the school yard by community effort, if the school board cannot supply it. Many potential tendencies are developed into actual diseases among our children from want of breathing and postural exercises. Any intelligent teacher should be able to put her children through "setting up" exercises daily and should be required to do so if other means are not supplied. All such work should be in the open as much as possible. To me it is of serious import when our children do not know how to breathe, sit, or walk correctly, and have no desire for play, as play, indeed, have no the healthy animal's impulse to exercise his muscles.

There is no longer a question mark after the necessity for physical inspection and supervision of all classes of school children. The war has brought the question of man-power and its lack through neglect in the present generation too forcibly before the eyes of the average voter to make necessary any lengthy educational campaign to have him approve this one form of public health

work. It appeals to the average man almost as much as the extensive use of state and federal funds for venereal disease control. In fact, his intelligence on the subject seems to have outstripped that of some of the public health officials. Herein lies the hope of the extension of this type of basically constructive public health work for the professional politician counts votes, not issues, and permits or allows to exist what the voter demands. Rural communities need organized physical inspection of their school children more than the urban. A thorough yearly examination of each pupil by a trained inspector should be the minimum requirement. Daily inspection in addition is the ideal. There should be a sufficient nursing force for family visiting, case work, "follow-up" work, social service and regular visits to the school. While most of this work seems too great at first consideration for many counties, and it is usually practical to take the county as a unit, it can be shown that through communicable disease control and prevention, checking of potential defects, correction of corrigible defects, raising of the general physical standard, classification of irremediable defects (and the direction of children so affected into proper channels for care and education) it gives the greatest interest on the least capital invested of any type of public health work. The school is practically the only organization we have in which large numbers of children are gathered into groups; therefore, much of the expense of organization work necessary in other types of child welfare work is eliminated. School boards become interested when the number of days of school saved in the year per child and the lessened average number of years to a grade per child are cited. That is the concrete thing that everyone can understand.

When we consider that twenty to forty per cent of those graduating from the grades are practically unfit physically; that sixty per cent of the children of every community, regardless of birth, breeding, wealth, or geographic location have physical defects needing skilled care, we must realize that our educational system has been builded upon the shifting sands, indeed, when the physical has been ignored. It is passing strange that in autocracy or democracy, the children of Judy O'Grady and the Colonel's Lady grade about the same.

If it is necessary to have health education and physical inspection of masses of adults in camps, how much more necessary is it to have both for immature humanity massed compulsorily in schools?

How the work of physical inspection is done must largely depend upon the finances and needs of the district and the amount of interest aroused in the people. Periodic physical inspection without a nursing system is almost devoid of good, particularly in rural communities. Indeed, if it is a question of the two, the nursing system should be the one installed rather than the medical. Dr. Thomas A. Wood says, "In rural districts, school examinations may often be advantageously done by the school nurse with the help of the teacher." I have seen it unquestionably proved.

Physical inspection should serve as the beginning of many other phases: in fact, should be the opening wedge of other activities. If these activities are to be successful, the nurses must be socially as well as institutionally trained. The school work may, through home visiting, become the opening wedge for pre-natal and pre-school age work. It is often the beginning of an awakening of an interest in personal hygiene and home sanitation in the children, and the cause of both being taught in the school. It may also be the beginning of the teaching of proper diet and food habits and through the children's interest, the beginning of the mothers'. I have seen the mothers of several country communities band together with the teachers in Parent-Teachers' associations, furnishing hot lunches in the schools for the children. In these cases, better dietary habits have been followed at the home when the weighing and measuring of the children showed to parents the degree of malnutrition that had been reached. I have seen whole classes of country school children double their chest expansion in a year, having demanded physical exercises daily after their first physical inspection. I have seen proper sanitary arrangements installed through the insistence of the children of the family after they had learned of hookworm disease, its results, and prevention, a whole corps of sanitary men could have grown gray before the householders would have heeded it. As quickly, children can be taught to grasp communicable disease prevention. With all adults, knowledge far outstrips practice, but children are literal-minded creatures and act instinctively upon what they learn if the lessons are practical and vivid. Herein is the hope for home sanitation and raising of the family's living standard. The possibilities are boundless. The parent must be drawn into these school activities. Associations, which exist today even in remote country districts, volunteer workers, trained through the Red Cross classes and other organizations, should be given definite pieces of work in the health program.

There still remain the children in need of special care, which is difficult to provide in rural districts. For the pre-tuberculosis, the tuberculous, the markedly malnourished, the hopelessly crippled and the mental defective, there is seldom a place save in the grade school.

But the impetus for new things in school hygiene in rural communities has started; in certain sections, it is outstripping that of the cities. The country people themselves are awakening to the disadvantages under which their children are growing up, they are asking for them in matters of health an "equality of opportunity." To provide this quickly and economically, a national program for rural school hygiene should be laid down.

SOME IMPORTANT FACTORS IN THE PREPARATION OF CULTURE MEDIA

LEWIS DAVIS,

Research Laboratory, Parke, Davis & Co.,

Detroit, Mich.

Read before Laboratory Section, American Public Health Association at New Orleans, La., October 30, 1919.

This investigator favors the steam pressure method of sterilization. High temperatures can effect undesirable chemical changes, while long continued heating may be destructive to food accessory factors. Emphasis is laid on the proper selection of bacteriologic peptone.

The importance of placing the preparation of bacteriologic culture media on an accurate, scientific basis, has long been recognized. The fact that a majority of the pathogenic microörganisms has similar food requirements makes such a step especially desirable. In spite of numerous attempts to formulate procedures striving towards uniformity, substantial progress in this direction has been slow. While it is aimed to record the biological characteristics of an organism with more or less precision, one of the most essential requirements, that of a proper cultural environment is, in most cases, left in a state of uncertainty.

Very frequently, failure to obtain some important biochemical reaction, toxicogenicity, or even growth with an organism, is explained as an individual idiosyncrasy. As a matter of fact, the cause may be readily apparent when examination is made of the bacterial food or the method of its manufacture. It is the purpose of this paper to discuss some of the factors concerned in the preparation of culture media, with particular reference to the nutritive and toxicogenic requirements of the more common pathogenic organisms.

Urgent attention recently directed toward bacteriologic peptone by reason of the actual need for a domestic supply has shown that proper selection of this important culture medium constituent is imperative. It will be readily conceded that for the simple cultivation of many organisms, ordinary beef infusion or even beef extract is able to furnish all of the necessary food constituents. In fact, Davis and Ferry[1] have succeeded in obtaining growth of the highly susceptible *B. diphtheriæ* in a medium consisting entirely of an aqueous solution of amino acids, purine bases and mineral salts. For the more complex requirements, however, such as production of toxins or even in the growth of delicate organisms, bacteriologic peptone plays a specific role by supplying the essential accessory factors in the form of easily assimilated, hydrolyzed protein. As stated in a previous investigation by Davis,[2] whch led to the development of a satisfactory bacteriologic peptone, the value of this product in bacterial nutrition is governed entirely by the presence of amino acids and other components which can be utilized by the bacteria. While some of these basic constituents are absolutely necessary for the maintenance of bacterial life and development, others in turn will be utilized, if present, for the production of toxins or certain by-products not essential to metabolism. Not only should a biologically utilizable peptone have the proper composition, but these amino acids and other components should be present in the most available form. Extended, comparative studies have also indicated that, among other factors, a peptone hydrolyzed to a much greater degree than the formerly imported product, possesses increased nutritive values.

The superiority of beef infusion over beef extract for the cultivation of pathogenic bacteria and particularly for the devlopment of toxins is generally admitted. The method formerly recommended in infusing the meat for 24 hours in the refrigerator with distilled water is practical only on a small scale. For operations involving large quantities of infusion, an equivalent, satisfactory product can be obtained by bringing the meat and requisite quantity of water to the boiling point in the course of an hour and a half and then expressing the liquid through flannel in a suitable press.

Regardless of which method is employed to prepare the infusion, fat should be removed as thoroughly as possible. Even the presence of small quantities is undesirable in the final broth to be employed in the production of diphtheria toxin or the propagation of certain surface growing organisms, B. tuberculosis, for example. Experience in the routine production of diphtheria toxin, observations on which will be communicated in a later article, has shown that a marked diminution in the elaboration of toxin occurs in those flasks of bouillon containing only traces of fat. I am inclined to agree with the opinion of Larson, Cantwell, and Hartzell[3] regarding the influence of the surface tension of media on the growth of bacteria. It is very probable that this deleterious action of the fat is exterted by depressing the surface tension of the medium. This would cause B. diphtheriæ to grow beneath the surface with consequent decrease of pellicle and toxin formation.

One of the most important steps in the preparation of culture media is undoubtedly the adjustment of the reaction, which establishes the optimum concentration of H ions for bacterial growth and metabolism. In spite of the numerous and convincing data brought forward within the past few years to prove the fallacy of the "hot titration" method, this inaccurate procedure is still common practice. As is known, the committee of this association clearly states in the Bacteriological Section of the Revised Standard Methods for the Examination of Water and Sewage,[4] "that a new method of titrating and adjusting the reaction of culture media which will give a more accurate indication of the hydrogen ion concentration is desirable." The colorimetric determination of hydrogen ion concentration as proposed by Sörensen,[5] Walpole[6] and more recently by Clark and Lubs,[7] offers a rapid and reliable method for ordinary, bacteriologic, laboratory requirements. Estimations demanding greater accuracy should be carried out by the electrometric method. With the simple electrode recommended by Bovie[8] and the direct reading ionometer of Bartell,[9] the hydogen ion concentration can be rapidly determined by the accurate gas chain method. A description of the "set up" required for such measurements is given in a previous article on hydrogen ion concentration determinations with diphtheria toxin (Davis).[10]

For a large number of pathogenic species including Bact. diphtheriæ, and the more delicate micrococci, we have observed that reactions of the sterilized medium ranging between $P_H=8.0$ and $P_H=8.3$ ($C_H=1.0\times10^{-8}$ and $C_H=5.0\times10^{-9}$) give very satisfactory results. The general procedure given below, which employs the colorimetric method for checking the reaction, is followed with such modifications as will be subsequently discussed.

A. Add the peptone and salt as required to the fat-free infusion. Agitate thoroughly and heat for 15 minutes in streaming steam or bring to a boil to ensure thorough solution. Sugars for carbohydrate media should not be added at this point, but just before sterilization.

B. Remove exactly 10 cc. of the broth from A to a small (preferably 100 cc.) Erlenmeyer flask. Dilute with about 40 cc. of cold, distilled water, and add 0.5 cc. of a 1 per cent solution of phenolphthalein (in 95 per cent alcohol) as indicator. Titrate to a deep pink color against an N/10 NaOH solution, freshly prepared, when required, as an exact 1/100 dilution of a stock 10 N solution. The burette reading gives directly the amount of the strong (10 N) solution required to neutralize per liter of medium. Steam again for 15 minutes or bring to a boil, and estimate the hydrogen ion concentration.

C. For determining the actual hydrogen ion concentration, the simple "comparator" of Hurwitz, Meyer and Ostenberg[11] is employed, with standardized boric acid-potassium chloride-sodium hydroxide mixtures of $P_H=8.0$, $P_H=8.2$, and $P_H=8.4$, prepared as directed by Clark and Lubs.[7] Flat bottomed test tubes, 17 mm. in diameter, of uniform bore, and with capacity of about 30 cc. have been found satisfactory for comparison purposes. Transfer exactly 10 cc. of the neutralized bouillon from B to one of the comparison tubes, dilute with 10 cc. of distilled water, and mix well. Remove 10 cc. of the mixture to another tube and add 0.5 cc. of an 0.02 per cent solution of phenol sulphonephthalein in 50 per cent alcohol. Prepare three other tubes containing 10 cc. respectively of the standardized $P_H=8.0$, $P_H=8.2$, and $P_H=8.4$ mixtures with 0.5 cc. of the phenolsulphonephthalein solution in each tube. The comparison technique is that described by Clark and Lubs.[7]

As a rule, the value will very closely approximate $P_H=8.2$. In the few cases where the color in the tube containing medium plus indicator is lighter than that of the compensated $P_H=8.0$ stand-

ard, N/10 NaOH can be run directly into the former tube until the desired tint is reached. Since the equivalent of 5 cc. of the medium is employed, twice the burette reading gives the amount of 10/N NaOH necessary to correct each litre of broth.

Media which are to contain sugars must be adjusted to a higher value than $P_H=8.2$ before sterilization to anticipate the increase in the concentration of hydrogen ions as a result of sterilization. Where the amount of carbohydrate to be subsequently incorporated is small, this may be accomplished by titrating to a deeper shade with phenolphthalein in the preliminary adjustment, and then standardizing to a final P_H value greater than $P_H=8.2$. As an instance, broth for the cultivation of the influenza bacillus, which has among other ingredients, 0.2 per cent of dextrose, should have a reaction coming within the narrow limits of $P_H=8.1$ to $P_H=8.2$. By adjusting to $P_H=8.3$, as above, the desired value is attained after sterilization.

When the medium is finally to have present a larger amount of sugar, the consequently greater increase in H ion concentration makes a different indicator than phenolphthalein necessary for the preliminary titration. The 2 per cent dextrose bouillon employed for toxin elaboration with B. tetani furnishes a good example. Experimentation has shown that in order to obtain the final optimum reaction value of $P_H=8.0$ to $P_H=8.2$, after sterilization, the broth before addition of the glucose must be adjusted to a P_H value of 8.6. This is easily accomplished by using 0.5 cc. of the .04 per cent solution of thymol sulfon phthalein recommended by Clark and Lubs,[7] as the indicator in the preliminary titration and adding the N/10 NaOH solution to a blue shade. Color comparison of the adjusted medium is then made in the usual manner with a standardized $P_H=8.6$ mixture, by using 0.5 cc. of an 0.02 per cent solution of ortho cresol sulphon phthalein indicator for both standard and broth, in place of phenol sulfon phthalein, as before. This is due to the fact that the range within which phenol sulfonphthalein is useful lies between $P_H=6.8$ to $P_H=8.4$.

The acid phosphate-glycerin bouillon recommended for the cultivation of *B. tuberculosis* is of interest in this connection. Preliminary cultivation experiments indicated that maximum growth of the organism can be obtained if the medium before sterilization has a hydrogen ion concentration equivalent to $P_H=7.2$. Using the hydrogen electrode for the "exploratory" work, a routine procedure was soon established. In this case, the preliminary titration is carried out according to the usual technique, to a deep pink shade with 0.5 cc. of the 0.02 per cent solution of phenol sulfonphthalein as indicator. The H ion concentration of the adjusted and steamed medium is now determined colorimetrically in the "comparator" with standardized KH_2PO_4—NaOH mixture of $P_H=7.0$ and $P_H=7.2$ (Clark and Lubs).[7] Very satisfactory color comparisons are obtained by adding 0.5 cc. of an 0.04 per cent solution of dibromthymolsulfonphthalein to the tubes containing both the broth and standards.

Solid media can be adjusted to definite H ion concentrations with no special difficulty. As has been pointed out by Clark and Lubs,[7] pure agar has practically no buffer effect in those ranges of reaction where it is usually employed, and its addition to an adjusted bouillon should have no appreciable effect on the hydrogen ion concentration of the latter. Agar, like sugars, can be incorporated in a medium just before sterilization. Since gelatin remains fluid at moderate temperatures, it can be added when necessary before the bouillon is adjusted. Serum, spinal fluid and other exudates which already possess an optimum H ion concentration should be added to media only after the reaction adjustment has been made.

A factor most frequently neglected in the preparation of culture media is proper sterilization. Theoretically, filtration through unglazed porcelain would be an ideal method for sterilizing culture media. On a practical scale, however, recourse must be had to some form of heat, generally flowing steam, or steam under pressure, as in the autoclave. As would be expected, the use of too high a temperature for this purpose can effect chemical changes in a medium which seriously impair its value for bacterial food. This is especially true where sugars or other carbohydrates are present, due to possible cleavages which may take place, particularly in alkaline solution.

Prolonged heating even at temperatures otherwise harmless should be equally avoided. This is especially of importance in the production of large quantities of media in bulk containers where a longer heating period is required to ensure sufficient heat penetration. A long distance recording thermometer of accepted type, which may be inserted directly in the liquid, will materially assist in determining the actual temperature. Contrary to the usually accepted belief, it appears that the deleterious action in this case is not due so much to a final increase in H ion concentration, as to a possible destruction in the medium of food hormones, probably of a vitamine character. The alkaline reaction generally present would also render these compounds more unstable. Experimentation in progress on the role of food accessory factors in the nutrition of *B. diphtheriæ*, which will be reported upon in a subsequent article, appears to substantiate this belief.

In general, even with sugar media, autoclave heating at a temperature not exceeding 120 degrees C. and for a period not more than 30 minutes, has been found to give a more satisfactory microbial food than intermittent sterilization in flowing steam. Media having a supernatant layer of oil for production of anaërobiosis are preferably sterilized by the intermittent method. This avoids the danger of boiling over so frequently encountered when such media are heated by steam under pressure. Actual electrometric determinations of the same medium sterilized by both methods shows less increase in the H ion concentration of the final product of autoclave sterilization. Where a biological index is possible, as in the production of toxins, the intermittent method is more likely to give weaker products.

SUMMARY.

Culture media preparation is discussed with special reference to the requirements of the more common pathogenic microörganisms. Importance is placed upon the proper selection of bacteriologic peptone. The value of this product in bacterial nutrition is governed entirely by the presence of amino acids and other components in a form utilizable by bacteria.

The presence of small quantities of fat in beef infusion has a deleterious action which is ascribed to a probable depression of the surface tension in the medium.

Hydrogen ion concentration of culture media is discussed with special reference to the colorimetric method of determination. A general procedure is outlined showing the application of this method and the modifications which are necessary in special cases of acid and alkaline media.

Comparison of sterilization procedures favors the steam pressure method. High sterilization temperatures can effect chemical changes in a medium, while prolonged heating even at safe temperatures may have a destructive action on the food accessory factors present.

REFERENCES.

1 Davis & Ferry: Jour. Bact., 1919, iv, 217.
2. Davis: Jour. Lab. and Clin. Med., 1917, iii, 75.
3. Larson, Cantwell, and Hartzell: Jour. Infect. Dis., 1919, xxv, 41.
4. Standard Methods of Water Analysis, A. P. H. A., 1917, 94.
5. Sörensen: Ergebn. Physiol., 1912, xii, 393.
6. Walpole: Biochem. Jour., 1914, viii, 628. Jour. Chem. Soc., 1914, cv, 2501.
7. Clark and Lubs: Jour. Bact., 1917, ii, 1, 109, 191.
8. Bovie: Jour. Med. Research, 1915, xxxiii, 295.
9. Bartell: Jour. Am., Chem. Soc., 1917, xxxix, 4, 630.
10. Davis: Jour. Lab. and Clin. Med., iii, 358.
11. Hurwitz, Meyer and Ostenberg: Bull. Johns Hopkins Hospital, 1916, xxvii, 16.

□

Acute Encephalo-myelitis.—The investigation which the authors report concerns an epidemic disease prevalent in certain parts of New South Wales during the summer of 1917 and 1918 which at first was thought to be acute poliomyelitis. The disease in question, however, shows important discrepancies both in its symptomatology and histological picture. An extensive series of experiments was undertaken using monkeys, sheep, calves, dogs and guinea pigs. The results indicate that the disease is an acute encephalo-myelitis akin to but not identical with that of acute poliomyelitis. The disease was rapidly communicated with fatal results to monkeys by intracerebral inoculation of an emulsion of nervous substance (brain, cerebellum, pons, medulla, spinal cord) from a human subject dead from the disease. The disease was also communicated (intracerebrally) from monkey to sheep, from sheep back to monkey and on again from monkey to monkey. In the case of the sheep there was a failure to induce the disease by swabbing the nostrils with virus containing emulsion. The virus is held back by filtering through a Berkefeld filter.—J. B. Cleland and A. W. Campbell, Jour of Hygiene, Oct. 1919, 272-316. (D. G.)

HEALTH HAZARDS OF THE DYE INDUSTRY

A. K. SMITH, M.D.,

Medical Director, E. I. du Pont de Nemours & Co.,
Wilmington, Del.

Read before Section on Industrial Hygiene, American Public Health Association, at New Orleans,
La., October 29, 1919.

The first step in prevention of poisoning in the dye industry
includes well-ventilated, properly equipped buildings. Selection
of workmen is important and the use of the best methods in
manufacturing. These investigations, which are based on 2,500
employees, whose blood was tested periodically, yield some
minor diagnostic material.

The hazards of the dye industry are those connected with any industry plus the poisonous chemicals necessarily handled in the production of dye stuffs.

Prior to 1917 the making of aniline products in this country for use as dye stuffs amounted to next to nothing. Our company had, however, been making aniline products since 1907, and in no inconsiderable quantities, for use as explosives; so that while the dye industry is fairly new to us, the nature of aniline and a number of its allied products is fairly familiar.

The first hazard we meet in the dye industry is from strong acids, such as nitric and sulphuric or a mixture of these two known as mixed acid. These are used to nitrate the benzine or toluene, etc. Their destructiveness to the human tissues is well known and every precaution is taken to prevent these acids from getting on the skin of the workmen. When acid does get on the workman he quickly knows it by the pain it causes, and he immediately drowns it with water and seeks a soothing dressing for his burn.

Nitrous fumes may also be considered under this hazard and are the reddish brown fumes, nitric peroxide, together with some finely atomized acid. Exposure to these fumes must be considered in the nature of an accident and occurs as the result of a nitrator fire or a large spill. Their effects are those of an irritant to the mucous membrane of the respiratory tract and they may cause anything from slight bronchial irritation to a fatal pulmonary edema.

The second hazard we meet with in the dye industry is from the products formed by the action of mixed acid on the benzene series of hydrocarbons, namely; benzene, toluene, xylene, mesitylene, cymene and hexa-methyl-benzene, forming the compounds known as the nitro aromatics, and also the hydrocarbons, napthalene and anthracene and derivatives from these.

A typical nitro compound is mononitro-benzene, and a typical amido compound is aniline which is made from mono-nitro-benzene by treatment with nascent hydrogen.

There are an amazing number of these nitro and amido compounds and a description of each individual compound would be impossible at this time. It is their general character we are after and this depends largely on their physical properties, their solubility and molecular instability.

Some are clingy, oily liquids, others quite insoluble solids and from the adherent, thin, easily absorbable compounds we expect quicker poisoning than from the more stable less soluble solids.

On ingestion any of these compounds may do serious harm. It is more their effects by absorption through the skin and the inhalation of fumes that concern us in the dye industry.

When aniline or aniline oil gets on the skin or clothes no immediate pain is noticed but the workman must be trained to have it removed quite as quickly as he would the strong mineral acid; otherwise he will later have the headache, giddiness, flushed face, rapid heart action, nausea and cyanosis due to its poisonous effects.

At one of our plants where from 2500 to 3000 men are employed and between 90 and 100 different dyes are produced, there were 114 cases of aniline poisoning in the past six months. It is quite often difficult to fasten the poisoning to any particular chemical, as very often there are many different chemical compounds in the course of handling in the same area.. It is for this reason we give the main product of an area credit for producing the poisoning unless its origin is definitely known. Of these 114 cases di-nitro-benzol is credited with 29; ortho and para toluidine 22; diamine 19; phenyl glycin 16; magenta and rosaniline colors 11; napthalene intermediates 6; auramine 5; azo colors 5; and dry mixing and grinding house 1. Some of these materials are fairly harmless, such as phenyl glycin, but aniline oil is used in its preparation and that accounts for the cases. Mono-nitro-benzol is not credited with any cases, and that is simply because it has not caused us any trouble at these works.

Some nitro and amido compounds are exceedingly irritating to the skin, such as para-nitro-aniline, tetra-nitro-methyl-aniline and di-nitro-chlor-benzol. Even the fumes of di-nitro-chlor-benzol can cause a dermatitis. These chemical inflammations of the skin closely resemble the dermatitis caused by poison oak or ivy and are readily amenable to treatment. Some workmen can work in a compound, notoriously irritating to the skin, month after month and suffer no skin inflammation, while other workmen handling the same compound will show an active dermatitis in twenty-four hours. Workmen with such sensitive skins should be permanently removed from contact with such irritants. The skin of an habitual drinker of alcoholic liquor becomes easily inflamed on exposure to these chemicals.

For a time periodic blood examinations were carried on at intervals of two weeks and many thousands of these examinations were made. The results of these examinations showed no great departure from normal, but there was a slight increase in the number of small lymphocytes, a small increase in the number of transitionals, and a slight increase in the number of eosinophiles. Such changes were only found in those workmen who had been exposed to nitro or amido compounds for a period of four or five weeks or longer. In acute cases there is a diminution in the amount of hemoglobin and a formation of methemoglobin.

The earliest symptoms we get in the workmen are headaches, giddiness and a "down and out feeling," as the men describe it, and then upon careful examination a certain amount of cyanosis will be discovered. He is then given an acetic acid bath which is vigorously done by an attendant and sufficient liquid is used to wash away all of the offending chemical; then he is given an effervescent saline laxative and put to bed. Rest and fresh air are very essential in the treatment. If stimulation is needed we use camphor in oil and avoid the use of alcohol. Milk has been found to be useful in these cases, serving as food and a diuretic at the same time. Examination of the urine shows it to be cloudy but without any other change, and the clearing of the urine is taken by our hospital doctors as a guide to the patient's condition. We have had no fatalities from aniline or its allied compounds due to poisoning and we have had no·chronic cases of aniline poisoning unless the slight blood changes noted before and which cause no other symptoms may be considered chronic cases. Usually the acute cases which we have recover in a few hours to three days.

There are perhaps a number of other chemicals used in the production of dyes which should be classed as hazards, such as cyanogen and phosgene or carbonyl chlorid. Any trouble from these compounds, whose effects are well known, can only come about through an accident to their containers, and the dye worker is not exposed to them under ordinary conditions. It is important to keep under observation for at least twenty-four hours any workman who has been exposed to phosgene gas.

Properly equipped buildings, well ventilated, and constant improvement in the methods of production and handling, together with proper selection and care of the workmen will reduce the hazards in the dye industry to those of any other industry. Even at the present time when the dye industry in this country may be said to be in its infancy, and when large numbers of new dyes are being constantly produced, no great difficulties are being experienced, a condition which we attribute to constant care, supervision, and improvement in our methods.

□

Tuberculosis Agencies.—It has been found after long experience that efforts directed principally against infection itself in tuberculosis have not been as successful as was hoped might be the case. We are realizing that there are other lines of attack in the combat against tuberculosis quite as important as the direct one. We must strike on the flanks of the enemy as well as on the front, and we need the forces of Boards of Health, the Red Cross, the public health nurse, the school physician, the social worker, the visiting nurse, and all the various agencies which have to do with industrial conditions, housing occupational diseases, and factory hygiene, for our combined attack.

The special task for the tuberculosis association or worker is outlined in the following program:

1. To search out in every community each case of tuberculosis and to see that it is properly disposed of.

2. To afford the local physician opportunity for a diagnosis of his suspected cases, either through a tuberculosis dispensary or a tuberculosis expert.

3. To educate the community on the importance of the prevention of tuberculosis and to promote wise legislation.

4. To persuade employers of labor as to the economic value of having their employes periodically examined for tuberculosis, to provide means for these examinations and to urge all other organizations to do the same.

5. To urge the importance of having all school children thoroughly examined each year for tuberculosis.

6. To see that provision is made in sanatoria and hospitals for those suffering from active tuberculosis and for children with latent tuberculosis, as well as open-air schools or fresh-air classes for pre-tubercular children.

7. To follow up discharged cases from these sanatoria so as to prevent relapses.

8. To do what we can to provide suitable occupation or proper hygienic conditions under which the arrested case can follow out his original vocation.

9. To provide well-trained visiting nurses or social workers to supervise and keep in touch with those consumptives, who for some reason remain at home.—E. O. Otis, *Jour. of Mass. Tuberculosis League,* Dec. 1919. (*D. G.*)

A Stronger A. P. H. A. Means More Help to You. Do Your Bit.

EDITORIAL SECTION

AMERICAN JOURNAL OF PUBLIC HEALTH
EDITORIAL OFFICE: 169 MASSACHUSETTS AVE., BOSTON, MASS.

A. W. HEDRICH, C. P. H., Editor   J. RITCHIE, Jr., Associate Editor

Editorial Assistants

E. R. HAYHURST, M.D.	DAVID GREENBERG	JAMES A. TOBEY
R. P. ALBAUGH, M.D.	M. P. HORWOOD, M.S.	FRANCIS H. SLACK, M.D.
E. B. STARR, M.D.	P. M. HOLMES, M.D.	JAMES M. STRANG

Board of Advisory Editors

PETER H. BRYCE, M.D., Ottawa, Canada	PROF. M. J. ROSENAU, Boston, Mass.
CHARLES V. CHAPIN, M.D., Providence, R. I.	PROF. W. T. SEDGWICK, Cambridge, Mass.
EUGENE R. KELLEY, M.D., Boston, Mass.	PROF. GEORGE C. WHIPPLE, Cambridge, Mass.
W. A. EVANS, M.D., Chicago, Ill.	PROF. S. M. GUNN, Paris, France.

All expressions of opinion and all statements of supposed facts are published on authority of the writer under whose name they appear, and are not to be regarded as expressing the views of the American Public Health Association, unless such statements or opinions have been adopted by vote of the Association.

NOTICE TO SUBSCRIBERS: Subscription Price, payable in advance, $4.00 per year for United States and possessions; $4.50 for Canada and other foreign countries. Single copies, 50 cents postpaid. Membership in the American Public Health Association, including subscription to Journal, $5.00 per year. **In Change of Address** please give both old and new address, and mail before the tenth of the month to take effect with the current issue. Mailing Date, 5th of each month. **Advertisements** accepted only when commendable, and worth while both to reader and advertiser. **News Items,** interesting clippings and illustrations are gladly received, together with name of sender. **Copyright, 1919,** by A. W. Hedrich.

AN AFTERMATH OF THE WAR.

The armies of the combatants in the recent war have offered the greatest clearing house for infections that the world has ever seen. Gatherings of pilgrims at religious shrines and the great fairs of India and other countries have been marked by the public health administrator as dangerous through their possible agencies in the interchange of disease, and before the war serious effort was made in Hindustan to lessen the risks by discouraging the gatherings. The war against Germany has presented similar dangers, but on a much vaster scale. In the pilgrimage centers and at the fairs, the people of the same or of kindred countries exchanged maladies with which they were more or less accustomed. In the war every soldier ran the potential risk of infection with any of the world's whole category of communicable diseases. The risk was increased by absence of natural immunity to foreign diseases, but a factor of comparative safety lay in the control and watchfulness of the army medical corps. So close a concentration of all the kinds of communicable diseases in the world presents opportunities for distribution as the demobilized troops return to their home countries and the routes are again opened to travelers and emigrants. This is the reason why Switzerland meets with suspicion and with a quarantine the demobilized soldier who seeks to cross her frontier; it is the reason that malaria, trench fever, dysentery and cerebro-spinal meningitis are receiving much attention at the hands and in the codes of British health administrators.

These facts should not be without their suggestions to public health officers in this country. There is no occasion for alarm, but much need for watchfulness. The best opinions in Europe and the United States counsel such watchfulness. There seems to be no feeling that any "epidemic following war" is to be feared, but care may be necessary and keen scrutiny of incoming strangers to prevent minor outbreaks.

Danger lies in the introduction into the country of carriers of disease who have acquired their germs abroad. No one knows precisely what virulence these microbes may present. There have been observations of imported cerebro-spinal meningitis that suggest unusual virulence. This is by no means a new story in the transmission of disease, for imported smallpox invariably results in fatalities. In Canada there has been noted a Gallipoli strain of dysentery. The disease is included in the list of the notifiable in only one-quarter of the States of the Union, and its spread may be unmarked, almost unnoticed; but it is a very important one in the armies of the Allies. It is necessary to keep it from our territory, the imported strain, since there may be potential risk to our people.

Such signals as these suggest the necessity for the highest standards of watchfulness at the ports of entry of the country, the most rigid quarantine; and on the part of state and local health officers, the closest attention to notification. While there is comparatively little to fear from the common infections through interstate transmission, because they are the kind already so well in hand, there should be the closest watch for any variations from regular forms of disease. It is the germ from abroad that is at the moment most important to guard against, for no one can predict what will be its course. The influenza epidemic emphasizes that fact.

In this country of easy transportation, health officials should now be on their guard against smallpox. The divided practice in vaccination leaves a number of endemic centres in North America in which it lurks, ready to invade other districts on the slightest relaxation of vigilance, or the barrier provided by a vaccinated community. Cases have been reported from a number of states, and local health officers should be, not alarmed, but forearmed and ready.

WHY NOT SANITARY SCHOOLHOUSES?

Contributors to the main articles in the JOURNAL this month have taken for their subject "School Hygiene." There seems to be no matter in the whole list of things that ought to be done in the interests of public health of more consequence than the sanitation of the schoolhouse. The first steps towards a sensible policy in this have not yet been taken in this country. The little boy who a few years ago asked his father, who was traveling with him on a train, why it was wicked to take a drink in one state and perfectly good form in the adjoining one, asked a difficult question. The same little boy could have overwhelmed his father with questions about the inconsistencies of the states in their schoolhouse legislation.

To quote one single item as a type of the whole system or lack of system; the fine schools of Rochester, N. Y., acknowledgedly exceedingly successful for their purpose in western New York, would be condemned as unfit for school uses in Vermont and in others of the States of the Union.

There is no one factor to health in the schoolhouse that is standardized. The problems of heating and ventilation have, in general, had no broad consideration; they are in the hands of the architect or the school committee, and may or may not be committed to some favorite in the business of heating and ventilation. The matter of illumination has received some attention from scientific investigators, but schoolhouses respond but indifferently to the standards.

The lavatories of schoolhouses in the principal cities of the country show no standards of space requirements, no standards of equipment, no standards of care. The rest room problem has been considered in a few instances, but no definite requirements are made. The same is true of space for the fast developing medical and dental attention that communities are furnishing for their school children.

Schoolhouse planning construction has been and is today a matter of local option, and one does not here need to stop for proof of political influence. The architect is not infrequently a friend of the governing forces, and may have been interested in schoolhouses only through his reading. The contractor more frequently, even, is a citizen of the town; in many places it is a written or an unwritten requirement. In a small city such a man is likely to know little of the special needs of schoolhouses, but from just such men the city gets its building and equipment. One might be pardoned for thinking that in constructing buildings for the education of children, there would be required something in the way of special education of those responsible for the schoolhouses. This, however, has been even till now a forgotten or ignored method of procedure.

Realizing the chaos that exists in schoolhouse construction, under varying policies in the different states, some of which do not even provide standards of security to the scholars against fire, the National Education Association has entered upon a determination of minimum needs in the various factors to health and educational progress. It is a splendid and far-seeing piece of research, reports on which are already available in part. But it is high time for the health officer to come into co-operation with the N. E. A., and use his influence towards the establishment of proper health requirements in school building, places to which attendance is compulsory for one-third of the child's waking hours. In the campaign for the health of the child, there is hardly any more important movement than the reformation of the schoolhouse. This will require the plain statement of the case, the education of the parents and the establishment of a common sense basis for health legislation and regulations for schoolhouses. Every health agency in the country ought to be interested in an effort to make the schoolhouse a fit place in health and sanitation for the children on whom the future of the country must depend.

A SUCCESSFUL SCHOOL OF PUBLIC HEALTH.

Of Schools of Public Health there are many kinds, ranging all the way from that old-fashioned apprenticeship, in which a zealous pupil works with and under the immediate direction of a master, to those organized and maintained by universities, with fixed and extensive curricula and sessions covering one or more entire academic years. Some state health departments have an annual school lasting for a week or less and intended for the better information and special instruction of health officers in actual practice.

As a rule, the successful School of Public Health, like every other successful school, depends largely upon the personality of one or more of the instructors, and now and then we hear of one which owes its effectiveness to a single leader endowed with vision and enthusiasm and gifted with personal magnetism and the power of inspiration. Such a school is that conducted by Dr. Frederick W. Sears, Sanitary Supervisor of the State Board of Health of New York and Professor in the Medical School of Syracuse University.

In a recent issue we published an account of the Syracuse School prepared by Dr. Sears himself and lately given by invitation before the Harvard-Technology School of Public Health in Boston. We have it on the best authority that this school has been unusually successful and that those who have taken the various courses and have reached the requisite standards have developed an enthusiasm for Public Health and obtained a practical knowledge of its problems and practice, which have redounded not only to their personal advantage but also to a marked improvement of Public Health Administration in the towns or districts under their care. It is to be noted that all of them were physicians or nurses not previously trained for Public Health work.   W. T. S.

DR. HUGH SMITH CUMMING

The nomination by President Wilson of Dr. Hugh Smith Cumming as Surgeon General to the United States Public Health Service is especially significant as an expression of the development of public health within that Service. Commencing his career a quarter of a century ago in what was then the Marine Hospital Service, Dr. Cumming was in the forefront of the expansion under Surgeon General Wyman of national quarantine. This constituted a broad school in which he gained experience in various parts of the United States and in the Orient.

In the next great expansive movement, when by the recognition of sanitation, the Service became a truly Public Health Service Dr. Cumming was placed in charge of the investigation of the Potomac River and the Coastal Waters. It was in this work, by gathering around himself an efficient staff of specially trained sanitarians that he became recognized as one of the leaders in the field of Sanitation. With the outbreak of the War his services were requisitioned by the Navy to take charge of important health work which war activities made vitally necessary. His success in this work took him to Europe at the time provisions for embarking the huge American Army for return to the United States required assured methods to prevent the introduction into America of the numerous diseases that were afflicting war torn Europe. The remarkable feat accomplished in the return of 2,000,000 men who had been in intimate contact with the festering conglomeration of peoples from all parts of the globe, with all their heterogeneous diseases, without any detectable outbreaks in America bears testimony to the efficiency of the methods adopted.

While in Europe Dr. Cumming gained experience in all the public health activities throughout the Continent, and has been one of the leading American representatives in the important international Public Health Councils held in those countries. It is therefore logical that on his return to America, Dr. Cumming should be chosen leader of the great work in the Public Health Service which is developing so rapidly in this country. Sanitarians will welcome this recognition of the important progress which Sanitation has made in the field of Public Health.

CORRECTION

In the article in the January JOURNAL, "A Study of the Toxicity of Diphtheria Bacilli Isolated from Immediate Contacts," the statement appears: (Page 43, Col. 1, top) "In this particular instance only about 1 in 10,000 persons were potential sources of diphtheria infection when thrown in contact with non-infected persons."

Instead of "1 to 10,000" this should be "about 1 in 1,000."

BOOKS AND REPORTS
REVIEWED

The Narcotic Drug Problem. *Ernest S. Bishop, M.D., F.A.C.P., New York: Macmillan Company. 1920. Pp 165. Price $150.*

To the readers of the AMERICAN JOURNAL OF PUBLIC HEALTH Dr. Bishop needs no introduction, for the reason that his papers on narcotic addiction disease have been presented at various recent meetings of the Association and have found place in the JOURNAL. They all focus on one important principle, that this addiction is a disease, that it should be treated as a disease, and that public opinion, the opinion of medical men in general and the usual attitude assumed towards the victims of the disease are fundamentally wrong, and so far as these have been the basis of legislation, that that is largely wrong too. It is a piece of missionary work to which Dr. Bishop has devoted himself, to undertake the education of the people, so that the wrong may be righted.

"The tendency and effect of legislative, administrative, police and penological activities in general," writes Dr. Bishop, "have been to place the sufferer from addiction-disease in the position of the criminal and vicious. The tendency of the psychologist and psychiatrist is to analyze him from the viewpoint of mental weakness, defect or degeneration, and to so classify and regard him....The addict himself, whose testimony has been all too little consulted or sought, will tell you that he is sick with some kind of physical condition which causes suffering and incapacity whenever a sufficient amount of narcotic is not administered."

"My present definition of narcotic drug addiction," continues Dr. Bishop, "is as follows; a definite physical disease condition, presenting constant and definite physical symptoms and signs, progressing through clean-cut clinical stages of development, explainable by a mechanism of body protection against the action of narcotic toxins."

Color, nationality, social or economic position, age, mental and moral attributes of whatever sort are no bar to the development of the condition. Judges on the bench, ministers in the pulpit, physicians, men in prominent positions, may be sufferers, while there are instances of record of addicted babies only a few hours old, born of addicted mothers.

As to origin, Dr. Bishop asserts that there is only one way to acquire the disease, namely through the continued administration of a drug that causes addiction. The details of their original administration vary, and a proportion of the cases must be charged to physicians in following customary opiate administration methods. "Unwisely prolonged opiate medication makes more opiate addicts than we have realized." The individual who is primarily normal, mentally, morally and physically, whose addiction condition is a result of ignorant, misguided or unavoidable medication, either professionally or self-administered, is worthy of study. The number of these is far greater than is generally appreciated. "They are social and economic assets whose interests we cannot ignore when we are considering the disposition and handling of the narcotic addict."

Dr. Bishop discusses the mechanism of addiction, the methods of treating victims of the disease, the rational handling of the disease, the laws and popular opinion. He notes that the discussion of the different methods employed in treating victims would require another volume, but briefly outlines the three broad principles underlying one or the other of them. Slow reduction and sudden withdrawal leave the patient subject to the physical torture which is the reason for their continuance as addicts, the latter process not infrequently ending in death. In the attempted cure by the substitution of other drugs, the substitutes are of such nature that it is difficult to attribute to them specific properties in an addiction disease.

With reference to the Harrison law, Dr. Bishop states that in its purpose and drafting it was a wise piece of legislation. "It sought to limit and control the use of opiate drugs and cocaine by making their possession and distribution illegal by other than those of professional and other status designated in the law, as qualified for their intelligent application and responsible distribution." The reaction within the medical profession was unfortunate, and instead of seeking to clarify the situation, the scientific men left the consideration and handling of the addict to lay officials.

These officials, unbacked by any knowledge that addiction is a disease, adopted the popular idea of degeneracy and criminality in the so-called "dope-fiends" and the immediate result was the cutting off of the supply to those to whom it was necessary. This action has resulted in the increase in illicit distribution of drugs. The dominant theme has been not that of therapy, but of "stamping out," and the honest physician who strove to meet the needs of his patient, an innocent addict, incurred the danger of severe criticism, possibly even jeopardy to his liberty under the interpretation of his acts as perpetuating a "habit."

This will call attention to some of the main points brought out by Dr. Bishop, who is calling for a reversal of public opinion in this matter through better information of the medical profession itself, which has in its ignorance of the real conditions, lent strength to the popular misapprehension. He is a disciple preaching the doctrine that "narcotic drug addicts are sick men who would be given medical treatment, and not criminals or degenerates who should be subjected to the drastic terms of the laws." He furnishes to the general reader a plain view of the subject, his volume has the information that can make the addict hold up his head and realize just what his condition is, it will serve to reinstate some of the unfortunates in the opinions of their families, while it is technical enough so that the physician may learn the truth.

As to the needs of the hour, they are education. No important courses in medical schools have been devoted to this disease, and laboratory work is almost negligible. "Education and training are the best hopes we have as a foundation for the alleviation of present conditions and the prevention of their further spread." "A campaign of medical and lay investigation and education will require a much shorter time than a continuous trying out of various panaceas, medical, legislative and administrative." The narcotic wards of our great hospitals should afford means of real study and the addict, himself, should be given much more extended hearing.

It is a missionary book, written by a skilled diagnostician, who in his study of the patients in public institutions has become impressed

with the erroneous attitude of the world. The volume is intended to prove the entering wedge towards better conceptions, real appreciation and proper treatment of the innocent men and women afflicted with narcotic addiction disease.

✤

The Feeding of Nations. *E. H. Starling, London: Longmans, Green & Co., 1919. Pp. 146. Price $1.90.*

This little volume contains two lectures—the Oliver Sharpey foundation—by one of the most distinguished of English physiologists. The writer was an influential member of the Inter-allied Scientific Food Commission. No one is better qualified to review the great problems of food supply in war-time or to point out the principles to be applied in any future emergency. Here we have outlined the unsuccessful attempt of the Central Powers to maintain health and morale upon a diminished ration and the better control of a critical situation by the Allied Governments.

The following salient observations may be noted. Carbohydrates cannot be substituted for fats to an indefinite extent. A nation facing food shortage should pursue a middle course with regard to its live-stock, neither slaughtering in haste nor seeking to maintain the maximum number of animals. The nutritive requirements of children must be estimated very liberally. At a time when most foods are rationed there should be at least one type which can be had in unrestricted amount. This "elastic reserve," utilized to bring various diets up to the necessary energy value, is best represented by bread. The book is concise, clear, and informing. It is most interesting to read that despite high prices the present wage scales have greatly reduced the number of underfed families in the United Kingdom.

PERCY G. STILES, PH. D.

✤

Organization of Public Health Nursing. *Annie M. Brainard, New York: The Macmillan Co. 1919. Pp. 144. Price, $1.35.*

"Organization" is the hope of the present. No natural or local result along any line can be hoped for without the right kind of organization. It is therefore an encouraging sign of the times that so vital a problem as public health nursing is being organized for greater efficiency. A book which deals with this organization problem in a helpful, practical way is the recently published volume, "Organization of Public Health Nursing," by Annie M. Brainard.

The public health nurse is not an innovation. We have had her with us for many years, in one of several capacities—as a district nurse, school nurse, tuberculosis nurse, factory nurse, visiting nurse, baby welfare nurse, etc.—and the field is constantly enlarging. But now a greater effort is being made to utilize this public health nurse and secure the greatest good to the whole community. This means organization. There are, of course, many snags in the way of developing public health nursing into a strong, efficient civic agency. The author points out these snags, especially emphasizing the necessity of keeping out of politics and of avoiding sectarian issues.

In addition to discussing the various types of organization, the author does not shirk the difficult task of showing what part the individual nurse may and should play in organizing the work in her own community. All too often the nurse, like the teacher, feels that the enthusiastic performance of her routine duties is the only service which should be expected of her. In fact she usually feels unqualified to undertake anything so ambitious as organization. But, as the author points out, the nurse can and should show her initiative and executive ability in helping put public health nursing upon a substantial basis.

Chapter V.—The Nurse's Part in Organizing—is an especially valuable discussion as is the following chapter on organizing public health nursing in a new community. From the first page to the last the book is practical, suggestive, and stimulating. It should find a large field waiting for it.

MAY BLISS DICKINSON, R. N.

✛

Courage. *Jeannette Marks, New York: The Womans Press. Pp. 140. Price $1.25 net.*

An inspiring and helpful little book for those who need to be reminded that mental courage and a healthful attitude of mind, together with the spirit to "carry on," are essential to the living of a successful life. Its message implies that every victory of will, however small or partial, helps in the training of complete self control, to be strong in

one's self. To be unafraid, to have a will power obedient and sensitive, is to have achieved the greatest of victories.

The writer emphasizes the value of sleep as a means of bringing calmness and of reinforcing the courage needed to meet life fearlessly and bravely.

The importance of enthusiasm in work to be done, and the application of ourselves to the task at hand; as well as an open-minded and open-hearted attitude toward our fellowmen, is the message that this little book brings. With its appropriately selected poems, and its blue and gold cover, the author has not only presented a helpful little volume, but also an attractive one.

✛

Standard Methods of Bacteriological Water Analysis. *Boston: American Public Health Association. Fourth Edition. Waterproof cloth. Price $1.25.*

The revised edition of Standard Methods of Bacteriological Water Analysis which will come from the printer about March first, contains but few changes from the methods in the 1917 edition. Among the most important additions is the adoption of a method of adjusting culture media to a definite hydrogen-ion concentration instead of the old method of titration with phenolphthalein, although the latter method is still retained for the convenience of those who are not yet ready to adopt the newer and more accurate method. All recent work in bacteriology points to the fact that it is real acidity rather than titratable acidity that determines the conditions for bacterial growth. It is logical, therefore, to adopt a method which determines this real acidity as measured by the hydrogen-ion concentration. In the sugar fermentation reactions the amount of sugar used is reduced from one per cent. to one-half of one per cent. which is in line with recent practice. A restatement of the method of making Endo plates, and of carrying out the indol and methyl red tests is made, which it is hoped will lead to better and more accurate results. An optional method of sterilizing sugar media is added for the benefit of those whose autoclaves require a longer exposure to heat than one-half hour to reach the required time and pressure. Most of the other changes are of minor importance.

Health Almanac for 1920, Bulletin No. 98, U. S. P. H. Service.
Miners' Safety and Health Almanac for 1920. Miners' Circular No. 26, Bureau of Mines.
Almanac 1920, Louisiana State Board of Health.

If the wording of the Old Farmer's Almanac type of publication were followed, one would see recorded in health announcements at this season of the year, "About this time look for health almanacs." This group of three represents three different types of the little volumes that have become more or less familiar in these later years. In size and general appearance they are similar to the almanacs from the country drug store, which were kept handy by the kitchen fireplace. Like these there appears on each right hand page a calendar for the month, surmounted by a little sketch or legend or slogan appropriate to the season. Notable events, interspersed health maxims are mentioned beside the proper dates, and instead of the advertisements of "Dr. Dopem's Tonic," one will find the modern doctrines of prevention set forth.

The U. S. P. H. Service almanac presents on its front cover a picture of Uncle Sam, M. D., in colors. It is plentifully supplied with short, pithy articles on public health, there are illustrative sketches of that problem of exceeding importance, the privy, and the accompanying text is helpful in its nature. The almanac takes occasion to set forth an outline of the work of the service, the names and addresses of its district supervisors, and a list of helpful publications is appended. Instead of the stereotyped instructions "Begin sowing buckwheat," "Start spring plowing," or "Overhaul the tractor," this almanac suggests the value of fresh air, the need of avoiding overeating, the necessity for keeping stables clean, with slogans on fighting venereal disease.

The Miners' Almanac is special in that it points directly at means of preventing accident as well as conserving health. It follows more closely the stereotyped Government form of publication and is not so attention-compelling as the almanac of the State of Louisiana, for example. Miners' diseases are discussed, the value of the wet drill as preventing dust is set forth, there is a story about children's diseases, and flies, drinking water, physical examination of the family, typhoid, school inspection, venereal disease, sanitary housing and scores of other health topics are discussed. The privy here is of enormous consequence, so that an illustrated article on the proper construction of this essential finds place in the pamphlet. There is also a sketch of the work in mine rescue, and lists of helpful health publications, those of the Bureau of Mines and of the U. S. P. H. Service, the latter of which has aided in the preparation of the almanac. The compiler is R. C. Williams, Assistant Surgeon in the U. S. P. H. Service.

Suited to the eye and the circumstances of citizens in general is the Louisiana State Health Almanac. Its cover bears the old farmer but he is sowing the seeds of health. There are astronomical data sufficient for ordinary family use, together with a statement of the holidays. Each page of the calendar devotes itself to some general subject, avoiding accident, remedies, antidotes both for poisons and for bites and stings, first aid suggestions and the like, plentifully interspersed with health maxims. There are plenty of attractive little pictures modern in fashion, emphasizing the short lessons and stories that are given. An occasional poem and once in a while an item that is humorous, serve to lighten the tone of the little book. It will be kept throughout the year in many a household with a constant appreciation of the lessons that it is so quietly giving.

□

Coming Soon
The Membership Campaign for 7,500
You Will Be Able to Help

ASSOCIATION NEWS

HEALTH EMPLOYMENT BUREAU

Help-wanted announcements will be carried free in this column until further notice. Copy goes to the printer on the fifteenth of each month. In answering keyed advertisements, please mail replies separately.

The Health Employment Bureau also sends lists of applicants to prospective employers without charge.

Technician for laboratory work in bacteriological research under direction of commercial producer. Some knowledge of chemistry useful. Ability to carry on independent work will be recognized. Address B. W. J., 331, care of this JOURNAL.

Full time Health Officer. Must be M. D., energetic, experienced in sanitation and communicable disease control; school experience desirable. Salary $3,000 per year, with transportation while on duty in the County. Population of County about 60,000. Good roads. Address Norfolk County Health Department, 318 New Kirn Bldg., Portsmouth, Va.

Man for position of full-time Health Officer in well established Health Department. Must be capable and energetic. Meat and milk inspection work; fully equipped laboratory with full-time bacteriologist, public health nurses, and sanitation all under his jurisdiction. Must be available on or before April 1st, 1920. $3,000 to efficient man. References required. For details apply to T. C. Hudson, Chairman, Board of Health. Control, Columbus, Ga.

Laboratory assistant or bacteriologist for routine work in private commercial laboratory. Man 18-25 years. Previous experience unnecessary. State education and name salary desired. Address H. A. Felder, South Bend Medical Laboratory, South Bend, Ind.

□

PROPOSED FOR ELECTION TO THE

A. P. H. A.

FROM JANUARY 13, 1920 TO FEBRUARY 10, 1920

SPONSORS*
and
NEW MEMBERS

MISS IDA MAY STEVENS, Berkeley, Cal.
  Miss Margaret Beattie, Instructor in Public Health, Berkeley, Cal.
MILBANK JOHNSON, M. D., Los Angeles, Cal.
  Donald J. Frick, M. D., Los Angeles, Cal.
HORATIO N. PARKER, Jacksonville, Fla.
  Frank C. Gephart, Ph. D., Chemist, New York City.
GRACE WHITFORD, M. D., Ozona, Fla.
  M. Josie Rogers, M. D., State Chairman Dept. of Public Health, Daytona, Fla.
H. O. JONES, M. D., Chicago, Ill.
  Mrs. Emma E. Koch, R. N., Chicago, Ill.
HARRY L. O'CONNOR, M. D., Chicago, Ill.
  Florentino N. Gonzales, Bacteriologist, Akron, Ohio
E. A. CRULL, M. D., Fort Wayne, Ind.
  Gertrude Barber, R. N., Exec. Sec. Anti-Tuberculosis League, Fort Wayne, Ind.
M. V. ZEIGLER, Asst. Surgeon, U. S. P. H. Service, Indianapolis, Ind.
  J. M. Bulla, M. D., Richmond, Ind.
L. D. BRISTOL, M. D., Augusta, Me.
  Olin Sewall Pettingill, M. D., Health Officer, Greenwood Mountain, Me.
A. W. HEDRICH, Boston, Mass.
  W. C. Bailey, M. D., Health Officer, San Jose, Cal.

*States arranged in alphabetical order.

F. J. Camboss, M. D., New Orleans, La.
Henry S. Capps, M. D., Health Officer, Beaumont, Texas.
Ettore Ciampolini, M. D., Cambridge, Mass.
A. S. Daggette, M. D., Pittsburgh, Pa.
Cyril Dickinson, Bacteriologist, Raynes Park, London, S. W. 19, England.
Chas. F. Freiburger, Sec. Detroit Dept. of Health, Detroit, Mich.
Alice G. Masaryk, M. D., President of the Czecho-Slovak Red Cross, Prague, Czecho-Slovak Republic.
Elizabeth Morford, B. A., Bacteriologist, Houston, Texas.
Rowlett Paine, Mayor, Memphis, Tenn.
B. C. Roloff, Exec. Sec. Ill. Social Hygiene League, Chicago, Ill.
MISS FRANCES D. PARTRIDGE, Port Huron, Mich.
  Ella J. Fifield, M. D., Medical Examiner, Port Huron, Mich.
C. W. F. HOLBROOK, M. D., Newark, N. J.
  Louis H. Osborn, Bacteriologist, Newark, N. J.
JOHN TOMBS, Regional Secretary, Nat. Tub. Association, Albuquerque, N. M.
  New Mexico Public Health Assn., Atten. of Clinton P. Anderson, Albuquerque, N. M.
C. E. WALLER, M. D., N. M.
  M. D. Taylor, M. D., Health Officer, Aztec, N.M.
F. L. RECTOR, M. D., New York City
  Eloise Meek, M. D., New York City.
M. EDGAR ROSE, M. D., New York City
  Mathilde S. Kuhlman, R. N., Supervising Nurse, New York City.

266

□

WHY NOT 7,500 A. P. H. A. MEMBERS?

When Dr. Frankel became President of the American Public Health Association he initiated the "Member per Member" campaign, which was so successful that it had the effect of doubling the existing membership. This numerical increase enlarged the scope of the Association, giving it the advantage of added members and consequent prestige, experience, ability and bettered financial condition. This excellent work President Rankin finds to be only the portal to increasing strength and he proposes to carry further the splendid work begun by his predecessor. The Association has now 4,500 members and subscribers, and Dr. Rankin has set the goal for this campaign at 7,500 members and subscribers, which he believes the Association can attain the present year. Accordingly he is taking the preliminary steps to this end. The intensive part of the campaign will come during the month of April.

The new "drive" will not for a moment lose sight of the great value of the efforts of the interested member, but proposes to conduct the campaign with each state as a campaign unit. Dr. Rankin, being himself a state health officer, realizes the advantage of enlisting other state health officers as campaign managers. The details of the movement will be set forth later. It is the hope to secure the help of every state health commissioner in the country. To each state

Golden Gate Park Memorial Museum, San Francisco, Cal., an architectural gem

will be assigned a quota of new members to be secured, proportionate to the possibilities of the state, and under the supervision of the State Campaign Manager committees will work in the pledging of members in their districts. In this way, and in skillful hands, the 1920 campaign for new members will be undertaken, and it will have no such word as "fail" in its vocabulary.

It will be incumbent on members to help by joining heartily in the work and reporting to their state health officers at the earliest moment. To every member there will be furnished presently the name of the campaign manager for his district, and instant activity is urged the moment the "drive" is on.

open sea and the vast expanse of the bay, must feel the tempering influences of the partly enclosed basin. Its latitude, between 37 degrees and 38 degrees N., about the same as that of Richmond, Va., is a further natural factor to an equable climate, while the presence of the mighty mountain ranges no great distance to the east, which act as condensers of the cloud-borne moisture, assure healthful humidity, fertility and a sound economic basis to the country.

Greater San Francisco has added to its natural advantages the conserving ones of the preservation of breathing spaces for its people, and the Golden Gate Park and the Twin Peaks drive are evidences in the city of the public spirit of its people, supple-

A picturesque spot in San Francisco. Fisherman's Wharf with its scores of boats and acres of drying nets

A WORD ABOUT SAN FRANCISCO

Whatever else may be said in favor of San Francisco as the meeting place for the Forty-eighth Annual Convention of the American Public Health Association, it has in its situation, its development and the spirit of its institutions the real environment for health administration of the most effective character. The situation of the State on the shore of the great Pacific Ocean bespeaks for its whole coast line a climate almost ideal for health. San Francisco, itself, on its narrow foothold between the

mented by the University Park and green hills of Berkeley and Oakland's "Heights," its beautiful Lake Merrit and its easily accessible Piedmont. There are to be added to these the facilities of three great universities and the existence in the city itself of no less than 17 hospitals, most of them dating since the fire, and utilizing the most modern fireproof construction and up-to-date equipment. Such factors as these cannot fail to constitute an attraction to the health officer, who is already well informed as to the specialty of health administration in the city and the state.

Golden Gate Park, whose Memorial Museum stands an architectural gem in a setting of greenery, is one of the most remarkable examples in the world of the results of a determination of the people to preserve for themselves a playground. Here the desert has been made literally to blossom, for upon absolutely barren sand dunes has been superposed every ounce of the soil from which now spring groves and undergrowth, with bowling greens and grassy meadows, the resort of tens of thousands of the citizens. An uneven district, its tree-embowered lake standing at a height of nearly 300 feet above sea level, Nature has been coaxed to make here her haunts, the reversal of the customary procedure whereby the municipality takes to itself an established beauty spot of wooded hill and dale.

San Francisco's civic pride has already been evidenced in the JOURNAL in the splendid City Hall, which is the pivot of its civic center. Here in the heart of the city have been assembled a group of municipal structures that no other city of the country can match. City Hall, Municipal Auditorium, Opera House and Public Library, in harmonious beauty, here enclose a park with splashing fountains, decorative shrubbery and delightful setting. The dignified building dedicated to the education of the people through their reading, the San Francisco Public Library, finds itself in good company.

At the Civic Center the San Francisco Public Library finds itself in good company

One other matter of greatest health interest to be touched upon briefly is that of food supply. Ocean, bay, river and farming lands are at hand to contribute. Of the quality and freshness of its fish supply the JOURNAL can present a bit of pictorial evidence, Fisherman's Wharf, with its scores of smacks and acres of nets spread out to dry. These little boats are in the service constantly and every day glide to their grounds to tap the inexhaustible finny wealth of the Pacific. And as for San Francisco's markets, they need but be seen to be appreciated.

□

LITTLE ROUND-UP OF TUBERCULOSIS ITEMS

Traveling Clinic of the Washington (State) Tuberculosis Association. — Although the traveling tuberculosis clinic, moving about over a state or a district with the freedom that the motor truck affords is not, strictly speaking, a novelty, it still seems worth the while to note the development of such a movement in the far Northwest as this has been accomplished in the state of Washington under the care and management of the Washington Tuberculosis Association of Seattle. The focusing of fresh minds on a problem, especially under conditions that are not common, has in it at times facts of value even for those who have begun and carried forward similar enterprises. This report has been pre-

pared for the JOURNAL by Mrs. Bethesda Beals Buchanan, Executive Secretary of the Washington Association.

Washington, of all states in the Union, might be conceded by anyone even slightly familiar with its topography and history, to offer the greatest scope for the work of a traveling tuberculosis clinic, at the same time presenting the greatest number of difficulties to overcome.

From the brilliant, sub-tropical weather of the eastern and southeastern part of the state, and the Columbia River Valley, where hot winds blow across thousands of acres of volcanic ash soil rapidly being put under cultivation; across the almost impassable barrier of the Cascade range running across the state from north to south, to the Puget Sound district, where 3,000 square miles of salt water lie within the borders of the state, where rains, fogs, many immense glacial rivers, primeval forests, tide lands, and hundreds of islands make up the country, there are a thousand variations of temperature and climatic conditions.

To the physician, there is presented in this state innumerable types of environments, in each of which are found groups of people subject to what might almost be termed endemic conditions—as for instance the high percentage of goitre-afflicted natives of the northwestern part of the state; or the rapid growth and inadequate housing and sanitary states of many lumber and mill camps, fruit growing areas and fishing villages.

Aside from geographical variations, there is the insistent problem of assimilation of the steady stream of new peoples pouring in from all quarters of the globe; the influence of the Oriental commerce and population, against a background of pioneer stock which has, for the most part, forgotten the hardships of early days, and which resents any new fad or cult out from the east. These influences, now faced by the second generation of hardy Americans who are today building the substantial towns and cities, and who are to the fore in educational and cultural movements, together with the thousands of returned Alaskans now resident here, may furnish some idea of the task which confronted the Washington Tuberculosis Association when it determined to send a traveling clinic over the state, a task to which its 21 affiliated leagues gave signal assistance.

The outfit which was to travel as many miles as possible in a given length of time was most carefully planned and reduced to the simplest needs, not only for its clinical work, but for purposes of hard and rough traveling. A Ford truck of the one-ton capacity was purchased and equipped, bearing on its canvas cover the double-barred red cross, and the words, "Traveling Clinic and Exhibit of the Washington Tuberculosis Association." A lighting system with engine was carried for a while, but was later detached, since no town was visited which did not have an electric lighting system, owing to the abundance of hydroelectric power in the state. The moving

picture and stereopticon show was condensed into traveling cases, the doctor's "office" was packed in a cracker box and bed rolls, blankets and a cot provided for emergencies. An educational exhibit was furnished, consisting of 180 National Child Welfare League pictures and collapsible racks for hanging, together with literature, records, maps, charts, etc.

The publicity was of an elementary sort, what might be termed as the advance agent type. Window cards, hand bills and descriptive folders supplemented by newspaper articles, talks before committees, commercial clubs, with superintendents of schools, the mayor, or the health officer or leading physician of the town, and to groups of women interested in educational

Arrival at the Commercial Club was not unnoted by the people of Mount Vernon

matters. The professional side of the matter was by no means neglected.

Where anti-tuberculosis leagues existed, its offices assumed charge of all arrangements, and saw the clinic through its one-day visit. Where there was no league, the names of people who had assisted in seal sales, and done war work were furnished, and Miss Harding usually asked that a representative group be called together, who were then formed into a committee on arrangements.

In the schedule of work was first the determination of those places in which such a clinic was most needed, and next the finding of a place suitable for it and the accompanying exhibitions. The program was roughly divided into four parts, the clinic, the exhibit, the infant welfare demonstration, and the evening meeting. The attendance was remarkable. Children who came to see the pictures went home to get their brothers and sisters. Whole school classes were sent by their teachers. Women who came to the infant welfare meetings stayed to ask questions. The evening lectures were well attended and by a very general company from young couples to returned soldiers and old people. Everywhere the clinic found itself welcome, in the larger places the chambers of commerce were especially helpful, while in smaller places oftentimes some business enterprise, a mining or a lumber company, furnished the hall and did whatever was possible towards being helpful.

The personnel of the party accompanying the exhibit included Dr. Raymond J. Cary, Miss Edith E. Farrar, R. N., and Miss Hilba J. Solibakke, who were aided by the officers of the Association. The larger one of the illustrations shows the exhibit as set up in the hall of the Commercial Club, Mount Vernon, with Miss Solibakke speaking, while the smaller one gives evidence of the interest that its arrival excited before the door of the club house.

Miss Farrar is in the doorway, with Dr. Cary close at hand. The ladies with Miss Solibakke at the curb are Miss Payne and Miss Byrnes of the local force.

The statistics compiled by Dr. Cary testify to the seriousness of the work. Sputum tests were made at the laboratory of the state board of health, and every effort made to check the diagnosis in order that the work might stand the most crucial test. No X-Ray work was attempted, but in each case where indicated the patient was advised as to what was best to be done in his case. Out of 39 counties in the state, 24 were visited, so that a territory was invaded as large as Ohio and Indiana, the exact population of the towns visited being 322,858. 580 examinations were made, classed as "Under 15," "15 to 20," "20 to 30," "30 to 40," and "Over 40." It was found that of the 230 men and 350 women examined, 410 came to the clinic by reason of publicity; 110 referred by nurses, and 60 by local physicians. The result shows 356 non-positive cases, 78 positives, 88 arrested, 47 suspects, 37 of the total showing a positive family history.

EXHIBIT SET UP IN THE COMMERCIAL CLUB AT MOUNT VERNON, WASH.

The educational statistics show there were given 63 Tuberculosis lectures, attended by 6,659 people; 58 infant welfare lectures, attended by 1,746; 15 child hygiene lectures, attended by 1,774; 6 miscellaneous lectures (oral hygiene and others), attended by 352; that the moving pictures were shown 49 times with an attendance of 6,493; and that the number of people attending exhibits and demonstrations was 10,051.

✦

Chicago Ambulatory Motor T B Clinic.— Some of the details of the Ambulatory Motor Clinic of the Chicago Tuberculosis Institute have already been presented in the JOURNAL (Nov., 1919, page 892). The opportunity is now afforded to give a view of the interior of the "main room" of the motor truck. This has the usual dispensary equipment in steel furniture enamelled in

white, the various items being clamped to the floor. There is a wash stand with running water, a table for the doctor's use, and a desk for the nurse's records. A chair for the patient and lockers furnish the seats, the lockers being used for storage of the outfit. The back of the auto has two doors, which give free passage, and they open upon a tail-board piazza from which steps descend to the ground. The front is partitioned off from the main room by curtains and can be used for dressing room, while the seat of the chauffeur can be converted into a bed. Ventilation is secured by means of hinged sashes at the tops of the sides.

✦

Connecticut Tuberculosis Commission.— The system established in the state of Connecticut for fighting tuberculosis has the reputation of being one of the most effective in the country, and has certain points of

advantage over those which consist of volunteer organization and association. At its head is a State Tuberculosis Commission, organized a decade ago, which acts in coöperation with all state, municipal and community health units. The following facts with reference to the work of this Commission have been kindly furnished to the JOURNAL by Hubert M. Sedgwick, Field Secretary of the Commission.

The Commission, long firmly committed to the policy of preventing, as well as curing tuberculosis, is energetically developing a plan for discovery of early cases, their prompt treatment, and the examination of suspected and contact cases.

With an estimated number of 15,000 cases in the State, only about 700 are housed for special treatment in the six sanatoria for lung tuberculosis at Hartford, Meriden, Norwich, Snelton, Wallingford and Wildwood, respectively, and 60 in the new bone tuberculosis sanatorium which has just been opened at East Lyme.

With only one out of 20 of the tuberculous patients in the state receiving sanatorium treatment, the problem of handling the remaining cases calls for an educational and preventive program that is extremely efficient and energetic.

Beginning with prudent and progressive sanatorium administration, the Commission has expanded its activity along several interesting and important lines. It has installed bacteriological research in every state sanatorium and conducted experiments, particularly in heliotherapy, and varying power and appearance of the causative agent of the disease.

It has loaned its staff of tuberculosis experts in the several sanatoria for holding clinics and giving lectures in the congested cities, the factory centers, and to medical societies and health organizations. It has assisted in the formation of tuberculosis units throughout the state. By itself and through its local agents it raised a Christmas Seal fund of $75,000 for preventive and educational work in Connecticut during 1920.

The clinics held by its sanatoria superintendents and their assistants have included:

1. The largest cities of the state.

2. Factories in which progressive Connecticut manufacturers have established

dispensaries, in connection with factory nursing. .

3. Temporary clinics in the larger towns of the state.

This extension of the preventive program is responsible for the discovery of hundreds of early cases, and the work is regarded as one of the most valuable contributions ever made to Connecticut anti-tuberculosis warfare.

In this connection, an educational program has been undertaken which comprises placing effective anti-tuberculosis literature in the large factories of the state, especially those which maintain nurses.

A group of 55 local units or agents of the State Commission has been organized to coöperate with it in carrying out its community plans. These include tuberculosis societies, visiting nurse associations, Red Cross local chapters, and miscellaneous health organizations, such as mothers' clubs, sunshine societies, D. A. R. chapters, and other similar societies which represent the health work of the locality. Into their local programs has been breathed the spirit of active, progressive prosecution of the State Commission plans for searching for the early cases and for the protection of the contacts.

A new sanatorium, "The Seaside," for the treatment of tuberculosis of the bones, has been established at East Lyme, a shore village on Long Island Sound not far from New London. A former hotel has been purchased by the state, remodeled and equipped and has a capacity of 58 patients.

✦

Prevent the Migration of Tuberculates Without Funds.—In an effort to save to many unfortunate persons each year the discomfort and hardship which must accompany their migration to another state, the Denver Anti-Tuberculosis Society plainly sets forth the conditions in the state of Colorado as a warning. The same general condition is true of other places which have for one reason or another chosen to advertise the health-giving qualities of their several climates.

It is estimated that several hundred tuberculous persons without funds come to Denver every year. Practically all of them come because they have the mistaken idea that climate will cure tuberculosis.

They arrive, almost penniless, without having made any inquiries, or any provisions for their needs. Since Colorado has no state, and Denver no municipal tuberculosis sanatorium (merely a ward at the County Hospital for thirty-five very sick tuberculous residents), the care of such indigent persons is limited to a few free private sanatoria, which are continuously so overtaxed that admittance is a long and difficult matter. These sanatoria comprise: the two Jewish, which accept only a small number of Gentiles; a tent colony of men with a capacity for seventy "down-and-outers"; and a small home for a dozen destitute tuberculous women.

These tuberculous poor who migrate to Denver, finding no place where they can be cared for, look for light work in order to maintain themselves and often their dependent families; but the demand for such work is far in excess of the supply. Driven to any work they can get, with neither friends nor care, anxious, homesick, hopeless, they rapidly grow worse, and usually soon die. They die for lack of proper rest, food, fresh air, and medical attention, those essentials of treatment, which many of them could have had at home—or here with sufficient funds for two years' care. Without these essentials climate is of no avail. If it were. Denver would welcome these tragic health-seekers instead of urging them, for their own best chances, to stay at home.

Denver also urges that the states throughout the country plan definite programs to retain their indigent tuberculous, giving them effective treatment in state sanatoria or in their own homes.

✦

The Weaker Sex

The weaker sex
Is that portion
Of the human race
Who goes downtown
In zero weather
In a half-masted lace waist
And pumps
To buy a muffler
And woolen socks
For her husband
So he can go to work.

PUBLIC HEALTH NOTES

Primary Causes and Hygienic Treatment of Constipation.—Constipation is very prevalent and is frequently the cause of malaise and general ill health. In a constipated individual, the waste products of the body have not been properly eliminated. This leads often to autointoxication with the poisonous materials resulting from the decomposition of the excreta in the body. The causes of constipation are carelessness, ignorance and laziness combined. Every individual should make an effort to eliminate, immediately after rising in the morning. Constipation is preventable, and can be prevented by forming the habit of daily elimination, by drinking plenty of water, and by including sufficient roughage in the diet. Children should be taught the importance of having regular and daily eliminations. Cathartics will not cure constipation, but are more likely to aggravate the condition. They should, therefore, not be employed. A plain water enema is the least harmful of anything, and should be employed where bowel movements are not regular.—Dwight H. Murray, M. D.—*N. Y. Med. Jour.*, Nov. 8, 1919. (*M. P. H.*)

✢

Treatment and Disposal of Sewage.—Attention is called to an article in *Public Health Reports* for January 16, 1920, which describes briefly and satisfactorily the methods, processes and structures used in the treatment and disposal of sewage in the United States. At the end of the discussion of each method, an excellent and up to date bibliography is given. The article discusses the following methods of sewage treatment: dilution, grit chambers, screening, plain sedimentation, chemical precipitation, septic tanks, Travis tanks, Imhoff tanks, sludge disposal by dumping at sea by air drying in open beds, and by pressing, contact filters, trickling filters, intermittent sand filters, disinfection, broad irrigation, activated sludge, Miles' acid process and the electrolytic process.—(*M. P. H.*)

✢

Venereal Disease Clinics in Massachusetts.—On February 1, 1918, Massachusetts required that all cases of venereal disease be reported. From February 1, 1918, to August 1, 1919, 19,218 cases of venereal disease were reported, of which 13,444 were cases of gon-orrhea, and 5,774 were cases of syphilis. These cases were reported by only one-quarter of the physicians in the state, so that it is believed there are many more cases of venereal disease which have not yet been reported. In order to treat venereal diseases, 16 state approved clinics have been established in various parts of the state. The purpose of these clinics is to furnish special treatment for patients suffering from venereal disease, to provide consultation service for physicians who wish assistance, to distribute arsphenamine free to physicians who know how to administer the drug, and providing no charge is made for its use. The question of need for arsphenamine is determined as far as possible by confirmatory Wassermann tests. An attempt is also made to follow up cases of venereal disease, and to keep track of each case until it is terminated.—*Boston Med. and Surg. Jour.*, Jan. 1, 1920. (*M. P. H.*)

✢

Meningococcus Carriers.—According to the authors the sites of carrying in the chronic meningococcus carrier are Luschka's tonsil, the fossa of Rosenmüller, the retronasopharyngeal wall, and the faucial tonsils. The anterior and upper parts of the nose and the nasal sinuses are not, as a rule, infected. The presence of lymphoid hypertrophy and nasal obstruction, although it may favor the production of a "chronic carrier," is not necessarily the cause. Meningococcus carriers are divided into two groups: (1) Acute or temporary carriers, those carrying under eight weeks; (2) chronic carriers, those carrying over eight weeks. Acute or temporary carriers remain infectious on an average for 24 days; the maximum discharge rate occurs during the third week. Chronic carriers remain infectious on an average for 5½ months. Eighty per cent of carriers are acute or temporary, 20 per cent chronic. Treatment of the carrier appears to prolong the carrying period. The meningococcus remains in the "carrying site" until ousted by some other bacterium. The best method of freeing a meningococcus carrier from infection is Nature, open air and exercise.—D. Embleton, W. S. Bryant and G. H. Stevens. Lancet, Oct. 18, 1919, 679, Abstr. Jour. A. M. A., Nov. 22, 1919, 1642. (*D. G.*)

Comparison of Antigens in T. B. Fixation.—The serums of 97 clinically normal individuals, 37 questionably tuberculous, and 84 incipient, 75 moderately advanced and 31 far advanced cases of pulmonary tuberculosis, using for comparison the autolysate antigen of Corper, the methyl alcohol soluble antigen of Petroff and the Wilson bacillary antigen gave the following results:

The three antigens did not differ greatly in the percentage positive findings in known cases of pulmonary tuberculosis, Petroff's antigen giving 66 per cent, the autolysate antigen 63 per cent and Wilson's antigen 57 per cent, the last being the least efficient of the three.

The percentage of positive findings obtained in the various classes of cases by the three antigens were 11 per cent of clinically normal individuals, 58 per cent of questionably tuberculous, 56 per cent of incipient, 64 per cent (66 per cent sputum positive cases) of moderately advanced, and 71 per cent of far advanced cases. Moribund cases gave a lower percentage positive, 44 per cent, than any of the other definite cases of tuberculosis, corroborating the findings by previous reliable investigators.

A fairly high percentage of serological positive luetic serums, 50 to 60 per cent, gave cross fixation with the three tuberculosis antigens.—H. C. Young and J. P. Givler, Am. Rev. of Tub., Oct., 1919, 476 (D. G.)

✛

Condition of Patients 20 Years After Discharge from T. B. Sanatorium.—The table below indicates the condition of patients after their discharge from the Trudeau Sanatorium for a period of 20 years or more.

Summary of Traced Patients of 816 Dead

	Incipient		Moderately Advanced		Far Advanced	
	No.	Pct.	No.	Pct.	No.	Pct.
Active	15	71	251	95	154	98
Inactive ..	56	44	163	74	24	86

Died of Tuberculosis. Known Deaths, 174

	Incipient		Moderately Advanced		Far Advanced	
	No.	Pct.	No.	Pct.	No.	Pct.
Active	5	100	61	95	48	98
Inactive ..	4	67	35	81	1	100

Traced Patients, 814

Alive after twenty years....148 = 18.2 per cent
Dead ....666 = 81.8 per cent

(Includes non-tuberculosis and doubtful.) Six incipient active not discharged long enough.)—F. H. Heise, Am. Rev. of Tub., Oct., 1919, 497 (D. G.)

City Plan for Tuberculosis.—Dr. Craster, the Health Officer of Newark, N. J., has laid out a plan for tuberculosis control in a city, the outline of which is indicated below:

A. Control of Infection—
    Reporting by physicians
    Hospital and sanatoriums
    Day camps and tents; field nurses
    Laboratory; enforcement of anti-spitting laws; milk supervision.

B. Social Progress—
    Publicity
    Social insurance
    Anti-tuberculosis societies program
    Home visiting and relief

C. Economic Improvement—
    Improved housing
    Industrial hygiene
    Open air school
    Vocational training
    Employment bureau

D. Associated Activities—
    Control of epidemics (measles, whooping cough, etc.)
    Convalescent homes
    Child hygiene
    Mental hygiene

—C. V. Craster, Jour. A. M. A., Jan. 31, 1920, 302 (D. G.)

✛

Untilled Fields of Public Health.—In an address before the Section on Physiology and Experimental Medicine, of the American Association for the Advancement of Science, Professor C.-E. A. Winslow, summarized the great accomplishments in public health, and the probable advance to be attempted in the future. Much has been accomplished through the sanitation of the environment. Typhoid fever has been greatly diminished. Cholera is almost non-existent in this country. Malaria, yellow fever, plague, typhus fever and smallpox can be adequately controlled through known methods. The discovery of many of the causative agents of disease, and the development of antitoxic sera and vaccines have materially aided in overcoming disease. Infant mortality has been greatly reduced. There remain alone, such causes of death as heart disease, tuberculosis, pneumonia, Bright's disease, cancer and other diseases which are dependent on the personal conduct of the individual life which have not yet been adequately controlled. The control of these diseases depends primarily on good personal hygiene. Through the greater spread of school medical inspection, school nursing, medical inspection and aid in industry, and the elevation of the standards of living for thousands of families, much has already been done to combat disease. The organization for adequate public health protection has, however, not yet been realized. The time is coming when the protection of the public health will be as amply supported as public education, and when health centers will be as numerous and as adequately equipped and supported as school houses are in our communities today. In order to meet this growing demand for properly qualified health workers, all persons intending to pursue public health lines should be adequately trained. —*Science,* Jan. 9, 1920. (*M. P. H.*)

+

What We Have Learned in Dietetics From the Army.—At the beginning of the recent war, General Gorgas organized a Division of Food and Nutrition, whose function it was, to make frequent inspections of food conditions in the camps and in the field, to improve the cooking and serving of the food, and to study constantly the suitability of the ration. As a result, the average requirement of food for the soldier in training is known for the first time. The following facts are also known; the amount of food the soldier eats outside of the mess; the average composition of the food eaten in the mess; the variation of food consumption in different seasons of the year; the variations in food consumption in different companies of the same regiment, owing to various psychological factors; and the average consumption by different classes of patients in the army hospitals. Through this thorough study it has been possible to work out an average ration. It was found, however, that where the soldier had a free choice of foods, he ate less meat, bread and potatoes than are prescribed in the ration, and more beans, fruit, milk, butter, coffee and sugar.—John R. Murlin, Ph.D., *Mod. Hospital,* Jan., 1920,(*M. P. H.*)

+

Teaching Health in the Schools.—The period of childhood is undoubtedly the best period in life in which to teach the principles of healthy living. It is necessary, however, to arouse the interest of children in healthy living in order to enable them to form good habits relating to health. Since children like to wear badges and belong to clubs, it has

been possible to arouse their interest in good health through the organization of health leagues, and the Modern Health Crusade movement. Group competition based upon weight and height, should be employed to stimulate interest. Health pictures and posters should be employed. Mothers should be kept regularly informed regarding the health progress of their children. The teaching of health should be a part of the regular cirriculum and should not be confused with physiology or physical training. Medical inspection and school nursing should be extensively introduced. The medical examination should be thorough and regular, and should determine the facts regarding the nutrition of the children, as well as the ordinary physical defects. The child should receive a thorough medical examination at least once a year.—L. Emmett Holt, M.D. *American City,* Dec., 1919. (*M. P. H.*)

+

Chlorination of Water Supplies.—The sanitary engineers of this country are responsible for the introduction of chlorine disinfection of water supplies. The first experiments were conducted with calcium hypochlorite by George A. Johnson at the Union Stock Yards in Chicago. This was then followed by the treatment of the Jersey City water supply at Boonton, N. J. The use of calcium hypochlorite was so popular that in 1911, 500 plants were in operation in the United States. Owing to the difficulty of preparing uniform disinfecting solutions from the calcium hypochlorite, and because the chemical deteriorated on standing, liquid chlorine was introduced to replace it. The amount of chlorine added can be determined more accurately with liquid chlorine than with calcium hypochlorite. In 1918 approximately 2,500 water purification plants in the United States were using liquid chlorine. It is used very often as an adjunct to filtration, and is exceedingly valuable in cases of sudden infection. The cost of using liquid chlorine is about 40 cents per million gallons of water treated. For a municipality of 5,000, the cost of such treatment per year, including depreciation would be only $150. There is no doubt that chlorination of water supplies has reduced the typhoid fever death rate remarkably, and that if smaller communities adopted chlorination on a larger scale, the typhoid fever death rate would be diminished still further.—*Editorial, Journal A. M. A.,* Dec. 27, 1919. (*M. P. H.*)

New Regulations Regarding Quarantine Periods.—The New York City Health Department has altered some of its quarantine regulations to read as follows: The minimum period of quarantine for (a) diphtheria shall be 12 days from onset, during which time no cultures will be examined; after which, until two consecutive cultures, taken not less than 24 hours apart, and preferably from both nose and throat, fail to show the presence of diphtheria bacilli.

(b) For Scarlet Fever: 30 days after the onset of the first symptoms, provided discharges from nose and ears have ceased.

(c) For Cerebro-spinal meningitis: 14 days from the onset.

(d) For Acute Anterior Poliomyelitis: 3 weeks from the date of onset.

(e) For Typhoid Fever: Until 10 days after the patient's temperature reaches normal, and thereafter, until two specimens of feces, collected at least 24 hours apart, are found to be free from the presence of typhoid bacilli. —*Weekly Bulletin, N. Y. C. Dept., Health,* Jan. 24, 1920. (*M. P. H.*)

✛

Excellent Anti-Tuberculosis Work in Rensselaer County, N. Y.—The Rensselaer County Tuberculosis Association was organized in March, 1919, with Joseph Herzstein, of Troy, N. Y., as Executive Secretary. The first annual meeting of the Association was held January 28, 1920, at which time the work of the preceding ten months was reviewed. Besides effecting a reorganization, Mr. Herzstein has built up a technical staff consisting of a medical director and two public health nurses. A tuberculosis dispensary was established, at which clinics were held three times a week. Altogether 595 free medical examinations were given, and 95 persons were found to be tuberculous. Sanatorium treatment was procured for 68 cases. The nurses made over 2,200 visits to the homes of patients suffering from tuberculosis. The active tuberculosis campaign created such a good impression that a special appropriation was made in the 1920 budget for Troy, for the employment of a tuberculosis nurse among the personnel of the health department. An active health education compaign was conducted by the executive secretary in the school, the factories and

through the public press. Besides distributing literature on health, 39 lectures were given, most of them illustrated with lantern slides. Motion pictures and exhibits were also employed.—*Troy Record,* Jan. 29, 1920. (*M. P. H.*)

✛

Scarlet Fever in Massachusetts.—Scarlet fever in Massachusetts is increasing daily, and likewise the deaths from scarlet fever are also increasing. There had been a continued decrease of the disease from 1915 to 1919. As a result, there are a large number of children in the state who have not had the disease, and who are not immune. It is, therefore, expected that the disease will be unusually prevalent this year.

The control of scarlet fever depends on the detection of all cases, especially the mild ones, during the acute stage of the disease. All cases should be quarantined for 28 days after the onset of the disease and until infective discharges from the nose and throat, ear and abscesses, have ceased. All contacts should be excluded from school for 8 days, unless they are immune, through having had the disease previously. The children in the school where a case of scarlet fever has occurred, should be examined by the school physician or the public health nurse. Children having sore throats, discharges from nose or ears, or suppurating glands or abscesses, should be excluded. The school nurse should follow up every case, every day, and should investigate all cases of absence, in order to detect all mild cases. No person who is ill with scarlet fever, or who has been exposed should be permitted to handle milk or other food supplies, until the maximum incubation period has elapsed or until release has been obtained from the board of health. It is interesting to note that milk is becoming an infrequent factor in spreading scarlet fever in Massachusetts. From 1909-1914, 845 cases of scarlet fever were traced to milk, while from 1915 to 1918, only 140 cases are known to have originated from infected milk. Besides conducting an epidemiological investigation of every case of scarlet fever that is reported, all persons who have been exposed, and whose daily work brings them into contact with children, should not return to work without permission from the local board of health.— Stanley H. Osborn, M.D., *Commonhealth,* September-October, 1919. (*M. P. H.*)

Hospital and Health Survey in Cleveland.
—An extensive hospital and health survey is to be made by the city of Cleveland, Ohio, under the direction of Dr. Haven Emerson. Mr. Malcolm McBride is chairman of the committee in charge of the work, and Mr. Howell Wright is secretary. The survey is to consist of two parts. One will be a survey and study of the existing hospital and health facilities, both public and private, and the other will be a study of the community. The former will consider the following points:

1. Existing facilities for medical education.

2. A study of the present nursing educational system including the training schools and facilities for special education and training.

3. The relationship of the Department of Public Health to the hospitals, dispensaries, medical institutions, medical profession, and the care of cases of communicable disease.

4. A study of the existing hospital facilities in order to determine the number of pay or private room patients, part-pay and ward patients and free patients. An attempt will also be made to determine what the normal needs of the community should be for each of these groups of patients.

5. A study of the available facilities for the care of the following cases; contagious, including venereal, acute surgical, acute medical, chronic surgical and orthopœdic, chronic medical, convalescent, insane and mental diseases, aged and infirm, maternity babies and children, accident and emergency.

6. A study of dispensaries with special reference to their location, availability, the type of cases treated, and the efficiency of each.

Under the section of the survey dealing with the community, there is to be a detailed study of the vital statistics, including morbidity, accident and mortality rates, race distribution, age distribution, occupations, and perhaps, also, a sickness survey. The care secured by the sick will also be studied. Under this head, such factors as financial status of the sick, home conditions, knowledge of existing relief and welfare agencies, will be considered. The capacity and facilities of existing agencies to give relief will also be studied. An attempt will be made to estimate the reduction in sickness that would occur, through the extension of preventive medicine and health insurance. Finally, the relationship of the medical and nurses' training schools to present and future hospitals, to dispensaries, to sickness prevention and to the health department will also be considered.—*Modern Hospital*, December, 1919. (*M. P. H.*)

✠

Supervision of the Pasteurized Milk Supply in New York State.—It is interesting to note that during the past year and a half, the supervision of the pasteurizing plants has been under the direction of the Engineering Division of the New York State Health Department. Theodore Horton, the chief engineer, compares a pasteurizing plant to a water purification plant and brings out many similarities. There are about 600 milk pasteurizing plants in New York State, 350 of which operate almost exclusively for New York City, and the other 250 for the municipalities up-state. The latter plants have been inspected from 2 to 7 times during the past year and more. Conditions at these plants were found to be deplorable. On the average each plant was urged to make 15 to 18 improvements. By repeated inspections and cooperation on the part of the owner, about 40 per cent of the original recommendations have been carried out. Each plant is required to conform to certain rules and regulations. After each inspection, a report is left with the owner, the health officer and the sanitary supervisor. Pasteurization is accomplished by the holding method, and each plant is urged to install a self-recording time thermometer.—*New York State Health News*, November, 1919. (*M. P. H.*)

✠

Nursing Situation from the Public Health Point of View.—Recently a committee was appointed with Professor C.-E. A. Winslow, as chairman, to study the public health nursing situation in this country. At the present time there are 15 educational institutions which train students in the theory and practice of public health nursing. The demand for public health nurses has been so great that it has been impossible to meet it. What the investigation hopes to bring out in a clear and definite way, are the functions of the public health nurse, the existing facilities for training public health nurses, and the various fields which are open to public health nurses. According to Miss Anne H. Strong, the present training of most public health nurses is inadequate and inefficient. She also believes that bedside nursing should play an important part in this training, and that each public health nurse should have adequate experience, not only in the usual medical, surgical, obstetrical and pediatric services, but also in eye, ear, nose and throat work, in mental and nervous diseases, and in communicable diseases, including tuberculosis, syphilis and gonorrhea. She should also be experienced in the outpatient department as well as the wards. It is also important that the requirements for admission to a school of public health nursing should be higher than they are now.—*Modern Hospital*, December, 1919. (*M. P. H.*)

✢

The Mohawk-Brighton Plan of Health Protection.—The reason why even well organized and efficient health departments do not succeed in materially diminishing the death rate and preventing disease is because our means of approaching and actually bringing to the people our knowledge about disease prevention and healthy living are seriously deficient and unsuccessful. It is because the general interest of the people in good health is not aroused except during periods of epidemics. If it were possible to stimulate the people sufficiently, so that they would be interested in good health and would demand adequate health protection, greater strides in disease prevention would be made. In the Mohawk-Brighton district of Cincinnati, 12,000 people were organized, and educated sufficiently so that they became thoroughly interested in initiating and controlling all activities aiming to better their personal and community health. Besides coping with the problems of fly and mosquito control, garbage collection, housing, sanitary food control in stores and restaurants, general nuisances, and other matters dealing with municipal sanitation, the following modern health systems were introduced:

1. Most of the expectant mothers were reached and given prenatal advice after the third month of pregnancy.

2. There was early and continuous supervision of all babies and adequate care of the mothers immediately after confinement.

3. Medical examination of children in the pre-school age was cared for and the correction of many physical defects.

4. The discovery and control of all active cases of pulmonary tuberculosis was begun.

5. Medical and nursing care of the sick was secured.

6. Unusual care was taken of cases during the influenza epidemic together with the general education of the community.

7. Correction of gross sanitary violations was undertaken, and improvement in the general cleanliness of premises.

8. The attention of parents has been called to the need and desirability of adequate health protection for their children.—Haven Emerson, M.D., *N. Y. Med. Jour.*, December 13, 1919. (*M. P. H.*)

✢

Prevention Versus Education.—In an advertising story H. W. Mowery in *Safeguarding Industry* brings up very vividly the difference between Mr. Dollar Foolish and Mr. Universal Safety, the former of whom has accidents in his plant that cost money, but he considers them covered by insurance. He is ignorant of the causes of accidents and thinks to stop them by posting bulletins instead of removing the causes. He hopes that people will remember only their safety and he permits hazards to remain instead of accepting the principle, that "conditions shall be such that people may pursue safely their normal activities without abnormal care." He talks in high sounding phrases, but neglects safe conditions.

On the other hand, Mr. Universal Safety knows what are the prolific causes of injury and he knows further, that merely educating foremen and workmen is not enough, if the causes remain. This story is woven skilfully about figures that show slipping to be one of the most important causes of accident in industrial establishments.

✢

Makes Swimming Safe.—The leading article in a *Red Cross Bulletin* is the first of three in a series telling of an effort that is to be made to prevent a portion at least of the enormous toll from drowning. There are about 8,000 deaths a year in the country from this cause and the A. R. C. avows its intention of taking the fear out of swimming and making the waters of our shores a safer playground for the young people. The work was taken up by the Red Cross in 1914 and the result has been an organization with life saving corps at different stations along the coast. There are three sections now in operation, for boys, women and for men, the latter of which has now 500,000 members. The slogan of the corps is: "Everybody a swimmer and every swimmer a life saver."

Fourteen Points About Cancer.—The American Society for the Control of Cancer sets forth the truth of the matter ingeniously in 14 points.

1. During the Great War the United States lost about 80,000 soldiers. During the same two years 180,000 people died of cancer in this country, Cancer is now killing *one out of every ten persons over forty years of age.*

2. Many of these deaths are preventable, since cancer is frequently curable, if recognized and properly treated in its early stages.

3. Cancer begins as a small local growth which can often be entirely removed by competent surgical treatment, or, in certain external forms, by using radium, X-ray or other methods.

4. Cancer is not a constitutional or "blood" disease; there should be no thought of disgrace or of "hereditary taint" about it.

5. *Cancer is not a communicable disease.* It is not possible to "catch" cancer from one who has it.

6. *Cancer is not inherited.* It is not certain even that a tendency to the disease is inherited.

7. The beginning of cancer is usually painless; for this reason its insidious onset is frequently overlooked, and is too easily neglected. *Other danger signals must be recognized, and competent medical advice obtained at once.*

8. Every persisting *lump in the breast* is a warning sign. All such lumps are by no means cancer, but even innocent tumors of the breast may turn into cancer if neglected.

9. In women, *continued unusual discharge or bleeding* requires the immediate advice of a competent doctor.

10. *Any sore that does not heal,* particularly about the mouth or tongue, is a danger signal.

11. *Persistent indigestion* in middle life, with loss of weight and change of color, or with pain, vomiting, or diarrhea, call for thorough and competent medical advice as to the possibility of internal cancer.

12. *Radium* is a useful and promising means of treatment for some kinds of cancer. No medicine will cure cancer.

13. *Open warfare by open discussion* will mean the prevention of many needless deaths from cancer.

14. *The American Society for the Control of Cancer* is always "on the job" with information and suggestions.

Does It Pay to Employ an Industrial Nurse?—Yes. Because:

1. She gives first aid in case of injury, thereby preventing infection and shortening the period of disability.

2. She cares for minor ailments, thereby enabling the employees to contine work.

3. She is on the alert to prevent the introduction and spread of contagious diseases through the plant.

4. She prevents illness by giving instruction in ways of keeping well.

5. She advises regarding the correction of physical defects.

6. She teaches the common rules of hygiene and sanitation and advocates suitable precautions in the dangerous trades and operations.

7. She visits and arranges for the care of those absent because of illness, thereby making possible an earlier return to work. She helps and advises in case of family illness or trouble, thereby relieving the mind of the worried employee and enabling him to give his undivided attention to his work.

8. She is at all times the friend and coworker of the comployees and interprets to them the plans of the employer for industrial betterment.—*Circular of National Org. for Public Health Nursing.*

✚

Health and the Industries.—It is now becoming recognized by employers of industrial labor who have given careful consideration to the subject, and also by industrial physicians and surgeons that, the work-producing capacity of a person depends more largely upon their physical and mental condition than almost any other factor. Broadly speaking, the hazards which confront industrial workers in a great many different lines of industry are of two kinds; hazards which cause accidents resulting in injury, and dangers which threaten the health of persons exposed to them.

The first or mechanical hazards are problems for the safety engineers, but the dangers which impair the health and cause sickness and death from various diseases are problems for the industrial physician, and if we are to secure and maintain high efficiency in a working force, both of these fundamental problems must receive the necessary and proper attention.—*Safeguarding Industry.*

The Social Unit in Cincinnati.—The committee appointed by the National Social Unit Organization to appraise the social work aspects of its activities during the past three years in the Brighton-Mohawk District of Cincinnati arranged with Dr. Edward T. Devine to study and report on the work for the committee. The following is Dr. Devine's conclusion as to the results: "Summing up the evidence in regard to results achieved, I am of the opinion that definite tangible and substantial results have been obtained; that they can be measured in the testimony of coöperating agencies and in the information applied by the executives and workers in the social unit and by the families in the district; but that they are not capable of a quantitive statement in statistical form. I have no doubt, from my observations and from the interviews which I have had with workers, residents, outside friends, and critics, that the social unit has added substantially to the physical and moral well-being of the residents of the district; that it has led to more efficient and discriminating relief, to more thorough and constructive diagnosis of the needs of families in trouble; that it has prompted neighborliness and sociability; that it has made the ordinary family residing in the district more hospitable to visitors who come with a helpful purpose, and more discriminating as to the probable effect of sanitary and social measures brought forward for their benefit." It is interesting to note the enthusiastic evidence of the residents of the district, who, in the face of newspaper criticism by the mayor of the city, recorded their desire by a vote of 4,434 against 120 that the social unit shall continue its work. —E. T. Devine, *Survey*, Nov. 15, 1919 (D. G.)

✠

Needs in Fighting Tuberculosis.—The tuberculosis worker who confines his interest and attention to the tubercle bacillus, its habitats and its habits, and particular measures directed against it and its effects and whose eyes are closed to all the non-specific factors, the inefficient teeth and the throats of children, the faulty habits and environment of the human being, the excesses of ordinary existence, whether they be excesses of labor, of play or of the passions, is not serving his cause well. He has failed to grasp the location and nature of the enemy's stronghold.

We shall get the grip on tuberculosis when

we create a universal and correct public sentiment concerning it; then, and no sooner. To exhibit pictures of bacteria and cross-sections of the human torso and columns of figures to the dweller of the tenement whose belly cries for food and whose eyes are heavy with smoke and dirt, is brainless business, busy though we may seem to be. To show this man how his surroundings may approximate yours and to prove to him that you are working with him to make them so is making progress.

Our organizations must be enlarged ten and a hundred fold, and in every hamlet the preacher of public health must be as familiar and active a figure as the school teacher. We must enlist every newspaper syndicate in our cause and have them day in and day out lay the facts of the disease and its prevention before their readers.

I would repeat that tuberculosis, when associated with the matter of a programme against it, cannot be considered apart from the society in which it exists. And its real conquest must originate in the demands of the whole people that it be done away with; and these demands will never be made until everyone appreciates the situation.—A. K. Krause, Amer. Rev. of Tuberculosis, Nov., 1919. (D. G.)

✠

Reduction of Resistance to Tuberculosis. —The objects of the experiments reported by the author were to note the effect of trauma and of various mechanical and chemical irritants when applied locally upon the spread of tuberculosis in guinea pigs.

Using the microscopic anatomic tuberculosis as an index of the acceleration of tuberculosis in the guinea pig it was found that regional gland crushing, and the subcutaneous injection of turpentine, croton oil, tincture of cantharidin, and tincture of capsicum, used as local irritants just prior to the subcutaneous injection of virulent human tubercle bacilli in various sized doses, had no appreciable influence upon the progress of the infection as compared with that obtained in control guiena pigs. Lamp black injected subcutaneously co-incident with the tubercle bacilli had a distinctly retarding influence, while finely pulverized glass had a markedly accelerating influence, though not sufficient to be available for practical use in accelerating the guinea pig diagnosis for the presence of tubercle bacilli in pathological fluids.—H. J. Corper, Am. Rev. of Tuberculosis, Dec., 1919, 605. (D. G.)

Child Welfare.—The following is an abstract of the report of the Child Welfare Section of Red Cross Societies at the International Conference held at Cannes, April 1, 1919.

The work relating to child welfare may be divided into six parts, corresponding to the period of child life to which it is directed:

First. Eugenic consideration affecting the prospective parents.

Second. The prenatal period in which the child is saved through care for the mother. The essential feature in prenatal care must be the supervision and education of the expectant mother by trained public health nurse, midwife or health visitor, from an early period of her pregnancy, aided when possible by the advice and assistance of a physician. The work is greatly facilitated by voluntary registration of pregnant women, which should be encouraged everywhere, and it should be connected closely with maternity and child welfare centers.

Third. Obstetrical care, which should include the services of a nurse as well as those of a physician or midwife.

Fourth. Birth to school age. This period is sometimes divided into infancy—including the first year or possibly two years—and a pre-school age, extending from this time up to the fifth or sometimes the sixth year. The important concern during the first two years is the child's nutrition; and the essential thing is that the child be kept under continuous observation and supervision.

The principal methods are: (1) Group instructions and individual advice from some such central place as a "milk station," a child welfare station, a "consultation," etc., and (2) home visiting by public health nurses.

The problem of infancy up to the school period is much the same and can be carried on with the same organization—quarterly visits to the home or by the child to the central stations and a full medical examination once a year should be the minimum.

Permanent institutional care for infants and young children should be discouraged on account of the almost insuperable difficulties in maintaining nutrition in infancy under these conditions, and because of the great susceptibility of young children to infection, preference should be given to placing such children in suitable families.

Fifth. In the school period. From the sixth to the fourteenth or sixteenth year, the problem is to secure normal growth and physical and moral development, to recognize and correct defects which interefere with these, and to reduce to the minimum the risks of contagious disease. The school physician, the school nurse and the school teacher all have important functions. The school, furthermore, offers an opportunity, the value of which is only beginning to be appreciated, to interest, instruct and train the child himself in health matters. Health work for the school children is inextricably bound up with the problems of general education, and all teachers should receive training which would qualify them to teach the simple facts of health and personal hygiene.

Progress in the pupil's health is best shown by the weight chart; thus an incentive can be furnished for the observance of health rules which are taught. Health records, at least a record of weight and growth, should be kept during school life. In an ideal scheme, a medical examination should be made once a year of every school child, and those who are found to be physically below normal or who do not make a normal gain in weight should receive special attention and supervision during their school life.

Sixth. Industrial period from the fourteenth to the eighteenth year. In connection with legislation relating to child labor, the following fundamental principles should be embodied:

(a) No child should be allowed to enter industry without first passing a physical examination by a competent physician, showing that he is able to perform the work intended, and (b) no child should be permitted to continue in any form of work which prevents his normal growth and physical development as determined by accepted standards, and periodic examinations made up to the age of eighteen years.—*Amer. Jour. Dis. of Children,* Oct. 1919, 306. (D. G.)

Mental Defects in a Southern State.— The Georgia Commission on Feeblemindedness in coöperation with the National Committee for Mental Hygiene has made a survey of mental deficiency in this state which is summarized below:

Feeblemindedness was disclosed in 40 per cent of the inmates of almshouses; in 28.7 per cent of children in an orphange; in 17.5 per cent of the male inmates and 43 per cent of the female inmates of the State prison farm; in 34 per cent of the inmates of two typical county jails; in 44 per cent of 122 immoral women examined; in 17 per cent of delinquents studied in the juvenile court; in 15 per cent of those in a reformatory, and in 27 per cent of the inmates of the State Training School for Girls. It is these feebleminded delinquent children that later on become the chronic recidivists, as is seen in our jails, adult criminal courts, and state prisons. Finally, 3.5 per cent of the children examined in the public schools were found to be feebleminded. These are the children who are to become the "grist" of our future courts, jails, reformatories, and state prisons, and to form the very backbone of the vast and grim procession of paupers, criminals, and prostitutes of tomorrow.

The recommendations made include (1) a training school and farm colony for feebleminded persons, (2) special classes in the public schools, (3) mental clinics, (4) state-wide supervision and (5) laws for the commitment of the feebleminded.—V. V. Anderson, *Mental Hygiene*, October, 1919, 527. (*D. G.*)

✛

Intestinal Flora and Nutritional Disorders in Children.— As a result of a clinical study the authors show: (1) that children, whose diet is well balanced and whose nutrition is normal, have an intestinal flora consisting of fermentative and putrefactive types without preponderance of either; (2) that children fed on large quantities of cow's milk have a more complex flora made up of various types, most of which are facultative putrefactors; (3) that in children who suffer from certain of the types of alimentary intoxication with malnutrition, the intestinal flora departs in a uniform manner from the normal, and that this departure is always characterized by the establishment of bacterial types predominantly putrefactive; (4) that the return of these children to normal health is coincident with a regression of the intestinal flora generally toward fermentative types and a later swing to balance between the two types; (5) that such changes in the intestinal flora can be brought about in the intestine of the human infant by withdrawing animal protein and persistently feeding large amounts of lactose (from 2 to 4 ounces daily), and other carbohydrates; that the period which may be necessary to produce this variation is from ten to forty days. While feeding acidophilus cultures has in a few cases aided a more rapid establishment of aciduric flora in the baby's intestine, this influence was not very great; (6) that the progressive cessation of symptoms of intoxication and a return of toxemic patients to nutritional health coincides with the recognizable dominance of a fermentative flora (7) that lactose and dextrines are the carbohydrates most effective in encouraging the rapid establishment of a fermentative flora in the intestines of infants and children.—Porter, L., Morris, G. B., and Meyer, K. F., *Amer. Jour. Dis. of Children*, Oct. 1919, 254. (*D. G.*)

✛

Diet and Intestinal Bacteria.— Through the leadership of Metchnikoff and his followers it was believed that the bacterial flora of the intestinal tract could be controlled by consuming bacterial cultures of specific organisms. This theory is being replaced by another which is much more tenable, namely: that the diet determines the bacterial flora in the intestine. The incorporation in the regular diet of an individual of 8 to 10 ounces of lactose per day changed the normal flora of bacteria in the excreta, so that *B. acidophilus* predominated.—Jour. A. M. A., December 13, 1919. (*M. P. H.*)

☐

Your State Campaign Manager Will Need Your Help in the Membership Campaign. Respond With Your New Member When He Calls.

STATE HEALTH—LEGISLATION

National.—S. 3829, introduced by Mr. Phipps early in February, purposes making an appropriation for the investigation of subterranean waters, especially the shallow underground waters and artesian wells of eastern Colorado.

✢

Colorado.—The State Board of Health, Division of Venereal Disease, has issued in pamphlet form the regulations of the Division. These include the declaration of these diseases to be dangerous to the public health, the requirement of reporting, which is to be by number, the duties of physicians in keeping records, the duties of patients in reporting change of physicians and the various duties of different individuals, health officers, druggists, etc., in reporting. Dentists are included in the list of those who must report if they have reason to suspect infection. Remedies are to be sold only on prescription. Inmates of jails and institutions shall be examined. There are certain forbidden occupations, including food handling, laundry work, use of public swimming pools or tanks, and teaching, the prohibition last named including every kind of school or college. The regulations concern themselves next with clinics, in which the details of administration and technique are given and there follow sections with reference to unusual prevalence, placarding, permits necessary for change of residence, repression of prostitution and a punishment for giving false information.

✢

Maine.—The new health laws require the employment by every community, either alone or in conjunction with some other community, of a local health officer, one-third of whose salary up to $800 may be paid by the state. Full time health officers, for groups of towns if necessary, are recommended by Dr. Leverett D. Bristol, commissioner.

An important decision has been rendered by the courts of Maine in the case, Ralph O. Stockman et al. vs. Philip F. Chapman et al. and Board of Health of the City of Portland, Me. This case involves the validity of the ordinance of the City Board of Health regulating the production and preparation of milk for sale within the city limits. The provision is that the Board shall "guard against all introduction of contagious and infectious diseases by the exercise of proper and vigilant medical inspection and control of all persons and things coming within the jurisdiction from infected places, or which for any cause are liable to communicate contagion." The last general clause invests the Board with very wide powers, namely, power to make provision against anything, which, "for any cause" is liable to communicate contagion. The phrase "liable to communicate contagion" gives full authority to prevent at the source, in the opinion of the sitting Justice, A. M. Spear.

The plaintiffs attacked six paragraphs of the Board of Health ordinance, related to Grade A milk and cream and Grade B milk and cream. Grade A milk is to be from tuberculin tested cows of below 100,000 bacterial count, put into the final container at the place of production; the cream Grade A shall be from Grade A milk with not more than 500,000 bacteria and the pasteurized milk Grade A shall have not more than 10,000 bacteria per cubic centimeter when delivered to the consumer. Grade B Milk shall be from cows passed by a qualified veterinarian with not more than 500,-000 bacteria raw or 50,000 pasteurized when delivered to the consumer. Grade B cream shall never have passed 1,000,000 before pasteurization, and on delivery, not more than 200,000 for bacterial count.

The opinion lays stress on the fact that the regulations are for the purpose of controlling the healthfulness of the milk, and in no way to affect the price. They are necessarily drastic and place the burden of compliance on the party to be restricted or prevented, and these elements of personal or private interest must yield to the public welfare.

Many opinions are quoted in support of the principle upheld by Justice Spear that the State had a clear constitutional right to pass the statutes in question and the right to confer the exercise of its power to the municipal officers. The ordinances are not discriminatory, the conditions required can be complied with by every owner of a herd of cows, "nor" notes the Justice, "can I believe that any fair minded man would object to the employment of methods of cleanliness in the care and milking of his cows that will prevent, as far as possible, the introduction of injurious bacteria from negligent or insanitary conditions."

✢

Massachusetts.—Through the operation of Chapter 350 of the General Acts of 1919, the name, "Department of Public Health" and "Commissioner of Public Health," are established for the department and its chief executive, and certain changes have been made in the way of additions to its divisions. The control of the four state tuberculosis sanatoria together with the other functions of former Board of Trustees of Hospitals for Consumptives has been given to the Department of Public Health, and with this is to be combined the other work in this disease undertaken by the Department. A new Division of Tuberculosis has been created within the Department and Dr. William J. Gallivan has been appointed Director.

There are two bills before the Legislature which have bearing on the health of the community. The first of these is the proposed Health Education law, which provides for a director of health education and physical activities in the State Department of Education, local supervisors to help the director, one or more school nurses in every town and courses in the State normal and public schools in simple health habits.

A second bill has reference to school nurses, and provides that the school committee of .every city and town in the Commonwealth shall appoint one or more school physicians, nurses, etc.

+

Ohio.—Legislative attacks upon Ohio's model health law—the Hughes Health District Act—just before it was to go into full operation· resulted in numerous important amendments to the measure. Chief among the effects of the new legislation are these:

(1) District boards of health may now employ part-time health commissioners if they so desire and are not required to maintain any other employes than the health commissioner.

(2) Civil Service provisions no longer govern appointments, general (county) district boards being without restrictions in this regard other than the requirement that the health commissioner must be a licensed physician and city district boards being without any restrictions.

(3) Performance of most of the duties required of district boards of health under the original law is now left to their option.

(4) All cities (which means all municipalities of more than 5,000 population in 1910) are now separate health districts; under the Hughes Law cities under 25,000 in population were combined with their respective general, or county, districts.

Two considerations influenced the changes

in the health district law—financial stringency in many counties and a supreme court decision which indicated that the original law would be held in part unconstitutional.

Most local political units in Ohio are short of funds, because of the inadequacy of existing tax laws to provide enough money for necessary activities and also, in consequence, because of the growing burden of debt. The shortage of funds for health purposes was in part artificial, caused by the failure of local officials, in formulating their 1920 budgets last summer, to make provision for the change in health organization, despite notices filed with them in ample time by the State Department of Health.

The supreme court decision involved a law making a classification of cities similar to that of the Hughes Act, which latter measure provided different forms of health organization for cities above and below 25,000 in population. The similar classification was held to be in violation of the constitutional classification into cities and villages, and it was apparent that the Hughes Law district organization would be thrown out on the same ground if it were attacked in court.

Under the Griswold Law—the amended Hughes Law—the question of providing adequate health organization is left to the district board of health. Reorganization is now in progress, and among the earliest counties reporting are several which have provided for whole-time health commissioners and for one or more public health nurses. Health commissioners' salaries in the full-time positions are fixed in most instances at $3,000 and $4,000. In most districts the boards are making a sincere effort to obtain qualified men.

While the smaller cities under the amended law will in most cases be unable to obtain full-time service from their health commissioners, the provisions for voluntary union between a city and the surrounding general district offer a way out of this difficulty. Two general districts may also combine if they choose.

The State Department of Health feels that the new health system, even as amended, is a notable advance over the old township, village and city health district system, and that in the course of time it may produce results as good as those which were expected from the original plan laid down by the Hughes Law. The process of educating the public to a general appreciation of the benefits to be derived from adequate health organization will necessarily make the process of development slow in some localities.

(*V. E. McV.*)

In its consideration of the new state health law in Ohio, Toledo in its *Toledo City Journal* makes the following statements with reference to its operation in cities possessing charters.

The Hughes Health Law, as amended by the Griswold Act, recently passed by the General Assembly of Ohio and allowed by Governor Cox to become effective without his signature, makes possible radical changes in the health administration of the state and of the cities of the state. Because it may be used by the City of Toledo at any time the following digest of its provisions is given here:

The act provides for a division of the state into health districts, each city constituting a city health district, and the townships and villages of each county comprising a general health district. Any two districts within the same county may be combined.

Procedure for organizing these districts is outlined in the act, but where a city charter has provided its own form of health administration, as in the case of Toledo, no change in that organization need be made.

Every district board of health is charged with the duty of studying and recording the prevalence of disease within its district and of providing for the prompt diagnosis and control of communicable diseases. It may also provide for the medical and dental supervision of school children, for the free treatment of venereal diseases, for the inspection of schools, public institutions, jails, workhouses, and other charitable and correctional institutions. It may also provide for the inspection of dairies, stores, restaurants, hotels and other places where food is manufactured, stored or offered for sale, and for the medical inspection of persons employed therein. It may also provide for the abatement of public nuisances dangerous to the public health and comfort.

The question of employing a part-time or full-time health commissioner is made optional with each district. In any case, when a health district has been organized according to the provisions of the act, and this fact has been certified to the State Commissioner of Health, the state will pay every six months one-half of the expenses entailed by that health administration, provided that the amount to be paid by the state shall in no case exceed $2,000 per year.

STATE HEALTH NOTES—GENERAL

National.—Over 200,000,000 tiny particles of dust, as sharp as ground glass, are breathed into the lungs and air passages with every cubic foot of air in some of the factories in the United States, according to a survey made by the Public Health Service here.

Such dusts breathed into the lungs are never expelled. Photomicrographs show the tiny particles to be exceedingly sharp and jagged and chemical tests prove them to be practically insoluble. Work under such conditions invites respiratory diseases and makes a real health hazard. Similar investigations in chemical factories showed that laborers were frequently exposed to poisonous fumes and gases.

As a result of a survey at Niagara Falls industrial hygiene engineers devised means of removing the dust from the air and minimizing hazards from fumes and poisonous gases. In spite of the fact that the installation of such devices was expensive, factory managements immediately put them into use.

At least 32,000 white children are born out of wedlock in the United States each year, and probably not more than 70 per cent of these children survive the first year of life, says a report on "Illegitimacy as a Child Welfare Problem," just issued by the Children's Bureau, U. S. Department of Labor. This report, which contains a general treatment of the prevalence and significance of the problem in this and other countries was written as an introduction to a more exhaustive study of the meaning, to the child and to society, of birth out of wedlock.

The most striking fact brought out is the very high infant mortality rate among these children, which in most European countries was found to be about twice that among children of more fortunate birth, and in three American cities was three times as high.

The children who do survive infancy are likely to be deprived of normal home life and a mother's care. Rarely do they receive the support from their father to which they should be entitled. In a large proportion of cases the public must assume the burden of the support of these children.

The American boy is a product of the American school. He is at the age then, between 15 and 20 years, when he will make himself physically strong, or weak, and form the ideals and habits that go with him through life. It is for this reason that the United States Public Health Service has started a campaign in America to reach all of the boys between the ages of 15 and 20 years and interest them in a campaign to keep themselves physically fit. This is not with an idea of raising the boys to be soldiers, but because there is one young man in every three physically unfit, not only to be a soldier, but anything else that requires strong, vigorous manhood. This was revealed when the army had to reject one man in every three for physical disability.

✢

Cuba.—There have been established services of Child Hygiene in the cities of Pinar del Rio, Cardenas, and Santa Clara y Cienfuegos, with the intention to establish others from time to time. For executive officers the Secretary of Health has designated Señorita Martina Guevara, Chief of the Infirmary Department.

In July last there was imported from Spain on board the "Venezzia" the first case of smallpox registered in the island. Altogether 58 cases were found in the city of Havana, 5 of them in the Spanish sections. There were deaths of two children whose cases were concealed for several days from the authorities. Steps were taken towards the punishment of the persons responsible for the concealment.

For the study of the etiology of yellow fever Dr. Mario Lebredo has been named, he being the Director of the National Research Laboratory. Dr. Antonio Barreras, Director of the Service of Child Hygiene, has been delegated to study the problems of maternity and infancy as developed in the United States. The Secretary of Health has organized sanitary conferences in the work shops and factories of the Republic, at which many of the employees gather daily. Lectures are given with illustrations and motion pictures.

In consequence of the discovery of cases of bubonic plague in New Orleans the Cuban Department of Health has intensified its campaign of deratization. All ships are compelled to discharge away from wharves, and are subject to rigid regulations. Warehouses are watched and guarded, and especial attention is given to drains and sewers.

A campaign against malaria has been undertaken under the supervision of Dr. Florencio Villuendas, who through the local chiefs will put into effect some of the standard anti-Anopheles measures.

California.—The State Health Department has lost by death Mr. George D. Leslie, Statistician and Registrar of Vital Statistics since 1905, which occurred early in January. He has been succeeded by Mr. L. E. Ross who has been with the Department for a year, coming to it with large experience in public statistical work.

✢

Connecticut.—In the reorganization of the State Health Department a Bureau of Sanitary Engineering was created. For the information of the public, a statement is made by the Department enumerating the larger responsibilities imposed by statute on this Bureau.

(a) Advising and assisting any public official in regard to sanitary drainage, ventilation or other sanitary matters.

(b) Supervision over all matters pertaining to the purity of water and ice supplies.

(c) Investigation and supervision of existing and proposed sewerage systems and refuse disposal plants.

(d) General oversight of all inland and tidal waters in relation to pollution.

(e) Expert examinations and inspections of public institutions, buildings, structures and works.

Definite programs have been drawn for carrying out these various lines of work and considerable progress already made. Ten engineers, chemists and inspectors are now employed in this bureau on a full-time basis.

Previous to the establishment of this bureau all the engineering advice or assistance that could be given was that which the members of the State Board offered by letter or by consultation at their convenience. This was because the board did not employ an engineer and such service as was rendered by the board was gratuitous.

✢

Delaware.—On January 13th strong opposition to vaccination developed, in Georgetown, Del., manifesting itself in the "running out of town" of Mr. C. H. Wells, Special Health Commissioner. The situation has developed in an interesting way. The local Justice of the Peace ruled against the State Board in the complaints against leaders of the mob, and the fight is now on to prove the authority of the State Board to control epidemics in incorporated towns. As the situation stands, the question of vaccination is now of minor importance, the real question being whether the State rule or regulation can be over ridden by any local incorporated town.

✦

Illinois.—An example of community co-operation has been shown in Chicago by the Stock Yards Community Clearing House. This is an organization for fostering community work in the Stock Yards district of the city, seven of the large houses centering about the industries here having joined in sponsoring the plan and in assuming the financial responsibility. The Clearing House undertakes to afford a means of co-operation in all that pertains to community betterment, and undertakes a community study, to be an outlook from which to gain an unprejudiced view of conditions as they are, a means of inter-communication between the various industrial, civic, religious and welfare organizations and furnish a means of co-operation in matters of relief in times of crisis. Just such a time came during the influenza outbreak and the Clearing House was able to establish an emergency hospital for forty patients, supply more than 8,000 meals to unfortunate families and furnish administration for the relief work.

The Chicago Municipality Dispensary has adopted the following standard in searching for the facts about the child's health:

(a) The diagnosis of tuberculosis in a child.

(b) "Contacts," all children now in association with an open case of tuberculosis, and children who have a definite history of prolonged exposure to tuberculosis.

(c) Those children falling under Classes III and IV in Dunfermline nutritional scale.

(d) Anemic children showing a hemoglobin under 80 per cent.

(e) Children below normal height and weight, and presenting associated conditions, which means a pathological state.

(f) Children who present conditions which cause them to be classed as "suspect," "pre-tuberculous," or "scrofulous," should be recommended for open-air school treatment.

✦

Indiana.—The Bureau of Venereal Disease of the Indiana State Board of Health was organized in July, 1918. Dr. William F. King, Assistant Secretary of the State Board of Health and Acting Assistant Surgeon, U. S. Public Health Service was made Director of the Bureau.

In the beginning a state wide educational campaign designed to ultimately reach every citizen of the state was planned. This campaign has been carried out by means of lectures, exhibits, distribution of educational pamphlets, moving pictures, and by securing the co-operation of all organizations and groups wherever possible. For the calendar year ending December 31, 1919, approximately 400,000 educational circulars have been distributed upon request and through general distribution. More than 300 lectures have been given before approximately 60,000 people. The moving picture film "Fit to Win" and "End of the Road" have been shown free to 25,000 people. "Keeping Fit" exhibits have been displayed in Y. M. C. A.'s and before high schools a total of approximately 500 days to 85,000 people. More than 100,000 small folders giving the social facts of the veneral diseases have been distributed to industrial employes through pay envelopes.

A campaign to secure the full co-operation of doctors and druggists throughout the state has been carried out with success.

Public Health Associations have been organized in 20 counties of the state, and this organization work will be continued in the hope of securing a similar organization in every county. It is realized that public education must be the final determining factor in veneral disease control, and for this reason the educational phase of the campaign has been given special emphasis.

Under the head of Repression, an attempt has been made to secure the co-operation of city and county officials, police departments and courts in the repression of prostitution. A model venereal disease control ordinance, in which is incorporated every essential provision for the control of the venereal diseases has been enacted in 65 of the 95 incorporated cities of the state.

Under the supervision of the State Investigator, a system of reporting, notification and transfer is being carried out through the entire state. No case of venereal disease in an infectious state is permitted to go from one health jurisdiction to another without permission of the health authorities at the point where travel begins and notification of others at the destination. A system of notification and follow-up through local investigators and local health authorities is carried out by means of which cases of venereal disease are required to be regular in their attendance at the free venereal disease clinics or to be regular in carrying out treatment under private physicians under penalty of arrest and quarantine. The right of health officers to quarantine cases of venereal disease and to require attendance upon treatment has been up-held by city courts in several instances. The State Investigator co-operates with social workers and social service departments and in this way it has been possible to reclaim and re-establish a large number of individual cases as well as families.

. Under the head of treatment, free venereal disease clinics have been established and are being maintained in most of the larger cities of the state.' At the present time 18 such free venereal disease clinics are in operation. In the larger cities these clinics are maintained on a full time schedule, while in the smaller cities, the clinics operate only on part time, but on an average of two days and two evenings of each week.

This work has been carried on under an allotment made by the Federal Government through the Interdepartmental Social Hygiene Board of $29,366.20 annually for a period of two years. An additional appropriation of $29,366.20 made by the Indiana Legislature, and appropriations made by cities, and county councils for free venereal disease clinics, totalling $32,000 for the past year.

✛

Maine.—In preparation for more widespread health work in Maine during 1920, and in accordance with the new health laws enacted by the 1919 legislature several new district health officers have been appointed. The three original health districts created in 1917 have been increased to eight and the five new health officers are Dr. Clarence F. Kendall, with headquarters in Biddeford, his native city; Dr. G. H. Hutchins of Mechanic Falls, with headquarters at Presque Isle; Dr. E. P. Goodrich of Winterport, headquarters in Lewiston; Dr. J. W. Laughlin of Damariscotta, whose headquarters will be in his home town; and Alton S. Pope of Manchester, with headquarters in Waterville.

The State Department of Health has appointed a special investigator for the Division of Venereal Disease, selecting for the position Miss A. Eugenie MacDonald, who is a graduate of the Maine General Hospital. Following a war experience at Camp Stuart, Va., Miss MacDonald has been public health nurse with the Portland Board of Health.

Missouri.—In the latter part of 1919, the State Board of Health requested the U. S. Public Health Service to undertake studies and demonstrations in Child Hygiene activities and to organize this Division as provided.

One of the important activities will be the stimulation of birth registration from data obtained from house-to-house canvass, obtain better results and thus enable the state to be accepted in the Birth Registration Area.

Second, Field investigators will canvass localities selected to obtain information relative to the children of the infant and pre-school age.

Third, Modern health centers will be established to give children the benefit of medical attention. Prenatal supervision will be provided wherever possible or desirable. With the inauguration of a health center, it will be the purpose to have communities employ special trained nurses for permanent work in infant welfare. With the co-operation of the school authorities, social organizations, health supervision of school children will be established. They will be examined and where necessary, suitable treatment for defects will be recommended and facilities provided to make such treatment accessible.

One of the most important innovations will be the establishment of nutrition clinics conducted in the schools for the benefit of under-nourished children.

✛

Nebraska.—Dr. W. H. Wilson, epidemiologist for the Nebraska state bureau of health, was appointed by the United States Public Health Service as collaborating epidemiologist with that Service for the state of Nebraska on December 4, 1919. Under this arrangement, the county superintendents of public instruction in this state, who are by law made secretaries of the county boards of health, are made assistant collaborating epidemiologists and are given the franking privilege. This enables the physicians over the state to report their contagious diseases to the county superintendents without the payment of postage, the county superintendents in turn reporting weekly to the state bureau of health.

✛

New Mexico.—The only hospital in the State solely for women and children has recently been opened in Albuquerque. It has beds for 26 patients. The State Health Department has established a bacteriological laboratory to be conducted in co-operation with the Department of Hygiene of the State University. As a health movement the New Mexico Public Health Association is endorsing the campaign to establish at the University a building to be devoted to domestic science, the idea being, that bettered home surroundings and well cooked food are factors towards the promotion of health. A committee from the Albuquerque Woman's Club waited on the city commissioners recently asking an amendment to an ordinance in the interests of stricter supervision of those engaged in the business of handling food. The amendment requires not only an examination of the employee, but that a certificate of health for every one shall be posted in a conspicuous place in the establishment in plain view of the public.

✚

New York.—New York City uses the Dunfermline scale of defective nutrition in its school medical inspection service. One year's grading resulted as follows:

51,238 (31 per cent) were found excellent (or No. 1).

87,823 (53.2 per cent) were found good (or No. 2).

19,564 (11.9 per cent) were found requiring supervision (or No. 3).

6,403 (3.9 per cent) were found requiring medical treatment (or No. 4).

In its report of work accomplished the Rensselaer County Tuberculosis Association notes that in the past 9 months 595 free examinations were made of the lungs with 95 positives. In co-operation with the State Department of Health and the State Tuberculosis Committee, 11 occasional clinics were held during the summer. A total of 2,200 visits were made by the nurses of the Association. In its educational work about 9,000 children were enlisted in the health crusade, 2,500 health primers were distributed and 1,000 copies of influenza and tuberculosis posters, together with 20,000 pieces of educational literature. The press work included some 250 notices. A lecture a week was given to the public including factory employees and lantern slides and motion pictures were also used.

In a recent investigation made by the New York State Department of Health of the sanitary quality of the public water supply for the City of Syracuse, an interesting question arose as to the elimination of tastes and odors due to algae growths. In the report of the Engineering Division on this investigation, suggestions were made for certain research and studies to be carried out in solving this problem. The question also arose as to whether the algae growths occurred in the lake or in the distributing reservoir or both and the novel method of applying copper sulphate at the upper end of the 20 mile conduit followed by aeration at the distributing reservoir was suggested as a promising remedial measure.

The public water supply of Cobleskill it was found that the Board of Water Commissioners are considering the installation of a closed coagulation and sedimentation basin to be operated under pressure in connection with the pressure mechanical filters now used to purify the supply.

✚

Ohio.—There is the greatest interest throughout the State in fulfilling the requirements of the Griswold Act. By the middle of January seven counties had perfected organizations. Columbiana, Warren, Morrow, Geauga, Pike, Auglaize and Belmont counties.

An accurate summary of the activities of Ohio hospitals will be made available for the first time through annual reports for the year 1919.

A midwife of Warren has been fined $50 for violating the State law with reference to ophthalmia neonatorum. The woman failed to apply to the eyes of a baby at whose birth she officiated the prophylactic solution which a midwife is required by law to use at every birth, and failed also to report to the health authorities the eye inflammation which followed her failure to safeguard the infant's eyes. A physician to whose attention the case was brought several days later reported it, bringing about an investigation by a state nurse.

Progress in the campaign against venereal diseases in Ohio is recorded in a report just compiled by the State Department of Health, covering activities of the past year and one-half in this regard. Thirty-three free clinics in the state treated 7,466 patients during this period. Nine hundred and fifty patients deemed dangerous to the public health were quarantined. Nearly 1,000 lectures were given by officials to audiences totaling more than

120,000. More than 20,000 high school boys were reached through the "Keeping Fit" exhibit, conducted in co-operation with the state Y. M. C. A. organization. Three-fourths of a million pieces of literature were distributed.

While reports to the State Department of Health indicate a widespread prevalence of influenza, the disease has so far been milder in type than last year and no large number of cases of pneumonia have been reported. Although the epidemic is in practically all parts of the state, the department thinks it will spend itself in a comparatively short time.

With the return to the state of many physicians and nurses who were in military service last year, most communities have been able to provide adequate medical and nursing aid. In some localities, however, this service is inadequate and to these communities the State Department of Health has advised the formation of an emergency committee for making the best use of available physicians and nurses and for caring for those families who are unable to afford a private nurse. The number of cases is so large in many communities that any further increase would make necessary the opening of an emergency hospital. Should this need arise, the State Department of Health has advised all boards of health to make preparations for such action.

Breathing of exhaust-gas fumes in closed garages has killed two Ohio motorists this winter, according to reports reaching the State Department of Health. One of the recent victims was from Youngstown and the other from Van Wert. The Van Wert man started the engine to recharge his batteries. When his wife became alarmed at his failure to return, she called neighbors, who broke open the tightly closed doors and found him dead on the floor. The Youngstown case was similar, the victim being found dead, with garage doors shut, several hours after he had gone to the garage to repair his car.

✦

Utah.—This state has established the annual medical examination of school children as an essential part of the health education work of the schools. It urges the importance of the examination of children's teeth every six months. Both of these recommendations are defensible on the ground of safeguarding the welfare of the next generation, and if persisted in throughout life, will tend definitely to prolong the period of existence and increase the happiness of all who follow them.

Reports on the weight of school children are now being sent to the homes by the schools. An effort is being made to get children interested in their own growth and nutrition and to find out which children are definitely undernourished. It is desirable that parents know more about just what the schools are trying to do and the significance to be attached to serious under-weight.

Leaflets are distributed to the children in school giving to them some of the elementary principles of health. Here is a quotation from one of them:

Little Things that Keep you Well:

1. Have your own handkerchief. (a) In your pocket—not on the desk where it will get dirty. (b) Use it for keeping your nose clean —not for cleaning your desk or wiping apples. (c) Use it yourself. (d) Do not loan it to any other person; you may get some disease.

2. Use your own book. (a) Another may have disease germs on it.

3. Wear your own hat or coat. (a) Disease is easily spread this way. (b) Pediculosis thrives.

✦

Virginia.—A Health Conference was held in Richmond during the week beginning December 29, 1919. It was primarily intended for a post graduate course for those directly or indirectly employed by the State Board of Health. For the first three days sessions were held with the public health nurses. During the forenoon joint sessions were held, and in the afternoon there were section meetings to discuss subjects in which certain groups were especially interested. The conference lasted a week and proved of such value that it is the intention to make it a permanent institution, and to call into it all the health workers in the state. One of the speakers was Dr. L. L. Lumsden, U. S. P. H. S., on "The National Health Campaign." There were discussions on public health nursing, public health posters, health stories and plays regarding child hygiene, Red Cross Nurse, and Junior Health League. There were two symposiums for nurses taking up infant welfare work and inspection of school children; social service aspect of public health nursing, classes in home nursing and industrial nursing. Dr. Williams presented a story of the activities of the State

Board of Health and a second one on the prevention of diseases and classification of diseases from the standpoints of prevention. Water supplies, vital statistics, rural dispensaries, rural sanitation, public health organizations and tuberculosis were other subjects considered.

+

Wisconsin.—The State Board of Health has adopted a code of rules governing the construction and maintenance of public comfort stations, which by a new law are compulsory in all cities and villages. This is the first state requirement of the kind on record. Many municipalities are already complying.

The State Board of Health voted in January not to recommend use of influenza vaccine or any other mixed vaccines for prevention of pneumonia or influenza. It endorsed, however, the efforts of the state laboratory of hygiene in supplying physicians of the state free of charge with vaccine for the prevention of types 1, 2 and 3 pneumonia. The board expressed its desire to establish at least one or two more co-operative laboratories.

A disease not akin to any previously encountered in the state, and of an intestinal nature, was rampant in parts of Sawyer and Bayfield counties, widely distant from each other, during January. Investigations made by the State Board of Health disclosed the principal symptoms to be abdominal cramps, vomiting, diarrhea, moderate fever, and profound prostration. Usually the illness was of a few days' duration and no deaths are known to have resulted.

Child health conservation measures instituted by the new bureau of child welfare are rapidly being adopted. Among recent advances have been the establishment of child health centers in a number of cities and the holding of state examinations for county nurses, or health instructors, required in all counties under a new law.

□

Conventions, Conferences and Meetings

March 22-23, New York City, New York State Medical Society.

April 6, Newark, N. J., N. J. State Nurses' Association.

April 6-8, Atlanta, Ga., National Organization for Public Health Nursing.

April 6-8, Jefferson City, Mo., Missouri State Medical Association.

April 12-17, Atlanta, Ga., National Organization for Public Health Nursing.

April 14-21, New Orleans, National Conference of Social Workers.

April 14-21 New Orleans, American Association of Hospital Workers.

April 19, Charlotte, N. C., North Carolina State Health Association.

April 20-21, Austin, Texas, Conference of County and City Health officers.

April 20-22, Charlotte, N. C., Medical Society of North Carolina.

April 20-22, Anniston, Ala., Medical Association of the State of Alabama.

April 22-24, St. Louis, Mo., National Tuberculosis Association.

April 26-30, New Orleans, La., American Medical Association.

April 29-30, Bismarck, N. D., North Dakota State Nurses' Association.

May 11-12, Indianapolis, Ind., Indiana State Health Association.

May 12-14, Des Moines, Iowa, Iowa Medical Association.

May 12-14, Des Moines, Iowa, Trudeau Society.

May 20-24, Brussels, Belgium, Congress of Royal (English) Institute of Public Health.

May 24-26, Omaha,. Neb., Nebraska State Medical Association.

May 24-26, Omaha, Neb., Nebraska State Health Association.

May 25-26, Toronto, Ont., Ontario Health Association.

May 25-27, Columbus, Ohio, Ohio Hospital Association, New Jersey.

June 1-4, Cleveland, Ohio, American Medico-Physiological Association.

June 3, Providence, R. I., Rhode Island Medical Society.

June 3-5, Portland, Ore., Oregon State Medical Association.

June 9, Boston, Mass., Massachusetts Medical Society.

June 15-16, Minot, N. D., North Dakota State Medical Association.

June 22-24, Vancouver, B. C., Canadian Public Health Association.

June 23-25, St. Paul, Minn., Catholic Hospital Association.

INDUSTRIAL HYGIENE AND OCCUPATIONAL DISEASE

Abstracted by Drs. E. R. Hayhurst, R. P. Albaugh, P. M. Holmes, and E. B. Starr.

Medical Service an Industrial Stabilizer.—Under this title appears a very important article by Dr. Selby. Among many answers which he quotes in reply to the question "Why do you have a medical department?" which was asked of factory managers whom he saw in person, is one as follows: "It is as necessary as a cost department or any other nonproducing department." The effects of such a department in reducing labor turnover and in increasing wages are shown by statistics. Seven reasons are given why such a department is good business. In addition, service for small plants and the creation of community bureaus for the same is discussed. To be effective, industrial medicine must not be limited to the care of injuries but its value is determined largely by its use in the prevention of disease among workers. *The medical department had best be answerable directly to the plant head* rather than subsidiary to any other department of the plant. Physicians who intend going into industrial service should seek special training in that direction. Trained nurses are in greater demand in industrial dispensaries than any other class of attendants. Industrial medicine is not only humane but essential to production. It is beneficial to workers and profitable to employers. It offers splendid advantages to physicians for the development of careers in a field of rapidly growing importance, vital with opportunity for service to humanity. A recommendation is made that medical colleges be induced to provide courses of instruction in industrial sanitation and medicine, and that affiliations be arranged between the colleges and industrial plants.—C. D. Selby, *Hospital Management*. December, 1919, pp. 58-64.

✛

Special Investigations of Industrial Skin Diseases.—The special committee of the Health Service Section of the National Safety Council has undertaken the investigation of industrial skin diseases, and a questionnaire has been sent to members asking information on this subject. Dr. Carey P. McCord, Department of Industrial Medicine and Public Health, University of Cincinnati, is the chairman of the committee and any having informa-

tion or desiring information on the subject should communicate with Dr. McCord. A list of the industries and trade processes in which industrial skin diseases are known has been prepared and is distributed by the *National Safety Council*, 168 North Michigan Avenue, Chicago, Illinois.

✛

Twenty Suggestions to Industrial Physicians and Surgeons.—It would pay any industrial physician or surgeon to read Dr. Selby's four-page article in the original upon this subject. How to place workers, hygienic supervision of working conditions, the opportunity for research, the necessity for securing sufficient authority in the plant are laid down in the suggestions.—C. D. Selby, *Modern Hospital*, June, 1919, pp. 455-458.

✛

The Journal of Industrial Hygiene devotes an entire issue to papers delivered before the Health Section of the National Safety Council, at its Congress recently held in Cleveland.—(*Jour. of Ind. Hyg.*, Dec., 1919.). The papers include the following: "Industrial Health Hazards," Charles A. Lauffer, M.D., Medical Director, Relief Department, Westinghouse Electric and Manufacturing Company, East Pittsburgh, Pa.; "Scope of the Physical Examination in Industry," C. D. Selby, M.D., Toledo, Ohio; "Industrial Dermatoses, Their Sources, Types and Control," William Allen Pusey, A.M., M.D., Chicago, Professor of Dermatology, University of Illinois; "The Treatment of Burns," W. Irving Clar, Jr., M.D., Medical Director, Norton Company, Worcester, Mass.; "Industrial Clinics in General Hospitals," David L. Edsall, M.D., Harvard Medical School, and Chief of East Medical Service, Massachusetts General Hospital; "Health Education in Industry," W. A. Evans, M.D., Health Department, Chicago Tribune, Chicago; "The Co-ordination of Industrial and Community Health Activities," C. E. Ford, M.D., Medical Director, General Chemical Company, New York City; "Malingering—Involving the Problem of Getting the Sick or Injured Employe Back to Work," Judson C. Fisher, M.D., New York City.

What the Workingman Thinks of Health Welfare.—James H. Maurer, president of the Pennsylvania Federation of Labor, sends a letter to the Editor, Department of Industrial Welfare, *Modern Hospital*, (August, 1919, pp. 136-137) which the Editor prints in full, at the same time disagreeing with some of Mr. Maurer's conclusions. Space does not permit recopying President Maurer's letter here, but he maintains that such service is not free but that the consumer pays for it. The work is often abused as when a company physician causes a worker to lose two weeks' working time without compensation because of a slight injury, on the plea that to remain at work might cause infection. Compulsory physical examination means discrimination to many maimed workers and those suffering from occupational disease. No one would seriously object to the efficiency aimed at, if such handicapped persons were properly placed and then not exploited because of their infirmities. Concerns that demand physical examinations seldom have in mind the placing of defectives; they want the physically sound. There are shining exceptions, however, to this common rule and where real physicians are employed in examining employes at regular periods to keep them in the best possible physical condition, such is to be commended. "Compulsory physical examinations by the employers' doctors and the plant stuck full of safety-first signs does not appeal to the worker who sees all around him unguarded machinery, pitfalls, death-traps and general all-around insanitary working conditions and whose income may compel him to live in some disease-breeding shack or tenement. The first great step in the conservation of human life and energy is not free medical or surgical treatment but to learn the mystery of our own bodies, tear aside the cloak of sham and modesty, learn how to live clean lives, quit driving the workers to the point of exhaustion, eliminate the profiteer, stop the exploitation of labor and there will be little need for the medical service."

✦

The Influence of Alcohol on Manual Work.—The British Medical Research Committee arrived at the following conclusions: Small doses of alcohol, well within the limits of what would be deemed by all moderation, do not sensibly affect the *speed* of performance of such semi-automatic operations as typing a memorized passage or setting down and adding a row of figures on a mechanical calculator, but gravely depreciate the *accuracy* of performance. Two glasses of port wine in a person accustomed to drink a glass of wine have this effect when the wine is taken with food. Less than this is sufficient to produce a result if taken on an empty stomach. Should the task set be very familiar to the subject, the foregoing conclusion does not hold.—*London Letter, J. A. M. A.,* Sept. 20, 1919, p. 926.

✦

Sanitary Survey of Schools and Factories in Framingham.—Among the various activities of the Framingham Tuberculosis Demonstration has been included effects of school and factory life. The first twenty pages of the bulletin at hand, which is illustrated, is devoted to the schools, another forty-two pages to factories and appendices showing classifications and forms used. In factories, special attention is given to the subjects of dust and ventilation and safety and general sanitary features. The dust and ventilation studies show it is necessary to take into account visibility, weight, count, size and character of the properly collected dust particles. The dust hazards were found greatest in woodworking industries, next in foundry work and least of all in the woolen industries, judged almost altogether from the point of view of the probable relationship of abrasiveness to pulmonary tissue irritation. Much improvement is needed in the matter of protective devices against mechanical hazards, in fire-drills, in first-aid and rest rooms and in safety organization in the plants. Special defects included hazards of which dry-sweeping methods, poor illumination, incidental subjection to lead, common drinking cups, etc., are examples. "It is evident from the several industrial surveys that from one-third to two-thirds of the plants present poor, dangerous, or inadequate facilities or equipment with regard to practically all of the hygienic factors considered." The biggest problem is found in the smaller industries. No great industrial poison hazards existed. The solution depends largely upon the personal factor, and therefore on an effective program of education as to personal hygiene. The plants also need more adequate personnel for medical, nursing and clinic service.—Donald B. Armstrong, Executive Officer, *Framingham (Mass.) Tuberculosis Demonstration,* (Monograph No. 6).

PUBLIC HEALTH
LABORATORY NOTES

Abstracted by Francis H. Slack, M. D., and Mr. James M. Strang.

Value of Complement Fixation Test in Gonococcal Infections.—The article is based on 840 tests made on 625 persons.

A positive result is, in the opinion of the authors, strongly indicative of active gonococcal infection. Only one case of known gonorrhea remained negative on second test. A single negative finding is not conclusive but a second negative in two or three weeks is strong presumptive evidence of absence of infection.

A continuously strong positive reaction indicates the presence of an active focus of the disease.—H. B. F. Dixon, *Lancet*, London, Nov. 29, 1919, p. 964.

✛

A New Stain for Diphtheria Bacilli.—Two solutions are used:

Solution No. 1

Toluidin blue	0.15 gm.
Acetic acid (glacial)	1.00 cc.
Alcohol (95%)	2.00 cc
Water (distilled)	100 cc.

Solution No. 2

Iodin	1 gm.
Potassium Iodid	2 gm.
Water (distilled)	300 cc.

Smears are made, fixed with heat and stained with solution 1 for five minutes. The slides are then drained without washing and the iodin solution applied for one minute. Wash with water, dry and examine. The granules of the bacilli are stained black, the bars take a color varying from dark green to black, and the intermediate portions, as well as other bacteria, take a light green.—Henry Albert, M. D., *Jour. A. M. A.*, Jan. 3, 1920, p. 28.

✛

A Benzidin-polychrome Stain for Blood.—This method is advantageous for the accurate classification of endothelial leucocytes, the granules of which stain dark brown as do those of the eosinophils. All the other blood elements are colored as in the simple Wright's stain. The stain is applied to the smear as follows: On a 22 mm. square cover glass

(No. 1), 4 drops of 80 percent. methyl alcohol, to 25 cc. to which there has been added 100 milligrams of benzidin (Merck or that obtained from the Will corporation) and one drop of hydrogen peroxid, are placed for thirty seconds; this is diluted with 8 drops of distilled water and 4 drops of polychrome stain (Wright's blood stain), are added. The diluted stain is allowed to act for four minutes and then it is washed, blotted, dried in the air, and mounted in balsam. The benzidin solution keeps for several weeks. The depth of the granule stain is much increased by diluting the benzidin reagent with a phosphate solution having a hydrogen-ion concentration of P_H 6.4.

The author gives directions for the preparation of the phosphate solution and also for the preparation of a glycerinized polychrome stain which keeps indefinitely.—F. A. McJunkin, M. D., *Jour. A. M. A.*, Vol. 74, No. 1, 1920.

✛

Diagnosis of Diphtheria by Direct Microscopic Examination.—Dr. Lowry emphasizes the advantages of a direct microscopic examination in the diagnosis of diphtheria. The details of his technic are given in full, of which the following is a summary. The swab is first inoculated on the blood serum at the bottom of the culture tube which is allowed to soak into the cotton. After one to two minutes the serum fluid is expressed from the cotton by a special flat stick and spread on two slides. As the slides dry gradually, the liquid is stirred up to break the clumps of bacteria. One slide is stained in a slightly modified Neisser with Vesuvial counterstain, the other with Raux. A description of the K-L bacilli with these stains is given, also the pseudo forms. In 100 recent examinations, 65 cases were found positive by the direct method and 78 by the culture. Fifty-eight percent. of the positive diagnoses were therefore obtained within half an hour of their arrival at the laboratory, an increase of 5 percent. over the previously described direct method.—Lowry, *Ann. Inst. Path.* 1919, 33, 713.

Experiments on the Role of Flies in Dissemination of Trachoma.—A fly coming in contact with a trachoma infected eye is able to transmit this infection at any time within the following twenty-four hours. It can similarly transmit the disease if it comes in contact with infectious material (handkerchiefs, pillow cases, etc.) that have been infected within six hours. Under the same condition and with the same delay, flies are incapable of transmitting acute conjunctivitis. Without doubt the fly plays an important role in the spread of trachoma. It is important therefore to recognize the necessity for screening hospitals in which trachoma patients are cared for. Nicolle, Cuenod & Blanc, *Revue Sci.,* Dec. 20, 1919. (*H. N. C.*)

✛

Preparation and Conservation of Sera and Vaccines by Dessication in an Absolute Vacuum.—The authors have studied the methods of conserving dried vaccine reduced to a fine powder and sealed in vacuum tubes. They mention several methods of obtaining this vacuum, noting that it is important to keep the condensation apparatus at a temperature of less than minus 80° C. D'Arsonval-Dewer tubes containing 5, 10, or 15 grams of dried vaccine in absolute vacuum have been prepared which allow it to be transported, maintaining its original activity, to regions where the daily temperature is in excess of 55°.—C. F. Borgas, *Revue Sci., Oct.* 18, 1918, (*H. N. C.*)

Achalme and Phisalix at a recent session of the Academy of Sciences, Paris, report a confirmation of this and cite their experiments followed in 1908-1909. They mention that this method is in constant use in certain African Colonies, particularly in English East Africa, where the laboratory prepares, each year, by this method, a quantity of vaccine.

✛

Action of B. Typhosus on Xylose and Other Sugars.—A detailed account is given of the work done at the Army Medical School with reference to the subdivision of *B. typhosus* into groups. Fermentation of xylose has been shown to be present in 116 strains from various sources. Where fermentation of xylose was so slow as to be reported absent by earlier workers, the authors have demonstrated the presence of this power, and that rapidly fermenting subcultures could readily be prepared. Cultures which produced acid in arabmose

broth very slowly, or apparently not at all, have developed this power on sub-culturation. In view of these experiments, and the many contradictions found in the literature, the authors conclude that there is no justification for the subdivision of *B. typhosus* into separate groups.—Teague and Morishima, *Jour. Inf. Dis.* 26, 52.

✛

Experimental Researches on Streptococcic Immunity.—The authors obtained a more active serum by injecting a single large dose of streptococcus culture into a house than by any other method. The serum protected mice against the same strain of streptococcus and to a slight extent against other strains.—Vinaver and Frasey, *C. R. Soc. Biol.,* 82, 1919, 606; *Bull. Inst. Past.,* 17, 1919, 22.   ✛

Non-Lactose Fermenting Organism from the Feces of Influenza Patients.—Attention is called to the relatively high percent. of euteriditis-like organisms which are found in the feces of influenza patients but not of normal controls. The authors feel that their findings warrant more extensive investigations of the gastro-intestinal tract during the disease.—Sherwood, Downs, McNaught, *Jour, Infec. Dis.,* 1920, 26, 16.

✛

Bacteriology of Chronic Empyema.—In studying the bacteriology of chronic empyema, the author used a modification of the West tube for obtaining representative samples of the flora of the pleural cavity. The results with this method were more consistently satisfactory than with unprotected needles. The tube is also an important element in the standardization of the technique.—J. E. Gendan, *Jour. Inf. Dis.* 1920, 26, 23.

✛

Living Microörganisms in Paper.—During the various processes which paper pulp undergoes in its manufacture, microörganisms are not destroyed. All paper contains in its fibres bacteria which can be cultivated. Time apparently has no effect on these intracellular organisms. A fragment of papyrus of the epoch of Ptolemy, that is to say nearly 200 years B. C., was soaked in water for three hours. From this were obtained intracellular organisms which held immovable for so many centuries where shown to be still possessed of movement.—Galippe, *Revue Sci.,* Nov. 15, 1919 (H. N. C.)

(Continued on Page XX, Advertising Section)

American Journal of Public Health

Official Monthly Publication of the American Public Health Association

Publication office: 124 W. Polk Street, Chicago, Ill.
Editorial office: 169 Massachusetts Ave., Boston, Mass.

Subscription price, $4 per year.   American Public Health Association membership, including subscription, $5 per year.
Subscriptions and memberships may be sent to the A. P. H. A., 169 Massachusetts Ave., Boston, Mass.

| Vol. X | APRIL, 1920 | No. 4 |

THE AMERICAN PUBLIC HEALTH ASSOCIATION, PRESENT, PAST, AND FUTURE

W. S. RANKIN, M. D.,

President, American Public Health Association, Raleigh, N. C.

It will take you only twelve minutes to read what your President has to tell you. He gives you the facts concerning the A. P. H. A. and its program. Every member should read it.

This statement has been prepared with the singleness of purpose of supplying the reasons which may be presented to public-spirited citizens in general and to students and workers in the field of public health in particular, in asking their loyal support of the Association. It is assumed that the Association, to be entitled to one's interest and membership, must do three things: First, it must make clear that the field of service which it occupies is essential to the public welfare, and that it has a program of such general interest and proper proportions as to hold a legitimate claim to the larger and more intelligent thought of our people. Second, the Association, having existed fifty years, must make its appeal for support and loyalty not altogether on what it is, but also upon what use it has made of past opportunities, upon public service already rendered. Third, the Association must

offer to its members, present and prospective, a program of future development, alluring in its possibilities and reasonably assured by the present condition and the past achievements of the Association.

WHAT THE ASSOCIATION IS

Essential Machinery: The American Public Health Association is an essential part of the public health machinery of the country. Upon the essential character of service which it renders, the Association, without the slightest misgivings, may rest its right to existence.

The Association is essential in the handling of the public health problem for the reason that it furnishes, and it alone furnishes, the common ground on which all of the various public health interests, both the scientific and the administrative agencies, investigators and officials, come together in a great clearing house of experience

297

and into dynamic contact with the inspiration of mass psychology.

Permanent Field: The American Public Health Association occupies a permanent field of service; permanent in that as long as time lasts it will be necessary for some agency to bring together the individual workers, separated in thought as in space, for conference, for collection and compilation of data, for reaching safe conclusions, and for adopting the best methods of work.

Program of General Interest: The American Public Health Association furnishes a program of general interest; general in that its program embraces the prevention, not of some particular disease or group of diseases, but of all preventable diseases; general in that its program embraces, not only disease prevention, but the much larger and more important field of health promotion; general in that it considers everything in the way of heredity and environment, in the way of habits and customs, that leads to disease or promotes health. The platform of the Association is, in length, breadth, and thickness, sufficient to accommodate all who are interested in human conservation.

Program of Symmetrical Growth: The Association believes in the relative values of special health problems; it has no hobbies; its ideal is an orderly, symmetrical, and closely coordinated public health program for the several branches of the Government, coupled with and supported by a broad and deep interest on the part of society in the general public health problem in all of its varied, but at the same time inseparably related, aspects.

THE PAST, OR WHAT THE ASSOCIATION
HAS DONE

Since 1872, the Association has brought together regularly every year the diverse interests and varied experiences of those engaged in the work of human conservation, and has thus provided that each individual worker should share the knowledge and the idealism of the entire membership.

To reflect upon what would have been the course of related events had some particular agency of large and general influence not existed, is perhaps the best way of approximating its contribution to progress. If the work for which the Association is to be credited had not been done, what would be the present status of public health work? Would it be the same that it is today? Would it be one, two, three, four, five, or ten years behind its present state of development? To answer these questions is to weigh the influence and the work of the Association during its existence of fifty years. It seems safe to say that had the work not been done the present development of public health work would be at least five years behind where it is, that instead of working with the resources of popular interest, men, and money, that are available today, January, 1920, we would be using our equipment of January, 1915.

In rendering the above service to the public, the Association has exercised an influence that has been a very real service to all health departments—federal, state, and local. There is not a health officer in this country, conscious or unconscious of the fact, that has not been tremendously helped in his work through the influence of the Association; there is not a laboratory for diagnostic examinations or for the preparation of biological products, not a public or private laboratory, that has not had its field of service enlarged and its work more appreciated as a result of the influence of the Association; there is not a chair of hygiene or sanitary science in the colleges and universities of this country that has not had larger classes as a result of the influence of the Association; there is not a school of sanitary engineering, there is not a sanitary engineer interested in the construction of waterworks and sewerage that has not received very large and very material assistance through the influence of the Association; there is not an industrial establishment that employs public health nurses or medical officers in industrial hygiene that is not a debtor to the Association; there is not a life insurance company in this country that is not indebted to the Asociation to the extent of thousands of dollars for added premiums and unclaimed policies. And so it is clear that both those with special interest, the technical group, and those with general interest, the public, have been for years the beneficiaries of the Association; its blessings, like the life-giving dew of Heaven, have fallen on all, the just and the unjust, the appreciative and the unappreciative.

THE FUTURE OR WHAT THE ASSOCIATION PROPOSES

The future of the Association is dependent upon one thing,—its food supply. Its staple article of diet is attention, the attention of its members. In the metabolism of its growth attention is converted into vision, the vision of what the Association is, and what it has accomplished, and of the unlimited possibilities of its future; vision is transformed into interest, the interest of its members; and interest becomes oxidized or vitalized into energy, and so the Association lives and moves and has its being. But remember this: that the starting point in the growth and the work of the Association is attention, for vision and interest and energy and life are the intermediate and end-products of its metabolism.

The Association today is hungry. As an infant cries for its milk, so it appeals for its wanted food. Give it

some. Give it ten minutes attention. The Association today weighs 4,500 members and subscribers. When it has completed its infancy, finished cutting its milk teeth, it ought to weigh 7,500 members and subscribers. By that time it will have assimilated the more easily digestible food supply, namely, those persons who have a special interest in public health work. The completion of this period should be reached by autumn, 1920. The Association by that time should have completed a healthy infancy; should be ready for weaning; should be capable of assimilating a greater variety of food; should be able to attract and interest the general public.

PARTICIPATION OF THE PUBLIC

Dr. Frederick R. Green, of the American Medical Association, has well said that the public health movement has outgrown the stage where it could be regarded as a physician's problem and likewise had developed beyond where it could be considered as the legitimate charge of the wet-nurse, philanthropy. The time is at hand when the public is no longer to be thought of as beneficiaries in the public health movement, but are to be welcomed and trusted as participants. Participants, that is the word. Why shouldn't the public participate in the councils of their own elected officers and public servants; participate in the support of a great movement that in the most fundamental way concerns their present and their future? This is the day of democracy, of popular government. We profess to believe in it; let us show our faith by our works.

The public can be interested. The National Geographic Society has demonstrated this beyond the shadow of a doubt. That Society has a membership of 630,000, and must have something like an annual income from members and advertising of not less than $3,000,000. If the intelligent people of this country can be interested and organized around a geographic idea, they can certainly be interested in a great public health program and organization.

But someone says the explanation of the National Geographic Society's size and strength is the magazine. That is exactly so, but it is easily possible to produce another magazine, devoted to health and life, as attractive and as interesting, and even more valuable than the excellent publication of the National Geographic Society. Moreover, sufficient funds to underwrite the publication of such a magazine, until the enlarged organization can be placed firmly upon its feet, are in sight, almost within touch, provided only the American Public Health Association can see its opportunity and line up solidly behind this larger idea of including the public within its membership.

Two separate public health organizations, one composed of those with special training, the teachers and the official directors of the public health movement of this country, and the other composed of the general public. is out of the question. The two groups should be combined, the technically trained group and the experts in various fields of public health work to furnish the facts and to suggest the policies, and the other to approve the policies suggested and to furnish the necessary support for their realization. The eyes and ears cannot be separated from the balanced judgment and the nerve and sinew of the social organism.

The two groups can be properly related under a carefully considered constitution and by-laws. An example of this possibility is the separation and the relation in the American Medical Association of those in charge of the scientific program, the Sections, and those in charge of the administration and the determination of the policies of the Association, the House and Delegates.

An American Public Health Association of from one hundred to three hundred or four hundred thousand members, tied together, kept in monthly touch with the organization through a splendid public health magazine; the average state with an affiliated state society of from five to thirty thousand members, and the average county or district with a society of from one hundred to one thousand members, a unit of the state society, all the people actively interested in the conservation of life, in the promotion of health, and this great problem will no longer be dependent upon the care of the physician or have to lean on artificial props of philanthropy, no longer an infant crawling and creeping, but rejoicing "like a strong man to run a race." This is the dream, the vision, and the reality. The only question is the date when the vision shall become the reality. The determination of that date rests with the members of the Association.

□

The first step is to increase the Members and Subscribers to 7,500. Your individual quota is One New Member. The A. P. H. A. does not ask more; it can't ask less. Decide whom you will invite to Membership.
Do it Now!

PROTECTIVE VALUE OF TYPHOID VACCINATION AS SHOWN BY THE EXPERIENCE OF THE AMERICAN TROOPS IN THE WAR

GEORGE A. SOPER, PH.D.,

Formerly Major, Sanitary Corps, U. S. A., New York City

Read before Section on Public Health Administration, American Public Health Association, at New Orleans, La., October 27, 1919.

It has recently been publicly argued that the Army reports demonstrate the failure of inoculation against typhoid fever. Major Soper distinctly contradicts this claim, states plainly how efficient it really was and explains some so-called failures. These were due to infection before vaccination, errors of haste in insufficient dosage or wrong counting, or worn immunity.

THE experience of the United States troops in the World War not only shows the value which attaches to typhoid vaccination, but affords a warning that this is not the only measure which should be taken to avoid typhoid and paratyphoid fevers.

That some typhoid occurred, in spite of the fact that the army was vaccinated against it, has led some to infer that vaccination proved to be a failure, whereas the opposite is the fact. When properly employed, and used in connection with other measures of prevention, vaccination was shown to be capable of affording a very large measure of protection.

It is to the unreasoning confidence which has been placed in typhoid vaccination, often to the entire exclusion of other precautions, that many of the seeming failures are attributable. But its strongest and wisest advocates do not pretend that it is a substitute for every other means of avoiding typhoid.

That typhoid did not assume any greater prevalence than it did in France, when under the stress of military necessity, all other safeguards were broken down, speaks well for this form of preventive treatment. The exposure of the troops to excremental infections was often very great. How great, may be inferred from the fact that there were times and places when 75 per cent of the men were more or less affected with intestinal diseases such, for example, as diarrhea and bacillary dysentery.

AMOUNT OF TYPHOID IN THE AMERICAN EXPEDITIONARY FORCES.

The following statistical data relating to the A. E. F., France, are taken from telegraphic reports. Although it is probable that some correction will have to be made in the figures when the final statistics are compiled from the clinical records, it is believed that the data are, in the main, reliable.

For the 101 weeks from October 18, 1917, to September 25, 1919, there were 1,529 cases of typhoid and 303 cases of paratyphoid, with 169 deaths. The average number of our troops which were in France during this period was 858,238. But, as will be explained presently, this average strength does not properly indicate the number of men from which the cases were derived, being much too small.

Of the 1,529 cases, 1,390 occurred within a period of about 9 months. That is, over 90 per cent appeared between July 25, 1918, and May 2, 1919. There were but 47 before this time, and 92 in the 5 months following.

The disease was not, therefore, evenly distributed in point of time. It was at first sporadic and then epidemic. Nine-tenths of the cases appeared during the epidemic period. During this period the number of our troops in France constantly increased. At the beginning of the epidemic the strength was 1,164,264 and at the end, 1,935,000. On the day when the greatest number of cases occurred the strength was 1,741,177. To say that the cases were derived from the average number of our troops in France during practically the whole expeditionary period is erroneous and gives an exaggerated idea of the typhoid rate. Nor is it fair to refer all the cases in the epidemic to the average number of troops during that time, for the beginning of the conditions which brought about the epidemic long antedated that period.

As to location, the epidemic was not confined to any limited area. Unlike most outbreaks in civil life, it was not due to any single water supply or other common source of infection. There were many sources. There were many outbreaks of small extent, and it was the aggregate of the cases in all of these outbreaks which made up the total count.

The epidemic was less conspicuously associated with place and season than with what may be termed the mode of life of the soldier. Among so many men it was inevitable that some should be potential foci and it was the mode of life which permitted some of these foci to become active. Thousands of young men of an age which is peculiarly susceptible to typhoid were compelled to live under conditions wherein no precautions were, or could be taken, to insure a rigid separation of their food and excrement. Under such circumstances frequent contamination of water and food with excremental virus was to be expected. The result was that all who could contract disease in this manner were attacked.

WHY THE EPIDEMIC GAINED HEADWAY.

It is easy to understand how the epidemic, once started, gained headway. Typhoid was not expected, and when it appeared it was not always recognized. Probably no disease more often fails of recognition in its early stages in civil life, and there the conditions are much more favorable for its diagnosis than they were among our fighting army in France. Among the sick and wounded there occurred many cases of typhoid before the nature of the disease was suspected. These cases increased the number of foci from which other cases sprung. The distribution of the disease was increased by reason of the fact that many of the infected men were sent from the front to more or less distant places for treatment.

It is almost always thus with outbreaks of contagious diseases. One case, or a few cases, if promptly recognized and properly cared for, are not particularly dangerous. But if a number of cases occur and remain undetected for some time, they lead to other cases and these to others in rapidly increasing ratio. Finally the infection becomes so general that it cannot be controlled and something like a conflagration follows.

The value of sanitation plus vaccination in protecting soldiers against typhoid and paratyphoid is shown in a way by the record of our troops in the United States during the war, although the exact measure of this benefit is obscured by a number of factors. It appears that some of the men were in a fair way to become sick when they entered the army; opportunities for infection were by no means absent in some of the cities and towns to which the soldiers resorted when on leave.

Much less typhoid occurred among the troops in the United States than among those in France. For the 108 weeks from September 1, 1917, to September 25, 1919, there were 466 cases of typhoid and 45 cases of paratyphoid, with 54 deaths. A considerable part of these cases appeared, before the three doses of vaccine were all given, and under circumstances which pointed to the infection of the men before they reached camp. The average number of troops for the period stated has been given as 967,591.

For the year 1918 there were 240 cases of typhoid in the army in the United States, the average strength of which was 1,381,429.

These strengths do not represent the total number of troops from which the typhoid cases were derived, for about three million men passed through the camps in the course of a year.

It is believed to have been due both to vaccination and sanitation that there was so little typhoid among our troops when they were mobilized on the Mexican Border in 1916. The custom at that time was to vaccinate against typhoid only, while in the World War the vaccination was against paratyphoid A and B as well. Between May 1, and October 18, 1916, there were but 24 cases of typhoid, whereas more than ten times that number of paratyphoid cases occurred. There is no reason to suppose that the virus of typhoid did not exist to a greater extent than did the virus of paratyphoid, for among any large number of people this is almost invariably so. But the virus of typhoid did not lead to a general infection as it did in France apparently because the men lived under less insanitary conditions on the Border and the medical officers were more alive to the possibility of its appearance.

It is interesting to compare the records of our troops on the Mexican Border and in the World War with our army experience in the Spanish War of 1898, before typhoid vaccination was introduced. In the Spanish War there were 20,926 cases of typhoid and paratyphoid with 2,192 deaths among 147,795 troops in about 8 months. During the following year there were 2,184 cases and 258 deaths among 105,260 regular and volunteer troops. In 1900 there were 978

cases and 164 deaths among 100,389 troops. It was in 1911-12 that antityphoid vaccination became general in the army.

REASON FOR SEEMING AND REAL FAILURES
IN VACCINATION.

There are various reasons why vaccination sometimes seems to fail, and there are reasons why it does fail, occasionally.

There have been instances in which the patient has fallen ill before the three doses of vaccine has been administered, infection having taken place beforehand.

In some cases the correct details of procedure have not all been complied with. In the haste which accompanied the mobilization of our army, in view of the great number of men to receive treatment, and considering the untrained personnel which was available to administer it, it is likely that mistakes now and then occurred. That something less than the standard dosage was sometimes given to the soldiers and that occasionally the records indicated that all three doses had been given to men who had, in reality, received only a part, or none at all, of their vaccination, are facts which must not be overlooked.

In considering the apparent failures of vaccination to protect, due allowance should be made for these exceptions. How often such mistakes were made is not known with certainty—it will always remain a matter of opinion.

Apparent failures of vaccination in civil life sometimes are attributable to the fact that the immunity conferred has worn off with the passage of time. In the United States Army the custom is to revaccinate every three years; but among civilians it is doubtful if the treatment is always so thorough or so rigorously repeated. Cases of outworn immunity should not be charged against preventive inoculation.

Some instances of failure in civil life are doubtless chargeable to imperfect vaccine and faulty technic of administration. Unfortunately, preventive inoculation is not so generally employed that every doctor possesses the degree of knowledge and skill necessary to administer it. But when all is said and done to excuse the failure of vaccination to protect, there remain a certain proportion of cases unaccounted for. In the army in the World War there were many soldiers who appear to have been vaccinated according to the best technic and who, nevertheless, were attacked within a year of two by typhoid or paratyphoid fevers. These need to be explained.

They can be explained on two hypotheses: either the prophylactic treatment did not render everyone who took it equally immune to ordinary doses of the virus, or those who were attacked were the victims of unusually large, and perhaps fresh, doses of the bacilli.

Most of the cases are believed by the regular army surgeons to have been due to "massive infection." They were instances in which such overwhelming doses of the virus were taken as to overcome the protection which had been conferred. It is needless to discuss this phenomenon here. Something like it happens now and then in smallpox and other infections. It appears to be a fact that very large doses, or perhaps very fresh ones, when taken singly or repeated, will produce typhoid in some persons who have been properly vaccinated or are believed to possess immunity by reason of having already had an attack of the disease.

Vaccination is not an infallible procedure. The idea is too prevalent among persons who have been vaccinated that they are completely and permanently immune and consequently need take no other precaution against it. This is an unwarranted supposition and one which is combatted by the Army Medical Department. The most recent pronouncement upon this point is contained in Special Regulations No. 28, War Department, Washington, March 11, 1919, as follows:

"The triple typhoid inoculation confers a high degree of protection against typhoid and paratyphoid fevers, but it does not give absolute protection against massive infection with the causative organisms. The use of the triple inoculation has enormously reduced the incidence of enteric fever in armies, but it does not warrant neglect of the other well-known sanitary precautions against the diseases. One of the most ready means of causing massive infection with typhoid and paratyphoid organisms is through the agency of a carrier employed in the handling of food."

TYPHOID NOT ASSOCIATED WITH THE IN-
SANITARY CONDITIONS OF BATTLE
FIELDS.

It would be of value to know whether it was "massive infection," incomplete immunity, or some other cause which produced typhoid outbreaks in the army which were not associated with the insanitary conditions of battle fields.

In an epidemic described by Hawn, Hopkins and Meader,[1] the first case appeared when the company left Camp Cody. Other cases occurred in a straggling way until the main outburst took place in a rest camp in England. By the time the organization left this camp there had been 38 cases. Later, there were more; so that, in a strength of 248 men there were 98 cases in all. All the men seem to have been vaccinated, save one. The cause of the typhoid was not definitely ascertained.

Four cases among 175 vaccinated men were described by Bradbury[2] as having occurred in the last three weeks of November, 1918, in the Eleventh Engineers, in France. The source was not found, but was assumed to have been a carrier in the kitchen.

Twelve cases were reported by Brown, Palfrey and Hart[3], at Camp Greene, in the United States. Nine were in a single organization. Investigation showed

[1] An Outbreak of Typhoid among American Troops in England; C. B. Hawn, J. D. Hopkins and F. M. Meader: Jour. A. M. A., Feb. 8, 1919, p. 402.

[2] Typhoid in a Company of Immunized Soldiers; Samuel Bradbury: Jour. A. M. A., Aug. 17, 1918, p. 582.

[3] Typhoid Fever Occurring after Prophylactic Inoculation; Claude P. Brown, Francis W. Palfrey and Leonard Hart: Jour. A. M. A., Feb. 15, 1919, p. 463.

that all the men had had the prophylactic treatment at various camps at proper intervals and within a year of their attack. The cases occurred coincidently with a mild epidemic in the neighboring city of Charlotte. The cause of the typhoid among the soldiers was not ascertained, but it was supposed to be due to "massive infection."

A careful review of the reports indicates that the type of infection which occurs by contact is the one most often associated with these outbreaks. The type is sporadic not explosive. Whether the infection be called "massive" or known by some other and more inclusive term, there seems to be something about crowding or close personal contact, which is particularly dangerous. It was a feature in connection with most, if not all, of the cases referred to in the three accounts just cited. It would not be surprising to learn that it was a no less prominent feature among the much greater number of cases in France. Apparently we are dealing here with contact infection, pure and simple. It may be well that it is less the massiveness of the dose than the relatively short direct route by which the virus passes from those who produce it to others that constitutes the danger.

☐

IMPORTANCE OF CONFIRMATORY B. COLI TESTS IN FAIRLY SAFE DRINKING WATER

N. NOVICK,

Bacteriologist, U. S. P. H. S. Hospital, East Norfolk, Mass.

During the latter part of 1918 the writer was sent by the Bureau of Sanitary Service of the American Red Cross to assume the duties of bacteriologist of Sanitary Unit No. 33, stationed in Charleston, S. C., and working under the supervision of the U. S. P. H. S. The various health activities conducted by this organization were those generally known as Extra-Cantonment Zone sanitation. Since the protection of the uniformed men of the army and navy around the military posts was the chief object of the Extra-Cantonment activities, the safeguarding of the city water supply was, therefore, to be an important duty of the bacteriologist. Furthermore, the town being "dry," a considerable amount of so-called "soft drink" was being consumed. This appeared to bring in another factor which called for a careful watch on the supply of water used for drinking purposes.

The present paper has for its object the purpose of revealing some data bearing upon the value which may be derived from confirmatory *B. coli* tests if properly conducted in the routine examination of presumably good water.

Shortly after my arrival, it was found upon investigation that while the city water was examined daily by a local authority, the work was apparently conducted without sufficient regard for bacteriological standards, and seemingly no attempt was made to confirm the results to any extent.

Accordingly, on November 21, 1918, an examination of the water was made by the writer, with the following results: Sample city water (Goose Çreek), bacteria per cc. 24 hours, 37° C. 210; 9 acid colonies on lactose-litmus agar plates, 1 cc. portion. Lactose bile fermentation tube showed more than 10 per cent gas in 2 cc. portion. A complete confirmatory test was immediately made and the organism isolated was identified as a member of the colon group. (Group 4, MacConkey.)

For the reason stated above, no data bearing upon the previous examination of the water supply were available for deductive comparison. A sanitary survey of the stream, from which practically the entire population of the city (there are some artesian wells in addition to the main supply) obtains its drinking water, seemed to bear favorably upon the sanitary quality of the water. Furthermore, during the time in question and in months previous, the city had suffered a scarcity of rainfall to such an extent that the level of the stream supplying drinking water had fallen to more than 3 inches below normal observations. The Water Works Commission requested the city, through the local daily press, to conserve water, and finally water was to be had only during certain hours of the day. It occurred to the writer that the supplying stream had apparently lost its normal diluting capacity which would probably account for a rather high bacterial count disregarding the apparently good sanitary condition of the source. However, a report of a water as cited above was open to suspicion. This report slightly alarmed the authorities, and corrections at the chlorination plant were made in due time.

During the subsequent months a regular and frequent e x a m i n a t i o n (almost every day), of the water was instituted, the results of which are recorded in the accompanying table. Unfortunately other bacteriological duties arose, and more frequent examinations

could not be made. Limited as the number of examinations was, the accompanying table shows that 75 to 100 per cent correct presumptives were o b t a i n e d, although the bacterial count ran low and the quality of the water from the sanitary point of view had been assumed as good.

While the presence of members of the colon group carries the thought of possible pollution, the search for specific pathogens is never lost sight of by workers in the field of sanitary bacteriology. Recent literature* contains reports which would seem to indicate that properly conducted confirmatory tests are valuable and always called for in routine examinations.

The method of examination used during this work was that recommended by the Committee on Standard Methods of Water Analysis of the American Public Health Association (Standard Methods, 1917). Lactose bile in fermentation tubes, although not recommended in Standard Methods was used for a short time, but was later abandoned as it was not deemed necessary to use that medium which is, primarily, to block out non-colon species, for the water in question did not show an unusual bacterial count afterwards. Lactose broth was substituted. Lactose litmus agar in duplicate was used for direct plating along with the plain agar in order to gain tentative information as to the quality of the water in 1 cc. portions, and also to serve as a check on the fermentation tube receiving a similar portion. Gas

*E. M. Myer, Jour. Bact., Vol. 3, No. 1.
C. L. Ewing, Am. Jour. Pub. Health, Vol. 4, No. 4.

Period 1919	Number waters examined	Average bacteria per cc. 24 hrs. 37° C.	Highest count	Lowest count	Presumptive pos. tests	Confirmatory pos. tests	Percent correct presumptives	Percent pos. B. Coli	Direct plating lactose litmus agar 1 cc.	Number times abrog. found	Extent possible pollution
Jan.	11	39	100	9	7	4	57	36	—*	3	1 cc. portion
Feb.	12	15	28	6	4	4	100	33	—	1	1 cc.-5 cc. portions
Mar.	12	15	24	6	3	2	66	16	—	0	5 cc. portion
Apr.	8	19	48	5	1	0	0	0	—	0	5 cc. portion
May	14	15	42	6	4	3	75	21	—	1	5 cc. portion
Total	57	......	......	......	19	13	Total %	22.8		5	

*—=No acid colonies present.

production was waited for not longer than 48 hours: .1, 1, 5, and 10 cc. portions were tested as a routine procedure; the smaller portions being inoculated into Smith fermentation tubes filled to the usual level, and the larger, into large test tubes holding an inverted vial and containing about 30 cc. of the broth, so as not to reduce the nutritive constituents of the medium, and particularly in order to conform to the Standard Methods. The medium was controlled both as to its sterility and its ability to produce changes, should the colon organism be present in the sample under test, the former by being incubated for 24 hours and the latter by receiving a broth culture of a known colon strain. For confirmatory tests, two loopfuls from the smallest portion of the water showing more than 10 per cent gas, were diluted in 10 cc. sterile water or saline solution, from which one loopful was pour-plated in lactose litimus agar at 45°C., and incubated for 24 hours at 37°C. The writer has always obtained a fairly good colony distribution in this manner, when the plates were found to be positive, several colonies of ovate form were shown surrounded by a light acid zone (colon group), which could not be missed when the plate was held at the proper angle to the light. The typical or semi-typical colonies were further tested in lactose broth fermentation tubes. Morphology and staining were determined from agar slant. A straight wire dipping from the same colony was also stabbed into a lactose litmus agar tube holding about 12 cc. of the medium, to note whether disintegration due to gas production was violent or not. This is a point of some importance. The strains which were isolated during this work were found not to break up the media severely,— a characteristic attributed to true colon strains.

B. lactis aërogenes was isolated several times, occurring in almost pure culture,

the significance of which could hardly be determined; in view of the fact that the number of waters examined was, indeed, limited and the time of my stay rather short. The organism was differentiated by its mucoid consistency of colony, strong acid production in lactose, yeast-like odor, absence of dye absorption which reduces the metallic lustre of the colony on Endo plate, and finally by its inability to break up dulcite and positive Voges-Proskauer reaction.

It seems that this portion of the southeastern section of the United States may claim this organism frequently in its water.

Summary: Fifty-seven waters from a fairly safe source from the sanitary point of view have been tested as a routine procedure for the presence of B. Coli. 22.8 per cent positive tests have been obtained during a period of five months. A study of the table will show that while the average bacterial count has been quite low, as low as would be desired in a good water, the presence of the bacillus of the colon group has been detected not too infrequently. While any conclusion to be drawn from such a number of waters could hardly seem justified, it is evident, however, that the chlorination plant of the supply in question should be controlled and supervised by proper routine bacteriological examinations.

It is also suggested that such routine procedure of the water examination should constitute one of the features of the municipal laboratory. Records of such examinations on proper forms should be kept in a systematic way for study and reference.

NOTE. The writer desires to express his sincere thanks to Dr. G. McF. Mood, City Bacteriologist of Charleston, S. C., for his kind coöperation and assistance in placing the laboratory facilities at his disposal.

BACTERIOLOGICAL EXAMINATION OF SOFT DRINKS

WILLIAM ROYAL STOKES, M. D., Sc. D.,

Bureau of Bacteriology of State and City Departments of Health, Baltimore, Md.

Read before Laboratory Section, American Public Health Association, at New Orleans, La., October 30, 1919.

Prohibition has boomed soft drinks so that more than ever there is need of rigid inspection. Dr. Stokes finds beverages with five-figure counts and empty "sterile" bottles always with some bacteria, sometimes with millions. This paper should attract the attention of health officers to their soft drink problems.

THE recent search for that evasive substance known as a ptomain has emphasized the fact that most of the cases of so-called ptomain poisoning are either due to bacterial infection or to such other causes as oxalic acid poisoning, over-eating, tartar emetic poisoning, acute and chronic nephritis and other similar conditions, as shown by the work of Rosenau* and his assistants.

These bacterial infections are usually produced by various members of the intermediate or hog cholera group such as the Alpha and Beta paratyphoid bacillus and *B. enteritidis*. *Proteus vulgaris*, an intestinal organism, can also produce intestinal disturbances, and all of these infections are due to the increase of the organisms in the intestine and definite infection at times accompanied by bacteremia with the presence of the organisms in the blood.

B. coli, a normal inhabitant of the intestine, seems to produce certain poisons in the foods before they are eaten, and the *B. botulinus*, a deadly anaërobic organism, also produces its soluble toxin in sausages, meat puddings and canned corn products when these materials have been subjected to inefficient sterilization. These two latter organisms do not produce direct infection by increase in the intestine but produce their poisonous products of metabolism in the food. When the food is consumed the poisons produce serious and even fatal intestinal diseases.

Owing to these facts the State Department of Health through Dr. Frederick C. Blanck, State Food and Drug Commissioner, instituted an examination of the various soft drinks which are being sold throughout the state. Many of these drinks were sold in large quantities at the various cantonments during the war, and this suggested an additional reason for their careful supervision. A great many of these drinks contain the various carbohydrates, and it is well known that the intestinal organisms develop favorably in such media, even splitting up the sugars into various gases and minute traces of alcohol.

Allen, LaBach, Pinnell and Brown,** of the Kentucky Agricultural Experiment Station, made a thorough investigation of the bacteriological condition of the various non-alcoholic, carbon-

*Med. Clinic of North America, Vol. 2, p. 1541.   **Bull. No. 192, June, 1915.

ated beverages sold in Kentucky. They also made a number of examinations of various materials involved in the processes of production. Their article contains a complete tabulated report upon a large number of examinations of these beverages as well as the city or filtered water used in the manufacture of the beverages, the rinse water used for the bottles, the water from caps, old caps, and the supposedly clean or sterile empty bottles before filling. The city waters examined showed counts ranging from 100,000 to 300,000 bacteria per cubic centimeter, the filtered water from 120,000 to 700,000 per c.c., the water used for rinsing bottles from 180,000 to 960,000 per c.c., the water off caps (one examination) 750,-000 per c.c. old caps (one examination) 165,000 per c.c., and the clean or sterile empty bottles from 1,900 to 310,000 bacteria per c.c. The various beverages showed counts ranging from 10,-000 to 850,000 bacteria per c.c.

Although the water used for manufacture very often showed a high bacterial count yet the products often showed very low bacterial counts, and they accounted for this result by the destructive or inhibitory effect of carbodioxide upon bacteria.

The unfiltered water contained a maximum B. coli count of 5,190 and a minimum of 0; the filtered water contained no colon bacilli. The rinse water showed a maximum of 106 and a minimum of 0; the empty bottles had a maximum of 1,440 and a minimum of 0 and the beverages showed a maximum B. coli count of 450 and a minimum of 0.

They believe that the bottles should be cleaned of all possible dirt by the proper kind of bottle washer and then sterilized with live steam for from 30 to 40 minutes, and the bottler should guard against any possible recontamination brought about by cooling with contaminated water. If filtered water be used the filter should be frequently examined in order to see that a pure filtrate is obtained, and it goes without saying that the water used should be free from colon bacilli and with a low bacterial count.

Our investigation is explained in detail in the following tables, the object of this investigation being to determine the number of bacteria present in the samples and to see whether any of these goods contained intestinal organisms. No special search was made for organisms other than the colon bacillus, the normal inhabitant of the intestine, but the presence of this organism in the fluids certainly suggests danger from the other pathogenic intestinal bacteria. The results which were obtained are set forth in detail in tables 1 and 2.

I am indebted to Mr. S. Caskey for much assistance in the routine examination of the above products named below. (See next page.)

CONSIDERATION OF RESULTS OBTAINED.

An examination of table No. 1 will show that in a number of instances the maximum count of these soft drink products was innumerable whilst other maximum counts show results of five figures. A large number of the samples also showed the presence of sugar-splitting or fermentative bacteria, as shown by positive presumptive tests in 10 cubic centimeters, 1 cubic centimeter and even 1/10 of a cubic centimeter. In the final attempt to isolate the colon bacillus, as expressed by the final test, it can be seen that we were often unable to isolate this organism, but the fermentation may have been produced by yeasts, the lactose splitting aërobic spore-bearing organisms recently isolated from water, the anaërobic spore-bearing organisms, or other aërobic gas producing bacteria. In many instances we were unable to obtain any colonies from the plates examined, but no special attempt was made to isolate other organisms besides the colon bacillus.

We tested out a number of empty bottles for sterility and found a maximum count of innumerable and a minimum count of 500 bacteria per bottle.

Colon bacilli were isolated in a number of samples even in as small a quantity as 1/10 of a cubic centimeter. This is an interesting point, since it may be that improperly sterilized bottles are often a cause of the bacterial contamination of the soft drinks, and we

TABLE No. 1

TABLE OF SOFT DRINKS SHOWING BACTERIAL COUNTS AND COLON TESTS

Flavor	Bacterial Count 37°		No. Exam.	Colon Examinations Presumptive Test			Final Test		
	Max.	Min.		10 cc.	1 cc.	0.1 cc.	10 cc.	1 cc.	0.1 cc.
Ginger Ale	In.*	0	92	43	22	1	17	8	0
Lemon	In.	0	83	41	13	0	10	4	0
Sarsaparilla	In.	0	83	40	26	4	16	14	3
Orange	2,800	0	42	19	11	3	4	2	0
Strawberry	In.	0	44	24	17	5	12	8	3
Root Beer	350	0	14	3	2	0	2	2	0
Birch Beer	20,000	0	7	3	3	1	0	0	0
Vanilla Soda	450	5	6	4	2	0	2	2	0
Chocolate	In.	0	10	3	3	0	0	0	0
Grape	38	0	8	3	3	0	0	0	0
Coca Cola	600	3	6	4	2	0	0	0	0
Champagne	275	0	8	2	2	2	0	2	2
Raspberry	3,200	20	6	4	0	0	1	3	0
Miscellaneous	38,000	0	47	8	5	0	4	3	0

EMPTY BOTTLES FOR STERILITY

	Per Bottle								
Bottles	In.	500	26	17	12	8	15	12	8

*In. indicates Innumerable.

TABLE No. 2

TABLE OF SOFT DRINKS SHOWING NUMBER OF BACTERIAL COUNTS ACCORDING TO GROUPS

	0	1-50	51-100	101-250	251-500	501-1000	1001-5000	50001-10000	10001-20000	20001-50000	Innumerable
Ginger Ale	8	54	7	4	4	4	8	1	0	0	2
Lemon	10	47	5	4	2	4	10	0	0	0	1
Sarsaparilla	10	26	12	3	2	0	8	5	0	0	5
Orange	10	23	3	2	2	0	2	0	0	0	0
Strawberry	6	23	5	1	1	0	3	3	0	0	2
Root Beer	5	7	0	0	1	0	0	0	0	0	0
Birch Beer	2	2	0	0	0	0	0	1	1	1	0
Vanilla	0	2	0	1	1	0	0	0	0	0	0
Chocolate	3	2	0	1	0	0	1	0	0	0	3
Grape	2	6	0	0	0	0	0	0	0	0	0
Coca Cola	0	4	0	0	0	1	0	0	0	0	0
Champagne	2	3	0	1	1	0	0	0	0	0	0
Raspberry	0	0	0	3	0	0	1	0	0	0	0
Miscellaneous	15	17	6	5	2	0	1	0	0	1	0

EMPTY BOTTLES FOR STERILITY

Bacterial Count Per Bottle

	1-500	501-1000	1,001-50,000	50,001-1000,000	100,001-250,000	250,001-500,000	500,001-1 mil.	1 m.-5 m.	5 m.-20 m.	In.*
Bottles	1	1	2	1	2	2	5	3	2	2

*In. indicates Innumerable.

usually found a small amount of fluid in the bottom of the bottles. Even a few bacteria remaining after sterilization might increase in this fluid and thus produce the high bacterial counts often obtained from the washings from the bottles. These bottles were washed out with 100 cubic centimeters of sterile water and the dilutions were made from such an amount.

An examination of table No 2 will show the bacterial counts arranged according to groups between certain fixed limits. A certain number of the soft drinks tested, therefore, showed no bacteria present; others showed bacteria varying between a count of 1 to 50, and these groups are continued to as high a limit as from 20,000 to 50,000. A few of the plates showed innumerable colonies and could not therefore be estimated.

An examination of the bacterial counts for sterility shows that some of the bottles contained millions of bacteria per bottle, and, as mentioned before, this is probably explained by the great increase which may take place in the small amount of water often left in the bottle after sterilization.

CONCLUSIONS

1. Many soft drinks contain variable numbers of bacteria and this large bacterial content may be partially explained by the improper sterilization of bottles.

2. A few bacteria remaining in the bottles may increase in the small quantity of water often left in the bottles after sterilization. Dust organisms getting into the bottles may also resist sterilization even if the bottles are properly dried.

This matter may be of some importance in relation to the possibility of intestinal infection, since the organisms which produce so-called food poisoning often find a favorable culture medium in the carbo-hydrates of these soft drinks.

□

Poland 200 Years Behind in Therapy.— The native doctors in Poland are using the drawing of blood for their principal curative method, just as was the custom generally a couple of hundred years ago. In just the same way these doctors usually combine the profession of the barber with that of "leech," just as in the olden time, and indeed the striped barber's pole is merely a sign of the blood-letting capacity of this artificer when the sign was invented. And just as these men applied leeches for the purpose, whereby the name of the worm became a synonym for the practicer of medicine, so their modern disciples in Poland have been in the habit of using the leech. If the man got well the barber-doctor had made a miraculous cure; if he died, it was but the will of God.

Recently this ancient system of practice has been violently overthrown. American Red Cross doctors and nurses came into the district and found typhus and many other diseases flourishing, with no medical attention except that which the barber could bestow. An American hospital with all modern medicines and equipment was installed and the barbers soon lost the medical and surgical end of their practice. Their aid was enlisted, however, in closely shaving be-whiskered men and clipping short the hair of those who were infested with vermin. Just now, after weeks of strenuous medical campaigning, headway is being made against the disease which the barbers' leeches had so long failed to cure. Leech-craft has gone out of Poland.

TREATMENT OF BEET SUGAR PLANT SEWAGE

LANGDON PEARSE AND SAMUEL A. GREELEY,

Chicago, Ill.

Read before Sanitary Engineering Section, American Public Health Association, at New Orleans, La., October 28, 1919.

Beet sugar is an industry yearly attaining greater and greater importance. Likewise the disposal of the wastes is a problem of increasing consequence in various sections of the country. This paper and the discussions constitute an unusual assembling of the facts, valuable to local authorities and those commercially interested, alike.

1. INDUSTRIAL SEWAGE PROBLEM.

THE treatment or disposal of industrial sewages is constantly assuming greater importance in this country. The location of industries is determined, among other factors, by the proximity of raw materials and the availability of transportation. Plant locations have quite generally been determined from these factors rather than on the disposal of the sewage. In some instances, an ample supply of water is an important element. Thus, industries which require large amounts of water and which in turn produce considerable volumes of sewage are frequently located close to rivers or streams. In many instances, particularly in the middle west, the streams at certain seasons of the year do not have sufficient flow to carry away without nuisance the sewage discharged into them from the manufacturing processes. As the population adjacent to rivers increases and as sanitary standards develop, public attention is directed toward the prevention of stream pollution, and thus to the treatment of industrial sewage. In this way, problems of sewage treatment, not contemplated in the original design of a manufacturing plant, have been forced to the attention of the plant managers.

2. THE BEET SUGAR PLANT INDUSTRY.

The manufacture of sugar from beets is an industry firmly established in this country, particularly throughout the Mississippi Valley. In 1917 there were, all told, about 96 beet sugar plants in this country, which handled 5,919,673 tons of beets with a production of sugar of 820,657 tons. A production of beet sugar in this country in 1901 of 184,606 tons had increased in 1917 to 820,657 tons. In 1917 the total acreage planted to beets was 865,308.

The process of making the sugar from beets is quite complicated, a diagrammatic outline of it being shown in Figure *1*. The beets are delivered from freight cars and teams into large storage bins, from which they are generally carried by water in flumes to the plant. The flow of water is in sufficient quantity to carry the beets through proper devices so that beet tops, earth and dirt are washed away. The clean beets are then cut into cossettes, which are carried by conveyors through the various plant processes. It is roughly estimated that from 100 tons of beets handled, the following approximate quantities are produced: Dry pulp, 5 tons; sand, dirt, grit, etc., 3 to 4 tons; sugar, 12.5 to 13 tons; and water, 70 tons. The loss due to improper cutting and topping is 3 to 4 tons.

3. SOURCES OF SEWAGE.

The principal sources of sewage in a beet sugar plant are the following:

a. The wastes from the flumes and beet washing processes which contain earthy materials mixed with beet roots and tops.

b. Water used in flushing out the diffusion cells. This is found to amount to about 110 per cent by weight of the beets sliced. This waste contains from 0.1 to 0.5 per cent of sugar in solution in addition to other organic compounds from the beet cells.

c. Press water from the pulp presses. This is stated to amount to about 67 per cent by weight of the beets sliced.

d. Waste water used in washing the filter presses which carries away the press cake to the sewers. This waste contains the precipitated calcium carbonate ($Ca\ Co_3$) which is estimated at 50 tons of dry matter per 24 hours per 1,000 tons of beets.

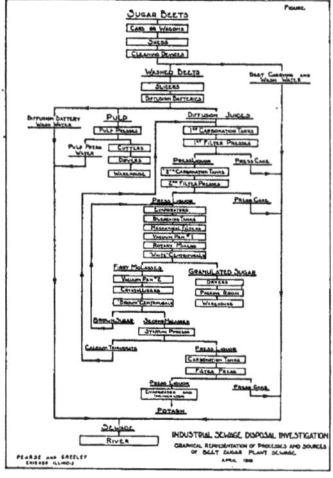

e. Water from the condensers which is used in the flumes for carrying the beets.

The beet carrying and washing waters are the largest by volume, but contain the least amount of organic matter. They contain a great amount of inor-

ganic, earthy material, which varies largely from day to day, ranging from 2 to 20 per cent by weight of the beets. The sewages which are strongest in organic matter are those from the diffusion batteries and the pulp presses, and waste containing the press cake.

4. QUANTITY OF SEWAGE.

The quantity of sewage from these various sources varies considerably from day to day, but bears an approximate relation to the quantity of beets sliced. The hourly variation is quite marked, ranging from 50 to 150 per cent of the average.

A summary of the total sewage from several beet sugar plants is given in Table *I*.

TABLE 1

THE TREATMENT OF BEET SUGAR PLANT SEWAGE—QUANTITY OF TOTAL SEWAGE

Plant	Gallons per 24 hours per 1000 tons of beets sliced
Holland-St. Louis Sugar Co.	
Holland, Mich., 1918..............	3,340,000
Decatur, Ind., 1917..............	3,640,000
1918..............	3,250,000
Caro, Michigan......................	4,070,000

5. CHARACTERISTICS OF THE SEWAGE.

The sewage from a beet sugar plant may be divided for study purposes into two classes, (1) the wastes from the diffusion batteries and pulp presses, and (2) the wastes from all other sources. The first class are the stronger in organic matter and the smaller in volume. The term "crude sewage" as used in this paper refers to the mixed sewage from the diffusion batteries and pulp presses. In appearance it is gray in color with a sweet musty odor, similar to that of cooked beets. It is distinctly turbid, containing bits of beet pulp. A summary of the analyses of this sewage compared with other industrial sewages is given in Table *2*.

Several special characteristics of beet sugar plant sewage appear from the data in Table *2*. The oxygen consumed is comparatively high, whereas the total organic nitrogen is low. Of a very large content of total solids (6,112 p. p. m.) only 974 p. p. m. appear as suspended matter. Thus a very large proportion of the organic matter is in solution. In addition, the sewage is strongly acid. The sewage most nearly resembling beet sugar plant sewage is that from a starch factory.

6. REVIEW OF EXPERIENCE.

The beet sugar plants are located mostly in the United States and throughout the north central part of Europe. Thus the principal source of information relative to the sewage treatment problem is found in German and American literature, with some references in the French technical journals.

During the winter of 1910, T. S. Ainge, of the Michigan State Board of Health, made a special trip through Germany to investigate treatment of beet sugar plant sewage. He summarized the situation in Germany as follows:

"A general plan for the sanitary disposal of the liquid wastes from beet sugar factories has not been worked out in Germany.

"Some years ago, Herr Von Boettcher, Ober-President of the Province of Saxony, tried to govern the disposal of the wastes from beet sugar factories by means of general regulations but found the plan impracticable.

"While some of the settling basins and other places into and through which the liquid wastes from the beet sugar factories flow, smell quite badly at times, very few complaints are received and that, in dealing with such complaints, owing to the importance of the industry, the Government officials act with the utmost conservatism so as not to unduly hamper the industry.

"Sugar factory owners are not permitted to allow the beet pulp to accumulate upon their premises, and must dry or remove the same, or arrange for its removal, as fast as it is produced. This rule is rigidly enforced."

The authors' search through German literature does not reveal anything more conclusive as having developed during the few years following 1910. At some of the plants where fresh water is scarce, the wastes are retained in large settling tanks and used repeatedly in the plant processes. At other plants, the sewage is first settled in large ponds and then treated on underdrained fields. At one plant the crude sewage from the diffusion batteries and pulp presses is treated in large settling tanks with lime, the effluent being further treated in underdrained fields. At Schofstadt, the sewage from 660 tons of beets per 24 hours is treated in this way, the area of the field being 12.6 acres.

Calmette, Director of the Pasteur Institute, Lille, France, states that if the diffusion battery sewage is diluted with about an equal volume of beet-carrying water, and then screened and settled, it can be treated on sprinkling filters at the rate of 1.07 million gallons per 24 hours, and a non-putrescible effluent produced. The writers' experience indicates that dilution with the beet carrying water is very helpful, as suggested here. In the United States the principal development has been at the sugar plants in the use of settling ponds.

7. CARO, MICHIGAN, DATA.

An opportunity to inspect the sewage treatment plant of the beet sugar factory at Caro, Mich., was afforded the writers by Frank Sielands, superintendent. This plant was first built in 1911 and has been subsequently enlarged from time to time. A general plan is shown in Fig. 2. There are 3 settling ponds.

The sewage flows through the settling ponds and thence onto underdrained sandy areas totaling 16.2 acres. The first installation of sand filter units covered only 8.9 acres which was found to be very much too small so that the soil clogged. The second filter of 7.4 acres was then added.

The total sewage flow is estimated at 3.25 million gallons per 24 hours. On this basis the displacement period in the three settling ponds at 2.0 feet liquid depth is about 3 days and 15 hours. The rate on the first sand filter built is about 365,000 gallons per acre per day. The net rate on both sand filters together is about 200,000 gallons per acre per day. This rate is stated to give a satisfactory effluent.

8. TESTING STATION.

The problem of sewage treatment being active at the Decatur plant of the Holland-St. Louis Sugar Co., it was concluded that sufficient information was not available for the design of a plant, and as no local sandy areas were available it was decided to build a testing station, Fig. 3, to study out other methods of treatment. The tests were run on crude sewage from the diffusion batteries and pulp presses. The testing station included the following apparatus:

a. A small cylindrical screen 2 feet in diameter and 4 feet long, supporting a fine screen with 30 meshes per lineal inch. Water was sprayed from a perforated pipe on to the outside of the screen near the top. The screen was operated at 8 r. p. m. The screenings were removed by a screw conveyor inside.

b. Two settling tanks were built, each of 2-inch staves, 10 feet long and 8 feet in diameter. The bottoms were formed inside with lean concrete to a 45 degree

slope. The sewage entered at the center at a level with the top of the hopper bottom and flowed upward and outward to a gutter around the circumference of the tank. The capacity of each sludge compartment was 450 gallons.

c. There were 2 sludge beds, each 7x4 feet. These were underdrained and contained 6 to 9 inches of graded gravel, on which was placed 3 inches of medium sand.

d. An apparatus was provided for adding milk of lime and there was a wooden mixing box 9.5x4 feet, containing 6 channels, through which the screened sewage and lime flowed at a rapid velocity.

e. There were two sprinkling filters, each of 2-inch staves, 10 feet long and 13 feet outside diameter. On top of an underdrain system was placed 7.5 feet of broken stone, ranging in size from 1¼ to 2¼ inches. At the center of each filter was a nozzle of the Worcester type.

.f. Two sand filters, each 5 feet 10

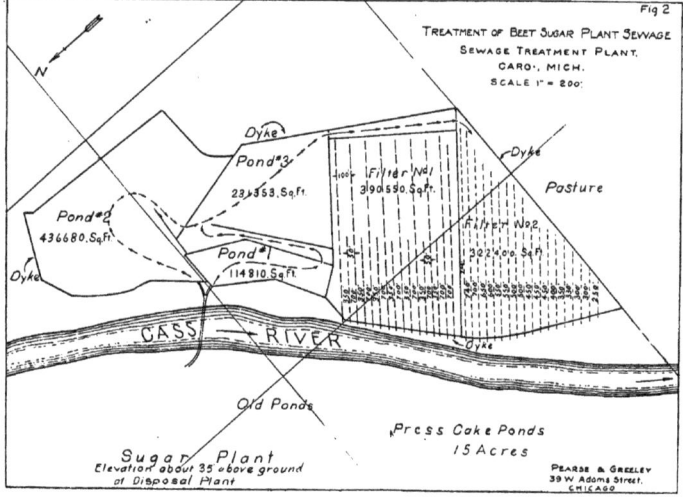

Fig 2

TREATMENT OF BEET SUGAR PLANT SEWAGE
SEWAGE TREATMENT PLANT.
CARO., MICH.
SCALE 1" = 200'

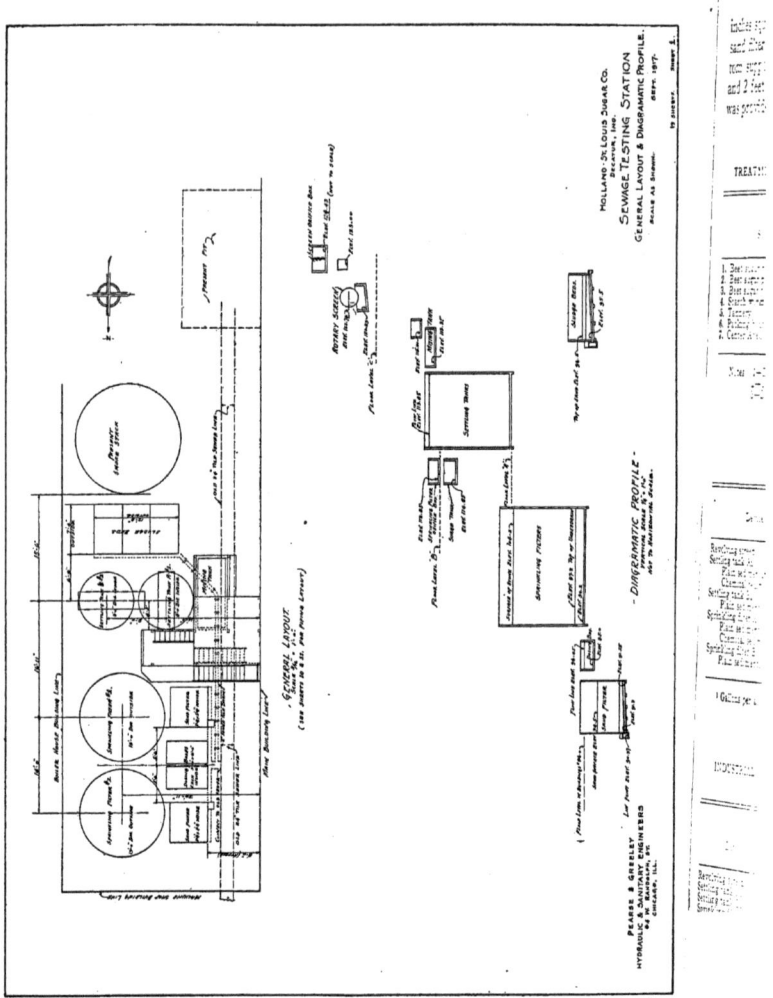

inches square, were built of wood. Each sand filter contained a sloping false bottom supporting 3 to 6 inches of gravel and 2 feet 6 inches of sand. Each filter was provided with a dosing tank operated by hand, as the dose was applied only once or twice during 24 hours.

g. The usual orifice boxes, dosing apparatus and other accessories were included.

TABLE 2

TREATMENT OF BEET SUGAR PLANT SEWAGE—ANALYSES OF CRUDE SEWAGE P. P. M.

Sewage	Solids		Total Organic N	Biological Oxygen consumed	Oxygen consumed	Alkalinity as Ca CO₃	Acidity
	Total	Suspended					
1. Beet sugar plant..........	12456	974	37.2	1000	1276	....	302
2. Beet sugar plant..........	12456	10007	50.0	....	119	29	....
3. Beet sugar plant..........	2065	....	....	....	1850	....	....
4. Starch works..............	5000	1500	138.7	1600	1000	....	....
5. Tannery..................	....	4000	30.0	....	....	233	....
6. Packing house............	5574	808	85.0	....	440	....	....
7. Center Ave., Chicago......	....	605	79.0	990	268	291	....

Notes: 1—Diffusion battery and pulp press sewage, Decatur, Ind.
2—Total sewage, Decatur, Ind.
3—Diffusion battery sewage, Caro, Mich.

TABLE 2a

TREATMENT OF BEET SUGAR PLANT SEWAGE
GROSS AND NET YIELD OF VARIOUS DEVICES 1917

Device	Gross rate gallons per 24 hours	Average hours of operation per 24 hours	Number days operated	Net yield gallons per 24 hours	Average Detention period hours
Revolving screen..............	75,000	16.0	52	36,400	....
Settling tank A₂					
Plain sedimentation........	16,100	15.7	17	10,640	4.2
Chemical sedimentation....	13,800	15.0	21	8,620	5.1
Settling tank B₂					
Plain sedimentation........	13,800	16.2	59	9,300	4.8
Sprinkling filter A₃					
Plain sedimentation........	782,000¹	17.8	17	581,000¹	....
Chemical sedimentation....	782,000¹	17.8	21	581,000¹	....
Sprinkling filter B₃					
Plain sedimentation........	782,000¹	18.9	59	617,500¹	....

¹ Gallons per acre per day.

TABLE 2b

HOLLAND-ST. LOUIS SUGAR CO.
INDUSTRIAL WASTE DISPOSAL INVESTIGATION GROSS AND NET YIELDS OF VARIOUS DEVICES 1918

Device	Period	Gross rate gallons per 24 hours	Average hours of operation per 24 hours	Number of days operated	Net Yields	
					Gallons per 24 hours	Average detention period hours
Revolving screen......	....	75,000	19.5⁵–22.9⁶	71½–54½⁵	....	....
Settling tank A₂......	....	20,000	17 –22.9	41 –23	....	3.65–2.779⁶
Settling tank B₂......	....	19,000	19.3 –22.9	71½ –54½	....	3.21 –2.77
Sprinkling filter A₃....	to Nov. 3	550,000¹	12	13	275,000¹	....
	to Nov. 26	550,000¹	23.1	23	531,000¹	....
Sprinkling filter B₂....	to Nov. 3	550,000¹	12	13	275,000¹	....
	to Nov. 23	550,000¹	23.2	20½	537,000¹	....
	to Dec. 11	245,000¹	22.7³	18 ⁴	240,000¹ ²	....
	to Dec. 27	168,000¹	23.0	14½	160,000	....
Sand filter A₄........	to Dec. 25	92,000¹	24	18	92,000	....
Sand filter B₄ (2).....	to Dec. 27	92,000¹	23½	50	90,000	....

Notes: ¹ Gallons per acre per 24 hours.   ² Sand filter B₄ was operated on Nov. 26 and Dec. 5 at 46,000 gallons per acre per 24 hours.   ³ Does not include period of overdosing.   ⁴ Includes overdosing time.   ⁵ Rate computed for total period of operation.   ⁶ Rate computed for period after Nov. 3rd.

Although this testing station has been operated for two campaigns, the shortness of the campaigns made it necessary to supplement the large scale tests with some smaller tests made in 4-inch tin tubes as described later. The gross and net yield of the various devices are shown in Tables 2a and 2b for the 1917 and 1918 work respectively.

9. FINE SCREEN.

The operation of the fine screen was very successful. The results of operation are shown in Table 3. The screenings were mostly small pieces of beet pulp having a somewhat slippery surface, so that cleaning the screen was easy. During the 1917 period, no attempt was made to limit the amount of wash water or determine its quantity. In 1918 it was found that almost no wash water was required. The screenings did not become offensive for several days and were returned to the plant for manufacture into cattle food.

10. SEDIMENTATION.

During the 1918 tests, one settling tank was operated as a plain settling tank, and the other as a chemical precipitation tank, using lime. It was soon found that excessive foaming occurred in the plain settling tank and during the 1918 tests, lime was added to both tanks as shown in Table 4. The results of sedimentation are shown in Table 4 (a). With the use of lime, it is estimated that upwards of 60 per cent of the suspended matter can be removed. The reduction in B. O. C. is indicated at 50 to 70 per cent. These determinations were somewhat irregular, however, and methylene blue tests indicated that the settling tank effluents would not stand for over a few hours. The oxygen consumed test, indicating less than 30 per cent reduction, is a better index.

Sludge data are shown in Table 5. The amount and character of the sludge varied with the amount of lime added.

TABLE 3

THE TREATMENT OF BEET SUGAR PLANT SEWAGE—RESULTS OF FINE SCREENING

Sewage	Year	Screenings, Pounds per mil. gallons		Percent moisture in screenings	Wash water percent of sewage screened	Rate of screenings gallons per Sq. Ft. per 24 hours	Percent removal of suspended matter p. p. m.
		Wet	Dry				
Beet Sugar Plant							
(1) Testing station.........	1917	14300	786	94.5	10.1	5700	12.0
	1918	11960	578	95.2	0.1	5700	6.3
(2) Anaheim, Cal..........	1913	33500	......	......	......	......	11.3
(1) Stock Yards, Chicago....	1913	7300	950	86.4	4.1	4000 to 8000	17.0

Notes: (1) 30 mesh screen.
       (2) 40 mesh screen.

TABLE 4

THE TREATMENT OF BEET SUGAR PLANT SEWAGE
RESULTS OF SEDIMENTATION

Description	Detention period	Lime added grains per gallon	Percent reduction over applied liquor		B. O. C.
	Hour		Suspended matter	Oxygen consumed	
1917					
Plain settling............	3.2	None	44.0	28.0	....
Lime settling............	3.2	70	35.0	14.0	....
1918					
Lime settling............	2.79	153	71.0	....	50.0–70.0
Lime settling............	2.79	34	69.0	....	70.0

It flowed readily out of the tanks into the sludge beds and dried to a spadeable condition within two weeks in autumn weather.

11. SPRINKLING FILTERS.

Dosing sprinkling filters at the rate of 500,000 gallons per acre per 24 hours or more was very much too high. When the rate was reduced to 168,000 gallons per acre per 24 hours, a very much bet-

TABLE 4
TREATMENT OF BEET SUGAR PLANT SEWAGE
RATE OF APPLICATION OF LIME 1918 TESTS

Week ending, 1918	Lime added, Grains per gallon	
	Tank A	Tank B
Nov. 9	254	37
16	160	35
23	110	30
30	90	34
Dec. 7	...	26
14	...	44
21	...	28
28	...	35
Ave. 1918	153	34
1917	70	

ter effluent resulted. The B. O. C. was reduced from 1,000 p. p. m. in the crude sewage to 282 p. p. m. in its effluent. The effluent took from 11.9 to 40.9 hours to decolorize methylene blue. The effluent contained about 30.1 per cent dissolved oxygen. The suspended matter in the effluent was reduced to about 40.0 p. p. m.

required an average of 24.8 hours to decolorize methylene blue. Several samples stood for from 60 to 204 hours, averaging for the period, December 8th to 21st, 35.5 hours.

13. SMALL SAND FILTER TESTS.

An attempt was made during the 1918 tests to operate half the testing station with a mixture of the beet carrying and wash water. This could not be worked out within the time available, so that tests were made of the mixed sewage on sand filters contained in 4-inch tin tubes. These filters comprised gravel supporting 30 inches of medium sized sand with a drip cock at the bottom of the tubes. They were dosed with varying liquids after quiescent settling at the rates shown in Table 6. The effluent of the filter receiving a "one to one" mixture was as satisfactory as that receiving a "one to three" mixture. In both cases it required upwards of 100 hours to decolorize methylene blue with a rate of operation of 100,000 gallons per acre per 24 hours.

14. SUMMARY.

A summary of the results of the two-year tests is given in Table 7. It would have been desirable to make further tests with a mixture of the diffusion battery and pulp press sewage and an equal

TABLE 5
TREATMENT OF BEET SUGAR PLANT SEWAGE
SLUDGE DATA

Kind of settling	Lime added average grains per gallon	Sludge cu. yds. per million gallons	Moisture contents percent	Percentage calculated to dry weight	
				Volatile matter	Mixed solids
1917 Plain	0	1.7	94.3	48.7	51.3
Lime	70	53.1	91.7	38.2	61.7
1918 Lime	153	109.9	86.4	20.4	79.6
	34	72.9	90.7	31.1	68.9

12. SAND FILTERS.

The sand filters were not operated during 1917, but during the 1918 tests they were dosed with sprinkling filter effluent at an average rate of 92,000 gallons per acre per 24 hours. The tests did not indicate any marked reduction in B. O. C. over the sprinkling filter, but it

volume of beet carrying water. A review of the evidence, and the results of the tests, however, indicated certain loadings as likely to work out in practice. Fine screenings and sedimentation are indicated as necessary for any type of treatment plant. The effluent of the settling tanks can be treated on sprinkling

TABLE 6
TREATMENT OF BEET SUGAR PLANT SEWAGE
SUMMARY OF RESULTS OF OPERATION OF 4-INCH SAND FILTER

Period ending 1918	Rate gallons per acre per 24 hours	Crude Sewage			Rate gallons per acre per 24 hours	1 crude to 1 pond effluent			1 crude to 3 pond effluent		
		D. O. % Sat.	B. O. C.	Hours to decolorize		D. O. % Sat.	B. O. C.	Hours to decolorize	D. O. % Sat.	B. O. C.	Hours to decolorize
Dec. 7	150,000	....	.....	35	150,000	....	.....	40	....	.....	40
11	150,000	....	40	30	150,000	....	20	52	....	20	57
14	50,000	....	830	55	100,000	....	330	38	....	330	45
15	50,000	....	.....	69	100,000	....	.....	.....	....	.....	.....
21	25,000	3.9	301	75	100,000	9.5	159	100	....	185	59
28	25,000	....	.....	134	100,000	17.2	129	114	....	80	157
31	25,000	....	.....	228	100,000	40.3	20	240	....	20	180

Note: Figures are weekly averages of daily samples of effluents of sand filters dosed with liquors indicated.

TABLE 7
TREATMENT OF BEET SUGAR PLANT SEWAGE
TYPICAL ANALYSES OF EFFLUENTS OF VARIOUS PROCESSES. p. p. m.

Sewage and year	Suspended matter	Oxygen consumed	Biological Oxygen consumed	Acidity	Alkalinity	Hours to decolorize methylene Blue	Notes
1917 Crude...............	976	1276	....	302	....	....	....
Screened...............	862	992	....	414	....	....	....
Plain settling...........	487	717	....	419	....	....	....
Lime settling...........	469	787	....	165	275	....	....
Spk. filter............	125	302	....	71	....	4.5	581,000 g.p.a.d.
Sand Filter............							
1918 Crude	1095	....	1000	249	....	....	....
Screened...............	1026	....	....	....	....	....	....
Lime settling	319	....	351	177	380	....	168,000
Sprinkling filter	145	....	285	290	....	....	g.p.a.d.
Sand filter..............	88	....	282	116	....	24.8	92,000 g.p.a.d.

filters. Our conclusions from the tests and data were, that sprinkling filters for the crude concentrated sewage could be dosed at about 200,000 gallons per acre per 24 hours, and sand filters at about 75,000 gallons per acre per 24 hours.

Should the concentrated sewage be mixed with an equal volume of beet-carrying water, the data indicate that a settled effluent could be treated on sand filters dosed at the rate of 100,000 gallons per acre per 24 hours.

These rates of filtration result in quite costly installations, and every effort should be made to keep the cost down by utilizing local conditions of stream flow and soil to the utmost. These results are not wholly conclusive, but indicate the great difficulty of treating beet sugar plant sewage.

DISCUSSION

Discussion of the foregoing paper on "Treatment of Beet Sugar Plant Sewage" by W. H. Dittoe, Chief Engineer, Ohio State Department of Health.

Mr. Dittoe noted that the paper just presented gave much valuable information not before available. He cited an experience in Ohio with the problem.

In 1910, a beet sugar plant with a capacity to handle 900 tons of raw beets per day was constructed at Paulding, Ohio. This plant is located immediately upstream from the village on Flatrock Creek, a stream draining 80 square miles, and having a low discharge during the dry months of the year, which, during extreme low flow, is entirely diverted to the plant for water supply. When operating at capacity, the plant produces from 2,500,000 to 3,000,000 gallons of wastes per day, which, in addition to the typical beet sugar plant wastes, contain also wastes from the Steffens process. This process is a method of handling the molasses or mother liquor coming from the centrifugal machines, by which the sugar is extracted and returned to the main plant processes. The wastes from the Steffens process are very concentrated, one catch sample showing in parts per million 7,800 parts oxygen consumed, 19,000 parts total organic solids, and 13,000 parts of alkalinity. These wastes have a volume of 150,000 to 200,000 gallons per day and appreciably increase the concentration of the wastes from the plant as a whole.

When the plant was constructed, an attempt was made to improve the character of the wastes, as follows: (1) A settling pond was provided for the clarification of about one-third of the water used for beet transportation and washing, the settled water being used again; (2) A settling pond was installed to receive the heavy lime cake wastes from the presses and also the Steffens waste, the overflow entering the main sewer of the plant conveying all other wastes; and, (3) A settling pond of 300,000 gallons capacity was provided for the combined wastes of the plant conveyed by the main sewer, the overflow being discharged into Flatrock Creek. This method of modification of the wastes was not efficient, due partly to the small capacity of the final settling pond and a serious nuisance was created in the creek which was the cause of much complaint during the campaigns of 1910, 1911 and 1912. An examination of the stream in December, 1912, showed the creek to be grossly polluted for several miles below the plant. Heavy sludge deposits, marked discoloration, and odors were noted. The following is an analysis of a catch sample of the effluent of the final settling basin at the point of discharge into the creek:

Determination	Parts Per Million
Turbidity	1,500
Oxygen consumed	1,688
Kjeldahl nitrogen	182
Alkalinity (filtered)	296
Total Calcium	2,402
Suspended solids—	
Total	9,647
Loss on ignition	1,254
Dissolved solids—	
Total	2,569
Loss on ignition	1,539

It is not surprising that such an effluent would cause a nuisance in a small stream.

In 1913, an attempt was made by the manager of the plant to improve conditions through coagulating the combined wastes by the use of sulphate of iron and enlarging somewhat the final settling pond capacity. This was found to improve the character of the effluent to some extent and the method was continued in use in 1914 and 1915. The removal of suspended solids was satisfactory until the settling basin filled with sludge, but no beneficial effect upon the dissolved organic solids resulted. Owing to the rapid filling of the settling pond with deposits, continued efficiency in clarification was not secured. In 1915, an examination of the creek showed foul conditions and heavy sludge deposits. In February, 1916, the State Board of Health ordered the company to improve conditions, and before the 1916 campaign the company made extensive improvements for the treatment of its wastes. These improvements, which were designed for a flow of 3 m. g. d., consisted of a mechanical screen, equipment for application of solutions of lime and sulphate of iron, and enlarged settling basins. The screen is a 12-foot drum screen, manufactured by the Sanitation Corporation, and is driven by a 5 h. p. motor at a speed of 2 r. p. m. It has bronze plates with V slots 5/64-inch wide and is cleaned by revolving brushes assisted by water sprays. The chemical treatment used in 1916 corresponded to 13 grains per gallon of lime and 2 grains per gallon of iron. After treatment, the wastes enter a pump well and about one-third of the flow is pumped to basins having a holding capacity of 3,800,000 gallons, or 3.8 days' flow. The effluent from these basins is used as a water supply for transporting beets. The remaining two-thirds of the flow passes to the main sewer, into which is also discharged the overflow from the basin receiving the Steffens waste and the lime cake from the presses. These wastes are kept separate from the general plant wastes up to this point to avoid the deleterious effect upon the water supply of the plant which would result. The mingled wastes in the main sewer then pass to a settling basin of 1,800,000 gallons' capacity, or 22 hours' retention, and the effluent from this basin is discharged into the creek.

The operation of these treatment processes was observed in November, 1916, and November, 1917. It was found that the effluent of the final basin was very dark in color. The creek was discolored but no sludge deposits or offensive odors were noted. The following is an analysis of a sample of the effluent of the final basin collected in November, 1916:

Determination	Parts Per Million
Kjeldahl nitrogen	66
Oxygen consumed	370
Alkalinity	386
Total suspended solids ..	122
Dissolved solids—	
Total	1,920
Loss on ignition	995

This analysis indicates a satisfactory removal of suspended solids but a high content of dissolved organic matter. During the 1916 campaign, the screen removed 2.5 tons of screenings per 24 hours, and the final settling pond retained approximately 4,000 cubic yards of sludge, filling it about half full. It is worthy of note that no complaints have been received by the State Department of Health since these improvements were installed.

The experience in the treatment of the wastes of the Paulding plant has demonstrated that efficient clarification can be secured by chemical precipitation and sedimentation, which treatment, however, does not accomplish a beneficial change with reference to the dissolved organic impurities in the wastes. Obviously, oxydizing processes would be required to accomplish this and a large expenditure would be involved. It does not appear that such expenditure would be justified unless it could be shown that public health is involved or that the rights of riparian owners demand more complete treatment. The absence of complaints from riparian owners would seem to indicate that the treatment processes used at the Paulding plant have accomplished sufficient improvement to meet the demands of property owners affected.

DISCUSSION (CONTINUED)

Discussion of the foregoing paper on "Treatment of Beet Sugar Plant Sewage" by *Robert Spurr Weston*, Boston, Mass.

Mr. Weston spoke of the value of the original paper, which throws light on a problem whose solution has not been fully reached.

Certain wastes from what may be termed the carbohydrate industries, which wastes ferment with the production of acetic, lactic, butyric, propionic and other organic acids, cannot be treated successfully by methods employing biological oxidation alone, because the acids produced by killing the oxidizing bacteria check the oxidation before the destruction of the organic matter is complete.

A few examples will make this clear. The most familiar one is ordinary cheese. In the process of making this, there are present both the bacteria which "ripen" and produce the flavor and also those which would ultimately destroy the curd by putrefaction. Indeed, some notorious cheeses like Limburger, are in a state of arrested putrefaction. Usually the acid by-product stops the destructive process before the cheese curd is appreciably attacked, and by killing the excess of bacteria, makes the cheese a safe food.

In the manufacture of lactic acid from any saccharine liquid, like glucose and water, by the growth of lactic acid bacteria, like *B. bulgaricus*, it is impossible to produce, by fermentation, a concentration of more than 3 per cent of lactic acid, but by the addition of chalk or lime, the acid may be neutralized to form calcium lactate, when the fermentation continues. The calcium lactate is then recovered from the mash by concentration and crystalization, and the lactic acid recovered by decomposition of the lactate with sulphuric acid.

Because the fermentation process is not perfect, there results a trade waste containing both nitrogenous and carbonaceous organic matter—with calcium lactate, various organic acids, and unfermented saccharine bodies present. If this waste be discharged into lagoons along with calcium or other sulphates, the calcium lactate breaks down, with the formation of butyric acid, and the organic matter putrefies, with the formation of hydrogen sulphide, thereby producing a condition of indescribable nuisance.

Not much greater success attends the efforts to treat this waste on biological beds, for, unless the amount of organic matter be so small that oxidation may be completed without the production of an excess of acid, the process soon comes to a standstill, and a putrescible effluent results.

In the Tropics, and even in this country, there are many sugar factories so located that disposal of their wastes by dilution in streams is impossible. Frequently the only dilution medium is the distillate from the cane juice itself, and there are many localities in Cuba where the combined waste must be drained into a practically dry *arroyo*. The effects of such discharges offend every æsthetic sense, and there is evolved almost every stinking compound in the chemical dictionary, among which butyric acid and hydrogen sulphide predominate. The problem is more difficult in the Tropics than in the beet sugar region because of the lack of the beet wash-water. In fact, the warm, combined cane-sugar waste begins to ferment before it leaves the factory, and fifteen minutes afterward literally boils. At this stage, however, the fermentation is aërobic and inoffensive.

We made one attempt in Cuba to treat cane-sugar waste by an Imhoff tank and trickling filter, and with little success. In the first instance there was little or no sludge deposited, and the tank seethed like a cauldron until its contents became acid, after which no apparent effect, either of subsidence or of digestion, upon the waste passing through, could be noticed. The addition of lime to the inactive tank restarted violent action, but no single treatment with lime served to carry fermentation to a point where the tank effluent could be applied to a well-constructed trickling filter and produce a non-putrescible effluent.

In the second instance, the process was varied by aerating and lagooning the waste, between tank treatment and filtration, but this did not suffice. The best results were obtained by successive tank fermentations and lime treatment, followed by lagooning

and filtration, but even then there remained the lime salts of the organic acids, prone to decompose into butyric acid and other offensive compounds.

How to transform carbohydrates into carbon dioxide gas and water is the problem. Professor Charles E. Coates of Louisiana State University has told the writer that one of his former students has attained success at one plant in Cuba by treating the factory waste with yeast in fermentation tanks preliminary to passing it through Imhoff tanks and trickling filters.

The experience of George W. Fuller of New York City[*] with the waste of a New Jersey factory producing butter substitutes and other edible fats throws a great deal of light upon the problem. The waste of this factory was handled successfully by a modification of the activated sludge process. Undismayed by the absence of sludge in the waste, Mr. Fuller built up that necessary factor in the process by adding cow manure and other similar substances. The process produced a well-clarified and non-putrescible effluent without resorting to subsequent filtration. The waste was rich in acid-producing constituents; yet Mr. Fuller states that "although it is a fact that the process is somewhat interfered with at times, it is much less sensitive to acids than one might suppose." The chief gain is the use of forced aëration and contact which evidently destroys not only the ordinary organic matter, but even the interfering organic acids themselves.

It seems to the writer that there are three means of purification to try out in these cases: Yeast treatment to remove sugar, activation to effect the destruction of the organic matter, and lime treatment as practiced by Mr. Greeley, to correct acidities which interfere with subsequent treatment. These means, singly or together, are the ones which seem most likely to succeed in solving problems of this perplexing class.

[*]Municipal and County Engineering—September, 1919.

Remember the date, August 30-September 3, 1920.

The Great A. P. H. A. West Coast meeting.

WHAT SHOULD BE THE BASIS OF THE CONTROL OF DEHYDRATED FOODS?

SAMUEL C. PRESCOTT,

Professor of Industrial Microbiology, Massachusetts Institute of Technology, Cambridge, Mass.

Read before Section on Food and Drugs, American Public Health Association, at New Orleans, La., October 28, 1919.

Since the War gave impetus to the preparation of dried or dehydrated fruits and vegetables, proper standards for inspection become necessary. Such standards are set forth by Professor Prescott. Dehydrated vegetables supply the same roughage values, the same fuel values and the same salts that fresh ones furnish, and their use is to be encouraged.

DEHYDRATED foods occupy, at the present time, a place of relatively small importance in the commerce of foodstuffs. The problems of those interested in this oldest of all processes of food conservation have hitherto been the problems of improvement of methods, by which it would be possible to secure a dried product which when properly cooked should be comparable in flavor, texture and food value to the same kind of food cooked from fresh materials. This problem has occupied mildly the attention of a few manufacturers during the past fifteen or twenty years, but rarely, until stimulation of the industry as a result of war conditions, has there been any very careful or scientific study of the processes involved, or much care as to the real quality of the product. Aside from the evaporation of fruits, dehydration as an industry hardly existed in this country previous to 1917, although there were isolated small factories producing a few tons of dried vegetables. The relation of this material to the whole general food supply was so insignificant that no special attempts at control had been made, and none were necessary. With the entry of the United States into the war it soon became evident that dehydration offered special advantages as a means of preparation for the fruit and vegetable components of the commissary supplies, and plants were installed hastily to meet this growing demand. At the beginning of the war no dehydrated products were considered by the Quartermaster Corps as desirable for the army ration, but within the year contracts for about 20,000,000 pounds were made. Dehydrated Irish potatoes, turnips, carrots and onions were purchased by the army, while of course "evaporated" and dried fruits have long been used in commissary supplies. The following year these figures were more than doubled or nearly trebled. With the cessation of the war, much of this production has ceased; but there remain a number of firms, who, while preparing much smaller tonnage, are giving marked attention to production of special lines of vegetables and fruits, to the fundamental problems of manufacture, and the cultivation of the markets, with the expectation that this method of food conservation will soon take an important position among the food industries, along with refrigeration, canning and preserving.

It at once became evident that there should be certain tentative qualifications required for these products, both as a means of protecting the government and the consumer and as guides to the manufacturer, and it was my good fortune to prepare the first set of such requirements. These were later adopted, with slight modifications, as the standards for dehydrated products by the office of the Director of Purchase and Storage of the War Department. The standards accepted by the army applied primarily to vegetables. No standards for fruits have been officially set forth, as already certain understandings relative to evaporated fruits were fairly definitely maintained.

The basis for any control of such foods is twofold: the first is economic, to prevent fraud or deception; the second is hygienic, to guarantee sanitary quality and wholesome material, i. e., to ensure protection of health. Thus the marketing of dehydrated products made from stock of poor quality, or rendered inferior as a result of excessive age, wilting, fermentation or attacks by organisms of plant disease should be prevented. Similarly, products made from originally suitable material but which has become undesirable, unpalatable and nutritionally of low value through the use of insanitary or objectionable methods of handling, or as a result of infections with objectionable organisms, such as yeasts, molds, bacteria, insects, etc., should not be permitted to be sold.

The War Department also rejected materials which might have deteriorated from age. While it is possible that such deterioration may take place, we are still lacking definite data as to the effect of long storage on properly prepared and suitably packed materials.

It is evident that without good raw material a product of high quality cannot be secured as there is no process of conservation in which the finished material is of better grade than the materials employed in manufacture. It will also be evident that if materials of high quality are employed they may be seriously injured during the process of

preparation unless special care is taken to maintain them as nearly as possible in their original quality. Furthermore, it is entirely possible to use high class materials, to prepare them by the most careful and intelligent methods and yet to have the product deteriorate through improper storage, insanitary methods of handling the finished goods, or exposure to excessive moisture, dust contamination or incursions of insect and microbic pests. Special studies are necessary in order to insure for each kind of material the highest quality of product. For example, methods of preparation of Irish potatoes may be quite unsuitable for leaf products or for certain other kinds of vegetables. Fruits may require a different procedure from the standpoint of pre-treatment and drying than the majority of vegetables. These are matters which the food manufacturer must study for himself before he can expect to place upon the market products which are sure to receive the approval of the consuming public. It is along this line also that the general inspection of dehydrated materials should, in my opinion, be conducted by food inspectors or by those charged with the problem of insuring to the consuming public, foods which are of the proper quality and free from objectionable material, which might conceivably be a menace to health. It seems to me, therefore, that the inspection of this new type of food material must begin with the factory and end with examination of the finished product as it is exposed for sale.

Specifications which have been prepared for the use of the army, constitute in a general way the foundation upon which the plans for control of dehydrated foods may be built. These may be expressed in relatively brief statements, as follows:

1. Raw material. All fruits and vegetables used for dehydration shall be of good quality, free from disease, sun-scald, frosting or other injury whereby they are rendered unsuitable in the fresh state for table use.

2. Preliminary treatment. All fruits and

vegetables so used shall be thoroughly washed and given such other treatment, as peeling, trimming, hot and cold dipping, as may be necessary to secure the best quality of product, and these processes shall be performed with the same care as that used in the preparation of vegetables for the table or for canning.

If pre-treatment by blanching or scalding is necessary to secure high quality products, this treatment shall be conducted promptly and in a clean and sanitary manner. All utensils used for this purpose should be of suitable construction to insure sanitary handling.

3. Process of drying. No detailed process of drying can be specified, but the process should be so arranged and handled that the products will not deteriorate while in the dryer, from spoilage or either as a result of action of yeast, molds or other microörganisms, or from physiological changes taking place in the material as a result of enzymes occurring naturally in the food itself. The process of drying should be so controlled that the food will not be seriously affected in color or have the flavor destroyed by scorching or for other reasons. The foods should lose only water during the process of dehydration and should not be so changed in physical structure that they will not return to approximately their natural form and appearance on being soaked in water. On proper soaking they should, within three hours at the ordinary temperature of the room, be restored to approximately their full size and natural appearance.

4. Protection against spoilage. After dehydration, fruits and vegetables which have been dried for human food should be packed at once in suitable, tight receptacles or stored in bins which have been specially prepared and which have adequate protection against vermin, insects, and molds and other microbic enemies. Such storage receptacles or containers should prevent access of moisture in sufficient amount to render the food material capable of fermentation or decomposition.

5. Insects. The greatest enemies of the dehydrated products are certain forms of weevils and other insects which may gain access to them, lay their eggs in the material and render them undesirable for food because of the development of worms and larvæ. All dehydrated products should be specially examined for such insects and their webs or cocoons, feces and eggs.

6. Sanitation of factory. The preparation of all dehydrated vegetables for army purposes should be conducted under cleanly and sanitary conditions and should be subject at all times to inspection by properly authorized officials. The methods of handling the finished product in the factory should be such as to preclude infection from boots, floors, and implements of any other external source. Care should be taken to impress upon the manufacturer that he is dealing with a food material and that it is essential for the welfare of the consuming public that such food materials should be placed before the consumer in a wholesome and uninfected condition.

EFFECT OF DEHYDRATION ON FOOD VALUE

The interest in commercial dehydration, as in domestic or community drying, has led to a number of interesting studies on the effect of dehydration in preserving the so-called vitamine substances which give to fresh vegetables their special nutritive or protective values and growth-promoting energy. The dietetic effect of green vegetables in preventing and alleviating scurvy and in supplying to the body certain other curative and growth-promoting substances has long been known. It has been suggested that dehydration tends to diminish the quantity of these substances by permitting certain chemical changes. The results of investigations to determine this point have not been entirely in accord and until generally accepted conclusions are reached, it seems undesirable to make any requirement pertaining to such effects a part of any system of inspection. While it is possibly true that dehydrated vegetables, like canned vegetables, contain less antiscorbutic material than the original vegetables in fresh condition, this does not appear to constitute an argument against their use, as so far as can be determined they supply the same roughage value as fresh vegetables, the same salts and the same fuel values. From the practical standpoint, therefore, the use of dehydrated vegetables is certainly to be commended, providing they can be prepared from the best quality of raw material and by methods which conserve the food values to the highest possible degree. The great advantages of dehydration in making possible the utilization of materials which now goes to waste, in reducing the cost of carriage, in their easy transportability to all parts of the world, in the saving of expensive containers and in the stabilization of agriculture and the price of materials, seem incontrovertible and argue strongly for the development of this industry which we believe now to be only in its infancy.

SOCIOLOGICAL ASPECTS OF HOUSING

IRA S. WILE, M. D.,

New York City.

Read before Sociological Section, American Public Health Association, at New Orleans, La., October 27, 1919.

Infant mortality is twice as great in homes without bathtubs, although the infants do not use them, and increases with lower rentals. Housing is also not to be separated from typhoid and respiratory disease. Health, education, standards, inspection, control of rent profiteering and a living wage are health factors related to housing.

ACCORDING to the lexicographer: "A house is a place of abode or shelter, a structure designed as a habitation; specifically, a building intended as a home or place of work for human beings."

From this definition it is evident that housing is not to be considered merely as a form of shelter against the ravages of the elements, but must be thought of in so far as it fulfills its purpose of serving as a home or place of work for thinking, active, living human beings. We are prone to overlook this phase of housing which is conducive to the development of normal family life.

During the war various schemes for housing were proposed, many of which were lacking in a recognition of the fact that many beings were to live within the confines of the hastily erected structures. At the conclusion of the armistice, most of these larger and more intelligent plans were discontinued, so the possibility of wholesale constructions were not realized. Since the armistice, the housing situation has been more acute; and as a result, careful attention to housing sanitation and hygiene has woefully declined.

While it is true that standards of house construction have been rising during the past decade or two, and that building laws have become more stringent, there are still no adequate standards by virtue of which rents may be gauged.

The needs of protection against fire hazards, as well as the necessity for adequate air space and lighting, are matters well understood. In spite of the present information and the moderately developed degree of regulation, the housing situation is generally unsatisfactory from the standpoint of public health.

By many it would be claimed that housing conditions exist by reason of the working of the economic law of supply and demand, but this is insufficient to justify the existence of housing conditions inimicable to public welfare. As a matter of fact, housing conditions are largely determined by family income, and the problem is the same, whether rural or urban conditions. If criticism is to be leveled against any particular form of housing, it must be most severe upon urban conditions where the coöperative interests increase the need for better living conditions. The isolation of houses in rural communities may threaten the health of the individual occupant, but in a sense it serves as a safeguard to those who are almost too remote to be regarded as neighbors. Even under these conditions, however, the matter of income determines whether the house and barn are to be practically under one roof, and as to whether outhouses and wells shall exist which are a source of danger.

In urban sections, whether one discusses detached houses or tenements, the character of the dwellings may be judged by the rent paid, and this in turn reflects the character of the income of the occupants. It is true that the relation of houses to parks and playgrounds, industrial centers, noisy or smoky areas; or their proximity to districts given over, willingly or unwillingly, to vice and crime, help to determine the rental value. These and numerous other factors, however, enter into the public health aspect of housing, and determine in part the healthfulness of the neighborhood.

It is unnecessary to cite an array of figures to demonstrate that homes vary with income. The amount of money to be given over to the provision of shelter is affected by the size of the family and the size of the income. In general, it may be said that the larger the family, the larger the percentage of income paid out for rent. It is equally true that the lower the amount of the income the higher percentage of it is spent for rent.

The matter of location, the type of house, whether old or new, the variation in the number of rooms, are not as significant in the determination of housing costs as the possibility of running water, running hot water, toilet facilities, and bath and heat. As an illustration of this, I am quoting the figures of D. W. Ogburn, *Monthly Labor Review*, September, 1919; taking as a basis five-room apartments. Those with bath and running water, but no heat, vary in cost from $13.00 to $32.29 per month; those with water but no bath or heat, from $9.02 to $15.12; those with no bath or heat, but with running water, $8.50.

The desire for a comfortable and sanitary home is normal to all save a negligible portion of the community, but the ability to secure healthful housing conditions is limited by the income. It may be said that housing is a commercial problem and that landlords cannot provide the types of dwellings desired without the ability of the tenant to give

an adequate return upon the investment. There are ample data available from the experiences of philanthropic self-supporting building associations to indicate that a reasonable return upon investment is compatible with the erection and maintenance of sanitary, hygienic, modernized dwellings.

From the broadest viewpoint of public health, the state of the family income should not be permitted to jeopardize communal welfare. The financial weakness should not be penalized by a further impoverishment, that of health. The interests and health needs of the community should serve as a powerful force to bring about a finer type of housing than has thus far been developed for the masses. The relation of housing to health comprises various factors influencing the physical, mental and moral development of the family and family life. Whatever benefits each unit of family inures to the advantage of the public. Housing is not to be regarded as a simple matter of personal selection but its minimal standards should be an item of public concern. In its broadest sociological aspect, housing is a determiner of personal, family and communal health.

I admit at once that no agency can determine what rental is to be paid, for this is a matter of arrangement between landlord and tenant, principally landlord. I also grant that there are numerous laws, ordinances and regulations governing houses with a view to securing health and safety, but they are unfortunately more distinguished in the breach than in the observance.

It is patent that from the physical standpoint housing problems include air, light and heat, ventilation, bathing and toilet facilities, sewage disposal and protection from fire hazards; but the question of insects and rodents, modern plumbing, proper protection against the elements and the numerous subsidiary factors growing out of an intimate rela-

SOCIOLOGICAL ASPECTS OF HOUSING 329

tion to them should not be deemed unimportant.

Mental health finds itself threatened by congestion, lack of privacy, impaired opportunity for home study, and the crowding of family life, with the numerous strains due to faulty physical surroundings. The moral health of a community merits greater attention than has been given, and is closely linked up with problems of room congestion, darkness, dampness, a lack of bathing and toilet facilities and the general unattractiveness so common in the homes and dwellings of those with limited income.

The influence of housing upon public health is manifested in the infant mortality question. As has been said, the house and home is largely determined by the income of the tenant and his ability to pay for hygienic surroundings. Some evidence as to the effect of housing upon infant mortality may be found from figures authorized by the Children's Bureau.

In Manchester, N. H., the mortality rate on the basis of rental was as follows:

175 babies. Less than $7.50............211.4
703 babies. $ 7.50 to $12.49............172.1
300 babies.   12.50 to   17.49............156.7
62 babies. Over $17.50 ....100.0
168 babies. Homes owned 86.0

The infant mortality decreases as rental increases. I recognize, of course, that there are other factors beside housing which enter into the mortality rate. In Johnstown, Pa., the infant mortality in homes with bathtubs was 72.6, and without bathtubs, 164.8. The number of rooms in the home relates itself to overcrowding. The greater the room congestion, the lower the standard of living; and, one may generally deduce a relatively lower wage. In Manchester, with less than one person per room, the infant mortality rate was 123.3. With one to two persons per room, the rate was 177.8, and with two to three per room it was 261.7. Lest it be urged that this is a

condition which does not obtain in communities where higher wages are paid, it may be pointed out that in Brockton, Mass., where high wages exist, the infant mortality rate, where less than one person was found to the room, was 86.5, and where there was more than one person per room, 110.2.

Osler refers to tuberculosis as the house disease. Williamson, in the British Journal of Tuberculosis, 1915, commented upon the fact that 60 to 70 per cent of tuberculous persons came from houses of three rooms or less, and that the number of cases was larger in two-room houses-than in three-room houses, and larger in one-room houses than in two-room houses.

House over-crowding is difficult to deal with, because, as Porter remarks in his Elements of Hygiene and Public Health, "It is the poor who overcrowd, and they only do so because they have not the means to pay for real and proper accommodations. Amongst the conditions associated with overcrowding are anemia, rickets, tuberculosis and probably other infectious diseases, since the resistance of persons exposed to overcrowding is apt to be reduced, either on account of it or of the attendant poverty."

The influence of crowds upon contagious diseases is fully appreciated, and administrative success in lessening the spread of contagion, requires an elevation of the standards of living, which includes better housing. In the words of Rosenau, "In addition to raising the standard of living, better houses diminish the chances of contact infection, afford better air and more sunshine, and tend generally to the well-being and uplift of mankind."

The problems of typhoid fever, malaria, plague, and venereal diseases are certainly not to be disassociated from housing questions.

The control of pneumonia and influenza and various other respiratory diseases, involves problems of house sanitation in no small degree.

By some it is believed that there are places in which cancer is more likely to occur, although the evidence in this direction is unconvincing. Even the statement of Watkins-Pitchford that "Cancer houses usually appear to be unwholesome dwellings, often affording special facilities in their immediate neighborhood for the irradiation of their anemic inhabitants," is open to question.

From the standpoint of society, the improvement of housing calls for serious consideration; not merely as a part of the general plan for allaying economic unrest and the discontent now rampant, but also as a measure of promoting a higher degree of physical welfare in the community. It appears to be necessary to secure a more effective enforcement of health laws dealing with buildings to be utilized for living purposes. It would appear to be desirable to establish regulations to ensure the development of minimal standards of housing based upon the health needs, as determined by modern knowledge concerning the relation of housing to public health.

Raising the standards for home making is being attempted through various educational agencies and devices, but the obstacles to obtaining the desired results are numerous. Habits of cleanliness are difficult to instill with the absence of running water and home toilets. It is difficult to secure coöperation in matters of open windows if the possibilities of heating are insufficient, particularly when there are infants in the household. The possibility of home nursing is greatly lessened when room congestion exists and privacy is impossible. The seriousness of this is accentuated by the impossibility of providing hospital care for all who, for home reasons, require it. Administrative attacks upon rodents, bed-bugs, and pediculosis are greatly handicapped when the tenants cannot be held responsible for the conditions leading to their presence in large number, despite all efforts at cleanliness and control.

It is time that the mental and moral effects of housing problems received their full measure of study. The influence of these conditions is more usually manifest at the time of epidemics when the problem of communal psychology assumes unusual proportions. Physical health and freedom from preventable disease are in part determined by the maintenance of a high degree of what is so generally spoken of as "morale." Housing morale is not a negligible factor.

It is patent that housing is a primary need, and, as such, is of paramount importance. To improve housing conditions is to influence the standards of living favorably. Higher standards of living, in turn, advance public welfare and decrease physical and mental defects and diseases and raise the moral qualities essential for effective citizenship. Poor housing breeds disease and crime; disease and crime lower potentially earning capacity, with consequent inability to pay for hygienic surroundings; thus a vicious circle is established.

In order to secure the maximum benefits of housing, several steps are necessary: First, an appreciation of the sociological and health significance of hygienic dwellings; second, the education of the public as to the natural value and importance of sanitary dwellings; third, the rigid enforcement of laws, ordinances and regulations dealing with home construction and house alterations; fourth, the promulgation of minimum standards of housing construction, and particularly the regulation of standards of maintenance and repair; fifth, the establishment of some form of supervision or control that would prevent the exploitation of tenants through profiteering rentals and unwillingness to make necessary repairs required in the interest of family health and safety; sixth, the determination of rules and regulations for proper disinfection and fumigation following the presence of contagious diseases, when such might prove a source of contagion to a new occupant; seventh, the encouragement of subsidized or non-subsidized programs of housing construction that would make available modern hygienic dwelling places at low rentals; eighth, the support by health departments of those measures tending to increase family incomes so as to bring about a minimum standard of living wage, consistent with the cost of living, in a manner that is conducive to health and comfort.

In dealing with housing, we have passed the stage of theorizing and have entered into a stage of practical performance. The house is no longer to be considered as a place of shelter, but as our definition states, "A building intended as a home or place of work for human beings." In our views upon the subject we have, therefore, aimed to stress the primary ideas which should dominate minds of public health workers.—"home" and "human beings."

☐

TRAFFIC REGULATION AS A MEANS OF PREVENTING INJURY AND DEATH FROM STREET VEHICLES

S. J. BYRNE, M. D.,

Asst. Registrar of Records, City of New York Dept. of Health, Brooklyn, N. Y.

Read before Section on Vital Statistics, American Public Health Association, at New Orleans, La., October 27, 1919.

Mortality in New York City from auto accidents increased 735 per cent in 1917 over previous averages, and 940 per cent in 1918. Figures are duplicated elsewhere. Dr. Byrne urges radical measures of restriction and calls for a campaign for standard regulations with real penalties. He considers education of pedestrians and children very necessary.

When we endeavor to analyze the various causes of sickness and death in the registration area after eliminating those due to old age and prenatal conditions, we are confronted with a considerable number that should be, with proper education and care, preventable. Among these we would call attention to the rapidly increasing number of accidents and deaths due to the operating of street vehicles of all kinds, but, particularly, on account of their large and increasing percentage to those due to the self-propelled type.

With the introduction of every new method of human advancement intended to broaden the activities of everyday life and crowd days of energy into hours,

and miles into feet, we meet with the same result—an unnecessary sacrifice of life and health due to neglect of care, or lack of knowledge, both of the new method and of the dangers to be met at each step forward. While recognizing that dangers must be met and risks must be taken in trying out each new method of shortening space and saving time, we have to admit that comparatively little attention has been given in the past to controlling the action of those who are careless, not only of their own lives and well-being, but who are also criminally neglectful of the health and safety of others.

When, however, we consider the immense advances already made and still in progress in the mad rush, if I may say it, to bridge time and space by all classes of people and for all kinds of purposes; when we realize the increasing number of vehicles in proportion to population, together with the immense amount of money invested, not only in the vehicles themselves, but also in the building and improving of roads for their easier movement; we awake to the fact that the time has arrived to start a widespread movement to regulate and keep under control this increasing traffic for its own good as well as for the good and welfare of all.

For this purpose there should be well-defined regulations, as few and simple as possible, but with all the force that law can give them. We should not, however, lose sight of the fact that we are dealing with an industry which has proven itself of the highest value during the war, and which promises to be of the greatest importance in the transportation problems of the future. It will, therefore, be necessary to have laws so framed, which, while protecting the health and lives of the public as much as possible, will not place any unnecessary burden on commerce or block the way of progress.

That regulations of a rigid sort are, however, becoming more necessary than ever will be easily appreciated if we consider a few figures showing the increase of accidents and death due for the most part to avoidable errors or criminal neglect during the past few years. Taking the city of New York as an example, from the moderately settled to the most congested districts, we find that the mortality tables of the Department of Health show that the average number of deaths from automobile accidents during the five years of 1912 to 1917 was 377. In 1917 alone, it rose to 530 and in 1918 another increase brought it up to 677. This is the more striking when we compare the number of accidents and deaths from motor vehicles with those of other classes of street vehicles. In the city of

New York there were reported to the police department 19,216 persons injured by street vehicles during the year 1918; 13,285 of these injuries were the result of the operation of motor vehicles. While the injuries by motor cars represent 69 per cent of all from street vehicles, the mortality from self-propelled vehicles represents 83 per cent of the total known dead from vehicular street traffic. In examining the records of other cities in the registration area we find this same condition prevailing, but in an even greater proportion. This might be readily assumed when we consider the very efficient traffic organization of New York City, and taking into account the fact that at traffic points in the most congested districts under care of traffic officers accidents are proportionately far less than at uncovered places, it will impress upon us the more forcibly the necessity of radical measures in dealing with those who make a menace of a great utility. As an illustration that moderate treatment is of little avail, I might quote the case of one offender who, in the course of nine months, was arrested four times for speeding and paid over two hundred and seventy-five dollars in fines without any apparent taming of his mania. He then received a sentence of ten days in jail. Whether this will result in a cure remains to be seen, but without criticism of the court, I believe a year's probation on a guarantee not to operate a motor vehicle would have a better result, at least as far as the public is concerned. The reports of accidents and mortality as a result of the operation of self-propelled vehicles received from many other cities, as well as the industrial and insurance experience tables issued by the Prudential and Traveler's Insurance companies fully bear out the same result as that of the city of New York. They all show the same constant and rapid increase in accidents and fatalities. In view of these facts, it would be well to start a campaign to have standard regulations for all states to control the use of highways in the driving or operating of street or road vehicles. They should provide that vehicles should not be driven on public streets or highways without a license issued to the driver or operator after a strict examination as to his or her character, ability to drive or operate, and proper knowledge of the rules and regulations governing the driving or operating of a vehicle on a public street or highway. They should also provide for safe and reasonable speed regulations for different classes of vehicles. Proper regulations of the use of lights at night should be made, as this is an essential to safe night traffic; and while still open to discussion, could probably be met by requiring a shade on the left-hand light, so arranged as to throw the beam of light in alignment with that side of the vehicle. They should establish a limit to the width of a car or truck consistent with safety on narrow roads and streets.

Penalties should be fixed for the punishment of offenders so that licenses would be revoked or suspended according to the character of the offense. A questionnaire of standard type, with which every applicant for a license would be required to make himself thoroughly familiar, should be established for general use and information, so as to leave no room for argument as to what should or should not be done under any given circumstances. This could be readily edited by the proper officials with the aid and advice of the officers of the various automobile associations.

For cities and towns, regulations of a standard character should be made to meet conditions of city life, and in congested zones, an officer in charge at a convenient point. His directions should have the force of law and subject those who refuse obedience to arrest and imprisonment.

As children are largely sufferers from the result of street traffic, all educational establishments should be required to call the attention of their students repeatedly to the necessity of observing due care on public streets and highways. Educational campaigns should also, from time to time, be given to the public through motion picture houses and through the press, of the dangers to be expected from street vehicles and the proper way to avoid them.

The matter of control of the action of pedestrians in regard to street vehicular traffic is one well worthy of serious consideration; but it is of such character and presents difficulties requiring special study and thought too broad for the scope of this article.

Finally, should it not be a function of the American Public Health Association to take the matter up with the different state and municipal authorities, to bring about a result beneficial and satisfactory to all?

☐

The 1920 Membership Campaign is on. Your individual quota is one member. Decide whom you will invite to membership and present his name.

DIPHTHERIA BACILLUS STAINS WITH A DESCRIPTION OF A "NEW" ONE

HENRY ALBERT, M. D.,

Professor of Pathology and Bacteriology, University of Iowa, Iowa City, Iowa.

Read before the Laboratory Section, American Public Health Association, at New Orleans, La., October 28, 1919.

Identification from younger cultures and consequently a quicker diagnosis of diphtheria, uniformly good results, ability to discern equally well by daylight and by artificial light, and easier recognition through the strengthening of the granules, are the claims made by Dr. Albert.

THE report of one or several "new" stains for diphtheria bacilli almost every year since 1895 would seem to indicate that none of those previously recommended have been entirely satisfactory.

To get an idea as to the number of stains that have been tried and recommended, one has but to consult a contribution by Graham-Smith,[1] which appeared in 1908 and another by Neisser and Gins,[2] which was published in 1913. The alkaline methylene blue originally recommended by Loeffler[3] is still regarded by some bacteriologists as the most satisfactory stain for the diphtheria bacillus. It stains the granules and bars of the bacillus well, but since it also stains other bacteria rather intensely, it does not offer sufficient contrast to enable the bacteria to be readily observed.

Practically all of the efforts at finding a more satisfactory stain have aimed to secure more contrast between the granules of the diphtheria bacillus on the one hand and the remainder of this microorganism and other bacteria on the other. Greater contrast, due to difference in the intensity of the staining, may be brought about by the addition of acetic acid. Thus, according to the stain described by Mallory,[4] the granules take an intense blue stain, whereas the remainder of the bacillus and other bacteria are of a lighter blue color. An important objection to the use of this stain is the time required for the reagent to act—namely, 15 to 30 minutes.

Most of those who have experimented with the staining of this bacillus have aimed to secure a polychrome effect, i. e., to have the granules stain one color and the remainder of the bacillus and other bacteria, another color.

This may be accomplished to a certain extent by using a well-ripened solution of methylene blue which gives to the granules a reddish hue, especially when viewed by artificial light. The ripening of the solution may be brought about by exposure to sunlight for several months or by the addition of a rapidly acting oxidizing agent. The polychrome effect is due to a change of some of the methylene blue into azure. Other stains that give a polychrome effect are toluidin blue, and cresyl violet. Toluidin blue is the basis of the stains recommended by Pugh,[5] Ponder,[6] and Sutherland.[7] The use of cresyl violet was recently described by Greenthal.[8] These stains have been found to be very good. Combinations of various dyes have also been employed to produce a polychrome effect. Crouch[9] combined dahlia and methyl green, and Schauffer[10] mixed methylene blue and pyronin. The stain of this type which has proved most satisfactory in our hands is the one described by Kinyoun.[11] He used toluidin blue, azure and methylene blue.

Double and even triple staining has also been used with the idea of getting polychrome effects. Neisser[12] was the first to bring out a double stain of value. The method consisted of first staining the preparation with an acid solution of methylene blue and counter-staining with an aqueous solution of Bismarck brown.

The results obtained by the Neisser stain are so variable that many modifications of it have been made. In practically all of these Bismarck brown is retained as the counter-stain. Bronstein[13] used dahlia as the principal stain; Falières[14] used boraxed methylene blue; Ljubinsky[15] recommended pyoktannin, and Beck[16] the use of gentian violet. Debré and Letulle[17] have recently described a modification of the Neisser stain in which the first solution is heated. They renew the claim that their stain differentiates between the true and pseudo-diphtheria bacilli. We have found that this stain does not differentiate between virulent and non-virulent forms.

One of the principal objections to the Neisser stain, or its modifications, is that they do not stain the barred forms of diphtheria bacilli very well.

Of the stains which have heretofore been described, the following have been found most satisfactory:

a. Loeffler's methylene blue well ripened preferably by prolonged exposure to sunlight.

b. Toluidin blue or cresyl violet acidulated with acetic acid as described by Ponder and others.

c. Beck's modification of Neisser's stain.

d. Kinyoun's stain.

The staining effects produced by these several stains are represnted in Table 1.

The chief objections to Loeffler's methylene blue are: (1) other bacteria are stained too intensely and there is, therefore, not sufficient contrast; and (2) it is difficult to secure a proper polychrome effect with many preparations of the dye.

The toluidin blue stains are more satisfactory as "granule" but less so as "bar" stains. Barron[18] was able to improve its "bar" staining properties by the addition of potassium carbonate. The end result is, however, a too diffuse staining of the bacillus.

The Beck stain misses many of the barred forms of the diphtheria bacilli. Kinyoun's stain if allowed to act for five

TABLE No. 1—DIPHTHERIA BACILLI BY VARIOUS STAINS

Stain	Diphtheria Bacillus			Other bacteria	Remarks.
	Granules	Bars	Intermediate substance		
Loeffler's methylene blue	Reddish purple	Dark blue	Very light blue	Blue	Granules best seen by artificial light.*
Beck's modif. of Neisser's stain	Dark purple	. . . .	Brown	Brown	Bars do not stain as such.
Ponder's toluidin-blue	Reddish purple	Light blue	Very light blue	Light blue	Granules best seen by artificial light.*
Kinyoun's stain	Reddish purple	Bluish purple	Very light blue	Bluish purple	Granules best seen by artificial light.*
Author's stain	Black	Dark green to black	Light green	Light green	Granules stand out in marked contrast. Bars stain well—many appear like granules.

*Without the use of the blue glass.

minutes brings out the barred forms quite well. As a granule stain it is better than Loeffler's methylene blue. The Kinyoun stain has been our favorite for the past three years.

Of all the stains which have been described it may be said that they have either one or both of two defects from the standpoint of practical use in the diagnosis of diphtheria cultures. Some do not afford sufficient contrast to enable the diphtheria bacilli to be recognized with readiness. This applies to Loeffler's methylene blue, Ponder's, Kinyoun's and many other good stains. Others, although affording good contrast, fail to stain the non-granular forms of the diphtheria bacilli which results in missing some of them.

With the idea of overcoming, if possible, these defects, we tried out a large series of stains, and combinations of such, and compared these stains with those previously described. As a result of these experiments we have developed a stain which we believe to be superior to those in use at present.[19] Two solutions are used. Solution No. 1 has the following formula:

Toluidin blue .... 0.15 gram
Acetic acid (glacial) .... 1.00 cc.
Alcohol (95%) .... 2.00 cc.
Water (distilled) ....100 cc.

Solution No. 2 is the same as the iodine solution used in the Gram stain. The formula is:

Iodine .... 1.00 gram
Potassium iodide .... 2.00 gram
Water (distilled) ....300.00 cc.

Smears are made on slides or cover glasses in the usual manner; fixed by heat and stained with the toluidin blue solution for five minutes. The stain is then drained off without washing and the iodine solution applied for one minute. It is then briefly washed with water and dried, preferably by means of filter paper. It is now ready for examination.

Occasional lots of toluidin blue stain the diphtheria bacilli too uniformly. One

that stains the granules well should be selected.

If staining is done in staining dishes, the iodine solution should be replaced with a fresh supply daily, since a precipitate results from the introduction of the toluidin blue stain carried over on the slide. The stained preparation should present a light greenish appearance to the naked eye.

By the use of this stain the granules of the diphtheria bacilli are stained black and stand out in marked contrast to other elements in the microscopic field. The bars of the bacilli take a dark green to black color, and the intermediate portions as well as other bacteria, a light green. The granules of diphtheria bacilli stand out very much more prominently than they do by Loeffler's methylene blue and other stains commonly employed. The bars stain with varying intensity. Sometimes they stand out better; sometimes not as well as with the Loeffler stain. They are, however, easily recognized. In this respect it is very much better than certain stains such as the Neisser, which sometimes stain the granules very well.

The advantages claimed for this stain over others that have been described are:

1. Diphtheria bacilli are more readily recognized by virtue of the fact that the granules of the bacilli stand out in very sharp contrast to other portions of the bacillus and more especially to other bacteria which are but feebly stained.

2. Diphtheria bacilli may be recognized in younger cultures and hence the diagnosis made earlier.

3. The bacilli may be seen equally well by daylight and by artificial light.

4. The results of staining are uniformly good.

It is interesting to note that many structures which appear as bars by Loeffler's methylene blue, take a granular stain by the method described. It is also noteworthy that this stain shows up both a granular and a barred structure in many diphtheria bacilli. The significance of these phenomena is now being studied.

REFERENCES

1. Graham-Smith, G. S.: The Bacteriology of Diphtheria, edited by Nuttall and Graham-Smith, p. 139, 1908.
2. Neisser and Gins: Ueber Diphtherie. Handbuch der Pathogenen Mikroörganismen, edited by Kolle and Wassermann. Vol. 5, p. 942, 1913.
3. Loeffler: For formula for Loeffler's methylene blues, see any text book on bacteriology.
4. Mallory, F. B.: Pathological Technique, Mallory and Wright, Seventh Edition, p. 311, 1918.
5. Pugh, W. T. G.: A note on the examination of cultures and smears from the throat and nose. Lancet II. 80, 1905.
6. Ponder: Lancet, London, clxxxiii, 22, 1912.
7. Sutherland: Lancet, London, Feb. 8, p. 218, 1919.
8. Greenthal, R. M.: New Stain for Diphtheria Bacillus. Am. Jour. Dis. Children. 18, p. 25, 1919.
9. Crouch, H. C.: The Microscopic Diagnosis of Diphtheria by a New Staining Method. Proc. A. P. H. A. xxi, 19, 1896.

10. Schauffter, W. G.: A New Stain for Diphtheria Bacilli. Med. Record. (Rev. Phila. Med. Jour., p. 909), 1902.
11. Kinyoun: A. J. P. H., Vol. 5, p. 246, 1915.
12. Neisser, M.: Zur Differentialdiagnose des Diphtheriebacillus. Zeitschr. f. Hyg., xxiv, p. 443, 1897. The formula for this stain may be found in any text-book on bacteriology.
13. Bronstein, J.: Zur bacterioskopischen Diphtheriediagnose. Berlin klin Wochenschr., xxxvii, p. 141, 1900.
14. Falières: Des granulations polaires du bacille diphthérique (Dissertation), 1902. (Quoted in The Bacteriology of Diphtheria by Nuttall and Graham-Smith, p. 144).
15. Ljubinsky: 1905 (Quoted in The Bacteriology of Diphtheria by Nuttall and Graham-Smith, p. 146).
16. Beck, F. A.: Method for Staining the Diphtheria Bacillus. Jour. A. M. A., July 13, 1918, p. 109.
17. Debré and Letulle. Presse Médicale, 27, 1919, p. 515.
18. Barron, M.: Jour. Lab. and Clin. Med. Vol. III, No. 6, pp. 432-434, 1918.
19. Albert, H.: A New Stain for Diphtheria Bacilli. Jour. A. M. A.

☐

INDIANA'S WARFARE ON TUBERCULOSIS

Presented here is the outfit of the Tuberculosis Division of the Indiana State Board of Health, with members of the State Board, the personnel of the Division and members of the Indiana Tuberculosis Association grouped about it under the shadow of the State House in Indianapolis. It attests the seriousness of the campaign in this state.

INFANT MORTALITY IN THE REGISTRATION AREA
FOR BIRTHS

WILLIAM H. DAVIS, M. D.,

Chief Statistician, Bureau of the Census,
Washington, D. C.

Read before Section on Vital Statistics, American Public Health Association, at New Orleans, La.,
October 29, 1919

"A high infant mortality rate today is a greater disgrace than a high typhoid rate," writes Dr. Davis. It reflects on clergy, physicians, nurses, school teachers and editors alike, and gives a low rating for the intelligence of the people. Breast feeding is the first line of attack. Mothers should be taught how to care for their children.

ORGANIZED efforts to save infant life by teaching and helping mothers have been very successful in the last decade. Health reports of many cities and states show notable reductions in the infant mortality rates between 1910 and 1917. New York City, for example, had a rate of 126 per 1,000 births in 1910 and in 1917 a rate of 89. Philadelphia in 1914 had a rate of 121 and in 1917 a rate of 108. Boston in 1910 had a rate of 127 and in 1917 a rate of 99, and so on wherever the propaganda was spread and earnest efforts were made the infant mortality rates were lowered. In fact, there is every reason to believe that 1918 would have shown many record low infant mortality rates had it not been for the pandemic. In Indiana, for example, the rate for 1918 was 87 against 86 for 1917. But if the excess deaths from influenza and pneumonia in the last four months of 1918 could have been prevented the rate would have been only 81. Similarly in Kansas the rate of 81 for 1918 would have been reduced to 77, and in Philadelphia the rate of 124 would have been reduced to 114. But we can not point to these rates with complete satisfaction, for the rates for Norway, Sweden, and Australia, for example, are still so much lower than the rates in this country that

we must conclude that there is much work yet to be done to eliminate that part of our infant mortality rate which is preventable. We do not need to go to foreign countries, however, to find such low rates for the annual reports of the Bureau of the Census show that a few cities in the birth registration area have had rates below 50.

In 1917 the lowest infant mortality rate for any state in the birth registration area was 67 for Minnesota, with Utah and Washington close behind, each 69. In 1918 Utah had the lowest rate (64) well below the 1917 rate of 69, but no other state shows a lower rate for 1918 than for 1917.

The trend of infant mortality, even since the establishment of the birth registration area in 1915, has been most encouraging and I think we have every reason to believe that the downward trend will still continue, for it is coming to be recognized more and more that the big factor in reducing infant mortality is breast feeding. There are other factors to be sure; prenatal care, heredity, the family pocket book, motherly care and proper obstetrical care, all are important, but the *great factor is breast feeding.*

Let us analyze briefly a few rates which show marked declines between 1915 and 1917.

In 1915 New York City had a rate of 99 and. in 1917 a rate of 89, a decline of 10 per 1,000 births and yet no part of this decline can be credited to any saving of lives under 1 month of age. In the eight months interval between the ages of 1 month and 9 months there was a decline of 8.4 per 1,000 to be credited about equally to each month of the interval, while the decline between 9 months and 12 months was less marked, amounting to only 1.7 per 1,000 births

INFANT MORTALITY RATES
IN THE BIRTH REGISTRATION AREA
1915 TO 1917
AND PROVISIONAL RATES FOR 1918

Area Cities of 100,000 Population in 1910	Deaths under 1 year of age per 1,000 births			
	1915	1916	1917	1918
Bridgeport, Conn........	97	106	87	100
New Haven, Conn.......	87	88	84	90
Washington, D. C........	111	106	97	112
Indianapolis, Ind........	...	...	95	93
Louisville, Ky..........	...	...	97	114
Baltimore, Md..........	...	...	118	150
Boston, Mass	103	105	99	115
Cambridge, Mass.......	93	91	75	107
Fall River, Mass........	167	173	159	180
Lowell, Mass...........	156	146	140	160
Worcester, Mass.......	93	101	95	97
Detroit, Mich..........	105	112	103	100
Grand Rapids, Mich.....	71	75	83	86
Minneapolis, Minn......	71	82	71	73
St. Paul, Minn..........	78	68	74	87
New York..............	99	93	89	92
Bronx Borough......	81	72	80	77
Brooklyn Borough...	93	88	85	91
Manhattan Borough..	106	102	94	97
Queens Borough.....	103	95	93	93
Richmond Borough..	109	93	91	106
Rochester, N. Y.......	84	86	84	93
Syracuse, N. Y.........	98	100	102	119
Cincinnati, Ohio........	...	...	¹88	104
Cleveland, Ohio........	...	...	109	98
Columbus, Ohio........	...	...	88	101
Dayton, Ohio..........	...	...	96	87
Toledo, Ohio...........	...	...	95	94
Philadelphia, Pa.......	104	105	108	124
Pittsburgh, Pa..........	110	115	120	139
Scranton, Pa...........	119	131	148	141
Providence, R. I.......	106	110	102	...
Richmond, Va..........	...	...	136	¹47
Seattle, Wash..........	...	...	61	62
Spokane, Wash.........	...	...	62	78
Milwaukee, Wis........	...	...	100	106

for the three months. Examining now the causes of death which figured in this decline, congenital debility is found to have declined from 13.7 per 1,000 births to 9.2, and diarrhea and enteritis from 23.7 to 20.8.

In 1915 Connecticut had a rate of 107 and in 1917 a rate of 94, a decline of 13 per 1,000 births; 1.9 for the first month of life; 2.1 for the second month of life; 3.1 for the third month of life, the decline for the first three months of life

thus accounting for over 50 per cent of the total decline. The decline of 13 per 1,000 births was almost entirely due to a decline of 8.4 per 1,000 births for diarrhea and enteritis and a decline of 3.8 for congenital debility.

So in an examination of almost any series of infant mortality rates the one great fact which stands out is that the infant mortality rate follows the rate from diarrhea and enteritis. If a city has a high infant mortality rate you may be sure that it has a high infant mortality rate from diarrhea and enteritis, and if it has a low infant mortality rate you may be sure that it has a low infant mortality rate from diarrhea and enteritis. For example, Fall River in 1917 with a rate of 159 shows a rate of 64 from diarrhea and enteritis, while Seattle with a rate of 61, shows a rate of 4 from diarrhea and enteritis. Again, if a great decline has occurred in an infant mortality rate, you will find that there has been a great decline in the rate from diarrhea and enteritis. And the point I wish particularly to emphasize is that until this factor is practically eliminated from the infant mortality rate, our energies should be directed towards its elimination because that field of endeavor still offers the best promise for great success.

New Zealand in 1907 had a rate of 89, of which one-fourth was from diarrhea and enteritis. In 1916 the rate from this cause was less than six and the infant mortality rate had been reduced to 51.

Some idea of the directions in which a reduction of the infant mortality rate is to be expected and to be sought can be obtained by a study of the tables which accompany this paper.

What has been done can be done again. If Seattle was able to show a rate of 4.9 for age period 3 to 6 months, then it should not be considered impossible for other places to reduce their rates for that age period to the same low mark. If Seattle was able to show a rate of 4.3 for diarrhea and enteritis, then it should

[Rates in bold face type are based upon less than 5 deaths. Numbers after the causes of death correspond to those of the abridged International List.]

Age and cause of death	The birth registration area	Connecticut		Maryland			Minnesota		Virginia			Fall River, Mass.	New York, N. Y.		Seattle, Wash.	Washington, D. C.		Commonwealth of Australia
				Total	White	Col.			Total	White	Col.							
	1917	1917	1915	1917	1917	1917	1917	1915	1917	1917	1917	1917	1917	1915	1917	1917	1915	1915
Age																		
Under 1 year	93.8	107.1	93.7	119.8	100.9	201.0	70.2	67.4	97.4	80.4	136.5	158.9	89.8	98.8	60.5	97.4	111.1	67.5
Under 1 day	15.0	14.0	13.9	18.4	17.4	22.5	16.5	15.3	14.9	14.7	15.3	15.2	12.0	12.7	13.9	16.3	18.7	23.9
1 day	4.6	6.2	5.4	4.6	4.3	5.9	3.6	2.9	3.6	3.6	5.7	6.0	3.7	3.7	3.5	7.7	7.4	—
2 days	3.5	3.6	2.8	4.0	3.3	6.8	5.7	3.0	3.3	2.8	4.6	4.3	2.9	2.8	3.5	4.5	4.6	3.9
2 to 6 days	6.0	6.3	6.0	6.2	6.1	10.1	5.5	5.7	3.8	3.8	9.8	4.7	2.7	3.2	3.8	7.4	5.8	4.9
1 week	4.2	6.3	6.3	4.3	4.0	11.0	3.5	3.5	3.9	3.8	4.0	5.8	3.8	3.7	3.7	4.8	5.6	4.1
1 week, but less than 1 month	3.4	3.6	3.5	3.3	3.7	6.7	2.5	2.5	3.1	3.8	4.0	6.6	3.2	3.7	3.1	2.1	2.6	3.4
1 month	3.4	5.0	3.6	3.9	3.7	20.2	2.8	2.4	3.4	2.4	4.4	6.6	3.1	2.9	4.9	1.2	2.6	2.1
2 months	4.4	8.6	6.1	10.9	6.5	19	3.1	3.5	5.9	3.8	12.1	12.9	6.0	6.6	2.6	1.6	2.6	5.6
3 to 5 months	6.6	9.2	8.6	9.0	6.5	20.2	4.0	4.0	8.6	3.5	12.4	15.2	6.2	13.2	1.9	9.1	8.8	4.1
6 to 8 months	15.1	10.7	13.0	22.8	18.1	42.8	5.3	8.3	16.5	4.5	25.6	31.3	11.8	18.3	5.1	18.2	14.7	8.5
9 to 11 months	9.2	11.4	9.1	17.1	14.4	29.0	4.3	5.5	11.9	7.2	20.0	26.0	12.1	12.8	3.3	10.8	11.7	6.9
Cause of death																		
All : ms[1]	93.8	107.1	93.7	119.8	100.9	201.0	70.2	67.4	97.4	80.4	136.5	158.9	89.0	98.8	60.5	97.4	111.1	67.5
Measles—5	0.1	0.5	0.1	0.7	0.7	0.9	0.4	1.0	1.4	1.3	1.6	6.0	0.1	0.9	1.0	0.4	0.3	0.4
Scarlet fever—6	0.2	—	—	—	—	—	—	—	—	—	—	—	—	—	—	—	—	—
Whooping cough—8	2.4	2.6	1.6	2.3	1.7	4.5	0.4	0.2	4.1	2.6	7.4	3.7	1.7	1.5	1.6	0.7	1.4	0.9
Diphtheria and croup—9	0.3	0.3	0.3	0.2	0.2	0.3	0.2	0.4	0.6	0.5	1.1	1.1	0.9	1.0	0.2	0.7	0.3	—
Influenza—9	0.3	0.6	0.1	0.2	0.2	0.1	0.1	0.1	0.7	0.3	1.5	0.5	0.4	0.3	—	0.4	0.1	—
Dysentery—(12)	0.5	0.2	0.3	0.2	0.3	0.2	0.1	0.1	0.5	0.3	1.0	0.3	0.1	0.1	0.2	0.1	0.1	—
Erysipelas—(12)	0.1	0.2	0.2	0.1	0.1	0.3	0.1	0.1	0.1	0.1	—	0.2	0.1	0.1	—	0.1	0.4	0.3
Tetanus—(37)	0.7	0.1	0.2	0.7	0.4	2.3	0.1	0.3	0.6	0.3	1.0	0.6	0.5	0.6	0.8	0.4	0.7	0.5
Tuberculosis of the lungs—13	0.7	0.4	0.5	0.4	0.3	0.6	0.1	0.1	0.1	0.1	0.2	0.5	0.6	1.0	—	0.7	1.1	1.8
Tuberculous meningitis—14	0.2	0.6	0.5	0.3	0.3	0.4	0.7	0.7	0.1	0.1	0.2	0.3	0.1	0.1	1.8	1.1	—	0.8
Other forms of tuberculosis—15	1.2	0.5	0.7	0.4	0.4	0.3	0.5	0.5	0.3	0.3	0.5	1.6	0.5	1.6	0.6	1.3	4.0	2.1
Syphilis—37	1.1	1.1	0.7	1.2	0.3	6.1	0.2	0.1	0.1	0.1	0.1	0.4	0.3	0.4	—	0.4	0.4	1.5
Meningitis—17	1.1	1.1	1.1	1.6	1.2	3.0	0.9	0.7	0.8	0.8	0.5	1.1	1.1	1.0	1.8	4.1	4.1	2.0
Convulsions—(37)	0.3	2.2	2.6	0.5	0.5	7.3	1.2	1.2	0.3	0.3	0.7	3.6	3.6	3.1	0.6	0.6	3.4	2.6
Organic diseases of the heart—19	2.2	2.7	4.1	3.5	2.7	8.8	2.2	2.2	1.1	0.7	2.9	2.1	4.3	4.0	0.6	1.9	4.1	2.0
Pneumonia—20	8.3	9.1	8.3	8.8	5.5	26.2	2.4	2.9	2.0	1.9	8.9	6.6	4.5	4.9	4.3	2.4	1.9	2.6
Bronchitis—20	1.2	0.9	0.9	1.2	0.8	2.6	0.7	0.7	0.7	0.7	0.8	3.1	0.8	0.3	1.7	4.3	1.6	3.7
Bronchopneumonia—(23)	20.0	30.8	22.4	32.8	28.8	49.8	8.8	8.0	17.1	13.9	24.2	63.8	20.8	23.7	17.4	24.4	21.2	16.3
Disease of the stomach—24	2.2	2.4	4.5	2.4	0.8	8.8	1.0	0.9	2.2	1.0	4.9	1.1	0.3	0.3	4.3	4.3	1.5	—
Diarrhea and enteritis—25	8.8	4.1	8.4	21.8	8.4	27.0	18.6	16.2	17.1	13.9	24.2	17.4	4.7	4.6	17.2	27.5	28.7	3.1
Malformations—(33)	19.1	17.5	18.7	21.8	11.0	20.6	16.8	17.0	11.0	8.8	18.0	17.4	4.7	13.7	6.2	4.6	4.4	2.7
Premature birth—(33)	3.8	5.1	5.6	3.6	3.5	3.5	0.7	0.7	3.0	1.5	3.6	5.5	5.5	3.9	1.6	27.5	28.7	29.4
Congenital debility—(33, 37)																		
Injuries at birth—(37)	2.9	0.9	1.9	0.4	0.4	1.3	1.3	1.1	1.6	0.3	3.1	2.5	2.5	2.5	1.9	6.1	4.1	} 35.
Violent deaths (suicide)—(37)																		
Unknown or ill-defined diseases—38																		
All other causes	4.8	4.7	5.3	4.4	3.6	13.6	1.8	1.6	4.7	4.2	16.9	5.3	4.1	4.8	3.3	4.9	5.8	5.7

[1] Exclusive of stillbirths.   [2] Less than one-tenth of 1 per 1,000 births.   [3] Included in "All other causes."

INFANT MORTALITY RATES
IN THE BIRTH REGISTRATION AREA
1915 TO 1917
AND PROVISIONAL RATES FOR 1918

Area	Deaths under 1 year of age per 1,000 births			
	1915	1916	1917	1918
Connecticut............	107	101	94	107
Rural...............	119	101	96	111
Cities.............	103	101	93	106
Indiana................			86	87
Rural...............			78	77
Cities.............			100	102
Kansas.................			77	81
Rural...............			73	75
Cities.............			98	107
Kentucky...............			87	95
Rural...............			85	91
Cities.............			103	120
Maine..................	105	108	93	104
Rural...............	104	102	89	102
Cities.............	109	128	107	111
Maryland...............			120	141
Rural...............			121	135
Cities.............			123	147
Massachusetts..........	101	100	98	113
Rural...............	92	87	91	106
Cities.............	103	103	99	115
Michigan...............	86	96	88	89
Rural...............	78	87	80	81
Cities.............	96	106	97	97
Minnesota..............	70	70	67	71
Rural...............	67	66	64	68
Cities.............	77	78	75	79
New Hampshire..........	110	115	110	114
Rural...............	89	97	86	102
Cities.............	131	133	132	124
New York..............	99	94	91	97
Rural...............	89	83	85	94
Cities.............	102	97	93	98
North Carolina........			100	104
Rural...............			96	99
Cities.............			159	170
Ohio..................			92	94
Rural...............			79	87
Cities.............			103	100
Pennsylvania..........	110	114	111	128
Rural...............	110	114	109	127
Cities.............	110	114	113	129
Rhode Island..........	120	111	108	
Rural...............	129	93	101	
Cities.............	118	116	109	
Utah..................			69	64
Rural...............			71	63
Cities.............			66	66
Vermont...............	85	93	85	93
Rural...............	80	86	81	88
Cities.............	116	128	108	120
Virginia..............			98	104
Rural...............			91	94
Cities.............			129	146
Washington............			75	69
Rural...............			62	68
Cities.............			78	80
Wisconsin.............			78	80
Rural...............			69	69
Cities.............			92	100

not be considered impossible for other places to show a like rate. Extreme poverty may be an important factor in some cases, but in this country the problem is largely one of education—every mother and every prospective mother must be taught how to care for her child, and the city which is most successful in inducing mothers to breast-feed their children will be the city to show the lowest infant mortality rates. Moreover, this campaign of educating mothers must be carried on not only this year and next, but every year so long as there are babies to be protected.

A high infant mortality rate today is a greater disgrace than a high typhoid rate, for a high typhoid rate may be due to one milkman's carelessness, or to the laxness of a few city officials in not properly safeguarding the water supply or the milk supply, but a high infant mortality rate reflects upon the clergy, reflects upon the physicians and nurses, reflects upon the school teachers and editors, all of whom have a joint responsibility not only to instruct mothers, but also to induce them to care for their babies properly. Furthermore, a high infant mortality rate today reflects upon the intelligence of the people.

Now that the war is over and the epidemic is past, no better or nobler work can be found for health officers and others than to stir up general interest in campaigns to reduce infant mortality.

Let every locality strive for a record infant mortality rate.

□

Anent the 1920 Membership Campaign! You, Mr. Member, have in mind some to propose for Membership in the A. P. H. A. You have (see page 370) the name of your State Campaign Chairman. You have only to bring the two together.

THE PURIFICATION OF OYSTERS AS A CONSERVATION MEASURE

WILLIAM FIRTH WELLS, M. D.,

Biologist and Sanitarian, New York State Conservation Commission, Albany, N. Y.

Read at hearing of Oyster Growers before the Commissioner of Health of New York City, March 1, 1920.

Give the oyster a chance to cleanse itself and typhoid will be as preventable here as with domestic water supplies. This is the motif of this paper by Dr. Wells, who is no new hand at discussing shellfish problems. "It can be considered a conservation measure," he urges.

A RECENT statement of the Metropolitan Life Insurance Company shows a reduction in general mortality at ages 1-74 in eight years of 17.9 percent. This actual saving to policyholders should convince all of the commercial value of modern methods of sanitation. Chief among infectious diseases is the reduction in typhoid fever of 69 percent due to improved water and food supplies. Thus the end has justified the means, and unquestionably sanitation has come to stay.

The first board sanitary movement was the improvement in water supplies. It was found necessary with the growth of population to take measures to prevent the pollution of natural waters as far as possible, and to seek carefully for the purest sources available for water supplies. The next movement came in the production of clean milk. Former slovenly methods of dairy practice were condemned, and a new standard was raised for dairy farms. This, at first, came as a distinct hardship to the industry, but gradually adjustments have been made until the production of milk under improved conditions is just as natural as was the production twenty-five years

ago under conditions which we could not tolerate today. Likewise the oyster industry shared the general attack of sanitarians, and consequently, former practices of taking up clean oysters and placing them in rivers receiving the sewage of large cities in order to float or plump them, have been universally condemned and abandoned. Contaminated grounds which formerly were tolerated as maturing grounds for oysters have been condemned, and as a result it may be generally stated that oysters today can be eaten with impunity, and with full satisfaction that they are produced from reasonably clean areas. The activities of the Boards of Health thus give assurance to the public that whatever products they receive with the endorsement of the health authorities are safe.

Sanitation, however, has not stopped here. However much improvement in our water supplies has been secured by the treatment of sewage discharged into natural waters, or by changing to supplies less polluted by sewage, it is now generally recognized that such methods are not complete. Science has produced methods for the treatment of water supplies by which all vestiges of suspicion may be removed. Likewise with the milk supply; however clean .may be the conditions under which it is produced such milk is not considered absolutely safe. Possibilities always exist for the accidental infection of milk in the process of handling, and here science has produced a simple and effective way of pasteurizing milk so as to remove the last faint possibility of suspicion.

The same problem exists in the oyster industry today. Whereas oysters generally may be considered free from contamination, there are practically no conditions under which oysters are naturally produced where contamination is not possible. The waters over the beds are open to navigation, and not absolutely free of access to accidental or occasional pollution. While under ordinary circumstances these possibilities may be considered negligible, it is true that they are possible, and while such a condition exists the Board of Health must always give its endorsement with reservations, and in the minds of the consuming public will linger a faint lack of confidence which they enjoy in full in their water and milk supplies. Until measures similar to those used in the purification of water and the pasteurization of milk are utilized in the oyster industry, the public is bound to lack the satisfaction in oysters which it should rightfully have.

Looked at from the standpoint of the Board of Health, what standard should be demanded of the oyster? A general statement has been made that oysters should be grown in waters as pure as those which would be tolerated for drinking. But if we apply this standard, which seems reasonable, we could make a general statement concerning oysters that practically none are grown in waters which would be endorsed without treatment from a sanitary point of view for drinking.

Health boards make the general rule that all surface waters are open to pollution, and therefore, all such supplies should be treated. Oysters are grown in surface waters, and to be consistent with rigid water supply standards all oysters should be purified.

The United States Public Health Service in its investigation of coastal waters, with special reference to the shellfish industries, soon discovered this fact, but from a practical point of view it did not seem reasonable to enforce such a standard, which would make oyster production practically impossible, until some simple and efficient method of purification was available. The Service carried out experiments to discover how rapidly oysters purified themselves if transferred to clean water. The remarkable ease with which oysters became polluted or cleansed, according to the conditions of their environment, convinced the authorities that transfer to clean surroundings would be an economic means of removing any possible pollution. Carrying these experiments further, I proposed a method whereby the oysters would be allowed to purify themselves by natural function in artificially purified water. These experiments have been thoroughly tested, both scientifically and practically, and been found to be a feasible means of guaranteeing the character of the oyster. Dr. Cumming, under whom these experiments have been demonstrated, and who since has been nominated Surgeon-General by the President, unqualifiedly endorsed the method and recommended its use in Raritan Bay.* There is no question, therefore, but that the oystermen and the health authorities have a common meeting ground on which the one can produce

*U. S. Public Health Service, Public Health Bulletin No. 86, page 41.

oysters, and the other can guarantee them.

I have successively proposed this method as a scientific, sanitary measure (Under U. S. Public Health Service), and as an economic measure of production (Under the U. S. Bureau of Fisheries), and it is true that the purification of oysters can be considered as a conservation measure, and the reason for my discussion is interest in this phase of conservation. The present food shortage and high cost of living requires that every available source of food be developed which can be legitimately utilized. It is not merely a question of oyster culture, but a question of food production. The same problem arises in many of our other food producing industries. Careless use or abuse of the waters has been causing them to be less and less valuable for the natural production of fish. The increased contamination is bringing about a condition in the shellfish industries similar to that which has made the purification of waters used for drinking purposes necessary. This creates a legitimate field for the method of purifying oysters, whereby it will be possible to give a guarantee to the oyster and retain in production many valuable beds.

Briefly stated this method of purification consists of nothing more than assuring conditions of cleanliness under which the oyster can, by its natural function, remove any pollution received from the water. Ordinarily the oyster is very active in filtering out and digesting fine particles which are drifting in the water. If kept in clean surroundings, the oyster is just as active in returning these substances into the water. Under ordinary conditions an oyster passes fifty gallons of water a day through his gills, and a particle of food deposited on those gills will pass on to the mouth and be eliminated from the oyster within five hours. If conditions are maintained such that pollutions are removed, and new ones are not permitted to enter the oyster, it is possible to cleanse a polluted oyster within a remarkably short period. Twenty-four hours has been found sufficient under ordinary conditions of practice. With slightly polluted oysters less time is required than for grossly polluted oysters. The latter, which it would not be proposed to treat, might require a longer period than twenty-four hours.

The only reason why this process has not been more rapidly developed commercially has been the difficulty of bringing about an agreement between the different parties interested. If anything can be done to bring about the development of a large, well-operated, carefully supervised plant, the condition of oysters so desirable to establishing the confidence of the people in oysters can readily be guaranteed. No one proposition today promises more to put the oyster back on the bill of fare in the proud position which it formerly enjoyed.

□

7,500 A. P. H. A. Members will easily be reached, if every present Member will only help.

STUDIES ON THE VIABILITY OF THE TUBERCLE BACILLUS

J. B. ROGERS, M. D.,

Percy Shields Laboratory, Cincinnati Tuberculosis Sanatorium and Department of Bacteriology, University of Cincinnati Medical School, Cincinnati, Ohio.

These observations suggest that open cases of tuberculosis should not be admitted to wards of a general hospital and emphasize the need of housing advanced cases under good control. Dust rising from dry-swept floors, even where phenol was used, produced the disease in guinea pigs.

THE establishment by Koch, of the etiologic relation of the tubercle bacillus to all forms of tuberculosis, led to much scientific investigation in regard to its habitat outside of the human body, its viability and the method of transmission from one individual to another.

· The earlier investigators were inclined to place the tubercle bacillus among the more resistant spore-forming micro-organisms, and searches were made in divers places entirely away from the human body in attempting to prove its ubiquity.

The question was eventually settled by Cornet and co-workers, that the tubercle bacillus is found in appreciable numbers only in close proximity to the individuals who suffer from the disease, and is present in smaller numbers in places less frequently visited by the diseased individuals. He was the first to recognize the deleterious influence of such factors as light, dessication, temperature, and the length of time outside of the human body on the organism. These either lower the vitality and render it innocuous or destroy its power to grow at all, either in favorable media or susceptible animals.

A thorough review of the literature of numerous investigators, as to the length of time the bacillus can remain alive and virulent outside of the human body was made by M. J. Rosenau (1), of the Harvard Medical School, and presented at the Sixth International Congress of Tuberculosis, and in summarizing the work, together with his own investigations, he concludes that the organism deprived of its environment is no more resistant than other non-spore forming bacteria.

E. R. Baldwin (2) states that the length of time that the tubercle bacillus can remain alive and virulent in human sputum depends on the size and thickness of the mass, its place of deposit, its quality, and most important its exposure to light and air. When the sputum is of tenacious character, and forms hard, glue-like masses, and is kept in a cool, dark place, such as a basement, the maximum period of vitality is from six to eight months.

Park and Williams (3) state that under ordinary conditions sputum will usually retain its infectious power for two or three months, and exceptionally as long as one year.

Twitchell (2) found that sputum placed on a handkerchief will remain infectious as long as seventy days and on a carpet, lesions resulted in guinea pigs after thirty days, but not after seventy days. Direct sunlight caused the death of the organism after several hours.

When pure cultures of the bacillus are subjected to detrimental agencies, an entirely different result is obtained. Thus it has been shown by John Weinzirl, (4) Department of Bacteriology, University of Washington, that diffuse light will kill the tubercle bacillus usually in about three or four days.

Theobald Smith (5), formerly of Harvard Medical School, has shown that cultures on nutritive media will remain alive from seven to nineteen months.

Our investigations in regard to the viability of the tubercle bacillus were undertaken for the purpose of determining whether or not the organism can be dried to dust form under natural conditions and still remain living and virulent.

Experiment I. Dust was collected from the floors of the open wards, and about two drachms first treated with 45 cc. of sterile 2% NaOH solution, incubated at 37°.5 C for 20 minutes and centrifugalized in a high power electric centrifuge for 10 minutes. At the end of this time, the coarser particles had settled to the bottom, leaving a thick, yellow emulsion above. This was removed with a pipette and washed twice with sterile .89% sodium chloride solution. The remaining sediment was emulsified and injected into the right lower quadrant of a guinea pig and each pig placed into a separate cage. Eleven pigs were injected November 25, 1918. They were etherized and examined at different times. Out of eleven pigs, seven were negative and four showed tuberculosis. (See tables.)

Experiment II. Dry dust and small particles of dirt were collected from the morgue floor and prepared for injection as in Experiment I. Four pigs were injected November 22, 1918. On February 26, 1919, all pigs were etherized and examined. Three presented generalized tuberculosis, and one tuberculosis of the inguinal gland on the injected side.

Experiment III. Dust was collected from the windows and shelving of the morgue and from the tops of specimen jars, and prepared as in the two previously described experiments. Five pigs were injected November 22, 1918. They were etherized and examined at different times. Two pigs presented generalized tuberculosis and three were negative.

Experiment IV. Ten pigs were placed in a sterilized wire cage and kept about three feet above the morgue floor, which was dry swept every morning. The animals remained in the morgue on an average of five hours daily for a period of eighteen days. After each exposure, they were removed, given a bichloride bath, and

RESULTS OF EXPERIMENTS

EXPERIMENT I

Date of Autopsy	Pig.	Results
1-15-19	1	Negative.
1-15-19	2	Negative.
1-15-19	3	Negative.
2-17-19	4	Tuberculosis of the inguinal and cervical glands, spleen and lungs.
2-17-19	5	Tuberculosis of the spleen, lungs and bronchial glands.
2-21-19	6	Negative.
2-24-19	7	Generalized tuberculosis.
2-24-19	8	Generalized tuberculosis.
2-25-19	9	Negative.
2-25-19	10	Negative.
2-25-19	11	Negative.

EXPERIMENT II

Date of Autopsy	Pig.	Results
2-26-19	1	Generalized tuberculosis.
2-26-19	2	Generalized tuberculosis.
2-26-19	3	Generalized tuberculosis.
2-26-19	4	Tuberculosis of the inguinal gland on the injected side.

EXPERIMENT III

Date of Autopsy	Pig.	Results
2-21-19	1	Generalized Tuberculosis.
3- 5-19	2	Generalized Tuberculosis.
3-15-19	3	Negative.
3-15-19	4	Negative.
3-15-19	5	Negative.

EXPERIMENT IV

Date of Autopsy	Pig.	Results
12- 1-18	1	Negative.
2- 8-19	2	Generalized Tuberculosis.
3-19-19	3	Negative.
3-19-19	4	Generalized Tuberculosis.
3-19-19	5	Generalized Tuberculosis.
3-19-19	6	Generalized Tuberculosis.
3-19-19	7	An occasional hard tubercle in both lungs.
3-19-19	8	Negative.
3-19-19	9	One hard tubercle in the left lung.
3-19-19	10	Hard tubercle in the left lung.

fed in a sterile cage in another room. Both cages were scrubbed with "Neko" each day. The bath, however, was discontinued after the first week, as we felt that too much handling of the pigs would be injurious. On dissection, three of the animals were negative and seven showed tuberculosis. An attempt was made to grow the organism from the dust on gentian violet egg medium. Five hundred tubes were inoculated but all were contaminated with spores.

SUMMARY AND CONCLUSION

Experiment I shows that dust material containing living tubercle bacilli can withstand drying and the effect of diffuse light and still retain virulence, and in sufficient numbers produce tuberculosis in a guinea pig.

The wards from which the samples of dust were taken are occupied by advanced, open cases of tuberculosis, many of these patients being of the middle and lower social strata. An attempt is made to prevent coughing with uncovered mouths and to observe other rules of. cleanliness, but unless constantly watched, the rules are ignored. The wards floors are mopped daily with a strong solution of "Neko" and in some of the samples of dust and dirt collected, this could be detected by its odor. The bed clothes are changed daily, and it is our opinion that the cleansing of the wards is as thorough as is practical in public institutions. Theoretically, if the pa-

tients observe the rules carefully, the bacteria should not be scattered by the patients, but from the bare facts of the case, it would appear that it is extremely hard to prevent to some extent at least the scattering of the microorganisms. It emphasizes the importance or absolute necessity of housing advanced cases where this dissemination can be reduced to a minimum, and would suggest rather than prove that open cases of tuberculosis should not be admitted to the wards of a general hospital.

Experiments II, III and IV, indicate that blood and other organic matter coming from the body at postmortem, protect the organism from natural germicidal agents and that even the process of sterilization, using strong solutions of "Neko" and phenol, a number of bacteria will escape and remain virulent and can be blown around in dust, be inhaled by guinea pigs and produce tuberculosis.

BIBLIOGRAPHY

1. Rosenau, M. J. "The Viability of the Tubercle Bacillus." Sixth International Congress of Tuberculosis. Vol. I, part I., page 5.
2. Ibid.
3. Park, W. H. "Sources of Tubercle Bacilli, Producing Human Tuberculosis." Ibid page 157.
4. Weinzirl, John. "The Action of Diffuse Light Upon the Bacillus Tubercle Bacillus." Journal of Medical Research, Vol. I. 1914.

□

Kill two birds with one stone. Go get your new Member, and at the same time persuade him to go with you to the San Francisco A. P. H. A. Meeting, August 30-September 3, 1920.

EXCESSIVE MORTALITY FROM INFLUENZA-PNEUMONIA AMONG BITUMINOUS COAL MINERS OF OHIO IN 1918

E. B. STARR, M. D.,

Director, Division of Industrial Hygiene, Ohio State Department of Health, Columbus, Ohio.

THE dearth of mortality statistics is probably the most disappointing feature associated with the study of disease in its relation to occupational employment. Among other obstacles which stand in the way of gathering reliable mortality statistics the following may be mentioned: (1) The relatively few occupations in which employment remains fixed; (2) the difficulty of obtaining figures representing race and age distribution and the number employed in the various occupations; (3) the prevalent carelessness with which occupational data is noted on death certificates, and (4) the infrequency with which the occupation of the deceased is recognized and assigned as a direct or predisposing cause of death.

There are a few occupations such as coal mining, pottery working, printing trades, etc., in which there is little disposition to occupational shifting. For some of these occupations it will be possible in the near future, we believe, to overcome the most serious obstacles which now stand in the way of the preparation of mortality statistics for the state of Ohio.

The Department of Investigation and Statistics of the Ohio Industrial Commission has for six years been compiling the annual statistical returns required by law of Ohio employers. These returns while at first incomplete are becoming more perfect each year and even now represent quite accurately the number employed in a few of the trades, more accurately in all probability, than can be expected from the Federal Census enumerators.

Unfortunately it has not been found

feasible as yet to gather statistics of race and age distribution in any of the trades. However, even this may be accomplished in due course, and the Commission now has under consideration the question of including on its schedule an item regarding the race of the employed. Many employers are now keeping individual records showing the race and age of employes and the custom is becoming more general each year. A few of the highly organized trades are likewise keeping systems of records which in time should prove valuable in compiling mortality statistics. An instance of the latter is the United Mine Workers organization in the state of Illinois. This organization has for the past ten years kept account of the number of coal miners in the state, and in addition, a complete record of each death as a prerequisite to the settlement of death claim insurance maintained by the state organization. It was these records that enabled Hayhurst[1] to include in his Survey of Coal Mining in Illinois and Ohio a study of mortality among the Illinois coal miners.

This Department and the State Bureau of Vital statistics are now planning to carry on a campaign among undertakers of the state to interest them in the important matter of inquiring into and more accurately noting the occupational data on death certificates, and it is the purpose of the Bureau hereafter to scrutinize more carefully that portion of the death certificate provided for occupational

1. Hayhurst, E. R.: *Report of the Health Insurance Commission, State of Illinois,* May 1, 1919, pp. 376-402; *Journal of Industrial Hygiene,* 1, No. 7, (November), 1919, pp. 360-367.

data, and to discourage the use of meaningless terms. Though the fruits of such efforts may be long delayed and imperfect, even slight improvement in such fundamental data should appreciably enhance the value of Ohio's statistics.

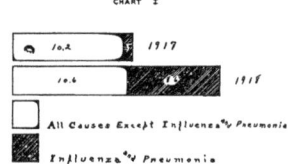

CHART I

All Causes Except Influenza & Pneumonia

Influenza & Pneumonia

Illustrative of the Influenzal Factor in the Death Rate Among Bituminous Coal Miners of Ohio ?

From statistical returns obtained by the Industrial Co m m i s s i o n and through the almost complete unionization of the bituminous coal miners, we have a pretty accurate annual count of the number of Ohio coal miners in employment. Both of these agencies agree on the figures 51,286 and 53,092 as representing with a considerable degree of precision the number of coal miners in Ohio in 1917 and 1918 respectively. This would seem then to furnish an occupational group as well suited for study as any at present.

No attempt will be made to draw any conclusions from the attached tables because of the limited period covered, except that the striking mortality from influenza-pneumonia among Ohio coal miners in 1918 would seem to justify their presentation at this time.[2]

"The coal fields of Ohio lie in the eastern part of the state, extending from near the shore of Lake Erie in Geauga and Lake counties south-west-

ward to Scioto and Lawrence counties on the Ohio River. An area of about 12,650 square miles, nearly one-third of the state, is underlain with coal-bearing rocks." Bituminous or soft coal only is mined. The population is chiefly rural.

The total deaths from all causes among Ohio coal miners in 1918 was 1,023, a rate of 19.2 per thousand employed, as against a total in 1917 of 571 deaths or a rate of 11.1 per thousand employed. The latter rate is not far from that found by Hayhurst[1] among Illinois coal miners for the six and one-half year period, February 1, 1912, to July 21, 1918; namely, 10.8 per thousand employed.

Of 39,565 deaths from all causes among males 15 years of age and over, in Ohio in 1918 (excluding coal miners), 11,989, or 30.3% were due to influenza-pneumonia, whereas 458 deaths or 44.7% of the total deaths among Ohio coal miners were due to influenza-pneumonia. Though these percentages certainly indicate a preponderance of influenza-pneumonia mortality among coal miners they do not in themselves represent the true relation when one considers the distortion resulting from the large mortality among

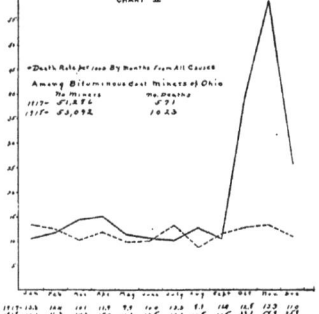

CHART II

*Death Rate per 1000 By Deaths from All Causes Among Bituminous Coal Miners of Ohio
          No. Miners   No. Deaths
1917- 51,286   571
1918- 53,092   1023

? Death Rates computed on an Annual Basis

2. Louis I. Dublin, Statistician, Metropolitan Life Insurance Company, has recently published figures representing mortality from influenza-pneumonia among bituminous coal miners, based upon 64 deaths occurring among 4,700 insured miners in the period October to December, 1918. *Journal Industrial Hygiene*, Vol. 1, No. 10 (Feb.) 1920, p. 493.

miners due to deaths from violence. By reference to Table I it may be seen that 20% of the total deaths among miners in 1918 was due to violence, whereas only 8.7% was due to the same cause in males of 15 years and over in the state at large. By eliminating this distortion,[3] due to violence, the relation betwen influenza-pneumonia mortality percentages in coal miners and males of the state at large appears in a truer light. The percentage of total deaths due to influenza-pneumonia among coal miners is then 55.9 as against 33.1 among males of 15 years and over in the state at large.

If one may hazard the statement of a death rate from influenza-pneumonia among males of 15 years and over, in the state at large (excluding miners), based upon an estimate of 1,886,000 males,[4] we may compute a rate of 635 per 100,000 as against a rate of 862.6 per 100,000 from the same cause among miners.

Of the total deaths from influenza-pneumonia among coal miners, 17% occurred in the age period from 15 to 24 years, 37% in the age period 25 to 34 years and 28% in the age period 35 to 44 years. Eighty-three per cent of

3. Figured by computing the percentages with deaths from violence excluded.

4. Arithmetically computed as of July 1, 1918, upon the growth in population of this group between the 1900 and 1910 census.

DEATHS AND DEATH RATES AMONG BITUMINOUS COAL MINERS OF OHIO BY SELECTED CAUSES
1917   and   18

TABLE NO. I

Cause of Death	International List Numbers	No. of Deaths Coal Miners		Per Cent of Total Deaths Coal Miners		Per Cent Total Deaths Among Males 15 yrs. & over State at Large* 1918	Death Rate per 100,000 Coal Miners Employed	
		1917	1918	1917	1918		1917	1918
Typhoid Fever	1	10	14	1.7	1.3	0.9	19.5	26.3
Tuberculosis All forms	28-35	48	66	8.4	6.4	9.7	93.4	124.8
Cancer	39-41 43-45	29	28	5.1	2.7	4.5	56.5	52.7
Apoplexy & Other Diseases of Nervous System	60-76	54	58	9.4	5.6	10.2	105.2	109.2
Cardio Vascular Diseases	77-85	106	93	18.5	9.1	14.4	206.6	175.1
Influenza and Pneumonia	10 & 91-92	45	458	7.9	44.7	30.3	89.6	862.6
Other Respiratory Diseases	86-90 93-98	11	8	1.9	0.7	1.1	21.4	15.0
Genito Urinary (Non-Venereal)	119-127	33	29	5.7	2.8	7.2	64.3	54.6
Suicide	.155-163	15	12	2.6	1.1	1.3	29.2	22.6
Other Violence	164-186	165	205	28.8	20.0	8.7	321.7	386.1
All Others	2- 9 11- 27 36- 38 46- 59 99-118 142-154 187-189	55	52	9.6	5.0	11.0	107.2	97.9
TOTALS		571	1023	99.6	99.4	99.3	1114.6	1926.9

*Exclusive of Coal Miners.

the deaths from influenza-pneumonia occurred in the age period 15 to 44 years. Of the total deaths in the age period 15-24, 57% died of influenza-pneumonia. Of the total deaths in the age period 25-34, 66% died of influenza-pneumonia. Of the total deaths in the age period 35-44, 54% died of influenza-pneumonia. The peak of the mortality curve came in November, a month later than that of the larger cities of the state.

For the two years under study the death rate from tuberculosis, cancer and Bright's disease were decidedly under the average for the U. S. death registration area, while the death rate from typhoid fever was nearly twice and that from violence, more than three times that of the registration area. The most conspicuous factor in .the high death rate due to violence among Ohio coal miners is ascribed to "Traumatism in Miners" and "Railway

Accidents," there being 121 deaths from these causes in 1917 and 161 in 1918.

Of the less conspicuous causes of death among coal miners during 1917 and 1918 the following may be mentioned: Four deaths due to dysentery; 2 to erysipelas; 2 to rheumatism, 8 to diabetes; 1 to exophthalmic goiter; 8 to aenemia; 19 to alcoholism; 4 to meningitis; 4 to tabes dorsalis; 13 to general paralysis of the insane; 5 to other forms of mental alienation; 2 to epilepsy; 4 to asthma; 5 to appendicitis; 4 to hernia and 19 to cirrhosis of the liver. There were no deaths in either year ascribed to malaria, tetanus or occupational poisonings.

It is our expectation as circumstances permit, to develop further mortality statistics for Ohio coal miners and for other occupational groups which may lend themselves to such purposes.

DEATHS AMONG
BITUMINOUS COAL MINERS OF OHIO
BY SELECTED CAUSES AND AGE GROUPS

TABLE No. 2.

Cause of Death	International List No.	Number of Deaths 1917	1918	15-24 1917	1918	25-34 1917	1918	35-44 1917	1918	45-54 1917	1918	55-64 1917	1918	65-74 1917	1918	75-84 1917	1918	85 and over 1917	1918	Unknown 1917	1918
Typhoid Fever	1	10	14	2	5	5	5	-	3	3	1	-	-	-	-	-	-	-	-	-	-
Tuberculosis All Forms	28-35	48	66	5	8	10	14	9	14	7	15	11	8	5	4	1	1	-	·1	-	1
Cancer	39-41 41-45	29	28	-	-	-	4	4	3	6	7	13	4	4	8	2	2	-	-	-	-
Apoplexy & Other Diseases of the Nervous System	60-76	54	58	1	1	3	3	5	8	13	8	5	12	16	15	7	11	4	-	-	-
Cardio Vascular Diseases	77-85	106	93	4	4	6	3	11	9	20	14	22	24	26	28	10	9	5	2	-	-
Influenza and Pneumonia	10 and 91-92	45	456	1	80	2	170	9	129	15	28	7	25	6	21	3	3	2	2	-	-
Other Respiratory Diseases (Non-venereal)	86-90 93-98	11	8	-	-	-	-	2	-	1	2	3	-	2	4	3	1	-	1	-	-
Genito Urinary (Non-venereal)	119-127	33	29	-	-	1	-	1	6	4	8	8	4	12	3	7	6	-	2	-	-
Suicide	155-163	15	12	2	1	5	6	1	1	3	2	3	2	1	-	-	-	-	-	-	-
Other Violence	164-186	165	205	21	39	43	47	39	59	38	37	16	13	8	9	-	1	-	-	-	-
All Others	2-9 11-27 36-38 46-59 99-118 128-154 187-189	55	52	3	2	8	6	9	6	10	12	10	12	11	8	4	4	-	2	-	-
TOTALS		571	1023	39	140	83	258	92	238	120	134	98	104	91	100	37	38	11	10	-	1

EARLY SCHOOL OF PUBLIC HEALTH AT LYONS, FRANCE

WILLIAM T. SEDGWICK, PH.D., Sc.D.,

Chairman, Administrative Board, Harvard-Technology School of Public Health, Cambridge, Mass.

My attention has recently been drawn, by Professor Selskar M. Gunn, to an interesting pamphlet entitled "Instruction in Hygiene at Lyons," which is a reprint from the Revue d'Hygiene et de Police Sanitaire (p. 893), of last October. I wish that space permitted lengthy extracts from this important brochure, but I must content myself with a very concise account of it and refer those interested to the original paper. It may be helpful to some to remark that on the continent the term "hygiene" is used much as is in Great Britain and the United States, the term "public health."

"At a time when our country is exhausted by war, our population diminished by almost three millions in five years, and our birth-rate shows a decrease more painful than ever, in short, at a time when we must produce more Frenchmen besides preserving those which exist, the problems of Hygiene stand first among those interesting sociologists and physicians. How shall we teach Hygiene to physicians? How disseminate and popularize a science indispensable for the future of our country, that is our first problem"—so begins this historical document. The authors then proceed to set forth their views on the teaching of hygiene and show that public health has been sadly "neglected" in France, but that in 1900 Professor Jules Courmont established at Lyons a remarkable School or Institute of Public Hygiene and Health and enlivened its teaching.

Courmont was, apparently, a very unusual man, "an apostle of hygiene," for his leading idea was that hygiene is not only a medical but a social science, that "Hygiene overflows Medicine," that "The Professor of Hygiene must not confine himself exclusively to medical teaching, and that everything ought to be done in the way of such teaching "first for physicians, but also for specialists such as directors of bureaux and for those whose profession requires thorough knowledge of the subject," among whom are named architects and engineers. And Courmont not only established an Institute of Hygiene, but also a Mu-

seum of Hygiene, and what interests us particularly a *Certificate of Hygiene* based upon methodical and appropriate courses.

We need not dwell upon the Institute itself or the Museum or the methods of instruction, although in these last it is interesting to know that in 14 years 286 students have thus far been registered, 209 Certificates of Hygiene given and 209 specialists prepared for the different functions of laboratory work, officers of bureaux of public health, etc.

The courses upon which the Certificate in Hygiene is based are given in part at the Veterinary School, in part at the Law School, in part in the Faculty of Science, and in part by the Faculty of Law. "Some Courses are given by chemists, others by physicians." "Hygiene overflows medicine."

The great point is that these improved courses are not only for physicians and medical students, but also for druggists, veterinarians, architects, engineers, chemists, inspectors of public health, etc. Jules Courmont wrote: "More and more the social function of the physician will be hygienic and prophylactic as well as curative." Again it is stated, "Against opposition met in the medical environment, Courmont insisted that a complementary education in Hygiene was necessary not only for physicians, but for all who, from their functions ought to be instructed in hygienic matters."

The certificate bears the title *Certificat d'Hygiène*, but after what has been said it will be obvious that it is really equivalent to the American Certificate in Public Health and those readers of the AMERICAN JOURNAL OF PUBLIC HEALTH who are interested in the development of schools of public health will perhaps be surprised, as was the author of this article, to learn that what is virtually a *Certificate in Public Health* was established in Lyons as early as 1905, and that in 1919 209 persons had received the certificate, 135 having been physicians or medical students and 74 non-medical men—pharmacists, chemists, architects, engineers, etc.

DISCUSSION OF "A STANDARD BUDGET."

Discussion of Dr. Haven Emerson's paper,* "A Standard Budget: the Health Officer's First Need," before the Section on Public Health Administration, American Public Health Association, at New Orleans, October 28, 1919, by *Ernst Christopher Meyer, Ph.D.*, of the International Health Board, New York City.

Several points touched upon in Dr. Emerson's excellent summary of the importance of a standardized budget deserve emphasis. Standardization means little without a degree of universality in the use of a standard. A standard of weights and measures, for example, is useful only if it is very generally adopted. The same is true of the standardized health budget. During recent years much progress has been made in the standardization of budgets in our cities. Nearly two-thirds of our states also have already adopted so-called standardized methods of budgeting. The movement is gaining headway rapidly. The method used in the past will, however, not produce the results which are sought by those who have in mind general uniformity in budget making. The budget systems adopted in the several states are not constructed on a standardized plan as between the states. The classifications of the functions and objects of expenditure used in California differ from those used in Wisconsin. The classifications used in Wisconsin differ from those used in Maryland, and so on. The result of this lack of uniformity is that comparative statistics on expenditures as between the particular states concerned are not produced by accounting methods based on the present standardized budget plans of these states.

What the state governments have had in mind in introducing standardized budgets is standardization of the procedure as between the different departments and bureaus of the particular state government concerned. This is in itself, of course, an immensely important matter. Standardization of method for this purpose is valuable, but the large benefits of standardization cannot be enjoyed unless there is coöperation and mutual agreement expressed in the adoption of a uniform budget

*For Dr. Emerson's paper, see A. J. P. H., March, 1920, page 221.
For Dr. Meyer's paper, "Methods for the Defense of Public Health Appropriations," see A. J. P. H., March, 1920, page 201.

by the different state governments, or by the different cities, not only within a given state, but throughout the country.

Without such uniformity of plan, comparative statistics can not be produced. The value of standardization depends upon the possibility of comparison. Our standards of efficiency and of cost of work are relative standards. There are no absolute standards either of the cost of health work or of efficiency. It can not be said, for example, that it should cost just $1.03 per day to maintain a patient in an isolation hospital. It is only by comparison of the cost and service between different institutions that a relative standard can be established. This point must be emphasized as the present movement towards standardized budgeting in all state governments wholly overlook it. A great deal of work will need to be done over again when the necessity of uniformity, at least along the broadest lines of classification, comes to be more generally recognized.

The point in question is well illustrated by the experience of the U. S. Bureau of the Census through its Division of Statistics of Cities and States which annually encounters great difficulties in the collection of financial data dealing with receipts and expenditures. Trained accountants of this division are compelled to spend from a few weeks to a number of months in various cities gathering up from the public records the details of financial statistics and juggling them into some form of uniformity of arrangement. To do this work it is often necessary to go back to original vouchers and to detailed accounts to re-classify the information and to adapt it for use in the uniform comparative plan of presentation that the Census Bureau has adopted. In spite of the fact that many cities have adopted standardized budgeting and have good systems of accounting, the lack of uniformity as between the cities makes it exceedingly difficult to get the necessary data.

The result of this nation-wide work, it may well be emphasized. Here is the production of the only comparable statistics on expenditures for health work in the country with the exception of those issued by a few state agencies, notable among which is the Municipal Division of the Bureau of Statistics of the State of Massachusetts. Statistics of cities have appeared annually since 1902; those of states since 1915. Statistics of cities cover all cities of 30,000 and over. Statistics of cities of 8,000 to 25,000 appeared in the report on Wealth, Debt, and Taxation of 1902, and in a special report for cities for 1903. In 1903 and 1913, statistics of cities of 2,500 and over were published in Wealth, Debt, and Taxation and in 1913 also in the report on Municipal Revenues, Expenditures, and Public Properties.

The volume on Statistics of Cities for 1917, by way of illustration, contains 373 quarto pages. We find here a classification of the expenditures of city governments for all purposes in minute detail. Those concerning health conservation are given under the following headings:

I   Health Department Administration
II   Vital Statistics
III Prevention and Treatment of Communicable Diseases
    1. Tuberculosis
    2. Other communicable diseases in hospitals
    3. Other treatment of communicable diseases
IV   Conservation of Child Life
    1. Medical work for school children
    2. Other conservation of child life
V   Food Regulation and Inspection
    1. Milk and dairy control
    2. Other food regulation

Under the present budgetary legislation health officers are in a position to introduce classifications of functions and of objects of expenditure without interfering with the broad outline of uniformity called for under the law. It is possible, therefore, for health officers to come to an agreement to introduce the necessary uniformity as between the cities and the states. The Committee on Uniform Accounting* can be a steering committee in this work. The classification of functions and of objects of expenditures as agreed upon by the Advisory Committee which is provided for in the report of the Committee on Uniform Accounting to the present session of the American Public Health Association will be brought to the attention of health officers and may be used by them for their guidance in the preparation of future budgets.

Just one other point should be emphasized. The installation of the systems of uniform accounting even on a broad basis of uniformity as suggested above will be largely sterile of results unless the standardized presentation of facts in the reports prepared by health officers follows. Without standardized reporting the information produced by uniform systems of accounting will not appear before the public in comparable form.

It is necessary, too, in providing for such standardized reporting that the physical statistics of work done be presented on a uniform basis so that the units for the measurement of cost and efficiency may be properly developed through the correlation of standardized financial statistics of the cost of work and standardized physical statistics of work done.

*See Report, A. J. P. H., Feb., 1920, page 172.

HEALTH CENTER AT THE JACKSON SCHOOL, BRIDGEPORT, CONN.

These mothers are Hungarians.

FIRST CONFERENCE OF NEW SURGEON GENERAL, U. S. P. H. S.

Many public health officers will recognize most of the staff of assistants in conference with Dr. Cumming. Left to right, sitting: Dr. J. W. Schereschewsky, Dr. J. C. Perry, Dr. Hugh S. Cumming, Dr. C. C. Pierce, Dr. W. G. Stimpson. Left to right, standing: Dr. R. H. Creel, Dr. A. J. McLaughlin, Dr. B. S. Warren, Dr. Charles Bolduan.

HEALTH WORK IN BRIDGEPORT, CONN.

This is one of the Health Stations in Bridgeport, Conn., and gathered here is a group of Italians assembled at the local center, which is homed in the Waltersville schoolhouse. These mothers can attend a clinic, which is in touch with the central one of the Health Department, and they gather here for little talks by the nurses on health essentials.

EDITORIAL SECTION

AMERICAN JOURNAL OF PUBLIC HEALTH
Publication Office: 124 W. Polk Street, Chicago, Ill.
EDITORIAL OFFICE: 169 MASSACHUSETTS AVE., BOSTON, MASS.
A. W. HEDRICH, C. P. H., Editor   J. RITCHIE, Jr., Associate Editor

Editorial Assistants

E. R. HAYHURST, M.D.   DAVID GREENBERG   JAMES A. TOBEY
R. P. ALBAUGH, M.D.   M. P. HORWOOD, M.S.   FRANCIS H. SLACK, M.D.
E. B. STARR, M.D.   P. M. HOLMES, M.D.   JAMES M. STRANG

Board of Advisory Editors

PETER H. BRYCE, M.D., Ottawa, Canada   PROF. M. J. ROSENAU, Boston, Mass.
CHARLES V. CHAPIN, M.D., Providence, R. I. PROF. W. T. SEDGWICK, Cambridge, Mass.
EUGENE R. KELLEY, M.D., Boston, Mass.   PROF. GEORGE C. WHIPPLE, Cambridge, Mass.
W. A. EVANS, M.D., Chicago, Ill.   PROF. S. M. GUNN, Paris, France.

All expressions of opinion and all statements of supposed facts are published on authority of the writer under
whose name they appear, and are not to be regarded as expressing the views of the
American Public Health Association, unless such statements or opinions
have been adopted by vote of the Association.

NOTICE TO SUBSCRIBERS: Subscription Price, payable in advance, $4.00 per year for
United States and possessions; $4.50 for Canada and other foreign countries. Single
copies, 50 cents postpaid. Membership in the American Public Health Association, including subscription to Journal, $5.00 per year. In Change of Address please give both
old and new address, and mail before the tenth of the month to take effect with the current issue. Mailing Date, 5th of each month. Advertisements accepted only when commendable, and worth while both to reader and advertiser. News Items, interesting
clippings and illustrations are gladly received, together with name of sender. Copy-
right, 1919, by A. W. Hedrich.

RED CROSS AND PUBLIC HEALTH WORK.

One of the objects which every competent public health official seeks to attain
is the establishment of an enlightened public opinion leading to the support and
co-operation of all the citizens. This is one of the most difficult problems of all
health administration on account of the human factor involved. It is human
nature to seize on all incidents, no matter how trivial or perverted, which offer a
support for condemnation or abuse. On the other hand, credit is seldom placed
where it is due and justly merited. In many communities the only persons who
support the health officer wholeheartedly are those who are themselves concerned
with health, such as members of the medical profession or private social and health
agencies. Yet even such agencies not infrequently are lined up against the public
official rather than in his support.

Sometimes there is just cause for opposition to the health authorities,
especially when they are admittedly incompetent, or under the influence of politics.
Such influence is likely to cease only when the public acquires a knowledge of the
principles underlying good health administration. This knowledge is to be gained
through various agencies and the foremost health administrators set a high value
on work in health education.

With the entry of the American Red Cross into the field of public health,
it would seem as if there were an excellent support for the health officer and
means for the education of the people ready made to order. The organization
clearly sets forth the offer of its services, in co-operation with existing public
health bodies, without desire or effort to supplant them or usurp their duties. As
a supplementing body it has almost unlimited opportunities. It recognizes the
necessity of administering public utilities by public health officers and it plans to
work with that in view.

The American Red Cross has enunciated a plan for the co-ordination of
official and extra-governmental health work, that seems to be well-considered,

sound and practical. It seems as if it might be the cement that can bind together all these agencies, for it has had wide expecience, it has the machinery of organization and it has gained the sympathy and support of the people. As a force in the health education of the American citizen and in the interests of the "team play," which is to accomplish results, the American Red Cross has an extraordinary opportunity.

ADVERTISING OF DISINFECTANTS

One of the effects of the influenza epidemic was the boom in the disinfecting business. It was a common thing to see disinfectants advertised along with Father John's Medicine and other cure-alls as preventives of influenza and pneumonia.

As a result of the advertisements, many a householder was led to "disinfect" his garbage pail, closet bowl, sinks, and floors, with the greatest assiduity.

Any one who has studied the etiology of the respiratory diseases, knows that these measures are not worth anything so far as preventing the disease is concerned. While we know very little concerning the practical measures for preventing influenza, we know positively that it is not transmitted by means of garbage pails, sinks, closet bowls, and floors—and we have no doubt that the manufacturer of disinfectants knows this also.

There is a measure of reasonable doubt in the case of the use of throat disinfectants as a preventive, although authorities seem to be pretty well agreed that the practice is not helpful and is perhaps harmful in some instances. It may be placing somewhat of a strain upon the instincts of a commercial manufacturer to ask him to refrain from advertising products concerning the utility of which the medical and public health professions are merely in doubt, in which the manufacturer, however, has faith. But no honest person, whether manufacturer, advertising agent, or sanitarian, can sanction the advertisements which have appeared and seem to thrive after the epidemic like sharks at a shipwreck.

The sale of these disinfectants for unwarranted purposes is not merely a swindle; it is harmful in that it creates false ideas concerning the transmission of disease and concerning the means of preventing it. The person who relies upon disinfectants must first have that obsession removed before he can be taught the really effective modes of avoiding infection. It is pretty difficult to teach a person to avoid the fresh nose and throat discharges of a scarlet fever patient when every newspaper screams forth a warning to beware of filth in sinks and garbage pails.

Many a health department is compelled to dissipate its funds in the ceremony of fumigating rooms after scarlet fever, diphtheria, and whooping cough, when the money could be spent to much better advantage in teaching people not to use common drinking cups, and to avoid the sneezes of others.

The American Public Health Association is sending a circular letter to advertising agents and to manufacturers of disinfectants, informing them that war has been declared against the unwarranted claims concerning disinfectants. Health officers will do well to supplement these efforts whenever possible in their health bulletins and their public addresses.

In Memoriam

EDOUARDO LICEAGA.

News has just been received in this country of the death of Dr. Edouardo Liceaga, of Mexico City, former president of the American Public Health Association, and, in these later years, honorary member.

It was in 1889 that a delegation of officials of the Federal Board of Health of Mexico first attended as guests the annual meeting of the American Public Health at Charleston, S. C. In 1890 Mexico was admitted into the Association and Dr. Edouardo Liceaga, president of the Federal Board of Health of Mexico, then first appeared as one of the delegation. In 1892 the association held its annual sessions in Mexico City and received the most magnificent entertainment probably ever accorded to it. The general director in all this illustration of the attention being extended to public health in Mexico by the government then existing, was Dr. Liceaga, the president's personal friend and physician; while the members of the American Public Health Association were made to appreciate fully the true meaning of the Mexican welcome, which says that "the house is yours."

Dr. Liceaga was a statesman in the truest sense of the word, and realized that the prosperity of Mexico depended upon freeing her seaports from the danger of epidemic diseases and the opprobrium of yellow fever. On the East lay Vera Cruz, the post of entry to Mexico, notorious as a pestilential swamp, breeding malaria and with yellow fever endemic there. To this problem Dr. Liceaga and his Board directed their first energies, determined to solve the problem of maritime sanitation. In the City of Mexico, on the other hand, situated within a basin of the table land, engineers were set the task of lowering the ground water to some eight feet below the ancient city, the Venice of Montezuma, by boring the Notchistonga tunnel through the moun-

tain rim. Within a few years the seaport of Vera Cruz saw constructed miles of concrete breakwater, the city had been drained, streets paved and sewered and a splendid water supply brought in for miles from the mountains. All the ideas known to modern quarantine were adopted at the port. A weekly bulletin of the presence or absence of yellow fever was published by the Federal Board and modern sanitation in the best sense was established as a daily routine.

The American Public Health Association again visited Mexico in 1906 and those that then passed in at the eastern gateway, Vera Cruz, found there a beautiful seaport, with rapidly developing foreign trade, with yellow fever and malaria only remaining as a memory; while in the City of Mexico the ground water had been lowered, typhus fever had disappeared, new colonies or towns had been planned, areas had been extended, and the old city of 200,000 population had become the modern city of 400,000, boasting of one of the most beautiful locations and urban developments on the continent of America.

These two works which illustrated the two principal permanent public sanitation works of the government, were followed by sanitation generally extended to the other towns and districts of the several states of the Republic. Model general hospitals were constructed, through encouragement of municipalities by the Government, while medicine as well as sanitation were being ever modernized largely through the practical wisdom of Dr. Liceaga. Physical training became a routine in the schools of the country, while charities were enlarged, prisons and reformatories improved, and modern progress of a social sort was continually moved forward through the efforts of the Federal Board of Health. Dr. Liceaga became vice-president of the American Public Health Association in 1893, and president in 1896, and for many years took a most active part in the work of the Executive Council of the Association. Scarcely a year passed which did not have a paper presented by Dr. Liceaga, or a report of some important phase of public health within the Mexican republic. Dr. Liceaga was ever fertile in methods for extending the field of applied sanitation and was proud to report Mexican advances in every department of public health.

During the last ten years of Dr. Liceaga's life, national misfortunes and personal losses deprived the association of his welcome presence, to which were added the inhibitions of failing health and advanced years. In Dr. Liceaga the Association beheld the finest example of Latin dignity associated with that courtesy and affability spontaneous in the cultural Spanish gentleman, and in his loss, as that of Dr. E. Pelletier of Montreal, last year, the American Public Health Association is not only made conscious of its fifty years of age, but also

that other times and other manners are year by year dominating more and more its procedures and meetings. We have with us still Dr. Stephen Smith, Dr. Holt and Dr. Montizambert; but the days of *les grande seigneurs* are rapidly passing. We may replace general culture by more exact scientific knowledge, and wide generalizations by the statistical precision of modern days; but the Association will suffer real loss if in these high pressure days, that true courtesy and those delicate attentions which constitute the gentlemen of the type of Dr. Liceaga, are allowed to disappear in the "Sturm and Drang" of modern competition.

To the family of Dr. Liceaga, those members of the Association who had the privilege of knowing him, will extend their most sincere sympathy; while every member of the Association will send to Mexico and our members there, condolences upon the great national loss which it has sustained through the passing of their most renowned leader.

BOOKS AND REPORTS REVIEWED

Anaphylaxis and Antianaphylaxis. *Dr. A. Besredka, Prof. Pasteur Institute, Paris. Prefaced by Dr. E. Roux, Director of Pasteur Institute, Paris. English Edition by S. Roodhouse Gloyne, M.D., D.P.H., London, England.* St. Louis, Mo.: C. V. Mosby Company, pp. 143. Price $2.25.

There is hardly anyone more competent to discuss the subject of anaphylaxis than Dr. Besredka. With the ever-increasing practice of serum and vaccine therapeusis, the subject is bound to gain in importance, and any scientific contribution coming from such a source should be carefully scrutinized by the profession. Rarely has a term been so often misapplied as the term "anaphylaxis." A bewildering amount of literature has a tendency to

confuse the mind of the student who is not in a position to follow the subject systematically. A bird's-eye view of it is therefore very welcome.

The rich experimental experience of the author supplies the text with a personal flavor not common to publications of this character. The foreign literature is not overlooked, however, and altogether this publication may be safely put down as the latest compilation of everything pertaining to this intricate subject. The last chapter, VIII, is written by S. Roodhouse Gloyne and deals with the "Recent Work on Anaphylaxis." Chapter II deals with the historical development.

References are richly supplied.

ARTHUR LEDERER, M. D.

Child Welfare in Kentucky. *An inquiry by the National Child Labor Committee for the Kentucky Child Labor Association and the State Board of Health. Edward N. Clopper, Ph. D., New York City: National Child Labor Committee. Pp. 322. Price $1.25.*

Improvement of health conditions in Kentucky (and such betterment is typical of what should be undertaken in many states) is urged in the recommendations for a state program made by the National Child Labor Committee for the Kentucky Child Labor Association and the State Board of Health. The account of this investigation made under the direction of Edward N. Clopper, Ph. D., and published under the title "Child Welfare in Kentucky," is one of the most valuable publications of its kind yet issued. It does not blink at the dark and disgraceful facts that stand to the discredit of many communities of an old American state, and yet it sees evidences of a public disposition to correct these evils. The director thinks it worth while to make detailed recommendations for a broad health program.

These provisions have been suggested in a special chapter on health by H. H. Mitchell, M. D., in which the laws of health as they relate to human life everywhere are admirably summed up. What Dr. Mitchell would do in Kentucky "for such growth of the public service as will protect the health and develop the capacities of her children," would be a valuable program for similar constructive action in almost any American state. Her plan in brief calls for State Bureau of Child Hygiene, to put into practice those provisions for care of mothers and babies that are well understood in the medical profession and too often neglected by the general public. This includes prenatal centers; extension of the services of public health nurses; closer supervision of midwives; establishment of maternity hospitals or wards in general hospitals; better vital statistics; children's health centers; health propaganda; physical examination and correction of defects among young school children; hygienic school houses and other evident necessities for healthful childhood.

Unless such health recommendations as have been outlined with wonderful clearness in this report can be put into effect in the near future, the outlook for Kentucky children would not seem to be very promising. As Dr. Clopper in-

dicates "Kentucky neglects her children," or at least has done so up to now. The investigation shows a state in which about 1,200,000 are being brought up, 80% in rural districts. These are subject to more diseases than affect the children in large and congested cities. Many of them live in primitive houses with polluted water supply. The rural schools in general are none too good. A child labor law —one of the best in the country—is on the statute books, but in most places it is not enforced because of lack of inspectors. Marriage of girls of twelve years old, and boys of fourteen, is permitted with consent of the parents. The condition of childhood, in brief, in all too many communities of the state is "aggravated by disease, deformity and illegitimacy."

This unfortunate situation, which is not at all peculiar to Kentucky, cannot be ignored in any child welfare report. One is glad, nevertheless, to find that this document is far from being fault-finding; it is not critical of the good people of the state, but finds them too often complacent and satisfied with the way things have been done. At the same time many Kentuckians are awake to the need of better protection for the children of the state and the investigating committee was given a cordial welcome on the part of the Commonwealth by Governor A. O. Stanley.

The separate chapters of the report cover such topics as schools, by Elizabeth Bliss Newhall; recreation, by Raymond G. Fuller; rural life by Charles E. Gibbons; child labor, by Loraine B. Bush; juvenile courts, by Mabel Brown Ellis; and law and administration, by W. H. Swift. These chapters contain so much specific and unusual information of a vital character that the report should be in every library of the country and in the hands of every public officer.

MAY BLISS DICKINSON, R. N.

✦

Public Health and Reconstruction.— *Report of the Public Health Committee of the New York State Reconstruction Committee, October 24, 1919.*

This excellent and comprehensive report is divided into six sections as follows: I, Individual and Public Health; II, Health of the Child Before School Age; III, Health of the School Child; IV, Health of the Young Adult; V, Health Insurance, and VI, Recommendations.

The first section is introductory.

Under section II the need for prenatal care is discussed and it is stated that maternity centers and visiting nurses are the best means to overcome ignorance and lack of care of prospective mothers. Stricter requirements for midwives are urged and the need for clinics and child welfare stations is stressed.

The third section gives a resume of present medical inspection of school children in the state and of the child welfare work of the State Department of Health and the municipalities of New York. Nutrition is discussed and the conclusion reached that too many children are under nourished. School lunches are urged. The importance of playgrounds for schools is set forth and better school sanitation is also urged. It is stated that an active campaign of education is the first essential in any plan for reconstruction and that health education to be successful must begin in the school room.

The discussion of the health of the young adult, to which nearly half of the pamphlet is devoted, is further divided into the following topics: (1) The general health of young male adults; (2) Pulmonary tuberculosis, (3) Pneumonia, (4) Typhoid fever, and (5) The venereal diseases.

The data are taken largely from the draft statistics. The New York rejections show, in general, that city men suffer more from alcohol and drugs, developmental defects, diseases of the ear and eye, flat foot, hernia and tuberculosis. In the rural districts there is a preponderance of disease of the bones and joints, venereal, genito-urinary diseases, bad teeth and diseases of the thyroid gland. The army experience shows the necessity of frequent physical examinations. The committee mentions the need for reorganization of health districts and expansion of the state department of health. More institutional care for tuberculosis is asked for. It is stated that only the well-to-do and the charity patient can avail themselves of proper nursing facilities. Health Centers, which aid and correlate all existing agencies, are strongly urged and where lack of funds prevents such organization, the State should assist.

Health insurance is endorsed and the committee states its belief that the Davenport-Donohue health insurance bill will give to workers of the state a measure of essential and enforcable health protection.

Among the recommendations not already cited are: A plan of boarding out destitute children on the unit system, using the institutions which exist as clearing houses; adoption of ordinances requiring pasteurization of milk; appointment in every school district of a full-time health officer who shall have full charge of all the health work; stringent child labor laws; maintenance in every one of the larger cities of a public health laboratory; support of the national program for combating venereal diseases by liberal appropriation from the State and local municipalities; continued support by the State of the Institution for the Study of Malignant Diseases at Buffalo.

The chairman of the committee is Dr. Henry Dwight Chapin. J. A. T.

✤

Tubercle, the new English magazine (83-91 Great Titchfield St., London), is performing an excellent service in assembling the news with reference to this disease from all the quarters of the earth. The January issue touches on the relationships to life assurance, war time, gaseous inhalations, and the industries, assembles facts and figures from Spain, the Malay States, and Egypt, presents notices of recent meetings, statements about hospitals and sanatoria, and sprinkles in a goodly seasoning of brief news items from everywhere. The Malay story states that the rate in Singapore was 4,840 per million of inhabitants in 1916 and in Perak, 2,170 per million in 1915. It is a disease on virgin soil where bovine tuberculosis is unknown, and out of 250,000 hogs slaughtered in the Ipoh abattoirs, not a single infected animal was found. Egypt is likewise a country with little immunity against the disease. The review in gaseous inhalations is a review of a report to the Medical Research Committee. It would appear that in certain trades in which gas is evolved had an unusual immunity among their employees from influenza. Experiments were tried which seem to confirm this fact. While it does not affect directly the tubercle bacillus, this treatment may lead to the control of secondary infections.

✤

The kitchen is the most important room in the house from a health standpoint, says the United States Public Health Service. Keep everything about it and every one in it scrupulously clean.

Health Centers. *American Red Cross.*

The American Red Cross has recently issued a twenty-page pamphlet entitled "Health Centers: A Field for Red Cross Activity." This pamphlet is the preliminary and general statement of a part of the peace-time program of the Red Cross, which is concerned with Public Health. It is the plan of the Red Cross to offer its services in assisting the establishment of health centers in those communities where they are needed. The demand for team play in Public Health is stressed and the health center is offered as the next step in the evolution of community welfare. The health center acts as a clearing house for Public Health information and offers opportunity to coördinate all the public and private activities which exist in a community. It is suggested that here should be housed the city health officer, his laboratory, and that space should be provided for various clinics such as infant welfare, tuberculosis, venereal disease, mental hygiene, dental hygiene and industrial hygiene, together with an auditorium which could serve as a meeting place for conferences and lectures and gatherings of local medical societies.

CONVENTIONS, CONFERENCES, MEETINGS

April 19-20, Charlotte, N. C., North Carolina State Health Association.

April 20-21, Greenville, S. C., South Carolina Medical Association.

April 20-22, Anniston, Ala., Medical Association of State of Alabama.

April 20-22, Charlotte, N. C., Medical Society of North Carolina.

April 22-24, Houston, Texas, Texas State Medical Association.

April 22-24, St. Louis, Mo., National Tuberculosis Association.

April 24-26, New Orleans, La., Louisiana State Medical Association.

April 26-30, New Orleans, La., American Medical Association.

April 29-30, Bismarck, N. D., State Nurses' Association.

May 4-6, Austin, Texas, Texas Graduate Nurses' Association.

May 4-6, Cedar Rapids, Iowa, State Dental Society.

May 10-15, Rosedale, Kansas, Kansas Health Officers' School and School for Public Health Nurses.

May 11, American Association of Eugenics.

May 11-12, Indianapolis, Ind., Indiana State Health Association.

May 12-14, Des Moines, Iowa, Iowa Medical Association.

May 12-14, Des Moines, Iowa, Trudeau Society.

May 20-24, Brussels, Belgium, Congress of Royal (English) Institute of Public Health.

May 24-26, Omaha, Neb., Nebraska State Health Association.

May 24-26, Omaha, Neb., Nebraska State Medical Association.

May 25-26, Toronto, Ont., Ontario Health Association.

May 25-27, Columbus, Ohio, Ohio Hospital Association.

June —, New Orleans, La., American Association of Industrial Physicians and Surgeons.

June —, Duluth, Minn., Minnesota Hospital Association.

June —, Cour d'Alene, Idaho State Medical Association.

June 1-4, Cleveland, Ohio, American Medico-Physiological Association.

June 3, Providence, R. I., Rhode Island Medical Society.

June 3-5, Portland, Ore., Oregon State Medical Association.

June 9, Boston, Mass., Massachusetts Medical Society.

June 15-16, Minot, N. D., North Dakota State Medical Association.

June 21 .., Vancouver, B. C., Canadian Public Health Association and five other Canadian National Associations.

June 21-25, Montreal, Can., American Water Works Association.

June 23-23, St. Paul, Minn., Catholic Hospital Association.

SURGEON GENERAL CUMMING DISCUSSES EUROPEAN HEALTH CONDITIONS

Dr. Hugh S. Cumming, the new Surgeon General of the United States Public Health Service, succeeding Dr. Rupert Blue, returned from his duties in Europe to assume his new position in Washington, arriving on March 10. For two years he has been abroad, sitting as the representative of this government on various international health

boards and observing conditions of disease and public health. He has made especial study of the outbreaks of typhus raging in many Oriental countries.

With reference to this disease, Dr. Cumming notes that it is far from checked, but seems to be on the increase, and there is imminent danger of its invading Europe on a large scale, unless strict quarantine and other measures of control are enforced. Once intrenched in European ports, its next step would be across the Atlantic. Even if it should invade this country, Dr. Cumming does not think it would be difficult to keep in check, because of the essentially different living conditions here. Likewise,

it is important the bubonic plague be kept out of the country. This is at the present time in practically all of the Mediterranean ports and constitutes a serious menace to this country.

With reference to the quarantine regulations of the country, the European authorities, according to Dr. Cumming, regard them with highest appreciation, and indeed they have been recommended for adoption by other nations.

As to international health relationships, the new Surgeon General of the Public Health Service stated that an agency would soon be established under the League of Nations which would coördinate and strengthen the health work of all nations, and would materially improve international reporting of diseases and the maintenance of quarantines. This matter is the subject of serious discussion at the meeting in London of April 12, one of the purposes of which is to formulate a permanent organization.

RUPERT BLUE

Former Surgeon General of the United States Public Health Service

Surgeon General Rupert Blue, since 1892 connected with the U. S. Public Health Service, is the son of John G. and Annie M. Blue, and was born in Richmond County, North Carolina, on May 30, 1867. After studies at the University of Virginia he attended the University of Maryland and received the degree M.D. in 1892. In 1909

Blue began with his entrance into the corps of the Public Health Service in 1892 as interne. The following year he was commissioned Assistant Surgeon by the President. In 1897 he was advanced to the grade of Passed Assistant Surgeon, and in 1909 was made Surgeon. On January 8, 1919, he was appointed by the President

this university conferred on him the degree D.Sc. Continuing his studies in Europe, Dr. Blue graduated from the London School of Tropical Medicine in 1893. In 1913 the University of Wisconsin conferred on him the degree D.Sc., and in the same year he was made D.P.H. by the University of Michigan.

Dr. Blue was elected President of the American Medical Association in 1915 and in the same year became President of the Association of Military Surgeons of the U. S. A.

The public career of Surgeon General

of the United States to the position of Surgeon General of the Public Health Service, in which position he has just been replaced by Dr. Hugh S. Cumming.

When the bubonic plague was detected in San Francisco in 1903-04, Dr. Blue was placed in charge of the eradicative operations in that city. His efficient service here led to a similar detail in 1907-08 when the disease again broke out in California. The energetic measures for the suppression of the disease which were inaugurated by him and the success that followed his vigorous campaign placed him in the foremost ranks of sanitarians in the country. Dr. Blue likewise served with distinction through the outbreak of yellow fever in New Orleans in 1905.

During his career in the Public Health Service Dr. Blue has served at stations of the service at ⁻Cincinnati, Galveston, Charleston, S. C.; San Francisco, Portland, Ore.; Milwaukee, New York, Norfolk, New Orleans and abroad at Genoa, Italy.

What has been accomplished under his leadership by the Public Health Service is noted elsewhere in this issue of the JOURNAL is a résumé of its work.

UNITED STATES PUBLIC HEALTH SERVICE

At this moment, when the term of office of Surgeon-General Rupert Blue, as head of the United States Public Health Service has terminated, and his successor has been named, it seems opportune to review briefly some of the accomplishments of the Service in the past few years.

The Public Health Service today is the evolution of a number of years, during which a series of Congressional enactments has increased from time to time its functions and changed its name.

⁻From 1879 to 1902, the Service was known as the Marine Hospital Service. In the latter year Congress changed its name to the Public Health and ˳Marine Hospital Service and greatly increased its function to keep pace with the progress of public health. From 1902 to 1912, the Service experienced a further period of expansion until in the year last named its name was changed to the Public Health Service and its public functions very materially broadened.

The early function of the Service consisted chiefly in rendering medical and hospital assistance to seamen of the merchant marine. However, the excellently trained personnel of the Service offered an agency through which public health studies and investigations could be carried on. This opportunity for progress had been recognized by Surgeon-General Blue for some years prior to his appointment to the office of Surgeon-General. Accordingly one of his first official acts after nomination was to urge upon Congress the enactment of a bill to change the name of the Service and increase its function and authority over public health matters.⁻ This bill, which became a law within eight months following Dr. Blue's appointment, vested full authority in the Public Health Service to "study and investigate the diseases of man and conditions influencing the propagation and spread thereof, including sanitation and sewage and the pollution either directly or indirectly of the navigable streams and lakes of the United States."

Since 1912 Congress has recognized the public health needs of the country to a greater extent than ever before. Under the progressive administration of Surgeon-General Blue the appropriations of the Service have increased steadily, making it possible to undertake much new work of great importance to the health of the country.

Following the law authorizing the Public Health Service to "study the diseases of man," etc., above mentioned, Congress appropriated in June, 1913, the sum of $200,000 for specifically carrying out this purpose. In 1917 this appropriation was increased to $300,000. Much scientific work of far-reaching importance has resulted.

In 1914, studies in industrial hygiene were begun to determine the sanitary conditions surrounding the factory workers of the country, and to collect statistics on the subject, in order that remedial measures might be taken where unsanitary conditions were noted. Much has been accomplished in this work.

Soon after his appointment to office, Surgeon-General Blue took steps to check the serious menace of malaria in the South. With the end in view of ameliorating these deplorable conditions malaria investigations were started in 1912. In some sections of the South, where malaria previously existed as a constant menace, the disease has now practically been eliminated, and in all sections proper methods have been demonstrated to the local authorities for its elimination.

With the increase of the public health functions of the Service, it became apparent that the facilities of the Hygienic Laboratory of the Service in Washington—at which all the laboratory work connected with public health studies is carried on—would necessarily be enlarged. Consequently the Surgeon-General requested Congress for increased appropriations to take care of this situation, with the result that in June, 1913, $25,000 was appropriated for this purpose.

Another achievement lies in the effective work the Service has performed along the lines of interstate sanitation. Realizing that the effective prevention of epidemics is possible only when strict measures against their spread through the instrumentality of interstate traffic are enforced, Surgeon-General Blue began soon after his appointment to devise means to cover this heretofore untouched field. In fact, no other health agency has authority or could efficiently occupy this field and accomplish the work with resulting benefit to the whole country. At least two great epidemics have been checked in a comparatively short time by reason of the authority vested in the Service. Without this authority these epidemics might have spread and become national in proportions.

The U. S. P. H. Service demonstrated its value and its ability to make good use of its authority and its funds in the outbreak in 1916 of poliomyelitis. It has established a complete system of certification of drinking water used by interstate carriers, and to an extent has supervised the sanitation of the cars of the railways. Pellagra, studies in which were already instituted when Surgeon-General Blue was appointed, have been investigated with vigor under a special appropriation, the outcome being that the disease has been classed as a nutritional one, and means for its prevention, in a nourishing, well-balanced dietary, have been established.

One of the important pieces of work prosecuted by the Service has been the investigation of rural health conditions. For the first time a comprehensive survey of the conditions has been possible, and already much has been accomplished in ascertaining causes and in prevention. The leper has been another of the problems which the Service has undertaken to solve, and with funds at its disposal for a central home for these unfortunates is awaiting only the selection of the proper site for such a home and the construction of the buildings.

With the increase in the use of vaccines, viruses, serums, etc., in the prevention and cure of disease, it is evident that a pure and potent product is essential to the safeguarding of the health of the nation. Although by the Act of 1902, the Service was charged with the regulations of the sale and traffic in these products in interstate traffic, it was difficult to enforce the law without funds to inspect the plants and the products and to determine by laboratory examinations and inspections whether the law was actually being complied with. Various appropriations have been made for this purpose. During the war this branch of the work was especially valuable.

The appearance of the bubonic plague in New Orleans in June, 1914, was the signal for active measures of repression, which were entirely successful. There were but few cases of sickness and death, and a disease which might have become epidemic in proportions was here quickly and quietly stamped out.

Of particular value was the work of the Service in dealing with the pandemic of influenza in the fall of 1918 which was imposed on the Service because of the entry of more than 30,000 physicians, practicing in the United States, into the military service. With the spread of the pandemic over the country urgent calls for assistance were addressed by stricken communities to the Public Health Service. Despite the dearth of physicians and nurses, Surgeon General Blue organized a mobile corps of nearly 1,100 physicians and a large number of nurses and detailed them to render the required medical attention to prostrated communities. To carry on this fight the Surgeon-General also asked Congress for $1,000,000, which was granted within a few days after the disease was recognized in epidemic form.

During the fiscal year ending June 30, 1919, the Bureau experienced the greatest expansion in its history. The executive order of July 1, 1918, centralizing all civil health activities connected with the war under the supervision of the Public Health Service was the forerunner of important and far-reaching legislation, namely (1) the act creating the Division of Venereal Diseases in the Bureau (contained in the Military Act of July 9, 1918), and appropriating $1,200,000 for the control of venereal diseases in co-operation with the States; (2) the Act of October 27, 1918, creating a Reserve Corps of the Public Health Service; (3) the Act approved November 1, 1918, appropriating $1,000,000 for the suppression of influenza, and, (4) the Act of March 3, 1919, authorizing the Public Health Service to provide hospital and sanatorium care for discharged disabled soldiers, sailors and marines. These enactments have contributed greatly to the remarkable expansion of the Public Health Service, and it is believed that these health activities would have been permanently lost to the civil authorities if the suggested transfer of the Bureau to the War Department had taken place in 1917-1918.

Remaining as it did as a civil organization, the Service was able to render invaluable assistance to the country during the war period. Foremost among these activities may be mentioned its extra-cantonment sanitation, industrial hygiene, production and supervision of biological products, the campaign against veneral diseases, and as a result of the war, the medical and surgical relief to discharged soldiers.

Mention of the increased activities of the Service during the term of office of Surgeon-General Blue would be incomplete without pointing out a further piece of constructive legislation which became a law in October, 1918. The Act creating a Reserve Corps in the Public Health Service is now referred to. Without this authority to expand its regular corps in time of emergency, it is not believed that the medical care of the discharged soldier could be successfully carried on by the Service.

The greatest good accomplished by the Public Health Service in all of its spheres of operation, consists of the aid which the Public Health Service renders to the state and municipal health authorities, either directly or by the publishing of information relating to the prevention of diseases, which constitute a basis upon which these authorities can take necessary sanitary precautions in their respective jurisdictions.

There are, however, two outstanding accomplishments in this connection which warrant, it is believed, special mention:

(1) During the past eight years the Service has realized the great value to be derived from acting as a clearing house for information regarding the prevalence of diseases, and by the publishing of information in bulletin form each week all the state authorities have been kept currently advised of the appearance and progress of disease in the country, thus enabling them to more intelligently combat its spread.

(2) In a further respect the Public Health Service, it is believed, has rendered extremely important aid to the state and municipal authorities by detailing officers for the purpose of making surveys with a view to publishing the result of these investigations and recommending certain changes believed to be necessary and desirable to meet the needs of the respective localities.

The U. S. Public Health Service has good reason to look back with pride on its accomplishments under the leadership of Surgeon-General Blue.

CLINIC FOR SCHOOL CHILDREN AT BRIDGEPORT, CONN.

ASSOCIATION NEWS

HEALTH EMPLOYMENT BUREAU.

Help-wanted announcements will be carried free in this column until further notice. Copy goes to the printer on the fifteenth of each month. In answering keyed advertisements, please mail replies separately.

The Health Employment Bureau also sends lists of applicants to prospective employers without charge.

Prosperous and growing city of the Middle West will require well equipped full time health officer. Salary to right man not less than $5,000 to begin. Address P. W. J., care of this JOURNAL.

Assistant chemist for sanitary analysis of water and sewage. Technical graduate with one year's experience or equivalent wanted. Work located in Chicago. Address 342, care of this JOURNAL.

A sanitary engineer for State Health Department. Desire a man familiar with water purification and sewerage practice and competent to examine plans and specifications. State training, experience, and salary expected. Address L. E. N., care of this Journal.

A nurse for industrial position in Chicago. State qualifications and references. Address 344, care of this Journal.

Competent man for position of sanitary engineer of State Board of Health. Usual duties, especially inspection and operation of water works, water purification and sewage disposal. Salary $150 per month. Address, with full record: Bureau of Engineering, Alabama State Board of Health, Montgomery, Ala.

Woman director for city laboratory. Salary to begin, $1,500. Address R. L. Carlton, City Health Officer, Winston-Salem, N. C.

Bacteriologist and Serologist for Cincinnati Health Department. Salary $2,000 to experienced man or woman. Work consists of bacteriological examination of diphtheria culture, Widal test for typhoid, sputum analysis, preparation of antigen and amboceptor and Wassermann test, gold curve, urinalysis, examination of fæces, spinal fluid, pneumococcus determination, examination of brain tissue for Negri bodies, etc. Address Wm. H. Peters, M. D., Health Commissioner, City Hall, Cincinnati, Ohio.

Two physicians for U. S. P. H. Service at the port of Boston. One temporary. Salary $150 to $200 per month. Address A. J. Nute, M. D., U. S. P. H. Service, Long Wharf, Boston, Mass.

A sanitary engineer for State Health Department. Man familiar with water purification and sewerage practice and competent to examine plans and specifications. State training, experience and salary expected. Address L. E. N., care of this JOURNAL.

A national organization interested in public health has openings for a number of properly trained public health experts. Duties are of organizing and advising in public health field. Salaries $4,000 or more. Physicians with experience in social and public health desired. In replying give full details as to training and experience. Address 343, care of this Journal.

The Texas State Board of Health offers unusual opportunities to nurses with public health training. A large and interesting field. County school nursing and community nursing. Pioneer work for the nurse with originality and initiative. Minimum salary $125 a month with a month's vacation on full pay. Address Mrs. Ethel Parsons, Dir. Public Health Nursing, State Board of Health, Austin, Texas.

A physician as medical assistant to Chief of Bureau of Venereal Disease Control, State Department of Health. Salary $2,400 per year with traveling expenses. Must be graduate of Class A, Medical school, with one year's internship. State license not required and experience not necessary. Address, Dr. A. J. Casselman, Chief, Bureau of Venereal Disease Control, 807 American Mechanic Building, Trenton, N. J.

Industrial physicians wanted. Salaries $2,500 to $3,000. State full particulars. Address 351, care of this JOURNAL.

Field Director rural sanitation in Southern state. Salary $2,700 to $3,600 with $800 expense allowance. Address 352, care of this JOURNAL.

CAMPAIGN FOR 7,500 A. P. H. A. MEMBERS

So closely is the future of the American Public Health Association related to a large and influential membership, that President Rankin has undertaken to advance the membership figure a step forward. Judging from the "drive" of last year, which carried the number of members and subscribers to the figure of 4,500, the goal set at 7,500 members and subscribers for the Membership Campaign of 1920, is not only a reasonable one, but one of comparatively easy attainment. It requires only that each existing member secure one new member, there being 3,600 members and 900 subscribers in the Association.

In the modern great movements, the potential qualities of the states are more and more recognized, and the evidences of this fact are not lacking in such matters as the coöperation of the U. S. Government with the state health departments in a number of important movements.

Following along the same line of thought, President Rankin has suggested and put into operation the 1920 Campaign for 7,500 members, enlisting the interest and invoking the aid of the health commissioners throughout the different states. This method of leadership gives especial local interest in the campaign. To lay out the work so that it might be most easily accomplished, quotas were named for the different states, figures approximately proportionate to the population.

In most of the states the State Health Officer has accepted the Chairmanship of the Campaign in that state. He has accepted the quota which the state is to raise, and he must rely on the A. P. H. A. members in his state to see that the goal is reached. In the few states where the State Health Officer found himself unable to be the chairman, the duty has been assumed by some other well known public health authority in his state.

In order to inaugurate the Campaign, President Rankin has addressed to each of the chairmen a letter of suggestion based on previous experience in the enlisting of new members. The chairmen will doubtless have individual plans for their respective states; for example, in those states where the annual conference of public health officers is due, a splendid opportunity will be afforded for setting forth before these specialists, the benefits of the A. P. H. A. In other states, where there are large cities, teams may be organized—a plan which proved very successful last year in some places.

Another letter goes forward from President Rankin to each member, giving him the name of his Chairman, and inviting him to serve on the State Committee. This will put him in touch with his Chairman, and have him prepared to name his member. Cards for nomination of new members will be enclosed to him.

State chairmen will always be in close touch with the Boston office and vice versa. In order to keep up the interest in the friendly rivalry between the states, reports will be collected and will be sent out periodically from Boston to all State chairmen. In some of the states the chairmen expect to send similar bulletins to members in their respective states.

States in the East will have their District Center in Boston, to which reports will be sent, and from which these will be distributed to the State chairmen. In the Far West, the Mountain and West Coast states, the District Center will be in the office of Dr. I. R. Bancroft, State Health Commissioner of California, who will care for the duties of this center in addition to those of California Chairman. His reports will be communicated to Boston by telegraph, and information for distribution will be sent to him by the same method. A similar center will probably be established in New Orleans for Southern states.

It is hoped to carry on the major portion of the Campaign during April, and to finish up by May 15th.

Future issues of the Journal and News Letter will show the results of the Campaign.

On the next page are presented the names of the State Chairmen of Committees. A few are missing, not yet having accepted the Chairmanship.

STATE CHAIRMEN OF CAMPAIGN COMMITTEES

Alabama—J. D. Dowling, M. D., Health Officer, Birmingham.
Alberta—W. C. Laidlaw, M. D., Provincial Medical Health Officer, Edmonton.
Arkansas—C. W. Garrison, M. D., State Health Officer, Little Rock.
California—I. R. Bancroft, M. D., State Health Officer, Sacramento.
Colorado—C. G. Hickey, M. D., President, State Board of Health, Denver.
Connecticut—J. T. Black, M. D., State Health Officer, Hartford.
Delaware—Mr. C. H. Wells, Special Health Commissioner, Wilmington.
Florida—R. N. Greene, M. D., State Health Officer, Jacksonville.
Georgia—T. F. Abercrombie, M. D., Secretary, State Board of Health, Atlanta.
Illinois—C. St. Clair Drake, M. D., Secretary, State Board of Health, Springfield.
Indiana—J. G. Royse, M. D., Director of Education, State Board of Health, Indian-
    apolis.
Iowa—Prof. E. L. Waterman, State University of Iowa, Iowa City.
Kansas—J. J. Entz, M. D., President, Kansas Health Officers' Association, Hillsboro.
Kentucky—A. T. McCormack, M. D., State Health Officer, Louisville.
Louisiana—Oscar Dowling, M. D., President Louisiana State Board of Health, New
    Orleans.
Maine—L. D. Bristol, M. D., State Commissioner of Health, Augusta.
Massachusetts—B. W. Carey, M. D., Deputy State Health Commissioner, Boston.
Maryland—C. Hampson Jones, M. D., Health Officer, Baltimore.
Michigan—R. M. Olin, M. D., Secretary, Michigan State Board of Health, Lansing.
Mississippi—W. S. Leathers, M. D., State Director of Public Health, Jackson.
Missouri—G. H. Jones, M. D., Secretary, State Board of Health, Jefferson City.
Montana—J. J. Sippy, M. D., Epidemiologist, State Board of Health, Helena.
Nebraska—I. H. Dillon, M. D., Chief, State Bureau of Health, Lincoln.
Nevada—S. L. Lee, M. D., State Board of Health, Carson City.
New Hampshire—Mr. Carl O. Seaman, Health Officer, Manchester.
New Jersey—A. Clark Hunt, M. D., Chief, State Laboratory of Hygiene, Trenton.
New Mexico—C. E. Waller, M. D., P. A. Surgeon, U. S. P. H. S., State Commissioner
    of Health, Albuquerque.
New York—H. M. Biggs, M. D., State Health Commissioner, New York City.
North Carolina—W. S. Rankin, M. D., President, American Public Health Association,
    State Health Officer, Raleigh.
North Dakota—C. J. McGurren, M. D., Secretary, State Board of Health, Devils Lake.
Nova Scotia—W. H. Hattie, M. D., Provincial Health Officer, Halifax.
Ohio—A. W. Freeman, M. D., State Commissioner of Health, Columbus.
Oklahoma—A. R. Lewis, M. D., State Health Commissioner, Oklahoma City.
Rhode Island—B. U. Richards, M. D., Secretary, State Board of Health, Providence.
Saskatchewan—M. M. Seymour, M. D., Commissioner of Health, Regina.
South Carolina—J. A. Hayne, M. D., State Health Officer, Columbia.
South Dakota—P. B. Jenkins, M. D., Superintendent, State Board of Health, Waubay.
Tennessee—Olin West, M. D., Secretary, State Board of Health, Nashville.
Texas—C. W. Goddard, M. D., State Health Officer, Austin.
Utah—T. B. Beatty, M. D., State Health Commissioner, Salt Lake City.
Vermont—C. F. Dalton, M. D., Secretary, State Board of Health, Burlington.
Virginia—Ennion G. Williams, M. D., State Health Commissioner, Richmond.
Washington—J. B. Anderson, M. D., State Health Officer, Seattle.
West Virginia—S. L. Jepson, M. D., State Commissioner of Health, Charleston.
Wisconsin—C. A. Harper, M. D., State Health Officer, Madison.
Wyoming—C. Y. Beard, M. D., Sec'y, State Board of Health, Cheyenne.

REGIONAL SUPPLY OFFICERS

WESTERN STATES—Mr. Guy Jones, State Health Department, Sacramento, Cal.
SOUTHERN STATES—Miss Agnes Morris, State Health Department, New Orleans, La.
CENTRAL STATES—H. O. Jones, M. D., Department of Health, Chicago.

LIST OF NEW MEMBERS
PROPOSED FOR ELECTION TO THE
A. P. H. A.
FROM FEBRUARY 10, 1920, TO MARCH 12, 1920

SPONSORS*
and
NEW MEMBERS

C. W. Garrison, M. D., Little Rock, Ark.
G. K. Stephens, M. D., Newport, Ark.
James R. Scott, M, D., Los Angeles, Cal.
Garnet B. Grant, M. D., Asst. Prof. Univ. Southern Cal., Los Angeles, Cal.
W. H. Kellogg, M, D., Sacramento, Cal.
W. J. Hanna, M. D., Health Officer, Sacramento, Cal.
Burton Lowther, Denver, Colo.
George F. Gilkison, D. P. H., Chief Chemist, Water Department, Kansas City, Mo.
James A. Tobey, Washington, D. C.
Margaret F. Byington, American Red Cross, Washington, D. C.
James N. Rule, B. S., Director Junior Red Cross, Chevy Chase, D. C.
Jesse F. Steiner, Ph. D., Social Technologist, Washington, D. C.
E. E. Loubaugh, M, D., Boise, Idaho
Mrs. Catherine R. Athey, Exec. Sec. Idaho Anti-Tuberculosis Assn., Boise, Idaho.
Mr. L. B. Mangun, Kansas City, Kan.
Frank P. Strickland, Jr., City Chemist, Kansas City, Kan.
Thomas Tetreau, M. D., Portland, Me.
Clarence F. Kendall, M. D., Health Officer, Biddeford, Me.
A. W. Hedrich, Boston, Mass.
S. Boucher, M. D., City Department of Health, Montreal, Que.
Eugenio S. de Jesus, M. D., District Health Officer, Davao, P. I.
Alonzo B. Eckerdt, M. D., Pathologist, Warm Springs, Mont.
J. C. Geiger, M. D., U. S. Public Health Service, Washington, D. C.
Lawrence Griffith, City Engineer, Yonkers, N. Y.
Charles T. Haynes, Chief Sanitary Inspector, Auckland, New Zealand.
Ralph Hendricks, M. D., Health Officer, Spokane, Wash.
Vicente Kierulf, District Health Officer, Cotabato, P. I.
W. G. Long, M. D., Lake Providence, La.
J. D. Maguire, M. D., Health Officer, Lexington, Ky.
H. B. Roshon, V. M. D., Reading, Pa.
Wickliffe Rose, Ph. D., New York City.
Thomas W. Salmon, M. D., Medical Director, Nat'l Comm. Mental Hygiene, New York City.
R. R. Sayres, Chief Surgeon, U. S. Bureau of Mines, Washington, D. C.
Frank S. Shaw, State House, Des Moines, Iowa.
J. F. Siler, M. D., Col. Med. Corps, U. S. A., Washington, D. C.
Alan C. Sutton, M. D., Med. Corps, U. S. A., Washington, D. C.

---

*(States arranged in alphabetical order.)

Carl H. Verner, M. D., Director, Darlington Co. Health Dept., Darlington, S. C.
John Ritchie, Jr., Boston, Mass.
Bernard W. Carey, M. D., Dir. Div. Communicable Diseases, State Dept. of Health, Boston, Mass.
B. R. Rickards, Albany, N. Y.
Charles S. Prest, M. D., Director Health Service, American Red Cross, New York City.
Victor Heiser, M. D., New York City
J. S. C. Elkington, M. D., Chief Quarantine Officer, Brisbane, Queensland, Australia.
Frederick D. Hopkins, New York City
Murray A. Auerbach, Regional Secretary, Nat. Tub. Assn., Atlanta, Ga.
Henry W. Lehmkuhl, Rochester, N. Y.
R. T. Will, The Will Corporation, Rochester, N. Y.
Prof. Warren C. Taylor, Schenectady, N. Y.
Arnold H. Goodman, B. E., Chemist, Schenectady, N. Y.
Frederick W. Sears, M. D., Syracuse, N. Y.
Henry A. MacGruer, M. D., Commissioner of Health, Syracuse, N. Y.
George H. Shaw, M. D., Camillus, N. Y.
H. B. Larner, Goldsboro, N. C.
A. W. Fuchs, Sanitary Engineer, U. S. P. H. S., Goldsboro, N. C.
Chas. E. Low, M, D., Wilmington, N. C.
R. P. Huffman, D. V. M., Food and Dairy Inspector, Wilmington, N. C.
Mr. I. W. Mendelsohn, Grand Forks, N. D.
Samuel Claman, M. S., Health and Sanitation Officer, Grand Forks, N. D.
Harold J. Knapp, M. D., Cleveland, Ohio
W. D. Pack, Asst. City Chemist, Cleveland, Ohio.
Harold L. Lang, Pittsburgh, Pa.
Cecelia Murdoch, Technician, Sewickley, Pa.
Grace C. Taggart, B. A., Laboratory Technician, Pittsburgh, Pa.
C. W. Goddard, M. W., Austin, Tex.
M. E. Parker, M. D., Secretary State Board of Health, Austin, Tex.
E. B. Porter, Sec. Territorial Board of Health, Honolulu, Hawaii
Clifford Charlock, Chief Sanitary Inspector, Hilo, Hawaii.

✢

NEWLY ELECTED OFFICERS
Roger I. Lee, M. D., of Harvard University, Cambridge, Mass., has been elected Treasurer of the Association to take the place of Guilford H. Sumner, M. D., of Des Moines, Iowa, resigned. Roger G. Perkins, M. D., of Western Reserve Medical School, Cleveland, Ohio, has been elected Vice-Chairman of the Laboratory Section in place of W. G. Bissell, M. D., deceased.

371

PUBLIC HEALTH NOTES

Abstracts by D. GREENBERG, M. P. HORWOOD and MAYO TOLMAN.

Death Rate in 1918 Highest on Record.
—The Federal Census Bureau has recently compiled the mortality statistics for the death registration area in the United States for 1918. The death registration area comprised 30 states, the District of Columbia and 27 registration cities in non-registration states. The total estimated population in this area is 81,868,104, or 77.8 per cent of the estimated population of the United States. The Territory of Hawaii is now a part of the registration area, but the figures given below relate only to the continental states.

The total number of deaths reported was 1,471,367, making a death rate of 18.0 per 1000 population, the highest rate on record in the Census Bureau. The high rate was due chiefly to the pandemic of influenza, which swept this country in 1918. There were 477,-467 deaths from influenza and pneumonia (all forms) during 1918, or 32 per cent of the total deaths. Of this number 380,996 deaths occurred during the last four months of the year. The death rate for influenza and pneumonia (all forms) for 1918 was 583.2 per 100,000 population. Influenza caused 244,681 deaths and pneumonia (all forms), 232,786 deaths. In 1917 the death rate per 100,000 for influenza was 17.2 and for pneumonia (all forms) 149.8.

The next most important causes of death were organic diseases of the heart, tuberculosis (all forms), acute nephritis, Bright's disease and cancer. Together they were responsible for 391,391 deaths, or nearly 27 per cent of the total number. The death rate from organic diseases of the heart showed a slight decrease over 1917 when it was 152.2 per 100,000 population. In 1900 the death rate from this cause was 111.2 per 100,000 of population.

Tuberculosis (all forms) caused 122,040 deaths, of which 108,365 were due to tuberculosis of the lungs. The death rate for tuberculosis (all forms) was 149.1 per 100,000 population. The death rate for tuberculosis (all forms) has declined continuously since 1904, when it was 200.7 per 100,000 to 141.6 per 100,000 in 1916. The decrease has been nearly 30 per cent. Since 1916 the rate has increased slightly. Until 1912 tuberculosis was the chief

cause of death. Since then the number of deaths from heart disease has surpassed that from tuberculosis.

Typhoid fever resulted in 10,210 deaths and had a death rate of 12.5 per 100,000 population. The death rate from this cause has shown a remarkable reduction since 1900 when it was 35.9 per 100,000. The decrease has been 65 per cent.

Cancer and other malignant tumors were responsible for 65,340 deaths, of which 24,783 or nearly 38 per cent, resulted from cancer of the stomach and liver. The death rate from this cause was 79.8 per 100,000. In 1917 the rate was 81.6 per 100,000 of population.

Diarrhea and enteritis caused 59,109 deaths, the death rate being 72.2 per 100,000 of population. The rate in 1917 was 79.0 per 100,000 population. More than four-fifths of the total deaths due to these two causes in 1918 occurred among children under 2 years of age.

Arterial diseases of various kinds, such as atheroma, aneurism, etc., caused 19,027 deaths, the death rate being 23.2 per 100,000 of population. In 1917 the death rate from the same cause was 25.3.

Whooping cough and measles together were responsible for 22,534 deaths, the death rate being 27.6 per 100,000 of population. The rate for whooping cough was 16.8 and for measles 10.8.

There were also 10,330 deaths, due to accidental falls, equivalent to a death rate of 12.6 per 100,000 of population; 9,937 deaths due to suicide; 8,610 deaths due to railroad accidents and injuries; 7,525 deaths due to auto accidents and injuries; 12,927 deaths due to diabetes; 12,783 deaths due to bronchitis; 11,280 deaths due to diphtheria, and 8,064 deaths due to meningitis.—*New York Times,* February 8, 1920.—(*M. P. H.*)

✦

New York City Has Lowest Infant Mortality Rate.—The New York City Health Department reports that during 1919 the infant mortality rate was only 82 per 1,000 births. This is the lowest rate in the history of the city. The infant mortality rate in 1918 was 91.7 and in 1917, 88.8. These low infant mortality rates doubtless indicate the efficiency of the child welfare campaign, which the city has been conducting for many years. The results are the more remarkable for a community like New York, which has its share of poverty, of overcrowded conditions and of the uneducated, ignorant, foreign population. It is believed that one of the primary causes for the low infant death rate is the elevation of the standard of living among the poorer classes and the ability of these people to live up to the better standard.—*Weekly Bulletin, New York City Health Department, January 31, 1920.—(M. P. H.)*

✛

Botulism and Ripe Olives.—Several outbreaks of botulinus poisoning have recently occurred in Alliance, Ohio, Detroit, Mich., Kalispell, Mont., New York City and Memphis, Tenn. In most cases the fatalities were traced to the consumption of ripe olives. Some cases were also traced to home canned string beans, asparagus and corn. The ripe olives had come from California and had been packed in glass. On further investigation it was found that the jars had been heated for approximately one-half hour to the temperature of boiling water, a temperature which is insufficient to destroy the *Bacillus botulinus*, if the organism is present in ripe olives. The public is urged to refrain from using ripe olives packed in glass, and all other foods showing the slightest unnatural odor or color or sign of decomposition. Until this year *B. botulinus* was more commonly found in string beans and asparagus. It has also been found in sausage and cheese. The important thing to remember, however, is that it is never found in food which is not spoiled.— *Public Health Reports, February 13, 1920.— (M. P. H.)*

✛

Some Forward Steps in the Oklahoma Tuberculosis Campaign.—A recent pamphlet issued by the Oklahoma Tuberculosis Association contains numerous interesting papers delivered at the second annual meeting in September, 1919. Among these are "Occupations for the Tuberculous," by H. A. Pattison, M.D., "Indian Health Problems" by W. A. Van Cleave, M.D., "Health Conservation Among Indians," by L. W. White, M.D., "Public Health Nursing Needs in Oklahoma," by Miss Edith Swaine and the annual report of the General Society, Jules Scheritz. Mr. Scheritz tells of the sanatorium campaign

which led to state provision for the establishment of two sanatoria for white people and one for negroes, and which established a bureau of tuberculosis in the State Health Department. Extensive publicity in combating tuberculosis has been conducted through exhibits, lantern slides in moving picture theaters, the daily press, display advertisements, day camps, special literature, special talks and public health nurses. Eight of the larger cities and counties in the state have already been organized to combat tuberculosis and are employing from one to three public health nurses each. Tuberculosis dispensaries are maintained in at least three cities in the state. Public health surveys were conducted in eight of the larger cities.

The Modern Health Crusade movement has been fostered and over 200,000 children enrolled. A monthly publication known as the Oklahoma Pow-Wow, is sent to all those interested in health work throughout the state. An intensive child welfare campaign, with examinations and demonstrations, was conducted in three counties during the summer of 1919. The association has also recently appointed a medical field secretary, an industrial field secretary, a public health nurse to work among the Indians, and a negro field secretary. In this way it is hoped that the anti-tuberculosis campaign will be pushed with greater vigor and along scientific lines.— *(M. P. H.)*

✛

Typhus in Esthonia.—Steps to combat the serious outbreak of typhus in Esthonia have recently been taken by the American Red Cross representatives in Europe. Early this year a dangerous shortage of doctors and nurses and an almost complete demoralization of hospital service was reported in face of a rapid spread of the epidemic. Lieut.-Col. Ryan, American Red Cross Commissioner for the Baltic States, has in addition to relief measures taken on the ground, arranged with the French Service de Santé for a detail of twenty French doctors for two months to assist in fighting the disease. In the vicinity of Narva the Red Cross is already caring for 15,000 typhus, dysentery and influenza patients.

Sixty-two American Red Cross nurses are now on duty in Serbia and Albania to battle against a recurrence of the typhus epidemic, which swept across the Balkans last year.

Exchange Professor of Public Health.— As has been announced, Professor William T. Sedgwick is to spend the summer in England as the first exchange professor in biology and public health that has entered into coöperative work of this kind. Soon after the visit of the British Educational Mission to this country in December, 1918, the late Dr. Richard C. Maclaurin, president of the Massachusetts Institute of Technology, suggested to the vice-chancellors of the Universities of Cambridge and Leeds that better educational understanding and international good fellowship might be promoted by the creation of a system of exchange professorships between the institute and the universities. In the development of this plan Dr. Maclaurin named Dr. Sedgwick to be the first professor sent out by the institute. Dr. Sedgwick is senior professor at the Institute and head of the department of biology and public health. He will divide his time between the universities named, returning to this country in September. It is not probable that the return professor will be sent from England before next year.

✠

Experimental Influenza.— Blake & Cecil describe results obtained during an investigation of experimental pneumonia in monkeys by intratracheal injection of *B. influenzæ* undertaken with the hope of throwing light on its relation to the influenza epidemic. The strain of *B. influenzæ* employed was originally isolated ·from a case of influenzal pneumonia in a child and its virulence was enhanced by passage through animals. Twelve monkeys received inoculation of *B. influenzæ* in the nose or nose and mouth, every one of which developed within from three to six hours a respiratory disease apparently identical with influenza. Five of them developed an acute purulent sinusitis of the antrum of Highmore, from which *B. influenzæ* in pure or mixed culture was taken. Nine animals were killed and in the great majority the influenza organism was found either in pure culture or mixed with other germs. Of ten monkeys injected intratracheally with the same strain, seven developed pneumonia, showing the same pathologic picture as in man. The author's conclusions are: "1· *Bacillus influenzæ* can initiate in monkeys an acute infection of the upper respiratory tract which may be compli-

cated by acute sinusitis, tracheo-bronchitis and bronchopneumonia. 2. This disease appears to be identical with influenza in man. 3. *B. influenzæ* when injected intratracheally will produce in monkeys a tracheobronchitis and bronchopneumonia, the pathology of which appears to be essentially identical with that which has been ascribed to pure influenza bacillus infection of the lungs in man. 4. In view of these facts and the constant association of *B. influenzæ*, it seems reasonable to infer that *B. influenzæ* is the specific cause of influenza. —F. G. Blake and R. L. Cecil, *Jour. A. M. A.,* Jan. 17, 1920, 170.—(*D. G.*)

✠

Free Diagnostic Clinic at Buffalo, N. Y. —The Board of Managers of Hospitals and Dispensaries of the city of Buffalo announce the opening of a clinic for diagnosis only to which physicians may. refer their patients. Patients will receive preliminary examination, proper histories will be executed and necessary laboratory specimens taken. Any child or adult resident of Buffalo or of Erie county is eligible for examination. These clinics are set for Mondays throughout the year at one of the health centers of the city, and on the following Wednesdays applicants may make ʾ return visit to the Buffalo City Hospital, at which time and place patients furnished with the preliminary data will be presented to specialists representing some 17 divisions. The reports of the ʾfindings will be mailed to the physician. No treatments will be given, nor will patients be examined save on written recommendation of a regularly licensed doctor of medicine. The clinic is intended for the use of patients' pay patients, to whom the cost of a consultation would be a burden, but no investigation of the financial standing of any applicant will be attempted. Physicians are warned that if they refer cases obviously able to pay a consultation fee to the clinic or exact from patients thus referred a fee larger than is customary for ordinary visits, such act will be construed as abuse of privilege and will result in barring the physician from the clinic. The organization and maintenance of this clinic are loyally administered by departments of the University of Buffalo as a benefit to the community.

Congress of the American School Hygiene Association.—One of the most interesting and popular meetings, held in Cleveland, O., on Friday, February 25-27, in connection with the annual convention of the Department of Superintendent of the National Education Association, was that of the American School Hygiene Association. There were nine sessions with fully 3,000 people, representing nearly every section of the United States, and many from Canada, in attendance.

The entire first day, Wednesday, was devoted to the consideration of health education as conducted in the United states, in Canada, in cities, in rural communities, in universities, in normal schools and in other special fields.

School health service commanded the attention of large audiences during all of the second day of the Congress. Medical inspection in schools, physical education, speech improvement, conservation of vision, the simplification and standardization of health records for school children, and the correlation of medical inspection and physical training, were some of the timely subjects presented before these sessions.

The Thursday morning session had sex education for its subject. Speakers of national prominence presented the following subjects for consideration: An Emergency Solution for an Emergency Need; Suggested Plan for Systematic Sex Education; Seeing Boyhood Through; and Sex Education in Home and in School.

On Thursday afternoon a symposium was given on "Relation of School and Health Authorities with Respect to School Health Service." This was participated in by representatives of health and educational departments and by others.

Mental Hygiene was discussed on Thursday evening. An audience of 450 people was in attendance at this session.

The session on mouth hygiene on Friday morning presented many practical and valuable contributions toward modern methods of dealing with dental conditions among school children. The speakers represented the Federal Government, the National Dental Association, the Rochester Dental Dispensary, the American Red Cross, colleges and magazines.

The closing session on Friday afternoon was devoted to nutrition of school children. This session was opened by a clinic with school children illustrating a practical plan for dealing with nutrition among children. A valuable contribution was made by one of the speakers who presented a State program for nutrition of school children, while another speaker gave many practical suggestions on interesting school children in health habits. Equally interesting were the papers in this session on school lunches in cities, in villages and in rural communities.

The proceedings of the Congress containing the papers will be published as soon as possible and can be obtained from the Secretary of the Association, Harry B. Burns, M.D., Director of School Hygiene, Pittsburgh, Pa. William A. Howe, M.D., of Albany, N. Y., State Medical Inspector of Schools, was elected President and Hiram Byrd, M.D., of the University of Mississippi, Vice-president.

✠

Eighty-three Health Agencies in New York County.—There are fully 83 kinds of health in New York County. This is the first finding of the preliminary activities of the new Department of Health Service, New York County Chapter, American Red Cross. And, though this tentative list includes 53 local and 30 state and national organizations, most of them have headquarters in the city itself.

Such a list the Red Cross believes has never been compiled before and has been made now by the Health Service as a beginning on the Chapter's reconstruction program to meet after-war issues and to start peace-time work. It is the first step of this newest Red Cross department to strengthen and supplement the work of existing public health agencies.

It is a preliminary list of organizations engaged in preventive and educational health work, ranging all the way from associations to prevent and control tuberculosis, cancer, and venereal disease to welfare societies for mothers and babies, nursing associations, relief societies that have definite public health activities, clubs that have active public health committees and settlements that maintain public health work.

The first draft of the list has been sent to all these 83 health agencies for their suggestions and when in final form will be available to everybody, through the Information Bureau of the Department of Health Service, American Red Cross, which expects to begin to turn its information over to the public early in the spring.

Health Centers.—The American Red Cross, in passing from a war to a peace time basis of activity, has taken as one of its goals the unification of community health activities so that there may be greater coöperation among existing health agencies and less duplication of effort. To this end it is fostering the establishment of health centers in all communities. The health center should be the point from which all the health activities of the community radiate. It should be the headquarters of the health officer and his staff, of the tuberculosis clinic, the child and infant welfare clinic, the venereal disease clinic, the mental hygiene clinic and the clinic where cases of industrial disease are examined. In addition, it should be the location of the dental clinic, the clinic dealing with eye, ear, nose and throat defects. The local hospital should attempt to establish much of its out-patient work at the health center. In addition to some of the clinics already mentioned the hospital might locate at the health center, the general medical and surgical clinic, the orthopedic clinic, the obstetrical clinic, the gynecological clinic and the dermatological clinic. The health center could also be the headquarters for after care work growing out of epidemics of influenza and poliomyelitis. The health center should also be the source of all the health educational activities of the health agencies aiming to instruct the people in hygiene, sanitation and the prevention of disease. Here the propaganda for frequent periodic medical examinations could be carried on. Here, too, the medical profession should be provided with meeting rooms and a consultation service. There should also be adequate and excellent facilities for holding public meetings for the purpose of instructing the people in the principles of healthful living. The health center would provide a place for the early diagnosis of disease. Here, too, the forces necessary to combat epidemics or other public emergencies would be mobilized and kept ready for action. Finally, the health center should be the home of the best library in the city, in books and pamphlets and circulars dealing with matters pertaining to the public health.—(*M. P. H.*)

✠

Panama Canal Health Service Work.— The quarantine officials of the Canal Zone are employing two novel methods whereby to effect their inspection of vessels and at the same time subject the vessels to the minimum of delay.

1. The trapping of vessels from ports within the yellow fever zone on their arrival at the Canal. This is done regardless of whether the vessels have been fumigated or not at the port of departure. Trapping is done by two attendants who go over all accessible parts of the ship with a spotlight and killing tube. In the long fight against malaria on the Isthmus this method of catching mosquitoes has been developed to the point where the trapper gets practically all of the mosquitoes in a given place if allowed sufficient time. As adapted to vessels it requires two experienced men about two hours per ship. Mosquito trapping is a check upon the efficiency of the previous fumigation, and in addition shows if the vessel has been where mosquitoes could get on board and the exact kind of mosquitoes. It is believed that this work, which already has a direct bearing on the treatment of the individual vessel, will furnish knowledge that may allow modifications in the general yellow fever quarantine.

2. The use of army gas mask in fumigation. When a vessel is opened up after fumigation, whether this be done with sulphur dioxide or hydrocyanic acid gas, there has been a delay waiting for the gas to be removed sufficiently so that the attendants could enter the apartments and open up completely. With the use of the gas mask the attendants enter immediately without any danger, and after opening all ports, doors, etc., proceed to gather up their apparatus without further delay.

✠

School for Nurses in Bohemia.—Prague is to have the first training school for nurses in Czecho-Slovakia. Realizing that the shortage of native doctors and nurses caused by the war was a very serious problem and that the best way of solving it was to train native personnel, the new government, through Dr. Alice Masaryk, daughter of the president of the republic, appealed to the American Red Cross for assistance. A plan has been worked out for which the Red Cross appropriated $20,000, and is already in operation. Two American Red Cross nurses, Miss Marian Parsons, former chief nurse of General Hospital No. 22, British Expeditionary Forces, and Miss Alotta Lentell, who served with the Red Cross in Flanders, have recently arrived in Prague to establish the school. Miss Parsons will be the superintendent and Miss Lentell will be her assistant.

During the three years that these American nurses remain in Czecho-Slovakia two young Czecho-Slovakian women will be sent to the United States to enter an American training school and prepare themselves to return to their own country and carry on the work initiated by the American nurses. The Massachusetts General Hospital, Boston, has agreed to accept these pupils as soon as they arrive in this country.

✚

How the Other Half is Born.—Under this striking caption the Children's Bureau of the U. S. Department of Labor presents the facts deduced from a set of studies in six rural areas in four states.

In a northwestern county and in a southeastern county there were nearly twice as many persons per physician as the average for the United States; in a southern mountain county there were four times as many. A vast area in the far northwest, larger than the state of Connecticut, was served by three registered doctors. Moreover, most of the doctors in every rural county were located at the county seat, while the remoter parts of the county were entirely without medical service.

More than one-third of the families in the far northwestern county studied were 20 miles or more from the nearest doctor, 10 being from 50 to 100 miles away. In a southern county more than one-fourth of the families were 10 miles or more from a doctor, and in another county 25 miles was not an uncommon distance.

Such distances cause delay on the part of physicians, who arrive too late to be of best service to their patients, and, discouraged by repeated experiences, the people of small communities are tempted to do without one altogether, and frequently do not take the initial steps till the patient's condition becomes critical.

In a southern county only 68 out of 160 mothers had a doctor at their last confinement; in only 8 out of 66 confinement cases in a northern county was a physician secured, and in still another county more than two-thirds of the women did not have a physician when their babies were born. Three were entirely alone and 46 had only their husbands in attendance.

Women would in many cases leave home for confinement if hospitals were within reach. But one 5,500-mile area had no hospital; neither had the southern mountain county. Reaching a hospital meant a journey of several days by wagon trail or one by stage across the roughest of mountain roads.

In a large number of cases the mother has no nursing care except that given by an untrained hired girl, a relative or a neighbor. Figures gathered from five rural counties are small in number but appalling in significance: 45 out of 89 babies, 22 out of 28, 12 out of 15, 10 out of 16, 10 out of 14 babies died *before they were a month old.*

✚

Red Cross·in American Hospitals.—Red Cross Home Service workers are looking after disabled men in thirty-nine of the forty-three Public Health Hospitals of the country. During December the total number of men received was 10,487 and 8,270 had out-patient care. Problems varying from compensation claims to straightening out love affairs were taken by these men to Red Cross workers.

✚

Eye Strain and the Movies.—If your eyes trouble at the movies, do not blame it on the pictures, but consult your doctor about your eyes. This is the advice given by the U. S. Public Health Service.

The fact that millions of people go to motion picture shows throughout the United States daily without experiencing any discomfort to their eyes, or that such eye trouble that is found is not traceable to "over-indulgence" in the movies, would seem to indicate that motion pictures are not injurious to the vision.

In this connection it may be pointed out that employes of motion picture playhouses who spend a large part of the day looking at the pictures, do not seem to be troubled with their eyes any more than the average individual.

It is safe to say a person may witness a picture play lasting about an hour and a half each day without straining the eyes or experiencing any discomfort, provided the eyes are good and there are no hidden defects to the vision. Indeed it is not unlikely that a motion picture show might be the means of advising one of a faulty vision.

A Record Health Year Was 1919.—According to the *Statistical Bulletin* of the Metropolitan Life Insurance Company, the year 1919, despite its very unpromising beginning, closed with better health conditions than have prevailed during any year on record. Between January and March, the United States and Canada were still feeling the effects of the wave of influenza. Many cities were having their worst attacks in those months. The outlook generally was gloomy. Based upon what happened after the epidemic of 1889, health officers expected a return of the influenza during the course of the year and a high death rate from diseases of the heart and kidneys. The country was full of persons who had been left weakened as the result of the influenza, and many of these were expected to die and thus increase the death rate. But the expected did not happen; beginning with the month of April and continuing for each month thereafter up to the end of the year, mortality rates fell sharply below the average of the preceding years. The death rate of the summer of 1919 was unusually low, and the extraordinarily favorable record continued throughout the autumn. In fact, the death rates for the last quarter of the year instead of showing the marked increases usual for the early winter, were as low as some of the best summer and autumn rates on record. From the health standpoint, the year 1919 has been one full of agreeable surprises.

These conditions prevailed in the general population and also among the twelve million policy-holders of the Metropolitan Life Insurance Company. An investigation of the records for policyholders of this company shows an unusually low prevalence of such diseases as tuberculosis, typhoid fever, measles, whooping cough, diseases of the heart and kidneys, diarrheal complaints and of accidents. During the last quarter of the year, there has been an increase in the death rates from scarlet fever and from diphtheria; but these were not of sufficient importance to influence the total death rates. A very remarkable feature of the insurance experience has been the marked improvement in the mortality among negroes.

✛

Influenza Among the Tuberculous.—After a careful analysis of the cases of tuberculosis registered at the Baltimore Health Department the author has written an interesting preliminary note on the incidence of epidemic influenza among the actively tuberculous. Of the 2,375 tuberculous persons, 595, or 25 per cent had influenza, while 1,780 or 75 per cent did not have this disease during the epidemic. Of the 8,820 non-tuberculous individuals living in the same households as the tuberculous, 1,971, or 22.3 per cent had influenza and 6,849, or 77.7 per cent did not have it.

Another table shows: 1. That a little more than one-half (1,104) of the total number of households (2,060) comprised in the statistics had no case of influenza in them during the epidemic. 2. That only about one-fourth (2,-572) of the total persons (11,055) included in the statistics had influenza. 3. That in households where only one case of influenza occurred, 37 per cent of the tuberculous persons living in such households had influenza, while but 15 per cent of the non-tuberculous living in such households had influenza. 4. That in households where two cases of influenza occurred, 48 per cent of the tuberculous persons, and 34 per cent of the non-tuberculous living in such households had influenza. 5. That in households where three or more cases of influenza occurred, 68 per cent of the tuberculous persons and 66 per cent of the non-tuberculous living in such households contracted influenza.—Raymond Pearl, *Quart. Pub. of the Amer. Stat. Assoc.*, Dec., 1919, 536. (D. G.)

✛

Destroying Lice in Clothing.—The observations reported by Hutchison show that if the penetration of steam is sufficient to produce a temperature of 75°C. (167°F.) in the center of a barracks bag (or other load of infected goods) all eggs and active stages of body lice will be destroyed. If the disinfectors are operated efficiently on the time schedule now employed (viz., a 10-inch preliminary vacuum; 15 pounds steam pressure for 15 minutes, reckoned from the time the steam is turned on; followed by a 10-inch drying vacuum), the requisite temperature (75°C.) is attained in every case. By efficient operation is meant (1) the maintenance of a full head of steam so that the 15 pounds pressure in the disinfector is produced within 5 minutes, thus allowing at least 10 minutes for exposure; (2) overloading must be guarded against; (3) the individual bundles must not be rolled too tightly. Little, if any, shrinkage of woolen goods is caused by this treatment. —R. H. Hutchinson, *Jour. Paras.* Dec., 1919, 65.—(D. G.)

STATE HEALTH NOTES—LEGISLATION

National—Health officers will be interested in the scope of the Federal Food and Drugs Act, which contains definitions of "food" and "drug" which differ somewhat from the popular understanding of these terms.

The term "food" includes "all articles used for food, drink, confectionery, or condiment by man or other animals, whether simple, mixed, or compound."

The term "drug" includes "all medicines and preparations recognized in the United States Pharmacopoeia or National Formulary for internal or external use, and any substance or mixture of substances intended to be used for the cure, mitigation, or prevention of disease of either man or other animals."

✛

All articles included within these definitions are subject to the provisions of the Federal Food and Drugs Act which (1) are shipped or delivered for shipment from any State or Territory or the District of Columbia into any other State of Territory or the District of Columbia; (2) are shipped or delivered for shipment from any State or Territory or the District of Columbia to any foreign country; (3) are being imported into the United States; or (4) are manufactured, sold, or offered for sale in the District of Columbia or any Territory of the United States.

✛

The provisions of the Federal Food and Drugs Act do not apply to articles which are manufactured and produced in one State and are not thereafter shipped outside of that State. Any person selling or delivering any food or drug to any person in the same State may, however, incur the penalties prescribed by the Act if, in accordance with section 9, he guarantees that the article is not adulterated or misbranded within the Act and the article thereafter enters interstate or foreign commerce.

Requests for information as to the scope of State food and drug laws should be addressed to State officials.

✛

Indiana.—Although the legislature does not meet till January, 1921, the Indiana

State Board of Health has prepared two bills to be presented early in the session. One of these is to establish full-time health officers and the other, to make compulsory school health supervision of children. It is believed that public opinion will support these bills and that they will be passed and with them good appropriations and wide powers for the State Board.

✛

Kentucky.—In the September Bulletin of the State Board of Health are presented the "Food and Drug Laws Rules and Regulations" as amended in 1918. These include sections referring to misbranding, inspection, bacteriological examination, sanitation of food establishments, offenses against the public health, dairies and dairy cattle, bakers and bakeries, handling of eggs, abattoirs and retail meat establishments.

✛

Massachusetts.—It is expected that the Committees on Public Health and of Education of the Massachusetts legislature will report a bill for the establishment of a State Director of Physical Training in Public Schools. An informal counting of noses shows the majority to be in favor of reporting. Child health legislation will be important during the session. There are two bills proposed, one for the establishment of minimum rules and regulations for the teaching of hygiene in the public schools and for the physical training of school children, the bill carrying appropriations for the purpose. The other makes it imperative on the authorities in cities and towns to instal school nurses.

✛

The *Boston Medical and Surgical Journal* in a report of a joint committee of the Massachusetts Medical Society and the Massachusetts Homeopathic Medical Society, notes the status of three bills before the legislature on maternity benefits. These bills, which vary in details, are aimed at the advising and assisting of pregnant women who have been for one year at least residents in the state. The Spencer bill provides two months' notice by the woman, that any money benefit, not to exceed $12 a week, shall be paid directly to the mother, and that no stigma of pauperism shall follow the payment of such benefit sums. The Carey bill mentions no period in advance of confinement for the application, but in other respects is similar to the other bill. The Young bill makes the date of application three months before the expected date of confinement. Here the State is to pay the physician. There are various minor differences, the Young bill omits reference to illegitimacy, the Spencer bill puts the burden on the State Board of Health of determining the financial condition of applicants, but provides no control over the physician provided he accepts the stipulated fee. The Young bill provides that he must not only accept the fee but abide by the rules issued by the State Board of Health. "In this clause," notes the *Boston Medical and Surgical Journal*, "lies the opportunity to bring about better conditions of obstetrical practice."

✦

New Mexico.—The special meeting of the State Legislature held February 16-21, 1920, passed Senate Bill No. 5, "An Act authorizing employment of health employes and the levying of special taxes for certain health purposes." The act passed the Senate 17 to 5, and the House of Representatives 34 to 0, and was approved by Governor O. A. Larrazolo, February 21.

This act will make possible the employment of full-time county and municipal health officers with a sufficient staff of sanitary inspectors, public health nurses, etc., in local health departments, and provides for the levying of a special tax not to exceed one-half mill on a dollar of assessed valuation of property within the county or municipality, to provide for the salary and expenses of local health departments.

In 1919 the regular session enacted a very complete and progressive health law providing for the creation of a State Department of Health and made appropriations for its maintenance. The State Department has adopted regulations requiring the reporting of births, deaths and morbidity. These regulations follow the model law. In order to carry out the provisions of the law it was found that full-time health officers would be necessary and funds. The special levy for this purpose is supposed to be the first one of its kind in the country, namely, a levy in excess of the regular

maximum which is to be devoted to health work.

In the passage of the Act the New Mexico Public Health Association was very active.

✦

North Dakota.—The State Board of Health has issued its regulations governing water supplies in the state, and sewerage and refuse disposal. The water supply that is furnished to more than 25 persons shall be subject ot bacteriological examinations and must satisfy the standards of the U. S. Public Health Service as set forth for interstate common carrier supplies. Sewage disposal by flowing it into streams is regulated, sewage being interpreted to be industrial wastes as well as those from humans and animals. Garbage regulations control retention in houses, disposal in various ways, and forbids filling land by dumping, excepting with the approval of the health officer. Special note is made of garbage retainers, which must be water tight, covered, fly and rat proof, set at least 9 inches above ground, and they must be emptied at least once every 48 hours.

Plans for water supply systems or sewage disposal must be approved by the State Board of Health in their sanitary features, elaborate regulations control the details of the drawings to be submitted, and plans must look well into the future. "The sewers should have a capacity when flowing half-full, sufficient to carry twice the future average flow 25 years hence, plus a sufficient allowance for ground water infiltration."

The regulations interfere little with sewage systems existing January 1, 1920, in municipalities, but require that when any city or village builds a municipal sewer, all abuttors to the sewer line where the property has been platted into lots, shall, under penalty, install toilets, connected with the water supply and sewer.

STATE HEALTH NOTES—GENERAL

Connecticut.—The leaflet published by the Bureau of Preventable Diseases of the Connecticut State Department of Health urges the use of the Schick test for determining immunity to diphtheria to be followed by the toxin-antitoxin treatment, pointing out that only 30 per cent of children between one and two years of age are naturally immune, though this percentage increases until nearly 85 per cent are immune at 20 years of age.

The use of the toxin-antitoxin treatment following the Schick test, apparently insures 100 per cent immunity, and it is pointed out that had this treatment been used in 1918, many of the 201 deaths among Connecticut children from diphtheria could have been prevented.— (*M. T.*)

✠

Indiana.—The State of Indiana has purchased two automobiles especially for the fight against tuberculosis. It is proposed to conduct an intensive campaign in a few of the counties that are entirely rural. The principle of the work will be to get at the children, for the reason that probably 80 per cent of all consumption is acquired in childhood. The lectures, literature and exhibits will be focused on this point. The remedy proposed is education in right living. The director of this work is Dr. H. W. McKane.

The State Health Department has another auto for the Division of Child Hygiene, which will likewise be devoted to touring the rural sections. Its slogan is, "Save the child and you will save the man." The outfit includes an exhibition, posters and literature and in its personnel are two nurses. The company will stay in any county long enough to visit every township and see that every home receives instructions with reference to tuberculosis and child hygiene. The schoolhouses will be centers for much of this work.

✠

Maine.—More than 600,000 visitors came to Maine during the summer of 1919, spending in this state from $27,000,000 to $30,000,000, according to figures included in the report of A. S. Dean of Portland, hotel inspector for the past season. Inspection of hotels during the summer season when vacation resorts as well as year round commercial houses are open to guests, is conducted annually under the supervision of the State Department of Health to determine whether or not such places are sanitary; use unpolluted water and pure milk, and otherwise keep the health regulations.

In the 253 hotels visited by the inspector, the majority of them along the coast with a few commercial establishments in Bangor, Portland and several smaller towns, sanitary conditions were noted as excellent in but 22. Twenty-three hotels were listed as "very

good," 146 as "good," 45 as "fair," and 17 as frankly "poor."

More than $36,000 was saved to the people of Maine during 1919 through the 10,000 free tests which were made by the diagnostic laboratory of the State Department of Health for such diseases as diphtheria, typhoid, tuberculosis, cancer, syphilis, gonorrhea, and other germ diseases. The record for the year shows an average of 27 examinations daily at an average commercial value of $3.68 each or a daily total of $9,715. The tests made include 1,063 for diphtheria, 1,827 of sputum for tuberculosis, 243 for malignancy, 380 for typhoid, and 5,837 for venereal disease. These figures show an almost 50 per cent increase over the preceding year and are interpreted by the commissioner, Dr. L. D. Bristol as highly indicative of the value which Maine people are putting upon the services of the department.

✠

Minnesota.—The general death rate for Minnesota is declining. The table below giving the total number of deaths year by year since 1910, also the rate, that is, the number per 1,000 population. In order to compare the number of deaths from year to year, it is to be remembered that the population is increasing.

1918 was an exceptional year, and the influenza epidemic gave the state the highest death rate it has had.

In 1919 there were 2,500 influenza deaths, about 25 times the usual number, but in spite of this, the improvement in other causes brought the rate down to 10.4, which is about normal.

MINNESOTA'S DEATH RATE FOR THE PAST DECADE
Deaths from all causes per 1,000 of population

Year	No. of Deaths	Rate
1910	22,868	11.05
1911	21,893	10.35
1912	20.502	9.57
1913	22,799	10.43
1914	23,382	10.6
1915	22,755	10.15
1916	24,295	10.81
1917	23,955	10.4
1918	31,342	13.3
1919	24,794	10.4

The "Keeping Fit" campaign instituted by the U. S. Public Health Service in its efforts to reach by placards, slides and literature all the boys of high school age in the country, is being vigorously carried on. The Minnesota State Board of Health, however, is the first to present an exhibit of like character to the girls. Dr. Mabel S. Ulrich has prepared for this purpose several sets of placards, 41 in each set, 31 of which are appropriately illustrated in color. The exhibit is primarily an educational health appeal, no particular stress being laid on either disease or sex—the title of the exhibit being "Better Womanhood."

The State Board of Health of Minnesota has issued the following instructions to the physicians of the state with reference to venereal diseases. The Division of Venereal Diseases was organized during the war when many of the physicians were in service. Since these men have had no opportunity to become acquainted with the Minnesota practices, a special letter is addressed to them.

The physician is interested primarily in the diagnosis and treatment of his patient, the State Board of Health is interested primarily in protection of the public health and in the individual patient only as it may protect the public through the diagnosis and treatment of that patient. These two angles are not incompatible, and it is hoped physicians will become more and more interested in the latter one.

The important items in regard to reporting cases are: Reports of infectious and contagious diseases are necessary for two vital reasons—1st, we must know our problem, in other words, how many cases there are. 2nd, we must know the location of these cases in order that control measures be taken if necessary.

It follows then that every case of gonorrhea, syphilis and chancroid must be reported.

It makes no difference whether infective or not.

It makes no difference whether previously reported or not.

It makes no difference if our laboratory has a positive finding on its records.

Report every case you diagnose or treat.

If you see them only once and they fail to return, report name and address to this division, and an investigation will be made.

If a patient has been previously reported, report him again so we will know where to locate him.

If you see a case and expect to refer it to someone else, report it—patients do not always go where sent, and we are in a position to find out and take action.

A positive laboratory report does not constitute a report of a case. All cases must be reported on a card supplied for the purpose.

New Mexico.—Dr. C. E. Waller of the department of public health, together with the forest officials, have worked out a plan whereby every forest ranger in the state will be made a representative of the department of health.

The forestry officers will advise the people of the law and assist them in familiarizing themselves with it, report to the state officers any violations. This will apply in the small remote settlements where, under present conditions it is very difficult for the state officer to enforce or even teach sanitation and health regulations.

Such an arrangement has been in effect in Arizona for some time and the results attained are very gratifying.

Walter M. Connell, chairman of Albuquerque City Commissioners has been appointed vice-president of the New Mexico Public Health Association to fill the vacancy made by the death of Dr. Oliver T. Hyde.

✛

Seventy persons attended the annual meeting of the New Mexico Public Health Association held in Alburquerque, January 27th.

At the business meeting, H. O. Bursum of Socorro was elected president, Dr. O. T. Hyde of Albuquerque first vice-president, Col. Bronson M. Cutting of Santa Fé second vice-president, M. W. Murray of Silver City third vice-president, Dr. Frank N. Carrier of Santa Rita secretary, and Dr. David R. Boyd of Albuquerque treasurer.

The following new directors were chosen to take the place of those whose terms had expired: Bernalillo, J. T. McLaughlin and Dr. J. E. J. Harris, Albuquerque; Chaves, Clark Dilley, Roswell; Colfax, Ernest D. Raynolds, Raton; Curry, E. W. Bowyer, Clovis; Dona Ana, W. A. Sutherland, Las Cruces; Grant, W. O. Hall, Silver City; Guadalupe, Frank Faircloth, Santa Rosa; Luna, E. D. Martin, Deming; McKinley, Mrs. C. C. Manning, Gallup; Otero, R. R. Pratt, Alamogordo; Rio Arriba, H. L. Hall, Chama; San Juan, Sherman R. Coon, Aztec; Santa Fe, Dr. Robert O. Brown, Santa Fe; Union, T. E. Mitchell, Albert.

✛

New York.—The Bureau of Venereal Diseases of the New York State Department of Health offers a prize of $100 to the person who best interprets the expression "Healthy parents head happy families," in a colored drawing that can be reproduced as a poster for public health work.

Drawings may be made any size, but must not be smaller than 12 by 18 inches.

Drawings may be signed by artist. Signatures will be covered before seen by judges. Judges will be announced later by Dr. Hermann M. Biggs, commissioner of health.

Winner will be chosen from among those whose drawings are received at the New York state department of health, Albany, N. Y., before 5 p. m. May 1, 1920.

Drawings will be returned if artist will submit postage. It may be desirable to purchase for use elsewhere certain of those not winning the prize.

The bureau reserves the right to reject all drawings if in the minds of the judging committee none satisfactorily meets the requirements.

Posters in use by this bureau at present picture the horrors following in the wake of the venereal diseases and it is felt that for the sake of constructive work a poster depicting full robust health should be employed.

Dr. Joseph E. Clark, sanitary supervisor of the New York State Department of Health for Oneida, Herkimer and Madison counties, died at the Utica Hospital on March 4th after an illness of nearly a year.

For a number of years, Dr. Clark was chairman of the Board of Health of the City of Medford, Mass. In 1914, following the reorganization of the New York State Department of Health, he was appointed a State Sanitary Supervisor and continued in that capacity up to the time of his death.

The post-graduate course in infectious diseases and public health, given by the Albany Medical College in coöperation with the State Board of Health· opened on March 4 with 51 registrations, a number of the men being of the school of last year, who wish to keep up with the times. The order of exercises at the opening of the course included an address by Dr. Charles C. Duryee, director of the course, followed by a lecture on general bacteriology and technique by Dr. Augustus B. Wadsworth, director of the division of laboratories and research of the state board. After luncheon Dr. Hermann M. Biggs, state health commissioner, addressed the men and there was a general conference on tuberculosis led by Dr. H. Edgar Rose of the state department of health. The students will meet one day each week until the middle of June. This can be done by them without neglecting their regular duties.

The commencement exercises of the Buffalo post-graduate course in preventive medicine and hygiene for health officers were held at the Lafayette Hotel on January 29th, 21 members of the 1919-20 class receiving diplomas. Dr. Charles S. Jones, dean of the medical department of the University of Buffalo, presided.

The Rotary Clubs of Syracuse recently gave a party to 82 children of that city who are crippled as a result of infantile paralysis. After the entertainment, refreshments were served and toys were distributed. Helena T. Mahoney, state supervising nurse, and Miss Abby Cornell, social worker of Syracuse, were in charge of the details.

Another list of towns in New York state which have inadequate medical service or where it is lacking altogether, has been published by the New York state health department, to which application should be made for further details. The towns and their respective counties are:

Town	County
Bloomville	Delaware
Cameron	Steuben
Cannonville	Delaware
Fremont	Sullivan
Gardiner	Ulster
Gilboa	Schoharie
Groveland	Livingston
Halcottville	Delaware
Lewis	Essex
Mariette	Onondaga
Meridale	Delaware
Medford	Suffolk
Newton Falls	St. Lawrence
North Bangor	Franklin
North Java	Wyoming
Piercefield	St. Lawrence
Putnam	Washington
Richfield Springs	Otsego
Rock Rift	Delaware
Rockwood	Fulton
Sidney Center	Delaware
Spafford	Onondaga
Starkville	Herkimer
Sterling	Cayuga
Treadwell	Delaware
Westford	Otsego
Willsboro	Essex
West Hebron	Washington.

The Red Cross and city health department

coöperating, have started a mental clinic in Plattsburgh. Dr. John R. Ross, medical superintendent of the Dannemora State Hospital, is the specialist in attendance.

A summary of the Oneida county tuberculosis clinics, which have been held under the auspices of the New York State Department of Health and the State Charities Aid Association, shows that 1,287 patients were examined, of these 214, or 16.6 per cent were found positive, 390 or 30 per cent suspicious, and 683 negative. The clinics were held at accessible clinic centers, extending over a period of six months.

Thirty-three nurses, having completed the four months' public health nursing course at the University of Buffalo, have received their certificates in public health nursing.

✦

North Carolina.—The Bureau of Venereal Diseases of North Carolina has instituted a "Keeping Fit" campaign among the boys and young men of the state under the care of Mr. Henry P. Coor, educational director, U. S. P. H. S. The campaign is expressly for older boys ranging in age from 14 to 20, and has been arranged with much consideration and thought. Quotas have been set for the different counties, the goal is 50,000 boys, and proceedings are well under way, Wilson county having already secured one-third of its quota and Guilford county one-fifth. Exhibits, lecture material, and instructions have been widely distributed.

At a conference of representative colored people of the State of North Carolina held in Raleigh, February 6, 1920, under the auspices of the North Carolina State Board of Health and the United States Public Health Service, the following resolutions were unanimously adopted:

WHEREAS, This conference recognizes the fact that the venereal diseases constitute a serious problem demanding careful thought and attention; and,

WHEREAS, The control of venereal diseases requres the coöperation of all persons and agencies in each community; and,

WHEREAS, Proper provision for the expression through natural outlets of the play and adventure instincts of life is necessary for the security of health and morals, and,

WHEREAS, An essential factor in preventing the venereal diseases is social betterment through the removal of negative, predisposing conditions and the development of positive, corrective agencies; and,

WHEREAS, It is the conviction of this conference that all institutions having to do with the developing of leaders in human society should give to their students adequate knowledge of the meaning of sex as a factor in life and should acquaint them with the best psychology that would assist them in bringing this knowledge to the attention and aid of those whom they serve; therefore, be it

Resolved, That the following recommendations be made:

1. That all medical men and women, including physicians, pharmacists, dentists and nurses in their private practices and in the institutions, organizations and businesses with which they are identified do regularly and efficiently render their best service in the treatment and control of venereal diseases.

2. That all directors and members of public welfare departments, supervisors and attendants of places of amusement and recreation, probation officers, social workers, and others engaged in activities for community welfare do render every possible service for the removal of the negative, underlying and predisposing conditions for social ills and for the development of wholesome community life.

3. That citizens in communities which have no social welfare work be encouraged to employ social workers and establish social centers and to request the local authorities to aid in the establishment and maintenance of such persons and institutions.

4. That the church and fraternal organizations, because of their large and interested membership, and the press, because of its large number of readers, do deliver the message covering this problem and, through their own work and in support of other activities for community betterment, contribute in a practical way to its solution.

5. That all business men and organizations do seriously consider the ways in which this problem affects the health and efficiency of workers, and use their influence to improve conditions by urging and assisting movements for better sanitation and hygiene in their communities and for the provision of wholesome recreation.

6. That all colleges and normal schools preparing teachers make provision for adequate instruction in the problem of sex education, which will prepare these teachers more

effectively to meet the demands of the various communities which they serve.

7. That the theological schools preparing ministers recognize the tremendous bearing which sex has upon every aspect of moral and religious life and that they take the necessary practical steps to enable the future ministry to use this great endowment of the human race intelligently and constructively.

8. That the Board of Nurse Examiners make adequate knowledge of social hygiene and venereal diseases a requirement for certification as a registered nurse.

9. That the members of this conference and others whom they may interest and associate with them in this program do keep in communication and co-operation with the local health authorities and the state board of health and welfare agencies, in order that there may be a constant development, and follow-up of all activities for the solution of the great and important problems of venereal disease control and sex hygiene.

The chairman of the committee is Dr. D. C. Suggs and the secretary, Mrs. Charlotte Hawkins Brown.

The State of North Carolina and the U. S. Public Health Service in coöperation with the local health authorities have established venereal disease clinics in eleven cities and towns, Ashville, Charlotte, Clinton, Fayetteville, Goldsboro, Greensboro, High Point, Raleigh, Rocky Mount, Wilmington and Winston-Salem. Most of these will have a clinic six days per week. In order to supplement this work the state has issued instructions to physicians, outlining what it furnishes and does and giving information with reference to prices and means of obtaining supplies. The state will make free Wassermann tests, will furnish arsphenamine, has a "Red Book" of instructions, and is planning for meetings and conferences to bring the facts to the attention of the men engaged in the work.

The North Carolina Bulletin for June, 1919, calls attention to the terrific toll that ignorance and carelessness exact in the field of smallpox alone. With this disease carelessness is apparently the biggest factor in its prevalence. Science has known how to absolutely prevent smallpox for 125 years; yet in North Carolina alone there were 1,688 cases in one year with 265 in a single city. If it were not for the preservation of the industrial efficiency of our nation, perhaps it would be well to let those

who are careless suffer this loathsome disease as a price of their indifference.

The time is not far distant when local health authorities will be held responsible for an epidemic of typhoid fever.

In four years the North Carolina health department has succeeded reducing the typhoid death rate in the state from 35.4 to 23.6, and this in face of some counties who pay so little attention to the disease that they permit a rate of 75.6.

During the coming summer a campaign for complete vaccination is to be conducted in 30 counties of the state. This campaign should result in a still greater reduction of the typhoid rate. Complete vaccination combined with sanitary privilege would gradually eliminate the disease.

A recent bulletin of the North Carolina state department of health points out that the pulpit and the press are practically silent on the moral responsibilities of each man for the health of his neighbor. Certainly a man's duty towards the health of his fellow-man is fully as great as his duty towards the morals of his fellow-man.

✦

Ohio.—In co-operation with all the states of the Union, the Ohio state department of health opened its "Keeping Fit" campaign on March 1. This fight against venereal diseases has been prompted by conditions revealed during the examination of the second million drafted men.

An exhibit consisting of a series of cards has been prepared and these, together with other literature, is used to instruct the public concerning the prevention and spread of social diseases. Pamphlets have been compiled for the boy and girl of high school age, for parents and educators and will be distributed through the commissioners of health in the various counties, through ministers and school superintendents.

Several counties have already planned the carrying out of the campaign and have arranged to have lectures accompanied by lantern slides especially prepared to show the effects of the diseases, so that the public may do its share in effectively stamping them out.

Measures for the prevention of quarantinable diseases which are now prevalent, though not widespread, in the state, have been sent to the health commissioners of the various counties. These diseases include smallpox, scarlet fever and diphtheria.

Thoroughness in treating a patient with one of these diseases will most always reveal the source of the infection and will often expose concealed and obscure cases. If the source is found and the exposures dealt with promptly and correctly, diseases will not spread. Quarantine is always necessary and should be made as light a burden as possible; the reason for it should be carefully explained to the patient's family and absolute adherence to the rules should be demanded.

In diphtheria, the patient should be isolated and this quarantine should be continued until he is no longer capable of communicating the disease. Swabs should be taken from the throats of other members of the family. If the swabs from the throats of the breadwinners prove negative they may be allowed to work, providing the patient is properly isolated. If this is not possible, strict quarantine of all members of the family should be enforced. When two successive throats swabs of patient prove negative and swabs from the other members of the family, taken not less than forty-eight hours apart are also negative, the house may be disinfected and the quarantine raised.

Where a patient is suffering with scarlet fever, he should be quarantined until no longer capable of communicating the disease. breadwinners who are immune by reason of a previous attack may be allowed to work, provided they do not come in contact with the patient or the food supply. When disinfection has been performed, children who have not had the disease should remain under quarantine for at least 10 days.

In the case of smallpox, the patient should be quarantined until there is no longer danger of the spread of the disease. Quarantine in a case of smallpox includes everyone in the house except those who have had the disease or who have been recently successfully vaccinated.

Complying with the provisions of the Griswold Act which amended the Hughes Health Law, 50 of the 88 counties of the state have organized and 39 new health commissioners have been appointed. Twelve of these are to serve full time. In three districts the city and county have agreed on the appointment of the same commissioner. Of the 50 districts already organized 25 have made provisions for a public nurse and 30 nurses have already been named.

While in some districts difficulty has been encountered in providing finances for 1920, in practically all of these the auditor and the advisory council have been working in coöperation and have been able to provide at least a minimum amount for the current year. The budget for 1921 will be adopted in April in time for submission to the budget commission so that provision may be made in the tax levies for financing the organizations on a permanent basis.

+

Utah.—The Division of Health Education of the State Department of Public Instruction has sent out widely its suggestions for protecting the mental health of children. These follow eminently sensible lines.

Parents and teachers alike should be advised as to the points in child training that are valuable as promoting and preserving mental health.

Give your child opportunity for a variety of wholesome activities and interests.

Train your child to work hard in some regular occupation suited to his ability and talents, but to avoid fatigue by alternation of work and rest.

Train your child to give attention to the present situation rather than to the future.

Train your child to strict obedience in a few important matters and let him alone in regard to the unimportant things.

Avoid conditions that tend to produce overstrain or precocity. The special business of a young child is to be a child—to grow and to play with other children.

Protect your child from shocks. Do not frighten him yourself or let other people do so.

Encourage frankness and directness.

Give your child a variety of well cooked wholesome food in ample quantity at regular intervals.

Train your child to avoid drugs and stimulants of all kinds.

Train your child to healthful habits of sleep in fresh air, giving opportunity for at least nine hours, and for more than that before the age of twelve.

If your child shows any difficulty in adaptation—sleeplessness, emotional storms, fears, irritability, persistent delinquency—consult a competent physician at once.

Take advice of a competent person concerning the peculiar, sensitive, or nervous child, in order to correct a possible unfavorable inheritance by proper education and environment.

The best method of training is by example.

✛

West Virginia.—A conference of all State Health Agencies with representatives from State Agricultural Extension Department, State Department of Schools, National Red Cross and National Anti-Tuberculosis Association, was recently called by the state health commissioner of West Virginia for the purpose of coöperation, and coördination of forces, in order to avoid overlapping, duplication and consequent waste of time, energy and money in health work in the state. The definite outcome of this was a plan for several intensive county health campaigns during the year in which all the organizations will unite their forces, upon invitation from a county, with the specific purpose of establishing a health center in the county with a full-time health officer. The campaign is already on in Upshur county and making good progress and Logan county is now organizing to begin their campaign in March.

At the annual convention of West Virginia, Federation of Women's Clubs, the following resolution was presented by the public health committee and endorsed by the convention:

Realizing that physical development is the foundation for mental development, and deploring the appalling percentage of maternal and infant deaths and the astounding number of undernourished children, be it

Resolved, That the West Virginia Federation of Women's Clubs endorse the "Child Health Organization" program, which provides for standard bar scales in every public school, and the record chart recording weight, in each room; and be it further

Resolved, That the West Virginia Federation of Women's Clubs stimulate interest for the appointment of a public health nurse in every community, and interest high school graduates and college women to enter training schools for nurses and fit themselves for the public health field.

Be It Further Resolved, That the national committeemen in the two dominant parties be instructed to advise the creation of a "United States Public Health Department," with a national secretary of public health.

The West Virginia state health department has planned a conference of all health officers of the state to be held in Huntington April 13-14th. The public health nurses of the state have been invited to attend and take part in this conference and are represented on the program.

A plan for coöperation and coördination in public health nursing has been worked out in West Virginia between the American Red Cross and the state department of health that seems to be ideal. The supervision of the Red Cross public health nursing service has been put under the division of public health nursing of the state health department, the director of the division sending in a monthly report and holding a monthly conference with the director of the bureau of public health nursing, Potomac division. Because of the added responsibility and increase of work that this entails and because of the limited appropriation of the state health department, the Red Cross has assumed the salary of an assistant until July, 1921, when necessary funds from the next legislature should be available. The Red Cross is also paying one-half the salary of a full-time stenographer for the division, because of the increased clerical work.

The San Francisco Meeting Is Only Five Months Away
August 30-September 3—Note the Date ·
Are You Making Your Plans?

PUBLIC HEALTH
LABORATORY NOTES

Abstracted by Francis H. Slack, M. D., and Mr. James M. Strang.

Investigations of the Etiology of the Influenza of 1918.—Since Pfeiffer's bacillus is found so inconstantly in cases of grippe, Burckhardt does not regard it as the causative factor. The diplococci causing pneumonia, pleuritis and other complications, as well as gram-negative cocci, are also excluded. Although a variant of the streptococcus family, as yet unknown, may be concerned, the author is inclined to attribute the disease to a filterable virus.—Burckhardt, *Centralbl. f. Bact.* 1919, 68, 425.

✛

Cerebro-Spinal Meningitis from a Micrococcus.—A case of meningitis caused by *Micrococcus tetragenus albus* is described. The morphology and cultural characteristics of the organism are given in detail. Several illustrations and a noteworthy bibliography are included.—Riemsdyk, *Zeit, f. Hyg. u. Infekt.,* 1919, 89, 146.

✛

Observations of the Culture of Paratyphoid B.—The authors have demonstrated by several series of experiments that paratyphoid B may be easily isolated and grown on a selective medium which is essentially a Drigalski agar rendered alkaline by the addition of NaOH or KOH. Ten to twelve cubic centimeters of normal KOH added to 100 of medium give the best results. Coli and other fecal organisms, with the exception of *Coli capsulatus*, are very strongly inhibited, while the conditions for the development of paratyphoid B are greatly improved. The number of colon organisms present apparently has slight effect upon the growth of this bacillus. *C. capsulatus* is not always inhibited, but can be distinguished from paratyphoid B by the shape of the colony. Organisms from other sources which grow readily on alkaline media are rarely found on these plates.

In 308 cases investigated for the presence of paratyphoid B in the feces, 110 were found positive by the ordinary media and 58 more by this special medium. Rarely does this organism grow on ordinary media and not on the alkaline. Cultures which give a typical colonies on such media rapidly become normal

on successive cultivation on the medium described.—Felseneich, *Zeit, f. Hyg. u. Infekt,* 1919, 89, 88.

✛

The Cultural Differentiation of Beta Hemolytic Streptococci of Human and Bovine Origin.—Hemolytic streptococci are common in good dairy products and are usually harmless to the consumer. They may be distinguished from hemolytic streptococci pathogenic to man by (1) Their action on blood in fluid media; (2) Their appearance in the blood agar plate; (3) Their fermentation reactions; (4) Limiting Hydrogen-Ion concentration in dextrose bouillon; (5) Their growth in milk; (6) Their reaction to methyl blue. None of the procedures described serves by itself to differentiate streptococci of human and bovine origin with certainty, although each of them serves as a strong presumptive test. Most strains fall easily into the human or bovine group by all the tests. —J. H. Brown, *Jour Exper. Med.,* Jan., 1920, 35.

✛

Dairy Infection with Streptococcus Epidemicus.—The authors' report on the investigation of a streptococcus epidemic due to *S. epidemicus.* The infection was traced to the milk from a single quarter of the udder of a cow in a dairy of 112 cows producing an otherwise excellent grade of milk. The streptococcus isolated from the cow was in every respect like streptococci isolated from patients and milkers, and different from those usually found in normal cows, or cows with garget. Certain recommendations are made to safeguard producers of raw milk against the occurrence of such epidemics.—J. H. Brown and M. L. Orcutt, *Jour. Exper. Med.,* Jan. 1920, 49.

✛

Culture Media from Fish.—The authors summarize experiments on the use of fish in the preparation of culture media in place of the more expensive meat juice and peptone. The ordinary bacteria, both ærobic and anærobic, were found to grow very well on these media.—Harde and Hause, *Comptes Rendus,* 1919, 82, 1259.

388

INDUSTRIAL HYGIENE AND OCCUPATIONAL DISEASE

Abstracted by Drs. E. R. Hayhurst, R. P. Albaugh, P. M. Holmes, and E. B. Starr.

The Empty Sugar Bowl—A Benefit to Health.—Before the war the average person consumed about 75 to 80 pounds of sugar per year, hence its increase or decrease in the dietary has some importance. Sugar requires practically no digestive manipulation in the human body. Sugar is utilized by muscle cells to generate heat and to produce muscular energy for both mental and physical processes. Starchy foods are eventually changed by the digestive fluids into sugar, but this requires the action of the digestive fluids and requires a longer time. It is believed that this is healthful, it gives the digestive mechanism employment. Sugar is a concentrated food and represents considerable fuel in a small package. Sugar is digested better by those who do hard manual labor than by those doing office or clerical work. Excess of sugar in the stomach ferments and the toxic substances result in digestive disturbances, constipation, bad complexions, pimples, etc. All sweet foods should be eaten sparingly. Eating sugar is a habit, and one that is in most instances decidedly detrimental to health. Forty years ago we were using 8 pounds of sugar per capita; today there are twice as many men dying between the ages of forty and fifty. The sugar shortage no doubt will be a blessing in disguise to many of us and it will work hardship on no one. An abnormal craving for sweets can be satisfied with fruits.—H. H. Smith, Chief Surgeon, *American Rolling Mills Company Bulletin*, December, 1919, Middletown, Ohio, pp. 44-45.

✦

New Basis for Measuring Accident Frequency and Severity Rates.—The International Association of Industrial Accident Boards and Commissions has adopted the following resolution: *Resolved*, That accident rates, both frequency rates and severity rates, be computed on the basis of 1,000 hours' exposure instead of 3,000 hours' exposure, as heretofore. The unit of measure for both frequency and severity accident rates, which has come to be generally used, is the "300-day worker," sometimes called "full-time worker." This hypothetical worker is supposed to work

10 hours a day for 300 days in the year, or 3,000 hours per year. The committee on statistics and compensation insurance cost at its first meeting considered very carefully the question of a proper unit for measuring accident rates and decided to adopt the only unit then in actual use, namely, the "300-day worker." The 300-day worker was chosen as the standard measure for accident rates because (1) it is absolutely necessary to have a common unit for measuring accidents in all occupations, all industries, all states and all countries; (2) the 300-day worker had been recommended as the standard unit for computing accident rates by the Permanent International Committee on Social Insurance and the International Institute of Statistics and was in use in Germany and Austria at the time the committee on statistics took up the matter of standardization of accident statistics; (3) it was alleged that most workers did work about 10 hours a day and about 300 days in the year. It was further argued that while the 300-day worker did conform closely to the normal worker, still he was merely an abstraction, a unit of measure, and would measure exposure to accident just as accurately for an 8-hour day as a 10-hour day, for a 200-day year as a 300-day year. The use of this unit, it was maintained, did not suggest a 10-hour day or a 300-day year as the ideal and proper working day and industrial year.

In view of the fact that the working time, both the hours per day and the days per year, varies widely from plant to plant, from industry to industry, from city to city, from country to country, and from year to year, it was thought best by the committee to cut loose entirely from a unit of measure that could be misunderstood as, in any way, implying what the proper working time should be. The adoption of 1,000 hours' exposure rids us forever of any such implication and gives a unit which is convenient in size and will remain unaffected by changes in the working day or variations in the working year. The 1,000-hour exposure is a stable, scientific, mathematical unit of measure, which is what is needed for the measurement of accident rates. It has the

389

further advantage that accident rates measured by any other unit of exposure may be readily expressed in terms of the 1,000-hour unit and vice versa.—*U. S. Monthly Labor Review*, U. S. Bureau of Labor Statistics, Jan., 1920, pp. 218-219.

✦

A Standard Method of Industrial Sickness Reporting.—Two plans have been prepared by the Public Health Service in coöperation with the American Public Health Association and the asistance of certain government bureaus. The first plan is considered preferable as offering possibilities for much greater detail in personnel records. In both it is considered essential that a diagnosis of each case of sickness causing disability be recorded.

PLAN A.

According to Plan A, a card is kept for each individual employed. It is 4 by 6 inches in size, and is shown below, both the face and the reverse.

From these cards, monthly tabulated statements can be made which show the number of workers, the number of cases of sickness ocuring among them and the sickness rate per 1,000 persons for any group of workers. Tabs or signals in certain divisions of the top of the card are suggested, to designate sex, color and age group. Thus a blue signal in the left third of the top of the card might indicate "white male, under 25 years," in the middle third, "25 to 44 years," and in the right third "45 years and over." A distinct signal, for any

1. Name of Employee	2. Check No.	3. Date This Record Begins	4. Firm No.	5. Date Employment Ended
6. Color and Sex	7. Year of Birth	8. Marital Condition	9. Speaks English	10.

11. Departments and Occupations in Plant.

From	To	Months	Department	Occupation	Possible Injurious Conditions
....	....	....	....	....	....
....	....	....	....	....	....

12. Former Occupation Outside of Plant.

From	To	Months	Occupation	Industry	Possible Injurious Conditions
....	....	....	....	....	....

13. Remarks.

The reverse side as follows:

Record of Absences from Sickness and Non-industrial Injuries.

14. Dates of Absence Beginning	End	15. Days Lost Through Illness	16. Sickness or Non-industrial Injury Causing Disability (Diagnosis)	17. By Who Diagnosed
....	....	....	....	....
....	....	....	....	....
....	....	....	....	....
....	....	....	....	....
....	....	....	....	....
....	....	....	....	....
....	....	....	....	....
....	....	....	....	....
....	....	....	....	....

18. Remarks:

Form A-1-1919—U. S. Public Health Ser.

illness, attached at the time to the card and removed at the end of the month, will facilitate the keeping of the sickness record.

PLAN B.

This is a simplified plan for those plants and sick-benefit associations which find it impossible to keep a personnel card for each employee. It affords a method of handling employees in groups.

Knowledge of hours of work in relation to fatigue and output.

Knowledge of the security and continuity of employment during slack periods and while recuperating from accidents or disease.

Knowledge of working conditions, such as safeguards from all dangers, social and physical; plant beautification, community conditions.

....(Name of plant or sick-benefit association)............................

Number of employees (or members) on the last day of...19........

(Month)

Department (or occupation)	Total (both sexes)				Males				Females			
	All ages	Under 25	25 to 44	45 and over	All ages	Under 25	25 to 44	45 and over	All ages	Under 25	25 to 44	45 and over
Total..........												

The Public Health Service invites establishments and employes' sick-benefit associations to take up this question direct with the service. —*Monthly Labor Review*, U. S. Bureau of Labor Statistics, January, 1920, 220-223.

✤

Qualifications of an Ideal Medical Officer for a Modern Manufacturing Plant.—In a recent discussion at Atlantic City on the scope of industrial surgery, Dr. C. E. Ford mentioned the following qualifications as required, in his opinion, by an ideal medical officer for a modern manufacturing plant:

Five years' general practice "to acquire a knowledge of a man and his foibles."

Knowledge of the special problems arising from the employment of women and children.

Knowledge of the workings of pensions and insurance.

Working knowledge of plant organization.

Knowledge of employment methods, including job analysis.

Knowledge of wages in relation to the cost of living according to local standards.

Ability to direct athletic and social activities.

Ability to replace injured to best advantage.

Working knowledge of company stores.

Knowledge of housing conditions and problems with ability to remedy defects.

Knowledge of labor turnover and its causes.

Ability to direct general education and Americanization of employes.

Such a medical man would indeed be a "superman" in almost any walk of life and deserve the salary of a popular opera tenor.— J. B. R., in *Pennsylvania Medical Journal.*

✤

Health Truths

Think of public health first and low taxes afterward.

A well organized health department can save more lives and more dollars than fire or police departments.

A person who thoughtlessly or willfully spreads communicable disease which causes death certainly commits a crime. What is manslaughter?—*Our Communal Health.*

American Journal of Public Health

Official Monthly Publication of the American Public Health Association

Publication office: 124 W. Polk Street, Chicago, Ill.

Editorial office: 169 Massachusetts Ave., Boston, Mass.

Subscription price, $4 per year. American Public Health Association membership, including subscription, $5 per year.

Subscriptions and memberships may be sent to the A. P. H. A., 169 Massachusetts Ave., Boston, Mass.

Vol. X   MAY, 1920   No. 5

RELATIVE FUNCTIONS OF STATE AND LOCAL HEALTH DEPARTMENTS

CARL E. McCOMBS, M. D.,

New York Bureau of Municipal Research,
New York City

Read before Section on Public Health Administration, American Public Health Association. at New Orleans, La., October 28, 1919.

City health work antedates that of the state by about fifty years. The municipality is the powerful agency for local improvement through intensive cultivation of community interest. The state should care for legislation, health surveys, demonstrations and research, and should supplement local appropriations, but municipalities should control their own health administration.

THE fact that this subject is one on which state and local health officers do not often agree, is probably responsible for the action of the Chairman of this section in passing it along to one who is neither a state nor local health officer. I realize fully that in attempting to present my own views, I shall probably risk the disapproval of some of my hearers; but, if out of the discussion which may follow, some, at least, of the principles can be established on which the relation of state to local health departments should be based, I shall feel that the risk was well taken.

I do not think that any one can say definitely what these principles are or ought to be. The times are changing, and there is a growing tendency throughout this nation and other nations for govern-ments to assume greater and greater responsibility for the individual, as well as the community welfare of its citizens. The adoption, in many states, of state controlled health insurance, and its active and aggressive promotion in others, illustrates very well this tendency. How far this movement will go remains to be seen; but as the relation of the government to the individual changes there is invariably a change in the relation of citizens at large as represented by the state, to smaller groups of citizens as represented by local government units. In the midst of such kaleidoscopic changes in the relation of governments to people it would be folly to be dogmatic. What seems reasonable and proper today may be found to be the mistake of tomorrow. I can only hope, therefore, to present for

393

your consideration certain phases of the problems as they appear to me to affect public health administration at this time

Public health work in this country began in the cities and towns, and in certain of our larger cities we find evidence that constructive health work was being done very early in the nineteenth century. As far back as 1805, New York City had a board of health of which DeWitt Clinton was president. The reports of the activities of this board make very interesting reading. Dr. Charles F. Bolduan, former Director of the Bureau of Public Health Education of the New York Health Department, and now Chief of the Section on Public Health Education of the United States Public Health Service, gives an excellent resumé of the health administration in New York City in a monograph entitled "Over a Century of Health Administration in New York City," which may be obtained from the New York City Health Department. We learn, for example, in Dr. Bolduan's monograph, that in 1805 a special committee of this board submitted a very comprehensive report on health conditions in New York City, and made recommendations relative to the provision of an ample supply of potable water, construction of common sewers, drainage of marsh lands, construction of a sea wall along the city water front, the planting of trees and healthy vegetables, interment of dead bodies, prohibiting the habitation of damp cellars and the use of certain houses in which deaths from malignant fever had occurred, provision of increased hospital accommodations, and better control of port quarantine.

Municipal health work thus antedates state health work by at least fifty years, for it was not until 1855 that a state board of health was created in Louisiana. But this board concerned itself chiefly with quarantine, and had, at that time, no general health program or policy. About ten years later, in 1869, the State Board of Health of Massachusetts was

established and began to develop what was for that time a broad public health program. In the following 50 years, state health departments or state boards of health were established in all states.

In its beginning, therefore, and up to the immediate present, public health work in this country was especially a function of local government, and full credit ought to be given to local health boards and health officers for putting the United States on the public health map. The interest which has been aroused in public health throughout the nation is the result of the educational work done chiefly by local health departments and state health departments have relatively little share in the credit. The individual initiative of local health officers has made public health service what it is today. Chapin of Providence is responsible for revolutionizing our ideas of contagious disease work; Darlington of New York City has the credit of establishing the first bureau of child hygiene in this country; Goldwater of New York established industrial hygiene work as an essential local public health service; Levy of Richmond should be credited with demonstrating the importance of proper disposal of excreta in the prevention of diarrheal diseases of infants; Goler of Rochester was far ahead of his time in providing effective measures for the control of venereal diseases and for the supervision of midwives. It is not necessary to go farther with the list; simply add the names of hundreds of other local health officers whom you know who are scattered through the cities and towns of the United States. No disparagement of the excellent work done by many state health officers is intended, but you will no doubt agree with me that the national public health movement is chiefly the result of the intelligent and progressive work of local health officers. They have put their stamp upon it in no certain way.

As indicated, there is a general tendency toward centralization of responsibility ·for public administration in both national and state governments. The movement for the creation of a national health department is on its way and it appears that this meets with the favor of the majority of public health executives and workers. Nationalization of health service in England is now a fact accomplished through the creation of a ministry of health with county health officers under the direct supervision of the Minister of Health. In the field of state health administration in the United States there is also ample evidence of this trend toward strong centralization of the public health service under state control. New York State as early as 1913 following in general the Massachusetts plan, enacted a law which provided for the creation of twenty or more districts, excepting cities of the first class, each under the supervision of a sanitary supervisor, appointed by the health commissioner of the state on the basis of a civil service test. These sanitary supervisors were not, however, made directly responsible for the organization and development of local health work within their districts, but were authorized to coöperate with and assist local health officers in the discharge of their duties and to make certain investigations outside the jurisdiction of local health units. The tendency of the present day is clearly toward this type of organization and toward even a stronger centralization of authority and responsibility in the state health department.

The recent laws of Ohio and Vermont, with which you are familiar, are excellent examples of this movement toward state control, which has been carried by these states still farther than in New York State. These more recent plans for highly centralized state control meet with the approval of many health executives who have despaired of securing efficiency of local health services under the old plan of part time service, political

meddling, inadequate appropriations, lack of uniformity of procedure and general incompetence. In this movement toward centralization under state control there appears to many a broad beam of hope and proposals are now being made in other states for the adoption of the plan of centralized control as in Ohio and Vermont. Certainly these plans have much in them which is commendable. They do fix responsibility for health work and they do guarantee, in a measure, that the failures of local health services will, at least, be revealed; and that those who fail as leaders will be held responsible for their failures.

It would be presumptuous for me to criticise the laws of Ohio and Vermont and the similar laws proposed for other states; but there is a phase of this movement toward strong centralization which I feel has not been given sufficient consideration. I am a "Home Ruler" and a believer in the principle of self-determination, possibly because of my Irish extraction. With such convictions, I feel naturally, that the gain which we may make in strengthening state health departments and in centralizing all health work under the control of the state, if truly a gain, is not unaccompanied by loss. Experience under centralized state control only can determine whether or not this view is correct, but over-centralization of control of local health work in the hands of the state must certainly mean limiting the initiative of local communities. It also means, I believe, a loss of community spirit and individual enterprise. The most efficient local health services in this country today, at least within my own knowledge and experience, are those which have been developed through the intensive cultivation of local or community interest in health matters. The American Red Cross, looking about for other fields to conquer, has stepped into the public health field and is attempting to capitalize this community spirit for the development of a very ambitious health program. The National Social Unit Organization which met in conference at Cincinnati recently, has the same purpose in view. As expressed in the prospectus of this organization, the movement is toward a "coöperative democracy in which all the people study their own needs and meet them through their own organized effort." Whether or not we approve of the public health activities of these private agencies, we must admit that they have seized an opportunity which most health executives have ignored.

Every citizen, whether he is willing to admit it or not, has a pride in his community. Perhaps his pride is not a justifiable pride, but nevertheless he has it. Our town government, our city government, our country government, is to most of us a personal and tangible thing, but the state is a nebulous thing which does not immediately concern us. Every change in government which takes us away from this real, personal and intimate contact and control of our own community affairs means a loss of that more or less indefinite thing which is called community spirit.

The record of work done by our United States Public Health Service in rural sanitation in the South illustrates very well what power may be exercised for the public health and welfare by the development and encouragement of community spirit. No high-powered, high-geared machinery of centralized control in Washington or elsewhere could have accomplished in such a short space of time and at such small cost what has been accomplished through the health demonstration work of Dr. Lumsden and his assistants of the United States Public Health Service. They sought not to force a health program upon a community, but to demonstrate health needs, and ways of meeting such needs through community coöperation. There was an appeal to the community "get together" spirit which brought immediate results

in the correction of unhealthful conditions, and in the formation of permanent and efficient local organizations to carry on the work after the officers of the Public Health Service had gone.

Admitting the inefficiency of local health services, admitting the lack of uniformity of procedure, admitting the too frequent hampering of local health work by petty local politics, there is no assurance that centering c o m p l e t e authority in the state is the only remedy or even the best remedy. I am not willing to concede that we would have progressed more rapidly along public health lines if we had long ago adopted the now widely acclaimed plans for state control of local health work. On the contrary, much of the splendid pioneer work which has been done by local health officers with full responsibility for their own communities' health would not have been done. The all-powerful state organization toward which we are tending will tie the hands of the local health officer, make him largely a rubber stamp and blight individual and community initiative. I do not contend that this has been done in the states which I have cited for purposes of illustrating this tendency toward state control of health administration, but I do contend that we would do well to take thought of this matter. Definition of the basic principles upon which the relation of state to local health services should be established is a subject worthy of consideration by the best minds of the American Public Health Association. It may be that strongly centralized state control is the right thing, and a thing that we should all support whole heartedly, but there are certainly some limitations upon the right of the state to control local health work.

In order that my paper may not be purely negative in its treatment of this matter, I shall summarize briefly what seem to me to be the essential functions of a state health department. The functions of local health authorities may then be considered as all not specifically mentioned as responsibilities of the state.

The first responsibility of the state health department is legislation. There must be, of course, some basic health law which will be applicable to all local units of the government. It would not be proper for me to forestall the report of the Committee of the American Public Health Association on uniform health legislation, but as a member of this Committee, I can say that the guiding principle in the work of the Committee has been to limit itself to broad health principles in drafting a uniform health code, with the idea of leaving it largely to the local health authority to work out the most effective method of applying such basic law to his own community. This to my mind is most essential, for our modern conception of municipal health work is based largely on the methods and procedures developed by pioneers working alone in their own local fields and able to think and act with freedom according to their own convictions. The state health authority should have the power, and it should be its duty, to promote the enactment of public health laws covering broadly all local health work, but it should not so define and detail local procedure that the local health officer does not have to think for himself. He will be a better health officer if he does think for himself, and the community will be a better community if its powers of initiative are not too greatly curtailed.

The second responsibility of the state health department in relation to the local health department is to make surveys of local health administration. Just as the United States Public Health Service sends its officers on request into local health departments to survey their activities and make constructive recommendations, so the state health department should be prepared to make expert surveys of the local health services of the state. The state should be even better

able to do this than the United States Public Health Service, because it is familiar, or ought to be familiar with local conditions; and it is familiar also with the general and special laws of the state which govern the activities of the local health departments. The survey method should be applied also by the state health authority in rural districts where no organized health service exists. The facts obtained through the survey, if made known to such rural communities, would go far toward providing the needed service.

The third important duty of the state is health demonstration work carried on along the same lines as the demonstration work of the United States Public Health Service and as Dr. Dowling has so effectively done in Louisiana. The importance of this work in developing that community spirit and enterprise of which I have spoken cannot be over-estimated.

Research is the next important function of the state health service and one which has been neglected in many states. By research I mean not only laboratory research, which is of prime importance, but research in child hygiene, tuberculosis, contagious diseases and all other lines of health work, for the purpose of developing facts which local health boards cannot develop except in a very limited way. The results of such research work should, of course, be made available to all local health departments.

The establishment of standards of record keeping and procedure is another responsibility which the state may well assume. The establishment of standards of accounting procedure, standard record forms for recording vital statistics, facts regarding health inspection, investigations, etc., would be of great value to local health departments. The adoption of such records should not be obligatory for local health departments, but if the standards are well devised and helpful to the local health officers, they will be quite likely to adopt them. They will be even more likely to adopt them if standard record forms are furnished them by the state. Uniformity of record keeping is a long step toward uniformity of procedure and increased efficiency of service.

The state should also be prepared to furnish special service when called upon to do so. It should be prepared to send an expert diagnostician to the local health department when one is needed; it should be prepared to furnish a sanitary engineer to advise the local health authority with respect to water supply, sewage disposal, disposal of garbage and refuse, and other matters requiring technical engineering knowledge; it should be prepared to send an epidemiologist to investigate outbreaks of disease in local communities and assist the local authorities in controlling them. In short, the state should be prepared to furnish, on request, any special service which the local health department may require.

The state should conduct an efficient laboratory service which may be freely available to local health units for diagnostic work. It should encourage the establishment of local laboratories wherever possible; furnish free, or at cost, sera and vaccines, which it should make in its own laboratory; devise standards of laboratory technique and procedure which may be available to local health laboratories; and finally, as already suggested, conduct special laboratory research and make the results of its work known to local health authorities.

The state health department should also be responsible for conducting periodical conferences of local health officers, at which the local health officer may be given an opportunity to hear his own voice. Such conferences should not be conducted with the view to giving some noted health authority an opportunity to utter health platitudes, but with a view to finding out what the local health officer thinks about his own job, and in order to give the state health authority an opportunity to get acquainted with the workers in the vineyard.

Another important service which the state health department should render is that of conducting special courses for local health officers. This work has recently been undertaken by the State Health Department in New York and has proved a success from every point of view. This same thing can be done in any state and at comparatively small cost. If instruction can be given free so much the better, but many local health officers would be glad to pay the cost.

Education of the public along general health lines is an essential function of the state health department. Bulletins, pamphlets, boiler plate material for the press, and particularly the rural press; traveling exhibits, special lecture service where desired—all of these activities can be carried on most successfully under state auspices. The state could well afford also to supply printed educational material to local health departments for distribution under their own imprint. The effectiveness of propaganda would be greatly increased by such procedure.

The state health authority should be the scorekeeper for local health departments. Having established standards of service and encouraged in all possible ways the adoption of such standards, the state authority could stimulate competition between local units by presenting comparative scores. The community which found itself a tail-ender in the health race would be likely to inquire why, and having found out why, would in all likelihood take the necessary steps to get out of its unenviable position.

Finally, the state should be able to aid local health services through supplementing local appropriations for health work, in the same way that the Federal Government makes grants to states for certain agricultural projects, and as the United States Public Health Service has recently aided the states in the venereal diseases campaign. The Ohio law also provides for subsidy of local health services by the state. Could this be done in all states the problem of raising the efficiency of local health services would be largely solved, for the state could then set the conditions upon which the allotment of funds would be made. It was this system of conditional grants of money which resulted in the establishment of Carnegie libraries from one end of the country to the other. Communities found themselves able to raise unheard of sums of money when they found they could get an equal amount as soon as they had raised their own share. It is too much to hope that this system can be universally effective for the improvement of local health administration except by the Federal Government, and provision should be made in any bill for a national health department for conditional grants to states which the states in their turn can apportion conditionally among the local health units.

Perhaps I have not covered all the services which the state should render to local health units, but if I have pre-

sented the idea clearly enough you can fill in the gaps. As you see, my ideal state health department is one that legislates along broad lines; advises, coöperates with and assists local health services in every possible way, educates its local health officers and the public, and is at the service of the local health department whenever it needs service. It is a state health department which seeks to stimulate and encourage local community spirit and enterprise and not to limit unduly or stifle such spirit. It is not an over-centralized, impersonal, all-powerful machine for state-wide control of health work, but a community service station prepared to meet community needs and to coöperate splendidly in meeting them.

In conclusion, may I suggest that, if it is the sense of this section, a special committee of the section or of the Association as a whole be appointed to consider this problem of the relative functions of state and municipal health departments, and to make recommendations which may be the basis for future legislation.

☐

Des Moines Health Center.—The city of Des Moines announces the establishment of a health center, which as the announcement of the opening states, 'is owned and managed by the people of the city and Polk County, for the benefit of every one in the community." Its purpose is set forth as being, "To keep the well well, to treat the ill, to remove 100% of all remediable defects and to co-ordinate health agencies." On the downstairs floor of City Hall in Des Moines the new center has been located in a number of rooms grouped about an entrance hall, which serves for waiting room and for recording and filing offices, while in the adjoining offices are the staff and equipments for various clinics and laboratories. The services which are to be maintained here include a medical clinic and dis-

pensary, a psychological clinic and a child conservation service, intended for the study, treatment and supervision of children hampered with remediable chronic physical and mental ailments. Interested in the center and indeed its mainspring is a Health Center Association which is really a federation of local public spirited societies. There are a dozen of these, Polk County Medical Society, Methodist Hospital, Women's Clinical Society, Public Health Nursing Association, District Dental Association, Council of Social Agencies and the city government, schools, courts, etc. The interest of the courts comes through the fact that so many of the cases of backward children are brought forward here. Twenty-five of the city physicians are sufficiently interested to be conducting each a free clinic in his specialty.

REDUCTION OF DEATHS FROM INFANTILE DIARRHEA BY CARE OF THE BOWEL DISCHARGES OF INFANTS*

E. C. LEVY, M. D.,

Director of Public Welfare,
(Formerly Chief Health Officer)
Richmond, Virginia

Read before Section of Public Health Administration, American Public Health Association, at New Orleans, La., October 27, 1919.

Utilizing the principle that care of bowel discharges is the most important single measure for the control of fatal infantile diarrhea in the South, the Richmond authorities have reduced the mortality from this cause from 150 per 100,000 in 1911 to 36 in 1919. Public health nurses have done this through health education of the family.

CONCLUSIONS reached in the following paper were arrived at from work done for the control of infantile diarrhea in the City of Richmond during the past 13 years. The writer wishes to make it plain at the outset that, in connection with the epidemiology of many diseases, geographic l o c a t i o n comes strongly into play. Conclusions which are reached must, therefore, for the present, be regarded as having particular application to Southern cities, exactly as the rôle of the privy in the control of typhoid fever is of special importance in that section of the country.

Furthermore, for the sake of exactness, it should be stated that the conclusions which are reached relate particularly to *fatal* infantile diarrhea, for, although since 1911 the morbidity rate has declined equally with the death rate, infantile diarrhea in Richmond was not reportable until that year, and hence morbidity data are not available for comparison prior to that time.

From 1909 to 1911 one thing after another occurred which pointed directly to the importance of infection as the chief element in fatal infantile diarrhea in

*At the request of the author, publication has been postponed until complete figures for the year 1919 were available.

Richmond. Within the limits of this paper I can give only one or two examples.

In March, 1909, there were four deaths from infantile diarrhea in the entire city. Of these four, three occurred in a single institution—the Virginia Home for Infants. In this institution there were at that time only about 30 babies. The three deaths occurred in one group of eight babies who were under the direct supervision of one nurse. There were neither cases nor deaths among the other 22 babies in the institution. The milk for all babies in this institution was received from a single source and prepared by one nurse. Evidently, therefore, the milk was not responsible.

Upon looking further into this matter, it was found that there had been a mild case of infantile diarrhea in the group of 8, but that the nurse was one who had only recently come to this institution. The Superintendent of this institution had had thoroughly impressed upon her the fact that infantile diarrhea must be regarded as an infectious disease, and that the diapers of all babies suffering from this disease must be specially disinfected. This nurse, being new, did not report the mild case nor give it any special attention. In consequence, three other babies in this group of 8 contracted the disease and died.

A second instance was the following: In August, 1911, there were 21 deaths from infantile diarrhea in the city of Richmond during the first 15 days of the month. There were only two days during this period without a death from this cause. There was one death on the 13th, two on the 14th and three on the 15th. There was then a period of 9 days, from August 16 to August 24, inclusive, without a death from infantile diarrhea, and there were only three deaths from this cause during the entire latter half of August, against 21 during the first half. It appeared for a time as if fatal infantile diarrhea was almost over for the year 1911, but in September there was a sudden sharp increase in the prevalence and fatality of the disease, and during that month there were 31 deaths. October followed with 26 deaths, or two more than had occurred in August. This was, and still is, without precedent in the City of Richmond. In this September and October prevalence breast-fed babies had almost as heavy a death rate as bottle-fed babies.

In connection with the above, it was a matter of almost universal comment in 1911 that flies, which had been quite prevalent up to the middle of August, suddenly almost disappeared; but there was a return in September, and during this month and October, flies were unusually prevalent for that season of the year. This corresponded exactly with the decline and subsequent rise in the infantile diarrhea death rate.

It was just about this time, namely, late in the year 1911, that, considering the evidence which had been gradually accumulating, the following conclusions were reached:

1. *Infection from case to case is the most important single factor in fatal infantile diarrhea in the South.*

2. *Infantile diarrhea being an infectious disease and the infecting organism being thrown off in the bowel discharges, we must by every analogy believe that carriers play an important rôle.*

3. *In view of the above, the proper disposal of the bowel discharges of ALL infants, sick and well, is the most important single measure for the control of fatal infantile diarrhea in the South.*

Of the above conclusions, No. 1 was not, of course, anything new; but, so far as I know, no one had previously suggested that carriers played any important part in the spread of infantile diarrhea, and hence no one had previously directed attention to the importance of proper care of the bowel discharges of *all* babies as a measure of value in controlling the prevalence of infantile diarrhea.

Along with the above conclusions came also the realization that sanitarians had up to that time utterly ignored the fact that when a city is sewered, or when it is provided with sanitary privies, these measures do not automatically dispose of the bowel discharges of the entire population. Under normal average birth rate and death rate of infants, four to five per cent of the population of any community consists of infants under two years of age, and the bowel discharges of this part of the population do not enter promptly into our sewers or sanitary privies. The diaper is its immediate destination, and what happens thereafter depends upon individual care.

As soon as the above conclusions were reached, the nursing force of the Richmond Health Department was informed of the conclusions, and it was strongly impressed upon its personnel that henceforth in their instruction of mothers they were to lay the greatest possible emphasis on the proper disposal of the bowel discharges of infants. They were told that this was, in the opinion of the Chief Health Officer, the most important single measure for the control of fatal infantile diarrhea. It must be made plain that they were also instructed that all former teachings regarding proper diet, preparation of the baby's food, clothing, fresh air, avoiding exposure to heat, etc., were measures the importance of which was in no degree lessened, but that transcending all these in importance was proper disposal of the baby's bowel discharges.

When all this was done, the diarrhea season for 1911 was already over, and it was too late for any effect to be brought about during that year, but, as shown in tables Nos. 1 and 3, the effect of these teachings appeared promptly and markedly during the first summer thereafter. During the five years from 1907 to 1911, inclusive, the average annual death rate

from infantile diarrhea had been 135, and the lowest year during this period had been 122. In 1912 the first year when the new teachings were put into effect, the rate promptly dropped to 100, and in the entire period of eight years during which these teaching have been increasingly emphasized every year, with a single exception, has shown a lower death rate from infantile diarrhea than did the previous year, reaching its lowest level in the present year, 1919, with a rate of 36.

It will be noted from table No. 1 that the infantile diarrhea death rate for 1917 was higher than for either of the preceding years.

Table No. 3 shows that through the month of June the number of deaths from infantile diarrhea in Richmond was lower than in any preceding year. I cannot speak from personal knowledge as to why the rate then went up, as I was not connected with the Richmond Health Department after May 1, 1917. I am rather inclined to believe, however, that the emphasis laid upon the proper disposal of the bowel discharges of babies was somewhat lessened.

The chart which is presented shows in graphic form the figures which are given in Table No. 1. As stated on this chart, dairy inspection started in May, 1907, too late to have any appreciable effect on the infant mortality for that summer. In 1908 dairy inspection had progressed to a point where the entire milk supply of the city was safe for infant feeding. In that year the rate fell to 122 per 100,000

TABLE No. 1.
Annual Number of Deaths and Annual Death Rate per 100,000 Inhabitants from Infantile Diarrhea, Richmond, Va., 1907-1919.

Year	Deaths from Infantile Diarrhea (under 2 years)	
	Number of Deaths	Death Rate per 100,000 Inhabitants
1907	161	142
1908	140	122
1909	147	126
1910	169	132
1911	196	151
Annual Average	163	135
1912	132	100
1913	112	84
1914	97	72
1915	101	65
1916	102	65
Annual Average	109	77
1917	113	71
1918	82	51
1919	59	36
Annual Average 1915-1919	91	58

TABLE No. 2.
Comparison of Annual Death Rate from Infantile Diarrhea in Richmond During the Five-Year Periods 1907-1911; 1912-1916; 1915-1919.

	Five-Year Period 1907-1911	Five-Year Period 1912-1916	Five-Year Period 1915-1919
Annual Average	135	77	58
Highest Year	151	100	71
Lowest Year	122	65	36

TABLE No. 3.
Deaths by Months from Infantile Diarrhea in Richmond, Va., 1907-1919.

Year	Jan.	Feb.	Mar.	Apr.	May	June	July	Aug.	Sept.	Oct.	Nov.	Dec.	Total
1907	4	4	5	3	12	39	44	22	15	10	1	2	161
1908	0	1	2	1	19	34	33	28	9	8	3	2	140
1909	2	1	4	3	14	39	34	16	14	8	2	7	147
1910	1	1	2	1	15	49	50	30	8	9	3	0	169
1911	1	3	0	1	5	53	45	24	31	26	3	3	196
1912	3	0	3	4	2	22	45	17	14	12	7	3	132
1913	4	1	1	2	14	31	17	14	16	7	4	1	112
1914	1	1	0	1	2	31	25	13	11	8	4	0	97
1915	0	1	4	0	6	21	28	17	12	8	3	1	101
1916	2	0	1	1	4	17	30	17	13	9	5	3	102
1917	3	0	0	5	2	14	35	28	16	6	3	1	113
1918	1	2	0	2	4	13	28	16	9	3	2	2	82
1919	1	1	1	1	1	10	21	10	7	6	0	0	59

from 142 in 1907, but in 1909, although improvement of the milk supply had further progressed, the rate went up slightly and was 126.

In 1910 one nurse was employed for instructive work among the mothers of babies who, for one reason or another, were believed to be especially handicapped in their struggle for life. In the following year two additional nurses were employed. In spite of this, the death rate from infantile diarrhea in 1910 was 132, which was higher than for

which the illness could properly be attributed to any fault of the general milk supply of the City of Richmond. Whatever rôle dirty milk may have played in infantile diarrhea in Richmond, the work which has been done since dairy inspection started in 1907, has utterly eliminated the milk supply as a causative factor.

Study of the chart must convince all trained sanitarians that in the year 1912 a new factor in the control of infantile diarrhea came into play in Richmond. The steady decline in the death rate from

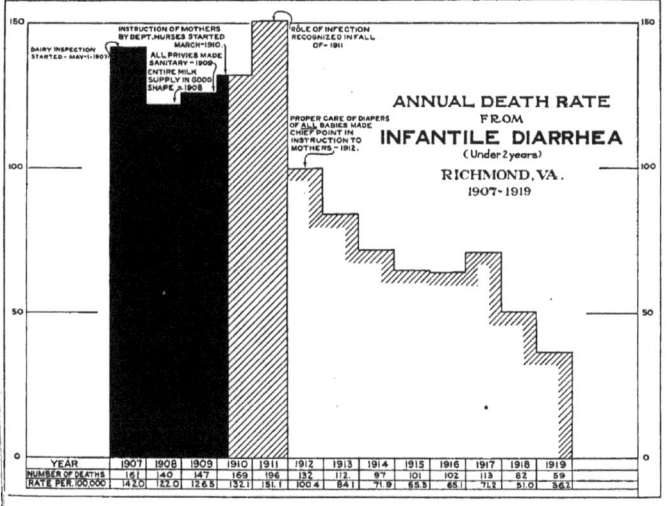

ANNUAL DEATH RATE
FROM
INFANTILE DIARRHEA
(Under 2 years)
RICHMOND, VA.
1907-1919

YEAR	1907	1908	1909	1910	1911	1912	1913	1914	1915	1916	1917	1918	1919
NUMBER OF DEATHS	161	140	147	169	196	132	112	97	101	102	113	82	59
RATE PER 100,000	142.0	122.0	126.5	132.1	151.1	100.4	84.1	71.9	65.3	65.1	71.2	51.0	36.2

either of the two preceding years, while in 1911 the rate was 151, which was the highest for any year of the five-year period.

As soon as an instructive nurse for infant welfare was added to our force, it was made one of her duties to investigate every fatal case of infantile diarrhea, and from that time (1910) to the present date, there has not been a single death from infantile diarrhea in Richmond in

this disease for a period of eight years tributed to any fault of the general milk can have no other interpretation. This factor is, beyond question, recognition and application of the three principles above set down.

Limitation of space prevents thorough discussion here of the details of control of the babies' bowel discharges. Briefly, our nurses instruct mothers along the following lines:

Every baby should be taught at as early an age as possible to indicate, by crying, the fact that it is about to have a bowel discharge, rather than indicate in the same way that this has actually occurred. This is not difficult and is accomplished chiefly by always promptly attending to any indication that the baby has actually had a bowel discharge. A baby, learning thus that it can get relief from the discomfort of a soiled diaper, soon learns to cry a little in advance, and if this crying is understood and promptly attended to, soiling of the diaper can usually be avoided.

Effort is made, after the babies have reached the age of a few months, to have their bowels move over the seat or chamber vessel, at regular intervals, by placing the baby over the seat at such times and encouraging the movement of the bowels by gently touching the parts with a moistened cone of castile soap or a spill of paper moistened in olive oil. It is no uncommon thing for our nurses to have in their care babies five or six months old with whom the soiling of a diaper by bowel discharges is quite the exception.

Where babies have not been trained to this point, the best that can be done is to remove promptly all soiled diapers and dispose of their contents harmlessly.

In conclusion, I wish to reiterate that in my opinion the proper control of the bowel discharge of all babies is the most important single measure for the control of fatal infantile diarrhea in any Southern community. This conclusion was reached late in the year 1911 and put into practical application the following year. Since then there has been a steady decrease in the death rate from infantile diarrhea in Richmond which cannot possibly be attributed to any other cause.

☐

HOW CONNECTICUT REACHES THE CHILDREN
"The First Lesson in Sanitation"

Reproduced through the courtesy of the Connecticut State Department of Health

BY-PRODUCTS FROM SEWAGE SLUDGE

Robert Spurr Weston,*

Boston, Mass.

Read before Sanitary Engineering Section, American Public Health Association, at New Orleans. La., September 27-?0. 1919.

Economy and conservation have worked for years at the problem of profit from sewage. Mr. Weston notes that many American cities have potential by-products enough to make recovery worth trying. English cities have found the American Miles process profitable. It will at least lessen the cost of sewage disposal.

FOR more than a generation economists have recognized that enormous quantities of fat and fertilizer are contained in and wasted with sewage which is disposed of by dilution, oxidation, or other methods involving the dispersion and destruction of these valuable constituents. The problem of recovery has been attacked time and again, and until recently, without reasonable prospect of success. The failures at Frankfurt-am-Main and Cassel come easily to mind, and the plant at Bradford, England, frequently referred to as a success, does not treat a true domestic sewage, but a trade waste consisting largely of wool scouring liquors from the center of the British woolen-cloth industry.

Notwithstanding its apparent hopelessness of solution, many engineers believed that the problem would be solved whenever the usual methods of recovery could be adapted to sewage, and money obtained from the sale of the by-products could be applied to reducing the cost of sewage disposal below the cost of existing methods. The best informed engineers do not believe that the recovery and sale of by-products can ever, under normal conditions, make the disposal of sewage a profitable business, but if they can reduce the cost to below that of other methods, which are equally efficient as far as the effluent is concerned. a success will be attained.

Several causes may be given for the renewed interest in fat and fertilizer recovery:

(a) The discovery of the activated sludge process;

(b) The discovery of the Miles process;

(c) The shortage of fats and fertilizers during the great war.

THE ACTIVATED SLUDGE PROCESS

It is redundant to describe the activated sludge process, beyond stating that it is an oxidation process in which the sewage sludge itself, activated and suspended in the sewage by aeration, is the carrier of the bacteria which effect the nitrification of the organic matter, and the contact medium which brings about the coagulation of the suspended matter and the consequent clarification of the sewage.

THE MILES PROCESS

The Miles Process, the most recent attempt to reduce the cost of sewage disposal, is another cause of the renewed interest in the subject of this paper.

Beginning about the year 1900, Mr. George W. Miles, a well known Boston chemist, with the co-operation of the officers of the Boston Sewer Department. suggested the use of acid to accelerate the precipitation and separation of sludge, and proposed to recover fats and fertilizer from the sludge so produced. The most important factor in the new process

*Of Weston & Sampson, Boston, Mass.

consists in the application of the acid to the sewage itself, rather than to the sludge precipitated therefrom; and it lays emphasis upon the decomposition of the soluble soaps and the liberation of the fatty acids, which latter do not appear as fats when unacidified sewage is tested by standard methods, and are only partially precipitated with the sludge in plain subsiding basins. Furthermore, Miles has suggested the use of sulphur-dioxide gas rather than the sulphuric acid made from it, thereby avoiding several expensive steps in its manufacture and greatly reducing the cost, besides bringing into play the disinfecting action of the sulphur-dioxide gas upon the sewage itself. If desired, a combination of sulphuric and sulphurous acids may be used.

Sodium acid sulphate (niter cake) is the waste product from the nitric-acid plants, and, as a result of the war, there are enormous quantities of this material piled near nitric acid plants, for which there is now little use. At the present time this is the cheapest source of sulphuric acid. Before the war the cheapest source was either sulphur or pyrite (ferrous sulphide).

Several experiments have been made with this process. The first one was conducted by Mr. E. S. Dorr and other officers of the Sewer Division of the City of Boston, at different times between June 20, 1911, and June 29, 1914. The results of these experiments are presented in a report published by the writer in connection with his own study of the process for the Sanitary Research Laboratory of the Institute of Technology. In the Technology experiments two continuous runs were made, one of seven days in July, and one of three days in November, 1915; and the volume of sewage treated averaged 8,241 gals. daily. The experiments are described elsewhere*, but the results obtained during the city's

*Weston, R. S., 1916. Tests of a New Process of Sewage Purification with Grease Recovery and Apparent Profit. American Journal of Public Health, 6, 334. Reprinted in Boston City Record. March 3, 1917.

experiments were almost duplicated, as the following table shows:

TABLE I
COMPARISON OF AVERAGE RESULTS OF TREATING SEWAGE WITH SULPHUROUS ACID, AS SHOWN IN EXPERIMENTS BY E. S. DORR AND M. I. T. SANITARY RESEARCH LABORATORY, 1912-1914 and 1915, RESPECTIVELY

	Experiments by E. S. Dorr	Experiments by M. I. T. Sanitary Research Laboratory
Average daily flow of sewage during experiments, gallons	92,514,647	103,498,049
Average amount of dry sludge, pounds per million gals. of sewage	1,738	1,909
Average percentage of grease in dry sludge	21.7	22.66
Average amount of grease precipitated from sewage, pounds per million gals.	436	430.1
Average amount of sulphur dioxide used, in pounds per million gals.	*2,300	1,963

*Approximate.

During the summer of 1914, Mr. Langdon Pearse, division engineer of the sanitary district of Chicago, made experiments* to learn whether acidification could increase the yield of fat from the Center Avenue sewage. Tests in barrels and in a tank holding about 1,500 gallons were made under his direction. A three-hour period of subsidence was used and the alkaline sewage required about 3,200 lbs. of 100 per cent H_2SO_4 per million gallons. Sulphur dioxide was not tried.

Pearse's results showed that acid treatment produced a higher recovery of fat, namely 69 per cent of that in the sewage as compared with 47 per cent obtained by plain subsidence for three hours. The sludge, which amounted to 2,275 lbs. per million gallons, contained, on an average, 93 per cent of moisture and 25 per cent of fats. The results also showed a great reduction in oxygen demand—170 per cent of that obtained by an Emscher tank. They also showed a removal of 71 per cent of the suspended matter.

Much more extensive experiments have been conducted by Professor C.-E. A. Winslow, of the Yale University Medical School, and Dr. F. S. Mohlman, now chemist of the Connecticut State Depart-

*Sanitary District, Chicago, Report on Industrial Wastes, 1914, pp. 191-194.

ment of Health. The results of these experiments have been embodied in a paper read in September, 1918, before the American Society for Municipal Improvements at its meeting in Buffalo and abstracted elsewhere.* The experiments were conducted at New Haven with sewages from the East street and Boulevard sewers. In these experiments, the sewage was acidified with sulphur-dioxide gas, and a four-hour period of subsidence was provided. The alkalinity of the East street sewage was very low, so that it was necessary, to secure an excess acidity of 50 p.p.m., to add about 700 pounds of gas per million gallons of sewage treated. With the Boulevard sewage, 1,130 pounds of acid per million gallons of sewage were required to secure the same excess acidity (computed in terms of calcium carbonate).

The treatment removed from 61 per cent to 66 per cent of the total suspended, and 90 per cent of the settleable solids. The removal of bacteria was all that could be desired, the two last experiments with the East street and Boulevard sewages respectively, indicating removals of over 99 per cent of the total bacteria, and of the gas-forming organisms.

The use of acid accelerated the precipitation of the suspended solids by about 50 per cent, only 40 per cent being removed from the untreated sewage by plain subsidence as compared with 60 per cent when the Miles process was used. The average data regarding the production of sludge are as follows:

TABLE II
CHARACTER OF MILES ACID SLUDGE AT
NEW HAVEN

	Totals and Averages
Length of runs days.	192
Total Gallons Sewage Treated.	1,654 940
Pounds of Wet Sludge per Million Gals. Sewage	3,485
Specific Gravity	1.057
Percent Moisture	87.8
Pounds Dry Sludge per Million Gals. Sewage	430
Ether Extract, Percent Dry Sludge.	28.0
Ether Extract, Pounds per Million Gals.	121.
Volatile Matter, Percent Dry Sludge.	59.6
Nitrogen, Percent Dry Sludge	2.1

*Engineering News-Record. 81, 1034-1036. Also 82 32-3u.

Opposed to these very favorable results is the presence in the grease extracted from the sludge of a large proportion of. unsaponifiable material (waxes, mineral oils and similar substances). Substances of this kind are practically worthless, and their removal is attended with a great deal of expense. Winslow and Mohlman are advised by experienced users of grease that it would be necessary to distill the crude extracted product in order to produce a salable grease.

Conditions at New Haven are favorable to the Miles process, to Imhoff tanks combined with chlorination, and to fine screening combined with chlorination, respectively. The activated sludge process would not work because of the presence of copper salts in the sewage.

The operation costs of the various disposal plants are estimated in the following tables:

TABLE III
ESTIMATED COST OF TREATMENT OF NEW HAVEN SEWAGE
Dollars per Million Gallons

Process	Miles Acid Process	Imhoff Tanks and Chlorination	Fine Screens and Chlorination
East St. Sewage—			
Gross Cost	15.50	11.99	11.03
Revenue	6.57	0.00	0.00
Net Cost	8.93	11.99	11.03
Boulevard Sewage—			
Gross Cost	20.98	12.14	12.35
Revenue	10.66	0.00	0.00
Net Cost	10.32	12.14	12.35

The results of these experiments have warranted the New Haven Committee in recommending the Miles process for adoption by the City of New Haven, and that a plant be built first at the East street sewer, which discharges 16,000,000 gals. daily, and, if this plant be successful, the sewage from the other outfalls should be treated.

The Miles process has now reached a stage where a large experiment to determine the cost factors for dewatering, drying, and degreasing sludge, and marketing the products, is desirable. In this the Miles process would have one disadvantage over the activated sludge process, in that the fertilizer produced will not be of quite so high a grade. On the other hand, the sludge contains not only the precipitated free fats, but a large part of the fatty acid set free from the dissolved soaps by acid treatment. When compared with most other sludges, particularly with the activated sludge, the problem of dewatering and drying is much less serious, as the following table indicates:

TABLE V

Kind of Sludge	Average Percentage of Moisture in Sludge	Relative Volume of Sludges Containing the Same Amounts of Dry Matter
Activated Sludge	98.5	100
Subsiding Basin Sludge.	91.5	18
Miles Process Sludge...	90.0	15
Imhoff Tank Sludge....	89.0	13.6

While the economy of the Miles process may not be known for any particular case without a large scale experiment, there have been some experiences in England which are illuminating, notably at Wolverhampton where, during the war, the sludge from plain subsiding basins was treated with acids and fats, and fertilizer recovered with great economy, and at Morley where Mr. F. Turner, the Burrough Engineer,* has put what is essentially the Miles process into practice, although under unusually favorable conditions.

At Morley the chemical precipitation of sewage was first practiced with the result that in six years twelve acres of land had been covered with sludge to an average depth of three feet. The dried sludge contained 16 per cent of grease and farmers would not accept it as a gift. Recently 80 per cent sulphuric acid (brown oil of vitriol, "B.O.V.") was substituted for lime. This effected a 25 per cent reduction in the volume of sludge and increased the grease from 16 per cent to between 30 and 45 per cent of the dried sludge. These percentages are of course unusual, being nearly twice what might be found in typical acid-treated, municipal sewage, but the economies effected therewith are indicative of what might be secured in a lesser degree with the weaker sludge. The treatment is as follows:

Six presses are required to make 30 pressings per week. The amount of sludge handled daily is 176,000 lbs. and the work requires seven men on eight-hour shifts.

During 1918 the works operated at a profit of $683.77 per week.

Comparing these efficiencies and costs at Morley with those corresponding to Boston sewage on a strictly pro-rata basis, we obtain, for 12,500,000 gals. weekly, the following:

Receipts:

12 Tons Fertilizer @ $2.43........	$29.16	
2 Tons Grease @ $195.21.........	390.41	
		$419.57
Expenses (prorated)		551.22
Deficit		$131.65
Per million gals.		10.51

This would be a low cost of obtaining a well disinfected, clarified effluent and would probably be lower than the cost of screening or Imhoff-tank treatment, followed by chlorination.

The conditions at Morley were exceptionally favorable. Not only did the sludge contain from 25 to 40 per cent of grease, but the sewage itself was exceptionally strong. On the other hand, the press cake contained but 2.36 per cent of nitrogen, corresponding to 2.80 per cent of ammonia. The amount of dry sludge recovered was about 85 per cent of that which could be obtained from Boston sewage.

The one great problem in the utilization of sewage sludge is its economical drying. For this work a new dryer, known as the B. T. W. dryer, has been tested out at the sewage works at Tadcaster, in York County, England, and the results have been so successful that a large dryer has been ordered for the City of Halifax where the company which controls the dryer commercially has recently concluded a lease with the Halifax Corporation to take all their sewage sludge press cake for a term of fifteen years. In May, 1919, it was hoped that this Halifax plant would be running by now.

It is hoped that this dryer has solved

the problem of drying the sludge from say 75 to say 20 per cent of moisture. To reduce the sludge from the condition which obtains when it comes from the settling tanks, to one containing 75 per cent of moisture, is very difficult. Filter presses and centrifugal machines have been tried, but so far have introduced a great element of cost, even if the process can be called successful in conjunction with the sludge recovery process as a whole. The problem of dewatering the Miles process sludge is much more simple than dewatering the activated sludge, because it is so much drier, as shown by the figures given above.

Recently a chemically cleaned subsiding tank known as the Dorr thickener, originally designed for the concentration of suspensions of ores, known as pulps, has been adapted to sewage disposal work, particularly for the removal of suspended matter from tannery and other similar wastes. It is quite possible that this device might be used to advantage to partially dewater the sludge, particularly if the same be treated first with an additional amount of acid for further coagulation and dehydration.

Because the problem is simply one of stiffening the sludge so that it will not be too fluid for a heated dryer at the beginning of the operation, Mr. E. S. Dorr* has suggested mixing in some dried substance, and for this purpose the best substance would be the previously dried sludge. A few figures show how much of this would be required. For instance, 500 lbs. of 10 per cent (moisture) sludge added to 2,000 lbs. of 85 per cent would give a sludge containing 70 per cent of moisture; or 700 lbs. of 10 per cent added to 2,000 lbs. of 85 per cent, would give 65 per cent sludge. This proposition would involve the addition of simple mixing devices and the use of a larger battery of dryers. On the other hand, but little more fuel would be

*Sewer Division, City of Boston.

required as there would be just the same quantity of water to be evaporated whether the sludge were dried in one or two operations. The excess fuel would only be that required by the greater radiation of a larger plant. By this process it would be possible to dry crude sludge by heat alone and thus eliminate the filter presses and centrifugals.

Summary

The most promising of the sludges from the standpoint of the recovery of by-products therefrom, are those of the activated sludge and the Miles processes. The cost of aeration and acid treatment are not far apart, and the more valuable Miles process sludge contains less water and is much more stable than the bulkier and partially de-fatted activated sludge.

Repeated experiments have shown that many American sewages contain enough fats and fertilizer constituents to make the problem of their recovery worth consideration. This is as far as the art has progressed in this country, but in England, during the war, certain cities using the Miles process, recovered grease and fertilizer at a profit. Furthermore, a dryer has been brought out which promises success with American sewages, and Dorr has suggested a method for avoiding the process of dewatering sludge to a point where it can be handled in a heated dryer. This brings the process to a point where a large scale experiment is necessary. In this experiment, various processes for making sludge and for handling the same should be tried side by side, and devices like the Dorr thickener and the B. T. W. dryer should be valued. This experiment would cost about $50,000 and it is hoped that some municipality or corporation can undertake the work as a means of at least reducing the cost of sewage disposal over that demanded by existing methods, even though the disposal of sewage at a profit be an unrealized dream.

NEED FOR STANDARDS FOR RECORDING AND CLASSIFYING DEFECTS AND IMPAIRMENTS

JOHN S. BILLINGS, M. D.,

Formerly Medical Director, Eastern Group of Telephone Companies,
Bell System.
New York City.

Read before Section on Industrial Hygiene, American Public Health Association, at New Orleans,
October 29, 1919.

Standardization is one of America's greatest needs, for there
are many active agencies that undertake related investigations
independent of one another, and overlap and duplicate effort.
Out of a very large experience Dr. Billings presents standard
forms for records of initial and follow-up physical examinations
of industrial employees.

THE observations and recommenda-
tions here submitted are based on an
experience of fifteen years with the
Department of Health, New York City;
the New York Public Library, the New
York Stock Exchange, and the Eastern
Group of Telephone Companies of the
Bell System.

In industrial medicine, particularly
that branch concerned with the selection
of sound, healthy employees, and with
keeping them in good health, some system of medical book-keeping must be
devised to determine the value—mone-
tary if you will—of the results obtained.
Records of illness incidence and time lost
are, of course, of the first importance.
But proof is also needed: (1) that the
general rank and file are in need of
medical advice for the correction of impairments and defects; and (2) that
they benefit by such advice.

Medical examination of supposedly
healthy individuals is becoming the rule
rather than the exception. This applies
not only to industrial organizations, but
to the general public, the most noteworthy example being the examinations
for the Army and Navy during the late
war. Much information of value has
been obtained, but on the other hand,
much of it is useless for comparative
purposes, each set of observers adopting
its own system of classification. No two

sets of results are comparable. The objection may be raised that comparative
figures will be of little value because of
the varying circumstances; e. g., results
of the Army examinations applying only
to men of the average age of 20; examinations by such an organization as
the Life Extension Institute, to individuals of a much greater average age;
and of those in telephone companies to
girls between the ages of 17 and 19.
Occupation must also be considered.
Yet the same objections apply to morbidity and mortality statistics, which are
of great value, although the influence of
age grouping, sex, occupation and other
conditions, must also be considered.

As a rule, the defects and impairments
found are recorded under the individual
name of each defect. The total number
of items given usually averages about
50. In one instance over 200 headings
were used.

There is no agreement as to what constitutes a defect or impairment, or if
the two terms are synonymous. The
question of degree plays little part. A
single cavity in an otherwise sound and
complete set of teeth has the same
weight as a defect, as an advanced case
of Riggs' disease. In some instances,
temporary ailments (colds, headaches,
etc.,) are classed as defects.

At the completion of the first 20,000

examinations made by the Medical Departments of the Eastern Group of Telephone Companies, an attempt was made to compare the results with those obtained by other observers. A considerable amount of material was apparently available, but the comparative figures were very disappointing. No two sets of figures could be used as they stood. An attempt was made to condense the results within the limits of a standard 15-group classification of defects and impairments, in the hope that the various sets of statistics could be reduced to some uniformity. Yet only a few could be adapted for use.

The figures of the Federal Draft Boards giving the 500,000 rejections from the Army in 1918, valuable as they are, were of little service, and represented only rejections. The only statistics which could be compared with those of the Telephone Companies, were the figures of the New York City Health Department, and those given by the Life Extension Institute as a result of examination of 2000 industrial and clerical workers. Even in these, the variations were often so wide as to be ludicrous. The following are examples:

Dental Defects 17% in one group against 58% in another.
Nervous Defects 0.7% in one group against 17.6% in another.
Visional Defects 9% in one group against 52% in another.
Hearing Defects 1.8% in one group against 25% in another.
Renal Defects 0.4% in one group against 42% in another.

The only consistent figures were those for heart and blood vessels, ranging between 4 and 9 per cent, and pulmonary conditions, ranging between 2 and 4 per cent.

In the three Medical Departments of the Eastern Group of Telephone Companies, it was attempted, with apparently fair success; (a) to define and standardize defects and impairments so that they can be readily tabulated; and (b) to devise a standard classification of impairments, with a minimum number of

groups, into which all impairments will fall, and which will be of real service to the executives.

DEFECTS AND IMPAIRMENTS

If all variations from the normal are to be considered as defects, fully 90 per cent of all persons examined will be found to be physically imperfect, and the majority of statistics of physical defects seem chiefly intended to demonstrate this fact. Many examiners thus go too far in their attempt to demonstrate the value of medical examinations of supposedly healthy persons. They should bear in mind that where the same defect exists in the majority of individuals, the presence of that defect is normal and not abnormal. The true object is to determine, not the total number of variations from the normal, but only those in which such variations really impair function. The former may be termed "Defects;" the latter "Impairments."

Defects are variations from the physical normal; they may or may not be impairments, either actual, potential or corrected. They should not include acute ailments or accidents, except as to their sequelæ.

Impairments are defects which appreciably interfere with the proper performance of duty; either directly, (faulty vision or hearing, loss of time because of illness); indirectly, by lowering the general working powers (chronic dyspepsia, general debility); or potentially, in the future (hernia without a truss, etc.)

All impairments are defects, but all defects are not impairments.

Impairments well corrected, whether temporarily or permanently, should be classed as defects for the time being.

For purposes of medical bookkeeping, only uncorrected impairments should be considered, and these should be classified as "correctable" or "non-correctable." The examining physician determines whether a defect is an impairment; if it is correctable, and in the latter case,

MEDICAL HISTORY AND EXAMINATION

Name   Occ.   Dept.   Bus. Addr.   In Service   Previously

Address   Age   Sex   Race   M. S. W. Children   Perv. Occ.

Referred By   Physician; Name   Address   Phone No.

Reason for Visit

Diag. and Comp.

Family History

Year of Diseases:

Hosp. or San. History

Obstetrical

Accidents   Operations   Vaccinations

Habits: Alc.   Tob.   Tea   Col.   Sleep, Character   Hrs.   Exercise

Appetite   Digestion   Constipation   Headaches   Menses

Symptoms: (Duration, Cause)

Chief Complaint

Absent from Duty—Yes, No   Since

Development and Appearance   M. M.   Voice   T.   R.   P.   Quality   Rhythm   Height   ft.   in.

Arteries   Blood Pressure: Reflexes   Weight: Usual   Present

Ears   R.   L.   Eyes   R.   L.   Glasses   Pupillary Reactions

Tongue   Teeth   Tonsils   Pharynx   Nasal Passages

Tremor   Flatfoot: R   L.   Skin: [Cold, Warm], [Dry, Moist]   Eruption

Heart

Lungs

Abdomen   Glands   Vaccination

Deformities   Hernia

Date   Sp. Gr: Alb.   Sugar   Micro   Date   Sp. Gr.   Alb.   Sugar   Micro.

Date   Sp. Gr.   Alb.   Sugar   Micro   Date   Sp. Gr.   Alb.   Sugar   Micro.

Blood, Sputum, etc.

Correctable Impairments   Treatment Recommended Yes No

Non-Correctable Impairments

Remarks

Examined by   M. D.

REVERSE OF ABOVE CARD

Present Health and Gen. Cond. Since Last Exam:

Habits	Sleep	Exercise	Appetite	Digestion
Constipation	Menses	Pulse	Weight	Reflexes
Blood Pr. S. D.	Hearing: R. L.	Vision: R. L.	Pup. Reactions	Tongue
Teeth	Tonsils	Pharynx	Nasal Pas.	Glands
Lungs		Heart		Abdomen
Urinalysis: Sp. Gr.	Alb.	Sug.	Microc.	Other
New Imp. Non-Correctable		Correctable		Treatment Recommended Yes No
Present State of Previous Imp. Non-Correctable			Correctable	Treatment Recommended Yes No
Remarks			By	M. D.

Present Health and Gen. Cond. Since Last Exam:

Habits	Sleep	Exercise	Appetite	Digestion
Constipation	Menses	Pulse	Weight	Reflexes
Blood Pr. S. D.	Hearing: R. L.	Vision. R. L.	Pup. Reactions	Tongue
Teeth	Tonsils	Pharynx	Nasal Pas.	Glands
Lungs		Heart		Abdomen
Urinalysis: Sp. Gr.	Alb.	Sug.	Microc.	Other
New Imp. Non-Correctable		Correctable		Treatment Recommended Yes No
Present State of Previous Imp. Non-Correctable			Correctable	Treatment Recommended Yes No
Remarks			By	M. D.

Present Health and Gen. Cond. Since Last Exam:

Habits	Sleep	Exercise	Appetite	Digestion
Constipation	Menses	Pulse	Weight	Reflexes
Blood Pr. S. D.	Hearing: R. L.	Vision. R. L.	Pup. Reactions	Tongue
Teeth	Tonsils	Pharynx	Nasal Pas.	Glands
Lungs		Heart		Abdomen
Urinalysis: Sp. Gr.	Alb.	Sug.	Microc.	Other
New Imp. Non-Correctable		Correctable		Treatment Recommended Yes No
Present State of Previous Imp. Non-Correctable			Correctable	Treatment Recommended Yes No
Remarks			By	M. D.

gives the necessary instructions and advice. It is possible, therefore. to tabulate the number and kind of correctable impairments found in a number of individuals by the different members of the medical staff. The results of examination a year later, can be tabulated in the same way, and a comparison of the figures will show a greater or less diminution year by year in the number of correctable impairments found.

Exaggeration of the importance of defects must, of course, be avoided. An excellent rule is to consider whether a given defect in one's own person would impair efficiency. Very few persons have perfect vision or hearing, yet such defects are frequently not impairments.

STANDARD CLASSIFICATION OF IMPAIRMENTS

The following standard classification of impairments, correctable and noncorrectable, has been in use about one year. Thus far, it has given satisfaction. and all defects found fall readily within

one or the other of the fifteen groups, which are as follows:

1. Teeth
2. Pharynx, tonsils, nose, etc.
3. Nervous disorders
4. Vision
5. Development
6. Malformation
7. Digestive disturbances
8. Heart and blood vessels
9. Lung conditions and tuberculosis
10. Menses
11. Hearing
12. Hernia and varicosities
13. Skin affections
14. Kidneys
15. Miscellaneous

PROCEDURE

The results of examination are recorded on a standard Medical History and Examination Card, all defects being entered on the body of the card. Severity is indicated by one or more + marks. + signifies negligible; ++, of moderate severity, calling for eventual correction; and ++-+, urgent, calling for immediate correction.

At the lower margin of the record of

TABULATION OF IMPAIRMENTS.

the first examination, are spaces for true impairments, correctable and non-correctable. The record of later examinations shows the same items, with spaces for present state of previous impairments.

The impairments are brought together on a standard tabulation sheet which shows, horizontally, the results of the successive examinations of the same individual, and what has been done in the way of correction. Vertically, the totals give the impairment figures for groups of individuals, as many as desired. As before stated, the work of the individual physicians can be controlled.

CONCLUSION

An attempt has been made to show the need for standard definitions of defects and impairments, and a standard method of classifying and tabulating the same. Certain simple, somewhat arbitrary methods which have given satisfaction, have been described. The matter would seem to be of sufficient importance to warrant a recommendation that a committee of the A. P. H. A. be appointed to take up the matter in joint conference with a similar committee of the Association of Industrial Physicians, and to submit recommendations as to the best methods of securing uniform results.

□

CONFERENCE OF NORTH CAROLINA HEALTH OFFICERS, JANUARY, 1920

Not long since an illustration was given showing the New York health officers attending the Health Officers' Class at Syracuse University. Here is a group of men in similar work in another part of the country, being the County Health Officers of North Carolina, who have been called together at Raleigh by State Health Officer W. S. Rankin, M. D., for a conference, with all that such an occasion means in the exchange of experiences.

MEAT INSPECTION LAW FOR MUNICIPALITIES

W. PARKER JONES, ATTORNEY-AT-LAW,

*Formerly Assistant Solicitor, U. S. Department of Agriculture,
Washington, D. C.*

Read before Section on Food and Drugs, American Public Health Association, at New Orleans, La.,
October 29, 1919.

Less than one-third of our cities of 5,000 population or more have any regulation of meat inspection, and in many of these the inspection is incomplete. This affects communities using local meats, which are more likely to be infected than are interstate meats. Public health demands serious reforms in this matter.

TWENTY years' experience of our National Government has demonstrated conclusively that an adequate system of inspection is necessary to make the meat supply safe for human consumption, and that it is entirely practicable to inaugurate and maintain a complete and thorough inspection at a relatively small expense. To the lasting credit of our country, it is generally conceded that the Federal Meat Inspection, under the Act of 1906, supplemented by the Act of October 3, 1913, as they are administered by the Federal Bureau of Animal Industry, have been potent factors in making American meat and meat products the best in the world.

While the quality and the wholesomeness of the meats we send to foreign countries and ship across state lines for domestic consumption is of the best, it is unfortunate that the same may not be said of the meat and meat products derived from animals which are slaughtered and disposed of within the borders of any one state. This is because the scope of the Federal Meat Inspection Law is limited to meats and meat food products which are transported in interstate or foreign commerce, and does not extend to meats and products prepared and sold entirely within the borders of a state.

For a number of years the number of cattle, sheep, swine and goats slaughtered under Federal Inspection has approximated 60,000,000 head. About half this number, or approximately 30,000,000 head, of all the animals slaughtered in the United States, do not move in interstate or foreign commerce and, therefore, do not have the benefit of Federal Inspection. Perhaps the most effective illustration of the service which has been performed by the Federal Meat Inspection system is that although the recent war made unprecedented demands for the movement of a steady supply of meat products to maintain both American and foreign armies at home and in the field, and none but U. S. inspected and passed meat and meat products were purchased by this Government, there has been no serious question raised as to their quality or wholesomeness. Through co-operation, the American meat packers and the Federal Inspection service were able to keep a steady supply of wholesome meats flowing to the points where they were most needed. The supply for our civilian population was ample to meet its demand, which was abnormally high. This was a most remarkable achievement, and one which undoubtedly contributed greatly to the success attained by the American and Allied armies.

Notwithstanding the shining example of Federal Meat Inspection, a recent survey shows that less than one-third of the cities of the United States having a population of 5,000 or more, maintain any kind of Meat Inspection, and even in those having inspection it is frequently incomplete. The absence of a thorough system of inspection for meats slaughtered and disposed of locally is a distinct menace to the health of the citizens of the respective communities. In localities where there is Federal Inspection, owners of diseased or suspicious-looking animals often send them for slaughter to an abattoir which does not have inspection, in preference to an inspected establishment where they would have to meet the tests of rigid inspection. The establishments which have Federal Inspection draw a large proportion of their cattle from the ranges and feed lots of the west, where tuberculosis is rare. Hence, the percentage of diseases found in the Federal service is far below that which occurs in animals of the dairy regions where tuberculosis is much more prevalent. It is estimated that not less than 10 per cent of the dairy cows in this country are affected with tuberculosis, and it is a well-known fact that dairy stock forms a much larger proportion of the animals killed at the small local establishments than they do at Federally-inspected establishments. Further, the local establishments which do not have inspection frequently pay relatively low prices for food animals, and since they are not required to maintain their establishments, or to operate them in accord with the strict sanitary requirements of Federal Inspection, are free from many items of expense. This enables the uninspected local houses to sell their products at a comparatively low price, resulting in the consumption of their products, to a considerable extent, by persons of small means. This not only produces unfair competition and deprives many of our people who most need it of protection from diseases of animals communicable to man, but removes a powerful incentive from the owners of diseased live stock to improve the condition of their herds. If there were no market for diseased cattle, sheep, swine and goats, the work of Federal

and State officials in endeavoring to improve the quality and condition of our food animals would be easier. In considering what provisions must be incorporated in a municipal meat inspection law, it is not necessary to look beyond the standards of the Federal Meat Inspection Law, because they are not excelled in any foreign country.

The Meat Inspection Law of June 30, 1906, is primarily a health and secondarily a labeling law. Inspection of meats derived from cattle, sheep, swine and goats, prior to entry into interstate or foreign commerce, is mandatory, except in the cases of retail butchers and retail dealers supplying their customers and of animals slaughtered by farmers on the farm.

It provides for the maintenance by the Department of Agriculture of a system of inspection of establishments in the United States in which cattle, sheep, swine or goats are slaughtered or the carcasses or meat or meat food products of which are prepared for interstate or foreign commerce. When the articles are found to be wholesome, the department inspectors must mark them "inspected and passed"; if the articles are found to be unwholesome, they must be marked "inspected and condemned." No meat or meat food products are permitted to be brought into federally inspected establishments unless derived from animals which have had both ante-mortem inspection and post-mortem inspection at the time of slaughter, except farm-slaughtered animals, with the heads and certain viscera attached, which must be inspected at the time of admission. By a recent regulation, the carcasses of cattle which are slaughtered on the farm, and which are examined by Bureau inspectors at the time of slaughter, may be marked "inspected and passed" by the inspectors, when upon inspection they are found to be sound, healthful and wholesome and fit for human food. Inspection may be withdrawn from establishments which violate the law or the regulations prescribed by the Department. The withdrawal of Federal inspection from an establishment a m o u n t s to prohibition against its longer engaging in interstate or foreign commerce in articles with which the Act deals.

Transportation in interstate or foreign commerce of any meat or meat food product not bearing the mark of Federal inspection and approval is an offense, punishable by a fine of not more than $10,000 or imprisonment for not more than two years, or both. The sale or offer for sale or transportation for intertsate or foreign commerce of any diseased, unsound, unhealthful, or unwholesome meat or meat food product, or of such an article which is otherwise unfit for food, with knowledge that the same is intended for human consumption, is punishable by a fine of not exceeding $1,000 or by imprisonment for not exceeding one year, or both.

In addition, all meats and meat food products entering interstate or foreign commerce, or manufactured or sold in the District of Columbia or in the territories, are subject to the provisions of the Food and Drugs Act. While the meat inspection act does not provide authority to seize such articles outside of federally inspected establishments, the power of seizure conferred by the Food and Drugs Act is applicable to them.

The Meat Inspection Act exempts from its inspection requirements any animals slaughtered by farmers on the farm and retail butchers and retail dealers in meats and meat food products supplying their customers, but provides that if any of these persons ships his products in interstate or foreign commerce, knowing that it is intended for human consumption, and it be unfit for food, he is guilty of a violation of the law.

As originally enacted in 1906, the meat inspection act did not deal with imported meats. They were subject only to the Food and Drugs Act. By the tariff act of October 3, 1913, the importation of meats was made conditional upon their being wholesome and free from unwholesome substances and complying with regulations of the Secretary of Agriculture. To ascertain wholesomeness, the Secretary of Agriculture investigates foreign systems of meat inspection and requires import consignments to be accompanied by ante-mortem, post-mortem and sanitary inspection certificates, issued by accredited officials of the National Governments of the countries of origin. Importations are prohibited from countries which do not maintain systems of inspection the substantial equivalent of our own, and articles found upon inspection at ports of entry to be unwholesome or to contain unwholesome substances must be refused admission into the United States. After admission, with marks of Federal inspection and approval, such imported products may be carried into federally inspected establishments and must be otherwise treated as domestic articles which have been inspected and passed.

The Federal Meat Inspection Law contains three fundamental requirements. The first requirement, and one which is indispensable in any adequate system of meat inspection, is that meat and meat products to receive the stamp of inspection and approval must be derived from the carcasses of animals which receive post-mortem inspection at the time of slaughter. The second requirement is that the meat and meat products must be derived from animals which receive ante-mortem inspection prior to their being admitted into slaughtering establishments. The third requirement is that the animals must be slaughtered and the products handled in sanitary establishments and in a sanitary manner.

No system of meat inspection is complete without ante-mortem inspection, or without adequate requirements for sanitation, but these are not so important as the post-mortem inspection.

Ante-mortem inspection is less important because the diseases of animals communicable to man which may be detected on ante-mortem inspection but which may not be detected on post-mortem inspection are generally comparatively few. Sanitary conditions of establishments are of less consequence than post-mortem inspection because it does not follow necessarily that because an establishment does not comply with modern ideas concerning sanitation, the quality or wholesomeness of the meat and meat products prepared therein will be injuriously affected.

. Nevertheless, we find on examination of the municipal ordinances relating to meat inspection that the great majority stop a.' imposing requirements concerning the sanitary conditions of slaughter houses, and that few provide for compulsory post-mortem inspection of carcasses of animals. The omission from municipal meat inspection ordinances is especially noted of provisions by which it is made certain that meats and meat products from animals which are condemned for disease will be destroyed. Under these ordinances there is no assurance that the meats will be actually withheld from distribution. Further, in very few of the municipal laws is there any provision made for efficient administration by men who are trained and are competent in the work of meat inspection. The great success of the Federal Meat Inspection Laws is largely due to the competency and the industry of the trained officials engaged in administering them.

In some cities local meat inspection consists merely in a reinspection of meats which have been inspected by the Federal Government and approved and marked. The possibility of deterioration of inspected and passed meats, in view of the rapidity with which they go into distribution after they have received the Federal mark, is slight, and a system of municipal inspection which covers merely the reinspection of meats and meat food products which already bear the Federal stamp accomplishes little. Much more is to be accomplished by a system which directs its activities toward the inspection and

disposition of the products of animals, which are killed and distributed locally.

There are a few of our American cities which have adequate municipal meat inspection and which also provide adequate forces for administering the laws. The City of San Francisco has provided for the inspection of meat and meat food products offered for sale within the city and county of San Francisco in Ordinance No. 1265, approved August 1, 1910. This ordinance reads as follows:

Be it ordained by the people of the city and county of San Francisco as follows:

Section 1. No person, firm or corporation shall expose or offer for sale, or sell or otherwise dispose of, or have in his possession within the city and county of San Francisco, any meat of any cattle, calf, sheep, lamb, goat or swine which does not have upon it the meat inspection brand or other official mark of identification of the Board of Health of the city and county of San Francisco, or the meat inspection brand or other official mark of identification of Boards of Health of the state of California whose meat inspection standard is equal to and recognized by the San Francisco Board of Health, or the meat inspection brand or other mark of identification of the United States Department of Agriculture. If any carcass of any animal hereinbefore named, or part thereof, is found, offered for sale or exposed within the city and county of San Francisco, which does not bear any of the meat inspection brands or marks recognized by the Board of Health of the city and county of San Francisco, said Board of Health shall take possession of and destroy such meat.

Sec. 2. No person, firm or corporation shall ship, send, bring or cause to be brought into the city and county of San Francisco the meat of any cattle, sheep, lamb, goat or swine which does not bear the meat inspection brand or other mark of identification recognized by the Board of Health of the city and county of San Francisco.

Sec. 3. The carcasses of calves in good healthy condition and over four weeks of age may be brought into the city and county of San Francisco, and each of said carcasses of such calves must be inspected and stamped or marked by the San Francisco Board of Health at the point of arrival of said carcasses of such calves in the city and county of San Francisco.

Sec. 4. An ante-mortem examination shall be made under the direction of the Board of Health of the city and county of San Francisco of all cattle, sheep, swine or goats about to be slaughtered before they shall be allowed to enter the slaughtering pen. All animals showing symptoms of or suspected of being affected with any disease or condition which under the regulations of the Board of Health of the city and county of San Francisco would probably cause their condemnation in whole or in part when slaughtered, shall be marked by affixing to the animal a metal tag bearing the words, "San Francisco Board of Health Suspect." All such animals shall be slaughtered separately.

Sec. 5. A careful post-mortem inspection under the direction of the Board of Health of the city and county of San Francisco must be made of all animals herein named at the time when slaughtered in the city and county of San Francisco. The head, tongue, tail, thymus gland and all viscera of each animal shall be retained in such a manner as to preserve their identity, until after the post-mortem examination has been completed, in order that the parts so retained may be identified in cases of condemned carcasses. Suitable racks or metal receptacles shall be provided in and by each slaughtering establishment for retaining said parts.

Sec. 6. All carcasses, meats or meat food products which are unsound, unhealthful, unwholesome or otherwise unfit for food, shall be stamped or otherwise marked by the Board of Health of the city and county of San Francisco, "San Francisco Board of Health, Inspected and Condemned," and shall be destroyed.

Sec. 7. All meats or meat food products offered for sale in the city and county of San Francisco shall be subject to reinspection and condemnation at any and all times by the Board of Health of the city and county of San Francisco.

Sec. 8. The Board of Health of the city and county of San Francisco is hereby authorized and directed to adopt rules and regulations governing the sanitation of slaughter houses and establishments where meat food products are sold or manufactured, the inspection of meats and the ultimate disposal of condemned meats, in addition to the provisions of this ordinance, as will enable the said Board of Health to enforce and carry out the meaning and intent of this ordinance. The standard of meat inspection shall be that adopted by the United States Department of Agriculture.

Sec. 9. It shall be unlawful and a violation of this ordinance for any person, firm or corporation, or officer or agent, or employe thereof, to forge, counterfeit, simulate or falsely represent, or without authority to use or detach, or knowingly or wrongfully alter, deface or destroy any of the stamps or marks or brands or tags recognized by the Board of Health of the city and county of San Francisco, on any cattle, calf, sheep, lamb, goat or swine, or any carcass, or on any part or parts of any carcass or carcasses of any animal named in Sections 1, 2 and 3 of this ordinance.

Sec. 10. Any person, firm or corporation, or other agents, violating any of the provisions of this ordinance or failing to comply with any direction or order of the Board of Health of the city and county of San Francisco, given pursuant to the provisions of this ordinance by the health officer or any other agent of said Board of Health, shall be guilty of a misdemeanor, and upon conviction thereof shall be punished by a fine not less than fifty ($50) dollars, nor more than five hundred ($500) dollars, or by imprisonment in the county jail for a period of not less than ten (10) days nor more than three (3) months, or by both such fine and imprisonment.

Sec. 11. Each day that the violation of this ordinance or the failure to comply with the directions of the Board of Health of the city and county of San Francisco, given in accordance with this ordinance, shall continue, shall constitute a new and separate offense, and be punishable accordingly, as herein provided.

Sec. 12. All ordinances and parts of ordinances in conflict with this ordinance are hereby repealed.

Sec. 13. This ordinance shall take effect immediately.

This ordinance is modeled after the Federal Meat Inspection Law and adopts the standards of the Federal Meat Inspection Law, so far as they are applicable. It provides that no meat shall be allowed to be sold in the City or County of San Francisco unless it bears an identification mark of a board of health whose meat inspection standard is equal to a standard adopted by the ordinance. The ordinance makes both post-mortem and ante-mortem inspection compulsory, and it confers the power upon the city board of health to make necessary regulations for giving effect to its provisions. The regulations which have been adopted by the San Francisco board of health conform to those which have been adopted by the United States Department of Agriculture. The power conferred to make regulations leaves sufficient latitude to provide requirements which will meet the progress of science and new developments in the meat industry.

San Francisco is not the only city which has effective municipal meat inspection. In New York City, in Philadelphia and in Boston, local meat inspection is quite thorough and efficient. Among the smaller cities a notable example of accomplishment in meat inspection is Columbus, Ga. The record of our American cities as a whole, however, in this respect, cannot be commended and there is room to perform a valuable public service by arousing public sentiment to secure the enactment generally of municipal ordinances similar to the San Francisco ordinance.

The enactment of appropriate ordinances alone will not suffice. To bring about substantial improvement, adequate funds must be provided for administration, the service must be divorced from politics, and trained men must be employed who can devote their entire time to the work of meat inspection. The compensation of employes should not be made to depend upon fees, nor should they be permitted to collect fees. The expense should be borne by the community as a whole, and if a town or city is unable to bear it alone, the expense might be defrayed by two or more jointly or by a county.

The adoption of ordinances containing the requirements of the Federal Meat Inspection Law, so far as applicable, with proper provisions for enforcement, is urged as an immediate and pressing public necessity, to make safe for human consumption the meat and meat food products of the 30,000,000 or more head of cattle, sheep, swine and goats against which our municipalities, with comparatively few exceptions, now afford no satisfactory protection.

□

Trachoma Survey in Cincinnati.—The United States Public Health Service, under the auspices of the State Department of Health, co-operating with the Cincinnati Board of Health, has undertaken a survey to learn if there is any trachoma in the city.

Trachoma is not a new disease. Our knowledge of it extends back for centuries. Some publicity has been given to the disease recently, but we have not stressed enough its prevalence, its effect upon vision, its communicability—and in this respect, trachoma is a menace to America—and the relatively simple method of prevention.

Trachoma is a slow but sure communicable disease, characterized in the beginning by granulated eyelids. The slow and insidious development of the disease robs it of the terror that usually accompanies the acute infectious diseases. Indeed, some of the victims do not complain, probably because they do not know how a good eye feels. In general, however, the patient is uncomfortable by day or night on account of the itching and burning and sensitiveness to light. Untreated, it continues on like a smouldering ruin until it burns itself out, but the damage done is irreparable.

We do not know exactly how trachoma became implanted in the United States, but it is most probable that the disease was brought in from European countries.

In the State of Kentucky, after the United States Public Health Survey, it was estimated that there were 33,000 cases of trachoma. It is also prevalent to a large extent in Virginia, Tennessee and West Virginia.

The General Assembly appropriated $20,000 for a two year campaign in the State of Ohio. Cincinnati is the first large city to benefit by the survey, which will be conducted under the personal direction of Surgeon John McMullen, United States Public Health Service, who has devoted the last twenty-two years directing the anti-trachoma work of the Government. Dr. Frank Boudreau, Director of Communicable Diseases; Dr. Robert Lockhart, Director of Trachoma Clinics; Dr. Ralph Tate and Dr. Ross Hopkins of the State Department of Health; Dr. Louis Stricker, consulting oculist to Cincinnati schools, and Dr. Oscar M. Craven, Chief Medical Inspector of Cincinnati, will assist Dr. McMullen.

Note Revised Date for San Francisco Meeting, A. P. H. A. September 13-17, 1920

FEDERAL MEAT INSPECTION AS A SAFEGUARD TO PUBLIC HEALTH

JOHN R. MOHLER, V. M. D.,

Chief, Bureau of Animal Industry, U. S. Department of Agriculture,
Washington, D. C.

Read before Food and Drugs Section, American Public Health Association, at New Orleans, La.,
October 30, 1919.

There is no Federal inspection for one-third of the meat consumed in this country. Further than this, there is much needed in constructive work on the part of states and municipalities, in which this one-third is produced and slaughtered. Cities plead lack of funds, and there is also lack of knowledge and lack of interest. Meat is too important a feature in our lives to be thus neglected.

IT is common knowledge that the Federal Government maintains through the Bureau of Animal Industry of the United States Department of Agriculture a system of meat inspection, but comparatively few persons are familiar with its scope or the manner in which it protects public health. The work is scientific and technical and gives consumers comfortable assurance that the inspected products they buy are healthful and wholesome. The inspection proceeds by logical steps, beginning with the careful ante-mortem examination of the animal, continuing with the inspection of the carcass while being dressed, the supervision of the curing, pickling, smoking, cooking, or canning, of all meats, and finally with the proper, honest labeling of all meat or meat products.

MORE THAN SEVENTY MILLION ANIMALS INSPECTED LAST YEAR

The extent of the Federal Meat Inspection Service is definitely shown by the number of cattle, sheep, goats and swine slaughtered under federal inspection. For a number of years the totals have approached 60,000,000 annually, or nearly two-thirds of all such animals slaughtered for food in the United States in the same periods. Figures for the fiscal year ending June 30, 1919, show a remarkable increase over previous years. Altogether more than 70,000,000 animals were slaughtered under Federal inspection. This inspection included in round numbers: cattle 11,241,000; calves 3,674,-000; sheep 11,268,000; goats 125,000, and swine 44,398,000. The statement that so many animals were inspected means that all were examined while alive and that the organs and different parts of each animal were inspected at the time of slaughter to determine their fitness for food. However, this double inspection, complete and important as it is, is but the first of several steps in the federal system. The subsequent handling, processing, preparation, storage and labeling, are given supervision, and the meats are reinspected as often as may be necessary. The federal system has been aptly described as extending "from the hoof to the can," or "from the live-stock pen to the finished meat or product in the labeled package ready for shipment to the consumer."

WIDE RANGE IN INSPECTORS' DUTIES

The scope and purpose of federal meat inspection are to place the federal mark of approval upon all meats and products which competent examination shows to be sound, healthful and fit for food, and to condemn and destroy those which are

421

found to be dangerous, unsound or otherwise unfit for such use. The inspection also includes supervision of the establishments with respect to sanitation, construction, and suitable methods of handling all meat and their products. Furthermore, the consumer of meats is protected against the use of harmful dyes and chemicals, and against false or misleading names or statements on labels. In short, the meat inspection service seeks to protect the public health and the rights of consumers, and to do this without infringing upon the just rights of the producer, and without waste of the nation's meat food supply.

Federal meat inspection is being maintained at 825 establishments in 230 cities. These figures undergo some increase or decrease from time to time, but they represent a reasonably permanent average. Stated in round numbers, about 2,600 inspectors are regularly employed. Of this number about 800 are graduate veterinarians; the remainder are lay inspectors who, through experience and training, acquire the technical knowledge and skill necessary to a proper performance of their duties. The appointing of inspectors is controlled by and is in accordance with the requirements of the United States Civil Service Commission.

Sometimes the question is asked why federal meat inspection is not made to cover every slaughter house and meat-preparing plant in the United States instead of a limited number. The answer is that the Federal Meat Inspection Act is based on the commerce clause of the constitution, which restricts the application of federal inspection to establishments engaged in interstate or foreign trade and to meats and products which are to be sold or shipped as articles of interstate or foreign commerce. The inspection cannot be extended to those establishments which confine their sales and shipments to the state in which located. However, when federal inspection is inaugurated at an establishment it is maintained there in respect to the whole establishment and applies to all animals slaughtered, and to all products prepared therein. This is necessary to the completeness of the inspection and to a proper enforcement of the regulations. The result is that very great amounts of meats not shipped or sold in either interstate or foreign commerce, but consumed locally, are, nevertheless, inspected and bear the marks of federal inspection.

The inspection has been extended as far as contemplated and permitted by the law and as far as has been possible with the funds provided by Congress for its maintenance. If the entire meat food supply of the country is to be properly inspected, it will devolve upon the several states or municipalities to establish and maintain an adequate inspection to cover the field to which federal inspection cannot be extended. Many of our cities do maintain such an inspection.

The great need of an efficient meat inspection is shown by the number of animals and the quantities of meats and products which are condemned yearly on account of disease, unsoundness, or other conditions of unfitness, and thereby excluded from the food supply. The complete figures for all classes of animals and the various reasons for condemnation involve considerable detail. However, a general statement regarding them should serve the present purpose. For instance, on the post-mortem inspection alone there was condemned in the fiscal year 1919 a total of 212,245 cattle, sheep, swine and goats; while organs and parts of carcasses condemned on account of localized disease run into the hundreds of thousands.

TUBERCULOSIS AND HOG CHOLERA CAUSE MOST CONDEMNATIONS

Tuberculosis in cattle and tuberculosis and cholera in swine were responsible for more condemnations than all other diseases and causes combined. In addition to the condemnations on the post-mortem inspection it was necessary to condemn in that year a total of more than 17,000,000 pounds of meats and products on account of their having become tainted, rancid, unclean, or otherwise unwholesome in the course of shipment, processing, preparation, or storage. The condemnations aggregate an enormous amount of material; fortunately, however, it represents but a relatively small part of the total of animals and meats inspected. By some the condemnations might be regarded as evidence that disease prevails to an unusual degree in American live stock, or that on account of undue strictness the inspection is wasteful of potentially good food. Neither of these deductions is in accord with the facts. Disease is less prevalent in the live stock of the United States than in the various European countries. As regards the inspection it must be maintained in the interest of the public health with a due measure of strictness. Necessarily this entails loss, but such loss cannot be called waste. Moreover, the basic rules and regulations by which condemnations on the post-mortem inspection are determined were prepared with great care by competent officials and then were submitted to an independent committee, composed of scientists and hygienists of the highest reputation, for consideration, and received that committee's approval.

INSPECTION BEFORE SLAUGHTER

The first examination is the ante-mortem inspection, or inspection of the animals prior to slaughter. They are scrutinized while at rest in the pens or as they are moved from the scales. If the condition of an animal is such as to cause the inspector to suspect that it is diseased or affected by any condition which will cause its condemnation in whole or in part on the post-mortem inspection, the animal is set apart and marked "U. S. Suspect" by means of a serially numbered metal tag affixed to the ear. Such animals are held for separate slaughter and for an especially careful post-mortem examination. The diseases and conditions for which animals are most frequently so tagged are cholera, actinomy-

cosis, emaciation, advanced pregnancy, and severe or excessive injuries. Animals which show symptoms of rabies, tetanus, milk fever, railroad sickness, and hogs which manifestly are sick with cholera are condemned and their carcasses destroyed without admission to the slaughter room. Such animals are marked by the inspector with a numbered metal tag bearing the legend "U. S. Condemned."

POST-MORTEM INSPECTION INCLUDES EXAMINATION OF ORGANS

The post-mortem or slaughter inspection is the most important of the several inspection procedures because it affords greater opportunity to discover the existence of most diseases. This calls for careful examination throughout. Accordingly, the inspectors first examine those glands, organs or parts in which disease most frequently occurs. For instance, in both hogs and cattle certain of the lymph glands of the neck usually are the first to show evidence of tuberculosis; therefore, these glands in every animal are cut and carefully viewed. The cheek and heart muscles of cattle are the seats where the beef measle, which produces tapeworm in man, is found most frequently. Accordingly these parts are sliced in every instance so that no cow or steer effected with measles shall escape detection. These particular procedures are cited simply to indicate the pains taken to make the post-mortem inspection a thorough one. All the organs, as well as the carcass, are covered by this examination. If, on the completion of this inspection, the meat is found to be sound and fit for food, the carcass is passed, and marked "U. S. Inspected and Passed" with the official number of the establishment at which it was slaughtered. The brand used for thus marking the carcasses is circular with the above legend in abbreviated form, and is stamped with a purple ink on the principal parts of the carcass. The ink is absolutely harmless.

ALL CONDEMNED MEAT DESTROYED IN
· GOVERNMENT-SEALED TANKS

If an animal is affected with disease
or other objectionable condition, whether
it be slight, extensive, local or general,
the inspector marks it with a serially
numbered U. S. Retained tag. Carcasses
and parts so marked are officially in the
custody of the inspector and are transferred to what is designated the final inspection room or place where all the
facilities necessary for the thorough examination of such carcasses are provided.
The final inspection and disposition of
retained carcasses and parts is a very important duty; therefore, only those veterinary inspectors who are the most experienced in the work are assigned to its
performance. If the final inspection
shows the meat to be unfit for food, the
carcass and the parts are condemned and
plainly marked "U. S. Condemned," by
means of a large metal brand. All condemned meats and products remain in
the custody of the inspectors and are destroyed under Bureau supervision by
conversion into fertilizer and grease in
government-sealed rendering tanks. If
the condition for which the carcass is
retained is found to be local, the affected
parts are condemned and the remainder
of the carcass is passed.

LABELS MUST BE APPROVED

The products inspection, as it is termed,
covers the inspection and reinspection of
meats and products from the time of
slaughter through the succeeding processes of preparation and storage, including supervision of all operations to insure the sanitary handling of all edible
materials. This supervision also extends
to the spices, curing agents and other
ingredients used in the products. None
but those permitted under the regulations
may be added. In order to see that the
regulations are strictly observed, a system of frequent collection of samples for
laboratory examination without notification to the establishment is maintained.
The products inspection also includes supervision of the branding and labeling of
meats and products. The use of labels
bearing false or misleading names or
statements is prohibited; in fact, only
those labels which have first been submitted to the Bureau and approved by it
may be used. The contents of the package must conform to the statements on
the label.

The sanitary requirements prescribed
and enforced under the meat inspection
regulations constitute a highly important part of the federal system. The
Meat Inspection Act confers upon the
Secretary of Agriculture authority to
prescribe and enforce such regulations
at all establishments at which inspection
is maintained. The more important of
these requirements are adequate and
proper toilet and lavatory and dressing-
room accommodations, and also smooth
and impervious surfaces for operating
rooms and equipment. Other requirements include good light, adequate ventilation, modern plumbing, efficient drainage, complete separation of rooms in
which edible products are prepared from
those in which inedible materials are handled, and pure water with ample facilities
for its distribution. The requirements
enumerated indicate the character of the
sanitary regulations. Their purpose is to
insure strict cleanliness in the preparation and handling of meats and meat food
products, and for the maintenance of
clean and wholesome conditions in and
about the establishment. Since the present meat inspection act became effective
the establishments in the United States
at which federal meat inspection is maintained have expended in the aggregate
many millions of dollars in order to conform to the standard set by the regulations. It has been money well spent.
The difference between a modern sanitary plant operating under inspection and
the country type of slaughter house operating without inspection of any kind can
hardly be described. It needs to be seen
to be adequately and properly appreciated. The regulations governing sanitation were framed on progressive lines,

so that they not only serve the present needs, but also provide for the attainment of still better standards for the future. When new plants are to be erected or old ones reconstructed it is aimed to have the best standards followed; accordingly, it is required that the plans and specifications for the same be submitted to the Bureau for examination and approval.

IMPORTANT FACTOR IN FOREIGN TRADE

While federal meat inspection is primarily a service in hygiene and sanitation, it occupies, nevertheless, an important position in our trade economics, and is the agency through which a very important part of our export commerce has been maintained. Without its certificate of inspection the export trade in meats and meat food products would be seriously impaired. The amount of beef, pork and mutton certified for export in the fiscal year 1918 exceeded a total of 2,500,000,000 pounds, while the certification for the fiscal year 1919 will approximate 3,400,000,000 pounds. The figures do not include the shipments made to the American expeditionary forces in France. Exports have been tremendously stimulated by the war; however, under normal conditions the United States imports as well as exports great quantities of meats. All the imported meats are subjected to an adequate inspection under the federal system.

An economic importance possessed by federal meat inspection, but to which only casual reference can be made at this time, is the relation of its post-mortem records to the locating of territories in which food animal diseases prevail to an unusual extent, and the eradication of which is to be attempted.

A further point in regard to the economic value of federal meat inspection is the moderate cost at which it is maintained. The first aim is to make the service efficiently fulfill the purpose for which it is intended; the second, to administer it with due regard to economy. In computing unit cost of maintenance the federal system has the advantage of a very large volume of operations, and it will be gratifying to the taxpayer to learn that largely owing to this advantage the service is maintained at a cost of less than six cents for each animal inspected. This sum covers the expense of all the inspections from that of the live animal to the final examination of the finished products.

STUDY OF LOCAL INSPECTION

Lately the Bureau has completed a survey of municipal and state meat inspection. About one-third of the meat consumed in the United States is slaughtered and sold within state boundaries and, therefore, is not subject to federal inspection. This is a condition which local authorities must handle. The results of the survey include some highly interesting facts and figures, and to make them available to members of the association I have requested our Mr. Roberts to furnish the association with a copy of the findings.* You will learn that the majority of cities have no inspection of their meats. The reasons for the absence of local supervision in many cities include lack of funds and lack of sufficient interest. Apparently health considerations alone have failed to rouse cities to the importance of having local meat establishments inspected. It is not within my authority to say what should be done, but this much is certain; the inspection is needed as the facts show and as all who are familiar with average slaughter-house conditions will quickly admit. Their interest in health alone fails to get results; possibly some additional fact may be found and used as a means of obtaining and holding the necessary support.

Municipal and state meat inspection is a field where a great deal of constructive work remains to be done. It is paramount for health reasons and the health side appeals to many people. Yet the economic side may appeal to a great many more. This briefly is the thought I want to leave with you. Human welfare is

---

*The paper by Mr. Roberts, "State and Municipal Meat Inspection," is to appear in a future issue of the JOURNAL.

the common cause we are serving. Methods of livelihood have produced what are commonly called "industrial classes" and also terms like "producer," "consumer," and "distributer." Each group has its problems in which it is deeply interested and many of which are vital to human happiness. In attempting to carry certain lines of scientific work before the public we may wisely study the aims of these groups, thus meeting with coöperation which may simplify many a knotty problem and hasten the successful solution of others.

☐

OBSERVATIONS ON THE DIPHTHERIA VIRULENCE TEST IN PUBLIC HEALTH WORK

E. M. WADE, M. A., AND G. E. VAUGHAN, M. A.,

Division of Preventable Diseases, Minnesota State Board of Health, Minneapolis, Minn.

Presented before Laboratory Section, Amer. Pub. Health Asso., at Chicago, Ill., December, 1918.

These authors advocate tonsilectomy where virulent diphtheria bacilli persist in throats with adenoids or enlarged tonsils. Diphtheria bacilli of well persons are rarely virulent unless these persons have associated with cases of diphtheria. Organisms are almost always virulent in persons sick with the disease and their associates.

Definite detailed study of the bacteriology of the diphtheria bacillus following its discovery and identification by Klebs-Loeffler in 1883-4 was prompted and augmented by the publication in 1899 by Wesbrook, Wilson and McDaniel[1] of their classification of the diphtheria bacillus. This classification gave a common ground for the discussion and comparison of different types. With this classification for a basis the Massachusetts Association of Boards of Health appointed, in 1900, a committee with an extensive representation in the various public health laboratories of that time, to determine the relationship of the different types, their prevalence and significance. The report[2] of this committee in 1902 showed tremendous variations in the diagnostic value of the different types and in their prevalence in both the sick and the well as reported by the various laboratories. For example, in well persons the presence of diphtheria bacilli was reported in 22% in Washington, D. C., but only 9% were granular organisms. In Providence, R. I., there were .43% granular organisms, 3% including barred forms and 25% including all forms, but there were actually reported positive 9%. In Boston 1.01% were reported positive. In Minnesota at that time there were reported positive 3.72% in institutions where cases had occurred and 3% in institutions in which no cases had recently occurred.

In 1910 this Association appointed a committee to study the same subject with an idea of standardizing diphtheria diagnosis. The committee was never able to complete its work.

Two extensive studies on the occurrence of diphtheria bacilli in well persons have been made since this time, one in Boston[3], in 1911, and the other in Detroit, Michigan,[4] in 1915. In Boston

4444 school children were cultured at the opening' of schools in September and 2.3% found to harbor diphtheria or diphtheria-like organisms. In Detroit a house-to-house culturing campaign was made and of 4093 persons cultured .928% were reported positive.

A study of the virulence of the organism in each case was planned in each of these studies, but for various reasons only a few of the cultures were tested for virulence in the Boston study. In Detroit one-half of the 38 cultures were tested and 2 found to be virulent. Supposing 2 more virulent cultures would have been found out of the other 19 positives there would be .097% of the total persons examined found to be harboring virulent diphtheria bacilli.

The value of the virulence test depends upon the non-variability of the organism. Goodman[5] in 1908 claimed he could produce from the same colony by artificial cultivation 2 strains widely divergent in acid production. In 1912 Berry and Banzhaf[9] showed that the divergence in Goodman's study was due to environment. They could get no true change in acid production or in virulence. Dr. Anna Williams, after much work, never succeeded in changing the virulence of diphtheria bacilli. Schofield[7] endeavored to change virulent organisms to non-virulent by exposure to drying and sunlight, but got no change after 30 days' exposure to sunlight and 60 days to drying in the dark. Kolmer[8] reporting on a large series of virulence tests concluded that an avirulent organism never became virulent; those of low virulence might become more virulent by passage from person to person and that exceptionally virulent organisms become non-virulent. However, it is occasionally found that both virulent and non-virulent organisms are present in the same throat culture, which might account for an apparent change of virulent to avirulent forms.

The present study covers two groups of persons; the first group being persons admitted to the State University Hospital for various ailments other than infectious diseases, and the second group being persons exposed in schools or in public gatherings to persons having diphtheria.

Group I. From Feb. 1, 1914, to Sept. 30, 1918, there have been cultures taken from 6960 persons on admission to the hospital, and of these 152, or 2.18%, have shown diphtheria or diphtheria-like organisms. Three clinical cases occurring in the hospital during this time are omitted. Virulence tests have been made on 132 of the 152 and of these but 10 or .14% of the total persons examined showed the presence of virulent organisms. The history of these 10 cases is as follows:

Two had abnormal condition of tonsils—enlarged and inflamed.
One had enlarged tonsils with membrane formation which was undoubtedly true diphtheria infection.
One had mild pharyngeal disturbance with chronic nasal catarrh.
Two came from families where clinical diphtheria existed.
One was exposed to a clinical case removed from next seat in school and had had sore throat.
One was admitted to hospital with paralysis, which increased; had had sore throat previously, without medical attention.
One in hospital because of heart disease, gave no history of known exposure at any time and had no symptoms; worked as night watchman in a coal yard. Cultures were positive over a period of three weeks; then three negative cultures were obtained.
One in hospital with carcinoma of tongue. No history obtained.

Group II. In this group of persons exposed more or less intimately in public places to clinical cases there were cultures taken from 12,897. In 393 cases, or 3.05%, the diagnosis was returned positive. Because of stress of work, virulence tests were not made in all of these cases, but when made it was found generally true that only those persons most intimately associated with the sick person, usually in the same family, or school companions, harbored virulent organisms. This is illustrated in one of our State institutions where delay in the cultural control of an epidemic of diphtheria occurred. In that case our proportion of virulent cultures increased to .6%.

This same relationship of virulence to symptoms, or to direct exposure to persons sick with diphtheria, is shown very clearly in a tabulation of all of our virulence tests made in routine work. Since January 1, 1914, there have been 1082 cases tested by the subcutaneous inoculation of guinea pigs, using as far as possible two strains from each case. The tabulation of these cases as given below shows 85% of the virulent cultures to come from persons having had clinical diphtheria, 14.1% from persons intimately associated with clinical cases and .9% only from well persons. Of the non-virulent cultures 97.4% were from persons without symptoms and without close association with clinical cases, .5% from persons exposed to clinical cases and 2.1% from persons with symptoms of diphtheria.

	Positive	Negative	Total
Clinical cases	561	9	570
Exposed to clinical cases	93	2	95
Nonclinical or well persons	6	411	417
Total	660	422	1,082

The six well persons with virulent organisms include three persons with some abnormalities of the upper air passages, one person without any symptoms or any known exposure to virulent infection and two persons in whom there were no symptoms but whose history regarding exposure was not obtained.

The two persons harboring non-virulent organisms and who were exposed to clinical cases do not need consideration, as it is quite possible to conceive of well carriers of non-virulent organisms being exposed to cases of diphtheria without becoming infected from the sick person. The 9 cases found to be harboring non-virulent organisms in the presence of symptoms give the following histories: Six had mild symptoms of tonsilitis varying in duration from 2 to 3 days; two had tonsilitis with exudate present 1 and 2 days, respectively; and one had a mild attack of diphtheria 47 days previously.

We may conclude then that virulent organisms are found almost invariably in persons with clinical symptoms of diphtheria and in well persons intimately associated with them. In well persons who have not associated intimately with infected persons, the organisms, while diphtheria-like, are avirulent. This agrees with the conclusions drawn by Weaver[9] on a series of 50 cases in Chicago.

TONSILECTOMY IN RELATION TO CHRONIC CARRIERS

The clearing of diphtheria infection from the upper air passages of chronic carriers has been a very serious problem to most physicians. After a fairly extensive trial of various bacterial sprays, the most frequently used being *Staphylococcus pyogenes aureus, B. Bulgaricus* and various yeasts, these were discarded. In 1915 Ewart[10] in England tried jasmin oil, running it into the nose down over the nasopharynx and filling the sinuses with it. In 1916 kaolin was advocated. Extensive use of this material was made by Rappaport[11], who showed that its value depended wholly upon its adsorptive properties. Therefore, the drier the kaolin the better the results. He recommended drying the kaolin in an oven and blowing it while warm into the nostrils and throat at two-hour intervals, washing out the old kaolin before each administration with a weak antiseptic solution. While this procedure gave good results at times it was not effective where tonsils were found enlarged or adenoids present. In such cases surgery must be resorted to. Ruh, Miller and Perkins[12] report tonsilectomies in 19 cases without ill results.

We have a series of cases beginning February, 1915, in which cultures taken before and after the operation have been examined in this laboratory. The results have been so satisfactory that we do not hesitate to suggest tonsilectomy to any physician caring for a chronic carrier.

Our series of cases may be divided into two groups: (A) Those encountered in our routine work and scattered over the State; and (B) patients in a State Hospital where, following an epidemic of diphtheria, tonsilectomy was performed on all persons with enlarged tonsils who had harbored diphtheria bacilli.

In group A there are 22 persons, 8 males and 14 females, varying in age from 9 to 36 years. Fifteen of the cases had had clinical symptoms and 7 had not been sick, but had been exposed intimately to clinical cases. The virulence of the infecting organisms was tested in all but two of the cases and in each instance the organisms were found to be virulent for guinea pigs.

From date of first symptoms, or in cases of exposure without symptoms from date of first positive culture to tonsilectomy, the lapse of time varied from 14 to 276 days. Omitting two cases in which the periods were 14 and 20 days, respectively, the average duration was 124 days. Of the 22 cases, 13 cleared up at once and cultures taken, 1, 2, 3, 3, 3, 4, 7, 7, 7, 8, 10 and 23 days later respectively, were negative as well as later cultures from each case. In six cases tonsilectomy was followed by 1 positive culture 4, 5, 6, 8, 9 and 10 days later, respectively, later cultures being negative. In three cases the results of the operation were not as marked; one having positive cultures on the 3rd, 7th, 15th, 18th and 24th day later, becoming negative on the 30th day; and a sister of this one having a positive culture on the 7th day and on the 18th day a positive nose culture (throat being negative), and becoming negative on the 24th day. In both of these cases, cultures from the nose gave the positive findings largely and it is quite possible that all adenoid tissue was not removed at operation. In the third case cultures were taken at irregular in-

tervals, but were positive on the 14th, 29th and 95th day after operation and were negative on the 115th day and later.

Group B includes cases in which tonsilectomy was performed in all cases that had harbored diphtheria or diphtheria-like organisms an excessive time following the cessation of an epidemic of diphtheria in the institution. The epidemic was confined to the women's side. Some cases with enlarged tonsils were operated upon, although cultures had become negative, but these are not included in this series. Twelve cases not sick and not exposed intimately to diphtheria infection, mainly among the male patients, but who had diphtheria-like organisms in cultures, were also operated upon because of abnormal throat conditions and these are dealt with separately later.

In this group there were 7 cases, all of whom had been sick or had associated with clinical cases. All were females. In 6 the organism was shown to be virulent by animal tests; in one no virulence test was made. The lapse of time from first symptoms or first positive culture to operation varied from 52 to 159 days, averaging 92 days. In 6 the cultures following tonsilectomy were all negative, four taken on the 6th day, one on the 25th and one on the 35th. It is unfortunate that cultures were not taken earlier from the two last named. In one, cultures were positive on the 6th, 7th, 8th, 16th and 19th day and negative on the 20th day and later.

The twelve cases referred to above, without symptoms and without association with cases, are interesting to compare with the above series of cases. There were 9 males and 3 females; virulence test was negative on 10 and not made on two of the males. Duration from first positive culture to tonsilectomy averaged 175 days. In only one of the twelve cases was the operation followed promptly by negative cultures. In six cases examined from 1 to 3 months later, cultures were still positive, in one examined 3½ months after operation, culture was negative, and the remaining three were not examined later than the 5th to 10th day at which time they were positive.

CONCLUSIONS

(1) While diphtheria or diphtheria-like organisms are found in from 2% to 3% of well persons these organisms are very rarely virulent unless the individual has associated intimately with persons sick with diphtheria.

(2) The organisms are virulent almost invariably in persons convalescent from diphtheria and in persons intimately associated with cases or convalescents.

(3) Where virulent diphtheria bacilli persist in persons with enlarged tonsils and adenoids, operation is usually an efficient method of getting rid of the infection.

1. Wesbrook, Wilson, McDaniel, Trans. Assn. Amer. Physicians, 1900.
2. Jour. Mass. Assn. Bds. of Health, XI. 1.
3. Slack, Arms, Wade and Blanchard. Jour. A. M. A., LIV., p. 951.
4. Goldberger & Williams. Hyg. Lab. Bull. No. 101.
5. Goodman. Jour. Inf. Dis., 1908. 5 p. 134.
6. Berry & Banzhaf. Jour. Inf. Dis. X. 3. p. 409.
7. Schofield. A. J. P. H.. VI. 12. 1303.
8. Kolmer, Woody, Moshage. Am. Jour. Dis. Child., 11. 4, p. 255.
9. Weaver. Jour. Inf. Dis., XX. 2. 125.
10. Ewart. B. M. J. 12. 11. 15 II, p. 2867.
11. Rappaport. Jour. A. M. A., LXVI 13, p. 943.
12. Ruh, Miller & Perkins. Jour. A. M. A. LXVI. 13, p. 941.

☐

APPRECIATION OF PUBLIC HEALTH NEEDS AT GREEN BAY

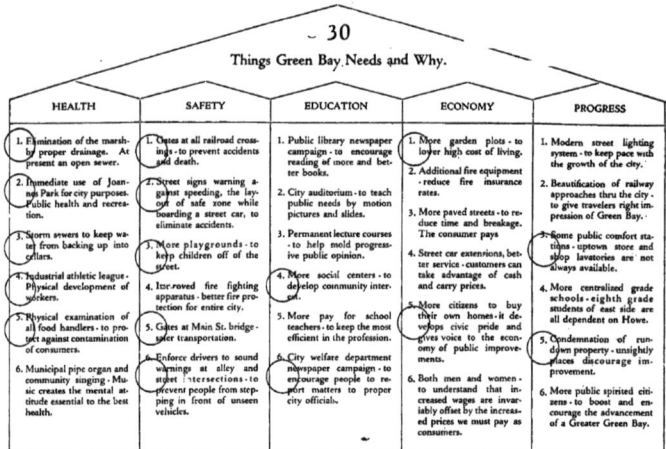

~ 30
Things Green Bay Needs and Why.

HEALTH	SAFETY	EDUCATION	ECONOMY	PROGRESS
1. Elimination of the marshy by proper drainage. At present an open sewer.	1. Gates at all railroad crossings - to prevent accidents and death.	1. Public library newspaper campaign - to encourage reading of more and better books.	1. More garden plots - to lower high cost of living. 2. Additional fire equipment - reduce fire insurance rates.	1. Modern street lighting system - to keep pace with the growth of the city.
2. Immediate use of Joannes Park for city purposes. Public health and recreation.	2. Street signs warning against speeding, the layout of safe zone while boarding a street car, to eliminate accidents.	2. City auditorium - to teach public needs by motion pictures and slides.	3. More paved streets - to reduce time and breakage. The consumer pays	2. Beautification of railway approaches thru the city - to give travelers right impression of Green Bay.
3. Storm sewers to keep water from backing up into cellars.	3. More playgrounds - to keep children off of the street.	3. Permanent lecture courses - to help mold progressive public opinion.	4. Street car extensions, better service - customers can take advantage of cash and carry prices.	3. Some public comfort stations - uptown store and shop lavatories are not always available.
4. Industrial athletic league - Physical development of workers.	4. Improved fire fighting apparatus - better protection for entire city.	4. More social centers to develop community interest.	5. More citizens to buy their own homes - it develops civic pride and gives voice to the economy of public improvements.	4. More centralized grade schools - eighth grade students of east side are all dependent on Howe.
5. Physical examination of all food handlers - to protect against contamination of consumers.	5. Gates at Main St. bridge - safer transportation.	5. More pay for school teachers - to keep the most efficient in the profession.	6. Both men and women - to understand that increased wages are invariably offset by the increased prices we must pay as consumers.	5. Condemnation of run-down property - unsightly places discourage improvement.
6. Municipal pipe organ and community singing - Music creates the mental attitude essential to the best health.	6. Enforce drivers to sound warnings at alley and street intersections - to prevent people from stepping in front of unseen vehicles.	6. City welfare department newspaper campaign - to encourage people to report matters to proper city officials.		6. More public spirited citizens - to boost and encourage the advancement of a Greater Green Bay.

Green Bay, Wis., has 30 things that it really needs, according to the *Northern Lights*, published in that city, from which the attractive listing of them here presented is taken. Of these 16 items, which the *Journal* has emphasized with the ring, are practical factors to health and safety. It is an up-to-date community that can consider seriously such matters as these, but Green Bay goes further and considers important improvements in other departments of public work.

SOME EPIDEMIOLOGICAL POINTS REGARDING ACUTE RESPIRATORY DISEASES

FRANK OVERTON, M. D., D. P. H.,

Patchogue, N. Y.

Customary measures for control of infections often shut the stable door after the horse is gone. Epidemics are frequently not recognized till the mischief is done. People must learn to practice the hygienic measures that will protect them. Real prevention needs the intelligent coöperation of every individual in a community.

ACUTE respiratory diseases have commonly been named according to the anatomical location of their lesions. Medical text-books confuse students by making separate entities out of rhinitis, pharyngitis, tonsilitis, bronchitis, and pneumonia, as if they were unrelated conditions. The modern conception of these diseases is that they are infectious; that they are caused by a number of different varieties of organisms; and that any organism may produce a lesion of any part of the respiratory tract and of any degree of severity. The scientific method of nomenclature would be to name each acute respiratory disease according to the species of organism which causes it, as in naming the acute infections of the intestine. The epidemiologist would like to know the identity of the organisms of every case of acute respiratory disease, in order to isolate and control those patients who harbor virulent organisms. Since he is usually unable to secure this identification, his alternative choice is to seek to secure some control over every case of acute respiratory disease. Even if accurate diagnostic methods were available, a delay of at least a day or two will always be necessary before the tests can be reported; and in the meantime there should be some

degree of control over the case. The control of every case, or of the infective material from it, offers the only prospect of preventing diseases of the respiratory organs. This is impracticable and impossible at the present time, owing to the ignorance of most people regarding the infectiousness of colds and other forms of acute respiratory diseases. Physicians do not usually treat the diseases as infectious processes, and still less do the people generally consider them to be transmissible. The basis for their control must be the education of the people regarding their infectious nature and the means of their transmission. The present failure of public health measures to control influenza is due principally to the ignorance of the people and their inability to understand the reasons for the preventive measures.

MEANS OF SPREAD

Physicians and the people need to be taught that the only way in which coldness, dampness, and fatigue influence the onset of acute respiratory diseases is by producing susceptibility to them, and preparing the soil for the growth of the infecting organisms. It is necessary to emphasize the two facts that the diseases will not develop unless the organisms are planted in the body, and that the organisms come from the discharges of the noses and throats of affected persons. The likelihood of transmitting the infection increases with the virulence and abundance of the organisms, and the closeness of the contact with the infecting case, as it does in any other disease. It was found at Camp Upton, for example, that if a case that developed into pneumonia was left in a barrack until a diagnosis of pneumonia was made, there would usually be other cases of pneumonia and also a series of milder cases of diminishing severity down to what appear to be mild colds; but if the original case was discovered and controlled early, few other cases developed.

A case of acute respiratory disease can transmit the disease from the time of the onset of symptoms. A person coming down with a cold usually goes to business for hours or days, mingles with others without restraint, sneezes, coughs, and spits promiscuously, and spreads infective material widely and indiscriminately. By the time he is disabled and goes to bed, he has exposed an unknown number of other persons to infection. Public measures and physicians cannot reach mild cases, or severe ones in their early stages. The remedy is education to such a degree that the majority of persons habitually consider colds to be infectious, and sneezing and coughing to be public warnings of danger to the community.

PERIOD OF INCUBATION

It is well established that influenza has an incubation period of two days. It is probable that most other acute respiratory diseases also have a two-day incubation period. Contrast this period with the two-week period of incubation of measles and most other common infectious diseases. At the end of two weeks when secondary cases begin to follow a primary case of measles, a primary case of influenza

may have been followed by the seventh generation of cases. An epidemic of influenza two weeks after the appearance of a primary case is usually in the same stage as an uncontrolled epidemic of measles three months after the primary case. The usual course of events in an epidemic of influenza is shown in the accompanying table from *Health News*, New York State Department of Health, September, 1919.

There is nothing to call special attention to the development of an epidemic until about the 10th day when a death occurs. A few cases of pneumonia are then recognized and rumors begin to spread that colds are prevalent. Yet the epidemic is then at its height, and nearly every susceptible person has been infected. Only a few scattered cases of influenza have been discovered, and yet a total of 364 cases may have been infected, if each case infects only three others. On the 12th day the funeral of the primary case makes an impression, a number of pneumonia cases are reported, and public health agencies begin to be active. The explosiveness of the outbreak is often mentioned, and yet cases have developed through an orderly series of six or seven generations. There are heated discussions regarding the value, or futility, of preventive measures; but the onset of new cases naturally stops because nearly all susceptible persons have been exposed, and about all that remains to be done is to treat the pneumonia cases that remain.

PREVENTION

The preventive measures against acute respiratory diseases are the same as those against other communicable diseases, and include the discovery of cases in their early stages, their isolation to some degree, and the careful and strict disposal of the excretions of their noses and mouths. The disease most analogous to acute respiratory diseases is measles. Success in preventing this disease depends on recognizing cases in their incipiency three or four days before the eruption appears. This is notoriously difficult in measles, and is still more so in such a disease as influenza. The situation in influenza is still more complicated by a two-day period of incubation. If we wait for severe symptoms to appear, as we have been doing, we will be about two generations behind in our discovery of cases. Our efforts will be of no avail if every case which we discover has left an undiscovered series of secondary and tertiary cases behind it. Speed is absolutely necessary in preventing or controlling an epidemic.

The protective measures are based on preventing the transfer of excretions of the nose and throat from one person to another, and include isola-

tion, the disposal of sputum, covering the nose and mouth during coughing and sneezing, and cleanliness of dishes, toilet articles, and the person. A whole page of rules might be written regarding what to do and avoid, but they may be summed up in the rules of *good manners and good housekeeping.*

Preventive measures against acute respiratory diseases require the intelligent cooperation of every individual in a community. The attitude of each person must be to report sickness, rather than conceal it; to respect suspicious signs of sickness, rather than ignore them; to impose some degree of self-isolation, rather than mingle closely with others; and to observe personal hygiene, rather than assert an excessive degree of personal liberty and independence. Prevention at present depends upon individual in-

SEQUENCE OF EVENTS IN A TYPICAL OUTBREAK OF INFLUENZA: SUPPOSING THAT EACH CASE INFECTS ONLY THREE OTHERS.

1st day	2d and 3d days	4th and 5th days	6th and 7th days	8th and 9th days	10th and 11th days	12th and 13th days
1 Primary case	3 Secondary cases.	9 Tertiary	27 Fourth series	81 Fifth series	243 Sixth series	729 Seventh series
The original or primary case comes to town with a slight cold	The primary case begins to feel sick.	Primary case sends for physician.	Primary case goes to bed.	Primary case reported as pneumonia.	Primary case dead.	Funeral of primary case.
		Secondary cases begin to have slight cold.	Secondary cases send for physician.	Secondary cases go to bed.	Secondary cases begin to have pneumonia.	Secondary cases begin to die.
			Tertiary cases begin to have slight colds.	Tertiary cases begin to feel sick.	Tertiary cases send for a physician.	Tertiary cases go to bed.	Tertiary cases begin to have pneumonia.
				Fourth series of cases begin to have slight colds.	Fourth series of cases feel sick.	Fourth series of cases send for a physician.	Fourth series of cases go to bed.
					Fifth series of cases begin to have slight colds.	Fifth series of cases feel sick.	Fifth series of cases send for a physician.
					Sixth series of cases begin to have slight colds.	Sixth series of cases feel sick.
					Health officer gets the first reports of a few of the worst cases. Rumors that everybody in town has a cold. Outbreak is really at its height.	Seventh series of cases begin to have slight colds. H. O. gets a number of reports of cases. H. O., Red Cross and other public health agencies begin to get busy. The number of new cases begin to diminish on account of the lack of susceptible persons.

itiative rather than public measures, but in future years we may expect a growth in education and public sentiment which will lead to the adoption and enforcement of public measures that are now left to the undeveloped consciences of individuals. The time will come when the majority of persons know as much about the elementary facts of the diseases as the few advanced thinkers now know.

Public health workers are prone to emphasize what is not known about acute respiratory diseases, and hesitate to apply a comprehensive plan of prevention based on what is already known. We do not need to wait to discover a short cut to prevention and to devise new measures the observance of which will atone for our personal sins of omission and commission along hygienic lines. The history of all vaccines and serums demonstrates that people generally use them only as a last resort. The prevention of typhoid fever, for example, still depends principally on sanitary measures. It would still be necessary for individuals to observe general hygienic measures for the prevention of acute respiratory diseases even if a potent vaccine or serum were discovered. The time is ripe for departments of health and education to develop a plan for public education regarding the elementary facts concerning the diseases, and to arouse the people generally to practice the hygienic measures which will protect them from the diseases.

□

ENDEMIC GOITER AS A PUBLIC HEALTH PROBLEM; ADDITIONAL NOTES

MAYO TOLMAN,

Health Director, Community Councils of National Defense, New York City

The article appearing in the July, 1919, Journal of the American Public Health Association on "Endemic Goiter as a Public Health Problem," seems to have stimulated considerable interest, as the writer has received numerous inquiries regarding his experience with goiter in West Virginia, and, in fact, has received applications from sanitary experts to make special investigations on a regular fee basis. Also he has received a correction regarding one of his statements, which correction should be quoted in full:

The author refers to Edmonton, Province of Alberta, Canada, as being a location of the highest endemicity of the disease. * * * The region to which his remarks may properly apply is not Edmonton, the capital of the province, but a district in the province near the foothills west of Calgary, and not less than 230 miles from Edmonton. This is the district surrounding a small town called Cochrane, where goiter does seem to be more than ordinarily prevalent. * * * Mr. Tolman's information was probably derived from the statements made by Dr. Ritchie of Cochrane, recently deceased, who has been responsible for making grossly exaggerated and unscientific statements regarding the prevalence of goiter in Alberta, and which were shown to be such by a special investigation ordered by the Dominion government. Dr. Sheppard of McGill University, who carried out this investigation, in his report did not support Dr. Ritchie's statements regarding goiter in Alberta and by resolution carried unanimously at the meeting of the Alberta Medical Association, held in Calgary in 1918, the medical practitioners of the province expressed absolute disagreement with the extreme views of the prevalence of goiter published by Dr. Ritchie as being unscientific and unreliable and not in accordance with facts.

The writer has not been able to locate his original source of the statement regarding Edmonton, although he does find the statement that the city is in a goiterous area in a Mineralogical Bulletin published in Massachusetts in 1884.

Quite recently Drs. McCord and Walker of the University of Cincinnati prepared an extensive and valuable article, which was printed in *Modern Medicine* for February, 1920. This article quotes the work of Clark and Pierce in West Virginia, where they made studies in 11 counties. Consequently, it may be of interest to present at this time a map of West Virginia showing the relative intensity of goiter as determined by a survey made by the State Department of Health in 1918. Return postcards were sent to every doctor in the state requesting a statement as to

the number of cases of goiter in his practice. Replies were received from some 60% of the physicians, and the reported cases were plotted in the area covered by the particular physician's practice.

While it is recognized that this is not an accurate method, it is felt that the results obtained at least have some value. The counties along the eastern edge of the state are largely in a limestone area, while the belt through the central part of the state is underlain by coal measures. The western edge of the state is not in the coal measures, except in the northwest corner, where it may be noted that the intensity of goiter again becomes very high. As stated in the earlier articles, this greater intensity in the coal

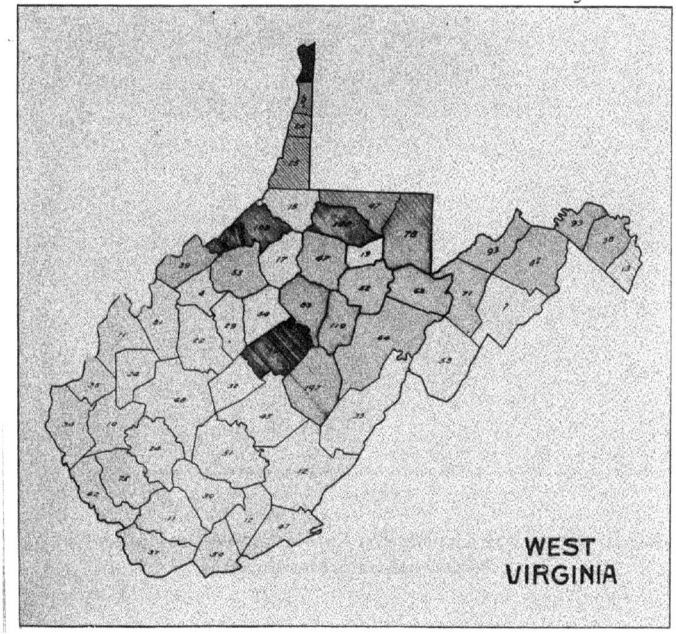

WEST
VIRGINIA

areas over that in the limestone region is contrary to the general experience of most investigators.

The July article referred to the house-to-house survey in Braxton County. The accompanying map shows the results of this survey, and it can readily be seen how closely it follows the stream beds. Of course, the majority of houses are to be found along the streams, but still there are enough people dwelling well up on the mountain sides to make the greater incidence along the creeks quite noticeable. It is interesting to observe that the

northeast corner of the county is but slightly affected. This area is entirely out of the coal measures, being largely in a red sandstone.

It seems to the writer possible that a careful spectroscopic study of the vapors of water from known goiterous wells and from wells known to be free from the goiter-producing characteristic, might be productive of interesting results, and it is suggested that some one thoroughly familiar with the use of this instrument undertake such an investigation.

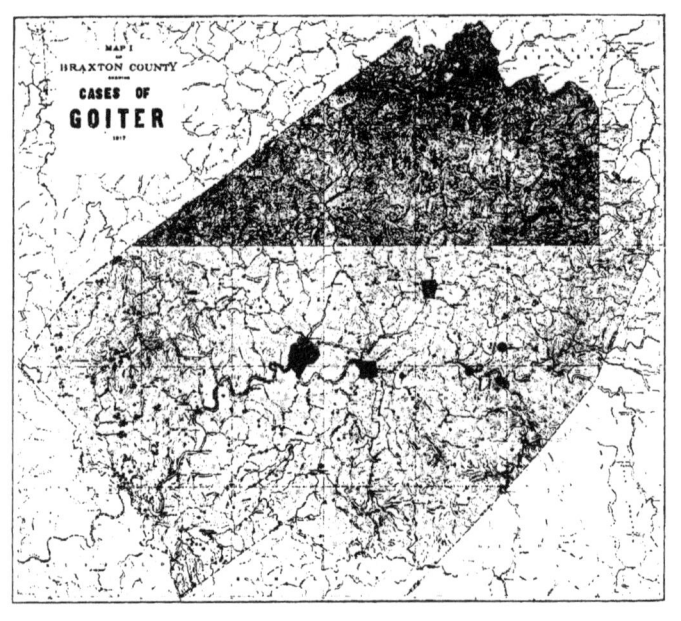

For latest news of Membership Campaign, see last pages of text, following Public Health Notes.

WATER TREATMENT AT ST. LOUIS, MO.

Edward E. Wall,

Water Commissioner,

St. Louis, Mo.

Read before Sanitary Engineering Section, American Public Health Association, at New Orleans, La., October 28, 1919.

With three kinds of water, Mississippi, Missouri and Illinois rivers, of different natures, and coming in an infinite variety of mixtures, St. Louis has peculiar water supply problems. This outline of methods will interest water engineers. Of the success of the St. Louis methods, the low mortality rates of the city are evidence.

FROM the date of the first daring attempt to clarify the Mississippi river water by coagulation followed by plain sedimentation; to the present time when water from the same source is settled, softened, coagulated, settled a second time, coagulated again, filtered and sterilized; there has been throughout all the wide range of study and experiment accompanying this evolution the same continuous variation in the numerous elements both chemical and physical entering into the composition of this impure and objectionable fluid.

It is true that the variation in all these elements is confined within certain limits, but the possible combinations between quantities and kinds are innumerable, so that any treatment to be successful must be of such a nature as to be readily modified in order to meet the changes resulting from the irregular mixing of the waters of the three great rivers that meet a few miles above St. Louis, viz., the Mississippi, the Illinois and the Missouri.

The upper Mississippi river receives the overflow from an immense area of lakes and swamps in northern Minnesota and Wisconsin, which gives the water its high color due to dissolved organic matter leached out of fallen leaves, twigs, limbs, pine needles, the cones of cedar, hemlock and tamarack and from the grass and undergrowth of those flat lands. Farther down it drains prairies, forests and fields, receiving the underground water from the sandstone and limestone districts.

The Illinois river drains a prairie district, an almost level agricultural area, so that both it and the Mississippi flow with a less rapid current than the Missouri and carry a much smaller quantity of suspended matter, but more finely divided than is the case with the Missouri.

The upper Missouri river flows through a forested region of mountain valleys and deep canyons into gradually widening bottoms, draining an area lower down where there are no trees, carrying at all times large quantities of sediment because of bank and bed erosion. It also carries a considerable quantity of dissolved matter taken up in the flow of surface drainage over and through alkaline soils.

The quantity of rainfall each year and its distribution, in point of time and season, over each of the drainage areas of these rivers determines the character of the water at the St. Louis intake.

In general the variation in the river water at the St. Louis intake follows certain lines, so that a knowledge of river and weather conditions prevailing at any time enables the chemist to predicate the treatment at least twelve or fifteen hours ahead with a reasonable degree of confidence. Occasionally sudden and remarkable changes occur, which upset all calculations, and conditions arise which differ from all previous experience. For example, in the autumn of 1911 heavy rainfalls in northern Illinois and Wisconsin, with little or no rain over the drainage area of the Missouri river, brought down from the forest and swamp lands of the upper Mississippi valley a flood of highly colored water, which the treatment at that time failed to reduce to a point where the water could be considered as unobjectionable. No such an unusual amount of color in the river water has occurred since.

The difference in color, turbidity, hardness, suspended and dissolved solids for the three rivers are indicated by the following table of averages:

	Color	Tur-bidity	Carb. Hard	Non-carb. Hard	Susp. Sol.	Dis. Sol.
Mississippi.	74	173	141	15	119	203
Missouri ..	15	1,931	143	53	1,890	346
Illinois ;...	20	188	161	40	145	267

The above averages give no idea of the wide range over which each of the above characteristics vary; e. g., color in the Mississippi water is sometimes as low as 30 and again as high as 250; suspended solids in the Missouri river water, range from 200 to 6000; dissolved solids at the St. Louis intake from 160 to 390 parts per million.

It is apparent that water entering the St. Louis waterworks' intake, composed as it is of a mixture of the waters of three rivers draining areas entirely distinct and unlike in character, must show at different times the predominant characteristics of each of the three streams according to their respective stages. The turbid water of the Missouri river, whose mouth is only about five miles above the St. Louis intake, at almost all times flows down the west side of the channel and is but imperfectly mixed with the clearer waters of the Mississippi and the Illinois.

Always, there is a very distinct difference in appearance, sharply dividing the two, just below the mouth of the Missouri, which often continues as far south as Sawyers Bend, three miles below the intake.

For this reason the water supply of St. Louis prior to 1915 consisted for a great part of the time of Missouri river water with only a comparatively small amount of mixed Illinois and Mississippi river water added, except at such times as the latter rivers were at higher stages than the Missouri.

This made it all the more difficult to adjust the treatment on those occasions when the Mississippi or the Illinois, or both combined, suddenly brought down water of a high color carrying very fine suspended matter, both of which characteristics being foreign to the Missouri river water, introduced new factors into the problem and often temporarily made it impossible to clarify the compounded waters by coagulation and simple sedimentation.

At the outset of the attempt to clarify the water supply in the spring of 1904, the quantities of chemicals (lime and sulphate of iron), to be applied, were determined empirically, by actual trial on samples taken from the river several times during the day. An excess of lime was always added, which removed all the temporary hardness and left the water slightly caustic. This treatment was capable of producing brilliantly clear water, but had some drawbacks, viz., a rapid coating of the inside of distribution pipes and valves, incrustation on train gears of meters, absolute death to fish in aquariums, through depositing carbonate of lime on their gills and slowly suffocating them; and, so the doctors declared, was productive of stomach troubles in the human family.

The determinations of suspended matter during the first year's attempted clarification, show an average of 30 p.p.m. with a maximum of 97 and a minimum of 0.

Prior to 1904 the water supply of the city, so far as appearance was concerned, was scarcely different from the water in the river. In reality it had passed through the system of settling basins, which ordinarily reduced the suspended matter to probably 150 p.p.m., although there were times, usually in winter or early spring, when the river water was comparatively clear and carried as low as 50 or 60 p.p.m. of suspended matter, and there were also other times of rising water when the suspended matter in the river water reached a figure of 8000 p.p.m. and then the consumer was served with a fluid containing 600 or 800 p.p.m. of sediment, of which Mark Twain said: "Every tumbler full holds an acre of land in solution."

Remembering that the people of St. Louis had been accustomed to using this turbid water for 70 years, it is not surprising that they were exceedingly well pleased with the partially clarified water served in 1904-1905. Each succeeding year saw improvements made in the method of treatment and a better quality of water furnished, until the consumption reached a figure where the settling basin capacity was too small to allow sufficient time for clarification, and there would be periods when an imperfectly clarified water was delivered to consumers. These periods occurred more and more frequently as the consumption increased, and in 1912 the proposition to build filters was seriously considered for the first time, although it had been brought forward and discussed at various times during the half century prior to this date.

For eight years following 1904, the process of clarifying and purifying the river water engrossed the attention of the engineers and chemists of the department. The deficiencies and objectionable features of the treatment, and the resulting troubles, had all been carefully studied and nearly, if not quite all of them, partially remedied or entirely elim-

inated. But throughout all their earnest and enthusiastic work, and in spite of their strong prejudice in favor of a process first tried out on a large scale at the St. Louis Waterworks, and afterwards elaborated there, and brought to its greatest efficiency; they always came up against the one insurmountable obstacle barring the way to perfectly satisfactory results, viz., the absolute impossibility of continually producing a uniformly clear, potable water. For a great part of the time the treated water was unobjectionable, but lapses from this high standard would occur on account of sudden and unexpected changes in weather or river conditions. After sending the water through the basins in a certain order for some time, high winds or sudden changes in the quantity of water being pumped had a strong tendency to increase the turbidity of the treated water. So that with all the inclination in the world to defend and to perpetuate the St. Louis purification process, the men who were most interested in making it successful were at last forced to admit that it was inefficient and inadequate.

The prime object of treating the Mississippi water was at first to remove the suspended matter. Other advantages resulting from its clarification, such as reduction of bacteria, softening and color removal, were merely incidental. Scarcely any weight was attached to the purification of the water, as the popular idea at that time was that the muddy water was particularly healthful. Its appearance was the objectionable feature. The great commercial value of softening the water was not realized for some time after the initiation of the process, but later became one of the salient features of the treatment, and has been continued in conjunction with the operation of the Chain of Rocks filters.

A very few comparative analyses of the raw and treated water were made during the first year (1904) of the purification process, and but half a dozen doubtful counts of bacteria made. The department was poorly equipped with laboratory facilities, having neither the necessary apparatus nor competent men to do the work. During the following year considerable equipment was added to the laboratory and monthly analyses made of the river and treated water. The Health Department made monthly sanitary analyses of the water and regular counts of bacteria were made by the City Bacteriologist.

Although the general statement was made that the quality of the water furnished by the Department in that year was practically all that could be desired, the record shows many times when the treated water was turbid; other times when it carried high counts of bacteria and that it showed caustic alkalinity during the greater portion of the year. The use of 8 and 9 grains of lime and 3 and 4 grains of sulphate of iron per gallon of water was of frequent occurrence.

In 1906 many improvements were made in the methods of handling and applying chemicals, the facilities for chemical and bacteriological analyses were largely increased and the working of the whole process systematized. Caustic alkalinity was frequent in the treated water during the first half of the year, but not allowed afterwards. This year marks the beginning of the scientific study of the problem, of accurate and systematic analyses of the water, and of undertaking to determine the quantities of chemicals required, from actual knowledge of the quality of the river water, rather than from a series of empirical tests.

For more than 8 years afterwards the routine of the chemical and bacteriological work continued along the same lines; viz., determination of the governing characteristics of the river water, from which the dosing of the water was determined, and making daily bacterial examinations of the river and treated water. Turbidity, color, neutral carbonates and bi-carbonates were determined many times every day, and often the charges of lime and sulphate of iron were changed with each determination.

As illustrative of some of the conditions suddenly arising, and which the ordinary treatment failed to meet successfully, may be mentioned the period in 1911 when after general rains over the drainage areas of the upper Mississippi, the Illinois and the lower Missouri rivers, there first came a rush of very muddy water from the rapid run-off from the steeper slopes of the Missouri, followed by a flood of highly-colored upper Mississippi water mixed with the outflow of the rising Illinois, which crowded the diminishing stream of muddy Missouri water over against the west bank, leaving the intake completely surrounded by a coffee-colored fluid, which condition continued for sixteen days. The sulphate of iron added to the river water for the purpose of coagulating suspended matter was not very efficient for removing color. In the presence of dissolved organic coloring matter, iron is held in solution and its precipitation as ferric hydroxide is considerably retarded, even though excess quantities of lime be used in the treatment.

The very fine suspended matter which characterizes the upper Mississippi water does not readily respond to increased doses of iron sulphate, and the treated water is likely to retain in solution and suspension as much as five parts per million of iron, which is sufficient to discolor the flow from hot water faucets, stain the seams of white goods in laundries, and in many ways be a source of annoyance to household consumers.

Lime is effective in precipitating calcium and magnesium carbonates, producing a softening incidental to coagulation. Increasing the charge above that required to react with the carbonate hardness until enough lime has been added to give a strong caustic reaction, will precipitate a portion of the magnesium as hydroxide. This was not an unusual practice in the earlier months of the process and resulted in producing a perfectly clear and colorless water. This was discontinued because of the presence of caustic alkalinity throughout the distribution system, and the consequent incrustation in the mains, service pipes, valves and meters, due to after reactions. The action of lime in precipitating calcium carbonate does not effect any color reduction, but the precipitation of magnesium carbonate does reduce color, provided it is not redissolved from the precipitate.

The operation of the clarification process was hampered at times throughout its entire use, from 1904 to 1915, by its inability to remove color, and also due to the fact that the presence of high color prevented perfect coagulation and resulted in the production of an imperfectly clarified water. Since the completion of the filter plant, it has been possible to use aluminum sulphate for secondary coagulation and for color reduction. The clarification process was often hindered and sometimes rendered entirely inefficient because of high winds agitating the surface of the water as it entered the basins, breaking up the coagulation and preventing sedimentation. As there was no way in which a second treatment of the water could be applied, this imperfectly clarified water had to pass on into the distribution system.

Obtaining uniformly clear and pure water was also often seriously interfered with, because of the stirring up of the light and finely divided precipitate after it had settled to the bottom of the basins. Any marked change in the velocity of the flow through the basins, lifts up the light sediment and redistributes it through the water, making the final effluent turbid with finely divided matter in suspension that will not again readily settle out. Changes in the direction of currents in the basins, caused by differences of temperature between the incoming water and that in the basins, induces new directions of flow which disturb and move the surface deposits on the basin floors. In the autumn, as the air temperature falls, the sediment and water next to the bottom of the basins is sometimes one degree or more (Fahrenheit) warmer than the river water. This tends to change the course of the currents of the incoming water, deepening the flow and increasing the tendency to stir up the sediment. Under the most favorable conditions of operation, the effluent, while appearing very clear to the casual observer, contained small amounts of suspended iron compounds, also small particles of calcium and magnesium compounds, as well as some silt and silicious matter too fine to settle out during the comparatively rapid flow of the water through the settling basins.

A large portion of this material settled out in the distribution mains at points where the velocity was low, only to be flushed out through fire hydrants and house faucets at times of heavy draught. This caused numerous complaints of cloudy water from different quarters of the city, usually occurring after some local disturbance to the regular flow in the mains, such as would be produced by an unusual draught in extinguishing a considerable fire, or from the bursting of a large pipe.

All of the above objectionable features, together with many other difficulties, the department employes studied and endeavored to overcome, with more or less success, but they were finally forced to the conclusion that a satisfactory water could not be uniformly produced from the variable and erratic mixture flowing past our intakes, unless the final step of filtering through rapid sand filters be added to the process used and studied for more than ten years.

After the filter plant was built and placed in operation in May, 1915, there was nothing to complain of, as far as the consumer could judge, but there were occasions when the operating difficulties were greatly increased and the effluent was not all that the chemists and engineers desired. In January, 1916, a flood of water carrying a large amount of extremely fine suspended matter came out of the Illinois river. On account of the heavy floating ice, water had to be taken through both intakes. The Mississippi water with its high color, mixing with the turbid flood from the Illinois, formed a combination of finely divided silt in suspension with organic coloring matter, which did not readily yield to treatment with lime and iron sulphate, so that the prepared water entering the filters had a turbidity as high as 98 p.p.m. representing the very finest of the suspended solids. Some of this fine material found its way through the filters.

Throughout the following year (1917) no especial troubles were encountered, the attention of the working forces being especially directed towards greater economy of operation. Not until February, 1918, was there experienced any trouble similar to that just noted, when again the highly colored water of the Mississippi mixing with the muddy Illinois (both rivers being at high stages), made the water extremely hard to handle. After treatment with lime and iron sulphate the amount of aluminum sulphate required to give the necessary flocculation of the suspended matter ran as high as four grains per gallon. Even with this large use of aluminum sulphate the maximum color of the filtered water was 24 p.p.m. Since that time there has been nothing exceptional in the way of extreme conditions; the usual fluctuations in color, turbidity, alkalinity and dissolved solids occurring and recurring with the changes of the weather and seasons.

In the latter part of 1913 an apparatus for applying liquid chlorine to the clarified water was installed, with the idea that its use would not be commonly required, but would be available in emergencies and on occasions when presence of bacteria of the B. Coli group was suspected. Within a year, however, the application of chlorine became continu-

ous and has so remained until the present time.

This somewhat hurried review of the history of water purification at St. Louis would not be by any means complete if mention were not made of the fact that St. Louis was foremost among American cities to investigate and propose filtration of its water supply. In 1865 the Board of Water Commissioners sent its chief engineer, Mr. James P. Kirkwood, to Europe to examine filters in use there and report on the feasibility of modifying those systems for purifying the Mississippi river water. A year later Mr. Kirkwood made a voluminous report recommending slow sand filters and outlining a design for their construction. The Board did not accept his recommendations and the scheme was abandoned, but from time to time afterwards dissatisfaction with the muddy water culminated in propositions of various kinds for improving its appearance, but little thought seems to have been given to its purity or lack of it.

After the opening of the Chicago Drainage Canal in 1900, the typhoid death rate per 100,000 gradually increased from 23 in 1899, to 47.09 in 1903. Early in 1904 the clarification process was inaugurated and although throughout the whole year the work was in the experimental stage and the results often uncertain and unsatisfactory, yet the typhoid death rate was reduced to 36.23 per 100,000, with a further reduction in 1905 to 18.97. After 1905 the rate never reached this figure again, but was steadily reduced during the succeeding years, reaching the comparatively low figure of 12.43 per 100,000 in 1914, the year preceding the opening of the filter plant. The value of this water treatment to the people of St. Louis, inefficient and unsatisfactory as it was, calculated from a health basis alone runs into figures that are staggering.

If conditions had remained the same it is likely that the typhoid rate of 1903 would have steadily increased, but assuming that it would have remained stationary after 1903, if the water supply had not been clarified, a total of 2536 deaths from typhoid were avoided during the 11 years that the treatment was in use prior to filtration. If the value to the community of the life of each individual be estimated at $3000, and if we assume that the cost of medicines, nurses' and doctors' services and funeral expenses in each fatal case would have been $250, and that the time lost from work in each case would have been six weeks; valued at $150, we will have a total sum of $3400 saved for each death avoided, or a grand total of $8,622,400 as representing the money value to the city of St. Louis of the lives saved through the partial purification of its water supply during 11 years.

It has been calculated from a careful examination of statistics that for every death from typhoid there were from three to four cases which did not terminate fatally. The reports for St. Louis of the number of cases for those 11 years show that out of 7120 cases 1245 deaths occurred; that is, a little more than one-sixth of the cases reported were fatal. To be conservative, let us assume that in avoiding 2536 deaths from typhoid, there were also avoided 7500 cases where the patients recovered. The actual expenditure avoided in each case for medicines, doctors and nurses, including the value of time lost from work, could not have been less than $250, which applied to the 7500 cases amounts to $1,875,000.

Adding this to the amount already calculated as the value of the lives saved, we have more than $10,000,000, or almost $1,000,000 for each year the purification process was in service, as the money value conservatively estimated from the health standpoint alone. The value to the community through being served with a clarified and softened water, *which permitted* the use of a diminished quantity of soap, which assured much greater

convenience and economy for use in steam and hot water p l a n t s , which brought about the disuse of private filters and made the purchase of bottled table waters unnecessary, and which relieved the citizens of the necessity for apologizing to their visitors for the appearance of the water in the toilet and bath, can hard.y be comprehended, much less calculated in cold figures.

The typhoid death rate dropped to 7 per 100,000 in 1915, the first year the filters were operated, rising in 1916 to 9.44; which increase was largely due to cases traced back to persons using water from impure wells and springs outside of St. Louis; in 1917 and 1918 the rate dropped to 7.5; which is, according to some authorities, about as low as could be expected for any large city.

In comparing typhoid statistics of different cities, the writer's attention has been called to a possibility that may tend to vitiate some of these returns; that is, in their zeal to make a good showing for their respective communities, some physicians and health officers record many typhoid cases as intestinal or diarrheal diseases, thus reducing the typhoid rate at the expense of the other disease rate.

A comparison of the published mortality statistics of 12 of the large cities, including St. Louis, seems to bear out this contention. On the deaths from typhoid as reported, St. Louis stands eighth in the list, but if the deaths from diarrheal diseases as reported be combined with those reported from typhoid, St. Louis comes among the first three cities. Again taking the annual death rate from all diseases, St. Louis shares honors with New York for third place.

While it is often said that statistics can be quoted to support almost any contention, it must be accepted as an incontestable fact that the purification of the water supply of St. Louis has added greatly to the healthfulness of the city and made it a more desirable place in which to live.

PERSONAL HYGIENE*

ALISON HANAFORD,
Mansfield, Mass.

To keep children well and happy one must know about personal hygiene. Personal hygiene is the care of our bodies. One should stand erect so that the organs of the body will have plenty of room to do their work.

In walking one should throw the weight of the body forward onto the balls of the feet. The correct position of the foot is pointing straight ahead.

In carrying school books one should carry them under the right arm one day and under the left arm the next day, or divide the books and carry the same number under each arm.

When one reads, the light should shine over the left shoulder or from overhead. One should not read long without looking at some distant object in the room, to rest the muscles of the eye.

The teeth should be cleaned after each meal, to remove any particles of food that remain.

One should take a bath at least once a week in the winter and every day in the summer.

The bowels should move at least once a day, and if not, physic is needed.

Exercise is needed to keep the blood circulating; exercise also gives strength.

Home sanitation is the keeping clean and airing of a house. A house looking south or placed with its corners to the points of the compass has great hygienic value. One should always have plenty of fresh air in their rooms. Sunshine makes the rooms healthier and more cheerful. People living in dark rooms soon grow thin and pale. Oxygen is something in the air that sustains life. Without oxygen one could not live. Impure air is very bad for a person. It is caused by over-crowding, oil stoves, and gas stoves. Good ventilation is needed to keep the room healthful. The best way to ventilate a room is to open the windows both top and bottom.

Housewives should know where their drink-

ing water comes from, and the pipes it goes through. Clear, sparkling water is not always pure.

The rooms should be well cared for, and the windows should be securely screened top and bottom. Screens should be put on before flies and mosquitoes are around and left on until they are gone.

Broken dishes and tin cans should be kept in separate barrels. The garbage should be taken away often.

The dish cloth and towels should be washed and hung in the sunshine after using, and not put away in a dark, warm place.

The hands should be washed before and after eating, after going to the toilet and before touching the baby.

The temperature of the baby's bath water should be between 98° and 100°. The baby's nose, ears, eyes and mouth should be kept clean, and a separate piece of cotton should be used for each nostril, eye and ear. If the baby's scalp is scaly, one should rub it with warm oil or vaseline. The baby's nails should be cleaned with a tooth pick every day, and should be cut often with small scissors. The baby should be dressed warm enough in winter and not too warm in summer. If a baby cannot have breast milk, cow's milk is the next best. The milk should be delivered in sealed bottles. Milk peddled in open cans should not be given to babies. Certified milk is examined by the state and found to be pure —and is the best for baby. If one is not sure the milk is pure, they can pasteurize it. This is done by heating the milk to 145° F. and letting it stay at that temperature for thirty minutes, then quickly cooled. The baby's milk should not be left on the steps, but put in the ice box.

I think there are quite a few things I could do to help save the babies from death, blindness and deafness. Many mothers do not know all they should about babies and they are not all foreigners. I wish that all mothers and girls could have the chance that some other girls and I have had.

*This is one of a group of essays written by pupils of the seventh grade in the public schools of Mansfield, Mass., following the regular instruction of the school system in Sanitation and Hygiene. It seems worth while to present it to show what is really done through public school work.

IMPROVEMENT IN VACUUM METHOD OF FILLING CAPILLARY TUBES

THOMAS A. WATSON,

Bureau of Laboratories, Department of Health,

New York City

The vacuum method, being a government requirement, is now generally used for filling capillary tubes with vaccine virus. In this method the capillary tubes sealed at one end are placed with the sealed ends uppermost in a cylindrical container together with a glass tube $\frac{3}{16}$-inch in calibre and open at both ends. This large tube is placed in the center of the capillary tubes and is used for introducing the virus. (See illustration.) After the glassware has been sterilized the required amount (6.5 cc. of virus to 300 capillary tubes) is poured through the larger tube and the container placed in a vacuum apparatus. The air is carefully withdrawn until a vacuum of 18 inches is produced. By allowing the air to re-enter very slowly the virus rises to the desired position, usually slightly above the center, and is retained there.

Difficulty has been experienced from time to time in getting the desired amount of virus inside the maximum number of tubes, instead of outside of them, with a resulting loss of virus and labor. The trouble is, however, not constant. It has been traced finally to two factors; first, the difference in the finish of the ends of various batches of capillary tubes; second, the arrangement of the capillary tubes in the cylindrical container.

(1) Some batches of capillary tubes have the ends cut smoothly and evenly across, while others are more or less irregular. It is the smooth-cut ends which give rise to trouble by fitting too closely to the bottom of the glass container. This may be overcome by using a disc of wire gauze of No. 20 or No. 40 mesh in the lower part of the container to raise the ends of tubes from the bottom.

(2) In filling the container with capillary tubes it is advisable not to pack them tightly, for with tight packing the virus

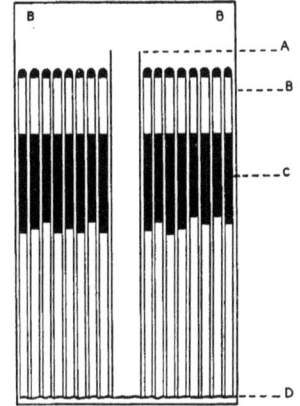

Cross section of cylindrical container with capillary tubes.

A - Filling Tube   B - Cylindrical Container

C - Virus   D - Wire Gauze.

tends to rise between the tubes, possibly on account of capillary attraction.

In the older method the loss by imperfect filling of the tubes was as high as 40 to 50 per cent; with the use of the improved method this loss is reduced to about 4 per cent.

EDITORIAL SECTION

AMERICAN JOURNAL OF PUBLIC HEALTH

Publication Office: 124 W. Polk Street, Chicago, Ill.
EDITORIAL OFFICE: 169 MASSACHUSETTS AVE., BOSTON, MASS.
A. W. HEDRICH, C. P. H., Editor   J. RITCHIE, Jr., Associate Editor

Editorial Assistants

E. R. HAYHURST, M.D.   DAVID GREENBERG   JAMES A. TOBEY
R. P. ALBAUGH, M.D.   M. P. HORWOOD, M.S.   FRANCIS H. SLACK, M.D.
E. B. STARR, M.D.   P. M. HOLMES, M.D.   JAMES M. STRANG

Board of Advisory Editors

PETER H. BRYCE, M.D., Ottawa, Canada   PROF. M. J. ROSENAU, Boston, Mass.
CHARLES V. CHAPIN, M.D., Providence, R. I.   PROF. W. T. SEDGWICK, Cambridge, Mass.
EUGENE R. KELLEY, M.D., Boston, Mass.   PROF. GEORGE C. WHIPPLE, Cambridge, Mass.
W. A. EVANS, M.D., Chicago, Ill.   PROF. S. M. GUNN, Paris, France.

All expressions of opinion and all statements of supposed facts are published on authority of the writer under whose name they appear, and are not to be regarded as expressing the views of the American Public Health Association, unless such statements or opinions have been adopted by vote of the Association.

NOTICE TO SUBSCRIBERS: Subscription Price, payable in advance, $4.00 per year for United States and possessions; $4.50 for Canada and other foreign countries. Single copies, 50 cents postpaid. Membership in the American Public Health Association, including subscription to Journal, $5.00 per year. In Change of Address please give both old and new address, and mail before the tenth of the month to take effect with the current issue. Mailing Date, 5th of each month. Advertisements accepted only when commendable, and worth while both to reader and advertiser. News Items, interesting clippings and illustrations are gladly received, together with name of sender. Copyright, 1919, by A. W. Hedrich.

PAPERS FOR NEXT ANNUAL MEETING.

The American Public Health Association at the New Orleans meeting last October took into consideration the important matter of programs. In a conference of the officers of the sections tentative standards were formulated and these will be tried out at the California meeting, August 30-September 3, 1920.

One point which was brought out in the discussion is that the number of papers in all the programs should be limited. In past years, in an endeavor to present as many view points as possible as many as 12 to 14 papers have been presented at a single session. This is obviously a mistake, for the delegate who sits through a session so filled with papers leaves the hall fatigued and with confused impressions. For this reason it is recommended that hereafter the maximum of papers for any one session be 6 and that for most of the programs it be confined to three or four. It is quite possible that the limitation of papers will cause some measure of dissatisfaction among members whose papers can not be heard for want of space. While the Association is desirous of presenting opportunities for the expression of new information and fresh opinions regarding public health, it is felt that crowding the programs defeats the real purpose of the Annual Meeting. It is better for the delegate to carry away a number of clear conceptions related to his work than to go home tired and confused.

Important here are the discussions of the papers, and it is well known that they constitute a factor to the meeting that is quite as interesting and quite as important as the original papers. These discussions must usually be cut out when the sessions are crowded with announced papers.

It was further decided at the conference of section officers, that programs should be made up on a unified plan, and that a number of papers focused on a subject of vital interest should be presented in symposium form. When possible, speakers should be invited who can best furnish the information desired.

It is possible, of course, to drive such a method to an extreme, but this must be avoided. There will always be excellent papers spontaneously offered. There are interesting speakers with good material who might not be thought of by the program committees. The plan of pre-arrangement would avoid including in the programs, papers that have no close relationships to the central theme. Such a method, however, should not be carried to the extreme. There will be, on that account, space reserved for papers offered spontanously, since they may be of importance.

Another matter which experience has shown as exceedingly important in connection with the annual meetings is the presentation of manuscripts to the section program committees. This should be done by the authors at least 30 days before the meetings and if possible, 45 days. Extemporaneous papers or those hastily prepared on the train *en route* for the meeting are usually not of high standard. The early presentation of the manuscript affords to the publication committees the chance to read all the papers and to prepare publication schedules to go into effect immediately after the meeting.

The presentation of manuscripts has another distinct advantage : the program becomes more stable and members are assured that the papers listed will be read. The speakers are pretty certain to be present and the audience will be spared the annoyance of coming to a meeting only to find that the announced speaker has neither come himself nor sent his paper. Those who attend the large meetings of associations know this to be a real difficulty with some programs. There is a bit of gossip that in one program of eight papers, not one of the speakers appeared. To avoid this difficulty there are a number of associations which absolutely refuse to publish names in the programs unless manuscripts are in the hands of the proper officials.

One further matter that is worthy the attention of those who propose to present papers before the A. P. H. A., is that of press abstracts. The author who sends to his program chairman well in advance of the meeting an abstract of his paper of from 150 to 200 words, has reasonable chances that his paper will be noted by the daily press of the country, an advantage that every one who has seen the recent campaigns for publicity during the war, should appreciate.

IS THERE HOPE FOR THE HEALTH OFFICER?

At the present moment the financial sky for most health officers is quite cloudy. The cost of living at the present time is 82% higher than it was in 1914. The income of the public health worker has been increased in no such ratio.

The situation, however, should not be considered hopeless. Competent statisticians predict that within the next few years there will be a marked decline in the cost of living. The existing high costs are due chiefly to two causes : the shortage of goods on account of the war and the increase in labor costs. Even if labor costs should not be greatly reduced, the supply of goods must before long catch up with the demand. History shows a constant alternation of undersupply and oversupply of commodities. During normal times the peaks of oversupply are four to five years apart, and the minima of supply show about the same periodicity.

Economic study of the periods succeeding each of the wars demonstrates a great scarcity of goods with extremely high prices during and immediately following the war. The earnings of manufacturers and distributors are increased very largely, with the result that optimism rules and a boom of overproduction follows.

Presently the shelves of the dealers are filled and buying moderates. Active competition soon begins to reduce prices and, once on the downgrade, prices are inclined to tumble. Dealers hasten to dispose of stocks while they can still obtain fair prices. This process must continue until normal, and even subnormal prices are established.

In the meantime, the health worker will do well to sit tight. If, as a number of economists have asserted, we are to experience a financial flurry within the next few years, the man in the official position will have the advantage over the servant of industry. The latter in retrenching may have to cut deeply.

☐

In Memoriam

HENRY B. BAKER

On Easter morning Henry B. Baker, physician, sanitarian and active administrator in public health passed to his long rest. By his death the list of past presidents of the American Public Health Association is diminished by a man never afraid to work, and never inactive in the face of duty.

Dr. Baker was born in Brattleboro, Vt., in 1837. He was of the number sent by his native state to fight in the War of the Rebellion, and served with the Army of the North from 1862 till the end of the strife. A few years later he took up the practice of medicine, for which he had been trained, and while thus occupied he became convinced of the value of sanitation and prevention. Established in the West, he was a leading spirit in 1870 in the introduction and support of a bill in the Michigan Legislature for the establishment of the State Board of Health. Three years later the bill was enacted, and he was appointed Secretary of the new Board, a position which he held till 1905. At that time he removed from Lansing to his farm at Holland, Mich., which was his home till his death.

A member of the American Public Health Association from the second year of its existence he quickly became influential in its work. His name appears in the successive lists as member of the Advisory Council, of the Committee on Statistics and later on of the Committee for the Restriction and Prevention of Tuberculosis. He was elected President of the Association in 1899, serving till his successor Dr. Frederick Montizambert was installed the next year. In his presidential address at the Charleston meeting of the Association, Dr. Baker showed prophetic vision. He then discussed the causation of diseases and advocated prevention. He considered the causation of diphtheria, of yellow fever, and immunity through inoculation. In speaking of the quarantine by Government authorities, he dwelt on its value, but advocated its extension. "Something more than merely continuing the present methods of quarantine is needed," he said. "Diphtheria and scarlet fever should be excluded by quarantines; but the entire country is permeated with those diseases, and with the still more important one—consumption, and a Health Department of the Interior needed to be established at Washington." Today, twenty years later, the country has waked to the real necessity of what he then voiced, and the laws which have in view such a department are now before Congress.

President Baker's address foretold the practical application of sanitary science and emphasized the importance of state boards of health. These topics were a measure of the man, and today what he advocated as a pioneer has in considerable part become the knowledge of intelligent people. His address of December, 1890, is a standard whereby to measure the strides forward of public health since that day.

In the past twenty years Dr. Baker has kept constantly at work spreading the gospels of prevention and health education, and his work has been sincere and without ostentation or the craving for public office.

□

CONVENTIONS, CONFERENCES, MEETINGS

May 18-20, Parkersburg, W. Va., West Virginia State Medical Association.

May 19-20, Rockford, Ill., Illinois Medical Society, Public Health Section.

May 19-20, New Haven, Conn., Connecticut State Medical Society.

May 24-25, Washington, D. C., Conference Royal (English) Institute of Public Health.

May 24-25, Washington, D. C., State and Provincial Health Authorities of North America.

May 24-25, Charlotte, N. C., Southeastern Sanitary Association.

May 24-26, Omaha, Neb., Nebraska State Health Association.

May 24-26, Omaha, Neb., Nebraska State Medical Association.

May 25-26, Toronto, Ontario, Ontario Health Association.

May 25-27, Kalamazoo, Mich., Michigan State Health Officers' Association.

May 25-27, Kalamazoo, Mich., Michigan State Medical Society.

May 25-27, Columbus, O., Ohio Hospital Association.

May 26-27, Washington, D. C., Conference of last-named with Surgeon General, U. S. P. H. Service.

May 31-June 2, Highland Park, Ill., American Pediatric Society.

June —, New Orleans, La., American Association of Industrial Physicians and Surgeons.

June —, Duluth, Minn., Minnesota Hospital Association.

June —, Coeur d'Alene, Idaho State Medical Association.

June 1-3, Toledo, O., Ohio State Medical Association.

June 1-4, Cleveland, Ohio, American Medico-Physiological Association.

June 3, Providence, R. I., Rhode Island Medical Society.

June 3-5, Portland, Ore., Oregon State Medical Association.

June 8-9, Boston, Mass., Massachusetts Medical Society.

June 8-9, Eureka Springs, Ark., Arkansas Medical Society.

June 15-16, Minot, N. D., North Dakota State Medical Association.

June 21, Vancouver B. C., Canadian Public Health Association.

June 21, Vancouver, B. C., Canadian Medical Association.

June 21, Vancouver, B. C., Canadian Health Officers' Association.

June 21, Vancouver, B. C., Canadian National Tuberculosis Association, Vancouver, B. C.

June 21, Vancouver, B. C., Dominion Committee for Venereal Diseases.

June 21, Vancouver, B. C., Dominion Committee for Mental Hygiene.

June 21, Vancouver, B. C., British Columbia Hospital Association.

June 21-25, Montreal, Can., American Water Works Association.

June 23-25, St. Paul, Minn., Catholic Hospital Association.

July —, Regina, Sask., Saskatchewan Medical Association.

July 1, Antigonish, N. S., Association of Health Officers of Nova Scotia.

July 12-13, Helena, Mont., Montana State Health Officers' Association.

July 16-17, Seattle, Wash., Washington Health Officers' Association.

September 13-17, San Francisco, Cal., American Public Health Association.

ASSOCIATION NEWS

For Campaign News and the Lists of Proposed New Members, See Last Pages of Text at the End of the Notes Section

---

REPORT (FOURTH SUPPLEMENTARY) OF THE COMITTEE ON STANDARD METHODS FOR THE EXAMINATION OF THE AIR*

The Committee on Standard Methods for the Examination of Air was first appointed in 1907. It presented two preliminary progress reports, in 1909 (American Journal of Public Hygiene, XX, 346) and in 1912 (American Journal of Public Health, III, 78), and a final report in 1916 (American Journal of Public Health, VII, 54).

It seems desirable at this time to review the progress that has been made in certain directions since the last report was presented.

REVIEW OF PREVIOUS RECOMMENDATIONS

In its "final" report of October 27, 1916, the committee recommended the use of:

1. Continuous recording thermometers (supplemented when necessary by the use of accurate mercury thermometers without backs)

*Presented before Laboratory Section, American Public Health Association, at New Orleans, La., October 27, 1919.

and of standard sling psychrometers for the study of temperature and humidity.

2. The katathermometer for the measurement of the rate of heat loss.

3. The Pitot tube and anemometer for the measurement of the rate of air flow.

4. The Palmer apparatus for the study of the dust content of the air.

5. A sand filter of the Ruehle type for the study of bacteria.

6. The Petterson-Palmquist or Haldane apparatus for the study of carbon dioxide.

All of the recommended procedures have been more or less continuously in use by members of the Committee and others, and so far as the Committee is aware have given reasonably satisfactory results. In regard to two points only, the use of the katathermometer for the measurement of heat loss and the determination of the dust content of air, is there anything material to be added to the 1916 report?

USE OF THE KATATHERMOMETER AS A MEASURE OF THE RATE OF HEAT LOSS

Studies of the rate of heat loss by the use of the katathermometer have been made by ·Leonard Hill in England and by investigators working with the New York State Commission on Ventilation and the Division of Industrial Hygiene of the United States Public Health Service in this country. The instrument has in the main proved itself delicate and reliable, but the recent investigations have brought out certain points in regard to the interpretation of the results obtained which are deserving of comment.

The value of the katathermometer lies, of course, in the fact that it measures heat loss from a warm surface as determined by air movement as well as by atmospheric temperature and humidity. It does not necessarily follow, however, that the relative influence of air movement and air temperature on the exposed kata bulb will be the same as that upon the human body which is so largely protected by clothing. Investigations of the New York State Commission on ventilation, not yet published, indicate that the katathermometer reading which coincides with comfort is distinctly higher when there is much air movement than when the air is stagnant. In other words, the katathermometer responds more readily to air movement than does the clothed human body. The same point has been brought out in another unpublished series of investigations carried out in the Di-

vision of Industrial Hygiene of the U. S. Public Health Service, in which it appeared that a kathathermometer heat loss of approximately 5 millicalories per square centimeter per second coincided with comfort under stagnant atmospheric conditions indoors, whereas the value was nearer 6 when comfort was compared with katathermometer records in actively moving air. Similar differences have been brought out by Leonard Hill in his monograph the *Science of Ventilation and Open Air Treatment, Part I,* which has recently been published as *Special Report No. 32* of the Medical Research Committee of Great Britain.

Dr. Hill in chapter 2 of this monograph reviews results of LeFevre in regard to the rate of cooling of a pigling (whose body is practically unprotected) as compared with a scanty-haired monkey and a heavily fur-coated dog, and of the naked and clothed body of man, and compares the rate of cooling of the ordinary kata bulb and of a kata bulb protected by a cloth envelope. His figures and curves indicate clearly the greater relative effect of air movement upon the naked body and the unprotected kata bulb as compared with the clothed body or the fur-coated animal.

We desire to call attention to these facts because they introduce appreciable difficulties in the establishment of definite standards of heat loss, as measured by the katathermometer, which can be assumed to correspond with comfort. For indoor conditions with fairly stagnant air, however, heat loss from the dry kata corresponding to 5 millicalories per square centimeter per second may be assumed as reasonably satisfactory.

In view of the importance of humidity in determining human comfort we had hoped that results attained with the wet kata bulb might be particularly significant, and in the practical work conducted for the U. S. Public Health Service it was found that the wet kata even in uncomfortably warm air falls so rapidly that it is somewhat difficult to obtain significant results. When the results of the wet kata are expressed in millicalories the values are large and look impressive, but a variation between a heat loss of 12 millicalories and one of 17 on the wet kata in still air corresponds only to a time difference between 43 and 30 seconds,—a difference which local and temporary air currents might account for. We have found, however, as Hill suggested in one of his earlier papers, that a heat loss of 20 millicalories on the wet kata is a limit that is not exceeded under comfortable conditions.

DETERMINATION OF THE DUST CONTENT OF THE ATMOSPHERE BY THE HILL DUST COUNTER AND THE KOTZÉ KONIMETER

In the earlier reports of the Committee various methods of determining the dust content of air were reviewed and our investigations finally led us to the conclusion that the Palmer water spray apparatus would furnish the most satisfactory device for this purpose. Since our last report was published several new procedures have been suggested which deserve consideration at this time.

Graham Rogers and others have in the past made numerous attempts to collect dust particles suspended in the air by causing a current of air to impinge against a surface covered with glycerin or some other adhesive material. The earlier procedures of this kind proved unsatisfactory, but a device of this type has again been advocated by Dr. E. Vernon Hill of the Chicago Department of Health (*Heating and Ventilating Magazine*, June, 1917, p. 23). Dr. Vernon Hill's dust counter consists of an exhaust pump for producing the movement of the air and a small capsule or shield fixed at the end of the pump, carrying a cover glass covered with adhesive material for catching and retaining the dust. Dr. Hill has tested the accuracy of this apparatus by setting up six or more capsules in succession in series and causing the air to impinge upon one plate after another in succession. From this test he concludes that the first place takes out 62% of the dust present. It seems obvious, however, that the removal of a particle of a given size and weight by an apparatus of this kind will depend primarily upon the velocity with which the air current approaches the adhesive plate. Large and heavy particles will be thrown against the first plate. Small and light particles, whose momentum is so light that they are carried around the first plate, will be carried around any number of plates that may be placed in series, so that this method of controling results obtained is of little value. The actual counts obtained by Dr. Hill are so exceedingly low (from 500 to 1,500 per cubic foot in clean outdoor air, and from 10,000 to 30,000 in ordinary schoolroom air) as to make it reasonably clear that his

apparatus collects only a fraction of the dust particles actually present.

The exceedingly significant investigations of the Miners' Phthisis Prevention Committee of South Africa (Pretoria 1919) have made it clear that it is precisely the small particles of dust which are most important from the standpoint of health, and the South African Committee criticises both Hill's dust counter and the Palmer water spray apparatus on the ground that they fail to reveal these small particles. So far as the Palmer water spray method is concerned this criticism appears to be based on a misconception, as it states that Palmer and his associates did not count any particles smaller than 10 microns in diameter, whereas the Palmer method includes all particles down to a visible size. The Hill dust counter, however, certainly fails to collect the fine particles which are of chief sanitary significance and seems to us of very limited value in ventilation investigations.

The South African Committee has, however, devised and used a dust sampling device described under the name of the Kotzé konimeter, which is based on exactly the same principle as the Hill dust counter but in which the nozzle through which the air passes is very small and the air being forced through this small opening by a piston rod moved with great rapidity by a brass spring. The velocity of the air impinging on the plate is sufficient to give a practically complete sample of even the minute particles of dust. The strength of the piston spring is sufficient to give a calculated velocity of air to the impinging nozzle of not less than 30 or more than 80 m. per second, and the slide for collecting the dust is coated with vaseline. This apparatus is described in detail in the final report of the South African Commission, and results obtained by the use of the instrument have been recently presented by Inness, J. Chem. Met. Min. Soc., South Africa, 19, 132.

The Kotzé konimeter seems to be an admirable piece of apparatus for determining the number of dust particles in the air. If one must choose between the determination of weight and number, the number of particles, as the South African Committee points out, is undoubtedly the more important point; but the Palmer apparatus has the advantage of making it possible to determine both the number and the weight.

DETERMINATION OF THE DUST CONTENT OF THE
ATMOSPHERE BY ELECTROSTATIC
PRECIPITATION

In our last report we called attention to some preliminary studies made by Dr. Mac-Millan of the New York City Department of Health on the precipitation of dust in air by the use of a high tension pole. A method of this kind has been extensively studied during the past two years by Dr. J. P. Bill in the laboratory of Preventive Medicine at Harvard Medical School, and Dr. Bill has very courteously furnished the Committee with the statement quoted below in regard to the comparative value of his apparatus and the Palmer water spray sampler. The dust in Dr. Bill's experiments was collected by drawing air by a motor at the rate of 273 cu. ft. per hour through a 12-inch length of aluminum tube 2½ inches in diameter. The dust was precipitated in this tube by a rectified alternating current of about 20,000 volts.

"Seventy-one tests, each of one hour's duration, were made with this apparatus and a Palmer water spray sampler in the various buildings and departments of a large plant rubber goods. The following determinations were made for each test:

"Relative and absolute humidity, barometric pressure, weight of total sediment in 50 cc. sample of 100 cc. aqueous suspension of particles collected in both machines, weight of organic and inorganic fractions of each 50 cc. sample, the weight of the aluminum collector before testing, with its accumulated dust charge, and with the dust portion still retained after rinsing out to make up a 100 cc. aqueous suspension. Counts were made on each suspension.

"The high tension weight figures were reduced to figures comparable with the rate of air passage through the Palmer machine (240 cubic feet per hour) by multiplying by the fraction 240/273. The resulting figures when compared with the weight figures of the Palmer and high tension suspensions, show, on a percentum basis, that the Palmer apparatus collected 59.9 per cent of total particles counted in the high tension suspensions, 63.3 per cent of the total sediment, 66.6 per cent organic portion, and 55.2 per cent inorganic portion collected by the electrical machine. Based on total sediments collected per 240 cubic feet of air in each process whose air was sampled, the Palmer collected 63.0 per

cent of the amount retained by the electrical method.

"The conclusions are that the Palmer apparatus under similar conditions is 61.6 per cent as efficient as the electrical method (average of above figures). The electrical apparatus used is too bulky for ordinary field work, and suggestions are made for its simplification. It is felt that the findings warrant further study of the electrical precipitation method as applied to the sanitary analysis of air."

CONCLUSIONS IN REGARD TO A STANDARD
METHOD FOR THE DETERMINATION OF
THE DUST CONTENT OF THE
ATMOSPHERE

It seems evident to your committee that there are three distinct methods which may be used with reasonable success for the determination of the dust content of the air. Their special advantages and disadvantages appear to be as follows:

The Palmer water spray apparatus is fairly convenient and portable and permits the determination of the total weight of dust as well as the number of particles in a given sample. It yields, however, only about 60% of the total dust present in the air.

The Kotzé konimeter is even more convenient and portable than the Palmer water spray apparatus, but it is not possible by its use to determine the weight of dust as well as the number of particles present. Exact comparative data as to the proportion of dust obtained by these two methods are not at present available.

The Bill electrostatic method yields more accurate results than those obtained by the Palmer apparatus and could of course be used for determining counts as well as weights of dust. On the other hand the apparatus is not as yet in form sufficiently convenient for ordinary field work.

With all the facts in mind we are inclined to recommend that the Palmer water spray apparatus be retained for the present as the standard method for the determination of the dust content of air. It seems probable that the failure to collect all the dust actually found to be present by the electrostatic method will not seriously affect the relative values obtained in different environments. Recent studies of actual atmospheric conditions in industrial plants (Miller and Smyth, Jour. A. M. A. 70, 599; Winslow, Greenburg and Amgermyer, *Public Health Reports*, March 7, 1919; Winslow, Greenburg and Greenberg, *Public Health Reports*, May 30, 1919) have shown that the Palmer method yields clean cut and satisfactory results, high counts being obtained in shops which are dangerously dusty and low counts being uniformly obtainable by the application of recognized methods of dust removal.

If later studies should indicate that the Kotzé konimeter yields materially higher results than the Palmer water spray apparatus, or if the Bill electrostatic collector should be made portable and convenient for field work, one or the other of these two devices should be adopted; but for the present we believe it is wisest to retain the Palmer apparatus for ordinary sanitary use.

C.-E. A. WINSLOW, Chairman.
T. R. CROWDER
W. P. MASON
E. B. PHELPS
G. C. WHIPPLE.

□

BOOKS AND REPORTS REVIEWED

Pellagra.—*H. F. Harris, M. D., New York: The Macmillian Company, 1919. Price $5.00. Pp. 421.*

The author's object in the preparation of this monograph was to make accessible to the English reader as complete a résumé as possible of the foreign literature on pellagra. In reviewing this literature it is amazing to note that such a considerable amount of study has been devoted to this disease. As to the theories of the causation of pellagra it is to be noted the studies in the past were not entirely limited to the maize hypothesis and that of the theories which have recently been put forward scarcely one is fundamentally new. Harris' view is that heredity is an important factor in the etiology of the disease. His conception of endemic pellagra is as follows:

Pellagra is an extremely chronic endemic affection common in tropical and subtropical countries, from habitual consumption of Indian corn, probably more directly the result of the action of certain phenol poisons produced by moulds while growing in this cereal and possibly of albuminous and ferment toxines contained in sound maize, all of which together acting from one generation to another and not unlikely intensified by bad hygienic conditions and insufficient and imperfect food, ultimately culminate in a frank outbreak of the classical symptoms of this disease. The malady is probably always hereditary.

Much space is devoted to consideration of the pathological anatomy and symptomatology of the disease. Harris groups the symptoms into three stages:

(1) Early stage—in which there is a progressive physiological deterioration of the entire body accompanied by dyspeptic nervous symptoms.

(2) An intermediate period in which the clinical features are more severe, there being recurring attacks and with intervals of fairly good health.

(3) A final stage in which one or more of the severer clinical phenomena persists throughout.

The matters of diagnosis prognosis and treatment are taken up in great detail. In the problem of prophylaxis the author's view is that in order to prevent the disease the consumption of maize must be greatly restricted and since the disease is hereditary we can not expect a complete cessation of the malady until at least one generation has passed following the institution of such measures. Some of the measures proposed are the cultivation of the best varieties of maize, development of proper methods of milling and the detection and rejection of spoiled maize.

This volume is complete in every detail in the consideration of a problem which is of such great moment to public health authorities, particularly in our Southern States.

D. GREENBERG.

SAN FRANCISCO CITY AND COUNTY DEPARTMENT OF PUBLIC HEALTH

Members of the American Public Health Association who will attend in numbers the Annual Convention in San Francisco, Cal., September 13-17, 1920, will have an opportunity to become well acquainted with the Department of Health of the city and county, of which William C. Hassler, M. D., is Health Officer.

The Board of Health consists of seven members, three physicians and four laymen, appointed by the Mayor for a term of seven years each. Annually one member retires and is either re-appointed or a new member takes his place.

The Department of Health has the management and control of the City and County Hospital (San Francisco Hospital), Almshouses, (Relief Home for Aged and Infirm), ambulance service, municipal hospitals and receiving hospitals. The latter three are embodied in what is known as the Emergency Hospital Service, which consists of five emergency stations located in parts of the city where the same will serve the greatest number of people. Four of these hospitals are equipped to give first-aid and have a personnel of 3 physicians, 3 hospital stewards and 3 ambulance drivers. Connected with the hospital is an ambulance that serves the district outlined for the particular hospital. One Central Emergency Hospital is maintained, which cares for all cases that require detention or restraint, and is also equipped to do any major surgery that may be brought there from one or the other ambulance stations when the case requires special attention.

The Health Department is charged with the duty of the preservation, promotion and protection of the life and health of the inhabitants of the city and county, determines the nature and character of nuisances and provides for their abatement. It has sanitary supervision of the municipal institutions of the city and county other than those named above, including jails, schoolhouses and public buildings; of the disposition of the dead; of the disposition of garbage, offal and other offensive substance. It has the control and disposition of all expenditures necessary in the institutions under its immediate control and annually fixes the salaries and duties of all appointees of the Department.

It maintains a Social Service Department with two city physicians attached thereto, whose duties are to investigate and treat any cases of sickness reported when the persons are unable to afford private physicians or private hospital treatment. Through this Department all indigents, and others requiring hospital treatment and unable to pay for same are admitted to the San Francisco Hospital or the Relief Home.

The Executive Officer of the Department is the Health Officer who has general supervision over all institutions under the direction of the Board of Health. In addition he has supervision over the following bureaus and divisions:

Bureau of Sanitation and Laboratories. In this Bureau there is a plumbing division with five inspectors who have charge of the installation of all plumbing in new buildings and all alterations made in old structures.

Division of Epidemiology which deals with communicable diseases and the abatement of nuisances.

Division of Child Hygiene which licenses foster-homes for children and has supervision of the health centers.

Division of factory and work shop inspection, disinfection, tenement house inspection, and market inspection, which supervises the anti-mortem and post-mortem inspection of all animals killed for food in the city and county of San Francisco. The force is composed of five veterinarians and ten lay market inspectors.

Division of Food, Milk and Dairy Inspection.

Division of School Health Inspection, consisting of 11 nurses, 3 physicians and one chief inspector.

The annual appropriation to the Health Department for the fiscal year 1919-20 for the maintenance of the institutions, laboratories and inspection divisions under its care and control amounted to $1,268,000.

Anent the San Francisco Meeting, September 13-17, 1920. Note the Revised Date. How about going on the A. P. H. A. Special Train? See last text pages of this Issue for Itinerary.

SAN FRANCISCO HOSPITAL

The JOURNAL is fortunate in being able to present a picture of the San Francisco Hospital of which the Department of Health has the management. The original hospital was erected in 1872, and as larger quarters became necessary, additional buildings were added until there were in all some 16 structures in the group.

In 1908, following a special election for authority to incur the indebtedness, a bond issue of $2,000,000, the construction of the new hospital was begun. It was evident later that the sum voted would not be sufficient, so that in 1917, the main group of buildings having been declared ready for occupancy in 1915, a further sum of $1,500,000 was voted for the hospital.

The general hospital, the ward wings of which are shown in the illustration, has a capacity of 512 beds with the possibility of a maximum of 752 if needed. The wards run east and west and are connected to a wide corridor which extends the length of the site and unites all the structures. The wards are 110 ft. by 26 ft., 26 beds each, with two separation wards of two beds each, the allowance of air space being 1500 square feet for each patient. In the administration end of each ward there is a diet kitchen with dining room attached, a laboratory, a dressing room where minor operations may be performed, utility rooms and a large solarium. An elevator large enough to take a bed with four attendants is in operation in each ward building. Administration, receiving building, nurses' home, communicable diseases and the necessary power plant, laundry, etc., are provided for in commodious and convenient quarters, while the tuberculosis group is an adjacent unit of several buildings, connected with the same long corridor. The accommodations here are for 250 patients. The wards are so liberally provided with windows that it is possible to make of any one of them an open ward.

One feature that might be specially dwelt upon in connection with the conduct of the San Francisco Hospital is that this institution has a training school for nurses, the number at present being about 120, and has a capacity for training about 144 nurses. The medical and surgical staffs for the treatment of patients are recommended by the faculties of the University of California and Stanford University Medical Schools and appointed by the Board of Health.

In connection with the acute Tuberculosis Hospital in the San Francisco Hospital group, the city is now negotiating for the purchase of a country sanatorium which will care for 100 adult cases and connected with this institution will be a place for the care of approximately 50 children.

PUBLIC HEALTH NOTES

Abstracts by D. GREENBERG, M. P. HORWOOD and MAYO TOLMAN.

Artificial Tuberculosis Infection Through Respiratory Route.—In an experimental study on the artificial tuberculosis infection of guinea pigs through the respiratory route, in which by way of the mouth was excluded, the author found: That a single spraying of five minutes with a suspension of tuberculous sputum, produced pulmonary tuberculosis in 100 per cent of guinea pigs when they were exposed to the spray. The tubercles became visible in the lungs microscopically on the 7th day, at which time the tracheobronchial glands showed distinct involvement. After the 18th day tubercles were frequently found in the liver and spleen. Microscopically, after 24 hours, localized interstitial cellular infiltrations were found and after 48 hours the infiltrations became generalized. On the 11th day, large consolidated areas were present. Inoculation experiments showed that when guinea pigs were kept in a spray of tuberculous sputum for five minutes, tubercle bacilli were present in the lungs 15 minutes later. In order to eliminate the possibility of the microörganisms having been absorbed from the nasal mucous membrane, the following parallel experiment was made on the same day. Twelve adult male guinea pigs were selected, and the same sputum used in the above spraying experiment, but undiluted, was placed inside their noses with a small wooden applicator and the pigs kept in a separate group. They were etherized and examined 18 days later with the following results: A single tubercle was found in the lungs of one pig; in the remaining 11 the lungs were entirely free. The cervical glands were involved in every pig. The spleen showed involvement in 5, the liver in 2 and the mesenteric glands in 5.—J. B. Rogers, *Am. Rev. of Tuber*, February, 1920, 750. (*D. G.*)

✛

Maternal Mortality.—The records of life insurance companies show that for all women under 45 years of age who are insured, the diseases of pregnancy and the puerperal state are the second greatest cause of death. It is believed that a considerable percentage of these deaths from childbirth were recorded on the death certificates as being due to tuberculosis, heart disease, etc., and that the applicant for insurance remembered the asso-ciated childbirth and not the cause of death given in the death certificate. Our present mortality records do not show the frequency with which childbirth is a contributing cause of death. The present maternal mortality may be greatly reduced by application of our present obstetric knowledge. Systematic education similar to that used in combating tuberculosis is needed. Increased hospital facilities and nursing service must be provided. The state should furnish assistance in giving poor women the proper care during pregnancy, labor and puerperium. For the present, more hospital beds may be made available by sending women home by ambulance early in the puerperium and caring for them through an out-patient nursing service.—C. H. Davis, *Jour. A. M. A.*, Feb. 21, 1920. (*D. G.*)

✛

The Eye a Channel of Infection in Respiratory Diseases.—Only recently has it been demonstrated that the eye might be an important channel of infection in respiratory diseases. Maxcy (Jour. A. M. A., Mar. 1, 1919) showed that *B. prodigiosus* introduced into the conjunctival sac can be recovered from the nose in five minutes, from the throat in 15 minutes, and from the stools in 24 hours. Corper and Enright have attempted to corroborate and elaborate on these experiments. The experiments were carried out on tuberculous patients, capable of expectorating sputum. The time factor after instillation, the course followed, the distribution after indigestion were all tested, *B. prodigiosus* being used, and the authors conclude that the eye must be considered as one of the most important portals of respiratory infection. Although the greater part of infectious material entering the eye was subsequently swallowed and taken into the gastro-intestinal tract they found that a small, but definite portion reaches the larynx and trachea, where it may persist as long as a week. In passing from the eyes it traverses a definite channel, according to the eye it has entered. Infectious material that has been ingested is far less liable to reach the respiratory tract than that entering by way of the eye or nose.—H. J. Corper and J. J. Enright, *Jour. A. M. A.*, Feb. 21, 1920. (*D. G.*)

Feeding Brazilian Babies.—From the report of the activities of the Instituto de Puericultra at Buenos Aires, Brazil, it appears that the only women who profit by Well Baby Clinics are those who get artificial food there for their children. Mothers who nurse their own children soon tire of bringing their babies merely to be told that they have increased so much in weight. Thus a premium is put on artificial feeding. It has been suggested that small monthly prizes be given to those mothers whose babies show the greatest progress, the woman's pride in being recognized as a model mother being a greater stimulus than the prize itself, and the amount given does not have to be large.

This station is now supplying breast milk in bottles. At the present time it is furnished only for in-patients, but it is expected that the practice of furnishing the milk can be extended so that it may be given out for use in the home. It is claimed that an infant thrives as well on bottled breast milk as it does when fed at the breast.—(*M. T.*)

✛

War Emergency Lessens Infant Death Rate.—A report from workers in France reveals an interesting situation at Lille during the German occupation. The cows were all carried off and no milk was available, and as factories were not running, the women could not find wage-earning work, and had to stay at home. The consequence was that women were driven to nursing their infants and that the infants had their mothers with them at home, resulting in an infantile death rate that was far lower than had ever been known before in the town.—(*M. T.*)

✛

A report on the physical condition of men of military age by the National Service Medical Boards in the period from 1917-1918 contains valuable statistical data. The number of medical examinations of men of military age made during the period under review was 2,425,184. This figure does not, however, represent the actual number of men examined, as it includes re-examination. Those examined were classed in four grades, as follows:

Grade I.—Those who had attained the full normal standard of health and strength and were adjudged capable of enduring physical exertion suitable to their age.

Grade II.—Those judged capable only of

undergoing such physical exertion as does not involve severe strain.

Grade III.—Those presenting marked disabilities, or such evidences of past disease that they were not considered fit to undergo the physical exertion required for the higher grades.

Grade IV.—Those totally and permanently unfit for any form of military service.

The result of the examinations was as follows:

	Number	Percentage
Grade I	871,769	36.00
Grade II	546,276	22.23
Grade III	756,859	31.32
Grade IV	250,280	10.00

Medical examination thus showed that of every nine men of military age in Great Britain, on the average three were perfectly fit and healthy; two were upon a definitely infirm plane of health and strength, whether from some disability or some failure in development; three were incapable of undergoing more than a very moderate degree of physical exertion and could almost (in view of their age) be described with justice as physical wrecks; and the remaining man was a chronic invalid with a precarious hold upon life.

An analysis of medical examinations of different groups of men between 18 and 25 in Yorkshire, made with a view to revealing the influence of occupation upon health, gave the following remarkable results:

	Percentages			
Occupations.	Grade I.	Grade II.	Grade III.	Grade IV.
Agriculturists	71.9	15.5	8.8	3.8
Miners	68.9	15.1	10.5	5.5
Agriculturists	62.0	23.0	11.6	3.4
Engineers	60.9	23.9	13.4	1.8
Iron and steel workers	60.2	23.6	11.2	3.0
Lace workers	45.0	26.9	22.7	5.4
Woollen trade	54.6	10.9	24.0	10.5
Woollen trade	37.5	31.7	27.0	3.8
Tailors	33.9	21.4	33.5	11.2

—*Medical Officer*, Mar. 13, 1920, 106. (*D. G.*)

✛

Salaries of Assistant Medical Officers.—The recommendations made at different times by the British Medical Association with regard to the salaries of medical men employed by health authorities have contained, with their excellent intentions, more than one anomaly.

This has embarrassed alike authorities in offering conditions of remuneration, candidates in applying for vacancies, and medical journals in accepting advertisements. In respect to the last, we have decided not to accept advertisements in these columns for the future where the pay offered for assistant medical officers is less than £500 per annum or its equivalent.—*Lancet,* March 13, 1920. (*H. N. C.*)

✦

Death of Founder of Ministry of Health in England.—The *London Times* of March 15, 1920, announced the death from pneumonia of Sir Robert Morant. Sir Robert was permanent secretary to the Minister of Health. late chairman of the National Health Insurance Commission and formerly permanent secretary to the Board of Education. For years before any official action was taken. he worked toward his great object, a Ministry of Health. On many occasions, just when hope that the ministry would be established and seemed brightest, some obstacle supervened and the scheme was dropped. Morant never waivered and never despaired. At last his patience prevailed and the Prime Minister was won over to the plan. Although not a medical man at all, he was frequently referred to in Great Britain as "the biggest medical man of his time," according to the *Times.*—(*J. A. T.*)

✦

Deratisation by Chloropicrin.—The possibilities of using chloropicrin as a deratisation agent are set forth in a paper presented before the Paris Academy of Sciences by M. Roux. Bertrand and Brocq-Rousseu claim that rats and their parasites are very sensitive to the action of the fumes of this substance. These are without effect on fabrics or colors.—*Revue Scientific,* February 28, 1920. (*H. N. C.*)

✦

Dangers to Child Bearing.—In its *Statistical Bulletin* for March the Metropolitan Life Insurance Company furnishes some figures in this very important matter, which bear significant value to the health officer who has here a means of prevention, if his community will support him in his endeavors.

An inquiry sent out recently by this company to health officers of all the states and larger cities having good birth registration has resulted in the following information for the year 1919:

1. More than five women die from disorders of pregnancy or childbirth out of each 1,000 births registered. This is equivalent to one maternal death out of every 185 confinements.

2. Forty-five babies out of every 1,000 total births, or one out of every 22, are born dead.

3. Forty babies out of every 1,000 born alive die before they are one month old.

Such are the dangers to mother and infant at the present time.

As against the above figures are the following which prevail among women who receive prenatal and maternity care under skilled direction:

1. Only *two* women instead of *five* die out of every 1,000 confinements.

2. Only *twelve* babies instead of *forty-five* are still-born in every 1,000 births.

3. Only *ten* babies instead of *forty* per 1,000 born alive die under one month of age.

Results such as these have been achieved in Boston, in New York City and elsewhere. They can be obtained anywhere if adequate nursing and medical care are available to women during pregnancy, at confinement and during the first month of the infant's life. Such is the great promise in life conservation held out by prenatal and maternity care for women.

✦

First Chinese Medical College.—During the war between Japan and Russia in 1904 the Chinese Red Cross was formed to look after thousands of Chinese who were left homeless and destitute in the regions where fighting raged for many months. After the situation was relieved, a considerable sum of money remained over, and upon decision of members of the General Council. ground was purchased near Shanghai and a building erected as the Chinese Central Red Cross Hospital and Medical College for Chinese students. The hospital is completely equipped with the most modern apparatus and furnishings. Instruction in the college is in English only. under the direction of S. M. Cox, M. D. The first year there were twenty registrants. Each received his degree as a competent practitioner.

The Chinese Red Cross is today an organization with 25,000 members, whose interest in world relief work is evidenced by the entrance of the society into the League of Red Cross Societies. The Chinese have been much impressed with the work of the American Red Cross both during and after the war, and China now desires to take her place beside the other nations of the world in the work of relieving human suffering.

Review of the Milk Problem.—In the issue for March 24, 1920, *Municipal Reference Library Notes* brings together world-wide studies on milk, which is worthy the attention of public health officers. An abstract of it is here presented.

The Milk and Dairies Act of Great Britain, which was passed before the outbreak of the war, but has never become operative, is to have a bill of amendment to it introduced soon, according to an editorial in *The Municipal Journal* (London), Feb. 13, 1920. It is expected that the bill will include (1) the licensing of milk traders; (2) powers to grade and define milk; and (3) power to local authorities if they so desire to distribute or to supervise to a greater extent than now the distribution of milk.

The committee on the production and distribution of milk, of which the Hon. Waldorf Astor, M. P., is chairman, has been studying the milk problem for some years. The committee has issued three interim reports, the first in June, 1917, and the third in November, 1918, and its final report in 1919. The amending bill is to be based on the recommendations of these reports.

Of particular interest is the scheme for the control of milk distribution. This includes dividing the country into suitable areas for distribution, a milk superintendent for each area, a national milk clearing house to control the wholesale milk trade, the government to obtain option to purchase the business of wholesale traders with a view to the State becoming the sole wholesaler of milk, producers to be encouraged to form themselves into coöperative associations and every means utilized to produce clean and wholesome milk.

The Ministry of Food has also prepared several memorandums on milk control and the milk supply, and a "Report on action taken towards the control and distribution of milk" in which "is described the action which has been taken by the Ministry up to 31st January, 1919, to initiate control of the wholesale trade in milk and to ensure a more effective distribution of supplies throughout the trade and to the public."

In the interesting *Report of the Medical Officer of Health* (1918. 100 p. 614.09G7b) of the city of Birmingham, England, reference is made to this subject in these words: "There is abundant evidence in peace time, and even more in war time, that the use of milk by the artisan classes is far too limited. The large

staff of women workers employed by the Public Health Committee, who are in intimate contact with the feeding conditions of the children of Birmingham, all tell the same story, viz., that the supply to the toddlers and other children is most inadequate, and that this is due to a want of appreciation of the value of milk and in a few cases to inability to pay for a supply. Leaflets are distributed on various subjects dealing with the need of milk for children."

Several states in this country have realized the need of education. Massachusetts, through its State Department of Agriculture, Dairy Division, and the Boston Milk Campaign, has recently carried on an extensive educational campaign. The organization consists of milk producers, dealers and the civic bodies, while the executive committee is composed of three members from each class. The funds are provided by the producers, who pay on the basis of 15 cents for each $100 worth of milk sold to the dealer, and the dealer matched this amount. The general scheme of publicity is carried out by exhibits and posters, with a staff of six experts who spread the doctrine of the healthfulness of dairy products in the schools and industrial plants of Boston.

California, through the help of the Dairy Council of the State Board of Health, conducted a school survey in the state and found in the larger cities that from 40 to 48 per cent of the school children were not drinking any milk. These figures "indicate the extensive field for educational advertising on the part of an industry that is suffering because of false economy on the part of consumers— an economy that is aggravated by ignorance of the true facts."

The Oklahoma Public Health Surveys publish in the Volume on Oklahoma City a story of the milk supply of the city, which contains a study of the conditions of supply and delivery, bacterial content and butter fat content, and physical condition of persons handling the milk.

Toledo has been studying its milk problem for some months and various reports have been printed in the Toledo City Journal; the most recent is that of February 21st, which is an exposition of the bacterial content of the milk, showing that the present conditions are a menace to the community, and that there is need for a new milk ordinance.

New York state and city have been struggling with their milk problems also. The Fair Price Milk Committee for the city of New York has recently issued a report. In the last three years the following efforts have been made by the city to bring milk within the reach of the poor: Mayor's Committee on Milk, by the county through the district attorney's office, an inquiry before Judge McAdoo, through the Wicks committee, the Reconstruction Commission, the Glynn-Finley Commission and the Battle Commission of the state, and lastly this Fair Price Milk Committee of which Dr. R. S. Copeland is chairman. The committee concludes "that the creation of a State Commission is essential, in order that all concerned may be treated fairly, and particularly that the public may have assurance that it is being rightly dealt with as regards the most vital of its foodstuffs." Definite and detailed recommendations are made by the committee.

✦

The Bolshevik as a Health Officer.—The *Review of the International Red Cross* publishes in its issue of October, 1919, extract of a document originating from the Commission of Public Health of the Russian Soviet government. This document outlines and recounts some of the work and gives the organization of the commission. The Soviet government is organized with commissions similar to our executive departments. The head of each commission enjoys the rank and privilege of a minister. All sanitary and medical work of the republic is in charge of the Commission of Public Health.

This commission is composed of fourteen sections as follows: Medical, sanitary and epidemiological, balneology, maternity and child welfare, general material and supplies, medical material, pharmacy, military medicine, naval medicine, railway medicine, medicine for waterways, finance, general administration, and elementary instruction in hygiene. It is interesting to note that a special section is devoted to the subject of baths. In the provinces there are apparently local medico-sanitary commissions which concentrate in themselves the sections on medicine, sanitation and epidemiology, supplies, etc. These local commissions have also taken over the work of the old federal, departmental and municipal departments of medicine.

The document states that the general death rate in Russia in 1914 was 26.7 per thousand, whereas in the rest of Europe it varied from 14 to 17 per thousand and that in that year the Russian birth rate was 43.7.

During the organization of the Commission the country was being ravaged by epidemics. As an example of its accomplishment, the Commission mentions that in 1908 the cholera epidemic claimed more than 200,000 victims, while a similar epidemic produced from September to April, 1918, only 35,619 cases. The preventive measures adopted by the Commission were principally prophylactic injections, hospitalization and chlorination of water. In the influenza epidemic of 1918 the Commission cites 700,000 cases. (Craig and Dublin estimate for this epidemic 6,000,000 deaths in India, 400,000 deaths in Italy and from 450,000 to 600,000 deaths in America.) In Russia "special missions were organized to study influenza and they obtained very interesting results on the nature and character of this malady." The typhus epidemic starting in the fall of 1918 and reaching its height in the spring of 1919 apparently occupied more of the Commission's attention than did either of the other epidemics. In eight months (November to July) it reports 1,299,262 cases with a mortality of 6.8 per cent. The Commission endeavored to interest the people themselves in an attack on this disease. Local committees were appointed and given the necessary rights and powers. 9,000 hospital beds were established in Moscow and 10,000 elsewhere. Public baths, washhouses and disinfection chambers were installed for the free use of the people. In all 200,000,000 roubles were expended in this work. Research was undertaken and the work of Professor Marzinovsky is quoted in which he claims to have recognized the cause of typhus in a certain protozoa. Smallpox, for which there are reported 81,861 cases from November 1, 1918, to July 1, 1919, also occupied its attention. By a decree of the Council of Kommissars (in which is vested supreme authority) vaccination was made compulsory for the first time in this country. To carry this out, steps were taken to increase the production of vaccine, which was distributed free to the people.

The Commission also takes credit for introducing other reforms. It fixed the obligation (upon whom, it does not state) for reporting infectious diseases. It instituted government inspection of vaccines and sera and by degrees gave to institutes and laboratories preparing these priority for supplies of food, forage, etc.

By decree also, all medical service of the country passes into the hands of the state and pharmacies have been nationalized. Again by decree the sanitary inspection of dwellings and lodgings was provided for and it is necessary for all such inspectors to first take courses in the subject. In Moscow a model laboratory is in operation showing the purification of water. One section of the Commission is occupied with the medical inspection of school children and infants. This has provided assistance for abnormal children, instituted school gardens and arranged summer colonies for city children. The nourishment of all school children is incumbent upon the state.

In educational work the Commission on Public Health claims that it has been particularly active. Besides establishing courses dealing with disinfection, tuberculosis and other subjects and printing "several million" pamphlets on medicine and hygiene there have been held special conferences on various epidemics and general congresses on bacteriology, epidemiology, sanitation, pharmacy, dentistry, school hygiene, military medicine and other subjects. In Moscow a museum of social hygiene has been established, an exposition dealing with epidemics and infectious diseases has been set up and workshops maintained for making exhibit material. In Moscow also a large number of buildings have been set aside for the use of an Institute of Public Health. This institute is to be the highest scientific authority on hygiene, bacteriology and epidemiology.—*Homer N. Calver.*

✛

Advice to Miners Valuable to Others.— Physical examinations at regular intervals is advocated for miners by the Bureau of Mines, Department of the Interior, and it adds that if this applies to miners it ought to be proper for every person.

"Every miner and his family should keep in the best possible physical condition," declares the bureau. "A good miner always takes care to keep his working tools in excellent shape, in order that he may do effective work. He also carefully observes the danger signs that are seen at various places.

In order to keep in good physical condition, every person should undergo a thorough physical examination at least once every year, better still, once every six months. This applies not only to the miner but to every member of his family as well. These periodical physical examinations should be made even if the person is apparently in good health.

Many diseases begin without sufficient symptoms to attract attention. Tuberculosis, Bright's disease, and some diseases of the heart may progress for some time before the victim is aware of it. Thorough physical examination at regular intervals is the best means of detecting diseased conditions. Early knowledge of a disease coming on enables the person affected to take the proper steps in the correction of diet, habits or occupation to arrest the progress of the disease.

Complete periodic physical examinations are important for every person.

✛

A Federal Department of Public Health for Brazil has been created by the law approved by President Pessoa January 20. Under the supervision of the department will be a Board of Health for Rio de Janiero, a board of rural sanitation and a board of maritime and fluvial prophylaxis. Besides these there will be sections dealing with sanitary statistics; sanitary engineering; the supervision of drains; the prevention of leprosy and venereal diseases; the supervision of the practice of medicine, pharmacy, dentistry and obstetrics and hospitals for contagious diseases and child welfare. The federal government also takes charge of meat and food inspection. Under the law a supreme council of hygiene and public health is appointed. Part of the expenses of the administration of the law will be met by taxes on alcoholic drinks, gambling houses, clubs and casinos at health resorts, sera, vaccines and drugs.—*Jour. A. M. A.*, Feb. 21, 1920. (*H. N. C.*)

✛

Red Cross of Seven Nations Fighting Typhus.—With the response of the Red Cross societies of Belgium and Sweden to the appeal of Poland for aid in her anti-typhus fight, the number of Red Cross societies participating in the war on the disease is increased to 7: United States, Spain, Rumania, Portugal, France, Sweden and Belgium.

The report of the medical mission sent by the League of Red Cross Societies to investigate typhus conditions in Poland, dwelt on the inexpediency of isolated action in dealing with the disease, and recommended concerted action. Individual nations are therefore assisting the League in the effort to coördinate the relief activities and thus render them more effective.

Present Foreign Operations of American Red Cross.—The American Red Cross continues to· carry on relief work in various European countries, and much of it is concerned with public health. The work of certain European commissions has been brought to a close in Switzerland and in Czecho-Slovakia, for example. In others, as in England, Italy, Greece and Roumania, the personnel has been withdrawn except for the few representatives necessary to wind up affairs and place upon a permanent local basis certain activities.

The conditions still existing in Serbia, Montenegro and Albania are of such a nature as to require the continuation of actual relief operations; but these are being turned, as rapidly as possible, into a constructive health program of such a character that it can be carried on to a major degree, at any rate, by the respective peoples themselves.

¯The country which, at the present time, is receiving the greatest proportion of the available resources of the Commission for Europe is Poland, where not only the appalling ravages of typhus and other epidemic diseases (during the last twelve months, 160,000 cases of typhus have been reported in Congress Poland, and 75,000 in Galicia), but the rigors of an unusually severe winter and the failure, in large part of last summer's harvest, combine to bring about conditions of extraordinary distress. The ravages of war had left this people without the resources for self help which have been developed in the sister republic of Czecho-Slovakia.

Under the Commissioner for Europe there are now two active Russian units, one in South Russia, where relief has been extended as far north and went as Denekin's lines have penetrated, and where additional supplies will be distributed as opportunity offers; the other in the Baltic States and that part of Western Russia not under soviet control. Here operations are rendered extraordinarily difficult by the complexity · of the political situation, but the Red Cross unit has made a wonderful record of courage, energy and initiative in carrying on relief and sanitary work in Finland, Latavia, Esthonia and Lithuania and is so organized that, when opportunity comes, it can render immediate and effective aid in Petrograd and other parts of soviet Russia.

The health conditions in this part of the world, already deplorable, are rapidly growing worse, but the Red Cross is doing its share in righting them and national headquarters at Washington is now engaged in recruiting an additional unit of forty doctors in response to a cable just received.

During the first year of its work, the Commission established fourteen hospitals for sick and wounded Czech and Russian soldiers and sent eighteen heavily loaded relief trains from Vladivostok to Western Siberia. In its anti-typhus campaign the American Red Cross equipped and maintained an anti-typhus train which shuttled back and forth along the line of the Trans-Siberian railway, playing a leading part in the fight against the spread of the scourge.

In Paris is the headquarters of the Jardin des Enfants, which is the Red Cross organization having particularly to do with the care of French children. Among its most useful activities is the moving of thousands of city children, suffering from malnutrition and lack of fresh air and sunshine for long vacations in the French countryside.

In France, as elsewhere in Europe, the Red Cross does not hesitate to give material relief where this is the thing most needed, but, wherever possible, emphasis is placed on the constructive medical program and particularly upon the care of mothers and children. There is the greatest need, owing to the primitive housing conditions, for small maternity hospitals.

Political conditions in the Balkans are still unsettled, and, as a result, the leadership and coöperation of the American Red Cross is peculiarly welcome, particularly in the field of public health, and the personal relations between the authorities and the Red Cross personnel are cordial to an unusual degree. The trust and affection of the common people is so intense as to be almost embarrassing. Even the Mohammedan Slavs, who have been isolated by their religion from the rest of Europe for centuries, recognize the disinterestedness of the American Red Cross, and welcome the women doctors and nurses into their homes, learning from them the much-needed gospel of cleanliness and fresh air.—The Red Cross Bulletin, February 16, 1920.—(*J. A. T.*)

STATE HEALTH NOTES—LEGISLA-
TION

Massachusetts.—The Senate of the State
has accepted the adverse report made by its
Committee on Public Health on the bill presented by the Medical Liberty League which
sought to provide for the abolition of compulsory vaccination.

By a unanimous vote the Joint Committee
on Social Welfare and Public Health of the
Massachusetts Legislature has reported a new
draft of the bill of Edna Lawrence Spencer
providing for a system of maternity benefits.
(The different bills are outlined in the
JOURNAL for April, 1920, page 379). The bill
reported provides for prenatal care, but not
postnatal. It carries also a system of cash
benefits somewhat different from that originally proposed in the Spencer bill.

Hundreds of leading · physicians, surgeons
and specialists in and about Boston, Mass.,
have signed a petition to the State Legislature
in which they ask relief from the present Federal restrictions on the manufacture, prescription and sale of alcoholic beverages for
medicinal purposes.

+

Mississippi.—The Legislature has under
consideration, with a fair presumption of its
passage, a law appropriating $20,000 for work
in venereal diseases. A State Detention Home
is also considered as one of the probable out-
comes of present legislation.

+

New Jersey.—The New Jersey State
Chamber of Commerce has been instrumental in introducing into the State Legislature four bills for the control of venereal
disease.

1. A bill to amend the marriage law, which
will prevent the issuance of marriage licenses
to persons suffering from gonorrhea and
syphilis.

2. A bill for the issuance of certificates to
prospective applicants for marriage licenses
limiting the fee to a maximum of $10, and
providing for certification at public expense.

3. A bill to amend the existing venereal
disease reporting bill to allow the names of
persons reported to the State Department of
Health to be disclosed to interested health
officers for follow-up work.

4. A bill to give the representatives of the
Surgeon General of the United States Public
Health Service the power of control over carriers of venereal diseases, which control is
now, by New Jersey law, limited to the representatives of the Surgeon General of the
Army or Navy.

+

New Mexico.—By the signature of Governor O. A. Larrazolo, the health levy bill
fostered by the New Mexico Public Health
Association has become a law. The bill received a favorable report by the senate finance
committee and was passed by that body, 17 to
5, with only a few amendments. The house
judiciary committee presented a unanimous
report favoring the passage of the bill with
the senate amendments. The bill carried in
the house 36 yes and none no. The bill allows
the governing bodies of counties and cities to
make special levies of not to exceed one-half
mill in excess of limitations for health work.

+

New York.—The Chamber of Commerce
of the State of New York, at its regular
monthly meeting in April, put itself on record
by the following vote: Resolved, That the
Chamber of Commerce of the State of New
York is opposed to the passage of what is
known as the Davenport Bill, Introductory
Bill No. 986, and urges upon the members of
the Legislature the duty of opposing its enactment into a law. The title of the bill is, "To
conserve the human resources of the state by
establishing for employees a system of mutual
health insurance funds." The bill if enacted
would make health insurance compulsory upon
practically every employee in the state without physical examination. The Chamber of
Commerce is convinced that compulsory health
insurance attacks the problem from the wrong
point of view and asserts that it is opposed
to public policy in a number of ways, that it
is a delusion, that it does not promote the
health of the individual and that experience
abroad had shown its fallacies.

There is now pending in the State Legislature the Sage-Machold bill, to establish a
state-wide system of health centres. This
provides for annual State grants for the construction of hospitals and their clinics and for
the operation of these, the amounts paid to
supplement local funds appropriated by the
communities. Provision · is made for pay
patients, whose fees will contribute towards
the maintenance of health centers. It further
authorizes the establishment of health centers
by a city, a county, or a consolidated health
district. The effect of the bill will be to make
more available the medical and surgical re-

sources of the state, to standardize medical service and to effect its better distribution. The health centers will bring to the doors of those who need them the services and ministrations of physicians, scientists and nurses, which are today available only to persons of considerable means and living in or near the large centers of population.

In discussing the measure Homer Folks, Secretary of the State Charities Aid Association of New York, stated that the bill is "epoch-making." He considers it the most important and progressive health measure since the enactment, in 1913, of the new Public Health Law of the state which has since become a model for many other states. "The bill recognizes," said Mr. Folks, "that it is to the public interest that every citizen receive intelligent medical attention; that it is a public calamity when preventable disease is not prevented or curable disease is not cured; and that only vigorous, efficient, organized public action can correct the serious evils which now exist."

Five State Departments have united to seek from the present Legislature an overhauling of the laws of New York State relating to children. The ideas of the departments of Education, Health, Charities, Probation and the Industrial Commission have been crystallized in a bill introduced in the Senate by Senator Charles W. Walton of Kingston, and in the Assembly by Assemblyman Marguerite L. Smith of New York. This bill creates a Children's Code Commission consisting of two senators, three assemblymen, five persons representing the State departments, and five citizens to be appointed by the Governor to make a thorough study of the confused, conflicting and scattered laws relating to children, with a view to revising the statutes and modernizing the methods of child care throughout the state.

In the words of the bill, the Commission "shall collate and study all laws relating to child welfare, investigate and study the operation and effect of such laws upon children, ascertain any overlapping and duplication of laws and of the activities of any public office, department or commission thereunder, and make recommendation to the Legislature of remedial legislation which it may deem proper as the result of its investigations."

The following have been pointed out as faults in the existing children's laws of New York State:

The laws are negative rather than constructive, and are diffused, indefinite and contradictory. As a whole, they are merely patches upon old laws based upon the theory that all poor persons, including children, were to be committed by town overseers of the poor to almshouses for support. Almost every section has been enacted separately, with little consideration of other provisions, and without any definite plan for complete child protection. Important passages are obscurely hidden in unexpected sections, and are located with difficulty. Definitions of terms are omitted entirely, or are inadequate.

✛

Ohio.—An amendment to the occupational disease reporting law provides a penalty for physicians who refuse or neglect to report occupational diseases to the State Department of Health. The law is effective May 4.

Every physician, the bill states, who is attendant on or called in to visit a patient whom he believes to be suffering from lead poisoning, poisoning from phosphorus, arsenic, brass, wood alcohol, mercury or their compounds or from anthrax or from compressed air illness and such other occupational diseases and ailments as the State Department of Health shall require to be reported must make such report to the State Health Commissioner within forty-eight hours from the time of the first visit. In this report must be the name of the patient with his address and occupation and also the name, address and business of his employer and the nature of the disease.

The amendment declares, "Whoever, being a practicing physician in the state of Ohio, neglects or refuses to make and transmit to the state commissioner of health any report provided for in section 1243-1 of the General Code (which names the diseases to be reported) shall be fined not to exceed $100 or imprisoned for not to exceed 90 days, or both, but no person shall be imprisoned under this section for a first offense and the prosecution shall always be as and for a first offense, unless the affidavit upon which the prosecution is instituted contains the allegation that the offense is a second or repeated offense."

These reports are to be made on, or in conformity with the standard schedule blanks provided by the State Department of Health. Above blanks can be obtained from the State Department free of cost—upon request.

STATE HEALTH NOTES—GENERAL

Alabama.—The twelve points of attack in the anti-tuberculosis program for Alabama include the following:

1. Help the Children: It is in childhood that the seeds of tuberculosis are sown. Teach hygiene by the Modern Health Crusade method.

2. Work for better housing and feeding and living conditions, at home and in school.

3. Watchfulness of children who show any signs of consumption. Open air schools for suspected cases.

4. An Anti-Tuberculosis Association in every county and large town.

5. Supervision of returned soldiers found to have tuberculosis.

6. Preventoria for anæmic children with inadequate home care.

7. A visiting nurse to reach every tuberculosis patient, so as to cheer the patient, instruct the home, promote recovery and insure safety.

8. Training in healthful occupations of persons recovering from tuberculosis.

9. A traveling dispensary, with doctor, nurse and exhibit, to reach remote districts.

10. Free expert examination of all needy cases of suspected tuberculosis.

11. Promotion of hospitals at public expense, to care for advanced and dependent cases of consumption.

12. A sanatorium available for all early cases, however poor, however proud.

Help us put it across—money talks!

The Alabama Bureau of Venereal Disease Control has ten clinics, see table below. In addition the following plan is used to reach the smaller centers:

The Bureau offers to furnish the salvarsan, mercury, etc., and the necessary equipment for the administration of salvarsan, and to teach the physician the technique if he is not already qualified.

The physician agrees to treat at the nominal fee of $2.00, thus placing a complete course of treatment in reach of all at about the usual cost of one "shot of 606." It is the purpose of the Bureau to secure the co-operation of one physician in each center of population. Thirty appointments have been made to date.

✦

Arkansas.—The seventh annual Conference of the health officers of the State was called to order in Little Rock on March 23, 1920, the sessions extending over into the next day. In addition to his speech of welcome, State Health Commissioner C. W. Garrison, M. D., discussed "Morbidity Statistics," and Dr. C. W. Goddard, State Health Commissioner of Texas, addressed the meeting, telling them "The Way We Do Things in Texas." Col. A. Murray, medical officer in charge of Camp Pike, was one of the speakers, and altogether there were 19 papers and addresses, the titles of which, together with the speakers, are here given:

Mortality Statistics, Mrs. Mary Ellis Brown; How the Arkansas Public Health Association Can Assist Health Authorities, Miss

COMPARATIVE WORK OF ALABAMA FREE CLINICS, FEBRUARY, 1920

| City | Syphilis | | | | Gonorrhea | | | | Total Patients | Doses Arsph. | Total Treatments |
| | Male | | Female | | Male | | Female | | | | |
	W	C	W	C	W	C	W	C			
Anniston	2	..	..	2	6	8	..-	8	139	10	506
Bessemer	2	18	1	3	5	8	..	2	55	42	171
Birmingham	51	126	16	71	41	41	13	21	628	525	2322
Florence	3	4	1	2	9	10	3	4	90	59	554
Huntsville	8	5	..	2	2	10	..	..	111	89	377
Mobile	13	26	7	14	22	37	18	21	228	128	2027
Montgomery	1	17	1	9	9	13	3	1	144	100	470
Talladega	8	5	3	2	2	16	7	2	160	87	599
Tuscaloosa	5	32	1	13	..	4	..	..	145	185	407
Riderwood	2	4	..	..	..	3	..	..	10	10	30

Wassermanns 822.

	Syphilis	Gonorrhea	Chancroid
Cases Reported by Doctors	167	220	19
Reported by Clinics	....	....	18

Total Cases Reported by Clinics...1905
Total Patients Reported by Clinics...1710
Total Treatments Reported by Clinics..7463

Letters Mailed..........36950
Bulletins Mailed........54431

W. C. BLASINGAME, Director Bureau V. D. Control.

Erle Chambers, executive secretary, Arkansas Public Health Association; Securing Coöperation, Dr. D. Norton; Venereal Disease Publicity, Mrs. J. O. Blakeney; Publicity and Human Health, Mr. Clio Harper; Relation of Local Health Officers to Venereal Disease Control, Dr. J. T. Clegg; Keeping Fit, Mr. John L. Hunter; Necessity for State Supervision of Public Health Nursing, Miss Linnie Beauchamp, state supervisor, Red Cross; Water and Sewage Disposal, Mr. M. Z. Bair; How Health Officers and Railroads Can Coöperate, Mr. H. W. Van Hovenberg, sanitary engineer, Cotton Belt Railroad; Malaria Control in Arkansas, Dr. F. M. Faget, U. S. P. H. S.; Organization of Clinics, Dr. C. M. Lutterloh; What Constitutes an Efficient Health Department, Dr. John Thames; Instructions as to Collection and Transmission of Specimens, Dr. M. King; and Legal Powers of Arkansas Health Authorities, Judge John W. Wade.

✛

Connecticut.—Announcement is made of the organization of the Health Center in New Haven, Conn., under the combined leadership and financial support of the four chief health agencies of the city, the Municipal Department of Health, the Visiting Nurse Association, the New Haven Chapter of the American Red Cross, and the New Haven Medical Association.

The Health Center will aim to build up the health as well as to detect the physical defects of the 20,000 inhabitants in the selected district, who are largely Italian stock. Free medical examinations, nursing care in the home, and intensive educational work will constitute the main lines of activity. Medical treatment will not be given at the Center, but individuals will be referred to the abundant medical facilities of the city. It is expected that the Health Center will be in full operation by July 1. Its temporary quarters are 194 York street.

The Board of Control is composed of the following members: Prof. C. E. A. Winslow, chairman; Dr. F. W. Wright, health officer; Mr. A. T. Hopkins, treasurer; Drs. C. J. Bartlett and N. Mariani of the Board of Health; Miss M. T. Dana and Mrs. L. M. Daggett of the Visiting Nurse Association; Mr. Thomas W. Farnam and Mrs. E. O. Buckland of the New Haven Chapter, American Red Cross, and Drs. R. B. Beck and F. M. Sperry of the New Haven Medical Associa-

tion. The director of the Health Center is Mr. Philip S. Platt, M. A., C. P. H.

✛

Delaware.—About 100 citizens of Delaware, interested in public health, met at the capital, Dover, on March 10, and effected a permanent organization entitled, The Delaware Public Health Association. The following were elected to serve for officers during the coming year.

President, Henry Ridgeley; vice-presidents, Henry P. Scott, Mrs. H. D. Boyer, O. A. Newton; secretary-treasurer, A. D. Warner, Jr.; executive committee, Mrs. Ella C. Emery and Albert Robin, M. D.

No one of these officers is an executive officer or employe of any of the boards of health in the state, the idea being that of a democratic, public organization composed of citizens, an organization of the people themselves.

The business of the meeting consisted in the appointment of a Committee on Constitution and the selection of the date, June 2, for the ratification meeting, which is to be held in Wilmington. Representatives of a dozen boards and societies spoke to the gathering, explaining the work of the different societies, the general tenor of the addresses being suggestions towards coöperation. In addition to the local speakers, Assistant Surgeon General T. Clark of the U. S. P. H. Service outlined the health work of the service.

✛

Georgia.—The Venereal Disease Control work in Georgia has been keeping pace with its program in the State very well. The interest in the county unit plan has been intensified and the representatives of the State Board of Health in their respective counties are doing great work. The Department of Venereal Disease Control has mailed to the physicians a supply of report blanks in the past few weeks. It is hoped that physicians will be prompt in making reports. The law is given on the cover of the book of forms, and it is believed that reports on venereal diseases will soon reach a satisfactory basis. It is the law, and it is the physician's duty to report his cases. The "Keeping Fit" exhibit has been demonstrated to 12,734 boys in the state in the past month. Thirty-five lectures were delivered and much interest shown. An exhibit for girls is being perfected, and will be put on the road. A great deal of work is being done in an educational way in Georgia with the young boys of the state along the line of sex matters.

✚

Indiana.—The State Board of Health has recently issued a series of little folders addressed to the mothers of Indiana. These present in very popular and attractive form a number of messages in the interests of babies who are to have full health and development. One set of rules is that given by the baby to its mother, another group suggests the advice that a competent physician would give to the mother. Other taking features are to be seen in the folders, notably an attractive picture for the first page.

There are ten rules that Baby is supposed to suggest to its mother that seem to be worth wider distribution than the limits of any one state.

BABY'S RULES FOR MOTHER

1. Bathe me every day. Oftener in hot weather. Test the heat of the water with your elbow. Pat me dry. Then I'll laugh and crow for you.

2. Keep me in a cool, clean, airy place. Dirt and heat make me ill and cross. Out of doors let me watch the sunlight and shadows dance. But shield my eyes from a direct light. It hurts them.

3. Let me sleep sixteen to twenty-two hours out of twenty-four. I detest waking to show auntie the color of my eyes. When I sleep, I grow. That is my business.

4. Feed me REGULARLY at three to four hour intervals. My stomach needs to rest between times If you give me too much I'll spit it up. I like mother's milk the best of any.

5. Let me kick and cry sometimes. I MUST get some EXERCISE. Play gently with me, but do not toss me high. I may fall and break my bones.

6. I love to cuddle in your arms, but please, mother, rocking me to sleep makes me dizzy. Turn me over often. I am vain about the shape of my head.

7. Let me hear soft tones of beautiful music. They soothe me. Sudden, loud or harsh noises get on my nerves. I love to hear you sing.

8. Support my head and back while I am tiny. PLEASE let me take my own time in learning to walk. I want my body to grow straight and strong.

9. Do not expect me to talk too soon. It takes quite a while to learn your foreign language. I can understand my own much better and I must think and think before I speak.

10. Protect me from persons who want to kiss my mouth. I am not strong enough to fight all their germs. Besides, it isn't done in the BETTER BABIES' families.

Keep all these rules for me and some day I may do something for you.

Yours for health and happiness,

BABY.

More recently the State Board of Health has issued "The Indiana Baby Book," a most attractive publication worthy of consideration and review as a real book.

✚

Kansas.—In the January Bulletin of the Kansas State Department of Health there is a little article on influenza masks headed "Bite the Knot." The reviewer recalls several practical nurses in an Emergency Hospital at Charleston, West Va., who literally "bit the knots." On account of the scarcity of influenza masks, these were washed and sterilized and used again. As many of the knots for tying the masks around the head were hard knots, the nurses picked them out with their teeth. Then a few days later, when they came down with influenza, the question arose whether the mask had any value at all. There are a great many such insidious and unconsidered ways that the organisms are waiting to take advantage of if the opportunity is afforded. Nature does not waste any time in considering what to do, it presents the most perfect example of the principle, "Do it now."

A bulletin of the same department states that probably 50 trained public health nurses could be placed in Kansas were they only available. It further points out that the time has come when every county and every municipality of importance should have one or more thoroughly trained, competent public health nurses as an integral and permanent part of its health organization. No work has been productive of such immediate results in mitigating human suffering among the poor, and the prevention of sickness and premature death has been attained through the rapid strides made by the public health nursing.

✚

Kentucky.—The August, 1919, Bulletin of the State Board of Health is devoted entirely to pellagra. The cause and prevention are discussed, and pellagra-preventing bills of fare are given. It is pointed out that in six states alone in 1916 pellagra caused some 3,700 deaths. As its fatality rate is probably not in excess of 5 per cent, the disease must rank practically first in importance as a cause of sickness and lowered physical efficiency of the people in the area affected. In six years pellagra caused the death of 865 people in Kentucky. So it can be seen that the disease represents a distinct public health problem for this state, even though the state is ordinarily considered too far north to be in the pellagra area.—(*M. T.*)

✦

Maine.—Dr. L. D. Bristol, State Commissioner of Public Health, in emphasizing the fact that guarding a city's or town's health is a full-time job, briefly summarizes in twelve points the duties of a full-time health officer, which duties indicate to every thinking man and woman the necessity for having some responsible person qualified to perform them. They are:

1. First and most important to receive regularly from all physicians reports of births, deaths and contagious diseases.

2. Quarantine for diphtheria, scarlet fever, smallpox, infantile paralysis and other diseases must be rigorously enforced when the cases first appear and vaccination against smallpox must be systematically done. Thorough cleaning of the premises after the death or recovery of the patient is imperative.

3. Water supplies must be carefully safeguarded and analysis made to see that all water used for domestic purposes is unpolluted.

4. Sewage disposal must be made as perfect as possible, as contagious diseases are spread from this source.

5. Nuisances, such as stables, pig pens, bad drains, etc., must be given attention.

6. Milk must be inspected.

7. Food of all kinds and soft drinks must be inspected for careful handling and sanitary conditions where they are made and sold.

8. Baby welfare, especially among the poor, must be religiously looked after.

9. Schools must be inspected and defects in children discovered and if possible corrected.

10. Housing conditions of the poor must be remedied. Conditions making for dirt, dampness and disease must call for the health officer's attention.

11. A laboratory should be established where specimens of milk, water and material from people suspected of contagious disease can be examined.

12. Cordial relations between the public and health workers must be established through every existing agency, especially the newspapers as the best informed people are always with the health officer in spirit.

✦

Missouri.—In co-operation with the Missouri State Board of Health, Division of Child Hygiene, the U. S. Public Health Service is making a demonstration of work in child hygiene. Local health organizations, including the Missouri Tuberculosis Association and the American Red Cross are aiding, the former being responsible for the preparation and distribution of much in the way of circulars and notices.

Missouri was chosen for the first work on this line by the government, it was stated, because conditions in Missouri were generally typical of the remainder of the country and also because the state legislature had provided for a state child hygiene bureau to work with and coöperate with the government in this campaign.

There will be six practical lines of work undertaken by different combinations of the coöperating agencies, the first of which is a field investigation. This is to be a house-to-house census by the U. S. P. H. Service and the State authorities in matters of birth registration, enrolling of children of pre-school age and parental supervision. Under the head of school hygiene, the physicians, nurses and teachers will undertake physical examination of the children, height and weight recording and a modern health crusade. Health centers are to be provided in which all the agencies will combine, and these will require a full-time health officer for each of them with a staff of Red Cross and Tuberculosis Society nurses. The various communities will arrange to furnish office and clinic rooms. Especial efforts will be directed towards the establishment of a good system of birth registration, literature will be supplied by various agencies, the Agricultural Extension Service here helping by pamphlets on the nutrition of children, and health education of the people is planned by means of adequate publicity.

In conducting the demonstration in Missouri each community will be asked to make the work permanent, particularly that part of the work which provides for a health officer continually on duty in the community, and for the regular examination and treatment of the children.

✛

New York.—The State Department of Health devotes a large portion of its *Health News* for February, 1920, to cancer, presenting a comprehensive article on the subject written in collaboration by ten specialists. This emphasizes the principles of early recognition and treatment as the real hope. The headings of the successive paragraphs in the main discussion suggest the thoroughness of the consideration of the subject. First there is the fact of the increase in the mortality and that cancer causes one death out of every 10 in persons above the age of 40 years. It is increasing apparently throughout all civilized countries, the annual increase in the United States being about two and one-half per cent.

The principal means of fighting is education of the people, impressing on every one the fact that on the detection of certain symptoms there should be no delay in going to a physician for examination. The disease is not contagious and not hereditary. There are certain known predisposing conditions which should be avoided, such as irritations, pigmented warts and the like, which by one cause or another are kept more or less constantly sore. Information regarding such matters, together with the somewhat detailed considerations of cancer in different portions of the body, together with a group of conclusions, form a treatise on the subject that is most valuable.

In Greenwich and Easton an inspection of the schools has been carried out by the health officer, Dr. Lewis R. Oatman, who thus reports on the findings of his investigations:

"Have examined 16 district school buildings (all of them in the town of Easton). All in comparatively good condition. Every schoolhouse has a drinking fountain with faucet, and each child its own drinking cup, and in all the schools have impressed the children with the necessity of always using their own. Have urged all trustees to install muslin screens for at least two or three windows and have advised teachers the best way to get good ventilation without draughts. There have been no serious epidemics the past year. This is wholly a rural town. No settlement large enough to be called a village.

"Investigated building for suitability for school building, while new building is being erected. Have investigated school buildings in town of Greenwich urging all trustees to install drinking fountains. Investigated water supply at Thomson school and sent sample to State Department. Conducted State Engineer to same supply later and he also took samples. Met with trustees of said school twice in considering a new water supply for said school. Also its heating and ventilation. Investigated installation of chemical closets for large rural school. Investigated Stevens and Thomson paper mill water supply (drinking). Sent sample to state laboratory."

Athens protects the public against fake remedies. The following regulation is incorporated in the Sanitary Code of the village of Athens, N. Y., and has been enforced for the past two years.

"Regulation 10. No corporation, association, firm or individual shall sell or offer for sale in the Village of Athens, N. Y., any medicine, or so-called remedies, or any so-called medical appliances other than by licensed pharmacists and physicians, unless before offering their commodities for sale they shall receive a permit from the local health officer.

"Any wilful violation of this regulation shall be punishable by a fine of $50.00 for each offense."

Tests of air in one of the factories at Niagara Falls, conducted by officers of the U. S. Public Health Service, revealed the fact that each cubic foot of air contained more than 200,000,000 tiny particles of dust, almost as hard as diamond dust and extremely dangerous to the lungs and air passages.

✛

North Carolina.—The North Carolina State Department of Health is conducting a far-reaching campaign for improving the condition of the teeth of the school children of the state. Three years ago a complete medical inspection of 3,847 school children in one county revealed 1,187 who had serious decay of permanent teeth, and 315 who were badly in need of operations for the removal of diseased tonsils.

The dental work is conducted without regard to the ability of the patient to pay. Skilled dentists are being sent into rural communities with the instructions to care for all teeth, regardless of the financial status of the parents. The North Carolina Department points out that nothing could be more undemocratic, un-American and unchristian than to divide the public into those classes who are able to pay and those who cannot, and then to give service to the latter group only.

Clearly one of the most inviolable duties of the State is to see that every child is given an even start in the race, regardless of class, color, social or financial standing.

A permanent equipment in the high school building of each county, a city-wide organization of capable dentists who should do all the work necessary for all school children between six and 12 years of age in each county every year, can be maintained for a sum of money far less than is now annually spent by the public each day for Coco-Cola and tobacco in North Carolina alone.

✛

North Dakota.—During an examination of the school children of the state many defects have been found which the *N. D. Pennant*, a local health publication, sets forth. In one school out of 221 pupils examined by the nurse, 128 had defective teeth and 106 had abnormal tonsils. Of the whole only one child in five was getting a chance to do his best at school, and on the others the public funds were being wastefully expended. In another school of 112 only 16 were found to be without defects, while in a third one the ratio of pupils below full efficiency was approximately the same.

The *Pennant* turns to the real health view of the situation after discussing the economics. It says:

"But the money loss to the nation, staggering though it be, is small when compared with the loss of human life and the lack of human efficiency that is a result of our low standard of health. Let us face the facts and set about removing the lack of knowledge and the lack of the 100 per cent ideal of health which lies back of our present waste of money and greater waste of human life."

The North Dakota State Department of Health has recently adopted one of the most complete sets of rules for the submitting of plans and specifications for water supplies, sewerage systems and garbage disposal systems that there is in any State. Careful compliance with the rules set forth should insure first-class water supplies for North Dakota in the future, and provide many needed remedies to existing plants.

Ohio.—One hundred and forty Ohio health commissioners have been appointed assistant collaborating epidemiologists by the U. S. P. Health Service. These are commissioners who have been appointed in both the municipal and general districts of the state under the Griswold health law.

With their appointment they also receive the privilege of using franked mail for their morbidity reports, and these reports may be submitted to the State Department of Health in the franked envelopes. As other districts, which have not as yet appointed their commissioner, make the choice, each will be given the same privilege as the ones now holding it. The men who have been chosen by the U. S. Public Health Service will receive $1 a year for their work.

Franked report cards have been placed in the hands of 8,089 Ohio physicians that their reports of communicable diseases may be submitted to the State Department of Health more quickly than formerly.

With the organization of the State according to the Griswold health law almost completed, there are 405 public health nurses now at work in Ohio, not including nurses employed by industrial plants. Using as a basis the census of 1910 for the state, this gives one public health nurse to every 14,320 population. Of the 88 counties of the state, 33 have as yet no nursing service, although thirteen have made definite provision for the employment of one and are only waiting until one can be found, leaving but 20 counties without any provision for nursing service.

Final plans for the state-wide campaign increasing the efficiency of Ohio youth have been completed by the State Department of Health, working in coöperation with the Y. M. C. A., and thousands of Ohio boys are being taught the "Keeping Fit" lesson. The campaign in Ohio is part of a national movement which is designed to reach every boy in the United States.

This fight was at first directed to boys of high school age only, in the hope that education along this line to younger men would bring about a more effective prevention of the spread of the diseases. Later plans included instructing the older boys and young men of the rural districts and those employed in large manufacturing plants over the state.

✛

South Carolina.—C. H. Verner, M. D., health officer of Darlington county, S. C., has hit upon the plan of interesting the children in the public schools in an anti-fly educational campaign, by offering prizes for the most attractive posters showing the house fly as a carrier of disease. Two sets of prizes of $20, $10, and $5 are offered to the schools of the whites and the negroes, so that six happy school children will be the immediate result, followed by the excitement of a follow-up, practical warfare on the flies. Any pupil of the schools of Darlington county is eligible, the judges will decide without knowledge of the contestant's names and the contest closes in time for its benefits to be exerted during the present fly season. The state distributes literature about the fly to any who request it.

Texas.—Following is the personnel of the Texas State Board of Health:

Commissioner—C. W. Goddard, M. D., president State Board of Health and Collaborating Epidemiologist, U. S. Public Health Service.

Heads of Departments: W. H. Minton, M. D., assistant state health officer; Oscar Davis, M. D., director, bureau venereal diseases; Aleck P. Harrison, M. D., director, bureau county health work; V. M. Ehlers, C. E., director, bureau sanitary engineering; Douglas Largen, M. D., director, bureau communicable diseases; M. E. Parker, M. D., director, bureau vital statistics; Mrs. Ethel Parsons, R. N., director, bureau child hygiene and public nursing; G. M. Graham, M. D., director, laboratory; H. L. Wright, M. D., director, bureau public health education.

Whole-Time County Health Officers: H. Garst, M. D., Bell county; H. S. Capps, M. D., Jefferson county; F. P. Smith, M. D., Tarrant county; W. H. Hossler, M. D., Williamson county; Arthur W. West, M. D., Wichita county.

Specialists: George Parker and E. H. Magoon, sanitary engineers; W. E. Hardenburg, in charge of malaria control work; Samuel L. Hildebrand, specialist on fish control of malaria, and J. L. Goodwin, M. D., trachoma specialist, the two last-named being on temporary assignment from the U. S. Bureau of Fisheries and the U. S. Public Health Service, respectively.

Since January 1, 1920, four new bureaus have been added to the State Health Department, viz., Bureau Communicable Diseases, Child Hygiene, Public Health Nursing and Public Health Education. A close coöperation has been established with the U. S. Public Health Service and International Health Board of the Rockefeller Foundation through which very effective malaria control work has been established in three groups of four cities each under the direction of three sanitary engineers who are experts in this line of work. The franking privilege has been obtained from the government for all communicable disease work. An affiliation with the American Red Cross has been established through which a large number of specially trained public health nurses are being placed throughout the state. A very valuable indexical survey of certain selected counties has just been completed which has furnished much important information. The Bureau of County Health Work has just completed the inauguration of five permanent county health departments with whole-time health officers in charge, a yearly budget of $10,000 each and an adequate working staff. It is intended that these five counties shall be the nucleus from which this work will be spread as rapidly as possible over the other counties of the state.

The Bureau of Public Health Education has under its direction the carrying on of the publicity work of all of the bureaus of the State Health Department; getting out pamphlets, literature, health exhibitions and supplying the news of the department to the press.

✛

Wisconsin.—The Dane County Medical Society concluded a winter series of five free public lectures on preventive medicine and public health. The last, by Dr. A. S. Lovenhart, chairman of the Court in Pharmacology at the University of Wisconsin, was an appeal for more stringent legislation against fraudulent advertising of alleged cure-alls. "There is no such thing as a patent medicine in the first place," he said, "for there is only one medicine, a remedy for syphilis, that has ever been legally patented. These nostrums are merely protected by trade marks and the majority of them contain nothing save a few well-known substances with a little coloring matter."

In coöperation with the United States Public Health Service, the State Board of Health during March conducted intensive surveys of the 1920 influenza epidemic in selected cities, to gain data for common deductions concerning the course of treatment of the disease. The cities were Antigo, Edgerton, Fort Atkinson, Platteville, Rhinelander and Sparta.

PUBLIC HEALTH
LABORATORY NOTES

Abstracted by Francis H. Slack, M. D., and Mr. James M. Strang.

The Campaign Against Diphtheria in Belgian Luxemburg.—In the diagnosis of diphtheria time is lost by the necessity of cultural examination of the swab; direct examination being negative in 80 per cent of cases. Fatty material which is on the swab prevents anything like a representative film of the bacteria present being made. The author proceeds to show how, by improved technique one can obtain about 70 per cent of positives instead of the usual 20 per cent, by direct examination. On receipt of material the swab is inoculated on to serum medium. The tube of medium should contain at least ½ cc. of "condensation water," in which the swab is soaked and then drawn over the surface of the medium in the usual way. The fluid in the soaked cotton wool of the swab is then squeezed out on to a slide by means of flat forceps and spread into a film which is stained by Neisser. Lomrey found that frequently one could judge of the probable result of the examination by the appearance of this fluid; if it proved to be milky in appearance, a positive result was almost invariably obtained and vice versa. The presence of a large saprophyte and a mould may give a little trouble owing to their bipolar granules which are stained by Neisser. The presence of two large terminal granules and a smaller central one, equally spaced, shows that one has to deal with true diphtheria.—R. F. Lomrey, Ann. Inst. Past, 1919, 717. Abstr. in Jour. State Med., Feb., 1920. (D. G.)

✛

Biologic Principles in Public Health Work.—According to the author the underlying ideas of almost any public health program are so seductively logical that it is only in recent times that any one has attempted in any systematic and strictly objective way to see what the program is actually accomplishing. The true test of the success of public health programs consists in analyzing what logically ought to happen and what actually is taking place. Intensive investigation of the fundamental biologic factors in the problems of public health are essential to further real progress toward their solution. As an illustration the author abstracts the results of a carefully conducted study on the last influenza epidemic, noting that the primary factor in causing variations between different communities in respect of reaction to the influenza epidemic was the organic fitness of these communities. Communities in some degree organically unsound as indicated by relatively high normal death rates from phthisis, organic heart diseases and nephritis were less able to meet successfully the attack of the epidemic than were those in which these organic diseases were not so prevalent.—Raymond Pearl, Jour. A. M. A., Feb. 7, 1920, 375. (D. G.)

✛

A Method of Standardizng Bacterial Suspensions.—The opacity of a bacterial suspension is measured by the length of the column of the suspension required to cause the disappearance of a wire loop. By a simple formula the measured capacity is translated into terms of bacteria per cc. and so made comparable with that of other suspensions of the same organism. An instrument for measuring the capacity of bacterial suspensions is described in detail. Jour. Exper. Med., Jan. 1920, 105.

✛

Grouping of B. Influenzæ by Specific Agglutination.—Ten strains of B. influenzæ were tested for their specific and cross agglutinating powers. Nine of the strains studied had the typical cultural and staining qualities of B. influenzæ, the tenth was less regular in its properties. The immunization of rabbits, preparation of antigen and agglutination tests was carried out in the usual manner, the tubes being incubated for 16 hours at 55° before reading.

The cross agglutination tests showed a marked grouping of related strains. Seven of the strains fell into two groups, group one having three strains; group two, four. The remaining strains did not cross—agglutinate, although they reacted to their own specific sera. This work demonstrates the possibility of the grouping of B. influenzæ organisms by immunological methods. —Small and Dickson, J. Inf. Dis., 1920, 26, 230.

HEALTH CENTERS

Harold B. Wood, M. D., Dr. P. H.

Providence, R. I.

The advantage of coördinate work in public health activities has long been recognized, but systematic coöperation has not been attained. The various associations working along these lines need not only to work in harmony but in coöperation. Each association should be well acquainted with the objects, activities, methods and results obtained by each other association working for the advancement of public health and the improvement of social and industrial conditions. The necessity of harmony has repeatedly been emphasized, yet rarely has there been an attempt made to coördinate the separate agencies, except at some tuberculosis conferences and at meetings of the American Public Health Association.

There are many official and other bodies and associations working for the improvement of public health conditions. These include state and local public health officials, the tuberculosis, child-welfare and public health nursing association, the civic leagues and charity aids. To these should be added the various official bureaus for the inspection of factories and mines,—the former a vast field for most beneficial work but largely a wasted opportunity with misplaced funds in many states, owing to inadequate laws.

Joint meetings of all these bodies should be held frequently to discuss methods for coöperative work in order to prevent the misusing of needed funds and the overlapping of activities and to determine the material assistance which each association can render the others. In unity there is production, and coöperative interest and work will produce a much greater result for the limited available funds. Public health nurses can be of more efficient service when working with an active health department than when working separately. When working with or under the local health department school medical inspectors can better systematize their work, especially as far as the detection and control of communicable diseases are concerned. A tuberculosis association can do better and more systematic work when it has the morbidity and mortality records of the health office available. The same unity of effort is needed between all the other health agencies; and the school, tuberculosis and charity workers can be of material assistance to one another.

The whole object of the existence of these associations is the help of mankind, and the most systematic is the best way to accomplish it. Personal glorification in past deeds and personal credit for accomplishments have no right to be considered; the "job is the big thing" (Pershing).

The problem to solve first is the practical method for coördinating these health agencies. The primary step is the matter of location of the offices of the organizations; the Health Center is the solution.

A Health Center is a building to which the general public may go to learn how to preserve health and from which are operated the various matured plans for protecting the public health. In it should be located the offices of the health officer and school medical inspector, of the tuberculosis association, the child-welfare association, the public health nursing association, of the civic league and charity aid organization, and similar philanthropic health associations. In the building should be a room reserved for health exhibits, always to be open to the public and frequently changed in their display material. These exhibits should treat of certain separate specific subjects, as baby welfare, tuberculosis or industrial accidents and diseases, other exhibits being more general in character. A room, with sufficient seating capacity, should be provided for conferences and public meetings. Where deemed satisfactorily located, the Health Center should be provided with proper rooms and equipment for health clinics at which people may learn how to keep well. These clinics would be equipped for work in infant-welfare, tuberculosis, industrial hygiene, venereal disease and in other public health problems receiving official recognition. In the South, hookworm and malaria clinics would be required. The people are not only examined and perhaps treated for their diseases, but given instruction upon how to avoid and how to prevent the various infectious diseases. Within the building the school medical inspector should establish a medical and a

474

dental clinic for the school children. The city laboratory should be housed in the same building.

The establishment of a Health Center is financially practical. Combining the offices in the same room or building is economic, since a sharing of the expenses for fuel, light and janitor service will save funds. In some localities the municipality furnishes the building. In others, Chambers of Commerce and other business or social clubs, realizing the need and the resulting social and industrial economy, will contribute toward the project.

The Health Center is most applicable for cities from 25,000 to 300,000 population. It is advisable; it is systematizing; it is productive; it is economic. The details of its operation vary with local conditions. Where already established, the Health Center has been eminently successful.

☐

WORLD-WIDE WORK OF INTERNATIONAL HEALTH BOARD
COSTA RICA

Anti-hookworm campaigns of the International Health Board and state and national governments owe a large part of their success to the influence exerted by school children. Everywhere the child in school receives a large share of the attention of the staff, and through him the interest of parents and of the community at large is awakened. Here is a group assembled in front of a Costa Rican schoolhouse to hear a lecture on hookworm disease.

Note.—In the JOURNAL for September, 1919, page 645, the heading reads, "Anti-Malaria Measures in Viti," and a reference is made in the text to malaria. There is no malaria in Viti, so that the device is not an anti-malarial one.

STORIES FROM THE
DAY'S WORK

Brief stories of helpful experience are solicited—EDITOR

Automatic Health Teachers.—A stereo-motorgraph set up in the men's waiting room of the Grand Central Station, New York City, constantly acts as teacher to the group waiting for the 5:13 or some other train. A series of slides depicting healthy methods of living and contrasting them with the unhealthy are automatically thrown on the screen for the benefit of John Doe of Keokuk, Richard Roe of Atlanta, and other men and boys from all parts of the country.

In order to learn the effect of this publicity method a tactful questioner has visited the exhibit at various times and entered into conversation with one or more onlookers, not disclosing his relationships with public health, however, or connecting himself with the exhibit in any way.

One of the first of these talks was with a khaki-clad youth who had done his "bit" overseas and was on his way home to Indiana. "They are certainly making a big fuss about a small matter, aren't they?" was the opening interrogatory assertion advanced by the reporter.

"Say, Buddie; if you believe that syphilis and gonorrhea are small matters you're dead wrong," was the prompt comeback of the doughboy. "I didn't pay much attention to them before I went into the Army—the fellows back home were too blamed ignorant about them and no one told when he had one. In the Army, though, it was different. We were closer to each other and got pretty chummy.

"Then was the time when we all spoke right out in meeting and you would be surprised at the number who owned up to having gotten one of these diseases when they were in civies.

"We learned a whole lot about them in the Army and I'm glad that the men who come in here are getting some straight dope. They need it as much or more than we did."

Similar conversations were had with a number of other ex-service men, most of them agreeing in the sentiments expressed by the first. More than one emphasized the fact that the "wise guy" who used to consider gonorrhea as a joke and syphilis as an exceedingly rare disease, had come out of the Army with real knowledge as to the seriousness and prevalence of both infections.

An elderly white haired man was the next one spoken to. He was busy, apparently, in reading a paper, but as each click of the machine announced a new picture or caption he would quickly transfer his attention to it. "What do you think of the idea," he was asked. "Well," he replied, "it doesn't affect me much, but I was just thinking what a fine thing it is for the boys. There was nothing like it when I was a youngster, but then—these are days when people are realizing that a great deal of disease is unnecessary," his way, undoubtedly, of expressing the more trite "knowledge is power."

Two middle-aged men on a nearby bench were discussing the slides. One evidently disapproved of them. From the portions of his talk which could be overheard, his arguments were to the effect that "such things shouldn't be shown in public," "if a man has one of these diseases it's nobody's business but his own," and "what right has the Government to 'butt in' on them." His companion listened for a while, then slapped him on the back and said, "You've certainly gotten to be a strong believer in 'personal rights,' Bill, since the prohibition amendment was passed." They then went on to their train, but perhaps Bill's companion convinced him that the doctrine of personal rights does not carry with it the right to endanger public health through failure to treat an infectious disease.

At the Pennsylvania terminal where a stereomotorgraph is also installed a negro porter was asked what it was for. When he had described its workings the reporter asked in a scoffing way, "Why don't they fight influenza or some more common disease instead of these?" The porter scratched his head for a moment. Then he answered, "Well, I s'pose it's because there's a *time* for the 'flu' but these other diseases come *all* the time."

"Then again," he continued, "you'd have to be a pretty close friend of my own before

476

you'd talk to me about syphilis or gonorrhea and I'd have to know you mighty well before I'd listen—but this machine talks *right out loud* to *everybody."*

As many as seventy men have been counted, crowded around one of these machines in a railroad terminal and, judging from the typical impressions told of above it seems safe to say that they are agencies of great potential value—agencies which state boards of health and other public and private social hygiene organizations might use to good effect.

✛

Making the Sewer Reach the Diapers.— Dr. E. C. Levy used to say that one reason why diarrheal diseases spread is because the sewer system does not extend to the baby's diaper. It is an altogether too common practice for careless mothers to allow soiled diapers to lie about on the floor, or elsewhere, where flies can get at them and where there is ample opportunity for contact infection. It is the custom in some places, though many health officers do not seem to be aware of this fact, for the nurses to teach mothers to rinse the soiled diaper as soon as it is taken from the child. The diaper is held firmly by the corner and thoroughly rinsed in the water closet, the closet being flushed once or twice at the same time. Of course care must be taken not to let go of it in the closet. It is then put to soak in a pail of water.

C. V. C.

✛

Experimental Proof of Infection by a Healthy Diphtheria Carrier.—A large part of the work of Health Officers consists in control by cultures and quarantine of healthy diphtheria carriers, as well as clinical cases. The general public is still very skeptical about the danger of such healthy children causing true diphtheria, and it is comparatively rare that we have reliable evidence of cases caused by such carriers. For this reason I think the following story of two cases of clinical diphtheria caused by a healthy carrier in a family is worth reporting.

This was a Mexican family called A., living in Belvedere which consisted of the following members: Mr. A., age 56; Mrs. A., age 60; Mrs. H., age 35; Maria, age 22; Manuel, age 18; Joe, age 15; Ascencion, age 14, and a baby.

The first case was Mrs. H., who started December 9th. She stayed at home. The two brothers, Manuel and Joe, were away from home at this time, and were not exposed until considerably later. Ascencion, a school child, was found to be a carrier on December 19th, when cultures were taken from all the family for release. She had had no throat symptoms or general illness, but had the signs of a mild nasal diphtheria. The house was still under quarantine and placarded, but in spite of this, Manuel came home January 6th and came down with diphtheria on the 13th. He was quite well when he came home, and it seems tolerably certain that he was infected by his sister, the healthy carrier.

Positive cultures obtained on the following dates from this carrier, Ascencion, proved that she was infectious at this time: December, 19, 23, 29; January 8, 15, 23, 31.

Manuel was promptly sent to the County Hospital January 16th. In spite of this evident result of Manuel's coming into the infected house, another brother, Joe, committed the same folly on the 20th and also came down with the diphtheria in a few days, namely on January 23d. A negative culture was obtained from Ascencion on the 19th, but the two positives obtained just before and after, indicate that she probably was infectious at some time soon after his arrival. This chronic carrier had been treated with the usual mild antiseptics and also silver nitrate 5 per cent, without success until January 31st. On that date and again on February 2d, I treated her nose and throat with a 2 per cent solution of gentian violet, and two subsequent cultures taken on February 2d and 4th were both negative. Apparently this new treatment was effective in her case.

WILLIAM L. HOLT, M.D.,

Los Angeles, Cal.

GOOD HEALTH AND GOOD CITIZENSHIP

The National Child Hygiene Association of New York City has devised one of the most striking and practical developments in public health education of recent years, in what it terms its "Parcel Post" exhibit. This comes ready for exhibition in a form suitable to almost any possible conditions or space limitations. Here are 25 panels ready for hanging on any handy wall or screen or for exposition in any store window. They are in groups of 5, each group centering about some pithy and important title, such as: "The good citizen is clean," "the good citizen is thrifty," "The good citizen values human life," etc.

and emphasize the need of loyalty and of cooperation for the common good. For those who would like to become missionaries in health education and good citizenship, the Association has placed these sets of panels on sale, demanding for them merely a nominal price.

They all emphasize the factors to good citizenship which thinkers realize lie in the proper appreciation of hygiene and sanitation.

The panels were prepared by the Association on consultation with specialists and their text is concise, attractive and direct. One group, copies of some of the panels being here reproduced, emphasizes the value of a clean mind in a clean body, the necessity of a clean house and clean premises, and that good citizenship has one of its outward and visible signs in the preservation of a clean city. These panels lay stress on "do," rather than "don't."

A. P. H. A. MEETING IN SAN FRANCISCO

CHANGE OF DATE

The attention of the members of the American Public Health Association is especially called to the change of date of the Forty-ninth Annual Meeting of the Association. After much consideration it has been set for the five days, September 13-17, instead of the previously announced date at the beginning of September. The fundamental reason for the change was the fact that there would be an important state election in California on September 30. This would have interfered with attendance, would have diverted the attention of many active workers among West Coast health officers from the meeting, and would have interfered with publicity through the press, both before and at the time of the meeting.

Another factor in determining the selection of the days named, September 13-17, was the meeting of the Association of Industrial Accident Boards and Commissioners at San Francisco the week following the A. P. H. A. meetings (September 20-24). It is not unlikely that the Southwestern Tuberculosis Conference will meet at San Francisco the week preceding the A. P. H. A. meeting. If not here it may be at Cheyenne, Wyo., the decision not yet having been made.

Definite announcements with reference to these meetings will find place in the Calendar of Conferences in the June issue of the JOURNAL.

SPECIAL TRAINS TO THE COAST

The NEWS LETTER for April has already presented the main suggestions with reference to a special A. P. H. A. train from Chicago to San Francisco, with the promise of details in this issue of the JOURNAL.

Chicago is the convenient center for the dispatching of such a train and plans have been formulated for a special A. P. H. A. train to leave the terminal of the Chicago & Northwestern Railroad in Chicago on the evening of Wednesday, September 8, 1920, at 10:30 p. m. Members who intend to take the transcontinental trip with their fellow health workers on the special train must report in Chicago in time to board it, having previously secured their reservations on it. Information with reference to local Travel Chairmen and rates follows.

The route from Chicago to San Francisco has been carefully chosen with reference to climatic conditions, and the itinerary arranged to view the Royal Gorge and its related scenic attractions and the Feather River Gorge, both by daylight and at convenient hours. The itinerary of the special train is the following:

ITINERARY OF A. P. H. A. SPECIAL TRAIN TO SAN FRANCISCO

Lv. Chicago	10:30 p.m.,	Wednesday,	September 8th,	via C. & N. W.	Central Time
Ar. Omaha	12:30 p.m.,	Thursday,	September 9th,	via C. & N. W.	
Lv. Omaha	1:00 p.m.,	Thursday,	September 9th,	via U. P.	
Ar. Denver	2:00 a.m.,	Friday,	September 10th,	via U. P.	
Lv. Denver	2:30 a.m.,	Friday,	September 10th,	via D. & R. G.	
Ar. Colorado Springs	4:30 a.m.,	Friday,	September 10th,	via D. & R. G.	Mountain Time
Pass through the Royal Gorge					
Ar. Salt Lake City	9:00 a.m.,	Saturday,	September 11th,	via D. & R. G.	
Spend the forenoon in Salt Lake City					
Lv. Salt Lake City	2:00 p.m.,	Saturday,	September 11th,	via S. Pac.	Pacific Time
Ar. San Francisco	6:00 p.m.,	Sunday,	September 12th,	via S. Pac.	

This itinerary is a special one for the A. P. H. A. train, and cannot be checked up by the regular folders of the railways. The scenic attractions include Colorado Springs, Pikes Peak, Royal Gorge, Canon of the Eagle River, Glenwood Springs, etc. At Salt Lake City a stop-over of five hours is arranged, enabling members to make sight-seeing tours of this interesting city, including the Mormon Temple and Tabernacle, a trip to Salt Air Beach, and perhaps an opportunity to attend an organ recital at the Tabernacle.

TICKET RATES FROM CHICAGO TO SAN FRANCISCO AND RETURN

Going via the above route to San Francisco and returning via Ogden and Salt Lake City, *(Continued on page 484)*

It is important to form your party for these special cars at the earliest possible moment.

Preliminary Returns of Membership Campaign

NEW NAMES PROPOSED FOR MEMBERSHIP IN THE

A. P. H. A.

FROM MARCH 13, 1920, TO MAY 4, 1920

NOTE—Names of sponsors are set in Bold Face type.
Names of proposed members are set in Roman.
*Asterisks indicate memberships received before the
beginning of the campaign.

ALABAMA

Jewell J. Smith, Fort Payne.
  G. H. Dubois, Fort Payne.
H. G. Perry, M. D., Montgomery.
  R. M. Kimbrough, M. D., Health Officer, Livingston.
J. Smith, Fort Payne.
  G. H. Dubois, Chemist, Fort Payne.

ARKANSAS

Edwin F. Voigt, Fort Smith.
  Susan A. Taylor. R. N.,, Tuberculosis Nurse, Fort Smith.
  *G. May D. V. S., Chief Dairy Inspector Fort Smith.
C. W. Garrison, M. D., Little Rock.
  *Cyrus F. Crosby, M. D., Heber Springs.
  *Thomas Douglass, M. D. County Health Officer, Ozark.
  *C. W. Hall, M. D., Greenwood.
  *M. E. Howard, M. W., Perryville.
  *J. M. Jelks, M. D., Searcy.
  *C. H. Newkirk, M. D., City Health Officer Corning.
  *J. S. Westenfield, M. D., Health Officer, Conway.
  *J. M. Williams, M. D., County Health Officer, Malvern.

CALIFORNIA

Margaret Beattie, Berkeley.
  M. Dorothy Beck, Berkeley.
R. F. Goudey, Berkeley.
  E. A. Reinke, Asst. Engr., State Board of Health, Berkeley.
  Charles R. Gerth, Bacteriologist, Betteravia.
Frank L. Kelly, M. D., Berkeley.
  Edward T. Ross, Chief Sanitary Inspector California State Board of Health, Sacramento.
Ida May Stevens, Berkeley.
  E. Francis Rodgers, Berkeley.
Clyde F. Smith, Berkeley.
  Ralph Hilscher, Chief Engr., Cal. State Board of Health, Berkeley.
F. E. Twining, Fresno.
  John F. McKenna, D. V. S., City Veterinarian, Fresno.
  Neal Hultslander, Bacteriologist, Fresno.
L. M. Powers, M. D., Los Angeles.
  *Irving R. Bancroft, Sec., State Board of Health, Sacramento.
C. A. Kofoid Ph. D., Oakland.
  Albert H. Rowe, M. D., Oakland.
Louis Olsen, A. B., Palo Alto.
  Donald W. MacNair, State Dairy Inspector, Saratoga.
I. R. Bancroft, M. D., Sacramento.
  Rozzie Manning, R. N., Public Health Nurse, Woodland.
  George E. Ebright, M. D., Pres., Cal. State Bd. of Health, San Francisco.
Guy P. Jones Sacramento.
  A. G. Bailey, M. D., Suisun City.
  Walter E. Bates, M. D., Health Officer, Davis.
  Charles R. Blake, M. D., Commissioner of Health, Richmond.

Stephen F. Butler, Health Officer, Salinas.
M. A. Craig, M. D., County Health Officer, Lakeport.
George W. Desrosier. M. D., Health Officer, Colusa.
Thomas J. De Vaughn, M. D., Health Officer, Huntington Park.
S. P. S. Edwards, M. D., Health Officer, Ontario.
J. L. Fanning, M. D., Health Officer Roseville.
Stephen P. Galvin L. L. B., Health Officer, Los Banos.
Jerome T. Gardner, M. D., Health Officer, Corcoran.
W. J. Guinan, M. D., Health Officer Marysville.
Anna C. Jamme, R. N., Director, Bureau of Registration of Nurses, San Francisco.
T. H. Kuser, M. D., Health Officer, San Rafael.
W. C. Jenney, M. D., County Health Officer, Vacaville.
Samuel C. Long, M. D., Bakersfield.
W. T. Lucas, M. D., Santa Maria.
William H. Marshall, Health Officer, Chico.
Benjamin T. Mouser, M. D., Health Officer, Piedmont.
Charles E. Pearson, M. D., Health Officer, Turlock.
Elgar Reed, M. D., Health Officer Chino.
C. A. Robinson M. D., Health Officer, Madera.
L. E. Ross, State Registrar of Vital Statistics, Sacramento.
Fletcher Greene Sanborn, M. D., Health Officer, Arcadia.
O. T. Schulze, M. D., Health Officer, Napa.
James Roe Snyder, M. D., City Bacteriologist, Sacramento.
Frederick L. Stein, M. D., Health Officer, Yosemite.
*J. W. Thayer, M. D., Health Officer, Gilroy.
Ethel M. Watters, M. D., Director, Bureau of Child Hygiene, San Francisco.
William B. Wells, M. D., Health Officer, Riverside.
William W. Worster, M. D., Health Officer, San Gabriel.
Paul Wright, M. D., Physician and Surgeon, Sisson.
J. C. McGovern, D. D. S., Health Officer, South San Francisco.
Donald MacCulloch Gedge M. D., San Francisco.
  P. A. Millar, M. D., San Francisco.
Edward E. Johnson, M. D., San Francisco.
  Pacific Wasserman Laboratories, Attn. Geo. Gilman, Director, San Francisco.
Agnes Walker, M. D., San Francisco.
  Alice L. Thompson, M. D., Bacteriologist, Board of Health, San Francisco.
E. W. Schultz, M. D., Stanford University.
  *C. V. Burke, Ph. D., Bacteriologist, Palo Alto.
  Lucille J. Mahoney, A. B., Bacteriologist, San Francisco.

COLORADO

Olive A. Chapman, Denver.
  *Agnes Cogan, State Supervisor Public Health Nursing, Cheyenne, Wyoming.
Clinton G. Hickey, M. D., Denver.
  Ray Lawrence Drinkwater, M. D., Denver.
  Roy Wiest, M. D., Estes Park.
  Minnie C. T. Love M. D., Denver.
  Edward James Horan, M. D., Glenwood Springs.
  Arthur T. Monismith, M. D., Fort Lupton.
  A. L. Stubbs, M. D., La Junta.
  Daniel J. Horton, M. D., LaSalle.
  Herman C. Homer, M. D., City Health Officer, Cheyenne Wells.

Mary Tower Bigelow, M. D., Denver.
S. R. McKelvey, S. B., A. M., M. D., Denver.
Wilbur T. Cannon. Pure Food & Drug Commissioner (State), Denver.
J. W. Morgan, M. D, Denver.
Clinton G. Hickey, M. D., Denver.

CONNECTICUT

LeRoy A. Wilkes, M. D., Bridgeport.
Edward J. Lynch, M. D., Supt., State Tuberculosis Sanatorium, Shelton.
Maria H. Ludlum, School Nurse. Brideport.
G. H. Noxon, M. D., Darien.
Charles B. Keeler, M. D., Darien.
Philip S. Platt, C. P. H., New Haven.
Mrs. E. G. Ruckland, New Haven Board of Health, New Haven.
Alexander C. Tener, LL. B., Member of Board of Health, Sewickley. Pa.
Dorothy Holland, New Haven.
William S. Sturges. Bacteriologist. New Haven.
Prof. C.-E. A. Winslow, New Haven.
Frank U. Thatcher, Epidemiologist. New Haven.
H. B. Hanchett, M. D., Torrington.
Coe-Brass Branch, American Brass Co., Atten. Robert Thursfield. Torrington.
The Torrington Co., Standard Plant, Atten. H. J. Cook. Torrington.
Torrington Manufacturing Co., Atten. H. G. Ellis, Supt., Torrington.
Borough of Torrington, Civil Engineer's Office, Torrington.
Turner & Seymour Mfg. Co., Torrington.
Harriet A. Parker, R. N., Torrington.
Alice J. Wedge, R. N., School Nurse, Torrington.
E. Brodsky, M. D., Westport.
Anna M. Cullen, R. N., Bridgeport.

DISTRICT OF COLUMBIA

W. C. Fowler, M. D., Washington.
A. C. Patterson, M. D., Chief, Bureau of Vital Statistics, Washington.
E. A. Peterson, M. D., Washington.
Charles B. Mack, M. D., D. P. H., Washington.
James A. Tobey, Washington.
Taliaferro Clark, M. D., Asst. Surg. General U. S. P. H. S., Chevy Chase. Md.
Harrieth S. Douglas. Red Cross Nurse, Washington.
Katharine W. Holmes, R. N., Public Health Nurse, Washington.
James L. Fieser, Asst. Gen. Mgr., American Red Cross, Washington.
*Myra M. Hulst, Statistician, Washington.
Fred C. Croxton, Asst. Gen. Mgr., American Red Cross, Washington.
William A. Kemper, Washington.
Frederick C. Munroe, Gen. Mgr., American Red Cross, Washington.
Margaret Sawyer, Dietitian, Washington.
Charlotte E. Van Duzor, R. N., Glencarlyn, Va.
Mabel T. Boardman, Sec. American Red Cross. Washington.
Ivan C. Weld, Washington.
George B. Taylor, Bacteriologist, Washington.

FLORIDA

R. L. Arms, M. D., Jacksonville.
*Arthur G. Grover, M. D., Prof. Pathology and Bacteriology, Los Angeles, Cal.
E. M. L'Engle, M. D., Jacksonville.
St. Luke's Hospital Assn., Jacksonville.
Ralph N. Green, M. D., Jacksonville.
George C. Kingsbury, M. D., Largo.
S. M. Worley, M. D., A. A. Surgeon. U. S. P. H. S., St. Augustine.

GEORGIA

M. F. Haygood, M. D., Atlanta.
F. W. McCorkle. M. D., Commissioner of Health Bainbridge.
J. D Applewhite, M. D., Valdosta.
Gertrude Anderson, R. N., Public Health Nurse, Marietta.

ILLINOIS

Maximilian Kern, M. D., Chicago.
S. M. Edison, U. S. Research Laboratory, Chicago.
S. G. West. M. D., Chicago.
Esther Werner, R. N., Springfield.
Baxter K. Richardson, State Dept. of Public Health, Springfield.
Minnie Hahn, R. N., Danville.
C St. Clair Drake, M. D., Springfield.
*S. N. Trockey, M. D., Chicago.
*Herbert W. Gray, M. D., Chicago.

INDIANA

J. N. Hurty, M. D., Indianapolis.
Charles S. Hurd, Consulting Sanitary Engineer Indianapolis.
Frank R. Doll, M. D., Whiting.
Pauline E. Kuehler, R. N., Whiting.

IOWA

Amy Beers, R. N., Fairfield.
Merle M. Wright, R. N., Public Health Nurse, Jefferson Co., Fairfield.
Prof. Earle L. Waterman, Iowa City.
John W. Teed, Chmn, Davis County Tuber. Assn., Bloomfield.
Geo. H. Steinle, M. D., Health Officer, Burlington.
B. Courahon, M. D., Health Officer, Sioux City.
Mrs. Max Mayer, Asst. in Social Welfare, Univ. of Iowa, Iowa City.
Iowa Child Welfare Research Station, State University of Iowa, Iowa City.
W. J. McDonald, M. D., Iowa City.
Charles R. Thomas, M. D., Asst. Director Student Health, Iowa City.
R. L. Laybourn, Iowa City.
Leon C. Havens, M. D., Asst. Epidemiologist, Univ. of Iowa.
Arthur M. Brown, M. D., Asst. in Prev. Med. & Hygiene, Iowa City.
Sarah R. Kelman, M. D., Keokuk.
Marianne Zichy, R. N., Public Health Nurse. Keokuk.
Margaret C. Henke, R. N., Public Health Nurse. Keokuk.
A. J. McLaughlin, M. D., Sioux City.
P. B. McLaughlin. M. D., Sioux City.

KANSAS

J. J. Entz, M. D., Hillsboro.
Ione S. Clayton, M. D., Arkansas City.

MAINE

L. D. Bristol, M. D., Augusta.
*E. P. Goodrich, M. D., District Health. Officer, Lewiston.
*W. A. Harris. Ex. Sec. Maine Anti-Tuber. Assn., Augusta.
*G. H. Hutchins, M. D., District Health Officer, Presque Isle.
James W. Loughlin, M. D., District Health Officer, Damariscotta.
Hiram W. Ricker, Maine State Health Council, So. Poland.
*J. F. Stevens, M. D., Health Officer, Millinocket.
A. G. Wiley, M. D., Health Officer, Bar Mills.
C. Edw. Britto M. D., Practising Physician. Stockton Springs.
Frans Leyonboro. M. D., Health Officer, North Haven.
A. M. G. Soule, Augusta.
Brooks Drown, State Dairy Inspector, Augusta.

W. A. Hennessy, Bangor.
  Henry D. McNeil, M. D., Health Officer, Bangor.
Mrs. S. R. Prentiss, Bangor.
  Louise P. Hopkins, Visiting Nurse for Tuber-
  culosis Assn., Bangor.
  Ralph Whittier, Bangor.
  Carl R. O'Brien, Bangor.
H. D. Worth, Bangor.
  A. L. Smith, M. D., Physician, Machias.
  F. D. Weymouth, M. D., Health Officer, Charles-
  ton.
Chester S. Kingsley, A. B., Bath.
  Wyman P. Wadleigh, Health Officer, Bar Harbor.
Thomas Tetreau, M. D., Portland.
  *Ludovic Joseph Dumont, M. D., Health Officer,
  Lewiston.

MARYLAND

John H. Gregory, Baltimore.
  Ronald T. Abercrombie, M. D., Health Officer,
  Baltimore.
C. Hampson Jones, M. D., Baltimore.
  J. Frederick Hempel, M. D., Asst. Commissioner
  of Health, Baltimore.
R. H. Riley, M. D., Baltimore.
  J. S. Bowen, M. D., Deputy State Health Officer,
  Mt. Washington.
  E. A. Jones, M. D., Deputy Health Officer, Cam-
  bridge.
  H. W. McComas, M. D., County Health Officer,
  Oakland.
Abel Wolman, Baltimore.
  Lillian C. Burroughs, Chemist, Maryland State
  Dept. of Health, Baltimore.
  S. J. Caskey, Bacteriologist, Maryland State
  Dept. of Health, Baltimore.
  W. F. Reindollar, Chemist, Maryland State Dept.
  of Health, Baltimore.
  W. H. Schulze, Chemist, Maryland State Dept.
  of Health, Baltimore.
  Harry B. Siegmund, Baltimore.
  John Wayner, Bacteriologist, Maryland State.
  Dept. of Health, Baltimore.
  Harold E. D. Willis, Bacteriologist, Maryland
  State Dept. of Health, Baltimore.

MASSACHUSETTS

Charles E. Marshall, Amherst.
  Harold H. Plough, Ph. D., Assoc. Prof. Biology,
  Amherst College, Amherst.
J. P. Bill, M. D., Boston.
  *Arthur M. Fagan, M. D., Roxbury.
J. Bronfenbrenner, Ph. D., D. P. H., Boston.
  Robert W. Lamson, Bacteriologist, Harvard
  Medical School, Boston.
Merrill E. Champion, M. D., Boston.
  *Mrs. Mabel Greeley Smith, Cambridge Anti-
  Tuberculosis Assn., Cambridge.
B. W. Carey, M. D., Boston.
  Frank C. Grangon, M. D., Randolph.
  Albert A. Carter, M. D., Boston.
  Horace J. Soule, M. D., Town Physician, Win-
  throp.
Prof. C. M. Hilliard, Boston.
  Helen Gunn, Boston.
A. W. Hedrich, Boston.
  *Roger I. Lee, M. D., Prof. of Hygiene, Harvard
  University, Cambridge.
Mrs. Wm. E. McNamara, Boston.
  Mrs. F. Lothrop Ames, Boston.
  Sister Georgiana, Superior, Notre Dame Aca-
  demy, Roxbury.
Harold E. Peebles, Boston.
  *W. Porter Pratt, M. D., Quincy.
Aaron P. Pratt, Brighton.
  *Mildred Lauder, B. A., Concord, N. H.
  *Mildred E. Wilson, B. A., Richfield, Kan.

M. P. Horwood, Cambridge.
  Sanford B. Hooker, M. D., Boston.
Oscar H. Perrin, Charlestown.
  George L. Gould, Dairy Inspector, Eagle Bridge,
  N. Y.
Burton G. Philbrick, Salem.
  Leo B. Bunker, Bacteriologist, Deerfoot Farms
  Dairy, Southboro.
W. H. Young, Springfield.
  L. L. Williams, Jr., M. D., P. A. Surgeon, U. S
  P. H. S., Springfield.
Laetitia M. Snow, Wellesley.
  *Mabel Bishop, A. B., Prof. of Physiology, Hood
  College, Frederick, Md.
E. H. Trowbridge, M. D., Worcester.
  Leslie P. Leland, M. D., Worcester.

MICHIGAN

A. W. Nelson, M. D., Battle Creek.
  *Manuel S Tarpinian, Bacteriologist, Battle
  Creek.
J. E. Mead, M. D., Detroit.
  Ford Motor Company, Highland Park.
Roy W. Pryor, Detroit.
  Ruby R. Green, Bacteriologist, Detroit Board of
  Health.
F. C. Potter, M. D., Kalamazoo.
  Grace C. Robinson, Laboratory Technician, Paris,
  Texas.
W. C. Hirn, Lansing.
  *Cornelius John Addison, M. D., City Health Of-
  ficer, Muskegon.
C. C. Young, M. D., Lansing.
  *Minna Crooks, Bacteriologist, Lansing.

MINNESOTA

P. M. Hall, M. D., Minneapolis.
  Otto F. Bradley, Exec. Sec., Hennepin County
  Tuberculosis Assn., Minneapolis.
E. C. Rosenow, M. D., Rochester.
  Walter F. Bleifuss, M. D., Health Officer, Roches-
  ter.

MISSISSIPPI

G. G. Hampton, M. D., Tupelo.
  Walter C. Hausheer, M. D., International Health
  Board, Tupelo.

MISSOURI

Geo. H. Jones, M. D., Jefferson City.
  Carlisle P. Knight, M. D., Director, Div. Child
  Hygiene, Missouri State Board of Health.
  Richard L. Russell, M. D., Director, State Divi-
  sion Venereal Diseases, Jefferson City.
Nella M. Woods, R. N., Jefferson City.
  J. T. Mathews, M. D., Heber Springs.
  Elazebeth Bass Reed, M. D., A. A. Surgeon, U. S
  P. H. S., Jefferson City.
Thomas Parran, Jr., M. D., Springfield.
  Guy D. Callaway, M. D., Health Officer, Spring-
  field.
Joseph A. Corby, St. Joseph.
  E. A. Logan, City Bacteriologist, St. Joseph.

NEBRASKA

Mrs. K. R. J. Edholm, Omaha.
  Alice Marshall, Sec., Omaha Tuber. Committee,
  Omaha.

NEW JERSEY

R. Clifford Errickson, Long Branch.
  Juliet M. Doherty, R N., Supervisor, Public
  Health Nurses, Long Branch.

Jacob G. Lipman, M. D., New Brunswick.
Thurlow C. Nelson, Asst. Prof. of Zoology, New Brunswick.
Laurence Runyon, M. D., New Brunswick.

NEW MEXICO

Thomas P. B. Jones, Deming.
Sally A. Gorman, R. N., U. S. Public Health Service, Deming.
Harold F. Gray, Santa Fe.
*Magdalene Banzhof, R. N., Santa Fe.
Henry M. Brown, M. D., Health Officer, Hagerman.
*Augustus Davis, M. D., Bernalillo.
C. W. Gerber, M. D., Health Officer, La Cruces.
C. E. Waller, M. D., Santa Fe.
M. M. Crocker, M. D., County Health Officer, Lordsburg.
A. F. Brown, M. D., Health Officer, Ft. Sumner
W. F. Wittwer, M. D., Los Lunas.
George S. Luckett, M. D., Santa Fe.
*Alice A. Blake, Presbyterian Missionary, Trementina.
J. H. Linder, M. D., Health Officer, Socorro.

NEW YORK

Theodore Horton, Albany.
C. A. Holmquist, Asst. Engr. State Dept. of Health, Albany.
Henry Ryon, Asst. Engr. State Dept. of Health, Albany.
Prof. B. R. Rickards, Albany.
C. Josephine Durkee, R. N., Asst. Editor, Health News, N. Y. State Dept. of Health, Albany.
A. B. Wadsworth, M. D., Albany.
*Ruth I. Stephens, County Bacteriologist, Auburn.
Edward H. Marsh, M. D., Brooklyn.
Wm. N. Miller, M. D., Health Officer, Croton-on-Hudson.
Lee K. Frankel, Ph. D., New York.
*Helen R. Y. Reid, Montreal, Canada.
Hermann M. Biggs, M. D., New York.
*J. H. Fotheringham, Buffalo.
*Lewis F. Frissell, M. D., New York City.
Helen L. Palliser, M. D., Poughkeepsie.
Augusta T. Freeman, Public Health Nurse, Poughkeepsie.
A. W. Schoonmaker, Poughkeepsie.
Frederick W. Sears, M. D., Syracuse.
Edmund C. Boddy, M. D., Sanitary Supervisor, Albany.

NORTH CAROLINA

William M. Jones, Greensboro.
Greensboro Health Dept., Atten. B. B. Williams, M. D., Greensboro.
Millard Knowlton, M. D., Raleigh.
Mrs. Josephine Washington, Guild Agent, Bureau of Venereal Diseases, Raleigh.
W. S. Rankin, M. D., Raleigh.
*D. A. Fitch, State Sanitary Inspector, Fayetteville.
*University of North Carolina, Atten. E. C. Branson, Chapel Hill.
Chas. E. Low, M. D. Wilmington.
W. A. Davis, Expert, U. S. P. H. S., Savannah, Ga.
John C. Weasell, M. D., Member of the Board of Health, Wilmington.
L. P. Williams, M. D., Asst. Health Officer, Wilmington.

NORTH DAKOTA

C. J. McGurren, M. D., Devils Lake.
Edwin L. Goss, M. D., Carrington.
W. D. Jones, M. D., Devils Lake.
A. F E. Schierbaum, M. D., Hebron.
H. W. Emanuel, M. D., Supt. Sargent County Board of Health, Milnor.
Ed. S. Fitzmaurice, M. D., Mohall.

S. W. Hill, M. D., County Health Officer, Regent.
W. A. Thomas, M. D., U. S. Indian Service, Solen.
W. L. Gordon, M D., County Health Officer, Washburn.
A. G. Long, M. D., University.
Caroline Steele, S. B., Bacteriologist, Grand Forks.
Edwin M. Stanton, Bacteriologist, Bismarck.
Charles R. Allen, B. S., Bacteriologist, Minot.
Miss Della Johnson, Bacteriologist, Fargo.

OHIO

Frank I. Mayer, Chillicothe.
G. E Robbins, M. D., Commissioner of Health, Chillicothe.
Frank Woodbury Jones, Cleveland.
Glenn Green, Sanitary Chemist, Cleveland.
Alfred A. Burger, Sanitary Engineer, Doylestown.
E. K. Kline, A. M., Columbus.
Leuty Vanetta Neville, R. N., Instructor of Hygiene, Toledo.
A. W. Freeman, M. D., Columbus.
*J. M. O'Neal, M. D., Muskingum County Health Commissioner, Zanesville.
*Alexander Joseph Gilbert, Bacteriologist, Newark.
*Clara Viola McWhirk, Bacteriologist, Toledo.
M. B. Floyd, M. D., Dayton.
Frederick G. Barr, M. D., Physician for N. C. R. Co., Dayton.

PENNSYLVANIA

Paul Serre, Dixmont, Pa.
Myra R. McBride, R. N., Dixmont.
Myrtle C. Van Lur, R. N., Dixmont.
J. L. Bower, M. D., Glenolden.
*S. C. Basney, M. D., Glenolden.
A. G. Sandblad, M. D., McKeesport.
J. Clarence Kelly, M. D., McKeesport.
H. S. Arthur, M. D., McKeesport.
David F. Owen, Hospital Supt., McKeesport.
D. E. Hottenstein, M. D., Millersburgh.
Charles P. Polk, President, Board of Health, Millersburgh.
S Gertrude Bush, New Bethlehem.
Wm. C. Keller, M. D., New Bethlehem.
C. C. Ross, M. D., County Medical Director, Clarion.
Joseph A. Robinson, M. D., Pres., Local Board of Health, New Bethlehem.
Lawrence M. Rosenfeld, P. D., Philadelphia.
Ralph G. Sharadin, P. D., Bacteriologist, Kutztown.
George H. Shaw, Philadelphia.
*Norman H. Taylor, M. D., Asst. Director, Dept. of Public Works, Philadelphia.
Henry Field Smyth, M. D., Philadelphia.
Caspar G. Burn, Moore.
C. Lincoln Furbush, M. D., Philadelphia.
*J. F. Polk, M. D., Slidell.
*Lawrence M. Rosenfeld, Bacteriologist, Philadelphia.
A. S. Daggette, M. D., Pittsburgh.
William T. Johnson, Pittsburgh.
Prof. J. E. Rush, Pittsburgh.
*Grover E. Rickard, Sanitary Engineer, Pittsburgh.
Emil L. Nuebling, Reading.
Ira J. Hain, M. D., Health Officer, Reading.
Miss Heloise Carroll, York.
J. Frank Small, M. D., Health Officer, York.

SOUTH CAROLINA

James A. Hayne, M. D., Columbia.
Mrs. Ruth A. Dodd, Supervisor, Bureau Child Hygiene, Columbia.

Ira V. Hiscock, C lumbia.
Mrs. R. E. Wheeler, R. N., Public Health
Nurse, Columbia.
Mrs. J. T. Giltman, R. N., Public Health Nurse.
Columbia.
Dr. G. A. Wheeler, M. D., Spartanburg.
Charles L. Booth, M. D., Medical Officer in
V. D. Clinic, Spartanburg.

TENNESSEE

Homer N. Calver, Knoxville.
Frederick A. Ault, Chairman Knox County
Chapter American Red Cross, Knoxville.
Robinson Bosworth, M. D., Memphis.
W. B. Cleveland, Chairman, Memphis & Shelby
County Tuberculosis Hospital, Memphis.
Hon. Rowlett Paine, Memphis.
Bolton Smith, Memphis.

VIRGINIA

A. W. Garnett, M. D., Danville.
Samuel Newman, M. D., Danville.
Prof. Aubrey H. Straus, Richmond.
Thomas L. Driscoll, M. D., P. A. Surgeon, U. S.
P. H. S., Richmond.
Loyd C. Bird, State Board of Health, Richmond.

WEST VIRGINIA

Charles E. Gabel, M. D., Charleston.
Maude D. Wood, Technician, Charleston.
S. L. Jepson, M. D., Charleston.
L. H. McCuskey, M. D., County Health Officer,
Moundsville.
J. B. Walkinshaw, M. D., County and City Health
Officer, Wellsburg.
A. J. Pickering, M. D., Health Officer, Hunt-
ington.
R. E. Gaynor, M. D., Parkersburg.
Charles P. Anderson, Supt. Solvay Collieries Co-.,
Kingston.
Ford Huff, M. D., County Health Officer, Parsons.
J. T. Phillips, M. D., Nashville, Tenn.
George Coleman, Wheeling.
J. A. Campbell, M. D., City Bacteriologist,
Wheeling.

WISCONSIN

L. M. Field, M. D., Beloit.
E. B. Brown, M. D., Beloit.
Justine L. Thorp, R. N., Public Health Nurse,
Beloit.
Henry F. Miller, Kenosha.
Irma Rasmussen, R. N., County Nurse, Kenosha.
Edward A. Babcock, Madison.
H. E. Purcell, M. D., Health Officer, Madison.
Miss Edna Within, R. N., Public Health Nurse.
Merrill.
John Le Feber, Milwaukee.
*Union Milk Company, Ltd., Atten. of F. M. Car-
lyle, Calgary, Canada.
Bertha V. Thomson, Oshkosh.
Laura M. Johnston, Oshkosh.
R. A. Maddock, Oshkosh.
John F. Snieder, M. D., Oshkosh.
A. J. Koehler, M. D., Oshkosh.
Prof. H. W. Talbot, Prof. of Biology and Bac-
teriology. Oshkosh.

CANADA

W. H. Hattie, M. D., Halifax, N. S.
P. S. Campbell, M. D., Medical Health Officer.
Port Wood. N. S.
Clarence Miller, M. D., Medical Health Officer,
Stellarton, N. S.
M. G. Tompkins, M. D., Dominion, N. S.
M. M. Seymour, M. D., Regina, Saskatchewan.
Angus M. S. Allan, Sanitary Inspector, Regina.
Bertha Dymond, M. D., Medical Inspector, Re-
gina.
Frederick C. Hill, Regina.
Augustine Joseph Marwood, Moosejaw.
Francis G. McGill, Regina.
Alex Mitchell, Sanitary Inspector, Regina.
Millen A. Nickle, F. R., C. S. E., Weyburn.
Gerald G. Roberts, Bacteriologist, Regina.
Thomas Watson, Sanitary Inspector, Regina.
Alice M. Wiggins, R. N., Public Health Nurse.
Regina.
A. W. Hedrich, Boston, Mass.
*Department of Public Health, Atten. A. R. Turn-
bull, M. D., Moose Jaw, Saskatchewan.

HAWAII

E. B. Porter, Sec., Territorial Board of Health, Hilo.
*Clifford Charlock. Chief Sanitary Inspector. Hilo.

A. P. H. A. MEETING IN SAN FRANCISCO

(Continued from page 479)

or Los Angeles and thence to Salt Lake City, Albuquerque or El Paso, $96.12.

Returning via Portland, Ore., and Huntington; or Portland, Seattle, Spokane, Minneapolis; or via Portland, Vancouver and Minneapolis, $115.56.

Rates from other central points to San Francisco and return, using the special A. P. H. A. train from Chicago west, are not available at the moment, but will be published later, and also information with reference to routes for the return.

PULLMAN RATES FROM CHICAGO—ONE WAY

Lower berth	$17.01
Upper berth	13.61
Drawing room	60.48
Compartment	48.08

War-tax is included in these rates.

FROM YOUR HOME TO CHICAGO

In order that the benefits of the trip may be utilized to the utmost, parties may be made up which can travel together, perhaps in a special Pullman, from central points in different districts. Cars will be run from Boston and New York, and arrangements can be made to secure them from other centers if there is sufficient demand. For New York, Dr. S. Dana Hubbard, Health Department of the City of New York, will act as Travel Chairman for the district about the metropolis, while members in the New England states should address, Secretary, A. P. H. A., 169 Massachusetts Avenue, Boston, Mass. For the Middle West, Dr. W. A. Evans, 906 Tribune Building, Chicago, Ill., will act as Travel Chairman, and will be able to give necessary information.

Remember the new date, San Francisco, September 13-17, 1920.

American Journal of Public Health

Official Monthly Publication of the American Public Health Association

Publication office: 124 W. Polk Street, Chicago, Ill.
Editorial office: 169 Massachusetts Ave., Boston, Mass.

Subscription price, $4 per year. American Public Health Association membership, including subscription, $5 per year.
Subscriptions and memberships may be sent to the A. P. H. A., 169 Massachusetts Ave., Boston, Mass.

| Vol. X | JUNE, 1920 | No. 6 |

COMMUNITY MEDICINE AND PUBLIC HEALTH

ERNST CHRISTOPHER MEYER, PH. D.,

Director of Surveys and Exhibits, International Health Board of the Rockefeller Foundation, New York City

Read before Public Health Administration Section, American Public Health Association, at New Orleans, La., October 29, 1919.

Only the rich and the poor get adequate medical attention today; the middle class are, to a large extent, less fortunate. In this the medical organization of the country has failed to accomplish its purpose. Dr. Meyer suggests lower cost of medical service through better administration and community medicine or pay clinics.

THE United States is abundantly supplied with physicians. On an average there is one doctor for every 750 citizens. England and France are less than half, and Germany and Austria were less than a third as plentifully supplied. Rural regions of the United States, of course, have fewer physicians than the cities. Their supply approximates the ratios just referred to for European countries.

PREVALENCE OF SICKNESS

Something is known, fortunately, concerning the extent of sickness, though the surface of this vital matter has hardly been scratched. The important investigations here are the sickness censuses taken by the Metropolitan Life Insurance Company, under the direction of Doctors Lee K. Frankel and Louis I. Dublin; the New York City Department of Health, under the supervision of Doctors William H. Guilfoy and Shirley W. Wynne; the State Charities Aid Association, under the guidance of Dr. J. J. Weber; the Framingham Community Health and Tuberculosis Demonstration, under the management of Dr. Donald B. Armstrong; the report on "Disabling Sickness among the Population of Seven Cotton Mill Villages of South Carolina in Relation to Family Income," by Doctors Edgar Sydenstricker, G. A. Wheeler and Joseph Goldberger, of the Public Health Service; the report on disability by age and occupation by Dr. Boris Emmet in "Modern Medicine," September, 1919.*

These censuses included 16,717 cases of sickness among more than 715,000 people. The first mentioned census alone covered over 13,000 cases of sickness in a population of 630,000, which were distributed among seven states. By "sick-

* This report is being issued officially by the United States Bureau of Labor Statistics.

ness" was understood "an illness so serious that it either necessitated or should have necessitated the patient's going to bed or securing medical aid." The censuses also determined the proportion of the sick who were disabled, i. e., too ill to work. The sickness rate was found to be about 22 per thousand; the disability rate about 18 per thousand. The population of the United States in 1918 was roughly 105,000,000. At any one time, assuming a sickness rate of about 25 per thousand among the population as a whole,† there are hence some 2,600,000 persons sick. The average duration of cases of sickness from onset of sickness to date of the census is about seven days.‡ The 365 days of the year may hence be divided into about 52 successive periods of sickness. On this basis we have in this country annually about 135,-850,000 cases of illness of the serious type just defined. This is more than one case for every inhabitant per year.

When minor or trivial illnesses are included, and particularly ailments which would profit by medical or dental advice or treatment, the number of cases per year, according to certain somewhat limited findings of the censuses, are more than doubled.

The losses to society due to sickness are known to be many and heavy. Medical care and drugs must be paid for. Sickness is apt to have far-reaching effects in impairing the living and working efficiency of families burdened with it. Then there is the sorrow, the physical and mental suffering. Above all, the loss in actual working days, that is, in earning power. This latter item has been variously calculated and represents an enormous total. Thus in North Carolina, a most progressive state in matters of public health, with a male population

† According to the sickness survey findings the morbidity rate would seem to be slightly higher in parts of the country not covered by the surveys. Hence a rate of 25 rather than 22 per thousand was chosen.

‡ This is based on the important findings of Dr. Boris Emmet. The investigation covered 40,000 wage earners and 42 occupations. The average period of disability was found to be 6.6 days.

over 15 years of age slightly in excess of 700,000, it has been estimated that no less than 5,250,000 working days are lost per year by the male population alone, and over 7,650,000 by the female population over 15 years of age. You may attach your own value to the worth of a working day.

PRESENT MEDICAL CARE OF THE SICK

What medical service do these huge numbers of sick receive? What interest have you as health officers in this? The Metropolitan Life Insurance Company surveys shows that no less than 27.2 per cent of the cases of sickness classed as "disabled," i. e., unable to work, were found to be wholly without the medical care of a physician. The States Charities Aid Survey showed 24 per cent of the disabled without medical care—a striking similarity in findings. Of the seriously sick, whether disabled or not, it would seem therefore that at least a fourth are without a doctor's aid. The total cases of serious sickness per year in the country was estimated at 135,850,-000. On this basis about 34,000,000 cases of sickness which should have medical care go without medical care every year. And if we add to this number the more trivial cases which would profit by medical or dental advice, the number may, according to the census findings, be more than doubled.

The sickness censuses of the Metropolitan Life Insurance Company already referred to revealed that of the total number sick 72.8 per cent were cared for. Of these, 61 per cent were cared for in the homes, 9.8 per cent in hospitals, and 2 per cent in dispensaries. On this basis, taking the country as a whole, 101,887,-500 cases were cared for. Of these, 91,228,500 were cared for in home, 7,942,-000 in hospitals, and 2,717,000 in dispensaries. In his book, *Dispensaries*, Dr. Davis states that between four and five million persons received medical care through the clinics and dispensaries of the country within a single year. If the present estimate that about 2,000,000 of the seriously sick annually get care at dispensaries is correct, then it would seem that probably 1,000,000 cases of the class of minor illnesses, excluded by the censuses, seek and get the benefits of free, or nominally charged for, medical service today; whereas, several millions of the more seriously sick, who could pay something for medical service, do not seek or get it.

Nor do all cases which have medical care seem to receive adequate care. The State Charities Aid Association Survey, the only one that went into the question of adequacy or inadequacy of care, revealed that 20 per cent of the cases cared for in hospitals and 45 per cent of cases cared for in homes received inadequate care. By "adequate" care was understood care which resulted in the patient's recovery where recovery could be expected, and which was of such a character that neither the patient nor the community incurred avoidable risks. The statistical basis of this part of the survey was too meager to warrant application of these percentages to the country as a whole. Suffice it to say that evidently a very large proportion of the 91,228,500 cases cared for in homes had inadequate care due largely to poverty, improper surroundings, homes unprepared for convalescence, ignorant attendants, and insufficient medical attention. The inadequacy of hospital care was due largely to lack of social service follow-up work.

The round number figures which have been presented must, of course, be taken with a grain of salt. It can be said for them that they are the best obtainable. They seem sufficiently broad in scope and sound in method of derivation to suggest the advisability of their presentation, with the expectation that they will be used advisedly.

Two big things appear to stand out: a very large proportion of the seriously sick seek or get no medical attention whatever; a considerable proportion of those who do come in contact with the doctor in private practice or through the hospital get inadequate care. To the extent to which this is true the present organization of medical service in the United States has failed to accomplish its purpose from the point of view of public interest if not from that of the physician himself. Wherein may the remedy lie?

CHEAPER MEDICAL SERVICE

Quite evidently there is no lack of doctors. It would seem, too, that neither the time nor the equipment of private medical practitioners are used to the fullest extent. The difficulty seems to lie largely with the failure of the public to appeal for medical service.

How may the public be induced to ask for more medical service? One way would be to tempt it with a still better quality. However, under the present organization of medicine, better quality would seem also to mean still higher cost. Higher standards in medical schools, still greater specialization, more and finer equipment, and more plentiful, prompt and accessible service—these things, under a system characterized solely by individualism, will increase cost.

Another way is to maintain or improve, if possible, the quality but lower the cost. The experience of dispensaries and clinics everywhere goes to prove that as cost decreases demand increases. But cost can be reduced only through saving in the administration of medical service. And such saving must be effected, as in business activity elsewhere, through improved organization of the physical plant and of the human element, the physician. Economies in the use of the physical plant, i. e., particularly the scientific instruments and equipment, lie in better quality, greater usefulness, and more extensive use. Economies in the use of the physician lie in exactly the same things —the skill of each used where most useful, and used to the fullest capacity as to the time and strength of the individual.

In other words, present hope for a solution of the problem of inadequate medical service or lack of service seems to lie in the improvement of the organization of medicine, or in a re-organization, if that term describes better the necessary change. •

POSSIBILITIES OF COMMUNITY MEDICINE

The term "Community Medicine" for the purpose of this paper is an abbreviation for all those forms of medical service expressed under the designations "co-operative medicine," "group medicine," "clinics," and "dispensaries." It is used in opposition to the individualistic practice of medicine as represented by the disassociated private practicing physician. We find it expressed pre-eminently in such institutions as the great Boston Dispensary (public) and the Mayo Clinics (private) of Rochester, Minnesota. The form most in the mind of the speaker, and the one from which he expects to develop his main line of thought, is the self-supporting, efficiently organized pay dispensary, set in some form of local health centre.

CHEAPNESS AND EFFICIENCY OF COMMUNITY MEDICINE

There seems to be general agreement that community medicine is cheaper and more efficient than is medical service rendered by the private practicing physician. The organization of plant, equipment, and personnel under the community medicine plan effects considerable savings. The patient comes to the doctor instead of the doctor to the patient. The time thus saved can be devoted to clinic practice. The scientific equipment installed at clinics may be employed during a maximum number of hours per day. This can rarely be true of equipment in the office of the private practicing physician.

The experience of the Boston Dispensary, under the able direction of Dr. Michael M. Davis, goes to show that "the total cost to the patient in treatment over an average period is no greater, and is often less, than the amount which the patient would have to pay for drugs alone if purchased at the price charged in drug stores." This statement relates particularly to the Syphilis Clinic. It was found, too, in the Eye Clinic that the usual retail prices of glasses alone was greater than the total expense of the administration fee in the dispensary clinic, plus the glasses, the latter being sold at a slight advance above cost.

Not only does community medicine appear to be far cheaper to the public than medical service under existing conditions of private practice, but it would also seem to be more efficient. Few doctors can afford the sort of scientific equipment which may be brought together for use in a community clinic. This equipment is apt to be both of a higher grade and to cover a wider range of service. The efficiency of community medical clinics is also increased by the fact that patients may be passed from specialist to specialist and thus in a very brief space of time receive the benefit of expert scientific diagnosis and advice. This feature is illustrated in an unusual degree by the Mayo Clinics of Rochester, Minnesota. (Those who are interested in reading a general account of the operation of the Mayo Clinics and prefer to reach such an account with a smile on the lips, are referred to an article by Dr. John A. Hornsby which appeared in the Modern Hospital Journal in May, 1918. Dr. Hornsby, it seems, had himself "put through the mill" to see if anything wrong could be found with his physical and mental make-up. His story of the procedure bears witness to the fact that humor is still alive in the medical profession.)

INCREASED DEMAND FOR MEDICAL SERVICE

Wherever community medicine, whether as dispensary, clinic, or other form, has been put in operation the popular demand for medical service seems to have been greatly stimulated. The rich can have medical service under all circumstances. They will probably always wish to have their own family physicians and their own specialists. The poor are being reached by growing facilities for medical service through the medium of an increased number of free clinics and dispensaries generally attached to public and private hospitals. But the great middle class, with ability to pay something for medical service, but unable, or unwilling under existing conditions, to pay for medical service on the terms offered by private practicing physicians, appears to be in great need of a cheaper and yet equally, if not more efficient, form of service. The pay clinic would seem to meet the need of this large part of the population. And the need would appear to be particularly urgent today, because of the universal shortage of physicians.

Even so intelligent a class as university students in our greatest universities do not seek medical service as frequently as the need of their own health would seem to require. This has been demonstrated in institutions where medical service for students has been inaugurated. It is stated that at the University of Wisconsin, as the result of free medical supervision supplied by the state, students consult physicians on an average probably four or five times as often during the year as they would have done if they had had to pay for each consultation.

DECREASES MORBIDITY AND MORTALITY

It has been customary to present the value of dispensaries and clinics in terms of the number of persons treated. Statistical data showing what improvement may be expected in a given population through the establishment of community medicine are very largely lacking. This is due to the fact that the population served in this manner is merged in the general population of the community. Such saving in sickness and death as is brought about loses itself in the general morbidity and mortality statistics of the community.

An interesting illustration which has produced statistical data of some definiteness may, however, be cited from the University of Wisconsin. I quote from an address by Professor John R. Commons on "A Reconstruction Health Program" which appeared in the *Survey* of September 6, 1919:

"At the University of Wisconsin we have free medical supervision for five thousand students. No medical fee is charged. The state is taxed for health supervision of the student exactly as it is taxed for their education. As a result, the students consult the physicians on an average probably four or five times as often during the year as they would if they had to pay at each consultation, besides getting the thorough physical examination at the beginning of the year. The result has been a great reduction in sickness, a reduction in absenteeism from classes, and greatly increased student efficiency. The loss of time due to bed illness has been reduced 40 to 60 per cent, due to the early treatment of preventable conditions. The frequent consultations have reduced serious illness and its complications by at least 50 per cent. During the eight years of this medical supervision the university death-rate has been reduced to only one-fourth of the general expectant rate, exclusive of tuberculosis, at the same age period, and even the death-rate from the recent influenza epidemic was believed to be only one-fourth of the general death-rate attributable to that cause."

INCREASES ECONOMIC AND POLITICAL STABILITY

Community medicine would appear to be one way of attacking the present high cost of living. It decreases the cost and increases the demand for medical service. It decreases sickness and decreases deaths. It thereby signally increases productive capacity, actual production, and total net savings. This increase in economic efficiency, as a necessary corollary, means increased economic stability. And increased economic stability, as a necessary and under existing conditions most important corollary means increased political stability. These considerations are of genuine significance to the individual, to society, to the nation at large.

INCREASES THE EFFICIENCY OF HEALTH ADMINISTRATION

The experience of the Boston Dispensary and of clinics and dispensaries elsewhere points to their exceptional value as aids to the local health administration in the control of communicable diseases.

Large numbers of people come to these health centres. They receive expert examinations and diagnoses. Communicable diseases are apt to be promptly discovered. They can be effectively treated and centres of infection speedily located.

Wherever accurate and complete records, standardized if possible, are kept, community clinics occupy the position of an automatic, spontaneous, and continuous survey of community health conditions. The recurrence of similar case histories, a condition readily brought out by statistical records, will point to weak spots in the community's health. Occupational diseases may be located and responsible conditions remedied.

DECREASES THE NEED OF HOSPITAL SERVICE

Prompt and efficient medical service to an increasing number of members of the population is bound to prevent the development of numerous serious and more or less permanent complications in health. This reduction in the number of chronic sicknesses and in physical disability will necessarily mean a reduction in the need of community hospital service. This fact suggests, too, with considerable force, the wisdom of developing community health centres first, and community hospitals at some future time when the mass benefits of community medical service have come into operation, and hospital cases within the community have come to approximate the irreducible minimum. When this stage has been reached, assuming public sentiment to be in favor, the time may have come for the construction of a community hospital.

Serious thought need be given to whether it is wise to tie up public or private funds in a hospital structure at the outset rather than to turn financial support to the relatively inexpensive community clinic. These clinics, as has been demonstrated in Boston and elsewhere, can readily be made self-supporting. The community hospital has on occasion, it is said, proven to be a white elephant on the hands of a well-intentioned but ill-guided community which lacks the financial strength to maintain such an institution and to do in addition the other necessary public health work.

How far the success of a dispensary may be dependent on its connection with a hospital is still a mooted question. You are referred for argumentation to Dr. Davis's book, *Dispensaries*, and to such other sources as Dr. S. S. Goldwater's *Dispensaries, A Growing Factor in Curative and Preventive Medicine.*

COMMUNITY MEDICINE AND HEALTH INSURANCE

If health insurance is a good thing, then community medicine would appear to tend to encourage a good thing. Those who are interested in community medicine point to the experience of England, under its new health legislation, where the inadequacy of medical service through the panel doctors has proven unsatisfactory to all parties concerned. Properly organized clinics would tend to surmount such a difficulty, and by making service both cheaper and more efficient would appear to stimulate the movement toward health insurance.

Why health officers who are interested in the building up of a strong and efficient department of health should wish to concern themselves with the progress of the movement towards health insurance, is forcefully brought out by Professor John R. Commons in the already referred to paper. Professor Commons draws an interesting parallel between the relation of accident insurance and the safety-first movement on the one hand, and health insurance and what may be called the "health first" movement on the other.

COMMUNITY MEDICINE AND THE PHYSICIAN

It is stated that the main opposition to the development of community medicine comes from the ranks of the medical profession. On the other hand, there is much evidence in recent literature on the subject that a large fraction of the profession is giving its enthusiastic support to this movement on the theory that its benefits to the physician considerably outweigh its objections.

It is claimed by some that the income of the capable doctor will be cut. There is much evidence, however, that his income will be increased. Emphasis is, of course, placed on the adjective "capable." There appears to be general agreement that the incompetent physician and the quack are the ones who will be most likely to suffer through the establishment of community medicine.

As already noted at the outset of this paper, community medicine appears to greatly increase the popular demand for medical service. By doing so it reduces the amount of self-administration of medical service and cuts down the consumption of patent medicines. This is an important item from the economic point of view. Huge sums of money, it is estimated, are thus devoted by the public to approved forms of medical service which otherwise would increase the income of the quack and of the patent medicine vendor.

Dr. Davis, of the Boston Dispensary, calls attention to the fact that the total cost to the patient of treatment at the pay clinics over an average period is no greater, and is often less, than the amount which the patient would have to pay for the drugs alone if purchased at prices charged in drug stores. He also points out that fully one-half of what the patient pays is paid back by the dispensary to the physician. This amount, if the patient were treated privately, would all have gone to the drug store or to the quack.

What large sums are involved in this deflection of private expenditures to the economic gain of the medical profession is suggested by the fact that, according to estimates of the Life Extension Institute, $500,000,000 are annually spent for drugs in this country and that most of them are at present self-administered.

The per capita expenditure for patent medicines, it is calculated, has increased from about 35 cents in 1880 to $1.50 at the present time.

Dr. Goldwater in 1915 stated that a representative of a large retail drug firm in the city of Boston told him that the business of his firm alone amounted to $3,000,000 a year, largely in patent medicines.

Enormous quantities of quinine, estimated at two billion doses, are annually consumed in this country. Much of this, it is claimed, is not needed. Much of it is said to be harmful. Even after making due allowances for all possible errors in round number estimates of this sort, it will be evident to all of you that the money put into patent medicines and drugs in this country from year to year represents a huge total.

It has been pointed out by Dr. Michael M. Davis that a physician who, while in attendance at a pay clinic, gets a net income of $5.00 for a two-hour clinic, receives an equivalent of $5,250 per year on a seven-hour day basis. This, it is estimated, is equal to an income of $10,500 from private practice on what appears to be the generally accepted theory that 50 per cent of the gross income of the doctor goes toward meeting the expenses of doing business—expenses which a physician attending a pay clinic does not have to bear.

It is necessary, too, to bear in mind the point already emphasized, that a large portion of patients who take advantage of community medicine would not, in the absence of such clinics, seek medical service from private practicing physicians. This is demonstrated by the considerable increase in medical service in a community after clinics are established and by the large proportion of the disabled sick —over 25 per cent—according to the sickness surveys already referred to, who at present get no medical service at all.

The most serious consideration, from the point of view of the doctor, in connection with the community medicine program, would seem to lie in the fact that a certain proportion of the local medical profession is apt to be excluded from practice at the clinics and is thereby placed at a serious financial disadvantage. The remedy for this, it has been suggested, is the organization of additional clinics. In other words, the number of clinics in a community is to be enlarged until all doctors, or at least all efficient doctors, are members of the clinic staffs. The least competent physicians are bound to be at a continuous disadvantage. The most competent men will be sought out when the first clinics are established. As additional doctors are needed the selection is apt to be progressively downward in the scale of competence. While this may be highly unfortunate for the less competent doctor, he is being served in no other manner than are the less competent in every other department of life.

There can be no question that in this movement the spirit of individualism is in conflict with the spirit of coöperation. Nor can we deny the immense value of individualism to our progress in every field of activity. We have always pointed with pride to the fact that our phenomenal development was due to a spirit of freedom and enterprise born of an indomitable spirit of individualism. Medical men, undoubtedly, share in full measure in this same spirit. Every doctor wants a chance to stand or fall on his own merits. He wants the greatest opportunity of individual success and is willing to pay the price of individual failure.

We are learning, however, today that the world appears to be moving on to a new phase of coöperation where community interests take the place, largely, of individual interests. This change would seem to be evolutionary and being evolutionary quite irresistible. This new spirit and method in medicine finds an eloquent apostle in Dr. Davis who, in the closing paragraph of his book, *Dispensaries,* forecasts the future necessary relationship of the medical profession to coöperative medicine as follows:

"The medical profession must frankly face the changes which medical science is bringing upon medical practice. The leaders in the medical profession bear the responsibility of making the rank and file understand that there is now a scientific necessity for the co-operative provision of diagnostic equipment, and of facilities for reception and care of patients, and that there must consequently follow a large development of co-operative medical service through various forms of institutional organization. Individualism in medicine should continue, so far as it implies a sense of direct responsibility for the patient, but individualism must not be and cannot continue to be in antagonism to working as part of an organization, with graded responsibilities established therein. We may be confident that whatever is clearly demanded by the public interests as a whole should and will over-ride the special interests of any vocation or group; and also that there lies ahead of the medical profession a future of enlarged dignity and of more secure economic remuneration, if there is a broad community organization of the wonderful resources of medical science and of the skill of its representatives in the medical profession—an organization such as will render the very best of these resources accessible to all the people on a democratic basis. The great War is calling to everyone's attention the power of medicine to prevent disease among great masses of individuals whose countries were swept by pestilence, and to heal wounds and illness among the victims of the battlefields as these have never been healed before. The public will not fail to remember, however, that these wonders have been accomplished by organized rather than by individualistic medicine."

One cannot help but view the present situation with greatest optimism. The process of readjustment appears to be going forward apace with economic forces, as usual, in the saddle. Doctors are coming more and more to see that the economies of organization will permit of a larger average remuneration for the medical man; that lowered cost and increased efficiency mean greater demand for medical service; that greater demand for medical service means greater per capita expenditures for such service; that it means the deflection of huge sums of money heretofore spent on patent medicines and drugs largely self-administered to the pockets of practicing physicians.

Brilliant specialists and general practitioners will undoubtedly continue to hold sway with remunerative practice among the rich. In increasing measure they will, it would seem, give part time free to the poor as they have so generously done in the past. The incompetent doctors will continue to struggle along in the rear as incompetents in all human endeavor have done since time immemorial. They will continue to divide their time neither with the rich nor the poor, but just with themselves. The great body of sterling, capable physicians seem to be increasingly recognizing the fact that prosperity, congeniality, and stimulation attend closer affiliation with the expanding mechanism of community medicine. The speed of this readjustment will depend on the efficiency with which the leaders in the community medicine movement develop its advantages, and the effectiveness of the educational campaign among doctors through which they may in increasing numbers learn to see where their permanent interests appear to lie.

□

MALARIA CONTROL FROM THE ENGINEERING POINT OF VIEW

W. G. STROMQUIST,
*Associate Sanitary Engineer, United States Public Health Service,
Memphis, Tenn.*

Read before Sanitary Engineering Section, American Public Health Association, at New Orleans, La., October 28, 1919.

Control of malaria is vital to the industrial development of the South and other warm regions and the engineer is vital to malaria control. The public must coöperate by understanding and by supporting improvements. Here is a plain educational statement of high value. It views the problems from many practical sides and suggests fundamental considerations.

MALARIA is the South's greatest problem. It affects 3,000,000 people and causes an estimated economic loss of $1,000,000,000 yearly.

Economically its insidious influence is felt by the banker and merchant, and by every business man whose prosperity is dependent upon the prosperity of the region he serves. The lumberman, the farmer, and every other employer knows that malaria is lowering the efficiency of his laborers, is reducing his production, and decreasing his profits. Rarely a fatal disease, it so lowers vitality that the fatality rate of other diseases is increased. But, most serious of any of its effects, is the handicap it places upon the child. To be enervated by malaria, during the years when the body should be developing into a sturdy, dependable machine, the mind and will growing and strengthening to correspond, means an appalling loss that can neither be calculated nor recovered. The solution of the problem lies with the engineer.

In studying the control of malaria, we must first consider the factors of its transmission, which are: A person infected with malaria—the anopheles mosquito—and the well person who may become infected. Thus we derive four lines of attack: Mosquito eradication to eliminate the transmitting agent; protection of well persons against infected mosquitoes by screening; protection of infected persons against non-infected mosquitoes by mosquito bars and screens; and reducing the number of infected persons by quinine treatment. The first three methods are essentially engineering problems.

Since the Stone Age, the problem of diseases and man's bodily ills has been apportioned to the doctors; but, together with typhoid, malaria must now be assigned to the sanitary engineer, with the prophylactic measures left to the physician.

An effective campaign against malaria requires the coöperation of the public, for funds must be provided, and without the support of local officials and individuals the work would be seriously handicapped. The actual direction of the control work should have the closest team work by the physician, the biologist, the laboratory technician, and the engineer.

The physician studies the characteristics of the disease, its means of transmission and its cure. In malaria control, he is the principal factor in prophylactic measures. The biologist studies the habits of the mosquitoes, their choice of breeding places, food requirements, etc. He also investigates the natural enemies of the mosquitoes and their value as active agents in mosquito eradication. In the laboratory, the technician studies the organisms of the disease and the conditions which favor or prevent its development.

The sanitary engineer engaged in antimalaria work uses the data on malaria and its various factors, which have been collected by the physician, biologist, and in the laboratory, to devise the most effective and the most economic methods of controlling the disease.

Mosquito eradication eliminates the connecting link between the infected and the well person, and has proved a most desirable method of malaria control. Not an unimportant consideration is the popular favor which the work gains by adding to the comfort of the people. Though the physician observes the reduction in malaria, the average person notices the comparative scarcity of mosquitoes, and his comfortable evenings on the porch make him feel that he is getting something for his money.

The most effective method of mosquito eradication is the elimination of breeding places. This may require the drainage of extensive swampy areas where the reclamation of land for cultivation will make it economically feasible. Under other conditions the desired results may be accomplished by ditches, or the clearing of small streams, which would seem child's play to the drainage engineer accustomed to big projects. The important feature is not the size of the project but the thoroughness with which the work is done. No one part of the problem may seem great or difficult, but taken in its entirety, it presents a mass of details which must all be solved in order to make the work successful.

Where drainage is not practicable because the cost would be excessive in ratio to the benefits derived, other means must be employed, such as oiling, or fish control. The engineer must determine the most suitable materials and devise the best methods where oiling is used, and it is often necessary to clear the water surface in order to make the methods effective.

The top water minnow, *Gambusia affinis*, is a deadly enemy of the mosquito because of his voracious appetite for mosquito larvæ. Ideal conditions for this method of control are not often found in nature and the engineer is frequently called upon to help the minnow, either by removing vegetation and other protection of the larvæ, or by providing protection for the minnow against larger fish which would devour it.

For the engineer of an inventive turn of mind, malaria control offers a wide field. In mosquito eradication, as well as in other lines of engineering, many local problems will be met which must be solved on short notice and at low cost, without precedents to guide the engineer. This was particularly true of the work in the extra-cantonment areas. No two zones presented the same problems. In one, tide gates were required to allow the drainage of swampy areas at low tide and to prevent their flooding at high tide. In another, vertical drainage was used to drain isolated water sheds with no surface outlet. In yet another, subdrains were installed to provide permanent drainage of marshes. All these are problems which will continue to present themselves, and for which more efficient and less costly methods can undoubtedly be devised.

There is a crying need for ditching machines suitable for mosquito control work, for which a special type of ditch is necessary. The drainage engineer is particularly interested in flood flows, and designs a large ditch, the purpose of which is to carry large quantities of water. The sanitary engineer engaged in mosquito control work is interested in the minimum flows. At such times, the wide flat-bottomed ditch which carries the flood waters will be a series of shallow pools, admirable breeding places for Anopheles. To prevent mosquito breeding a small V-shaped ditch in the bottom of the larger ditch is necessary. Trenching machines used in laying water mains or sewers make a straight-sided, flat-bottomed ditch, which would not be suitable for a permanent ditch. The cost of mosquito control could be reduced, and thereby the work greatly promoted by the development of a small, portable ditching machine, which could worm its way through streams, or ditches, or dig new ditches of the type necessary for this work.

Another problem is that of aquatic growths. It is often necessary to remove pond lilies, moss or other water plants from ponds in order to make oiling or fish control effective. Hand labor is a tedious and expensive method. Aquatic saws are on the market but they are costly and are not entirely satisfactory. In some extra cantonment areas an emergency was met by improvising an aquatic saw from the "licker-in" wires used at cotton mills. This is another opportunity for the inventive engineer.

The original work is the more expensive but maintenance is an expense which will remain, and any means of reducing this cost will do much to advance malaria control. A study should be made of the possibilities of lining ditches, possibly by placing wire netting and applying a thin wall of concrete with a cement gun. The initial cost would be increased, but maintenance cost would be eliminated by preventing the growth of vegetation in the ditches.

A kerosene burner for burning grass and weeds in ditches proved very successful in Panama, but the cost of this method as compared with hand cleaning, has not been determined in this country. With the increasing prices of oils, the question of the most economical as well as efficacious material to use, and the most satisfactory means of applying it, are important problems.

A few problems which present themselves to the sanitary engineer in mosquito control work have been enumerated in order to show that although the possibility of reducing malaria by the eradication of mosquitoes has been proven time and again; there remain opportunities in developing methods and reducing costs.

Screening has been mentioned as a method of malaria control. This is also work for the engineer, and though not a complicated engineering problem, it is another case where thorough work and close attention to detail is necessary. It may be added, that to effectively and economically screen some plantation tenant houses, without building a new house, is a problem which is beyond even the most ingenious engineer.

In malarious sections the control of this disease has an intimate relation with all engineering enterprises. In fact, it may determine the success or failure of an undertaking. We have an excellent example of that in the Panama Canal. The chief reason of the French failure was the demoralization of their forces by yellow fever and malaria. When Mr. John F. Stevens was the chief engineer, he made the statement that there were three epidemics on the isthmus; yellow fever, malaria and cold feet. It was the sanitation of the Zone which made the canal possible.

The same is true, to a variable degree, of any enterprise in a region where malaria is prevalent. On a closely estimated engineering project the availability and efficiency of labor may be the determining factor between profit and loss. With a large percentage of the laborers infected with malaria there is a great loss of time on the part of the laborer, which reduces the available man-power. A considerable percentage of the men who are infected will not be sick enough to remain in bed, but will continue to work. However, their efficiency will be greatly reduced and the employer will be fortunate if he gets thirty cents' worth of work for a dollar in wages from such men. Labor overturn is also an important factor, for the securing of new labor is often expensive. Every employer knows that he will get greater efficiency—which means increased production at less cost—from healthy employees who are working under conditions which keep them satisfied. Such conditions are not possible where malaria prevails.

Engineers are largely responsible for increased malaria in many places. Storage reservoirs for water power projects have been built without considering the vast increase of mosquito breeding places, which could be prevented at reasonable cost, and as a result areas near some of these reservoirs have been practically depopulated. In building railroads and highways, the engineer leaves borrow pits which are not drained; places culverts too high so that ponds are formed above the embankments; and these provide excellent, but entirely avoidable, breeding places for Anopheles and are the cause of unnecessary "man-made malaria."

The control of malaria is vital to the full development of the vast resources of the South. It affects the agricultural, lumber, mining and manufacturing interests, probably more than any other one factor. There are sections in the South which have been practically abandoned by white people because of malaria. As affecting the development of agriculture, it may be stated that the most fertile lands are often found in the sections where malaria is most prevalent, such as the Mississippi Delta.

The lumber camps and saw mills have men idle or working at low efficiency because of malaria. The same is true of cotton mills, steel mills and other industries. With under-production on the farms and in the factories the revenues of the railroads are kept down. Many of the progressive corporations are conducting anti-malaria campaigns. The Tennessee Coal & Iron Company has reduced malaria cases among its employees and their families from about 3,000 to 50 per year. One result of this work is more efficient and contented employees, a condition which must have a wholesome influence on production records.

The railroads are growing more interested in the malaria problem, as it is becoming more evident to them that the disease is causing great inroads on their revenues. The financial benefits derived from malaria control have been shown by the St. Louis-Southwestern Railroad, known as the "Cotton Belt Route." Practically the entire system lies in a malarious region. Beginning in 1917, this railroad has conducted anti-malaria campaigns among its employees and in cities along its lines. One mill operator reported that the output of his mill had been increased 20% by the reduction of malaria. This resulted in an increase of $60,000 in the annual freight revenues of the railroad from this mill. Many similar cases could be cited.

The various industries of the South, the railroads, and the financial interests are rapidly awakening to the importance of malaria control. The engineer is directly concerned with all development, being in many ways the pioneer with the possibilities of new ventures left to his judgment. With the control of malaria, he eliminates a factor which might prove his undoing. From the field party making the preliminary survey for a railroad or a water-power development project, to the employees of a saw mill or a city factory, malaria is a problem which confronts the engineer in the South at every turn. It is a problem which is of the utmost concern to every engineer and not only to the sanitary engineer who is directly engaged in the work.

At the present time an effort is being made to strengthen commercial relations with the South American countries and to build up an extensive foreign trade. Some parts of these countries have a high malaria rate and whether or not measures are taken to control the disease may mean the success or failure of many of the investments made of American capital in these countries.

The engineer is vitally interested in malaria control from a personal and professional point of view. This does not only apply to the sanitary engineer who is charged with the protection of the public health, but is equally true of any engineer who is located in a malarious region, or is connected with enterprises in a section where malaria is prevalent. Human efficiency is a great factor in the success of an engineer or of his undertakings. Human efficiency and malaria cannot occur together. The engineer must secure maximum results at minimum expense, which cannot be done with labor infected with malaria.

The engineer is interested in results, and delights in progress charts which show his accomplishments. If he is engaged in anti-malaria work he will often be discouraged at the lack of visible evidence of results of his efforts for he cannot see his bridge span the stream—his building rise toward the skies—or his dam gradually stem the flow of the river. But he must have vision to see the decrease in human suffering — the saving of life. He must see the child, who instead of starting out in life infected with malaria and the handicaps which that implies, is given an even chance as a result of the fight against this insidious disease. When he can see this, he sees the most important progress chart and he sees malaria control from the engineering point of view -- the greatest benefit to humanity at the least cost.

☐

National Mine-Rescue Competition at Denver.—With a view of stimulating still further the safety movement among the mines and metallurgical plants of the country, a National First-Aid and Mine-Rescue Contest will be held under the auspices of the Bureau of Mines, Department of the Interior, at Denver, Colo., August 20 and 21, 1920. Mining teams from the principal mining companies of the country will participate, and especially those teams of the west that were unable to attend the national meet, held last year at Pittsburgh, Pa., in which more than 100 teams took part. The contest will be for the national championship in first-aid and mine-rescue work, honors which are coveted by every miners' team in the country. National contest cups, medals and prizes will be awarded to the winners.

D. J. Parker, in charge of the rescue work of the Bureau of Mines, has immediate supervision over the arrangements for the contest. Mining companies intending to enter are urged to get in touch with him at the U. S. Bureau of Mines, Pittsburgh, Pa. The contests will be decided solely according to Bureau of Mines standards and by judges thoroughly familiar with first-aid and mine-rescue work and with Bureau Mines practice.

AN INFERENTIAL INDEX OF SWIMMING POOL PURITY

GORDON M. FAIR,
*Instructor in Sanitary Engineering, Harvard University,
Cambridge, Mass.*

Score cards for swimming pools is the suggestion of this paper. Figures about these establishments are today in the class with crude statistics, and may lead to unreliable conclusions. Here are suggested various indexes which may be of service in framing minimum requirements for these pools. This article is an effort to clear up a complicated matter for which there are not now accepted standards.

NOT long ago Mr. Stephen de M. Gage directed our attention in a very instructive paper on the "Sanitary Control of Swimming Pools"* to a new way of stating the probability of contamination of these bodies of water. For the purpose of comparing different pools he invented the term *bathing load,* which he defined as the number of bathers divided by the capacity of the pool in thousands of gallons. Since the number of bathers using a swimming tank fluctuates from day to day and the operation schedule of the pool is most often based on a weekly cycle, he proposed for general use the *weekly bathing load,*—namely, the number of bathers per week, divided by the capacity of the pool in thousands of gallons. Previous to Mr. Gage's suggestion the probable contamination of swimming tanks was often ascertained by assuming the water to be equally divided among the persons using the pool in a given time. By this method, for example, a tank of 50,000 gallons capacity and a weekly attendance of 1,000 bathers presents a capacity of 50 gallons of water per bather per week, while the same tank with a weekly attendance of only 500 bathers presents a capacity of 100 gallons per bather per week. The relative probability of contamination is, therefore, expressed by the inverse ratio of the term under con-

sideration. The *bathing load,* on the other hand, constitutes an expression, the values of which are in direct proportion to the probability of contamination, with a magnitude of 20 in the first case, for example, and one of 10 in the second.

The *bathing load* is a term very much like the crude or general death rate which reveals to some extent the health of a community but does not form a reliable basis upon which to compare the health of different cities. Similarly, the *bathing load* gives an excellent idea of the relative care which should be exercised to maintain in a sanitary condition, pools of different capacities and varying attendance, but without indicating the actual safety of the water. The existing contamination, so far, has been inferred from the results of bacteriological analyses of the pool water. It is, however, a question just what bacterial findings shall constitute a safe or dangerous condition of the same. Very few sanitarians have been willing to commit themselves to proposing a fixed standard of bacterial purity, and it is only recently that one of our Western state boards of health has adopted a tentative standard of a total bacterial count of 1,000 colonies per cubic centimeter on agar incubated at 37.5° C., for 48 hours and a *B. coli* count of one per cubic centimeter, determined by the usual standard methods. This progressive action is indeed commendable, but it is debatable whether or not

---

*Stephen de M. Gage. The Sanitary Control of Swimming Pools. Jour. Boston Soc. Civil Engrs., Vol. 5, pp. 229.

this tentative standard has the approval of the great number of investigators. In the above mentioned paper*, for example, Mr. Gage states on the one hand that he considers satisfactory a swimming pool water complying with the United States Treasury Standards for drinking water, but he further qualifies his opinion by saying that, under certain conditions, one may obtain counts of several million bacteria and yet consider a pool safe. This, the writer believes, is a very logical stand to take relative to the problem of bacterial purity of swimming pool water. As in all other questions of water analysis, the actual purity of pool water is often very different from the safety inferred from bacteriological tests. An acquaintance with existing conditions is frequently of more value than a few bacteriological analyses which, if correctly interpreted, serve a very good purpose in strengthening the evidence collected *in situ*, but which, under most conditions of public supervision, are limited in number and often not representative. The writer holds no brief against bacteriological standards for water and does not wish to deprecate the efforts of those investigators who are attempting to formulate a standard of bacterial purity for swimming pools, but he does believe that our present understanding and present methods are not sufficient to warrant the adoption at this time of even a tentative standard of bacterial purity unless the same can be made very broad indeed, and then it will be rather hard to formulate. Aftergrowths of harmless water organisms following disinfection and immense variations in the bacterial flora caused by keeping swimming pools at high temperatures, for example, might be sufficient to condemn, under our present system of interpretation, a pool which is really perfectly satisfactory. Furthermore, it is practically impossible to compare, on a basis of total counts, a tank operating at from 68° F., to 70° F., with one in which a temperature higher than 72° F., is

maintained. Yes, even with expert supervision and analytical control sudden increases in bacterial growths are frequently unavoidable. The presence of coarse suspended matter, hair, lint, etc., and other foreign substances such as sputum and epithelial cells, may also contribute large numbers of organisms to the samples, thus leading to false inferences and making the errors of sampling very large indeed. While, therefore, bacteriological analyses may be of doubtful value in establishing a standard of swimming pool purity, they still have their very good place in the checking of disinfection and water treatment and will always remain of inestimable value in the sanitary control of private and public bathing places.

For these and other reasons the writer has tried to attack the problem of an index of swimming pool purity from a different angle, based in its elementary conception upon the *bathing load*. If, for example, it is possible by considering the ratio between the number of bathers using a pool in a given time and the tank capacity, to conceive an idea of the probability of contamination of the pool, it is likewise possible, by considering not only the number of bathers and the tank capacity but also the number of times that fresh water is added to the tank or tank water is purified by disinfection or filtration, together with the quantities dealt with in each case, to obtain an indication of the actual purity of the pool, just as an analysis of a general death rate is made by computing the component specific rates. Assuming again a pool of 50,000 gallons capacity, a weekly attendance of 1,000, a resulting *bathing load* of 20 and daily disinfection of the pool body, we can reason that the actual contamination is directly proportional to the relative amount of disinfected or otherwise pure water furnished each bather. We thereby define the *index of contamination* as the expression obtained by dividing the number of bathers using the pool in a given time by the amount of disinfected water in thousands of gallons, remaining at liberty to determine a weekly, daily, or hourly *index of contamination*. In the case assumed, the value of the weekly index is equal to one-sixth of the bathing load, or 8.3, increasing to 16.7 if disinfectants are applied only three times a week. The Committee on Sewerage and Sewage Disposal of the American Public Health Association* recently defined contamination as *the introduction into a water of bacteria or other substances which tend to render it unsuitable for domestic use.* If we retain the spirit of this definition, the index of contamination therefore becomes a term denoting the bacterial purity of the water. An index of low value signifies that effective measures for disinfecting the water or otherwise displacing it by uncontaminated water are in force, and one of high value reveals that the processes of pool operation are unsatisfactory.

This method of analysis, however, does not disclose the esthetic condition of the pool or the physical safety of the water. Favorable bacterial counts may be obtained by frequent disinfection of an otherwise stagnant pool rendered unsightly by the presence of surface scum and collections of sediment, hair, lint, etc., and made dangerous by the darkness of color or quantity of suspended matter contained in the water. For this reason, it might be well to continue our study for the purpose of finding a different expression from which can be inferred the esthetic condition of a swimming pool. Such a term might be called an *index of pollution,* for the above mentioned committee* defines pollution as *the introduction into a water of substances of such character and in such quantity that they tend to render the body of the water (or river) objectionable in appearance (or to cause it to give off objectionable odors).* Unfortunately, however, the words contamination and pollution are still loosely

*Report of Committee on Sewerage and Sewage Disposal. A. J. P. H., 1917, Vol. 7, pp. 847.

used interchangeably to express the same condition. It might therefore be better to call the expression an *index of stagnation.* This method of reasoning is based upon the fact that it is the stagnation of the swimming pool which brings about the unsightly and dangerous conditions mentioned above, which in turn constitute a state of pollution. If, once more, we assume a pool of the same description as before, the water of which, however, is recirculated at a rate sufficiently high to turn over the pool once a day, the water being filtered during recirculation, we obtain by a similar method of reasoning as before an *index of stagnation* equal to the number of bathers divided by the amount of filtered water in thousands of gallons,—in this case one-sixth of the bathing load, or 8.3, increasing to 16.7, when the pool is recirculated only once in two days.

A consideration of the three expressions—*bathing load, index of contamination,* and *index of stagnation*—furnishes us with important information as to the sanitary condition of a swimming pool and makes possible comparisons between pools of different capacity, attendance, systems of disinfection, methods of operation, temperatures, etc. The use to which these expressions may be put is illustrated in Table I, the data for which are taken partly from Mr. Gage's paper and partly from unpublished or hypothetical sources.

The method of obtaining the figures in Columns 11 and 12 of this table is illustrated by a consideration of the data relating to the natatorium at Brown University. The water in this pool is recirculated and filtered at a rate of 0.96 times a day, a total of 432,000 gallons of repurified water being added per week. At the same time the pool is raised two inches six times per week for the purpose of removing scum collecting on the surface of the pool, or to replace water lost by splashing or displacement, a total of 14,100 gallons of fresh water being added per week. The sum total of clean water added per week is therefore 446,100 gallons, representing an *index of stagnation* of $\frac{450}{446}$ or 1.0. The pool is furthermore disinfected twice a week, 75,000 gallons of water being treated each time. The total amount of disinfected or otherwise uncontaminated water coming in contact with the bathers is therefore 150,000 plus 14,100, or 164,100 gallons, thus establishing an *index of contamination* of $\frac{450}{164.1}$ or 2.7.

The *indices of contamination and stagnation* in Table I have been worked out for weekly cycles of pool operation. After a closer study of this subject it may be found necessary to decrease the length of time over which the index extends and to compute a daily or, better, an hourly index, as illustrated in the following example. Assuming a pool of 50,000 gallons capacity with a weekly attendance of 1,200 bathers, the water in the pool being uniformly recirculated and disinfected for eight hours at a rate of three turnovers, or 150,000 gallons, per day, we obtain the following expressions for an eight-hour bathing day.

Weekly bathing load 24.0
Weekly index of stagnation.............. 4.0
Weekly index of contamination.......... 4.0
Daily bathing load........................ 4.0
Daily index of stagnation................ 4.0
Daily index of contamination............. 4.0
Hourly bathing load...................... 0.5
Hourly index of stagnation.............. 4.0
Hourly index of contamination........... 4.0

Presupposing an even attendance, therefore, the *indices of stagnation and contamination* must remain the same for all time intervals, while the bathing load suffers a decrease proportional to the time interval. If, on the other hand, the water in the pool is recirculated and disinfected for 16 hours, at a rate of only one and one-half turnovers, or 75,000 gallons, per day, the total amount of water recirculated and disinfected during a day remaining the same as above, the *hourly index of stagnation* increases to 8.0, together with the *hourly index of contamination*, but the other expressions remain unchanged. The true daily and hourly indices vary furthermore with the different numbers of bathers using the pool in the time intervals under consideration. It is a question whether the figures given by the weekly indices are or are not of sufficient practical value to be used in the stead of indices based upon shorter intervals of time.

The relation of the quality of pool water to the *indices of contamination and stagnation* is illustrated in Table II, the data for which were derived from Mr. Gage's much quoted paper.

A consideration of the figures in this table establishes the fact that the correlation between average bacterial counts and the indices is quite noticeable. With the exception of the Pawtucket Boys' Club Pool, 20° C. counts higher than 1000 and 37° C. counts higher than 4 were not obtained for an *index of contamination* less than 7.8 and an *index of stagnation* less than 4.9. Similarly, positive *B. coli* results were obtained only for *indices of contamination* more than 9.3 and *indices of stagnation* more than 4.9. The exception established by the Pawtucket Boys' Club may be explained by the fact that small boys are proverbially dirty and that the pool is operated apparently without disinfection on the fill and draw principle. The use of data relating to the bacterial purity of tank water might seem inconsistent with the writer's attempt to establish a new and different index of swimming pool purity, providing that the figures given in Table II were not averages of many analyses and providing that many objections to a standard of bacterial purity to which every single chance sample examined must conform, were not met in a study of averages.

Certain special cases may arise in which it may be necessary to modify the procedure of determining the various indices. If, for example, the amount of disinfectant added to the pool body or the recirculating water is only sufficient to

TABLE I.

1	Capacity Gals.	Bathers per Week	Time Between Refilling Days	Times per Week Fresh Water Added	Height Pool Raised When Fresh Water Added Inches	Times per Day Pool Turned Over by Recirculation and Filtration	Times per Week Pool Disinfected	Capacity of Pool Gals per Bather per Week	Weekly Bathing Load	Weekly Index of Stagnation	Weekly Index of Contamination
	2	3	4	5	6	7	8	9	10	11	12
Boston Y. M. C. A.	78,000	500	...	6	...	1.5	During recirculation	156	6.4	0.65	0.65
Brown University	75,000	450	120	6	2.0	0.96	2	167	6.0	1.0	2.7
Pawtucket Boys' Club	65,000	130	5	1	...	...	not known	500	2.0	2.0	not known
Providence Y. M. C. A.	50,000	1200	105	6	6.0	0.72	2	42	24.0	4.9	9.3
Newport Y. M. C. A.	45,000	600	110	1	6.0	0.06	1	75	13.3	37.8	9.1
Pawtucket Y. W. C. A.	30,000	87	160	6	6.0	0.67	1	345	2.9		1.9
Woonsocket Y. M. C. A.	30,000	240	1	1	...	not known		125	8.0		7.8
U.S.N. Training Station (N oph.)	30,000	135	...	6	...	...		222	4.4	0.64	0.75
Pawtucket Y. M. C. A.	28,000	600	45	3	0.5	0.04	1	47	21.4	0.75	20.9
Newport A. & N. Y. M. C. A.	28,000	300	80	1	0.4	not known	6	93	10.7	83.6	10.2
Moses Brown School	21,000	325	80	3	0.7	not known	not known	65	15.5		2.6
Aborn St. Baths, Providence	18,000	88	14-21	1	...	...	not known	205	4.9	9.8-14.7	...
Lundin St. Baths, Providence	9,500	75	3-7	0.5-0.33	...	...	6	127	7.9	3.9-3.9	3.3
Hypothetical Fill & Draw Operation	50,000	1000	several-months	2-1	6.0	1.0	dur. recir.	50	20.0	3.0	3.0
Hypothetical Recirculation	50,000	1000	1	6	6.0	1.0	6	50	20.0	3.0	3.0
California State Board of Health Recommendations (a)	50,000	1000	1			800-2000 gals. added per bather 1.0	0	50	20.0	0.5-1.2	0.5-1.2
(b)1	50,000	1000	sev. days or months			1.0	6	50	20.0	0-3.3	3.0-3.3
(b)2	50,000	1000	"			1.0	12	50	20.0	3.0-3.3	1.6-1.7
(c)	50,000	1000	"			1.0	dur. recir.	50	20.0	3.0-3.3	3.0-3.3

reduce the bacterial counts by 50 per cent, the index of contamination must be computed by dividing the number of bathers by one-half the amount of disinfected water. As suggested before, it is in the study of conditions similar to this that bacteriological methods are of value.

The two *indices of contamination and stagnation* become *standards of contamination and stagnation* when a certain definite value is assigned to them. After extensive studies covering many different types of swimming pools, for example, those state boards which have the power to regulate public bathing places may find that a value of, say, 0.5, 1.0, or 2.0 for the *index of contamination* and the *index of stagnation* is usually found in swimming pools which are satisfactory from the standpoint of public health. It would then be possible to call the respective value a *standard of contamination* and a *standard of stagnation*. These specific standards, however, must always remain only part of an actual standard of swimming pool sanitation, for it is evident that the sanitary condition of these bodies of water is not controlled merely by the purity of the pool water, but is dependent upon the

many other questions of preventive sanitation, pool construction, supervision, etc., which together tend to produce an harmonious whole. We must, therefore, expect to continue our analysis for the purpose of incorporating requirements relating to the methods and facilities of preventive sanitation, conditions of drainage, methods of cleaning, etc.

The writer believes that all these specific standards or indices may be incorporated to good advantage in a score card in which the methods and facilities of the pool shall be rated as parts of a perfect score adding up to a certain minimum which will be the true standard of swimming pool sanitation. Regulations of public restaurants and other establishments in which food is handled do not confine themselves to an examination of the number of bacteria found on the knives, forks, and plates, but are generally incorporated in a score card such as the one described above. Scores for dairies and schools, etc., have also been in use for some time. We may, therefore, look forward to the introduction of a score card for swimming pools in which the *indices* or *standards of contamination and stagnation* shall form two of the major divisions; the details of such

TABLE II

1	Bathing Load	Index of Stagnation	Index of Contamination	Average Bacteria per cc.			B. Coli		
				20° C	37° C		0.1 cc.	1.0 cc.	10.0 cc.
					Total	Red.			
1	2	3	4	5	6	7	8	9	10
Brown University.....	6.0	1.0	2.7		3	1	0	0	0
Pawtucket Boys' Club	2.0	2.0	2.0	1,300	10	0	0	0	+
Providence Y. M. C. A.	24.0	4.9	9.3	17,000	2	0	0	0	+
Newport Y. M. C. A..	13.3	37.8	13.1	17,000	2	1	0	0	0
Pawtucket Y. W. C. A	2.9	0.64	1.9	150	0	0	0	0	0
Woonsocket Y. M. C. A	8.0	.....	7.8	5,500	4	1	0	0	0
Pawtucket Y. M. C. A.	21.4	83.6	20.9	32	6	1	0	0	+
Newport A. & N., Y. M. C. A........	10.7	.....	10.2	28,000	65	3	0	0	+
Moses Brown School..	15.5	.....	2.6	380	1	1	0	0	0
Aborn St. Baths......	4.9	9.8-14.7	....	13,500	30	17	0	+	+
Lundin Baths........	7.9	3.9- 7.9	....	140	23	11	0	0	0

a score card, however, are not within the scope of this inquiry.

SUMMARY

The salient points of this discussion are summarized as follows:

1. The *bathing load* gives an idea of the relative care which a pool must receive to make it sanitary.

2. It is extremely hard to formulate a standard of bacterial purity for swimming pools.

3. The *index of contamination*, equal to the number of bathers using a pool in a given time divided by the amount of disinfected water added to the pool during that time, establishes a conception of the actual bacterial purity of the swimming pool.

4. The *index of stagnation*, equal to the number of bathers attending a pool in a given time divided by the amount of clean or refiltered water added to the pool during that time, gives an idea of the cleanliness of the pool water and consequently of the esthetic condition and physical safety of the pool.

5. It is impossible to regulate a public bathing place merely by prescribing a certain standard of bacterial purity or similar expression. A system of scoring the entire sanitary equipment of these institutions and the establishment of a minimum score is therefore recommended.

PUBLIC HEALTH ASPECTS OF CARTAGENA, COLOMBIA

ALFREDO DE ZUBIRIA S,

*Massachusetts Institute of Technology,
Cambridge, Mass.* .

Mr. Zubiria, a native of Cartagena, gives this outline of the sanitation of a country concerning which little has been observed or published. In view of constantly increasing trade with Latin America, such information may be of practical value.

THE city of Cartagena, or "Cartagena de Indias," as it was called before the Independence (1810) by the Spanish government, to distinguish it from Cartagena of Spain, is one of the most important cities of Colombia, South America, not only because of its commercial enterprise, but because of its being a seaport of the country which receives from the city its second largest income through the customs duties. Cartagena is also a very old city with a thrilling history attached to every speck of dirt in the imposing ramparts, or walls, which completely surround the city, for the reason that Morgan, Drake and Vernon indulged in their favorite sport of attacking and sacking the city to extract from it the wealth which the Spaniards stored within its fortifications. It was founded in the year 1533 by Don Pedro de Heredia. It is situated on the shores of the Caribbean Sea, at 10°26'01" N. latitude and 1°29'33" west of Washington. The city proper is an island connected to the mainland by many short bridges which span the narrow canals separating it from the continent. The population consists of 41,583 inhabitants, according to the census taken in 1918. Of those about 20 per cent are blacks and 60 per cent "mestizos" or half-breeds, leaving about 20 per cent of pure whites, descendants of European races, mostly Spanish. Of the mestizos there are innumerable shades of color, from dark brown skinned to pale colored ones, which pass for whites. It is these latter who by sheer force of numbers form the backbone of the country, and who by their ambition for progress and self-advancement keep the pure white population on the alert lest their supremacy, gained by the merit of education and position, be seriously jeopardized.

Schools abound in the city. There are kindergartens, preparatory schools, public schools, and the University of Bolivar in Cartagena. In the public schools tuition is free, but the instruction is not obligatory, and the students must procure their own books and supplies. In matters of public education, however, Colombia stands forth among the 20 republics of Latin America.

The health problems of the city are many, for its sanitation at the present time is regulated by a very incomplete and antiquated body of regulations. The Board of Health is doing all in its power to cope with the situation, and in view of the fact that it consists merely of a "Director de Sanidad," Doctor of the Port, a Milk Inspector and a Food Inspector and a City Chemist, it is a wonder that the city is not visited more frequently by epidemics and pestilence. The budget allowed for the city's sanitation is much too meagre, and, therefore, the number of street cleaners and other minor employees and the equipment of the Health Board, leave much to be desired.

The activities, therefore, of the Board are necessarily limited. They have been hinted at above by the names of its members. The Director of Sanitation, as his title implies, is the executive in the health work of the city; the Doctor of the Port examines all the passengers of incoming steamers, and has the power to reject all those whose landing might seriously endanger the health of the people. The milk and food inspectors attend to the milk and food supplies. The former has a staff of agents who look after the milk distributors and milk selling stations, to prevent adulteration of the milk. The latter inspects the food products as sold in the public market place. The city chemist analyzes everything from milk and water to meat, beans and rum. He has a laboratory, but has no other chemist to assist him.

Water Supply: This consists of well waters and rain water. The former is used for household purposes; the latter for drinking water. Every home has at least a well; most homes have also an "aljibe," or cistern, which consists of a subterranean vault built under the front "patio," or garden, and having walls of cement and its bottom of brick or cement. This "aljibe" is filled by the rain waters which are collected by tin gutters and pipes. The gutters are placed in such a way as to collect the water flowing down the inclined tiled roofs. They empty into two vertical pipes which conduct nature's precious liquid gift down into the cisterns. Here the water is stored for use by the family occupying the house, which usually numbers from 5 to 30 people, including servants, and serves also to supply the neighbors when their supply is exhausted. As the rainy season lasts about six months and is followed by six months of dry weather, many "aljibes" do run dry, and that family has to obtain water from its more fortunate neighbors, or from its own wells, if necessary.

How the water is handled in the homes may be of interest to the visiting tourist. He need not be alarmed when his hospitable host offers him an earthenware cup from which to drink, nor when he takes the water out of the large earthenware "tinaja" with a tin vessel provided with a long handle to fill the drinking cup. The "tinaja" is a large-sized earthenware vessel, the shape of an egg, standing on its broad end and truncated at its narrower end. It may be two feet to four or five feet high, and have a diameter of a foot to three feet at its broadest place, with the opening of about a foot in diameter. It has been found to be the best means of keeping the water ready for drinking, for it cools it by the evaporation through the porous wall which furnishes an excellent insulation and at the same time acts as a bacterial remover (by absorption). Instead of a "tinaja," the water can be kept ready to drink in small earthenware bottles. All these and the drinking cups are kept covered at all times by earthenware covers. There is no better and safer means of keeping drinking water cool in the home in the hot climate of the tropics.

For the last twelve years Cartagena has been supplied with water for its increasing industrial and household needs, by the aqueduct of an English waterworks company. The water is brought from the springs of Matute, about ten miles outside of the city. It is a very hard water, containing sulphates and carbonate of lime and magnesium. The hardness is so great that at the present time the city is suffering from lack of water due to the inability of the mains to transport it from the source. The inside of the conduits are covered with a coating which has diminished the diameter of the pipes one-half. The problem will have to be solved by a new installation of larger pipes to transport the amount of water which ˙Cartagena needs today. The water is supplied to the city in its natural state and is quite fit to drink.

A˙ public square, Cartagena·

Milk Supply. The milk supply of the city comes from 20 to 30 different "haciendas," or farms, which are primarily intended for cattle raising, the milk being sold as a by-product. The ·milk is collected, shipped and distributed in the most primitive ways. Since most of the "haciendas" are situated at from 5 to 15 miles distance from the city and there˙ are no "milk trains," the farmers milk their cows at midnight, or in the early hours of the morning, in order to have their milk reach the city by sunrise, 6:00 a. m. The milk is collected in the "corrals" into open pails placed on the ground, and by not very clean or careful milkers. The pails are then emptied into the regular milk cans, which are then covered, the cover being made tight by introducing dry corn husks between it and the mouth of the can. Two cans are then mounted, one on each side of a burro or a mule, and on the back of these most useful beasts of burden are carried to the city. The cans are locked by careful milk dealers in order that the milk carrier may not adulterate the milk, watering being a favorite pastime among the latter.

The milk is distributed in the city at the doors of the customer's homes.

The milk carrier dips a small tin measuring cup into the milk, introducing the whole length of his arm if necessary, into the can and the tips of his fingers half of the time.

Why, with such insanitary practices, are there not more frequent and serious epidemics of typhoid and other intestinal diseases? The answer lies in the fact that milk is brought to a boil in every home before it is consumed, no matter how poor its inmates may be; for by some it is considered unthinkable that milk can be consumed raw; by˙ the others that such a practice would be unsafe. Milk that has already been boiled in the morning is again boiled at noon just before it is used, cold milk being an unknown luxury in the city.

Public˙ Market. In the public market, a large building situated at the water front in the harbour, meat, fish and fruit, as well as small eatable animals, are sold to the cook or other servant sent by the housewife to buy the day's provision early after sunrise. It is also the place where almost all the grocery stores which supply the city

Public Market at Water Front

are located. Here food is sold at competing prices, fresh and cheap. The food is brought to the market place by burro or mule back or in schooners from the nearby villages and farms. The fact that it is all to be found in one large building (covering a large city block) makes the task of food inspection comparatively easy. Meat must be sold within 24 hours of the slaughter of the animal, so this article, as well as many others, are always to be obtained fresh. There are no cold storage plants, so that decayed foods are easily detected through the active bacterial life encouraged by the climate.

Sewage and Garbage Disposal. Mechanical sewerage is as yet an unrealized dream in Cartagena. The streets are drained by uncovered gutters, which run all along the foot of and surround the city walls. In important places in the city there have been built underground sewers of a very primitive nature and grade of efficiency. The drainage canals empty into the harbor in various places.

Garbage collection is practiced regularly by the city, the refuse being disposed of in out-of-the-way dumping grounds by the sea. The sun's merciless rays take care of it. These places are very popular with the black buzzards, which are efficient consumers of any decaying animal matter. In the homes of the people themselves, it is a common sight to have three or four of these birds perched on the roof's edge, patiently waiting for the time when the family cook throws to them the trimmings of the chicken or beef, which is being prepared for the day. No sooner have these reached the ground in the back "patio" than the three or four buzzards have sprung on them and devoured them. It is a very quick way of disposing of meat trimmings which might otherwise attract flies in the garbage cans. Yet it is to be hoped that such a primitive way of disposing of the household refuse will soon be replaced by more sanitary and efficient methods.

Restaurants and Food Stores. There are only four properly called restaurants in Cartagena where the sale and service of food is the main business. It is a common practice, however, to have open air kitchens about the public market place where meat, fish, etc., as well as the staple food, rice, are cooked. These serve for the laboring man's meals. They can there see for themselves how their food is handled before accepting it. Of course, flies and other undesirable visitors are not uncommon, and thereby hangs the tale of woe of the health authorities. Walking ice cream and refreshment vendors are a common sight. However, very good restaurants are managed in connection with hotels, boarding houses and clubs in the city, where the food is handled

Uncovered Gutters run along the foot of the City Wall

in a satisfactory manner and cooked in the usual tropical style—plenty of grease and condiments—as well as in the European and North American ways.

Housing Conditions. Here again is a problem for the city to solve in the old colonial quarters, where the streets are very narrow and not exactly symmetrical, and where half of the people live in "accesorias" (also called "viviendas"), dark, damp rooms on the ground floor, into which light and air enter from the street windows, or from the door, which opens into the interior of the house. These conditions are maintained in the quarters enclosed by the city walls, and are at times in sharp contrast to the comfort and cleanliness of the family occupying the upper floors of the house. In the new parts of the city, which have now grown in the suburbs to be about twice as extensive as the original city proper, there are stately residences surrounded by gardens and equipped with modern comforts for all tastes, and where sanitary conditions are very satisfactory.

About nine-tenths of all buildings in the walled part of the city are of brick and stone, about half of them in the remote parts of the suburbs are built of wood and have palm thatched roofs, which make the rays of the tropical sun bearable and even keep the house cool. Most of the buildings, in fact, three out of five in the city, have a "patio" where flowers and small plants make a delightful garden to look at and enjoy from all parts of the house. This is situated, of course, on the ground floor. All the rooms of the house open out into the patio, a balustrated corridor intervening between the room doors and the garden. The roofs of the houses are of the Spanish red-tiled style, which make a picturesque contrast with the whitewashed (by a lime emulsion) walls. The houses of the well-to-do have also a "mirador," which translated literally, means a "lookout" tower. From the tops of these towers the whole city can be viewed and the surrounding blue water of the Caribbean admired. From here also one can appreciate the outdoor life which

The "Patio" from the "Mirador"

white washed walls and towers, one sees the broad green leaves of the banana plant or the palms of the cocoanut trees of the patio, the whole brilliantly illuminated by the sun of a tropical day furnishing a realized dream of the peace and quiet, which mark the life in the tropics.

Hospital Facilities. There is a very commodious "Hospital de Caridad" in Cartagena, managed efficiently by the Sisters of Charity. It occupies a whole large-sized block overlooking the sea. It has been in operation for the last fifty years and fills a great need for the poor of the city and of the surrounding districts. There are also special private clinics of physicians of the city which accommodate those who can afford them for especially serious surgical operations.

Medical facilities are afforded by many notable physicians, products of the country, graduated in the schools of medicine in the several universities of Colombia. Of these universities may be mentioned the "Universidad de Medicina" of Bogota (the capital), and the "Escuela de Medicina" of the "Universidad de Bolivar." Among the physicians of Cartagena may be mentioned Drs. Rafael Calvo, Tatis, Obregon, Pajaro, Barboza, Valiente (a graduate of the University of Illinois Medical School), Paz and many others.

The City and the Blue Caribbean

the people lead even in the walled city, for amidst the red-tiled roofs and

Leper Colony. On entering the harbor of Cartagena one is surprised, not to say shocked, by the sight of the leper colony. This consists of a small village of thatched roofed houses of some 800 inhabitants. Those people are, however, well cared for and comfortably lodged in clean houses and amid pleasant surroundings, attended by a physician paid for the purpose. This colony is maintained by the government, and the latter has in it a vital problem to solve, for there is much to improve in the life of those unfortunates who depend more on the unlimited charity of the ladies of Cartagena than on the appropriations of the national treasury. At the present time the matter is attracting a great deal of attention from the government.

Vital Statistics. Under the item of population the number and color classification of the inhabitants has been approximately given. The writer says *approximately*, because he regrets to say, statistics in Cartagena are very poorly kept and data published by the registrars there cannot be accepted without further analysis. He regrets also that he has no figures at hand which he can offer as positively exact. However, the following statistics may be accepted as fairly accurate, coming as they do from such an authoritative source as Dr. Felipe S. Paz, Professor of Statistics at the University of Bolivar in Cartagena. In a study by Dr. Paz on the population of Cartagena, published in *El Porvenir*, the oldest daily paper in Cartagena, with the title of *Apuntes Sobre la Poblacion de Cartagena*, we find the increase in the number of inhabitants of the city since 1871:

INCREASE OF POPULATION OF CARTAGENA

Year	Inhabitants
1871	8,603
1881	9,681
1882	11,975
1909	17,717
1918	43,583*

MORTALITY OF CARTAGENA
1872-1918

Year	Population	Deaths	Rate per 1,000 during the year
1872	8,603	877	101.94
1881	9,681	658	67.96
1882	11,975	664	55.44
1909	17,717	587	33.13
1918	41,583	729	17.53

Note: In 1918 the death rate may be considered a little too low since the population figure includes many outlying districts in which deaths and births are poorly and incompletely recorded. However, 20 per thousand would not be a bad estimate. It is a very high percentage, due to the utter lack of instruction among the lower classes of "mestizos" and blacks regarding hygiene, both municipal and personal.

The following table, taken from the excellent historical treatise of Urueta and Pineres, *Cartagena y Sus Cercanias, pp. 45-48 (Cartagena and its Suburbs),* gives an idea of the deaths and main causes of death in the city between the years 1872 and 1910.

NUMBER OF DEATHS BETWEEN 1872 AND 1882, ACCORDING TO SEX BY YEARS

Year	Deaths (Males)	Deaths (Females)	Totals	Population	Death rate per 1,000
1872	473	404	877	8,603	102
1873	117	132	249	....	...
1874	142	131	273	....	...
1875	141	139	280	....	...
1876	119	120	239	....	...
1877	196	171	367	....	...
1878	234	303	537	....	...
1879	212	249	461	....	...
1880	294	264	558	....	...
1881	306	352	658	9,681	68
1882	314	350	664	11,975	55
Averages	2,548	2,615	5,163 469.4	99,083 9,008	... 52

In this table there are excluded the deaths during the months of July and August, 1872, the time of the fierce cholera outbreak, which caused an appalling number of deaths. It was the epidemic commonly called "El Tablon." Columns 5 and 6 were added by the writer in order to calculate the average death rate for the period. The

*This last figure includes the population of all the suburbs and districts under the jurisdiction of Cartagena.

table shows for 1876 the lowest number of deaths, 239 during that eleven-year période. Assuming the population from 1872 to 1880 to have remained stationary (8,603), the 5,163 deaths between 1872 and 1882, which give an average of 469.4 annual deaths, give a total average death rate per 1,000 population of 52 for the eleven years considered. This figure, of course, is staggeringly high. Errors in the taking of the censuses may account for it, and it must be kept in mind that they are not infallible.

Sr. Pineres has concluded Sr. Urueta's statistical data up to the date when the second corrected and augmented edition of *Cartagena and its Surroundings* was finished (1910). He collected the later data from the records kept in the Alcalde's office (Mayor's office), corresponding to the years from 1899 to 1910. He estimates that the population of Cartagena doubles in that period what it was in 1882, but bases his figures on the common base of 20,000 inhabitants, which he claims to be somewhat under the right population figure for the year 1910. Sr. Pineres' figures follow:

NUMBER OF DEATHS BETWEEN 1899 AND 1910, ACCORDING TO SEX BY YEARS

Year	Deaths (all ages)		Totals
	Males	Females	
1899	298	244	542
1900	382	274	656
1901	455	418	873
1902	407	291	698
1903	341	257	598
1904	410	285	695
1905	361	364	725
1906	290	250	540
1907	296	225	521
1908	374	315	689
1909	304	283	587
1910	334	297	631
Totals	4,252	3,503	7,755

Average number of deaths per year for the 12-year period, 646. Death rate per 1,000, 32.3.

The high figure for the year 1901 is due to an epidemic of smallpox. The death rate has fallen from 55 in 1882 to 32 per 1,000 in 1910.

The following two tables taken from page 47 of the same book give the infant deaths and those of the old age groups; for the former 1-5 years is taken; for the latter, 60-110 years.

INFANT DEATHS 1-5 YEARS OF AGE BY YEARS. 1899-1910

Year	Deaths
1899	246
1900	230
1901	375
1902	280
1903	223
1904	242
1905	360
1906	258
1907	245
1908	392
1909	324
1910	315
Total	3,490

Three thousand four hundred and ninety infant deaths is approximately 45 per cent of the total deaths during the 12-year period studied.

The high infant death rate is likely to be due to improper feeding, as the milk supplied to Cartagena is of very poor quality.

The other table which gives the deaths among the people between the ages of 60 and 110 years, gives proof of the excellence of Cartagena's climate, which helped by reasonable personal hygiene, makes possible a high longevity. The city of Cartagena has an undeserved name as an unhealthy spot of "unbearable climate." This is in complete opposition to all facts, the city being a seashore resort, constantly refreshed by the cooling trade winds. The temperature fluctuates between 17°C. and 33°C. The former temperature is reached in the early hours of the morning; the latter at 3:00 in the afternoon. Between 10 o'clock in the morning and 3 o'clock in the afternoon it is hot, but as the people of the city rest between 11:00 a. m. and 1:00 p. m., most of the hot hours can be passed in comfort by those used to tropical living. The evenings, it must be admitted, are delightfully refreshing.

The figures in the table have been carefully compiled by Sr. Pineres:

DEATHS IN AGES BETWEEN 60 AND 110 YEARS CARTAGENA, COLOMBIA

(1899-1910)

Age Group	Deaths
60-70 years	338
70-80	317
80-90	264
90-100	104
100-110	7
Total	1,030

One thousand and thirty deaths of people between the ages of 60 and 110 represent 13.3 per cent of the total deaths.

Of the causes of death the following seven causes made up 47.43 per cent of all deaths in the same twelve years. (Page 48, Pineres).

CAUSES OF DEATH, CARTAGENA, 1899-1910

Causes	Total in the 12 years	Deaths per year
Tuberculosis	608	50
Fevers of several types	1,748	145
Infant tetanus	276	23
Gastro-enteritis	517	43
Dysentery	369	31
Small pox	103	8
Yellow fever	58	5
Totals	3,679	305

To quote Pineres: "Smallpox and yellow fever occurred in 1900, 1901 and 1902; the former in 1901 and 1902 with 32, with 45 cases in 1900. These were years of war (the last civil war in Colombia), and consequently, of much mobilization of troops from the interior of the country, who are the ones who suffer most from the second of these scourges. Between the years 1906 and 1910 there was recorded only one case of yellow fever." This fever, which is the terror of foreigners in Colombia, is a thing of the past and malarial fevers are of rare occurrence in Cartagena.

Epidemics are rare in the city. There was an epidemic of cholera in 1849, which hit Cartagena and many other towns of the Department of Bolivar, and of the interior of the republic. Since then only smallpox, which has broken out from time to time, and "El Tablon" once, have occurred in epidemic form. The 1918 epidemic of influenza also attacked Cartagena with a rather high case rate, but with almost no fatality. This seems to have been due to the warm climate prevailing there, for in Bogota and other cold high latitude places of Colombia the fatality was staggering.

The writer, after some hesitation, has decided to publish in a foreign country what he knows of health conditions in his own native city. He believes that the light of truth is the best disinfectant for the germ of lethargy which is so prevalent in his home city in matters of public health. He hesitated at first, because, naturally, discussing the health problems of his city, people of non-analytical minds might be led to think that such facts were the only facts to know about Cartagena, without considering that only unfavorable ones (the problems), have been brought out. He submits his observations unbiased even by his deep affection for Cartagena, to which he hopes to return to enjoy his later life.

The Railway Station is in an unimproved section

CAUSES OF TYPHOID FEVER IN MASSACHUSETTS

GEORGE T. O'DONNELL, M. D.,
*State District Health Officer, State Department of Health,
Boston, Mass.*

Read before the Section of Public Health Administration, American Public Health Association, at New Orleans, La., October 28, 1919.

To decrease its typhoid Massachusetts needs now to prevent contacts, use prophylaxis, and educate its citizens in personal hygiene. Municipal water supplies are practically safe. Flies, food (milk excepted), privies and sewage are together only a small factor in spreading the disease. The human contact factor is the one that must be controlled.

IN giving this short paper under this title, no thought is entertained of naming any new or hitherto unknown causative factor. The factors or agencies by which the disease is transmitted are well known already and are, of course, universally the same; that is, water, milk, food and contact with clinical case or carrier. But rather it will be an explanation of why a certain order of importance is given these factors in Massachusetts.

Geographically and geologically, Massachusetts differs from many other sections of the country, and this combination coupled with the fact that public health work had an early start, dating back fifty years, made it possible to settle water and sewage problems for extensive areas. These accomplishments had a most marked influence in changing the relative importance of the causative factors in typhoid fever. Gradually, but certainly, water has been relegated to a position among these factors which gives Massachusetts now very little concern as a cause of typhoid fever.

In 1907 the State was divided into 15 districts, each having a part-time health officer who would serve as a connecting link between local boards of health and the State Board of Health and who would serve as an in-

vestigator. In 1912 the number was reduced to 12 districts. In 1914 a reorganization of the State Board of Health took place and the State Department of Health was established with a Commissioner, and the state divided into 8 districts, each with a full-time District Health Officer. This group was made up largely from previous appointees and they, with their experience, carried out the recommendations of 1913 which resulted in intensive work on all typhoid case reports.

In 1914 a regulation was passed by the State Department of Health demanding that all typhoid fever cases as well as certain other milk-borne diseases, be reported at once if on the premises of milk handlers or producers.

This investigation is promptly and thoroughly carried out by the local boards of health and State District Health Officers and the part played by the carrier brought into the light.

It seems well to speak of the above in the fore part of this paper because of the fact that a pure water supply and adequate sewage disposal facilities are absolutely essential to the prevention and control of typhoid fever.

WATER

In 1848, just 21 years before the creation of the Massachusetts State Board of Health, the first metropolitan water supply was established at a point about 15 miles from Boston; a secondary or supplementary supply was completed in 1873, and these were added to at different periods up to 1898 when the Great Wachusett Reservoir, 40 miles from Boston, was finished. These great storage basins with their protected watersheds deliver water by aqueducts to distributing reservoirs at given points near the city. By this means, from storage reservoirs, water is supplied to what is practically one-third of the population of the state.

Should pollution, in the shape of typhoid fever infection, find its way into the water supply from some point on the water-shed, by the time this water reached the consumer no infection would probably be present; as it has been proven conclusively that one month, with its exposure to the sun, and accompanying natural and chemical precipitation, plus the fact that germs do not propagate in storage water, spell death to the infection of typhoid fever.

This plan or similar plan of public water supply has been carried out by most of our large cities and towns, and has resulted in a marked decrease in the incidence and death rate in typhoid fever. In recent years, dating from 1896, we have had no series of typhoid fever cases blameable to public water, with one exception, and that occurred in one of our cities which uses a filtered supply from a much polluted river. This was due to the freezing of the filter beds which allowed polluted water to enter the municipal water mains.

We still have in our rural districts the problem of the well water and the neighborhood pump. The continued examinations of our water laboratories bring out the fact that practically all of these are polluted, either by a privy on the premises or by very poor sanitary arrangements about the well head. They often are easy of access to the public and are used as a place to wash hands, the

drip-water returning to the well. There sulting in 22 cases, both of these occurring during the past summer.

SEWAGE

For the most part, those cities and towns which operate public water supplies, have also established concomitant sewage disposal plants which, of course, in a complementary way reduce to a very great degree the possibility of the pollution of the home and other water supplies. All of the municipalities bordering on the ocean dispose of the sewage by discharging it into the sea at a suitable distance from the shore. In addition, many inland towns, such as those in the metropolitan area, also empty their sewage into the sea by trunk sewers.

The rural community which gets its drinking water from private wells, has also the much complained of overflowing cesspools and privies, and therefore, as stated above, we still have present with us this condition which is slowly but surely improving due to our efforts in an educational way. This will be considered later.

MILK

In 1913, after much study and thorough investigation, there was recommended, and a year later established, a routine epidemiological investigation of each individual case of typhoid fever, using a special blank form upon which was recorded all data considered important. When a number of cases, sufficiently large to study, had been reported on these forms, the degree of importance attached to each factor was brought to light and the cause of milk infection was revealed. During the period of years 1915 to 1918, inclusive, the attempt to investigate every case was usually successful and 496 cases out of 6,331 were found to be due to the agency of milk, but only in one instance was an outbreak proved to be due to an acute case. This outbreak numbered 22 cases, and 46% of these milk-borne typhoid fever cases in this period were proven to be due to milk infected by a carrier. For the last are some cases of typhoid due to such infected water, among them a well which caused 11 cases and a public spring re- 10 years, only 8.1% of all the typhoid fever cases proved to have been milk-borne.

In 1918, 48% of our milk infection by typhoid fever bacilli was proven to be due to infection by carriers; but in the remaining 52% of the cases no clinical case was found and the milk was prob-ably infected by carriers.

In order that some of the matters just referred to may be made more clear let me explain that a State Board of Health was established in 1869, and long years passed when there was little or no co-operation on the part of local agencies and during which time reported typhoid fever outbreaks had to be looked into by special investigators. With no knowl-edge of the Widal and with no labora-tory facilities such as now prevail, it can readily be seen that the march of prog-ress in Massachusetts as in other sec-tions was slow and tedious during the early years.

CARRIERS

As nearly as can be ascertained, about 2% of all typhoid fever victims become carriers. This seems a small percentage. In the last 10 years, 41 permanent car-ciers have been found. This also may seem small, but when you learn that in the period of years, 1910-1914, 3 of these carriers were responsible for 125 cases of typhoid fever and from 1915-1919, 14 carriers caused 249 cases, a picture quite different is shown.

It is interesting to note that 18 of the 41 carriers were found as a result of out-breaks of typhoid fever among customers of dairies and on milk routes. The carriers infecting milk were in each in-stance permanent carriers; that is, they had the disease several years previous, one carrier giving a history of typhoid 45 years previous.

The temporary carrier is undoubtedly a greater source of infection than is at present realized and a cause of many of the typhoid cases of unknown origin. It is possible that in the near future two or more negative fecal and urine examina-tions may be required from convalescing cases to determine whether cases are carriers or not. This is now done in several of the large hospitals in Massa-chusetts.

CONTACT WITH THE CLINICAL CASE

This infection takes place usually be-cause of ignorance of personal hygiene on the part of the attendant or nurse. Failure to wash and disinfect properly the hands after tending a patient before handling food used by others is the direct way of infecting self and others. The returning of infected milk bottles to a non-infected supply, the failure to disin-fect stools properly and depositing same where flies predominate, are also com-mon methods of securing secondary contact.

HOUSEHOLD CONTACT

The case records in a group of 556 cases furnished an indication of the num-ber of persons constituting a household, the total being 3,051 individuals, or five persons to the household.

Considering that there were but 98 secondary cases in these households, it is rather a good showing, but a closer study shows that over one-half of these cases had their onset three weeks or more after the onset of the primary case. Also 31 families had two or more cases, one family having five and another seven cases.

The use of typhoid prophylactics on all the members of the household at the appearance of the first case would have prevented some of the secondary cases. It is this phase of typhoid infection which has proved to be unsatisfactory and difficult to deal with in our state. We are hoping that the educational work in the state will soon make the use of the typhoid vaccine in families more welcome and decrease the secondary cases in households.

EDUCATIONAL WORK

The State Health Department carries on throughout the year a program of illustrated lectures given by District Health Officers and public health nurses in which the story of public health is carried to the cities and towns, especially the smaller ones. By the use of illustrated talks, the method of transmitting infection, what contact really is, the elements of personal hygiene, clean handling of food and milk, the knowledge of the Widal Test and immunization are impressed upon the community life throughout the state.

Many of our small towns of from 1,500 to 5,000 inhabitants have seen fit to employ public health nurses who devote their entire time to public health and school work. The larger places, without exception, have one or more nurses who are performing a high order of work. This group is being increased constantly, and a plan is now being put into operation which will bring nursing activities to every corner of the Commonwealth.

This feature is mentioned because it is certainly one of the influences which is responsible for the decrease in the incidence of typhoid fever in Massachusetts.

MORBIDITY AND MORTALITY

As a result of the intensive work mentioned the following statistics are of interest:

The morbidity rate in Massachusetts has decreased from 102.1 cases per 100,000 of population in 1910, to 27.2 cases per 100,000 in 1918. Likewise, the mortality rate has decreased from 12.2 deaths per 100,000 in 1910, to 4.0 per 100,000 in 1918.

CONCLUSIONS

(1) The experience of the Massachusetts State Department of Health shows that flies, food (exclusive of milk), privies and sewage, are relatively a small factor in the spread of typhoid at the present time in the state.

(2) There are very few cases due to water, especially in recent years, and in general no municipal supply is considered as a dangerous source of typhoid infection.

(3) Milk as a means of spreading typhoid infection was responsible for 8.1 per cent of the total cases reported in Massachusetts during the past ten years.

(4) Contact with clinical cases of typhoid is the most frequent known method of spreading infection. Contact with known carriers has been responsible for a few cases in homes and neighborhoods.

(5) Carriers were proven to be responsible for 41.6 per cent of milk-borne typhoid in 1915 to 1918, inclusive. Carriers are a larger factor in the spread of typhoid than at present known, and are a cause probably of an appreciable number of typhoid cases of unknown origin.

(6) The early establishment of water supplies and sewage disposal plants was a fortunate thing for Massachusetts in eliminating polluted water as a factor. Finally, the prevention of typhoid fever in Massachusetts can be summed up under the following procedure; namely, investigation of the individual case; educational work, particularly along lines of personal hygiene and a more widespread use of immunization.

The A. P. H. A. Meeting at San Francisco is only two and one-half months away!

September 13-17, 1920.

Plan your vacation so as to be there!

SELF-IMPOSED INSPECTION OF THE NATIONAL CANNERS ASSOCIATION

H. M. Loomis,

National Director of Inspection, National Canners Association, Washington, D. C.

Read before the Food and Drugs Section, American Public Health Association, at New Orleans, La., October 27, 1919.

Here is where the manufacturers on their own initiative have instituted inspection to improve, standardize and certify their own canned products. The public health aspects are important and include good original material, proper processing, supervision of health of employees and improved sanitation of factories.

A DETAILED description of the National Canners Association inspection is beyond the scope of this paper, but in brief it is a voluntary movement on the part of canners in this country to secure some disinterested and competent agency to inspect their canneries and canning operations for the purpose of bringing the former up to high standards of sanitation, and of raising the average quality of canned foods produced in such canneries.

Subscribing canners sign an agreement with the National Canners Association that they will pay an assessment to defray the expense of inspection and that they will abide by the rules and regulations of the Association. The inspection is conducted without profit to the Association.

Minimum standards of quality are being established, and canned foods which come up to or exceed these standards, and which are packed under the sanitary conditions required, are entitled to receive the certificate of the Association showing that they are packed under its supervision, in accordance with its regulations.

These standards which provide for a clean, attractive and palatable can of food, are prepared by the inspection service, and, being tentative in character, can be revised when necessary with comparatively little trouble. Such standards have already been adopted for canned sardines, corn, tomatoes, string beans, lima beans, peas, pumpkin, sauerkraut, spinach and fruits. One of the rules for certification provides that "Beginning with the output of 1920 in all cases where a standard grade has been or shall be adopted by the Joint Committee on Definitions and Standards of the U. S. Department of Agriculture, the minimum standard for certification shall not be lower than such standard grade." Products falling below those standards will not be certified and in that way is to be attempted the gradual elimination of the poor quality goods which injure the market for canned goods.

The canners, in order to keep in close touch with the inspection service and the director of inspection, elect an advisory board from among their number, to advise the director on matters relating to the inspection. The directors of inspection, however, are appointed by the executive officers of the National Canners Association to whom they are alone responsible, and they in turn have entire charge of the appointment of their assistants and of questions relating to certification.

INSPECTORS AND INSPECTION METHODS

The inspection service of the Association has been divided into districts, and each district is in charge of a director of inspection appointed, as already stated, by the National Association. Eleven such directors have so far been appointed and nine of these have had long experience in either federal or state food inspection work. The other two are men thoroughly trained in scientific and practical canning. Under the Association rules, no relative of a canner nor any one financially interested in an inspected cannery can hold a position on the inspection force.

This inspection plan originated at a meeting of the officers of the National Canners Association with representatives of the Marine Sardine Canners in February, 1916. The meeting was called at the request of the latter to organize for the good of the industry and to ask the Association to put into effect some plan of inspection by which the average quality of the Maine sardine, as well as sanitary conditions in the factories, could be improved. A large majority of the Maine canners signed an agreement to live up to such inspection rules as the Association might adopt, and to pay an assessment on each case of cans bought by them. About two-thirds of the Maine sardine pack are put up under this inspection.

The plan was later followed out substantially in the inspection service for the California sardine industry, and for the fruit and vegetable canners inspection begun in Southern California in 1917, and in Iowa, Illinois, Wisconsin, Indiana, Ohio, Michigan, and New York, in 1919.

The Pacific Coast salmon industry has largely adopted this form of inspection, but owing to the difficulty of access to the various Alaska canneries and the lack of sufficient men trained for the work, the service this year has been limited to a thorough sanitary survey of the canneries, followed by recommendations from the Director of Inspection that will make it possible for each cannery to operate next year

in accordance with the sanitary requirements of the Association.

The whole plan may still be said to be in its infancy and many important details remain to be worked out or perfected.

This inspection will not be realizing all that is expected of it if it does not bring about a permanent improvement in standards of quality and sanitation. Only thus will the canners derive any lasting benefit from it, and far-sighted men in the industry see this and have refused even to ask for the certification of goods which they do not believe to be of suitable quality.

They realize that if such goods go out to the trade bearing the certificate of inspection, the harm done to the inspection, in the success of which they are vitally interested, will far outweigh any possible temporary advantage from such certification. Such abuse of certificates will prove a boomerang affecting not only the individual canner responsible, but all the canners who are backing this movement.

In some states so noticeable has been the improvement in quality effected by this inspection that buyers are demanding certified goods and many canners indicate the fact of such inspection on their invoices. It has been found in many districts that there is a decided reduction in the losses due to spoiled cans since the inspection was inaugurated.

To quote a sardine canner who has been connected with the inspection from the beginning: "Our sardine canning factories are in a much better condition than they were three years ago—neater, cleaner and much better kept in every way and there has been a decided improvement in sanitary conditions in and about the factories. The raw material is handled in a clean and sanitary manner, and a better article is being produced.

"As a result of the inspection system the men engaged in our industry have confidence in their product. They know that the packers who are under inspection are putting out good sardines. They know that none of the members of the Sardine Section are packing and selling sardines that will injure the industry generally. We know that the jobber and the retailer have more confidence in Maine sardines knowing that they are packed under inspection, because as a result of the three years' working of the inspection system they have come to know that sardines bearing the certificate of the National Canners Association are good sardines."

This letter expresses the effects of the inspection from a canner's viewpoint.

I desire here to make clear that before this inspection was started there have been and there always probably will be canners who maintain high standards for cannery conditions and quality of products. In most cases such canners realize that anything which will tend to place the industry on a higher plane will be of benefit to them, and they have been among our most loyal supporters.

Since the beginning of the inspection service the only form of certificate issued has been one to be attached to each case of approved canned foods and worded substantially as follows: This certifies that the product contained in this package has been packed under our supervision in accordance with our requirements. Signed National Canners Association and giving the name of the Director of Inspection.

However, the case certificate alone does not fully meet the wishes of the canners. Such certificates do not come to the attention of the consumer, except in rare instances, and if they did he probably would not know what they implied. Furthermore, as this inspection is rather a process of gradual evolution than an over-night revolution, by force of competition and example

many of the canners who are outside the inspection and who had been in the habit of putting out poor quality goods and operating insanitary factories, have been compelled at least to approximate the minimum quality set up by the inspection service and the sanitary conditions required thereunder.

The canners under inspection feel that to get the greatest benefit out of this inspection, and, to some extent, reimburse them for the large added expense under which they are operating, the certificate of inspection should appear on each can, so that it will reach the consumer. Then by a properly conducted campaign of education and publicity, the consumer can be induced to demand certified products. The working out of such a plan for some form of certificate or emblem on each can of food approved by the inspection service, is contemplated during the coming year.

SANITATION

The general sanitary requirements are about 30 in number and are based on the Association's experience and on sanitary laws. They provide for cleanliness of factory, utensils, raw materials and product, also for sanitation in habits and dress on the part of employees. In addition to this, in each branch of the industry special rules may be made which are applicable to that particular industry. In some instances, canneries have been dark and dreary places with a consequently depressing effect on the workers. The liberal application of white paint in such places has a marked effect on the feelings and attitude of the employees, and I have never yet found a case where a canner regretted the outlay of money for that particular purpose.

It is evident from the experience of the past three years that most canners do not realize at first that this inspection is not simply restrictive, but may be helpful and constructive in character, depending on their attitude toward it. Of course, in work of this sort much depends on the tact and common sense of the inspector, but the fact remains that while at first packers were apt to regard the inspectors with suspicion, and complaints were frequent that the inspectors spent too much time around their factories, there has been a steady and notable increase in the number of canners who desire closer and more continuous inspection by the Association. If that feeling becomes general, there will be almost unlimited possibilities for the extension of the service. Canners will realize that the inspection is a great help to them and that as they are paying for it, anything they may do to cripple it or to impair its usefulness will ultimately injure themselves.

Many canners have admitted that the spirit of competition or emulation stimulated among their employees by this inspection has been of great benefit to them. They are glad to have an inspector come in, and in a helpful way call attention to things which would easily be overlooked by the cannery management, particularly during the height of the canning season.

It was estimated last spring that about one-fifth of the total pack of canned foods would be packed under Association inspection this year, but the latest figures indicate that about one-third of the 1919 output will be so inspected. Certificates will not be issued in some districts on account of the delay in starting the inspection.

Several questions naturally arise in connection with this form of inspection which is not backed up by force of law, but merely by the pledged word of each canner signing the inspection agreement. How can the inspection be made really effective and how can the rules be enforced if a canner declines to live up to his agreement?

The answer to this is that the canners are putting their own money into this plan, and that means they wish it

to succeed. All, or nearly all, of them realize that it cannot succeed unless the rules are lived up to and the use of the certificate is safeguarded. To have poor goods go out under certificates will make the certificate of little value in the eyes of the buyer, and that makes it as important a matter to the canner as to each inspector that certificates should only go on goods that will be a credit to the industry.

The publicity to be given to the certified goods by the campaign planned will make certificates of real value and the possible loss of certificates on any lot of goods will be another incentive to canners to live up to the requirements.

This movement is not wholly a new idea. Probably the best known effort of a similar kind is that of the California citrus fruit growers, who formed a non-profit organization to make possible more efficient and prompt marketing of their perishable products and to standardize the quality of the latter when sold under copyrighted and extensively advertised brands. At the head of that organization was placed a scientifically trained man of proven executive ability who was experienced in fruit growing.

Two or three state laws have recently been framed providing for state inspection and certification of canned foods; in other states similar legislation is contemplated.

SCIENTIFIC WORK

In any attempt to put into effect a constructive system of inspection, account must be taken of scientific methods for controlling both the factory operations and the quality of the finished products, for the canning industry is based fundamentally on the science of bacteriology, with a less direct application of chemistry, physics and engineering.

The Research Laboratories of the Association in Washington under Dr. Bigelow are well equipped to handle most of the problems relating to the industry, but it is felt that smaller field laboratories in connection with the inspection offices would fill more exactly the local needs. Consequently, such laboratories have already been established in Maine and in California, and close connections with state or commercial laboratories have been established in four other districts. These laboratories are prepared to handle such problems as those relating to sterilizing or processing, quality of raw material, examination of finished products, accumulation of data on which to base definitions of grades or standards, proper fill of cans, and methods of retarding deterioration in case of perishable raw materials.

If this plan is to be a permanent success, it will not be bound down to certain limited and prescribed functions, like inspection, either state or federal, under the Meat Inspection Act or the pure food laws. Such official inspection is based on certain minimum standards of quality and sanitation below which a producer cannot fall without violating the law. Canners Association inspection, however, must continue to grow and develop along constructive lines.

⊡

VALUE OF PLANT RECORDS IN THE DEVELOPMENT OF PLANT HYGIENE

A. R. HACKETT, M. D.,

*Delray Industrial Hospital,
Detroit, Mich.*

Read before Section on Industrial Hygiene, American Public Health Association, at New Orleans, La., October 28, 1919.

PLANT medical records can be of much service in developing plant hygiene. A great many varied hygienic conditions are met with in industry. These vary according to different working conditions and also to the working conditions found necessary, or more often unnecessary in producing the product peculiar to the industry, such as lead poisoning, gas poisoning, T. N. T. poisoning, and so forth. These I would classify as preventable accidents, rather than occupational diseases. There are, however, a large number of conditions and diseases that may be traced to poor plant hygiene and there are also an equally large, or even larger number, of diseases that can be traced to personal hygiene rather than to any condition connected with the plant. To differentiate between these two is an all-important problem and in order to do it with any degree of accuracy some very careful work must be done. Records in themselves amount to very little as evidenced by the various forms of records used and there has been very little attempted at standardization. Recently I read of one plant which claimed to have obtained better results from their work by keeping absolutely no record of their sick cases whatever. This, of course, is carrying things to an extreme but I do believe, however, that the simplest form of records possible will accomplish the best results.

We have been surprised to find how many so-called occupational diseases, which are often blamed on poor plant hygiene, have, when a thorough history has been recorded and the laboratory findings tabulated, been found to have their origin in something entirely foreign to any condition connected with the plant. For instance, to find how many general systemic conditions can be traced to focal infections, such as diseased tonsils, abscessed teeth, and so forth, each case must be handled individually and the proper diagnosis aimed at.

It is an obvious fact that all hygienic supervision of the plant should originate in the medical director's office, and it depends largely on the records he keeps and the thoroughness with which they are worked out, whether they will be of very much value in this connection. In too many instances the medical director is called upon to do all the detail work of not only seeing all the sick and accident cases personally, and making all physical examinations, but has to do the clerical work as well. Naturally he has to be as brief as possible with this part of the work and will overlook a great many facts that are of vital importance in making the correct diagnoses and amassing accurate data that will help solve the hygienic problems of the plant.

To prove what I am saying, I want to cite several concrete examples that came under our observation recently.

The first case was that of Mr. L., an employee of the company for over 15 years, who had been working around the coke ovens for most of that time, and who had been subjected to coal gases—given off during the manufacture of the coke. He had reported at the dispensary on various occasions with indefinite symptoms, for which he received treatment, but which did not clear up. He was brought to the hospital with the impression that he might be suffering from a chronic gas poisoning. A thorough history was obtained and laboratory findings tabulated, which resulted in showing that the man gave a positive Wassermann and that he was suffering from cerebro-spinal lues from which he died very shortly. This case could have been very easily overlooked, without the proper laboratory work being done, and could have been classified as one of several occupational diseases.

The second case was that of a Mr. P., a man who had been but recently employed with the company, but who had reported at the dispensary for an injured ankle which he said had been received before being employed by us, but which he claimed was being aggravated by the kind of employment he had, as it necessitated his standing on his feet for a greater part of the time. He was brought to the hospital and given a thorough examination and laboratory tests applied which resulted in showing that he had a Charcot joint following a syphilitic infection. This ultimately necessitated amputation of his lower limb.

The third case was that of an engineer on one of the yard locomotives. He had been in our employ a long time and came into the hospital suffering with pain in his lower spine. We immediately thought he had an "engineers spine" and that we had a true occupational disease to deal with. However, during the course of general examination it was found that his teeth were in very bad condition and he was advised to consult a dentist. The dentist reported that nearly all of his teeth were abscessed at the roots. This again ruled out the occupational disease and put the diagnosis where it belonged.

The fourth case was that of a foreign employee who had reported at the Dispensary on several occasions complaining of indefinite pains in the abdomen. He also thought his work was too heavy for him and that a change of occupation would relieve his condition; however, during the examination it was found he was suffering from a severe pyorrheal infection and several of his teeth were loose. An X-ray of all his teeth was taken which resulted in showing that not only were some of his teeth abscessed at the roots but that a large percentage of them were partially eaten away and his gums in general were badly infected. Here again lay the cause rather than in an ulcerated stomach or heavy work. A man with a chronic infection like this is not able to do real work.

The old type doctor might truly be called an "all-around man." He attempted to do everything in the way of diagnosis and treatment, and often times surgical as well. As I have mentioned earlier in this paper this is the type of work that has characterized a great deal of the industrial medical departments in the past.

In order to do this work properly it has been our experience that not only is it necessary to have a competent medical staff and plenty of clerical help devoting all of their time to this work, but to have as well, a thoroughly modern laboratory and X-ray equipment with trained tech-; nicians in charge.

In a large number of the states the so-called occupational diseases are being put on the same basis as the industrial accidents. This will lead to a great number of these cases getting before the Industrial Accident Boards. In order to show that the plant hygiene is or is not

responsible for them it will be absolutely necessary that accurate records be kept and sufficient clinical and laboratory findings tabulated to show beyond a doubt what the correct diagnosis is.

This, however, is an expensive proposition and is beyond reach of the average small plant. The best solution to this, in our experience, would be to have several institutions in a given community join together and recognize and support a thoroughly equipped diagnostic clinic for this very purpose.

This, we believe, would not only save the companies themselves a large amount of money but would also save the individual much unnecessary medical attention and time lost in undergoing treatment which in a great many instances, if an early diagnosis had been made and the proper treatment instituted in the beginning, would have quickly cleared up the cases.

☐

WORLD-WIDE WORK OF INTERNATIONAL HEALTH BOARD
AUSTRALIA

Here is a group of Australian aborigines assembled for hookworm examination and treatment. These people were thought to be only lightly infected, but the campaign conducted by the State of Queensland with the assistance of the International Health Board has disclosed a high rate of infection (from 60 to 100 per cent) among them. Arrangements for their systematic treatment are being made.

RESUME OF METHODS FOR CONTROL OF MALARIA: INDICATIONS; RESULTS; COSTS

H. R. CARTER,

*Asst. Surgeon General, U. S. P. H. S.,
Baltimore, Md.*

Read before General Sessions, American Public Health Association, at New Orleans, La.,
October 29, 1919.

Eighty to ninety-nine per cent reduction in physicians' calls to
malaria patients has been the result of malaria control work in
the South. The author notes that there is no set rule for all
localities. Cost is a factor not to be ignored. Quinine is sometimes necessary, but usually mosquito control is adopted.

Knowledge of the mechanism of the transmission of malaria gives us the key to its control—*i. e., to prevent access of infected Anopheles mosquitoes to men.* For this our methods are:

(a) Get rid of Anopheles mosquitoes.

(b) Prevent the infection of Anopheles mosquitoes.

(c) Prevent access of any Anopheles mosquitoes to men.

Sufficient control of either host, human or insect, will control malaria.

For (a) we aim to prevent the production of Anopheles;

(b) to free all men in the community from malaria parasites;

(c) to keep men behind screens and mosquito bars during the flight of Anopheles.

I do not mention hand-catching of Anopheles in residences, or the use of quinine to prevent infection in the person taking it. The former is an efficient but little used and rather troublesome method of control; the latter has never been tried out in the United States and, although it unquestionably has given good results in Italy, Greece, Algiers and some other places, it seems to me rather a makeshift to be used until other measures can be instituted. It is however a makeshift I have used a few times, I believe, to my great personal advantage.

The first and second are community measures; the third may be either community or individualistic. The first implies control of the insect host, preventing the infection of man; the second, control of the human host preventing the infection of the mosquito; the third prevents both the infection of men—if the mosquitoes screened out are infective—and the infection of mosquitoes—if the men screened in are infective. (The action of hand-catching is analogous to screening.)

METHODS

Of the three methods, which is the best? There is no best method, or rather each of them is best under certain conditions. You do not ask what is the best laxative or the best stimulant! What is best under one set of conditions is not best under another.

I will say however, that where practicable, community measures are in general preferable to individual ones, just as it is better to sterilize the water supply for a city than to trust to individuals to do so, each one for himself. Yet if the city fails in this duty, that man is wise who boils his own drinking water. If community control is not enforced, protect yourself.

We will then compare only the two community measures. Until today at least, I expect you have heard mostly of the method by mosquito control, applied first by Ross at Ismalia; by Gorgas around Havana and on the Canal Zone, and, since 1914, by others in many places in the United States. Obviously, preventing Anopheles production is absolutely effective in controlling malaria. Often has it been so proven both here and abroad. And it is always physically possible to control the production of Anopheles. Why then should we consider any other method? Because this method of control is not everywhere possible within the *allowable limits of cost.* Some other method may be.

Now here I think I *can give you the* best method of Malaria Control or rather criteria by which you may in any given case determine it: *That method is the best which gives sufficient control of malaria at the least cost,* or, what is the same thing, *which gives greatest and sufficient control for the same cost.* It seems to me that all working sanitarians will agree with me here. Economy in sanitary measures is to be considered equally with their efficiency. To spend $1.00 for a result obtainable for 80 cents is not only bad business, but bad sanitation. We may even pay too much for sanitation. We speak of health as "priceless." This is hyperbole. Health has a money value and to spend $1.00 and gain 80 cents worth of health is again bad sanitation. I think we have usually gotten at least $10.00 worth for every $1.00 spent in malaria control.

The values of the different methods are then accurately proportional to the ratio of the benefit received to the cost; or, as it might better be expressed, of the injury removed to the cost. Obviously the number of people benefited multiplied by the percentage of the reduction of malaria among them expresses the benefit.

The advisability of methods then and their proportionate value to the sani-

tarian, may be measured comparatively by the fraction at the bottom of the page.

This fraction we take then as the measure of the value of our method.

The numerator of the last fraction is the injury removed for the average man, and the denominator, the cost to him for so doing; hence, the fraction represents his proportionate gain. Cost includes all expenditures in money, time and inconvenience, first cost and upkeep. Permanence of result is considered in percentage of control.

CHART I

CONTROL OF MALARIA IN SUNFLOWER COUNTY,
MISSISSIPPI, BY CURING INFECTED PERSONS

Mississippi State Board of Health

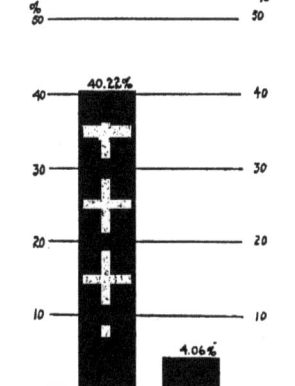

Reduction in prevalence of malaria in a 100 square mile area in Sunflower County, Mississippi, 89.9%, following intensive malaria control work in 1918. (The tall column represents, the proportion of the total population who had attacks of malaria during the twelve months previous to the first survey and treatment, and the short column the proportion who had attacks during the twelve months following.)

INDICATIONS FOR THE DIFFERENT
METHODS

Now it is obvious that in the method by control of mosquito production the cost will in general vary roughly with the

$$\frac{\text{Number of people benefited} \times \text{percentage of malaria reduction}}{\text{Total cost}} = \frac{\text{Percent of Reduction.}}{\text{Cost per head.}}$$

extent of the area requiring control and that therefore, the "Cost per head," the denominator of our last fraction *increases and decreases inversely to the density of the population*. This fraction then, the measure of the value of the method to the sanitarian, varies directly with the density of the population, the number of men per unit of area. This method then is generally less suitable to thinly settled farming communities than to villages and thickly settled communities. The difference of applicability does not obtain for the method by freeing infected men from parasites. Also, of course, the cost of control of the unit of area has to be considered in judging of the suitability of the first method. It may be prohibitive, as was the case at Lonoke, Ark., where even for a village we depended on the sterilization of the human host. A survey of the place where we purpose control to show the cost of the work and the probable con-

trol obtainable, is a necessary preliminary to a choice of methods.

Let me call your attention to one point in the last four Arkansas charts, (See Chart III) viz., the diminution of malaria in 1918 prior to the possibility of it being affected by the control measures. This means that in the early part of the season of 1918 malaria was naturally less prevalent than in previous years. Indeed, Taylor says that the year was less malarious than usual. LePrince, working at the camps in Miss., Ala., and at Memphis finds the same condition, and I judge we should allow a certain part of this reduction to 1918 being less malarious than usual in this part of the South. It is these places which should be compared with the Sunflower work because (1) it was the same year and (2) each involves only one year's reduction. Those preceeding them are valuable as showing how the control has invariably been kept up.

RESULTS AND COSTS
The Method by Quinine Sterilization given in a Farming Community:

Place	Population	Years	Reduction Blood Index	Reduction Physician's calls	Cost per head
Sunflower County, Miss.	8,000	1917-18	....	89%	$1.16*

*See Chart I.

THE METHOD OF CONTROL OF MOSQUITO PRODUCTION:

Place	Population	Years	Reduction Blood Index	Reduction Physician's calls	Cost per head
Roanoke Rapids, Va.	4,100	1913-16	97%	99.33%	$0.80 for 1914
					0.27 " 1914
					0.24 " 1916[1]
Electric Mills, Miss.	1,000	1913-15	91%	85%	1.21 " 1914
					0.24 " 1915[2]
Crystal City, Mo.	8,000	1915-17	83%	80%	0.90 " 1916
					0.54 " 1917[3]
Crossett, Ark.	2,029	1915-18	....	97%	1.24 " 1916
					0.63 " 1917
					0.53 " 1918[4]
Hamburg, Ark.	1,285	1916-18	....	97.4%	1.45 " 1917
					0.44 " 1918[5]
Lake Village, Ark.	975	1917-18	....	94.8%	1.25
Dermott, Ark.	2,760	1917-18	....	87%	0.54
Monticello, Ark.	3,023	1917-18	....	89.8%	0.46
Bauxite, Ark.	2,500	1917-18	....	78.4%	1.11

1. "We count ourselves free from malaria." says Dr. Long, Health Officer. See Chart II.
2. "Two-thirds of the cases reported in 1915 contracted elsewhere." Dr. Champenois, Health Officer.
3. Reduction given for 1916 only. "76% of cases reported in 1916, relapses from 1915." Statement of Health Officer.
4. Reduction first year 72½% blood index; 70.4% calls.
5. First year 89% reduction.

Similar work has been done, and with similar results, at Dallas, Tyler, Lufkin, ·Keltys, Sherman, Marlin and Waxahatchie, Texas, Emporia, Kress, and Wilson, Va., and some other places.

At Wilson a 100% reduction was obtained—a fluke of course—but malaria *was* eliminated in a single year. Wickliffe Rose states the same to have been the case at Ruleville, Miss., where both methods were used, although "control was based in the main on anti-mosquito measures."[*]

CHART II

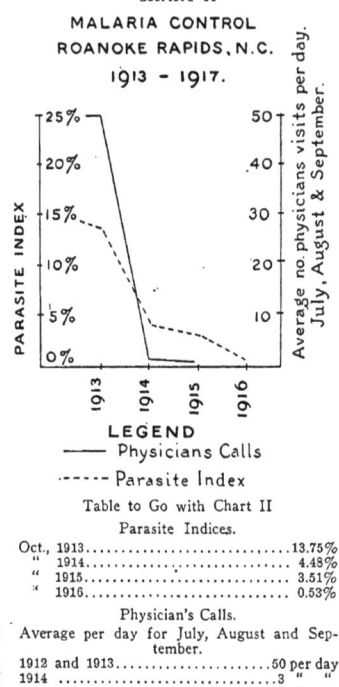

MALARIA CONTROL
ROANOKE RAPIDS, N.C.
1913 - 1917.

LEGEND

—— Physicians Calls

----- Parasite Index

Table to Go with Chart II

Parasite Indices.

Oct., 1913	13.75%
" 1914	4.48%
" 1915	3.51%
" 1916	0.53%

Physician's Calls.

Average per day for July, August and September.

1912 and 1913	50 per day
1914	3 " "
1915	⅓ " "

Costs.

1914	80 cents per capita
1915	27 cents " "
1916	24 cents " "

Both methods then give excellent results. They are not rivals—they supplement one another. Their indications are different. The first is especially applicable to a thickly settled community in which the cost of control of mosquito production is not excessive; the second to one more sparsely settled in which the control of production is excessive.[†]

Of the two community measures the first, where applicable, has some advantages, in that:

(1) The main work is done usually once for all, the up-keep is usually small —and in fact has, I think, always been kept up.

(2) The work is done with materials; earth, water, etc., not with people. Health officers well know that no material is as refractory to work with as people.

(3) Both the installation and up-keep are carried out directly under the supervision of the health officer and the result cannot be vitiated by individual carelessness, crankiness or bad faith.

(4) It is independent of the movement of the population into the controlled area from an infected one.

(5) Getting rid of mosquitoes as a pest is of no small advantage.

In many places, however, the method by quinine sterilization is the only one practicable, as a community measure. Then, of course, there can be no question of choice. It has also the advantage, and it is no small one, of preventing all relapses from infections of the previous year and of curing any infections due to Anopheles which have hibernated, neither of which are affected by the control of mosquito production at the time it is usually undertaken. It needs a painstaking, forceful and tactful administrator and director. It is best suited for a community either very biddable or

---

[*]Gilmerton, Va., and Red Leaf Plantation, Miss., were treated by screening, with good, but not brilliant results, i.e., the first cost was high.

[†]The individual protective measures—screening; hand-catching and immunizing quinine are to be used in case community measures are not practicable.

very intelligent and well instructed. In the South I would take my chance with the country negroes as being the first rather than with the white farmers as being the second. The immediate results have been most excellent. Time will show how permanent are its results and its cost of upkeep.

CHART III

MALARIA CONTROL IN ARKANSAS
THROUGH THE APPLICATION OF ANTI-MOSQUITO MEASURES

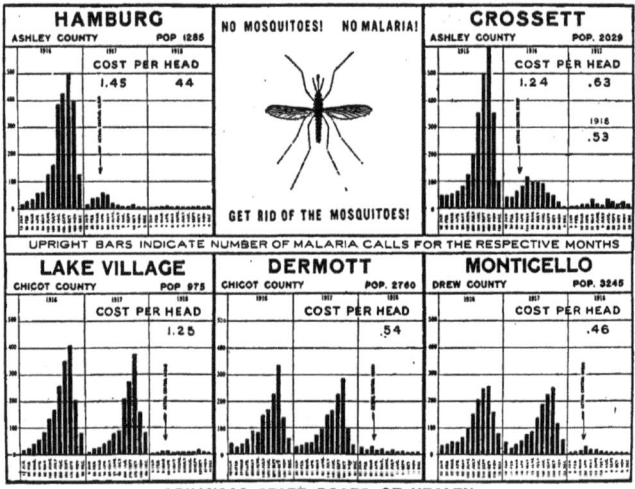

C. W. GARRISON. M. D., STATE HEALTH OFFICER   H. A. TAYLOR. M. D. STATE DIRECTOR.

Health Rules for Tuberculous Cases in Training.—Turner declares that the arrested case of consumption may become well from three to four years through the system propounded. His rules are: (1) Follow the simple life (regularity in eating, sleeping, working and playing; take plenty of time; don't hurry; make life a social event). (2) Sleep in the open air at least nine hours a day and in air which is in motion. (3) Limit work hours according to effects. Most inside jobs are suitable; most outside jobs are not—because they require too much manual labor. "Seek to accomplish the most work with the least amount of physical effort." Dusty and unsanitary places must be avoided. (4) In regard to play, take recreation of a quiet sort such as golf, croquet and short walks. Avoid active physical play like dancing, tennis, skating, swimming, hunting and horseback riding. Avoid gambling, as the mental excitement is too great. (5) Learn the danger signals of relapse: a sense of fatigue, loss of appetite, loss of strength, loss of weight, rise of temperature, night sweats, increased cough and sputum, spitting of blood and rapid pulse. Weigh yourself every two weeks. Cultivate a cheerful disposition; be an optimist; when in doubt consult your physician. Surgeon John W. Turner, *Vocational Summary*, March, 1920, pp. 204-206, *Federal Board for Vocational Education*, Washington, D. C.

NUMBER OF BACTERIA ON THE LIPS OF MILK BOTTLES AND THEIR SIGNIFICANCE

Roy S. Dearstyne,

City Health Dept., Charlotte; N. C.,

and

C. LeRoy Ewing,

City Health Dept., Baltimore, Md.

Read before the Laboratory Section, American Public Health Association, at New Orleans, La., October 30, 1919.

This communication proves to be a good argument in favor of the outside paper cap that covers the whole top of the bottle and is held on by a ring, although no mention is made of it. Possibilities for contamination of milk bottle lips under current methods of handling are set forth quantitatively as a help to the education of the public.

ONE of the principal aims of present day sanitation is concerned with the placing of a safe and clean milk supply before the consuming public. Much enlightenment regarding the importance of various operations, such as production, cooling, pasteurization, bottling, etc., has come about through laboratory findings. One of the factors which is of prime importance from a public health viewpoint and which has apparently been somewhat slighted in the past, is the cap and lip of the milk bottle. Unclean hands may deposit dangerous germs upon the cap or lip of the bottle; flies may carry their filth there: cats and other animals often lick the upper part of the bottle; finally street dust, with its varied bacterial flora settles upon the lip and cap. The sanitary significance of the cleanliness and bacterial flora of the bottle cap and top is therefore not to be underestimated.

The scope of this work was to ascertain the extent of possible contamination under various but normal conditions, by the numerical count of organisms on the lips of said bottles as delivered to the consumers. The technique employed was as follows: Cotton swabs were sterilized at dry heat for one hour at 175° C. The original packages of milk were taken from the producers as delivered to consumers. The cotton swabs were moistened in 100 cc. sterile dilution blank and the lip area of the bottle above the cap over which the milk must flow if poured from the bottle, was thoroughly swabbed. These swabs were then emulsified in the dilution blank, and after making suitable dilutions from this blank, agar plates were poured. The technique of this procedure, as well as the counting was carried out according to *Standard Methods of Milk Analysis*, American Public Health Association.

Fifty samples of pasteurized products, representing the maximum condition of safety in sterilizing bottles and handling the product after bottling, were taken in Baltimore, Md. The other 50 were taken in Alexandria, Va., these latter representing the average raw milk supply where the milk was bottled at the place of production, and the sanitary precautions exercised are undoubtedly typical where such conditions govern. The grouped counts per lip are given in Table I (Next page).

From the data tabulated in Table I, it is seen that from a sanitary standpoint the present system of capping milk bottles does not offer complete protection. The significance of these data lies not in the numbers of bacteria found on the lips of the bottle, but in the fact that there is a possible chance that these organisms may be of pathogenic nature.

TABLE I

Counts Per Lip—	Balti-more	Per Cent	Alex-andria	Per Cent
Under 1,000..........	10	20	..	..
1,000- 2,000......	6	12	1	2
2,000- 3,000......	2	4	0	..
3,000- 4,000......	4	8	0	..
4,000- 5,000......	2	4	0	..
5,000- 6,000......	5	10	0	..
6,000- 7,000......	3	6	0	..
7,000- 8,000......	1	2	0	..
8,000- 9,000......	2	4	0	..
9,000- 10,000......	2	4	1	2
10,000- 20,000......	4	8	6	12
20,000- 30,000......	2	4	4	8
30,000- 40,000......	1	2	4	8
40,000- 50,000......	1	2	6	12
50,000- 60,000......	0	..	1	2
60,000- 70,000......	1	2	5	10
70,000- 80,000......	1	2	1	2
80,000- 90,000......	1	2	3	6
90,000- 100,000......	1	2	2	4
100,000- 200,000......	1	2	9	18
200,000- 300,000......	..	..	..	..
300,000- 400,000......	..	..	..	..
400,000- 500,000......	..	..	1	2
500,000- 600,000......	..	..	2	4
600,000- 700,000......	..	..	2	4
700,000- 800,000......	..	..	1	2
800,000- 900,000......	..	..	0	..
900,000-1,000,000......	..	..	0	..
Over 1,000,000	..	..	1	2
	50	100	50	100

Assuming that the bottles have no bacterial growth on their lips when started from the dairy on the way to the consumer, wherein are the sources of contamination and what are the chances of gathering pathogenic micro-organisms from these exterior sources? The most tangible and obvious of these are as follows:

1. THE HANDS OF MILKMEN

Everyone has noticed the careless manner in which the milkman grasps the bottles by the neck, his hands covering the lip of the bottle and depositing upon this lip whatever organisms may be lying upon the surface of the skin. It is possible that this man has been handling horses, dogs, cats or other dusty or dirty objects, which would add to the natural bacterial flora of the skin. It is well known that any of the contagious skin diseases, as well as other communicable diseases may be transmitted in such a manner.

By swabbing a square centimeter of skin on the hands, under ordinary conditions, it was found that such a surface contained between 50 and 100 organisms which grew on agar at 37½° C.

2. THE AIR

Contamination gathered from the air varies according to general sanitary conditions. The carelessness practiced so generally by the milk consumer in allowing the bottle of milk to stay for hours on the doorstep, exposed to floating particles of street dust before removing, enhances the chance of pathogenic organisms being found on the lips of milk bottles. Practically all of our pathogenic bacteria can withstand desiccation for a short time, while others are able to retain their vitality for weeks and months.

In order to get an idea of the number of bacteria gathered from the air under average conditions, the following brief experiment was performed. Bottles were capped and sterilized at 175° C., for one hour and set on a doorstep in a dusty street with the following results, the technique in obtaining these counts being the same as in the original problem.

TABLE II.

1. Bottle (a) after 1 hour—Bacteria per lip of bottle........................ 30
   Bottle (b) after 2 hours—Bacteria per lip of bottle........................ 40
   Bottle (c) after 3 hours—Bacteria per lip of bottle........................150
2. Bottle (a) after 1 hour—Bacteria per lip of bottle........................ 30
   Bottle (b) after 2 hours—Bacteria per lip of bottle........................ 50
   Bottle (c) after 3 hours—Bacteria per lip of bottle........................100
3. Inside of Laboratory—
   Bottle (a) after 1 hour—Bacteria per lip of bottle........................200
   Bottle (b) after 2 hours—Bacteria per lip of bottle........................250

3. FLIES

This source of contamination is probably a factor of danger to be considered in this problem. The well known fact that the fly is a transmitter of typhoid and other diseases, and considering the enormous numbers of bacteria carried on his feet and body, make this insect one of the important factors in adding to the bacterial numerical content on the lips of milk bottles. All persons have observed the swarms of flies hovering over the milk bottle on the doorstep during fly season. Fortunately the anti-fly propaganda has been so far-reaching that this danger is evident, even to the layman.

4. ANIMAL CONTAMINATION

This source of danger—one that must not be underestimated—is due to the fact that animals are well known carriers of contagious diseases. Cats and dogs, both inside and outside of the house, express their fondness for milk by licking the top of the bottle, especially if there be a few drops of milk on the lip or cap of the bottle, which is frequently the case. Who has not seen a stray cat or dog greedily licking the mouth of a milk bottle recently placed on the doorstep in the early morning hours by the busy milkman?

We should account for the greater part of the contamination of the lips of bottles from these sources, at the same time. bearing in mind that part of the bacterial flora of the lip came from the milk itself, gathered on the lip during the process of filling the bottles.

PRACTICAL DEDUCTIONS

1. It is evident that from a sanitary standpoint, the present method of delivering and handling of milk in bottles is far from satisfactory. Street dust, dirty hands, animals and careless filling of bottles all contribute to deposit bacteria, some of which may be pathogenic, upon the lip and top of milk bottles.

2. Both the milkman and housewife are at fault. The latter should see that the bottle is brought into the house very soon after being delivered. The top and cap of each bottle should be thoroughly cleansed with a cloth and hot water before the contents are poured out.

3. The bacteria deposited upon the top and cap of a milk bottle stand a chance of being more dangerous than are those found within the bottle.

□

Success and Failure of Attendant Nursing Service.—Public health officials who are endeavoring to find a solution to the problem presented by the shortage of public health nurses will be interested in the results obtained by two communities with attendant nursing service. In Cleveland this service after a trial of more than two years has been abandoned. In Brattleboro, Vt., it is still satisfactory after a period of ten years. In the former city the service was a part of the Visiting Nurse Association and the principal difficulty found there was in the supervision of only partially trained workers so that the work of these attendants would be reliable and not reflect discreditably on the Association. The ability of these attendants to get fees higher than the pay allowed by the Nurses' Association also led many of them to leave, after short and insufficient training, and work independently using the name of the Association as a reference. Brattleboro evidently has not encountered these difficulties. It has on the contrary found its attendants satisfactory.—Thwing, *Public Health Nurse*, April, 1920. (*H. N. C.*)

Typhus Fever in Poland.—One of the worst typhus fever epidemics in the history of the world now threatens Poland, judging by present indications. The report of the American Typhus Fever Expedition says that the Polish Government fully realizes the seriousness of the epidemic which if unchecked will threaten the whole of Europe. This is the fourth year that the epidemic has raged and the present focus appears to be in Russia and Ukrainia. From there it has been spread by refugees, prisoners of war and by infected soldiers sent from the Bolshvik armies into Polish territory. Infection is also spread by the clothing of the dead which is stripped off and carried away to be sold. No one knows the number of cases and the mortality is variously estimated at from 10 to 60 per cent. In order to check the spread of the disease, Poland has purchased nearly four million dollars worth of material used by the A. E. F., including sterilizers, mobile laundries, beds, bedding, 100 tons of soap, bathing plants, trucks and an enormous amount of hundreds of other items.—*Medico-Military Review*, April 15, 1920. (*H. N. C.*)

EDITORIAL SECTION

AMERICAN JOURNAL OF PUBLIC HEALTH.
Publication Office: 124 W. Polk Street, Chicago, Ill.
EDITORIAL OFFICE: 169 MASSACHUSETTS AVE., BOSTON, MASS.

A. W. HEDRICH, C. P. H., Editor
J. RITCHIE, Jr., Associate Editor

Editorial Assistants

E. R. HAYHURST, M.D.
R. P. ALBAUGH, M.D.
E. B. STARR, M.D.

DAVID GREENBERG
M. P. HORWOOD, M.S.
P. M. HOLMES, M.D.

JAMES A. TOBEY
FRANCIS H. SLACK, M.D.
JAMES M. STRANG

Board of Advisory Editors

PETER H. BRYCE, M.D., Ottawa, Canada
CHARLES V. CHAPIN, M.D., Providence, R. I.
EUGENE R. KELLEY, M.D., Boston, Mass.
W. A. EVANS, M.D., Chicago, Ill.

PROF. M. J. ROSENAU, Boston, Mass.
PROF. W. T. SEDGWICK, Cambridge, Mass.
PROF. GEORGE C. WHIPPLE, Cambridge, Mass.
PROF. S. M. GUNN, Paris, France.

All expressions of opinion and all statements of supposed facts are published on authority of the writer under whose name they appear, and are not to be regarded as expressing the views of the American Public Health Association, unless such statements or opinions have been adopted by vote of the Association.

NOTICE TO SUBSCRIBERS: Subscription Price, payable in advance, $4.00 per year for United States and possessions; $4.50 for Canada and other foreign countries. Single copies, 50 cents postpaid. Membership in the American Public Health Association, including subscription to Journal, $5.00 per year. In Change of Address please give both old and new address, and mail before the tenth of the month to take effect with the current issue. Mailing Date, 5th of each month. Advertisements accepted only when commendable, and worth while both to reader and advertiser. News Items, interesting clippings and illustrations are gladly received, together with name of sender. Copyright, 1919, by A. W. Hedrich.

SUPERVISION OVER THE MANUFACTURE OF ARSPHENAMINE

The supervision exercised by the Federal Government over the importation of biological products and their sale in interstate traffic is generally understood. The law (July 1, 1902), provides that no viruses, serums, toxins, or analogous products for human administration are to be imported for sale or sold in interstate traffic unless they are manufactured in an establishment holding a license issued by the Treasury Department for the importation or sale in interstate traffic of the particular product. Such licenses can be issued only after an inspection of the plant and an examination of samples of the products. Where there exist assured methods for standardizing biological products, definite requirements as to potency are in force, but in most instances the requirements bear chiefly on questions of preventing contamination. License from the Treasury Department does not place the Government behind the claims of the concern producing a biological product, nor does the Department refuse to license certain preparations the therapeutic value of which is not scientifically determined; on the other hand, licenses are not issued for products which are obviously useless or which are marketed for fraudulent purposes. The act is administered through the U. S. Public Health Service.

Recently a far-reaching opinion was issued by the Solicitor for the Treasury Department, to the effect that arsphenamine (including, of course, salvarsan, neosalvarsan, and the many arsenical preparations allied to these) must be regarded as analogous to viruses, serums and toxins, as understood in the act of July 1, 1902. Therefore, such products cannot be imported for sale or sold in interstate traffic unless manufactured by firms licensed for their importation and interstate sale.

During the war the manufacture of arsphenamine was supervised by the Federal Trade Commission under regulations framed by the Public Health Service. The interpretation just mentioned permits the continuation of such supervision by the Public Health Service, and there is assurance, therefore, that adequate safeguards will continue to govern the manufacture of these important products. In fact, at the present time, the Treasury Department is issuing a group of regulations for the control of these preparations, the regulations having the approval of the Surgeons General of the Public Health Service, the Army, and the Navy.

There is vital necessity that American arsphenamine be manufactured in an efficient manner and that the toxicity be held to definite standards. Before the war arsenical preparations for the treatment of syphilis were almost exclusively German-made. Today, firms in this country are manufacturing a product which is regarded by the Public Health Service as being equal to, and probably superior to, foreign preparations. The improvement in the quality of the American article is probably in part due to the rigorous standards set by the Government.

As almost all arsphenamine is manufactured for interstate shipment, the product can be almost entirely controlled by the Federal Government under the commerce clause of the Constitution (the basis for the act of July 1, 1902). This is one of the fields where the Federal Government has assumed its definite duties and opportunities. In the case of many of the other products coming under the "biologics" law, a considerable amount of purely intrastate traffic is engaged in. In those cases the States should adopt laws which will reinforce the Federal provisions. This will permit a salutary supervision over a class of preparations which, if manufactured through careless means, could directly cause loss of much life and indirectly discredit one of the most effective known means of disease prevention and cure.

R. B.

TAKE YOUR VACATION IN SAN FRANCISCO

In September the Golden Gate will be a veritable Mecca for sanitarians. Here during the week preceding the meetings of the A. P. H. A. there will be the gatherings of the California Tuberculosis Association and the Southwestern Tuberculosis Conference, while for the week following the visit of the Association there is scheduled the meeting of the International Association of Industrial Accident Boards and Commissions, three almost solid weeks of health discussions.

Attractions like these make it the more advantageous for health officers to take their vacations at the time of the meeting and go to California. In case their time limitations do not permit their traveling on the special A. P. H. A. train with their fellow health workers, or making their stay in San Francisco conform to the precise dates of the Association meetings, there will be these other matters of interest on either side of the principal dates.

The forty-ninth annual meeting of the A. P. H. A. presents unusual attractions like these. There will be the welcome from San Francisco and California, the heartiness of which is proverbial; there will be the visit to states and cities which have established admirable administrations in public health; there will be the presentation by men who have worked in these fields of mixed populations of the problems and the methods whereby the solutions have been sought; and by way of background, there are the picturesque and social features of a visit to "the land of flowers."

The time of the meeting, September 13-17, is drawing near and the different programs have each their attractive features. Energetic and experienced leaders will not be wanting to make the plans successful, but the fundamental essential is the early decision on the part of members as to their individual intentions. Make up your mind now what you intend to do and get into communication with your local Travel Chairman.

BOOKS AND REPORTS
REVIEWED

A Laboratory Manual of Physiological Chemistry.—*Elbert W. Rockwood, M. D., Ph. D. Fourth Edition. Philadelphia, F. A. Davis Company, pp. 316. Price, $2.00.*

The first edition of this manual was published in 1899. The author has profited by long observation of the students' reaction toward the book and has developed the text in an interesting way. The procedures, qualitative and quantitative, appear to be up to date and the balance of material is excellent. As stated in the preface, much more is included than is likely to be used in a standard course of instruction. This allows the teacher considerable latitude in choosing the experiments most appropriate to his class. Suggestive questions and valuable references are appended.—*Percy G. Stiles, Ph. D.*

✦

Syphilis. *Henry M. Hazen, A. B., M. D., St. Louis, Mo., C. V. Mosby Co., 1919, pp. 647. Price, $6.00*

This latest treatise on syphilis as a whole is most excellent. Especially admirable is Dr. Hazen's arrangement in placing the bibliography so conveniently. The illustrations are adequate. Dr. Hazen has associated with himself a number of men who are responsible for various chapters. One of the best of the special articles is that on Syphilis of the Nervous System. Its clearness and freedom from prejudice is noteworthy.

In the chapter on Syphilis of the Eye the author, Dr. L. S. Greene, makes a statement concerning the treatment of interstitial keratitis that is at least open for discussion. He states that arsphenamine has signally failed in the treatment of interstitial keratitis. This is entirely at variance with the belief of many ophthalmologists and syphilographers based on long experience. Given early in the attack of interstitial keratitis arsphenamine is most valuable. Also, Dr. Greene implies, writing as he does on acquired syphilis, that interstitial keratitis occurs commonly in the acquired form of syphilis, when as a matter of fact it is extremely rare.

The concluding chapters on diagnosis, prognosis and treatment are informative and judicial. The knowledge they contain should be spread broadcast as an aid to prophylaxis.

The work is a distinct addition to the textbooks on syphilis—and should be of much help to practitioners as well as medical students.—*(C. M. S.)*

✦

The Transmutation of Bacteria. *S. Gurney-Dixon, M. A., M. D., Cambridge University Press, 1919, pp. 179. Price, $3.25.* This little book is a compilation of the literature available only up to the time of the beginning of the war in 1914. The author apologizes for the shortcomings of the publication in this respect. Certain chapters on viability and agglutination reactions which were meant to be included were destroyed by a shell explosion and could not be replaced. The author deserves credit for his courage in walking off the beaten track and focusing attention upon certain peculiar phenomena with which the bacteriologist is confronted from time to time. A study of the text furnishes a better explanation than could be given in any other way for the difficulty of classifying certain groups of organisms properly. It is evident that practically every character of bacteria is liable to vary at different times and under different conditions. Since there is no absolute criterion as to what constitutes a "species" amongst bacteria; dissimilarity in the several characters they present is the sole guide to classification. The conclusions of the author are of interest. He states that transmutation differs from variation and evolution in degree alone. The occurrence of transmutation between closely allied organisms in the human body is not capable of proof but is suggested by circumstantial evidence. Supposed instances of transmutation brought about by animal inoculation are shown to rest on non-conclusive evidence. The enzyme theory which is discussed in Chapter XI, suggests a means by which bacteria may exchange many of their characters and functions without themselves undergoing transmutation. The evidence is arranged very systematically in twelve chapters. Bacteriologists know how scattered the information pertaining to the subject is and will therefore appreciate this little reference book in their libraries.—*Arthur Lederer, M. D.*

ASSOCIATION NEWS

HEALTH EMPLOYMENT BUREAU

Health officer for the New Jersey Bureau of Venereal Disease Control. Training in public health and law desirable; good personality and ability in public speaking absolutely essential. Initial salary $2,100 with good future. Apply A. J. Casselman, Chief of Bureau, 807 American Mechanic Building, Trenton, N. J.

A qualified school nurse for year around position, salary to begin with $100 per month. Address R. W. G., in care of this Journal

A chemist and sanitary engineer are required by the North Dakota Public Health Laboratories. Salary $2,000 to start. Address A. G. Long, M. D., Grand Forks, N. D.

Bacteriologist. Applications will be considered from trained bacteriologists with view to appointment in large bacteriological laboratory in Massachusetts. Salary $1,500 to $1,800 per annum. Male resident of Boston preferred. Address 355, care of this Journal.

Field Director rural sanitation in Southern state. Salary $2,700 to $2,600 with $800 expense allowance. Address 356, care of this Journal.

□

CONVENTIONS, CONFERENCES, MEETINGS

June 21-25, Vancouver, B. C., Canadian Public Health Association.

June 21-25, Vancouver, B. C., Canadian Medical Association.

June 21-25, Vancouver, B. C., Canadian Health Officers' Association.

June 21-25, Vancouver, B. C., Canadian National Tuberculosis Association, Vancouver, B. C.

June 21-25, Vancouver, Dominion Committee for Venereal Diseases.

June 21-25, Vancouver, B. C., Dominion Committee for Mental Hygiene.

June 21-25, Vancouver, B. C., British Columbia Hospital Association.

June 21-25, Montreal, Can., American Water Works Association.

June 23-25, St. Paul, Minn., Catholic Hospital Association.

June 24-29, Colorado Springs, Col. American Home Economics Association.

June 25, Lake Tahoe, Nev., Nevada State Medical Association.

June 28, Fairmont, Minn., Southern Minnesota Medical Association.

July —, Regina, Sask., Saskatchewan Medical Association.

July 6, Kentville, N. S., Association of Health Officers of Nova Scotia.

July 12-15, Helena, Mont., Montana State Health Officers' Association.

July 16-17, Seattle, Wash., Washington Health Officers' Association.

August —, Florida State Health Conference.

August 20-21, Denver, Colo., National First Aid and Rescue Contest.

September 9, San Francisco, Cal., California Tuberculosis Association.

September 10-11, San Francisco, Cal., Southwestern Tuberculosis Conference.

September 13-17, San Francisco, American Public Health Association.

September 20-24, San Francisco, Cal., International Association of Accident Boards and Commissioners.

✛

HEALTH WORKERS HEADED FOR SAN FRANCISCO

San Francisco will see an unusual succession of health conferences in September, for no less than four important associations have registered for meetings in that city. To members of the A. P. H. A. the meeting of September 13-17 will be of prime importance, but during the preceding week the California Tuberculosis Association will hold its annual meeting on September 9 and the Southwestern Tuberculosis Conference will meet on Friday and Saturday, September 10-11. On the following Monday the A. P. H. A. will begin its conference running from September 13 till September 17, and from Monday, September 20, till Friday, September 24, the International Association of Accident Boards and Commissions will gather for its meetings. The Northwestern Tuberculosis Conference meets in Cheyenne at the same time that the Southwestern Conference is in session in San Francisco.

REPORT OF COMMITTEE ON SANITATION OF SWIMMING POOLS

Read before the Sanitary Engineering Section, American Public Health Association, at New Orleans, La., October 27, 1919.

The committee on swimming pools begs leave to submit at this time a progress report of work accomplished since the Chicago meeting in December, 1918, at which time this committee was first named.

The amount of detail work incident to the operation, control and engineering design of swimming pools and the consequent significance of each part of the problem has made it impossible, as well as unwise to attempt an investigation of all phases of the problem in one year. The committee has held the opinion that its first work should be general and superficial, setting aside the detail work for another year. It has been deemed advisable this year, to collect and submit data pertaining to the following points and thus emphasize the greater significance of the problem and show why it is a public health matter.

1. The present status of swimming pool control and supervision by state boards of health:

(a) By specific legislation statutes.
(b) By rules and regulations.

2. The present status of swimming pool control and supervision by city boards of health or other city departments.

(a) By specific ordinances.

3. Extent of investigation work conducted by state board of health, city board of health, state and private institutions.

4. Survey of the field of literature and compilation of a bibliography.

5. Preliminary census of swimming pools in the United States with general data concerning many of them.

The significance of swimming pool sanitation, and its relation to the conveyance of certain infections, has previously been pointed out by several investigators. The number of swimming pools in this country, the increasing numbers of people using them and the almost negligible control given them, despite their frequent conveyance of some infections, tend to make the problem an important one.

Letters were sent to each state board of health inquiring into the existence of statutes and rules or regulations for handling swimming pool matters. As a result of this inquiry it was ascertained that only two states possess a specific legislation statute giving the state board of health direct charge and supervision over all swimming pools and requiring pool operators to secure a state board of health permit previous to operation, also requiring the approval of all plans and appurtenances before construction. The two states having such a statute are California and Florida. The latter was successfully passed during the present year. One state, Louisiana, has specific rules and regulations pertaining to swimming pools, adopted by the State Board of Health; of the 48 states, thirteen made no replies to the inquiry, and of the 35 replies received 22 had no rules supervising swimming pools and had done nothing towards getting such supervisory rules. Ten State Boards had made some investigations with a view of later compiling some regulatory measure. Following are states having no rules, regulations or statutes pertaining to swimming pools, and in which no investigations or work of importance have been conducted:

Alabama	North Carolina
Connecticut	North Dakota
Illinois	Ohio
Indiana	Oregon
Kansas	Texas
Georgia	Utah
Maine	Vermont
Mississippi	South Carolina
Missouri	Washington
Montana	West Virginia
New Jersey	Virginia

In Massachusetts, New York, Maryland, Minnesota, Iowa, Wisconsin, Pennsylvania, New Hampshire and Rhode Island, special investigation work has been conducted but no statutes made available as yet.

The survey of the states clearly shows that the sanitation of swimming pools has been greatly neglected and it has not yet been considered seriously as a public health matter of prime importance. It is noted, however, that a tendency is prevailing to make the sanitary control of swimming pools more of a public health measure, and several of the states have expressed a keen desire to promulgate proper regulations; but to date, the problem, practically speaking, has been left untouched by the state boards of health.

Swimming pools in general are located in cities or at resorts near cities. Yet our investigation clearly indicates that cities have paid little or no attention to swimming pool control or operation. Aside from infrequent bacteriological examination of pool waters by some city boards of health, no work of significance, has been done. Several cities conduct detailed pool examinations at stated periods and thus maintain a control. Only six cities, Fort Smith and Little Rock, Ark.; Cleveland, Ohio; Seattle, Wash.; Appleton, Wis.; Chicago, Ill.; out of 261 cities investigated, state that specific ordinances are available for controlling pool sanitation. In these 261 cities, located in all parts of the country, and replying to our inquiries, there are located in excess of 493 pools.

The committee received data and preliminary information relative to 1,254 pools distributed by states as follows:

Alabama	14	Montana	4
Arizona	3	New Hampshire	6
Arkansas	7	New Jersey	53
California	221	New Mexico	1
Colorado	17	New York	114
Connecticut	31	Nevada	1
Delaware	1	North Carolina	12
Florida	8	North Dakota	4
Georgia	10	Ohio	103
Idaho	4	Oklahoma	11
Illinois	83	Oregon	8
Indiana	42	Pennsylvania	81
Iowa	30	Rhode Island	7
Kansas	13	South Carolina	8
Kentucky	12	South Dakota	3
Louisiana	6	Tennessee	15
Maine	5	Texas	20
Maryland	6	Vermont	2
Massachusetts	70	Virginia	25
Michigan	87	Washington	25
Minnesota	29	West Virginia	7
Mississippi	4	Wisconsin	37
Missouri	35	Washington, D. C...	3
Nebraska	16		

GEORGE W. SIMONS, Jr. Chairman
STEPHEN DE M. GAGE,
J. W. M. BUNKER,
M. C. WHIPPLE.

☐

REPORT OF THE COMMITTEE ON PROBLEMS IN CANNING OPERATIONS

Since our report of a year ago substantial progress has been made in the study of the problems of the canning industry. The record of the progress that has been made in the field is given in a considerable number of articles which have appeared during the year in scientific journals. The articles referred to do not mark the end of the investigations they represent, but rather indicate the increasing volume of work that is being done in the field and will doubtless be followed by other publications.

In addition to the references appended, a considerable number of articles has been published relating to methods for bacteriological work, which are not included because they are of general application. Some articles regarding home canning and home canned foods have also appeared, but are not included as it is understood that the scope of this Committee is limited to the commercial product.

Tin Plate Investigation.—The study of tin plate intended for manufacturing packer's cans has been continued by the National Canners' Association in collaboration with the American Can Company, The Titanium Alloys Manufacturing Company and the National Enameling and Stamping Company. Progress has been made in connection with this work, but much remains to be done. During the last year a new lot of plate has been made, the Committee giving special attention to the manufacture of the steel used for base metal.

This plate has been made into cans and typical acid fruits have been sealed into the cans to study the question of pinholing.

Black Patches in Canned Corn.—During recent years the canning industry has been troubled more than at any earlier period by the formation of black patches on the inner surface of corn cans. This matter is being made the subject of intense study both in the laboratory and in the field. The experimental packs that have been put up are now being studied in the laboratory and it will probably be some months before a definite announcement can be made.

Heat Penetration.[1]—During the last year several laboratories have shown an interest in the study of heat penetration in canned foods and have reported different forms of apparatus for its determination. Other forms of apparatus which have been used have not yet been publicly announced. Some of this work has been done in the laboratory, but much of it has been done in commercial canning plants where heat penetration has been studied under various conditions of the commercial canning. The work has been applied to laboratory autoclaves, to the pressure kettle ordinarily employed in commercial canning plants, and to an experimental pressure cooker with which it is possible to determine the heat penetration while the can is being heated at any desired pressure and rotated at any desired speed.

Bacteriological Investigations. — During the last year several laboratories have given attention to the bacteriological flora of canned foods and have made material contribution to the literature of the subject. This work has given us a more comprehensive and more exact knowledge of the particular bacteria to which various forms of spoilage are due. The work is now being extended to the determination of the time necessary at various temperatures and in different foods to destroy resistant bacterial spores to which spoilage due to understerilization is occasionally due.

Publications on this subject made during the last year are listed below and it is expected that additional publications will be made in the near future giving the new developments of the work.

Inspection of Canned Foods.—The recently inaugurated inspection service of the National Canners' Association has been described by Mr. Loomis, the head of that service. (*A. J. P. H.*, June, 1920, p. 521.) It should be noted in this connection, however, that there are many research problems which are being worked out in connection with this inspection service. These problems consist partly in the establishment of standards so that a more exact knowledge of the grade and character of the food may be stated on the label in such terms that the consumer may understand it, and partly in a control of the raw product and canning operations which will insure a product of greater uniformity and a higher degree of excellence. The establishment of systematic inspection service makes it possible to work out many such problems to a degree that would be difficult under other conditions.

Study of Food Poisons.—The study of food poisons with special reference to canned foods, which is being conducted under the direction of Dr. M. J. Rosenau of Harvard Medical School, has been mentioned in previous reports of this Committee and was described in some detail in a paper by Dr. Rosenau at an earlier session of this Section. No further mention will, therefore, be made of it here except to say that the investigation is proceeding in a satisfactory manner and much information has already been obtained from it. Eight publications giving results of the work have already been issued and others are either in press or in preparation.

[1]*Bigelow, Bohart and Richardson*—Paper before the Food Division of the American Chemical Society, May, 1919. Unpublished.

Bovie and Bronfenbrenner—Studies on Canning: An apparatus for measuring the rate of heat penetration. *J. Ind. Eng. Chem.* Paper before the Society of American Bacteriologists, Dec. 1918, 1919, *11*, 568-70.

[2]*Bruett*—Utility of blanching in food canning —effect of cold shock upon bacterial death rates. *J. Ind. Eng. Chem.* 1919, *11*, 37-9.

Cheyney—A study of the micro-organisms found in merchantable canned foods. *J. Med. Res.*, Boston, 1919, *40*, 177-197.

Donk—Some organisms causing spoilage in canned foods, with special reference to flat sours. Paper before the Society of American Bacteriologists, Dec. 1918. Published in abstract, *Abs. of Bact.*, 1919, *3*, 4.

Hunter and Thom—An aerobic spore-forming bacillus in canned salmon. *J. Ind. Eng. Chem.* 1919, *11*, 655-7.

Obst—A bacteriological study of sardines. *J. Infect. Dis.*, Chicago, 1919, *24*, 158-169.

Weinzirl—The bacteriology of canned foods. *J. Med. Res.*, Boston, 1919, *39*, 348-413.

WILLARD D. BIGELOW, M. D., Chairman,
C. E. MARSHALL, M. D.,
E. V. McCOLLUM, M. D.,
PROFESSOR JOHN WEINZIRL,
MR. WILLIAM G. TICE.

Remember the Meeting in San Francisco, September 13-17, 1920.
How about going on the A. P. H. A. Special Train?
How about taking with you your new member?

FINANCIAL DISTRICT

DOWN COLUMBUS AVE.   UNION SQUARE

FROM THE DRIVE

SAN FRANCISCO—THE A. P. H. A. CONVENTION CITY
September 13-17, 1920

SAN FRANCISCO MEETING—RAILWAY RATES

In the JOURNAL for May the railway rates from Chicago to San Francisco and return were given (page 479 and page 484). Further figures have since been furnished by the C. & N. W. R. R., applying to other central points east of the Mississippi, as follows:

Albany, N. Y. $144.05
Atlanta, Ga. 120.50
Boston, Mass. 157.03
Buffalo, N. Y. 126.68
Chicago, Ill. 96.12
Cincinnati, O. 111.28
Cleveland, O. 116.07
Detroit, Mich. 111.99
Indianapolis, Ind 104.22
Jacksonville, Fla. 129.31
Louisville, Ky. 107.69
Montreal, Quebec 149.31
New York, N. Y. 149.08
Philadelphia, Pa. 143.67
Pittsburgh, Pa. 123.42
Richmond, Va. 141.42
Toronto, Ont. 126.95
Washington, D. C. 140.57
New Orleans, La. 96.12*

These rates are for the round trip through Chicago to San Francisco and return, with the journey west of Chicago via Ogden and Salt Lake City in one or both directions. For the same figure the return from San Francisco to Chicago may be made via Los Angeles and thence to Salt Lake City; or

*This is the figure that accompanies the others in the list. It seems desirable to present it although it has not been possible to secure definite information before going to press. It seems not improbable that the rate given is for connection with the through trip to San Francisco at some other point than Chicago. Members in southern cities should therefore verify the rate by enquiry of their local railway agents.

Albuquerque or El Paso. For the return from San Francisco to Chicago via Portland, Ore., and Huntington; or via Portland, Seattle, Spokane and Minneapolis; or via Portland, Vancouver and Minneapolis, the price of the round trip ticket will be $19.44 more. This amount should be added to price here given for the local ticket by those who plan to vary their journey by taking one of these routes. War tax is included in these figures.

These fares become effective June 1, and tickets will be on sale daily until September 30, 1920, with the final limit of October 31, 1920, permitting stop-overs at all points en route within that time limit.

Information with reference to special A. P. H. A. trains to the coast is given in the JOURNAL for May, page 479, and reservations should be made through the district travel chairman. For New York, Dr. S. Dana Hubbard, Health Department of the City of New York, will act as travel chairman for the district about that city; members in New England should address Secretary, A. P. H. A., 169 Massachusetts Avenue, Boston 17, Mass., and for the Middle West, Dr. W. A. Evans, 906 Tribune Building, Chicago, Ill., will act as travel chairman, and will be able to give all necessary information.

The Pullman rates from Chicago to San Francisco one way are the following:

Lower berth $17.01
Upper berth 13.61
Drawing room 60.48
Compartment 48.08

War-tax is included in these rates.

The rate from your home to city of Chicago may be secured from your travel chairman or the local railway agent.

The San Francisco Meeting will be "The Best Ever"
The A. P. H. A. Special from Chicago the Wednesday evening before will be an unusual opportunity for Health Officers to exchange experiences. Secure your reservations for it early. The date of the meeting is September 13-17, 1920.

PUBLIC HEALTH NOTES

Abstracts by D. Greenberg, M. P. Horwood and Mayo Tolman.

Lobar Pneumonia Transmitted to Monkeys.—Previous attempts to transmit pneumonia experimentally to monkeys have either failed or met with only partial success. In no case were the experimental conditions similar to those which exist normally. Recently Blake and Cecil of the Army Medical School, succeeded in producing lobar pneumonia in monkeys, by intratracheal injections of pneumococci. The experiments were conducted with the four types of pneumococci, and it was possible to produce the disease in each case. An 18 hour culture of pneumococci was used in each case, and amounts varying from 0.000001 cc. to 1 cc. were introduced into the lumen of the trachea by means of a sterile needle. Out of 37 monkeys which received inoculations, 32 came down with lobar pneumonia, 2 died of pneumococcus septicemia, and 3 received such small doses that no disease was produced. Attempts to transmit the disease by subcutaneous and intravenous injections and by nose and throat inoculations failed. Symptoms of the disease appeared in from 12 to 36 hours after inoculation. The symptoms in monkeys were very similar to those in man. The temperature curves were similar to those seen in lobar pneumonia in man. Often there was a critical drop in temperature on the seventh to the ninth day. Blood cultures showed varying grades of pneumococcemia, which in non-fatal cases usually disappeared before the crisis, but which in some of the severer cases, increased enormously before death. Pneumococci were found in the blood as early as six hours after inoculation, even before the symptoms of the disease appeared. The organisms apparently penetrate the bronchial wall near the hilum and spread by way of the interstitial tissue and lymphatic system of the lung.

In the less severe cases, there was at first a low leukocyte count. This gradually rose, however, until the blood became free of pneumococci. In severe cases, the leukocyte count at first was increased. This, however, was followed by a fall, which was sometimes very rapid. It was also shown that the disease is spread by contact. Not only can we hope now that prophylactic immunization against the disease will be worked out, but it should also be possible to determine the value of antipneumococcic serums for curing the disease.—*Journal A. M. A.*, April 24, 1920. (*M. P. H.*)

✛

Higher Standard of Dying.—The postbellum cry for a higher standard of living has evidently penetrated now to the South African native. At any rate he is agitating for a higher standard of burial. Trouble is reported from Germiston, a Rand mining town, on the occasion of the funeral of three natives killed while cleaning out a municipal tank. The natives were, according to the municipal regulations, to be buried without coffins. Fellow laborers to the number of 200 strongly objected to their being so interred; the funeral was thereupon held up until coffins were obtained.—*London Lancet*, March 27, 1920. (*H. N. C.*)

✛

Defective Teeth in New York City Schoolchildren.—The *New York Times* for May 2, 1920, reports the findings of the New York Association for Improving the Condition of the Poor resulting from the examination of the teeth of 1,382 schoolchildren. The children examined live on the lower East Side of New York, and varied from 4 to 15 years in age. Of the number examined, 1,334, or 97 per cent, had defective teeth. The total number of cavities found was 9,307, or 6.8 cavities per child. Perhaps the most serious aspect of this dental survey is the vast amount of decay found in the first permanent molars, of which every normal 6 year old child is supposed to have four. This survey is part of the community health plan which the A. I. C. P. started two years ago. It is planned to follow up the survey with prophylactic and curative measures.—(*M. P. H.*)

✛

Other Public Health Notes are to be found on pages following the Lists of New Members.

State Health Notes, Industrial Hygiene and Public Health Laboratory Notes will be found on page 546 *et seq.*

STATE HEALTH NOTES—
LEGISLATION.

National.—A matter of interest to public health workers is the resolution on the distribution of government pamphlets, introduced by Senator Smoot of Utah and passed by the Joint Committee on Printing. The language of the resolution as reported in the Congressional Record of April 2, 1920, is as follows:

"That No person connected with any department of the Government shall furnish any publication for free distribution to any private individual, corporation, or agency in lots to exceed 50 copies without first making application to the Joint Committee on Printing, giving the name of the person or agency desiring the publications, the name of the publication, and the number of copies desired: *Provided,* That this regulation shall not apply to publications which are sold at a price to cover the cost of same; *Provided further,* That the clerk of the Joint Committee on Printing be instructed to furnish to each department of the Government and to the Public Printer a copy of this resolution with a request that the receipt of same be duly acknowledged."

The Sheppard-Towner bill or Senate Bill No. 3259 which is now before the Senate Committee on Public Health and National Quarantine provides for national support of maternity and child welfare. It authorizes an annual appropriation of $480,000, $10,000 of which is to be allotted to each state for the establishment and administration of infant and maternal hygiene boards. A Federal Board is provided for, consisting of the Secretary of Labor as Chairman; the Chief of the Children's Bureau, as executive officer; the Surgeon General of the United States Public Health Service, and the United States Commissioner of Education. An additional appropriation of $2,000,000 is authorized for the fiscal year ending June 30, 1921, and increasing about $400,000 annually for five years. This sum is to be apportioned among the states according to population, provided the state appropriates an equal sum.

Other senate bills on public health have previously been discussed in these pages. The France bill S, 2507, to establish a national health department is still in committee.

There are several bills before the House of Representatives which have not previously been mentioned in the JOURNAL. On April 20th H. R. 13229, to establish in the Department of Labor a bureau to be known as the Women's Bureau has been read twice and referred to the Committee on Education and Labor. This bureau is to formulate standards and policies which shall promote the welfare of wage earning women, improve their working conditions, increase their efficiency, and advance their opportunities for profitable employment. H. R. 13726 was introduced by Mr. Tilson on April 21 and referred to the Committee on Agriculture. It is a bill to regulate the shipment in interstate commerce of milk and cream, and for other purposes. It requires that no person shall ship such products without a permit from the United States Department of Agriculture. The permit will be issued for one year from January 1st and is revocable for cause. The cattle producing the milk and cream must be physically sound and have reacted negatively to the tuberculin test as prescribed by the United States Bureau of Animal Industry.

H. R. 13526 was introduced by Mr. Baer on April 9th and referred to the Committee on Judiciary. It is a bill to create a National Food Commission, to define its powers and duties, and to stimulate the production, sale, and distribution of live stock, and live stock products, and for other purposes.

H. R. 13677 making appropriations to supply a deficiency in the appropriations for the Federal control of transportation systems and to supply urgent deficiencies in certain appropriations for the fiscal year ending June 30, 1920, contains an item of $7,666,187.14 for the Public Health Service. The need for this sum is given as for medical, surgical and hospital services and supplies for war-risk insurance patients and other beneficiaries of the Public Health Service, including necessary personnel, regular and reserve commissioned officers of the Public Health Service, clerical help in the District of Columbia and elsewhere, maintenance, equipment, leases, fuel, lights, water, printing, freight, transportation and travel, maintenance and operation of passenger motor vehicles and reasonable burial expenses (not exceeding $100 for any patient dying in hospital).—(J. A. T.)

✢

Hereafter it will be "milk cow" and not "milch cow"—at least so far as the U. S. Department of Agriculture is concerned.

This decision marks the termination of a controversy in which etymologists in the department have had not a little interest. Those defending "milch" have pointed to scriptural use and certain of the classics as establishing precedents, while the opposition has contended that dairymen, ranchmen, and farmers in general use "milk" instead of "milch" almost universally. The advocates of "milk" also favored that word because, they contended, it was more strictly an English word, while "milch" was akin to German. Since Americanization of language as well as ideals is an article in every patriot's creed, it is thought that this last sally of the "milk" defenders helped as much as any to decide the question in their favor.—*Weekly News Letter*, April 21, 1920. —(J. A. T.)

✛

District of Columbia.—H. R. 13406, introduced by Mr. Mapes at the request of the Commissioner of the District of Columbia, is a bill to regulate the sale of milk, cream and certain milk products within the District. It requires dealers and producers to secure a license from the Health Officer which shall be issued only under certain requirements, including a negative reaction by cattle to the tuberculin test. The milk is graded and containers are required to be labelled according to grading, standards for which are contained in the bill. The penalty for the first violation is a fine of not more than $100 or imprisonment in the workhouse for not more than 30 days, or both, and for any subsequent offense a fine of not more than $300 or imprisonment in the workhouse for not more than one year, or both. The license may also be revoked.— (J. A. T.)

✛

Delaware.—For several months the State Board of Health has been considering a revision of its communicable disease rules, many of which were adopted years ago and are not in harmony with present-day practices. Moreover, many of the existing rules work an unnecessary hardship upon families in which cases of communicable diseases exist. The new regulations were adopted April 1, 1920.

The tabulation of the requirements is set forth in the *Delaware Health News* for April, making a convenient folder for general information. They include for the ordinary diseases: The length of time that the patient must be quarantined, the restrictions that are placed upon well school children and adults, the regulations concerning disinfection, the removal of laundry, milk bottles, etc., from the house while it is quarantined, and general information regarding the incubation period, how the disease is spread and when it is most contagious.

✛

Indiana.—The Indiana State Board of Health at its meeting April 7th passed milk rules, having the force of law, grading milk hereafter sold in the State of Indiana.

Grade A. Raw Milk.—Milk of this grade shall come from cows free from disease as determined by tuberculin tests and physical examinations by a qualified veterinarian, and shall be produced and handled by employes free from disease as determined by medical inspection by a qualified physician, and shall be collected, handled and delivered under sanitary conditions. Dairies from which this supply is obtained shall score at least 80 on the United States Bureau of Animal Industry score card.

Grade AA. Pasteurized Milk.—Milk of this grade shall come from healthy cows and shall be produced and handled under sanitary conditions. The heating apparatus used for this grade of milk must be equipped with an automatic mechanical control device and with a recording thermometer. The chart from same to be filed daily and subject at all times to inspection of the health authorities

NOTE—Pasteurized milk shall be pasteurized under official supervision. The method shall be heating to a temperature of at least 145° F. —then held for at least 30 minutes and then cooled to 50° F. or lower. To make certain the adequacy of the process of pasteurization, the responsibility rests upon Public Health Officials. Both the "flash" and "holding" methods of pasteurization are permitted if they are scientifically and thoroughly done, as determined by inspection. Dairies from which this supply is obtained shall score at least 65 on the United States Bureau of Animal Industry score card.

Grade B.—Milk of this grade shall be called cooking milk and shall come from healthy cows and shall be produced and handled under sanitary conditions. This grade must be sold in bulk and used only for manufacturing purposes.

These rules when promulgated will have all the force of law and the State Board will enforce them as rigidly as possible.

New Mexico.—At the March 27th meeting, the State Board of Health promulgated amendments to the "Regulations for the Control of Communicable Diseases," requiring the name of cases of venereal disease to be reported where adequate treatment is not continued, and requiring isolation of such cases under conditions where isolation is necessary to protect the public.

✠

New York.—New York State plans to modify the Public Health Laws. On March 25, 1920, an act was introduced by Mr. Sage in the New York Senate known as Bill No. 1533. The act proposes to amend the public health law, so as to provide for residents of rural districts, for industrial workers and for all others who cannot otherwise secure such benefits, adequate and scientific medical and surgical treatment, hospital and dispensary facilities and nursing care, to assist local medical practitioners, and in general, to improve the health of the inhabitants of the state by authorizing a county, city, or health district to create and maintain one or more health centers, to provide state aid for same, and to make an appropriation therefor.

In more detail, the act provides that health districts shall be established by the board of supervisiors of any county and shall appoint a board of health consisting of five members, at least one of whom shall be a graduate in medicine for at least three years. These members shall receive no remuneration for their services. They shall appoint a district health officer of proper qualifications to serve for six years on a full time basis, at a salary fixed by the District Board of Health. Local boards of health and local health officers who come within the district, shall continue to maintain their organizations and perform their regular duties, except in so far as these may be altered by rulings and ordinances of the District Board of Health. The local health officers shall act as deputy district health officers.

Any county board of supervisors may establish one or more health centers and shall specify the area each is supposed to serve. Under the provisions governing this portion of the act, the board of supervisors may provide as part of the health center, hospital facilities, either through arrangement with existing institutions or by the erection of new hospitals. Such facilities shall include special pavilions

for treating tuberculosis and other communicable diseases, for children, maternity cases, for mental diseases and other groups of diseases. Clinics for outpatients, such as maternity, prenatal and child welfare clinics, clinics for tuberculosis and venereal disease, clinics for mental and nervous diseases and defects, clinics for school children, dental clinics, and also general medical, surgical and diagnostic clinics shall be established. In addition provision should be made for clinical, bacteriological, x-ray and chemical laboratories to aid in the diagnosis and treatment of disease. Public health nursing for all parts of the district should be provided. Provision is also made for cooperation with the department of education to secure proper medical supervision and medical inspection for school children, and to assist in providing facilities to treat all school children showing physical defects or disease. Provision is also made for periodical medical examinations of all inhabitants in the district who desire it, and are willing to pay a proper charge therefor. The health center shall also serve as headquarters for all other public health, medical, nursing, and other public welfare agencies of the district that wish to utilize the same.

The bill also specifies the powers of the board of supervisors, among which are the following: To afford a board of managers of the health center which shall consist of seven members, one of whom shall be the county judge ex-officio, two of which shall be physicians, at least one, a woman. The board shall meet at least once each month. Each member shall receive $5.00 for each meeting in addition to his or her travelling expenses. The board shall appoint a properly qualified person as superintendent of health center. The latter may be the district health officer. The board shall also fix the salaries of all employes and exercise general management and control over the health center. The organization of health centers in cities shall be left in the hands of the mayor and other important city officials.

The State is to provide one-half the cost for constructing and equipping hospitals, the cost not to exceed $750 per bed. No State aid is to be given for establishing beds in excess of one to each 500 people in the district. The State is also to provide 75 cents per day for each free patient maintained at the health center hospital. Outpatient clinics are to be financed to the extent of one-half the cost of establishment, and is not to exceed $5000 per clinic. Free treatments in these clinics are to be financed to the extent of one-half the cost, and is not to exced 25 cents per treatment. One-half the cost of maintaining the laboratories of the health center, not to exceed $3000 per annum for each laboratory is also to be provided by the State. The State is also to provide $1500 towards the initial installation and equipment of such laboratory.

Where the local district has less than 1500 population, the State is to provide 10 cents per capita per annum towards the salaries of the deputy health officer, and 5 cents per capita per annum where the local district has a population from 1500 to 3000. Communities having more than 5000 population shall receive no State aid for more than one health center for every 5000 inhabitants.

The work of all health centers, including hospitals, clinics, laboratories, etc., shall be standardized by the State department of health, and shall be supervised and in many ways controlled by the State Commissioner of Health.

Provision is also made that the State Health Commissioner shall provide for occasional or periodical consultations and clinics at the health centers by specialists in medicine and surgery.—M. P. H.

✚

Ohio.—Regulations known as the Ohio Sanitary Code are to be effective July 1, 1920. On that date all rules and regulations which had formerly been adopted by the State Board of Health or by the Public Health Council are repealed.

The new code contains regulations governing the reporting of notifiable diseases in the state, naming the ailment according to its classification as a dangerous disease, and stating who is responsible for the reporting of it. It includes provisions for notification of such diseases as are found in institutions and for the reporting of deaths from notifiable diseases to the State Department of Health.

The necessary measures for the prevention and control of communicable diseases, such as quarantine, isolation of exposed persons and proper disinfection are embodied in the new code. Regulations for the transportation of the dead and for the inspection and examination of school teachers, janitors and children are also provided.

STATE HEALTH NOTES—GENERAL

California.—The California State Dental Association is active in serving the ever growing need of the public for Dental Education. A Bureau of Information has been established which is in charge of Dr. Guy S. Millberry, Chairman of the Publicity Committee, and Miss Charlotte Greenhood, Executive Secretary. It is the purpose of this Bureau to gather all information relative to dental clinics and will assist every organization endeavoring to establish such. The Bureau will cooperate with child welfare agencies, social service, charitable institutions, Red Cross chapters and health organizations.

✚

Indiana.—The Indiana State Board of Health, after thorough study of the subject, passed rules having the force of law, governing the production of sanitary milk and sanitary dairy products. The Indiana Dairymen's Association opposed the rules which graded milk and also wanted the score required for the dairies, to be lowered from 75 to 65. Some of the politicians of the state also opposed the rules. The Indiana Manufacturers of Dairy Products favored the rules in every particular. However, the opposition became so great that the promulgation of the rules, which under the law is necessary to put them in force, was postponed. Now letters are coming from the people, advocating the passage of the rules to secure pure milk and thus safeguard the child.

✚

Illinois.—In its annual budget the Council of the city of Evanston, Ill., has set aside the sum of $4,000 for infant welfare work. About one year ago the movement was initiated, and was financed by popular subscription. Its success was so evident that the city has now taken it over for a portion of the regular work of the Health Department. The development is in the hands of the Health Commissioner, Clarence T. Roome, M. D., and there are established two stations, two full-time nurses and about 500 children are enrolled that are under supervision.

✚

Iowa.—Workers from specialized tuberculosis and allied health organizations from thirteen Mississippi Valley states will meet at the Hotel Fort Des Moines, Des Moines, Iowa, September 22 to 24. The Conference program includes general and sectional discussions of health and tuberculosis problems from clinical, sociological, secretarial, nursing, sanatorium, and educational points of view.

Although it is a full program, it is arranged so all may be present at each session of general interest. The Iowa Trudeau Society, the clinical section of the Iowa Tuberculosis Association, is responsible for a series of six demonstration clinics in the early diagnosis of tuberculosis which will be held in conjunction with the Conference program. The clinical programs are also planned particularly for physicians not specializing in tuberculosis. Dr. B. R. Shurly, Detroit, is chairman of this section.

+

Kansas.—The Kansas State Department of Health shows considerable activity in its Division of Venereal Diseases. Since July, 1918, more than 3,300 cases of gonorrhea, 1,400 cases of syphilis, and 50 of chancroid have been reported. Treatment has been provided in five clinics and arsphenamine, to a cost of more than $3,600, has been distributed through the clinics and physicians. The laboratory, maintained in connection with the University Medical School has averaged 500 Wassermanns per month since its establishment in January, 1919. Quarantine has been enforced in the two years of 1918 and 1919 on 178 men and 598 women. The number of men showed an increase in 1919, while the number of women quarantined was a reduction of the figure for 1918. An active educational campaign through the use of motion pictures, card exhibits, slides, and the distribution of literature has been conducted.

In Marion County, Kansas, a health survey has just been completed in the rural schools by Dr. J. J. Entz and Miss Cora Gui. Dr. Entz is a member of the State Board of Health and president of important health organizations and Miss Gui was detailed for the work by the American Red Cross. Three thousand seven hundred and four children were examined, 69 per cent of them were found to be underweight, 19 per cent overweight and only 12 per cent normal. The use of milk for a food to a greater extent was suggested and a milk fund was raised to provide this drink for the school children at regular intervals and under supervision five schools undertook the experiment. In one of these the smallest gain in weight was 3 pounds, while one growing boy gained 15. One of the interesting procedures was the drinking of milk out of the bottles through straws.

+

Maine.—The first health union to be formed in Maine has just been organized by the towns of Milford, Old Town, Bradley, Orono and Veazie, under the name of the Motbov Health Union. A full time health officer, Major Albert W. Buck of Arland, has just been appointed and a committee of six, two from Old town and one from each of the other towns has been named to conduct the affairs of the Union. The committee consists of E. L. Warren of Old Town, Chairman; C. D. Woods of Orono, secretary; and A. A. Perkins of Old Town, W. G. Colter of Bradley, James Dudley of Veazie, and C. E. Longley of Milford. A salary of $2,400 is paid the health officer. The organization of this health Union is unique in the health history of Maine, for while Portland, Lewiston, Bath, and Auburn, each employs a full time health officer, and the little town of York supports one unassisted except by the state appropriation, this is the first union to be formed.

+

Michigan.—Detroit announces the establishment of a clinic for crippled children. This has been sponsored and is being supported by the Sigma Gamma Society of Detroit which will see that children are transported to and from the clinic by motor. The medical and surgical work will be under the direction of Doctors Carrol L. Storey and Nathaniel Ginsberg of the Health Department. The corrective training will be looked after by Miss Marian T. Sweeney, a graduate of Wellesley College, Department of Hygiene. Experience with this type of case, particularly post infantile paralysis, shows that great progress toward complete recovery of weakened limbs is possible by suitable muscular training.

The venereal clinic of the Detroit Department of Health registers a growth in attendance from 685 in January, 1918, to 5,297 in December, 1919. This work now involves the full time attention of one physician, six nurses and one clerk and the part time service of two physicians, one medical student and one nurse.

The "friend" is the most potent single influence in sending people to the clinic. Fifty-three per cent of males and 24 per cent of females were advised to seek relief from their affliction by friends who had been at the clinic previously. Fourteen per cent are referred to the clinic by private physicians. Twenty-five per cent of positive cases are referred by the clinic to private physicians.

The Detroit Department of Health has just established 28 antitoxin depots in fire and police stations, hospitals and drug stores. A complete equipment of various size doses and also tubes of culture media are maintained and regular collections of culture tubes are made several times during the 24 hours. Physicians now have antitoxin available within a short distance from their office or the case. This plan supersedes the previous one of sending antitoxin out from the main office in answer to each call. The growth of the city has necessitated this change in the distribution system.

The value of chlorine in the treatment of water and the neglect of city officials has been clearly demonstrated in the recent typhoid fever epidemic at Alpena, Mich. The water supply for this city is obtained from Thunder Bay about 2,000 feet from shore where the water is 16 feet deep and is always dangerously polluted with the city sewage. There was no purification prior to 1913 and the average typhoid death rate from 1900 to 1913 was 44 per 100,000 population. Hypochlorite of lime treatment was begun in February, 1913, but on account of poor supervision did not reduce the typhoid death rate. In October, 1915, a liquid chlorine machine was installed with laboratory control and the average typhoid death rate for 1916, 1917, 1918, and 1919, was 11 per 100,000 population.

✛

Minnesota.—A number of Public Health agencies in the State of Minnesota, are arranging with the State Fair Board to secure a building in the State Fair grounds to be devoted exclusively to public health. The Minnesota State Fair is the largest fair of the kind in the country, with an attendance of almost one-half million, and the importance of a concentrated public health exhibit at such an occasion as this, where all the health agencies of the State are represented, should furnish a substantial impetus to the whole movement of public health.

The Minnesota State Board of Health at its April meeting, determined that in its future activities for the control of venereal disease, greater emphasis should be put on the matter of educating the physician. Treatment through clinics and general educational publicity for the laity, have been developed to a considerable extent already. It is the opinion of the Board that the future development of the venereal disease control work in a state so largely rural as Minnesota, must include increasingly greater emphasis on contact with the physicians scattered throughout the small towns in the state, with a view to familiarizing them more thoroughly with the diagnosis and treatment of venereal disease, and the methods and purpose of its control.

✛

New Jersey.—The principal papers presented at the annual conference of New Jersey state and local health officials, held in Trenton in February last, are to be printed in the successive issues of *Public Health News*, the monthly bulletin of the State Board of Health. A great deal of the present work of the Board is in relationship to the midwives of the state. Supervision of these women is being rapidly accomplished. With its extensive foreign population, New Jersey is not in a position to try to dispense with the midwives, who are advisers to the families as well as obstetrical assistants. The experiment has been tried of combining the association of midwives of two or three counties.

✛

New York.—The New York County Chapter, American Red Cross, has opened a Bureau of Public Health Information as a part of its Health Service. It is located at the new headquarters of the New York County Chapter, and is for the use of every citizen of New York.

Up-to-date information on public health matters will be given free to all enquirers. The Bureau plans to serve as a central clearing house for the 83 public health agencies in New York County. At the Bureau will be lists of free clinics of all kinds, with information regarding when they are open and how they can be used.

Dr. H. H. Crum, Health Officer of Ithaca, is advocating the establishment in that city of a convalescent home for children crippled by infantile paralysis. He believes that such a home would be practically self-supporting and would result in the cure or improvement of many children thus affected who otherwise would not receive adequate care and might thus become community charges.

The examination of sanitary conditions at the following New York state institutions has recently been made by the Engineering Division of the State Board of Health, and reports containing recommendations for improvement transmitted to the institution authorities: New York State Hospital for the Care of Crippled and Deformed Children, West Haverstraw, N. Y.; New York State Reformatory for Women, Bedford Hills, N. Y.; Matteawan State Hospital, Beacon, N. Y.; State Homeopathic Hospital, Middletown, N. Y.; Rochester State Hospital, Rochester, N. Y.; New York State Woman's Relief Corps Home, Oxford, N. Y.; State Agricultural and Industrial School, Industry, N, Y.; Binghamton State Hospital, Binghamton, N. Y.

✦

Ohio.—The Board of Trustees of Ohio State University has appropriated a good salary for a competent woman to take charge of courses in Public Health Nursing and the combined five-year course of Science and Nursing. The position is to be an assistant professorship and will be in the Department of Public Health and Sanitation, which department is on a co-operative basis with the State Department of Health.

The courses will be under the care of Emery R. Hayhurst, M. D., who has been appointed Professor of Hygiene, retaining at the same time his position as Consultant in Industrial Hygiene with the State Department of Health.

According to the definition recently made by the State Commissioner of Health, concerning maternity or lying-in hospitals, any institution admitting maternity cases is now required to obtain a license from the State Department of Health to engage in maternity work.

For a number of years institutions engaged in such work have been licensed, this activity having been limited so far as hospitals are concerned to those institutions engaged exclusively in this work. With the definition of a maternity hospital as given by the Commissioner of Health, that any place receiving women for such care will be known as a maternity hospital, the regulations immediately govern hospitals operated exclusively for maternity cases, a department or ward of a general hospital or a private home used for this purpose.

Five new water filtration plants will be constructed in Ohio in the near future. Contracts will soon be awarded for plants at Defiance and Wauseon. It has been decided to build such plants at Delaware, Greenfield, Eaton and Fremont. Plants at Shelby and Wadsworth are finished and Ashland's is nearing completion.

Results of investigations carried on in various cities over the state to ascertain the reasons for the taste and odors of the drinking water show that the water is not contaminated, but that these arise from natural causes, resulting from the sealing of the river by ice for such a long period during the winter months.

Urging an intelligent use of the budgets which the various counties have appropriated for the carrying on of health work in the state and asking for co-operation among the health commissioners of the different districts, Dr. Allen W. Freeman, Commissioner of State Department of Health, indicated the general line of work to be carried on in Ohio to 21 new health officials who recently met in conference at the State Department of Health.

"The success of this new plan of health organization in Ohio depends upon you and not upon the State Department of Health," said Dr. Freeman. "It is not physically possible for the Department to do more than co-operate with you. The success or failure of the new plan depends upon the industry, intelligence, diplomacy and application of the men in the various districts."

"You cannot build this thing up rapidly. You cannot build a sound administrative machine up in to or three years, so do not be afraid of making haste slowly. Make your budgets reasonable, that the money may be spent intelligently and get the right sort of personnel for the work. Remember in spending money for public health you buy one and only one commodity, that is brains. In your work it is the quality of the men you hire and the quality of your own mind that makes for success or failure. As you view your job, view it only as a job of getting your own brains and training them on this job," the speaker said in conclusion.

Pennsylvania.—The Medical Division of the Pennsylvania Department of Health has been making some preliminary trials of the Schick test. Sixty-five volunteers in the Department were tested on April 13 and of this number 40, or 62½ per cent, tested positive. All doubtful re-actions, of which there were six, were counted positive.

On April 29 41 tests were made in the Messiah Orphanage, at Grantham, York County. Of these twelve, or 29 per cent, were positive, which includes three doubtful re-actions. In this institution diphtheria had been prevalent during the winter, there having been some 30 cases in a changing population. It is believed the low percentage of positives in this institution was due to a certain amount of immunity from having received antitoxin both for curative and prophylactic purposes. The test was not performed in any persons who had had antitoxin within two months. Toxin-antitoxin mixture is being administered to those re-acting positively who are willing to accept the treatment.

The Department is planning to extend the use of toxin-antitoxin mixture, beginning with institutions such as orphanages and having in mind eventually extending the work to the schools.

For the purpose of preventing the large number of dental defects that occurs in the school children of the Commonwealth, the State Department of Health has instituted a campaign to further the use of dental hygienists in the schools. A concrete ocular demonstration is being made in a number of the larger communities by means of a traveling dental clinic comprised of a dentist and two dental hygienists. The work of the hygienists consists in mechanically cleaning and polishing the surfaces of all the teeth while the dentist supplements the work by extracting and filling such teeth as require treatment. The demonstration is confined to a small group of children usually of the fourth grade. It has been possible by means of this traveling dental clinic to conclusively show local school authorities the practicability of prophylactic dental service in any public school system. The demonstrations have been very successful.

In pursuance of the plan of the State Department of Health to form Health and Morals Committees in every county of the state, and unusually strong, well balanced, sane committee has been formed in Pittsburgh. Tensard DeWolf, Judge of the Morals Court, Allegheny County, chairman of this committee, has succeeded in bringing together a representative group of men and women, each one of whom stands so high in his sphere that the committee is bound to demand the respect of the entire community.

The personnel of the committee is as follows: Tensard DeWolf, (Chairman), Judge of Morals Court; Rev. Thos. F. Coakley, Secretary to the Bishop of the Catholic Church in Pittsburgh diocese; Sherman Conrad, Executive Secretary, Co-operative Welfare Association; J. J. Buchanan, M. D., President Allegheny County Medical Society; H. B. Davis, Ph. D., President Colfax School; Col. Wm. Evans, in charge of the Salvation Army work in four states; Mrs. H. D. W. English; Frank R. Flood, former Captain in the Chemical Service, U. S. Army; Rev. Luther Freeman, Emery Methodist Episcopal Church; W. H. French, Social Welfare Department U. S. Steel Co.; William K. Heck, President Pittsburgh Labor Council; Rev. Ambrose Hering, Secretary of the Lutheran Inter-Mission Society; A. .H. Hanauer, Chamber of Commerce; William Frew Long, Manager of the Employers' Association; Miss Grace Lownes, Urban League; Mrs. Enoch Rauh, President Council of Jewish Women; A. W. Thompson, President Philadelphia Company and Edward A. Woods, Manager Equitable Life Assurance Society of the U. S.

✦

Tennessee.—Demonstrations of malaria control by mosquito eradication are to be made in at least two towns in Tennessee in 1920, the Tennessee State Board of Health, International Health Board, and the U. S. Public Health Service coöperating with the communities in this work. Brownsville has appropriated $1500 and Dyersburg $3000 for the first season's work, these sums to be supplemented by funds from the State Board of Health. Other towns may take up the work.

In addition the coöperative work done in these towns, the city of Memphis has appropriated $10,000, for anti-malaria work within the city limits, and Shelby County $15,000 for work in the suburban sections adjoining the city. This is an important manufacturing district and the officials of the plants are taking great interest in the work.

Texas.—"Local boards of trustees shall make provision for the fumigation of books before the reissue of the books," says the Texas State Free Text Book law.

To determine the most effective method of fumigation, a series of tests was ordered by Dr. C. W. Goddard, State Health Officer, at the request of Miss Annie Webb Blanton, State Superintendent of Education. There will be from six to ten tests made, different concentrations of gas being employed to kill tubercular, diphtheria and other pathogenic germs, placed between the pages of school books, and records of the experiment will automatically show which is most efficient. The result of the information thus obtained will be sent to school boards of the state by the Department of Education as a guide to carry out the requirement of the Free Text Book law.

✦

Utah.—The State Department of Public Instruction, Division of Health Education, has the past month addressed a health letter to the high school students in the state with reference to taking frequent inventories of their stock of health. The principle upon which this action is based is that in a very short time the high school students will have graduated and be practically dependent on their own responsibility, and they should therefore acquire habits that will in the future prove to be a safeguard to health. These are the questions that the students are given to consider:

1. What is the condition of my hair, my teeth, my eyes, my ears, my nose, my throat, my skin, my stomach, my liver, my heart, my lungs, my kidneys, my bowels, my hands, my feet, my nutrition?

2. Do I want to be attacked by some acute disease before calling for expert help, or do I periodically, say once a year, get that expert help in the way of a scientific examination by one adequately trained for such work?

3. What have I done to rid myself of such remediable physical defects as have been brought to my attention?

4. Have I acquired a set of health habits which will tend to keep me in abounding health and make for my efficiency in life?

5. As I look back upon my school work for the past ten years, is there anything that I have acquired in the way of an education that can be compared in value with a sound body free from defects, full grown, red-blooded, two-fisted, and safeguarded by the possession of the right kind of health habits?

✦

Virginia.—Virginia cities and towns have already provided or are about to make provision for improved water supplies the eventual cost of which will reach an aggregate of $7,500,000.

Of this sum by far the largest expenditure is that contemplated by Norfolk, the completed program of which for water supply will represent an investment of $6,000,000. For immediate investment for this purpose the city has provided the sum of $1,500,000, and will work out its full program during the next four or five years.

Every water supply made use of by a railway company for furnishing drinking water to its passengers must be certified to twice each year by the State Board of Health. These certificates are forwarded to the United States Public Health Service for approval. When the State Board declines to approve a water supply to the Public Health Service railroad companies are required by law to post notices at their station or stations at the places having the unsafe supply warning their patrons against the use of such water.

Gratifying evidence of the efficacy of rural sanitation work in preventing disease has been recently presented in the report of public health work in Fairfax County conducted under the supervision of E. L. Flanagan, M. D., field director for the State Board of Health, in close coöperation with local authorities and welfare organizations and with the financial backing of these agencies and of the State Board of Health and the International Health Board. Typhoid fever virtually has been wiped out in Fairfax County as a result of the health and sanitation work done in the years of 1918 and 1919.

In 1915 there were 30 cases of this disease reported with 4 deaths, in 1916, 26 cases and 3 deaths, while in 1917 the number of cases reported increased to 48 with 3 deaths. In 1919 there were but 8 cases reported and but one death.

On the eve of the season of high temperatures and increased menace from filth-borne diseases due to the presence of flies, State Health Commissioner Ennion G. Williams has declared that if Virginia would continue to secure reduction in the incidence of many forms of preventable disease no time should be lost in breaking up every possible breeding place of flies, at the same time making certain the fly-proofing of every toilet. While it is difficult on the farms to avoid furnishing the fly a breeding place in the piles of stable manure it is possible largely to reduce the number of such breeding places, the Commissioner declares, by keeping the manure-spreader busy.

At an enthusiastic meeting last month of the people of Salem and Roanoke counties, Va., held under the joint auspices of the chambers of commerce and the women's clubs, it was decided to take up actively a communal campaign of sanitation. The work has begun by a clean-up week, and by preparations to care for the sanitation of every schoolhouse in the counties. West Point has gone even further, for the town is divided into districts each one with some public spirited organization to look after it, and the effort is being made to have a fly-less, mosquito-less community. Educational work has been undertaken in the schools and the public is notified of the progress by window exhibits and cartoons.

✛

Wisconsin.—During January, February and March, 1920, 42,793 influenza cases were reported in Wisconsin, and 3,352 deaths from influenza and all forms of pneumonia were recorded, giving a ratio of one death to every 12.7 cases. This proportion is declared to be too high but represents the statewide condition with regard to reporting. Relatively, however, the state ranked high in reporting during the late epidemic.

Tabulations of 1919 mortality by the State Board of Health indicate that deaths from tuberculosis were fewer than in any year in the state's history. These deaths were 82.5 per 100,000 population. In 1908 this rate was 107.7.

Cities and villages in Wisconsin are complying rapidly with the new law requiring provision for public comfort stations. The code on this subject prepared by the State Board of Health is now in the hands of all city officials concerned, and a gratifying response to the demand has been shown by municipalities and the public.

Public health nurses, including county, school, industrial and Red Cross nurses, employed in Wisconsin, assembled at Madison in April for the first state conference called by the Bureau of Public Health Nursing, of which Mrs. Mary P. Morgan is director. A three days' program on all phases of the work gave the movement great impetus.

The State Board of Health has completed the chain of coöperative laboratories of hygiene by establishing one at Beloit, on the southern border. The state now has one central, one branch, and five coöperative laboratories.

Legislation of 1917 reinforced by an act of 1919 have made it obligatory for every city and incorporated village to provide and maintain comfort stations, and rest rooms. The phrasings of the law, definitions and rules and regulations are set forth in a pamphlet issued by the State Board of Health, which presents general plans together with pictures which are of value to municipalities proposing to establish similar conveniences.

✛

West Virginia.—The Division of Sanitary Engineering of the State Department of Health of West Virginia has issued a pamphlet entitled, *Sanitation in Camp and Country.* It is addressed particularly to the boys and girls who in clubs are accustomed to pass more or less time each summer under canvass or in wooden camps. It is estimated that there are more than 10,000 of such young people to whom such a treatise will be of greatest value. It is hoped that the impression thus conveyed to the boys and girls will be the foundation for bettered understanding of sanitation on the part of the parents.

INDUSTRIAL HYGIENE AND
OCCUPATIONAL DISEASE

Abstracted by Drs. E. R. Hayhurst, R. P. Albaugh, P. M. Holmes, and E. B. Starr.

National Safety Council Committee to Study Dermatoses.—Skin diseases or dermatoses are prevalent among workers in certain industries, and in some cases are caused by or aggravated by the conditions to which the worker is exposed. Such diseases cause a large amount of lost time in many plants, and have received a good deal of attention from industrial physicians, but there is very little accurate information as to their cause and methods of prevention. This led the Health Service Section of the National Safety Council to form a special committee to investigate and report on this subject. This committee consists of three men of the highest standing in the medical and industrial world—Dr. Carey P. McCord, director, Department Industrial Medicine and Public Health, University of Cincinnati; Dr. C. A. Lauffer, medical director, Westinghouse Electric & Manufacturing Company; Dr. C. F. N. Schram, medical director, Fairbanks, Morse & Co.

The report of this committee will be awaited with great interest, for it concerns not only the health of the employe, but the efficiency of the industrial plant.

✦

Report of the Industrial Conference Called by the President.—This Bulletin of 51 pages, signed by the various members of the President's Industrial Conference, considers among other features the hours of labor and employment of women and children in industry. As a basis it states that the nation is interested fundamentally in the progress and development of the physical, mental and spiritual well-being of its citizens. This well-being must be based upon a body of fact accurately ascertained from experience. If the conditions of an industry do not offer variety and continuing interest the worker should have hours short enough for some recreation and for greater contact with his fellowmen outside of working hours. Study should be made in each industry (preferably by the industry, but in its default, by the appropriate government agency) of the problem of industrial fatigue. In relation to

maximum production those schedules which are below the standard must necessarily reduce the total industrial production and consequently reduce the standards of living or increase prices. The Conference believes that some industries are now operating, in part at least, on schedules which have too long hours. There are large basic industries which still employ substantial numbers of men in exhausting work for 84 hours per week and longer. Such conditions are opposed to public interest and are a pregnant cause for industrial and political unrest. A universal standardization of hours is unnecessary and unwise. Undoubtedly there should be provision for one day's rest in seven. Where work is of repetitive nature a schedule of not more than forty-eight hours per week is advised. Overtime should not be permitted except in case of temporary emergency. Further reduction in hours may especially prejudice agricultural communities who already feel the growing competition of the cities in drawing away workers from the farm. For women special provision is needed to keep their hours within reason, to prohibit night employment in factories and workshops, and to exclude them from those trades offering particular dangers to women. Women should not be discriminated against in the matter of equal pay for equal work nor in respect to opportunities for equal training and advancement. The Federal Government has already recognized the unsoundness of permitting the entrance of young children into industry. This matter cannot wisely be left to the sole initiative of the separate states. Differentiation should be made between the various employments which children enter; at the same time, the time of the children should be taken up with their mental and physical development. Over 68 per cent of the 5,516, 163 illiterate persons of over ten years of age in the United States at the last census were native born. Prohibition of child labor and provision for compulsory elementary education are complementary. The ideal solution of the child labor problem is a reasonable uniformity by all the states in their legislation upon these topics. Experience has demonstrated that the economic interests of the country are best conserved by lengthening the period of education. The Conference proposes joint organization of management and employees as a means of preventing misunderstanding and of securing coöperative effort. Report issued, March 6, 1920, Wm. B. Wilson, Chairman (*U. S. Dept. of Labor*, Washington, D. C.).

✠

Industrial Sanitation in Massachusetts.— New laws in Massachusetts provide that employees who make a substantial change in clothing before working must have lockers. All industrial establishments must provide fresh and pure drinking water to each of their employees and easy of access during working hours. Sections strengthening laws governing compulsory school attendance including evening schools for illiterate minors, the hours of employment of women and children, the moving of heavy receptacles by female employees (75 lbs. or over must be moved with pulleys or castors), and medical chests in mercantile establishments where women or minors are employed are other features. Labor Legislation in Massachusetts 1915-1919, *State Bureau of Statistics*, Boston.

✠

The Removal of Carbon Monoxide from the Breathing Atmosphere.—This article is a summary of investigations on the removal of carbon monoxide from the air which was carried on at the American University Experiment Station established by the Bureau of Mines during the war and supported mainly by funds from the Navy Department. The result is the development and manufacture of a carbon monoxide mask primarily for naval use. While this gas is out of the question for any intentional use as a toxic war gas, yet it is a source of serious danger in marine and land warfare, and, as is well known, in industrial pursuits. The difficulty of removing carbon monoxide from air is its peculiar physical and chemical properties. It is insoluble in almost all solvents at ordinary temperatures. The requirements for a good absorbent are: (1) a quality of high activity in absorbing action and speed, (2) it must be able to act at law temperatures, (3) the amount which can be carried conveniently must have considerable absorbing capacity, (4) the absorbent must offer a low breathing resistance, (5) it must have a considerable

chemical and physical stability and be able to withstand long storage, and (6) it should be unaffected by the normal constituents of the air. A large number of absorbents were investigated until finally a combination of mixtures, consisting of the metallic oxides of MnO_2 5 per cent, CuO 30 per cent, CO_2O_3 15 per cent, and Ag_2O 50 per cent was developed and named "hopcalite." This substance practically meets all of the difficulties cited and is capable of practical manufacture. Its action is normally a catalytic one. Each canister through which the air passes must be provided with a drier to remove the moisture from the air before it passes into the hopcalite container. The drier finally recommended is a specially prepared dry, granular calcium chloride. The canister's function depends largely upon the amount of heat produced in the catalytic oxidation of a carbon monoxide air-mixture. A solution of this sulphate is used to control excessive heat production. The life of the canister is limited solely by the life of the drier, hence the gain in weight of the canister due to the absorption of moisture from the air is a criterion of its condition. Any canister which has gained more than 35 grams above the original weight stamped on it should be discarded, as there is then a possibility of more than 0.1 per cent of carbon monoxide gas leaking through it. Lamb, Bray and Frazer, *Jour. of Indus. and Engineering Chem.*, March, 1920, pp. 213-231.

✠

Women in Industry.—The Women in Industry Section of the National Safety Council has, through its Chairman, Miss Copp, elaborated an extensive program which includes a list of the occupations dangerous to women; keeping absenteeism down to a minimum; practical methods of reducing fatigue; specifications of a proper factory chair for women; the limits of weight which a woman should be permitted to lift; time needed for the lunch period; safety and health aspects of night work; first aid rooms; Americanization of women workers; the modifications of process or equipment which will result in greater comfort for employee and greater production; factory uniforms and clothing for women workers and also when and how physical examination of women should be conducted.—*Safety News*, March 8, 1920.

PUBLIC HEALTH LABORATORY NOTES

Abstracted by Francis H. Slack, M. D., and Mr. James M. Strang.

Serum Reaction in Bacillary Dysentery; Observations on Agglutination.—McLeod and Ritchie observed the agglutination reactions of sera (1) from the individuals from whose stools dysentery bacilli had been isolated, (2) from normal individuals, (3) from patients possibly suffering from dysentery, but with negative stools. They employed the macroscopic test of Dreyer, utilizing a freshly prepared emulsion of organisms.

In group one, 83 per cent of the sera from the Flexner-Y infections gave agglutination in dilutions of 1/40 or above and only three sera reacted with the Shiga emulsion even in very low dilution. Relatively few Shiga sera were tested, but all studied gave agglutination at 1/30. In group two, only four out of 540 apparently normal men gave agglutination of the Flexner-Y emulsion in dilutions of 1/40 or above, and two of these were proven to have previous histories. About 12 per cent of the doubtful cases in group 3 were shown to agglutinate the Flexner-Y emulsion above 1/40 hence were considered positive.

The authors advocate a standard dilution of 1/30 for Shiga sera and of 1/40 for Flexner-Y, rather than the higher and less satisfactory standards now in use. Freshly prepared emulsions of bacteria are considered to be more specific than those which have stood for some time.—McLeod and Ritchie, *J. Path. & Bact.*, 1920, 23, 217.

✛

Bacteriological Characteristics of Tubercle Bacilli From Different Kinds of Human Tuberculosis.—This paper is one of a series giving the results of investigations of cases of tuberculosis of different kinds with reference to the origin of the organism involved. Special emphasis is here given to cases of scrofulodermia or tuberculosis of the subcutaneous tissues.

Dr. Griffith found that this disease is caused by organisms of both human and bovine types of which the virulence was usually considerably attenuated. At the end of the paper a chart is given tabulating the results of the careful study of 1,068 cases of tuberculosis. The chart shows the number of cases and type of organism concerned in each of several age periods for the different forms of the disease.—A. S. Griffith, *J. Path. & Bact.*, 1920, 23, 129.

✛

Methods of Cultivating Anaerobic Bacteria.—Holker describes a very simple piece of apparatus which consists essentially of a glass arm which may be attached to the vessel containing the cultures and which communicates with a pressure gauge by means of a T-tube and with a suction pump and the gas tap through a two-way stop cock.

By alternately emptying the vessel by the pump and filling it with illuminating gas from the tap, a condition is reached at which the oxygen tension in the vessel is very low and a small amount of relatively unreactive coal gas remains. A special glass-stoppered test tube is figured in which several culture tubes can be incubated anaerobically at once.—J. Holker, *J. Path. & Bact.*, 1920, 23, 192.

✛

Agreement in Results of the Wassermann Reaction.—The blood serums of 3,000 patients were subjected to the Wassermann tests by two independent laboratories. An analysis of the results showed that there was complete uniformity in the findings of the two laboratories in 93.44 per cent. The 6.56 per cent variation included cases reported as positive by one laboratory and negative by the other. Considering only the variation of cases reported positive by one laboratory and negative by the other, the percentage variation was 4. This was 1.4 per cent positive in one laboratory and 2.6 per cent positive by the other. Some of these cases were known to be syphilitic so the negative reaction was the incorrect one. Considering then the cases that either laboratory may have reported as positive in non-syphilitic cases the percentage was 3.16. This is probably a higher percentage for false positives than actually occurred, as some of these cases were presumably syphilitic. This percentage variation is based on only one test. Repetitions resulted in a uniformity of findings in the majority of cases.—Harry C. Solomon, M. D., *Jour. A. M. A.*, Mar. 20, 1920, p. 788.

CAMPAIGN CRINKLETS—READ THEM

Eleven hundred new members from campaign so far.

✛

A third of our quota filled. Tide continuing strong.

✛

North Carolina and New Mexico see-sawing for the lead. Neither dares to stop.

✛

Dr. Kappleman of Ohio attends health meeting and sends in "57." All one variety: happy.

✛

State chairmen all working hard; but remember, no battle was ever won by the generals alone.

✛

Do your industrial and school physicians and health board members belong?

✛

See your prospective member before he leaves on vacation.

✛

Your association counts on you for one member.

✛

Send him in for the next news letter.

✛

Thank you.

✛

HOW DOES YOUR STATE RANK? PERCENT-
AGES OF QUOTAS FILLED TO
JUNE 1, 1920, INCLUSIVE

	Percentage of quota filled
Total	37
Western States	98
Southern States	44
Atlantic States	29
Central States	31
Canada	17
North Carolina	230
New Mexico	227
Utah	157
California	137

Saskatchewan	133
Maine	104
North Dakota	100
Colorado	92
Rhode Island	91
Montana	91
Nova Scotia	91
Vermont	76
Idaho	75
Connecticut	67
South Dakota	60
Ohio	56
Washington	54
Arkansas	54
Florida	54
Delaware	50
Minnesota	49
Michigan	44
Maryland and D. C.	43
Iowa	42
West Virginia	41
Alabama	40
Oklahoma	38
Wisconsin	36
Massachusetts	34
Tennessee	30
New Jersey	28
Missouri	25
Nebraska	21
New York	21
South Carolina	19
Indiana	18
Kentucky	17
Virginia	16
Kansas	15
Mississippi	15
Illinois	12
Pennsylvania	10

Note: States and provinces are omitted from which appreciable returns have not yet been received.

Each sustaining member is credited as the equivalent of five active members.

SEE LIST OF MEMBERS BEGINNING NEXT PAGE.

LIST OF NEW MEMBERS

Proposed for Election to the

A. P. H. A.

May 18 to May 29, inclusive.

Names of Sponsors are set in **Bold Face Type**.
Names of New Members are in Light Face Type.

ALABAMA

J. D. Dowling, M. D., Birmingham.
Mrs. J. D. Garner, Public Health Lecturer, Anniston.
Andrew J. Perolio, M. D., County Health Dept., Birmingham.
J. W. McQueen, Birmingham.
C. T. Fairbairn, Birmingham.
Henry David Perkins, Chief, Bur. Comm. Diseases, Birmingham.
Geo. G. Crawford, Birmingham.
George V. Truss, Statistician, Board of Health, Birmingham.
J. D. Lathem, Chief, Bur. Sanitation, Birmingham.
Frank H. Crockard, Woodward.

CALIFORNIA

Frank L. Kelly, Berkeley.
Dudley Smith, M. D., Oakland.
John N. Chain, M. D., Eureka.
California Central Creameries, Atten. S. V. Morrison, Eureka.
J. L. Pomeroy, M. D., Los Angeles.
H. E. Kirschner, M. D., Monrovia.
Kirby Smith, M. D., Oakland.
E. F. Jones, M. D., Health Officer, Oakland.
Chas. C. Wing, D. V. S., Asst. Health Officer, Oakland.
Irving R. Bancroft, M. D., Sacramento.
N. K. Foster, M. D., Oakland.
Emily J. Richards, R. N., Supt. Graves Mem. Disp., Los Angeles.
Allen F. Gillihan, M. D., Sacramento.
Charlotte Greenwood, Dental Hygienist, University.
Mary L. Cole, R. N., Dir. Pub. Hlth. Nursing, A. R. C., San Francisco.
Flora N. Bradford, R. N., Field Rep. A. R. C., San Francisco.
Mrs. Estella S. Edson, R. N., Exec. Sec'y, Tuber. Assn., Sacramento.
Mrs. Dorothy K. Stewart, R. N., School Nurse, San Bernardino.
Ida M. Thiele, R. N., State Board of Health, Sacramento.
Myrtle Sacry, Public Health Nurse, Santa Rosa.
Annie F. Fletcher, Public Health Nurse, Long Beach.
Margaret M. Lindsay, R. N., County Nurse, Riverside.
Laura A. Watkins, R. N., Public Health Nurse, San Jose.
Reba A. H. Ingols, R. N., Children's Agent, Sacramento.
Harry N. Jenks, Sacramento.
Gertrude N. Whitton, Supervisor, Children's Health Centers, Berkeley.
Guy P. Jones, Sacramento.
Frances E. Corey, M. D., Health Officer, Alhambra.
Prof. M. E. Jaffa, Univ. of Calif., Berkeley.
Ethel D. Watts, R. N., Public Health Nurse, Fresno.
Walter M. Dickie, M. D., Dir. Bur. Social Hygiene, Los Angeles.
Mabel A. Genung, M. D., Field Agent, U. S. P. H. S., Sacramento.

D. M. Gedge, M. D., San Francisco.
B. A. Mardis, M. D., San Francisco.
William Simpson, M. D., San Jose.
A. D. Browne, M. D., Medical Advisor, Stanford University.
A. W. Hedrich, Boston, Mass.
Foster M. Hull, M. D., Health Officer, Culver City.

COLORADO

C. G. Hickey, M. D., Denver.
Charles C. Donaldson, M. D., Aniba.
M. O. Shivers, M. D., Colorado Springs.
Charles N. Meader, M. D., Denver.
A. S. Taussig, M. D., Denver.
John W. Amesse, M. D., Denver.
Glyde W. Bumpus, M. D., Denver.
Frank D. Sanford, M. D., Garrison.
Charles E. Dumke, M. D., Sanitary Inspector, Louviers.

CONNECTICUT

George H. Jennings, M. D., Jewett City.
J. H. Hoover, M. D., Vciuntown.
J. F. Rogers, M. D., New Haven.
May Caughey, New Haven.

DISTRICT OF COLUMBIA

Bernard J. Newman, Washington.
William G. Beucler, Asst. Sanitarian, U. S. P. H. S., Washington.
W. C. Fowler, M. D., Washington.
William Gerry Morgan, M. D., Washington.
Caroll Fox, M. D., Washington.
James G. Townsend, M. D., P. A. Surgeon, U. S. P. H. S., Kensington, Md.
Chas. V. Hardliska, M. D., Washington.
D. C. Y. Moore, M. D., Chairman, Health Board, So. Manchester, Conn.

FLORIDA

Ralph N. Greene, M. D., Jacksonville.
Margaret Grace, Supt. of City Hospice, Jacksonville.
Joseph A. Hicks, Sanitary Patrolman, Pensacola.
W. A. McRae, Comm. of Agriculture, Tallahassee.
Alice H. Parmenter, R. N., Tampa.
Arthur M. Henry, Food and Drug Chemist, Tallahassee.

IDAHO

E. R. Dooley, Twin Falls.
T. L. Cartney, D. D. S., Filer.
Hal G. Blue, Supt. of Schools, Twin Falls.
Frederick E. Snook, D. D. S., Twin Falls.
W. A. Minnick, City Clerk, Twin Falls.
Brittomart Wolfe, Supt. of Schools, Twin Falls.

ILLINOIS

J. M. Furstman, M. D., Bloomington.
McLean County Tuber. Assn., Bloomington.
Isaac Abrahams, M. D., Chicago.
Simon P. James, M. D., Chicago.

N. H. Bundesen, M. D., Chicago, Ill.
    H. C. Becker, M. D. V., City Veterinarian, Chicago.
    James C. Brydge, M. D., Quarantine Officer, Chicago.
    George G. Davis, M. D., Chief Surg. Illinois Steel Co., Chicago.
    Frank Thomas Duffy, M. D., Quarantine Officer, Contag. Dis., Chicago.
    James P. Kilkourse, Chief, Bur. Food Inspec., Chicago.
    Erwin A. Kowohl, Atty. Health Dept., Chicago.
    C. A. Jennings, Chicago.
    Samuel F. Manning, Office Sec'y Dept. of Health, Chicago.
    L. S. Marsh, Engineer of Tests, Chicago.
    William C. Marti, Chemist, Dept. of Health, Chicago.
    Abe F. Nemiro, M. D., in charge V. D. Clinics, Chicago.
    Russell J. Poole, Dir. Bur. of Foods, Chicago.
    Mary E. Sharkey, M. D., Chicago.
    Robert G. Timms, M. D., Asst. Dir. Bur. of Laboratories, Chicago.
    J. H. Wilson, Supervisor, Dept. of Health, Chicago.
Bernard C, Roloff, Chicago.
    Marcus S. Oliver, M. D., Chicago.
C. W. Lillie, M. D., East St. Louis.
    Charles Schmidt, Sanitary Officer, East St. Louis.
C. St. Clair Drake, M. D., Springfield.
    E. C. Gaffney, M. D., Lincoln.
    W. B. Schowengerdt, M. D., Health Officer, Champaign.
    Frank Wieland, M. D., Med. Dir., Montgomery Ward Co., Springfield.

INDIANA

J. G. Royse, M. D., Indianapolis.
    Clara Faulkner, M. D., Health Officer, Hobart.
    Arthur L. Oilar, M. D., U. S. P. H. S. Clinic, Anderson.
    W. F. Peter, Supt., Seymour Water Co., Seymour.
    Mrs. Lida Outland, Health Officer, Upland.
    Fred C. Denny, M. D., County Health Commissioner, Madison.

IOWA

H. L. Saylor, M. D., Des Moines.
    Public Health Nursing Assn., Des Moines.
Prof. Earle L. Waterman, Iowa City.
    Elsie T Osborne, Visiting Nurse, Clinton.
    Leonore Addington, R. N., Supt. Samaritan Hospital, Des Moines.
    C. F. Starr, M. D., Park Hospital, Mason City.

KANSAS

J. J. Entz, M. D., Hillsboro.
    Clara O. Laury, R. N., County Nurse, Iola.
R. L. Kilborn, M. D., Topeka.
    Milton O. Nyeberg, M. D., City Physician, Wichita.

KENTUCKY

A. T. McCormack, M. D., Louisville.
    J. M. Alexander, M. D., Fulton.
    Fred Gernert, Louisville.
    W. S. Cramer, Chief Engr., Lexington Water Wks., Lexington.
    F. A. Stine, M. D., Member, County and City Health Boards, Newport.
John F. Hamilton, M. D., Owensboro.
    C. N. Caldwell, M. D., Dir. Scott Co. Health Dept., Georgetown.

LOUISIANA

Oscar Dowling, M. D., New Orleans.
    C. C. Conerly, M. D., Hornbeck.
    Solomon Wolff, New Orleans.

MAINE

L. D. Bristol, M. D., Augusta.
    Isaac B. Gage, M. D., Atlantic.

MARYLAND

W. A. Gunther, M. D., Cumberland.
    W. A. Gracie, M. D., County Health Officer, Cumberland.

MASSACHUSETTS

B. W. Carey, M. D., Boston.
    Lawrence T. Newhall, M. D., Brookfield.
    Louis A. Moll, M. D., School Inspector, Cambridge.
    Louisa P. Loring, Prides Crossing.
    Fritz B. Talbot, M. D., Boston.
    George W. Blaisdell, M. D., Board of Health, Manchester.
    Thomas E. Lilly, M. D., Chairman, Board of Health, Shirley.
    Albert F. Hunt, M. D., Chairman, Board of Health, Bridgewater.
    Frederick P. Murphy, M. D., School Physician, Lowell.
    William J. Cochran, M. D., Natick.
    Esther Dart, R. N., Matron, Stillman Infirmary, Cambridge.
    Milton S. Howes, Member Cummington Bd. of Health, Swift River.
    D. W. Hyde, Agent, Board of Health, North Adams.
    James E. Pendergast, Health Agent, Norwood.
    Whitin Machine Works, Atten. Mr. Wm. T. Norton, Whitinsville.
A. W. Hedrich, Boston.
    Carl P. Sherwin, M. D., Fordham University. New York City.
    Robert J. McMurray, M. D., Sebring, Fla.
    G. F. Zerzan, Holyrood, Kan.
    C. S. Kenney, Norton, Kan.
    New York Diagnostic Clinics, Atten. M. Joseph.
    Mandelbaum, M. D., Dir., New York City.
    Standard Steel Corporation, Atten. Geo. E. Ackerman, Milwaukee, Wis.
    Dorothy Hayden, Public Health Nurse, Greensboro, N. C.
    A. Souther Harkness, Bacteriologist, Springfield, Ill.
Victor Safford, M. D., Boston.
    Walter T. Fuller, M. D., Med. Dir. Boston Board of Health, Dorchester.
Percy G. Stiles, M. D., Boston.
    Boston School of Physical Education, Boston.
    Benjamin White, Ph. D., Boston.
    Carolyn R. Davis, Everett.
Geo. E. Bolling, M. D., Brockton.
    Fred C. Creedon, Exec. Officer, Board of Health, Brockton.
    James H. Drohan, M. D., Chairman, Board of Health, Brockton.
    Frank H. Kennedy, Sewer Dept., Brockton.
    Fred J. Ripley, M. D., Health Officer, Brockton.
Samuel B. Morris, Fall River.
    A. A. Keeley, M. D., Diagnostician, Fall River.
Frederick W. Howe, Framingham.
    Lyman L. Workman, Teacher of Hygiene, Framingham Center.
I. J. Clarke, M. D., Haverhill.
    Alice G. Symonds, M. D., Pres. Haverhill Health Center, Haverhill.
W. H. Allen, M. D., Mansfield.
    Esther Brown, R. N., School Nurse, Mansfield.
C. T. Pomeroy, Melrose Highlands.
    James J. Ray, Agent, Health Dept., Peabody.

MICHIGAN

Roy W. Pryer, Detroit.
    S. L. Morgans, M. D., Bacteriologist, Dept. of Health, Detroit.

Henry F. Vaughan, M. D., Detroit.
Francis Duffield, M. D., Detroit.
Thomas B. Cooley, M. D., Detroit.
Gustavus D. Pope, Member, Board of Health, Detroit.
Wilbur B. Payne, Bacteriologist, Kalamazoo.

MINNESOTA

J. Sundall, M. D., Minneapolis.
Elizabeth Fleeson, Students Health Service, Minneapolis.
Charles E. Smith, Jr., M. D., St. Paul.
Alex Ridgway, M. D., Belgrade.
E. W. Hammes, M. D., Health Officer, Hampton.
J. C. Rothenburg, M. D., Health Officer, Springfield.
John A. McIntyre, M. D., Chairman, Board of Health, Round Lake.
V. E. Verne, M. D., U. S. P. H. S. Examiner, Moorhead.
P. A. Walling, M. D., Commission Tri County Sanatorium, Park Rapids.
P. Boysen, M. D., Health Officer, Pelican Rapids.
W. H. Valentine, M. D., Health Officer, Tracy.
A. G. Kessler, M. D., Supt. Sunnyrest Sanatorium, Crookston.
H. T. Ground, M. D., Health Officer, Virginia.
Theo. Holtan, M. D., Health Officer, Kilkenny.
W. D. Stovall, M. D., St. Paul.
Elsie E. Dorward, Bacteriologist, State Lab. of Hygiene, Madison.

MISSISSIPPI

J. D. Green, M. D., Brooksville.
F. S. Spalding, M. D., Clay County Health Officer, West Point.

MISSOURI

Guy L. Noyes, M. D., Columbia.
Andrew W. McAlester, M. D., Commissioner of Health, Columbia.
Geo. H. Jones, M. D., Jefferson City.
Thomas J. Walker, Missouri Tuber. Assn., Columbia.
A. S. Harrison, M. D., Kennett.
M. B. Harutun, M. D., Commissioner of Health, Joplin.
R. C. Lamson, M. D., County Health Officer, Neosho.
Dora Stacy, School Nurse, Springfield.
Murray C. Stone, M. D., Springfield.
Ralph J. Brooks, City Bacteriologist, Springfield.

MONTANA

W. F. Cogswell, M. D., and John J. Sippy, M. D., Helena, Mont.
Roscoe C. Main, M. D., Health Officer, Billings.
Charlotte I. Wellcome, R. N., County Nurse, Hamilton.
J. H. Morrison, M. D., Health Officer, Libby.

NEBRASKA

I. H. Dillon, M. D., Lincoln.
Florence McCabe, Supt. Visiting Nurses Assn., Omaha.
Louise S. Westermann, R. N., Red Cross Instr. of Hygiene, Lincoln.

NEW HAMPSHIRE

L. W. Wellington, Berlin.
Elizabeth McManus, R. N., Tuberculosis Nurse, Berlin.

NEW JERSEY

Elmer C. Jackson, M. D., Harrison.
Elbert S. Sherman, M. D., Newark.
Charles V. Craster, M. D., Newark.
M. James Fine, M. D., Dir. Div. of Tuberculosis, Newark.
John Roach, Chief, Bur. Hygiene and Sanitation, Trenton.

Louis Schneider, M. D., Newark.
Ward Burdick, M. D., Bacteriologist, Denver, Colo.
Otto Lowy, M. D., Newark.
Arturo R. Casilli, M. D., Newark.
David B. Gershenfeld, M. D., Newark.
John W. Gray, M. D., Pathologist, Newark.
Edwin Steiner, M. D., Newark.
Jacob Ran, Member, Board of Health, Newark.
Jordan Green, Newark.
Ambrose F. Dowd, M. D., Res. Physician, City Hospital, Newark.
Carmine G. Berardinelli, M. D., A. A. Surg., U. S. P. H. S., Newark.
Henry B. Dunham, M. D., Supt. Essex Co. Sanatorium, Verona.
John O'Brien, Health Officer, Orange.
Joseph C. Salis, D. O., Osteopath and Health Officer, Bloomfield.
W. J. Wilsey, Perth Amboy.
Frank Born, Health Inspector, Carteret.
F. W. Sell, M. D., Rahway.
Sec'y, Board of Health, Garwood.
D. E. Buckley, West Orange.
Abbie L. Hanlon, R. N., Baby Welfare Nurse, Orange.

NEW MEXICO

D. B. Williams, M. D., Portales.
E. E. Hoagland, Portales.
Harold F. Gray, Santa Fe.
A. H. DeLong, M. D., Health Officer, Gallup.
C. E. Waller, M. D., Santa Fe.
Thomas F. Self, M. D., Health Officer, Roy.

NEW YORK

Anna C. Moore, Albany.
Broome County Health Assn., Binghamton.
Gilbert M. Tucker, Jr., Albany.
M. Louise Strachan, Exec. Sec'y Ontario Co. Tuber. Comm., Canandaigua.
Frederick Sprenger, Bronxville.
James D. Burt, State Dept. of Health, New York.
S. J. Byrne, M. D., Brooklyn.
Herman T. Peck, M. D., Asst. San. Supt. Brooklyn Dept. of Health, Brooklyn.
Edward Clark, M. D., Buffalo.
Frank O. Cole, M. D., Health Officer, Gasport.
Robert Selden, M. D., Catskill.
Ellen G. Murphy, R. N., Public Health Nurse, Catskill.
David Edwards, M. D., East Hampton.
John H. Nugent, Jr., M. D., Southampton.
John Nugent, Sr., M. D., Southampton.
Hugh Halsey, M. D., Health Officer, Southampton.
George H. Schenk, M. D., Southampton.
V. A. Moore, M. D., Ithaca.
Samuel A. Goldberg, Prof. of Pathology, Ithaca.
B. Eleanor Easton, Kingston.
Evelyn M. Bugg, Bacteriologist, Kingston.
Royal S. Copeland, M. D., New York.
George G. Hatzel, M. D., Med. Insp. Dept. of Health, New York.
Jessie S. Edwards, M. D., Health Dept. N. Y. City, Brooklyn.
William Wouschin, M. D., New York.
C. E. Denison, M. D., Med. Insp. Health Dept., New York.
Edward S. Godfrey, Jr., New York.
Horace J. Mann, M. D., Brockport.
J. A. Miller, M. D., New York.
Charles L. Dana, M. D., N. Y. Academy of Medicine, New York.
Howard C. Taylor, M. D., New York.
B. Sachs, M. D., New York.
Anna W. Williams, M. D., New York.
Hazel M. Hatfield, M. D., Bacteriologist, Health Dept., New York.

Euthimios H-D. Tchor-BaJ-Oglu, M. D., Otisville.
    H. Everett Russell, M. D., Health Officer, Otis-
    ville.
Harry E. Smith, Oxford.
    Mrs. Jesse Jacobs, Oxford.
Helen L. Palliser, M. D., Poughkeepsie.
    May L. Reynolds, Commissioner Board of
    Health, Poughkeepsie.
A. S. Downs, Saratoga.
    Harry Loop, M. D., Saratoga Springs.
F. W. Sears, M. D., Syracuse.
    Henry G. Meacham, Welfare Worker, Seneca
    Falls.
C. W. Buckmaster, M. D., Yonkers.
    Chauncey V. Umsted, M. D., Deputy Health
    Officer, Yonkers.

NORTH CAROLINA

Rose M. Ehrenfeld, R. N., Raleigh.
    Fairy Rosser, R. N., Public Health Nurse,
    Statesville.
K. E. Miller, M. D., Raleigh.
    John W. Ward, Chairman, County Board of
    Health, Rowland.
    D. S. Curry, M. D., Parkton.
    Mrs. Alf McLeod, Lumberton.
    Hon. W. R. Surles, Mayor, Proctorsville.
W. S. Rankin, M. D., Raleigh.
    Harold Glascock, M. D., Raleigh.
    William J. Alexander, City Manager, Gastonia.
    J. W. Jones, M. D., County Health Officer,
    Boone.
    William H. Williamson, Raleigh (sustaining
    member).
    P. J. Chester, M. D., Health Officer, Greenville.
    Hugo Muench, Jr., M. D., County Health Offi-
    cer, Windsor.
    William E. Warren, M. D., County Physician,
    Williamston.
    A. J. Crowell, M. D., Member, State Board of
    Health, Charlotte.
    Jerrerson Standard Life Ins. Co., Atten. Chas.
    W. Gold, Treas., Greensboro (corporate mem-
    bership).
    W. A. Bradsher, M. D., Quarantine Officer,
    Roxboro.
    V. F. Couch, M. D., Health Officer, Yadkin-
    ville.

NORTH DAKOTA

C. J. McGurren, M. D., Devil's Lake.
    A. R. MacKay, M. D., Bottineau.
    S. W. Hill, M. D., County Health Officer,
    Regent.
    M. G. Flath, M. D., County Health Officer,
    Stanley.
W. C. McMurtry, M. D., Wolford.
    North Dakota Tuber. Sanatorium, Atten. J. G.
    Lamont, M. D., Supt., Dunseith.

OHIO

J. A. Kappelman, M. D., Canton.
    G. W. Burnett, M. D., Health Commissioner,
    Greenville.
    Valloyd Adair, M. D., Health Commissioner,
    Lorain.
    Arlington Alles, M. D., Health Commissioner,
    Sidney.
    F. A. Ireton, M. D., District Health Commis-
    sioner, Batavia.
    W. H. Morgan, M. D., Health Commissioner,
    Newark.
    W. S. Tilton, M. D., Health Commissioner,
    Martins Ferry.
    I. S. Putnam, M. D., Health Commissioner,
    Millersburg.

G. B. Fuller, M. D., Health Commissioner,
Loudonville.
H. LuSern Hinkley, M. D., Health Commis-
sioner, Green Springs.
Irvin S. Workman, M. D., Health Commis-
sioner, Mount Vernon.
R. M. Schwartz, M. D., Health Commissioner,
Salem.
Health Board Miami Co., Atten. A. H. Ha-
worth, Troy.
U. D. Ward, Health Commissioner, Dover.
C. M. Peters, M. D., Health Commissioner,
Canton.
D. K. Jones, M. D., Health Commissioner,
Wooster.
N. Sifritt, M. D., Health Commissioner, Warren.
W. N. Caldwell, M. D., Health Commissioner,
Fostoria.
Minna T. Meyer, Health Commissioner, Co-
lumbus.
J. E. King, M. D., Health Commissioner,
Girard.
Lake County Pub. Health League, Painesville.
S. J. Ellison, M. D., Health Commissioner,
West Union.
J. J. Sutter, M. D., Health Commissioner, Lima.
Edward Blair, M. D., Health Commissioner,
Lebanon.
N. E. Brundage, M. D., Health Commissioner,
Delphos.
Emil C. Norwood, M. D., Health Commissioner,
Delaware.
H. Kenning, M. D., Health Commissioner,
Painesville.
S. B. McGavran, Health Commissioner, Cadiz.
John D. Boylan, M. D., Health Commissioner,
Youngstown.
W. H. Carey, M. D., Health Commissioner,
Bellefontaine.
Mart F. Helfrich, M. D., Health Commissioner,
Galion.
W. G. Rhoten, M. D., Health Commissioner,
Hillsboro.
C. B. Finefrouck, M. D., Health Commissioner,
Port Clinton.
Eleanor M. Loomis, R. N., Health Commis-
sioner, Painesville.
C. H. Skeen, M. D., Health Commissioner,
Napoleon.
O. C. Stutz, M. D., Health Commissioner,
Upper Sandusky.
B. H. Grube, M. D., Health Commissioner,
Xenia.
F. M. Houghtaling, Health Commissioner,
Huron.
Robert Conard, M. D., Health Commissioner,
Blanchester.
D. L. Cowden, M. D., Health Commissioner,
Kimbolton.
R. D. Worden, M. D., Health Commissioner,
Ravenna.
W. S. Yeager, M. D., Health Commissioner,
Leipsic.
D. W. Boone, M. D., Health Commissioner,
Bellaire.
G. E. French, M. D., Health Commissioner,
Elyria.
J. J. Hathaway, M. D., Health Commissioner,
Carrollton.
H. J. Wittenberg, M. D., Health Commissioner,
Norwood.
A. J. Pounds, M. D., Health Commissioner,
Delaware.
C. M. Valentine, M. D., Health Commissioner,
Linden Heights.
Ralph B. Tate, M. D., Health Commissioner,
Cincinnati.
H. H. Pansing, M. D., Health Commissioner,
Dayton.
J. J. Martin, M. D., Bucyrus.
J. P. Young, M. D., Health Commissioner,
Empire.

C. J. Loveless, M. D., Health Commissioner, Granville.

Pearl Kamerer, R. N., State Dept. of Health, Columbus.

W. E. Howell, M. D., Health Commissioner, Rio Grande.

F. W. Murrey, M. D., Health Commissioner, Summerfield.

H. J. Powell, M. D., Health Commissioner, Bowling Green.

Joseph Blickenoderfer, M. D., Health Commissioner, New Philadelphia.

Frank I. Mayer, Chillicothe.

W. C. Beaver, Bacteriologist, Whipple.

William H. Peters, M. D., Cincinnati.

Ayleshire Neal, M. D., Health Commissioner, Hamilton Co., Cincinnati.

A. H. McCrory, M. D., Bucyrus.

M. F. Vereker, M. D., Health Commissioner, Hamilton.

Richard A. Feiss, Cleveland.

S. Harold Greene, Boston, Mass.

A. W. Freeman, M. D., Columbus.

C. B. Bliss, M. D., Ohio Pub. Health Assn., Sandusky.

J. Sheldon Scott, Chemist, Water Purification Plant, Steubenville.

G. L. Lyne, M. D., District Health Commissioner, Wapakoneta.

Charles R. Keyser, M. D., Dist. Health Commissioner, Van Wert.

H. Dickson, M. D., Urbana.

E. B. Starr, M, D., Columbus.

P. C. Ramsey, M. D., Health Commissioner, Alliance.

Donald D. Shira, M. D., Commissioner of Health, Summit Co., Akron.

K. R. Teachnor, M. D., Health Commissioner, Hamilton Co., Hamilton.

G. T. Wasson, M. D., County Health Commissioner, Jefferson.

R. R. Richison, M. D., Health Director, Springfield.

C. C. Buttins, M. D., Health Commissioner, Wilsonville.

O. J. Walker, M, D., Youngstown.

O. P. Kimbal, M. D., Industrial Health Officer, Youngstown.

J. M. Woltz, Youngstown.

The DeVilbiss Mfg. Co., Atten. A. D. Gutchess, Toledo.

Whitaker-Glessnew Co., Atten. Safety Dept., Portsmouth.

OKLAHOMA

Ruth F. Horel, Oklahoma City.

Cecelia Conner, Washington Co. Tuber. Assn., Bartlesville.

A. R. Lewis, M. D., Oklahoma City.

B. W. Slover, M. D., County Health Officer, Blanchard.

O. H. Parker, M. D., Custer.

D. Armstrong, M. D., Durant.

F. Dinkler, M. D., Fort Cobb.

J. Angus Gillis, M. D., Frederick.

A. O. Meredith, M. D., County Health Officer, Kingfisher.

George A. Waters, M. D., Public Health Supt., Pawnee.

Harrell Hardy, M. D., County Supt. of Health, Poteau.

J. B. Murphy, M. D., County Supt. of Health, Stillwater.

R. L. Baker, M. D. ,Wynnewood.

J. P. Bortley, M. D., Duncan.

PENNSYLVANIA

Seneca Egbert, M. D., Philadelphia.

Maud Etheredge, M. D., Dr. P. H., Sevierville.

SOUTH CAROLINA

Katherine Marden, Spartanburg.

Sarah R. Connell, Nurse, U. S. P. H. S., New Orleans, La.

TEXAS

F. B. Porter, M. D., Fort Worth.

Wilby T. Gooch, Ph. D., Prof. of Chemistry, Baylor University, Waco.

UTAH

T. B. Beatty, M. D., Salt Lake City.

L. B. Laker, M. D., City Health Officer, Eureka.

William H. Rothwell, M. D., City Health Officer, Murray.

J. R. Ward, Chairman, Board of Health, Ogden.

T. J. Howells, M. D., County Physician, Salt Lake City.

R. W. Born, M. D., Health Officer, Sandy.

VERMONT

C. F. Dalton, M. D., Burlington.

John H. Blodgett, M. D., Member, State Med. Society, Bellows Falls.

Warren J. Howard, M. D., District Health Officer, St. Albans.

Victor P. Genge, M. D., District Health Officer, St. Johnsbury.

H. W. Eliot, M. D., District Health Officer, Manchester.

Charles W. Kidder, M. D., District Health Officer, Woodstock.

VIRGINIA

E. G. Williams, M. D., Richmond.

Joel Crawford, M. D., Yale.

Harvey Wallace, M. D., Staunton.

Miss Draper Fultz, South Boston.

WASHINGTON

John B. Anderson, M. D., Seattle.

H. H. Gray, M. D., Health Officer, Chimacum.

J. M. P. Chalmers, M. D., Vancouver.

WISCONSIN

C. A. Harper, M. D., Madison.

Royal F. Clark, Beaver Dam.

C. F. Schram, M. D., Industrial Surgeon, Beloit.

Myra W. Kimball, R. N., Supervisor of Nurses, La Crosse.

Ernest G. Ovitz, M. D., Laona.

Milwaukee Medical Society, Atten. Oscar Lotz, Sec'y, Milwaukee.

Lewis J. Daniels, M. D., Milwaukee.

D. E. W. Wenstrand, M. D., Asst. Med. Dir. N. W. Mutual Life Ins. Co., Madison.

E. J. Campbell, M. D., Oshkosh.

T. F. Thomson, M. D., Milwaukee.

S. L. Pilgrim, Chief, Div. of Food, Milwaukee.

CANADA

C. S. Mahood, M. D., Calgary, Alberta.

W. G. Golding, Milk Inspector, Calgary.

H. V. Graham, M. D., Halifax, N. S.

E. Ada Luxon, R. N., Victorian Order of Nurses, Halifax.

B. F. Royer, M. D., Halifax, N. S.

H. A. Payzant, M. D., Dartmouth.

W. D. Forrest, M. D., County Health Officer, Halifax.

A. G. Nicholls, M. D., Provincial Laboratory, Halifax.

Jessie L. Ross, Chief Nurse, Mass.-Halifax Health Comm., Halifax.

J. A. Doull, M. D., Provincial Inspector of Health, Halifax.

A. C. Jost, M. D., Divisional Health Officer, Guysboro.

Aboriginal Therapy in Europe.—Recently in the pages of the *A. J. P. H.* we were interested to read of Aboriginal Therapy in Africa and accepted the fact that medical science was in a primitive stage among such savage people. It is surprising, however, to read of similar practices being carried on in a European country. Social and religious customs, dense ignorance, superstition and poverty all combine to make the scientific practice of medicine in Albania very difficult. It is hard to realize that this country which has the native land of Aesculapius adjoining it on the south and that of Tippocrates just across the Adriatic should still in these days witness "herb doctors" who surround their widespread practice with all the hocus-pocus of charms, incantations and offerings to the gods. Even the wives and daughters of the so-called cultured classes must depend for treatment on ignorant midwives, for they are not allowed to have male physicians.—*Correspondence, London Lancet,* April 17, 1920. (*H. N. C.*)

✤

The Undernourished Child of the School Age.—Everybody is doubtless familiar with the fact that during the past two years many children have been weighed and measured, and that a large number was considered undernourished. A child was deemed to be undernourished if it was more than 10 per cent below the weight of the average child of its age. Such factors as the nationality or race of the child, the weight at birth, and the stature of the parents were not considered at all. Out of 500 children of the preschool age who were examined according to the former standard, 37 per cent were considered undernourished. But when the latter and more scientific standards were employed, only 7 per cent were considered undernourished.

Some of the causes of malnutrition in children are fatigue, constipation, syphilis, the results of rickets in infancy and the results of early contagious diseases such as measles, whooping cough, diphtheria and scarlet fever. Malnutrition in children is exceedingly easy to prevent, but extremely difficult to cure. One of the best means of prevention is proper feeding during infancy. This determines in a large degree the ehalth and vigor of the child in later years. During the first two years the brain and heart undergo their most important development. Rickets should be prevented since it causes not only anemia and deformities, but pre-disposes to malnutrition and tuberculosis. The best way to prevent malnutrition in the first year is to breast-feed every baby. Out of 5,000 mothers it was found that 88 per cent of all babies can be entirely breast-fed for six months, and 46 per cent can be partially breast-fed for six months. After the first six months, particular attention should be given to the presence of sufficient and proper vitamines and salts in the diet.

Other important factors in preventing malnutrition are to insure an adequate and satisfactory supply of fresh moving air for the infant and child at all times, and an adequate amount of rest, during the day and night.—Julius Levy, M. D., *N. J. Public Health News,* March, 1920. (*M. P. H.*)

✤

Health in Business.—A business man walked into a doctor's office the other day. He looked in the pink of condition.

"I want a thorough physical examination," he said.

The doctor accommodated him. Heart was sound, lungs were healthy, kidneys and all the other organs functioning properly.

"You're the most splendid specimen I've seen in a long time," said the doctor.

"Thanks; I intend to remain so," said the client. "You shall go over me like this every six months. And I propose to have every man in a responsible position in my organization undergo a similar examination twice a year.

'A competing firm recently put a man into an important job who looked as well as I. He broke down, and in the demoralization of the firm's business that came with his breaking, our firm has taken over one of their biggest and best accounts. A condition of twenty years' standing, which he thought completely overcome, caused that man's breakdown.

"I don't propose that my firm shall suffer through any such experience."

Cold, hard business applied to health. Doesn't personal interest recommend to every man such prudence?

How many men can you recall who have discovered a serious state of health too late to mend?—*Haverhill Gazette.*

Australian Maritime Quarantine Against Influenza.—Few countries were in a position to install a complete system of quarantine defence against influenza. The story of how Australia prevented the invasion of the pandemic of 1918 is set forth in the official report of the Director of Quarantine of that country. Vessels presenting a clear record as regards health and contact were not detained. Other vessels were detained for three or more days according to departure from an infected or non-infected port, presence or absence of cases on board, length of period at sea, etc. On detained vessels temperatures were taken daily and inhalation treatment with zinc sulphate was carried out.

That the quarantine system was effective was shown by several things. The immunity persisted until the end of January, 1919. The type of influenza that then became prevalent was much less fatal and of lower infectivity. In Australia the epidemic lasted more than four months, whereas in South Africa and New Zealand it was complete in eight weeks, there being a much higher mortality rate in the latter countries than in the former. There was no evidence that the influenza that appeared in Australia was due to a break through the quarantine. There was good cause, however, for believing that it was produced from the influenza already present in the county during July and August.—*Medical Officer*, March 13, 1920. (*H. N. C.*)

✦

Educating the Rural District in Social Hygiene.—In line with its purpose of bringing health education directly before the people, particularly in remote rural districts, and co-operating with all existing public health agencies and societies, the American Red Cross has just appropriated $10,000 as a donation to the American Social Hygiene Association to aid that organization in establishing a traveling exhibit on socal hygiene. The exhibit will be mounted on a motor truck and will consist of a motion picture machine with films and slides on social hygiene, a fireproof booth that can be set up in schoolhouses or churches, and large quantities of literature and posters.

The American Social Hygiene Association was formed in 1914 by the union of the American Vigilance Association and the American Federation for Sex Hygiene, and later merged with the New Morrow under the name of the Society of Sanitary and Moral Prophylaxis. During the war, having secured from private sources some half million dollars, it supplemented the governmental efforts in combating venereal disease by coöperating with official agencies that were promoting the campaign in and around military and naval establishments.

✦

Waste in Educating Imperfect Pupils.—"Our schools are wasting nermous sums in trying to educate children handicapped by ill health," so said Dr. Thomas D. Wood, professor of physical education at Columbia University, in talking to 120 of the leading educators of the United States who were assembled at Cleveland not long ago.

"Seventy-five per cent of the 16,000,000 school children of the United States have physical defects which can usually be remedied," he continued, "and the economic loss to the country through this means is a truly staggering total."

✦

Physical Unfitness in Great Britain.—That the United States was not alone in having a high proportion of its men of military age, physically unfit, is shown by a recent report to the British Parliament on the National Service Medical Boards. The medical examination of these boards showed that of every nine men of military age in Great Britain, there were on the average three perfectly fit and healthy; two were upon a definitely infirm plane of health and strength; three were incapable of undergoing more than a very moderate degree of physical exertion and the remaining man was a chronic invalid with a precarious hold on life. Statistical evidence is not available as to whether or not the test of active service bore out these findings. However, more recruits were de-graded than up-graded after they entered the army.

The report also includes investigation in particular places and among special groups, made with a view to determining the influence of occupation, overcrowding and bad hygienic conditions upon health and the incidence of particular diseases. In Yorkshire, agriculturists and miners showed up well while tailors were at the bottom of the list. In London the barbers showed the highest percentage in relation to almost every disease whereas clerks were comparatively healthy.—*Medical Officer.* (*H. N. C.*)

Malaria in the Balkans.—Americans in the Balkans have changed their opinions of the Turk character. They do not blame him now because he appears to be lazy, inefficient and despondent. Wherever he is to be found in Macedonia, Albania, Montenegro, Bosnia, and Herzegovina, his characteristics are the same as those of his Christian neighbors, with whom he lives in greater peace than do the constantly bickering Christian tribes and nascent nations among themselves.

Dr. Regina Flood Keyes, of Buffalo, New York, and American Red Cross physician who has lived in the Balkans for several years and who has been decorated by the French, Greek and Serbian Governments for operations performed under heavy bombardment, attributed the backwardness of the Balkan peoples to two causes, sand-fly fever and malaria.

"The Red Cross fight against typhus, smallpox, cholera and sex diseases in the Balkans attracts much attention in the press," says Dr. Keyes, "but our real work out here is the struggle to down malaria. More British soldiers died or were incapacitated by malaria in the Struma valley during the war than were killed in the taking of the Grande Couronne.

"The whole littoral of the eastern Adriatic from Fiume down to Avlona is a hot bed of malaria and sand-fly fever, while the northern shore of the Aegean from Salonica to Constantinople is even worse. America, if she is going to play her role in the world, must do for the Balkans what she did in the Panama zone. These peoples must be taught drainage, how to kill the mosquito and to maintain domestic sanitation. It is a work of years but we have made a good start in the last thirty months. Malaria causes the all too obvious despondency of the Balkan peoples. To enable them to rise we must kill the mosquito."

✠

Oyster Pollution.—The discovery that oysters in Poole Harbor were contaminated by polluted sea water rather than by sewage from the city of Poole was one of the important results of an investigation of these beds located on the south shore of England near the Isle of Wight. It was recognized for several years that oysters taken from Poole Harbor were contaminated but not until recent studies was it found out that this pollution comes in with the flood tide from the open sea and does not originate within the harbor.

It was also observed that the nearer the sea and the more rapid the current the greater was the pollution of the harbor water. After many examinations of water and experimental plantings a spot was found in the harbor perfectly free from pollution.—*Medical Officer,* April 3, 1920. (*H. N. C.*)

✠

Olive Growers to Study Botulism.—The olive growers and canners have raised a sum of money to study botulism. Particular attention will be given to the distribution of *Bacillus botulinus* in nature, the methods by which food materials may become infected with the organism, and the necessary steps required to destroy the organism after raw food materials have been infected. The work will be conducted at the laboratories of the Standard University and the University of California Medical Schools.—*Science,* April 23, 1920. (*M. P. H.*)

✠

An Operation in the Harem.—"I have had many strange experiences as a woman doctor in the Balkans," says Dr. Lulu Hunt Peters, of Los Angeles, who was recently decorated with the order of St. Sava by the Crown Prince of Serbia. "But the oddest operation I ever performed was in Gostivar, Serbia.

"Early one morning a well-dressed Turkish merchant called upon me. He explained that he wished me to operate upon two of his daughters, whom he wished to marry off, and also upon one of his boys. He spoke broken English and good French, but I could not understand what the operations required were.

"Seeing me hesitate, he offered me several valuable rings and bracelets. I assured him, however, that I would be glad to do what I could without compensation. Accordingly, I followed him to his harem.

After some parleying with one of his elderly wives, he finally called forth his daughters. They came from behind a curtain like two automatons, having evidently been kept in waiting there. Both girls upon command raised their veils. At once I saw why they had not married earlier. Both had hare lips. So had the little boy.

"Two days later I performed operations upon the two girls and the little boy, on my day 'off' from Red Cross work,

PUBLIC HEALTH NOTES

FROM FOREIGN LANDS

Translated by Mr. Homer N. Calver

Vaccination Against Tuberculosis.—A remarkable opportunity, which the author states is without precedent in the history of medicine, has been presented to investigate on a large scale the value of a new tuberculosis vaccine. An entire city of 24,000 people, inspired with an absolute confidence in the science of medicine has offered itself as a laboratory. It is not Framingham, Mass., but Alcira, Spain. A famous investigator whose studies cover a period of more than 20 years, is in charge of this massive experiment. The city council bears all of the expense of the work and all the 17 local doctors are happy to assist. A report of the studies made by Dr. J. Ferran on the non-acid-fast bacilli closely related to the bacillus of Koch includes a description of the vaccine used. This contained several strains of non-acid-fast bacilli which the investigator had observed, transformed by passage through animals into organisms resembling the bacillus of Koch; as well as bacilli that had lost their acid-fast characteristics after cultivation *in vitro*.

The entry of Dr. Ferran into Alcira, accompanied by distinguished physicians, professors and journalists is described as almost triumphal. A public meeting was held during which lectures were given on the history of tuberculosis vaccination and experiments in Spain and America. In 8 days 11,788 people of Alcira and 1,952 from adjoining villages had been vaccinated. The great number of outsiders submitting themselves for vaccination promised to complicate the statistics so that operations were suspended for a few days when a second inoculation was given to 9,723 people. Two weeks later a third inoculation was given to 7,601 individuals. In a little over a month 31,264 vaccinations and revaccinations were registered. The author estimates that the total number of inoculations made was in reality nearer 50,000.

The effects of these vaccinations are being carefully watched. Each person in this Spanish Framingham who has been vaccinated has, whether sick or well, his clinical record. The immediate effects were various. Local inflammation was produced in 15 cases. It frequently occurred that about 5¼ hours after the injection there was some discomfort such

as fever, headache, sweating, etc. In recognized cases of pulmonary tuberculosis symptoms were generally increased but during the whole series there was not a single death. Nine hundred and fourteen cases of a great many different kinds were given the tuberculosis vaccine and only in two instances were the particular affections exaggerated. The statistical analysis of this experiment is well presented and a clear description of the methods employed is given.

It is too early to judge of the prophylactic value of the vaccine but at later session of the committee it is hoped to present a more detailed report.—Pulido, *Proces-Verbaux des seances du comité permenent de l'office. Int. d' Hygiene Pub.,* October, 1919.

✠

Botanical Mosquito Control.—The continued spraying of pools and ponds throughout the mosquito breeding season is often a laborious task. An observer on the island of Corsica noted that stagnant pools covered with a growth of water-lentils, *Lemna minor,* commonly called duckweed, did not contain mosquito wigglers, whereas neighboring pools not so covered contained larvæ of the Anopheles. There was introduced into these pools manure and other decaying organic matter and they were seeded with duckweed. These plants developed rapidly covering the entire surface with the result that the larvæ unable to reach the surface for air disappeared. This seems to offer a valuable and inexpensive method of malaria control.—*Revue Sci.,* March, 1920.

✠

Experimental Trachoma in Rabbits.—The sensibility of rabbits to the virus of trachoma makes the experimental study of the disease more simple. The incubation period in these animals is from 11 to 13 days. The granulation that then takes place lasts at least 60 days. Two different viruses were passed through two different rabbits. In a baboon a typical infection was produced by the virus from one of these.—D'Arsonval, et al., *Revue Sci.,* March, 1920.

✠

Five minutes on the 'phone may do it. Why not call your prospective member now?

American Journal of Public Health

Official Monthly Publication of the American Public Health Association

Publication office: 124 W. Polk Street, Chicago, Ill.

Editoria loffice: 169 Massachusetts Ave., Boston, Mass.

Subscription price, $4 per year. American Public Health Association membership, including subscription, $5 per year.

Subscriptions and memberships may be sent to the A. P. H. A., 169 Massachusetts Ave., Boston, Mass.

| Vol. X | · | JULY, 1920 | No. 7 |

COMPENSATION OF HEALTH OFFICERS

JOHN A. FERRELL, M.D., Dr. P.H.,

International Health Board, Rockefeller Foundation,

New York City.

Read before the Conference of State and Provincial Health Authorities, Washington, D. C., May 25, 1920.

Hope for the health officer in point of salary is what Dr. Ferrell holds forth. Compensation, although inadequate, is steadily increasing, and there is demand for competent men. Salaries must depend on the good faith of a public that is learning the value of efficient professional service. .Health officers' associations carry weight in forming public opinion.

THE compensation scale for health officers has been a constant source of concern to those who have dedicated themselves to this field. The high cost of living has rendered the situation quite critical for a large part of the population, and health officers have been no exception to the general rule. Despite the fact that in the salary scale for health officers there has been a gradual increase from year to year, the diminished purchasing power of the dollar has rendered the present salary scale lower than that which prevailed five years ago. There is encouragement for these officers, however, in the nation-wide movement for lower prices, and in the fact that the public is beginning to discriminate, as to the justness of the claims of different groups that are seeking higher compensation.

If health officers are to be adequately rewarded for the duties and responsibilities resting upon them, the education of the public with regard to the meaning of thorough public health work must be accelerated. It is at present far from complete. Associations of health officers, through the various channels which can be employed for reaching the people, must take every measure necessary for thoroughly acquainting the public with the ideals and principles for which they stand. Work of this character is more advanced in some states and communities than in others. The results it has yielded, where it has been wisely employed, have been most satisfactory. The community has recognized that the real health officer must have broad sympathies and thorough academic, professional, and business training; and that he must understand the methods to be employed in dealing, not only with law-makers and other leading citizens, but also with the less fortunate classes, to whose welfare the health work usually makes its greatest contribution. The community knows that he appreciates the position of the taxpayers, and it depends upon him to supply them a full statement of the work he has accomplished and of the use which he has made of the funds placed at his disposal. The community is coming to regard him as its servant: an essential factor in the most important branch of human progress,—good health.

Unlike the physician in private practice, his material rewards are not dependent upon haphazard personal fees, but on the good faith of a public which is rapidly learning to pay adequately for efficient professional service. In the case of the health officer, this service consists of protecting the community by saving it from preventable sickness, death, and other losses. The community—whether nation, state, county, city, or town—is his patient. He makes a comprehensive examination, outlines the ailments, and prescribes the remedies. His duty does not stop there, however; he must see that the remedies are employed. His professional success depends upon the good health of the community.

An index showing the growth in public appreciation of health work is afforded by reviewing the phenomenal growth in state and local appropriations for the work during the past ten years. In the years 1908 and 1909, for example, each of several of the Southern States had state appropriations of less than $15,000 a year; at present they have approximately $150,000 or more per year. Then, the counties and the cities in the South, with rare exception, had no full-time health officers; now the full-time health officers in the local political units are quite numerous. Many of the counties and cities have not stopped with the employment of the full-time health officer, but have also established creditable health organizations. The movement throughout the nation is gaining

such momentum that the associations of health officers carry a large responsibility for giving it guidance.

Many localities remain, however, in which the public has far from a proper conception of the value of health work. In these communities the expenditures are generally small and the people have not been convinced of the wisdom of devoting larger sums to the conservation of health. The reasons lie partly in the influence of politics, partly in the unwise selection of health officers, partly in shortage of funds, and partly in a cause which concerns both the strong and the weak health organizations; namely, the shortage of qualified men. Regardless of the causes responsible for the unfortunate situation, the people cannot be expected, where it exists, to give public health work the legal and financial backing its success requires, nor to view with favor proposals to increase the health officer's compensation.

Although much remains to be accomplished in the field of public health before the rank and file health officers can feel certain of satisfactory tenure of office and adequate compensation, the outlook, in the light of developments during the past ten years, is most gratifying. Many states and cities are employing business *experts* at salaries higher than are allowed the highest paid elective officials. Moreover, the present assured income of successful health officers, when compared with the more or less uncertain net income of private practitioners, has many attractions for the young man who is completing his medical education.

SALARIES IN PUBLIC, SEMI-PUBLIC, AND PRIVATE HEALTH WORK

In the United States Public Health Service, as a result of recent legislation, the compensation of commissioned officers has been advanced fifteen to thirty per cent, with the result that salaries have been increased in amounts ranging from $600 to $840 per year. The new basis allows an income running from approximately $3,000 a year for past assistant surgeons to approximately $6,000 a year ·'for assistant surgeons general. *The Medical Journal* of England, at the suggestion of the Society of the Medical Officers of Health of the British Medical Association, has recently announced that it will reject all advertisements for assistant medical officers of health when the salary offered is less than £500. In referring to the personnel of the United States Public Health Service, it is gratifying to state, as an evidence of the upward trend in public health work, that the number of commissioned officers has grown from 128 in 1910 to 218 in 1919; that the number of scientifically trained staff members has grown from 1,350 in 1910 to 3,746 in 1919; and that the appropriation for compensating the personnel has grown from $660,620 in 1910 to $1,778,476 in 1919.

In state health work the compensation scale for the chief executive officers of health for the year 1919 ranged from $1,000 in Arizona to $10,000 in Pennsylvania. The great majority of salaries lie between $3,000 and $6,000 per year. A creditable number of states pay $5,000 or more. The salaries for assistant state health officers of state boards of health likewise vary widely from $1,200 a year for the assistant executive officer in North Dakota to $6,500 a year for the assistant executive officer in Pennsylvania. The majority of the· officials heading divisions receive from $2,500 to $4,000 per year. The wide differences in salary scales can be better appreciated if consideration is given to the fact that the total state appropriations for health work range from about $15,000 a year in New .Mexico and South Dakota to more than $2,600,000 per year in the State of Pennsylvania.*

For county health officers, the compensation scale in the various states

*The author is indebted to Dr. C. St. Clair Drake, State Health Officer of Illinois, for data given in the paper regarding salary scales and health appropriations of the several states. A summary of the facts collected by Doctor Drake appears at the end of this paper. (Page 574.)

where this kind of work has been developed ranges from $2,400 to $5,000 per year. Quite a large number of counties are now paying from $3,000 to $3,600 for health officers. During the present year a number of vacancies have occurred for which these salaries were offered

In city health work likewise, the scarcity of qualified health officers has resulted in the payment of increased salaries. Cities announced in 1919 a half-dozen or more vacancies for health officers carrying salaries ranging from $4,000 and $6,000 per year. Moreover, in institutions desiring to give courses in public health there have been numerous vacancies. One of these positions at least carried a compensation of $6,000.

Among private health agencies—such, for example, as the American Red Cross, the American Social Hygiene Association, and the International Health Board —vacancies now exist· for men who can qualify for positions carrying, immediately or ultimately, salaries ranging from $2,500 to`$7,500 per year.

The writer.has no immediate accurate knowledge as to the compensation scale nor the number of vacancies for executives qualified for the administration of general hospitals, hospitals for the insane, hospitals for the tubercular, and other state and private institutions of a ·similar nature. It stands to reason, however, since exceptional ability is necessary for the successful management of such institutions, that the compensation scale, in comparison with that paid by other agencies, must be attractive if suitable men are to be obtained.

An enumeration of the various branches of the government and of some public and private health agencies which are in the market for qualified health officers would be incomplete if we should neglect to mention the great field which is rapidly developing in industrial hygiene and sanitation. The compensation scale allowed by industrial organizations is usually not a matter of public information. We do know, however, that the executive officers of such enterprises do not hesitate to invest their money in brains. The compensation allowed for this work is said to range from $3,000 to $15,000 per year, and it is altogether probable that the salaries of the most successful men in this field equal or exceed those of health officers employed by public or semi-public agencies.

REMUNERATION OF HEALTH OFFICERS AND PRACTICING PHYSICIANS COMPARED

The greatest single obstacle with which the numerous health agencies are now confronted is a shortage of men. The agencies which are not restricted legally or otherwise will naturally pay the price necessary to secure the men they wish to have. This, in turn, will work at least a temporary hardship on less favored health agencies. Ultimately, however, the necessary adjustment will be made all along the line; and the health officer will doubtless come to be envied by professional men in other fields of endeavor, particularly by physicians, whose field will probably become more restricted as public health work grows in scope and in effectiveness.

Even now the average net income of physicians is not particularly attractive, if the limited published data on the subject is reliable. For example, a newspaper of Richmond, Virginia, reported in 1915 that the American Medical Directory credited Richmond with 330 physicians. According to the state income tax returns for that year, only 32 of these were able to report incomes of $4,000 or over. A similar basis for arriving at estimates has been published for Wisconsin. Of approximately 2,800 physicians in the state, it appears that for the year 1914 only about 1,642, or sixty per cent. filed income tax returns which were legally required of all persons having a net income of $1,000 or more yearly. The sixty per cent of the state's physicians who filed income tax returns reported an average income for the year of approximately $3,000. The net in-

comes of physicians are reported to be frequently less than half of their gross receipts.

DEVELOPMENT OF FACILITIES FOR TRAINING HEALTH OFFICERS

In addition to the factors which have already been mentioned as among those to which the associations of health officers should attend, including the education of the public with regard to the principles and practices of preventive medicine and the wide dissemination of reports dealing with striking achievements, one of the most important problems involves the production of a larger number of trained health officers. The demand for these officers has been growing year by year, until the situation has become acute. In a large number of instances, funds for health work are available, but cannot be used because of the impossibility of finding suitable executives. The associations of health officers should direct their energies to interesting a larger number of medical students, medical interns, and practicing physicians in the possibilties of public health work as a career, and should endeavor to have those men who are interested take the special training necessary to fit them for the work.

One step that would go far toward relieving the shortage of qualified men would be for health departments so to arrange their programs as to give employment during the summer months to medical students. Many of the students who are so employed acquire during this period their first intimate knowledge of the interests and possibilities of public health work, and not only choose the field as a career for themselves, but become in a sense missionaries for the cause among their fellow students.

The need of additional facilities for training health officers has been generally recognized. Already fifteen institutions in this country and four in Canada are offering courses in public health. Detailed information regarding the courses offered by each institution will

Data Concerning American and Canadian Medical Schools Offering Courses in Public Health Work

State	City	College	Degrees, Certificates or Diplomas Offered	Entrance Requirements	Time Required to Complete Course
Colorado	Boulder	University of Colorado	........†	A.B.,†	........†
Connecticut	New Haven	Yale University	Certificate in Public Health	A.B., B.S., or 2 years' medicine	1 year
"	"	"	Doctor of Philosophy	A.B.	3 years
"	"	"	Doctor of Public Health	M.D.	2 years
Illinois	Chicago	Chicago Hospital College of Medicine	........†	........†	........†
Kentucky	Louisville	Univ. of Louisville and State Board of Health	........†	........†	........†
Louisiana	New Orleans	Tulane University	Doctor of Public Health	M.D.	........†
"	"	"	Certificate in Public Health	M.D.	........†
"	"	"	Diploma in Tropical Medicine and Hygiene	M.D.	........†
Maryland	Baltimore	Johns Hopkins University	Teacher's Certificate	Teaching Experience	........†
"	"	"	Doctor of Public Health	M.D., A.B., or B.S. or its equivalent	........†
"	"	"	Doctor of Science in Hygiene	A.B. or B.S. Courses in Chemistry, Physics, and Biology	2 years and one summer
"	"	"	Bachelor of Science in Hygiene	2 years' college work, Certificate in Chemistry, Biology, and Physics	3 years
"	"	"	Certificate in Public Health Special Courses	M.D., A.B., or B.S.	2 years
Massachusetts	Boston	Harvard University and Massachusetts Institute of Technology	Certificate in Public Health	........†	1 year
"	"	"	Certificate in Public Health	M.D.	2 years
Michigan	Detroit	Detroit College of Medicine and Surgery	Doctor of Public Health	2 years in medicine, A. B. or B.S.	2 years
"	Ann Arbor	University of Michigan	Master of Science in Public Health	M.D.	1 year
New York	Albany	Albany Medical College	Doctor of Public Health	A.B., M.D.	1 year
"	New York	New York University	Diploma in Public Health	........†	14 weeks
"	"	"		M.D.	2 weeks (summer)
Ohio	Syracuse	Syracuse University		M.D.	2 weeks Correspondence
"	Columbus	Ohio State University	Master of Science in Public Health		Special Course
Pennsylvania	Philadelphia	University of Pennsylvania	Doctor of Public Health	A. B. or its equivalent	1 year
"	"	"	Certified Sanitarian	M.D.	1 year
Wisconsin	Madison	University of Wisconsin	Master of Public Health	2 years' college	1 year
"	"	"	Doctor of Public Health	M.D.	1 year
				M.D.	2 years
Canada	Kingston	Queens University	Doctor of Science	M.D.	2 years—Thesis with Special Research
"	London	Western University	Diploma in Public Health	B.S., M.D.	........†
"	Toronto	University of Toronto	Diploma in Public Health	M.D.	1 year
"	Toronto	University of Toronto	Diploma in Public Hygiene	M.D.	1 year
"	Montreal	Laval University	Doctor of Public Health	M.D.	........†

†Details not available.

be found in the accompanying tabulation. These schools need and should have the counsel and co-óperation of the health officers. A number of men already in public health work would be greatly strengthened in their work by such courses. Many of the state boards of health have been able to conduct courses of from one to two weeks for those now engaged in health work and those who expect to engage in it. These short courses serve a useful purpose and should be given more systematically and more frequently.

CONCLUSION

1. Although the compensation scale for health officers is too low, it has been steadily increasing year by year for the past ten years. The present shortage of men qualified to fill existing vacancies which carry attractive salaries would indicate that the compensation scale will continue to advance.

EXHIBIT A.
COMPENSATION SCALE IN DOLLARS—STATE BOARDS OF
HEALTH EXECUTIVE OFFICERS AND CHIEF OF DIVISIONS

STATES	Executive Officer	Asst. Executive Officer	Communicable Diseases	Laboratory	Sanitary Engineering	Vital Statistics	Child Hygiene	Education	County or Rural Sani	Venereal Diseases	Tuberculosis	Epidemiologist or Specialist	Resources of S. B. H.—1919 [2]
Alabama	$5000	$2000	$3000	$3000	$2520	$3300	$2400	$3000	$3000	$3000	....	$3000	$ 90
Arizona	1000	....	....	....	....	....	600	....	2400	1500	....	....	22
Arkansas	4500	....	....	....	3000	2100	....	....	....	....	....	2000	61
California	4500	2400	3600	....	4000	2400	3000	....	....	....	3600	....	307
Colorado	2000	....	....	....	....	....	....	....	....	3000	....	2500	48
Connecticut	4000	4000	3000	2500	2500	2500	2500	....	....	....	....	....	228
Delaware	3000	....	....	3000[3]	....	....	....	....	....	2100	....	....	23
Florida	3000	3000	....	3000	3000	2750	2750	....	....	3000	....	....	155
Dist. of Columbia	4000	2500	2750	....	....	....	1800	....	....	....	....	....	
Georgia	....	....	....	....	....	....	....	....	....	....	....	....	
Idaho	3000	2500	....	....	....	....	....	....	....	....	....	....	29
Illinois	6000	3600	3600	3600	4000	2400	4000	2400	2200	4200	....	3000	332
Indiana	3000	2750	....	3500	....	1800	1800	....	....	1500	....	2500	159
Iowa	3900	....	....	....	2500	....	....	....	....	6000	....	2400	78
Kansas	4000	....	3300	....	....	2400	2000[3]	....	....	2500	....	....	136[4]
Kentucky	1200	2400	....	....	....	3000	....	....	2400	2400	2400	2400	135
Louisiana	5000	....	....	....	3000	2500	2500	....	....	4500	....	2600	60
Maine	4000	....	2000	2200	2200	....	....	....	....	2500	....	....	76
Maryland	3750	....	3000	3000	3000	2400	....	....	....	....	....	3000	180
Massachusetts	7500	....	4000	1500	5000	....	3500	....	....	8000	....	4000	346
Michigan	4500	2500	3000	3000	3000	....	....	1800	....	....	....	1800	230
Minnesota	4500	3500	3500	....	3500	2000	180)	....	....	2500	....	....	148
Mississippi	3600	3000	....	2700	....	....	....	....	2700	3000	3600	....	144[5]
Missouri	2400	....	....	....	....	1800	....	....	....	3600	....	....	20
Montana	5000	4500	4200	3000	2400	....	....	....	....	2400	....	2400	131
Nebraska	....	....	....	....	....	....	....	....	....	....	....	....	
Nevada	....	....	....	....	....	....	....	....	....	....	....	....	
New Hampshire	3000	....	....	2000	3000	....	....	....	....	2400	....	....	33
New Jersey	4000	3600	3000	....	3600	3000	3000	....	3500	3000	....	2500	320
New Mexico	3000	....	2400	....	2400	....	....	....	....	....	....	....	13
New York	8000	6000	4000	5500	5000	4000	4000	....	....	4000	3500	....	922
North Carolina	5000	3000	....	4000	....	2500	3200	....	....	3000	3250	....	345
North Dakota	1200	....	....	....	....	....	....	....	....	3000	....	....	12
Ohio	6000	4000	3300	3000	4000	....	3600	....	....	3000	....	3000	198
Oklahoma	3600	2400	....	1800	2000	1800	....	....	....	3000	....	....	146
Oregon	4000	....	....	3000	....	1800	1800	....	....	2400	1800	....	17
Pennsylvania	10000	6500	4000	4000	6000	4000	4000	....	....	4000	3500	3500	2682
Rhode Island	3500	4000	....	....	....	....	3000	....	....	3000	....	....	48
South Carolina	3250	....	....	....	....	....	....	....	....	....	....	....	236
South Dakota	2000	1200	....	....	....	....	....	....	....	3000	....	....	21
Tennessee	3500	....	....	2100	....	3000	3000	....	3000	3000	....	....	72
Texas	3000	2400	....	2100	2750	2400	3000	....	3000	4800	....	....	98
Utah	4000	....	....	3000	....	....	....	....	....	2400	....	....	21
Vermont	3500	....	....	....	....	....	2000	....	....	2500	2400	2400	70
Virginia	4200	3600	....	....	3500	2750	2500	....	....	3600	3500	....	64
Washington	5000	3600	....	3000	....	....	....	....	....	3000	....	....	34
West Virginia	4800	....	2700	....	2400	2400	1800	....	3000	3600	....	....	38
Wisconsin	6000	....	3000	3250	4000	3000	2500	2000	....	3600	....	....	94
Wyoming	....	....	....	....	....	....	....	....	....	....	....	....	

[1] Information supplied by Dr. C. St. Clair Drake, State Health Officer of Illinois.
[2] In thousands. [3] Associate Commissioner of Health paid by private organization, $6500.
[4] Supplied in part by other branches of State government including University. [5] 1920.

2. At present, salaries for public health officers range from about $2,000 per year to $10,000 per year. Certain private agencies and industrial organizations pay even more to health officers who carry very large responsibilities. It is becoming very difficult to secure a man having practical experience for less than $3,000 a year for health work of any kind.

3. The associations of health officers should give direction to the movement which has already gained tremendous momentum, by keeping the public informed regarding achievements in the prevention and control of disease, by interesting in special training those medical students, medical interns, and other persons who can be used in the work, and by giving guidance and support to institutions which are offering creditable courses in public health.

□

WORLD-WIDE WORK OF INTERNATIONAL HEALTH BOARD
AUSTRALIA

No better illustration of what Dr. Dowling has commented on in his article on Hookworm in this issue of the JOURNAL could be desired than this picture kindly lent by the International Health Board. Hookworm disease is noted for the physical and mental retardation which it causes. The picture, taken in Australia by representatives of the Board, compares the physical development of two boys of the same age. The one on the left is free from infection and the other is heavily infected with Hookworm disease. Note the typical facial expression of the infected boy.

INFLUENZA-PNEUMONIA AS INFLUENCED BY DISH-WASHING IN 370 PUBLIC INSTITUTIONS

(Concluded)

LIEUT. COLONEL JAMES G. CUMMING, M. C., U. S. ARMY,

Washington, D. C.

This author places greatest emphasis on blocking the major avenue of saliva-borne disease distribution, which he says can be done effectively by the use of boiling water in dishwashing. He figures that the influenza-pneumonia mortality in institutions using boiling water was only half that of similar institutions with handwashed dishes.

IN a former article[1] it was reported that, among an institutional population of 252184 the influenza case rate for that group eating from machine-washed dishes was 108 per 1,000 inmates, while for the one eating from hand-washed dishes the rate was 324 per 1,000 inmates. On the basis of these rates for the two groups, and a consideration of the relative importance of the several avenues of contagion distribution, it appears, from the following consideration of the theory of case and source elimination that an epidemic can be either effectively controlled or, even prevented, by blocking the major avenue of transmission.

THEORY OF CASE AND SOURCE ELIMINATION AS A CONTROL MEASURE

We argue, first, that by blocking the major avenue of transmission, the greater percentage of cases, convalescents and carriers is eliminated, thereby reducing the number of sources of infection and their resultant secondary cases; and second, that by completely closing the major avenue of transmission, there is a marked reduction in the inanimate object contamination and the resultant hand to mouth infections, i. e., secondary cases. In this connection, it should be borne in mind that when the major avenue is closed, these secondary cases become the sources of further distribution only through the minor avenues of distribution, and since the minor avenues of distribution—i. e., hand to mouth—account for only a small percentage of infections, an epidemic may be brought under control in proportion to the thoroughness with which the major avenue of transmission is blocked.

The influenza rate per 1,000 for the protected group which ate from machine-washed dishes, is one-third the rate for the unprotected group which ate from hand-washed dishes. Let us first assume that none of the transmissions in the protected group was through eating utensils. Having assumed that the eating utensil is eliminated as an avenue of distribution, in this group there remains only hand to mouth transmission, through hands contaminated by inanimate objects, such as doorknobs, backs of chairs, pencils, etc., and by direct contact.

If in this protected group the rate of infection—108 per 1,000—results solely from hand contamination, the same rate of infection through the same route of distribution must be equally applicable to the unprotected group since in the large institutional groups under consideration, the law of averages equalizes any other factors influencing distribution.

1. Cumming: Influenza-Pneumonia as Influenced by Dishwashing in 370 Public Institutions. A. J. P. H., Nov., 1919.

This being so, and since the total rate of infection in the unprotected group was 324 per .1,000, then by subtracting the rate of the protected group—which comprises only hand to mouth distribution—from that of the unprotected group, the remainder is the rate of infection due wholly to distribution through contaminated eating utensils. Hence the rate of infection through eating utensils is 216 per 1,000 inmates in the unprotected group or, in other words, at least 66 per cent of the transmission is through eating utensils.

Perhaps we should be satisfied with this proof by which it is shown that 66 per cent of the cases could have been prevented by the use of scalded dishes, but on further analysis it is found that the blocking of the major route accomplishes more than 66 per cent reduction in cases. For applying the idea of eliminating, as sources of infection, those cases, carriers, and convalescents which arise through the major avenue of transmission, we find that 66 per cent of the sources of infection as well as 66 per cent of the cases among the total in this group, could have been eliminated by eating utensil sterilization. This being so, 66 per cent of the remaining 33 per cent would automatically have been prevented because of the elimination of 66 per cent of the sources of infection. This then makes a total reduction of 88 per cent of the cases and of the sources of inanimate object contamination.

But here again apply the theory of elimination of sources and the blocking of the major avenue of distribution to the remaining 11 per cent. If 88 per cent of the sources have been eliminated by the elimination of 88 per cent of the cases, convalescents and carriers, there is automatically eliminated 88 per cent of the remaining 11 per cent of total cases, or a reduction of the total 100 per cent of cases to 3.2 per cent of the total cases.

On this basis we have reduced the case rate in the unprotected group lower than in the protected group. But this reduc-tion in the unprotected group is impossible unless a portion of the cases in the protected group had their origin through the major avenue. This is doubtless so, for, as our investigation of public eating places shows, machine-washing may not always mean sterilization, as occasionally the temperature of the water is not sufficiently high to have a sterilizing effect. Therefore, the use of only warm water in the machines of public institutions may occasionally occur.

Consequently it is believed that in various public institutions where machine-washed dishes are used, a few cases may have had their origin through eating utensil contamination, and since it is reasonable to assume that in this protected group there were numerous transmissions through eating utensils, it is concluded that many of the cases in this group arising through hand to mouth infection, had their source of infection from those cases originally infected through eating utensil contamination, because the major avenue of transmission in the protected group was not completely closed. If in this protected group there actually had been no transmission through eating utensils, the cases and carriers which might have arisen from this source, would have been eliminated as sources of infection for those cases which were infected solely through hand contamination. There would, therefore, have been a reduction in the incidence equal to the extent of elimination of inanimate object contamination. This elimination of inanimate object contamination would be in proportion to the reduction in the number of cases having their origin in contaminated eating utensils, i. e., the major avenue of transmission. It is impossible to estimate to what extent this reduction of the incidence might be carried, on the basis of the total elimination of sources of infection arising from cases and carriers who become infected through the major avenue of transmission, i. e., eating utensil contamination.

It is sufficient to say that the complete closing of this major avenue of transmission would have eliminated the secondary cases which became infected through this route, thereby enormously reducing inanimate object contamination. In addition to this, such secondary cases as had their origin through hand to mouth infection would not be sources of further spread through that major avenue—the eating utensil—but only through minor avenues, which are relatively of insignificant importance.

If, on this theoretical basis, the total cases would have been constantly reduced it is obvious that the universal application of blocking the major avenue of distribution would have eliminated the majority of cases and sources, thereby limiting the recent epidemic of influenza.

In the control of the saliva-borne infections our aim must be that of universally blocking the major avenue of distribution. This blocking process must apply to not only the sick, but also to the well, for during epidemic periods of these infections there is a high healthy carried rate. The universal application of the principle of eating utensil pasteurization is mass prevention in contrast to prevention by the isolation of the sick and presumably only a small percentage of carriers. From the experience of recent epidemics, both in the civil population and the Army, it is indicated that control by the isolation method is of but little value, and the suggestions here offered are with the view of presenting a new and perhaps a more successful line of attack.

The case fatility rates, Chart III, for influenza-p n e u m o n i a in institutional

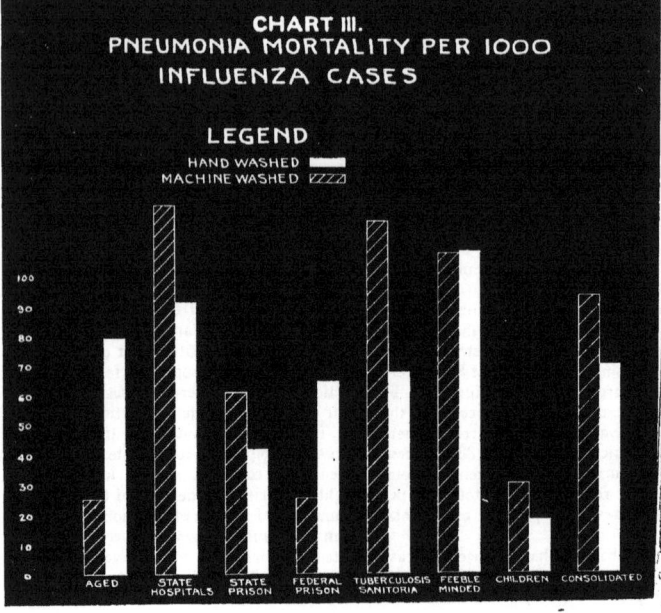

CHART III.
PNEUMONIA MORTALITY PER 1000
INFLUENZA CASES

LEGEND
HAND WASHED
MACHINE WASHED

AGED   STATE HOSPITALS   STATE PRISON   FEDERAL PRISON   TUBERCULOSIS SANITORIA   FEEBLE MINDED   CHILDREN   CONSOLIDATED

populations increase in the following order: (1) normal children, (2) the aged, (3) middle-aged adults, (4) feeble-minded children. These rates and their order of sequence are what might be expected in view of the age distribution and the laboratory findings.

In normal children there is the lowest pneumonia carrier rate because of their youth; the aged come next, because in this class the majority of the pneumonia carriers have previously died; next is that group of middle-aged persons in which, owing to their age and the prolonged exposure incident thereto, there is an increased carrier rate; and finally, the class of feeble-minded children which, notwithstanding their youth, have rapidly become infected to a high degree through hand to mouth distribution, owing to their low standard of personal hygiene. The intelligence of the individual and the intelligence of the race determine to a large extent the carrier rate. This in turn determines the case fatality rate as well as the virus infection rate.

In the further discussion of this chart it should be borne in mind that we are considering two infections: influenza on the one hand, and pneumonia on the other, and only the case fatality rate and not the population mortality rate.

In considering the deaths resulting from the influenza epidemic, it should be recognized that these deaths do not result from the virus infections, but from those groups of potentially dangerous organisms — pneumococci and streptococci — which are chronically harbored in the mouth and tonsils. From the standpoint of the carrier state, the investigation has proved most instructive. Although the case rate in the group eating from machine-washed dishes comprises only 25 per cent of the total influenza cases, it will be noted in Chart III that 57 per cent of the total case fatalities of both groups occurred in this protected group. Although the influenza case rate was less in the protected group, in this group there were more pneumonia deaths per 1,000

influenza cases than in the unprotected group. In considering this case fatality rate there should be no confusion with the population mortality rate as shown in Chart IV, in which only 31 per cent of the total deaths occurred among those eating from machine-washed dishes.

The influenza case rate in the protected group is low, the influenza case fatality rate resulting from pneumonia is greater in this group, while the population mortality rate is only 31 per cent of the total deaths of both groups.

Why should there be this excessive case fatality rate in that group which is presumably protected to a high degree against the acute virus infections and against the carrier state by reason of using machine-washed dishes? It is concluded that this group is protected because its incidence of influenza constituted only 25 per cent of the total institutional cases, and its group mortality rate only 31 per cent of the total institutional deaths. Obviously then, per 1,000 influenza cases of this group, more died from pneumonia than in that group in which there was no blocking of transmission through eating utensils. The former were protected against influenza, but died of pneumonia. There is then only one conclusion: that in the protected group, among those *few who became infected with influenza,* there was a higher percentage of carriers of pneumonia-producing organisms — pneumococcus and streptococcus—than in the unprotected group. But why should it appear that the influenza virus has a special predilection only for carriers in the protected group, while in the unprotected group non-carriers as well as carriers are attacked? There presents but one explanation; that the carriers of these potentially dangerous organisms have a special susceptibility to even small doses of the influenza virus, and although there is a special protection in the group eating from machine-washed dishes, yet in this group even the small doses of virus are sufficient to infect the carriers, but not the non-carriers. On the other hand, in the unprotected group not only the carrier—for the carriers of both groups are equally susceptible—but also the less susceptible non-carrier becomes infected, owing to the massive doses of influenza virus, which he received through the interchange of contaminated dishes. Hence in the unprotected group, because of the greater incidence of influenza among non-carriers, there is a lower case fatality rate than in the protected group. From the foregoing, it would appear that a carrier is susceptible to a dose too dilute to infect a non-carrier—in short, it is demonstrated that the carrier is more susceptible to influenza virus infection than the non-carrier.

As further proof of this theory attention is called to the following consideration of the population mortality rates of these two groups:

If the carrier and non-carrier were equally susceptible to influenza, the ratio of influenza cases and the ratio of mortality per 1,000 inmates for the two groups would be the same. (See Chart IV.) But this is not so. For, while the ratio of influenza cases in the protected and the unprotected groups was 1 to 3, the ratio of pneumonia deaths per 1,000 inmates in these two groups was 1 to 1.2, showing one of two possibilities; either that the pneumonia carrier rate was higher in the protected group or that the carrier is the more susceptible to the virus infection. The first possibility is remote, and since there was a marked reduction in the influenza cases in this protected group, it is reasonable to assume that there would likewise be a reduction in pneumonia carriers. It might be argued that the main route of transmission of pneumonia is by the hand to

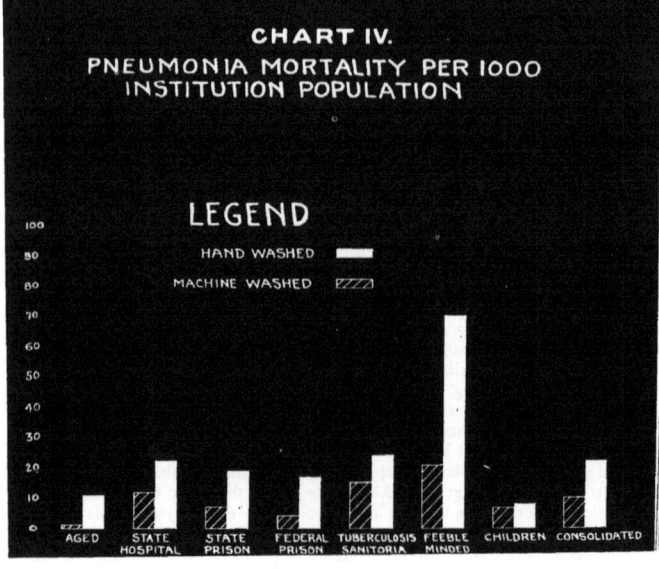

CHART IV.
PNEUMONIA MORTALITY PER 1000
INSTITUTION POPULATION

LEGEND

HAND WASHED

MACHINE WASHED

AGED   STATE   STATE   FEDERAL   TUBERCULOSIS   FEEBLE   CHILDREN   CONSOLIDATED
         HOSPITAL PRISON   PRISON   SANITORIA   MINDED

mouth route and that the method of washing dishes was not an influencing factor. But if this were so, the percentage of carriers would be the same in both groups and there would then be a sameness of ratios for the influenza case rates, and pneumonia mortalities in the two groups. Since this is not so, there appears additional evidence that the carrier is more susceptible to the virus infections than the non-carrier.

Can it be possible that the pneumonia carrier rate determines the occurrence of virus epidemics?

In a former report[2] on measles-pneumonia we attempted to establish the principle that the carrier state predisposes to the virus infections (measles, scarlet fever and influenza) and that these in turn pave the way for the pneumonia secondary invaders. This idea was based on the finding of 36 per cent of all measles cases positive for hemolytic streptococci on entrance to the hospital; while among normal troops at that time there were only 6 per cent hemolytic streptococcus carriers. This view was further supported in a subsequent report[3] of the examination of 2,135 hospital patients, including cases of measles, scarlet fever and mumps, among whom it was found that 59 per cent were positive for hemolytic streptococci.

The epidemiologic study of the case and fatality rates in public institutions supports this view as to the increased prevalence of the virus infections among individuals who harbor this potentially dangerous group of pneumonia organisms.

In Chart IV there is presented the pneumonia mortality per 1,000 institutional population for the several classes of institutions; these are divided according to the method of dish-washing. The marked difference in the mortality rates for the two groups in all classes of insti-

tutions indicates the value of using dishes disinfected by machine washing.

The rate for the protected group is 10.4 per 1,000 population, and for the unprotected group 22.9 per 1,000. Only 31 per cent of the mortalities occurred in that group protected by the use of machine-washed dishes.

The mortality rates for the aged, and for normal children are the lowest. In this connection it may be stated that although the generally accepted opinion is, that the case rate as well as the mortality rate among children in civil communities was low, it is questionable whether or not this was true. It is thought error has occurred because case rates in influenza have been calculated on the mortality rates among the several age groups. Our figures, so far as children are concerned, do not support this method of case rate calculation for of all the institutional classes, none has as low a mortality rate as normal children, and this despite the fact that in public institutions children have the highest influenza case rate. The mortality rate among normal children is low, not because they have a low influenza rate, but because the percentage of pneumococcus and streptococcus carriers is small in this age group. This might be more strikingly apparent in civilian children if the exact case and mortality rates were known.

Our investigations show that among 160 children, six years old, no carriers of the hemolytic streptococcus were found, while among a like number of the adolescent age, the percentage of carriers of the hemolytic streptococcus was 1.2 per cent, while in adults there was a still further increase to 5 per cent. Granting that we accept the prevalence of the hemolytic streptococcus as an index as to the possibility of the occurrence of pneumonia as a complication of the virus infections, in these percentages we have an explanation of the case fatalities as well as of the population mortalities for the different age groups. In general, it may be said that the older an individual

2. Cumming, Spruit, and Lynch. The Pneumonias: Streptococcus and Pneumococcus Groups, Jour. A. M. A., April 13, 1918.

3. Cumming, Spruit, and Aten. Streptococcus Pneumonia: Journal Am. Med. Asso., March 8, 1919.

is — provided he is non-immune — the more liable he is not only to the virus infections, but also to pneumonia complications. This is due to the increasing carrier state as age advances and explains the exceedingly low mortality from the virus infections among children, the frequent death of the oldest child only, in the family group of children, and the high mortality from the complications of these infections among adults. The carrier rate in the group of aged is, of course low, because, as has been said, the majority of carriers have previously died.

CONCLUSIONS

1. The successful operation of the theory of case and source elimination depends upon the identification and the blocking of the major avenue of saliva-borne disease distribution. Inasmuch as this blocking prevents more than half the cases, it consequently eliminates an equal number of sources, and since by its continuous operation there is a cumulative effect in eliminating cases and sources. for each successive human cycle of the infection we have in the universal application of this principle a means of eventually eradicating this group of infections.

2. Epidemiologic observations, in institutions, in the civil population, and in the Army, indicate that eating utensils are the major avenue of saliva-borne disease distribution.

3. This major avenue of distribution can be effectively blocked by the use of boiling water in the process of dishwashing.

4. Healthy adult carriers of the pneumonia-producing group of organisms are more susceptible than non-carriers to the virus infections.

5. The greater susceptibility of the pneumonia carrier, and the fact that this group of organisms is almost wholly responsible for the mortality of virus epidemics indicates that, as a public health measure, the prevention of pneumonia transmission is more important than of influenza transmission. Both these infections are saliva-borne so that control measures which apply to one apply likewise to the other.

6. In those institutions where machine-washed dishes were used the influenza-pneumonia mortality was 55 per cent less than in those where hand-washed dishes were used.

□

Coins as Possible Carriers of Disease.— In order to ascertain the possible risk of infection, tests were carried out to determine the viability on coins (copper and silver) of the commoner pathogenic organisms. Five were selected for the test—B. influenzae, a streptococcus, a pneumococcus, a staphlylococcus and B. typhosus. The results of the tests indicate that these microörganisms have a short life under the conditions of the experiment. This may be due in part to the laboratory strains used not being as resistant to an adverse environment as are those which have not been cultured on artificial media for some time, and also to other factors inseparate from experimental work; but the chief factor is undoubtedly the bactericidal action of the metals used. These results support the views of other investigators that coins do not offer a suitable nidus for the propagation of bacteria, and can be regarded as a negligible factor in the spread of infectious disease.—*Medical Officer*, May 1, 1920, 178, *(D. G.)*

BACTERIA OF THE AIR IN AN AMUSEMENT HALL

I. Forest Huddleson and Thomas G. Hull,

(*Formerly First Lieutenants, Sanitary Corps, U. S. A.*)

In view of the controversies over the closing of theatres and halls during the influenza epidemic this paper is illuminating. Such places seem, even under good conditions, to be clearing houses for oral organisms. Contamination of the atmosphere in them apparently relates itself to local epidemics. Here is food for thought for health officers.

THE first studies upon the microflora of the air and their relation to the spreading of infectious disease were in greater part conducted under artificial conditions. A common method employed consisted in inoculating the nose or mouth with various organisms and then causing the individual to speak, cough or sneeze for a specified length of time. Agar plates were exposed for various periods in different parts of a room to receive any organisms which might settle on them. Another method employed consisted in spraying organisms into the air of a room and exposing agar plates in a similar manner. .

Flügge,[1] Hübener[2] and Gordan[3] were among the first to study the microflora of the air and to point out their importance as a means of spreading infection. Their experiments were usually conducted under artificial conditions. Winslow and Robinson[4] conducted a series of similar experiments under artificial conditions and concluded that aerial infection is a minor factor in the spread of infectious disease. Wood[5] has shown that pneumococci when sprayed into the air, may remain suspended therein for a number of hours if the ventilation of the room is good, but they become harmless in a very short time, especially if exposed to a strong light. Graham-Smith[6] examining the air of the House of Commons found no organisms which could be associated with specific diseases in man. Chapin[7]

in summing up his chapter on "Air as a Means of Infection," says: "There may be pathogenic organisms actually present in the air, yet they may not be dangerous, either because they have wholly or partially lost their virulence, or because they are too few in number, or for some other unknown reason."

During the severe epidemic of respiratory diseases of 1917-8, among troops stationed in camp in this country, Beals, Zimmerman and Marlow[8] found the *Streptococcus hemolyticus* to be the predominating organisms in the respiratory organs of normal and diseased individuals. This organism was found present in from 20% to 86% of the men examined.

The experiments herein described were conducted for the purpose of determining the types of organisms actually existing in the air of a large amusement hall, and their relation to prevailing respiratory diseases. They were carried out in the "Festhalle," Coblenz, Germany, during the early days of American occupation. This building, which had been taken over by the Y. M. C. A., for welfare work, contained a large auditorium, holding about 2,000 men, in which entertainments and soldier shows were given, and which was filled to capacity every evening. Around three sides of the room was a balcony, not overhanging, but extending back over adjoining rooms. Ventilation was obtained by many small windows, near the roof of the building, all wide open. By an order of the Commanding General, the size of the audience was limited to the seating capacity of the room, no patrons being allowed to stand. Thus it was possible to conduct the experiments under comparable conditions in different parts of the room and at different times.

During February, 1919, there existed in the Army of Occupation what amounted to an epidemic of severe "colds" with extremely bad coughs and sore throats. Pneumonia cases were numerous. The first experiment was conducted on February 23. By the first of March the epidemic had practically cleared up. The second experiment, conducted March 3, clearly shows the difference in air contamination in the building.

The medium used in the experiments was dextrose blood agar in Petri dishes. The open plates containing this medium were exposed in pairs in the four corners of the room and in the balcony, just above the height of a man standing—one plate horizontally and one plate vertically. In this way organisms being swept by air currents were caught, as well as those settling by gravity. The plates were slowly revolved on a stick. Three periods of time were used—one minute, five minutes and ten minutes.

In Table 1 are given the results of the first experiment on February 23. It will be seen that in one minute an average of 82 organisms settled on the plates, and in five minutes, 151 organisms. Several of the 10-minute plates in this experiment were accidentally contaminated just before exposure, so the results are not given. In picking colonies indiscriminately from the incubated plates four type IV pneumococci were found, and many hemolytic and non-hemolytic streptococci, with numerous staphylococci and gram negative and gram positive diplococci.

Results of exposing blood agar plates to air during the height of the epidemic.

TABLE I

Plate No.	Exposed 1 minute No. of colonies	Exposed 5 minutes No. of colonies
1 R. F.	72	276
2 R. F.	23	17
3 R. R.	20	300
4 R. R.	34	10
5 L. F.	360	396
6 L. F.	27	39
7 L. R.	30	300
8 L. R.	58	13
9 B.	76	88
10 B.	124	76
Average	82	151

Note: Odd numbers, horizontal exposure; even numbers, vertical exposure. R. F. right front of hall, R. R. right rear of hall, B, balcony.

Eight days later, (March 3), the experiment was repeated. The details of operation were identical in every particular—the same medium being used and the same methods. On the plates exposed one minute and five minutes the organisms found were extremely few in number. On the plates exposed ten minutes an average of 16 colonies was counted. Among these, molds and staphylococci predominated; no pneumococci were found; 16% of the total number of colonies present were streptococci, which showed partial but not complete hemolysis (alpha type).

This great reduction from 82 organisms in one minute to 16 organisms in 10 minutes, which settled on the plates directly corresponded to the falling off of the epidemic. In either case, however, a man sitting through a performance of one and a half to two hours would inhale enough pathogenic organisms to give him any respiratory disease which might prevail among those sitting about him, provided he did not possess some natural or acquired resistance.

The prevailing organism present in the respiratory passages of men admitted to the hospital at this time was *Streptococcus hemolyticus.*

SUMMARY

1. During the height of an epidemic of bad "colds" and coughs the air of an

amusement hall filled with soldiers was so badly contaminated that an average of 82 organisms fell on blood agar plates exposed one minute. Among the organisms were pneumococci and numerous staphylococci.

2. Eight days later, after the epidemic had subsided, only an average of 16 colonies developed from the plates exposed under similar conditions but for a period of ten minutes. Sixteen per cent of these colonies were streptococci.

3. Excellent ventilation and prevention of overcrowding by limiting the size of the audience to the number of seats did not prevent enormous bacterial contamination of the air.

4. Any man susceptible to the prevailing respiratory diseases under such conditions could not help but contract those diseases by sitting through a performance of one and a half to two hours.

The authors wish to give credit to Dr. W. M. L. Coplin for suggesting these experiments and for his kindly interest in them.

REFERENCES

1. C. Flügge, "Ueber Luftinfection." *Ztschr, f. Hyg.*, 1897, Vol. 25, p. 179.

2. W. Hubener, "Ueber die Moglichkeit, der Wundinfection vom munde aud und ihre Verhutung durch Operationsuraken," *Ztschr, f. Hyg.*, 1898, Vol. 28, p. 348.

3. M. H. Gordan, Report on a bacterial test for estimating pollution of air. *Report of the Medical Officer*, 1902-3, 1904, p. 421.

4. C.-E. A. Winslow and E. A. Robinson, An investigation of the extent of bacterial pollution of the atmosphere by mouth spray. *Jour. Infect. Dis.*, 1910, Vol. 7, p. 17.

5. F. C. Wood, Viability of the pneumococcus after drying. *Jour. Expt. Med.*, 1905, Vol. 7, p. 592.

6. G. S. Graham-Smith. The microorganisms in the air of the House of Commons. *Jour of Hyg.*, 1903, Vol. 3, p. 498.

7. C. V. Chapin, Sources and Modes of Infection, 1912, p. 300.

8. L. S. Beals, B. F. Zimmerman and S. B. Marlow, Acute respiratory disease among troops with especial reference to empyema. *Jour. Infec. Dis.*, 1918, Vol. 23, p. 475.

□

MILLS-REINCKE PHENOMENON AND TYPHOID CONTROL BY VACCINE

HAROLD G. McGEE,

Akron, Ohio.

Assuming typhoid to be an index of conditions favoring other causes of death, this author calls attention to the likelihood that anti-typhoid vaccination, by attacking typhoid alone, really masks sanitary conditions and may permit unnecessary deaths. Complete eradication of typhoid through vaccination would not affect the three other deaths suggested by the Mills-Reincke hypothesis.

That the substitution of a bacterially safe water supply for a polluted one results in a considerably greater reduction in deaths from all causes than can be accounted for by the reduction in deaths from typhoid fever alone, is the tenor of the Mills-Reincke phenomenon and Hazen's theorem. Recently, the writer has met several public health officials who believe that this effect is due to coincident sanitary improvements of other kinds and that, consequently, the above conclusion is simply the result of malobservation. The significance of this attitude becomes apparent when considering the control of typhoid fever, as a health measure, by vaccination.

This paper offers some hitherto unpublished evidence tending to support the original proposition; and, assuming that its validity has not at least been disproved, questions the public health policy of eradication of typhoid fever by vaccination.

Alpena, Michigan, with a population of 12,706 by 1910 census, is located on Thunder Bay, an arm of Lake Huron, from which the public water supply is drawn. It is served by combined sewers, which discharge either into Thunder Bay River and thence into the bay, or directly into the Bay. The accompanying table and diagram indicate the typhoid fever and total death rates from 1900 to 1918, inclusive. During 1907-'08, the waterworks intake was moved from a point northeast of the mouth of the river to about 8,000 feet southwest thereof; and, during the summer of 1915, radical improvements were made in the means of sterilization of the supply.

During 1915, a careful study of the occurrence of the typhoid fever and of the water supply led to the conclusion that the latter was largely responsible for the former; improvements were recommended and acted upon, and a material drop followed. If it be granted that the change in intake location in 1908 resulted in a material deterioration in the quality of the supply, then the substitution of a polluted for a less polluted supply increased the typhoid deaths per 100,000 from an average of 31.7 to 67.7, a difference of 36 per year for the eight years prior and subsequent thereto; and at the same time and for the same periods, deaths from all causes increased from 1,370 to 1,520, a difference of 150, more

than four times the increase due to typhoid alone. Since 1915, the drop in deaths from typhoid has averaged 55.2; in deaths from all causes, 320, nearly six times the decrease in typhoid. However, this latter period is rather short to be significant, particularly in view of the complication introduced by the extreme death rate rsulting from the influenza epidemic of 1918.

TABLE 1. GENERAL AND TYPHOID DEATH RATES AT ALPENA, MICHIGAN

Year	Estimated Mid-year Population	Deaths per 100,000 from Typhoid Fever	Deaths per 1000 from All Causes
1900	11,810	59.3	17.5
1901	11,901	...	13.9
1902	11,993	8.3	10.3
1903	12,084	24.8	14.2
1904	12,176	24.6	13.2
1905	12,267	24.5	10.8
1906	12,359	56.6	15.4
1907	12,450	24.1	14.6
Average for period, 1900-07		31.7	13.7
Maximum for period, year 1900		59.3	17.5
Minimum for period, year 1902		8.3	10.3
1908	12,542	71.8	17.7
1909	12,633	63.3	17.6
1910	12,724	31.4	15.1
1911	12,817	93.5	16.4
1912	12,908	53.9	14.3
1913	13,000	91.3	13.9
1914	13,091	68.9	14.0
1915	13,182	67.3	12.7
Average for period, 1908-15		67.7	15.2
Maximum for period		93.5	17.7
Minimum for period		31.4	12.7
1916	13,272	7.53	12.1
1917	13,364	22.5	11.9
1918	13,455	7.43	*16.8
Average for period, 1916-18		12.5	12.0

*Total deaths from all causes 1918 not significant because of influenza epidemic; not included in average for this reason.

However, unless it be assumed that, coincident with a supposed improvement in the water supply, the general application of the principles of hygiene and the effectiveness of the public health administration suffered a setback, it seems logical to conclude that the same circumstances which caused an increase in typhoid caused a considerably greater increase in deaths from all causes. In other words, this case seems to be evidence of the truth of Hazen's theorem by converse.

In public health administration, the presence of disease may be considered as symptomatic of sanitary disorder. In particular, the presence of typhoid fever may be considered a symptom of fecal infection of water or food. If Hazen's theorem is accepted, then such infection of a public water supply (and why not private water supplies and food as well?) will result in about three deaths from causes not ordinarily considered water-borne to each death from typhoid fever.

Under such circumstances, does not the eradication of typhoid fever by anti-typhoid vaccine tend to hide and consequently to continue the true disorder,

fecal infection, and thereby degenerate into a mere treatment of symptoms? And would not complete eradication of the disease, if it could be effected thereby, perpetuate the loss of the three additional lives by the removal of our best index of polluted water?

This occasion is taken to acknowledge the assistance and encouragement given the writer in the above investigation by the State Sanitary Engineer and the Secretary of the State Board of Health; and the courtesy of the Michigan Department of Health in furnishing data accumulated since 1915.

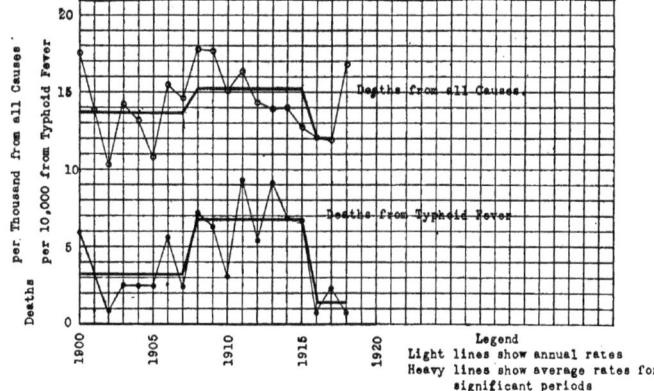

Alpena, Michigan,
Annual Death Rates from all Causes and from Typhoid Fever

Legend
Light lines show annual rates
Heavy lines show average rates for significant periods

□

Clinical, Etiological and Epidemiological Observations of Influenza.—The author considers the Pfeiffer bacillus to be the causative factor in influenza since he was able to isolate this organism from 60 cases without exception.—Schmidt, *Centralbl. f. Bact.*, 1919.

Experimental Typhoid.—Besiedha has shown that by the simple expedient of giving a rabbit a few cubic centimeters of ox-bile some hours before feeding it with typhoid bacilli renders the animal sensitive to that disease.— *The Lancet*, March 27, 1920.—*H. N. C.*

COORDINATION OF PUBLIC AND PRIVATE AGENCIES IN A STATE PROGRAM OF PUBLIC HEALTH NURSING

JESSIE L. MARRINER, R. N.,

Director, Bureau of Public Health Nursing,
Alabama State Board of Health

Read before the meeting of the National Conference of Social Work, at New Orleans, La., April 19-24, 1920.

Alabama has a State Program for Public Health Nursing. This service, stimulated by the war, has developed enormously everywhere. Most movements in this country are by independent agencies. Coördination is the urgent need. Miss Marriner outlines what Alabama is doing towards standardization and coöperation.

WHAT is public health nursing? Who can define it? Many have tried and each has interpreted the function in terms of his own need or the need of those for whose welfare he feels some responsibility. The private practising physician says it is paying nursing visits to the sick and aiding their recovery; the prevention of death or other serious consequences of illness. The health officer asserts that it is carrying out an educational program and measures for the control of communicable diseases, while some administrators of public school systems set up an interpretation which fits the need of the school child and the normal growth of education. The interpretations of managers of industrial plants are as varied and interesting as the personalities of the managers, and have about as much claim to uniformity. The executives of social service agencies claim the right to define the function of public health nursing in relation to their activities, because, they say, "We need the nurse."

Ask the public health nurse herself "What are you, and what do you do?" Her answer is, "I am the servant of all, trying as I am able, in whatever way I am permitted, to use the skill and knowledge I have acquired for the benefit of mankind." It is true that our leaders have made brave efforts at standardization of the various activities covered by the term public health nursing; that is efforts have been made to substitute knowledge and experience for ignorance and experiment in the administration of our special work, but thus far the utmost that has been achieved is a rather broad generalization which defines public health nursing as "any phase of social work dealing more or less directly with health problems or problems of health education in which the knowledge and skill of a thoroughly trained nurse renders the worker more efficient." (Quoted from memory from the *Public Health Nurse.*)

When we consider the wide range of possibilities included in this statement, both as regards the administrative side of the work, the service itself and the personnel available for carrying it forward, it is easy to understand the wide variation in standards and accomplishment, as well as the occasional disappointment, bitterness and misunderstanding which mar the rapid growth of this new expression of an aroused social consciousness.

Many successful attempts have been made to harmonize independent agencies in the local field, in the interest of economy of administration and efficiency of service. These demonstrations although of the utmost significance in connection with our subject cannot be discussed within the limits of this paper.

A movement still more far-reaching is the inauguration within recent years of state programs of public health nursing. These it is hoped, will effect a coördination of public and private agencies within the state in harmony with the program. Our next inquiry then will be: What are state programs? On what basis of legal authority or moral obligation do they rest? How do they work to accomplish desired ends?

EXAMPLE OF STATE PROGRAM (ALABAMA).

1. A-B. We may define a state program as a statement of fundamental principles governing an activity which closely concerns the public welfare. It has legal authority, when voiced by a government agency upon which rests the responsibility for public welfare in a stated field. It has the authority of leadership when set forth by professional bodies, in said field, in such a way as to win the understanding and support of the general public.

C. An Act of the State Legislature confers upon county boards of revenue the power to appropriate funds for the maintenance of a public health nursing service, to be administered by county boards of health. This law is permissive rather than mandatory and may need at some future time to be adjusted to more advanced conditions. The form such social legislation will take may be, in a large measure, determined by the state program, and its enactment secured, by appealing to an enlightened public opinion.

2. The State Program for Public Health Nursing of the Alabama State Board of Health recognizes:

A. That public health nursing is a highly technical service rendered by graduate nurses in the interest of health education and health protection. It is rightfully a government responsibility and should be maintained at public expense.

B. As a public function it will be best administered by executives of general health agencies, but in the absence of such agencies may be successfully administered by any good executive who will familiarize himself with the fundamental principles involved.

C. When private organizations assume this function they should do so for the expressed purpose of revealing a need and demonstrating the efficiency of an instrument for meeting the need. When the demonstration has proceeded far enough to convince government officials of its value and the government is ready to assume control, private enterprise should be diverted to other fields.

D. When public and private agencies covering the same or closely allied lines of public health nursing operate within the same territory, they should be coördinated on an equal basis with relation to a fixed function, usually the more comprehensive and fundamental health function exercised by the government. Their place and the scope of their activities in a unified program, may be determined with relation to the same fixed figure.

3. The State Program Advocates:

A. The maintenance of a Bureau of Public Health Nursing as a Division of the State Board of Health, the purpose of which shall be:

a. To serve as the administrative medium for all of the public health nursing activities of the State Board of Health.

b. To promote the development of public health nursing throughout the state.

c. To encourage nurses to take advantage of increased facilities for education in public health nursing.

d. To select and recommend candidates for positions.

e. To set up desirable standards of work.

f. To., encourage local executives to determine administrative policies only after consulting with state experts and investigating the published opinions of national leaders in this field as well as giving consideration to the personal capacity and major interest of staff nurses.

g. To conduct special studies of the public health nursing field in order to provide a basis for the construction of a local program and assist in the determination of policies of administration.

h. To conduct special efforts in public health nursing education.

B. That the relation of the State Bureau of Public Health Nursing to regional, county and municipal boards of health be one of voluntary non-authoritive supervision in its special field.

C. That it endeavor to create a demand for itself by being helpful; that the Bureau of Public Health Nursing should seek to become the agent in the State of the American Red Cross and the Anti-Tuberculosis League so far as the programs of these organizations include public health nursing; that the bureau offer the services of its personnel to both of these agencies in an effort to establish coöperatively the activities in which each is interested; that each be invited to place at the disposal of the Bureau the salary and expenses of a field nurse who would be responsible for work along these special lines.

That other agencies which are planning to undertake public health nursing work of limited scope be urged to delegate the supervision of such activities to the State Bureau under a coöperative agreement which should safeguard the standards and requirements of the initial agent, provide adequate funds for the prosecution of the enterprise and provide for adequate reporting of field activities to the agency which supplies the funds.

D. That bureaus which are or may be a part of the State Board of Health, engaged in the control of special health problems, such as child hygiene or V. D.

control should, when contemplating the use of public health nurses as field agents for demonstration or strictly educational work, be urged, in the interest of a harmonious and economically sound program, to place these specialists upon the public health nursing staff of the State Bureau; the direction of the special work to come from the special bureau through the head of the nursing bureau, whose office it would be to harmonize such special activities with the general plan and cause it to be of the greatest possible value to local nurses in the field.

E. That specialists in infant welfare, school nursing, industrial nursing, and public health education be added to the Bureau staff as soon as state appropriations will permit, thus completing a well-rounded staff of experts whose qualifications for leadership will by no means be limited to special fields but will prove stimulating alike to the general county nurse in the most isolated rural sections and the staff nurse in the urban center which has achieved an adequate and complete generalized service.

F. Consideration by executives of the claims of specialized versus generalized public health nursing is advocated. These may be briefly stated as follows:

a, Generalization,—a service in which each staff nurse serves all classes of cases and covers all phases of work within a limited district favors economy of administration and more constructive family work. It is impracticable excepting where an adequate staff is employed, and the work localized in a district of reasonable extent to make a creditable showing in percentage of community served and results gained.

b. Specialization,—that is, emphasis upon one class of cases or phase of community service in health education favors sound building of a program by developing one phase of work at a time and adding block by block to the structure. It also favors in practice a very high grade of technique, and attracts the organized suppórt of lay people who feel a marked interest in special problems.

A one-sided development or limitation of the service to one or two health problems sometimes results from specialization; it frequently leads to duplication of visits and unwarranted expenditure of time and money.

c. In rural and small town work a general program with emphasis upon one or two special phases of work will lend itself most readily to expansion as public understanding and support increases; the ultimate goal being an adequate staff doing generalized nursing over a carefully districted area.

d. In urban communities where transportation is not a problem, there are fewer objections to specialization during the building period. The consideration is that when a service is started with one nurse in a city of some size, either the area of operation, or the scope of the activity must be limited. There are usually fewer objections to a limitation of the scope of activities, than there would be to showing undue favoritism towards some section of the city, especially when tax money supports the work. A completed program may be built up by adding specialties step by step until the entire field is covered and a sufficient number of nurses employed to graduate into generalization.

G. That agencies employing more than two public health nurses place them under the expert supervision of a specially trained public health nurse who will be able to maintain the service at a desirable standard by means of educative methods of supervision. This function is entirely distinct from the function of administration and is far removed from the office of a boss who gives orders which must be carried out. The technical supervisor holds a position of leadership rather than one of authority and in addition to familiarity with the psychology of education she must possess expert technical skill in order to be truly helpful.

4-A. The State Program may also endeavor to establish a basis of coöperation between agencies:

a. By setting forth and emphasizing an identity of interest. An authority in political economy, Gladden' has said. "Men cannot coöperate successfully for any purpose if the sole bond between them is self-interest." By coöperation we mean actually working together, operating as a unit, for example, as Faucett has said in his *Political Economy*, "Industry is said to be carried on upon the coöperative principle when capital and labor are merged into one and when the capital which is needed for the production and distribution of wealth is supplied by those who provide the required labor." It is doubtful if this example of "pure coöperation" can be duplicated in the realms of social service, but it should at least be possible to avoid furnishing a justification of the pleasantry that "coöperation is something that everybody demands of the other fellow."

An example of a real bond of common interest among health agencies is that of public health nursing in the programs of the American Red Cross, the Anti-Tuberculosis League, public and private community nursing associations and the activities of state, regional, county and municipal boards of health.

The agreement between the Gulf Division of the American Red Cross and the Alabama State Board of Health approaches the ideal of "pure coöperation," in that it recognizes an identity of interest and provides coöperatively for the development and supervision of work in this field by a single agent carrying a dual responsibility, that is, the Bureau of Public Health Nursing of the State Board of Health, which takes directions from and makes reports to both agencies.

Present conditions indicate that an extension of this agreement to include the community nursing activities of the Anti-

Tuberculosis League would be in line with the best interests of all.

b. Facts, figures and demonstrations may sometimes be used to convince agencies of the practicability of combining operations without merging the essentials of organization identity. Some of these essentials are a consciousness of being "different," of having an individuality and the satisfaction of having a place in the world and a work to do, which will furnish tangible grounds for an appeal for public support, thus assuring a continuance of the organization.

To illustrate this we might cite the instance of the combination of public and private city agencies for public health nursing which provides for generalized work in districts by an adequate staff of nurses under the supervision of an expert public health nurse, the identity of the several participating agencies being preserved by a system of records and reports which give accurate credit for funds furnished and all work done, as well as results secured, in the special fields of each.

Organizations in their group consciousness are characterized by more or less personal motives and before they can be induced to coöperate (work together), they must, like individuals, be assured of the normal rewards of work well done; in other words, public acknowledgment of their accomplishments and their right to life, liberty and the pursuit of their objective.

c. The probability of clashes of self-interest may be minimized by fostering the mutual respect of organizations for individual organization rights within certain well-defined limits. Welfare agencies, like individuals, need to learn to live together on the earth by achieving a form of self-government which shall be just and fair and in harmony with the ideals of democracy.

d. Apparent disparities of interest, such as that between preventive and remedial medicine may be disproved by showing that good preventive work but offers to remedial medicine a wider reach and a better grasp of its own field, and makes possible the practice of medicine upon ever higher planes of effectiveness. In every country in the world where preventive medicine has been undertaken, experience has proved that in its final analysis it means, more and earlier medical attention for all the people, in other words, an increased dollar reward for the practising physician, and a more even distribution of skilled nursing.

e. Aims and purposes which have held undisputed sway over public conscience for a long time may be reinterpreted in harmony with higher ideals of service or upon a broader foundation of educative effort, as when welfare agencies are led to see that the Christian principles expressed in the Gospel of St. Matthew applies to organizations as well as to persons. The body that would save its life shall lose it, and that one which would lose its life for the sake of the program which was inaugurated with the words, "Thy kingdom come," shall save not only its own life from failure, but bring to the world "Life more abundant."

B. The State Program for Public Health Nursing will endeavor further:

a. To become itself coördinated with other state programs for civic betterment, such as those for relief, correction, protection of children, public education and recreation, Americanization and reconstruction and vocational education for the handicapped.

This era is said to be one of organization; in some fields of human endeavor it has the appearance of organizations running wild, and contending against one another for supremacy.

In urban centers the very complexity and stress of social activities have made some form of coördination imperative, and some "rules of the game" have been automatically set up and followed, in the interest of self-preservation.

The extreme individualism of rural life makes spontaneous efforts towards combinations of any sort unlikely, while the very commendable zeal of those responsible for state and national welfare programs, is urging them continually "into the open country," "where the need is greatest." There they establish themselves, if at all, upon an independent basis and continue to work independently; each contending for the supremacy in its field and each clamoring for special legislation in the interest of its program.

Small wonder if the rural and small town dweller becomes confused and resentful of interference and assumes an attitude of hostility toward all "new-fangled nonsense." There are two fundamental reasons for this attitude on his part; they are first the demand of the rural mind for directness and simplicity in community enterprise, and second, a very natural antagonism to proposed social legislation which the rural citizen does not understand and for which he feels no need.

In view of these considerations the State Program for Public Health Nursing proposes to become itself coördinated with other welfare programs, with special reference to rural and small town activities in the interest of a simplified and harmonized plan of work, which will be acceptable to the people with whom it has to deal.

b. This comprehensive, final proposal of the State Program for Public Health Nursing is confronted by one major difficulty: With relation to what fixed function shall state welfare programs become coördinated with one another?

No function of government comprehensive enough to fill the need and specific enough to differentiate itself from the general group of state departments has become a recognized feature of state government.

c. It is therefore proposed that this need be brought to the attention of lawmakers and that the legislative body be asked to recognize the coördination of state welfare programs as a function of State government and to provide for it officially and financially. This function should be limited to rulings with regard to the function and relationship of organizations engaged in or wishing to undertake some form of welfare work within the state.

It would seem desirable that this office be filled by an expert organizer, although it would entail no administrative duties or powers. In a state which is largely rural this function of coördination might be assumed upon authorization by the legislature by the Attorney General's office, rulings with regard to doubtful or borderline functions being made only after consultation with all department heads and executives of interested organizations.

Public and private agencies having achieved a state program by means of which they hope to influence human conduct and race progress would then submit their programs to the designated state official and ask for a ruling on the question, in case of doubt as to which of the administrative departments of the government its proposed function is most closely related.

5A. Results:

a. The results to be hoped for from this experiment, the working details of which it would be impossible to forecast, include the possibility of a unified program for the upbuilding of rural life; a program which shall coördinate local public health nursing forces on an equal basis with relation to the fixed function of public health administration and further coördinate state welfare programs of every creed and color, with relation to some comprehensive fixed plane of human service, yet to be determined and given concrete expression.

b. A more economical administration of work in all lines both as to expenditure of effort and funds, should become possible as a result of the elimination of non-essentials, duplication and mutual distrust.

c. The state programs individually and collectively should meet with increased responsiveness on the part of the public as a result of this effort at unity of action, and a more open-minded popular consideration be assured to proposed social legislation which is being advocated by the state program.

The above example of a State Program for Public Health Nursing has been outlined with special reference to conditions in one state and may serve only as a suggestion of how such a program may be built up within each state upon a basis provided by the state government. Where the health function has not yet been developed as a part of the govern-ment some private agency may temporarily assume the leadership in this field. When this is done, the surest criterion of usefulness of the private agency will be the promptness with which a government agency for health protection will be set up and put into operation, as a result of stimulation of public interest in health, and a sense of responsibility for its conservation.

The most striking example of the abrogation of self-interest to the public welfare will be furnished by that agency when it graciously accords the position of leadership to the government function which it has helped to create, and itself assumes the position of follower, supporter and advocate at the bar of public opinion.

□

NEW FORM OF JET DRINKING FOUNTAIN

Everyone who has had occasion to follow the development of the "bubble" drinking fountain, from the early form of Newcomb to those in use today, has realized that there are some difficulties in devising a fountain for public places which may not lend itself to the carrying of infection. The introduction of the oblique jet has solved most of the problems. The form of fountain here represented has been devised by C. M. Siever, M. D., Ph. D., in charge of the Department of Student Health, Kansas State Agricultural College. It has been on trial in the main building of the college for the past few months and has given excellent satisfaction. The small streams act as an automatic guard to keep the mouth away from the metal parts. In addition to the vertical streams, there are small ones directed across the fountain at the base of the others, so that the head of the fountain is continually washed.

SOCIOLOGICAL ASPECT OF HOOKWORM DISEASE

OSCAR DOWLING, M. D.,

President of the Louisiana State Board of Health
New Orleans, La.

Read before Sociological Section, American Public Health Association, at New Orleans, La.,
October 30, 1919.

Dr. Dowling finds a need so urgent for funds for fighting hookworm that he advocates using some of the school allotments
which even now are inadequate. The economic waste is evident
of trying to educate there defective children. More important
than economic losses, however, are the lowered ethical standards
incident to hookworm disease conditions.

HOOKWORM as a disease has a very ancient history. It is quite likely that certain passages in the Ebers papyrus refer to it, this record antedating Christ's birth by 1,550 years. The disease was probably recognized in Brazil about the middle of the 17th century. The cause, however, was not actually known until the discovery of the European species of the parasite by Dubini, an Italian, in 1843. It was then recognized as the etiological factor in Egyptian chlorosis. In 1880, it caused a high death rate among the workers in the St. Gothard Tunnel and was spread by these men throughout southern Europe and Italy.

Hookworm disease was probably first introduced into this part of the Western Hemisphere by African slaves brought to Porto Rico in 1760. It prevails extensively in the United States; but because of the mild climate and other conditions, the highest percentage of infection is found in the South. As has been pointed out by Stiles, the greatest prevalence is among the mountaineer dwellers of the Southern Appalachians and the Sandy regions along the Atlantic and Gulf Coasts. Between 1910-1913, more than 415,000 children in 413 counties of the Southern States were examined. The reports revealed 43% of them infected. Of 700,-000 persons of all ages for the same lo-

calities 35% were found to harbor the parasites. In Louisiana the percentage of the infection depends on the locality; one parish has an average of only 15-16% based on about 3,000 examinations. In Camp Nichols in 1917, 9% of the men examined were found infected. In a neighboring state there are said to be counties in which 75% of the population have the disease; in Louisiana six years ago there were some with an estimated percentage of 50.

The conditions which exist in some of the remote rural districts are exceptionally favorable to the spread of the disease. Sanitary conveniences are unknown or of the most primitive type. At the school both infected and non-infected children use the same retiring places. The rains come and the entire adjoining areas are infected with hookworm larvæ which await the first opportunity to enter the skin of the bare-footed child—it may be the bare-footed man or woman. "Ground itch" follows and as the process is repeated, the person becomes heavily infected. Marbles and other school games may be responsible for ground itch on the hands or food may be handled without thorough washing of hands and the hookworm is saved much trouble in reaching its normal habitat, the intestinal tract.

This disease is not confined to the rural districts. In many of the smaller towns and villages by far too large a ratio of the people are infected. In fact, where no sanitary measures are complied with or enforced, or where there is no sewerage systems or sanitary privies hookworm is almost sure to exist. In the larger modern-built cities there are probably no cases reported or even suspected, but at least the chances of infection are far less than in the rural districts.

The infection is in most instances so insidiously acquired by the unsuspecting victim that he and the members of his family, who probably are likewise infected, do not know just when the effects of the disease began to manifest themselves. In the course of a few summers, however, a once healthy family has become pale and puny; a once industrious family has become languid and backward in its work; a once prosperous family has fallen into debt; a once proud family owning valuable property has been reduced to poverty by an easily curable and easily preventable disease. The children once bright and well advanced in their school classes begin to lose their zeal and their mental alertness when gradually robbed of their vitality. They fall behind in the struggle with their healthier classmates, and finally discouraged, give up school work in despair.

Hookworm districts are always far below the average in every respect. Now and then there is a wealthy farmer, but the majority of the residents are barely self-sustaining and it is a usual condition of affairs to find them poverty stricken. Education is neglected, both sexes are poorly clad, listless and with pallid skin and stunted body, they drag out their existence. They are people who in the struggle for existence have lost their grip; human refuse which is the progenitor of more wreckage.

Such individuals cease to be a social asset; they become a social liability. This is a phase that should be emphasized.

That the disease has an economical bearing upon the progress and well-being of the body politic is very evident. If in any country or in any section of a country a portion of the people are below the standard physically they add to the economic burden of the whole. In such ratio as they are inefficient they are an economic loss; in such ratio as they are physically unfit, they are a liability. Dr. Ferrell cites the case of the Continental Coal Corporation of Pineville, Kentucky, whose miners were infected to the extent of 65%. When measures for treatment and for prevention of soil pollution had been instituted the same body of men accomplished 33% more work than was possible the previous year. Dr. Rose, as quoted by Dr. Ferrell, states that a physically sound coffee-picker in Porto Rico picks from 500 to 600 measures of coffee per day, but that the infected man can pick only 100 to 250 per day. Of 300 laborers in a cocoa plantation in Ecuador anemia had so reduced their efficiency that they could only work one-third of a day. The manager of a large British Guiana Sugar Estate reports that "treatment for hookworm had doubled the working power of the gangs." A mine in California claims to lose $20,000 a year by having "to carry on its payroll men sufficient to replace those unable to work because of hookworm anemia."

It is acknowledged that the labor of the southern mills is inefficient because so large a number are afflicted with uncinariasis.

On a basis of investigations which have been in effect in different sections of the South since 1910, it is estimated that there is an economic waste in the Southern States, due to hookworm infection, of between $250,000,000 and $500,000,000 annually.

It can be readily understood that physical deterioration and physical disability lessen tremendously the working capacity of those affected. It appears, likewise, that the class of people habitually ill become more and more helpless as working units. This condition constitutes a vicious circle. Physical degeneration produces poverty and poverty in turn creates conditions favorable to the spread of the disease. However, in passing, I might add that hookworm disease is not confined to the poverty stricken portion of the population; its prevalence among the better classes is illustrated by the work of Gage and Bass, who found 25% of hookworm infection among 315 university students. Of 259 students, not residents of New Orleans, 30.1% were found infected. Infection with other intestinal parasites brought the general average up to about 30%, which is remarkably high for people of this standing.

An important phase of the economic problem is the effect on children. A child with a stunted body and low vitality does not, cannot accept advantages offered by the schools. School and college records show that infected students even though not apparently ill, average lower in their studies than those free from infection. To quote again from Dr. Ferrell, "In a woman's college the average standing of 56 girls found infected was 77.75%, whereas 56 other girls in the same institution averaged 89.28%. In an academy 25 infected men and boys averaged 64%. A non-infected group 85%." If among students of colleges and other institutions for higher education the difference is so marked, it must be even more so among the children of the lower grades.

An examination of the pupils of two schools in Rapides Parish—one situated in a good-sized town, the other in a rural neighborhood—has just been made. A comparison shows the children of the town school on the average in much the better physical condition. For example, of the 74 of the country children examined, 35 gave evidence of malnutrition and 34 of anemia; 15, about 20%, had intestinal parasites and 47 of the 74 were

found infected with malaria. Not one of the 74 had been vaccinated. Of the 448 in the town school, 10 showed malnutrition, 84 anemia, 145 had been vaccinated. As the examinations for intestinal parasites are not yet complete, we can not make a comparison, neither for malaria. One of. the deplorable things revealed is the large number in both who give a history of smallpox, a serious arraignment of our knowledge of how this may be prevented.

There is a tremendous waste involved in maintaining schools, the advantages of which are not utilized by those for whom they are planned. A child who is too listless or anemic to become interested is a burden the same as his inefficient father. It would be far better to expend for examination, treatment if necessary, a portion of the school funds than to maintain schools which are an economic loss. I am not unaware that the schools everywhere are inadequately financed, but even so, their usefulness is limited if the children are unable to respond to the opportunities provided.

Without a healthy body, the best educational system must become illusory, but not only must the child be healthier but he must be kept so. No plan of campaign can have the slightest chance of success which does not take the instruction of the fundamentals of sanitation and hygiene into consideration.

The social importance of any disease which lowers the individual intellectually is almost beyond comparison as the infected children of infected parents today become the stunted, indifferent, mentally deficient, and physically inefficient adults of tomorrow, and so on ad infinitum. The eradication of hookworm is imperative. Not only for our present and future advantage, but from the very humane standpoint of alleviating misery is this a crying need of the rural districts of the Southern States and other portions of the country. To illustrate the improvement in normal and physical stamina, as related by a person who had no particular knowledge of the hookworm disease, an incident is pertinent. A family in a certain town of North Carolina, had for many years the reputation of being the most worthless, shiftless, and "no account" members of the community. It occurred to a physician of the town to try the effects of a course of hookworm treatment on this family, apparently, partly perhaps a matter of experiment, partly also from humane reasons. The results were all that could be desired. Within a year or two, all signs of shiftlessness had vanished, the parents and children had been transformed into worthy, industrious and self-respecting people, had acquired property, and had achieved a very creditable position among their fellow citizens.

May I again repeat, the economic loss from lowered vitality and lessened working capacity, is of infinitely less importance than the effect on the lowered ethical standards which follow. A nation may make up for an economic loss by one means or another, and although we may not accept the philosophy of the gentle Oliver Goldsmith, I think we can accept as true:
"Ill fares the land, to hastening ills a prey,
Where wealth accumulates, and *men* decay."

□

Vaccine Treatment of Diphtheria Carriers.—In spite of our rather complete knowledge of how to prevent and cure diphtheria the lack of a dependable method of rendering diphtheria carriers non-infectious forms a lementably weak spot in the cordon of control which is gradually being thrown around this disease. Medical science has been ingenious in devising new and extraordinary treatments, but much disappointment has followed the use of all of these.

To the author it appeared that investigation along the line of symbiosis and saprophytism might lead to definite results. Had it been discovered that there was some organism constantly associated with the diphtheria bacillus in the throats of carriers, it was intended to employ a vaccine against the supposed abetting organism. Failing to find such a symbion the idea appealed to the author of using a vaccine of the offending organism itself.

The vaccine used was made in the usual way and was not autogenous. It was tried on a series of 50 cases, male and female of various ages, who had been carriers for from three to 20 weeks. Thirty-nine were given one or two doses, the rest from three to eight. In most cases the dosage was from 10 million to 30 million, although two patients were given 200 million each.

All cases were cleared up, 37 in one week, including 19 during the first day. Seven more were negative in a fortnight.

Fully one-fourth of the patients were observed for from eight to 27 days without manifesting renewed "positivity" in spite of the fact that they remained in contact with other infected persons. The author states that no untoward effects were noted on the vaccinated patients. Pulse rates were moderately increased for a few hours, the respiratory rate was mostly unaffected and pyrexia or local pain was exceptional—J. L. Brownlie, *London Lancet,* March 27, 1920. (*H. N. C.*)

✛

"Commonwealth" Influenza Vaccine.— One of the important measures employed in the control of influenza in Australia was the use of vaccine. The vaccine employed was one compounded from different strains of the several organisms associated with influenza, and for convenience termed "Commonwealth vaccine." The official report of the Australian Director of Quarantine describes its composition, preparation and method of employment. The ratio of deaths in the inoculated and uninoculated groups is given as five to 240. Some of this advantage must of course be attributed to the earlier hospitalization of the inoculated.—*Medical Officer,* March 13, 1920. (*H. N. C.*)

AN EPIDEMIC OF PNEUMONIC PLAGUE

W. H. Kellogg, M. D.,

*Secretary, California State Board of Health,
Sacramento, Cal.*

Read before Section of Public Health Administration, American Public Health Association, at New
Orleans, October 28, 1919.

Dr. Kellogg calls on health authorities to wake from their apathy
with reference to plague in California, and instead of restrictive
measures to adopt an aggressive warfare. He points out that
there is real danger to the country and urges adequate appropriations to exterminate the animal disease carriers while this may
be done with certainty.

THE occurrence of a small epidemic
of pneumonic plague in Oakland
during the latter part of August and
the first part of September, 1919, serves
to remind us that the problem not only
is with us still, but that it must be
reckoned with in the future. This outbreak is of considerable interest, since
it is the first instance of an epidemic of
pneumonic plague on the western hemisphere. The great epidemic of Manchuria in 1911 is still fresh in our minds,
and the work of Strong and Teague will
be later referred to in a discussion of the
possibilities of such a visitation in this
country. In the report of the State
Board of Health for the biennial period
ending June 30, 1918, the writer made
the following statement:

BUBONIC PLAGUE AND SQUIRREL ERADI-
CATION

"The continued existence of bubonic
plague among ground squirrels of California, after ten years of work for their
extermination, should be a matter of
general concern and should prompt us
to redouble our efforts to eradicate them.
California is definitely on the map as
one of the endemic foci of this disease,
others being Arabia, Manchuria and
Thibet.

The work of squirrel eradication is
being carried on by the United States
Public Health Service in coöperation
with the State Board of Health, and the
amount of money being expended in the
work averages about $60,000 per year,
less than half of which is contributed by
the state through funds appropriated to
the State Board of Health. The work
is carried on by intensive poisoning operations in those localities shown to be
plague infected. This is determined by
sending hunters over the area under investigation, examining in the laboratory
squirrels shot, and concentrating poisoning operations in the places found to be
infected. This method is made necessary by reason of the lack of funds to
carry on more extensive work. In November, 1917, the Service surrendered
charge of eradicative work in Merced,
Stanislaus, San Benito and Monterey
counties to the State Horticultural Commission, and has since confined its operations to the counties of Contra Costa,
Alameda and San Mateo. Plague-infected squirrels were found in the latter
group of counties which surround the
bay of San Francisco, on which is located
the city of San Francisco, which was the
scene of a human plague epidemic in
1907.

Until plague-infected ground squirrels
are entirely eradicated from California
we shall always have a sword of Damo-

cles hanging over our heads. So long as infection persists among the ground squirrels, the possibility of an extension of the disease to the rats of the cities, and consequently to the human population, will exist. It may be one year, it may be five years, or it may be 20 years, before this lighting up of the virulence of the infection will occur, but we can surmise from the world history of plague and from its known tendency to slumber in endemic foci, 'such as we have in the vicinity of San Francisco Bay, that this will happen some time. We have now had a fair trial of the present method, extending over ten years, which is to spend just enough money to keep the disease in check, but not enough to exterminate it. The only rational plan is to proceed vigorously and to prosecute the work at such a rate that an entire ten years' allotment of funds is used up in a year or two. A reasonable basis would require an outlay of not less than $250,-000 per year, with the expectation that two years would finish the work."

HISTORICAL.

Plague is primarily a disease of rodents, principally rats, and in some parts of the world of native animals, such as the tarbagan in Manchuria, the marmot in Arabia, and the ground squirrel in California. It persists endemically among these animals, occasionally extending to the human population, usually by way of an epizöotic among the rats, but sometimes by direct contact of humans with the wild animal harboring the infection. Whether the excursion of the disease from tarbagan or squirrel to the rat, and then to the human, is a matter of chance, or whether it depends upon some temporary exaltation of virulence of the bacillus of plague is not known. The time interval between these human outbreaks is sometimes very long. It is believed that the disease lay dormant among the marmots of the west coast of Arabia during the many decades that elapsed between its disappearance from

Europe and the beginning of the last pandemic in the early nineties.

Plague probably entered the United States in 1899, as the first recorded case on this continent was discovered in Chinatown, San Francisco, in March, 1900.* It had already appeared at the Hawaiian Islands on its westward march and was undoubtedly introduced into San Francisco by plague-infected rats from the Orient.

In August, 1908, the first evidence was secured of the extension of the infection to the ground squirrels of California, the supposition being that the point of contact was in the vicinity of the grain warehouses of Port Costa. Since that time the State Board of Health and the United States Public Health Service have jointly carried on a campaign of extermination and a systematic examination for infected animals with what funds were available for that purpose. Since 1908 sporadic human cases have occurred as follows, one at each of the places named:

Los Angeles................August 11, 1908
Alameda County (rural)..September 24, 1909
Santa Clara County.........August 31, 1910
Oakland ....August 9, 1911
San Joaquin County......September 18, 1911
San Benito County.............June 4, 1913
Contra Costa County..........July 13, 1915

Following the apparent extermination of plague among the rats of San Francisco and Oakland, as a result of the work of those communities under the direction of the United States Public Health Service during the epidemic of 1907 and 1908, the usual feeling of security supervened, resulting in the complete cessation of rat exterminative measures in those communities.

PRESENT EPIDEMIC—(See Chart)

On August 15th, a man named Di Bortoli, residing at 960 Forty-fifth street, Oakland, was taken ill. His physician was called who found him with a temperature of 101.5°, a pain in his right side, with what he considered to be a congestion of the lower lobe of the right

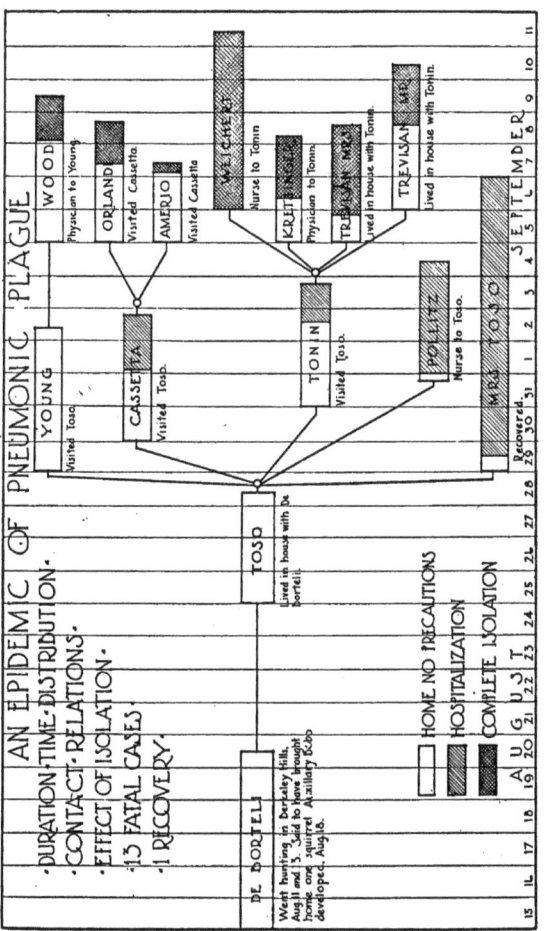

lung. A diagnosis of influenza was made. Di Bortoli felt somewhat improved for two days and then developed a severe pain in the right axilla. Upon examination at this time the physician found an axillary swelling that was exceedingly tender and a temperature of 100.5.° Another physician was called in consultation on August 15th and the swelling was incised. Nothing was found but a bloody serum. The bubo was again opened on the 19th. At this time the patient was suffering great pain and heroin was administered with no effect. At 4 o'clock in the morning of the 20th the physician again was called and found the patient pulseless. He died shortly after the doctor's arrival. The second case to develop was that of Toso, who lived in the same house with Di Bortoli and who was taken sick August 25th, dying August 28th. On August 29th Mrs. Toso was taken to a hospital, with a temperature of 105° and a diagnosis of influenza-pneumonia. She recovered and was discharged from the hospital on September 6th. In quick succession appeared the cases of Young, onset August 29th, died September 2d; Casetti, onset August 30th, died September 2d; Tonin, onset August 31st, died September 3d; Pollitz, onset September 1st, died September 4th. All of these cases had been in direct contact with Toso. Young was his landlord and had helped take care of him; Miss Pollitz was his nurse and Casetti and Tonin had visited him. From three of these cases seven more developed by direct contact. Contacts with Tonin were: Augustine Trevisan, onset September 5th, died September 8th; Assunta Trevisan, died September 10th; these two lived in the same house with Tonin. The third contact was Dr. Kretsinger, Tonin's physician, who was taken ill September 5th and died September 8th. The fourth contact was Mrs. Weichert, Tonin's nurse, who was stricken September 6th and died September 11th. The cases originating from contact with

Casetti were: Amario, his cousin, who rode in the ambulance with him to the hospital, and who died September 7th. Orlando visited him at the hospital; he was taken sick September 5th and died September 8th. One case resulted from contact with Young, his physician, Dr. Wood, who was taken sick September 5th and died September 9th.

The first three or four of this series were thought to be influenza with pneumonia, but the suspicions of Dr. Crosby, the Oakland Health Officer, becoming aroused, he ordered an autopsy in the case of Amario, which was performed by Dr. Tiffany, autopsy surgeon of the coroner; a representative of Dr. Crosby, in the person of Dr. Moore of the Western Laboratories, being present. It was reported to the Bureau of Communicable Diseases that at this autopsy Dr. Moore had made slides from the organs, but no cultures were taken for the reason that the body had been embalmed. It was also reported that the conclusion was that death was due to influenza-pneumonia. It later developed, however, that Dr. Moore's slides from the lungs showed numerous bipolar staining bacilli resembling plague. On September 11, Dr. Crosby notified Dr. Kelly, Director of the Bureau of Communicable Diseases, that another suspicious death had occurred the previous afternoon, and had been autopsied in the presence of Dr. Moore, the body not having been embalmed. He stated that Dr. Moore had found bipolar organisms in the lungs and spleen and had inoculated guinea pigs from the lung tissue. The bacteriological proof of the identity of this case (Mrs. Trevisan), as one of plague, was made by the Hygienic Laboratory of the Board of Health and by the Federal Laboratory, independently; cultures being obtained in both instances from one of the guinea pigs which died with typical gross lesions of plague, following the inoculation by Dr. Moore with material from the human case. The post mortem findings, as described by Dr. Moore in this case, were as follows, which description applied, according to the statement of Dr. Tiffany, the coroner's autopsy physician, to the other cases of the series which were autopsied by him:

No petechia were observed on the skin surfaces of the body. There was marked bilateral hydrothorax, both pleuras containing a considerable quantity of clear, straw-colored fluid, no blood or pus being evident. Pericardium contained from 100 to 150 cc. of dark straw-colored fluid; no blood. There was a bilateral, lobular pneumonia diffused over both lungs; on incision surface very moist and a thin bloody fluid exuded freely. Kidneys showed evidence of an acute parenchymatous nephritis, spleen from 10 to 12 inches long, being fully four times its normal size. Its substance was soft dark purple in color, of almost semifluid consistency. Peribronchial lymph nodes were enlarged, soft and hemorrhagic; no enlargement of lymph glands noted elsewhere in the body. Smears from the lung and spleen were made which showed upon examination, after staining with carbol-thionin, numerous typical bipolar staining organisms.

Although only one case has been positively identified as plague, the clinical history of the other cases, and the description of the post mortem findings, taken in connection with the very clear history of contact, as worked out by Drs. Force and Kelly of the Bureau of Communicable Diseases, leaves no room for doubt as to the identity of the entire series as cases of pneumonic plague; the first one of the series, Di Bertoli, being a case of bubonic plague with a supervening pneumonia, which was communicated in the usual manner, i.e., droplet infection and personal contact with the other victims, who contracted the pneumonic type by reason of the mode of entry of the virus. There is considerable doubt as to the identity of a case of plague in Miss Pollitz, the nurse to Toso,

because the reported clinical history might give rise to the suspicion of another cause of death, chronic nephritis being the assigned cause and no post mortem examination having been made.

Some question might also be raised in the case of Mrs. Toso, the sole basis of such question being the fact that she recovered. This is not a valid objection, as the recovery of pneumonic plague cases is not an unknown occurrence, although the mortality in this form of the infection is very high.

Another interesting incident was the sending of a specimen of sputum from the case of Dr. Wood to a reliable laboratory in San Francisco, which made the report of type identification of pneumococci, but made no mention of the presence of bipolar bacilli.

The finding of bipolar organisms in this sputum apparently excited no suspicions at the laboratory. The sudden termination of the series of cases in the fourth generation of infections was probably due to the hospitalization of all the cases with complete isolation and careful medical asepsis, which no doubt was more careful than would have usually been the case with pneumonia, because there was a feeling of alarm caused by the rapidly fatal character of the preceding cases. In this connection it may be profitable to discuss some of the future probabilities considered in the light of the apparently easy checking of this epidemic. Certain conclusions reached by Teague and Barber[*] in their work in Manchuria throw some light on this question.

The Manchurian epidemic, occurring during the winter of 1910 and 1911, was wholly of the pneumonic type and within three months 50,000 people died from the disease. In searching for reasons as to why this particular epidemic should be exclusively of the pneumonic type, whereas the great number of cases in India had been of the bubonic form,

[*]Philippine Journal of Science, 1912, page 157.

Teague and Barber observed that the most noticeable difference prevailing in the two instances of epidemic prevalence was one of temperature. In Manchuria, during the entire season of the epidemic, the temperature ranged around 30° below zero C., whereas, in India the temperature was in the neighborhood of 30° above zero C. Following the lead indicated by this difference in temperature, they carried out a series of experiments with plague and other cultures and experimental animals. The following is quoted from a summary of their article:

"Hence, it seems probable that the plague bacilli contained in fine droplets of pneumonic plague sputum would suffer death from drying in a few minutes unless they were suspended in an atmosphere with an extremely small water deficit. Infection in pneumonic plague follows the inhalation of droplets of pneumonic sputum, and obviously the longer these droplets remain suspended in the air, the greater is the danger of infection. As has just been stated, these fine droplets disappear very quickly except when they are suspended in an atmosphere with a very small water deficit. Such an atmosphere is, under ordinary circumstances, of common occurrence in very cold climates, whereas, it is extremely rare in warm ones. Hence, since the droplets of sputum persist longer, the plague bacilli remain alive longer in the air, and there is a greater tendency for the disease to spread in cold climates than in warm ones.

"In harmony with the above ideas, we find that the only great epidemic of pneumonic plague of modern times occurred in Manchuria during the winter of 1910 to 1911, when the atmospheric temperature was many degrees below zero Centigrade. The disease spread with amazing rapidity. Furthermore, although during the past fifteen years there have been millions of plague cases in India, and 2 to 5 per cent of these have been cases of plague pneumonia, yet this form of

the disease has not assumed epidemic proportions. The largest epidemic of pneumonic plague in India (1,400 deaths) occurred in Kashmir, in northern India, at an elevation of 1,524 meters above the sea level during very cold weather."

The above conclusions were based on a series of experiments on the effect of drying on the viability of plague and other organisms and on the length of life of these organisms suspended in droplets of moisture under varying conditions of humidity and temperature.

Adopting the conclusions of Teague and Barber, then, we may conclude that under the circumstances of temperature and low humidity existing in Oakland at the time of this outbreak, conditions were not favorable for the transfer of infected droplets, carrying plague bacilli from one person to another, excepting under conditions of the closest contact. The drying and consequent death of the bacillus was so rapid that the ordinary measures of prophylaxis, which were easy of application, sufficed to check the progress of the infection when all existing cases were being cared for in hospitals. With the same line of reasoning, we can surmise that if a different condition of temperature and humidity existed, the result would have been far different, and we are justified in drawing the conclusion that this epidemic teaches that we have still another danger to be looked forward to from the continued existence of plague among the ground squirrels in California. We have, heretofore, been accustomed to think principally of the possible occurrence of an epidemic of the bubonic type following the extension of the disease to the rat population of some of our cities. The gravity of the situation is enhanced considerably when we realize the possibilities of a human case in the incubation stage of the disease following contact with squirrel plague, journeying to some eastern state in the winter time and developing an infection such as that of Di Bortoli, in the proper climate setting for the development of a pneumonic epi-- demic which could easily be found in some of our eastern states in winter. The prospect of the consequences that could follow such a set of circumstances is not at all reassuring.

The State Board of Health took immediate action upon receipt of the first information suggesting the true nature of the cases, and was ably assisted by Dr. Crosby, the health officer of Oakland. The city council of Oakland promptly made an emergency appropriation, following similar action by the Governor of California, and a corps of inspectors and rat catchers, jointly paid by the Oakland city health department and the State Board of Health, was put into the field. Embalming of all bodies before authentic information as to the cause of death was obtained was immediately stopped and a system of inspection of bodies of persons dying under circumstances that might by any possibility be attributed to plague in any form was established. To insure that no case might be overlooked, the death certificates were scrutinized and countersigned by a deputy detailed for that purpose. The medical profession of the bay region was advised by special letter as to the exact situation and physicians were urged to report immediately all cases of pneumonia and all cases of acute infection of any sort, the diagnosis of which was not perfectly clear. All such cases were visited for the purpose of making a clinical and bacteriological examination.

It is very evident that the medical profession of the Pacific coast should be continually on its guard for cases of plague which may occur at any time so long as the infection exists among the rodents of the state. It should be remembered that in the early period of plague epidemics the first cases are very apt to be overlooked and mistaken for other conditions. The bubonic and septicemic form is frequently mistaken for typhoid fever, pyogenic infections, etc. All cases with acute enlargement and tenderness of the lymphatic glands should be looked on with suspicion, and bacteriological examination made wherever possible. The pneumonic form is particularly hard to identify, excepting by bacteriological tests. On the Pacific coast bacteriologists should be on the constant lookout for the presence of bipolar staining bacilli in the sputum of pneumonia cases.

SUMMARY

1. The third visitation of human plague in California occurred in Oakland, in August and September, 1919.

2. This epidemic was of the pneumonic type, the first instance of this form appearing epidemically on this hemisphere.

3. The epidemic was promptly checked by the adoption of measures of isolation.

4. The endemic prevalence of plague among ground squirrels of California constitutes a permanent menace not only to the State of California, but also to the whole of the United States.

5. The measures of extermination, which are at present being conducted by the State of California, as represented by the State Board of Health and the federal government, and as represented by the United States Public Health Service, should be financed to such an extent as to permit an extensive campaign of extermination that would offer some hope of the conclusion of the work within a period of one or two years.

6. The pneumonic type of plague is probably not a serious menace on the Pacific coast, owing to climatic conditions; but could readily become a serious matter in other parts of the United States by extension from the Pacific coast under the proper climatic conditions.

EDITORIAL SECTION

AMERICAN JOURNAL OF PUBLIC HEALTH

Publication Office: 124 W. Polk Street, Chicago, Ill.
EDITORIAL OFFICE: 169 MASSACHUSETTS AVE., BOSTON, MASS.

A. W. HEDRICH, C. P. H., Editor   J. RITCHIE, Jr., Associate Editor

Editorial Assistants

E. R. HAYHURST, M.D.	DAVID GREENBERG	JAMES A. TOBEY
R. P. ALBAUGH, M.D.	M. P. HORWOOD, M.S.	FRANCIS H. SLACK, M.D.
E. B. STARR, M.D.	P. M. HOLMES, M.D.	JAMES M. STRANG

Board of Advisory Editors

PETER H. BRYCE, M.D., Ottawa, Canada	PROF. M. J. ROSENAU, Boston, Mass.
CHARLES V. CHAPIN, M.D., Providence, R. I.	PROF. W. T. SEDGWICK, Cambridge, Mass.
EUGENE R. KELLEY, M.D., Boston, Mass.	PROF. GEORGE C. WHIPPLE, Cambridge, Mass.
W. A. EVANS, M.D., Chicago, Ill.	PROF. S. M. GUNN, Paris, France.

All expressions of opinion and all statements of supposed facts are published on authority of the writer under whose name they appear, and are not to be regarded as expressing the views of the American Public Health Association, unless such statements or opinions have been adopted by vote of the Association.

NOTICE TO SUBSCRIBERS: Subscription Price, payable in advance, $4.00 per year for United States and possessions; $4.50 for Canada and other foreign countries. Single copies, 50 cents postpaid. Membership in the American Public Health Association, including subscription to Journal, $5.00 per year. In Change of Address please give both old and new address, and mail before the tenth of the month to take effect with the current issue. Mailing Date, 5th of each month. Advertisements accepted only when commendable, and worth while both to reader and advertiser. News Items, interesting clippings and illustrations are gladly received, together with name of sender. Copyright, 1919, by A. W. Hedrich.

HEALTH A POLITICAL PLANK

There has been no better public acknowledgement in recent years of the fundamental necessity of proper administration of the public health than the formulation of a "plank" in its political platform by the convention of the Republican party assembled in Chicago. Principles for which the American Public Health Association has been outspoken are here accepted as among the needs of the country. How true it is that the dreams of yesterday are the realities of today.

"A thorough system of physical education for all children up to the age of nineteen," is one of the proposals, "including health supervision and instruction." Health supervision has been for years the goal towards which the school systems of the country have been turning their steps and health education is today a staff upon which the health administrator depends. These two factors, health supervision and health education, to quote the language of the "plank" still further, "would remedy conditions revealed by the draft and would add to the economic, industrial and economic strength of the nation."

Further still the "plank" realizes the necessity that the Government be a guide and an adviser. "National leadership and stimulation will be necessary to induce the states to adopt a wise system of physical training."

The "pull together spirit," so ably advocated by Dr. Vincent at the Chicago meeting of the Association, finds its place in the statement of the essentials of the best government, by a great political party, in these terms: "The public health activities of the Federal Government are scattered through numerous departments and bureaus, resulting in inefficiency, duplication and extravagance. We advocate a greater centralization of the Federal functions, and in addition urge the better coördination of the Federal, state and local health agencies."

Health officers throughout the country will welcome this appreciation of the importance of their profession and of the general line of thought of their leading men. Public health is certainly coming into its own as a power for the strengthening of the nation, so that in the tests for supremacy that the future is certain to present, it may hold with undiminished lustre the high place that it has ever assumed when the freedom and the advancement of its citizens have been considered.

Child labor and women in industry are other "planks" in the platform involving principles with which the health officer is familiar, while housing is treated by the platform in a large and comprehensive way. Although Lincolns come occasionally from log cabins and some sanitarians may question the direct effect of housing upon health, the fundamental fact remains that in the environment that surrounds the hovel, the health risk is almost inevitably greater. Better housing—and the country needs it sorely—is a measure that can be given its proper place by interest in it of the National Government.

With the emphasis of the U. S. Government on health supervision, health education, National leadership and example, coördination and coöperation, and betterment of conditions in the industries, the health officer may attack his local problems feeling that he will have a support and a sympathy that are essential to his work. The "plank" in the platform of the Republican party will cheer him and strengthen his hand.

TEAM WORK AMONG HEALTH AGENCIES

In an encouraging number of states we find the beginnings of coördination between the various health activities. For a long time, most of the agencies have pursued their ways, each for itself. It has been a rather common thing to find independent, overlapping, and even conflicting efforts between the organizations for child welfare, tuberculosis, public health nursing, mental hygiene, social hygiene, and the official agencies.

Organizations for coöperation now exist in Kansas, Maine, Ohio, Delaware, Massachusetts, and doubtless other states. The latest addition to the list is Massachusetts, where the Massachusetts Central Health Council of state-wide agencies was organized in May, 1920. Each of the constituent organizations sends two representatives to the Council. Every two months the latter meets and discusses the respective activities.

It is to be emphasized that the work of this Council is not repressive. Its functions are advisory, if anything, the programs of the constituent organizations will be expanded, because of the opportunities for service created through the suggestions of other organizations. The public health nursing organization, for example, will find that the cancer society has a message which should be carried to the public through public health nurses.

The initial activities of this organization will be to bring representatives from the various fields together to talk things over. Each organization will present its programs and problems for discussion. Other activities will, however, suggest themselves as time goes on. For example, the influence for legislation of the combined organizations will be stronger than of the constituent units. It may be found advisable later to conduct one campaign for funds instead of the rather bewildering number of the past. Finally, organization of this type tends to bring about a more wholesome relation between the official and the non-official health worker. The present regrettable condition in this regard has been largely due through failure to get together and talk things over. As a consequence there is no agreement as to what are the respective duties of the official and the voluntary health worker.

From starting out as forums for the discussion of problems of coming interest it is not inconceivable that some of the constituent organizations may find it advantageous to amalgamate, or to establish a federation involving firmer ties than at present. In the beginning, however, Councils like this will do well to leave to their constituent organizations a maximum autonomy.

BOOKS AND REPORTS
REVIEWED

Yours for Sleep. *William S. Walsh, M. D., New York: E. P. Dutton and Co. 1920.*

Insomnia may be corrected in so many cases by the exercise of enlightened common sense that a book of this character will be of real value to the person suffering from sleeplessness. It is for him that the volume is written, and it will therefore be of only secondary interest to the physician. The health officer will be interested only because of the fact that the living of a moderate, hygienic existence will usually prevent insomnia.

The various chapters take up the physiology of sleep, wakeful disorders of sleep, insomnia and its causes, worry, neurasthenia, indigestion and constipation, hypertension and arteriosclerosis, eye defects, diseases of the teeth and gums, value of exercise and fresh air, hygiene of the bed and the sleeping room, and remedies for sleeplessness.

Dr. Walsh's suggestions are concrete and generally sound.—*R. B.*

✦

Standard Nomenclature of Diseases and Pathological Conditions, Injuries and Poisonings for the United States. *Washington, D. C., Government Printing Office, 1920.*

Lack of standardization is a common failing of the age, and much time is consumed, much discussion aroused and much misunderstanding caused because of the employment of various names for the same thing or failure to realize the precise definition of certain words. The confusion formerly existing in stating the causes of death to the authorities for record has largely been swept away by the international classifications. For diseases and pathological conditions the definition of the terms has been undertaken and is set forth in the volume. Begun by the Council of National Defense, the list has been completed by the Bureau of the Census under the supervision of William H. Davis, M. D., Chief Statistician for Vital Statistics and Richard C. Lappin, Expert Special Agent.

The nomenclature is divided into three sections, diseases and pathological conditions; injuries, wounds, etc., by external causes;

and poisonings and intoxications. An expansive notation admits of additions in future reprintings of the list, and that these may be the more perfect, criticisms and suggestions are solicited. This little volume will certainly be most helpful.—*R.*

✦

Industrial Educational Literature. The *National Safety Council* is devoting more and more space in its educational leaflets and bulletins, which are distributed weekly, to the subject of industrial hygiene and the prevention of occupational diseases. Recently there have been issued by the Council illustrated leaflets on the subject of fatigue reducing chairs, correct types of acid containers, methods of opening acids drums, value of the thermometer in the workroom to keep temperature down, and similar material. Attention should especially be called to Safe Practices Bulletin No. 21, entitled *Accident Records, How to Compile Them and How to Use Them;* and also to Bulletin No. 32 entitled *Exhaust Systems.* The address of the Council is 168 North Michigan Avenue, Chicago, Illinois.

✦

The Modern Hospital, having outgrown its former quarters has removed its offices to its own building, 22-24 East Ontario Street, Chicago, Ill. In doing this the well known authority on all matters pertaining to the hospital is strengthening the growing group of medical centers in Chicago, for within a few blocks is the house of the American Medical Association while the new home of the American College of Surgeons is near at hand. Within the Modern Hospital Building will be gathered a goodly number of affiliated activities, *The Modern Hospital* and its *Year Book,* and *Modern Medicine,* together with the offices of the American Hospital Association and the National Catholic Welfare Council. Other developments are in the air which are likely to make this center more noteworthy to all who are interested in these particular fields of work.

BOOKS AS A HELP TO HEALTH

T. S. DaPonte.

The war probably did more than any other agency in all history to promote the use of books. Homesick men, tired men, wounded men, all took to books to keep their minds off their troubles and their pains. Men who formerly had scoffed at books, the pleasures they could give and the things they could teach, turned to them as they would turn to faithful friends. And the habit of reading acquired by men in active service and those incapacitated by wounds or disease has clung to them since, helping many to a state of mental satisfaction, and others to material success.

During the war the American Library Association distributed more than 7,000,000 volumes to men in service at home and overseas. Those who were active in camp and field had, of course, some time to read, but the most beneficial effects through books was achieved among men in the hospitals. For them the hours passed slowly, and books were necessary to help them in comparative contentment. Not only were tales of travel, adventure and fiction in demand, but there was an unceasing call for technical books and special kinds of reading matter such as might help a man to climb to a more advanced place in the world's workshop after army life was over. Many a soldier who, since the armistice, has achieved success in profession or trade, acknowledges that he was helped materially by books that he read while in the service.

Doctors in the military hospitals emphasized the therapeutic value of reading, and the A. L. A. rapidly marshaled its resources and was able to supply books, magazines and newspapers to more than 200 hospitals, and librarians to 75. Since the war's termination the Association has kept up this work to a very considerable degree, and still is supplying a book and magazine service to the 42 Public Health Service Hospitals. In nine of these the A. L. A. has full-time librarians stationed, and in others the Red Cross and the A. L. A. combine to pay the salary of a librarian who also acts as Red Cross Director, the Red Cross furnishing the quarters for the library, and the A. L. A. the books, newspapers and magazines. In some cities the public libraries consider it as part of their regular duties to give a special service to these hospitals.

This great work which the Association did during the war made it ambitious to accomplish even more for the benefit of civilization and the advancement of good citizenship, and it, therefore, has adopted an Enlarged Program which comprises the promotion of efficiency, contentment and industry by inculcating a desire for good reading, and placing books where they will be easy of access to all. The Association's slogan "Books for Everybody!" makes known its intent in a general way, but there are many special branches of this general program, such as urging that a more diversified literature be printed for the blind in the standard Braille type, and that publishers be shown the necessity of having books, which tell of American ideals and traditions, printed in foreign languages so that the new comers to this country can readily acquire an understanding of its aims, and the opportunities which it offers.

For these purposes as well as to urge the adoption of the county library system through which books will be put within easy reach of the most isolated communities, and to facilitate its present service to the Merchant Marine, coast guards, and lighthouse stations and patients in the Public Health Service hospitals, the Association is raising $2,000,000. This sum is being obtained through the personal efforts of librarians, library trustees and friends of libraries, and without recourse to a "drive."

Theodore Roosevelt once said: "After the church and the school the free public library is the most effective influence for good in America. The moral, mental, and material benefits to be derived from a carefully selected collection of good books, free for the use of all the people, cannot be overestimated. No community can afford to be without a library."

This view likewise has been endorsed by other great men and women, and almost universally by the press. Writing on the subject the *New York World* recently said editorially: "What has been done for a few towns by private generosity, with or without public co-operation, should be done for many towns and outlying regions, needing to be more closely knit to the intellectual life of the country as a whole, by public action at the public cost."

ASSOCIATION NEWS

HEALTH EMPLOYMENT BUREAU

Help-wanted announcements will be carried free in this column until further notice. Copy goes to the printer on the fifteenth of each month. In answering keyed advertisements, please mail replies separately.

The Health Employment Bureau also sends lists of applicants to prospective employers without charge.

Field Director Rural Sanitation in Southern State. Salary, $2,700 to $3,600, with $800 expense allowance. Address 352, care of this Journal.

Director for large teaching dispensary in North Atlantic State. Previous experience in hospital or dispensary administration desirable. Medical degree preferable, although not essential. Salary, about $6,000, according to ability. Address 359, care of this Journal.

Food chemist at the Health Bureau, Rochester, N. Y. Salary, $2,500 to $3,000, according to qualifications and experience. Apply to Health Officer, Rochester, N. Y.

Full time health officer is desired for Oakland County. Salary, $3,600, with allowance of $700 for auto maintenance. Address 361, care of this Journal.

Woman technician directress laboratory City Health Department, capable of doing water and milk analyses and routine bacteriology. Salary to begin, $1,500. Apply with full information to R. L. Carlton, M. D., City Health Officer, Winston-Salem, N. C.

Full time city and county administrative health officer in North Carolina; population approximately 40,000; salary, $3,500 to $4,000 to experienced man. Address 363, care of this Journal.

Recent medical graduate interested in bacteriological or serological research and qualified to teach hygiene in state university. Man with a medical degree preferred, but one without will be considered. Salary, $2,500 to $3,500. Address 364, care of this Journal.

Organizer for Venereal Disease Bureau in the Middle West. Medical degree required. Address 365, care of this Journal.

One chief medical officer. Salary, $3,600. Two public health physicians. Salary, $3,000 each. One laboratory technician. Salary, $2,400. Reorganizing Health Department. Wonderful opportunity. City of 90,000. Send for qualification requirements. Address John A. Kappelman, M. D., Health Commissioner, Canton, Ohio.

SAN FRANCISCO MEETING

Reservation Blank for Hotel—Tear off on this line

To Dr. Gayle G. Moseley,
No. 333 Pine Street,
San Francisco, Cal.:

Please reserve for me..............rooms for................persons for the A. P. H. A.
Meeting from September......till September.......
Place cross (X) after your preference.

With bath. Single room...... Double room...... Twin beds......
Without bath. Single room...... Double room......
Preferences in hotels. Name two or three..
Maximum rate per day for room.......... Minimum rate per day for room........
    Name ....
    Street address ....
    City .... State ....

TRIP TO CALIFORNIA

For the information of members of the A. P. H. A. who have in mind attendance at the Forty-ninth Annual Meeting in San Francisco, Cal., September 13-17, 1920, the JOURNAL assembles references to the principal facts which have already been given in detail. Blanks are also furnished, which may be convenient for securing Pullman car reservations, also rooms in the hotels. A list of hotels is here given together with the accommodations they offer and the rates for these accommodations.

The Palace Hotel is to be the Association Headquarters. Meetings will be held in the Auditorium, Civic Center.

For rooms at the hotels address Dr. Gayle G. Moseley, No. 333 Pine Street, San Francisco, Cal., Chairman, A. P. H. A. Hotel Committee, giving details of accommodations desired and the limits of cost of same. For a guide the form on page 610 has been prepared, which may be filled out, detached and sent forward. You will receive a reply confirming your reservation.

To secure your transportation make application to your local railway agent who will furnish tickets from your home city to San Francisco and return. He will furnish them in accordance with the route that you select.

SAN FRANCISCO HOTELS

		Room with Private Bath		Room Without Bath	
Palace Hotel, Association Headquarters	Single	$5.00 to	$ 8.00		
	Double	8.00 to	14.00		
Hotel St. Francis, Union Square	Single	5.00 to	8.00		
	Double	8.00 to	14.00		
Hotel Stewart, Geary St. at Union Square	Single	3.50 to	4.00		
	Double	5.00 to	5.50		
	Twin beds	6.00			
Clift Hotel, Geary St. at Taylor	Single	4.50 to	5.00		
	Double	7.00 to	8.00		
Hotel Plaza	Single	2.50 to	3.50	Single $2.00 to	$2.50
	Double	4.50 to	5.50	Double 3.00 to	4.00
	Twin beds	6.00			
Hotel Whitcomb, Civic Center	Sinble	4.00 to	6.00	Single 1.50 to	2.50
	Double	5.00 to	8.00	Double 2.00 to	3.00
American plan	Single	4.00 to	5.00	Single 3.50 to	4.50
Bellevue Hotel, Geary St. at Taylor	Single	3.50 to	4.00		
	Double	5.00 to	6.00		
Chancellor Hotel, Powell St. at Union Square	Single	3.00			
	Double	4.00			
	Twin beds	4.50			
Hotel Argonaut, Fourth St. and Market	Single	2.00 to	2.50	Single 1.50	
	Double	3.00 to	3.50	Double 2.00	

Reservation Blanks for Berth in Pullman Train—Tear off on This Line

DR. W. A. EVANS, Chairman A. P. H. A. Travel Committee,
906 Tribune Building, Chicago, Ill.

Reserve for me............berths on the A. P. H. A. Special Train to the Coast, to leave Chicago on Wednesday, September 8, 1920, at 10:30 P. M.

Name ....

Address ....

The rate from Chicago to San Francisco and return is $96.12. The rates from other important cities east of the Mississippi are given in the JOURNAL for June, page 544. The itinerary of the special A. P. H. A. train from Chicago to the Coast may be found in the May JOURNAL, page 479, and Pullman rates are in the same JOURNAL, page 484.

Those who intend to board the A. P. H. A. Special at Chicago will secure their round trip railway tickets (San Francisco and return) from their local agents, and provide Pullman accommodations from the point of origin to Chicago. For Pullman reservations on the A. P. H. A. Special, write to Dr. W. A. Evans, and then claim your reservations and make payment for the same at the station of the C. & N. W. R. R. in Chicago.

It is expected that there will be special cars from Boston and New York to be attached to the Special in Chicago. Final information will appear in the July NEWS LETTER.

Order your reservations of Dr. Evans NOW! (Use blank on page 611.)

□

PERCENTAGES OF QUOTAS FILLED
TO MONDAY NOON, JUNE 28, 1920

TOTAL NUMBER OF MEMBERS RECEIVED TO
DATE, 1,535, or 51% OF QUOTA

	Percentage of quota filled		Percentage of quota filled
Utah	457	Oklahoma	53
New Mexico	318	Delaware	50
North Carolina	273	Massachusetts	48
California	145	Iowa	48
Saskatchewan	142	Wisconsin	45
Colorado	127	Missouri	43
Idaho	125	West Virginia	43
Maine	117	New York	37
Florida	117	New Jersey	35
Montana	110	Tennessee	30
North Dakota	106	Manitoba	27
Nova Scotia	100	Arizona	25
Rhode Island	91	Indiana	23
Vermont	88	Illinois	23
South Dakota	85	Virginia	22
Maryland and D. C.	82	Nebraska	21
Alabama	78	South Carolina	19
Connecticut	69	New Hampshire	19
Ohio	60	Kansas	17
Michigan	59	Kentucky	17
Washington	58	Mississippi	15
Minnesota	56	Pennsylvania	14
Arkansas	54	New Brunswick	13
		Texas	12

LIST OF NEW MEMBERS
Proposed for Election to the
A. P. H. A.
June 15 to June 22, 1920, inclusive.

Names of Sponsors are set in **Bold Face Type.**
Names of New Members are in Light Face Type.

ALABAMA

J. D. Dowling, M. D., Birmingham.
Samuel A. Tarrant, Sanitary Officer, Board of Health, Birmingham.
E. E. Jackson Lumber Co. (sustaining member), Riderwood.
E. B. Johnson, Montgomery.
Gordon S. Bunkley, Local Director, Malaria Control, State Board of Health, Shelby.

CALIFORNIA

I. R. Bancroft, M. D., Sacramento.
G. C. Bellinger, M. D., Supt. Tuber. San., Salem, Ore.
Agnes Walker, M. D., San Francisco.
Annie D. MacRae, M. D., Bacteriologist, Health Dept., San Francisco.
Julia George, Social Worker, San Francisco.

COLORADO

C. G. Hickey, M. D., Denver.
Sarah E. Barkley, R. N., Public Health Nurse, Fowler.

IDAHO

E. R. Dooley, Twin Falls.
A. A. Newberry, M. D., Filer.
J. N. Davis, M. D., City Health Officer, Kimberly.

ILLINOIS

S. S. Winner, M. D., Chicago.
W. G. Sachse, M. D., Health Officer, Morris.
C. St. Clair Drake, M. D., Springfield.
E. H. Best, M. D., Commissioner of Health, Freeport.
C. E. Crawford, M. D., District Health Officer, Rockford.
Mary E. Wilson, R. N., Springfield.
Harry W. Schumacher, M. D., State Dept. of Health, Springfield.
Streator Red Cross Association.

IOWA

John W. Teed, Bloomfield.
Beulah Bennett, R. N., Public Health Nurse, Bloomfield.
Organized Welfare Bureau, Sioux City.

KANSAS

Edna Flanagan, Abilene.
C. F. Attwood, M. D., County Health Officer, Abilene.

LOUISIANA

Oscar Dowling, M. D., and Mary L. Railey, New Orleans.
Edgar J. Beranger, M. D., Acting Asst. Surgeon, U. S. P. H. S., New Orleans.
R. C. Williams, M. D., New Orleans.
R. R. Spencer, M. D., Medical Officer, U. S. P. H. S., New Orleans.

MAINE

Wilfrid A. Hennessy, Bangor.
John Wilson, Pres. Bangor Associated Charities, Bangor.

MARYLAND AND D. C.

C. L. Ewing, Baltimore.
Theodore C. Buck, Jr., Bacteriologist, Baltimore.
Wm. Royal Stokes, M. D., Baltimore.
John J. Dunn, Jr., Bacteriologist, Baltimore.

Carroll Fox, M. D., Washington.
James Leslie Busby, M. D., U. S. P. H. S., Takoma Park.
R. S. Carey, M. D., P. A. Surgeon, U. S. P. H. S., Washington.
Martin Cooley, M. D., U. S. P. H. S., Washington.
Charles S. Cowie, M. D., Hyattsville.
Sherwood Dix, M. D., P. A. Surgeon, U. S. P. H. S., Washington.
Ella R. Fales, M. D., A. A. Surgeon, U. S. P. H. S., Washington.
Thomas Foster, M. D., Surgeon, U. S. P. H. S., Glen Echo, Md.
E. D. Graves, M. D., U. S. P. H. S., Washington.
Gordon B. Hamilton, M. D., A. A. Surgeon, U. S. P. H. S., Washington.
Carl J. Harris, M. D., Surgeon U. S. P. H. S. (R), Washington.
Samuel B. Harris, M. D., Asst. Surgeon, U. S. P. H. S., Washington.
Henry Hayes, M. D., P. A. Surgeon, U. S. P. H. S. (R), Washington.
Earl K. Holt, M. D., Takoma Park.
J. S. Laird, M. D., A. A. Surgeon, U. S. P. H. S., Washington.
Horace M. Lowe, M. D., Asst. Surgeon, U. S. P. H. S., Washington.
George I. McKelway, M. D., U. S. P. H. S., Washington.
J. H. Mendelson, M. D., U. S. P. H. S., Washington.
Charles E. Ralph, M. D., P. A. Surgeon, U. S. P. H. S., Washington.
C. S. Rine, D. D. S., P. A. Dental Surgeon (R), Washington.
L. B. Rogers, M. D., A. A. Surgeon, U. S. P. H. S., Washington.
George A. Rowland, M. D., Surgeon (R), U. S. P. H. S., Washington.
Margaret R. Stewart, M. D., U. S. P. H. S., Takoma Park.
L. M. Wilbor, M. D., P. A. Surgeon (R), U. S. P. H. S., Alexandria, Va.
Carl E. Miner, M. D., Washington.
Henrietta Additon, Exec. Asst. U. S. Interdepartmental Social Hygiene Board, Washington.
Ormie C. Lance, Supervisor, Interdepartmental Social Hygiene Board, Washington.

MASSACHUSETTS

B. W. Carey, M. D., Boston.
Fred O. Elder, M. D., Peabody.
Wm. C. Woodward, M. D., Boston.
Allston Burr, Chairman, Metropolitan Chapter, A. R. C., Chestnut Hill.

MICHIGAN

J. H. Kellogg, M. D., Battle Creek.
M. May Allen, M. D., Race Betterment Foundation, Battle Creek.
William H. Riley, M. D., Battle Creek.
R. S. Eckman, Jackson.
Mayme Lewis, Dietitian, Foote Memorial Hospital, Jackson.
Blanch N. Epler, M. D., Kalamazoo.
Mabel Kiltz, R. N., Kalamazoo.
Harriet M. Stone, M. D., Kalamazoo.
Philip D. Bourland, M. D., Lake Linden.
Calumet & Hecla Mining Company, Atten. Jas. MacNaughton, Vice-Pres., Calumet.
Wm. F. Petrie, Lansing.
James A. Humphrey, M. D., Health Officer, Lansing.

R. M. Olin, M. D., Lansing.
  F. W. Edelmann, M. D., Saginaw.
  Anna M. Schill, R. N., Supt. Hurley Hospital, Flint.
Grace Amadon, St. Joseph.
  Emmanuel Missionary College, Berrien Springs.
  Elizabeth Fogg Upton, St. Joseph.
F. W. Edelmann, M. D., Saginaw.
  Wallis C. Smith, Chapter Chairman, A. R. C., Saginaw.

MISSOURI

M. P. Ravenel, M. D., Columbia.
  James R. Pyrtle, M. D., Deputy Health Commissioner, Centerville.
  R. W. Berry, M. D., Deputy Health Commissioner, Mexico.
  E. H. Brandt, M. D., Deputy Health Commissioner, Warrenton.
  John Franklin Chandler, M. D., Deputy Health Commissioner, Oregon.
  J. E. Gartside, M. D., Deputy Health Commissioner, Kingston.
  Willard H. Gooch, M. D., Elmer.
  J. H. Holman, M. D., Unionville.
  Austin McMichael, M. D., Deputy Health Commissioner, Rockport.
  Wilson Murray, M. D., Deputy Health Commissioner, Platte City.
Geo. H. Jones, M. D., Jefferson City.
  H. T. Phillips, Mo. Tuber. Assn., Warrensburg.

MONTANA

S. K. Campbell, M. D., Harlowton.
  J. U. Williams, Supt. of Schools, Harlowton.

NEW HAMPSHIRE

John C. Chase, Derry Village.
  Charles E. Newell, M. D., Derry Village.

NEW JERSEY

John Hall, Freehold.
  Harvey S. Brown, M. D., Health Officer, Freehold.

NEW YORK

Fenimore D. Beagle, Albany.
  Matie T. Jones, Community Nurse, Brockport.
F. J. Sherman, M. D., Ballston Spa.
  Grace H. Redmond, R. N., Community Nurse, Ballston Spa.
S. J. Byrne, M. D., Brooklyn.
  W. E. Ford, M. D., U. S. P. H. S., New York.
Halsey J. Ball, M. D., Glens Falls.
  Louis A. Parmenter, M. D., Health Officer, Corinth.
S. W. Sayer, M. D., Morristown.
  H. R. Thompson, M. D., Health Officer, Morristown.
C. R. Hervey, M. D., Oswego.
  J. D. Olin, M. D., Watertown.
  B. W. Severance, M. D., Health Officer, Phoenix.
Kenneth Allen, New York.
  James W. Routh, Civil Engineer, Dir. Bur. of Municipal Research, Rochester.
H. M. Biggs, M. D., New York.
  Dept. of Agricultural Chemistry, Cornell University, Ithaca.
Royal S. Copeland, M. D., New York.
  Herbert J. Stone, M. D., Medical Inspector, Dept. of Health, New York.
C. E. Ford, M. D., New York.
  J. R. de la Torre Bueno, Editor, Gen. Chemical Co. Bulletin, White Plains.
  Gilbert G. Fox, M. D., Works Physician, Gen. Chemical Co., Newell, Pa.
  C. D. Kunkel, M. D., Plant Physician, General Chemical Co., Pulaski, Virginia.
  B. F. Lowry, M. D., Plant Physician, Gen. Chemical Co., Cleveland, Ohio.

NEW YORK CITY

C. E. Ford, M. D., New York.
  John C. Phipps, M. D., Plant Physician, Gen. Chemical Co., Hudson Heights, New Jersey.
Rudolph Hering, D. Sc., New York.
  Allan W. Cuddeback, Engr. & Supt. Passaic Water Co., Paterson, N. J.

NORTH CAROLINA

G. E. Reynolds, R. N., Charlotte.
  Ethel Smith, R. N., Public Health Nurse, Charlotte.
Rose M. Ehrenfeld, Raleigh.
  Mrs. Lionel Weil, Goldsboro.
W. S. Rankin, M. D., Raleigh.
  Albert Anderson, M. D., Supt. State Hospital, Raleigh.
  W. W. Faison, M. D., Supt. State Hospital, Goldsboro.
  W. A. Hardenbergh, Sanitary Engineer, Charlotte.

K. E. Miller, M. D., Tarboro.
  Charles L. Outland, M. D., Health Officer, Tarboro.
  J. P. Brown, M. D., Fairmont.

OHIO

J. V. Greenbaum, M. D., Cincinnati.
  Hiram B. Weiss, M. D., Cincinnati.
J. A. Kappelman, M. D., and Ruth E. Young, R. N., Canton.
  Laurene F. Menke, Public Health Nurse, Canton.

OKLAHOMA

A. R. Lewis, M. D., Oklahoma City.
  C. M. Bloss, M. D., Health Officer, Okemah.

UTAH

T. B. Beatty, M. D., Salt Lake City.
  John R. Anderson, M. D., Springville.
  Steele Bailey, Jr., M. D., Health Officer, Mammoth.
  W. J. Bardsley, M. D., Health Officer, Park City.
  William H. Bash, M. D., Health Officer, Clear Creek.
  Geo. D. Bennett, Metropolitan Life Ins. Co., Ogden.
  Brigham Young University, Atten. G. H. Brimhall, Pres., Provo.
  F. J. Burton, M. D., Health Officer, Parowan.
  Geo. Eaton, Prin. East Side High School, Salt Lake City.
  F. R. Gledhill, M. D., Health Officer, Richfield.
  J. A. Hagan, M. D., Health Officer, Gunnison.
  Alma Hardy, Health Officer, Bountiful.
  C. J. Heath, M. D., Health Officer, Marysvale.
  E. S. Hinckley, State Industrial School, Ogden.
  Branch Agricultural College of Utah, Atten. Roy F. Homer, Prin., Cedar City.
  W. Karl Hopkins, Supt. Ogden Schools, Ogden.
  R. M. Jones, M. D., Health Officer, Hiawatha.
  Oscar A. Kirkham, Chief of Boy Scouts, Salt Lake City.
  H. Claude Lewis, Supt. of Schools, Cedar City.
  M. J. Macfarlane, M. D., Health Officer, Cedar City.
  S. L. McCorkle, Supt. Moab Schools, Moab.
  David O. McKay, Health Officer, Ogden.
  H. K. Merrill, M. D., City Physician, East Logan.
  Joseph R. Morrell, M. D., Ogden.
  Ogden Chamber of Commerce, Ogden.
  Henry Peterson, Supt. Logan Schools, Logan.
  Geo. S. Sears, M. D., Health Officer, Manti.
  E. A. Stranquist, M. D., Health Officer, Brigham City.
  A. Z. Tanner, M. D., Health Officer, Layton.
  E. R. C. Tracy, M. D., Health Officer, Delta.
  W. Visich, M. D., Health Officer, Morgan.
  F. J. Woodbury, M. D., Health Officer, St. George.
  F. D. Worlton, M. D., Health Officer, Lehi.

VERMONT

Bern D. Colby, M. D., Rutland.
  Mary A. Devlin, R. N., Public Health Nurse, Rutland.

VIRGINIA

L. J. Roper, M. D., Portsmouth.
  D. R. Smith, Meat and Milk Inspector, Portsmouth.
W. F. Draper, M. D., Richmond.
  Stanley B. Campbell, Sanitary Demonstrator, Richmond.
Roy K. Flannagan, Richmond.
  Mamie Rice, County Nurse, Darlington Heights.

WASHINGTON

Mae E. Larkin, Seattle.
  Katherine D. Stewart, City and County Bacteriologist, Yakima.

WISCONSIN

C. N. Harper, M. D., Madison.
  Charles H. Lemon, M. D., Milwaukee.
W. D. Stovall, M. D., Madison.
  M. Starr Nichols, Chemist and Bacteriologist, Madison.
R. A. Maddock, Oshkosh.
  Arthur J. Hall, City Chemist and Bacteriologist, Appleton, Utah.

CANADA

Harry Lytle, Saskatoon, Sask.
  T. W. Walker, M. D., School Medical Inspector, Saskatoon.

PORTO RICO

A. W. Hedrich, Boston, Mass.
  P. Gutierrez Igaravidez, M. D., Dir., Inst. of Tropical Medicine & Hygiene, San Juan.

PUBLIC HEALTH NOTES

Abstracts by D. GREENBERG, M. P. HORWOOD and MAYO TOLMAN.

Is the Tuberculosis Campaign Based on Sound Principles?—Recently Dr. Raymond Pearl has questioned the value of the public health campaign. He maintains that public health officials fail to recognize the supreme importance of the racial factor in the control of mortality and morbidity rates, and as a result millions of dollars are squandered every year for public health work. He believes that the reason why communities varied in the amount of influenza they had was due to the differences in the biologic constitution and organic fitness of the people in each community. Dr. Armstrong, on the other hand, has found that although the racial factor is exceedingly important in determining the tuberculosis mortality and morbidity rates of a community, that race habits are equally important. Furthermore, Dr. Dublin has shown that the mortality rate from tuberculosis of the lungs among the white policyholders of the Metropolitan Life Insurance Company, has decreased 42 per cent from 1911 to 1919 among those persons in the age group from 35 to 44. He believes that the reason for this can be found in the intensive campaign of public health education, which communities and private agencies have waged during this period. Increased knowledge of the principles of personal hygiene has aided in diminished death rates. The Journal of Outdoor Life concludes that the tuberculosis campaign is based on sound principles, and that the campaign should be broadened to include other fundamental factors which bear on the prevalence of the disease.—*Journal of Outdoor Life*, April, 1920. (*M. P. H.*)

✦

Summary of Sanitary Situation in Oriental Europe.—The Central Bureau for the Control of Epidemics of the League of Red Cross Societies reports under date of January, 1920, a resumé of sanitary situations regarding epidemic diseases in Austria, Hungary, Czecho-Slovakia, Poland, Ukrainia, Roumania, Jugo-Slavia, and Italy. Typhus fever is the most wide spread and the most severe, constituting a source of great danger not only for eastern Europe but for the whole continent. It is spread throughout Russia and the epidemic is most virulent in the territory constituting the recent theater of war on the eastern front. Smallpox is similarly especially prevalent in this area, but has been successfully combatted in all those states which have instituted vaccination, either voluntary or compulsory on a large scale. Up to the time of the report plague was officially reported only from certain places in western Asia and southeastern Europe. But it is rumored to be present also in Ukrainia and Czecho-Slovakia. Cholera, while wide spread in that part of Russia adjacent to Poland, has so far not obtained a foothold in that country itself.—*Revue Int. Croix-Rouge,* March, 1920. (*H. N. C.*)

✦

$15,000 for Health Work in the Dominican Republic.—An additional appropriation of $15,000 has been made by the American Red Cross for hospital work among the poor of the Dominican Republic, following an investigation of health and sanitary conditions there by Dr. John M. Swan. A physician will be provided by the Red Cross to administer the Seybo Hospital as well as nursing personnel for the Municipal Hospital at Santo Domingo City. Certain necessary hospital and medical supplies will also be furnished, and a training school for native nurses will be established in the city.—(*J. A. T.*)

✦

Health in the Virgin Islands.—What the American flag means to the Virgin Islands, expressed in terms of life and death, is shown in vital statistics for the first quarter of the present year revealing a decided decline in the death rate. Health and sanitation work is under the direct supervision of the American naval government. The American Red Cross, which, through its Insular and Foreign Division has in the last two years spent nearly $44,000 for the equipment of hospitals on the Island, has also been of great and timely assistance in improving conditions.

A statement by the chief municipal physician of St. Thomas and St. John shows that the death rate for the first three months of 1920 is the lowest on record in the municipality. It is about one-half of the death rates recorded for the other (English, French and Dutch) West Indian Islands, and is .4 below the 1919 death rate of the registration

615

area in the United States. In addition the birth rate exceeded the death rate by more than 133 per cent. while infant mortality was 76.9 or less than one-half of that recorded in the surrounding islands and considerably below the rate in the States. The record is all the more remarkable because December, January and February are the months when mortality is slightly higher than at other times.

Funds for the administration of the islands are limited but in spite of this in two years the general death rate has been lowered from 39.5 per thousand to 13.6 and infant mortality from 251.7 to 76.9.—(*J. A. T.*)

✦

Public Health in Tasmania.—Any country that has a death rate of 8.84 commands the interest as well as the respect of public health officials. The annual public health report of Tasmania demonstrates that this distant island is, as the geography states, "salubrious." With a population of a little over 200,000 and a birth rate of 25.91, diseases of early infancy caused 149 deaths, cancer 145, tuberculosis (all forms) 124 and influenze 37. The highest figure of all is for diseases of the circulatory system which caused 248 deaths. The only other disease which reaches three figures in the "causes of death" tables are those of the nervous system, 177; the respiratory system, 212; and the digestive system, 158. Deaths from infectious diseases are measured by units or tens.

A child welfare association conducts home visiting, lectures, talks and demonstrations at a center. Two-thirds of the total expenditure of the health department went for the prevention and treatment of influenza. The laboratory reports indicate that supervision of food, especially milk, is actively pursued and that the department is by no means slow to take legal action when occasion arises. The general tenor of the report gives one the impression that the Tasmanian health department is full of youthful vigor.—Editorial, *Medical Officer*, May 1, 1920.—(*H. N. C.*)

✦

Insanitary Post Offices.—"Many of the post offices of the country are not fit for the purpose for which they were erected. In addition, insanitary conditions prevail in some of the largest. A notable example is the Chicago post office, the sanitary condition of which has been a source of complaint for over a decade. Lack of ventilation, proper lighting, and even of ordinary cleaning have been continuously complained of without redress. Such surroundings contribute to a lowered efficiency, a higher sick and death rate, and an earlier superannuation. Uncleaned, even undusted, mail sacks not only spread germs through the offices but must contaminate the mail received by the public. Tuberculosis rises to the dignity of an occupational disease among post office clerks."—Speech by Mr. Nelson in the House of Representatives on April 29. Reported in the *Congressional Record.*—(*J. A. T.*)

✦

Influenza and Tuberculosis.—Amberson and Peters in a critical review of the recent writings on the effect of the influenza epidemic on tuberculosis, and in an analysis of their own cases have come to the following conclusions: (1) What evidence we possess does not lend any support to the belief that the usual severity of an influenza attack is less among the tuberculous than among the nontuberculous; on the contrary pulmonary complications seem equally frequent, and our statistical records indicate that the case fatality of influenza among the tuberculous was higher than among the general population. (2) In a certain number of individuals epidemic marks the inception of definite pulmonary tuberculosis which did not previously exist as clinical disease. The onset of pulmonary tuberculosis following influenza may be rapid and immediate or insidious and remote. We believe that to ignore or deny the possibility of pulmonary tuberculosis as a *sequela* is to defer diagnosis and treatment of a number of patients requiring treatment unduly, with resulting limitations of their chances for recovery. (3) Among those already tuberculous, influenza may to a varying degree have reactive, quiescent or apparently inactive lesions. Such reactivation may be marked by a temporary exacerbation of symptoms of short duration or by the classical evidences of a severe relapse. That a large number do not pursue such a course and do escape definite permanent damage is not denied.—J. B. Amberson Jr. and Peters Jr. *Amer. Rev. of Tub.*, Apr., 1920, 71. *(D. G.)*

SYMPTOMS OF ILLNESS IN CHILDREN

These directions, phrased in language which may be understood by the parent or teacher, have been issued by the New York State Department of Health, Hermann M. Biggs, M. D., Commissioner. They are so direct that they merit the widest circulation, and the JOURNAL is pleased to be a factor toward that circulation.

Symptoms of illness in children which should be observed by parents and school teachers and their significance

GENERAL SYMPTOMS

Any deviation from the normal in a previously healthy child.

Disinclination to study or play
Unusual "tired feeling"
Drowsiness
Lack lustre of eyes
Cheeks flushed or pallid

SYMPTOMS OF FEVER
May be the beginning of an acute infectious disease or simply stomach trouble, intestinal i n f e c t i o n or "cold."
These symptoms mark the beginning of most children's diseases.

Chills

The earliest symptoms of many acute infectious diseases; always demand attention.

Vomiting

May be due to simple gastro-intestinal disorder (indigestion). May be early symptoms of scarlet fever or other communicable disease.

Sweating

May be profuse and has probably followed a preceding chill or fever.

Nervousness
Restlessness
Irritability

May indicate beginning disease of brain or spinal cord, or a functional nervous disorder; St. Vitus dance or epileptic fits. May be due to eye strain, skin disorder, insufficient sleep, etc.

Cough

May be beginning:
Whooping cough
Tuberculosis
Measles
Simple cold or influenza (grippe)

Loss of weight

Particularly if associated with slight fever, swollen glands of neck, a limp, or pain in the back, may suggest tuberculosis.

Cold in the head

Especially with running nose and eyes: first symptoms of measles, or German measles. May be simple cold or influenza

Pallor

Indicates impoverished blood. With puffiness of the face may indicate kidney disease, especially after scarlet fever.

Frequent requests to go to the toilet

May indicate trouble with bowels, kidneys or bladder.

LOCAL SYMPTOMS

Swelling in the neck
May indicate:
Mumps
Tuberculous glands
Beginning of diphtheria
Suppurating glands after scarlet fever or measles
Bad teeth

Eruptions on the skin
May be one of acute infectious diseases.
May be one of communicable skin diseases, ring worm, impetigo.
If eruption is accompanied by scratching, may be, if on head, lice; if on hands and body, itch.

Discharges
If from nose, throat, ears or suppurating glands may be the result of measles or scarlet fever.
If irritating, creamy, or bloody from nose may be nasal diphtheria.
If from one nostril may be foreign body in nostril.

Scowling
Squinting
Headache
Holding book improper distance in reading
Symptoms of faulty eyesight

Eyes red
May be "Pink Eye," eye strain or beginning measles or German measles.

Eyes discharging
May be granular lids or beginning measles.

Sore throat
May be first sign of
Diphtheria
Scarlet fever   Measles
Tonsilitis   Septic sore throat

Earache
May be due to adenoids or beginning middle ear disease.

Running ears
Middle ear infection (otitis). May be complication after infectious disease.
May be due to adenoids.

Pain If referred to hip and accompanied by limp or inability to bear weight on limb: may be first symptoms of tuberculous hip disease.
If referred to back, may be beginning of Pott's disease.
If referred to right side of abdomen, may be appendicitis.
If referred to back of ear, may be beginning of mastoid disease.
If headache, may be beginning of meningitis; may be symptom of inflammation anywhere.

Salaries of Health Workers.—"A man faithful to his ideals frequently gets a thin time from some of the noble philanthropists who adorn our town councils." So writes a correspondent, evidently a health officer, to the *Medical Officer*. Health workers in Great Britain are apparently considerably exercised over the matter of salary. In this issue of the magazine devoted to their interests appear four items concerning remuneration and one on security of tenure of office. Previous issues have more than once dealt with these subjects. Under "Notes and Comments," this journal says, "It is becoming more and more a scandal that medical officers of health as regards their conditions of appointment and their remuneration should be almost entirely subject to the caprice of local authorities." The Ministry of Health has evidently taken a hand in the matter though its influence is apparently not a controlling one. The medical magazines have naturally voiced their sentiments for higher salaries and one at least has refused to publish advertisements calling for health officers where the salary offered was below a certain minimum. The attitude of the local governing body regarding this stand of the profession is reflected in a note relating to a meeting of the Worcestershire County Council. This county was offering the post of Assistant Tuberculous Officer at a salary of £450. Medical papers had declined to print the advertisement stipulating a salary of £450. The Ministry of Health in a letter endorsed this. The Chairman of the Council "objected very strongly to this sort of pressure" and "felt very much adverse to allowing the medical papers or the Ministry to dictate to them." The Council was apparently convinced that assistant medical officers of health could be secured for £450 and voted to advertise in the daily papers.—*Medical Officer.* May 1, 1920. (*H. N. C.*)

✦

Uncle Sam Keeping Candy Pure.—Candy in interstate commerce, the United States Department of Agriculture tells the manufacturers, must be pure and must carry a label that tells the truth.

On the question of purity, harmless colors that do not conceal inferiority are permitted. The use of shellac and other gums for coating is prohibited. The department holds that saccharin is injurious to health and its use in

candy is prohibited. Talc, terra alba, barytes, chrome yellow, alcohol, narcotics, drugs, and mineral substances of all kinds are specifically forbidden in confectionery by the terms of the law. The use of cocoa dust in the manufacture of chocolate goods is held to be objectionable. A harmless mineral oil may be used for a slab dressing if used in such way that little or none of the oil is incorporated in the finished candy. Any of the decisions or opinions relating to the application of the Federal food and drugs act to confectionary may be obtained upon request from the Bureau of Chemistry, United States Department of Agriculture.—(*J. A. T.*)

✦

John Bull Pays for Healthy Babies.—John Bull believes that healthy babies make strong men, and is willing to pay for them, according to reports recently received by the Children's Bureau of the U. S. Department of Labor. In 1918 grants made by the national government in support of infant welfare work in England and Wales amounted to about $1,150,00, which represents one-half of approved expenditure for welfare centers, "health visitors," maternity care and similar work for mothers and children.

The number of health centers increased from 850 in 1917, to 1,550 in June, 1919, over one-half of them supported entirely by public funds. Attendance at the centers has also shown a phenomenal increase.

As a result, it is thought, of public protection of maternity and infancy, the infant mortality rate for England and Wales for 1918 is 94. There was no increase over 1917 even under the adverse conditions of war and influenza.

The 1918 infant mortality rate for the U. S. birth registration area, just published, is 101, 7 points higher than the rate for the preceding year.

Children's Bureau investigations have shown that Uncle Sam's babies die because they and their mothers do not have skilled care.

✦

Do not take drugs to cure the headache, says the United States Public Health Service. Consult a physician, a dentist or an oculist, to see if the cause can be located. Often the eyes, or the teeth may be at fault.

Health Classes for Children.—The health class presents the possibilty of communal service along various lines. It is an agency for general family adjustment in the matters relating to childhood. It possesses a vantage point for the prevention of tuberculosis, cardiac diseases and the development of defects of sight and hearing; as well as the correction of postural errors, and incipient deformities of the feet and spine. In a remedial way, it eliminates or palliates dietetic errors and lessens the likelihood of malnutrition affecting other children of the household. Health classes to function properly should be articulated with a general hospital or dispensary, the home and various agencies which can supplement and augment the work of the class. To provide for these articulations, it is essential to have a social service nurse and one or more friendly visitors, who can correlate the various agencies and activities. The knowledge and experience of social service nurses, broad as they may be, are insufficient to enable them to deal satisfactorily with many home problems. For this reason a teacher of domestic sciences and arts is almost a necessity. In addition to her special work with the home, it is designed to arrange for various classes for mothers and older children, with a view to instilling a working knowledge concerning the numerous phases of home making that are so intimately related with family health.

In his own classes the author has established a certain amount of competition among mothers by having 3 types of admission cards, indicating 3 relative degrees of proficiency in carrying out the instructions given, and in coöperating towards a higher standard of health habits and methods of living. Mothers are promoted and their own efforts determine the rating deserved.—I. S. Wile, *Arch. of Pediatrics,* Mar. 1920, 162. *(D. G.)*

✢

Cats and Human Diphtheria.—Dr. Savage after examining bacteriologically the nose and throat of 8 healthy cats and 12 kittens which had not been associated with cases of human diphtheria found that all the kittens and 3 of the cats failed to show any bacilli which at all resembled diphtheria bacilli. In the case of the remaining five cats bacilli closely resembling the Klebs-Loeffler were recovered, but with one possible exception it was definitely considered that they were not true diphtheria bacilli. The exception was in the case of a cat which was examined three months after the first examination.

Very similar results followed experiments on cats which were associated with cases of human diphtheria, and finally Dr. Savage sought to infect kittens with the disease artificially, for as he observes if, as so often has been asserted, cats suffer from diphtheria, or even if it be merely advanced that they act as carriers of the diphtheira bacillus in their throat or nose, it should be possible to infect them artificially and set up either condition. Feeding experiments were unsuccessful, throat and nasal swabbing met with a like result and contrary to expectation diphtheria bacilli implanted into the nasal cavities were unable to survive beyond a very short period. Dr. Savage expresses the definite opinion that cats do not act as diphtheria carriers, and further states that it would appear that the mucous membranes of these animals are particularly inimical to diphtheria bacilli.—W. G. Savage, *Jour. of Hyg.* Feb. 1920, 152. *Medical Officer,* Apr. 17, 1920.

✢

The Fly a Carrier of Trachoma Virus.—The direct transmission of the virus of the granulomatous conjunctivitis of hot climates is an obvious method of infection, and experiments have shown that the most trivial lesion of the conjunctiva renders the surface susceptible to inoculation. The possibility of infection by flies is also obvious; and in Tunis fresh cases of conjunctivitis occur most frequently at the beginning of the autumn, when flies are most numerous and troublesome. An Algerian monkey *(Macacus innuus)* is readily susceptible to the virus and, when infected, presents a granular conjunctivitis of the type occurring in man, which develops quickly, and becomes cured in about two months. In two experiments flies were kept for three hours in tubes containing the secretion from cases of trachoma, and were then transferred to a clean cage. After an interval of 24 hours in one experiment, and six hours in another, the heads and feet were cut off and pounded up with normal saline solution. Inoculation of the lids of the monkey, after scarification, with this material was followed by a granulomatous conjunctivitis of typical character.— C. Nicolle, A. Cuénod, and G. Blanc, *Compt. Rend. Acad. Sciences,* 1919, vol. 169, 1124. *Medical Officer,* Apr. 3, 1920, 135. *(D. G.)*

A BOTULINUS OBSERVATION

This interesting photograph, reproduced through the courtesy of Matthias Nicoll, M. D., of the State Department of Health, presents a group of patients in one of the state institutions who were suffering from botulinus poisoning. The outbreak occurred during February, 1920. The pieces of paper adhering to the walls and to the persons of these patients have been magnetized by them. If left undisturbed they would adhere to the men or the objects for a long time.

In his report of the occurrence, Dr. J. B. Ranson, Chief Physician at the institution, writes:

"In connection with this particular outbreak there were several features which have never been identified with any other reported outbreaks of botulinus poisoning which make it of particular interest for reference and study. One was the development of patches in the nose and throat of many of the patients; another one was the development of a pecular static electric phenomena, in that these patients, and these only, were able to magnetize sheets of paper to a remarkable degree; the paper after being magnetized by these patients would adhere to any object, walls and rooms for hours and very difficult to shake; these same patients, by rubbing their hands and touching the electric bulb, would cause the carbon filament to vibrate rapidly, even to come in contact with the side of the glass wall of the bulb."

The phenomenon of the magnetization of paper by persons in normal condition in winter weather is well known to physicists and popular experimenters. If these observations point to a febrile condition that specially induces such magnetic condition, they will be of interest in suggesting closer study of the new effect. Unless the men were really the only persons affected, it seems strange that the observers did not find the same phenomenon in their own handling of the paper, and the fact of controls is distinctly mentioned by Dr. Ranson.

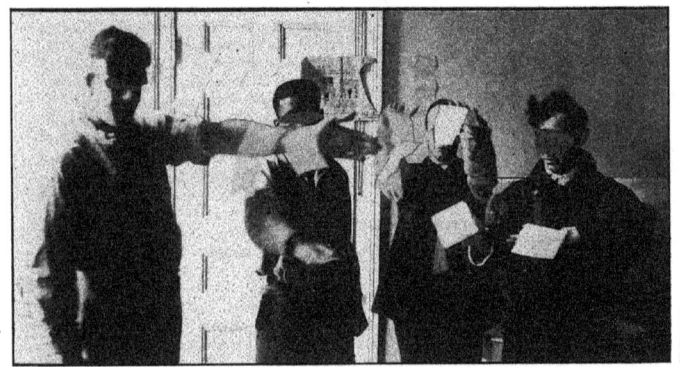

Can the Tuberculosis Rate Be Reduced?— The plan of the work reported by Cumming, who has already made several important contributions on the transmission of respiratory diseases, was: (1) to determine the presence or absence of tubercle bacilli on eating utensils after they were used by tuberculous patients; (2) to determine the presence or absence of these organisms on eating utensils after these were washed by the usual hand method in hot water; (3) to determine their presence on the hands of patients, and (4) to determine their presence in the air of tuberculosis wards.

He investigated spoon wash water, spoon rinse water, hand scrapings and air washings. Since tuberculous sputum passes through the oral cavity on its way from the lungs of the tuberculous to the exterior, this cavity becomes contaminated. Objects that enter the mouths of these patients become contaminated with the specific organism. As eating utensils are the most frequent inanimate objects which come in contact with the mouth, it is to be expected that guinea pigs injected with the wash water from eating utensils of the tuberculous patient would die from tuberculosis. Thirty-five per cent of the animals so injected died from the injection.

But the outstanding feature of this series of experiments is that the percentage of deaths, 25, from the rinse water injections was almost as great as that from the wash water injections. It is believed that the hand washing of the spoons in this series of experiments can be taken as representative of the usual method of washing eating utensils. If this is so, the difference in the percentage of deaths between the animals injected with washings and rinsings indicates that only about 30 per cent of the spoons used by tuberculous patients are rendered free from the organism by the usual hand method of washing.

This group of rinse water injections, with its 25 per cent mortality, demonstrates the facility of tuberculosis transmission and indicates that in families the eating utensil is the major avenue of distribution. The universal application of the principle of eating utensil asepsis will accomplish more in the control of tuberculosis than will any other single measure of practical application.—J. G Cumming, *Jour. A. M. A.* Apr. 17, 1920, 1072. *(D. G.)*

Prophylaxis of Infantile Diarrhea.—The author reports the remarkable record maintained at a home for infants, where for a period of 22 years no case of diarrhea originated in the home and there was not a single death from that cause. He attributes this result to a strict system of dealing with the children. (1) All incomers were isolated on arrival until such time as it was certain that their motions were normal. (2) A special room provided with washing apparatus and slop sink, was set apart to which all babies had to be taken whenever the napkins required changing. (3) As the napkins were removed they were immediately placed in a disinfectant, the nates were washed and bathed with a disinfectant, the nurse washed and disinfected her own hands, and those of the child and then put on fresh napkins. (4) A special nurse was detailed for this duty, she was not permitted to take part in the preparation and distribution of food to the children. (5) The food was kept in a larder and, except at meal-times, was out of all contact with the children and their service.—G. D. Sherwood, *Lancet,* Apr. 24, 1920, 906. *(D. G.)*

✠

Early Diagnosis of Tuberculosis with X-Ray.—There are two methods of X-Ray examination of the thorax, radioscopic and radiographic. With the former one can study the function and with the latter the structure of the lung. Since functional derangement frequently precedes visible structural change it will be evident that in many cases we must look for the earliest manifestations of disease in the radioscopic picture (fluorescent screen). The importance of observing any limitations of diaphragmatic movements as an early sign of tuberculosis has long been realized. In the experience of the author there is a stage even earlier than that of actual limitation, this stage can best be described as hesitation, and it is his belief that this is, so far as our present knowledge goes, the earliest sign of infection. In a typical case it will be seen that the diaphragm on the affected side commences its descent during inspiration a fraction of a second later than on the sound side. —M. Berry, *British Jour. of Tuberculosis,* Jan. 1920, 12. *(D. G.)*

THE PRIVY AND THE WELL

A PHILIPPINE STUDY IN CAUSE AND EFFECT

The happy days of childhood we often call to mind; we love to live them o'er again by memory's light refined—Zacate and camotes in the field of fragrant hay, the garden and the privy, and the well not far away. The back yard with its litter of manure all around about; the garbage heap where flies galore flew buzzing in and out; the pig-sty and the chicken coop; the dogs that played all day on the ground used for a privy, with the well not far away. We took our joys and sorrows as they chanced to come along; my brother had "makati" and he didn't grow up strong; Juanith died of fever—it was mighty sad that day—but we didn't blame the privy nor the well not far away. In those good old days mosquitoes used to sing the whole long night, but we would keep the house tight closed and thus avoid the bite; but Pedro got the ague and Maria pined away—mosquitoes— foul air—privy, and the well not far away. We used to think that death was just a punishment for sin—the sin of ignorance, I say! So let us now begin to try and get the windows screened but open night and day, and a sanitary privy with the well quite far away. Let's try and wash our face and hands, let's clean the back yard, too; let's rid ourselves of fevers and the chills and ague crew. Let in the air and sunshine but keep the fly away from the place used for a privy with the well far, far away.

—*Philippine Health Service Bulletin.*

□

CONVENTIONS, CONFERENCES, MEETINGS

July 16-17, Seattle, Wash., Washington Health Officers' Association.

August (—), Florida State Health Conference.

August 10, Portland, Ore., American Society of Civil Engineers.

August 20-21, Denver, Colo., National First Aid and Rescue Contest.

September, Oklahoma City, Okla., Oklahoma Tuberculosis Association.

September 6-7, Omaha, Neb., Missouri Valley Medical Society.

September 6-10, Holyoke, Mass., New England Water Works Association.

September 7-8, Ogden, Utah, Utah State Medical Association.

September 7-9, Saratoga Springs, N. Y., Convention of Health Officers of New York.

September 9, Providence, R. I., Rhode Island Medical Society.

September 9, San Francisco, Cal., California Tuberculosis Association.

September 9-11, Cheyenne, Wyo., Northwestern Tuberculosis Conference.

September 10-11, San Francisco, Cal., Southwestern Tuberculosis Conference.

September 13-17, San Francisco, Cal., American Public Health Association.

September 14-15, Springfield, Ill., Conference Illinois Officials and State Department of Public Health.

September 16-17, Springfield, Ill., Illinois Health and Welfare Association.

September 22, Kentucky Tuberculosis Association.

September 22-24, South Bend, Ind., Indiana State Medical Association.

September 29-October 3, Cleveland, O., National Safety Council.

October 4-10, Montreal, Canada, American Association of Occupational Therapy.

October 4-10, Montreal, Canada, American Hospital Association.

October 9, Ottawa, Canada, Canadian Association Prevention Tuberculosis.

October 11-13, St. Louis, Mo., American Child Hygiene Association.

October 13-15, Chicago, Ill., Association of Railway Surgeons.

October 22-26, New York City, American Dietetic Association.

**The A. P. H. A. Meeting at San Francisco is only Seventy days away!
September 13-17, 1920.
Plan your vacation so as to be there!**

STATE HEALTH NOTES—
LEGISLATION

National.—The bill (S. 3383 and H. R. 11927) to increase the pay of the Army, Navy, Marine Corps, Coast Guard, Coast and Geodetic Survey, and the Public Health Service was signed by the Vice President and the Speaker of the House of Representatives on May 15 and was approved by the President on May 19. The first section provides for increases as follows: commencing January 1, 1920, commissioned officers of the Army, Navy, Marine Corps and Public Health Service shall be paid in addition to all pay and allowances now allowed by law, increases at rates per annum as follows: Colonels in the Army and Marine Corps, captains in the Navy, and assistant surgeons general in the Public Health Service, $800, lieutenant colonels in the Army and Marine Corps, commanders in the Navy, and senior surgeons in the Public Health Service, $600; majors in the Army and Marine Corps, lieutenant commanders in the Navy, and surgeons in the Public Health Service, $840; captains in the Army and Marine Corps, lieutenants in the Navy, and passed assistant surgeons in the Public Health Service, $720; first lieutenants in the Army and Marine Corps, lieutenants (junior grade), acting assistant surgeons and acting dental surgeons in the Navy, and assistant surgeons in the Public Health Service, $600; second lieutenants in the Army and Marine Corps, and ensigns in the Navy, $420; Provided, That contract surgeons of the Army serving full time shall receive the pay of a second lieutenant.

Another bill which has passed the Senate and House and has recently received the signature of the President is H. R. 12775, an act to amend an act entitled 'An act for making further and more effectual provision for the national defense, and for other purposes." Section 10 concerns the Medical Department of the Army and provides for one Surgeon General with the rank of Major General and two assistants with the rank of brigadier generals. Hereafter members of the Army Nurse Corps are to have relative rank as follows: The superintendent shall have relative rank of major; the assistant superintendents, director, and assistant directors, the relative rank of captain; chief nurses, the relative rank of first lieutenant; and nurses, the relative rank of second lieutenant; and as regards

medical and sanitary matters and all other work within the line of their professional duties shall have and shall be regarded as having authority in and about military hospitals next after the medical officers of the Army.

H. R. 9521 is an act to prevent hoarding and deterioration of, and deception with respect to cold storage foods, to regulate shipments of cold storage foods in interstate commerce, and for other purposes. It was passed in the Senate May 17, with amendments and on May 18 the House disagreed with these amendments and asked for a conference. The act requires all goods kept in cold storage more than 30 days to be marked with the date placed in storage, and taken out of storage. It shall be unlawful for any person to ship, deliver for shipment, or sell, in commerce, any article of food that has been held in cold storage for twelve months or more. The Secretary of Agriculture is empowered to enforce the act. The punishment for violation is a fine not exceeding $1,000 or imprisonment for not more than one year, or both. The sum of $200,000 is provided to enforce the act.

H. R. 11841 amends an act granting additional quarantine powers and imposing additional duties on the Marine Hospital Service, approved February 15, 1893. It was introduced May 8, 1920, and requires vessels clearing for any port in the U. S. to obtain a bill of health from the consular officer or his medical officer.

H. R. 13627 is to amend an act to authorize the Secretary of the Treasury to provide hospital and sanitarium facilities for discharged sick and disabled soldiers, sailors and marines. It passed the House May 21 and is now before the Senate. It provides for the purchase of a building in the District of Columbia now leased as a hospital.

H. R. 14315 is a bill to authorize an appropriation to enable the Secretary of the Treasury to provide medical, surgical, and hospital services and supplies for patients of the Bureau of War Risk Insurance and of the Federal Board for Vocational Education, Division of Rehabilitation, suffering from neuro-psychiatric and tubercular ailments and diseases, and for other purposes. It was introduced in the House on May 29 and referred to the Committee on Public Buildings and Grounds. This bill provides for three hospitals for neuro-psychiatric patients, one each in the Central Atlantic Coast states, the region of the Great Lakes, and the North Pacific Coast states. It also provided two hospitals for tuberculosis patients, one in the Rocky Mountain states and one in Southern California. The sum of $10,000,000 is authorized for this purpose.

The Sundry Civil Bill (H. R. 13870), which passed the House on May 11 and passed the Senate with amendments on May 24 makes the following appropriations for the Public Health Service:

Pay, allowances and commutation of medical officers ....$	856,000
Pay of acting assistant surgeons...	275,000
Pay of all other employes	740,000
Freight, transportation and · traveling expenses	40,000
Fuel, light and water	135,000
Furniture and repairs to same	8,000
Purveying depot, purchase of medical, surgical and hospital supplies	85,000
Hygienic Laboratory	45,000
Marine hospitals	625,000
Medical Examinations, care of seamen, etc.	220,000
Preparation and shipment of remains of deceased officers	5,000
Journals and books	500
Total ....$	3,034,500

The following is also provided:

For medical, surgical and hospital services and supplies for beneficiaries (other than war risk · insurance patients) of the Public Health Service ....$	4,000,000
Quarantine service	255,000
Prevention of epidemics	355,000
Field investigations	300,000
Interstate quarantine	25,000
Rural sanitation	50,000
Pellagra	16,000
Biologic products	50,000
Division of Venereal Diseases	200,000
Hospital and Sanitorium facilities for discharged sick and disabled soldiers, sailors and marines	295,000

This bill also allows ....$1,015,000 to the Interdepartmental Social Hygiene Board.—(J. A. T.)

+

District of Columbia.—H. R 13846 was introduced on April 29 and referred to the Committee on the District of Columbia. It is a bill to regulate the practice of undertaking and embalming in the District of Columbia, and to safeguard the public health. The bill provides for a board of examiners which shall license all undertakers and embalmers in D. C. after a suitable examination.—(J. A. T.)

+

New Mexico.—Amendments have been passed to the Regulations Governing the Reporting and Control of ' Communicable Diseases by which the names of cases of venereal diseases are to be reported, under special circumstances, where treatment is not continued, or the patient so conducts himself as to be a menace to society. In the latter case the health officer is given authority to isolate such persons.

+

North Dakota.—By act of the last legislature, the budget of the North Dakota State Board of Health ceases to operate after July 1, 1920.

+

Pennsylvania.—During the year 1919 the Legislature ' of the State of Pennsylvania passed 11 acts affecting the public health in addition to a number of amendments concerning minor matters.

Act No. 136 authorizes the county commissioners in any county or the authorities of any city of the third class to erect joint hospitals for communicable diseases. Fifteen sections deal with the details of coöperation. By act 166 certain amendments were made to the laws concerning the health boards in cities of the third class. It is provided in these amendments that the council of the city shall have authority to appoint members of the board, their officers and subordinates. The second change in existing laws provides that the city clerk shall be *ex officio* secretary of the board of health.

Act 191 provides for the appointment by the Governor by and with the consent of the Senate, of a Deputy Commissioner of Health in the State Board, to be a physician of at least ten years professional experience and a graduate of a licensed medical college. The salary is to be $6,500 a year and necessary expenses.

Act 108 is to provide more effectual protection of the public health. It requires evidence of vaccination against smallpox or of immunity to the disease from every child seeking to enter or attend any of the schools, public or private. Certificates of vaccination must be in accordance with State regulations. Act 210 authorizes the financing by the boroughs of the construction of sewage plants or sewage purification plants.

Act 253 and Act 271 consider the details of medical inspection in the public schools, the act last named taking from boards of school directors the option they formerly possessed of deciding not to have medical inspection in the schools of their districts. Act 400 enumerates the communicable diseases, 26 sections being devoted to details of notification, quarantine, forms and records, technique, etc. Act 411 limits the keeping and slaughtering of animals save under permit of the department of health.

Act 442 makes it unlawful for any individual or association to advertise as being engaged in the business or profession of treating diseases of the generative organs of either sex. It is likewise unlawful for any publisher to insert advertisements of such nature in any of its publications. Penalty, $1,000 and imprisonment for not more than a year. Act 446 concerns itself with the education of children mentally or physically defective.

The text of these amendments together with the regulations of the Advisory Board of the Department of Health, Commonwealth of Pennsylvania, find place in the official publication of the Department, *Pennsylvania Health Bulletin*, No. 103.

☐

STATE HEALTH NOTES—GENERAL

Alabama.—Dr. L. W. Johnston, of Tuskegee, recently elected President of the Alabama State Medical Association, has been one of the most conspicuous members of the medical fraternity in the state for a number of years. He is a graduate of the Medical Department of the State University and has served for a number of years on the State Board of Censors and the Committee of Public Health of the State Medical Association.

A conference of the County Health Officers of Alabama was held in Montgomery, June 4 and 5, 1920. The State Health Officer, S. W. Welch, M. D., in addressing the group, quoted the statement of Dr. L. L. Lumsden, of the U. S. P. H. Service, made at the conference of the Surgeon General with the state and provincial health officers in Washington, D. C.: "According to data secured in January, 1920, by correspondence with state health officers, there are eighty-eight full-time county health officers employed in the United States, sixteen of whom are maintained by counties in Alabama." Dr. Welch was gratified that each of the 16 health officials was present in response to his invitation, and each was given an opportunity to report upon the activities of his unit, and the progress made during the past six months. These reports revealed a decided advancement in the technique of rural health work.

Two years of experience with numerous and varied types of sanitary latrines have led, by a steady process of elimination of the impractical and unfit, to the selection of four basic types which are now recommended by the department of health. These are—named in the order of their economic and sanitary value—the chemical toilet—the septic tank; the septic privy and the pit privy.

In towns of 200 or more homes not served by sanitary sewers, the box and can system with scavenger service may be successfully operated; a system of this sort which serves less than 200 homes cannot be self-supporting upon the monthly fee basis, and is therefor impractical in operation.

It had been recognized by many of those present that future success in achieving 100 per cent rural sanitation must depend upon standardized and commercialized equipment for these structures, combined with simplicity of installation. Dr. W. E. Burt, of Talladega county, has demonstrated the feasibility of this by securing from commercial sources the production of the following approved types of equipment, which may be purchased upon application to the health office: A septic tank and septic privy of cement construction, a wooden box for pit type, and cast iron, cement and wooden boxes for the box and can system. The commercialized product shows a distinct gain in economy and ease of installation; it also has the advantage of esthetic values which will encourage adequate care in operation. It is believed that when the farmer can drive into town and purchase from an intelligent salesman a sanitary appointment for his home, which has been selected as a result of personal inspection and understanding, he will be as eager to make this purchase as he now is to buy other house furnishings which he sees displayed in the shop window.

The Executive Secretary of the State Anti-Tuberculosis Association, Mr. J. M. Graham, gave the Conference his assurance of a complete understanding between the state and county health officials, and the Anti-Tuberculosis Association, which will result in the immediate future in the addition of a special tuberculosis nurse to the staff of the Bureau of Public Health Nursing of the State Board of Health.

The discussions which developed during the meeting were enlivened by comments upon the work now being accomplished by the various divisions of the State Board of Health.

Before adjournment it was decided that a second conference will be held in Birmingham at the end of six months.

✦

Kentucky.—The State Board of Health held its ninth annual Health Officers' Conference May 10 to 15, in Louisville, which included for the first time every public health nurse in the state, the meeting being a complete success. Prominent state and city officials, as well as many physicians and nurses from other states, were present. A paper on "The City Health Department" was read by Dr. Wm. H. Peters, Health Officer of Cincinnati.

✦

Maine.—The Maine Anti-Tuberculosis Association has recently reorganized into the Maine Public Health Association for the purpose of entering into a broader health work in Maine than was possible under the old name and by-laws. Such work as prenatal care, child welfare and venereal disease, as well as tuberculosis work, will be now included in its program. W. A. Harris is its executive secretary. One aim in the reorganization is to unify under one head all the private health organizations in the state and to work more closely with such state departments as the Maine Department

of Health, School Department, Department of Charities and Correction, and others.

Dr. A. L. Smith, of Machias, has been appointed District Health Officer for Hancock and Washington counties. This appointment completes the ranks of the district health officers in Maine, making eight for the state. Dr. Smith, who is a graduate of Jefferson Medical College, Philadelphia, has been a practising physician in Machias since 1896, and for fifteen years has been connected with the U. S. P. H. Service, with the rank of Acting Assistant Surgeon.

Miss Edith M. Soule has been appointed Director of the new State Division of Public Health Nursing and Child Welfare, and will assume her duties in July. Through the coöperation of the Red Cross and the Maine Public Health Association, this division has been made immediately possible to the State Health Department.

✦

Michigan.—The recently appointed health officers in Michigan are: Alpena, Dr. Duncan A. Cameron; Hastings, Dr. C. H. Barber; Charlevoix, Dr. F. F. McMillan; Escanaba, Dr. H. J. Defnet; Hancock, Dr. W. H. Dodge; and Saginaw, Dr. J. H. Powers.

A portable laboratory is under construction by the Michigan Department of Health, under the direction of State Sanitary Engineer Edward D. Rich and Director of Laboratories C. C. Young. It consists of a special body mounted on an automobile chassis and is equipped with the necessary apparatus and materials for bacteriological and chemical analysis of water and for the various kinds of clinical work that the State Laboratory is called upon to do. This summer a campaign to improve conditions affecting public health is to be started at the various summer resorts located in the state. By means of this truck it is believed that work can be done in a very effective and rapid manner. It can also be used in connection with investigation of typhoid fever epidemics and in stream pollution work.

For the purpose of obtaining comparative data in two counties of the state in which conditions are of a contrasted character, the Michigan Department of Health is conducting physical examinations of all the school children. The reports, when tabulated, should show some interesting findings in view of the totally different conditions in the localities chosen.

"Three Million Fingers" is the striking caption under which the Detroit Department of Health calls attention to the need for cleanliness in places which handle foodstuffs. The citizens receive their meals and supplies from 30,000 different persons, 80 per cent of whom are aliens. Many can neither read nor write the English language, and printed rules and instructions are not readily grasped. The difficulty of preventing disease transmission by food handlers at times of an influenza epidemic may be appreciated from the above.

About 200 children, anemic or tuberculously inclined, are attending special open air schools in Detroit. The Board of Education is arranging for the care of 900 more who have been discovered by the Department of Health nurses and for whom there are now no such provisions.

The Detroit Department of Health has found it necessary to ignore complaints of insanitary dwellings unless made in writing and with the signature of writer attached. Last year 1,213 complaints were found to be without cause and represented the efforts of people to 'vent their spite on unfriendly neighbors.

Those illegal practitioners of medicine who prey upon the sick, offering quick sure cures for all ailments, are 34 less in number than they were a year ago, according to a recent bulletin of the Detroit Board.

Thirty-seven per cent of the physical defects, exclusive of the teeth, found in school children in Detroit by Health nurses in 1919 were corrected during the year. Ten per cent are under treatment. The remaining 53 per cent are uncorrected.

✦

New Mexico.—A case of Malta fever has been reported in a goat herder in Chaves county. The patient denies the use of goat milk, but drank water from a cistern from which the goats drank and through which they walked.

The State Health Department, in investigating an outbreak of diphtheria at Dilia, in Guadalupe county, found seven carriers out of 47 persons examined. With the control of the carriers the outbreak rapidly diminished.

A special "Keeping Fit" campaign has been conducted. The exhibit has been shown in 20 high schools to 986 boys and adults. W. W. Raisner and J. V. Hopkins were the field representatives in charge of the exhibits.

Through a questionnaire to its physicians, to which less than half of these medical men replied, it has been determined that only a small portion of the patients with venereal disease in the state are receiving treatment other than by themselves with patent medicines.

✦

New York.—Prompt and vigorous action by the health officer of Fort Covington, Dr. McArtney, undoubtedly prevented a serious outbreak of smallpox in that community recently. Several hundred people who were promptly vaccinated escaped the disease, while the two persons who refused to be vaccinated developed smallpox.

The Bureau of Venereal Diseases of the State Department of Health has been conducting very active campaigns in the following cities: January, Utica; February, Schenectady; March, Binghamton; April, Elmira and Hornell; and May 3, Corning. In addition, work in the rural districts was carried on under the auspices of the Home Demonstration Bureau in the following counties during the months of April and May: Chemung (Elmira), Broom, Tioga, Chenango, Orleans, Monroe, Jefferson and Oneida. Since the bureau was established more than 100,000 people have been reached through its educational propaganda.

The Annual Conference of Health Officers of New York State will be held at Saratoga Springs on September 7, 8 and 9, with headquarters at the Grand Union Hotel.

The Wayne County Red Cross has established two public health nursing districts with Sodus the headquarters for the northern section and Lyons for the southern, the work in the respective districts being facilitated by the use of automobiles furnished by the chapter.

An outline of a lecture on tuberculosis for use before lay audiences in connection with the department set of lantern slides on this subject is now available, and may be obtained by writing to the Supervisor of Exhibits, State Department of Health. Albany, N. Y.

Dr. Minna Mary Rohn, Health Officer of the Lake George Health District, is now completing a sanitary survey of the shores of Lake George. This will be furnished to the summer residents on the lake.

Glens Falls has also completed a sanitary survey, the report of which is to be distributed to the citizens.

A survey which Dr. Alfred H. Sevenson, Professor of Preventive Dentistry at Columbia University, declares is the first of its kind ever made in New York City, is being undertaken by the Health Service Department of the New York County Chapter American Red Cross.

All the free dental clinics for children in the city are asked to coöperate in getting together complete and authoritative statistics on the extent and character of the dental needs among the children.

A letter sent by the Department to each of the 47 clinics on Manhattan Island asks their coöperation and requests them to add to their card indexes of cases a type of record card which has been prepared by the Department in consultation with the Association for Improving the Condition of the Poor and the leading dental authorities in the city. The card suggested is of the simplest kind and is designed to make a record of examinations only. It is not to supersede any existing methods of recording examinations and treatments, but it will be uniform for all 47 agencies.

On the basis of returns for twelve months, the Department plans to make a report, showing the scope and character of the needs for dental work among the children in New York City and any need that may exist for increased facilities for free treatment.

✚

Oklahoma.—The Medical School of the State University of Oklahoma was recently given "A" standing by the Council on Education of the American Medical Association. Dr. LeRoy Long is the dean.

Fully 400 physicians attended the 28th Annual Meeting of the Oklahoma State Medical Association held in Oklahoma City May 18-20, 1920, inclusive.

Pennsylvania.—The State Commissioner of Health is making preparations for the training camp to be held on the grounds of the Mont Alto Tuberculosis Sanatorium on June 28 and to continue until July 2. Those who are to attend are all of the county medical directors and certain of the state nurses. The subjects that will be emphasized include child health, school health, milk inspection and laboratory methods. Special stress will also be laid upon the coördinating of the activities of various civic organizations of each county in the carrying out of the county health work.

✚

North Carolina.—This state is taking steps through the distribution of advice, suggestions and legal forms of procedure, applicable under the Guilford County Public Morals Act, which was extended to the entire state by enactments of 1919, to combat various vices, especially prostitution. That statute makes using or leasing any building, when that building is devoted to immoral purposes, such as prostitution, gambling or illegal sale of intoxicating liquors, a public nuisance. It makes the building itself and the furniture and fixtures in it also a nuisance. There are two methods by which this nuisance may be abated:

First, If it is established in a criminal proceeding against the owner or lessee of such building that such nuisance exists, an order of abatement shall be entered as part of the judgment in the cause.

Second, By a civil action for injunction brought in the name of the State of North Carolina on the relation of a prosecuting attorney (in case the prosecuting attorney fails to act, by any citizen of the county wherein the alleged nuisance is to be found).

If the injunction is made permanent, a judgment making it so shall include an order of abatement, which order shall direct the removal from the building or place of all the fixtures, furniture, musical instruments or movable property used in conducting the nuisance and shall direct a sale thereof in the manner provided for the sale of chattels under execution. It shall further command the closing of the building, or places, against its use for any purpose, and so keeping it closed for a period of one year, unless sooner released.

This method of repressing prostitution does not involve the expenditure of public funds for the maintenance of persons convicted of violating the law. The cost of court procedure is at least partially covered by proceeds from the required sale of furniture found in such houses.

With a typhoid death rate that has been steadily reduced during each of the past five years, the State Board of Health is preparing for another intensive effort against this most easily preventable of all the preventable diseases that annually take the lives of North Carolinians. Through its field men this summer the State Board of Health will strive for the vaccination of a minimum of 50,000 persons.

The work will be directed by Dr. Charles S. Mangum, of the medical faculty of the University of North Carolina, and Dr. Luther T. Buchanan of the medical faculty of Wake Forest College.

✛

South Carolina.—The Darlington County Health Department, in coöperation with the County Board of Education, began a campaign against the house fly on April 6. A feature of this campaign was the contest for the school children. Prizes were offered to the school children of the county drawing the most attractive posters showing the house fly as a carrier of disease. Separate contests were arranged for the white and colored schools. The first prize was $20.00; second, $10.00, and third, $5.00.

The contest closed on April 30, with 129 contestants from the schools of white children and 31 from the negro schools. It is presumed that the smaller number of the latter was on account of the closing of the schools during the time of the contest. The prize winners in the white schools were all girls, while of the three in the schools for colored children, the second and third prizes were taken by boys.

For one of the results of the campaign 316 homes of white people have been screened against flies, and the houses of 77 of the darker race.

✛

Virginia.—During the first four months of 1920 there have been 1,821 reported cases

of smallpox in the state, with six deaths, against 7,0 reported cases in the same period of 1919 and ten deaths for the entire year of 1919. During 1917 the disease caused but two deaths, while in 1918 six deaths were attributed to it. In January, 1919, there were 129 cases, against 467 in January, 1920. In February, 1920, the disease reached its apex for the season, with 703 cases, against 113 for the corresponding month of last year. In March the figures were 326, against 261 for March, 1919, while in April they were 235 and 267 cases, respectively. During April of this year smallpox was reported in 34 of the 100 counties and during the year it has appeared in approximately half of the counties of the state.

Nearly three times as many women are dying from the perils of motherhood as would succumb if all of them had the benefit of the care of painstaking physicians. According to a study of Virginia vital statistics made by the State Registrar, Dr. W. A. Plecker, there is but one death out of 500 births where the mothers have proper and competent attention. On the other hand, under conditions as they exist, with a large proportion of mothers deprived of such painstaking care, the maternal death rate actually is one to every 185 births, making maternity second only to tuberculosis in its danger to women between the ages of 15 and 45 years.

State Health Commissioner Ennion G. Williams urges the more general use of whooping cough or pertussin vaccine in dealing with epidemics of this disease so dangerous to small children. Excellent results are obtained, even where the child has begun to cough. The use of the vaccine is recommended when whooping cough breaks out in the neighhborhood and is urged where the children have been exposed. Its use modifies the cough, even after the disease has become well-seated.

State health workers are very much pleased by health work undertaken voluntarily by the senior class of the St. Paul Normal and Industrial School, an institution for colored children at Lawrenceville. This class, following a course given it in physical inspection of school children by Dr. Mary Evelyn Brydon, of the Bureau of Child Welfare of the State Department of Health, inspected the 51 children in the primary grade of the school with the following results: Ten were found with defective hearing, 39 had defective teeth, and two were suffering from throat trouble.

✛

West Virginia.—The State Medical Association for the past two years has devoted one night exclusively to the discussion of public health questions. On the 19th of May a night meeting was addressed by Dr. Carl F. Raver on "The Necessity for a New Vital Statistic Law"; by Dr. S. L. Jepson, Health Commissioner, on "The Health Center as a Factor in Disease Control," and a great treat was given to the large audience by an address by Assistant Surgeon General A. J. McLaughlin on "Preventive Medicine."

✛

Wisconsin.—To acquaint medical men of the state more fully with their obligations as guardians of the public health, representatives of the Wisconsin State Board of Health recently visited a number of county medical societies and addressed them on public health movements whose success is largely dependent upon the practicing physicians. These speakers were Dr. Robert Oleson, acting Epidemiologist; Dr. W. D. Stovall, Director of the State Laboratory; and Dr. I. F. Thompson and Dr. G. W. Henika, of the Bureau of Social Hygiene.

Citizens of Appleton, Wis., and adjoining communities have subscribed $500,000 to build a new St. Elizabeth's hospital to enlarge the city's hospital facilities which are now totally inadequate for the demand.

Dr. A. J. Dana has been elected health officer of Fond du Lac, Wis., to succeed Dr. N. J. Malloy, resigned.

✛

Nova Scotia.—The Province is greatly encouraged at the approval of the program suggested by the Nova Scotia Provincial Branch of the Red Cross, by the League of Red Cross Societies, Geneva.

The splendid public health course for nurses outlined in this program, organized under the auspices of Dalhousie University in coöperation with various other bodies in the City of Halifax and financed by free scholarships granted by the Red Cross, is about to be very greatly supplemented. Col.

Frank V. Woodbury, who has recently been demobilized from the Army Medical Service, has been appointed by the Executive of the Nova Scotia Branch of the Provincial Red Cross to devote his entire time to the organization, selection of staff, and working out of details of equipment and transport for the two traveling clinics that are to go throughout the province during the months of July and August.

These clinics are to be organized on a semi-military basis and will carry with them trained specialists with operating room outfit and complete equipment for removing tonsils and adenoids and correction of other remedial defects found in school children in the remote sections of the province; a dentist with chair and outfit for cleansing and putting into hygienic condition the mouths of school children unable to get such service; a tuberculosis specialist, who will coöperate with the family doctor in helping determine the diagnosis where the local physician seeks advice; an eye specialist to give advice and to fit or prescribe lenses where advisable; a nursing corps to assist the doctors in their operative procedures, some trained to go into the homes of the tuberculous to establish such sanitary reforms as may be required; and some of the doctors and some of the nurses to be trained in health teaching. The entire personnel will coöperate closely with the local family doctor.

The plan of the Red Cross even contemplates carrying with these traveling clinics facilities for impressing sanitary lessons by educational moving picture films and in communities where moving pictures may not be shown, graphic lessons by projecting lanterns, the lecturers with the party being trained to elaborate and supplement such graphic lessons.

It is believed that the traveling clinics planned for Nova Scotia will have very far-reaching effects throughout this province and throughout Canada, both in promoting public health and in relieving life handicaps in isolated communities, such as the smaller fishing villages.

Full diaries are to be written up of the experiences of those associated with the traveling clinics, and publicity will be given in the press to the progress of the movement.

INDUSTRIAL HYGIENE AND
OCCUPATIONAL DISEASE

Abstracted by Drs. E. R. Hayhurst, R. P. Albaugh, P. M. Holmes, and E. B. Starr.

Devices to Protect Sand-Blaster Against Dust Hazard.—This is a study of the efficiency of certain devices used for protecting workers in the sand-blasting process. The study was made in a plant where the sand-blast was used upon automobile parts. The process was done in the usual cabinets having an exhaust and with hoppers below. The operators were provided with the usual "muzzle" type of rubber respirator with a piece of sponge and an air valve, also with helmets. The Palmer water-spray apparatus was used for dust counting; highest counts for dust ever reported were obtained from within the sand-blast cabinet (an average of over 16 million particles per cubic feet). It was found that the respirator removed about 92 per cent of the dust by count and 97 per cent by weight. The combination helmet respirator gave distinctly better results but counts were still far in excess of the limits to be considered safe. The combination of respirator and helmet provided with positive air pressure (from 2.3 to 3.7 cubic feet per minute) greatly reduced the amount of dust caught within the helmet and brought about a condition remarkably satisfactory. The writers recommend that for polishing shops the weight of dust should generally be kept below 0.06 milligrams per cubic foot and should not average over 0.03 milligrams. In fact, it was found that the helmet supplied with the positive air pressure alone without the respirator gave practically as good results. It is recommended that workers within sand-blast cabinets be provided with positive-air-pressure-helmets and with respirators of the generally used types.—Winslow, Greenburg and Reeves, *Public Health Reports*, March 5, 1920.

✛

Poultry Farming an Occupation Suitable for Consumptives.—The waste of human material caused directly by the tubercle bacillus calls for immediate action. Because in poultry farming, to be successful, workers must have a full knowledge of the subject, it must be conducted on a large scale and the building up of such a farm requires so much energy as to be out of the question for the average consumptive, but the consumptive may be an employee on such a farm to a great advantage. Several employees should be on each such farm in order to allow one to work fewer hours per week should his condition so require. Consumptives must have working hours regulated to their strength, absence of competition with healthy workers, an abundant dietary, ample opportunity to recuperate when a slight relapse occurs, and lastly, ever-ready help at hand should adverse circumstances be encountered. The conduct of such a farm at Papworth Colony is described. By careful study of each suitable industry along the lines indicated much waste of human material and human energy may be prevented. Varrier-Jones and Woodhead, *The Lancet*, April 3, 1920, pp. 793.

✛

Industrial Hygiene in Japan.—The Kanegafuchi Spinning Company, Limited, describes in a 106 page pamphlet how it cares for its employees and workers. In each of its mills are "hygiene inspectors" and nurses who endeavor to detect sickness in its early stages. Each worker before being employed is given a physical examination and after being hired is vaccinated and examined twice yearly. The temperature of all workers is taken from two to four times each month. At various times doctors stationed at the entrances of the mills watch the operatives passing, later calling up for examination those who show signs of ill health. The superintendent, home visitors, foremen, etc., are instructed to watch the operators for a similar purpose. Dormitories and other buildings are rat-roofed and a bacteriologist is employed solely in anti-plague study. In each mill an anti-plague corps is organized for an emergency. Each mill has a hospital to care for the sick and the company has sanitoria. At the hospitals are nurses with midwifery licenses who attend women employees. In addition the company makes available recreational and educational facilities and supplies at cost, quarters, food and clothing. It also conducts general welfare and relief work. Funds for the latter being partly derived from the Kanebo Mutual Benefit Association. (*H. N. C.*)

631

PUBLIC HEALTH LABORATORY NOTES

Abstracted by Francis H. Slack, M. D., and Mr. James M. Strang.

Bacteriology of Vital Pulps.—From pulps of 22 normal teeth all cultures were negative. From 40 teeth with pyorrhea only 17 positive cultures were obtained; from 23 teeth with caries, only 10 positive cultures; from 30 teeth with both caries and pyorrhea, 14 positive cultures. *Streptococcus viridans* was isolated from these vital pulps 29 times; *Staphylococcus albus* 8 times; diptheroid bacilli 3 times; spore bearing ærobes twice, and *Staphylococcus aurens, B. proteus, Streptococcus hemolyticus* and *B. coli* once each. It is concluded that in approximately one-half the number of vital teeth invaded by caries or surrounded by pyorrhea, the pulp is already infected by streptococci.—Arthur T. Henrici, and Thomas B. Hartzell, *Jour. Nat. Dental Assn.*, April, 1920, p. 375.

✛

Problem of the "Positive Throat" in Diphtheria Convalescents.—A vaccine made from diptheria bacilli, not autogenous, was administered in 50 consecutive cases of these persons who were carriers of the bacilli for an undue length of time following the disease. The series occurred in the ordinary course of practice in an isolation hospital. There was no selection and no accessory treatments were at any time employed. Twenty-four of these patients cleared up with but one dose of vaccine, 15 with two doses, five with three doses, one with four doses, three with five doses, one with seven doses and one with eight doses.

In a number of cases a culture characteristically positive 24 hours before vaccination became completely negative 24 hours after vaccination. Thirty-seven of these carrier cases cleared up within a week, 7 within a fortnight, while only 6 cases took longer.—J. L. Brownlie, M. D., *The Lancet*, Mar. 27, 1920, p. 706.

✛

Source and Significance of streptococci in Market Milk.—The saliva, skin and feces of 45 cows were examined for normal streptococci present in these locations, and 37 strains were isolated and studied of which 13 were from the skin and 21 from feces. Twenty-six samples of market milk were then studied from which 72 strains of streptococci were isolated and studied. Fifty-six of these strains were hemolytic, out of which 43 showed characteristics of the hemolytic types most frequently associated with bovine mastitis. Fecal and skin streptococci are practically absent in fresh milk if kept under proper conditions. The principal source of streptococci in milk is the cow's udder. All the streptococci from the vagina, saliva, skin and feces have been non-hemolytic.—F. S. Jones, V. M. D., *Jour. Expt. Med.*, April 1, 1920, pp. 347-361.

✛

Protein Fever. The Effect of Egg-White Injection on the Dog.—A series of experiments was carried out first on guinea pigs then on dogs. Repeated subcutaneous injections of egg-white in guinea pigs produce a constant fever associated with most of the signs of infection. Repeated subcutaneous injections of egg-white in dogs do not affect the temperature curve and do not produce fever. —Seymour J. Cohen, *Jour. of Lab. & Clin. Med.*, Feb., 1920, pp. 285-295.

✛

Wassermann Results With Anti-Complementary Sera.—It is suggested that such sera, instead of being discarded, should be titrated with varying amounts of complement to determine their complement fixing power, and the test then made with this additional amount of complement added. In most cases, clear cut results may be obtained without requesting additional specimens. — Miles J. Brener, M. D., *Jour. Lab. & Clin. Med.*, Feb., 1920, p. 327.

✛

Bacillus of the Colon—Typhoid Group Isolated From a Case of Furunculosis.—It is often considered that staphylococci are the sole causes of boils. The authors record a case where an organism having the morphological and cultural characteristics of the colon group was the causative agent. The cure of the patient by means of an autogenous vaccine showed the etiological relation of this organism.—Oliver and Schwab, *J. Inf. Dis.*, 1920, 26, 336.

American Journal of Public Health

Official Monthly Publication of the American Public Health Association

Publication office: 124 W. Polk Street, Chicago, Ill.
Editorial office: 169 Massachusetts Ave., Boston, Mass.

Subscription price, $4 per year. American Public Health Association membership, including subscription, $5 per year. Subscriptions and memberships may be sent to the A. P. H. A., 169 Massachusetts Ave., Boston, Mass.

| Vol. X | AUGUST, 1920 | No. 8 |

THE NATION'S GREATEST NEED: A NATIONAL DEPARTMENT OF HEALTH

SEALE HARRIS, M. D.,

Editor, Southern Medical Journal,
Birmingham, Ala.

Extracts from the President's Address, American Medical Editors Association, New Orleans, La., April 26-27, 1920.

NO one doubts the need for increasing federal activities in coöperation with the state public health authorities for the prevention of disease, but there is an honest difference of opinion as to how the desired results may be obtained. Personally I feel that a national department of health is the best plan for securing adequate protection for the more than 100,000,000 citizens whose health and lives should be safeguarded by our Government. The very fact that the Nation considered the prevention of disease of sufficient importance to create a department charged with carrying on health work would create in the minds of the people of the United States a respect for personal hygiene and public sanitation that would mean much in the coöperation by the public with the national health authorities in their effort to prevent disease.

Health and life are surely of as vital importance to the welfare of the nation as agriculture, commerce, and labor, the governmental functions of which are provided for in great departments, with officials at their head who sit in the President's Cabinet. Property and life are protected from foreign invasion by the War and Navy Departments. Is it not of as much importance to the welfare of the Nation to protect its citizens from preventable diseases, enemies that disable and kill more people in the United States every year than have been wounded and slain in all the wars in our history?

"Health is a purchasable commodity." is a trite saying; but it may be considered as a truism that the effectiveness of national public health work depends to a large extent upon the size of the government appropriations for that purpose. The United States Public Health Service has done magnificent work considering the penurious policy of the government in providing funds for the prevention of disease. It is now one of the small bureaus of the Treasury Department; and the Secretary of the Treasury probably devotes as much as eight hours a month to the consideration of the Bureau of Public Health, and then he feels that he is taking time that is needed for what he regards is more important business. Does any one doubt but that a cabinet officer devoting all his time to the duties of Sec-

633

retary of Health would be able to secure larger appropriations and more effective administration for his department than could be secured in any other way?

A cabinet officer must be close to the President, and he also must be a man of influence in the administration or he would not have received his appointment. It is therefore certain that the administration in control of both branches of Congress would support any measure that he might advocate. A physician in the President's Cabinet, in one year, could bring about more constructive legislation for the prevention of disease than we have been able to secure in a decade. From the viewpoint of practical politics, an important consideration when the public treasury has to be opened for appropriations, a department of health with a physician in the President's Cabinet is our best hope for adequate support for national public health work.

THE SUGGESTED COMMISSION OF HEALTH

There are those who favor a commission of health, somewhat like the Interstate Commerce Commission, feeling that such a plan would remove public health from the mire of politics. In the first place, it is impossible, and I am not sure that it is desirable, to eliminate politics from governmental activities; because all the commissions now in existence are entirely dependent upon Congress for appropriations. The practical politicians in the Senate and House of Representatives are not always impressed by the needs of the country, unless the party in power is responsible for the conduct of the particular matter under consideration. We have witnessed in the past few months the effort to destroy the usefulness of the Federal Trade Commission, and the Tariff Commission, by cutting their appropriations to a point where most of their activities would cease. A health commission would be without political influence and it would be difficult for it to get the money for efficient work.

Undoubtedly it would be ideal to have a number of trained sanitarians as life members of a health commission but in the opinion of many it could never expand and be the efficient force for public health on the large scale that is to be expected in a great country like the United States.

PREPARING THE BILL FOR A DEPARTMENT OF HEALTH

In my opinion there is little doubt that the great majority of physicians in the United States desire a national department of health. There are already several bills in the Senate and the House of Representatives providing for such legislation. The bills of Senator Owen, democrat, of Oklahoma, and of Senator France, republican, of Maryland, are best known to the medical profession. Both are good, though there are differences in their provisions. It seems to me that a committee consisting of three state health officers, the Surgeon General and two other surgeons of the U. S. Public Health Service, and three physicians representing the general medical profession should confer with the committees on health and sanitation in the Senate and House and agree upon a bill. This could be done in a week and the bill can be introduced both in the Senate and House. This bill should be as brief as possible, providing only for the establishment of a department of health with a cabinet officer at its head. There should be a clause providing that the present U. S. Public Health Service should be the nucleus for the department of health, and another providing for an appropriation for the first year sufficient for the proper organization, including the salaries of the secretary and his assistants, whose first duty should be to investigate the public health activities in all the departments of the government; and when they are familiar with them, they could work out a plan and prepare a bill correlating them under the department of health. The Secretary of Health and his immediate assistants would most likely be of the same political faith as the President and the majorities in the Senate and House. They would therefore be in a position to secure the legislation, and the appropriation to provide, for an adequate national department of health.

The Secretary of Health would also be associated with the heads of the other departments of the government that now carry on functions that should be in the department of health. For instance, the Departments of Agriculture, Labor, and Commerce are all engaged in activities that properly belong to the public health service; and the Secretaries of those departments will have to be dealt with diplomatically to keep them from opposing legislation that they might think would reduce the prestige of their departments.

It has been suggested that a committee be appointed by the President, and that Congress be called upon to appropriate sufficient funds for its maintenance, with powers to investigate all the governmental health activities; and that this committee would then be in a position to recommend comprehensive legislation providing for advanced public health legislation. This plan would involve a delay that might prove fatal to any proposed constructive legislation; and in its work the suspicion of the various heads of departments would be aroused and they might become hostile to any legislation that would take away any of their functions. Investigating committees are not very popular in Washington because they have been abused so much. It is also unfortunately true that Congress does not take investigating committees very seriously.

ORGANIZING THE FIGHT FOR A DEPARTMENT OF HEALTH

If a department of health or any other advanced legislation for public health work is enacted in the next few years, it is time that the organized medical profession begin a systematic campaign to pledge the support of the candidates for President, and all the candidates for the Senate and House of Representatives, as well as those now in office who will hold over next year. A man who is in the race for an office is naturally in a more receptive frame of mind than after his election. The best method of securing the support of a candidate or an office holder is for his friends and supporters at home to present the matter to him.

It is also desirable for him to know that the general public desires the proposed legislation. Public health is a business proposition and if the matter is brought to their attention most of the commercial bodies of the country would endorse a national department of health and transmit copies of their resolutions to the senators and congressmen in their states. Women will exert a wider influence on legislation than ever before, now that they will be granted suffrage. They are more interested in health matters than men and, if their support is enlisted they will let our national legislators know how the mothers and homemakers feel on the subject. I have had some experience with public men and I am convinced that most of them act from vinced that proposed legislation has the right motives. When they are convinced they will give it their hearty support. Surely there can be no more meritorious legislation than that which proposes to protect human life; and since the medical profession knows the need for a department of health, we should do our duty in presenting the case to our national legislators.

THE A. M. A.'s GREAT OPPORTUNITY

The American Medical Association has a great opportunity at this time to get the organized medical profession to work in the interest of a department of health. The various state medical associations, whose members make up the membership of the American Medical Association, have already passed resolutions favoring a national department of health; and the American Medical Association has funds that can be used for placing information regarding health matters before the public. Its Council on Health and Public Instruction should have added to assist its Secretary, Dr. Frederick R. Green, sufficient force to have committees appointed by every national, state, and local medical society in the country, who could take up the question with their congressmen and senators. These committees could also conduct publicity campaigns in their various localities. Through such committees and with the publicity department of the A. M. A., in a month every man now in the United States Senate and House of Representatives who will hold over until after next March, and every candidate for the next Congress, can be conferred with.

The state health officers in each state should be the chairmen of state committees and they could appoint committees in every congressional district which are in close touch with their senators and congressmen in their states.

SYSTEMATIC EFFORT NEEDED

The medical profession should go at this thing in a systematic, thorough and practical way, not as organized labor has done with threats to office-holders if they fail to support legislation proposed to help one class; but with the facts, pointing out that a national department of health would not benefit physicians any more than any other class of citizens, but that it would save thousands of lives every year.

An organization for presenting the question to our national legislators should be perfected at once. Anything like propaganda should be avoided because the word has been made odious by the Germans; and senators and congressmen are not impressed by it as formerly, but the needs for a department of health should be presented to our national legislators from as many sources as possible. This is not a partisan question, because it does not make any difference whether the department of health is sponsored by a democratic or a republican administration, every right-minded physician of both parties will favor it. It is not a question of who is right, but of what is best. It is, however, a broad political question and practical politics on the part of organized medicine will get results that will redound to the everlasting credit of those who "put over" the department of health.

GREAT BRITAIN'S MINISTRY OF HEALTH

Disraeli, in one of his most important messages to his countrymen, said: "Public health is the foundation upon which rests the happiness of the people and the welfare of the State. Reform directed toward the advancement of public health must ever take precedence of all others." Great Britain was a long time in following Disraeli's advice; but last year that great country led the world in establishing a Ministry of Health with a physician in the King's Cabinet. Britain's loss of man power by the war demanded measures for the conservation of life and her practical statesmen were not slow in meeting the need. Our war experience opened our eyes to our defects when 29% of the young men of the United States proved physically unfit for military service. One child out of three dies before it reaches five years of age and many of those that live are defective. There has never been in our country greater demand than now for able-bodied men and women; and we should follow Britain's example and meet the nation's greatest need by establishing an adequate national department of health.

A PROGRAM FOR ORGANIZING AND COORDINATING INDUSTRIAL CLINICS

BERNARD J. NEWMAN,

Consulting Hygienist, United States Public Health Service,
Washington, D. C.

Read before the Section on Industrial Hygiene, American Public Health Association, New Orleans, La.,
October 28, 1920.

To win success the industrial clinic must be neutral ground with domination exercised by neither the employer nor the employees. It is an industrial necessity where both parties must pull together. Further, it must be standardized. Towards this the clinic itself, as a clinic and research center, can aid. The author outlines plans of organization.

ECONOMIC CONDITIONS FORCING AN INDUSTRIAL HEALTH PROGRAM

THERE are certain facts in industrial life toward which is it worth while to direct attention because they indicate the need for a comprehensive industrial health program. In the first group are those which explain the reduction in the former over-supply of able bodied industrial workers, viz:

1. The results of the draft;[1]
2. The deaths from battle and diseases and the injured in war;[2]
3. The deaths in epidemics;[3]
4. The killed and injured in industry;[4]
5. The decline in immigration and the present increase in emigration—a loss not replenished from the ranks of native parentage.[5]

In the second group are those which have a more definite economic significance and which have arisen partly in consequence of the first group, such as:

1. High nominal wages—wages which, as now distributed, do not come out of profits so much as out of the prices that are charged to the consumer.

2. Shorter hours not always based on physical or cultural necessity, but at times on the uneconomic principle of more work for more

workers. Wage increases and shorter production hours have not, in some cases, tended to increase production, but rather to decrease it, thereby further increasing the cost of living.

3. Financial problems that confront capital and labor alike and that arise from the necessity of competing with foreign trade in the foreign field, complicated by the unreliable condition of European finances.

As conditions now stand, the industrial world is confronted by a decrease in the amount of available cheap labor and an increase in the cost of production. Its problem is, therefore, how to offset this decreased labor supply and how to lower production costs. It is this problem which helps to make an industrial health program an economic necessity. Heretofore industry has not given much attention to the health of the worker. The plant manager has been concerned about cheap raw materials, free power, immigrant labor, low wages, and, when it has been forced upon him, labor saving machinery. Frederick Taylor[1] introduced the idea of efficiency in production through standardized motions—regularized activity and periodic rest. Now shop committees[2] are being organized with the workers participating in profits gained by reducing wastage and increasing output.[3] It is partly due to this new program, which stimu-

1. See reports of Provost Marshal General, 1919.
2. Records Statistical Division, Adjutant General's Office, Washington, D. C.
3. Epidemiology of Influenza, Wade H. Frost, M. D., Vol. 34, No. 33, Public Health Reports; U. S. Public Health Service 1919; Health Insurance, B. S. Warren, M. D., and Edgar Sydenstricker, Public Health Bulletin No. 76, U. S. P. H. S.
4. The Safety Movement in the Iron and Steel Industry, Bulletin 234, Bureau of Labor Statistics; also other Industrial Accident Bulletins of the Bureau of Labor Statistics.
5. Report of Commissioner of Immigration 1919, U. S. Department of Labor.

1. *The Principles of Scientific Management,* Frederick W. Taylor.
2. American Company Shop Committee Plans, Bur. Indust. Res., New York City.
3. *Man to Man,* John Leitch.

lates maximum production at minimum cost and forces a recognition of the handicap of the half-well worker, and the loss resulting from sickness, injury, death or turnover of the skilled mechanic, and partly because of the increased value of the worker due to the decreased supply, that plans are being more frequently adopted for plant medical and surgical departments[1] and more emphasis is being placed on the necessity to eliminate occupational health and safety hazards.[2] Full credit muts also be given here to the influence of the agitation for accident compensation and for health insurance.

THE NEED FOR THE INDUSTRIAL CLINIC

Into this program for industrial health the industrial clinic fits, by virtue of the fact that it is a neutral agency for physical examinations and advice, and can be made a research agency for the determination of occupational health hazards. In some industries where plant medical and surgical departments have been organized the workers have developed a strong dislike for physical examinations because they allege such are used for the purpose of discriminating against the employment of union men on the one hand and of handicapped men on the other. Irrespective of the accuracy of their contention, the suspicion of any large part of the working group as to the honesty of such examinations forces a need for a neutral agency where medical council based on a comprehensive knowledge of their physical condition may be given to all workers. Moreover, there is a further reason for the industrial clinic arising from the necessity to acquaint the general practitioner in industrial centers with the diagnostic, therapeutic and prophylactic phases of occupational diseases, and to instill into plant managers and workers a knowledge of health hazards and the protective measures against such hazards. In addition, experience has shown that the legislative impulse, always strong, seeks, when aroused in a new field, to establish legal standards to control conduct. Such standards, unless founded on a scientific basis, are apt to cause injustice. It is almost invariably true that the impulse to the enactment of legal standards is emotional, founded upon injustice or an alleged injustice; or is a social reflex from either a real or an alleged antisocial act. In the field of occupational hazards the danger of establishing unworkable standards is present and may become real unless the information is supplied which will give a scientific background for the laws enacted. That states is seen in standards adopted governing the manufacture and use of certain hazardous and alleged hazardous elements and compounds.

PRESENT DETERMINATION OF OCCUPATIONAL POISONS UNRELIABLE

In the literature circulating in this country today relative to industrial poisonings the influence of the compilation of Sommerfeld & Fisher[1] is markedly shown. Some new names of occupational poisons appear in pamphlets and books, but all too often the basis for claims set up is usually one or two cases of alleged poisoning reported among workers engaged in handling suspected material. Often there is insufficient evidence that such cases have been followed through with enough thoroughness to eliminate other predisposing or exciting factors and thereby to justify the deductions announced.

As a matter of fact there is much uncertainty about the health hazards of the various trades. Many branches of industry have been listed where poisonous fumes, gases or liquids are present.[2] Some are known to be a serious menace to health; how many actually are a

1. Studies of the Medical and Surgical Care of Industrial Workers, Public Health Bulletin No. 99, U. S. P. H. S., C. D, Selby, M. D.
2. The Occupational Diseases, W. Gilman Thompson, M. D.

1. Bull. 100, List of Indust. Poisons, Bur. Labor Statistics.
2. Diseases of Occupations and Vocational Hygiene, Kober & Hanson, p. 740 ff. Industrial Health Hazards and Occupational Diseases in Ohio, Emery R. Hayhurst, M. D.; The Occupational Disease, W. Gilman Thompson, p. 665, ff.

menace is not known. Most dusts are injurious. Some markedly so, while the hazard from others is still in doubt.

How many processes unnecessarily cause an amount of sustained muscular strain or cause organic weakness sufficient to contribute to the incidence of disease is problematical. Fatigue through monotony; eye strain through faulty lighting; nerve deterioration through excessive noises; the impairment of muscular force through labor in damp places or amid insanitation, all are mooted problems in so far as the determination of the extent of their influence upon workers thus exposed is concerned.

THE INDUSTRIAL CLINIC AS RESEARCH CENTER

Various methods have been tried to secure information on mooted occupational health problems. One is straight research. This is efficacious, essential, but slow. It has some by-products in establishing principles which have an economic value. It often calls for extensive laboratory-methods without which no positive results would be obtainable. Without restricting the work of analysts in this field, the time has come when the specialists in the various fields of medicine and surgery practicing in industrial centers, should be brought together for consulting, if not practicing service, in what for lack of a better name may be called an industrial clinic. The details as to plan of organization, methods of work and rates of such an institution, may be matters of individual opinion, and may be determined as coöperating groups and local conditions may dictate. The fact remains that such clinics are essential in all industrial centers. Standardized as nearly as possible by the introduction and use of common forms for physical examinations, a common nomenclature, record system and methods of interpretation, with coöperative endeavor when specific problems need consideration, such clinics should be able to collect a mass of information which,

when analyzed, would uncover occupational diseases and hazards and, as previously stated, the diagnostic character and the therapeutic and prophylactic technique pertaining thereto. They would permit also of engineering research to eliminate or to reduce to a minimum the hazards discovered.

VALUE OF CLINIC TO WORKERS

Briefly stated, wherever clinics are organized the wage earners would have a right to expect the following services:

1. Complete physical examinations yearly or as often as conditions require;

2. Supplementary examinations by specialists when the preliminary examinations determine the necessity therefor;

3. Confidential advice in relation to physical fitness for occupations requiring special physical qualifications. If handicapped by defective vision, the loss of an arm or leg, valvular heart trouble or other infirmity, advice as to the kind of work best qualified physically to perform; or if otherwise disqualified and for causes that might, by treatment, be overcome, advice as to the necessary measures to be adopted.

4. If feeling indisposed, advice as to physical condition, and if symptoms indicate an ailment that requires treatment, further advice as to such treatment;

5. When employed on an alleged hazardous job, or when exposed to alleged poisonous compounds, advice as to the extent of the hazard and of the measures that may be taken to mitigate, or to eliminate it. If the former only is possible, consultation service as often as necessary to determine any ill effects from such exposure and to receive advice when, for the preservation of health, to change employment;

6. Advice as how best to safeguard the family from exposure in times of epidemic, or when exposed to a poison hazard that might be communicated by clothing or dust; or when a disease such as tuberculosis has been contracted which might be communicated to the home.

7. Advisory service when called upon to the family, especially maternity advice to the pregnant mother.

VALUE OF CLINICS TO THE COMMUNITY

In addition to the foregoing, the community would have a right to the following:

1. Well kept records of all physical examinations of cases of occupational diseases found, successful treatments applied and like data; the story of which, when told, would help to educate the public as to the nature and extent of such diseases, and more especially would they educate the general practitioner

to serve more efficiently his industrial patients;

2. An interpretation of such records so as to reveal the hazardous processes in industry and to determine the engineering improvements necessary to institute and maintain safe working conditions as well as the program for personal and plant hygiene which should be prepared and followed;

3. Through the physical examinations and by the recognition and treatment of early symptoms of occupational and other diseases to protect the worker from more serious illness with its attendant economic loss; and also through the reduction of absenteeism and turnover to save losses now recuperated either out of wages or out of increased prices for the finished product;

4. Through more scientific knowledge of industrial diseases and their causes and practical experience as to the efficiency of corrective programs to exercise a control over legislation relating thereto, both in the interest of the manufacturer and worker and for the protection of the public; for the fact must not be lost sight of that the cripples of industry are often the charity wards of society and are an unnecessary burden upon public and private philanthropic funds.

5. Service as a clinical laboratory in industrial hygiene for the local Health Board and to advise such local Board in all matters pertaining to industrial hygiene and medicine in the community;

6. The promotion of a sane educational program in the schools, public gatherings and newspapers, in the interest of safe and sanitary work places and the compliance by both employers and employees with the requirements of industrial hygiene.

WHERE CLINICS HAVE BEEN ESTABLISHED

Not many industrial clinics have been established. Some dispensaries are interested in certain phases of industrial work, notably those established to fight tuberculosis; others of a general character attached to hospitals functioning in industrial neighborhoods have the opportunity, but do not specialize in industrial diseases. Rarely, indeed, are they sufficiently conversant with neighborhood industries to serve them more than in a casual way.

The most thoroughly organized and equipped clinic, with the most comprehensive program so far reported is located in Milan, Italy. Prof. Devoto[1] defines its functions as primarily "for consultations with, and examinations of industrial workers, for treatment of patients, for experiment and research, and for a popular propaganda of occupational hygiene."

The physical equipment as well as the program of Dr. Devoto's clinic is beyond the reach of the average industrial city. The buildings house "five dispensary rooms, eight infirmaries, and six isolating rooms, three physiopathological laboratories and one room for experimental fatigue, three bacteriological, five chemical, five pathological, histological and micrscopical laboratories, three roentgenological laboratories, and anatomic museum and an autopsy room" as well as several other special rooms for research and teaching. Dr. Devoto defined his ambition for his institution when he characterizes it as "a clinic for the pathology of work," which is "more than a mere infirmary for persons affected by saturnism or mercurialism and other complex forms of occupational diseases."

Less elaborate, but unique, is the clinic of the Joint Board of Sanitary Control, New York City. Dr. George M. Price[1] describes this clinic as operating for the benefit of the Garment Workers' Union. One requisite for admission to this Union is to pass successfully a physical examination in the clinic. Dr. Price states that the Joint Board of Sanitary Control was organized in 1910 to supervise the sanitation and safety of the working conditions of 85,000 workers in 2,500 shops. In an effort to promote the health of these workers, a medical clinic with a diagnostic and therapeutic program was instituted in 1912. Between this date and 1918 inclusively the output of the clinic was 27,640 physical examinations.

In addition to this clinic the Joint Board has opened a Dental Clinic because it was found that "50 per cent of the workers examined suffered from diseased and decayed teeth" for the treatment and care of which they could

---

1. *Modern Medicine*, George. M. Price, Vol. I, No. 1, p. 49

1. *Diseases of Occupation and Vocational Hygiene,* Kober and Hanson, p. 765.

get only defective work at heavy costs from neighboring dentists.

Still another form of clinic has been evolved, rather than created, at the Massachusetts General Hospital out-patient department. Dr. Edsall[1] states that in 1913, medical students working in the male clinic of the out-patient's department were given occupational cards calling for a brief job analysis of present work of the patient, past work history, exposure to hazardous processes, poisonous material handled, and present physical defects for which treatment was sought. Careful follow-up work by a trained social worker was provided. Thus an ordinary hospital clinic, by the introduction of a special card, the direction of the attention of the examining staff to the occupational research possibilities and a little follow-up with its attendant analysis of records, became an efficient, though small, industrial clinic. Within the first eighteen months, out of 624 patients examined and recorded, 1,207 exposures were noted. Out of this has grown the industrial clinic of the Hospital, temporarily discontinued during the war period, but now in active operation again.

Other industrial clinics have been opened in connection with the University of Pennsylvania, and the Rush Medical College. There has been no concerted nor general movement, however, to open clinics in the various industrial centers throughout the country. In some cities such as Jersey City, Newark, Syracuse and Perth Amboy, movements in this direction are under way.

ORGANIZATION OF CLINICS

It should not be difficult to organize an industrial clinic. Necessarily the right location is in the industrial city and the right place there is in the industrial neighborhood where working-men live. In large cities, such as New York, Chicago, or Philadelphia, or even

1. *Monthly Rev.*, Bur. of Labor Statistics, Dec., 1917, p. 170.

where they are of lesser size but have large industrial populations, clinics should be opened in each residential area housing large numbers of wage earners. They may be fostered by the local health board, or in the event this is not feasible for political or other reasons, they may be operated by the Bureau of Hygiene of the State Labor Department or of the State Health Department. They may well be organized in connection with a medical school, utilizing, for much of the preliminary work of physical examinations and statistical interpretation, the fourth-year students who would thus get excellent field training to supplement their theoretical work. Where labor unions are strong, as in the garment trades in New York City, the unions may well sponsor a clinic, utilizing it for the benefit of their own members. Groups of small manufacturing establishments whose workers are not otherwise served would find it to their interest to organize and direct such a service.

PERSONNEL

Each clinic needs a full time medical director with such medical nursing, sociological and clerical assistants, as the work calls for. Moreover, practicing physicians in the city, and eye, ear, nose, throat, lungs and heart specialists, should be attached to the clinic in a consulting capacity. Governed by the need for their services, office hours at stated periods should be kept. If the city is fortunate enough to possess a diagnostician in occupational poisoning, his services should be retained. Where there is none the medical director himself should specialize in this field, or the volume of work not permitting, he should train up a specialist, who, in time, would be able to recognize and advise with authority upon the more prominent occupational diseases in the industries in the city.

ADVISORY COUNCIL

Wherever the organization of an occupational clinic is decided upon, whether by a city, state or other agency, there should be a representative board or council selected to have general advisory supervision of the plans proposed and the determination of the policies adopted. Such a body should not only have representative physicians serving upon it, but also representatives from industry, and from employees of the industrial community affected. It should also have engineers familiar with mechanical safety devices, qualified to make recommendations to reduce the number and severity of the hazards, and social workers competent to interpret the economic and social relations and consequences resulting from such hazards. Lest such council become a mere figurehead, stated meetings are necessary and definite advisory duties assigned its members. A working program should be followed which would assure the intelligent supervision and popular support of the clinic, the checking of any abuse of its privileges, and the massing of data capable of being interpreted and worthy of interpretation. Such advisory council might well become a medium for the intelligent interpretation of statutes relating to industrial hygiene and sanitation, for checking unwise legislation and recommending, in coöperation with other clinics in other cities and states, those statutory changes that might be necessary to make such laws in all states approximately uniform.

EQUIPMENT

The equipment needed for an industrial clinic will depend wholly upon its program. If opened in a hospital, the question of equipment simplifies itself. If in a new neighborhood and the program is largely one of physical examinations and advice, without treatment of any kind and without dispensary aid, the quarters needed would call for a cheery waiting room, an assistant's room with office equipment where a social worker or nurse may interview the patient and secure preliminary information. Opening from such a room should be small dressing rooms leading to the shower and toilet fixtures, beyond which, or adjacent to which, should be the examining room. The equipment of the examining room may be elaborate, if program and funds warrant. Lacking funds, it may be limited to such instruments and facilities as clinical scales, examining table, stethoscope, dynamometer, clinical thermometer, head mirror, tallquist's scale, sphygmometer, nasal, oral and throat speculæ, Snellen test cards and worsteds for color tests, and a tape measure. Where more refined procedures are needed, as in differential blood counts or other examinations, the patient should be referred to the laboratory of a neighboring hospital. As the program of the clinic develops so also would the equipment. The important point is that the preliminary outlay need not be expensive. It is quite probable that the need for additional equipment will be felt ultimately as workers appear who need special examinations for injuries to eyes, ears, nose, throat or other organs that call for intensive work at the hands of specialists.

FINANCING THE CLINIC

Wherever organized, clinics should be adequately financed either by appropriations from public funds, or be jointly and adequately subsidized by industrial plants, labor unions and public spirited citizens. Such funds should cover the initial expense of rooms and equipment with a sufficient additional amount to meet overhead, including the publicity necessary to acquaint the community to be served with the plans and purposes of the clinic.

It is neither wise nor necessary that the clinic should be run on the basis of charity. Self respecting wage earners would not wish it to be so run; free service will defeat the purposes for which it is organized. Moreover free service would subject it to the growing hostility among practitioners now concentrating on the abuses that have grown up with free clinics and free dispensaries. The charges, though, cannot be based on the fees which specialists now receive for their services. A nominal fee, determined by the advisory council, and sufficient to cover operation costs, can be charged. Some clinics collect small fees of 25 and 50 cents, others one dollar. A fair fee would be determined by the standard wage of the population served. Circumstances will determine whether the clinic should expand so as to function also as a dispensary. Even where the clinic is run by a union, though the periodic physical examinations of members and the special medical examination of all reported sick might, with reason, be free, yet when the dentist, oculist, ear, nose, and throat specialists are called in, fees should be charged. In the clinic of the Joint Board of Sanitary Control previously referred to, the rates vary from $1.00 for examination and advice to $2.50 when a full hour's service in dental work is rendered. Such charges brought this particular clinic $12,577.00 from 7,465 patients, or within $292 of the entire cost of the department.

RECORDS ·

Because so much of the value of the clinic depends upon the use to which the information gathered by physical examinations can be put, it is of the greatest importance that complete and intelligent records should be gathered. The records of ailments in any industry may indicate the hazards in that industry. Thus the fundamental physical examination schedules should be carefully determined before the clinic opens its doors. When these schedules are in use by a number of clinics, there is a chance for an early study of an occupation or even an industry. With supplementary sociological and industrial data gathered

by the industrial nurse or social worker, an interpretation of the social costs from occupational hazards may be made.

Some progress has been made in standardizing physical examination forms by the Office of Industrial Hygiene and Sanitation, U. S. Public Health Service. Two of these forms are appended to this article, Chart II is typical of the supplementary physical examination outline to be used when workers from a specific industry are being examined. Samples of the forms used when workers give a history of exposure to specific poisons are available on request to the office of Industrial Hygiene and Sanitation, U. S. P. H. S., Washington, D. C. The use of these forms is recommended for all industrial clinics. When changes are contemplated to suit local conditions they should be of a nature to amplify rather than to contract the information called for. Should local industrial areas find other occupational poisonings predominating, special forms for supplementary physical examination will be prepared by the Service upon request, duplicates of which will be forwarded to all other clinics coöperating in the collection of data.

In order to make an early interpretation of the data collected by such physical examinations, it is recommended that a progress sheet be maintained as the examinations proceed, whereon information may be visualized which will give an approximate idea of existent occupational disabilities. Such a progress sheet may be as concise or as elaborate as the clerical staff will permit. If indications point to the presence of unexpected hazards, special efforts should be made to direct additional workers from such occupations to the clinic that the suspected hazards may be verified. It is advisable in such cases to direct the social worker to obtain social data pertaining to family income and home conditions, that these possible factors may properly be evaluated and if circum-

CHART I

PHYSICAL EXAMINATION   Case No.........

City .... Plant ....
Name .... Address ....
Age.... Apparent age .... M. F........ M. S. W. D......... Race ....
Birthplace .... Birthplace
Father's nationality .... Cause ....
Father—living, dead .... Birthplace
Mother's nationality .... Cause ....
Previous occupations and time in each.

Present occupation .... How long ....
Where now employed .... Time........ Piece........
Character of work ....
Hours of work........
Hazards—Dust, heat cold, acids, fumes, gases, poisons. Others........
Exact description ....

Length and extent of exposure........

Date
Past history and habits .... Shop No.........

Present complaints ....

General Appearance .... Height ....
Wt.....Recent change........
Skin—Smooth, rough, clear, color........
Eruptions........
Scars and ulcers........
Evidence of........
Eyes—React to light........ Accommodation
Lids.....Inflamed........ Ptosis
React.—Vision—R........ L........
Ears—Discharge........ Hearing—R........ L........
Nose—Obstruction........ Disease
Mouth—Open........ Ulcers
Breath........ Other conditions..Disease
Gums—Color........ Disease
Teeth.....No. out.....No. decayed........ Malocclusion
Tongue........
Tonsils—Large, absent. Mucous patches........ Inflamed
Throat—Inflamed........

Glands enlarged ....

Deformities ....
Congenital .... Acquired
Spine ....
Flatfoot ....
Chest—Barrel........ Flat........ Pigeon
Heart   Lungs
Hypertrophy .... Murmurs ....
Pulse .... Temperature ....
Blood pressure—Sys........ Dias........
Arteries .... Sclerosis ....
Veins .... Varicose ....
Abdomen—Large, flat, tender, tympanitic........
Hernia .... Large.....Wear Truss
Spleen .... Large.....Tender
Liver .... Large.....Tender
Genito-Urinary Organs ....
Varicocele .... Hydrocele
Urethral discharge .... Gonorrhea
Other ....
Chancre ....
Chancroids ....
Menstruation .... Dysmenorrhea
Rectum .... Hemorrhoids ....Ulcers

Nervous System ....
Defective mentality ....
Station ....
Gait ....
Tremor—Tongue, eyelids, fingers........
Paralysis ....
Epilepsy ....
Reflexes .... R........ L
Dynamometer test........
Diagnosis ....

Remarks ....

Signed .... M. D.

Form B-1, July. 19, U. S. Public Health Service, Office of Industrial Hygiene and Sanitation.
If worker handles, or is exposed to an industrial poison, fill out the proper appendix card.

stances warrant, eliminated from the list of causative agencies for the disabilities discerned.

BRINGING WORKERS TO THE CLINIC

The patronage of the clinic by industrial workers and their families is largely a matter of how the clinic is operated. Where it is independent of any institution or organization, the clientele or personnel of which furnishes the patrons, the problem is largely one of acquainting the workers with its purpose and location. This may be done by lectures to shop groups at the noon hour, or by talks to unions or other organizations largely made up of wage earners. When such talks are given, cards describing the clinic should be distributed, each containing a note stating that the bearer upon presentation of the card at the clinic is entitled to a physical examination and medical advice as to his condition and counsel as to the treatment of any ailments discovered. Patronage of the clinic may be facilitated by securing the coöperation of the employers and their plant subordinates, or, it may be helped by enlisting the assistance of settlements, associations, and · the churches functioning among such workers or newspapers read by them. It is wise to placard shop bulletin boards and like strategic places with posters, giving the name and location of the clinic, the purposes it is to serve, and the fees, if any, that are to be charged. When special efforts are made to attract men and women, these should be directed to groups of like interests, i. e., to all foundry workers one week, all machinists another, all painters a third, and so on. Or the groups may be appealed to by industries or plants. The best results from a scientific point of view follow the appeal to occupational groups, for the data thus gathered lends itself more readily to coördination and interpretation.

JOB ANALYSIS

Close coöperation between the clinic and industrial plants, with a careful grading of workers according to their physical fitness, will permit the clinic to do constructive advisory service that will eliminate the more patent defects in the workers classified in the lower grades and thereby help to promote them from the lower to higher grades with the corresponding transfer in their employment; a mutual gain thus accruing to employee and employer. In order to accomplish this well planned and concise analyses must be furnished the clinic by local industries. Such job analyses should show:

a. The nature and scope of the work to be done;

b. The educational training and experience the worker should have in order to do the work;

c. The mental and physical requirement to be possessed by the worker assigned to the job;

d. The hazards associated with the work and the extent to which these may be reduced by prophylactic or other measures under control of the workers.

Such a job analysis might well follow one adopted by the Office of Industrial Hygiene and Sanitation, U. S. Public Health Service, in some researches made into occupational health hazards.

CONCLUSION

The purpose of the occupational clinic will be defeated unless discretion is shown in its organization and management. It must be a neutral ground where dominance is neither with the employer nor the employee. Both will have to pull together, with the records of the physical examinations treated confidentially except in special cases where job analyses are furnished, and workers are recommended as fit for special jobs. The community should benefit through the preservation of the health of its citizens; industry should benefit through the increased regularity and efficiency of the wage earner, and the wage earners should benefit through the knowledge furnished them about

CHART II

PHYSICAL EXAMINATION

FOUNDRY WORKERS   Case No........

Supplemental physical examination and history for workers in FOUNDRIES

City .... Plant .... Date ....

Name .... Address .... Shop No........

Job Description ....

Present illness (Develop history in detail and chronologically):—
....
....
....
....

Check the following symptoms if present or history, if same obtained:............

Heat stroke	Neuritis	Dizziness	Chronic cough	Diarrhea
Heat exhaustion	Striker's arthritis	Headache	Frequent colds	Constipation
Excessive fatigue		Chills	Nausea	Intestinal colic
Rheumatism	Neuralgia	Skin eruption	Vomiting	Hemorrhoids
Lumbago	Parasthesia	Jaundice	Gastric disturbances	
Sciatica	Insomnia	Bronchitis		

Supplementary physical examination. Note particularly evidences of the following:

Pallor	Conjunctivitis	Cardiac hypertrophy	"Sunburn" of arms and face Genu Valgrum
Emaciation	Cataract	Cardiac murmur	Spinal curvature
	Pyorrhea alveolaris		
	Impaired hearing		

Diagnosis ....

Signed........   ....M. D.

Form B-8, July, 1919, U S. Public Health Service, Office of Industrial Hygiene and Sanitation.

their health and the advice given as to how to treat complaints that may be found.

Definite detailed steps for the organization of an occupational clinic are not set forth here for the reason that clinics should be adapted to their environment and should be established only after a study of the industries, nationalities, and resources of the community to be so served both as to financial support and as to the available specialists who may be secured to assist. Wherever an occupational clinic is contemplated, the services of the Office of Industrial Hygiene and Sanitation, of the U. S. Public Health Service are available for consultation and advice, and possibly assistance in the preliminary research work necessary to determine the program to be followed.

Finally, too much emphasis cannot be laid on the importance to the nation of industrial clinics well coördinated. Such coördination cannot well take place un-less standardized forms for physical examinations are used. These the Office of Industrial Hygiene and Sanitation, U. S. P. H. S., is now prepared to recommend.

When clinics have been functioning long enough to have accumulated a sufficient number of physical examinations for an occupation or industry to justify an interpretation of its progress chart, and it thereby discovers what appears to be a specially hazardous process, such information, if supplied to the U. S. Public Health Service will enable the Office of Industrial Hygiene and Sanitation to circularize among all other clinics for comparative data; and if circumstances warrant it, to direct special researches into the nature and extent of the alleged hazard together with the diagnostic features of the poison and the therapeutic and prophylactic measures to be adopted to eliminate it, or at least to minimize its effects.

☐

WORLD-WIDE WORK OF INTERNATIONAL HEALTH BOARD

FIJI ISLANDS

Anti-hookworm staff in the Fiji Islands. The medical representative of the International Health Board is seated in the center, and about him are four Fijians—note their luxuriant heads of hair. At the left end are Hindu nurses and at the right a Hindu caretaker. In all countries the doctor recruits his staff from among the residents.

BIOLOGY OF THE PFEIFFER BACILLUS

PROFESSOR EDWIN O. JORDAN,

Department of Hygiene and Bacteriology, University of Chicago, Chicago, Ill.

Read Before Laboratory Section, American Public Health Association, October 28, 1919.

THE observations here reported deal with three cultural reactions of the Pfeiffer bacillus: (a) Indol Production; (b) Reduction of Nitrate to Nitrite; (c) Growth in Litmus Milk.

(a) *Indol Production.* I have recorded earlier* the fact that 10 out of 13 strains of Pfeiffer bacilli tested produced indol in blood broth. Twelve additional strains have since been subjected to the same test. These strains have been isolated from various diseased conditions of the human respiratory tract, four from influenza cases during the pandemic of 1918 and the rest from "colds" and "sore throats" during the past few months. Eight of these have produced indol, four, including two epidemic strains, have remained consistently negative. The total for the whole 25 cultures is therefore 18 giving positive indol production, 7 negative.

(b) *Reduction of Nitrate to Nitrite.* The presence of this reaction does not seem to have been previously determined in cultures of Pfeiffer bacilli. On finding in the fall of 1918 that cultures of the Pfeiffer bacillus in blood broth grew well and in some instances produced indol abundantly, I tested in the same medium the power of the strains then available to reduce nitrate to nitrite and found that all possessed the power of reduction. The medium used is blood broth containing 0.2 per cent potassium nitrate.

All of the 25 strains examined proved

*Jour. A. M. A., 1919, 72, pp.1542 and 1543.

to have the power of reducing nitrate to nitrite in this medium. Occasionally a strain has failed to give the initial reaction, but on reinoculating a fresh tube of the medium abundant nitrite formation has occurred, so that an occasional absence of the reaction may well be attributed to a failure to develop. The same failure of an inoculation to "take" has also been observed at times in indol-producing strains so that several negative tests have been considered necessary to establish the character of a strain. Nitrate reduction, however, has occurred under suitable conditions in all the strains of Pfeiffer bacilli thus far studied.

(c) *Litmus milk.* In a medium composed of equal parts of heated blood broth and litmus milk the majority of the strains examined turn the medium slightly alkaline. A few strains give irregular or doubtful reactions and at times seem to produce a small amount of acid.

These cultural characteristics separate the group of Pfeiffer bacilli very definitely from *B. pertussis* (4 strains) and *B. bronchisepticus* (3 strains). No one of the strains of *B. pertussis* and *B. bronchisepticus* produce indol, none of them reduce nitrate to nitrite, and all of them produce much larger amounts of alkali in litmus and brom-cresol milk. The development of alkalinity in cultures of *B. pertussis* is considerably later than in cultures of *B. bronchisepticus*, but far exceeds that observed in any cultures of the Pfeiffer bacillus.

HEALTH QUOTATIONS

COMPILED BY JAMES A. TOBEY,
Washington, D. C.

"A short saying oft contains much wisdom."—Sophocles.

Although sanitary science owes its greatest development to the achievements of modern scientists, health is a subject which has concerned the great minds of the world from the dawn of civilization. It has concerned not only the medical and its allied professions, but has also inspired noted authors and statesmen, some of whose writings have had an important influence on the public conception of health. Modern literature on public health is not always adorned with culture and modern writers on this engrossing subject could frequently enrich their productions with quotations from the writings of the past.

In the following pages are presented some selected quotations on health. While many of the citations may be found scattered in the various standard collections of quotations, this is believed the most complete compilation of quotations applicable to public health. It is hoped that it may prove of value to authors and speakers and for bulletins and pamphlets as well as a source of inspiration to the profession generally.

HEALTH

Refuse to be ill.—Lytton.

Love and health to all.—Shakespeare, Macbeth.

Have mind upon your health.—Shakespeare, Julius Caesar.

The first wealth is health.—Emerson.

Why should'st thou die before thy time?—Eccl. 7:17.

The tongue of the wise is health.—Prov. XII; 18.

Life is the gift of God and is divine.—Longfellow.

It is not life to live but to be well.—Martial.

He who has not health has nothing.—Rousseau.

Health and cheerfulness make beauty.—Cervantes.

It is not how long but how well we live.—Delille.

Gold that buys health can never be ill spent.—John Webster.

Oh, blessed health. Thou art above all gold and treasure.—Sterne.

He who has health has hope, and he who has hope has everything.—Arabian Proverb.

There is no kind of an achievement equal to perfect health.—Roosevelt.

Happiness lies first of all in health.—George William Curtis.

Let health my nerves and finer fibres brace.—James Thomson.

The healthy know not of their health, but only the sick.—Carlyle.

Give me health and a day and I will make the pomp of emperors ridiculous.—Emerson.

Good health and good sense are two of life's greatest blessings.—Publius Syrius.

Health lies in labor and there is no royal road to it except through toil.—Wendell Phillips.

Health is certainly more valuable than money; because it is by health that money is procured.—Johnson.

Health is the greatest of all possessions—a hale cobbler is a better man than a sick king.—Bickerstaff.

Beloved, I pray that in all things thou mayest prosper and be in health, even as thy soul prospereth.—III John 2.

In health there is a liberty. Health is the first of all liberties, and happiness gives us the energy which is the basis of health.—Amiel.

Health is the second blessing that we mortals are capable of—a blessing that money cannot buy.—Izaak Walton.

Health is the essential factor in pro-

Single copies of the reprint of this article may be obtained of the JOURNAL at 10 cents each; in quantities of 10 or more, at 5 cents each.

ductiveness, prosperity and happiness, and hence in the advancement of civilization.—Sir Frederick Treves.

The Public Health is the foundation upon which reposes the happiness of the people and the strength of the nation. The care of the public health is the first duty of a statesman.—Disraeli.

And as ye go, preach, saying, The kingdom of heaven is at hand. Heal the sick, raise the dead, cleanse the lepers, cast out demons; freely ye received, freely give—Matt. 10: 7, 8.

Our national health is physically our greatest asset. To prevent any possible deterioration of the American stock should be a national ambition.—Roosevelt.

I solemnly warn my fellow countrymen that you cannot maintain an A-1 empire with a C-3 population. You cannot bring up healthy people in unhealthy homes.—Lloyd George.

Health is the vital principle of bliss,
And exercise, of health. — James
Thomson.
Rich, from the very want of wealth,
In heaven's best treasures, peace and
health.—Thomas Gray.
Reason's whole pleasure, all the joys
of sense,
Lie in three words, health, peace and
competence.—Alexander Pope.

My mind to me an empire is,
While grace affordeth health.—Robert
Southwell.
You hoard not health for your own
private use,
But on the public spend the rich pro-
duce.—Dryden.
And he that will this health deny
Down among the dead men let him
lie.—Dyer.

Nor love, nor honor, wealth nor power,
Can give the heart of cheerful hour
When health is lost. Be timely wise;
With health all taste of pleasure flies.
—Gay.

CHILD WELFARE

Every child has the right to be well born.—John Ruskin.

God could not be everywhere, therefore he made mothers.—Jewish proverb.

What right have we to the word "civilized" till we give mothers and children a proper chance?—John Galsworthy.

The childhood shows the man
As morning shows the day.—Milton.

Do not try to produce an ideal child; it would find no fitness in this world.—Robert Spencer.

Give me intelligent motherhood and good prenatal conditions and I have no doubt of the future of this or any other nation.—Rt. Hon. John Burns.

The death of a child occasions a passion of grief and frantic tears, such as your end, brother reader, will never inspire.—Thackeray.

There should be no more thence an infant of days, nor an old man that hath not filled his days; for the child shall die an hundred years old.—Isaiah LXV: 20.

He who helps a child helps humanity with a distinctness, with an immediateness, which no other help given to human creatures in any stage of their human life can give.—Phillips Brooks.

PUBLIC SERVICE

The noblest motive is the public good.—Virgil.

The public safety is the supreme law—Bacon.

Seek the welfare of the human race.—Tarascon.

Answer a fool according to his folly.—Proverbs.

Lean, hungry, savage anti-everythings.—Holmes.

The vocation of every man and woman is to serve other people.—Tolstoi.

The health of the people is of supreme importance.—Chester A. Arthur.

There is something better than making a living—making a life.—Lincoln.

The Public is an old woman. Let her maunder and mumble.—Carlyle.

It is characteristic of Science and Progress that they continually open new fields to our vision.—Pasteur.

Physiological experiment on animals is justifiable for real investigation, but not for mere damnable and detestable curiosity.—Darwin.

When a man assumes a public trust, he should consider himself as public property.—Thomas Jefferson.

To raise the level of national health is one of the surest ways of raising the level of national happiness.—William E. H. Lecky.

He who serves the public is a poor animal, he worries himself to death, and no one thanks him for it.—Goethe.

The fate of a nation has often depended on the good or bad digestion of a prime minister.—Voltaire.

The whole sum of life is service—service to others and not to self. No man has come to greatness who has not felt in some degree that his life belongs to the race.—Phillips Brooks.

Men who are occupied in the restoration of health to other men, by joint exertion of skill and humanity are above all, the great of the earth. They even partake of the Divinity, since to preserve and renew is almost as noble as to create.—Voltaire.

DISEASE

Diseases crucify the soul of man.—Burton.

Ring out old shapes of foul disease.—Tennyson.

This strange disease of modern life.—Arnold.

For a desperate disease a desperate cure.—Montaigne.

I find the medicine worse than the malady.—Fletcher.

Disease is a retribution of outraged nature.—Hosea Ballou.

Disease is a crime, a man has no moral right to be sick.—C. G. Finney.

There are some remedies worse than the disease.—Publius Syrius.

Did you ever have the measels, and if so, how many?—Artemus Ward.

PHYSICIANS

Physician, heal thyself.—Luke 4: 23.

Time is the great physician.—Disraeli.

Physicians are many in title, but few in reality.—Hippocrates.

An ignorant doctor is the aide-de-camp of death.—Avicenna.

Keep the physician from the door as long as you can.—Flavius Volens.

They that are whole need not a physician, but they that are sick.—Luke 5:31.

No man can be at once physicist, biochemist, pathologist, practitioner and sanitarian.—Sir Clifford Albutt.

It is not much trouble to doctor sick folks; but to doctor healthy ones is troublesome.—H. W. Shaw.

He who cures disease may be the skilfullest, but he that prevents it is the safest physician.—T. Fuller.

Ignorance is not so damnable as humbug; but when it prescribes pills it may happen to do more harm.—George Eliot.

Physicians and politicians resemble one another in this respect that some defend the constitution and others destroy it.—Acton.

The physician is the flower (such as it is) of our civilization; and when that stage of man is done with, and only remembered to be marvelled at in history, he will be thought to have shared as little as any in the defects of the period, and most notably exhibited the virtues of the race.—Robert Louis Stevenson.

SANITATION

A very ancient and fish like smell.—Shakespeare.

Every state should provide pure water for its people.—Aristotle.

The sun, too, shines into cesspools and is not polluted.—Diogenes.

Water, air and cleanliness are the chief articles of my pharmacopeia.—Napoleon.

Give me the splendid silent sun, with all his beams full dazzling.—Walt Whitman.

Sanitary, civic and moral decadence was the worm at the root of every discredited and submerged civilization of the past.—Burkart.

He who overlooks a healthy spot for the site of his house is mad and ought to be handed over to the care of his relations and friends.—Varro.

As one who long in populous city pent,
Where houses thick and sewers annoy
  the air.—John Milton.

PERSONAL HYGIENE

Know thyself.—Socrates.

Cleanliness is indeed next to Godliness.—Wesley.

Pain is no evil, unless it conquer us.—Kingsley.

Throw physic to the dogs; I'll none of it.—Shakespeare, Macbeth.

Cleanliness may be defined to be the emblem of purity of mind.—Addison.

Cleanness of body was ever deemed to proceed from a due reverence of God.—Bacon.

Better use medicines at the outset than at the last moment.—Publius Syrius.

Martin, if dirt was trumps, what hands you would hold.—Charles Lamb.

Lord, I wonder what fool it was that first invented kissing.—Swift.

It is exercise alone that supports the spirits, and keeps the mind in vigor.—Cicero.

The weaker the body, the more it commands; the stronger it is, the more it obeys.—Rousseau.

If a man defile the temple of God, him shall God destroy. For the temple of God is holy, which temple ye are.—1 Cor. 3:17.

Rough, vigorous pastimes are excellent things for the nation, for they promote manliness.—Roosevelt.

A man's own observation, what he finds good of and what he finds hurt of, is the best physic to preserve health.—Francis Bacon.

Early to bed and early to rise,
Makes a man healthy, wealthy and
  wise.—Franklin.

Bid them wash their faces
And keep their teeth clean.—Shakespeare, Coriolanus.

Make the house where gods may dwell,
Beautiful, entire and clean.—Longfellow.

HEREDITY

Survival of the fittest.—Spencer.

Think of your ancestors and your posterity.—Tacitus.

In the field of destiny we reap as we have sown.—Whittier.

Before man made us citizens, great nature made us men.—James Russell Lowell.

In your children ye shall make amends for being your father's children.—Neitzsche.

Heredity is only the sun of all past environment, in other words environment is the architect of heredity.—Burbank.

□

Composite Industrial Poisons.—All who are familiar with and have occasion to refer to the list of 54 industrial poisons contained in U. S. Labor Bulletin No. 100 will be particularly interested in this review of a series of articles by Dr. Johann Mueller in which are listed numerous industries and their peculiar processes in which workmen are subjected to the influence of mixed poisons. For each industry there is stated in tabular arrangement the dangerous processes and products, the poisons used, poisonous by-products and impurities, and a final column headed "remarks." Many prominent industries are covered, such as the sulphuric acid manufacture, artificial fertilizers, india rubber, dyeing, gas industry, metal industry, tanning, tinning, porcelain, etc.—*Monthly Labor Review*, February, 1920.

TYPES OF FATIGUE

Percy G. Stiles,

*Assistant Professor of Physiology in Harvard University,
Harvard Medical School, Boston, Mass.*

Bad habits in the nervous system often lead to "vicious circles" in mental processes. Discipline is important here. Change of scene or sanatorium life is beneficial largely in its power to get the mind out of its "ruts." Psychotherapy may effect this. Recovery from mental fatigue is less a matter of correcting metabolism than of forming desirable habits.

CHEMICAL processes of two opposing orders are conceived to be going on in living cells. Activities of the first type are constructive and dependent ultimately on the appropriation of food. The converse processes are those in which organic compounds are broken down with release of energy. Such reactions underlie the production of heat and work, and, in some measure, the phenomena of secretion and absorption. It is evident that no organism can remain constant as to its mass and potentialities save as a balance between these two is closely preserved. A temporary excess of destruction (katabolism) over renewal tends to be self-limited and the disturbance of equilibrium in this direction may be said to constitute *fatigue*.

When the processes of repair are as active as possible and the katabolic changes still counterbalance them we have a condition in which the tissue is giving its maximum performance; it expends all it can without progressively falling off in capacity. The heart is our stock illustration of an organ in which expenditure and renewal are nicely balanced; we must note, however, that it does not commonly work up to its limit of power. In a rhythmic performance like that of the heart we may say that fatigue and complete recovery alternate at very short intervals, usually of less than one second. In the breathing muscles the space of time between these extreme phases is longer, say four seconds. The heart muscle is automatic, the respiratory muscles are not so, but actuated by a center in the medulla. It seems to be a physiological principle that as we pass from simple and elementary mechanisms to those which are more plex and highly organized the ordinary alternation of active and resting periods becomes slowed. Muscles that are much used under cerebral control appear to require long intervals of relative repose. They are capable of spurts so intense as to induce long continued depression. It is a familiar fact that when the utmost efforts have been applied to pulling an ergograph definite fatigue can be demonstrated for an hour or two, even though the work was done in two or three minutes.

The mechanisms that stand in closest relation to the cerebrum seem to have evolved with some conformity to the diurnal rhythm, their metabolism may be continuously above the mean for more than half the twenty-four hours, but for a considerable part of the night it must be reduced below this average. Where the highest departments of our organization are concerned a still longer span may intervene between the trough of fatigue and the crest of recuperation. The weekly cycle and the beneficent function of the Sabbath Day are naturally suggested. Possibly an annual decline and recovery may also be recognized.

If we regard fatigue as diminished capacity to respond to stimulation—an elevation of threshold—we at once realize its protective value. We see how the interposition of resistance at any point in a coördinated system prevents the wearing down of associated structures. Such a resistance appears to be developed at the junctions between nerve and muscle when they are repeatedly traversed. A corresponding obstruction in the line of flow is soon established at the junctions (synapses) between the minute units of the nervous system. The weaker links in the chain are probably most easily renewed. In the case of the synapses there seems to be a physical reason for this. They are regions of great attenuation of the conducting substance; protoplasm so organized should burn out quickly if it is the seat of active chemical decomposition. On the other hand, it should be speedily repaired because it has most extensive surface relations with the surrounding fluids.

A new picture of the intimate behavior of muscle under prolonged stimulation has been furnished by Pratt of Buffalo. It turns out that what we call a sustained contraction depends on the alternating activity of the fibers or fiber-bundles composing the muscle. The contractile elements in turn bear their part, drop out of action, and having rested, spring back to the work. They fall out because metabolic changes have caused their thresholds to rise. They resume because they have been granted time for at least partial recovery. This principle of working by shifts is favorable to endurance.

When fatigue is mentioned one thinks first of the muscles. This is natural enough. However much the mental may have entered into modern human life most people's activity is still measurable in terms of mechanical work. The muscles form about half the body and they account for perhaps four-fifths of its metabolism. When they are vigorously employed all the tissues are flooded with their waste-products so that there is a sympathetic depression of glandular function and probably of the cerebral currents which attend the intellectual processes. The massive proportions of the muscles must not be forgotten. Their metabolic influence can hinder the subtle performances of the cortical cells—in other words, bodily fatigue can unfit one for application to mental tasks—but the pursuit of mental work cannot develop great quantities of end-products that shall saturate and narcotize the muscles. A period of mental stress may make one disinclined to exercise but disinclination is not the same thing as incapacity. If there is any loss of power in such a case it is probably not represented in the muscles but at their seat of government.

Cerebral processes involve but very small masses of protoplasm and they are doubtless conducted with extreme economy. Is there a condition which can be accurately described as "mental fatigue?" We usually assume that this is a possibility. If, however, we analyze our own experiences we have to admit as a rule that what we call fatigue in connection with the steady performance of some monotonous mental operation is the tendency to seek relief in novelty—to admit new and irrelevant ideas. Unless the trial is carefully regulated there will be elements of eye-strain or postural discomfort which are neuromuscular rather than mental in nature. To be sure, we eventually need to sleep, but frequently the drowsiness comes sooner to the indolent than to the diligently working brain. Some of our ablest experimenters doubt whether we can surely demonstrate mental fatigue.

Such a doubt might encourage the belief that mental processes are definitely metaphysical and make no demand upon the material organization of the brain. This does not follow. It is much easier to conceive that even the most restricted and tedious kind of calculation employs many neurons in rotation and does not utilize particular ones so constantly as to impair their efficiency. Analogies in this field are decidedly clumsy, but the suggestion may be ventured that the multiple equipment of the cortex is at least remotely comparable to a typewriter in which each key is necessarily idle when another has its turn. This is a rather daring transfer to the higher levels of the brain of Pratt's picture of the tetanized muscle in which certain units are continually replacing others. We have said that this mode of working prolongs the endurance of muscle. If this is true of a tissue with a high metabolism it may well nullify fatigue in gray matter where the rate of disintegration appears to be low.

When an emotional element enters into the experience the inception of fatigue may be far more obvious than in calm, straightforward mental work. Excitement has its neuromuscular accompaniments and certainly means accelerated metabolism. An important feature is the involvement of glands of internal secretion, notably the adrenal and probably the thyroid. When these have been exercised depression is to be expected. The glands may be exhausted so that for a time the delivery of their products is subnormal. The muscles, having passed through a phase of stimulation due to these same products, may enter upon a period of reaction. If we may make any suppositions about the comparative employment of cortical cell-groups in orderly mental work and in emotional turmoil we shall be inclined to assume that the latter type of activity is more massive and probably less varied in distribution from moment to moment. If it is more nearly continuous in fixed paths it must be a severer tax than the unemotional process with its frequent shifting of channels.

Consideration of what is commonly called nervous fatigue suggests two factors in the condition which should be kept in view. The first of these is the prominent part played by inhibitory complexes in nervous systems of the highest order. Maturity in the individual and civilization in the race depend on the subjection of many primitive reactions to control. A late acquisition is a relatively insecure possession and its loss as a result of many forms of wear and tear is too often observed. A nervous system which has suffered this loss is said to be fatigued though it shows many signs of over-activity. It is, in a sense, a defect of the highest organization that it does not regularly incline to rest when rest is needed. This perversity can be explained in part on the basis of lessened inhibitory powers, but there is still another element which should be given due consideration. The property referred to is that of *canalization*.

The utility of this factor in adaptation to the circumstances of life is readily recognized. In the human nervous system, far beyond any other, reactions are more easily executed as they are repeated. The principle is that of habit-formation. A path may be pursued by nerve-currents until its synapses develop resistance to the continued transmission and the common type of central fatigue is manifested. But such fatigue is transient, and, when it has passed, the net result is a greater facility for conduction in the path that has been traversed. This adaptive quality is the basis of accomplishments of every kind as well as of mannerisms and unfortunate habits. Canalization in the association systems must be at the root of scholarly attainment as surely as, at lower levels, it is the condition of manual skill. It appears that the power to form pathways of ready transmission—in short, the power to learn—and the establishment of overruling complexes of an inhibitory order are alike characteristic of higher as contrasted with lowlier nervous systems. A simple organism may have a few standard reactions which will be serviceable in all probable contingencies and no provision for their repression may be necessary. The need for inhibition comes with the development of numerous alternative reactions and is especially valuable as a check on the canalization capacity which tends to make "ruts" in the brain. This is rather an academic statement of something which William James long ago showed to be a most practical matter.

Now the picture presented by the victim of what we call nervous fatigue suggests two difficulties. One is the want of inhibitory control. This is exhibited in the familiar unrest, and, on the afferent side, as hypersensitiveness. The second feature of the trouble is canalization. The "tired" nervous system has formed bad habits. These are discovered not only in conduct but in unhappy trains of thought, incessant anxiety and self-pity. Important as it may be in such cases to build up the general health, we can see that the critical need is *discipline*. Change of scene and sanatorium life may be chiefly useful as they favor the disruption of the nerve-paths so excessively employed. Psychotherapy may effect this. This application may be in the abstract terms of some idealistic system or the very same jostling from the grooves may be accomplished with a measure of harshness. The more insight one gains into the workings of the nervous apparatus the less one is surprised by the comparatively rapid readjustments which may often be accomplished in it. Perhaps the most injurious canalizations have the character of closed circuits in which every discharge reacts upon the cells originally concerned and compels them to renew their activity. This seems to be the material concomitant in the numerous cases which yield to Freudian psychoanalysis. The circular flow of nerve-impulses needs to be diverted to some channel of expression that it may no longer return persistently to its own source.

Summary. Fatigue, in general, is depression of working capacity, owing to a katabolism running above the average for the tissue. In muscle it is just this. Muscular fatigue, because of the large masses of active protoplasm involved, can extend its influence to other systems. In narrowly localized brain activity the metabolic process cannot be large and true cerebral fatigue is probably far less common than is supposed. The use of different cell-groups in rotation may minimize the demand upon each member. The ordinary cause of diminishing mental efficiency is the desire for a change. In a reasonably trained system this is a wholesome impulse. What we call nervous fatigue, referring to a condition which is pathological and often of long duration, is due primarily to lessened inhibition. Many of its features are symptomatic of bad habits established in the ill-controlled system. Unusual outflowing currents may pervert the action of the endocrine organs. Recovery from nervous fatigue is less a matter of correcting the metabolism than of desirable habit formation.

□

Only Forty Days to the Meeting
at San Francisco!
September 13-15, 1920.
Shall you be there?

ANTHRAX PROBLEM IN MASSACHUSETTS

STANLEY H. OSBORN, M., D., C. P. H.,

Director, Bureau of Preventable Diseases, Connecticut State Department of Health, Hartford, Conn.; Formerly Epidemiologist, Massachusetts Department of Public Health

Federal regulations do not prevent importation of anthrax infected material. This author suggests anthrax surveys in countries of origin of materials, quarantine of all hides, wool and hair from suspected areas, disinfection of these at places of origin and sanitary care here of wastes from hide and wool industrial establishments.

ANTHRAX is a disease primarily of animals, but easily transmitted to man by contact with animal cases, or as usually happens in Massachusetts, by contact with animal products, such as hides, hair and wool that are infected with anthrax spores.

Anthrax in animals is more or less common in certain areas of pasture land, particularly meadows, in Massachusetts, but only one case was infected by a native animal anthrax case during the period 1916-1919, inclusive.

This article is a brief study of the 126 anthrax cases reported in Massachusetts from 1916 to 1919 inclusive. The plan of investigation, inaugurated in 1916 by Dr. Charles E. Simpson, State District Health Officer, and Dr. Walter H. Brown, epidemiologist of the department, in locating the source of infected hides in the countries from which they came, has been followed and elaborated. The cases have been personally investigated by a district health officer or the epidemiologist and have shown that in spite of federal regulations anthrax-infected material is still arriving in the United States.

There are no records of anthrax in Massachusetts in the Colonial days. In the annual report of the State Board of Health for the year 1871 Arthur H.

Nichols published an account of the prevalence of "charbon" in the State. In this report Dr. A. L. Pierson of Salem is quoted as having treated anthrax that had been caused by foreign hides. Dr. Silas E. Stone of Walpole reported 26 cases in Walpole from 1853-1869 that were due to hair, 24 of which worked in a hair factory. Qf the 26 cases, 16 were external, malignant carbuncle cases and 6 died. The remaining 10 were internal forms, probably pneumonic, and 8 were fatal.

From 1865 to 1906 inclusive, the State Registration Reports have a record of 128 deaths from anthrax, and although there are morbidity records, the cases must have at least doubled that figure, for the fatality rate was 40 to 50 per cent.

ANTHRAX CASES IN MASSACHUSETTS

Year	Cases	Deaths	Fatality Rate Per cent
1907	1	4	
1908	5	2	40.0
1909	7	1	14.3
1910	7	2	28.6
1911	6	2	33.3
1912	11	2	18.2
1913	8	3	37.5
1914	8	1	12.5
1915	11	4	36.4
1916	31	5	16.1
1917	54	10	18.5
1918	23	7	30.4
1919	18	1	5.6
Totals	190	44	

657

In August, 1907, anthrax was made reportable to boards of health and the cases since that year are as in the table on the preceding page.

It is apparent that conditions brought about by the war were responsible for the great increase in cases since 1914. The abnormal increase in the demand for leather, and the shutting off of certain districts that formerly shipped hides caused dealers to go farther inland in China and South America for hides. This is particularly true of the Hankow market, which in addition furnishes the better grade of cow hides. The result was that hides from Thibet, Kansu, and other districts far in the interior of China, where it is impossible for disease conditions to be known, were shipped to Hankow and thence to the United States and other countries.

A consular certificate is demanded by the Federal Bureau of Animal Industry* certifying that hides are from a nonanthrax infected region or that the hides are disinfected before they are admitted to the United States. The consular certificate is obtained whenever possible because the process of disinfection is apt to be injurious to the hides. This certificate was given in the majority of hide shipments that apparently infected hide handlers in Massachusetts. Because of these conditions, manufacturers of leather in Massachusetts sought new methods of hide disinfection sufficient to kill the anthrax spores, and thus prevent the workers from contracting the disease.

Etiology: Anthrax is caused by a microörganism, a rod-shaped bacillus, which is easily killed, but is capable of assuming spore forms which resist all of the usual methods of disinfection. Bacilli are present only in a live or freshly killed animal and assume spore forms in the presence of oxygen at a temperature approximately 85° F.

---

*Joint Order No. 2, U. S. Department of Agriculture and U. S. Treasury Department.

The spore forms, because of their great power of resistance to heat, cold and acids, are the chief means for keeping anthrax epidemic in certain areas, by "seeding" the ground. The spores are apparently responsible for 125 of the 126 cases studied, for only one case was due to the patient handling an animal anthrax case.

Mode of Infection: The unbroken skin surface protects, but any abrasion, scratch or cut, offers an opportunity for dirt to be rubbed in, and if the spores are present in the dirt a case of anthrax will probably result.

It is the infected hides particularly that have proved to be the most difficult problem in eradicating human anthrax in Massachusetts.

Source of Infection: Infection is usually from anthrax spores on dried or pickled cow hides, goat skins, horsehair and wool in the external type of the disease.

Horsehair and wool, because of the spore infected dust that rises in handling them, cause the pneumonic type or "wool sorter's disease" at times.

Types of Anthrax: There is an external and an internal type of anthrax.

(1) External anthrax, the most common in Massachusetts, exhibits the skin lesion of the disease, as a papule, vesicle and carbuncle accompanied by much edema, fever and prostration, but there is practically no pain. It is the result of direct contact with anthrax spores, or, rarely in this state, with anthrax bacilli.

(2) Internal anthrax may be the intestinal form, where anthrax infected meat has been eaten, or the pneumonic or lung form (wool sorter's disease) where anthrax spores have been breathed in and the lung infected. There are no cases of the intestinal form on record in Massachusetts as far as is known. There have been a few cases of the pneumonic type. This type can be diagnosed by finding anthrax bacilli in the

sputum, but usually is not diagnosed until death and an autopsy held. During the period 1916-1919 there were 3 pneumonic cases, all of which were fatal, out of 126 cases of anthrax. Recently British investigators* have reported cases of meningitis due to the anthrax bacillus, but the diagnosis was not determined until lumbar puncture disclosed anthrax bacilli in the spinal fluid:

Method of Investigation: Practically all of the cases have been personally investigated and visits made to hospitals, factories, tanneries, hide dealers and brokers in checking up and following the thread of information leading to the country from whence the hides were shipped.

When the first case reported from a hide infection, has been a worker on the docks, the factories and health department at the place where the hides are to be shipped have been notified of the probably anthrax infected lot. In other instances shipments were separated into several lots and forwarded to various dealers. If such a lot was suspected to have been infected, information to that effect was sent to the buyers so that they would be informed and the hides disinfected before workmen had an opportunity to become infected.

Seasonal Incidence: The appearance of anthrax cases does not bear any relation to the seasons, as respiratory diseases do, but depends solely on when an anthrax infected shipment of hides, hair or wool arrives in the state and when the material is handled.

The seasonable incidence for the four-year period is summarized below:

SEASONAL INCIDENCE OF ANTHRAX IN MASSACHUSETTS 1916-1919

Month	Cases
January	2
February	7
March	15
April	11
May	17
June	17
July	6

*Local Government Board Report, 1916, by Francis J. H. Coutts, M. D.

August	5
September	13
October	14
November	10
December	9
Total	126

Most of the hides from China are sun-dried cow hides and during the rainy season in that country great difficulty is encountered in drying hides, particularly if they are required to be disinfected in the bichloride solution before shipment. Unless hides are thoroughly dried they will "sweat" in the hold of the steamer and this will seriously decrease their commercial value. Obviously then, the temptation to avoid disinfection of hides in the rainy season is great and a consular certificate will be accepted in lieu, if obtainable. Thus during the rainy season the hides from China should be particularly suspected of being infected.

The majority of cases during the year, apparently infected by China hides, received their infection from hides shipped from China during the period of March to June.

Ages: The age distribution of cases and deaths of anthrax were as follows for the years 1917-1919 inclusive:

AGE OF ANTHRAX CASES 1917-1919

Age	Cases	Deaths	Fatality Rate Per cent
10-19	6	1	16.6
20-29	26	0	0.0
30-39	17	2	11.8
40-49	21	7	33.3
50-59	11	4	36.4
60-69	5	2	40.0
Unknown	9	2	20.2
Total	95	18	18.9

From the study made, the individual who is over 40 years old has much less chance of recovering from anthrax than one under that age. The three pneumonic type cases were individuals aged 30, 35 and 47 years in this period, so it is apparent, when these cases are excluded from the above table, that the older the individual the smaller are his chances of recovery.

Means of Transmission of Disease: A study of the cases, to determine the most common means of causing the infection, shows that cow hides, particularly dried hides, and goat skins are the chief offenders. Hides of one kind or another apparently caused 111 cases or 88 per cent. of the anthrax cases.

MATERIAL CAUSING ANTHRAX CASES

Material	Cases	Deaths	Fatality Rate Per cent
Hides	111	17	15.3
Hair	5	2	40.0
Wool	7	2	28.6
Native animal case	1	0	0.0
Unknown	2	2	100.0
Totals	126	23	18.3

It will be seen that because hides cause the external type of the disease there are fewer deaths, proportionately, than those due to hair or wool, which are more apt to be of the pneumonic and more fatal type of the disease.

Origin of Infected Material: A summary is given showing the foreign origin of material handled by the anthrax cases and apparently causing the disease. In a few cases, material from two or more countries had been handled, and such cases are given under both countries; for this reason, the totals exceed the cases under consideration.

COUNTRIES EXPORTING THE INFECTING PRODUCTS

(Number of cases handling materials)

Countries	Hides	Hair	Wool
ASIA			
China			
Hankow	68	0	0
Shanghai	2	0	0
Tientsin	1	0	0
India			
Amritza	14	0	0
Dacca	1	0	0
Angra	1	0	0
Russia			
Manchuria	0	7	0
Totals	87	7	0
SOUTH AMERICA			
Argentine	17	0	6
Brazil	3	0	0
Venezuela	1	0	0
Totals	21	0	6
NORTH AMERICA			
Mexico	0	0	1
United States	5	1	1
Totals	5	1	2
Unknown origin	8	1	1

Hair: In the cases infected by hair, the material was usually horsehair from Manchuria, which is a dirty mixed hair. The cases were workers in brush factories prior to 1917, but that year a case appeared, apparently due to a new low-priced shaving brush. There have been four cases of suspected shaving brush origin in the period under discussion. Unfortunately, all the brushes were destroyed before bacteriological studies could be instituted.

Occupations: The occupations of the cases were such, in the majority of cases, that the victims came in contact with animal products such as hides, hair, wool, or with the sludge from hide vats. The occupations are known in 124 of the cases, as follows:

LEATHER INDUSTRY

	Cases
Beamhouse laborers	79
Tacker	1
Embosser	1
Housewife	1
Hide Broker	1
Shoe cutter	1
Shoe dealer	1
Carpenter	1
Plumbers	3
	89

BRUSH INDUSTRY

	Cases
Carders	1
Laborers	3
Foreman	1
	5

MISCELLANEOUS

	Cases
Farmer	1
Restaurant	1
Unknown	2
	4

FREIGHT HANDLERS

	Cases
Teamsters	3
Longshoremen and stevedores	10
Hide weighers	4
	17

APPARENTLY INFECTED BY SHAVING BRUSHES

	Cases
Barber	1
Soldier	1
Carpenter	1
Clerk (drug store)	1
	4

WOOL INDUSTRY

	Cases
Wool sorters	5
Wool salesmen	2
	7

The leather industry claimed 89 cases or 71 per cent of the total number. All except 5 cases, classified under this heading, handled hides or leather in some manner. In addition, 3 plumbers or steam fitters and 1 carpenter were infected apparently from sludge about hide vats where they were working. A housewife digging dandelions on land where the effluent of. hide vats had flowed, also became infected.

The group of freight handlers, such as longshoremen, teamsters, stevedores, dock laborers and hide weighers are next in importance and had 17 cases or 13 percent. These men unloaded hides, hair and wool from ships and shifted them about the docks. In every case it was hides which apparently infected the individual and not hair or wool.

The wool industry plays a comparatively small part at present in the state as a cause of anthrax, only 7 cases being found probably due to this cause. The cases were in wool sorters and wool salesmen.

The brush industry claimed 5 anthrax patients and, indirectly, apparently by infected shaving brushes, 4 cases more. Only one of these shaving brush cases had bacteriological diagnosis, although the other 3 cases had just purchased a new brush prior to the onset of the typical anthrax carbuncle on their faces. The material handled by three of the remaining four cases of the 126 cases studied is unknown. The remaining case was a farmer who was infected by material from an animal that died of anthrax and which he had buried. This is the only case during the four-year period due to anthrax bacilli and not to anthrax spores.

Treatment of Anthrax Cases: A patient who is operated on and has the anthrax carbuncle excised, has a smaller chance of recovering than the patient who is given rest, quiet, liquid diet, corrosive poultices and anthrax serum. In operating, the opportunity of an anthracemia is offered and there are but few cases of an anthrax patient recovering after this occurs.

The fatalities from operating are summed up in the accompanying table, which gives anthrax cases in Massachusetts which had the clinical diagnosis supported by animal inoculation with material from the lesion or by smear examination, showing "large square ended bacilli" at the laboratory.

The importance of the non-operative form of treatment in preventing fatalities is so great that the comparison between the operative and non-operative treatment is given in detail.

FATALITY RATE OF OPERATIVE AND NON-OPERATIVE ANTHRAX CASES IN MASSACHUSETTS 1916-1919

Location of Lesion	Diagnosis Confirmed by Laboratory		
	Cases	Deaths	Fatality Rate %
Operative Cases—			
Neck	4	1	25
Chin	1	1	100
Forehead	1	0	0
Ankle	0	0	0
Forearm	0	0	0
Totals	6	2	33.3

Location of Lesion	Clinical Diagnosis Only		
	Cases	Deaths	Fatality Rate %
Neck	6	2	33
Chin	1	0	0
Forehead	0	0	0
Ankle	1	0	0
Forearm	1	0	0
Totals	9	2	22.2

Location of Lesion	Diagnosis Confirmed by Laboratory		
Non-Operative Cases—			
Neck	20	6	30
Forearm	10	0	0
Cheek	9	1	11
Chin	4	0	0
Eyelid	2	0	0
Hand	1	0	0
Forehead	0	0	0
Upper leg	0	0	0
Upper arm	2	0	0
Nose	1	0	0
Ankle	1	0	0
Back	0	0	0
Unknown	0	0	0
Totals	50	7	14.0

Location of Lesion		Clinical Diagnosis Only	
Neck	15	3	20
Forearm	10	0	0
Cheek	8	1	13
Chin	2	0	0
Eyelid	0	0	0
Hand	3	0	0
Forehead	4	1	25
Upper leg	2	0	0
Upper arm	0	0	0
Nose	1	0	0
Back	1	0	0
Ankle	0	0	0
Unknown	2	1	50
Totals	48	6	12.5

Information is available for 113 cases. Of this number, 56 cases had their diagnosis confirmed by bacteriological examination of smears or animal inoculation. It is of interest to note that the fatality rate of the cases that have bacteriological diagnosis approximate the rate of cases that have had no laboratory examination made, indicating that the symptoms are so typical in most cases that clinical diagnosis is usually correct.

The most successful treatment of cases in Massachusetts has been rest in bed, liquid diet and bichloride poultices combined with anthrax serum. The first dose of the serum* is 45 cc., injected subcutaneously, repeated, if necessary, after intervals of 24 hours with injections of 25 cc. In advanced stages the serum should be administered intravenously and doses up to 100 cc. may be given.

None of the pneumonic type of cases were treated with anthrax serum, so the effects of the serum in these cases is unknown.

Public Health Aspects of Anthrax: In 1916, when the cases began to increase, the manner by which workers should be protected, particularly in industries handling hides and hair, became a problem.

There will probably be an increasing demand for leather in the future and the areas that sent out infected hides during the war will continue to ship them un-

*This treatment is that advised by the Federal Bureau of Animal Industry when using the serum furnished by that bureau.

less some method of control is established.

In addition to preventing cases, the Massachusetts Department of Public Health furnished anthrax serum for all anthrax cases requesting it, through the kindness of the Federal Bureau of Animay Industry which manufactures it.

Tanning processes wash off or mechanically dislodge anthrax spores rather than disinfect, but for this reason there is little danger of anthrax in workers who handle finished leather. The spores, washed off, exist in the sludge and infect persons coming in contact with this material, as plumbers and carpenters. It is the laborers, hide trimmers and beamhouse workers who face the anthrax peril. The dust produced during the handling of dry hides on ships, in warehouses, storehouses, at the factory and under like conditions is always a possible cause of anthrax pneumonia. In any industry involving raw hides, hair and wool, where there is dust, there is danger of anthrax. There are probably more cases of internal anthrax, particularly of the pneumonic type, than are realized at present. Probably the reporting of this type of case will increase in the future as it becomes the custom to examine sputum in pneumonia cases.

Every case of pneumonia in a longshoreman, wool worker, hide handler or other worker among animal products, should be considered a possible pneumonia due to the *bacillus anthracis*, and diagnosis determined by sputum examination rather than later by autopsy.

Method of Importation of Hides: Federal regulations* permit the entrance of hides and skins without disinfection when accompanied by a United States consular certificate, stating that anthrax is not prevalent and that neither foot and mouth disease nor rinderpest exist in the locality in which the hides or skins originated. One of the chief troubles

*Joint Order No. 2, U. S. Treasury Department and Department of Agriculture, January 1, 1918.

in importing hides is this consular certificate, for obviously in a large country as China, where hides come into the Hankow market from areas thousands of miles away drained by the Yangste River, it is an impossibility for an official to be informed correctly regarding the prevalence of disease. The fact that the hides come from myriads of small farms and are collected by local hide collectors and passed on, instead of originating in a central abattoir, makes the certification of hides an impossibility.

Protection at Factories: Workers in leather tanneries, hair and wool factories can be protected by furnishing rubber gloves, rubber aprons, dust removing appliances on carding machines and instant treatment when an anthrax pustule appears, but why wait for the "fire"? Why not prevent at the source. All of these methods have been tried and have been found wanting—cases still occur.

It would seem far better to disinfect hides as near their source of origin as possible, to minimize the number of contacts and anthrax cases. The disinfection of hides after the workers have been infected occurs far too often. The anthrax problem is a national affair and not a state task. All disinfection should be carried out on animal products prior to shipping or on their arrival at a port in the United States and not at leather tanneries and hair factories, as is the case at present.

Preventive Methods: There have been many precautions taken during recent years by the different leather, wool and hair factories to prevent anthrax infection among their employees. These are, briefly:

(1) Issuing of rubber aprons, rubber gloves and cotton gloves to employees handling hides.

(2) Installation of dust-removing appliances, as on carding machines.

(3) Education of employees by lectures and pamphlets on the dangers, and requiring them to wash with hot water and soap before leaving the factory.

(4) Medical examination of injuries and disease at factories.

(5) Hospitalization of anthrax cases.

(6) Disinfection by steam of all hair handled in the factory where cases have occurred.

(7) Disinfection of hides on their arrival at the factory. This provision is required, under certain conditions, by the United States Department of Agriculture, Bureau of Animal Industry, and, in a few instances, carried out voluntarily by the factories.

(8) Disinfection of walls and floors before sweeping a building used for storing hides, hair or wool.

Disinfection of Animal Products: The experience in the practical disinfection of animal products in Massachusetts shows that steam disinfection is practicable for hair but not for wool or hides. The wool fibre and hides are seriously damaged by the action of the steam. The most successful disinfection of hides is by Professor Schattenfroh's method or slight modifications of it.

Disinfection of Hair: In carrying out disinfection of hair for anthrax spores, certain conditions are necessary for successful disinfection.

The hair must be loose, the bales opened and all parts of the material exposed to the action of wet steam. A temperature of 212° F. should be maintained for 15 minutes after all parts of the hair have reached that temperature.

A Local Government Board Report (New Series, No. 112) states "that for steam disinfection to be successful the cases and bales should be opened, the bundles removed, and most of the strings cut, unless the temperature inside the steam disinfection apparatus is maintained at 230° F. for half an hour."

The Federal Bureau of Animal Industry recommends* that hair be disinfected by proper exposure to a tem-

*Joint Order No. 2, United States Treasury Department and Department of Agriculture, January 1, 1918.

perature of "not less than 200° F. for at least 15 minutes, or in such manner as may be directed by the Chief of the Bureau of Animal Industry."

Disinfection of Wool: The disinfection of wool has not been studied as much in Massachusetts as that of hides and hair, because there have been few cases of anthrax among wool handlers. In England, however, the wool question has been thoroughly investigated and a practical method of disinfection of wool for anthrax has been found and, according to Dr. T. M. Legge, is in use at the present time.

This method of disinfection of wool is described fully in the report of the Departmental Committee appointed to inquire as to the precautions for the preventing of the danger of infection by anthrax in the manipulation of wool, goat hair, and camel hair (Vol. II, cd. 9171).

Disinfection of Hides: The disinfection process appears on the surface to be a relatively simple matter but experience has shown that the use of acids and disinfectants sufficient to kill anthrax spores, in most instances injure the hides.

Disinfection of hides by bichloride of mercury and the Seymour-Jones method of using formic acid are not looked on with favor by leather manufacturers, for the hide is apparently injured by such treatment.

The Schattenfroh method is used successfully, at times with slight modifications, in Massachusetts. This method consists of a solution of 10 percent. sodium chloride and 2 percent. absolute hydrochloric acid (hydrogen chloride), the hides being kept in soak for 40 hours at a temperature of 60-70° F. Great care must be used in preparing the solution for the strength of commercial acid varies as follows:

HYDROGEN CHLORIDE IN COMMERCIAL HYDROCHLORIC ACID

18 degrees hydrochloric acid contains 27% hydrogen chloride.

20 degrees hydrochloric acid contains 31% hydrogen chloride.

22 degrees hydrochloric acid contains 34.5% hydrogen chloride.

Experiments by Dr. Francis H. Slack of the Sias Laboratories, carried out for a leather firm under practical conditions, showed that the solution of 10 percent. sodium chloride and ¾ of 1 percent. absolute hydrochloric acid is on the border line of successful disinfection and that 1 percent. acid and 10 percent. sodium chloride solution is satisfactory for killing anthrax sphores on hides. A temperature of 60-70° F. must be maintained and the hides kept in soak for 40 hours.

At present, as far as is known, the acid and salt method is used only in Massachusetts for routine disinfection of upper leather, although it is probably suitable for all leathers at different strengths of the solution.

Experiments by Dr. Slack made for the Massachusetts Department of Health showed that the following solutions will kill anthrax spores at 68° F.:

SOLUTIONS CAPABLE OF KILLING ANTHRAX SPORES

2% absolute hydrochloric acid and 10% sodium chloride.

2% absolute hydrochloric acid and 5% sodium chloride.

1.5% absolute hydrochloric acid and 10% sodium chloride.

1.5% absolute hydrochloric acid and 5% sodium chloride.

1% absolute hydrochloric acid and 10% sodium chloride.

1% absolute hydrochloric acid and 5% sodium chloride.

¾% absolute hydrochloric acid and 10% sodium chloride.

The solutions using less than ¾ percent. of hydrochloric acid failed to kill anthrax spores and for this reason it is desirable not to use less than 1 percent. of the acid.

Results of Disinfection of Hides by Acid and Salt Method: Wherever this method has been used no anthrax cases have been caused by the hides treated, although in one instance the strength of the acid used was only ¾ of 1 percent.

Results of Investigation:

(1) Anthrax infected hides, hair and

wool are being imported from foreign countries.

(2) Anthrax infected hides are shipped chiefly from Buenos Aires, Argentine, Hankow, China, and Calcutta, India.

(3) Federal regulations do not prevent the importation of infected material.

(4) Hides bearing the consular certificate have apparently caused anthrax cases.

(5) Hides, hair and wool can in most cases be successfully disinfected for anthrax spores.

(6) Anthrax cases operated on have a fatality rate double that of the non-operative cases.

Recommendations for the Prevention of Anthrax: There are several ways by which anthrax may be prevented.

(1) Quarantine of all hides, wool and hair from anthrax infected and suspected areas or areas about which information is lacking.

(2) Disinfection of all hides, wool and hair from anthrax infected and suspected areas or areas about which in-

formation is lacking. This disinfection should be done in the country where the hides, wool and hair are collected, preferably at the market center, where, by mass disinfecting, a trained corps of workers could disinfect material efficiently, successfully and at the lowest possible expense.

(3) An anthrax survey should be made by a corps of trained men, acquainted with anthrax and the hide and leather industry. This survey should consist of field investigations, to ascertain the prevalence of anthrax in regions where hides, hair and wool are collected for export, and the manner of collecting and preparing the different products for shipping. The collecting of this definite data by permanent investigators would enable a consul to have a far better knowledge of the hides, particularly on which he is requested to issue the "consular certificate."

(4) The disposal of sludge from hide vats should be cared for in such a way that no material can overflow the land and thus "seed" it with anthrax spores.

MILK IN FEEDING ANIMALS

A striking illustration of the value of milk for food for young animals is given in this picture which the JOURNAL presents through the courtesy of the New York State Department of Farms and Markets. These calves were shown together with similar couples of pigs, dogs and other creatures at a recent exhibition in the Grand Central Palace, New York City. These calves are two months old. The weight of the milk-fed one is 245 pounds, while the weight of the other is 145 pounds. The obvious moral is that milk is good for growing animals. Dogs which tell precisely the same story are shown on page 672 of this JOURNAL.

APPLICATION OF VACCINES IN PUBLIC HEALTH WORK

GEORGE W. McCOY, M. D.,

Director, Hygienic Laboratory,
Washington, D. C.

Read before the Conference of State and Provincial Boards of Health, at Washington, D. C.,
May 26-27, 1920.

An important service to health officers is this dispassionate appraisal of the practical advantages of vaccines. They are useful, but constitute no royal road to health. Aside from antienteric vaccines and the toxin-antitoxin mixture public health administrators need expect little help from the use of the bacterial vaccines that are known today.

I SHALL not consider the two vaccines that are on the most satisfactory scientific and practical basis, for the efficacy of smallpox vaccination is so well known that it is not an appropriate subject for discussion, and antirabic vaccine has importance only for the individual who has been bitten by a rabid animal.

Coming to the *bacterial vaccines*, we must appreciate primarily that to put a prophylactic vaccine of this kind on a sound basis two things are necessary: first, we must know what organism is the cause of the disease, and in addition we must know whether one can induce immunity by means of the killed organism. We have no rational basis for any influenza vaccine, considering now only the primary disease, because we do not know what particular organism causes the disease; even if we did know this we would still need to know that the organism was one against which it is possible to induce immunity.

The best illustration of our inability successfully to vaccinate against a disease, the etiological agent of which is well known, is tuberculosis. For many years we have known the organism which causes the disease, and we know a great deal about it, but we know no method of immunizing against infection.

Let us turn to the more encouraging fields. The evidence in favor of typhoid and paratyphoid vaccines appears to be almost perfect and I shall not attempt to review it even briefly, but will point out several features of special interest for this group.

1. Even a well-vaccinated personnel may show a rather high typhoid incidence if the infection is very heavy; in other words, the immunity is relative. It is not as complete, for example, as is the case with smallpox.

2. Vaccination should be repeated at shorter intervals than has been the custom. The old teaching that a single series of inoculations would protect for four years was probably too optimistic, since in military service it was found that vaccination in one or two years was required.

3. The civil experience with typhoid vaccine is rather meager; really we do not know how valuable it is under such conditions, and these are the conditions with which this body is concerned primarily. There are such effective methods of reducing typhoid fever practically to the vanishing point in a community without reference to vacci-

nation that under ordinary civil conditions we need not rely upon this, though it should be employed as a valuable adjunct in anti-typhoid work.

There are some exceptional circumstances, as with people going to a place where the hazard is very high, or with those inhabiting camps or other temporary communities where the proper safeguards do not exist that justify reliance to a large measure oh typhoid vaccine.

There are two other intestinal infections which appear to be controllable, in part at least, by prophylactic vaccination, though the evidence at hand is not very extensive. I refer to cholera and to bacillary dysentery. In respect to the latter the evidence is particularly encouraging.

Neither of these diseases has any special significance for us in this country, though our dysentery problem is, I think, one worthy of more serious attention than it has had.

A vaccine against plague has, of course, been in use for a long time and almost all of the reports are encouraging, not to say optimistic, though not all will stand critical analysis. But the incidence of plague in the United States is so small, and we have such effective means of controlling it that, in my judgment, recourse to vaccination as a public health measure will never be required.

We must consider now the group generally designated as respiratory infections, and we will take up first the most promising of these. This is the toxin-antitoxin mixture which has been so extensively popularized in this country by Dr. Wm. H. Park. The indications all are that in the case of this preparation we have a reliable means of controlling diphtheria. Indeed, the results reported by Dr. Park and those working with him show that it is possible to eradicate diphtheria f r o m schools and institutions. It has the disadvantage of requiring several doses, three or four, and the immunity re-

sponse is not prompt; therefore, it is not a procedure for emergency immunization.

The subject of vaccination against whooping cough is one that is so often the subject of inquiry and there is so much optimism, unwarranted I believe, that I want to express the opinion that this is in a purely experimental stage.

Vaccination against influenza has interested, not to say agitated, us all in the past eighteen months more than any other one subject of this sort, I suppose. We have seen "success" obtained in the vaccination of what were really the naturally insusceptible persons in a group, and we have seen failure charged to a vaccine which did not have a fair trial because sufficient time had not elapsed to permit of the development of any immunity that the vaccine might conceivably be capable of evoking.

Our own experiments and those carried out by persons closely associated with the Hygienic Laboratory were all carefully controlled and in every instance failed to show any evidence in favor of the vaccine; whether the latter was made from Pfeiffer's organism alone or included, in addition, pneumococci and streptococci. We feel that we should say in passing that some of the most careless work we have ever encountered has been in connection with this subject of vaccination against influenza and its complications.

With respect to lobar pneumonia the experiments reported have been most encouraging. Our own work in this connection is not yet complete, but taking the most optimistic view of it possible restricts us to saying that there appears to be protection for a period limited to a few weeks, perhaps six or eight.

In connection with the subject of influenza and pneumonia we must not ignore a vaccine that we once hoped would prove a great advance in bacterial vaccines. I refer to the oil suspensions which are generally designated as lipovaccines. The reports from military sources were so encouraging that we were all hopeful that a very great advance had been made. Experience soon showed that there were unexpected obstacles to overcome and I regret that they have not yet been overcome. In the first place, it was very difficult to make the vaccine sterile. It is surprising how high a degree of heat organisms will resist in the oil suspensions, but differences of this kind can be overcome. A more serious matter was the discovery at the Hygenic Laboratory of the fact that oil suspensions of organisms were definitely less effective in provoking measurable immunity response in laboratory animals (and presumably in man) than were saline suspensions of the organisms. Thus far the defect has not been overcome. The Hygenic Laboratory has felt that it is unwise to recommend license for oil suspensions of organisms until these two serious defects had been overcome. If we were unduly conservative I hope that we may be pardoned.

From what I have said I am sure that I am justified in expressing the opinion that aside from antienteric vaccines and the toxin-antitoxin mixture we need expect little help in practical public health administration work from the use of bacterial vaccines.

Public Health administrators with whom I have discussed the subject have expressed the fear that the popularization of vaccines may interfere with substantial progress along other lines, but I see no indication that the public is enthusiastic enough about vaccines to warrant this fear; indeed, surprisingly few people will submit voluntarily to vaccination, even when every encouragement, including free administration, is offered.

GOOD WORK OF NATIONAL SAFETY COUNCIL

In the JOURNAL for January, 1920, mention was made of the methods whereby the National Safety Council is conducting its work of education. Further presentation of the posters, which are a most excellent means of impressing fundamental truths upon the people is made here. Under the caption, "Glad Feet," are a few simple rules. There are not many individuals who realize how dependent they are on their feet till something happens to them. The second poster contains excellent advice with reference to food. The National Safety Council places such posters before millions of people in this country.

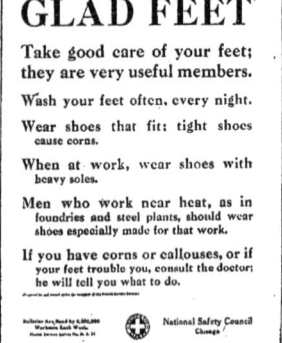

RELATION OF SCHOOL AND SPECIAL FEEDING TO DEFECTIVE NUTRITION

JOHN C. GEBHART,

Director, Department of Social Welfare,
New York Association for Improving the Condition of the Poor,
New York City

This author sets forth the futility of attacking undernourishment principally as a school problem. Experience both in this country and in England shows that school meals are merely palliative if unaccompanied by measures to raise permanently home standards of food and hygiene. The school measures must be fitted into the larger social machinery for dealing with the defect.

THERE is an unfortunate tendency to confuse defective nutrition with underfeeding and to assume that the mere provision of adequate food is sufficient to promote normal growth and development. School lunches and other ·forms of special feeding in the past, while temporarily assuaging hunger have contributed little toward an effective program for dealing with undernourished children. The experience of the past ten years, however, has thrown much light on the real causes of disturbed nutrition and has aided us in formulating a program for their removal.

England was thoroughly aroused to the physical condition of her youth during the Boer War, when she was obliged to reject two-fifths of her recruits because of physical disability. An investigation of the defects for which these young men were rejected indicated that defective nutrition during childhood was chiefly responsible for undermining their physique. School feeding was immediately heralded as the remedy par excellence for the deterioration of the British stock. As a result, in 1906 the "provision of meals" act was passed which provided for the public feeding of school children. The language of the act itself indicates clearly that undernourishment and underfeeding were regarded as

synonymous. The act states that "no child shall be deprived of his education for lack of food."

The guarantee of government subsidy resulted in a vast extension of school feeding which prior to that time had been a popular form of philanthropy. In 1914, 29,560,316 meals were served. The high wages paid in war industries and government allowances for soldiers' families resulted in a marked falling off in the number of meals served until in 1918 only 6,503,140 meals were served. Children are selected for the meals on the basis of two tests: (1) the poverty test and (2) the physical condition of the child. The poverty test is the one most frequently used and often without any reference whatever to the child's physical condition except that he appears to be underfed. The Chief Medical Officer of the English Board of Education and other careful observers in England are keenly sensitive to the anomaly of this situation and are constantly urging the local authorities to employ the physical rather than the poverty test for the selection of the children.

A feeding experiment was conducted in Bradford, England, in 1907 to determine the effect of school feeding on undernourished children. Forty children who appeared to be most in need of food were selected from two of the poorest schools in the city. From April 17th to July 24th this group was supplied with a hearty breakfast and dinner every school day. From the same schools 69 children were selected as a control and these received all of their food at home. At the end of the feeding period the children who had received the school meals showed an average gain of nearly two pounds in excess of the control group. The experiment proves conclusively that if underfed children are supplied with adequate food they will increase their rate of growth. But the experiment also showed that during the holidays when no school meals were served, the children not only failed to gain but actually lost most of the weight which they had acquired during the preceding weeks. While the latter disclosure was used as an argument for continuing the school meals during the holidays, an arrangement which has since been effected in that city, it also clearly indicates that the effect of the school meals if unaccompanied by other measures which permanently raise the food and hygienic standards of the home is merely temporary and palliative.

American practice in school feeding has never sanctioned the wholesale serving of school meals as the sole remedy for defective nutrition. Whereas in England 90% of the meals are served free, in America the same proportion are sold at a price which at least covers the cost of the food. School lunches were first introduced in Philadelphia, New York, and Boston, because large numbers of children were either going without lunch or were purchasing buns, pickles or other delectables from pushcarts and candy stores with the pennies that their mothers had supplied for their noon meal. The "penny lunches" as they were then called were simply intended to make it possible for children to purchase soup, cocoa, and other nourishing foods with the money that they were already spending for trash.

The importance of providing special feeding for groups of anaemic children and those threatened with tuberculosis has long been recognized and has been carried on extensively both in Europe and in this country. In England and on the continent such children receive a liberal provision of food which is far in excess of the normal requirement in order to enable them to build up resistance to disease and to bring them up to normal weight. After the child has been restored to normal health he is returned to his former environment. In America such children remain at home but attend school in special open air class rooms. The amount of food supplied varies from nothing at all to three-fourths of the child's required nutrition. The feeding is regarded simply as supplementary to what the child will or ought to receive at home. In this city, crackers and milk or cereal and milk are frequently furnished during the middle of the forenoon and afternoon. In many cases the child also receives a regular noon lunch at school.

The same difficulty has been encountered in special or supplementary feeding as in the regular school lunch. As long as an abundance of food is provided good gains are made but at the end of the feeding period the children lapse into their former state. Dr. Leopold Marcus, director of open air classes in this city, found that in one school the children were receiving two-thirds of the total food required but in spite of this extra feeding they did not make even the average gains. A study of the home conditions proved that the parents had cut down on the accustomed diet of the children at home because they were fed so well at school.

School feeding both in England and America has, therefore, failed to secure definite and lasting results when it has regarded the undernourished child as a detached unit who mysteriously appears at school at 8:30 in the morning and disappears as mysteriously at 4:00 in the afternoon. The factors which determine the child's nutrition are indissolubly tied up with the home environment and standard of living of the family. Clinical experience with undernourished children indicates that an unregulated diet, bad hygienic habits, uncorrected physical defects, such as diseased tonsils and adenoids, chronic indigestion and other ailments, prevent children from making a normal gain.

The awakened interest in the seriousness of defective nutrition has resulted in various efforts to get at the fundamental causes and to deal effectively with them. Hospitals and other agencies have developed nutrition clinics where undernourished children are kept under medical supervision and where other physical defects likely to affect the child's nutrition are given attention. Nutrition classes which combine group instruction in food and health habits, with periodical visits to the home to secure the interest and co-operation of the parents, are conducted either as adjuncts of the nutrition clinic or in the public schools. These efforts even where no feeding is provided are producing most encouraging results in the building up of undernourished children. The school-feeding movement to be an effective weapon for combating defective nutrition must be made to fit into the larger social machinery now being developed for dealing with the defect.

As a preventive measure a school lunch in all neighborhoods where children are for any reason whatever not likely to receive the proper lunch at home can render a real service. Many of these children are not now victims of defective nutrition and may be prevented from falling into this class if they can be supplied with a warm nourishing meal during the noon hour at their school. The school lunch can be made the point of departure for sound educational procedure in the relation of food to health. The food served at the lunch counter should serve as a practical demonstration of the kind of food which normal children should receive daily. This work must not stop with the children, but various expedients must be used to interest the parents in what the school is doing and to get them to prepare similar food for the children at home.

The meals should be planned so as to provide a maximum of food value at a minimum cost. In this respect school lunches in American cities have suffered from the competition of the pushcarts and candy stores where food of very poor quality is sold. Milk products and fresh vegetables ought to be used liberally in the school menu but to introduce these elements will, of course, necessitate an increase in the prices charged. Cocoa made with water and a little condensed milk could be sold last year for two cents a cup at a slight profit; cocoa made with whole milk if sold for two cents entailed a loss. The increased price will drive some children to the pushcarts where apparently they get better value for their money. Such features must, therefore, be introduced gradually, increasing in quantity as a better appreciation of food values on the part of the children is developed.

One advantage of the English system of school feeding is that it is definitely linked up with the undernourished child, while in America this vital connection is usually left to mere chance. In selecting the schools for a lunch service, preference should be given to those schools in which the amount of defective nutrition is greatest. Moreover, in these schools, the children who are found to need nutritional care (grades III and IV of the Dunfermline scale) should be set aside for intensive work not only to insure their attending the school lunch regularly but to carry over to the home the entire nutrition program. For example, there are in a school of 2,000 children, 600 undernourished children. The principal or the school doctor should notify the parents at once of the child's condition and impress upon them the necessity of the child's attending the lunch every day and of carrying out the instruction of the school nurse or school dietition. These children should be weighed weekly and a failure to make at least the expected gain will call for further study of the home conditions and a physical examination of the child to determine what is retarding him. The problem must then be taken up with the parents to see that the necessary corrections are made either in the child's habits or physical condition.

In many cases it will be wise to provide supplementary food for undernourished children, but this must always be done in such a manner as to impress the mother with the fact that the food supplied at school, whether purchased by the child or served gratis, is simply intended to supplement the normal food allowance which he should be getting at home. One of the schools in this city has been able to accomplish excellent results with its undernourished children by supplying them with either milk and crackers or cocoa and crackers during the forenoon and afternoon. Besides this the principal keeps in very close touch with the home conditions of all such children. In addition to the feeding she has secured the removal of diseased tonsils and adenoids, has had the mouths put in a hygienic condition and has influenced the mothers to provide better food at home.

School feeding is given a lesser role in the program for dealing with defective nutrition than the one ascribed to it in earlier days, but it is one of strategic importance. The school lunch can be made the center from which radiate various activities dealing with the child's nutrition. There is something very concrete and appealing about a real meal which carries its message over to the child much more effectively than any amount of preaching on the subject. As long as the school lunch or special feeding are administered in a truly educational spirit and are co-ordinated with all other well-considered efforts their contribution to the work with defective nutrition will be most important.

☐

MILK-FED VS. NO MILK

These dogs tell their own story of the food value of milk. They were shown at the Grand Central Palace, New York City, by the New York State Department of Farms and Markets, to which the JOURNAL is indebted for the picture. See also page 665.

WHAT IS THE MATTER WITH PUBLIC HEALTH?

DISCUSSION *

HIBBERT W. HILL, M. D.,

Executive Secretary, Minnesota Public Health Association,
St. Paul, Minn.

Millions for tribute; not one penny for defense.

The fundamental difference between the view of the Health Officers' duties which Dr. Mccombs so lucidly champions (A. J. P. H., Dec., 1919) and that view he calls for convenience "Dr. Hill's" (A. J. P. H., Nov., 1919) seems to be brought out best as follows:

Dr. McCombs assumes that the health officer now has responsibilities concerning both compulsory and voluntary public health activities and he condemns "my" plan because it (he thinks) proposes dividing these responsibilities between the health officer and the voluntary public health agencies (the latter, of course, taking the voluntary activities, i. e., all related to personal hygiene and to therapeutics).

As a matter of fact 'my'" view is quite the converse, and, remember, I am speaking of the duties and responsibilities of the health officer, not of those of the Government as a whole, which is a quite different matter.

My view is that the health officer has undivided, and indivisible, responsibilities, but concerning compulsory public health activities only, i. e., against *preventable* disease; and that he has none whatever concerning voluntary activities above outlined. For the health officer to "pass over to voluntary agencies" his voluntary responsibilities is, in my view, impossible; simply because, in my view, he has no such voluntary responsibilities to pass over. The situation is, in my view, that the health officer in some instances has secured or is attempting to secure voluntary activities that do not belong to his office and that he has assumed them, not for the reason that they are properly his, but, as Dr. Mc-Combs frankly and clearly agrees, because these voluntary activities have a popular appeal and may bring to the health officer the public sympathy, support, and prestige which he now, alas, lacks.

*For previous presentation of views see Dr. Hill's original article in the A. J. P. H. for Nov., 1919, page 827, and the reply by Dr. Carl E. McCombs, A. J. P. H., December, 1919, page 951.

I have not succeeded yet in putting my own point of view of the situation more clearly to my own mind than by a parable; and perhaps I will be pardoned for repeating that parable here.

General Pershing was authorized, equipped, and sent to Europe for the one purpose of combating the Germans and defeating them. Suppose that, instead of his doing this, he had decided that the relief and reconstruction of the devastated areas were more popular, would get him more public sympathy, greater prestige, etc.

The relief work in Europe was enormous, infinitely insistent, humanitarian, a moral duty than which there was no duty higher. But though it was perhaps the moral duty of the American people to relieve the distress, it clearly was not General Pershing's duty, moral or otherwise. He had his own work set out clearly before him.

The health officer of today, as Dr. Mc-Combs agrees, has not made good in his admitted primary duty—defense against infectious disease. He has not in most instances seriously attempted it even. If Pershing had not seriously attacked the Germans; had fought a battle or two; had been defeated and had then sat back, lamenting; with what face could he have come to the American people and said, "Because of my failure in the duty you authorized, equipped, and sent me to do, I have decided that I want still other duties, enormously varied, expensive, not military at all, for which I am not authorized or equipped; but I find the Germans do *not* want to be defeated; and I find the war-orphans *do* want to be relieved! Also, I find fighting too dull, too difficult, and, to be frank, not popular enough—let me handle relief! True, I have totally failed in the one job you gave me, but I now promise to do the same job, and another one with it, to your eminent satisfaction."

The parable is not perfect—no parable can be in every detail. I want to set forth the moral and not the technical situation, and have doubtless exaggerated the situation a little; but there are some useful analogies to be drawn.

Pershing *could* fight the Germans—and as we all know, he beat them; but he did not do it by directing his energies, his men, and his money to reconstruction work! The voluntary agencies, on the other hand, could not fight Germans—they were not authorized, equipped, or sent for that—but they could and did the thousand things that Pershing could not, and their relief and reconstruction work has become a monument for all time.

Dr. McCombs very broadly and quite properly defines Public Health to include everything relating to the health of the public. My own definition makes Public Health apply "to all mankind, in every physical relation." But his *non sequitor* (as I conceive it)—is—that because Public Health includes all health activities, therefore, the *Health Officers' duties* include all health activities too. As well quite properly define morals to include every form of public moral welfare, and then say—the *Police Department* must therefore handle everything relating to morals, education, etc., schools, universities, asylums, jails, and all social uplift agencies, private or public. The Police Department was not created to promote moral welfare, but to prevent crime—a very different thing indeed. The promotion of morals is a great duty, but it is not their duty. The policeman's duty may be an unpopular, difficult duty, but is that the reason he should abandon it, and go teaching Sunday school, or become a university professor of ethics?

Public health, defined to include everything relating to physical welfare, must include, therefore, the hygiene and sanitation of all human beings, sick or well; that is, it includes hygiene, the practical application of physiology to the physical operation of every human body at every age and stage; sanitation, the adjustment of the surroundings of all humans to their bodies' needs; and therapeutics, which is the hygiene and sanitation of the sick.

Now, if I understand Dr. McCombs aright, he assumes that the control and direction of this enormous field is the duty of the health officer, who therefore must not only control infection (an intricate specialty) but also maternal welfare (an intricate specialty), infant welfare, pre-school supervision, medical school inspection, hospitals, tuberculosis sanatoria in all their detailed details, eye-clinics, venereal clinics, playgrounds, water supplies, milk supplies, foods, drugs, drug addiction (all intricate specialties) and how much more? Where will the health officer of today, or the superhealth officer of tomorrow, find the brains, the time, the energy, to say nothing of the funds or the authorization, thus to control the therapeutics and the day-by-day lives of all the race?

Surely such minute supervision embodies a splendid ideal—but an ideal not agreed in by the Christian Scientists, the various medical cults and fads, and all the others who believe they know therapeutics as well as the health officer does, and how to live hygienic lives much better! Do our health officers, as a matter of fact, know therapeutics and hygiene so perfectly that they may set up compulsory standards for them? Dr. McCombs well says that as a class they have not intelligently or efficiently exercised the knowledge or the powers they now have relating to disease!

Is it not well known that we have no Federal Department of Health, partly, at least because of the belief that that department when formed would not confine itself to control of infection (I think almost everyone would endorse that program) but would extend its field to control of treatment and to compulsory hygiene? The cry of its opponents, successful so far, has been that the propagandum for a Federal Department of Health was nothing but a camouflage, in guise of public health, to impose therapeutics on the country! Untrue? Yes, but repeated by Hon. Joseph G. Cannon no less, in last September Harper's—a view not to be pooh-poohed as the opinion of the densely ignorant, since such a leader makes it, and Harper's gives it circulation everywhere.

Dr. McCombs' article supports a view interpretable as our enemies would wish it interpreted, i. e., that public health is not for control of disease, but for control of therapeutics and hygiene.

I cannot forbear protesting against the attitude that the control of the infectious diseases is a mere bagatelle, not worthy the time of a health officer—a disagreeable police duty without field for exercise of professional training or skill or shrewdness. This attitude is not uncommon. It is the outgrowth of the sad fact that, as it is too often now conducted, control of infection is not only an administrative but also a professional and technical farce, not over 1% efficient, if so much. If health officers really devoted their attention to infection—not conducting the campaign by a mere routine placarding of reported cases, which routine placarding they expect to continue, and their successors after them, forever and ever—but as a very lively war with an enemy requiring to be sought out and conquered, no health officer would be able to complain of lack of employment or of dullness in his duty. We have only begun to study and to handle the venereal diseases—and tuberculosis we have not really even begun to study, from the epidemiological standpoint. Yet the control of the infectious diseases is regarded as a small side issue, something anyone can do—already largely done—hardly worth while! Even the fundamental error that the control of infection rests upon reporting by physicians is repeated over and over—yet no health department can pretend to be 50% efficient even in locating cases, while it relies upon such reports; nor until it reverses this situation and is finding the cases itself and is reporting them to the physicians—until it knows more of the ramifications of infection in its community than all the physicians of the community know, all put together.

This attitude of mind recalls the inversion, as quoted in the Boston Health Department Bulletin of April, 1920, of the Great Revolutionary slogan, "Millions for defense, not one penny for tribute." The devotion of health department activities to hygiene, therepeutics, correction of preventable defects, coupled' with their neglect of prevention inverts the slogan to read—

"Millions for tribute to disease—
Not a penny to fight it."

SUMMARY

1. "My" plan does not propose that the Health Officer divide his present responsibilities, but only that he assume no more—at least until the present duties concerning infection are really done, not merely talked about.

2. This leaves to the voluntary associations the largely experimental, wholly voluntary, and quite uncontrollable public health activities which the law has not and probably will not assign to the health officers except here and there; activities for which health officers are by no means equipped and which merely distract them from their proper duties. I mean those voluntary activities involving therapeutics and personal hygiene.

3. Health Officers should accomplish their notoriously neglected first duty, the control of infection, and then and not until then, come into court with clean hands, if they wish to ask the popular sympathy and support, which contrary to Dr. McCombs' theory of the public feeling, the public do grant to really competent and efficient policing; which really competent and efficient policing, however, they rarely get from health officers as a class today.

4. Health officers as a class should not engage themselves in educating the public—few health officers know what to teach, still fewer how! The universities and the schools are the proper places for education, and the voluntary agencies do it as well as any one does it at present, particularly since the schools, the universities, and most health departments have fallen down on the job.

5. Finally, I am not arguing that the Government should not conduct therepeutics and hygiene to the very limit—if the public will let them—but I do argue that the health officer is not the Government; and that he is not authorized to do these things now, is not able to do them now, and that it would be very unwise for him to attempt them now. I am speaking of health officers as a class—as they exist all over the United States—not of a few super-health officers, acting under peculiar circumstances in certain small areas to whom special legislation has granted uncommon powers.

To secure the A. P. H. A. Special Train to the Coast, 125 reservations are necessary. These must be ordered this month. Do not have the train cancelled for just a few belated reservations. Get your place in it and

GET IT NOW!

EDITORIAL SECTION

AMERICAN JOURNAL OF PUBLIC HEALTH

Publication Office: 124 W. Polk Street, Chicago, Ill.
EDITORIAL OFFICE: 169 MASSACHUSETTS AVE., BOSTON, MASS.

A. W. HEDRICH, C. P. H., Editor   J. RITCHIE, Jr., Associate Editor

Editorial Assistants

E. R. HAYHURST, M.D.   P. M. HOLMES, M.D.   FRANCIS H. SLACK, M.D.
DAVID GREENBERG   JAMES A. TOBEY   JAMES M. STRANG
M. P. HORWOOD, M.S.   HOMER N. CALVER

Board of Advisory Editors

PETER H. BRYCE, M.D., Ottawa, Canada   PROF. M. J. ROSENAU, Boston, Mass.
CHARLES V. CHAPIN, M.D., Providence, R. I.   PROF. W. T. SEDGWICK, Cambridge, Mass.
EUGENE R. KELLEY, M.D., Boston, Mass.   PROF. GEORGE C. WHIPPLE, Cambridge, Mass.
W. A. EVANS, M.D., Chicago, Ill.   PROF. S. M. GUNN, Paris, France.

All expressions of opinion and all statements of supposed facts are published on authority of the writer under whose name they appear, and are not to be regarded as expressing the views of the American Public Health Association, unless such statements or opinions have been adopted by vote of the Association.

NOTICE TO SUBSCRIBERS: Subscription Price, payable in advance, $4.00 per year for United States and possessions; $4.50 for Canada and other foreign countries. Single copies, 50 cents postpaid. Membership in the American Public Health Association, including subscription to Journal, $5.00 per year. In Change of Address please give both old and new address, and mail before the tenth of the month to take effect with the current issue. Mailing Date, 5th of each month. Advertisements accepted only when commendable, and worth while both to reader and advertiser. News Items, interesting clippings and illustrations are gladly received, together with name of sender. Copyright, 1919, by A. W. Hedrich.

WHAT IS A HEALTH CENTER?

"What is a health center?" is a question that many have asked and not a few have answered. The answers, unfortunately, vary. Two things are apparent: that there is no meeting of minds on the part of those who have assumed to answer this question; and second, a multiplicity of definitions has served to confuse the inquirers, and perhaps retard the growth of this valuable and fairly new phase of public health work. It may not be possible at this time to devise standards for the work of health centers or for those in the field of public health to agree on just what these institutions are or should be. Certainly, health centers must be as diverse in kind and scope as are local health departments. There does exist a fairly uniform conception of what the health departments are or at least what they should endeavor to become. It seems not unreasonable, therefore, to hope for a similar uniformity in the conception of health centers.

Dr. McLaughlin, in his "Standardization of Municipal Health Organizations" recently stated, "The term 'health center' has been loosely used as a name for everything from a milk station to a miniature health department." This is literally true. The term health center has been applied to child welfare stations, tuberculosis dispensaries, infant welfare stations, the offices of public health nurses, groups of dispensaries, venereal disease clinics, the out-patient departments of hospitals, settlement houses, sub-stations of local health departments, recreation centers, gymnasiums, at least one commercial bowling alley, and with the exception of the last, it has been given to manifold varying combinations of two or more of these. Seventy-five different activities have, in fact, been listed that are at present conducted in health centers, and this figure probably does not account for all existing activities nor exhaust the possibilities.

In the face of this condition it is not surprising that the definitions that have been offered are numerous as well as diverse.

1. Health Centers are the manifestation and result of coöperation within the municipalities. (Editorial, *Am. Jour. Public Health*.)

676

2. A Health Center is a place where people may come to learn how to keep well. (Editorial, Massachusetts Bulletin, *The Commonhealth.*)

3. The Health Center is an institution which coördinates in a centrally-located building all the public health and relief agencies of the community. (Alameda Co. Health Center.)

4. The Health Center is a means by which the community is in actual touch with the health nurse and social workers. (Krusen.)

5. The Health Center idea means doing things for everybody and doing things together within a given district. (Davis.)

6. It is a small combination of the health, hospital, and dispensary departments, affiliated with the charity organization society, tuberculosis association, district nursing associaton, and other eleemosynary organzations the aggregation operating as a conjoined whole. (Fronczak.)

7. A Health Center is the physical headquarters for the public health work of a community. (Red Cross.)

8. By combining the administrative health functions with other essential auxiliary duties and health-promoting efforts, the health center could be made the radiating source of all local health activities, both public and private. (Hoffman.)

9. A Health Center is a building to which the general public may go to learn how to preserve health and from which are operated the various matured plans for protecting the public health. (Wood.)

10. A real Health Center should be a complete health department. (McLaughlin.)

Some of these statements have doubtless been made as descriptive of particular health centers and are not proposed as generic definitions. There are, however, three general ideas evident in practically all the literature on this subject. These are, first, a health center is a physical headquarters at which, or from which, is conducted some form of activity that attempts to prevent disease or promote health; second, there is an effort to coördinate activities and, if possible, to bring about a coöperation of agencies; and third, there is an emphasis on the attack of public health problems from the standpoint of a district or a community, rather than from the standpoint of a particular affliction. There is a concurrence of opinion among most health workers on these three points as elements of the health center idea. More than this probably cannot be agreed upon in the present conception of a health center. The use of the term health center as a camouflage for a venereal disease clinic or the use of the advertising value of this term to bring trade to a milk station, a bowling alley, or any other institution of such limited scope, either public, philanthropic or commercial, does not enter into the present discussion. H. N. C.

SUCCESS AND FAILURE IN MENTAL HEALTH

President William H. Burnham of the Massachusetts Society for Mental Hygiene, in a recent address emphasizes the importance to mental health of a great deal of success and of occasional failure. He points out that one of the greatest defects in present-day education is that some of the children are doomed to persistent and repeated effort. Ambition is thereby dulled and mental development retarded, if indeed serious mental defects are not invited.

In his "Measure of Mentality," Dr. Arthur Sweeney brought to attention in a public address the fact that all men have not the same degree of mentality, nor as high a standard as is generally supposed. Based on an army test of three million American soldiers, he says, "It is somewhat of a shock to realize that the average of human intelligence in this country is that of a child of about twelve years of age." Applying these results to the population of the country means that more than forty million of our population have a mental age of not greater than our highest grammar school requirements. There is little wonder then that among children within the schools the same mental age is not reached by all. The result of this is that many of the children are not able to carry on the standard grade of school work. It follows that such children soon enter a rut of continuous failure from which there is little chance to emerge. Five or six years of continuous failure of this type is certain to leave a permanent effect.

Another condition which leads to such failure of school children is the endeavor to bring about symmetrical development regardless of the natural aptitudes of the child. To illustrate this, President Burnham quotes Professor Dolbear's interesting myth of the antediluvian animal school. The purpose of this school was to produce graduates that could swim, climb, fly, and run equally well. The duck was penalized for not walking and climbing gracefully. The eagle could make no headway in climbing to the top of a tree although he could get there by flying, so the monarch of the air was degraded. An abnormal eel with large pectorial fins was found who could run, swim, climb trees, and fly a little, so he was made valedictorian.

This little fable does illustrate a condition in schools, which one of our leading college presidents once jocosely suggested is to be met only by a separate school for each individual student. This principle is not absolutely absurd, excepting, of course, in an extreme application, and there are tendencies in the modern methods to care for certain classes of students, notably those termed deficient, by giving them special attention so that they will not hold back the normal pupils in the school. There have been so many of the great scholars and scientific men who were failures in their early school days that it is a question whether the difficulty does not lie in the effort to make the child fit the curriculum, rather than to provide a course of studies that will develop the child. In these times standardization is a desideratum, and standardization in pedagogy has doubtless brought with it many advantages, but the educational profession is recognizing and will continue to recognize the necessity for the system of teaching an unusual child in an unusual way. The subnormal child will thus be relieved of the discouragemet of continual failure.

A little failure, no doubt, as President Burnham points out, is of distinct value. Invariable success tends to an overbearing nature, the more so if it is met during the earlier and formative period of life.

Note.—President Burnham's paper is entitled, "Success and Failure as Conditions of Mental Health," published in *Mental Hygiene*, Vol. III, No. 3, and Dr. Sweeney's paper is entitled, "The Measure of Mentality," published in *Minnesota Medicine*, November, 1919.

□

In Memoriam

WILLIAM CRAWFORD GORGAS

Major General William C. Gorgas, formerly Surgeon General of the United States Army, died in London, England, on July 4. His last appearance at a public function was at the Brussels Health Conference in the latter part of May, where he was decorated by King Albert. Returning to London on May 29, he immediately suffered a stroke of apoplexy, with the result of his death.

General Gorgas had accomplishments second to no other man in this country in public health work. Improvement of health conditions in Panama and Cuba are two of his major achievements. He it was who fought and defeated the malarial mosquito that had made the task of cutting the Panama Canal an insuperable one to the Frenchmen. His work in combating yellow fever in Cuba rid the northern hemisphere of that century-old focus of infection. Previous to his coming, the death rate had been 200 to 1,200 annually, but now the island is virtually free from the disease.

General Gorgas made himself felt in many insanitary quarters of the globe.

Under the direction of the United States Government and the International Health Board, he supervised campaigns against yellow fever in Central America, Peru and Ecuador. On the invitation of the British Government, he went to South Africa in 1913 to establish sanitary conditions in the Rand. For this work he received high honors from the medical profession in London, and Oxford University conferred a degree on him.

He was decorated by the French Government and made a Commander of the Legion of Honor. He was knighted by King George of England.

He reached the age limit while still on duty in France in 1918 and was retired from active service in the army at the conclusion of the war. In 1919 he was appointed head of the Yellow Fever Commission of the International Health Board.

General Gorgas became a member of the American Public Association in 1901, and, although not serving as an officer, was ever active in its councils and a frequent contributor to the pages of the JOURNAL. Together with General George M. Sternberg, Dr. Henry D. Holton, Dr. Stephen Smith and Dr. Frederick Montizambert he was elected to honorary membership in the Association at the Rochester meeting, September, 1915.

BOOKS AND REPORTS REVIEWED

Food Inspection and Analysis. Albert E. Leach. Revised by Andrew L. Winton. New York: John Wiley & Sons Co. Fourth Edition, 1920. Pp. 1090+XIX and 41 plates. Price, $8.50 net.

The scope and plan of this standard work is so well known to food chemists and all who have had occasion to make analyses of food materials as to need no comment. In the present edition, which represents somewhat of an increase in size over the previous one, the general outline and method of treatment is still retained. The principal changes consist in some omissions of obsolete methods and the elimination of the alphabetical bibliographies at the ends of the chapters, and in the addition of considerable material in special lines, in order to bring the work more nearly in accord with present practice.

Of these additions, the most noteworthy and commendable are probably the sections devoted to meat extracts; the table of the constants of edible oils, which is much improved; the chapter on wine, especially the portion devoted to the detection of watering; and the detection of adulteration in vinegar; which has been brought up to date. The chapter on the detection and separation of animal and vegetable colors has been practically rewritten and greatly improved, full advantage being taken of Mathewson's work on colors. Some new methods are noted in the examination of flavoring extracts.

A deletion that is perhaps just as well is the procedure for the detection of spoilage in ketchups by miscroscopical examination, which has been severely and justly criticized. On the other hand, more might well have been added in regard to egg substitutes and nut butters, food products which are quite in vogue at present. These might well have been accorded some of the space still retained for numerous processes for the detection of preservatives in milk, a form of adulteration of probably greater historical than practical interest in these times.

The discussion of the detection of watering and of skimming of milk, especially the latter, is still entirely inadequate, as it was in the previous edition. It certainly seems strange that nothing is said in a standard book, published at this day, about the significance of protein-fat or fat-sugar ratios in the examination of milk, except for the few words tucked away in the discussion of the milk serum. The formulæ for the calculation of sugars in jams and jellies are still retained, even the meaningless one for total invert sugar, although they are of little practical value, and are not "perfectly accurate" in any case.

Several slight errors of commission and omission, noted in going through the work, are perhaps worth mentioning, although they would not lead astray anyone familiar with food analysis. The Massachusetts milk standard (p. 147) is no longer a variable one, and the statements made are quite in error as to its meaning. The normal weight for the Laurent instrument is given as 16.19 on page 135 and as 16.29 on page 606. The footnote on page 789, referring to Anderson's work, should be to Journal of Industrial and Engineering Chemistry, not to Technology Quarterly. On page 827, the reference to Mulliken should be to Vol. III, not Vol. VI.

To those who were familiar with Leach and his work with the Massachusetts State Board of Health, it is very pleasant to see characteristic portions of his book retained in sufficient proportion to give it still the early charm it had, and at the same time well-chosen additions made that bring it right "up to the minute," and make it a safe guide in almost any path of food examination.

A. G. WOODMAN.

✛

Instruction Camp of 1919. Department of Health, Pennsylvania, Bulletin 104, Harrisburg, February, 1920. 345 pages.

During the summer of 1919, the Pennsylvania Department of Health established the novelty of a camp of instruction of public health, which its employees were asked to attend. The camp was arranged to continue for one month and the courses given there were divided into two consecutive periods of approximately two weeks each, half of the physicians and nurses attending at one time. This did not interfere with the continuity of regular work of these officers.

The report is valuable because, in addition to the story of the camp itself, there are presented, entire or in abstract, the lectures given to the students. Under the circumstances, these were, of course, condensed stories touching closely on the very many phases of the health officer's work, not forgetting that of the nurses. The main subjects included administrative policies, engineering, contagious diseases and hospitals, a special section devoted to tuberculosis, laboratory procedures, a symposium on milk and food values, sanitary education, hygiene and sanitation in the

public schools, child welfare, mental hygiene, home economics, and the social diseases. More than 75 papers are assembled in this report, and although these were addressed especially to the personnel of the Pennsylvania Department they bear equally good lessons and quite as valuable instruction to others engaged in this very necessary work of public health. The discussion of housing was accompanied by the distribution of literature. The functions of the tuberculosis dispensaries were made the subject of a discussion, as were a number of papers in this particular section. Laboratory work was not forgotten, and especial information was given with reference to the method of preparing and sending forward the specimens. Municipal milk control and pasteurization were dominant topics in a discussion of milk, with Professor E. V. McCollum, of Johns Hopkins University, to speak a few words on the subject of its nutritive value. Taken altogether, the volume will be important for the information of those engaged in practical health work.

✛

LATEST TUBERCULOSIS BOOKLET IN FRENCH

The Rockefeller American Commission for Preservation against Tuberculosis in France, in its campaign in coöperation with the French Government, has issued a delightful booklet, "Principes d'Hygiene," which is in the form of a primer, although addressed to adults. Its profusely and strikingly illustrated bits of advice, however, appeal to children and grown-ups alike.

The first section is devoted to the "Care of Children," with advice to mothers on care of themselves, the baby's food, air, and exercise; with warnings to avoid divers vices, which are pictured, such as raising dust while baby sleeps, spitting, and using unclean milk. Correct breathing, proper care of the teeth and eyes, too, have their illustrations.

Then follows a treatment of the subject of tuberculosis itself, picturing its woeful effects, giving bits of advice as to its care, and a list of aphorisms for its prevention, for example, "Cough into your handkerchief," "Avoid crowds," "Use an individual cup," "Wash hands often," "Open your windows," and "Keep clean."

There are four charming full-page illustrations: one with ruddy-cheeked children, picturing the benefit of open air classes; another telling of the disappearance of illness and the advent of health, which comes with the visiting nurse of the hygiene bureau; and the two illustrations accompanying this article—the healthfulness of playgrounds, and the coming of health "like good luck, during sleep—with open windows."

From the mediaeval herald on the front cover announcing to the people the good news of good health to the last page with its symbol of tuberculosis warfare shedding its illuminating rays, the little book is a succession of attention-compelling features, with text that shows the rare skill of the paragrapher and illustrations in that artistic spirit inseparable from the French.

es terrains de jeux c'est la santé des enfants.

Pictures of the curse of alcoholism, of the ravages of disease-bearing flies, of the necessity of placing wells in ground which will not receive drainage from stables and outhouses give their warning or their good advice. A section on the "Health of Workmen" advocates, not only for the benefit of the workman himself, but also of the employer, society, and the country, sanitary, safe, well-ventilated and lighted factories and workshops, with provision for recreation and care in accident or illness. Here there is profit for the workman, the employer, society in general, and the State.

The community is told its duty—to organize a Health Service, which will preserve it from disease by inspecting the milk, by isolating persons with contagious diseases, and by analyzing milk and water in bacteriological laboratories.

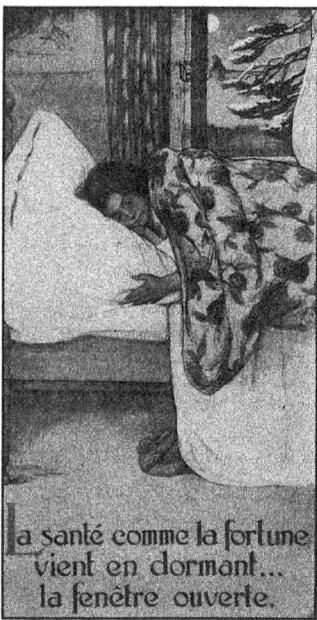

La santé comme la fortune vient en dormant... la fenêtre ouverte.

ASSOCIATION NEWS

HEALTH EMPLOYMENT BUREAU

Help-wanted announcements will be carried free in this column until further notice. Copy goes to the printer on the fifteenth of each month. In answering keyed advertisements, please mail replies separately.

The Health Employment Bureau also sends lists of applicants to prospective employers without charge.

Chemist (male) wanted for Panama Canal; Must be graduate in Chemistry or Sanitary Engineering, and have had satisfactory experience in water purification work. Must be an American citizen under 50 years and in good health. Entrance salary $181 month increased to $200 month after three months' satisfactory service. Free steamship transportation to Isthmus. For further particulars write "Chief of Office, The Panama Canal, Washington, D. C."

Some good health officers with pep—no fossils or corpses need apply. Salary $3,000. Georgia State Board of Health.

Health officers wanted for county organizations in New Mexico. Initial salary $2700 to $3000 per annum.. Experienced men preferred. New and interesting field. Climate and living conditions excellent. Address State Commissioner of Health, Santa Fe, New Mexico.

Full time health officer is desired for Oakland County, Mich. Salary, $3,600, with allowance of $700 for auto maintenance. Address 361, care of this JOURNAL.

Supervising nurse, Protestant faith, qualified to handle staff of five nurses—organization comparatively new, must be capable of handling some phases of pioneer work. Salary $150 per month. Address J. G., 377, care of this JOURNAL.

Competitive examination to fill two vacancies in district health office force. Will be held by the Mass. State Dept. of Public Health at the State House, Boston, September 20th and 21st, 1920. All persons interested and possessing necessary qualications are requested to communicate with Dr. E. R. Kelley, Commissioner of Public Health. Initial salary, $3,000.

□

SAN FRANCISCO MEETING

Members who wish to avail themselves of the special A. P. H. A. train from Chicago to San Francisco or the special cars from New York and Boston connecting with this train are requested to write immediately to the nearest of the A. P. H. A. Travel Chairmen. These are:

Chicago—Dr. W. A. Evans, 906 Tribune Building.

New York City—Mr. F. C. Foy, care of General Passenger Agent, N. Y. Central R. R., Grand Central Terminal.

Boston—Secretary, A. P. H. A., 169 Massachusetts Ave.

Reservations should be ordered at once in order that the minimum guarantee requirements may be obtained. Should the minimum number of reservations not be secured before the end of August, it may be necessary to cancel the special train.

Programs of the meetings will be sent out with the JOURNAL appearing August 20, the date having been moved forward in order to secure their early distribution. All final notices will appear in the same JOURNAL.

MEMBERSHIP CAMPAIGN

The Membership Campaign up to the time of going to press has resulted in the addition of 1,700 names to the membership lists and it is reasonable to believe that the total accessions will touch 2,000 new members before the time of the Annual Meeting. The total of memberships and subscriptions now stands at 6,000.

Since the report in the July JOURNAL, page 612, California has increased her percentage of quota filled from 145 to 164, while Maryland and D. C. has gone over the top, jumping from 82 to 104. The actual number of new members is 1,687, or 56 per cent.

LIST OF NEW MEMBERS

Proposed for Election to the

A. P. H. A.

June 23 to July 20, 1920, inclusive.

Names of Sponsors are set in **Bold Face Type.**
Names of New Members are in Light Face Type.

ALABAMA
Capt. H. Y. Carson, Birmingham.
W. H. Bell, M. D., Birmingham.
J. D. Dowling, M. D., Birmingham.
H. A. Irvin, Chief Sanitary Inspector, Fairfield.
C. H. Kibby, M. D., Chief of Bureau of Sanitation, T. C. I. & R. R. Co., Fairfield.
W. F. Rainey, Sanitary Inspector, Ensley.

ARKANSAS
M. Z. Bair, Little Rock.
Mollie King, M. D., Director Hygienic Laboratory, Little Rock.
William Ropes, Sanitary Engineer, Little Rock.
C. W. Garrison, M. D., Little Rock.
H. A. Ross, M. D., Arkadelphia.

ARIZONA
T. C. Cuvellier, Phoenix.
Jane H. Rider, Director, State Laboratory, Tucson.
A. W. Hedrich, Boston, Mass.
T. C. Cuvellier, Exec. Sec. Arizona Anti-Tuberculosis Association, Phoenix.

CALIFORNIA
Charles W. Anderson, M. D., Calexico.
Walter L. Ellis, M. D., City Health Officer, Calexico.
C. P. Bagg, M. D., Los Angeles.
Frank N. Chessman, M. D., Los Angeles.
Kirby Smith, Oakland.
Jersey Milk, Cream & Butter Co., attention M. R. Pinheiro, Oakland.
S. P. S. Edwards, M. D., Ontario.
Frank P. Abbott, M. D., President Anti-Tuberculosis Association, Ontario.
Calvert L. Emmons, M. D., Member of Ontario Board of Health, Ontario.
I. R. Bancroft, M. D., Sacramento.
C. W. Anderson, M. D., Calexico.
California Tuberculosis Association, Fresno.
Charles C. Browning, M. D., Los Angeles.
Mrs. Esther A. Jobes, Director Oregon Tuberculosis Association, Portland, Oregon.
Reba A. Ingols, R. N., Sacramento.
Miss Matilda Jacobsen, Deputy Health Officer, Corona.
Guy P. Jones, Sacramento.
J. Loughridge, M. D., Health Officer, Folsom.
A. J. Messier, Assistant to Secretary California State Board of Health, Sacramento.
A. J. Messier, Sacramento.
George H. Roth, M. D., Assistant Health Commisioner, Los Angeles.
William C. Hassler, M. D., San Francisco.
Arthur H. Barendt, San Francisco.
Guy E. Manning, M. D., Member of Board of Health, San Francisco.
George B. Somers, M. D., Member Board of Health, San Francisco.
Ruth O. Pierson, San Francisco.
Florence Adele Harrelson, R. N., San Francisco.
W. C. Bailey, M. D., San José.
Finley M. Eastman, Pathologist Santa Clara County Hospital, San José.
B. F. Knause, M. D., Santa Monica.
Mary G. Hills, R. N., Supt. Dist. Nurses' Association, New Haven, Conn.

COLORADO
Burton Lowther, Denver.
Frank B. Young, Sanitary Inspector, Denver.
C. G. Hickey, M. D., Denver.
Agnes B. Courtney, R. N., Public Health Nurse, Antonito.
J. N. Hall, M. D., Denver.
William Whitridge Williams, M. D., A. A. Surgeon, U. S. P. H. S., Denver.
Chester S. Morey, Denver.
George K. Olmsted, M. D., State Board of Health, Denver.
Cuthbert Powell, M. D., Denver.

Nell F. Notestine, R. N., Public Health Nurse, Ft. Collins.
Genevieve M. Pallea, R. N., Meeker.
C. W. Thompson, M. D., Medical Supt. Woodcroft Hospital, Pueblo.
George H. Curfman, M. D., Salida.
C. Rex Fuller, M. D., Salida.

CONNECTICUT
J. T. Black, M. D., Hartford.
James J. Costanzo, M. D., City Health Officer, Stamford.
W. S. Cutney, M. D., Milford.
Milford Visiting Nurses Assn., Milford.
Frank W. Wright, New Haven.
Julius Goodwin Henry, M. D., Epidemiologist, New Haven.
Miss Anna I. van Saun, City Bacteriologist, New Haven.
A. W. Hedrich, Boston, Mass.
Colonel Frederick Fuller Russell, Medical Corps, U. S. A., Norwalk, Conn.

FLORIDA
B. L. Arms, M. D.
H. H. Hyman, Manager Miami Water Co., Miami.
Ralph N. Greene, M. D., Jacksonville.
George W. Ward, De Funiak Springs.
C. M. Tyre, M. D., City Health Officer, High Springs.
H. F. Watt, M. D., City Health Officer, Ocala.
Perry G. Wall, Tampa.
S. C. Colly, M. D., City Health Officer, Tavares.
A. H. King, M. D., City Health Officer, West Palm Beach.

GEORGIA
T. F. Sellers, Atlanta.
E. Carroll James, State Board of Health, College Park.
J. D. Applewhite, Valdosta.
E. D. King, Jr., D. V. M., Meat & Milk Inspector, Valdosta.

IDAHO
E. R. Dooley, Twin Falls.
Prof. William M. Gibbs, Dept. Bacteriology, U. of I., Moscow.

ILLINOIS
Isaac Abrahams, M. D., Chicago.
Simon P. James, M. D., Chicago.
W. A. Evans, M. D., Chicago.
Arvill Wayne Bitting, Chicago.
J. F. Norton, Ph. D., University of Chicago.
T. T. Crooks, Instructor, Ricketts Lab., University of Chicago.
William J. Garard, M. D., Galesburg.
B. L. Ditto, Health Officer, Burlington.
Prof. S. G. Winter, Bacteriologist, West State Laboratory, Galesburg.
A. L. Mann, M. D., Elgin, and
C. St. Clair Drake, M. D., Springfield.
Percival E. True, Elgin.
C. St. Clair Drake, M. D., Springfield.
H. P. A. Carstens, M. D., Forest Park.
W. P. Davidson, M. D., Sullivan.
W. M. Freeman, M. D., Health Commissioner, Woodstock.
John Richardson Thompson, M. D., Bridgeport.
Lethe E. Morrison, Urbana.
Miss Miriam Dougherty, Monmouth.

INDIANA
J. C. Royse, M. D., Indianapolis.
Paul R. Tindall, M. D., Secretary Board of Health, Greensburg.

IOWA
Prof. Earle L. Waterman, Iowa City.
Matie Simonsen, R. N., Public Health Nurse, Waterloo.
W. D. Hayes, Sioux City.
J. E. Swanson, M. D., County Physician, Sioux City.
Anna Forbes, R. N. School Nurse, Sioux City.

683

KANSAS

Earl G. Brown, M. D., Topeka.
Alberta Bailey, R. N., Supervisor T. P. A. N. Association, Topeka.

LOUISIANA

R. M'G. Carruth, M. D., New Roads.
M. O. Beenel, M. D., Health Officer, New Roads.

MARYLAND AND DISTRICT OF COLUMBIA

James W. Armstrong, Baltimore.
Edward S. Hopkins, Sanitary Chemist, Orangeville.
Rosa E. Prigosen, Baltimore.
Arnold L. Swancara, Bacteriologist, U. S. P. H. S. Hospital, St. Louis.
R. H. Riley, M. D., Baltimore.
Maryland Social Hygiene Society; attention of Alan Johnston, Jr., Baltimore.
J. J. Murphy, M. D., County Health Officer, Annapolis.
F. O. Reinhard, M. D., Baltimore.
R. C. Salter, State Bacteriologist, Baltimore.
A. L. Sullivan, Food & Drug Commission, Baltimore.
E. E. Wolff, M. D., City Health Officer, Cambridge.
H. F. McPherson, M. D., County Health Officer, Centreville.
Prof. Edward F. Webb, Supt. Public Instruction, Cumberland.
W. N. Palmer, M. D., County Health Officer, Easton.
H. P. Fahrney, M. D., County Health Officer, Frederick.
W. N. Kirkman, State Board of Health, Halethorpe.
Merritt Brice, M. D., County Health Officer, Millington.
H. Arthur Cantwell, M. D., County Health Officer, North East.
H. M. Slade, M. D., County Health Officer, Reisterstown.
William T. Pratt, County Health Officer, Rockville.
Lewis K. Woodward, M. D., Secretary Board of Health, Carroll County, Westminster.
William Royal Stokes, M. D., Baltimore.
Stanhope Bayne-Jones, M. D., Associate Professor Bacteriology & Pathology, Johns Hopkins Medical School, Baltimore.
E. G. Kastenhuber, Jr., Easton.
A. E. Goodrich, Resident Engineer, State Department of Health, Easton.
J. S. Bowen, M. D., Mt. Washington.
C. L. Mattfeldt, M. D., Health Officer, Catonsville.
Lewis O. Tayntor, M. D., Salisbury.
C. C. Ward, M. D., Health Officer, Crisfield.
James A. Tobey, Washington.
Edward R. Hunter, M. D., American Red Cross, Washington.
Carroll Fox, M. D., Washington.
Blanche E. Myers, Washington.
B. J. Lloyd, M. D., Washington.
James E. Miller, M. D., U. S. P. H. S., Marine Hospital Division, Washington.

MASSACHUSETTS

Mary Beard, R. N., Boston.
M. Grace O'Bryan, R. N., Associate Director, Instructive Dist. Nursing Association, Boston.
B. W. Carey, M. D., Boston.
Annie Lee Hamilton, M. D., Boston.
Russell B. Sprague, M. D., Foxboro.
Mary H. Goerlach, Supt., Frederic S. Coolidge Memorial, Pittsfield.
Joseph E. Lamb, M. D., Member Board of Health, Revere.
Laurence S. Howard, Clerk of Board of Health, Somerville.
A. W. Hedrich, Boston.
Mary Beard, R. N., Director Instructive District Nursing Association, Boston.
Prof. C. M. Hilliard, Boston.
Miss Tryphosa R. Worcester, Manchester, N. H.
Prof. J. O. Jordan, Boston.
Prof. Theodore James Bradley, Dean Mass. College of Pharmacy, Boston.
R. U. Spencer, Boston.
Adelbert L. Safford, Supt. of Schools, Reading.
Prof. C. E. Turner, Boston.
R. J. Campbell, Old Town, Maine.
B. E. Roberts, M. D., Springfield.
Chicopee Board of Health, attention Charles J. O'Brien, Agent, Chicopee.

MICHIGAN

Fred. O. Adams, Detroit.
Miss Elsa T. Schueren, Detroit.

Mrs. L. E. Gretter, Detroit.
Henry G. Stevens, Detroit.
M. W. Robinson, R. N., Ypsilanti.
Marvle W. Rayburn, Public Health Nurse, Ann Arbor.
Charles Pillsbury, M. D., Health Officer, Ypsilanti.

MINNESOTA

Wm. F. Reasner, M. D., Minneapolis.
W. F. Kunze, Member Board of Public Welfare, Minneapolis.
Linda James, St. Paul.
Clay County Public Health Association, attention of Mrs. Albert Thysell, Sec., Hawley.
C. E. Smith, Jr., M. D., St. Paul.
C. L. Scofield, M. D., Vice-President State Board of Health, Benson.
Riverside Sanatorium, attention Sara W. Dunton, Superintendent, Granite Falls.
Prof. S. Marx White, Prof. of Medicine, University of Minnesota, Minneapolis.
G. G. Hampton, M. D., Tupelo.
A. D. Tisdale, M. D., County Director of State Board of Health, Ripley.

MISSISSIPPI

MISSOURI

George H. Jones, M. D., Jefferson City.
T. A. Son, M. D., Member State Board of Health, Bonne Terre.
T. H. Wilcoxen, M. D., Bowling Green.
Edith B. Lowry, M. D., U. P. H. S., Jefferson City.
M. B. Harutun, M. D., Commissioner of Health, Joplin.
Emmett P. North, M. D., St. Louis.
Wilson J. Ferguson, M. D., Sedalia.

MONTANA

W. F. Cogswell, M. D., and
John J. Sippy, M. D., Helena.
Margaret Irish, R. N., Billings.
J. X. Newman, Missoula.
Florence W. Dixon, Missoula.

NEW JERSEY

Louis Schneider M. D., Newark.
William B. Watson, Member Board of Health, Belleville.
Josephine S. Pratt, Newark.
Evelyn G. Chase, Supervisor, P. H. Nursing Service, Nashville.
A. Clark Hunt, M. D., Trenton.
Edward Guion, M. D., Bureau of Health, Atlantic City.
Charles Englander, M. D., Pathologist, Cedar Grove.
A. W. Hedrich, Boston, Mass.
Rutgers College Library, New Brunswick.

NEW MEXICO

D. B. Williams, M. D.
Mrs. J. P. Stone, Portales.

NEW YORK

G. C. Supplee, Adams.
Louis J. Auerbacher, New York.
Edmund C. Boddy, M. D., Albany.
Harriott P. Churchill, R. N., Exec. Sec. Oneida County Tuberculosis Commission, Utica.
Frank W. Laidlaw, M. D., Albany.
George F. Wilklow, M. D., Health Officer, Ellenville.
Edward C. Rushmore, M. D., Health Officer, Tuxedo Park.
James S. Walton, M. D., Amsterdam.
B. F. Bishop, M. D., Garrattsville.
H. S. Baketel, M. D., Brooklyn.
A. E. Sherndal, Ph. D., Brooklyn.
Edward Clark, M. D., Buffalo.
W. G. Sprague, M. D., Health Officer, Barker.
Herman F. Senftner, M. D., Epidemiologist, State Health Dept., Buffalo.
Arthur O. Hahl, M. D., Clarence.
Edwin Shoemaker, M. D., Health Officer, Newfane.
Chancellor H. Whiting, M. D., Health Officer, Medina.
Anne L. Hansen, R. N., Superintendent District Nursing Association, Buffalo.
Rachel M. Palmer, Geneva.
Elizabeth M. Hennessy, R. N., Industrial Nurse, Geneva.
Halsey J. Ball, M. D., Glens Falls.
C. J. Crippen, M. D., Health Officer, Constable.
Katherine Lee, County Tuberculosis Nurse, Cortland County.
J. B. Washburn, M. D., Health Officer, Delmar.
Morris Maslon, M. D., Glens Falls.
Marjorie M. Bucknam, R. N., Public Health Nurse, Glens Falls.

John A. Conway, M. D., Hornell.
George H. Fox, M. D., Binghamton.
Clayton M. Axtell, M. D., Health Officer, Deposit.
F. C. Annabel, M. D., Health Officer, Elmira.
Charles N. Hammond, M. D., Health Officer, Elmira.
Eugene Bauer, M. D., Oswego.
W. W. Bachman, M. D., Prattsburg.
J. F. Trant, M. D., Prattsburg.
B. R. Wakeman, M. D., Hornell.
James P. MacDowell, M. D., Dundee.
H. M. Humphrey, Health Officer, Penfield.
Addison T. Halstead, M. D., Pushville.
F. J. Colgan, M. D., Health Officer, Rochester.
Ida B. Sammis, Huntington.
Mrs. Frederick D. Bidwell, Chairman Child Hygiene, Albany.
B. Eleanor Easton, Kingston.
E. E. Norwood, M. D., Kingston.
Mary C. Hurlbut, M. D., Lockport.
Lemuel R. Hurlburt, M. D., Lockport.
LeRoy W. Hubbard, M. D., Mt. Vernon.
John H. Tallman, M. D., Health Officer, Mt. Vernon.
Edwin G. Ramsdell, M. D., Health Officer, White Plains.
Herman M. Briggs, M. D., New York City.
Frances M. Hollingshead, M. D., Director Buffalo Foundation, Buffalo.
C. E. Ford, M. D., New York City.
S. B. Buckley, M. D., General Chemical Co., Denver, Colo.
Charles E. Cord, M. D., General Chemical Co., Chicago Heights, Ill.
William F. McNary, M. D., E. St. Louis, Ill.
S. Pirosh, M. D., General Chemical Co., Baltimore, Md.
John G. Kraus, M. D., General Chemical Co., Elmhurst.
A. Quackenbush, M. D., General Chemical Co., Northpines, Ontario.
W. W. McChesney, M. D., General Chemical Co., Monarat, Va.
H. Sheridan Baketel, M. D., New York.
Gustave P. Metz, Ph. D., Vice-President, H. A. Metz Laboratories, Inc., Brooklyn.
Miss Harriett Staples, New York.
Mrs. Walter P. Bliss, New York City.
C. R. Hervey, M. D., Oswego.
Robert Simpson, Jr., M. D., Fulton.
John R. Murlin, Ph. D., Rochester.
Harold H. Baker, M. D., Rochester.
Fitch, Prince & Palmer, attention Ralph P. Fitch, M. D., Rochester.

NORTH CAROLINA

G. E. Reynolds, R. N., Charlotte.
Bunyan McLeod, D. D., Charlotte.
W. S. Rankin, M. D., Raleigh.
Foy Roberson, M. D., Durham.
N. C. Landowners Association, attention Mr. W. A. McGirt, Vice-President, Wilmington. (Sustaining membership.)

OHIO

G. W. Moorehouse, M. D., Cleveland.
H. J. Luff, Sanitary Engineer, Cleveland.
H. O. Way, Cleveland.

Miss Harriet Boewig, Asst. Bacteriologist, Board of Health, Cleveland.
H. T. Phillips, M. D., Cleveland.
William C. Groeniger, Columbus.
A. E. Smith, State Dept. of Health, Columbus.

PENNSYLVANIA

W. S. Stevenson, F. E. Daniels and J. Warner Fortenbaugh, Harrisburg.
George T. Hammond, Brooklyn.
D. E. Hottenstein, M, D., Millersburg.
Louvilla Snyder, Community Nurse, Millersburg.
W. L. Stevenson, Philadelphia.
Ivan M. Glace, District Engineer, Department of Health, Harrisburg.
A. W. Hedrich, Boston, Mass.
Roland F. Wear, M. D., Berwick.

SOUTH CAROLINA

C. E. Smith, M, D., Columbia.
Jean B. LaBorde, M. D., Health Officer, Columbia.
R. A. Murphy, Chief Sanitary Inspector, Columbia.

SOUTH DAKOTA

F. W. Freyburg, M, D., Aberdeen.
C. J. Lavery, M. D., Aberdeen.
P. B. Jenkins, M. D., Waubay.
F. E. Files, Geddes.
Mary G. Fraser, State Supervisor of Nurses, Waubay.
H. J. Herman, M. D., County Supt. Board of Health, Webster.

TEXAS

V. M. Ehlers, Austin.
Ines A. Newman, R. N., State Advisory Nurse, Austin.
Henry E. Elrod, Sanitary Engineer, Dallas.
George Parker, Sanitary Engineer, Washington, D. C.
R. M. Grimm, M, D., San Antonio.
J. R. Hawkins, M. D., A. A. Surgeon, U. S. P. H. S., Freeport.
R. A. Wilson, M. D., A. A. Surgeon, U. S. P. H. S., Terlingua.

UTAH

T. B. Beatty, M, D., Salt Lake City.
Hon. Frank T. Burmester, Mayor, Grantsville.
L. S. Merrill, M. D., Ogden.
The Industrial Commission of Utah, Salt Lake City.
M. J. Seidner, M. D., Health Officer, Storrs.
Wellsville Board of Health, attention W. O. Christenson, M. D., Wellsville.

CANADA

A. W. Hedrich, Boston, Mass.
Department of Health, attention of Dr. George G. Melvin, Fredericton, N. B.

HAWAII

A. W. Hedrich, Boston, Mass.
Major James S. Simmons, M. C., Officer in Charge, Dept. Laboratory, Honolulu, H. T.

PUBLIC HEALTH NOTES

Abstracts by D. GREENBERG, M. P. HORWOOD, JAMES A. TOBEY and HOMER N. CALVER.

Problem of the Skinny Child.—This was the subject of an address by Dr. Caroline Hedger before the `American Home Economic Association in June. She maintained that a large part of the skinny children in the country are from families other than the poor and the foreign born.

That parents do not have a vital sense of the seriousness of this condition in their children ,was brought out by the fact that they, in most cases, defend their child with such excuses as, "But Johnny is growing" or

"Johnny looks like his father's family" without the slightest realization that Johnny is a physical and financial menace to society.

The rapid growth of a child is only one of the three childhood demands for proper nourishment, the speaker · maintained. The second is a reserve force for future development and the third is a ceaseless activity which is necessary if a child is to keep well and develop control over muscle, nerve and brain.

Proper feeding is the remedy for this condition in children, according to Dr. Hedger who was for four years director of the Infant Welfare Commission of the Board of Health of Chicago. During the war she was for six months in conquered regions of Belgium where she made a survey of the feeding of children, and is now medical director of the Elizabeth McCormack Memorial Fund in a large child welfare agency in Chicago.

"We have always supposed that given a good home the child will eat. This is not so. I know of absolute cases of semi-starvation which have had nothing to do with poverty. We are up against new demands which we have never faced before. We are face to face with the demand for better and stronger children.

"Does your child possess that something which makes him feel like jumping up and down on the sidewalk when he starts out for school in the morning?" questioned the speaker. "This is life. This is health. This is the unconscious and harmonious working of the body, the reserve vigor which is life's essential. Health makes your child resistant to disease. It is the skinny child who gets tuberculosis."

✦

Antiscorbutic Orange-Juice Powder.—According to a paper on "The Antiscorbutic Properties of Concentrated Fruit Juices," by Harden and Robison published in the April number of the *Biochemical Journal*, the drying of fruit-juice has been successfully carried still further. The technical procedure has followed the lines of milk-powder production by the spray process, which avoids a temperature likely to reduce, if not to kill, the potency of the antiscorbutic agent. From the results obtained it is reported that a highly active dried orange-juice can readily be prepared on a commercial scale which will keep after prolonged storage under suitable conditions. The orange-juice, mixed with corn syrup, was forced as a fine spray into a chamber where it met a current of air heated to 75°-80° C. The drying was almost instantaneous, and the product when tested on guinea-pigs was found to afford complete protection from scurvy. As the authors point out, the peculiar value of such a substance lies in its adaptability for infant feeding and for the use of expeditions of long duration, where fresh fruit and vege-

tables are unobtainable and when transport must be reduced to a minimum. It would appear that orange-juice is decidedly superior to vegetable juices in regard to keeping its activity when exposed to relatively high temperatures. In spite of this observation the investigation of the effects of storage on dried orange-juice at tropical temperatures remains to be determined.—Editorial, *Lancet*, May 29, 1920. (D. G.)

✦

On the Control of Measles.—In a special report, the medical officer of health for the borough of Whitehaven gives his observation on the value of home nursing for cases of measles occurring in young children.

In discussing the subject of home nursing Dr. McIntosh lays stress on two points, the benefit of individual sufferers, and prevention of the spread of disease. The nursing of measles he considers is a definite part of welfare work, because the heaviest incidence of the disease is amongst young children, *i. e.* those under five years of age, and also that measles if not properly treated at the onset, paves the way for serious and often fatal complications. As to prevention of spread, he attaches considerable importance to the nurses' visits in detecting missed or concealed cases as well as their impressing on the parents the dangers of the disease.—*Medical Officer*, June 5, 1920, 221, (D. G.)

✦

Carries Health to Little Czechs.—More than 10,000 Czecho-Slovak children will be taught to play and started on the road to health this summer by an American teacher, Miss Emily Pipal, of Des Moines, Iowa, who has sailed for Prague where she will assist in setting up children's health camps of the Junior Red Cross of America. Miss Pipal is of Czech extraction and speaks the Czech tongue. Junior Red Cross playgrounds and summer camps have been established throughout the new country of which Prague is the capital, and thousands of under-nourished and sick children will be sent to them for holidays of a month or longer. Plenty of exercise, some simple instruction and nourishing food will be the means of restoring these youngsters to health.—(J. A. T.)

STATE HEALTH NOTES— LEGISLATION

National.—The Sixty-sixth Congress adjourned on June 5, 1920. The only bill of any importance to public health passed since the last article on national legislation appeared in the JOURNAL was H. R. 13,229, which created a Women's Bureau in the Department of Labor. The Vocational Rehabilitation Bill (H. R. 4438) was also passed and signed by the President on June 2. The Shepard-Towner Bill to give Federal aid to states for maternal and infant welfare work was reported favorably by the Senate Committee on Public Health on June 2 with an amendment to Section 8 which provided that work shall "be carried on in such manner as may be mutually agreed upon by the Federal Board and any state receiving the benefit of the act." No action on this bill was taken before adjournment. The France bill to create a Federal Department of Health did not get out of committee. The Cold Storage bill (H. R. 9521) also failed of passage. A bill (H. R. 385) to prevent the shipment in interstate commerce of food liable to botulism was introduced on June 3 and referred to the Committee on Interstate Commerce, where it remained until adjournment.—(*J. A. T.*)

✦

Public Health in the Platforms of the Two Leading Parties.—*Republican.*—A number of matters of interest to health workers are contained in the Republican platform, which was adopted in Chicago during the Convention in June. The party is pledged to the solution of social problems. A thorough system of physical education for all children up to the age of 19, including adequate health supervision and instruction as a remedy for conditions revealed by the draft, is advocated to add to the economic and industrial strength of the nation.

A plank also refers to the public health facilities of the government. The language is as follows: "The Public Health activities of the Federal Government are scattered through numerous departments and bureaus, resulting in inefficiency, duplication and extravagance. We advocate a greater centralization of the Federal functions, and in addition urge the better coördination of the work of the Federal State and local health agencies."

The platform condemns child labor and demands Federal legislation to limit the hours of employment of women engaged in intensive industry, the product of which enters into interstate commerce. It commends to Congress the permanent establishment of the Women's Bureau in the U. S. Department of Labor to serve as a source of information to the states and to Congress. The information on housing and town planning collected by the Government during the war is urged to be made available.

Democratic.—The Democratic platform, adopted on July 2, also contains several matters on public health. It urges coöperation with the States for the protection of child life through infancy and maternity care; in the prohibition of child labor and by adequate appropriation for the children's bureau and the women's bureau in the Department of Labor. A continuation of appropriations for education in sex hygiene is also urged.—(*J. A. T.*)

✦

Massachusetts.—The Legislature of 1920 passed an important law authorizing cities and towns to establish and maintain dental, medical and health clinics and to conduct health campaigns in connection therewith. Two or more towns are authorized to unite in obtaining such service.

✦

New. Mexico.—Regulations governing the sanitation of public school buildings have recently been passed by the State Board of Health. The State Health Department is also coöperating with the Department of Education by having all county and city school superintendents include the salary and expenses of at least one school nurse in the budgets for the next year.

✦

Legislation in Favor of Physical Education.—During the past year and the first four months of 1920 progress in legislation favoring physical education has taken a remarkable step forward. Three Southern states have been added to the list having such laws and the total number of states with such provisions is 19.

Between 1914 and 1918 the following States passed laws: New York, New Jersey, Rhode Island, Illinois, North Dakota, Maryland, Delaware, Nevada, Alabama and California. In 1919 Washington, Oregon, Utah, Maine, Michigan and Indiana "went over the top."

Alabama.—The Alabama State Board of Health devoted the end of June to a conference of all physicians and clinicians interested in venereal disease control. Speakers were secured for the morning, which was given over to lectures, while in the afternoon there was a clinic at which there were more than 100 patients. The conference was in charge of W. C. Blasingame, S.A., U. S. P. H. S., Director of the Bureau of Venereal Disease Control.

✦

Connecticut.—The spring meeting of the Connecticut Public Health Association was held in New Haven, June 2. Dr. Thomas F. Joyce, physician in charge, spoke of the Treatment of Drug Addicts at the New York Department of Health; Professor Lafayette B. Mendell, of Yale University, on Practical Hints on Diet, and Dr. Walter H. Brown on the Health Center in Community Life. A demonstration was given of the technique of the Schick test for diphtheria diagnosis.

On June 10 the New Haven County Public Health Association held a meeting in New Haven. E. M. Bailey, Ph.D., spoke on Food in Health and Disease, Miss Marion Sherwood on Typhoid and Carriers, and Stanley H. Osborn, M.D., on Practical Work in Detection of Typhoid Bacillus Carriers.

The Child Hygiene Institute met in the State Capitol, June 3-4, Dr. John T. Black, State Health Commissioner, presiding. In the four sessions a dozen papers were presented, visits were made to the Bany Health Station, the children's pavilion at the Hartford State Tuberculosis Sanitorium, and the Isolation Hospital. For the education of the public, films, "An Equal Chance," and "Our Children," were shown at a local theatre in the evening.

✦

Kansas.—The Diagnostic Laboratory of the State Board of Health and the Public Health Laboratory, formerly at Rosedale, have been combined in a Public Health Laboratory in Topeka, the Director of which is Dr. Kenneth F. Maxcy, from Johns Hopkins University. Mr. C. A. Haskins, for ten years Sanitary Engineer for the Board, has resigned, to be succeeded by Albert H. Jewell. Lieut. Jewell was Camp Sanitary Engineer, Selfridge Field, Mt. Clemens, Michigan, from November, 1917, to August, 1918. From August,

1918, to March, 1919, he was Water Supply Officer of the 26th Engineers in France.

✦

Kentucky.—Dr. F. A. Stine of Newport, Ky., has been appointed to the State Board of Health in place of the late Dr. I. A. Shirley, of Winchester. Dr. Oscar Dilly, of Louisville, Ky., Dean of the College of Pharmacy of the University of Louisville, has been appointed member of the State Board of Health under the recent law adding a pharmacist to the Board. Dr. Dilly was formerly Superintendent of the City Hospital in Louisville.

Under the model law of 1918, full-time health departments have been created in the under-named counties, each of which has an annual appropriation of at least $10,000. The following Health Officers have been appointed:
Daviess County, J. H. Hamilton, M.D., Owensboro; Boyd County, Robert D. Higgins, M.D., Ashland; Scott County, C. N. Caldwell, M.D., Georgetown; Harlan County, Ralph J. Malott, M.D., Harlan; and Muhlenburg County, Ben Wilson Smock, Greenville.

For Mason County no officer has yet been named.

✦

Louisiana.—Dr. George J. Dempsey of New Orleans, has been appointed State Registrar of Vital Statistics, in place of Dr. John H. Ellis, deceased.

✦

Florida.—At Perry in Taylor county the State Board of Health, in coöperation with the local Board, the U. S. P. H. Service, and aided by industrial corporations, has undertaken an important anti-malarial project, the cost of which is to be about $30,000. The importance of this may be judged by the fact that it represents a per capita cost of $16 or $17, while the usual cost of such work has not been above a maximum of $2. The plans call for about five miles of large channels for drainage, 20 feet wide at the top, and 7 feet wide at the bottom, with a general depth of 5 feet.

✦

Maine.—A remarkable decrease in the number of deaths from measles in Maine, during the past year, has been brought to light in the compiling of vital-statistics for 1919 by the Maine Department of Health. There were but four such deaths during the past twelve months, as compared with 102 measles deaths in 1918. The death record for the past year is further remarkable in that a decided decrease is noted in every disease except cancer and whooping cough. In the case of whooping cough, a jump from 34 deaths in 1918 to 104 in 1919 is shown, while with cancer, the number of deaths has increased by over fifty.

✦

Massachusetts.—With reference to lethargic encephalitis, Dr. Eugene R. Kelley makes note to the JOURNAL that, early in 1919, the advisability of making the disease reportable was considered by the Massachusetts State Health Department. The Committee on Preventive Medicine of the Department decided that it was not desirable at the present time, on account of the small number of cases, the transitory duration of the disease, difficult diagnosis, and the moral effect on the public of making it reportable. In May, 1920, the Department requested the opinion of the Massachusetts Association of Boards of Health; and as a result the recommendation is given forth to all doctors to report all suspected cases of the kind to local boards, so that investigation may be started. The Department still does not deem it necessary to add this disease to the list of reportable ones.

Dr. Mary Putnam, of Cambridge, Mass., has been appointed Clinic Physician in the Division of Hygiene of the Massachusetts Department of Public Health. Dr. Putnam will conduct clinics for children, especially in the rural parts of the State. No treatment will be given; cases needing medical care will be referred to the family physician. The emphasis will be laid upon the prophylactic examination of the well child, offering an opportunity to discuss with the parent the health needs of the child. This clinic will be conducted in as simple a manner as possible, in order to encourage the local communities to carry on the work themselves.

Dr. Milton J. Rosenau has resigned as Director of the Division of Biologic Laboratories, State Department of Health, and has been succeeded by Dr. G. Benjamin White, formerly Assistant Director. Dr. James E. Henry has been appointed epidemeologist to the Department.

✦

Michigan.—Mr. Albert E. Kunze, a recent graduate in Sanitary Engineering at the University of Michigan, has been appointed an Assistant Engineer in the Michigan Depart-

ment of Health. G. C. Stucky, of Louisville, Ky., formerly assistant at the Trudeau Foundation Laboratory and since then connected with the University of Michigan Medical School, has been appointed Bacteriologist in the Laboratories of the Michigan State Board.

✦

Minnesota.—To encourage study of the means for the prevention and cure of tuberculosis, the Hennepin County Tuberculosis Association of Minneapolis, Minn., announces that it has set aside a fund for the support of a tuberculosis research fellowship in the Graduate School of the University of Minnesota. The candidate for the fellowship must be a graduate of a Class A medical college. He will be expected to devote himself to research in some problem concerned with the causes, prevention, or cure of tuberculosis. No teaching or other service will be required. The fellowship yields $750 the first year and progressively increasing amounts to be appropriated for the second and third years, as conditions warrant. Inquiries and requests for application blanks should be addressed to the Dean of the Graduate School, University of Minnesota, Minneapolis, Minn.

In and about Minneapolis and St. Paul there are three tuberculosis sanatoria and a children's preventorium. These, with the University's laboratories, its hospital, clinics and dispensary, and the thirty hospitals of the Twin Cities, constitute an inviting field for the medical research student who wishes to study the anti-tuberculosis problem either from its bacteriological, clinical, or social aspect.

The State Board of Health now offers its assistance anywhere in the state in diagnosis or treatment of venereal diseases. It is ready to demonstrate the preparation and administration of arsphenamine or neo-arsphenamine, the taking of blood, the examination of smears, etc.

✦

New Jersey.—At the Child Hygiene Conference, Asbury Park, New Jersey, June 12-14, 1920, Dr. Julius Levy, of Newark, presiding, a program with reference to mothers, babies, care of babies and children, and their food and treatment was given. One of the interesting items in Surgeon General Cumming's speech was that of the value of dried milk powder. He called attention to the cooperation of the Public Health Service with the Boston Baby Hygiene Association, the Department of Pediatrics of the Massachusetts General Hospital, and the School of Preventive Medicine, Harvard, and noted that an investigation had been conducted in Boston. The perfection of a process for making milk powder will not only utilize quantities of otherwise wasted milk, but will furnish wholesome milk to babies all over the world, and safeguard baby lives. Another point touched upon by Surgeon General Cumming was the examination of juvenile delinquents, in which he spoke of the custom in the District of Columbia of making physical and mental examinations of such children for the information of the Court. This examination is followed up by the necessary medical-social work for proper correctional and training methods.

The policy in operation in the State of New Jersey is the control and education of midwives. The large foreign population makes this treatment a desirable one, and the principle of the Department is to give all a chance to improve and to eliminate those unable or unwilling to be taught. There are 450 licensed midwives, of whom 30 are untrained; about half the remainder are carefully trained but do not always carry out the good technique they were taught; and the rest are poorly trained but follow the instructions from local physicians. Only four possessed ample sanitary outfits.

Mrs. Katherine T. Fitzgerald, Supervisor of "Related Family Problems," reported to the conference on three important subjects: unmarried mothers, day nurseries, and boarding homes for children. Of the 800 cases of unmarried mothers referred to the Bureau, 397 were sent to private or public organizations in their counties for supervision, and 150 mothers and their babies were returned to the homes of relatives or friends, 12 were placed in domestic service, 12 mothers were married, and 3 remained in hospitals. Day nurseries should use the services of a trained worker, and should help keep the family together, rather than disintegrate it. Not infrequently the nursery is used as a storage place for the baby at times when the mother's absence from home is not necessary. With reference to boarding homes, the interest and aim of the Department or Health is to find out the kind of children boarded, to try to do preventive work by supervision of the unmarried mother problem, and those of desertion of children, and boarding children for profit only.

In outlining the aim of the State work for babies, Miss Charlotte Ehrlicher, Supervisor of Nurses, stated that the first principle is prevention—to keep well babies well, and next to teach mothers how to care for their sick babies where there is no visiting nurse. The staff of this Division includes 60 nurses and 73 doctors, whose services are voluntary. There are 75 baby "Keep-Well stations." Four automobiles are provided, and the State gives supervision to two municipal groups, saving the cost of this supervision to local authorities.

✦

New Mexico.—The State Health Department is giving a course to cover a period of four weeks in the subjects of child hygiene and community nursing at the State Summer Normal School. Mr. Harold F. Gray, of the Department, is in charge.

It is planned to establish three and perhaps five full-time county health organizations in the state during the coming year. Under the provisions of a special act passed by the Legislature in February last, counties and cities may levy a half-mill tax for health work. The Department seeks men to fill the positions of full-time county health officer.

✦

New York.—Lethargic encephalitis has been added to the list of reportable communicable diseases in New York State, by action of the Public Health Council of the State Department of Health.

Fifty-seven graduates of the 1919 and 1920 Post-Graduate Course in Infectious Diseases and Public Health, which has been conducted under the joint auspices of the Albany Medical College and the State Department of Health, Dr. C. C. Duryee, Director, met at the former institution on June 24 for the purpose of organizing the "Eastern New York Post-Graduate Public Health Association." The following officers were elected: Honorary President, Dr, Charles C. Duryee, State Department of Health; President, Dr. M. D. Dickinson, Troy; Vice-President, Dr. W. C. Treder, Scotia; Secretary and Treasurer, Dr. W. G. Keens, Albany; Executive Committee: Dr. J. H. Collins, Schenectady; Dr. G. S. Eveleth, Little Falls; and Dr. Wm. Van Doren, Mechanicville.

It was decided to have two meetings annually, one of which is to be held in conjunction with the State Annual Conference of Health Officers. Dr. Hermann M. Biggs, State Commissioner of Health, and Dr. Thomas Ordway, Dean of the Albany Medical College, were elected honorary members of the Association.

The Jewish Agricultural and Industrial Aid Society is planning to install a permanent exhibit on its property at Ellenville, N. Y., to demonstrate to the farmers and summer boarding house proprietors' in the vicinity how wells, springs, cesspools, sewage disposal plants and privies should be constructed and maintained in rural districts. The exhibit will consist of full size models built in accordance with the best modern practice and arranged so as to be readily accessible for inspection. The plans for the models were submitted to the Engineering Division and several changes were made in them to conform to the suggestions of that Division.

Acting on information from the State Department of Health, the district attorney of Jefferson County recently caused the arraignment of a young lady living in West Carthage for breaking quarantine while carrying virulent diphtheria organisms. Evidence was presented showing that subsequent to occurrence of a diphtheria case in her home and the obtaining of a positive culture from her throat she went to Schenectady, where she was later discovered and taken to the Isolation Hospital. On her release she was taken to Carthage, arraigned and held for action by the Grand Jury.

Dr. Hermann M. Biggs, State Commissioner of Health, has been given the honorary degree of Doctor of Science by Harvard University, in recognition of his work in combating tuberculosis.

✛

New York City.—Twenty-one thousand employees in 27 factories in the Bush Terminal section of Brooklyn will be given an opportunity of learning the primary problems of public health this summer through an arrangement just made by the Health Service Department of New York County Chapter American Red Cross.

A series of five health lectures for five weeks, in each of a number of factories, making a total of 148 such health talks, has been arranged by the Speaker's Bureau of the Health Service Department of the Chapter.

The speakers who are giving their services in this public health campaign are specialists. The list comprises Dr. Eric S. Green, field representative for the First Aid Department of the Brooklyn Chapter; Capt. Walter W. R. May, of the U. S. Public Health Service; C. G. Brook, City Physical Director for Industry, of the Brooklyn Y. M. C. A.; Prof., Charles E. Barr, of the Atlantic Division, American Red Cross; and Dr. Helen W. Brown, of the American Social Hygiene Association.

✛

North Carolina.—Reports from the 100 counties to the State Board of Health for the month of June show the smallest number of typhoid fever cases since accurate statistics have been kept in the state. For the month a total of 152 cases were reported as against 432 cases reported during June of last year, a reduction of 280 cases this year.

The Board has been concentrating in its efforts against typhoid fever through anti-typhoid vaccination and the installation of sanitary privies. These efforts are bearing fruit as shown in the decrease in the number of cases and in the steadily decreasing number of deaths from this cause. In 1919 there were 427, a reduction of more than fifty per cent in five years.

To enforce strict compliance with the State sanitary privy law the engineering division of the State board of health is placing additional inspectors in the field for the purpose of checking up communities which have previously been inspected by the regular field men of the health department. Where previous instructions for the construction and maintenance of sanitary privies have not been followed prosecutions under the law are being made.

Among recent prosecutions were three of the largest property holders in the town of Henderson. Each defendant entered plea of guilty and judgment was suspended for 30 days pending their compliance with the law. At Norwood six property owners were convicted for failure to provide sanitary privies.

"Your name has not been found among the 773 physicians who reported 8,274 cases of venereal disease to this office during the year ending March 31, 1920, though a careful search of our records has been made."

This is the way in which Dr. Millard Knowlton, Medical officer in charge of the Bureau of V. D. calls the attention of North Carolina physicians to the fact that they are not reporting in accordance with the requirements of the law. This and letters addressed to the physicians has resulted in a marked increase in reporting.

Other letters addressed to the doctors have resulted in an average attendance of 50 per cent at the meetings throughout the state in a campaign of special instruction to physicians.

✛

Ohio.—A course in Industrial Medicine is to be given at Ohio State University under the supervision of the Department of Public Health and Sanitation of which Dr. E. R. Hayhurst is in charge. The course, which is open to physicians who are recent graduates of Class-A schools, will begin with the college year in September. It will offer a certificate of Graduate in Industrial Medicine. Remunerative internships are a part of the plan.

Arrangements have been completed at Ohio State University for the teaching of Public Health Nursing in both the one term and a one year course, the latter leading to a certificate. A five year course in Science-Nursing lead to a B. S., as well as the graduate nurse degree. The nursing courses are under Assistant Professor, Mrs. Norma Selbert, in the Department of Public Health and Sanitation and are to be given in conjunction with the local and State Health Departments and nursing associations.

✛

Virginia.—The State Registrar of Vital Statistics is to take drastic action against those physicians who fail persistently to comply with the law requiring the reporting within ten days of the birth. In Augusta County more than 60 percent of the births are not thus properly registered. Legal action is to follow the future neglect to comply with the law.

Mecklenburg County with the financial coöperation of the local branch of the Red Cross has guaranteed a fund of $5,000 to be strengthened by an equal sum from the State Board of Health and the International Health Board for the establishment of a county health unit. A preliminary year's demonstration has been given by the U. S. Public Health service. The intention is to secure a medical health officer, undertake public health nurse work, look after school inspection, improve water supplies and undertake intensive health measures.

At a Farmer's Union picnic in Brunswick in June, funds were raised for the employment of county health nurse and plans were set on foot for a child welfare conference in the near future.

In Pittsylvania County out of 5,978 school children inspected, 1,353 were found to have defective sight, 546 have incipient deafness, 2,214 have enlarged tonsils, 1,091 are suffering from adenoids, and 4,609 have decayed teeth. The summing up of all the defects averaged about two to a pupil.

Virginia had 1,838 more births and 886 fewer deaths the first quarter of 1920 than in the corresponding period of 1919.

The aggregate number of births reported is 15,148 for the quarter ending March 31, 1920, while for the like period in 1919 the number was 13,310.

Deaths for the 1920 period stated reached an aggregate of 9,853 while for the first quarter of 1919 the total was 10,639.

✛

West Virginia.—In coöperation with the State Board of Health, an Oral Hygiene Unit of the Public Health Service is making a state-wide survey of dental hygiene problems in West Virginia, with special reference to school children. The unit is visiting every county seat in the state and making inspections of the mouths of a number of children attending school, demonstrating to the community the extent of the dental needs of the school population, and assisting the local communities in perfecting measures whereby dental services can be provided where such do not now exist. At the same time teachers are being instructed in the principles of dental prophylaxis. Eventually it is hoped to have the proper authorities establish mobile dental clinics to visit the schools throughout the state. The American Red Cross is interested in this work and has furnished sufficient funds for the dental unit to give necessitous children tooth brushes and tooth paste.

✛

Nova Scotia.—Dr. D. A. Craig, for five years medical superintendent of the Queen Alexandria Hospital, London, Ontario, and during the war consultant in diseases of the chest for Military District No. 1, of the Canadian Army, has been appointed tuberculosis examiner by the Massachusetts-Halifax Health Commission. He will give his entire time to tuberculosis work and to educational phases of public health contemplated by the Commission. He will supervise the three tuberculosis clinics being organized in the health centers and serve as a free tuberculosis consultant to physicians in Halifax and Dartmouth.

Dr. B. Franklin Royer, Executive Officer, has also announced the appointment of Dr. Gordon Wiswell as the physician to be immediately in charge of the prenatal, baby, preschool age and malnutrition services in Health Centre No. 1; and of Dr. Hugh W. Schwartz as the physician immediately in charge of the nose and throat services. Dr. M. J. Carney, who organized the first tuberculosis clinic in Halifax, will continue in charge of at least one of the Health Center tuberculosis clinics.

The Commission recently announced the names of a consulting staff,which will coöperate with Dr. Royer, in determining the policies in health centre work. Their names are as follows:

Col. John Stewart, Dean of Dalhousie Medical School.

Dr. Frank Woodbury, Dean of Dalhousie Dental School.

Dr. Arthur Birt.

Dr. George M. Campbell.

Dr. S. J. MacLennan.

Dr. R. Evatt Mathers.

□

CONVENTIONS, CONFERENCES, MEETINGS

August 10, Portland, Ore., American Society of Civil Engineers.

August 20-21, Denver, Col., National First Aid and Rescue Contest, U. S. Bureau of · Mines.

September 2-4, Duluth, Minn., Mississippi Valley Conference on Tuberculosis.

September 6-7, Omaha, Neb., Missouri Valley Medical Society.

September 7-8, Ogden, Utah, Utah State Medical Association.

September 7-9, Saratoga Springs, N. Y., Health Officers Association of N. Y.

September 7-10, Holyoke, Mass., New England Waterworks Association.

September 8-10, La Crosse, Wis., Wisconsin State Medical Society.

September 9, San Francisco, Cal., California Tuberculosis Association.

September 9, Cheyenne, Wyo., Northwestern Tuberculosis Conference.

September 10-11, San Francisco, Cal., Southwestern Tuberculosis Conference.

September 13-17, San Francisco, Cal., American Public Health Association.

September 14-15, Springfield, Ill., Illinois Health Officials and State Department of Public Health.

September 15, Minneaplis, Minn., American Roentgen Ray Society.

September 16-17, Springfield, Ill., Illinois Health and Welfare Association.

September 20-24, San Francisco, Cal,. International Association of Industrial Accident Boards and Commissioners.

September 22, Louisville, Ky., Kentucky Tuberculosis Association.

September 22, South Bend, Ind., Indiana State Medical Association.

September 24—October 3, Cleveland, Ohio, National Safety Council.

October 4-10, Montreal, Can., American Association of Occupational Therapy.

October 4-10, Montreal, Can., American Hospital Association.

October 7-8, Augusta, Me., Maine Public Health Association.

October 9, Ottawa, Can., Canadian Association for Prevention of Tuberculosis.

October 11-13, St. Louis, Mo., American Child Hygiene Association.

October 13-15, Chicago, Ill., Association of Railway Surgeons.

October 15-16, Roswell, N. M., New Mexico State Medical Society.

October 22-26, New York City, American Dietetic Association.

INDUSTRIAL HYGIENE AND
OCCUPATIONAL DISEASE

Abstracted by Drs. E. R. Hayhurst and E. B. Starr.

Opportunities for the Employment of Handicapped Men.—An excellent series of bulletins has been prepared by the Harvard Bureau of Vocational Guidance and published by the Red Cross Institute for Crippled and Disabled Men. Each bulletin has been prepared by a person conversant with the industry. Those at hand include opportunities for handicapped men in the following industries: shoe, optical goods, coppersmithing, brush and rubber. As an example, that for the rubber industry describes the various processes in different branches of the industry and states for each one what type of disabled men may be employed. An appendix at the end lists the various common disablements, both surgical and medical, such as those of the arms, legs, hands, sight, hearing, nervous disorders, heart diseases, pulmonary diseases, etc. Bulletins vary from 35 to 120 pages, which, mostly, are illustrated and have a wealth of practical information for placing handicapped workers.—*Division of Education,* Harvard University, Cambridge 31, Mass.

✦

Occupation in Relation to Tuberculosis.— From the predisposing causes of tuberculosis we know that while the tubercle bacilli are widely scattered yet there is a large proportion of persons exposed to infection who do not develop the disease. Hence a suitable soil is a factor, and such soil is usually found in persons of feeble physique, enfeebled through any one of a great variety of causes. Vulnerability may be acquired by indoor life and dust occupations, especially with exposure to dampness, temperature extremes, and industrial poisons. Statistical data upon the relation of various forms of dust to the death rates, carefully selected from original monographs in the literature, constitute a chief part of this paper. One table shows quite clearly that tuberculosis is infrequent in occupations involving outdoor life combined with muscular activity as well as in liberal professions, presumably because of higher standards of living. The influence of weak stock, disease of digestive organs, alcoholism, venereal disease, industrial poisoning and

dust exposure are shown. "Fortunately the effects of legislation and factory sanitation, together with the gospel of personal hygiene and higher standards of living conditions, which have been emphasized in the educational campaign against the great white plague, are strikingly shown by a most marked decrease in the mortality from tuberculosis in eight of the so-called dangerous trades in the State of New Jersey. * * * * It is less than 15 years since attention has been paid to industrial hygiene in this country; but in view of what has been accomplished during that brief period, I venture to predict that no country will make greater progress in social and industrial betterment than our own beloved United States. In the meantime no opportunity should be lost in the general campaign to emphasize the importance of personal hygiene and general sanitation." —Geo. M. Kober, *Public Health Reports,* March 26, 1920.

✦

Educational Work in United States Public Health Service Hospitals for Tuberculous Ex-Soldiers.—Several of the Army hospitals which have been turned over to the U. S. Public Health Service are being made over into sanatoria for tuberculous ex-soldiers. Occupational therapy embracing mental work and manual handicraft has been instituted which will lead to vocational training under the Federal Board for Vocational Education. At the present time an educational director and teachers have been stationed at eight points in the country.—*Public Health Reports,* May 14, 1920.

✦

Mortality Statistics of Wage Earners and Their Families. — This bulletin concerns wage earners residing almost entirely in urban communities and covers a period of six years (1911-1916), during which time there were 635,000 deaths for all age groups. Up to 25 years there is no marked variance in the mortality of wage earners when compared with that of the general population. After that age the mortality of male wage earners becomes excessive. Excessive mortality for female wage earners shows itself after the age of 35. Among the causes given for these excessive death rates are arduous labor, hazardous occupations, large families with small incomes, low standards of diet, housing, clothing and medicinal services. The death rate of the colored policy holders is more than 50% in excess of that of the whites. The more important diseases are discussed in special chapters.—Dublin and Kopf, Metropolitan Life Insurance Company, New York City.

✠

Reports from Committee on Mortality from Tuberculosis in Dusty Trades.—Two preliminary reports have been prepared by this committee, which was appointed on December 31, 1917, by the National Tuberculosis Association, and is composed of Frederick L. Hoffman, Edward R. Baldwin, Alice Hamilton, H. R. M. Landis, A. J. Lanza, O. W. McMichael and Alfred Stengel. The reports reprint the correspondence of members and present various valuable abstracts from the literature. An outline for the investigation of the effect of marble and granite industries on tuberculosis is given. Mortality statistics showing an excessive death rate from tuberculosis and pneumonia for the granite cutting districts (1910-1918), and suggested plan of work for Niagara Falls and the county in which it is located are given.—U. S. Working Conditions Service, U. S. Dept. of Labor, or National Tuberculosis Association, New York City.

✠

Industrial Explosion Hazards.—This is No. 34 of "Safe Practices" dealing with gases, vapors, flammable liquids and dusts. The 12-page illustrated pamphlet is in the nature of an exposition of standards and procedures recommended. Dangers from the chief hazardous industrial explosives from such factors as ignition, heat, containers, storage tanks, gravity, displacements, conveyors, drying and cleaning processes are detailed. For dusts the following statement is made: "Comparatively few persons realize that nearly all finely divided organic or metallic substances are liable to explode when mixed with air and when ignited. As a general rule, the finer the dust and the more complete its mixture with air the greater is the danger of explosion." A list of thirty-eight dangerous

dusts, mostly organic, is given.. Building design, ventilation and cleanliness standards are stated with various diagrams.—National Safety Council, Chicago, Ill.

✠

British Provision for Tuberculous Ex-Soldiers.—A memorandum issued March 25, 1920, by the British Ministry of Health states that sanatorium treatment for tuberculosis has been found to be inadequate. Patients who return to their homes and former occupations are unable permanently to earn a living or maintain their health. Patients should pass through a threefold course: first, sanatorium treatment; second, training; and third, permanent settlement in suitable surroundings. The village settlement should be a natural development of the sanatorium and training colony where the patient may take up his permanent residence with the understanding that his earnings would have to be supplemented; but the community would gain by the prevention of the spread of infection and the fact that the patient would remain a productive worker. Measures have been taken to increase the capital grants for combating tuberculosis exactly along the lines indicated, with further time for looking into the question of village settlements.—April 30, 1920, *Public Health Reports.*

✠

Drinking Water Facilities in Industrial Plants.—An intimate relation exists between drinking water and health. Large sums of money are spent in the installation of drinking facilities in many manufactures. The basic requirements are four: (1) purity, (2) quantity, (3) palatability, and (4) distribution that will insure proper temperature at the time of consumption, convenient accessibility and preclusion of the transmission of disease from one person to another. The article discusses the physiological requirements of an adult person for various temperatures and degrees of activity, the amounts varying from two to ten quarts per day. Sanitary types of angle stream fountains are discussed and pictured; also the method of making a sanitary drinking cup out of a square piece of paper six inches in dimension. Standards for care in refrigeration are stated as well as types of systems for small plants and portable drinking fountains.—J. A. Watkins, *Safety Engineering,* February, 1920.

PUBLIC HEALTH
LABORATORY NOTES

Abstracted by Francis H. Slack, M. D., and Mr. James M. Strang.

Epidemiology of Influenza-pneumonia.— The authors conclude both from their epidemiological studies and from laboratory research that indirect spread through the hand or hand auxiliary to the mouth is by far the most important and major route of contagion dissemination. Granting that this is true, preventive measures will not consist of periodic masking of the populace, but rather an intensive application of the rules of personal hygiene, hand hygiene, and especially the sanitation of eating utensils and the protection of food. They advocate actual sterilization of eating utensils, both in the army and in civilian life, and the use of boiling-water for dishwater.—Lynch and Cumming, *Jour. Lab. & Clin. Med., March,* 1920.

✛

On the Resistance of Ascaris Eggs.— The eggs were collected from the patients' feces by mixing with water, filtering, and centrifuging, and tested against a variety of disinfectants and acids. The influence of the reagent on the eggs depends on the permeability of the egg covering. Formalin and sulphuric acid act to coagulate the albumin coating, thus preventing penetration. After long action, glacial acetic acid, hydrochloric acid, and nitric acid destroy the albuminous coating, but do not easily penetrate the inner chitinous membrane. Carbolic acid penetrates the egg membrane more easily and effectively than any of the other reagents used.

It is a most important and interesting fact that ascaris eggs are unable to develop and ultimately die in human urine which contains several ferments which act to dissolve the albuminous membrane. This action is more effective at 31° C. than at 10° C.—Sadao Yoshida, Osaka, Japan, *Jour. Parasit., March,* 1920.

✛

Influenza Studies.—A study of successive influenza outbreaks during 1918 and 1920 at the Great Lakes Naval Station, containing 5,500 to 6,000 men, and in Camp Grant, containing 4,400 men, show an incidence of the disease during the second outbreak among those who had previously suffered equal to that among those with no history of influenza, and indicate that no marked immunity to the disease exists 12 to 15 months after a previous attack. There is no evidence that immunity may not be present at an earlier period.—E. O. Jordan and W. B. Sharp, *Jour. Inf. Dis.,* May, 1920.

✛

Bacteriological Characteristics of Tubercle Bacilli from Different Kinds of Human Tuberculosis.—The author examined bacilli from cases of tuberculosis meningitis, phthisis pulmonalis, and miscellaneous cases. The bulk of the article, however, deals with a careful study of tubercle bacilli isolated, from 52 cases of scrofulodermia. Of these, 32 yielded cultures with the characteristics of the human type of tubercle bacillus and 20 cultures with the characteristics of the bovine type.—S. S. Griffith, M. D., *Jour. Path. Bact.,* Feb., 1920.

✛

Streptolysin.—After careful quantitative studies, the authors have devised a medium with the idea of using the optimum serum concentration for maximal lysin production of a blood both efficient and accessible to general use. Sheep blood is believed to fill this need. To obtain maximal lysin production rather high concentrations of serum are necessary (20 percent). The number of red blood cells is kept down by making artificial combinations of heated serum and cells.

The serum cell mixture is made by combining four parts of heated serum with one part of cells. This mixture is then combined with liquid agar in the ratio of one part of the mixture to three parts of agar. The final concentration then is: serum 20 percent, cells, 5 percent, and agar, 75 percent. The proposed medium is not only a very suitable one for demonstration of the hemolytic zones of Beta streptococcus, but is in addition very efficient in the demonstration of multiple concentric zones of green production and hemolysis for Alpha streptococcus and pneumococcus.—de Kruif and Ireland, *Jour. Inf. Dis.* April, 1920.

American Journal of Public Health

Official Monthly Publication of the American Public Health Association
Publication office: 124 W. Polk Street, Chicago, Ill.
Editorial office: 169 Massachusetts Ave., Boston, Mass.

Subscription price $4 per year.   American Public Health Association membership, including subscription, $5 per year.
Subscriptions and memberships may be sent to the A. P. H. A., 169 Massachusetts Ave., Boston, Mass.

| Vol. X | SEPTEMBER, 1920 | No. 9 |

STATE AND MUNICIPAL MEAT INSPECTION

JOHN ROBERTS,

Editorial Office, Bureau of Animal Industry,
U. S. Department of Agriculture.

Another report of importance to health officers. It tells plainly where deficiencies lie in existing systems of meat inspection. With inspection there is much condemnation of meat so that the potential risk of consuming diseased meat is vastly greater in absence of inspection. Health officers realize the dangers and will welcome proper legislation.

IT is generally known that the Federal meat-inspection service covers not more than about two-thirds of the total meat produced in the United States. The remainder of course is subject to State and local inspection, but to what degree this is carried on has been wholly a matter of conjecture.

In these times of high meat production, it may be of interest first to ascertain just what the above proportions represent in pounds of meat. Estimates of total production, consumption, etc., of meat are made annually in the Bureau of Animal Industry, U. S. Department of Agriculture, and from these it appears that the total quantity of dressed meat, excluding lard, produced in the United States during the calendar year 1918 was 18,041,166,000 pounds. This was the largest production on record, and the in-

dications point to a similarly large output in 1919. Of the total production in 1918, it was estimated that 66.55 per cent was inspected by the Government. Therefore one-third, or 6 billion pounds, was not Federally inspected. Since only U. S. inspected meats and those specifically exempted from inspection by law can be exported, it necessarily follows that practically all this nonfederally inspected meat was consumed in this country. Furthermore, it is doubtless true that a large proportion of it was slaughtered not only without adequate inspection by State or city, but without any inspection whatever. And, finally, it is generally understood that such meat would be handled in slaughterhouses that receive a much larger percentage of diseased and suspicious-looking animals than is the case in Federally-inspected establishments. It can easily be seen, therefore, how dangerous uninspected meat may be to the public health.

The Bureau of Animal Industry has from time to time made efforts to stimulate the inspection of meat by State and local authorities as a supplement to the Federal system. It has been recognized, however, that the situation in this respect and in respect to the sanitary condition of the average country slaughterhouse still leaves much to be desired.

No accurate information as to either the quantity or quality of State and municipal inspection of meat has so far been available, so in order to obtain data on the present status of the matter, Dr. John R. Mohler, chief of the bureau, authorized a questionnaire to be prepared and sent to the States and to all cities and towns shown by the census to have a population of 5,000 or more.

It may here be stated that the questionnaire concerning State meat inspection resulted in a virtual blank. In some cases no replies have been received and in no case was there reported any system of State inspection that could be regarded as thoroughly adequate. The great majority of States reported no meat inspection of any sort. A few reported ante mortem examination only, or supervision of slaughterhouses and markets only, and in some of these cases the work had been suspended because of the war. This paper, therefore, will be confined to the discussion of municipal meat inspection.

The main facts brought out by the investigation are set forth in the summary table on the next page, following which is a brief résumé of the salient features.

NUMBER OF CITIES MAINTAINING INSPECTION

It is satisfactory to note that the mere fact of sending out the questionnaires has borne fruit in the way of improvement. The replies from several cities indicated that meat inspection was either just begun or was to begin shortly. In a number of other cases advice was asked on the subject, and these requests were promptly attended to by Dr. R. P. Steddom, Chief of the Federal meat-inspection service.

The questionnaire was sent to somewhat more than 1,400 cities of which 574 responded. It is assumed that most if not all of the remainder had no inspection. Of those responding 379 reported no inspection, which left 195 cities in which meat inspection of varying degrees of efficiency was conducted.

The summary table shows that Massachusetts easily leads in number of cities maintaining inspection, the most prominent of the other States in this respect being New York, New Jersey, California, Ohio, and Texas. The reports indicate, however, that the Federal standard of inspection is more uniformly maintained in California and New York than in the other States mentioned. It should be noted, too, that California is far ahead in number of inspectors devoting their whole time to the inspection of meat.

MUNICIPAL AND CENTRAL ABATTOIRS

One of the principal objects of the questionnaire was to ascertain how many municipal and central, or public slaughterhouses there were in the country and what was the nature of the inspection conducted in connection with them. It is recognized that the public abattoir, whether municipally or privately owned, affords the most practical way in which a community can properly protect its citizens against diseased and unwholesome meats, because only at such central places can the requirements of a thoroughly efficient system of meat inspection be economically carried out.

There were reported on the questionnaires 20 municipal and 28 central abattoirs. It is doubtful, however, whether in some cases the questions were properly understood. For example, in four instances both municipal and central abattoirs were reported in the same city, and at two of these places there was no inspection whatever by the city authorities. In other cases the answers showed there was a more or less cursory inspection of meat at the markets and shops only, with no examination of the carcasses and viscera at the time of slaughter. The latter is absolutely necessary to the proper detection of disease in the meat, to say nothing of the antemortem, or inspection of the live animal before slaughter.

After sifting the reports, it would appear that the number of cities where municipal or central abattoirs are maintained should be reduced to 35, and at five of these there is no inspection at the time of slaughter, while 11 more fail to report an antemortem inspection. The abattoirs are located in the following cities:

Municipal Abattoirs	Hartford, Conn.
Bridgeport, Conn.	Atlanta, Ga.
New Britain, Conn.	Augusta, Ga.
Albany, Ga.	Columbus, Ga.
Baton Rouge, La.	La Grange, Ga.
Raleigh, N. C.	Savannah, Ga.
Winston-Salem, N. C.	Terre Haute, Ind.
Devils Lake, N. Dak.	New Orleans, La.
Grand Forks, N. Dak.	Pittsfield, Mass.
Ogdensburgh, N. Y.	Detroit, Mich.
Beaumont, Tex.	Moorhead, Minn.
Paris, Tex.	St. Cloud, Minn.
Port Arthur, Tex.	St. Paul, Minn.
Taylor, Tex.	Meridian, Miss.
Winchester, Va.	Lincoln, Nebr.
Central (public)	Nashville, Tenn.
Abattoirs	Norfolk, Va.
Anniston, Ala.	Roanoke, Va.
Birmingham, Ala.	Yakima, Wash.

Summary, by States, of reports from cities concerning muncipal meat inspection.

State	Cities Reporting	Cities Maintaining Inspection	Slaughterhouses Municipal	Central	Private	Inspectors Engaged Whole Time	Part Time	Average Salary Of	Annual Cost Of Meat Inspection
United States....	574	195	14	21	1385	226	182	$1,442	$447,095
Alabama........	7	5	..	2	7	1	5	$1.533	$ 2,500
Arizona.........	6	1	..	..	9	..	1	1,620	810
Arkansas........	5	2	..	..	15	..	2	1,500	1,800
California.......	20	9	..	..	82	44	5	1,637	81,718
Colorado........	8	4	..	..	18	8	5	1,343	16,450
Connecticut.....	12	2	2	1	11	3	..	1,420	8,000
Delaware.......	1	1	..	..	6	1	..	1,350	1,350
Dist. of Columbia	1	1	..	..	12	2	..	1,100	2,200
Florida.........	5	4	..	..	6	2	2	1,360	2,580
Georgia.........	10	6	1	5	7	8	6	1,600	16,400
Idaho...........	3	..	..	..	6	..	..	....	....
Illinois.........	37	4	..	..	34	..	6	1,350	1,850
Indiana.........	28	3	..	1	57	4	4	1,050	6,800
Iowa...........	16	4	..	..	20	4	1	1,410	4,320
Kansas.........	14	1	..	..	31	..	2	1,500	1,000
Kentucky.......	8	3	..	..	44	14	2	1,330	16,200
Louisiana.......	6	4	1	1	10	18	3	1,740	19,120
Maine..........	7	1	..	..	7	1	..	1,500	1,800
Maryland.......	3	1	..	..	51	1	3	1,200	2,000
Massachusetts...	50	44	..	1	83	5	50	1,036	22,548
Michigan.......	21	6	..	1	100	5	5	1,455	11,455
Minnesota......	11	7	..	3	12	6	2	1,293	9,360
Mississippi.....	4	1	..	1	9	..	1	1,200	1,200
Missouri........	16	3	..	..	65	5	1	1,440	7,420
Montana........	5	3	..	..	14	1	2	1,620	1,800
Nebraska.......	11	2	..	1	25	6	..	1,450	11,200
Nevada.........	1	..	..	..	3	..	..	....	....
New Hampshire..	5	1	..	..	9	..	1	....	....
New Jersey.....	20	11	..	..	38	4	17	1,574	18,947
New Mexico.....	1	..	..	..	2	..	..	....	....
New York.......	38	14	1	..	53	11	10	1,400	22,117
North Carolina..	7	4	2	..	5	2	3	1,500	4,700
North Dakota...	3	1	2	..	2	..	1	....	600
Ohio...........	41	9	..	..	142	22	16	1,355	47,920
Oklahoma......	2	..	..	..	..	..	..	....	....
Oregon.........	6	1	..	..	9	5	..	1,896	9,480
Pennsylvania....	46	4	..	..	181	8	3	1,350	15,040
Rhode Island....	7	3	..	..	10	2	1	1,350	3,840
South Carolina...	2	1	..	..	2	..	1	....	900
South Dakota...	2	..	..	..	2	..	..	....	....
Tennessee......	5	3	..	1	27	4	2	1,140	6,550
Texas..........	18	9	4	..	33	11	6	1,353	20,720
Utah...........	3	2	..	..	10	8	..	1,485	12,200
Vermont........	4	..	..	..	4	..	..	....	....
Virginia........	7	4	1	2	10	2	3	1,733	6,300
Washington.....	8	2	..	1	14	6	..	2,040	13,500
West Virginia....	2	1	..	..	6	..	1	....	....
Wisconsin.......	20	3	..	..	79	2	9	1,600	11,800
Wyoming........	2	..	..	..	3	..	..	....	....

It may be noted that the abattoirs are widely distributed geographically and that the State of Georgia leads with a total of six. Texas has four, all municipally owned, and Connecticut, Minnesota and Virginia each has three.

The total number of private slaughterhouses reported from the 574 cities is 1,385. It goes without saying that many of these are extremely insanitary and a menace to the public health. It is greatly to be hoped that the number will be reduced and replaced by municipal and central abattoirs, where proper sanitary conditions can be more easily controlled and where all other operations can be carried on more efficiently and economically, both for the butchers and the city authorities.

On this point the questionnaire returned from Grand Forks, N. S., bears eloquent testimony. As shown on the list, there is a municipal abattoir at this place, although they are unable to support a qualified inspector. A letter accompanying the report contains this paragraph:

"Our operation of the municipal abattoir has proved a wonderful stride along sanitary lines. We have thus eliminated the operation of a number of private owned slaughterhouses where conditions were simply horrible. Outside of the lack of meat inspection, our slaughtering conditions are very satisfactory."

The Bureau of Animal Industry is prepared to give every assistance in its power to any city contemplating an improvement in its meat-inspection service, and to this end will be glad to furnish copies of its regulations and any other information or advice desired.' The bureau has a model plan and specifications and other details concerning the designing, construction, equipment and operation of municipal abattoirs that will also be furnished upon request.

NUMBER OF INSPECTORS, THEIR SALARIES AND ANNUAL COST OF INSPECTION

The reports showed that there were 226 inspectors devoting their whole time to municipal meat inspection and 182 others engaged part of their time. The latter, of course, are mostly in the smaller cities and towns where the inspectors' duties include supervision of milk, other foods, etc. The leading states where city inspectors devote their whole time to meat inspection are California (44), Ohio (22), Louisiana (18), Kentucky (14), New York (11), and Texas (11). The leading cities are New Orleans, La., (17); San Francisco, Calif., (14); Louisville, Ky., (14); Cleveland, Ohio, (14); Oakland, Calif., (12); Los Angeles, Calif., (11); Denver, Colo., (8), and Columbus, Ohio, (8).

The salaries of meat inspectors vary very considerably: the lowest, $900, is reported from several places, while the two highest are the chief of bureau at Cleveland, Ohio, who receives $3,150 and the chief inspector at New Orleans, La., with a salary of $3,000. The state averages are lowest in Massachusetts ($1,036) and Indiana ($1,050) and highest in Washington ($2,040), Oregon ($1,896), and Louisiana ($1,704). The average salary of all whole-time inspectors for the United States is $1,442.

The expenditures by cities for meat inspection aggregate $447,095. The total cost for the nine cities in California was $81,718, which is a far larger amount than was spent in any other state. The next three states in order are Ohio, nine cities, $47,920; Massachusetts, 44 cities, $22,548, and New York, 14 cities, $22,117. Of the individual cities San Francisco., Calif., ranks highest with $27,168, Cleveland, Ohio, next with $20,-860, followed by Los Angeles, Calif., $20,000; Oakland, Calif., $19,000; Columbus, Ohio, $15,640; Louisville, Ky., $15,000, and New Orleans, La., $15,000.

Only a few cities attempt to reimburse themselves for the expense of meat inspection by charging fees. Those reporting this system are Birmingham, Ala.; Richmond, Calif.; Tampa, Fla.;

Cedar Rapids, Iowa, and Saranac Lake, N. Y., while Des Moines, Iowa, reported receipts in fees amounting to about one-third of the total cost of inspection. The amount of the fees is not mentioned except in the case of Cedar Rapids, where there is no slaughtering in the city and the fees are paid by farmers, 25 and 50 cents per carcass, the total for the year being $360.

There is no objection to a city charging a fee for meat inspection, provided the fees do not go directly to the inspector as his salary. Cost of inspection should be included in the city's budget.

CHARACTER OF INSPECTION

Some important features of meat inspection included in the questionnaire, not shown in the summary table may be briefly mentioned.

Regarding the standard of inspection, 82 replies, representing 42% of the total cities reporting meat inspection, stated that they based the inspection on the Federal regulations. However, only 46 cities stated specifically that an ante-mortem as well as postmortem examination was conducted.

CITY MEAT INSPECTION ORDINANCES

Several cities sent copies of the ordinances under which the meat inspection is conducted, and these have been examined in the Meat Inspection Division. Some more or less serious objections are noted, as for example, in the case of a city in Michigan which does not provide for antemortem inspection and also permits the slaughterer to inspect and stamp meats. The antemortem examination is not taken into account in a number of instances, while in others the ordinances are not comprehensive enough for the requirements of a thorough inspection system.

Of the large cities, San Francisco and Philadelphia have good ordinances, although that of Philadelphia does not deal with the inspection of meats.

Of the smaller cities, the ordinance of Columbus, Ga., may be cited. In some respects it is quite strict; it does not take a chance even on imported meat that bears the Federal stamp, as such meat cannot be sold unless it has also passed the city inspection and has the city stamp on it. Again, section 419 (2) (c) seems to impose an equipment expense that would not be justified in small establishments. However, it lacks in the respect that it allows wooden floors in slaughtering compartments, which is contrary to Federal requirements.

CONDEMNATIONS — PERCENTAGE, CHIEF CAUSES AND DISPOSAL

The great majority of the cities were unable to supply data in pounds of the quantity of meat inspected and condemned in 12 months. Many kept records of the weight of meat condemned, but not of that inspected, while others had records in animals and in carcasses and parts of carcasses. There were 37 cities, however, that gave the weight of both inspected and condemned meat, and thus permitted the calculation of the percentages.

The percentages show great variations, ranging from 0.07 to 16.93. The latter figure, however, involves only a very small quantity of meat and may be considered abnormal and disregarded. The real maximum is the next highest on the list, 8.27%, reported from New York. Wilmington, Del., with the lowest figure, 0.07, reports that meat inspection can not be adequately performed as there is only one inspector to cover all markets and stores, as well as five slaughterhouses in which approximately 35,000 animals are slaughtered in a year. Hence the quantity of meat condemned is probably far smaller than it should be. The very low figure for Kansas City, Mo., 0.11%, may be accounted for by the fact that the work there consists entirely of "Reinspection of meat immediately after being hung in markets." Much of this meat may have previously passed the

Federal inspection when it was slaughtered.

It may be of interest to note here that the proportion of meat condemned in all establishments under the Federal inspection is probably within a very small fraction of one per cent. A calculation was made for the fiscal year 1917 which showed that the total condemnations, including reinspected products, were 1.08% by weight of the estimated total inspections. When this figure is compared with the above-mentioned New York percentage, 8.27, we may, perhaps, get some idea of the potential difference in quality between the animals that come under the Federal inspection and those that are marketed in places where it is known they will not have to run the gauntlet of the Government inspection.

Regarding the chief causes of condemnation reported on the questionnaire the usual cause of condemnation where market inspection is concerned is taint or decay of the meat. Where animals and carcasses are inspected it is a case of "tuberculosis first and the rest nowhere." Hog cholera is frequently mentioned, and other diseases and conditions which are given are pyemia, emaciation, immaturity of calves, septicemia, actinomycosis, pneumonia, measles, parasites, caseous lymphadenitis, icterus, milk fever and glanders. The latter is in connection with the slaughter of horses in New York.

The disposal of condemned meats is generally satisfactorily accomplished by tanking, denaturing, burning, burying, etc. A few of the questionnaires, however, denoted unsatisfactory methods or a lack of care in dealing with this important matter. The following are quoted as examples, "Sent away," "Fed to hogs," "Given to man who gathers fats, etc.," "Garbage," "Left with dealer," and "Dealer allowed to dispose of it."

ODDMENTS FROM THE QUESTIONNAIRES

Many of the replies to the questionnaire deplored the absence or inefficiency of the meat inspection in the respective cities. Here, for instance, is a note from the health officer of a town in Maryland, at which place there are 13 slaughterhouses and no inspection whatsoever:

"I wish you could stimulate the local governing body and persuade them as to the necessity of establishing meat inspection."

A similar plaint comes from the Food and Dairy Inspector of a city in Kentucky, where there are five slaughterhouses and no inspection:

"This is an important matter and I have been trying to bring about something of this nature. I will appreciate your help and suggestions along this whole field of slaughtering."

Even in an important city on the West Coast where there is a large force both of Federal and city meat inspectors, conditions are far from ideal because of the heavy work entailed in covering the markets, farmers, and private slaughterhouses. The chief city meat inspector, states that the ordinance providing for city meat inspection "makes provision for establishments to use a house mark on their products in case there is no inspector present at time of slaughter." He also adds, "We do not have sufficient help, and I am unable to give the slaughtering establishments the proper inspection they should have."

The Health Officer of a town in California throws out the following suggestion for meat inspection along coöperative lines in small cities:

"In my opinion, an inspection at the time of slaughter is badly needed, and should be taken up by some unit larger than the small city, i. e., by the county. Most cities of, say, from 5,000 to 10,000 population would refuse to put up the money necessary to maintain a satisfactory meat-inspection service. Several cities near together might unite on such a plan."

The report from a town in Pennsylvania (three slaughterhouses, no inspection), says, "It would be a fine thing to have an inspector here."

A city in Arkansas reports eight slaughterhouses and no inspection, and adds, "Our slaughterhouse conditions are bad; no inspection of meats provided for at all."

Losses of sheep caused by dogs are accentuated in the report from an important city in Massachusetts, wherein the official gives as one of the chief causes of condemnation, "Laceration of sheep from dogs."

A small town in Michigan at which there are three slaughterhouses reports through the mayor that there is no meat inspection "except when city physician is called." The only condemnation during the year was a cow that died during parturition. The mayor reports that the cow should have been made into fertilizer, but adds, "No trace can be found of what was done with the carcass."

The mayor of a small city in Missouri is humorously pessimistic. In answer to the question, "At what places are meats inspected?" he says. "By housewife or at kitchen," and to Question 14, "Method of disposing of condemned meat," he replies: "Let the people eat it."

The report from a city in New York says there is inspection of meats at places of sale only and is signed by the "Plumbing Inspector."

One of the larger cities of Rhode Island reports five slaughterhouses and no inspection, and adds, "Everything goes in this town."

ACKNOWLEDGEMENTS

The writer desires to acknowledge his indebtedness to Dr. R. P. Steddon, chief of the Meat Inspection Division, Bureau of Animal Industry, and to Mr. G. H. Parks, expert in sanitation, of the same division, for advice and assistance in connection with this investigation.

□

WORLD-WIDE WORK OF INTERNATIONAL HEALTH BOARD
SEYCHELLES

A lecture and demonstration on hook worm disease in the far-away Seychelles Islands. Not even regions as remote as this are left untouched in the coöperative campaigns which the International Health Board—Rockefeller Foundation—and local health agencies throughout the world are waging against that disease. The lecturer stands before the doorway.

RECOVERY OF STREPTOCOCCUS HEMOLYTICUS FROM RESTAURANT TABLEWARE

CLARENCE C. SAELHOF AND W. J. R. HEINEKAMP,

Departments of Bacteriology and Pharmacology, University of Illinois,
College of Medicine,
Chicago, Ill.

"Dangers of dirty dishes" this paper might be termed. It is a quantitative presentation of just what these dangers are in public restaurants. They constitute a vexing problem to every health officer, and he needs the plain facts for the education of his public. With these, his people will back him in efforts to improve such places.

THE following experiments were performed to determine how commonly hemolytic streptococci could be isolated from the' supposedly clean eating utensils obtained in a group of restaurants and cafés in Chicago.

Cummings (Am. Jour. Pub. Health, Vol. IX, No. 6, June, 1917, p. 424) reports that of 23 sets of tableware he recovered hemolytic streptococci in 91%; pneumococcus from 17% of nine sets of tableware; diphtheria from 2% of 26 sets of tableware; and *Streptococcus viridans* from two sets of tableware (100%). Lynch and Cummings (Am. Jour. Public Health, Vol. IX, January, 1919, p. 25) record that the average bacterial count in 54 specimens of water used to wash eating utensils was 4,000,000 per cc.

Our procedure for taking cultures was as follows: A large number of throat swabs were made and sterilized in test tubes in the hot air oven at 160° C. each day before being used. They were then moistened under aseptic conditions, in sterile, distilled water in order that the organisms might adhere to the swab.

The different articles, such as spoon, knife, rim of the water glass, surface of the plate, etc., were swabbed as they were placed before us on the restaurant tables. The swabs were brought back to the laboratory, and smeared over plain agar plates (made neutral by means of the colorimetric method, using bromthymol-blue as an indicator) to which 7 drops of fresh blood had been added. These plates were incubated for 24 hours at 37° C. and at the end of that time we made macroscopic and microscopic examinations of the different types of colonies.

In making a macroscopic examination of the different types of colonies, the size, shape, margin, texture and color were noted under the hand lens so as to determine the type of organism as far as possible. In this manner, such colonies as *Streptococcus hemolyticus, Bacillus subtilis, Staphylococcus aureus* and S. albus were easily determined. A subsequent microscopic examination of the same colonies was made to verify the macroscopic findings, using ordinary and, when necessary, special stains. Sub-cultures of all suspicious colonies were made for further identification and upon special media, such as the sugars, gelatin, etc. whenever necessary. For animal experiments broth cultures were used.

The articles from which we obtained organisms were as follows: spoon, knife, fork, butter-dish, glass and plate. They were from nine different restaurants. An extra swab as a control was exposed to the air for approximately the same length of time as was taken in swabbing the tableware. The data obtained are presented in Table I.

The groups of organisms encountered were not numerous. We were chiefly concerned with the hemolytic streptococcus. We found this organism in the percentages given in Table 2. Three different strains of hemolytic staphylococci were found; we did not test their pathogenicity on animals. Most of the strains of staphylococci isolated were *S. albus;* three strains isolated were *S. aureus.* The pneumococcus was typical of Type III, having the mucoid and slimy growth, a distinct capsule and fermenting mannit and inulin. The strain of *B. coli* was identified by its odor, the shiny white colonies with dentate edges, its reaction with dextrose and lactose and by its morphology. Other organisms were encountered but were not identified.

The *Streptococcus hemolyticus* colonies were of the typical pin-point variety, having a sharp, clearly defined zone of hemolysis about them, and, on inoculation in broth, produced long chains of six, eight, and ten cocci as a rule; one strain producing chains of 16 to 20 cocci.

Each of the four strains of hemolytic streptococci, grown in broth culture, was inoculated in 1.5 cc. doses intravenously in rabbits, weight approximately 1200 grams. There occurred in all a loss of weight, and swelling of the joints. Death occurred in 24 to 60 hours. Post-mortems of these animals showed congestion of the internal viscera and lesions of the joints and endocardium. Cultures made from the joints and the heart's blood in each rabbit gave organisms identical with those injected.

TABLE I.*

Restaurant	Character of place	Spoon	Knife	Fork	Butterdish	Glass	Plate	Control
1	Fairly clean	B. subtilis	Strep. hemolyticus. Staph. albus	B. subtilis	Staph. albus B. subtilis	Staph. albus	Strep. hemolyticus	.....
2	Clean	Staph. albus	B. subtilis	B. subtilis	B. subtilis...	Strep. hemolyticus	B. subtilis	.....
3	Very dirty	Staph. albus	Staph. albus		Staph. albus	Staph. albus	Staph. albus	Staph. albus	......
4	Reasonably clean	Staph. albus	B. subtilis	B. coli	Staph. aureus	Staph. albus	Staph. albus	......
5	Fairly clean	Staph. albus	Staph. albus B. subtilis	Staph. albus B. subtilis	Staph. albus	Staph. albus B. subtilis	Staph. albus	......
6	Dirty	B. subtilis	Pneumococcus Type III	Staph. aureus	....	B. subtilis	B. subtilis Staph. hemo.	B.subtilis.
7	Fairly clean	Staph. albus B. subtilis	Strep. hemolyticus B. subtilis	B. subtilis	Staph. albus	Staph. albus	Strep. hemolyticus	.....
8	Fairly clean	B. subtilis	Staph. albus	Staph. albus	Staph. albus B. subtilis	Staph. albus	Staph. albus B. subtilis	.....
9	Dirty	B. subtilis	Staph. albus	No growth	....	Staph. albus	B. subtilis ·	......

*Only the predominating organisms were classified.

TABLE II.

Bacteria	No. of Examinations	Number Positive	Percentage Positive
Streptococcus hemolyticus...............................	63	4	6.35%
Pneumococcus...	63	1	1.60%
B. coli...	63	1	1.60%
Staphylococcus aureus..................................	63	2	3.20%
Staphylococcus albus...................................	63	31	50.81%
B. subtilis...	63	23	36.50%

DISCUSSION

It is evident from these results that the dishes and eating utensils are not sufficiently cleaned and washed to render them sterile. The dishes after being washed and drained usually are stacked on an open shelf exposed to dust and droplets from the sneezing, coughing, and spitting of both the employees and customers who may be carriers of virulent bacteria.

Direct contamination of eating utensils from the mouths of persons harboring virulent bacteria of various kinds naturally must occur. Many persons have sore throats, colds, influenza, and other contagious diseases and go about their business regularly and eat in public places. This source of dangerous bacteria is probably the most important one in contaminating eating utensils. Lynch and Cummings (Am. Jour. Pub. Health, Vol. IX, No. 1, January, 1919, pp. 24-38) isolated 12,000,000 organisms, many of which were streptococci, from the ladle of a spoon used by a streptococcus carrier. Hands, clothes, handkerchiefs, etc. of the customers harbor germs and no doubt further aid in carrying infection.

Another source is from indirect contamination. Cummings. (Am. Jour. Pub. Health, January, 1919, Vol. IX, No. 6, pp. 415) found that 80% of the cases of influenza from 22,084 troops epidemiologically investigated occurred among troops using mess kits. The men invariably used their hands as mops to clean kits. He states that the distribution of influenza in this manner is by indirect contact and chiefly by the hand to mouth route of travel. Our findings corroborate his experiments. There is also the possibility of infection by the aerial route.

It is easily seen that pneumonia, influenza, diphtheria and other throat and lung infections might readily be disseminated through the medium of the dirty and greasy plate. During a pandemic such as we have just experienced, it is reasonable to suppose that a certain percentage of the cases were contracted from the eating utensils. Less attention has been paid to this possible mode of dissemination than it deserves.

People working about restaurants should take special care to avoid contamination of hands or clothes. All dishes and eating utensils should be thoroughly cleaned in hot water made alkaline with strong soap. It is not sufficient merely to pass the greasy dishes through hot water. The alkalinity is an effective germicide. Strong soapy water will do a great deal towards killing and removing pathogenic organisms. The surfaces of all dishes should then be subjected to live steam for at least five minutes. It is absolutely necessary that each dish be subjected to this procedure. If the plates, etc., are stacked in piles the steam does not reach the entire surface. Mannheimer and Yhavez (Am. Jour. Pub. Health, 1917, Vol. VII, pp. 614-618) suggest subjecting eating utensils to a temperature of 80° C. for one minute. We, however, think that the utensils should be subjected in a hot air oven to a temperature of at least 100° C., for 30 minutes.

The following suggestions seem pertinent.

(1) All dishes should be thoroughly scoured and washed and subjected to live steam at least five minutes and then dried in a hot oven.

(2) All dishes and utensils should be stacked in a covered oven or box and not in the open air.

(3) The floor should be washed down once a day and the fixtures at least once a week with a strong germicide. Lysol is probably as efficacious and as easy to use as any; its odor is objectionable to some people.

(4) The employees of restaurants should be examined by a health officer at regular intervals in order that carriers may be detected.

SUMMARY

(1) Hemolytic streptococci were iso-

lated from the "washed" dishes and tableware, in small restaurants and cafes.

(2) 6.35 percent of the articles examined yielded this organism.

(3) The strains of *Streptococcus* *hemolyticus* were virulent for rabbits. They correspond to the human type.

(4) For the protection of the public a better system of washing dishes is needed in the small eating place.

NEW YORK STATE HEALTH AUTO

The New York State Department of Health has recently purchased a model 16 G. M. C. truck for its work in public health education. It is called "Health on Wheels," and is carrying on an active campaign in disseminating good health propaganda in

various New York communities. A novel feature is its adaptation for out-of-door lantern exhibitions. A light frame is placed in position on the roof of the car on which slides or motion pictures may be thrown. This device does away with the necessity of setting up an outfit in each new place, either in the open air or in a hall. The health mobile is sure to be one of the most attractive features at the various county fairs, and its great radius of action will enable it to cover an exceedingly large field. The cut is presented through the courtesy of *Forbes*.

ON THE SOLUTION OF PNEUMOCOCCI BY BILE

F. B. KELLY,

*John McCormick Institute for Infectious Diseases,
Chicago, Ill.*

The lytic property of bile and its preparations with reference to
pneumococci appears to be of uncertain quality. A variance
seems to exist in the susceptibility of different strains of these
organisms to lysis by bile. Inhibition of growth on blood agar
is of value in determining lytic action.

BECAUSE of the variations in the solution of pneumococci by bile noted by recent workers[*] it seemed worth while to look with more detail into the subject of the bile-solubility of this organism.

Neufeld (*Ztschr. f. Hyg. U. Infectionskrankh.*, 1900, 34, p. 454.) was the first to describe this phenomenon. He accidentally noticed that on adding 0.1 cc. of rabbit bile to 2.0 cc. of a broth culture of a pneumococcus the mixture cleared up entirely. He found this to be true of the bile of other animals, including oxbile; that the property was retained after autoclaving; that solution was retarded by cold; that the process could be observed under the microscope, where in a hanging drop the various stages of a gradual decrease in the number of size of the cocci could be seen; that the power was carried over in the alcohol-soluble, ether-insoluble portion of the bile, which contains the taurocholic and glycocholic salts; and most important of all, that the lytic action was limited to the pneumococci and *Streptococcus mucosus*.

Levy (*Virchow's Archiv*, 1907, 187, p. 327) used sodium taurocholate restored to a dilution of 10% with broth as a lytic agent, claiming pure bile to be too variable in viscosity, color, and power of solution. He found that 0.3 to 2.5 per cent of the salt solution was required to dissolve various strains of pneumococci. He was the first to suggest bile solubility as a differential test of pneumococci and *Streptococcus mucosus* on the one hand, and hemolytic and green - producing Streptococci on the other, and emphasized it as superior to all other tests.

Mendelbaum (*Münch. Med. Wochenschr.*, 1907, 54, p. 1431) also used sodium taurocholate, 2.0 ccm. of a 10% solution in broth, with 2.0 ccm. of 24 hour cultures of pneumococci. He obtained clearing macrascopically with pneumococci and *Streptococcus mucosus*, whereas mixtures with streptococci retained a turbid appearance. He states that if after one hour a loopful of any of these mixtures was streaked on an agar plate the plate remained sterile. Under the microscope, by adding a little methylene blue to the hanging drop, he observed many involuted or degenerated forms otherwise invisible, showing the lysis to be incomplete even after 48 hours. Using oxbile, 0.5 ccm. with 2.0 ccm. of a broth culture, the mixtures became entirely clear, when pneumococci or *Streptococcus mucosus* were used. Microscopically, unstained, nothing could be seen; with methylene blue a few degenerated forms appeared, but even these were invisible after one hour. He therefore declares bile to be better than the sodium taurocholate, both because of its greater lytic strength, and also because he found that

[*]Nuzum, Jour. Am. Med. Ass'n., 1918, 71, p. 1562.
Keegan, Ibid., p. 1051.
Dunn. Ibid., p. 9128.
Howard, Bull. Johns Hopkins Hospital, 1919, 33, p. 13.

it could be kept better than a solution of the salt.

Neufeld (*Arb. Kaiserl. Gesndhtsamte,* 1908, 28, p. 572) confirmed his earlier results and the value of the test in differentiation. He found there was complete lysis with all freshly grown and virulent strains of pneumococci and *Streptococcus mucosus,* but that their solubility was in a large measure lost after artificial growth for some time. It was regained by passing the organisms through animals. In trying to account for the specificity of the phenomenon he found it could not be due to the capsule, as some strains of pneumococci without capsules dissolved, whereas other capsule-bearing organisms were resistant.

Nicolle and Adil-Bey (*Ann. de l'Institut Pasteur,* 1907, 21, p. 20) noted that the presence of either sugar or serum inhibits the lytic action of bile. Libman and Rosenthal (*Trans. N. Y. Path. Soc.,* 1908, 8, p. 40) found that every organism they had classified as either pneumococcus or *Streptococcus mucosus* dissolved in bile. The solution was microscopically clear at the end of 20 minutes. They used oxbile, adding either one part of it to four parts of culture, or two parts to three of the culture. Neutral solutions gave best results. Acidity inhibited growth of the organisms. Transfers were made to blood agar plates after allowing the mixtures to stand at room temperature for varying lengths of time up to 24 hours, the streptococci being recovered in every case and the pneumococci and *Streptococcus mucosus* occasionally, showing that the lytic action was not always complete. They attributed Mendelbaum's failure to recover the streptococci to his use of plain agar instead of blood agar. Glucose solutions were found disadvantageous for diagnostic work because the results were variable.

Grixoni (*Riv. Critica Clin. Med.,* 1909, 10, p. 17) found a great variation in the lytic action according to the character

of the bile used. Rabbit bile was more active than ox bile, while fresh sterile bile acted more readily than old and contaminated bile. He claims the lytic power is lessened by sterilization, but retained if the bile is kept on ice. Both sodium glycocholate and taurocholate proved effective, the latter being the more active. Both, combined, each in a 2% solution were less powerful than fresh bile, though they were better than bile heated at 120° C. for one hour. He found, like Neufeld, that freshly isolated organisms dissolved in less time than was required for the organisms after they had been grown for some time on an artificial medium.

Cole (*Monographs Rockefeller Inst.,* 1917, 7, p. 13), and his coworkers declare the solvent substance for pneumococcus in bile is cholic acid. They specify the use of whole bile or of 10% solutions of either sodium glycocholate of taurocholate dissolved in salt solution as a routine test, employing one-fifth to one-tenth volumes of bile with actively growing broth cultures. They say that heat-killed organisms are insoluble. In testing several hundred strains of pneumococci they never failed to get solution. They incubate their bile mixtures at 37° C., in a water bath for one hour as a routine measure.

Aschner (*Jour. Ing. Dis.,* 1917, 21, p. 409) used a neutral, sugar-free broth containing 1% Witte's peptone and incubated till a sufficient growth of organisms was obtained. To this he added one-fifth volume of filtered sterile ox bile and obtained complete solution in 20 minutes with pneumococci. He notes the difficulty in getting a sufficient growth of these organisms in plain broth, and that sugars and serum added to enhance the growth retard lysis by bile.

In my work the organisms used at first were a strain each of the four types of pneumococcus, of *Streptococcus viridans,* of a hemolytic streptococcus, and of two untyped pneumococci which had been found variable in bile-solubility. The ox bile was a mixture from a great number of animals, prepared, within a few hours after they were killed, according to the method of Cole and his co-workers and then kept on ice. All cultures used were 24 hours old. Plain broth cultures, 0.1% and 0.2% dextrose broth cultures, and suspensions in salt solution from blood agar slants were tried. The plain broth gave a very scant, scarcely noticeable growth with pneumococci; the 0.1% dextrose gave a slight growth; the 0.2% a good growth; while the salt suspensions could be made as dense as desired. In order to get greater uniformities in the cultures all were diluted to a definite opacity as determined by the visibility of a needle held against the opposite side of the tube. One part of bile was added to four parts of the culture or suspension. Two control tubes were used, the one containing one part of bile to four parts of the uninoculated clear medium; the other, one part of salt solution to four parts of culture or suspension.

The plain broth and the 0.1% dextrose broth cultures were both so clear that nothing could be told macroscopically concerning any changes in them. There was no apparent immediate change in the 0.2% dextrose broth or salt suspension. After incubation at 37° C. for 30 minutes there appeared to be a slight clearing up in both in the case of the pneumococci, but none with the streptococci. A 4 mm. loopful of each of the mixtures after their incubation, when put on blood agar plates gave no growths with three of the pneumococci strains from the plain broth-bile mixtures, with any of the six strains from the 0.2% dextrose broth-bile mixtures, and with four of them from the control tubes of the latter; while all the streptococci mixtures and the remaining pneumococci preparations produced colonies. The fact that so many of the controls from the 0.2% dextrose gave no growth, while all of the bile mixtures from the 0.1% dextrose did, shows

the failure of growth cannot be ascribed to the bile in the case of the bile mixture inoculations from the 0.2% dextrose broth.

No solution could be regularly obtained if the sugar was used to enhance the growth of the pneumococci. With salt suspensions from blood agar the bile mixtures became quite clear in 5 to 6 hours in the case of the pneumococci, and platings made at that time gave growths only occasionally from these tubes. Control tubes containing the organisms always gave a growth. The streptococci were always unchanged microscopically, and always gave growth when inoculated at the end of 6 hours.

Using salt suspensions only, different bile products were then compared with the bile in regard to their lytic effect. Two samples of sodium glycocholate, one of sodium taurocholate, one of desiccated bile, and four of inspissated bile were tried.

The bile, in a ratio of 1 to 4 to the suspension gave a clear solution with the pneumococci after 6 hours. Five of the six strains gave a growth when streaked on blood agar after 2 hours; one, even after 6 hours.

One sample of sodium glycocholate in a 10% solution showed no microscopic change after 6 hours, although there was absolutely no growths of the pneumococci on plates inoculated after 2 hours. A second sample of the salt gave no clearness after 2 hours, although two of the organisms gave no growths when plated at that time. When two parts of the solution was added to three parts of the suspensions the mixtures became clear within 5 minutes but gave a plate growth with three of the strains even at the end of two hours.

When two parts of a 10% solution of sodium taurocholate were added to three parts of the suspensions, there was macroscopic solution within 5 minutes, but two of the strains gave a growth on blood agar even after two hours.

The desiccated bile, in a 10% solution and in the ratio of one to four to the suspensions, made but slight change in the appearance of the mixtures, and gave growths on plates with all the strains of the pneumococci even after two hours. In the ratio of two to three it gave distinct clearness in five minutes and four of the strains gave no growths on plates inoculated at the end of 20 minutes. Within two hours all of the mixtures were decidedly turbid again.

Ten per cent solutions of the four samples of inspissated bile (Parke, Davis & Co.) in the ratio of one volume to four volumes of the suspensions gave absolute clearness in the case of the pneumococci in five minutes. With the first sample no growths on blood agar could be obtained after the end of 20 minutes. With the second sample two of the strains gave growths even at the end of one hour; with the third sample, all six gave growths at the end of one hour; and with the fourth sample, no growths occurred when plated after one hour. When two parts of the bile solutions were added to three parts of the suspensions, only one strain when mixed with the second sample gave a growth after one hour; only three strains when mixed with the third sample gave growths at this time.

In no case did the bile products affect the appearance of the streptococci, or prevent their giving growths when streaked on blood agar.

Using the last three samples of inspissated bile, their effect on the following organisms was observed, the previous strains being tested at the same time as controls:

4 strains of type I pneumococcus
4 strains of type II pneumococcus
3 strains of type III pneumococcus
10 strains of type IV pneumococcus
15 strains of untyped pneumococcus
21 strains of streptococi

The 10% solutions of inspissated bile were added in the ratio of two to three of the suspensions. Of the 36 strains of pneumococci, 27 gave a perfectly clear solution within 5 minutes with all three samples of bile. Of the remaining 9 strains, 4 had been of variable solubility before, while the rest had required $3\frac{1}{2}$ to 24 hours to dissolve. Now they showed variations in solubility both as compared with each other, using the same bile, and also each with itself using the different biles. Loopfuls from each were inoculated on blood agar after 2 hours. Growths appeared from mixtures with sample 2 with 22 strains, with sample 3 with 31 strains, while with sample 4 no strain gave a growth. The streptococci showed no change miscroscopically with any of the biles. In only one case did no growth result when the mixtures containing streptococci were inoculated onto the plates.

In reading the tubes, if they were held in front of a dark object, such as a book, there was always present a slight opacity, greaselike in appearance, even when the bile was added to clear salt solution. This disappeared if the tubes were held so that a clear sky formed the background. The brightness under this condition was often sufficient to penetrate and make a fairly opaque mixture appear as clear. The most dependable results were obtained by using an object such as a building some distance away from the window as a background. With all the various mixtures used, the coloring matter in the bile was a confusing element, making it somewhat uncertain at times what changes had occurred.

CONCLUSIONS.

The presence of sugar has an inhibiting action on the lytic property of bile on pneumococci. Suspensions in salt solution offer a good means of testing the organisms; first, because the concentration can be controlled; second, because they give colorless suspensions; and third, because they eliminate many extraneous factors. While some samples of bile give good results, not all have strong lytic action; and the various bile preparations also differ in their power.

Inspissated bile seems stronger than other products but even different samples of this vary in their strength. Apparently there is a variance in the susceptibility of different strains of pneumococci to lysis by bile. If a coccus dissolves it is undoubtedly a pneumococcus; but if a solution is only partial, this fact does not necessarily rule out the possibility of the strain belonging to this group. If growth on blood agar does not occur when it is inoculated from a suspension mixed with bile for a few minutes, provided the suspension alone does give a growth, the organism may be considered definitely a pneumococcus; but the organism may be a pneumococcus even if it does give a growth after mixing it with bile.

✛

CITY HEALTH BULLETINS: THEIR USE AND MISUSE, THE NECESSITY FOR ADDITIONAL MAILING PRIVILEGES

MAX J. COLTON,
Health Officer,
Cumberland, Md.

Presented before Section of Public Health Administration, at New Orleans, La.. October 29, 1919.

Pound rate postage for city health bulletins is the plea of this author, a city health officer. Bulletins can take up public health education in most valuable ways, notably venereal disease and patent medicine discussion, which newspapers can hardly touch. Pound rates would demand change in postal laws by Act of Congress.

AN essential factor in the improvement of the public health is the education of the people in health matters. They must be taught how to live healthy, how the spread of communicable diseases can be diminished, and the need for a sanitary and healthy community. There is no doubt that an expenditure on education will be amply repaid by a saving of lives and prevention of disease. The old maxim that "an ounce of prevention is worth a pound of cure" is never more realized than in public health. Education can be furnished through health bulletins, issued periodically and distributed to those fitted to receive them.

The value of any publication lies in its composition and distribution. This is especially applicable to health bulletins, because we are dealing with a subject that must be continually kept before the public, otherwise people grow very indifferent to public health matters. The need is, therefore, apparent, and the demand is at hand for properly written and judiciously distributed health bulletins.

There are excellent reasons why city departments of health should issue bulletins. The campaign of education should not be left wholly to local daily newspapers. Health bulletins, however, do not supplant newspapers but instead one is needed to support the other in the campaign for better health. The citizens of a community should be educated about many subjects, information concerning which newspapers will not print. Probably the two most prominent of these matters are venereal diseases and patent medicines. There should be a frank discussion on the venereal disease problem and the menace of quacks and patent medicines. Of the first mentioned, many newspapers still insist on calling them "social diseases" instead of plainly printing gonorrhea and syphilis, and about the latter, advertising secured from patent medicine concerns and quacks is too profitable for most newspapers to take chances of losing that money, by publishing the real truth concerning such matters.

Practically every profession and industry has its own journals, and many manufacturing and mercantile establishments issue what they call "house organs," in which they endeavor to inform their clients regarding all matters, but more especially featuring their own line of business. Health departments are no less public institutions than mercantile establishments, and they should stand ever ready to sell public health provided they can find the buyers. It therefore behooves the officials in charge to use all legitimate means of creating a demand and there exists no better way than through a health bulletin where the real truth and only the truth should be set forth, unvarnished and not written to suit the particular taste of any newspaper, faction, party or interest.

The complaint has been made regarding city health bulletins that they do not reach the class of people who most need the instruction and advice contained in them. That may all be true, but health bulletins to people of that kind are incomprehensible and even though a copy of each issue could be placed in their hands, the time, energy and money would be wasted. They can be instructed only by word of mouth and actual demonstration. The people for whom health bulletins are valuable are the better class, who can read, and know what they are reading (providing, of course, the material is properly prepared). It is to the citizens of this type that the appeal must be made for a more solid support of the health department, and to whom a dis-

cussion concerning the activities and proposed activities of the health department must be addressed.

In view of these facts and others not set forth, the need for city health bulletins is established, as evidenced by the publications issued by many of our large cities and numerous smaller ones. Unfortunately many of the publications issued are not worthy of the name "health bulletins," but instead are merely statistical reviews put up in a fashion all their own and oftentimes in a manner easily misinterpreted. The information contained in these statistical reviews may be merely the number of inspections, examinations, condemnations, etc., made by the various employees of the department and the number and causes of deaths. It is fair to assume that these tables are not read to any extent and the information contained therein is of no material benefit to the citizens of the community.

Information solicited from approximately fifty health departments that issue health bulletins shows a large expenditure of money both for printing and distributing. In many of the cities, as evidenced by the bulletins issued, the money expended for this purpose could be put to far better use through the publication of two or three popularly and properly prepared leaflets for distribution from house to house.

Perhaps a few illustrations of publications issued by health departments under the term "health bulletins," and supposedly for the benefit of a community, would not be out of place here.

Several cities issue a four-page review each month, in pamphlet form, of cumbersome size, setting forth nothing but statistics. In a few of these even an itemized statement as to the cemeteries where bodies were buried is given. A number of cities issue similar monthly statistical reviews, and include a full list of the Board of Health and all employees. Some bulletins are issued with blank pages. It would be far better, if the time and facilities were not at hand to prepare an article, to at least print a few terse statements which would be a lesson in themselves. Another defect is the issuing of the publication some months later than the time carried on the date line.

There are, of course, many excellent health bulletins, among which may be mentioned those issued by the health departments of Detroit, Cincinnati, Philadelphia, Chicago, St. Louis, New York, and a few among the smaller cities.

Bulletins to be of value to their readers, must be prepared in a live fashion, the material up-to-date, written in a clear, concise manner, set up in legible type, and containing information that is of benefit to the readers, and that can easily be digested by the average person. It should have a regular date of appearance and current material should be used. Furthermore, exaggeration should not be resorted to; only the truth should be set forth. The reading matter should be of a practical instead of a theoretical nature and the articles should not be lengthy. One main purpose of publishing bulletins is to secure the confidence and support of the citizens to whom the particular health department caters, and this can only be obtained by a plain statement of the facts and a frank discussion. Even though the bulletin be published mainly for physicians (which it should not be) the articles should be clear and concise, interspersed with pithy expressions, so that by spending a few minutes the gist of the matter can be obtained. An additional attraction in health bulletins is the publication of self-explanatory pictures or cartoons portraying existing conditions.

My main plea at this time is to stop wasting money on publications which cannot possibly do good in the community.

The need for more liberal mailing privileges for health bulletins issued by municipal health departments has been apparent for some time, and a number of members of this Association have had the matter under consideration. The gist of the proposition is this: Under the Federal postal laws and regulations, health bulletins issued by state departments of health are admissable for mailing at pound rates. This privilege does not embrace municipal health bulletins. The reasons for this condition is that postal regulations do not permit the mailing at pound rates of a publication that has to be distributed by the carriers at the same post office where the publication is mailed. This regulation was made in order to prevent daily newspapers from using the local post office as their distributing agents.

The point is, of course, well taken for newspapers, but there should be no reason why a health bulletin, issued for the benefit of all people and from which no profits are derived, should not be allowed to be distributed as cheaply as possible. Furthermore, under the pound rate privilege a health department can publish three or four times as many copies of the bulletin as under the present system, at no greater expense. This is mainly why pound rate privileges should be extended to include city health bulletins.

A change in the postal laws could afford the advantages of pound rates to municipal health bulletins, but such change would be only by Act of Congress. Should Congress be induced to make the necessary changes in the law, the benefits to be derived by municipalities all over the country which are at present issuing health bulletins are numerous, but mainly it will ensure the reaching of a large part of the population with that most essential feature of public health administration, popular health education.

IDEALS IN THE ORGANIZATION OF AN INDUSTRIAL MEDICAL SERVICE

EMERY R. HAYHURST, Ph. D., M. D.

Professor of Hygiene, Ohio State University,
Columbus, Ohio.

A COMMON observation in regard to industrial medical services as installed in various establishments is the fact that so many of them are one-sided, that is, are promoted and managed almost entirely by the employer. It is well known that organized labor has shown antipathy to welfare work in general, including even medical and health phases thereof. It is also plain to be seen that coöperation between employers and employes is essential for the success of this service.

One serious factor appears to be the fact that there is no established procedure for taking care of workers who, through physical examinations and other forms of inquiry, are found to be misplaced in their employment relations and who are very apt to suffer if any changes are made. It would appear that there are one or two solutions for this situation; for instance, the institution of compulsory health and disability insurance or the adoption of group insurance to cover the health and disability of the workers in a given establishment.

Industrial medical service cannot achieve its ideals until an inventory is made of each worker's capabilities and until he is placed in accordance with the findings of the inventory. Refinements are not necessary; rough groupings ought to suffice. A great extension of possibilities in placing him intelligently can be had through an analysis of the jobs at hand, including the checking up of their health-hazards. A reduction of these hazards naturally extends the field placements.

An industrial medical service is not complete which devotes itself almost exclusively to reconstruction and palliative measures. It must give much attention to such preventive measures as industrial hygiene and housing hygiene as well as physical examinations.

Hence, it appears that the medical department of an establishment should be managed by a committee representative of both employer and employes and with at least one official representative of the local board of health. The make-up of this committee should be such that proportionate representation is had with the further provision that in case of a divided opinion either the local health representative should have a deciding vote or, if of sufficient importance, a higher committee should have such jurisdiction, such, for instance, as one composed of a representative of each of the following: The local or state manufacturer's association, workmen's organization, the chamber of commerce and the state department of health.

The cost of an industrial medical service should also be divided. It is not good moral practice to bestow service free of charge where those being served have some personal responsibilities. The industry may justly pay for the equipment necessary, considering it a part of the plant, but maintenance should be charged partly to employes, and partly to the direct cost of production. It is obvious that an industrial medical service cannot be all capitalistic in either management or maintenance and be certain of more than the passing interest or lukewarm coöperation of those being served, yet from the nature of industrial relations capital must be the natural leader in its management as in other features of business.

ORGANIZATION OF CONTROL OF PASTEURIZATION

Frederick O. Tonney, M. D.

Director of Laboratories, Chicago Health Department,
Chicago, Ill.

Read before Joint Session of Section on Public Health Administration with Laboratory and Food and Drugs Sections, American Public Health Association, at New Orleans, La., October 29, 1919.

THE experience of the Chicago Department of Health in the enforcement of a comprehensive pasteurizing ordinance during the past seven years has presented an excellent opportunity for the study of methods of control. It has been possible during a long continued period of observation to test out the various control procedures and judge their efficiency by the ultimate results accomplished. The outcome of this period of experimentation has been the adoption of a general scheme of organization and the development of a stnadardized plan of procedure which now appear to be of proved value. The methods herein outlined, therefore, may be said to have been found effective as applied to the control of a milk supply of 215,000 gallons daily* derived from 18,000 farms, pasteurized in 456 pasteurizing plants and distributed through 603 milk depots. Ninety-eight per cent of the milk supply of the city of Chicago is now pasteurized. The remaining two per cent represents the amount of certified milk distributed in this market.

The control of pasteurization is basically a bacteriological problem. The effectiveness of such control will depend in last analysis upon the extent to which sound bacteriological principles are applied in its solution. Success is conditioned, therefore, upon the close coordination of the inspection division with the public health laboratory. Efficient laboratory service is required not only for the examination of routine samples but for the education of the inspecting personnel, and for the guidance of scientific matters

* As of the year 1918.

of those responsible for the direction and planning of the work.

ORGANIZATION OF FORCE

The inspection force proper will be considered in three general groups: the milk inspector, representing the rank and file of inspector; the field plater, who is selected for work requiring a certain amount of technical skill; and the bacteriologist, who is required to repeat and confirm the work of the other groups in selected instances.

The Milk Inspector.—The milk inspector, or rank and file of inspector, engages exclusively in field work. His duties include general inspection of depots, plants, and wagons, scoring of plants, and collection of routine samples. Many of these men necessarily have little or no technical training. They cannot be expected, therefore, to master fully the bacteriological technic of sampling. They should be assigned to the laboratory for a two-weeks' course of instruction before taking up their duties and should also receive instruction in field work at the hands of some member of the inspecting force. Such bacteriological work as is participated in by them must necessarily be accepted with reservation and subject to confirmation by more fully trained technicians. The number of such inspectors employed should be about one to each 25 pasteurizing plants, if we allow for other duties such as depot and wagon inspection.

The Field Plater.—Among the rank and file of field men there will always be found certain ones who possess aptitude for laboratory work by reason of preliminary education or natural technical ability. Such men are selected after a period of observation and are given a six weeks' course in the Bureau of·Laboratories where they are instructed in bacteriological plating methods and are specially trained in the technic of using the field plating outfit.[1] These inspectors may be regarded as intermediate from the standpoint of technical training between the milk inspector and the bacteriologist proper. Their duties include both field work and laboratory work and their time is chiefly spent in passing upon new installations and inspecting plants which are more or less unsatisfactory. The number of field platers is about one-third that of the milk inspectors.

The Bacteriologist—The bacteriologist is a member of the laboratory force, specially trained in milk bacteriology, who is detailed by the laboratory from time to time to the inspection division. His findings are used for final confirmation of the results of tests by inspectors and for preparation of cases for suit in court. One such bacteriologist is usually sufficient for a given health department organization.

The Supervising Inspector.—There should be one supervising inspector to each 25 inspectors, approximately. He is assigned to a supervisory district and is held responsible for the apportionment of work to inspectors, the reviewing of reports, and the checking of assignments. He reports directly to the division chief or person acting in the capacity of division chief. An office force is required to file reports, check thermo recorder charts, send out notices, report results of tests, and attend to miscellaneous correspondence.

PLAN OF PROCEDURE

Initial Installation of Pasteurizing Plants.—The initial installation of a pasteurizing plant gives occasion for the application of four general control measures: (1) approval of the plan of

construction and site of building; (2) inspection and scoring of the establishment after completion; (3) testing of the heating device, holding device, sterilizing facilities, and thermo recorder; (4) issuance of a license or permit under which the plant may legally operate.

The construction of a new plant or remodeling of an old one offers an opportunity for plan approval whereby errors in construction and sanitary arrangement may be avoided or corrected with a minimum of expense to all concerned. An expert plan examiner should be assigned to this work, and previously approved plans may be furnished for guidance in construction. The plans should be laid down with certain fundamental principles in mind such as:

(1) Convenience in arrangement facilitates the use of proper bacteriological methods.

(2) Smooth surfaced impervious materials are most readily kept clean.

(3) All pipes and apparatus should be arranged so as to be easily accessible for cleaning.

(4) Long runs of piping for carrying milk should be avoided because of their tendency to accumulate filth favorable to bacterial growth.

(5) When possible the sterilizer capacity should be sufficient to permit the treating of all utensils at one time as a last step in the daily routine, after the cleaning of equipment and premises is finished.

(6) Living quarters, locker facilities, and toilets must be separate from the rooms in which milk is handled.

(7) Adequate light and ventilation are prime essentials.

Inspection and Scoring.—Inspection and scoring of the completed plant is ordinarily carried out by the milk inspector. For this purpose a score card is provided for depots and pasteurizers. Plants should score at least 75%

---

1. Tonney & White—A Field Plating Outfit, etc. A. J. P. H., Vol. VIII, No. 8. p. 582.

before approval for operation is given. The inspector makes a detailed record of necessary structural changes and sanitary improvements and records a recommendation for approval or disapproval of the plant. Such orders and recommendations are transmitted to the supervising inspector for review and confirmation and are thereupon passed to the chief or assistant chief executive of the division for final disposition. Approved orders are then mailed to the plant or licensure proceeded with as the case may be.

Testing of Apparatus.—The testing of the heating and holding apparatus is commonly carried out by the field plater. He tests the temperature with a standardized thermometer, times the holder, and takes samples of milk at various steps in the process, using his field plating outfit. The plates are taken to the laboratory for incubation and are counted by the same inspector after the incubation period. If the equipment is thereby shown to be capable of giving satisfactory results, a recommendation for its approval is recorded by the inspector and transmitted to the inspection division. If not, the bacteriologist proper is assigned to confirm the findings of the inspector. His recommendations must be complied with and compliance verified by subsequent inspection and tests before license is issued.

The testing of the holding device when the milk is held "in batch" consists ordinarily of recording the time interval, and taking the temperature at the beginning and end of the heating period, using a standardized thermometer. In the case of continuous flow holders the methylene blue test is applied, the time being taken at the outset and again at the first appearance of the dye at the outlet of the machine. Many continuous flow machines have been discarded because of their inability to pass this test. The inspector also tests the recording thermometer by placing the thermometer of the instrument in a pail of hot water, varying the temperature by addition of cold or hot water, and checking the recorded temperature with his standarized thermometer.

Licensure.—When a satisfactory record is obtained with respect to the previously prescribed tests license is approved. For plants within the jurisdiction of the municipality a double licensure is recommended, i. e.,

(1) A general license issued by the mayor or chief executive for a fee, authorizing the sale of milk; and (2) a permit issued by the commission of health without fee for the operation of a pasteurizing plant. For plants located outside the municipal jurisdiction a permit only is issued. Both license and permit have a tenure of one year and are revocable for just cause by the issuing authority.

GENERAL CONTROL OF CITY PLANTS

For convenience in discussing city plant control the subject matter will be treated under the following headings: (1) Inspection and scoring. (2) The hearing board. (3) Reporting of contagious diseases. (4) Sampling. (5) Court process. (6) Revocation of license.

Inspection and Scoring.—A routine inspection and scoring should be made of each plant by the milk inspector once in two weeks on an average. Unsatisfactory plants should receive attention more frequently, whereas plants known to be conducted satisfactorily may be seen at longer intervals. The score is made upon the regular card. A score of at least 75% is required. The inspector records orders for the abatement of insanitary conditions or the correction of unsatisfactory methods. These orders are turned in to the supervisor for review and transmitted to the office for issuance, a time limit for compliance being set in the order. A reinspection is made after the expiration of the time limit and in case ot non-compliance the dealer is summoned to appear before the hearing board.

The Hearing Board.—The hearing board, which consists of representatives of the health department and legal department of the city government, is convened at regular intervals for the purpose of allowing violators of sanitary ordinances a preliminary hearing and making reasonable adjustments without resort to court procedure. At the hearing a further time extension may be allowed, or, in the discretion of the board, the case may be recommended for suit. The hearing board which was established in Chicago in 1915 by Dr. John Dill Robertson has adjusted many thousands of cases, thus securing early compliance without the costly and time-consuming court process. The number of cases heard by the hearing board, including food and sanitary cases other than milk, is 24,583 and the number of cases recommended for suit is 7,843.*

Reporting of Contagious Diseases. Under the terms of the Chicago ordinance, milk dealers are required to report to the health department the existence of any contagion developing among their working force or their families. In practice, however, it becomes necessary to rely chiefly on other sources for this information. Within the municipality the official reports of physicians to the health department, the laboratory findings on specimens submitted for diagnosis, and information obtained by quarantine officers and food inspectors constitute the main sources of information. With regard to major contagious diseases, routine tabulation of the milk supply is made from the reports of physicians and quarantine officers and when an excessive number of cases ap-

* As of Jan. 1, 1919.

pears chargeable to a given dealer a special investigation is made with the object of discovering contagion in or about the establishment.

When persons infected with contagious disease or who are carriers of disease are found they must be excluded from work in connection with the pasteurizing plant or its distributing agencies. When contagion exists in the family of a worker he may be permitted to continue work if he establishes living quarters away from the infected premises. When contagion exists on the premises where pasteurizing is done, continuance of business may be permitted provided that the milk is taken to another plant for pasteurization and all work done by persons who have not been exposed to contagion. When evidence of the existence of an unknown infecting focus appears in connection with a pasteurizing plant, the establishment is shut down pending investigation of the source of infection.

The Thermo Recorder.—The thermo recorder chart, taken in conjunction with routine inspection, may be accepted as evidence of the proper operation of the heating apparatus and holding device. When practicable, the charts should be collected by the inspector but may if necessary be nailed to the inspection bureau. On receipt at the Central office, they are checked up by an inspector who should be an experienced field man preferably familiar with the general layout of the plants whose records pass under his scrutiny. When deviations are found in the temperature records, the attention of the field force is directed to the plant and in the case of recurrence, a shut-down of the plant may be necessary.

Sampling.—Bacteriological sampling of milk for control purposes falls into three principal groups: (1) primary routine sampling by the milk inspector; (2) secondary "follow-up" sampling by the field plater and (3) final sampling by the bacteriologist.

The primary routine samples constitute the largest group of samples collected. They are taken by the rank and file of milk inspector. In Chicago from 50 to 75 such samples are collected daily from milk depots, stores, wagons, and receiving platforms. The results serve to indicate in a general way the plants which are in need of closer attention. These findings, however, because of the long interval between collection and examination of the sample and because of the limitation of the average inspector's technic must be accepted with reservation. They should be considered as confidential information for use of the department only and should not be given out to dealers or used as a basis for suit or revocation of license. In the laboratory the simplest possible technic is used, with the idea of examining as large a number of samples as possible. To this end, two dilutions only are plated from each sample. The actual count of the colonies, therefore, often falls above or below the limits of the dilution, making estimation necessary in lieu of counting. We have attempted to simplify further the laboratory technic of primary sampling by trying out the Breed method of direct examination of milk.[1] It was found, however, that the method is not adapted to milk of the age at which it commonly reaches the city and is especially unsatisfactory as applied to pasteurized milk. Its disadvantage lies in the fact that dead organisms apparently take the stain and cannot be distinguished from the living. The result is that the direct count shows enormously greater numbers of bacteria than the plate method required by the ordinance. In fact, in such milk as we have had to examine there is apparently no relation between the results of the two methods of counting.

1. N. Y. State Jour. of Med. Vol. 19, No. 4, p. 134.

For this reason, we have found it necessary to abandon the direct method as unsuitable for control purposes under the conditions encountered. Table No. I indicates the discrepancies observed between the direct count and the count by plating.

TABLE NO. I
SHOWING NUMERIC RELATION OF BACTERIA FOUND IN MILK BY DIRECT MICROSCOPIC METHOD AND BY PLATE METHOD

Laboratory Number	Direct Method	Plate Method	Ratio Direct to Plate Count
200	44,500,000	2,000,000	22 to 1
197	13,500,000	400,000	33 to 1
318	10,000,000	50,000	20 to 1
199	467,500,000	800,000	584 to 1
652	38,000,000	150,000	253 to 1
198	51,500,000	90,000	572 to 1
317	32,000,000	100,000	320 to 1
742	47,500,000	750,000	66 to 1
756	79,000,000	500,000	158 to 1
315	20,500,000	80,000	256 to 1
263	113,500,000	500,000	227 to 1
265	8,000,000	65,000	123 to 1
266	35,500,000	1,000,000	85 to 1
262	8,000,000	350,000	23 to 1
653	4,500,000	80,000	56 to 1
319	2,500,000	45,000	55 to 1
388	276,500,000	250,000	1106 to 1
386	25,000,000	1,000	25000 to 1
385	12,500,000	850,000	14 to 1
384	4,000,000	200,000	20 to 1
345	72,000,000	4,000,000	18 to 1

Secondary "follow-up" Sampling.— The secondary sampling is carried out by the field plater who is assigned to those plants which are indicated by the primary sampling to be in an unsatisfactory state. The number of such samples examined in Chicago is about twenty per day. The purpose of the secondary sampling is to locate the sources of contamination and to give instruction to the dealer in the proper methods of operation. The inspector remains at the plant during the entire process, observing methods, inspecting equipment, and sampling at each step. He plates his samples on the premises using the field plating outfit, thereby demonstrating the elementary principles of bacteriological technic for the benefit of the plant workers. The plates are brought to the laboratory and after incubation are counted by the same inspector. Later he returns to the plant for the purpose of eradicating the sources of contamination indicated by the results found. The results of secondary sampling may be considered more reliable than those of the primary sampling and may be reported to the dealer. They are not, however, suffi-ciently dependable for court purposes. It has been found that the majority of unsatisfactory plants may be success-fully handled by the field platers. The few remaining intractable ones are re-ferred to the bacteriologist for confirm-atory sampling, the results of which are used as a basis for court proceed-ing.

Final Confirmatory Sampling.—The final confirmatory sampling is carried out by the bacteriologist assigned from the laboratory. He confines his at-tention to persistently unsatisfactory plants which have resisted all previous efforts of correction. The technic of these tests is quite elaborate and all of the technical details specified in the ordinance are painstakingly carried out. Every possible precaution is used to safeguard against error. The sam-ples are taken in the final containers only, delivered iced to the laboratory within one hour, plated immediately in a range of five dilutions in duplicate. incubated for a timed period of forty-eight hours and accurately counted. Controls are run with all tests, the pipettes are callibrated and the amount of culture medium used in each plate is measured. The results will therefore stand the test of cross-examination by experts. On account of the amount of work involved in this test the number of such samples should be limited to about four daily if one bacteriologist is employed. It should be noted that the results obtained by this strict technic are commonly much lower than the previous results obtained in the same plants by the inspecting personnel. Table No. II shows the comparative results of primary sampling by the milk inspector and final sampling by the bacteriologist. The table has been abbreviated in the interests of economy of space.

TABLE NO. II
RESULTS OF PRIMARY ROUTINE SAMPLING AND FINAL COURT SAMPLING COMPARED

	Date	Rout. Samples	Date	Final court samples
	4-18-19	450,000		
Plant A	1-22-19	60,000	5-21-19	50,000
	6-14-18	Too numerous to count		
	4-28-19	200,000		
Plant B	4-9-19	650,000	5-21-19	400,000
	5-20-19	450,000		
	4-2-19	200,000		
Plant C	10-2-18	100,000	5-21-19	25,000
	9-10-18	70,000		
Plant D	4-18-19	400,000		
	12-17-19	380,000	5-22-19	400,000
	4-22-19	300,000,000		
Plant E	12-19-18	350,000	5-22-19	5,000
	12-19-18	100,000		
Plant F	4-23-19	200,000		
	3-28-19	40,000	5-22-19	120,000
Plant G	4-22-19	200,000	5-22-19	150,000
	3-22-18	50,000		
	4-22-19	5,000,000		
Plant H		4,000,000	5-23-19	100,000
	12-19-18	Too numerous		
	4-21-19	200,000		
Plant I	1-7-19	Too numerous	5-23-19	25,000
	1-7-19	40,000		

Court Process.—The number of in-stances in which court process must be resorted to under the plan outlined is small, since other means are pre-viously exhausted and only persistent violators resistant to other measures reach this stage in the program. About 30 suits for high bacterial counts have been brought to trial in Chicago during the two years passed. While the rule is that the ordinance is commonly up-held, it must be admitted frankly that the court process, as a control meas-ure, is not entirely satisfactory. The procedure is time consuming and costly in effort. There are many loop-holes of escape before the case is finally dis-posed of in court. The fines imposed also are frequently too small to be ef-fective. The method, however, as a whole, is of distinct value, as the know-ledge that suits are being brought has a corrective effect upon the industry.

Revocation of License.—A more sat-isfactory method of dealing with old offenders which has recently been used extensively with good effect by the Commissioner of Health of Chicago is the revocation of licenses. By this method pasteurizing plants which have long been unsatisfactory are suddenly confronted with summary interruption of business. The doors are padlocked and a police detail is stationed on the premises. The result is the display of remarkable alacrity in carrying out orders for the improvement of sanitary conditions. Repairs which have been pending for months are accomplished over night. Old nuisances are abated, flies are kept out of the premises, the methods of operation are improved and bacterial counts in the product which have been persistently above the legal standard suddenly drop to a satisfactory level. In fact, the prompt response and resulting necessity of early renewal of license has lately led the Commissioner of Health to adopt the practice of serving a 24 hour notice before revocation. It is found that this notice often obviates the necessity of revocation because of prompt compliance with regulations. It should be borne in mind further that the results cited are accomplished with a minimum of effort and in record breaking time.

The annual renewal of licenses also constitutes an effective means of enforcing sanitary requirements. It is the practice to secure an inspection and scoring of all premises shortly before the expiration of the license period. Plants found to be below standard are not given renewals until conditions are made satisfactory.

CONTROL OF COUNTRY PLANTS

The methods of control of pasteurization, as used within the city, require some modification when applied to plants located outside the boundaries of a municipality.

Inspection and Scoring.—A dairy inspector or creamery inspector is required to visit country plants at least once each month. The number of such inspectors should be about one to each 15 plants, approximately, if time is allowed for dairy duties and other assignments. The card used for scoring is similar to that used within the city.

A score of at least 75% should be required. Orders for abatement are forwarded to the department for issuance as in the case of city plants.

Reporting of Contagious Diseases.—Information with reference to contagion among employes of country plants or their tributary farms is obtained in a number of ways. The dealers themselves report a considerable number of cases. The dairy inspectors, the creamery inspectors, the local health officers, and physicians are important sources of information. Rarely the farmer himself reports the existence of contagion. A report of two or more cases in a given locality is followed by investigation in the neighborhood which often discloses additional cases in adjoining farms and nearby plants. Diseases in the herds are commonly reported by the local veterinarians. When a report is received of the existence of contagion in a pasteurizing plant or its tributary farms, the product of the plant is excluded from the market until such time as the case is removed from the premises or the tributary supply is cut off. The return to work of the employee concerned is not permitted until a formal certificate of recovery is obtained from the local health officer. In the case of tributary farms, the shipment of milk to the plant may be allowed if the herds are removed to other premises and cared for by persons not in any way exposed to contagion.

Thermo Recorders.—Thermo recorders are required as in city plants. The charts are required to be mailed regularly to the department of health.

Sampling.—Sampling consists chiefly of field plating at the plants and general primary sampling on arrival of the product in the city.

The "Shut-off."—Perhaps the most effective means of control of plants located outside of the municipal jurisdiction is the "shut-off." This procedure may be regarded as a temporary suspension of the permit to operate a pasteurizing plant. It is resorted to for reasons such as the following:

1. Non-compliance with orders for abatement of insanitary conditions.

2. Acceptance of milk from other shippers who have attempted to evade a "shut-off."

3. Failure to send thermo recorder charts to the department.

4. Falsifying thermo recorder charts.

5. Failure in the case of a new plant to apply for a permit before shipment.

6. High temperature of milk at the receiving platform in the city.

77. Excessive bacterial content of the milk sampled at the receiving platform.

The "shut-off" is accomplished in the following steps: (1) Written notice is sent to the consignor and consignee; (2) Telephone notice is given to the dairy inspector of the district; the inspector ascertains whether the plant is shipping and reports by telephone to the department, giving the railroad and time of arrival; (3) A milk inspector is assigned to the receiving platform in the city. On the arrival of the shipment, it is returned to the consignor by the milk inspector or held under condemnation tag. The shipper, in order to be relieved of the "shut-off," is required to come to the city or send a representative to interview the executive or assistant executive of the inspection bureau. Here the reasons for the "shut-off" are fully explained and the importance of securing compliance with orders emphasized. When all orders have been complied with and this fact has been verified by inspection of the plant, the "shut-off" is lifted.

Revocation of Permit.—Revocation of permit or refusal to renew the permit at the end of the expiration period is at times resorted to as a means of penalizing repeated disregard of sanitary regulations. This step closes the city market to the plant in question and usually results in prompt compliance with orders issued for abatement of insanitary conditions and improvement of methods.

□

Marriage and Disease.—The new Danish Marriage Law is up for its third reading in the Folketing (Lower House) after which it will go to the Landsting (Upper House) for consideration. It contains these provisions:

(1) If the person who wishes to contract a marriage does not suffer and has never suffered from venereal disease, he shall give a written declaration on his honor to that effect.

(2) In the opposite case, he must either put in a doctor's certificate, made within the previous fortnight that the danger of infection or its transmission to the children is most improbable; or

(3) If such a declaration cannot be made, he must prove that the other party to the marriage has been informed as to the disease, and that both parties have had oral instruction from a doctor as to the dangers consequent thereon.

Typhus on Decrease in Esthonia.—Mortality from typhus in the hospitals of Esthonia is on the decrease, according to announcement made by Colonel Edward W. Ryan, head of the American Red Cross Commission to West Russia. From 8 percent to 0.5 percent is the record drop in the number of deaths from typhus registered in five days in some of the hospitals.

The work of cleaning up in the hospitals in Reval has been completed and the commission has begun work at Narva. The Esthonian authorities have given the Red Cross officials every possible assistance. The chief of the commission has expressed himself as confident that the typhus epidemic will shortly be overcome, unless the disease suddenly grows unexpectedly widespread.

PUBLIC WATER SUPPLY CONTAMINATED BY AN INTER-CONNECTED PRIVATE WATER SUPPLY

Caleb Mills Saville,

*Manager and Chief Engineer, Water Department,
Hartford, Conn.*

Read before Sanitary Engineering Section, American Public Health Association, at New Orleans, La.,
October 28, 1919.

Private water supplies connected for emergency purposes to public supplies are a potential source of pollution. Check valves which a decade ago were considered safe have been subject to such changes in design as to be now condemned. Health officers should be on their guard against any commercial economy here that means health risk to their communities.

ORIGIN OF POLLUTION

THE amount of water which can be obtained from underground sources has been made the subject of numerous investigations. The quality of this water in its relation to health seems to have been somewhat overlooked. There seems generally to be a feeling that water which comes from underground is always of the purest quality and the deeper the well the better the chance of getting such water.

This opinion is probably based on the fact that water slowly percolating through fine gravel is purified in its journey and oftentimes appears in wells and springs, clear, cold and sparkling.

Reasoning from this, if water can be obtained from deep wells in gravel, it is undoubtedly a better water than that from near the surface. In wells driven into rock the popular fancy is that here is the best source of all. For what, seemingly, could be safer water than that obtained from the interior of a rock with an entrance of water from the surface, cut off by tightly sealing the hole around the casing pipe where it enters the rock.

Little thought is usually given as to the origin of this water supply said to come from solid rock many hundreds of feet below the surface.

A block of granite, or trap rock, or sandstone even casually examined, seems to have little capacity for containing water in any quantity, and the most superficial observer would hardly be convinced that water could flow through rock at the rate of from 20 to 30 gallons per minute, which is a common rate in the deep wells in Connecticut driven into rock.

By observing the exposed face of any rock quarry, however, we find that the supposedly solid rock is cut into blocks of greater or less extent, by a multitude of seams and oftentimes even by appreciable cracks.

These cracks appear to be at all angles, oftentimes even vertical or horizontal. They may be bedding planes as in the sandstones and shales, or due to pressure and contraction as in the igneous rocks. Whatever their cause, they readily may form channels down and along which surface water may move with more or less ease.

With this in mind it requires little imagination to understand that if there is at any depth a horizontal or nearly horizontal bedding plane intersecting these cracks from the surface, water from a considerable distance may flow freely under ground with none of the purification affected by its passage through beds of gravel or sand.

724

If one of the driven wells penetrating even several hundred feet through solid rock, at length enters a water-bearing crevice, there is every possibility that water drawn from it may be highly polluted from sources long distances away, and even from other surface drainage areas.

POLLUTION FROM PRIVATE SUPPLY.

An experience has recently been had concerning local pollution of a city water supply, which is both interesting and instructive. While, fortunately, it led to no serious results, the possibilities were such that a recitation of the facts may · be of value in hunting down a possible source of contamination to public water supplies not always apparent to public health officers searching for a cause for an epidemic of water-borne diseases.

All of the water for the regular public water supply of Hartford, Conn., is treated with chlorine gas and furnished practically sterile to the city. Secondary infection was discovered by the daily bacterological tests of tap water. The cause was sought and found in a connection with a private deep well supply to a large establishment located in the center of the city.

That the cause was discovered and the evil remedied was conclusively proven by the bacteriological tests before and after the closing of the connections and the fact that since then no suspicious conditions have been observed.

In the search for the origin of the pollution many hitherto unknown emergency connections to secondary supplies were discovered. At this time, and in connection with the search, an investigation was made of a number of secondary fire supply connections to factory property governed by so-called double check valves. A careful study was also made of the monthly inspection reports of these valves, extending over a period of about ten years, and a source of potential danger from these valves seemed

more real than had hitherto been supposed probable.

About the last week in June, 1918, the daily reports of the bacteriological examination of city water from the laboratory tap began to show positive results for B. coli, and in nearly every instance the differential test was confirmatory. At the same time no positive determinations were obtained from the samples taken at a testing tap a short distance below the chlorine gas station.

A careful study of conditions for a few days gave the following results: B. coli, raw water differential tests positive; treated water in 10 cc. differential tests negative; laboratory tap differential tests positive in 1 cc. The amount of chlorine gas used at this time was about 0.86 p.p.m. Soon after this the chemist reported that "the number of bacteria in the laboratory tap samples showed the usual effect of after growth and the presumptive test for the colon bacillus was positive twice in 0.1 cc., once in 1 cc., once in 5 cc. and once in 10 cc. Both tests in 0.1 cc. volumes and the one test in 1 cc. volume gave other characteristic growths of the colon organism. A positive test of the tap water was given special examination to determine whether the organism was a spore former, and a positive test from the raw water on the same date was carried through the same examination. Both organisms proved to be non-spore-forming types, the tap water sample showing 20% gas in lactose broth and the raw water sample 10% gas.

At this time three supply mains were bringing water to the city, the branching of these from the distributing reservoir being below the sterilization plant.

Although the B. coli determinations below this point had been negative, in order to eliminate any suspicion from the source of supply, samples were taken from each of the three mains at their entrance to the city. In all tests B. coli was absent in 10 cc. samples. This result seemed to indicate conclusively that the water became polluted after reaching the city and that the results from the laboratory tap were due either to carelessness in sampling or to actual local pollution.

In order to get an idea of the possible location of the source of the trouble, circles defining zones were drawn every ⅛ mile, using the laboratory location as a center. In these zones a number of samples were taken and subjected to intensive examination.

At the same time a careful inspection was made of all premises known or suspected of having secondary supplies in deep driven wells. Most of these supplies were used in connection with refrigerating plants because the water, while too hard for most domestic uses, was a number of degrees colder than the city water and therefore effected a saving in condensing processes. In most cases the connection was of small size governed by an ordinary gate valve with the city pressure from 30 to 40 lbs. higher than the well pressure. In all cases the city water was available in an emergency in case of failure of the private supply.

The result of the zone tests was very satisfactory and located the place of probable infection within an area about 2,000 feet square in the heart of the city business district and in the vicinity of the testing laboratory.

A careful inspection of the places in this area known to have auxiliary supplies, resulted in the elimination of a number where the secondary supply was without question carried always at a lower pressure than the city supply.

The search was thus narrowed to three suspected sources with evidence most strongly pointing to one of them. Tests of tap water for *B. coli* were taken in the vicinity of these three places, with the result that conclusive evidence of the origin of the trouble was located in the place expected. The cause of the trouble was as follows:

On account of drop in pressure in the city system during portions of the day when the draft was considerable, the city water failed to reach the upper stories of the building under consideration. This condition resulted in inadequate service to the sprinkler system, to remedy which a large tank was filled by pumping from a deep well driven into rock, a form of water supply quite common in Hartford, for certain purposes. The tank was connected with the piping from the city mains through two check valves, one of which was supposed to close when the city pressure rose to a point which would overflow the tank, and the other supposed to close when the city pressure became low, and so prevent water from the tank flowing into the city mains. The water pipes feeding the sprinkler supply were also tapped and connected so that water could be drawn from either system for supply to some parts of the building, the only safeguard between the two systems being a hand operated valve. Whether the cause of the injection of polluted water was due to leaking check valve or to some one carelessly leaving open the connection, is unknown. An interesting feature of the case, however, was a complaint received several months previously from a hair-dressing parlor, of the extreme hardness of the water on one or two occasions. As the city water has an alkalinity of from 20 to 25 and the well water about 200, the conclusion as to cause is now obvious, although at the time little attention was paid to the matter.

DOUBLE CHECK VALVE CONNECTIONS.

The order of the Board requiring complete severance of all connections with auxiliary supplies taken from sources other than the city supply resulted in a protest from several of the large manufacturing plants in the city. These establishments, in addition to the primary fire protection afforded by the city system, are required by the insurance underwriters to maintain an adequate secondary supply for emergency use.

Several of these plants take this supply from a very highly polluted stream running directly through the heart of the city and not only draining a populous area but also furnishing an outlet for some sewers and overflow for others.

These connections are supposed to be protected by the so-called double check valve system, which, in effect, is a pair of specially constructed check valves six or eight inches in diameter, with connections for draining the valves and testing their tightness predicated on observation of rise or fall in pressure under conditions of pressure on one side of the valve and none on the other.

Theoretically the scheme is perfect and without doubt the device is in general the most efficient one which has as yet been developed, if connection must be had between the city water and a polluted source.

Without question a secondary supply of ample proportion is necessary for the protection of important plants. This is required not only to protect property, but to safeguard life and insure continuity of employment to the inhabitants of a city, as well as to hold important industries where they are located.

There can, of course, be no argument but that no connection between a polluted source and a city water supply is a safer proposition, so far as protection of city health is concerned. In the case where a city supply is ample, both in quantity and pressure, for the primary protection, there seems no reason, except cost, why the secondary protection cannot be furnished by large cisterns underground or by elevated tanks, both filled with city water. I am aware of various objections which are offered to this method by some of the fire insurance companies, but it is a matter of fact that in localities where only city water is available, the underwriters accept the tank without increase in rates. This appears to be a good criterion on which to base opinion as to the efficacy of this method.

In the case of localities where the public supply is not adequate, it is necessary for the mill pumps to furnish the primary supply, the public supply acting as an auxiliary. In this case there may be some argument in favor of the connection between the two sources of supply. Without in any way minimizing the danger of the connection, the matter resolves itself into a question of expediency for local determination. That is, as a choice of two evils; which is the lesser danger to public health or risk of conflagration with its attendant hazard to human life and continuity of employment, not to mention loss of property?

Under the conditions just mentioned, if connection is decided to be necessary, without doubt the double check valve in its last design will afford the best protection at present available.

In cases where the city supply is ample, there seems no argument except that of cost of installation and maintenance of tanks. When public health is concerned, this argument does not appear valid, at least within reasonable limits of expense. What these reasonable limits are is one for local determination.

In the ten years' experience of Hartford, with twelve sets of check valves, the records show that eternal vigilance only can keep these valves even passably tight; that they do leak on the slightest provocation; that sometimes both valves have been found leaking at the same time; and that there is no assurance that they will remain tight even for a short period after test. The custom of inspection is a visit once each week to make pressure tests and once every four months for a thorough inspection of the entire valve.

In considering this matter, one of the best known sanitary specialists in the country, although endeavoring to see the matter as favorably as possible, yet felt constrained to say that while he believed such connections, (emergency supplies), could be made of little danger if installed by a properly designed check valve system; that the present design was not satisfactory; also that as a general rule, health officers and practical water works operators are opposed to connections of this character. The present design was considered eminently satisfactory when brought out ten years ago and hailed at that time and since as a panacea for all dangers from pollution at connections, yet since that time the device has been the subject of changes in design and is now unequivocally condemned. In view of these facts, the question naturally arises as to how far it is justifiable to proceed with the experiment for the sake of reducing cost, when the matter is one involving questions of health, particularly if it is possible to avoid these connections by other means.

□

CAMPAIGN AGAINST MALARIA IN CUBA, 1918-19*

F. VILLUENDAS, M.D.,

Special Commissioner of the Cuban Department of Health and Charities, Havana, Cuba.

ORGANIZATION

Division of the Territory. The territory of the two provinces was divided into 11 districts and two subdistricts, taking into consideration the complex circumstances affecting the topography, the lines of communication, the roads, the resources, inhabited areas, agricultural enterprises, etc. Some of the districts comprised a single municipaltiy, including the local health office (there is a local health office supported by the State in Cuba for each municipality); other districts comprised several of these, and others special extensions or areas of one or more municipalities.

Search for Paludics: Sanitary Police. There were created a number of offices of lay sanitary policemen in sufficient number in each district so that each of them could make the rounds of the district twice a week, following three different routes, which included the visiting of the hamlets, farms (sugar mills and cane plantations, etc.), groups of workers engaged in razing forests for

plantations, and country stores located on the roads and in the woods. These inspectors were furnished horses or railroad transportation. Every day after finishing his labor, each of these policemen was charged with making a written report covering the work done during the day, for which purpose a blank form was furnished him, and this report was in turn sent in to the local health officer or the medical inspector under whose orders the men worked. Their mission, which was explained in well-prepared written instructions, was to seek febrile cases, those suspected of being paludics, and others who through their appearance and worn-out condition should be suspected of being paludal, but without the recurrence of fever.

If the suspect was an ambulant worker without a family or permanent home in the locality, he was removed either to the infirmaries of the sugar mills or plantations, where mosquitoproof rooms were provided (protected with wire netting), or sent to the hospital, according to the locality where he was found.

If the patient had a home, or in cases of women and children, they were left

*A campaign lasting twenty months, beginning in January, 1918, and ending in August, 1919, was carried on against malaria in the provinces of Camaguey and Oriente.

in the home, but were provided with mosquito nets, given capsules of quinine, and subjected to rules and prescriptions which were rigidly enforced. If the rules were disobeyed the patients were then transferred to a hospital.

The policemen also had the duty of taking blood samples from the suspects and also from those entering the hospitals, before dosing them with quinine. The blood sample, to which a tag bearing the name of the suspect was attached, would then be sent to the Research Laboratory, and the result as to whether it was a positive or negative case was reported by telegraph. Positive cases were sent from the infirmaries to the special wards at the hospitals where the patients remained until examinations made at intervals of ten days should give negative result.

The sick who remained at their homes, especially women and children, were assiduously watched to prevent being bitten by mosquitoes, and were furnished with free quinine when necessary until they became well, as shown by the blood analysis made at the laboratories.

The majority of the owners of sugar mills and managers of cane plantations furnished the quinine required by their laborers, both for curative and for preventative purposes. The Sanitary Department also furnished quinine freely. Large signs in Spanish, English and French giving the laborers instructions to avoid mosquito bites, to take plain quinine which would be furnished them free, to communicate with the health officers in case of illness, and telling them what they should do in case they felt ill, were displayed at the railroad stations, restaurants, stores and places where people might gather. Pamphlets containing popular instructions were also distributed among them.

Examinations of the blood of children attending the boys' and girls' schools of the large as well as the medium and small-sized cities and towns

were conducted. In some cases from six to eight children among groups of from 60 to 80 were found to have the symptoms and infection, but without fever and attending classes. An investigation at the homes of these developed that there were other smaller children and women affected. Chocolate bonbons containing ten centigrams of tanate of quinine were used with success in cases of children. The teachers were left in charge of dosing them with three, four or five bonbons per day; others were treated at their homes, and in that manner much prevention was assured.

HUMAN ANTI-PARASITICAL CAMPAIGN

Anti-Anopheles Campaign (Against the Mosquito): The work in this connection was comparatively complex.

1. Agricultural concerns employing large numbers of men were made to install properly-isolated infirmaries well protected from mosquitoes, with a sufficient number of beds (in ratio to the number of laborers) in order to take care, without loss of time, of all suspects whether febrile or not. They were also required to employ nurses and a physician in order to obtain good blood samples and to apply quinine injections.

The sick were always transferred to these infirmaries during the day time, during which hours the anopheles mosquito is rarely found at large, but always under mosquito netting to avoid infection.

2. It was also demanded that the sleeping quarters of all residents of plantations, from the highest employees down to the field laborers, and whether located in large quarters or in small barracks, as well as the rooms of all merchants having their quarters at the large plantations, should be protected with wire nettings covering all openings and entrances with double or triple sets of doors, to prevent the ingress of mosquitoes. It was also demanded that all laborers sleeping in open quarters

in the field should be provided with mosquito nets.

3. The work also comprised the canalization, cleaning and removal of all grass and shrubs for a distance of two kilometers from all streams in and around the places where large groups of men had their quarters. At the large sugar mills, which are small towns in themselves, systems of sewage were installed in and around the mills; and at others the springs and water courses were lined with concrete for a distance of two kilometers from the mill.

The extensive and constant labor of leveling the ground to prevent the formation of pools and the canalization of the streams during the dry season was also carried out. Wherever it was possible, a well was dug near the location of large pools, until an absorbing stratum was reached and the water allowed to run into it. The pool was then filled in. In other cases the water from these pools was diverted into some large stream by means of costly canals.

The medical officers of the department are now obtaining topographical plans of the sugar mills grounds and the large plantations in order to point out to the proprietors the way to change the course of the streams and how to proceed with their canalization, refilling, etc.

4. Petrolization and O t h e r Resources. Besides the work carried out as above there was maintained an extensive as well as continuous campaign of petrolization of the stagnant waters and the small streams, which were kept free of the small weeds which are always sought by the anopheles. The most practical method of petrolization

was found to be the submerging in the streams of bags filled with sawdust which had been previously immersed in tanks filled with petroleum during 48 hours. These bags, which are made in different sizes in accordance with the width of the stream, are placed at a distance one from another in accordance with the strength of the current and volume of water. The bags are nailed to sprigs of wood, fastened to the bottom or bed of the spring and are renewed every eight or ten days. The oil escaping from the sawdust comes out on the surface perfectly atomized, and forms a film on top, which it has been found after having tried every system imaginable, is not obtained in any other manner. When it has not been possible properly to petrolize accidental volumes of water (at the mines and quarries), the proceeding adopted has been to dissolve salt in order to form a strong solution which has prevented the formation and development of mosquito larvæ.

The process of petrolization is singularly favorable during the dry season (the dry and rainy seasons in Cuba are irregular). By reducing the volumes of water where the anopheles may deposit their eggs the breeding of mosquitoes may be reduced, and when the rain season comes the strong currents carry away the small masses of larvæ remaining and there ensue periods when the number of mosquitoes is reduced to the minimum. The work performed has converted into healthy regions, zones which were formerly ravaged by endemic malaria. It is a hard labor which requires assiduity and tenacity, because any interruption might cause the advantage gained to be lost.

The A. P. H. A. Meeting is only a month away. San Francisco—September 13-17, 1920.

THE COUNTRY SLAUGHTERHOUSE; HOW TO BUILD IT

G. H. PARKS

Expert on Sanitation, Bureau of Animal Industry, U. S. Department of Agriculture, Washington, D. C.

Read before Section on Food and Drugs, American Public Health Association at New Orleans, La., October 28, 1919.

I T is estimated that in the year 1918 of all cattle slaughtered in the United States 3,921,000 were killed in establishments not operating under the Federal Meat Inspection Act of 1906; the estimate for calves is 4,310,000, and for swine 28,640,000 head. Of the number of animals enumerated some were slaughtered by the farmer on the farm, and the larger number were killed in the country slaughterhouse.

As such a large proportion of the animals are slaughtered in the country slaughterhouse, it is needful that the slaughterhouse shall be constructed so that sanitary conditions can be maintained.

In surveys made in several states the slaughterhouses were found in such insanitary conditions that if clean, healthful, wholesome meats were to be provided, extensive alterations in the buildings and surroundings were imperatively necessary. Methods of operation also required modification. The following descriptions of conditions disclosed by the surveys are taken from the files in the Bureau of Animal Industry of the United States Department of Agriculture. The slaughterhouses where animals are killed for local consumption are usually isolated and scattered about the town, either situated on some back street surrounded by stables and dwellings, or outside of the corporate limits where they are not subjected to undesirable observation.

One state reports that of 327 slaughterhouses inspected, only 23, or about seven percent, were found to fulfill sanitary standards adopted by the state. The Act approved contained the following: Insanitary conditions shall be deemed to exist wherever and whenever any one or more of the following conditions appear or are found, to wit: If the slaughterhouse is dilapidated and in a state of decay; if the floors and side walls are soaked with decaying blood or other animal matter; if efficient fly screens are not provided; if the drainage of the slaughterhouse or yard is not efficient; if maggots, filthy pools, or hog wallows exist in the slaughterhouse yard or under the slaughterhouse; if the water supply used in connection with the cleansing or preparing is not pure and unpolluted; if hogs are kept in the slaughterhouse yard or feed therein on animal offal, or if the odors of putrefaction plainly exist therein.

At nearly all slaughterhouses inspected, foul, nauseating odors were evident for yards around; swarms of flies filled the air and the buildings, and covered the carcasses which were hung up to cool. Beneath the houses was to be found a thin mud or mixture of blood and earth churned by hogs, which are kept to feed on offal. Maggots frequently existed in numbers so great as to cause a visible movement of the mud. Water for washing meat was frequently drawn from dug wells, which receive seepage of the slaughterhouse yards, or the water was taken from the adjoining streams, to which the hogs had access. Dilapidated buildings were the usual thing, and always the most repulsive surroundings and odors e x i s t e d. Slaughterhouses of fair sanitary condition were not found. They were abominably bad or else met the standard completely.

Reports from other states present similar conditions, but it is not necessary to give additional descriptions.

731

Another feature to be noticed in connection with the subject is that every slaughterhouse may be a potential center of disease, and naturally the poorer the condition of the premises the more dangerous it is. This fact is apparent from the character of the work performed. Even if only a few animals are slaughtered each week, the total number may amount to several hundred during the year and it is probable that some of the animals are diseased. If the offal from diseased animals is fed uncooked to the hogs which are raised upon the grounds the latter may become infected. Rats frequently overrun the place, and they in turn may become infected with trichinæ. Rats act as direct transmitters of trichinoisis to hogs.

If a slaughterhouse should be burned or abandoned as sometimes happens, the rats which inhabited the premises will wander to neighboring farms, and will carry with them the disease that they have contracted from eating diseased offal. If hogs suffering from hog cholera or swine plague are killed and the offal thrown into the yard draining into a creek, the creek becomes contaminated and the disease may spread to the farms lower down the creek.

A country slaughterhouse then to be operated under sanitary conditions should be planned to include essential features as follows: (first) suitable location; (second) abundant water supply; (third) buildings so constructed that they may be kept clean with the least amount of labor.

LOCATION.

The lot should possess natural drainage in order that pools of water will not be formed on the surface of the ground and remain sufficiently long to become stagnant. If the natural grade does not furnish efficient drainage, the lot must be graded and ditches or sub-soil drainage must be supplied.

The slaughterhouse proper should be so located on the lot that direct sunlight may be admitted on three sides of the killing room. This condition can be obtained if the cooler is towards the north, and the holding pens are towards the south. The east and west sides of the cooler may be shaded by other buildings or by trees, but the killing room should be in the open. Where the cooler is exposed on three sides, the arrangement shown is best, as the walls of the cooler are subjected to the least variation in temperatures and there is, therefore, a more even temperature maintained in the cooler with a resultant saving of ice.

WATER.

The water must be potable and must be obtained from a supply that is not subjected to pollution from any source, and the supply must be ample to permit of free use in cleaning the premises, both within and without the buildings, after killing operations have ceased for the day.

PLAN AND CONSTRUCTION.

The slaughtering plant may consist of one or more compartments. If of but one room, it will be a compartment in which the animals are killed and the carcasses dressed and prepared for food. An addition to serve as a cooler should be provided if it is necessary to hold the carcasses longer than a few hours and the temperature of the locality is higher than 45° F.

KILLING ROOM.

The killing or slaughtering room should be constructed with an impervious floor, and with tight, smooth walls and ceiling. Numerous windows should be installed in the outside walls so that an abundance of direct natural light can be admitted, as sunlight is of assistance in maintaining sanitary conditions.

The floor of the room should be made of concrete, asphalt, or vitrified brick, and the floor must be so constructed that it will slope or pitch to floor drains which may be either gutters or cast iron stable traps. There must be sufficient slope or pitch to the floor to allow all liquids to flow without interruption to the gutters or drains which must be of sufficient size to carry off the drainage quickly. A pitch of ¼ inch to the foot is sufficient for a properly constructed floor, but it is better to make the pitch ⅜ of an inch to the foot to overcome the inequalities of the floor due to faulty construction and faulty workmanship.

WALLS AND CEILING.

The walls and ceiling of the room should be as smooth as possible. The walls to a height of at least six feet from the floor should be made impervious to all liquids so that they can be readily washed and kept clean. Above the impervious portion the studs should be sheathed with matched and dressed lumber. Matched and beaded ceiling should not be used as the recesses formed by the beads furnish crevices for the lodgement of dirt and dust and also furnish breeding places for vermin. Portland cement plaster may be used on the walls, or galvanized metal sheets may be nailed to the wooden sheeting of the walls. If metal sheets are used all joints, both vertical and horizontal, must be soldered to prevent liquids and vermin from gaining access behind the metal sheets. The ceiling should be sheathed in order that there will be no accumulation of dirt, dust, and cobwebs, and the labor of cleaning the room thereby increased. Some ceilings will require less paint as the surface exposed is less than if the rafters or ceiling joints are left uncovered.

WINDOWS.

The windows of the killing room should be as numerous as the wall space will permit. They should be located so that the lower edge of the sash will be about five feet from the floor and the tops of the windows as close to the ceiling as construction will permit. The windows may be either sliding sash or casement sash that are hinged to swing like a door. The casement sash permits of the entire opening to be used and will therefore admit more air, which is an advantage in warm climates. All openings must be screened to prevent the entrance of flies and other vermin.

CONSTRUCTION.

The building may be constructed with a balloon frame superstructure and concrete foundation. The portion under the cooler is excavated to furnish a hide cellar. The portion below the killing room and fore-cooler is not excavated but is to be filled in with gravel or broken rock to a sufficient height to carry the concrete floor of the killing room. The purpose of the rock filling is to prevent ground water from being absorbed by the concrete floor, and it also permits the floor to dry more thoroughly. A storage space for hides is provided in the cellar under the chill room. The hide cellar should have an entrance from outside the building as this will prevent the odors from the hides permeating the building.

The offal and other refuse incident to killing operations should be removed daily from the premises and the premises should be kept clean to prevent maintaining a nuisance and also to eliminate fly-breeding places.

HANGING ROOM AND COOLER.

The hanging compartments are of two kinds, one in which the carcasses can be hung to dry and to remove a part of the animal heat. Animal heat will not be reduced materially below the temperature of the surrounding air. The other kind of a hanging room consists of a compartment in which the air is chilled by means of ice or mechanical refrigeration.

In localities where the temperature is higher than 45° F. the cooler or chill room will be necessary if the carcasses are to be held in storage longer than a few hours. The chill room is so constructed that the floor, walls and ceiling do not permit a rapid exchange of air from the inside to the outside of the building. The air of the room is, therefore, partially under control and can be maintained at a nearly even temperature by means of refrigeration.

Go with the Forty-niners to San Francisco, A. P. H. A. Meeting, September 13-17, 1920.

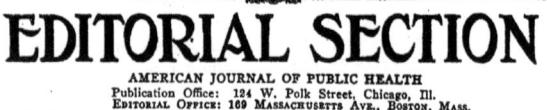

EDITORIAL SECTION

AMERICAN JOURNAL OF PUBLIC HEALTH
Publication Office: 124 W. Polk Street, Chicago, Ill.
EDITORIAL OFFICE: 169 MASSACHUSETTS AVE., BOSTON, MASS.

A. W. HEDRICH, C. P. H., Editor   J. RITCHIE, JR., Associate Editor

Editorial Assistants
E. R. HAYHURST, M.D.   P. M. HOLMES, M.D.   FRANCIS H. SLACK, M.D.
DAVID GREENBERG   JAMES A. TOBEY   JAMES M. STRANG
M. P. HORWOOD, M.S.   HOMER N. CALVER

Board of Advisory Editors
PETER H. BRYCE, M.D., Ottawa, Canada   PROF. M. J. ROSENAU, Boston, Mass.
CHARLES V. CHAPIN, M.D., Providence, R. I.   PROF. W. T. SEDGWICK, Cambridge, Mass.
EUGENE R. KELLEY, M.D., Boston, Mass.   PROF. GEORGE C. WHIPPLE, Cambridge, Mass.
W. A. EVANS, M.D., Chicago, Ill.   PROF. S. M. GUNN, Paris, France.

All expressions of opinion and all statements of supposed facts are published on authority of the writer under whose name they appear, and are not to be regarded as expressing the views of the American Public Health Association, unless such statements or opinions have been adopted by vote of the Association.

NOTICE TO SUBSCRIBERS: Subscription Price, payable in advance, $4.00 per year for United States and possessions; $4.50 for Canada and other foreign countries. Single copies, 50 cents postpaid. Membership in the American Public Health Association, including subscription to Journal, $5.00 per year. In Change of Address please give both old and new address, and mail before the tenth of the month to take effect with the current issue. Mailing Date, 5th of each month. Advertisements accepted only when commendable, and worth while both to reader and advertiser. News Items, interesting clippings and illustrations are gladly received, together with name of sender. Copyright, 1919, by A. W. Hedrich.

EDUCATION AND HEALTH ADMINISTRATION

A leading lawyer in an important city of Greater Boston narrowly escaped death or injury not long ago from an express train. He disliked to use the subway connection between the platforms, and made a practice of climbing the fence between the tracks to get from one side of the station to the other. He did this one day in the face of an oncoming express train and by the merest chance, thanks to the cries of the spectators, escaped a horrible fate.

It is probable that he has received many messages of congratulation, but it is very doubtful whether a single individual has expressed to him his disapproval of his practice. As an upholder and defender of the laws, it should have been his duty to take cognizance of the regulations and barriers established by a corporation to protect the users of its property from injury. In his neglect to observe the railway regulations he typifies an unfortunate failing of the American citizen—lack of discipline, and in this we are widely at variance with the people of European countries. It is said that in Paris a man who is run over by a street conveyance is fined because he had no business to be in the street in the way of the vehicle. Whether this is actually true or not, the principle exists in France, in Germany, in other Continental countries, of implicit obedience to formal laws and regulations. Their military training instills discipline into their daily actions. In this country, with its intense spirit of personal liberty, the citizen is apt to forget the regulations if out of sight of the policeman.

This characteristic independence, if it may so be termed, is one of the fundamental difficulties that confronts the health officer. He finds himself face to face with a carelessness or indifference or actual objection on the part of his citizens, and it is largely on account of this feeling that the police powers of the boards of health are necessary. Most of the routine work and most of the expenditure of money are required to oblige "law-observing" citizens to conform to those rules that have been formulated for the benefit of all.

Education of the people in public health has an importance that few are yet willing to ascribe to it. In the first place, public opinion formed through education is necessary in order that the health officer may properly formulate the regulations for his municipality. He cannot for any length of time maintain any standard in which he has not the support of his people. In the second place, education in public health and sanitation is necessary in order that the health officer may not spend his time solving the problems which a careless and unthinking public sets before him. Careless and unthinking individuals invite disease, help in its dissemination, and aid in establishing insanitary conditions, and they do this not with malice aforethought. Discipline, realization of the importance of obeying rules and regulations, is a first step towards their reformation. Public health education is a quick way to establish the proper state of mind. It should be a foundation stone on which the health administrator can confidently rest his preventive work.

MODERN MEDICINE

It is becoming more and more apparent to the medical profession that increase in knowledge in the medical sciences is so rapid and has come to cover such a variety of subjects that it has long since become impossible for any one man to keep abreast of all the branches of medical work. In a report submitted to the English Ministry of Health by the Consultative Council on Medical and Allied Services, the failure of the present organization of medicine to bring the advantages of medical science within reach of the people is noted: "Medical treatment, while becoming more effective, tends at the same time to become more complex. As the complexity of treatment becomes greater, it grows increasingly difficult for the individual practitioner to administer the full range of treatment requiring, as it does, access to such resources as those of bacteriology, bio-chemistry, radiology and electro-therapeutics, while the number of patients who can afford to pay for it diminishes."

The remedy seems to be as pointed out in recent articles on this subject in the organization of group diagnostic clinics. In such clinics the patient instead of traveling about the country and visiting specialist after specialist, receives, in one or two consultations, the coördinated efforts of a group of specialists working together. These clinics—and a great number are already established, the largest of which is that conducted at Rochester, Minn., by the Mayos—have been eminently successful in bringing to light the nature of certain difficult and obscure cases and relieving the patient of the necessity of paying exorbitant fees.

The New York State Department of Health realizing the value of such clinics to the residents of the state as a measure in health conservation, particularly in rural parts of the state where the most modern facilities for diagnosis of disease are not readily accessible, such as the laboratory and the X-ray, has undertaken the task of bringing these facilities to the public for its use. A description of the organization and operation of one of these clinics is described on another page of this issue. This is a most important and far-reaching step in the interest of health conservation and the prolongation of life and from the results obtained in New York State this group consultation clinic promises much for the future of public health in this country.

D. G.

INSIGNIA FOR THE A. P. H. A.

In the July, 1919, number of the Journal a prize offer was announced for an Association emblem intended for use on the membership certificate, stationery of the Association, for affiliated health organizations, and similar purposes. A few designs which could easily be reproduced are shown with this article. Many interesting ideas were submitted, but none were considered suitable by the Committee on Association Emblem. The idea suggests itself of extending the contest until the time of the annual meeting. This will permit members to think the matter over while on the train to the San Francisco meeting.

Emblems may be divided into two classes: first, simple designs, more or less geometrical in character, such as the Red Cross, Tuberculosis Cross, the Swastika, etc.; second, designs which tell a story or appeal to "human interest," such as coats of arms, the bell of the Bell Telephone Company, the picture of the two happy kiddies in the emblem of the Child Health Organization, etc.

Most of the designs offered to date fell within the second class. A considerable number showed maps of America as a prominent part of the design; others showed the American eagle; and still others showed a variation of the Caduceus. The Committee felt that these were not distinctive enough and that they probably would be confused with other emblems if, indeed, the Association would not be charged with plagiarism.

The greatest obstacle to date seems to have been the difficulty of emblemizing the idea of health. The goddess Hygeia has been suggested. The use of such a figure requires a label, as Hygeia to almost every one of us looks about the same as any other Grecian woman.

736

A few suggestions follow:

1. Simplicity is desirable. Highly complicated designs do not invite the attention of the observer.

2. If the idea of health or the fundamental object or characteristic of the Association can be suggested by the design, so much the better.

3. Ideas will be acceptable as well as designs, but a sketch will be helpful even if crude.

Designs should be mailed to the Secretary, addressed as follows: Secretary, American Public Health Association c|o Memorial Auditorium, San Francisco, Calif., or may be handed in the Registration Desk at the Association Headquarters in San Francisco, not later than Monday, September 13. Each suggestion should be labeled with a pseudonym, the key of which should be placed in a sealed envelope accompanying the design. The following prizes will be awarded by a committee at the San Francisco meeting:

$20 for the best suggestion.
$10 for the second best.
$ 5 each for the five next best.

BOOKS AND REPORTS REVIEWED

The Nation's Food. A Statistical Study of a Physiological and Social Problem. *Raymond Pearl. Philadelphia: W. B. Saunders Co., 1920. Pp. 274. Price, $3.50 net.*

This book consists primarily of a critical survey of the food resources of the United States, for which the author is rather exceptionally qualified, through his connection with the Statistical Division of the Food Administration.

The basis of the survey is mainly physiological, since it deals with the proportion of nutrients in food rather than gross totals, the food values being based on the well-known work of Atwater and Bryant. The material has been largely compiled from the census figures, the Department of Agriculture Yearbook, and marketing statistics from the Bureau of Markets. Estimates by those familiar with production have been relied upon in some instances.

Nutritive materials are classified as "primary," used as human food without intervention of animals, such as potatoes, fish or wheat; and "secondary," including edible products of animals used for human food, such as honey, eggs, milk and meats.

In the production of human foods the grains, meats and dairy products are the most important, in the order named. The United States is shown to be a grain producing nation. Of the ordinary grains, the survey shows conclusively the paramount importance of wheat. The energy content of the country's wheat crop is nearly double that of its nearest competing commodity. The wheat crop, the hog and the cow together account for 62% of the protein and carbohydrate used as human food, 69% of the fat and 65% of all the calories.

It is interesting to note that the relative importance of certain foods is not at all in accord with popular notions. A few commodities furnish a very large proportion of the nutritional intake of the people. The foods contributing most to the total calories consumed, in order, are wheat, pork, dairy products, sugar, corn, beef, oils and potatoes. It is rather a surprise to note the comparatively low rating taken by the corn crop, and to find that sugar, sometimes considered a pleasant but not essential part of the dietary, contributes more than 20 times as much to the carbohydrate intake of the nation as does rice. The only vegetable making a significant contribution to the food resources is the potato, and this amounts to less than 4%. Apples contribute about twice as much as rice and nearly three times as much as fish. As a natural corollary of the low rating of vegetables, it is shown that the home garden movement, patriotic and desirable as a war measure though it may have been, contributed to the total nutritional resources of the country only an extremely insignificant bit.

The statistical figures bring out clearly the discrepancy between theory and fact with reference to human food consumption. Theoretically, the American man may need only 50-75 grams of protein per day to sustain life; actually, he uses up about 120 grams. If the figures of the last seven years form any criterion, the latter figure is the one that we must count on supplying to each man equivalent of the population for some time in the future. There has actually been, in spite of patriotic pleas and "save food" slogans, only a very slight decrease in per capita gross food consumption since 1911. This decrease is probably due mostly to some reduction in the wastage of edible foods.

A. G. WOODMAN.

✠

The Woman of Forty. *E. B. Lowry, M. D., Chicago: Forbes & Company, 1919. Pp. 194. Price, $1.25.*

An important addition to the list of ten books in the sex hygiene series written by this author. He here focuses and brings to attention many self-evident truths which are abundantly worth while assembling. Dr. Lowry's admonition appears to warn against mental as well as physical obesity at forty. By keeping her interests keen, her philosophy sound, and her sympathies broad, the opportunity for the woman of forty to achieve health, happiness, and success is as great as ever. The author calls to attention the fact that a large percentage of famous women have become so after forty. The book is of vital interest to the women approaching middle age. It gives simple and reliable advice for the care of the health at this period, and is written in a clear and practical way.

✠

The Problem of Nervous Breakdown. *By Edwin Lancelot Ash, M. D., Macmillan, New York, 1920. Pp. 299. Price $3.50.*

This is a non-technical book of general interest and usefulness. In four well-balanced divisions it discusses the origin, the varieties, the prevention and treatment of nervous states, and the special cases produced by the war. The point of view is sane and superior to the advocacy of any

exclusive therapeutic method. Full justice is done to both psychological and physical systems. There is a wealth of classical and literary allusion reminding one of Osler's fascinating expositions. The author looks somewhat coldly upon the Freudians and ventures the opinion that the tide is setting against them.

Some passages are rather prolix and there are curious awkward phrases. What, for example is meant by "not unseldom?"—an expression repeatedly used. It is easy to overlook the defects of the text for it brings together in its moderate compass a body of material difficult to gather from the literature and of great value. Much first-hand observation is transcribed from Dr. Ash's own notes.

PERCY G. STILES.

✠

Pathogenic Microörganisms. *William Hallock Park, M. D., and Anna Wessels Williams, M. D., assisted by Charles Krumweide, Jr., M. D. 7th edition. Philadelphia: Lea & Febiger. Price, $6.00.*

This work has won a well deserved reputation both as a practical aid to the laboratory technician and as an excellent text-book.

The seventh edition contains much new material and it is evident that great care has been taken to make a thorough revision and to bring the subject matter as nearly as possible up to date.

Among other changes it is noted that the chapter on media making has been practically re-written and contains very complete directions for determination of the hydrogen-ion concentration or actual acidity of the media.

The Wassermann and other complement fixation tests are more thoroughly dealt with than in previous editions. The complement-fixation test for tuberculosis is recognized as a valuable diagnostic aid with the use of antigens made from moist suspensions of whole bacilli or from defatted dried bacilli.

There is a very complete résumé of the technique for determination of pneumococci types and also much additional matter in relation to streptococci and to influenza.

The new edition contains 786 pages as compared with 709 in the sixth. There are a number of new engravings. The plates are the same as in the previous edition though not quite so well colored.

As a practical reference book thoroughly covering the subjects of pathogenic micro-örganisms both bacterial and protozoan, their cultivation and care, the problems of immunity, the various laboratory tests and examinations; the book is a mine of information carefully compiled by experts who have thorough and practical knowledge of the subjects they present.

FRANCIS H. SLACK, M. D.

✣

A MAGAZINE IN FOUR TONGUES

The *International Journal of Public Health* which was issued in July for the first time is expected to become, in the words of the editor, "an authoritative medium for the diffusion of knowledge in the vast field of public health and preventive medicine, subject of rapidly growing importance and fraught with the greatest possibilities for the healing of the nations and the welfare of mankind." It is published as a bimonthly by the Department of Medical Information of the General Medical Department of the League of Red Cross Societies. It is the official scientific organ of that league, and is, of course, published in Geneva, Switzerland. The editor is Dr. Thomas R. Brown, Chief of the Department of Medical Information. The magazine will appear in four editions, English, French, Italian, and Spanish, each containing the same material. The names of the foreign editions are, respectively, *Revue Internationale d'Hygiene Publique*, *Rivista Internazionale di Sanita Pubblica*, and *Pevista Internacional de Sanidad*.

The *Journal* will be scientific and technical in nature, making its appeal to professional workers in the field of public health and preventive medicine throughout the world. The first three numbers, it is announced, will be distributed gratis in all parts of the world to organizations and individuals actively interested in any matter pertaining to public health. The magazine is a companion publication to the *Bulletin of the League of Red Cross Societies*—a popular periodical founded for the purpose of promoting "that education of the people which in all communities is a *sine qua non* for the introduction of effective public health measures and legislation."

There will be published in the *International Journal* original articles of scientific and practical import, critical reviews on subjects of timely interest, abstracts of important articles appearing in other special journals and in the general medical literature, and demographical notes and statistics bearing upon health conditions in all parts of the world.

Perhaps the most interesting feature of the first number is the series of signed reviews covering a large number of public health subjects under the general headings of communicable diseases, social hygiene, child welfare and nutrition, tuberculosis, hygiene and sanitation, nursing, and malaria. The original articles in this number are contributed by Prof. A. Calmette, Assistant Director of the Pasteur Institute; Dr. Richard P. Strong, General Medical Director of the League of Red Cross Societies and Professor Tropical Medicine at Harvard University Medical School; Prof. Ad. d'Espine, Professor of Pathology and Diseases of Children in the University of Geneva; Prof. George C. Whipple, Chief, Department of Sanitation, General Medical Department, League of Red Cross Societies, and Professor of Sanitary Engineering, Harvard University; Prof. Giuseppe Tropeano, Professor of Social Medicine, Royal University of Naples; and Miss Alice Fitzgerald, Chief, Department of Nursing, League of Red Cross Societies.

The publication of this Journal is one of the most significant developments attendant upon the decision of the Red Cross societies of the Allied nations to enter the field of public health in full strength. It typifies in its dignified and well arranged pages the organization which has spelled Red Cross strength in the past and which, on an international scale, may be wielded for great good in the field of public health.—

R. H. BRITTON.

For preliminary Programs of the San Francisco meeting, see the News Letter for August. If your copy has not reached you, send for another.

ASSOCIATION NEWS

HEALTH EMPLOYMENT BUREAU
HELP WANTED

Help-wanted announcements will be carried free in this column until further notice. Copy goes to the printer on the first of each month. In answering keyed advertisements, please mail replies separately and to editorial office in Boston, Mass.

The Health Employment Bureau also sends lists of applicants to prospective employers without charge.

Laboratory technician in state of Ohio. Must be able to do Wassermanns. Salary $1,600 to $1,800. Address 380, R. P. M., care of this *Journal* at Boston address.

Competitive examination to fill two vacancies in district health office force. Will be held by the Mass. State Dept. of Public Health at the State House, September 20th and 21st, 1920. All persons interested in public health work and possessing necessary qualifications are requested to communicate with Dr. E. R. Kelley, Commissioner of Public Health. Initial Salary $3,000.

Two assistant sanitary engineers for the Illinois State Department of Public Health. Salaries to start, $1,500 to $1,800 per year. Assistant analyst for the water and sewage laboratory at a salary of $1,500 per year. Recent graduates could qualify for these positions. The positions are under Civil Service but temporary appointments could be made, to be followed by examination which men who can suitably qualify should readily be able to pass. According to the State law, preference is given to men who have been in the military or naval service. For further information address Dr. C. St. Clair Drake, Director of the State Department of Health at Springfield, Ill.

Health Officer for a Southern town. Population about 12,000. Salary from $2,200 to $2,700. General health work including laboratory examinations, sanitary inspection, dairies, etc. Address Box 560, Goldsboro, N. C.

Position of Assistant in the Health Department of a large University in the Middle West is open. Young Physician with hospital training and knowledge of the principles of Public Health preferred. Communicate with No. 111, M. J. W., care of this *Journal*, Boston, Mass.

+

POSITIONS WANTED

Position - wanted announcements will henceforth be carried in this column. The charge is $2 per insertion. Copy should be received at this office by the first of the month.

Wanted: Health work by a graduate in medicine and public health; about ten years' experience, including county, state and municipal, both administrative and educational; will furnish any kind of reference required. Address 127, W. L. H., care of this *Journal*, Boston, Mass.

Will be at liberty to accept location as health officer or to do general sanitary and publicity work about October 1. Now have the rank of Major in Reserve Corps and commission in Public Health Service as P. A. Surgeon. Further details by correspondence. Address 128, care of this *Journal*, Boston, Mass.

Assistant Chief of Bureau of a State Health Department, with experience in organization, lecturing, clinic supervision and public health education; ex-officer, Army Sanitary Corps; other executive sanitary experience; B. S. degree; *wants position*, with salary of $3,600; requiring ability and experience worth more. Address No. 129, M. M. W., care of this *Journal*, Boston, Mass.

Wanted: Position as Medical Inspector of Schools by a Woman Physician experienced in this work. California preferred. References. Address H. C. M., No. 126, care of this *Journal*, Boston, Mass.

LIST OF NEW MEMBERS
Proposed for Election to the
A. P. H. A.
July 21 to August 3, 1920, inclusive.

Names of Sponsors are set in **Bold Face Type.**
Names of New Members are in Light Face Type.

CALIFORNIA
J. Severy Hibben, M. D., Pasadena.
Charles W. Arthur, Ph. B., City Bacteriologist, Pasadena.
I. R. Bancroft, M. D., Sacramento.
Katherine E. Reardon, R. N., State Bureau of Social Hygiene, Fresno.
Mrs. Robert T. Devlin, Red Cross Public Health Activities, Sacramento.
Mrs. Augusta L. Fraser, Social Service Worker, San Diego.
E. F. Glaser, M. D., San Francisco.
Edward T. Ross, Sacramento.
A. Wallace McWhinnie, Sanitary Inspector, Visalia.
William C. Hassler, M. D., San Francisco.
Joseph C. Astredo, Chief Probation Officer, San Francisco.
I. Irving Lipsitch, Supt. of Social Service, San Francisco.
Karl F. Meyer, M. D., San Francisco.
E. C. Fleischner, M. D., San Francisco.

COLORADO
Clinton G. Hickey, M. D., Denver.
Pliny O. Clark, Supt. Presbyterian Hospital of Colorado, Denver.

CONNECTICUT
Stanley H. Osborn, M. D., Hartford.
J. Frederick Baker, County Health Officer, New Haven.
Philip S. Platt, New Haven.
Alice Masaryk, M. D., President Czech-Slovak Red Cross, Prague, Czecho-Slovakia.

ILLINOIS
Maximilian Kern, M. D., Chicago.
Hugo Friedatein, M. D., Instructor Pediatrics, Chicago.
E. L. Lobdell, M. D.; and W. A. Evans, M. D., Chicago.
Jennie B. Clark, M. D., Chicago.
T. J. Brophy, Danville.
W. C. Dixon, M. D., Health Commissioner, Danville.
LeRoy Newlin, M. D., Robinson.
C. St. Clair Drake, M. D., Springfield.
George Hoffman, M. D., Chester.
W. H. Engbring, Commissioner of Public Health, Effingham.
E. D. Wing, M. D., Galesburg.
George J. Wohner, Kankakee.
Clarence N. McCumber, M. D., Lewistown.

IOWA
Professor Earle L. Waterman, Iowa City.
Alice J. Prattie, R. N., Red Cross Executive Nurse, Oskaloosa.

MARYLAND AND DISTRICT OF COLUMBIA
R. H. Riley, M. D., Baltimore.
Henry P. Fahrney, M. D., County Health Officer, Frederick.
Carroll Fox, M. D., Washington.
Howard W. Barker, M. D., P. A. Surgeon, Washington.
Alan C. Sutton, M. D., Washington.
Major George C. Dunham, Medical Officer, Army Medical School, Washington.
James A. Tobey, Washington.
Thomas E. Green, Ph. D., Director Speakers Bureau, American Red Cross, Washington.

MASSACHUSETTS
B. W. Carey, M. D., Boston.
Clifford S. Chapin, M. D., Great Barrington.

MICHIGAN
J. H. Kellogg, M. D., Battle Creek.
Lenna F. Cooper, Battle Creek.
Matilda W. Robinson, R. N., Ypsilanti.
Ursula Fulton, R. N., Red Cross Nurse, Ypsilanti.

MINNESOTA
C. E. Smith, Jr., M. D., St. Paul.
J. W. Hawkinson, D. O., City Health Officer and County Physician, Luverne.
Arthur A. Wohlrabe, M. D., Health Commissioner, Mankato.
Irving H. Kiesling, M. D., Health Officer, Nashwauk.
W. V. Lindsay, M. D., Health Officer, Wihona.

NEBRASKA
Professor H. H. White, Lincoln.
Drs. Welch, Rowe and Lehnhoff, Lincoln.

NEW HAMPSHIRE
A. W. Hedrich, Boston, Mass.
W. G. Weber, M. D., Alton Bay.

NEW JERSEY
Raymond S. Patterson, M. D., Trenton.
W. Henley Smith, M. D., Trenton.

NEW YORK
Halsey J. Ball, M. D., Glens Falls.
M. R. Engel, M. D., Health Officer, Hyndsville.
Mrs. Elmer Blair, Chairman, Public Health Dept., General Federation of Women's Clubs, New York City.
John A. Conway, M. D., Hornell.
W. T. Jones, M. D., Horseheads.
V. A. Moore, Ithaca.
M. Alves deSouza, M. S., Veterinary Inspector, Ministerio de Agricultura, Rio de Janeiro, Brazil.
LeRoy W. Hubbard, M. D., Mt. Vernon.
Elizabeth J. Nash, R. N., Supervising Nurse, Middletown.
Alyce M. McGaulley, R. N., Supervising Nurse, State Dept. of Health, Schenectady.
A. W. Hedrich, Boston, Mass.
Vincent A. Caso, Ph. D., Laboratory Director, Brooklyn.

NORTH CAROLINA
W. S. Rankin, M. D., Raleigh.
Frank G. Atwood, New Haven, Conn.

OHIO
Frank I. Mayer, Chillicothe.
L. C. Lehman, Versailles.
G. W. Moorehouse, M. D., Cleveland.
Malcolm L. McBride, Cleveland.
Correction: Minna T. Meyer, whose name appear in the list of new members for June as Health Commissioner, is visiting nurse for the City Board of Health, Columbus.

PENNSYLVANIA
I. M. Glace, M. D., Philadelphia.
A. S. Cantor, M. D., Dickson City.
A. W. Hedrich, Boston, Mass.
Joseph R. T. Gray, Jr., M. D., City Bacteriologist, Chester.

RHODE ISLAND
Fred F. Gorham, Providence, R. I.
Philip Hadley, Ph. D., Professor of Bacteriology and Director of Laboratories, R. I. State College, Kingston.
A. W. Hedrich, Boston, Mass.
Dorothy W. Caldwell, Rhode Island State College, Kingston.

WASHINGTON
Professor T. J. Murray, Pullman.
W. D. Hofman, M. D. V., Portland, Ore.

CANADA
A. J. Douglas, M. D., Winnipeg, Manitoba.
Mrs. W. J. T. Watt, City Health Department, Winnipeg, Manitoba.

HAWAII
C. Charlock, Hilo.
Alfred G. Souza, Assistant to Board of Health Pathologist, Hilo.

If you have not already sent in your member,
Bring him with you to San Francisco!

PERCENTAGES OF QUOTAS FILLED TO MONDAY NOON,. AUGUST 9, 1920

TOTAL NUMBER OF MEMBERS RECEIVED TO
DATE, 1,751, or 58% OF QUOTA

	Percentage of quota filled		Percentage of quota filled
Utah	472	Massachusetts	65
New Mexico	336	Oklahoma	53
North Carolina	285	Iowa	53
California	174	Missouri	51
Saskatchewan	142	Delaware	50
Colorado	142	New York	47
Idaho	125	Wisconsin	46
Florida	123	West Virginia	43
Maine	117	New Jersey	40
Maryland and D. C.	112	Manitoba	36
Montana	110	Tennessee	30
North Dakota	106	Illinois	29
Nova Scotia	100	New Hampshire	27
Rhode Island	100	Arizona	25
South Dakota	95	South Carolina	25
Connecticut	94	New Brunswick	25
Vermont	88	Nebraska	24
Alabama	78	Indiana	24
Minnesota	72	Virginia	22
Michigan	65	Kansas	20
Ohio	64	Kentucky	17
Arkansas	64	Mississippi	17
Washington	62	Pennsylvania	16
		Texas	14

☐

REPORT OF COMMITTEE ON STATE HEALTH SOCIETIES IN THE UNITED STATES

This report is the result of a letter sent to the national organizations doing health work as one of their principle activities. This letter asked the national societies for a list of states in which there were state societies organized by them or affiliated with them. After the replies to these letters had been received a list of the state societies in each state according to the information furnished by the national society was supplied to the health officer of the state for criticisms, comments, additions and subtractions. We admit that the list is not complete, but it is more nearly so than any other of which we know. Since new societies are being organized from time to time, a list dated March 1st would not embrace all the societies in existence on September 1st.

The information gathered from the two sources is tabulated in Table 1.

In the list of national societies there are 24 names. Three of these—the Conference. of Social Agencies, the National Woman's Federation and the Malaria Conference—were designated by one or more state health officers and are therefore included in the list, though they do not belong there.

This table shows that the number of state health societies runs from 2 in Wyoming to 12 in Maryland. In 24 states there are more than 6. In all there are 316 state health societies, including those of the District of Columbia. Some of these are separate organizations and some are sections or activities of other organizations such as the state medical society.

Three of the national organizations have attempted to form local rather than state organizations. These three organizations—the American Social Hygiene, National Safety Council and the American Child Hygiene—have 106 locals.

This is an average of about 6½ societies and 2⅓ locals per state.

On the one hand I am sure there are some health societies not listed. There are health societies in the list which have only a paper organization and some which exist on paper only. Several state health officers have written that certain state health societies on the lists sent are not active and even that some have no existence. Attention is called to these by a footnote to Table 1. This criticism is true in the main, but it is not entitled to the weight which might be given it.

With the exception of those organizations where a large annual meeting is an essential activity a society may be doing very effective work without having a large popular membership or a considerable organization or a convention of importance. For example, certain very active and effective national propaganda organizations have only nominal annual meetings with only a small attendance and only a small or a loosely tied membership.

Such points as this will be discussed more in detail later in this report.

Three of the states have two state health societies each, though one of these, New Mexico, has in addition three locals of the American Child Hygiene Association. Ten have four each. Eight have five societies each, three of these, West Virginia, Minnesota and Washington, having locals of other organizations in addition. The rather misplaced position of Minnesota in this scale is due to the development of various health society activities as sections of the Minnesota Public Health Association. Four have six societies each, Ohio having locals in addition. Eight have seven societies each, Iowa, Maine, Missouri, Montana, Nebraska and Wisconsin having locals in addition. Five have eight each, and of

the five Kentucky and Oregon have locals in addition. Four states have nine societies each and all except Kansas have locals in addition. Four states have ten each and each has locals in addition. Two have eleven each and both have locals in addition. One has twelve and locals in addition.

This is enough to make out a *prima facie* case for some kind of co-operation, affiliation, federation or amalgamation.

In Table 2 we attempt some kind of an analysis and grouping of the various national organizations. The American Public Health Association holds a large annual convention for the discussion of technical subjects, to educate and train those in attendance and to promote the interests of the organization and its members. It maintains a technical journal and it does propaganda work. It meets by itself except that one or more organizations, some well organized, others less so, meet with it. It organizes state health societies. Its membership is composed of health officers, sociologists, laboratory workers, statisticians, sanitary engineers, industrial hygienists and physicians, laymen and corporations interested in preventive medicine. Its work belongs to three types—education, propaganda, organization.

The American Medical Association holds a large annual convention for the discussion of technical subjects to educate and train those in attendance and to promote the interests of the organization and its members. It maintains a technical journal and does propaganda work. It meets by itself, though many organizations, some well organized, some less so, meet in the same city at or near the same date. It has a section on preventive medicine, though in the main its members are physicians engaged in the practice of medicine. It has a state medical society in each state and most of these have sections on preventive medicine. Most counties have county medical societies in affiliation with their state societies.

The American Red Cross does not have a large annual convention. It is difficult just at this time to classify its activities. It does not attempt to organize state societies, but does organize locals and group these into district organizations.

The National Tuberculosis Society holds a large annual convention for the discussion of technical subjects to educate and train those in attendance, and to promote the interests of the organization and its members. It maintains a technical journal and a popular journal and does propaganda work. In addition it holds regional meetings. It promotes the organization of state societies, some of which in recent years have taken the name public health societies. In some states these state societies have fairly large conventions, in others the annual meeting is only a nominal meeting. The National society meets by itself.

The State and Provincial Boards of Health meet with the Surgeon-General of the U. S. Public Health Service, and also by itself. They discuss technical subjects and organization matters. They are in close touch with the meetings of local and state health officers.

The National Child Hygiene Association has a large annual meeting for the discussion of technical subjects to educate and train those in attendance and to promote the interests of the organization and its members. It does propaganda work. It meets alone. Generally speaking, it organizes or affiliates local child hygiene societies and makes no attempt to organize state societies.

The American Social Hygiene Society holds a small annual meeting for the transaction of organization business. It maintains several publications. It is essentially a propaganda organization. It has organized a few local societies and has recently begun organizing state societies. None of these attempt popular annual meetings.

The Mental Hygiene Society holds a small meeting for the transaction of organization business. It does propaganda work. It maintains a periodical and issues other publications. It meets alone. It has organized a few state health societies, but these are propaganda organizations and none attempt large annual conventions.

TABLE 1

	Public Health Society A. P. H. A. Plan	State Medical	Tuberculosis	Parent Teachers	Blindness	Mental Hygiene	Physical Education	Health Officers	Nurses	Cancer	Social Hygiene	Safety Council	Industrial P. & S.	Child Hygiene	Sanitary Engineers	Women's Clubs	Miscellaneous	Summary
Alabama	0	+	+	+	0	+	0	+	0	0	0	0	0	0	0			5
Arkansas	0	+	+⁵	0	+	0	+	0	0	0	0	0	0	0	0			4
Arizona	0	+	+⁵	+	0	0	0	0	0	0	0	0	0	0				4
California	0	+	+	+	+	+	+	+	+	+	0⁹	0¹⁴	0	0²²	0		+³¹	10+6 locals
Connecticut	+¹	+	+	+	+	+	+	0	+	0	+	0¹³	0	0²²	0			9+5 locals
Delaware	+	+	+	+	+	0	0	0	0	0	0	+	0	0	0			6
District of Columbia	0	+	+	+	0	+	0	0	+	0	+	0	0	+	0			7
Florida	0	+	+	0	0	0	+	0	0	+	0	0	0	0	0			4
Georgia	0	+	+	+	0	+	+	+	0	+	0	0	0	0	0			7
Idaho	0	+	+	+	0	0	+	0	0	0	0	0	0	0	0			4
Colorado	0	+	+	+	0	0	0	0	+¹	+	0	0	0	0	0			5
Illinois	0	+	+	+	+	+	+	+⁸	0	+	0¹·	0	0²²	+				11+7 locals
Indiana	0²	+	+	+	0	+	+⁶	+	+	+	0	0¹⁴	0	+	0	+³⁰		10+2 locals
Iowa	0	+	+	+	+	+	+	0	+⁸	0	0	0	0	0²²	0			7+2 locals
Kansas	+	+	+	+	0	+	+	+	+	0	0	0	0	0	+			9
Kentucky	+	+	+	+	+	0	0	0	+⁸	+	0⁹	0	0¹³	+				8+3 locals
Louisiana	0	+	+	+	+	0	+	+	0	+	0	0	0	0²¹	+	+¹⁰		10+1 local
Maine	0	+	+	+	0	+	+	0	+⁸	+	0	0	0	0²²	0			7+2 locals
Maryland	+	+	+	+	+	+	+	+	+	+	+	0¹³	0	+	0			12+1 local

TABLE I—Continued

	Public Health Society A. P. H. A. Plan	State Medical	Tuberculosis	Parent Teachers	Blindness	Mental Hygiene	Physical Education	Health Officers	Nurses	Cancer	Social Hygiene	Safety Council	Industrial P. & S.	Child Hygiene	Sanitary Engineers	Women's Clubs	Miscellaneous	Summary
Massachusetts	0	+	+	+	+	+	+	+	+	+	+	O[13]	0	O[22]	+	....	....	11+11 locals
Michigan	+	+	+	+	+	0	+	0	+[8]	+	+	O[14]	0	O[16]	0			10+8 locals
Minnesota	0	+	+[5]	0	0	+	0	+	0	+	0	0	0	O[22]	0			5+2 locals
Mississippi	0	+	+	+	0	+	0	+	0	0	0	0	0	0	0			5
Missouri	0	+	+	+	+	0	+	0	0	+	+	O[14]	0	O[18]	0			7+4 locals
Montana	+	+	+	+	0	0	0	+	+[8]	0	0	O[13]	0	O[21]	+			7+1 local
Nebraska	0	+	+	0	+	0	+	+	+[8]	+	0	0	[0	0	0			7+1 local
North Carolina	0	+	+	+	0	+	+	+	+	.+	0	0	0	0	0			8
North Dakota	O[3]	+	+	0	+	0	[0	0	+	0	0	0	0	0	0			4
New Hampshire	0	+	+	+	0	0	0	+	0	0	0	0	0	0	0			4
New Mexico	0	+	+[2]	0	0	0	0	0	0	0	0	0	0	O[23]	0			2+3 locals
New Jersey	0	+	+	+	+	0	+	+	0	+	0	0	0	0	+			8
New York	0	+	+	+	+	+	+	+	+	+	O[16]	O[17]	O[26]	0				9+19 locals
Nevada	0	+	+[2]	0	0	0	0	0	0	0	0	0	0	0	0			2
Ohio	0	+	+	+	0	0	+	0	0	+	O[9]	O[16]	+	0	0			6+5 locals
Oklahoma	0	+	+	0	0	+	0	0	0	0	0	0	0	+				4
Oregon	0	+	+	+	0	+	0	+	0	+	+	0	O[23]	0				8+2 locals
Pennsylvania	0	+	+	+	+	+	0	+	+	0	O[15]	+	0	0				9+7 locals
Rhode Island	0	+	+	+	0	+	+	0	+	0	0	0	0	0				6....
South Carolina	0	+	+	0	0	0	0	+[8]	0	+	0	0	0	0				4
South Dakota	0	+	+	+	0	0	0	+[8]	0	0	0	0	0	0				4
Tennessee	0	+	+	+	0	+	+	+[7]	0	+	O[12]	0	0	+[27]	0			8
Texas	0	+	+[5]	+	0	0	0	0	+	0	+	0	0	0	0			5
Utah	0	+	+[5]	+	0	0	+	0	+	0	0	0	0	0				5
Vermont	0	+	+	+	0	0	0	+	0	0	0	0	0	0				4
Virginia	0	+	+	0	0	+[6]	+[8]	+	0	0	+	0	0	0	0			6
West Virginia	0	+	+	0	0	0	0	+	+	0	O[13]	0	O[21]	0	+[30]			5+1 local
Washington	0	+	+	+	0	0	+	0	+	0	O[9]	O[17]	0	0				5+6 locals
Wisconsin	0	+	+	+	+	0	+	+	+[8]	0	O[11]	0	0	O[22]	0			7+4 locals
Wyoming	0	+	+[5]	0	0	0	0	0	0	0	0	0	0	0	0			2
Summary	7	49	49[4]	37	18	22	29	23	28	21	11[19]	2[20]	4	2[26]	4[29]	8	3	1

1—Application A. P. H. A. doubtful. 2—Attempt to organize being made. 3—Same as 2. 4—8 of these are known as Public Health Societies 5—Known as Public Health Society. 6—Activity questioned by State Health Officer. 7—Said by H. O. to be inactive. 8—A section of State Nurses Association. 9—One local 10—Several locals. 11—2 locals. 12—Known as White Shield. 13—1 local 14—2 locals. 15—3 locals. 16—4 locals. 17—5 locals. 18—7 locals. 19—8 locals. 20—43 locals. 21—1 local. 22—2 locals. 23—3 locals. 24—6 locals. 25—8 locals. 26—14 locals. 27—Questioned by State H. O. 29—54 locals. 30—Mentioned by State H. O. 31—Health League.

TABLE II.

	Type of Annual Meeting	Principal Activities	Publications	Annual Meeting	Plan of Organization	Plans for Future	Number of State Societies	Do State Societies Hold Conventions
American Public Health Association	Large Convention	Organization, Education, Propaganda	Technical Journal, News Letter, Miscellaneous	A few organizations meet with A. P. H. A.	National, state and local health societies	Health Society in each state	7	Nominal mostly.
American Medical Association	Large Convention	Organization, Education, Propaganda	Technical Journal and many other publications	Many organizations meet with A.M.A.	At present, organization in each state	At present, organization in each state	49	Yes. Well attended
American Red Cross	Small meeting for business purposes	Clamot classify	Red Cross Magazine and others		Regional and local organization			
National Tuberculosis	Large Convention	Organization, Education, Propaganda	Technical Journal, Popular Journal, and other publications	Alone	National, regional, and state	Organization in each state now	49 and independent local societies in several states	A few large meetings. Mostly nominal.
State and Provincial Boards of Health	Convention	Conference, Education	None, unless we count state bulletin	Meet with U.S.P.H.S, once a year at least	National		22 state societies of health officers	Yes.
American Child Hygiene Association	Convention	Education, Propaganda	Transactions	Generally alone	National, a few state many local	Organizing state societies	4 and 54 locals	Nominal
American Social Hygiene	Small meeting for business purposes	Education, Propaganda	Several	Alone	National, a few state several local	Organizing state societies	11 and 8 locals	Nominal
National Committee for Mental Hygiene	Small meeting for business purposes	Propaganda	Journal and Miscellaneous	Alone	National, a few state a few local		22	Nominal
American Society for the Control of	Small meeting for business purposes	Propaganda	Miscellaneous	Alone	National, a few state		21	Nominal
National Committee for Prevention of	Small meeting for business purposes	Propaganda	Miscellaneous	Alone	National, a few state		18	Nominal
American Posture League	Small meeting for business purposes	Propaganda	Miscellaneous	Alone	National only		None	
National Organization for Public Health Nursing	Large convention	Organization, Education		Alone	National and a few state		28. 11 of these are sections of nurses society	
Parent-Teachers Association	Convention	Education		Alone	National and state		37	Nominal.
American Physical Education Association	Large Convention	Organization, Education	Journal	Alone	National and state		29	
National Safety Council	Large Convention	Organization, Propaganda, Education	Miscellaneous	Alone	National and in industrial centers	Organizing in industrial centers	2 state and 63 locals	Well attended.
American Association of Industrial Physicians and Surgeons	Convention	Organization, Education		Meets with A.M.A.	National and a few state	Organizing state societies	4	Fair attendance.

TABLE II.—Continued

TABLE II.—Continued

	Type of Annual Meeting	Principal Activities	Publications	Annual Meeting	Plan of Organization	Plans for Future	Number of State Societies	Do State Societies Hold Conventions
Conference of Social Agencies	Large Convention	Organization, Education		Alone	National and state			
National Federation of Women's Clubs	Large Convention							
Society of Sanitary Engineers								
Malaria Conference	Convention	Education, Propaganda		Meets with Southern Medical	National			
American School Hygiene Association	Convention	Organization, Education		Meets with N. E. A.	National		8	
National Child Welfare	Small meeting for business purposes	Propaganda, Education	Miscellaneous	Alone	National			
Association Medical Milk Commissions			Sometimes; Transactions	Meets with A. P. H. A.	National and local			
Nutritional Clinics for Delicate Children	Small meeting for business purposes	Propaganda	Miscellaneous	Alone	National			

The American Society for the Control of Cancer holds a small annual meeting for the transaction of organization business. It meets alone. It is essentially a propaganda organization. It issues pamphlets, but no journal. It has organized a few state societies, but these do not attempt large annual meetings and are essentially propaganda organizations.

The Society for the Prevention of Blindness. The analysis of the Society for the Prevention of Blindness is the same as that for the Prevention of Cancer. A few of the locals employ paid workers.

The American Posture League, is the same type of society as the Society for Mental Hygiene, except that the Posture League makes no attempt to organize local or state societies, being exclusively a propaganda group making no effort at organizing and not furnishing a forum for discussion of technical subjects.

The National Association for Public Health Nursing holds a large annual convention to discuss technical subjects and to promote the interests of the organization and its workers. It meets by itself. It uses the Journal of the Nurses' Association. In 16 of the 29 states having a state nurses' organization the organization is known as a public health nurses' society, while in 13 it is a section of the state nurses' society.

The Parent-Teachers' Association holds an annual convention to discuss technical subjects and to promote the interests of the organization and its members. Their national affiliation is with the national, state and local teachers' association. They issue what might be termed a year book.

The American Physical Education Association holds a large annual convention to discuss technical subjects, to educate and train those in attendance and to promote the interests of the organization and its members. It meets alone. Its membership is closely in touch with schools, teachers, gymnasiums and playgrounds and their employees. It issues a journal and does some propaganda work.

The National Safety Council holds a large annual convention for the discussion of technical subjects, to educate and train those in attendance and to promote the interests of the organization and its members. It meets alone. Its membership is more closely in touch with the industries and with the industrial hygienists. Its work is essentially propaganda in type. It organizes locals and state societies in some instances. Occasionally these subsidiary societies hold mass meetings. The membership of this organization is of the corporate type, in the main.

The Association of Industrial Physicians and Surgeons hold an annual convention to discuss technical subjects, to educate and train those in attendance and to promote the interests of the organization and its members. It meets with the American Medical Association. Its activities in the main are educational and organization in type. They are launching a campaign to organize state societies to meet with the state medical.

The Conference of Social Agencies hold a large annual convention. They have a section on Public Health. Many societies meet at the same time in the same place as does this conference. Their membership is drawn in the main from sociologists and social workers.

The American School Hygiene Association holds a large annual convention to discuss technical subjects, to educate and train those in attendance and to promote the interests of the organization and its members It meets with the National Education Association, Department of Superintendents. Its work in the main is educational.

The Federation of Women's Clubs has a section on public health. It organizes state federations and each of these has a health section. Its main functions are organization and education. Health is not one of its principal activities. The national has a large biennial convention. The state federations have annual conventions.

We have not learned whether there is a national association of sanitary engineers.

The Malaria Conference meets with the Southern Medical Association.

As to annual meetings we find that 14 hold large (more or less) annual meetings. Four or five have more than a thousand in attendance at a normal meeting. Seven hold small annual meetings for the transaction of business only. The remainder we cannot classify.

We group five as doing propaganda work only and five as doing propaganda work along with other work. Six are classed as doing organization work, three in conjunction with propaganda and education work and three with education work but not propaganda work. However, the line between education work and propaganda work is not always easily maintained. Several we are unable to classify.

Three issue technical journals, one issues transactions, three issue journals somewhat popular in type. The miscellaneous publications are numerous.

Fourteen of the organizations meet alone. One meets with the N. E. A., one with the Southern Medical, one with the A. M. A., one with the A. P. H. A. and one with the U. S. P. H. S. at least once a year.

Concerning organization as to locations, seven are given as national and state, three national only, one national and regional, one national, regional and state, one national, a few state and many locals two, national, and a few state three. Principally in industrial centers one, unclassified several. The answers to "Do state societies hold annual conventions?" are: Yes, 4; nominal, 9; No, 1. Several cannot be classified.

An interesting item relates to the natural affiliations of the bulk of the membership of several of the organizations.

PETER H. BRYCE, M.D.
C. J. HASTINGS, M.D.
W. A. EVANS, M.D., *Chairman.*

☐

EXHIBITS AT THE SAN FRANCISCO MEETING

In the past few years in increasing measure the exhibits at the Annual Meetings of the Association have been of value to health officers, who have been able through them to keep in touch with the most recent improvements in methods and equipment. At San Francisco, despite the handicap of distance and the uncertainty of railway freight deliveries, the exhibits are important. Below are noted some of the special features that will be shown.

✠

BAUSCH & LOMB OPTICAL COMPANY OF SAN FRANCISCO, CALIF., AND ROCHESTER, N. Y.
Visitors to Section 4 will have the opportunity of examining the new colorimeter recently added to the B. & L. line; also microscopes and accessories, microtomes, and photomicrographic and projection apparatus all of the superior quality that distinguishes the products of these pioneer makers of optical goods.

✠

HORLICK'S MALTED MILK COMPANY, RACINE, WISCONSIN
The exhibit of this company will occupy Booth 30, where a representative will be in attendance to distribute literature and answer all inquiries concerning the many dietetic uses of the well-known and reliable "Horlick's" products. The exhibit will include "Horlick's"—the *original* Malted Milk, in powder and tablet form, Horlick's Food and Horlick's Diastoid—products perfected by the experience of over a third of a century that are extensively endorsed by the medical profession, dietitians and health and food experts generally, because of their quality and advantages in the feeding of infants, invalids and convalescents.

✠

FRED I. LACKENBACH BIOLOGIC DEPOT
This San Francisco firm will install a special exhibit devoted to the most approved methods for the administration of Arsphenamine and Neoarsphenamine; will exhibit also an interesting line of serums, vaccines and viruses in collaboration with the Gilliland Laboratories of Marietta and Ambler, Pa.
At this exhibit also will be found the Red Cross First Aid Emergency Kit which is admirably adapted to the needs of automobilists and travelers. The price of the kit is $1.00. Mr. Lachenbach is interested in bringing these kits to the attention of the public.

✠

LYONS SANITARY URN COMPANY, INC.
Lyons Sanitary Milk Urn is the only urn that dispenses milk containing the proper percentage of cream in each and every glass served, without any mixing, stirring, or other agitating mechanism, and it makes no difference whether the milk remains in the urn 2 minutes or 24 hours. Place the day's supply of milk in the urn and draw it out through the faucet as you need it, and the milk will always be sweet, clean, cold, and fresh.

✠

METROPOLITAN LIFE INSURANCE COMPANY
The Metropolitan exhibit consists of a screen of illuminated photographs on glass depicting the Company's health conservation work for policy-holders and employees. The actual bedside work of the visiting nurse is shown on the left half of the screen. There are also illustrations of the instructive work of the nurses, and of the agents, in hygiene. The Company's educational literature on the prevention of illness will also be shown and copies distributed.
The actual work of medical examination, dispensary care, dental care, luncheon service, building sanitation carried out by the Company in its Home Office, constitutes the right half of this illuminated screen.
Two floor stands of six charts each, illustrate the effect of life conservation · work upon the total death rate of insured wage earners, the downward course of tuberculosis mortality, the extent to which typhoid fever is being eliminated as a cause of death, the trend of mortality of insured children ·in comparison with the general population of the United States, and the course of mortality in adult and after middle life. Three graphic charts of Visiting Nurse Service statistics will be shown. Three problems immediately facing the American public health movement are shown in charts—accident mortality, mortality in childbirth, and diseases of the heart.

✠

SPENCER LENS COMPANY
The exhibit of the Spencer Lens Company will consist of microscopes, microtomes, micro lamps, mechanical stages, delineascopes and various accessories for microscope and microtome work. Among the instruments shown will be the new high power Mon-Objective Binocular Microscope No. 2 H, with the distinctive feature of *convergent eyepiece tubes*, which the Company claims completely avoids the excessive and false conception of perspective usually produced. There will also be shown the Standard Clinical Microscope No. 44 H, with No. 485 mechanical stage, which may be fitted to any square stage microscope. Among the microtomes shown will be the Rotary No. 820 made with an inclined plane feed (the only Rotary Microtome ever made on this plan), which entirely overcomes the

inaccuracies usually encountered due to the up-and-down movement of the object. This microtome has gained an international reputation. The exhibit will also display samples of optical glass from the Spencer factory at Hamburg, N. Y., where 42 different types of optical glass are now made. This industry grew up during the war and played an important part in winning it.

✛

H. A. METZ LABORATORIES, INC.

Salvarsan (Arsphenamine-Metz) and Neosalvarsan (Neoarsphenamine - Metz), Novocaïn (Procaïne-Metz), Pyramidon, Parathesin and Holocaïn, all passed by the Council on Pharmacy & Chemistry, of the American Medical Association, will be exhibited in Section 10, Exhibit Hall, by H. A. Metz Laboratories, Inc., 122 Hudson Street, New York.

The technic of the preparation of solutions of Salvarsan and Neosalvarsan will be demonstrated by chemists from our laboratories.

Salvarsan is recognized by syphilologists as being the most important therapeutic weapon at their command, and in view of the campaign against the venereal peril now under way, this exposition should prove of decided interest to all physicians who are working in the field of public health.

✛

TAYLOR INSTRUMENT COMPANIES

Taylor Instrument Companies are displaying at Section 3 their new office type Tycos Sphygmomanometer. This instrument gives a very fine open reading and permits observation of detail that cannot be observed on smaller instruments.

In addition to the above, special circulars giving carefully prepared instructions for morning and evening baths are distributed.

The sedative values of water within narrow limits and influence upon the human body, make very interesting reading matter, as well as being exceedingly valuable.

There is also on exhibition the Pocket Sling Psychrometer, a convenient instrument for determining moisture conditions in homes, schools, office, factories, etc.

✛

U. S. NAVAL MEDICAL SUPPLY DEPOT

The exhibit of this Depot consists of a complete Navy Standard dental outfit, finished in white enamel, such as is now used in the hospital ships of the Navy. A dental officer will be present at all times to give such information as may be desired concerning use of the equipment and general duties of a dental officer aboard ship.

S. S. WHITE DENTAL MFG. CO.

The introductory installation of the Combination C, comprising the S. S. White Equipment Stand No. 3 and the Diamond Chair, was made in the Thos. W. Evans Museum and Dental Institute. Since then, a number of dental colleges and public institutions have installed this type of dental equipment. The essentials of design and construction which met with the unqualified approval in the original installation have made for the permanent success of the outfit.

PUBLIC HEALTH NOTES

Abstracts by D. GREENBERG, M. P. HORWOOD, JAMES A. TOBEY and HOMER N. CALVER.

Child Welfare Expense.—To convince the New Jersey taxpayers of the important uses made of their money and of the low cost of preserving life, it has been computed that the Child Hygiene Bureau's work costs about $1.20 for each individual cared for, on the basis of 100 mothers and 1,500 babies per district nurse, at a cost of $2,050. The work covers all counties, although not all of the 70,000 mothers, 70,000 infants born, 350,000 children of preschool age, or 650,000 children of school age are under supervision.

✛

STATE HEALTH NOTES—GENERAL

Alabama.—In a report to the recent Conference of State and Territorial Health Officers, Surgeon L. L. Lumsden, of the U. S. Public Health Service, states that "only about six percent of the rural population of the United States (January 1, 1920) is provided with whole-time local health service of any kind whatsoever." Between 30 percent and 35 percent of the rural population of Alabama is served by full-time local health workers.

Alabama has sixty-seven counties. In 14 of these, 20.9 percent of the total number, a full-time health officer is on active duty. In eight of these counties, units consisting of health officer, one or more inspectors, one or more nurses, and a laboratory diagnostician are maintained. In 11 of them regular inspection service is conducted as a phase of the health activities.

The University of Alabama has established courses in hygiene preparing its graduates to teach hygiene and health conservation in the higher institutions.

Arkansas.—At the annual meeting of the Arkansas Medical Society at Eureka Springs in June, Dr. Gus A. Warren, Black Rock, was elected President and Dr. William R. Bathurst, Little Rock, re-elected Secretary and Editor of the *Journal of the Arkansas Medical Society*. Hot Springs was selected as the place of meeting for 1921.

W. M. DICKIE, M. D.,
Newly Appointed State Health Officer
of California

California.—The State Board of Health has begun the issue of a weekly **Public Health News**, a mimeographed bulletin devoted to various health education matters, together with a communicable disease report. In the first issue plague and rabies are described and it is noted that the State grants by law an annual leave of 15 working days to everyone in its employ. Attention is called to the fact that the taxpayer pays the cost of the care of the feeble-minded and inferior individuals, and that he has the right to say whether his tax money shall be spent in prevention or in care, whether the State shall deal with causes or effects.

Connecticut.—In response to a public demand for an extension of the state program for venereal disease control, it has been necessary for the State Board of Health to establish three new treatment stations—at Willimantic, Meriden and Naugatuck, in addition to the six clinics previously in operation.

The city of New Haven opened on July 9 its local health center, which is to carry out a complete health program for the district in which it is situated in coöperation with local agencies.

Florida.—The State Board of Health is endeavoring to establish a venereal disease clinic in every county in the state. Ten are now in operation in addition to the ambulatory one.

The State Health Officer has had an interesting experience in reading the opinions of various "experts" during the recent plague outbreak at Pensacola. Here are some of the suggestions:

"Doctor, is it true that the fumigators asphyxiated a baby yesterday?"

"Doctor, at what hour will they burn the building containing the body of the plague victim?"

Prominent, but prejudiced citizen: "This plague scare is the biggest money graft I ever heard of."

Another enlightened educator: "This ain't no plague, it is nothing but blue-balls. These here doctors can't tell the difference between pox germs and plague germs."

Excited lady: "There is a ship coming into the harbor that has the bodies of three hundred people on board; they all died of plague." (Note.—No passenger boats enter the harbor of Pensacola, except small coastwise steamers.)

Sagacious Citizen, pencil in hand, demonstrating his opinion to eager throng: "This is the way the plague germ looks under the microscope (drawing as follows: '$')."

Elderly boatman: "Dock, if I had been in your place, I'da jest planted that guy and said nothing about his having died of plague."

Indiana.—The State Board of Health has established 20 venereal disease clinics in the state; and the average daily attendance is 100. 4,801 doses of arsphenamine were administered during the quarter ending June

30. 17 addresses and lectures were given in the quarter named, all of them illustrated with films and slides. The average attendance at these lectures was 274. During the fiscal year ending June 30, 1920, 7,688 cases of venereal diseases were treated, 11,481 Wassermann tests were made and 211,097 treatments given. Number of cases of venereal disease discharged from clinics as cured, 2,210. Average cost per cured case, based on state appropriation, $13.05.

The sanitary engineering department of the State Board during the quarter ending June 30, 1920, examined 279 public water supplies, 255 private water supplies, making a total of 534. Only 56 percent of these samples of water examined were found useable.

Trachoma is becoming a problem in Indiana, as inspection has discovered the disease practically present in every one of the 92 counties. The State Board has ordered the executive to organize the health officers in opposition to this infection.

At the last meeting of the State Board, 21 schoolhouses were condemned because of being insanitary and unfit for school purposes, and new ones ordered.

Maine.—A state clinic for physicians which will be devoted to the diagnosis of tuberculosis with special lectures and laboratory demonstrations on cancer and venereal diseases is announced for August 2-6, inclusive, to be held at Fairfield Sanatorium. This clinic, which is the first of its kind ever to be held in Maine, has been arranged by the Maine Public Health Association, in coöperation with the Maine Department of Health and the Maine Tuberculosis Sanatorium Trustees. Laboratory and X-ray demonstrations are scheduled for each morning, a course in physical diagnosis will be given in the afternoons and there will be technical lectures by prominent New England authorities.

Tuberculosis is on the decrease in Maine. Last year was marked by a lessening death rate for nearly all communicable diseases, and the total for tuberculosis was 786—638 of the pulmonary type. The figure for 1892, the year when the state was admitted into the registration area, 1,513 of which 1,352 were pulmonary, will serve for comparison, showing the notable decrease.

Dr. L. D. Bristol, State Commissioner of Health, has issued a warning to the seaport towns of Maine to be on their guard against the entrance of bubonic plague. There is some opportunity for this on account of very large amount of shipping coming into Maine harbors. Municipal authorities in the state are urged to give attention to ratproof construction and the extermination of the rat.

Michigan.—The Michigan Department of Health is conducting a series of clinics for the residents of Drummond Island, most of whom are Indians. The clinics, giving particular attention to tuberculosis and child hygiene, will be conducted under the direction of Dr. Kenneth Noble and a corps of nurses.

The new laboratory truck equipped by the Michigan Department of Health to test milk and water supplies and inspect waste disposal in Michigan summer resorts started its tour of the state July 15th. Demonstrations were given to the students at the University of Michigan and at the Michigan State Normal College before it visited Jackson county and Lake Michigan resorts.

Detroit, Mich.—After nine months' trial of the health center plan, certain changes are to be put into effect which experience has indicated to be practicable. The Delray district, which is that in which the preliminary tests have been made, has a population of more than 100,000 in an area of six square miles. It has been found that a single health center for the whole district is not practicable in Detroit. There will therefore be established a central office which is to serve as headquarters for the force of nurses, and to house the tuberculosis and general diagnostic clinics. It seems not practicable to locate the baby clinic and the prenatal one here, for they should be within walking distance of the mothers. Three clinics are to be established in school buildings within the populous sections. A further improvement is to relate the district medical inspector to one of the hospitals for experience in diagnostic work.

On the basis of a population of 994,000, the appropriation for the Detroit Health Department is $1.03 per capita. The distribution of this budget by activities is the following: Administration, 6.5 cents; sanitary engineering, 6.4 cents; records and accounts, including vital statistics, 3.7 cents;

food inspection, 7.8 cents; laboratories, 4.2 cents; hospitals, 31.3 cents; medical service supervision, 1.8 cents; tuberculosis, 7.1 cents; contagious disease, 9.3 cents; venereal disease, 2.9 cents; infant welfare, 8.0 cents; school inspection, 11.7 cents; dental inspection, 2.5 cents.

An interesting sidelight on the efficiency of disease reporting at times of an influenza epidemic is furnished by the situation in Detroit from January 20th to March 8th of this year. Approximately 12,000 cases of influenza and pneumonia were reported to the Health Department during this period. Of this number, 854 died, or about 7 percent. There also died during this same period from influenza or pneumonia associated with influenza, 1,302 people whose illness was never reported to the Health Department. There were 14 known cases 'to every death. At this ratio, the 1,302 deaths represent 18,000 cases. On this basis, Detroit had 30,000 cases of influenza and pneumonia in January and February—12,000 reported and 18,000 not reported.

. **Montana.**—The second annual meeting of the Montana Public Health Association at Helena, July 12 and 13, set forth a very ambitious program. There were 24 addresses, 34 papers, most of them followed by discussion, a number of round table talks, the showing of films and the consideration of business matters. Six sections held synchronous sessions with general sessions and joint meetings, together with a "get-together luncheon" and a reception, and the exhibition of health films. Among the distinguished visitors who spoke were Governor Stewart, S. C. Ford, State Attorney General, Surgeon General H. S. Cumming, U. S. P. H. S., and I. A. Hayne. Commissioner of Health of South Carolina.

Minnesota.—The State Board of Health has undertaken a campaign of information to the physicians of the state with reference to the use of the facilities furnished by the state in coöperation with the U. S. Public Health Service in the securing of Wassermann tests. Elaborate and definite instructions have been issued, and a warning is given that physicians must not make a charge for the work which the state does for nothing. In the months of April, May and June, 1920, the State Laboratory reported on a total of 3,100 Wassermanns, with a positive percentage of 12.6.

New York.—The State Department of Health has recently organized in the state two group consultation clinics based on the Mayo plan, whereby a group of specialists are brought together to assist local physicians in difficult diagnoses. This plan was the outcome of the shortage of medical assistance in rural communities. It practically gives such localities the facilities of the large cities.

To date, two clinics have already been conducted, and from the keen interest which physicians and the public have shown and the results which have been obtained, this undertaking promises to be an important measure in health conservation. In order to make the clinic a comprehensive one and to give it state-wide recognition, several state departments combined with the State Health Department, namely, the State Department of Education, the State Hospital Commission, the Commission for Feeble Minded, the State Charities Aid Association and the American Red Cross. The clinics have been in direct charge of Dr. E. C. Boddy, Sanitary Supervisor. Both clinics were held in typical rural communities, the first in Livingston County on June 8, 9 and 10, in the town hall, and the second in Chenango County on June 29, 30 and July 1, in the High School building.

In the preliminary organization a group of public health nurses under the supervision of Miss Mathilde S. Kuhlman traveled about the county visiting physicians, explaining to them the object of the clinic and inviting them to bring or send their difficult cases. Permission was also asked of the doctors to visit their patients and to invite them to the clinic. Cases known to the various state departments furnished leads upon which to work, and these cases, too, were invited to attend. Publicity was given to the clinics through newspapers, posters, clergy, grangers' meetings, etc.

The following departments of medicine, surgery and dentistry were represented: pediatrics, school hygiene, internal medicine, mental and nervous diseases, venereal diseases, orthopedics, prenatal care and gynecology, diseases in the chest, laboratories, X-ray, and dentistry.

The keynote of the whole undertaking is coöperation, which was ably demonstrated between the clinic staff, local physicians and local health agencies. The local Red Cross furnished examining tables, screens and conducted a canteen and a motor corps service for the benefit of patients who came from long distances.

A few preliminary results are now available. At the first clinic there was an attendance of 465 with 667 consultations. At the second clinic there was an attendance of 441 with 867 consultations, 221 laboratory examinations and 112 X-rays. The laboratory and the X-ray report, together with the findings on physical examinations, will be sent to each consultant who will then be able to correlate all these findings, make his diagnosis and send this to the patient's physician with suggested treatment and future course of procedure to follow.

Many of the local physicians of the county attended the clinic with their patients and took part in the consultations and were gratified by the advice they received and with the acquisition of the modern advance of the physicians.

The New York Milk Committee has established a Service Bureau as an aid to communities in need of better official control of their milk supplies. The Bureau is the result of a recommendation made by the National Commission on Milk Standards at its meeting held in New York City during the latter part of May. It is the purpose of the Service Bureau to help preach the gospel of clean, safe milk for infants and children by emphasizing throughout the continent the fundamental principles contained in the reports of the National Commission on Milk Standards. The sanitary character of a milk supply is a vital factor in the public health problem of every community and these reports contain suggestions that have been a great help in drafting effective milk legislation in the states of New York, California and all the cities therein, the Local Government Board of England, besides a great many other cities in America.

Through the meetings of this Commission, unanimous reports and recommendations have been obtained. These have been published at various times by the U. S. Public Health Service and furnished to American cities for the first time a basis for uniform standards and grades of milk.

The chief features of the work of this Commission have been as follows: A standard time and temperature for the pasteurization of milk; the recommendation that all milk be pasteurized excepting milk corresponding to certified milk in character; that milk be graded into at least three grades—A, B and C—according to its sanitary character and that each grade be distinguished by its own label on the final container; a standard method for determining the sanitary character of milk by the examination for the number of bacteria.

New York City.—A map of the health resources of Manhattan has been made by the Health Service Department of New York County Chapter American Red Cross which has for a distinguishing feature the use of color to indicate the character of activity in the health institution specified.

Types of institutions noted on the map are eight: hospitals, dispensaries of clinics, maternity centers, baby welfare stations, settlements and neighborhood associations which maintain health activities, nursing association headquarters, and health centers. Varied symbols, circles, triangles, squares, rhomboids, are used to indicate the type of institution, and twelve colors are utilized to denote within the symbols the kinds of health work done by the institutions.

Bellevue Hospital with its multifarious activity, involving all twelve colors, is, perhaps, the best example of this method of presenting the problem. The hospital symbol of two concentric circles is divided into twelve differently colored segments, so that with a very little pains the student of the map may learn that Bellevue cares for cancer cases, general and heart cases, contagious and venereal cases, tuberculosis, eye, ear, nose, throat and speech defects, nutritional conditions, child and infant welfare, welfare of women, skin troubles, orthopedic conditions and mental and neurological cases.

North Carolina.—The State Board of Health began the application of the laws requiring physicians to report births. One local doctor has been fined $45 and another $50, the latter being a second offense.

"It is the inherent right of every baby born in North Carolina to have its birth promptly and properly registered," declared Dr. F. M. Register, state deputy registrar of vital statistics, in commenting on the prosecutions being instituted by his division of the state board of health. "In this case the state board of health has extended 'its activities to the most northwestern county of the state. Its arm is long enough to reach across the mountains and say to the doctors and midwives who are derelict in their duty, 'you must treat every baby right, and register its birth.' Failure to comply with the provisions of the law will not be tolerated, and prosecutions will be instituted in all cases of violations, regardless of who may be affected."

In commenting on the recent prosecutions, Dr. W. S. Rankin, State Health Officer, in discussing the principle underlying the legislation which provides penalties for non-reporting, said:

'The laws with regard to the accurate keeping of vital statistics and the prompt reporting of contagious diseases are fundamental in health work. Their enforcement is a duty imposed upon the State Board of Health, and the board intends to continue its policy of making prosecutions when other methods of securing compliance with the law fails."

Nova Scotia.—Nova Scotia has adopted the spectacular feature of great public health caravans. Two of these, planning to tour the province, left the parade in front of the city hall on July 12 at noon. Dean Lloyd of the Anglican Church officially blessed the undertaking, and the cavalcades left the city. Each caravan is equipped with educational motion pictures and lantern slides. The personnel consists of six doctors, a dentist, and a corps of nurses. They will spend six weeks in visiting the coastal and fishing villages most in need of assistance. One of the caravans will move towards the north, along the shore of Minas Basin, skirting the northern coast of the Province, through Antigonish, Cape Breton, and thence to the extreme north of the island—a country rich in historic legend and second to none in Canada for its scenic beauty. The caravan that goes south moves through the historic Evangeline country by Grand Pré to Yarmouth, and thence it will travel along the east coast, ending its trip at Halifax.

These public health caravans are the largest traveling clinics and educational exhibits that have been utilized anywhere in the world, and for Nova Scotia to have

undertaken such a work indicates a great awakening of the public health effort. The plans are those of the Nova Scotia Provincial Branch of the Red Cross Society of Canada, which is in harmony with the peace-time program of the League of Red Cross Societies of the world.

A county health clinic for Hants Co. has been established at Windsor, while V. D. centers have been opened in Sydney, New Glasgow and Yarmouth.

Texas.—On account of the plague situation, the Bureau of Sanitary Engineering of the State Department of Health has been obliged to increase its force to meet the demands for information.

A survey of school children's health, which the public health nurse declares to be typical of the entire state and other states, has recently been completed by Miss Pearl N. Hyer, R. N., public health nurse of the Texas Public Health Association.

Examinations were made of 729 children in a certain North Texas town and 1,656 defects were found—more than two to each child. There were 385 that needed teeth treated, 20 who were over 10 pounds overweight, and 299 who were five pounds or more underweight.

"This survey seems typical of conditions throughout the greater part of Texas," said Miss Hyer, "and examinations show that more than 50 percent of the children have defective teeth, and even more have bad tonsils, while a large number have defective hearing or eyesight.

"Every community needs a public health nurse, so that these defects may be discovered and corrected in youth, and so that the children may grow up into strong, healthy, happy men and women. It is the duty of the people of Texas to provide this health insurance for the citizens of the future."

At the meeting in Austin of the Texas Water Works Association on July 19-20, 1920, most of the communications were related to health. State Health Commissioner C. W. Goddard spoke with reference to "The Importance to Public Health of a Safe Water Supply," while other papers considered Abilene's new reservoir and supply, relations of purity of water to public health, raw water settling basin, copper sulphate treatment and construction of purification plants. The proceedings were varied by business, election of officers, complimentary luncheons, auto rides about the city, a complimentary swim and a reception.

Virginia.—The State Board of Health has entered into coöperation with counties and communities in order to effect medical and physical inspection and correctional work through the public schools. The sum of $20,000 has been appropriated for this aid, the condition being that the community shall add to this sum an amount twice as large, the maximum for any one county being $1,000. Child welfare conferences were held during the week of July 24-31 at five stations in Roanoke County under the care of Dr. Mary E. Brydon, State Director of Child Welfare. A public health unit has been organized in Albermarle County and in coöperation with the Blue Ridge Sanatorium has established four tuberculosis clinics in the district. In Allegheny County under the auspices of the Virginia Tuberculosis Association a number of successful tuberculosis clinics have been organized. The Farmers' Union Picnic at Lawrenceville was the occasion for raising funds for the employment of a public health nurse for Brunswick County. Rockbridge County likewise has taken steps toward the organization of a county health department.

□

CONVENTIONS, CONFERENCES, MEETINGS

September 2-4, Duluth, Minn.—Mississippi Valley Conference on Tuberculosis.

September 6-7, Omaha, Nebr.—Missouri Valley Medical Society.

September 7-8, Ogden, Utah—Utah State Medical Association.

September 7-9, Saratoga Springs, N. Y.—Health Officers of New York.

September 7-9, Glenwood Springs, Col.—Colorado State Medical Society.

September 7-10, Holyoke, Mass.—New England Waterworks Association.

September 8-10, La Crosse, Wis.—Wisconsin State Medical Society.

September 9, San Francisco, Cal.—California Tuberculosis Association.

September 9, Cheyenne, Wyo.—Northwestern Tuberculosis Conference.

September 10-11, San Francisco, Cal.—Southwestern Tuberculosis Conference.

September 13-17, San Francisco, Cal.—American Public Health Association.

September 14-15, Springfield, Ill.—Illinois Health Officials and State Department of Public Health.

September 16-17, Springfield, Ill.—Illinois Health and Welfare Association.

September 16-17, Tacoma, Wash.—Washington State Medical Association.

September 20-24, San Francisco, Cal.—International Association of Industrial Accident Boards and Commissioners.

September 22, South Bend, Ind.—Indiana State Medical Association.

September 24-October 3, Cleveland, O.—National Safety Council.

September 29-30, Concord, N. H.—New England Tuberculosis Conference.

October 2, Lakewood, N. J.—New Jersey Anti-Tuberculosis League.

October 4-7, Waterloo, Ia.—Tri-State District Medical Society.

October 4-10, Montreal, Canada—American Association of Occupational Therapy.

October 4-8, Montreal, Canada—American Hospital Association.

October 7-8, Augusta, Me.—Maine Public Health Association.

October 7-8, Rutland, Vt.—Vermont State Medical Society.

October 9, Ottawa, Canada—Canadian Association for Prevention of Tuberculosis.

October 11-12—Wilmington, Del.—Delaware State Medical Society.

October 11-13, St. Louis, Mo.—American Child Hygiene Association.

October 12-13, Oklahoma City, Okla.—Oklahoma State Public Health Conference.

October 12-14, Chicago, Ill.—Mississippi Valley Medical Association.

October 13-15, Chicago, Ill.—Association of Railway Surgeons.

October 15-16, Roswell, N. M.—New Mexico State Medical Society.

October 22-26, New York City—American Dietetic Association.

October 28, Boston, Mass.—Massachusetts Association of Boards of Health.

November 8-11, Louisville, Ky.—Southern Medical Association.

November 13, Boston, Mass.—Massachusetts Society for Social Hygiene, Inc.

INDUSTRIAL HYGIENE AND OCCUPATIONAL DISEASE

Abstracted by Drs. E. R. Hayhurst and E. B. Starr.

Promoting Plant Efficiency.—The eight-hour day is not only more efficient than the ten-hour day in industrial plants, but is more economical.

This is the conclusion reached by experts of the United States Public Health Service after a careful detailed study of conditions and production in standard factories of both classes, which has been under way since 1917.

The plants surveyed were selected after a great deal of care. Each is a modern factory, employing such a large number of workers as to make any conclusions reached apply to industry in general. The other consideration was that the machinery, manufactured product and processes in the ten-hour plant should be sufficiently similar to the eight-hour plant to make a comparison fair.

The advantages are all in favor of eight-hour days, or shifts, as compared with the ten-hour day, and relate to maintenance of output, to lost time and to industrial accidents.

Here are the main conclusions summarized:

Maintenance of output: The outstanding feature of the eight-hour day is steady maintenance of output. The outstanding feature of the ten-hour system is the decline of output.

Lost Time: Under the eight-hour system work ends with almost full power begins and ends approximately on schedule, and lost time is reduced to a minimum. Under the ten-hour system work ceases regularly before the end of the spell and lost time is frequent.

Stereotyped Output: Under the ten-hour system the laborers seem artificially to restrict their efforts and to keep pace with the less efficient workers. Under the eight-hour day the output varies more nearly according to the individual capacity of the laborer.

Industrial Accidents: This phase of the study is of particular interest. Ordinarily accidents may be expected to vary directly with speed of production, owing to increased exposure to risk. But when fatigue is taken into consideration there is a marked modification of this rule. When there is a reduction of output due to fatigue there is an increase in the number of accidents; that is, in the

last hour of the ten or twelve-hour day, in spite of employees slowing up in work, more accidents occur. If for any reason production is speeded up in the last hours, when the laborers are fatigued, the rise in the number of accidents increases so rapidly as to leave no room to doubt that the higher accident risk accompanies the decline in working capacity of the employee.

The full report is contained in *Public Health Bulletin No. 106,* which is the first of a series to be published by the U. S. Public Health Service on the problems of industrial working capacity.

✛

Plant Dispensaries and their Equipment. —Factors which make for good service in factory dispensaries include accessible location, unit arrangement, and agreeable personnel. The writer emphasizes system in the dressing of patients and illustrates the time lost by a nurse in useless trotting to and fro and in the unnecessary expenditure of motions. Charts show daily variations in number of cases for the month of February in a typical plant in Toledo. The modern industrial dispensary is an evolution from the first aid cabinet. The modern plant dispensary has become the industrial clinic. The location is the first element in prompt service, the proper arrangement the second element. A design is shown for the plan of a typical industrial dispensary.—C. D. Selby, *Hospital Management,* April, 1920.

✛

Industrial Physicians Extend Their Organization.—Following the meeting of the American Association of Industrial Physicians and Surgeons at New Orleans which was held in connection with the American Medical Association, a campaign is announced to extend membership. The Association at last reports had 600 active members in what is now its fifth year. The membership has been a little larger but decreased some during the war. President Geo. E. Vincent of the Rockefeller Foundation recently stated that there were some 1,500 corporations in the country employing industrial physicians and surgeons, most of whom were full-time men. At the New Orleans meeting a program was set on foot to interest medical colleges and teaching institutions in extending their work to qualify their graduates for this important field. It is stated that the usual medical training does not fill the bill, and that about one more year of work of graduate character, devoted to such subjects as industrial psychology, statistics, sociology, public speaking, occupational therapy, functional re-education, industrial hygiene, occupational diseases, and the administration of industrial medical service is necessary. The officers elected for the present year are as follows: President, Dr. Otto P. Geier, Cincinnati, O.; First Vice President, Dr. Thomas R. Crowder, The Pullman Co., Chicago, Ill.; Second Vice-President, Dr. W. Irving Clark, The Norton Company, Worcester, Mass.; Secretary-Treasurer, Dr. Francis D. Patterson, Dept. of Labor and Industry, Harrisburg, Penn.; and Asst. Secretary-Treasurer, Miss M. S. Shane, P. O. Box 4055, West Philadelphia Station, Philadelphia, Pa. What is believed to be the first local chapter of the National Association is the Cincinnati Chapter, whose organization has been completed in the latter part of the early months of 1920 and which has adopted a constitution and by-laws. An innovation consists in making eligible to active membership only those who are full-time industrial physicians and surgeons and leaving to associate membership all others, among whom are included a number of specialists in medical practice. The Cincinnati Chapter has to date 58 members. At the meeting of the Ohio State Medical Association in Toledo during the first week in June, under the auspices of the firm of Heath, Selby and Hein, some 15 physicians of the state, prominent in this field, perfected a temporary organization for forming a state chapter. A committee was appointed to proceed with the organization and to adopt principles of organization. In this connection it is worth while to note that a similar organization of industrial engineers is prospective. Mr. Herbert N. Casson (*100% Magazine*, June, 1920) writes the following in answer to "Who Are Industrial Engineers?"—"(1) Industrial engineering is an art, a science, and a profession—all three. (2) Its scope is the whole field of industrial production—factories, mills,

mines, shipyards, etc. (3) It affects the other engineering professions favorably by offering them a new species of skilled service. (4) No man can qualify as an industrial engineer until he has spent at least five years successfully in the practice of his profession. (5) The position of the industrial engineer will be very similar to that of the architect." Some precepts from his statement might well serve as a guide for extension work in the National Association of Industrial Physicians and Surgeons.

✦

Mine Rescue Work.—Two men were recently rescued from death in Indiana coal mines through the bravery of fellow-miners and a knowledge the latter had gained in mine rescue work from the United States Bureau of Mines which had just completed a course of training among these miners. It is declared by the rescuers themselves that the two men would have lost their lives if the old methods had been employed.

The two lives saved in the Clinton, Ind., field are but two of the latest instances that have come to the Bureau of Mines and generally the owners and superintendents of the mines are free to acknowledge that the rescues are the result of the efforts of the Bureau in training the miners. It quite frequently occurs that the miners in a certain part of the country succeed in their daily work in saving the life of some miner before they have finished their course with the bureau. Already more than 50,000 men have been trained, and it is estimated that men are daily being saved by these voluntary rescuers and many wounds and suffering lessened and workers are able to return earlier to their work by reason of the skill of the first-aid crews.

In order to further this movement that involves more than a million men in the United States, the Bureau of Mines holds each year a great contest in which miners' teams enter for the championship. The next contest of this character will be held at Denver, Colorado, September 9-11, and teams in the East and West are now in training to enter. This time the contests will include Canadian and Mexican teams, and promises to be a great international affair in which the workmen of three countries will participate.

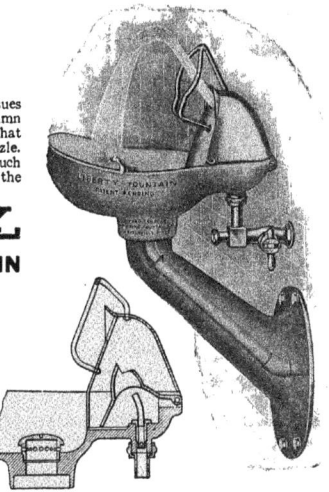

PUBLIC HEALTH
LABORATORY NOTES

Abstracted by Francis H. Slack, M. D., and Mr. James M. Strang.

Complement Fixation Test for Tuberculosis.—The results of 6,128 complement fixation tests made on 1,207 sera from 1,000 patients point to the fact that this is not a 100 percent test for the detection of tuberculosis. A considerable percentage of sera from incipient and far-advanced cases apparently contains insufficient antibodies to fix complement no matter what system or what antigen is used for the test.

About 70 percent positive results appear to be the average findings with all types of unselected active tuberculosis cases for many thousands of complement fixation tests made by many serologists using tubercle bacillus suspensions or tuberculins as antigens. Normal, non-tuberculous patients gave almost no positive results on repeated tests. Moderately and far-advanced cases in good condition showing constitutional symptoms gave an average of 85.2 percent positive fixation in this series.

The author concludes that the complement fixation test will not be very valuable, as an aid in diagnosis, to the tuberculosis specialist except as a confirmatory test. However, a positive fixation reaction will be of very great value to the general practitioner, not only as a confirmatory test but also as an aid in diagnosis and prognosis.—von Wedel, *Jour. Immun.* March, 1920.

✦

Biologic Studies of the Diphtheria Bacillus.—The morphologic characteristics of the diphtheria bacillus show a tendency to variations from time to time. The morphologic types are, therefore, apparently non-specific. The solid forms corresponding to types D_2 and E_2 are probably young forms of the more common granular types.

Solid-staining types of the diphtheria bacillus are sometimes virulent. They should not be regarded as avirulent on the basis of morphology alone. Virulence tests should be made to determine the status of carriers. Positive cultures from carriers whether convalescents or those in contact with cases should be considered virulent, regardless of morphologic characteristics until proven otherwise.

By use of the agglutination test two groups of the diphtheria bacillus have been determined. These groups are distinct, showing no evidence of cross-agglutination. The members of the two groups show no difference in morphology or in relative virulence. The antitoxins to these two groups are not so sharply differentiated as the agglutinins, as group antitoxins seem to exist in small amounts common to both groups, but the effectiveness of therapeutic diphtheric antitoxin would probably be enhanced by the inclusion in its production of a strain of the second or smaller group.—L. C. Havens, *Jour. Inf. Dis.,* May, 1920.

✦

Sterilization of Milk by Electricity.—In the conclusions of a report "On the Destruction of Bacteria in Milk by Electricity" (Medical Research Committee, Special Report Series No. 49) the authors say that milk can be rendered free from *B. coli* and *B. tuberculosis* by the electrical method without raising the temperature higher than 63° or 64° C.; that this temperature effect is very short in duration, and in itself is not the principal factor in the destruction of the bacteria; that though the milk is not sterilized in the strict sense of the word, yet the percentage reduction of the bacteria taken over a period of a fortnight is 99.93; and that the taste of the milk is not altered, and, so far as careful chemical examination can determine, the properties of the milk are not in any way impaired.

The authors scarcely consider the definite bactericidal action of the electrical current. They say that it is not due to copper liberated from the electrodes, for they found no trace of copper in the treated milk.—*Medical Officer,* May 22, 1920, 200. *(D. G.)*

The Preliminary Programs have been published in the August NEWS LETTER? Did you get your copy?

American Journal of Public Health

Official Monthly Publication of the American Public Health Association

Publication office: 124 W. Polk Street, Chicago, Ill.

Editorial office: 169 Massachusetts Ave., Boston, Mass.

Subscription price $4 per year. American Public Health Association membership, including subscription, $5 per year.

Subscriptions and memberships may be sent to the A. P. H. A., 169 Massachusetts Ave., Boston, Mass.

| Vol. X | OCTOBER, 1920 | No. 10 |

ENDEMIC DISEASES VS. ACUTE EPIDEMICS

MAZÿCK P. RAVENEL, M.D.

*Professor Preventive Medicine, University of Missouri
Columbia, Mo.*

Read before Public Health Administration Section, American Public Health Association, at San Francisco, Cal., September 15, 1920.

Epidemics are cared for through the incident terror of the people, and there is always money to fight them and investigate, but the far more important insidious endemics attract little interest or popular support. Attention to reduction in morbidity, rather than mortality, rates is the "stitch in time" plea of Dr. Ravenel.

EPIDEMIC diseases break upon a community often with little warning, strike terror into the community, demoralize business, reap their harvest of victims and pass on, leaving physicians, nurses and the general public exhausted as well as somewhat dumbfounded by what has happened. Perhaps a few chronic cases may be left behind, some other diseases may be aggravated, and some may carry their scars for years or even for life, but all of these are greatly in the minority. The vast majority of those stricken recover promptly and in a few weeks or months, at most, have returned fully to accustomed health and vigor. This was the history of the worst and most extensive epidemic that has ever visited this country, and one of the worst recorded in history for the whole world—the epidemic of influenza in 1918-1919. We have scarcely yet recovered our equilibrium and scientifically are still staggering under the impact of the blow, yet it must be admitted that in epidemic form the disease has accomplished its mission and has gone, leaving little behind physically except the graves of its victims to remind us of its visit. In spite of its appalling death-rate business was only temporarily disturbed, and those who survived speedily regained their normal health and strength. The scars left on the nation are the graves of the young who might otherwise have lived to a useful citizenship. The nation lost totally a deplorably large number of its citizens, but the loss ceased with the epidemic, and there are no maimed and wounded to be cared for, no burden to be carried for years to come.

Such is the history of epidemics generally—they come, rage and go on their way, leaving us little the worse except for the loss of life.

Entirely different is the picture presented by endemic diseases—a low death-rate as a rule, but a high sick-rate, a large proportion of the community more or less incapacitated for mental or physical work day after day, week after week, month after month and year after year, business and production slowed, vigor and manhood sapped, character and courage lost, progress stopped, districts depopulated, and as history shows, perhaps an entire people may fall before more vigorous enemies and disappear.

Two great civilizations of the past, both of which left treasures of literature, poetry and art, which have never been surpassed and seldom · equalled, have disappeared. One had its home in Greece, the other in Italy. It seems fairly certain that endemic disease, especially malaria, played a large part in the decline and fall of these ancient peoples, sapping their vitality, destroying their health and changing their character. A study of the facts we have been able to collect teaches an interesting and useful lesson.

Greece. Prior to B. C. 500, only two references to malaria—both of which are doubtful—are known in Greek literature. The writings of Hippocrates, as well as those of lay authors, prove that in 400 B. C. malaria was endemic in many parts of the Greek world, the types are clearly described, and the effects on the people noted. Malarial cachexia is well described—its victims are said to have large spleens but thin faces and shoulders; fatal dropsies are common; the birth-rate is injuriously affected by the physical condition of the women; aging is premature and the span of life is short. The inhabitants of malarial districts are described as being short, stout, dark-haired, dark-colored and bilious, lacking in courage as well as endurance. The statement that people in malarial districts were dark-haired may indicate that the fair northern element to which the Greeks seem to have owed their best qualities had disappeared or was disappearing. It seems probable that malaria was known in the medical schools even before Hippocrates, but this does not imply that it was prevalent in Greece itself, since it may have been observed in Asia Minor. Passages in Herodotus indicate that the Ionian Greeks had become infected by the latter half of the sixth century B. C. We are told that Dionysius attempted to train the crews of the fleet collected to resist the Persians. For a short time they persisted in the drills but soon became exhausted by the unusual exertion and heat, and refused to continue. Many became ill and many more were expecting to fall ill. While there is no certain evidence that malaria was the illness brought on by exhaustion and heat in this case, the story accords with what might have been expected among malarial carriers—the attack would be precipitated.

From both lay and medical writers we have abundant evidence that malaria was widespread in Greece from 400 B. C. and that its effects were pernicious. There is no positive evidence to prove that it did not exist before, or that it was introduced about this time. What evidence there is on these points is negative. That it became markedly more prevalent about this time seems fairly clear. A statue of "Health-Athena" was erected in the Acropolis at Athens between 429 and 400 B. C. The worship of the health goddess is usually referred to as connected with plague, but there is as good reason to believe that it was prompted by malaria. The worship of Æsculapius, the god of healing, was introduced into Athens from Epidaurus about the close of the fifth century. His festivals were in March and September, respectively, the beginning of the malarial season in Greece and its height. All evidence points to the increase of ill health during this period. Medical history shows a steady decline from the rational methods of treatment introduced by Hippocrates and an increasing belief in dream-oracles, charms and other superstitions, a mixture of religion, magic and empiricism.

Perhaps no other disease would tend to foster such practices as much as malaria. Quinine was not known, and no specific cure of the disease was possible. Spontaneous cure is known to occur in all types of malaria except the pernicious, and the chief factors in such cures are diet, rest and change. It is then easy to understand how such cures were attributed to supernatural agencies, with the consequent increase of faith in such procedures, just as at the present day we see the origin and growth of medical cults and practices founded on the fallacy "post hoc ergo propter hoc," and the adoption of these cults by otherwise intelligent persons.

The blighting effects of malaria on energy and character were recognized by the early Greeks. The word melancholy, meaning black bile, occurs soon after the Greek words for malarial fever became common. Melancholia was the disease caused by black bile, to which quartan fevers were attributed by many Greek physicians, and Galen stated that large spleens were due to an excess of the "melancholy humor." Certainly all melancholia was not malarial in origin, but there can be little question that malaria was the chief cause of the condition.

There is no doubt that contemporaneously with the increase in malaria, as shown in both medical and lay writings, Greek character began to change for the worse—decay set in. Their brilliancy left them, initiative was lost, vacillation and indecision, weakness, cowardly depression and cruelty marked their conduct. The philosophy of even their best writers became pessimistic, and their former lofty patriotism was lost.

It would be extreme to attribute to the spread of malaria alone the loss of physical excellence, mental and moral strength, and the many other fine characteristics of the ancient Greeks, yet it is possible that malaria might have been the fundamental cause. Other factors were certainly operative—chiefly prolonged and disastrous wars, perhaps made unsuccessful by the changes in Greek character. It is true that the most prolonged of these wars were civil, but the bad effects certainly extended beyond the states engaged. The flower of the young manhood was withdrawn from productive pursuits and many fell in battle. Agriculture must have come almost to a standstill, and with it drainage of the fields, which would become swampy and fertile breeding places for mosquitoes.

There is strong evidence that malaria occurred in epidemics and became endemic, though other epidemics are recorded, notably the "plague," which smote Athens after the Peloponnesian war.

With the decline of agriculture and increase in malaria there doubtless came the emigration of the more intelligent and energetic seeking healthier homes, and the degradation of those remaining, an effect of malaria recorded by Hippocrates. It is impossible to differentiate cause from effect with accuracy. A vicious circle was no doubt formed. In Greece as in Italy malaria increased as prosperity declined and prosperity declined as malaria increased. Pausanius, A. D. 180, states that the weakness of the Greeks in the third century B. C. was due to disease, and attributes the power of the Achæan League partly to the relative freedom from disease of its members. Plutarch says that the Greeks of his day were obliged to avoid fatigue lest an attack of fever should be brought on. "That malaria precipitated the decline can hardly be doubted; that it was the determining factor in most cases is scarcely less certain."

There is some authority as well as

good reason to believe that malaria played a part in the downfall of Sybaris, one of the most wealthy cities of ancient times and so populous that we are told they put an army of 300,000 men in the field. Their name has come down to us a synonym for love of ease and pleasure, yet the great wealth and influence of these people prove that they had energy and determination at one time. Their reputation for love of ease and effeminacy may have come from the precautions necessary to preserve health. The city was located in a hollow at the junction of the Crathis and Sybaris rivers, where it was hot at midday and cold at morning and evening. From this probably arose the saying that he who did not wish to die young must avoid seeing the sun when it rose or when it set—advice which might well be given in a malarial district. Probably here as elsewhere, malaria was only one of several factors in the decay of the people. The city was finally conquered by the inhabitants of Croton, who though vastly inferior in numbers to the Sybarites, turned the course of the Crathis to inundate the city, the ancient site of which is now a malarious swamp. It is of interest to note that ancient writers speak of Croton as being proverbial for its healthfulness, and this probably accounted in part at least, for their conquest over superior numbers.

Italy. The history of Italy is not so conclusive, though we have many remarkable facts which have not yet been explained in any way, and are satisfactorily accounted for by the increasing prevalence of an endemic disease weakening the people physically and morally. Without entering into controversial points as to the origin and identity of the Etruscans, it may be stated with certainty that they came from abroad ages before Rome was founded, and through superior skill and energy subdued the various people inhabiting the land, possessed themselves of the larger part of the Italian peninsula, remained dominant for many centuries, built populous cities fortified by mighty walls, attained a high degree of civilization, second only to that of the Greeks, developed navigation and commerce to an extent that made them for centuries "lords of the sea," became eminent in military tactics, agriculture, medicine, arts and other sciences, especially astronomy.

"Etruria was of old densely populated, not only in those parts which are still inhabited, but also, as is proved by remains of cities and cemeteries, in tracts now desolated by malaria and relapsed into the desert; and what is now the fen or the jungle, the haunt of the wild-boar, the buffalo, the fox, and the noxious reptile, where man often dreads to stay his steps, and hurries away as from a plague stricken land * * * of old yielded rich harvests of corn, wine and oil, and contained numerous cities mighty and opulent, into whose laps poured the treasures of the East, and the more precious produce of Hellenic genius."

This wonderful people disappeared leaving no history of itself. Of the internal life and customs of the nation we have learned only recently through exploration and excavation. Their great reverence for the dead and firm belief in a future life led them to store in their tombs treasures of art, articles of personal adornment, vases, urns, mirrors, et cetera, which have revealed much of their life to us.

"In five centuries the Pontine district was converted from a fertile land, so thickly populated with a warlike people as to excite the wonder of the historian, into a dreary marsh with few inhabitants and more or less unhealthy."

Without question more than one cause must have been operative in bringing about the downfall and disappearance of such a powerful and cultured people involving the destruction of beautiful cities, one of which, Veii, equalled in size Athens or Rome, and which for the magnificence of its buildings was so preferred by the Romans to the Eternal City itself, that only the eloquence of one man prevented its becoming Roma Nova,'and mistress of the world.

In attributing to malaria the primary or even an important role in the production of this desolation, we at once meet with the difficulty, as in the case of Greece, of showing that malaria did not exist, or was not prevalent, among these people during the period of their rise and greatness, and that it later became prevalent. This can be done only by inference. It is not conceivable that the Etruscans should have established themselves, built great fortified cities, and reached such heights of prosperity and civilization, in a country so fever stricken as this territory has been for centuries past. Even with our present knowledge malaria is perhaps the greatest obstacle to colonization and acclimation of European races in the tropical climates.

If malaria had been common, some reference to it would surely be found in the literature of the period, yet the first mention of it we find in Plautus, who died B. C. 184. Cato the Censor, B. C. 232-148, gives advice as to the location of a country house, and speaks of the unhealthfulness of marshy places. Since Cato wrote on many medical subjects, it seems that malaria would have been mentioned had it been known. It appears, therefore, that it must have been absent or so slight as to have escaped attention in his day.

Varro, B. C. 118-29, evidently knew malaria and suggested the etiology, which is perhaps the earliest statement concerning the relation of micro-organisms and disease. He says: "It is also to be noticed, if there be marshy places, that certain minute animals breed which are invisible to the eye, and yet, getting into the system through the mouth and nostrils, cause serious disorders."

Cicero, B. C. 106-43, mentions the tertian and quartan types of malaria, and Livy, B. C. 59-A. D. 17, gives evidence of having known the disease.

Suetonius tells us that Caesar, B. C. 100-44 when fleeing from Sulla, had frequently to change his hiding place "although aggravating his quartan fever." Pliny, the Elder, A. D. 23-79, frequently mentions tertian and quartan agues, describes the symptoms and gives remedies. Evidently malaria had become widespread in his day.

Though references to intermittent fevers by the classical writers are frequent and definite and show a familiarity with all forms of malaria, there is no mention of particular localities in which infection might occur, though Strabo, B. C. 63-A. D. 23, wrote "All Latium is fertile—except those places which are marshy and productive of disease."

No argument is needed to show the extent of malaria in Italy for several centuries past, nor the blasting effect it has had on the prosperity of that nation. Its effect on the character of the inhabitants has been equally as marked as in Greece. The more enterprising are apt to seek more healthy homes, leaving the poorer and less enterprising, who gradually sink lower and lower. North says of the people of the Roman Campagna, "The moral sense of the natives of these towns is so degraded that the death of a horse or a mule is said to be a matter of far greater concern to them than that of a child or relative."

Are we justified in holding that malaria was responsible for the disappearance of peoples, changes in the aspect of the country and in the types of the inhabitants of these districts? In all cases in which definite history has been obtained, some political cause can also be found which may account for the changes to a greater or lesser extent; such as insecurity of life and property, war and disease and famine following war, with destruction of the works of civilization. Fertile areas when abandoned soon become overgrown, drainage ceases, small water courses become clogged with the production of swamps and marshes where luxuriant fields once stood. We know that the Campagna wa[s] once in a high state of cultivatio[n] studded with towns, and contained man[y] luxurious villas, yet for cen[t]uries it ha[s] been a desolate waste. notorious fo[r] malaria. Sybaris, famous for its wealth and the luxuriousness of its inhabitants, has disappeared, and on its site a pestilential marsh, noted for malaria. now stands.

Doubtless wars, with their attend[a]nt miseries, played a large part in the disastrous history of ancient Italy, but it cannot be doubted that malaria made good use of the situation and has ever since held the subjugated districts. "The inhabitants reduced to the utmost state of destitution and misery, the soil untilled, the woods destroyed, the water courses neglected, nature uncontrolled has had her way for centuries with the result that a land which was the home of the greatest empire that the world has ever seen, occupied by a people who excelled in learning and the arts. as in luxury and vice, became a squalid pestilential desert. whose reclamation and restoration to anything approaching its former state will sorely tax the energies and finances of their successors."

Admitting freely that there are gaps in our information. and other causes undoubtedly played an important part. it seems certain that malaria was a prime factor in the decay and downfall of the two great peoples of ancient times, and that the histories of Greece and Italy have been profoundly modified by the implantation and spread of this disease in these countries.

Even the introduction of quinine and the discoveries of Laveran and Ross have not eliminated malaria as an important economic factor in these, as it is today in our own and other countries.

Hookworm. Since Ashford in 1899 demonstrated that the anemia of Porto Rico, which had been recognized as a scourge in that island for more than 100 years, and Stiles in 1902 showed that endemic uncinariasis existed in the [U]nited States, many researches have [b]een made and articles written on the extent and effects of hookworm. It produces profound anemia, retarded mental [a]nd physical development, permanent reduction in height and weight, muscular weakness with aversion to exertion, miscarriage and still-birth, and a high percentage of impotence in the male and sterility in the female. Its effects on the moral character are no less marked, causing. disobedience, cunning, lying, stealing, forgery and sexual perversions, while psychic retardation, irritability, depression and blunting of the higher sensibilities are believed by some to be results.

Infection is widespread in our Southern States, in which 35 per cent of those examined have been found to harbor the parasite. The young are particularly affected. 58.5 per cent being children under 16 in this country. The disease is of long duration, while the parasite may live 12 to 15 years.

The cost to the South in economic waste is estimated at between $250,000,-000 and $500,000,000 yearly. This gives an index of the large number of persons infected as well as the influence of the disease in lessening vigor and ability to carry on productive pursuits. Lack of physical development and physical disability lessen working capacity, while retardation of mental development with low vitality reduce capacity to learn—thereby fostering ignorance. Apathy and lack of ambition are typical of the infection, leading inevitably to shiftlessness, poverty and degradation. Geographically the infection is widespread throughout the tropical and subtropical countries. Endemic foci are often found in more northerly climates, especially in mines, workers in which have shown infection to the extent of 65 per cent.

The announcement of Stiles, followed by abundant proofs, excited much interest at the time, which was manifested by numerous discussions in the public press, and the humorists made much use of the material. At present physicians and health officers remember the existence and bad effects of the disease, but the press has apparently forgotten it, the public has become used to it and interest has lagged. This is the usual story with endemic diseases.

I have selected these diseases to illustrate the baneful effects of endemic diseases on national life and vigor because of the disastrous influence they have had on the history of the world both in ancient as well as modern times, and are even now exercising in our hemisphere. Who can estimate the deterrent effect they have had on settlement and development of new country, and progress in already settled areas? Their heavy hand has also been felt in our economic and political life.

It is very hard to excite a community over malaria or hookworm. Even health officers accept reports of many cases of these diseases with much more complacency than they would a single case of small-pox, yet small-pox has not in the past sixty years done as much damage as malaria does each year. Our Public Health Service, as the result of careful surveys, estimates that between six and seven million persons suffer from malaria annually in the United States. In given communities 40 to 60, and sometimes 90, per cent of the population become infected. Large areas of fertile land remain uncultivated and uninhabited largely because of malaria. In districts where malaria prevails crops are shortened, prosperity and progress lag, while the energies and the ambitions of the inhabitants are sapped. It is this effect on character that gives to the anemia-producing diseases their chief importance and from this arises their baneful economic influence. No nation in the world has become or remained

great except through the virility of its people. Death, which is the great fear in acute epidemics, is a lesser evil to a nation than a slow, insidious, widespread disease, which spares life but destroys efficiency.

When an epidemic occurs, health officers are given, or can take, almost unlimited powers, and public sentiment backs them up even in extreme measures, while the public treasury is opened with a free hand. It is quite the contrary, as a rule, with endemic diseases—money to combat them is withheld, there is no excitement or even interest aroused, and public sentiment is not awakened.

One might instance in further elaboration of this theme the complacency with which the general public accepts the loss of 150,000 lives each year from tuberculosis with the economic loss entailed, and the unknown, but certainly enormous toll exacted by syphilis. Both of these diseases are destructive of energy, virility and life, but as with malaria and hookworm, they are, like the poor, always with us, and we have become accustomed to their presence.

I am well aware that whatever force there may be in the facts and arguments I have tried to present will apply with unequal weight to the various sections of our country, depending on the greater or less prevalence, or absence of these diseases. The principle involved is, however, the same for all. My plea is that we cultivate in ourselves and the public a wholesome fear of these infections with a correct appreciation of what they mean to the nation, that in our public health work we emphasize reduction in morbidity rather than mortality rates, and lay less stress on death, which must eventually come to everyone, and more stress on happiness and efficiency.

WHAT CAN A COMMUNITY AFFORD TO PAY TO RID ITSELF OF MALARIA?

L. M. FISHER,

*Associate Sanitary Engineer, United States Public Health Service,
Columbia, S. C.*

Anti-malarial measures, like any others, have a limit beyond which they may be deemed economically unprofitable. Here are given formulæ by which ratios may be figured of costs relative to benefits. For sentimental reasons, however, a community may be willing to pay somewhat more than it could afford as an investment.

UPON the intelligent understanding of this problem will largely depend the rate of progress with which the malarious sections of the country will be cleaned up. In places where health work has been backward the health authorities probably do not realize that the community will tax itself very heavily to assure itself of good health, provided it has confidence in the ability of the health authorities to do what they say is necessary to clean up the community. Good health is the greatest human asset. The extent to which this is appreciated by the average man is evidenced by the fact that advertising concerns find it profitable to make health the "appeal" in a large percentage of the advertising matter put out. Hugo Munsterberg, in his "Psychology of Business," says: "Psychological experiments in which advertisements with different feeling appeals were graded by twenty men and twenty women showed on an average that the idea of health appealed to the personality most strongly. Next comes cleanliness." . . . This is an indication of the extent to which health authorities can draw upon public support when confidence is established by results accomplished.

A man in a desperate situation will pay any sum to escape from it. The only requirement is that it must offer at least a faint chance of success. If his situation is less desperate he will weigh the money cost more in detail. It becomes then a question of relative values.

If a community has much malaria and possesses little money, it can afford to spend little on malaria, for other demands upon its funds cannot be ignored. It must provide for its means of livlihood first. It must finance agriculture, industry, commerce, transportation, and keep business as active as possible. The money a community spends on malaria control should be considered as an investment. *Whether it is a good or a bad investment depends upon the money returns realized just as in the case of any other investment.* The more intelligent and public-spirited a community is the quicker will it be to sense the value of a good investment in malaria control work.

The economic significance of malaria has probably not been fully realized by many people. The insidious losses do not attract marked attention since they are practically an everyday occurrence and few people, comparatively, die of malaria. The losses occur in little leaks. Personal efficiency is reduced. The business man is not fully alive to his opportunities. The laborer cannot render full value for his wages. His employer loses thereby and recoups his losses by reducing the pay for labor, thus the loss is passed on to the laboring man. The professional man suffers like the business man—from decreased personal efficiency. In addition both suffer from the smaller volume of business and from poorer collections because of the reduced prosperity of the community.

The manufacturer loses because of the lowered efficiency of the operative, and because of idle machines due to illness.

The railroads lose because the community does not produce the freight it would produce if every worker were fully efficient.

Time is the essence of the computation of the amount of this loss. If a cotton mill, for instance, produces 5,000 pounds less manufactured goods a day than it would produce if there were no malaria, it loses daily the profit it would make on manufacturing 5,000 pounds of goods. The laborers lose each day the compensation they would receive for manufacturing 5,000 pounds of finished product. The railroad loses the revenue it would earn each day by hauling 5,000 pounds of freight from the community. The merchants lose because there is less money to spend that day. The doctor loses because the wage earner must spend his money for the necessities of life, leaving little or nothing for family medical attention. The children, who are the first in the community to suffer, acquire a defective education because of lost days at school, and inefficient days. This handicap projected over a period of years in the lifetime of the individual may become very formidable in dollars and cents. It is not practicable to name a definite figure indicative of this loss. The community, however, realizes that it is a very real loss.

The farmer loses a portion of his crops because his labor is in bed or only partly efficient. Some of the family lose time nursing the sick; money is spent for quinine and other medicines, for screens, mosquito lotions, chill tonics and so forth.

The property owner loses because of depreciated property values and low rents.

If all these losses are figured up for the year and capitalized, the result indicates from an economic and commercial view an amount for which the community would be justified in issuing bonds to effect permanent relief if a bond issue would have to be resorted to, or a cash expenditure, which would be justified if a bond issue would not have to be resorted to. From the result thus obtained, a sum must be deducted, the interest on which would pay for the maintenance charges on the permanent work.

Thus if the losses above referred to should amount to, let us say $8,000 a year, for the community, and figuring interest and sinking fund charges at 8%, the losses capitalized would amount to $100,000. Now if maintenance of ditches, etc., would cost $2,400 a year, this sum capitalized with interest at 6% would amount to $40,000. The community would, therefore, be justified in bonding itself for $60,000 or in raising and spending $60,000 in cash. Whatever additional value the community would place upon the comforts of being free from mosquitoes, enjoying a good reputation as a healthful, energetic, enterprising town, could be added to the sum of $60,000 above referred to.

The enormous drain malaria is upon the resources of a community tends to discourage those who must bear it, so that the enterprising ones will abandon the locality. What may be called a deterioration in the quality of the population is thus accentuated.

Carter observed that it is progressive, and commenting upon the above deterioration said in effect that in a country where malaria is prevalent the control of malaria is more important than the control of all other communicable diseases, including smallpox, cholera, bubonic plague, yellow fever, typhoid fever, dysentery, tuberculosis, etc.; that the population would move out of a malarious country and would not return,—they would return after the passing of a yellow fever epidemic or after cholera or after plague, but that malaria ruined a country economically.

Now if in the above assumption the community contained a population of 3,000 the per capita first cost would amount to $20, but if the results sought, namely, the elimination of malaria, were accomplished, the expenditure would undoubtedly be justified, although the per capita cost is high.

The first cost for malaria control work varies widely for different communities. In some localities it may amount possibly to some figure like $1.50; in others it may amount to twenty times as much or even more. *It may even amount to a figure which would make it cheaper to abandon the property created by the community and let the people move away, rather than pay the cost of eliminating malaria.* In such a case decision must be made between continuous malarial infection or abandonment of the property which the industry of the community has created. It is thus caught on the two horns of the dilemma. Some communities were perhaps abandoned where control measures intelligently applied would have cost less than the value of the property abandoned, but were abandoned because knowledge of just what was necessary to be done did not exist.

The best course to pursue depends in such a case upon three factors: the annual community loss, the first cost of permanent work, and the cost of maintenance.

Let us assume that:

1. P equals the population in the community and
2. C the per capita first cost of malaria control work, then
3. PC is the total cost of the work. Now if
4. I is the interest and sinking fund charge in percent, then
5. PCI is the total annual interest and sinking fund charge in dollars. If

6. M is maintenance in percent of first cost, then
7. PCM is total annual maintenance charge, and
8. PCI + PCM = Total annual cost, interest and maintenance. Let
9. R = percent of population infected, then
10. PR = number of infected persons in the community. Now if
11. V = the annual loss in dollars per person infected, then
12. PRV = total loss to community annually before control and equals average annual gain after complete control, and
13. $\text{PRV} - (\text{PCI} + \text{PCM}) = \text{Total}$ saving for community $= \text{P}(\text{RV} - \text{C}(\text{I}+\text{M}))$, and
14. $$\frac{\text{PRV} - (\text{PCI} + \text{PCM})}{\text{P}} = \text{Net}$$

average annual gain per capita $= \text{RV} - \text{C}(\text{I} + \text{M})$ and

15. $$\frac{\text{PRV} - (\text{PCI} + \text{PCM})}{\text{P}}$$

$$\frac{}{\text{C}} = \text{Annual dividend to community on first cost}$$
$$= \frac{\text{RV} - (\text{I} + \text{M})}{\text{C}}.$$

Now if only partial control is effected and we let

16. F represent the percentage of control, such as 65%; 80%; 90%, etc., then equation 12 will become.
17. PRVF = average annual gain under partial control; this factor F will appear in each of the remaining equations and equation 15 will take the form
18. $$\frac{\text{RVF} - (\text{I} + \text{M})}{\text{C}} = \text{Annual dividend to community on first cost.}$$

From this equation it is evident that the dividend varies directly as the percentage of the population infected, directly as the loss per person infected, directly as the percentage of control and inversely as the per capita first cost, i. e., the greater the infection, the greater the dividend; the greater the annual loss per person infected, the greater the dividend; the greater the percentage of control, the greater the dividend, and the less the first cost the greater the dividend. The percentage of infection alone does not determine the wisdom of undertaking the work nor does the per capita cost, but both must be considered together.

Now if we take two communities A and B, equal in population and assume interest charges the same in both places and annual·maintenance a fixed percentage of the first cost in each place, the annual loss per person infected the same in each place and 100% reduction in each place, but with only 10% of the population infected in A and 85% in B and with a per capita cost of only $1.50 in A whereas it is $10.00 in B; then substituting these values in equation 18 we have for A, Dividend =

$$\frac{10 \times 5 - (8 + 7)}{1.50} = 18\%$$

and for B, Dividend =

$$\frac{85 \times 5 - (8 + 7)}{10} = 27\frac{1}{2}\%.$$

These results are only illustrative but indicate that the dividends on the first cost in the case of B are greater than they are for A although the per capita cost for A was very much less than for B.

Therefore, in order to arrive at an intelligent decision as to the profit of proposed malaria work in a community the first requirement is that a malaria census be taken to determine the approximate annual loss suffered because of malaria. The next step should be the preparation of an estimate of first cost and of maintenance annually. From formula 18 the annual average dividend could be·approximated.

The sum that a community could *afford* to pay on the above assumptions may be very materially more than the sum it is *willing* to pay.

□

DETROIT SUMMER HEALTH CAMP

To help the most needy cases among children in getting back to normal, the Detroit Health Department opened in June, a camp on the site of the new Tuberculosis Sanatorium. This is an area of about a square mile in the country north of the city. The children are taken to the camp for a five-weeks' stay in relays of about 85, so that somewhere about 200 children who have been in the open-air schools during the past year are provided for, It is estimated, however, that open-air school space is needed for about 900 more.

The children at the camp are housed in army tents loaned by the Government, and spend the day in a regular order of sleeping, eating, swimming, games, and walking. A complete physical examination, including a culture from the throat, was made before the children were sent to the camp,

STATUS OF STATE BUREAUS OF CHILD HYGIENE

Anna E. Rude, M.D.

Director, Division of Hygiene, U. S. Children's Bureau
Washington, D. C.

Read at the Child Hygiene Session, American Public Health Association, at San Francisco, Cal..
September 14, 1920

CHILD Hygiene is an essential part of any general program in public health and preventive medicine, and the prominence which this subject is assuming in this as well as other countries is indicative of its fundamental importance. No other phase of public health today compares in popularity with the child hygiene movement. Much confusion seems to have arisen in defining the terms "child hygiene" and "child welfare." Popular usage understands "child hygiene" to mean something less than health, while in the social service field the term "child welfare" has grown to have a meaning which applies only to selected groups of unfortunate children, such as the dependent, defective, delinquent, or neglected. This use of terms is probably the result of a lack of correlation of many individual activities dealing with special phases of welfare, but a changed attitude is imminent in that the tendency now is to see that the great mass of children bears a normal relation to society, and that health, education, recreation, and suitable employment are essentials in the normal life of all children. Literally understood, "child hygiene" is a more limited term than child welfare, which includes all conditions affecting the general well-being of the child. In the development of all comprehensive public health programs it is noteworthy that recognition is given more and more to the social and economic conditions as having a direct bearing upon all matters of hygiene; therefore, "child welfare" probably better defines the present day movements

towards safeguarding the health of the child than "child hygiene."

While the effects of war, through a reduced birth rate, and an increased sickness and death rate due to a scarcity and high cost of food and general hardship and privation which lower resistance to all forms of disease, have compelled other countries to realize the imperative need of the conservation of the life and health of the child, our more fortunate country is none the less alive to the importance of the problem.

In this country, as in foreign countries, a history of the child welfare movement shows that philanthropic and voluntary effort have initiated the work, which, serving as a demonstration, has quite logically been taken over eventually by local authorities. Such a multiplicity of child welfare organizations have been started and grown with such incredible rapidity that at present the varieties and complications of activities are confusing if not bewildering, and definite constructive state-wide plans are necessary for efficiency and standardization:

The first State Child Hygiene Division in the United States was not established until 1912 and during the following 5 years only 8 States organized to assume the responsibility for state-wide child welfare work. The period 1918 to 1920 was a record-making time, with an increase of 23 state divisions, while 3 newly-established divisions during the present year make a total of 34 states now organized to carry on child welfare activities on a state-wide plan.

STATE DIVISION OF CHILD HYGIENE AND CHILD WELFARE

State	Date and official name	Director
Louisiana	1912 Subdivision of Division of Hygiene	Miss Agnes Morris, State Board of Health, New Orleans.
New York	1914 Division of Child Hygiene	Dr. M. Edgar Rose, State Board of Health, Albany.
Kansas	1915 Division of Child Hygiene	Dr. Florence Brown Sherbon, State Board of Health, Topeka.
Ohio	1915 Subdivision of Child Hygiene in Division of Hygiene	Miss Natalie Merrill, State Board of Health, Columbus.
New Jersey	1915 Division of Child Hygiene	Dr. Julius Levy, State Board of Health, Trenton, N. J.
Massachusetts	1915 Subdivision of Child Hygiene in Division of Hygiene	Dr. Merrill E. Champion, State Board of Health, Boston.
Montana	1917 Child Welfare Division	Mrs. L. J. Reid, State Board of Health, Helena.
Illinois	1917 Division of Child Hygiene and Public Health Nursing	Dr. C. W. East, State Board of Health, Springfield.
Pennsylvania	1918 Division of Child Health	Dr. Ellen C. Potter, State Board of Health, Harrisburg.
Florida	1918 Bureau of Child Welfare	Dr. Wm. B. Keating, State Board of Health, Jacksonville.
N. Carolina	1918 Bureau of Public Health Nursing and Infant Hygiene	Miss Rose M. Ehrenfeld, State Board of Health, Raleigh.
Minnesota	1918 Division of Child Conservation	State Board of Health, St. Paul.
Arizona	1919 Department of Child Welfare	Mrs. C. R. Howe, State Board of Health, Phoenix.
California	1919 Bureau of Child Hygiene	Dr. Ethel M. Watters, State Board of Health, 511 Underwood Bldg., San Francisco.
Colorado	1919 Child Welfare Bureau	Mrs. Mary E. Holland, Ex. Sec'y, Department of Public Instruction, Denver.
Connecticut	1919 Bureau of Child Hygiene and Division of Public Health Nursing.	Miss Margaret K. Stack, State Board of Health, Hartford.
Georgia	1919 Bureau of Child Hygiene.	Dr. Lydia Allen De Vilbiss, State Board of Health, Atlanta.

Idaho	1919 Division of Child Hygiene	Department of Public Welfare, Boise.
Indiana	1919 Division of Infant and Child Hygiene	Dr. Ada E. Schweitzer, State Board of Health, Indianapolis.
Kentucky	1919 Division of Child Hygiene	State Board of Health, Louisville.
Michigan	1919 Bureau of Child Hygiene and Public Health Nursing	Miss Harriet Leck, State Board of Health, Lansing.
Missouri	1919 Division of Child Hygiene	Dr. C. B. Knight, State Board of Health, Jefferson City.
Nebraska	1919 Child Welfare Bureau	Mrs. Emily P. Hornberger, Department of Public Welfare, Lincoln.
New Mexico	1919 Child Welfare Service	Dr. Sarah Coker, Department of Education, Santa Fe.
Rhode Island	1919 Division of Child Welfare	Dr. Elizabeth Gardiner, State Board of Health, Providence.
S. Carolina	1919 Bureau of Child Hygiene and Public Health Nursing	Mrs. Ruth A. Dodd, State Board of Health, Columbia.
Texas	1919 Bureau of Child Hygiene and Public Health Nursing	Mrs. Ethel Parsons, State Board of Health, Austin.
Utah	1919 State Department of Health Education	Dr. E. G. Gowans, Department of Public Instruction. Salt Lake City.
Virginia	1919 Division of Child Hygiene and Public Health Nursing	Dr. Mary E. Brydon, State Board of Health, Richmond.
W. Virginia	1919 Division of Child Welfare and Public Health Nursing	Mrs. Jean G. Dillon, State Department of Health, Charleston.
Wisconsin	1919 Bureau of Child Welfare and Public Health Nursing	Mrs. Mary P. Morgan, State Board of Health, Madison.
Maine	1920 Division of Public Health Nursing and Child Hygiene	Miss Soule, State Board of Health, Augusta.
Alabama	1920 Bureau of Child Hygiene and Public Health Nursing	Miss Jessie L. Marriner, State Board of Health, Montgomery.
Mississippi	1920 Bureau of Child Welfare and Public Health Nursing	Dr. Edith B. Lowry, State Board of Health, Jackson.

It is interesting in passing to note that though public health measures are so largely educational in character, these state child welfare divisions, with three exceptions, have been established under State Boards of Health, the exceptions being Colorado, New Mexico, and Utah, whose divisions are under Departments of Education, and Idaho and Nebraska, whose divisions are under Departments of Public Welfare, which presumably are substitutes for the regulation State Boards of Health. In Massachusetts, Ohio, and Louisiana the State Board of Health organization places child hygiene as a subdivision under departments of general hygiene.

While the pioneer work done in the 8 original state divisions undoubtedly helped to serve as a model for other divisions, it is the purpose of this paper to analyze in general the organization and different lines of approach which have developed in the more recently organized divisions. State undertakings have naturally varied with local conditions, which must serve as the foundation in developing work; therefore efficient organization from the beginning has been more or less dependent upon the extent to which previous child welfare activities had prepared the way.

The following topics serve to cover the general lines of development, which have been submitted in reports on state departments of child hygiene or child welfare:

Initial Survey.—Since intelligent action must be based upon an exact knowledge of existing conditions, a first step might logically be a preliminary survey of the state, made by personal visits or questionnaires, to determine existing agencies engaged in child welfare work and the character and extent of their work. Yet only in 6 states out of the 30 from which reports are available has the work been begun with a general census-taking of the state's activities dealing with child welfare problems. Two states limited their surveys to specific problems, namely, midwifery and infant mortality, rather than general child welfare activities; while other states have undertaken surveys of communities or counties and concentrated efforts on these smaller areas, which were intended to serve as demonstrations for the rest of the state.

Budgets.—State appropriations for child-welfare divisions show a great disparity, New Jersey leading with $150,000 as a 1920 budget and Idaho with only $3,800 for two years' work. This wide range in state appropriations indicates to a certain degree possible undertakings, but this is not an invariable rule, for in Minnesota where a state appropriation was entirely absent the child welfare activities were taken over by the State Public Health Association in cöoperation with the pediatric and gynecological societies of the state and most creditable work effected. In Missouri, where the legislature created a state division of child hygiene but made no provision for funds with which to develop and carry on the work, federal funds were made available, and, through effective cöoperation, state-wide child welfare activities have been developed. Although figures or budgets have been reported from only a limited number of states, the available data point to the fact that a number of the newer state child hygiene divisions which are best organized for effective work are functioning on initial budgets of $10,000 or $12,000 for their first year. Obviously larger appropriations are necessary to develop satisfactorily any state-wide plans, but the possibilities for beginning active work even on limited funds are well demonstrated by the majority of state divisions, and increasingly large appropriations will follow in natural order.

Organization.—A director and office secretary appear to be the only constant members of staff personnel. Other members are assistant director, supervising and public health nurses, organizer, child welfare visitor, lecturer, educational secretary, etc.

Adoption of Standards for Working Basis.—In a number of states, after a preliminary survey of activities, the Children's Bureau's Minimum Standards for Public Protection of the Health of Mothers and Children have been adopted and used in outlining work. While the realization of these standards is a distant goal in many states, Kansas is making an interesting demonstration through its State Women's Committee, which is organized in fifty counties and is measuring the present condition of Kansas children by these standards. The survey is general, covering all interests of children; namely, health of mothers and children; dependent, defective, and delinquent children; and children in industry. A series of club study outlines has been based on the standards and the Women's Bar Association is making an index to Kansas laws relating to women and children.

Standardization of Legislation.— Health legislation very definitely intersects all child welfare activities in many interesting ways as shown in laws on eugenics, birth registration, midwifery, ophthalmia neonatorum, boarding homes, institutional care, maternity benefits, mothers' pensions, social insurance, etc.

In several State Child Welfare Divisions popular demand for information regarding existing laws affecting the welfare of children has made necessary a survey of such laws, setting forth their inadequacies and limitations, and the need for new legislation to accord with progressive development. So-called "Children's Codes Commissions" have been organized in 18 states and the District of Columbia, and are functioning, not in the ordinarily accepted meaning of the term code, a digest of laws, but covering general existing conditions affecting children and purposing to coördinate and supply laws and administrative agencies to handle various aspects of child welfare that are handled inadequately or omitted. Laws on birth registration and midwifery are the ones

which have been given special prominence in state child hygiene reports.

The plan of the New Jersey State Child Hygiene Division serves as an excellent example of how, through coöperation, extra-official agencies can be utilized to further desired legislation. In coöperation with the State Child Hygiene Division and the State Bureau of Vital Statistics, the Women's State Council of Child Welfare through its county chairmen has conducted a state-wide birth registration campaign, with the ultimate aim of putting New Jersey in the birth registration area. Of the 34 states now organized for state child welfare work, 15 are still not included in the birth registration area. Not only is birth registration of primary importance for records of vital statistics, but early and accurate notification forms the nucleus around which centers all infant welfare activities.

Although 5 state departments appear to be actively attacking the problem of midwifery, South Carolina and New Jersey reports conspicuously emphasize improved legislation making training, supervision, and licensing of midwives compulsory.

Obviously, standard legislation and enforcement of it, is fundamental to any child-welfare program, and all efforts at legislative standardization, if not initiated by, should at least be very closely correlated with State Child Welfare or Child Hygiene Divisions.

Education.—Although public health and preventive medicine are primarily educational in character, child welfare is concerned with the specific education of parents and children.

Popular methods of carrying out child welfare educational activities have been participated in by all 34 functioning state child welfare divisions and practically uniform methods used which may be grouped as follows:

(1) Publicity, through press, pulpit, literature, lectures, slides, films, etc.

(2) Campaigns, such as health week,

birth registration day, Baby-Week, Children's Year, etc.

(3) Exhibits.

(4) Classes for mothers, Little Mothers' Leagues.

(5) Health Centers.

Probably today there is no state in the Union which cannot boast of a varying number of health centers, most of which have been developed under or in coöperation with its State Child Welfare Division and local or national organizations. In fact, the health center today figures as the objective in many phases of child welfare work and as developed in many communities is, strictly speaking, a community-educational center whose functions are not only to advise on the hygiene of the child but to conduct classes for teaching mothers as well.

Curiously enough, our early health centers were usually called infant welfare centers, and provided for the care of children only during the first one or two years of life, but as child welfare work has expanded we find many consultation stations and organizations changing their names to more inclusive terms covering the entire period of childhood. Need for periodic physical examinations, hygienic advice, and supervision of the preschool child is now considered quite as important as similar assistance during infancy. The possibilities for development in child welfare activities through such centers is only partially indicated by such developments as infant feeding classes, nutritional classes, prenatal work, dental care, etc. Increase in clinical and hospital facilities must ultimately form the link in the chain by making adequate care available to all mothers and children.

Coincidently with the development of the health center has been the development of public health nursing work. Additional teaching of mothers in their homes as well as in centers has been found necessary to secure the best results, and here lies one of the greatest opportunities for the public health nurse.

Public health nursing, like other phases of public health, is essentially educational and is fundamental to the success of the child welfare movement.

During the past few years many Public Health Nursing Divisions have been formed in State Departments of Health. In 12 states, Illinois, North Carolina, Connecticut, Michigan, South Carolina, Texas, Virginia, West Virginia, Wisconsin, Maine, Alabama and Mississippi, public health nursing divisions have been combined with child hygiene. In many instances this arrangement is only temporary, pending adequate appropriations allowing for directors of separate divisions.

A distinct directly educational approach in promoting child welfare is being made, either coincidently with or entirely apart from other activities, through existing educational channels, such as normal schools or other schools graduating teachers, and teachers' institutes. New Mexico, Virginia, and South Carolina reports especially emphasize this training of teachers, and several other states have prepared hygiene courses for use in elementary schools. Undoubtedly this line of approach is a logical one in many states where general public health work is in its infancy and where the school machinery is the only available organized institution through which to work. The need for the standardization of school hygiene has been given recognition in several states, where uniform record cards for physical examinations have been made in coöperation with the Department of Education.

Statistical Studies.—Careful analysis of the vital statistics of the state to determine the areas of greatest child mortality and morbidity is an effective method of visualizing local conditions with a view to stimulating interest.

The infant mortality rate is considered today to reflect the intelligence of the people of a community, hence careful statistical studies in all the State Child Welfare Divisions could be profitably made. Differentiation of stillbirths, premature births, deaths under one week and under one month affords a fruitful field in this country.

Research.—Only one state child hygiene division has reported research work as one of its functions. This study is on gastro-intestinal disorders of children and is undertaken in coöperation with three other state departments. It is planned to make continuous observations on a large number of infants in communities of various types for a period of some months. The study will include housing, sanitation, clinical observations, laboratory analyses, with a final careful study of data obtained.

The field of research as a necessary adjunct to a state child hygiene division is practically unexplored, and presents unlimited possibilities of correlation between child welfare and venereal disease, tuberculosis, and other communicable diseases, infectious diseases, stillbirths, and kindred subjects.

Coöperation.—A study of the organization charts of state and municipal child hygiene or child welfare divisions emphasizes not only the relative importance and signal pre-eminence which such state departments hold, but also shows the many lines of coöperation essential to the success of any state child welfare program. For effective service, mutually stimulating coöperation should exist between the child welfare or child hygiene division and the other state board of health divisions, namely: Vital Statistics, Laboratory, Communicable Disease, Sanitary Engineering, Social Hygiene, Public Health Nursing, Tuberculosis, Industrial Hygiene, etc. Among the state coöperating agencies are the State Department of Public Instruction, Board of Charities and Corrections, Board of Control, Department of Agriculture, Medical Association, Dental Association, Health Officers' Association, Tuberculosis Association, American Red Cross, University Extension, and Women's Organizations.

The topics in this paper are from necessity considered only along very general lines. Many state plans in detail are truly inspiring and promise excellent results. A bird's eye view of present child welfare activities shows a definite focusing of action on later infancy and the preschool period (through health centers) and on the school period, leaving the extreme periods of child life, early infancy and the industrial period practically untouched.

It is singular that action has so slowly extended toward the point at which it should have logically begun — eugenics and prenatal care; since health in infancy in a large measure determines the general health standard of the whole of life. That the general downward trend in infant mortality is not due to fewer deaths during the first month of life, calls for definite action centered on the protection of the infant by ensuring the welfare of the mother during pregnancy, confinement, and the lying-in period. Only 9 of the state child welfare divisions have reported definitely as doing prenatal work, which has consisted chiefly of distribution of literature, a series of prenatal letters being used in 4 states. One state division reports coöperation with its State Obstetrical Society for the purpose of developing prenatal clinics. While pediatrists are now stressing breast feeding as the most important single factor in the reduction of infant mortality only two state reports have emphasized this important subject. Such facts indicate some essential aspects of the problem which must be faced and solved. Federal stimulation and financial assistance to meet the problem of early infancy are embodied in the Sheppard-Towner Bill, known as a bill for the protection of maternity and infancy, now before Congress.

The examinations for the draft, and the causes for rejections, aroused a notable interest in health and hygiene. Health at all ages of life is now a matter of general interest. It is significant that even lay persons were struck by the fact that most of the disabilities causing rejection's in the draft might have been corrected in infancy or early childhood. In 1912 there was one state division of child hygiene; in 1920 there are 34. These figures indicate that at last we are realizing that child hygiene is the most important of all hygiene; that child welfare is the welfare first to be considered; that a child hygiene division is the center, the focus, of state public health work.

☐

NOVA SCOTIA'S HEALTH CARAVANS

Here is Health Caravan No. 1 in charge of Dr. Edgar Douglas leaving Provincial Red Cross Headquarters via Sam Slick's residence at Windsor, headed for Evangeline country, the Gaspereaux, Cornwallis and Annapolis Valleys, thence through the municipality of Clare, where direct descendants of the returned Acadians dwell. This is one of two caravans leaving Halifax to tour Nova Scotia, and after rounding the southwestern tip of the Province will journey northward along the southeast coast for a distance of four hundred miles, holding educational, diagnostic and operative clinics, and moving picture shows in all important and central fishing villages. A duplicate caravan goes along the northern shore of Minas Basin, the south shore of Northumberland Straits, through Cape Breton and the coal fields adjacent to Louisburg and other fishing villages in the far north and east. The shabby ambulance in the rear of the caravan is a war veteran, which has been purchased by the school children of Nova Scotia. It served on the battlefields of France where it carried thousands of wounded to the rear. The damage to the ambulance cover was received on the battlefield.

INDUSTRIAL HEALTH EDUCATION—A MEANS
AND AN END

JULES SCHEVITZ, B.S.

General Secretary, Oklahoma Tuberculosis Association
Oklahoma City, Oklahoma

Read Before Industrial Hygiene Section, American Public Health Association, at San Francisco, Cal.,
September 15, 1920

If health officers were backed in their work by business men
they would no longer worry about inadequate appropriations
or political interference. Business men already know the
economy of health in the factory. It is the duty of industrial
hygienists to furnish the missing link and educate the business
man to the value of bettered public health to his factory and
himself.

THE past ten years have witnessed a remarkable advance in the movement for the promotion of the health of the worker. The experience of large and small industrial enterprises has revealed the value of this movement, both from the point of view of reduction in amount of illness among the workers as well as in increased efficiency and production in the plant.

The first aid, accident prevention and safety first campaigns, were the logical forerunners of the modern industrial hygiene movement, and it was only natural that employers of labor recognizing the value of these earlier life-saving measures, agreed to try out the more constructive program of medical, surgical, nursing and other welfare services.

While the motives of the employers of labor may not have been primarily altruistic, great credit is due these leaders of enterprise who by their vision and far-sightedness were able to stimulate the entire industrial health movement to such a marked degree. More recently public and private agencies have become interested in the movement for the health conservation of the workers. Divisions of industrial hygiene in state and local health departments have been most active along these lines. These agencies have been able through education and by other means to interest an increasingly large number of employers to institute the methods of health conservation so successfully administered in other plants.

Contact with the head of industry is a valuable opportunity accorded many industrial health workers. If, in addition to proving to the employer that the expenditure for the administration of complete medical, nursing and welfare services is a good investment, paying large dividends, the health worker will attempt to win over the business man to the cause of health promotion outside of industry, he has done something which may in the long run be of greater service to humanity than the introduction or expansion of a health service in one particular plant.

What most health workers have been doing in the past has been to consider industrial health solely as an end in itself, namely, the prevention of occupational diseases and the promotion of the health of the worker. We apparently have been satisfied in accomplishing this end, and have gone no farther. Of equal, if not greater, importance to the entire public health movement is the capitalization of this demonstration to the employer and business man, that disease can be prevented, that health can be purchased, and that the same constructive methods will prove equally effective in the general health campaign. In other words, after having demonstrated the value of industrial health as an end in itself, why not use this demonstration as a means of gaining the enlightened and influential support of the business interests of this country in the general health campaign?

An experiment of the Oklahoma Tuberculosis Association in the field of industrial health—as a means and an end—will illustrate the advantages to be gained from such an effort. The Oklahoma Tuberculosis Association is a volunary health organization engaged in a statewide campaign of public health education, including an effort to stimulate business and professional men, state officials, commercial and civic organizations in the public health campaign.

Fortunately for the organization, from its very inception it has had the guiding influence and helpful supervision of business men of the highest order—men who apply to the conduct of this health organization the same sound business principles regularly used in their own successful enterprises. The longer these men were associated with the state association, the more pronounced were their convictions that the enlightened interest of the business and professional men was essential to an effective and well-supported public health program. This applies equally to the official health agency as it does to the voluntary organization.

The purposes of the experiment referred to above are two-fold—to prove to the business man that health conservation methods applied to his own industry mean a saving in man-power with consequent increase in production and efficiency, and second, when this is accomplished to enlist the interest of the business man in the general health campaign. First, we approach him on his own ground and talk to him in his own language, and later having obtained his confidence, the opportunities in the broader public health field are presented to him.

.An industrial health secretary carries on a health educational program in industry by means of talks to employees, distribution of literature in plants, "Health First" posters on bulletin boards, exhibition of motion pictures, and display of special exhibit material. This educational work is well received by the employer and may be the first step in bringing about the introduction of a complete industrial health service. In most instances, this is the employer's first contact with any public health work, despite the various forms of private and official health work carried on in his own community. He expresses a desire to coöperate in the educational campaign in his own plant and evinces interest and surprise when informed of the activities of the local health agencies. One frequent outcome of these dealings with the employer is the gaining of an additional supporter in the general health campaign. This may take the form of his definite affiliation with a voluntary health organization or leadership and interest in health committees of commercial and civic organizations.

These new contacts are carefully followed up by correspondence from the state office, by bulletins of particular interest to the employer, by our monthly health journal, the Pow-Wow, and as often as possible by personal interviews with officers and members of the staff of the state association. We have always maintained the attitude that the health campaign is of sufficient importance to command the attention and time of the highest type of business and professional men in the community, and have consequently selected the busiest and most influential persons to align themselves with us in our work.

At the coming State Public Health conference, we are planning to conduct a special "Business Man's" health session. dealing with the relation of the business man to the health movement, and we are hoping to have a very encouraging attendance as a definite sign of the business man's interest. With health playing such a vital part in community life and so thoroughly interwoven with commercial and civic advancement, it is only proper that the business interests should lend their best efforts to the health movement. This session will be attended by leading employers and business men and representatives of civic and commercial organizations in the state. The business man will be made to feel his responsibility and the need for his close coöperation in the health campaign. As a further effort to draw the business interests closer to the health movement, it is planned to have the question of health discussed before various commercial gatherings in the state.

Applied on a larger scale, this would mean that representatives of large business interests will take a part in national health gatherings and representatives of health organizations will participate in the programs of commercial gatherings. Such a relation would bring the question of health to the fore in public attention and among other results we may expect political conventions and legislative bodies to think of health as a live issue not to be cast aside until expediency deems otherwise, but to be considered along with other important national and state questions.

Local and state health departments are the constituted and recognized authorities for the protection and improvement of the public health. It should require no great array of facts to prove that the efforts of these agencies in the health campaign are very much handicapped and the attainment of their goal greatly delayed without the thorough understanding and whole-hearted coöperation of the business and professional interests of the country. We are all familiar with numerous instances of health laws and regulations unenforced because they lack the support of an enlightened public opinion. We can all point to health departments, local, state and even federal, that are trying to meet problems of the greatest magnitude with a mere stipend granted by the governmental bodies.

With the assistance and backing of business men, health departments will no longer have to worry about inadequate appropriations and political interference. The enforcement of health laws will be demanded instead of discouraged, and the campaign of public health education will take a long step forward.

To the industrial health worker is presented this excellent opportunity for advancing not only the industrial hygiene movement but the entire public health campaign. Will he take advantage of this opportunity?

□

Child Welfare Work in Belgium.—A national children's bureau has been established in Belgium. The bureau is directed by a board of forty members, called the "Conseil superieur des oeuvres de l'enfance." This board has the decision on all questions relating to the protection of children; it issues orders concerning the functions of subsidized agencies; it takes necessary measures for the protection of children within the limits of the law; and determines the use of funds at the disposal of the bureau.—*Journal A. M. A.,* April 24, 1920. (*J. A. T.*)

Electrical Purification of Air.—The possibility of precipitating liquid or solid particles floating in air has been appreciated for some time. An experimental bacteriological application of this fact was made by submitting to a current of 50,000 volts, air polluted with a homogeneous mineral powder in which had been seeded a culture of *Micrococcus prodigiosus.* This air was found to be sterile whereas the neighboring atmosphere showed a mean bacterial count of 150 colonies per cubic meter.—D' Arsonval, et al. *Revue Sci.,* March, 1920.

TRUTH IN ADVERTISING DRUG PRODUCTS

ARTHUR J. CRAMP, M. D.,

Director of Propaganda for Reform Department, Journal of the American Medical Association, Chicago, Ill.

Read before the Food and Drugs Section, American Public Health Association, September 16, 1920, at San Francisco, Cal.

Advertisements of patent medicines are not controlled by law, although the labels on the boxes and bottles are, to some extent. Statements made in patent medicine advertisements are often notoriously exaggerated. Dr. Cramp asserts that, so long as the individual can have proprietary monopoly in his product, it is hopeless to expect truth in the advertisements.

ADVERTISING as we know it today is a thing of recent development. The advertisement of 1920 differs widely from the advertisement of 1820, and even of 1880; it differs not only in its appeal, but in its intent. In the earlier day the advertiser was usually content to notify the public that he was in a position to supply certain of its demands. The modern advertiser goes much further. He does more than aim to supply a demand; he actually creates a demand. Twentieth century advertising may be said to be the art of awakening in the public a demand for things which, otherwise, it might not even know about, and for which it certainly has no craving. It is this changed conception of what constitutes legitimate advertising that has made some thoughtful students of the subject seriously question whether there is any proper excuse for advertising products that are used in the treatment of human ailments. One may produce plausible economic arguments in favor of such advertising, applied to ordinary merchandise, as will make the public buy more of these commodities than it actually needs or can properly afford. But there is nothing to be said in favor of so advertising drug products as to stimulate a demand for them in excess of their legitimate need.

THE DEMAND ELEMENT IN MODERN ADVERTISING.

The present trend on the part of many by no means unintelligent people toward the various so-called drugless-healing cults or fads is the not unnatural reaction to the over-drugging of the public, both by the public itself and by physicians. And this over-drugging has been brought about largely through the power of modern advertising. The use of drugs in the treatment of many human ailments is, in the present state of human knowledge, necessary, but there is no excuse for stimulating the use of drugs beyond the point where they are very definitely indicated. Yet that is exactly what must happen if the sale of drug products is to be stimulated in accordance with the tenets of modern advertising.

The advertising director of a large pharmaceutical manufacturing house recently contributed an article to a magazine devoted to the art of advertising. In explaining the method employed by the manufacturing pharmacist for stimulating a demand on the part of the physician for drug products, he said:

"He gets out expensive 'literature.' He advertises freely in the medical journals. He sends out letters and pamphlets through the mails. He trains a staff of 'detail men' and has them call personally on physicians. Other ways and means are employed with intelligence and discretion to create a demand among physicians for the new and improved products of the manufacturer."

Should the physician's experience and study tend to cause him to use drugs less and other therapeutic aids more, the advertising campaign of the pharmaceutical manufacturer may be counted on to counteract this tendency. Of such advertising the authority just quoted said:

"It keeps alive the practitioner's confidence in medicinal agents. It defeats the tendency frequently exhibited toward therapeutic nihilism."

The modern advertisement, then, is "selling copy"—an appeal that creates a demand—rather than "offering copy" or the mere notification of where already existing demands may be filled. But there is a further factor that puts the advertising of drug products on an entirely different footing from that of the advertising of other merchandise. As has been pointed out elsewhere[1] the man selling drug products has a tremendous advantage over the man selling ordinary merchandise. The seller of shoes, pianos or automobiles has Nature as his antagonist; wear and tear will show the purchaser whether or not he has been defrauded. But the exploiter of drug products has Nature as an assistant; the purchaser is seldom, if ever, able to be sure whether any beneficial effect that may follow the use of certain medicaments is due to the drug or to the healing power of Nature itself. The human mind is so constituted that it is much more prone to give credit to artificial agencies (in this case drugs) than to natural agencies; the seller of drugs reaps the benefit of this common weakness.

CLASSIFICATION OF ADVERTISED DRUG
PRODUCTS.

As a convenient, although arbitrary

1. Cramp, Arthur J.: Modern Advertising and the Nostrum Evil, Am. Jour. Public Health, October, 1918, p. 756.

classification, drug products that are advertised may be grouped thus:

GROUP 1: Non-proprietary pharmaceuticals; official or semi-official in character.

GROUP 2: Scientific proprietary products advertised to the medical profession for prescribing and dispensing purposes.

GROUP 3: Unscientific proprietary products nominally advertised to the medical profession for prescribing and dispensing purposes.

GROUP 4: Proprietary products advertised to the public as home remedies for the self-treatment of disease; colloquially, "patent medicines."

GROUP 1: Advertising of medicaments in this group can be dismissed in a few words. The products being non-proprietary in character, non-secret in composition, their standards of strength and purity being constant and maintained by state and national laws, the advertisements are likely to be of the "listing" or "offering" type only. Such products are made by most of the large pharmaceutical houses of the country, and in the nature of the case there can be no element of monopoly in their manufacture. Competition thus assures sale at a financial return so small as to make it unprofitable for manufacturers to spend any large amount in an advertising campaign for the purpose of increasing the sale of the preparations. It is true, of course, that even this group gets the benefit of that human weakness of mistaking sequence for effect. This must be true of all drug products, even if they were not advertised at all, and in effect this peculiarity of medicaments is in itself advertising — inherent, silent and subtle.

GROUP 2: The scientific proprietary products advertised exclusively to the medical· profession and comprising the second group will be found to rank in what may be called the highest class of "selling copy" advertising. The past twenty-five years has brought a marked change in the character of advertising of products of this class. A quarter of a century ago the medical profession was less critical of the claims made for products of this sort than it is today. It would accept with fewer questions the statements made by high-class manufacturers for their scientific drug products. On the other hand, the professional advertising "copy writers" had not been developed, and there was not, therefore, that tendency to exaggeration that exists under the modern system. The old-time advertisements, while based on less critical data than those demanded today, were comparatively free from the bombast and ill-suppressed hyperbole of the advertisements in the better class modern medical journals. In general, however, it may be said that the products making up Group 2 have, with a few exceptions, always been advertised with a due respect to truth.

GROUP 3: As might be expected, products in this group, unscientific products advertised to physicians, are advertised with little regard for scientific accuracy. The products themselves being unscientific and the manufacturers having a practical monopoly under our trademark law, there is every reason to expect exaggeration and misrepresentation in their sale. The advertising appeal is adapted, naturally, to the clientele to which the manufacturer caters. This nominally is the physician of the less discriminating type; actually, it is the layman reached through the physician. For this reason the preparation is put up in some distinctive form. The physician is always urged to prescribe the "original ·bottle," the inference being that otherwise a dishonest druggist will substitute some other preparation. The original

bottle, and the "literature" that accompanies it, coming into the hands of the layman convinces him that he is as competent to prescribe the preparation as the doctor himself.

Such physicians as prescribe unscientific proprietaries are satisfied with unmeaning generalities relative to the composition of such products. A few years ago, before the medical profession had been aroused to the fact that many published formulas for proprietary remedies were utterly fraudulent, it was no uncommon thing for manufacturers of this type of medicaments to publish formulas which were either meaningless or bore no relation to composition. Some would even give weird and imposing structural chemical formulas for their products; these, while laughable to chemists, might be counted on to mislead many physicians. All medical men in theory, and the better educated and more scientific members of the profession in fact, refuse to prescribe products whose composition is secret. There are, nevertheless, enough careless and thoughtless doctors to support a vast industry in these products of Group 3, many of which are essentially secret in composition. Many of these medicaments are little better than what are known colloquially as "patent medicines."

FACTORS MAKING FOR TRUTHFULNESS

Then began the campaign of education by *The Journal of the American Medical Association,* aided by the association's "Council on Pharmacy and Chemistry" and the findings of the Association's Chemical Laboratory. A year or two after *The Journal* began its propaganda for reform in proprietary medicines—an educational force that it continues to this day—there was born that great power for comparative righteousness in the drug field, the National Food and Drugs Act. The latter laid the manufacturer who made false statements regarding the composition of his preparations open to prosecution—provided he made these statements on or in the trade package.

The result of these two forces, so far as they affected statements of composition of products in this group, was the elimination by the manufacturer of all specific statements bearing on this point. In some cases, however, where the medicaments contained one of the few drugs whose presence the national law requires to be declared on the label, there were brought about some curious verbal gymnastics. A widely advertised so-called medicated wine had been specifically advertised as not a cocain preparation; following the passage of the pure food law a legend appeared on the label to the effect that each ounce of the preparation contained a stated amount of cocain. Another unscientific medicament, which before the law went into force was recommended to physicians on the ground that by using it they could "avoid acetanilid poisoning," was forced to declare the presence of acetanilid. Various proprietary products alleged to be cod-liver oil compounds, but which, in fact, never contained any cod-liver oil, were forced by the exigencies of the Food and Drugs Act to be rechristened. A number of most ordinary mixtures of simple, well-known drugs, which, previous to the passage of the act, had been exploited as synthetic compounds of awe-inspiring chemical complexity, toppled from their high estate and the new trade packages were suspiciously silent on the subject of composition. In not a few instances products which, up until the time of the Food and Drugs Act, had been advertised exclusively to the medical profession for alleged prescription purposes only, immediately went over into the "home remedy" or "patent medicine" field. This was largely due to the fact that prosecutions under the new law verified the disclosures already made by *The Journal of the American Medical Association* so that even the uncritical physician was forced to reject the product because of its obviously unscientific character.

THE UNINFORMATIVE TRADE PACKAGE.

In advertising preparations of this sort today the method is to say as little as possible about the composition or therapeutic action of the products, in or on the trade package. The advertising of a "selling copy" type is confined almost exclusively to those fields that are not subject to the legal restrictions of the Food and Drugs Act, such as the pages of commercially owned and operated medical journals. It is the advertising receipts from these products that keep alive a number of so-called medical journals whose demise would be a benefit alike to to scientific medicine and the public. The chief advertising asset of products of this sort is the testimonial, or, as it is more euphemistically termed, the "clinical report." These reports are descriptions of uncontrolled experiments from uncritical men. As scientific evidence, they have no more value than the testimony of the layman for the newest quack panacea.

The manufacturers of drugs of this group, while saying as little as possible regarding the composition of their products, attempt to shroud in mystery what little they do say. A widely advertised proprietary poultice whose chief ingredient is dried and finely powdered clay, is described as being composed of "anhydrous and levigated argillaceous mineral." A certain brand of aspirin is described, not as acetylsalicylic acid, but as "the monoaceticacidester of salicylic acid."

GROUP 4: In this group—proprietaries of the home remedy type, or the so-called "patent medicines"—truth in advertising is conspicuous chiefly by its absence. All the elements that foster falsehood and exaggeration in the advertising of the drugs in Group 3 are present in this group, with the additional element of a purchasing public which is totally undiscriminating because of its ignorance of the elements involved. As the purchaser of products of this group is also the user, there is added a factor which has brought discredit and disrepute on the entire "patent medicine" industry. That factor is fear through suggestion. Unscientific and misleading advertisements of the drugs in Group 3 cannot be charged with having directly affected the persons who take these drugs. Not so the advertisements of products in the present group. The "patent medicine" maker flourishes by playing on the fears of the public. As one nostrum maker put it, in a burst of candor, when urging druggists to stock his product:

"Fully 75 per cent. of all cough and kidney remedies are bought by people who THINK they have consumption or some serious kidney ailment . . . and not by people who actually have them."

When John Doe pays a dollar for a bottle of Dr. Quack's Quick Cure he does not realize that from one-half to three-fourths of his dollar goes to pay for the manufacturer's efforts to convince him that he is suffering from some ailment for which the Quick Cure is a panacea. The least expensive thing about the average "patent medicine" is the medicine. The most expensive thing is the advertising which creates the market for the medicine. As one "patent medicine" maker, high in the councils of his organization, once put it:

"The twenty thousand newspapers of the United States make more money from advertising the proprietary medicines than do the proprietors of the medicines themselves. . . . Of their receipts, one-third to one-half goes for advertising."

Here one has, then, out of the mouths of those who know, the admission that fully 75 percent. of those who purchase certain types of nostrums are merely neurotics who *think* they are suffering from the ailments that these nostrums are supposed to cure. From a similarly authoritative source comes the admission that from one-third to one-half the cost of a "patent medicine" goes for newspaper advertising alone; to say nothing of the cost of the millions of

"almanacs," window displays, circulars and other publicity features used in the business. It is no far-drawn inference that the three people out of every four who purchase "patent medicines" because they *think* they are ailing have been made to so think by the vast and utterly disproportionate sums spent on advertising these nostrums.

THE ADVERTISING APPEAL.

In advertising "home remedies" the style is adapted to the clientele sought. To the intelligent neurotic a subtle and cleverly worded appeal is made to convince him that a glorified cottage cheese mixture originating in Germany, patented and sold under an imposing trademarked name, is a "re-creator of lost health" with "specific nerve tonic action." To the farmer a cruder message is carried. "Scare" pictures "tell the story" that every passing soreness in the lumbar region is a symptom of incipient Bright's disease, for which "kidney pills" of a certain brand are a sure-fire remedy. To the tired housewife comes the alluring vision of new energy to be derived from some Female Tonic of alleged vegetable origin, whose virtues as a "repeater" are really due to the very definite alcohol content of the nostrum and the very indefinite promises of the exploiter. Still cruder is the picture conjured up in the mind of the youth with thoughts dwelling abnormally on his sexual apparatus, by the fearsome and horrific descriptions that make up the advertising stock-in-trade of the exploiter of nostrums for "lost manhood."

Yet even in the "patent medicine" field there has been improvement in advertising. The very stench of this Augean stable of the advertising world has resulted in some effort to cleanse it. Three factors have been potent in bringing about some betterment in the advertising ethics of the makers of home remedies. First, the searchlight of publicity turned on the business by the medical profession through *The Journal of the American Medical Association* and other medical publications, as well as by some of the better lay magazines and papers. Second, the activities of the federal authorities in enforcing the National Food and Drugs Act. Third, the work of the Better Business Bureau of the Associated Advertising Clubs of the World and of other organizations interested in truthful advertising and alive to the fact that every fraudulent advertisement menaces all advertising by destroying public confidence.

ELEMENTS OF REFORM.

The first factor—public education through publicity—while slower in its action, is more lasting in its results. With all due respect to the opinion of the late Mr. Barnum, the public does not like to be humbugged. It is humbugged to the extent that it lacks knowledge, and in the realm of therapeutics the public's ignorance is broad and deep. By turning the light on the methods of the nostrum vendors, by lifting the veil of secrecy which is the "patent medicine" maker's chief asset, the medical profession has given facts which have sunk deep into the public consciousness and which the public has not failed to take to heart. The Food and Drugs Act, which prohibits "false or misleading" statements regarding the composition or origin of a drug product and "false and fraudulent" therapeutic claims has done much to remove some of the cruder falsehoods. Its weakness lies in its limitations which confine its penalties to the statements made in or on the trade package. The newspaper advertisement, the "almanac" or the circular, in fact the very publicity avenues that sell the "home remedy" are, in fact, subject to no law regarding the truth or falsity of the claims made. It is true that, theoretically, most of the states have on their statute books laws prohibiting fraudulent advertising, but, insofar as these laws apply to "patent medicine" advertising

copy they are to all intents and purposes a dead letter.

But the federal law has brought about marked changes in the trade package. An "Indian Cough Cure" which was neither "Indian" nor a "cure," becomes a "Cough Remedy." A "Cure for Consumption" becomes "A Medicine for Coughs, Colds, etc." A "Walnut Juice" hair dye, which contained no walnut juice, becomes a "Walnut Tint" hair stain. A "Sure Cure for Falling of the Womb" becomes a product that is merely "Recommended for the Treatment of Non-Surgical Cases of Weaknesses and Disorders of the Female Generative Organs." An "Infallible Remedy for Consumption" becomes, by virtue of the power of the federal government, a mere "Tonic Appetizer and Aid to Digestion."

The change in many instances has been, it is true, a change in the letter rather than in the spirit. The "lie direct" has been discarded for the "lie with circumstances." Inferential rather than direct falsehood characterizes many of the claims on the trade packages today. In other avenues of advertising not subject to the penalties of the Food and Drugs Act there is many a fraudulent claim. One can with almost mathematical accuracy determine the falsity of modern "patent medicine" advertising: Subtract the claims made on the trade package from those made elsewhere; what remains—and the residuum will be large—is falsehood!

SUMMARY.

Summed up, it may be said that the advertising of non-proprietary drug products is invariably truthful and conservative; the advertising of scientific proprietary drug products sold for prescription purposes only also, in general, conforms to the truth, with occasional lapses due to over-enthusiastic copy writers. The advertising of unscientific proprietary products offered nominally to the medical profession, but virtually to the public, is invariably exaggerated and misleading and, in some instances at least, fraudulent. The advertising of proprietary products offered directly to the public, that is, of so-called "patent medicines," is notorious for its untruthfulness, not alone in its declaration, but also in its inference.

What is the remedy? For the untruthful advertising of drug products of Group 3—unscientific mixtures offered nominally to the medical profession—relief must be looked for in the better education, and its accompanying discrimination, of the physician of the future. The higher standard of medical education, both in the medical course itself and in the pre-medical educational requirements, will in time automatically bring about the extinction of the unscientific proprietary remedy offered to the medical profession. These factors are already at work. Each year shows a diminution in the number of drug products of Group 3. They either go out of existence entirely or frankly join the ranks of Group 4, the "patent medicines."

The outlook for any radical change in advertising methods of Group 4—the "patent medicines" is not, from the standpoint of public interest, so hopeful. The education of the public will continue to bring about a toning down of the cruder claims made for "patent medicines," and this agency for reform will be aided by

the forces at work in the advertising field making for greater truthfulness. The fundamental evil of the "patent medicine" business will continue to exist, however, so long as proprietaryship and secrecy of composition continue as the controlling factors of the industry. Every physician knows that the number of drugs or drug combinations that are needed to fill the legitimate need for self-treatment on the part of the public is extremely small, and such needs can be amply filled from official products already on the shelves of every druggist in the country. The place of the hundreds of laxative "patent medicines" now on the market could be filled adequately, and with greater safety, by half a dozen official drugs. The same holds true for "patent medicines" sold for other conditions that come within the scope of legitimate self-drugging. So long, however, as the individual putting out a "patent medicine" has a proprietary monopoly in his product, he must as a commercial proposition stimulate the sale of his preparation, first, by making claims that are wholly unwarranted, and, second, by creating an artificial demand for his particular preparation by playing on the fears and imaginations of the public. Under such conditions it is hopeless to expect anything approximating truth in advertising.

☐

Sanatorium Treatment of Tuberculosis.— The author defines the conditions under which the sanatorium can carry out its functions to the best advantage and produce good results.

(a) The cases admitted should be either in an early stage of the disease, or, if more advanced, have been found by observation in a chest hospital to have a reasonable prospect of being made fit for work. (b) Treatment should be prolonged, either in the sanatorium or first in the sanatorium and then in the

colony. Instead of two, three or four months, the recognized period of institutional treatment should be six, twelve or eighteen months. (c) The patient should be free from financial worry regarding the maintenance of his dependants during his treatment. (d) Some relief to the inevitable monotony of sanatorium life should be afforded by well directed schemes for providing a choice of congenial occupations for the patient, preferably one from which he can derive some financial benefit himself, or by which he can earn his living.

GEOGRAPHICAL AND SEASONAL VARIATIONS IN INFANT MORTALITY IN THE UNITED STATES, 1917-1920

FREDERICK S. CRUM, PH.D.

Assistant Statistician, The Prudential Insurance Company of America, Newark, N. J.

Read before Section on Vital Statistics, American Public Health Association, at San Francisco, Cal., September 15, 1920.

How to reduce infant mortality is one of the most pressing health problems of today. More babies saved means larger adult population. Dr. Crum establishes standards whereby to measure future improvement. His charts disclose irregularities related to season or location. They suggest means of closer study through separation of racial statistics.

THE present paper is a partial revision and continuation of the paper entitled "Infant Mortality in the United States During One Year of War," which was read before the Vital Statistics Section, American Public Health Association, at Chicago, December 11, 1918, and published in the American Journal of Public Health, Vol. IX, No. 4, April, 1919. · In the meantime, the 1920 populations of the 46 cities included in the earlier and the present papers have become available and the estimates of infant populations made in 1918 have been revised on the basis of the new, official Census figures. The changes affect principally the four cities included in the Central Atlantic group and the seven cities included in the Western group. For the Central Atlantic group, as a whole, the population estimates made in 1918 were too low, making the infant mortality index* too high; and the population estimates made in 1918 for the Western

group, as a whole, were too high, making the infant mortality index too low.

The revised basic index (no index for any week of the normal year 1917-1918 falling below this figure) for the Central Atlantic group of cities is 90.0 as against 100.0 according to the earlier estimate; and the revised basic index for the Western group of cities is 55.0, as against 50.0 in the earlier estimate. A comparison of the charts in the earlier papers with those presented here will show that the changes are of relatively slight importance in the weekly seasonal indexes and the general trend of the seasonal curves are not, of course, affected in the least, this being dependent upon the actual number of infant deaths as reported by telegraph weekly to the Census Bureau.

---

*The term "index" will be used throughout this paper to express the infant mortality per 1000 of estimated population under one year of age. Infant mortality rate has come to mean infant deaths per 1000 births, the deaths and births being for the same period—week, month or year, as the case may be. For comparative purposes the "index" as here determined is probably as accurate, if not more so, than the "rate" as births are nowhere so completely reported as deaths and the variation in the completeness of birth reporting is considerable, even in the large American cities.

TABLE I

Comparative Infant Mortality of 46 Large American Cities Year Ending September 28, 1918

Cities	Estimated Population Under 1 Year	Reported Deaths Under 1 Year	Index or Deaths per 1,000 Est. Pop. Under 1 Year
North Atlantic:			
Albany............	1,688	224	132.7
Boston...........	14,823	2,011	135.7
Buffalo...........	10,365	1,547	149.3
Cambridge.......	2,405	251	104.4
Fall River.......	3,318	625	188.4
Jersey City......	6,789	814	119.9
Lowell...........	2,435	483	198.4
Newark, N. J....	9,856	1,067	108.3
New Haven......	3,527	411	116.5
New York.......	126,232	11,593	91.7
Philadelphia.....	37,546	4,748	126.5
Pittsburgh.......	13,001	1,915	140 8
Providence.......	5,428	667	122.9
Rochester........	5,182	503	108.6
Syracuse	3,043	454	149.2
Worcester........	3,782	432	114 2
Total.	250,150	27,805	111 2

790

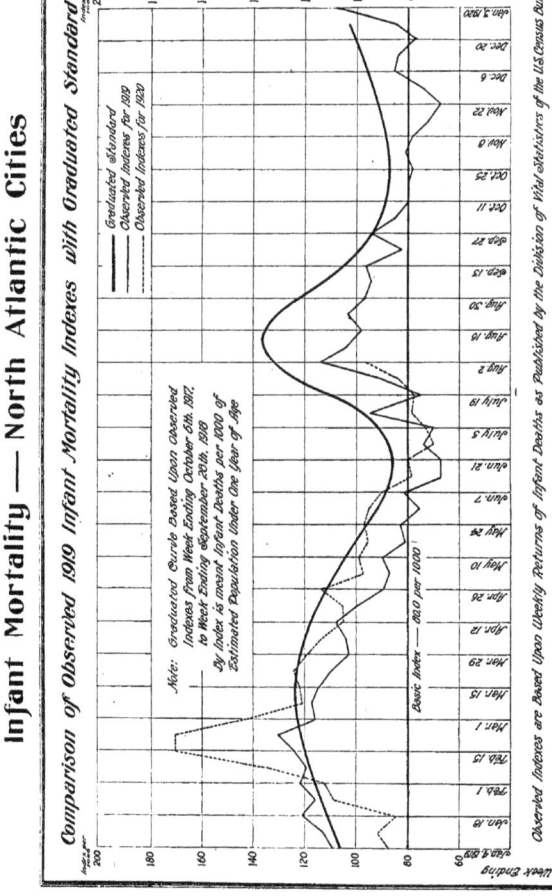

Infant Mortality — North Atlantic Cities

Comparison of Observed 1919 Infant Mortality Indexes with Graduated Standard

Chart No. 1.

Central Atlantic:			
Atlanta.........	4,148	380	91.6
Baltimore.......	12,812	2,036	158.9
Richmond.......	3,244	476	146.7
Washington......	6,903	844	122.3
Total........	27,107	3,736	137.8
Southern:			
Birmingham......	3,747	431	115.0
Louisville........	3,902	432	110.7
Memphis........	2,660	298	112.0
Nashville........	2,263	267	118.0
New Orleans.....	7,630	888	116.4
Total........	20,202	2,316	114.6
Middle Western:			
Chicago.........	58,343	6,093	104.4
Cincinnati.......	6,626	735	110.9
Cleveland........	18,469	1,800	97.5
Columbus........	3,520	410	116.5
Dayton..........	2,781	251	90.3
Grand Rapids....	2,815	217	77.1
Indianapolis.....	4,908	536	109.2
Kansas City, Mo..	4,648	514	110.6
Milwaukee.......	9,373	1,077	114.9
Minneapolis......	6,577	594	90.3
Omaha..........	3,004	251	83.6
St. Louis........	13,685	1,265	92.4
St. Paul.........	3,990	365	91.5
Toledo..........	4,475	484	108.2
Total........	143,214	14,592	101.9
Western:			
Denver..........	4,001	397	99.2
Los Angeles......	7,880	577	73.2
Oakland.........	3,611	214	59.3
Portland.........	3,694	328	88.8
San Francisco....	7,233	475	65.7
Seattle..........	4,384	299	68.2
Spokane.........	2,048	136	66.4
Total........	32,851	2,426	73.8

In Table I are presented the comparative infant mortality indexes (infant deaths per 1,000 estimated population under one year of age) for the year ending September 28, 1918, and on the basis of the Census populations of 1910 and 1920. The proportion of the total population of ages under one year is assumed to have been the same as in the Census of 1910, as the 1920 populations with distinction of age are not yet available. According to this summary the lowest index was for Oakland, Calif. (59.3) and the highest index was for Lowell, Mass. (198.4). Other relatively low infant mortality indexes in the normal year ending September 28, 1918, were 65.7 for San Francisco, Calif., 66.4 for Spokane, Wash., 68.2 for Seattle, Wash., and 73.2 for Los Angeles, Calif. In the cities of the Middle Western group Grand Rapids, Mich., had an index of 77.1 and Omaha, Neb., the relatively low index of 83.6. New York City had the lowest infant mortality index (91.7) of

any city in the North Atlantic group; and Atlanta, Ga., had the lowest index (91.6) of any city in the Central Atlantic group. In the Western group no one of the seven cities had an infant mortality index as here calculated as high as 100.0, while in contrast not one of the five cities of the Southern group had an index as low as 110.0, the average being 114.6, with no wide departures from that average in any city of the group. In the North Atlantic group Fall River, Mass., like Lowell, had a very high index (188.4), while Buffalo and Syracuse, N. Y., also had relatively high indexes of 149.3 and 149.2, respectively. In the Central Atlantic group of four cities the highest index was for Baltimore, Md., or 158.9, but Richmond, Va., also had a relatively high index for this group, or 146.7. Table I should be a valuable standard or norm by which to measure the subsequent improvement, or otherwise, in the infant mortality of the various cities, 46 in number, embraced therein.

TABLE II

Comparative Infant Mortality of 46 Large American Cities
Year Ending December 27, 1919

Cities	Estimated Population Under 1 Year	Reported Deaths Under 1 Year	Index or Deaths per 1,000 Est. Pop. Under 1 Year
North Atlantic:			
Albany..........	1,718	174	101.3
Boston..........	15,057	1,813	120.4
Buffalo..........	10,626	1,398	131.6
Cambridge.......	2,420	200	82.6
Fall River.......	3,322	417	125.5
Jersey City*.....	6,894	647	101.6
Lowell..........	2,455	385	156.8
Newark.........	10,107	867	85.8
New Haven......	3,625	301	83.0
New York......	129,342	10,630	82.2
Philadelphia.....	38,419	3,769	98.1
Pittsburgh.......	13,793	1,630	118.2
Providence......	5,553	514	92.6
Rochester.......	5,397	470	87.1
Syracuse........	3,138	358	114.1
Worcester**.....	3,891	360	94.3
Total........	255,757	23,933	93.8
Central Atlantic:			
Atlanta..........	4,297	359	83.5
Baltimore........	13,293	1,715	129.0
Richmond.......	3,349	410	122.4
Washington......	7,167	702	97.9
Total........	28,106	3,186	113.4

*Data available for only 48 weeks.
**Data available for only 51 weeks.

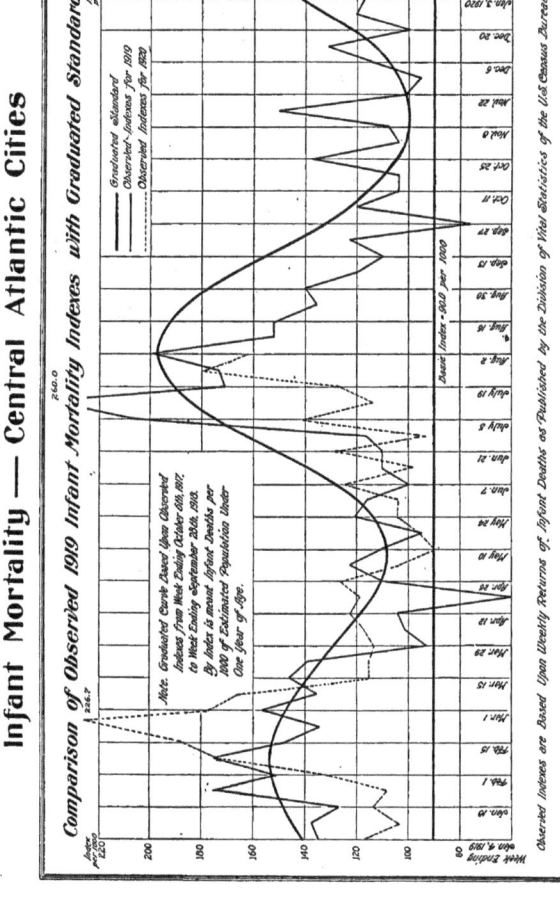

Infant Mortality — Central Atlantic Cities

Comparison of Observed 1919 Infant Mortality Indexes with Graduated Standard

Observed Indexes are Based Upon Weekly Returns of Infant Deaths as Published by the Division of Vital Statistics of the U.S. Census Bureau

Chart No. 2.

Southern:			
Birmingham	3,900	391	100.3
Louisville........	3,929	389	99.0
Memphis........	2,740	358	130.7
Nashville........	2,287	272	118.9
New Orleans.....	7,776	715	91.9
Total........	20,632	2,125	103.0

Middle Western:			
Chicago..........	60,080	5,746	95.6
Cincinnati........	6,720	615	91.5
Cleveland........	19,342	1,513	78.2
Columbus........	3,649	385	105.5
Dayton..........	2,886	279	96.7
Grand Rapids....	2,896	237	81.8
Indianapolis.....	5,106	518	101.4
Kansas City, Mo..	4,800	523	109.0
Milwaukee	9,638	1,010	104.8
Minneapolis	6,790	520	76.6
Omaha,..........	3,175	298	93.9
St. Louis........	13,917	949	68.2
St. Paul........	4,117	283	68.7
Toledo..........	4,694	440	93.7
Total.....	147,810	13,316	90.1

Western:			
Denver.........	4,105	357	87.0
Los Angeles......	8,457	605	71.5
Oakland.........	3,787	211	55.7
Portland........	3,808	325	85.3
San Francisco...:	7,435	502	67.5
Seattle..........	4,555	306	67.2
Spokane....	2,047	120	58.6
Total.......	34,194	2,426	70.9

In Table II an effort has been made to calculate the infant mortality indexes of the same 46 cities for the year ending December 27, 1919. The striking feature in the comparison of Table II with Table I (both for 52 weeks, or a full year) is the almost uniformly lower indexes disclosed in Table II. This is brought out clearly in the following summary, Table III, limited to a comparison of five geographical groups of cities:

TABLE III

Comparative Infant Mortality of Five Geographical Groups of 46 Cities

(Indexes or Deaths per 1,000 Estimated Population Under One Year)

Group	(1) Year Ending Sept. 28, 1918	(2) Year Ending Dec. 27, 1919	Decrease Actual	Per- centage
North Atlantic....	111.2	93.8	17.4	15.6
Central Atlantic....	137.8	113.4	24.4	17.7
Southern............	114.6	103.0	11.6	10.1
Middle Western....	101.9	90.1	11.8	11.6
Western.............	73.8	70.9	2.9	3.9

How much of this favorable showing for 1919 was due to the splendid organization work of the Federal Children's Bureau initiated in 1918 in co-operation with the Council of National Defense it is impossible to say, but it must have been in part responsible for these favorable results. The comparatively low 1919 indexes may in part have been due

also to the influenza epidemic in the last four months of 1918, which affected the infant mortality adversely and intensively for short periods during the last three months of 1918, and only to a much lesser degree in the early months of 1919, with the exception of the group of Western cities. These facts will be discussed in more detail subsequently, and chart No. 5 visualizes the effects of the 1918-1919 influenza epidemic on infant mortality. The recurrent epidemic of 1920 also had an unfavorable effect on the infant mortality, but for shorter durations than in 1918-1919. See Charts 1, 2, 3 and 4.

In Table IV are summarized the infant mortality indexes (yearly basis) for the first 31 weeks of 1920. On the basis of the facts presented comparisons of the 1920 mortality with the normal year, 1917-1918, can readily be made for the individual cities as well as for the geographical groups. All of these group indexes are lower for the first seven months of 1920 than for the normal or standard year ended September 28, 1918, with the exception of that including the Western cities, which was 89.4 in 1920, against 73.8 for the year 1917-1918.

TABLE IV

Comparative Infant Mortality of 46 Large American Cities for 31 Weeks Ending July 31, 1920

Cities	Estimated Population Under 1 Year	Reported Deaths Under 1 Year	Index or Deaths per 1,000 Est. Pop. Under 1 Year
North Atlantic:			
Albany..........	1,728	109	105.9
Boston.........	15,135	1,224	135.7
Buffalo.........	10,713	819	128.2
Cambridge.. ...	2,425	155	107.3
Fall River.......	3,324	250	126.2
Jersey City* ...	6,229	449	124.9
Lowell... ...	2,461	239	163.0
Newark.........	10,190	636	104.7
New Haven.....	3,657	232	106.4
New York......	130,332	7,293	93.9
Philadelphia.....	38,710	2,344	101.6
Pittsburgh......	13,857	1,005	121.6
Providence......	5,594	344	103.1
Rochester.......	5,468	355	108.9
Syracuse*.......	3,169	234	128.0
Worcester.... .	3,928	253	108.1
Total.... ..	256,920	15,941	104.2
Central Atlantic:			
Atlanta.........	4,346	294	113.4
Baltimore.......	13,454	1,138	141.9
Richmond.......	3,384	270	133.8
Washington......	7,255	496	114.7
Total.	28,439	2,198	129.6

*Data limited to 30 weeks

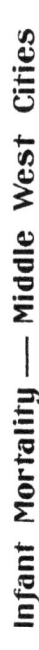

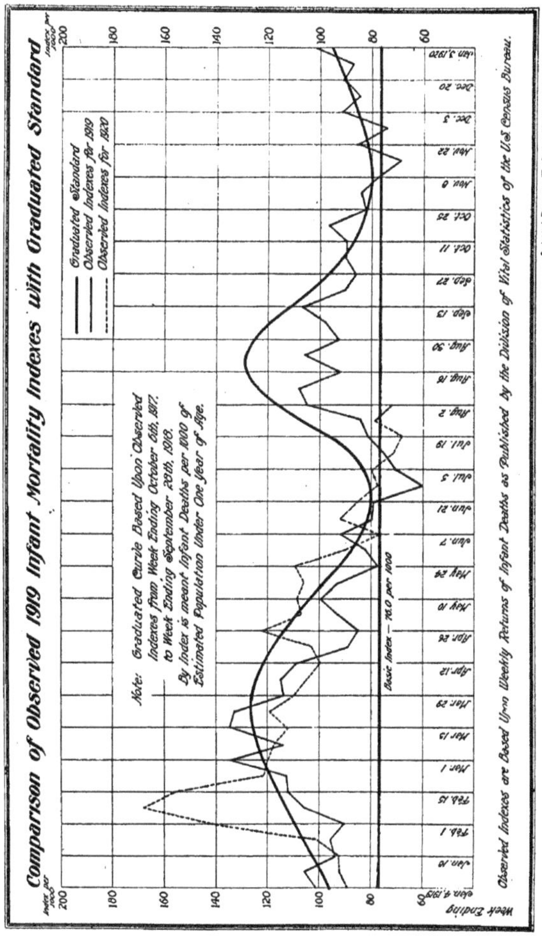

Infant Mortality — Middle West Cities

Comparison of Observed 1919 Infant Mortality Indexes with Graduated Standard

Graduated Standard
Observed Indexes for 1919
Observed Indexes for 1920

Note: Graduated Curve Based Upon Observed Indexes from Week Ending October 4th, 1917, to Week Ending September 20th, 1918. By Index is meant Infant Deaths per 1000 of Estimated Population Under One Year of Age.

Basic Index — 78.0 per 1000

Observed Indexes are Based Upon Weekly Returns of Infant Deaths as Published by the Division of Vital Statistics of the U.S. Census Bureau.

Statistician's Department, The Prudential Insurance Company of America

Chart No. 3.

Southern:

Birmingham......	3,949	322	136.8
Louisville........	3,938	191	81.4
Memphis*.......	2,166	242	151.6
Nashville........	2,294	187	136.8
New Orleans....	7,824	505	108.2
Total........	20,771	1,447	117.4

*Data limited to 30 weeks.

Middle Western:

Chicago.........	60,659	3,672	101.5
Cincinnati.......	6,752	408	101.4
Cleveland.......	19,633	937	80.1
Columbus.......	3,692	231	105.0
Dayton.........	2,921	177	101.6
Grand Rapids....	2,983	188	105.7
Indianapolis....	5,172	374	121.3
Kansas City, Mo..	4,850	422	146.0
Milwaukee......	9,227	631	108.8
Minneapolis.....	6,861	371	90.7
Omaha,.........	3,232	262	136.0
St. Louis........	13,995	702	84.2
St. Paul........	4,160	200	80.6
Toledo.........	4,767	294	103.4
Total........	149,414	8,869	99.6

Western:

Denver...:.....	4,139	274	111.0
Los Angeles.....	8,650	528	102.4
Oakland........	3,845	179	78.1
Portland........	3,846	184	80.2
San Francisco...	7,503	339	75.8
Seattle.........	4,612	240	87.3
Spokane........	2,047	108	88.5
Total........	34,642	1,850	89.4

The effect on infant mortality of the 1918-1919 influenza epidemic was interesting. The indexes and the weekly curves seem to indicate quite clearly that in a large part the effect was indirect, that is, that the excess infant mortality was due largely to lack of care and that infant attack by the disease was not wholly responsible. In most cities the highest infant mortality indexes occurred when the epidemic was at its height in the given city or group of cities, but these high indexes dropped more quickly to normal than the adult death rates. Lack of mother's care, scarcity of nurses and physicians, and possibly other social and economic maladjustments probably brought about a considerable portion of the excess infant mortality during the influenza epidemic.

Table V presents the facts roughly indicative of the excess in the infant mortality during the influenza period, 1918-1919, but Table VI brings out the details week by week for the four groups of cities for which reliable data are available. This table, supplemented by Chart No. 5, gives a very complete picture of the effect of the influenza wave on

TABLE V

Comparative Infant Mortality of 46 Large American Cities
For 22 Weeks Ending March 1, 1919

Cities	Estimated Population Under 1 Year	Reported Deaths Under 1 Year	Index or Deaths per 1,000 Est. Pop. Under 1 Year
North Atlantic:			
Albany..........	1,708	93	128.1
Boston.........	14,979	1,052	187.6
Buffalo.........	10,539	780	174.7
Cambridge......	2,415	127	124.4
Fall River.......	3,321	225	160.0
Jersey City*.....	6,859	247	156.0
Lowell.........	2,448	228	220.1
Newark........	10,023	507	119.6
New Haven.....	3,592	187	123.0
New York......	128,352	5,883	108.3
Philadelphia.....	38,128	2,427	150.5
Pittsburgh......	13,729	1,008	173.6
Providence......	5,511	344	147.5
Rochester.......	5,325	273	121.2
Syracuse........	3,106	218	166.0
Worcester**.....	3,855	133	99.7
Total........	253,890	13,742	129.9
Central Atlantic:			
Atlanta.........	4,247	191	106.3
Baltimore.......	13,133	931	167.6
Richmond****...	3,314	220	157.0
Washington......	7,079	878	125.6
Total........	27,773	1,718	146.2
Southern:			
Birmingham****..	3,848	193	124.2
Louisville.......	3,920	219	132.1
Memphis***.....	2,713	98	94.0
Nashville........	2,279	134	139.0
New Orleans....	7,727	400	122.4
Total........	20,487	1,044	123.0
Middle Western:			
Chicago........	59,501	2,946	117.0
Cincinnati.......	6,689	342	120.9
Cleveland.......	19,051	648	80.4
Columbus.......	3,606	156	102.2
Dayton.........	2,851	137	113.6
Grand Rapids....	2,869	110	90.6
Indianapolis....	5,040	238	111.9
Kansas City, Mo..	4,749	213	106.0
Milwaukee......	9,550	507	125.5
Minneapolis.....	6,719	250	88.0
Omaha****.....	3,118	174	138.1
St. Louis........	13,840	510	87.1
St. Paul........	4,075	150	87.0
Toledo.........	4,621	223	114.1
Total........	146,279	6,604	106.8
Western:			
Denver.........	4,070	144	83.6
Los Angeles.....	8,265	360	103.0
Oakland........	3,728	130	82.4
Portland........	3,770	169	106.0
San Francisco...	7,368	310	99.5
Seattle.........	4,498	183	96.2
Spokane........	2,047	83	95.7
Total........	33,746	1,379	96.6

*Data available for only 12 weeks.
**Data available for only 18 weeks.
***Data available for only 20 weeks.
****Data available for only 21 weeks.

infant mortality. In the North Atlantic cities the excess infant mortality was largest, followed by the Central Atlantic group. The Western group of cities came third, but there the unfavorable effect was longer drawn out than elsewhere, the cities in that group being so

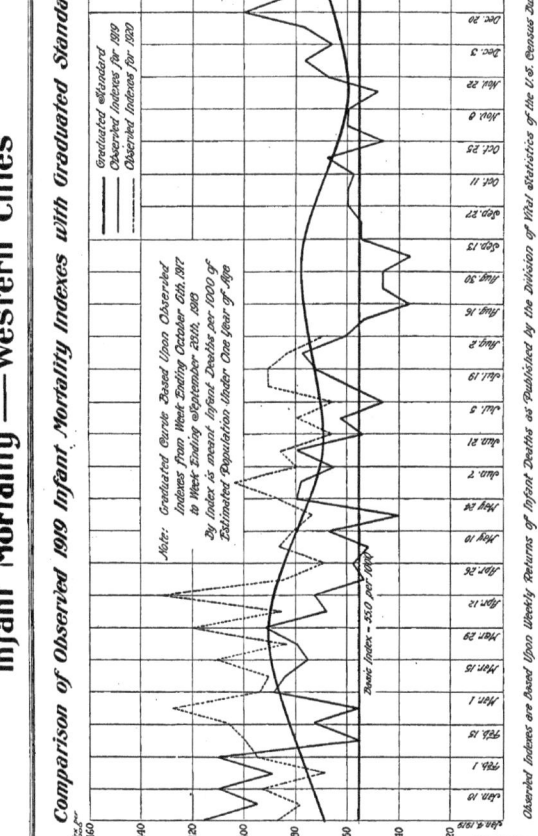

Infant Mortality — Western Cities

Comparison of Observed 1919 Infant Mortality Indexes with Graduated Standard

Chart No. 4.

far apart, apparently the epidemic wave traveled slower in that section.

The most valuable part of this paper, in my judgment, are the five charts showing the weekly fluctuations in the infant mortality indexes for four geographical groups of cities. Unfortunately, the Southern cities could not be successfully charted because of irregularities, due probably to the fact that the

TABLE VI

Comparative Infant Mortality
Influenza Epidemic Period 1918-1919, Compared with 1917
Infant Deaths per 1,000 Estimated Population Under
One Year of Age, Reduced to Yearly Basis

North Atlantic Cities

1917 (Standard)		1918		Percent Increase 1918 over
Week Ending	Index	Week Ending	Index	1917
Sept. 22	97.8	Sept. 21	110.3	12.8
" 29	93.5	" 28	113.3	21.2
Oct. 6	90.6	Oct. 5	127.8	41.1
" 13	88.2	" 12	159.1	80.4
" 20	87.2	" 19	200.9	130.4
" 27	86.8	" 26	246.3	183.8
Nov. 3	87.1	Nov. 2	205.5	135.9
" 10	88.0	" 9	141.5	60.8
" 17	89.3	" 16	108.9	21.9
" 24	91.2	" 23	99.3	8.9
Dec. 1	93.3	" 30	93.7	0.4
Sept. 22-Dec. 1	90.3	Sept. 21-Nov. 30	146.1	61.8

TABLE VII

Central Atlantic Cities

1917 (Standard)		1918		Percent Increase 1918 over
Week Ending	Index	Week Ending	Index	1917
Sept. 22	160.9	Sept. 21	129.0	—19.8
" 30	149.5	" 28	145.9	— 2.4
Oct. 6	138.9	Oct. 5	164.9	18.7
" 13	129.5	" 12	245.2	89.3
" 20	121.5	" 19	372.1	206.2
" 27	115.1	" 26	380.5	230.6
Nov. 3	111.1	Nov. 2	205.1	84.6
" 10	109.1	" 9	135.3	24.0
" 17	108.9	" 16	122.6	12.6
" 24	110.8	" 23	129.0	16.4
Dec. 1	114.5	" 30	80.3	—29.9
Sept. 22-Dec. 1	124.5	Sept. 21-Nov. 30	191.8	53.3

TABLE VIII

Middle Western Cities

1917 (Standard)		1918		Percent Increase 1918 over
Week Ending	Index	Week Ending	Index	1917
Sept. 22	103.4	Sept. 21	112.2	8.5
" 29	94.4	" 28	107.9	11.9
Oct. 6	90.8	Oct. 5	107.9	18.8
" 13	86.7	" 12	117.1	35.1
" 20	83.8	" 19	100.9	20.4
" 27	81.8	" 26	174.4	113.2
Nov. 3	80.7	Nov. 2	148.2	83.6
" 10	80.2	" 9	124.2	54.9
" 17	80.4	" 16	101.3	26.0
" 24	81.4	" 23	89.8	10.3
Dec. 1	82.7	" 30	93.9	13.5
Sept. 22-Dec. 1	86.2	Sept. 21-Nov. 30	116.2	34.8

TABLE IX

Western Cities

1917 (Standard)		1918		Percent Increase 1918 over
Week Ending	Index	Week Ending	Index	1917
Oct. 20	65.3	Oct. 19	67.8	3.8
" 27	62.9	" 26	112.6	79.0
Nov. 3	61.1	Nov. 2	102.5	67.8
" 10	60.0	" 9	119.8	99.7
" 17	59.4	" 16	102.5	72.5
" 24	59.5	" 23	85.1	43.0
Dec. 1	60.2	" 30	89.5	48.7
" 8	61.6	Dec. 7	92.4	50.0
" 15	63.1	" 14	99.6	57.8
" 22	64.9	" 21	108.2	66.7
" 29	66.8	" 28	73.6	10.2
Jan. 5	68.9	Jan. 4	115.4	67.5
" 12	71.1	" 11	95.2	33.9
" 19	73.4	" 18	109.7	49.5
" 26	75.6	" 25	88.0	16.4
Feb. 2	77.9	Feb. 1	109.7	40.8
		Oct. 19, 1918, to		
Oct. 20-Feb. 2	65.7	Feb. 1, 1919	98.2	49.5

white and colored infant deaths are not separately reported to the Census Bureau in the data here analyzed. The relatively high indexes and wide seasonal variations in the Central Atlantic group, may also be attributed in part to the large Negro element in the population of that group.

In the preparation of the data for charting and in the construction of the charts I am deeply indebted to Mr. Arne Fisher, who is almost solely responsible for that part, the most important, I think, of this paper. These charts are based upon the fact that infant mortality indexes by weekly intervals exhibit a cyclic periodicity. If the data here subjected to mathematical treatment (1917-1918 graduated curves) were available also with distinction of cause, it undoubtedly would be entirely feasible to plot the curves which would be typical of the geographical areas and of the seasons. Causes of mortality inherent in congenital debility would exhibit a very different series of curves than the respiratory and digestive causes. The last two groups are undoubtedly more affected by season. Even a casual study and comparison of these five charts will reveal the wide variations in infant mortality, due in large part to locality and season.

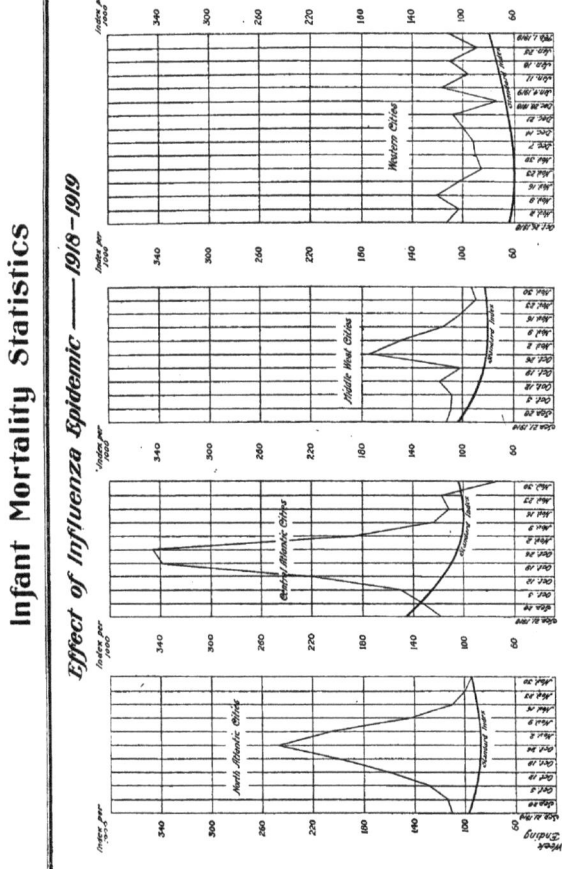

Infant Mortality Statistics

Effect of Influenza Epidemic —— 1918 – 1919

Chart No. 5.

EDITORIAL SECTION

AMERICAN JOURNAL OF PUBLIC HEALTH

Publication Office: 124 W. Polk Street, Chicago, Ill.
EDITORIAL OFFICE: 169 MASSACHUSETTS AVE., BOSTON, MASS.

A. W. HEDRICH, C. P. H., Editor   J. RITCHIE, JR., Associate Editor

Editorial Assistants

E. R. HAYHURST, M.D.   P. M. HOLMES, M.D.   FRANCIS H. SLACK, M.D.
DAVID GREENBERG   JAMES A. TOBEY   JAMES M. STRANG
M. P. HORWOOD, M.S.   HOMER N. CALVER

Board of Advisory Editors

PETER H. BRYCE, M.D., Ottawa, Canada   PROF. M. J. ROSENAU, Boston, Mass.
CHARLES V. CHAPIN, M.D., Providence, R. I.   PROF. W. T. SEDGWICK, Cambridge, Mass.
EUGENE R. KELLEY, M.D., Boston, Mass.   PROF. GEORGE C. WHIPPLE, Cambridge, Mass.
W. A. EVANS, M.D., Chicago, Ill.   PROF. S. M. GUNN, Paris, France.

All expressions of opinion and all statements of supposed facts are published on authority of the writer under whose name they appear, and are not to be regarded as expressing the views of the American Public Health Association, unless such statements or opinions have been adopted by vote of the Association.

NOTICE TO SUBSCRIBERS: Subscription Price, payable in advance, $4.00 per year for United States and possessions; $4.50 for Canada and other foreign countries. Single copies, 50 cents postpaid. Membership in the American Public Health Association, including subscription to Journal, $5.00 per year. In Change of Address please give both old and new address, and mail before the tenth of the month to take effect with the current issue. Mailing Date, 5th of each month. Advertisements accepted only when commendable, and worth while both to reader and advertiser. News Items, interesting clippings and illustrations are gladly received, together with name of sender. Copyright, 1919, by A. W. Hedrich.

HEELS AND TOES

One may well look at the feet of our women on the street and ask, "Are we in civilized America in the twentieth century or is it mediæval China with women's feet constricted and distorted?" The heels and the toes that fashionable shoes present should set the sanitarian to thinking.

It is not in America alone or merely now that these problems present themselves. At the beginning of the war, before this country became interested to the extent of taking a part in it, Dr. A. Ritschl, a German, voiced in the periodical literature of the day the following sentiments of disapproval: "But how badly the feet are treated by a majority of our people, partly from ignorance, partly through foolish vanity, by shoes too short or too narrow, with heels too high. What misshapen and deforming shoes they dare offer our women and girls even in this grave time of war, when it is the duty of every one to make himself strong and efficient." He further comments on conditions as they then existed by saying, "A glance at the people moving in a city street shows that crowds of these have bitten at the injurious bait:" Dr. Ritschl goes on to discuss the high-heeled, narrow shoe from the anatomical and medical points of view. He also comments on the heel that is too low.

The condition that set this German physician to thinking is the rule, almost, in this country. The streets of all our cities witness great crowds of women and girls shod in injurious foot gear. It is not that men have not injurious and insanitary fashions, but at the moment it is the high heel and pointed, wedge shaped toe, that are under discussion. High heels on the street furnish another example of what has been termed "the American failing of diamonds at breakfast," and while they may be demanded for a short while as a portion of party adornments, they are obviously out of place on the street. But they are there and furthermore are worn by women in occupations requiring continuous standing, by shop girls, restaurant waitresses, elevator attendants and factory employees.

It is important in this connection to realize that more and more it is known and taught that the human body is a connected whole, and local causes for what appear to be local ailments are less and less sought. "What affects one part of the body affects the whole" is an expression of the thought of today.

America is essentially a mechanical nation and the false mechanics of the high heel should appeal to every thinking individual. The principles of the arch apply equally well whether the structure be of stone and mortar or bone and muscle. The main arch of the foot supports great weight, the entire weight of the body, and it is important that the stresses be properly provided for and that the arch have a firm foundation. The high heel really violates both these principles; it shifts the strains and changes the foundation to an insecure one. Watch a French heel strike the sidewalk. See how uncertain it is when it comes into contact with the walk, see how it "wobbles" before coming to rest, and see how, even then, the lines of support are not the vertical ones of natural posture.

The tilted arch means undue strain somewhere, the indecision of the step means strain somewhere, and the final posture of rest means still other strains brought to bear on muscles not intended for the work. The high heel means disarrangement of the regular lines of support of the body above the foot. Every engineer knows that compensations are necessary. When the elevated heel throws the knee forward to maintain a comfortable angle at the ankle, it is balanced by a backward-tilted thigh and this again demands a forward-leaning backbone and body. Instead of the upright figure that is normal for the support of the weight, this is upheld by a line broken at three points, a mechanical disadvantage. Be these departures from natural conditions ever so small, they mean unfortunate leverages and the calling into play of muscles not intended for the work.

The toboggan slide of the sole upheld at one end by the high heel needs no discussion for those conversant with mechanics. It is inevitable that the foot, impelled by the weight of the body, slide down the inclined plane of the sole till restrained by the toe-end or the sides of the shoe. If deliberate intention had sought to create continuous inconvenience and final injury to the foot, it could hardly have hit upon a more cunning device for the purpose. It is no use to urge the well-known plea, "They are perfectly comfortable and miles too wide," for the mechanical conditions are there and injury will inevitably follow. Then of course there are important medical conditions in distortion and constriction to be considered, in which the foot is not the only sufferer.

It is a well-known military maxim that an army is as good as its feet and one especial care in the late war was to have the American soldier well fitted to shoes. Some original invention made this possible in a minimum of time. For the first time in the country the scientific measurement of the feet was undertaken for very large companies of men, and from these measurements it developed that half to three-quarters of the men of the country were wearing shoes from half a size to two sizes too small. This difficulty, so far as the army is concerned, was corrected in the interests of efficiency. The reports prove, however, that the men of the United States have not given the attention to their feet that good health and efficiency demand.

The person, man or woman, whose ability to walk is for any reason handicapped runs the risk of falling into a vicious circle. He loses the amount of exercise requisite for good health, and ill health tends continually to lessen the already insufficient measure of exercise.

There is much more in the proper shoeing of a nation than appears at first sight. In an enlightened age the feet are truly worthy of sane and proper treatment. Care of the feet demands today in good measure the attention of popular educators in public health.

QUARANTINE OF THE CRETIC

The Cretic incident in the port of Boston involves important principles of public health. It would appear that the steamship arrived in Boston without technically perfect health papers from the port of sailing. The crew of the steamship objected, it is said, to the practices and requirements of the quarantine officers. If the public press is to be credited, there was talk of withdrawing the steamer from the port in future sailings. This, however, has not been done. The matter of the stringency of the quarantine administration was discussed by the Boston Chamber of Commerce and it is said that a telegram of complaint was sent by it to Washington. The situation, whatever it may have been in reality, displays the need of information to various parties of what quarantine really means.

The story of the quarantine service in Boston is not without interest. Developed as a local enterprise, carried on for a good many years under the supervision of Boston's health department, it had the reputation of being second to none in the country in quality of administration. One by one the ports on the Atlantic and Gulf states came under Government quarantine supervision, with Boston and New York alone outstanding. Six or seven years ago in the interests of complete standardization of quarantine regulations, Boston made over its quarantine to the National Government, and it was presumed that the management in New York would be likewise standardized.

The bubonic plague and other Oriental infections are knocking at our doors. The tremendous movement of men from all quarters of the earth has focussed in middle Europe maladies heretofore endemic in Asia or Eastern Russia. Infectious diseases are nearer this country than ever before. The plague has made its appearance in a number of our Southern ports, and other undesirable diseases are known to be running in European cities of the Mediterranean and Baltic. Never before in the world has this country been called upon to exert so close a watch over its immigrants and incoming shipping as now.

It is not a new story for business to interest itself in quarantine. California has had an experience of the kind that should be a lesson to every other section of the country. It is a matter of history that commercial interests refused to acknowledge the existence of the plague on the West Coast until it had gained such a foothold that the results are with us yet. It is important that a similar mistake be not made elsewhere. The health of the people is of more consequence than the business of the few, and it is unfortunate that proper official acts should find criticism through the press.

The Boston Transcript, editorially, speaks of the relationships between business bodies and Governmental quarantine functions in these words, showing a firm stand on good and true health principles: "If the health officer of the port of Boston has been enforcing the laws passed by Congress for the protection of the public health with diligence and intelligence, he has been doing his duty as an officer of the Government. . . . In the discharge of that duty he deserves the whole-hearted support of the people of Boston, and the nation to which Boston is one of the chief gateways. . . . On this account it is to be hoped that the Surgeon General of the Public Health Service will not jump to the conclusion that the Boston Chamber of Commerce speaks for all the people of Boston in its telegram of complaint against alleged quarantine discrimination at this port. If Dr. Bryan, the representative here of Surgeon General Creel, has been derelict in duty, why did not the Chamber of Commerce so report? If he has not been derelict why does the Chamber of Commerce, instead of supporting him, appeal for an investigation of his office? What are the facts in the case? They should be published before the name of Boston is used in a way to weaken his authority."

It is most important that official business bodies and representatives of the press view the question of quarantine as a uniformly acting Government Service designed for the protection of the health of the nation.

BOOKS AND REPORTS REVIEWED

A National Plan for Health Service. *Report of the [English] Consultative Council on Medical and Allied Services.*

No country or great body of people has laid out or adopted for itself any well thought out or comprehensive scheme of universal service in curative and preventive medicine. This, in spite of the fact that there have been made in many countries broad and general applications of scientific knowledge in the industrial, agricultural and economic fields. The field of health is as yet, however, largely untilled and this condition exists in face of the tremendous strides that have been made in the last few decades by medical and sanitary science. Medical men and public health workers everywhere are beginning to realize that the day is past for a haphazard application of scientific principles to cure the ills of the race. Progressive men and women in our field are thinking about and looking forward to the time when for this country and perhaps for the world there will be put into operation an intelligent and all-including plan that may logically attack the problems of disease prevention and cure, infant welfare and depleted vitality.

It has fallen to England to take the first step in this direction. This country now has a plan for a systematized health and medical service established on a basis of locality but applicable area for area to the whole kingdom. The plan is given in the interim report of the Consultative Council on Medical and Allied Services, to the British Ministry of Health. The *Lancet* for May 20th and the *Medical Officer* of the same date outline and quote extensively this report. The document first prepares the reader for a complete pattern of organization designed to meet the needs of any community and notes the facts that have created this need. Medical services are classified into (1) those which are domiciliary as distinct from those which are institutional and (2) those which concern the section of the population and not the sick individuals. The periphery of the proposed scheme is constituted by the preven-

tive and curative services which revolve around the home, such as those of the doctor, dentist, nurse, druggist or midwife. Various other "communal" services, preventive and curative are brought together to form one organization in an institution called a health center. The domiciliary services of a given district are based on a local health center. Patients retain their own doctors but have in addition the advantage of an institution conducted by the general practitioners of the district in conjunction with an efficient nursing service and the aid of visiting consultants and specialists.

Just as a group of homes is based on a local health center, so a group of these centers is based on a primary health center. Here is extensive equipment and specialized personnel. A third institutional element enters into the scheme, namely a teaching hospital having a medical school. The hospital would receive cases of unusual difficulty and in addition the special departments and laboratories of the hospital would be courts of reference and would lead and inspire special services of the health centers attached to it.

The Report is evidently a lengthy one but it brings out several points of interest to health workers in this country. Not the least of these is the plan laid down for a new type of health authority to bring about unity of local control for all health services both curative and preventive. It is suggested that the "health authority" be invested in a body which is either a statutory committee of the existing local government or an independent body. Three-fifths of the members of this committee are to be elected by popular vote, the remaining two-fifths to consist of persons whose special knowledge would be of value in health questions. A majority of these should be nominated by the local medical advisory council. This council should consist of 10 to 20 persons elected periodically by and from the registered practitioners resident in the area. The health officer and his two chief assistants should be ex-officio members of this advisory council.

The plan outlined is comprehensive as well as extensive.

Whether or not it will be adopted remains to be seen. In any event the present report is not final. Regardless of these considerations, however, the fact remains that the time is not far off when in America it will be necessary to take cognizance of the lack of a uniform health service and to adopt a plan which will supply a uniform all-including program for the present dilatory methods and palliative measures which now exist.—*Homer N. Calver.*

✛

The Human Costs of the War. *Homer Folks, Harper & Brothers, 1920. 326 pages. Illustrated.*

Colonel Homer Folks as organizer and director of civil affairs for the American Red Cross in France and later as Special Commissioner to southeastern Europe, had an opportunity afforded to few to estimate at first hand the toll in sickness, suffering and death exacted as a part of the price of the world war. From his previous wide experience in public health and social economics, he was unusually well qualified to undertake such a task of human bookkeeping. Under the above title the author describes his investigations in detail.

Starting from France on Armistice Day, Col. Folks and his party made a survey of the war-stricken countries for the purpose of estimating the net results of the conflict on human welfare and of reporting how best the conditions found could be met.

The countries visited included Serbia, Belgium, France, Italy and Greece. In each of these countries the attempt was made to secure at first hand the actual facts regarding the condition of the people in respect to food, clothing, housing, health, including the ravages of the various communicable diseases, and also the number of widows and orphans left dependent as a result of the war.

Some conception of the terrific conditions facing the stricken countries can be gathered from the author's estimates that 10,000,000 people are homeless as a result of the war; that 42,000,000 more were subjected to the indignities and deprivations of enemy rule, that 9,000,000 soldiers died of wounds or disease; that there are 50,000,000 manless homes and 10,000,000 homes without children, where there would have been children under normal conditions.

The somber subject matter of the book is lightened by the power of the author to portray the scenes of desolation and the ghastly facts in a manner that holds the interest of the reader.

As the author is a prominent public hygienist his report of conditions in the devastated regions will be of particular interest to other workers in this field.—*B. R. R.*

✛

Medico-Military Review. This is a mimeographed publication of 15 to 20 pages, issued semi-monthly as a supplement to the Bulletin of the Surgeon General's Office. It was established December 1, 1919, and has a circulation of 750 distributed to reach all officers of the Medical Department of the Army. The circulation list also includes a few civilians, medical libraries, and medical journals, which have requested the addition of their names to the mailing list.

The Review is edited by the Division of Laboratories and Infectious Diseases of the Surgeon General's Office and serves as a medium through which news items of current interest, especially those of a medico-military nature, and information bearing upon the problems of disease control, abstracts of important articles appearing in Medical Journals and notes on investigations being carried on in the Army, can be placed in the hands of officers of the Medical Department. Each issue contains a statistical report of the U. S. Army hospital bed capacity and current admission rates of the important communicable diseases.

✛

Healthy Living. *Books I and II. Charles-Edward Amory Winslow, D.P.H. Enlarged edition. Each with a chapter by Walter Camp. New York and Chicago: Charles E. Merrill Co. $0.84 and $1.12 respectively.*

When Professor C.-E. A. Winslow wrote his little books on healthy living two or three years ago they were recognized at once as a wide departure from the stereotyped form of text book on health and hygiene. They appealed especially to the younger generation, although grown-ups were by no means excluded, through the novel presentation of the various subjects, the topics being the central thoughts of well-written little stories rather than of condensed paragraphs. Interest of children, for example, is excited in the preparation made by the knights of old who in their training were taught to conserve · health and strength for their future great work. Chapters on clothing impress the children with the relation of garments to health; classic stories of achievements of strong men are narrated to induce the young of today to preserve their health; and suggestions are made with reference to exercises and the methods of keeping in training.

Under the heading, "Fuel for the Body," children are told of the values of different kinds of foods, and it is thus early impressed upon them that the diet has most important duties in keeping the human machine going smoothly. In this connection, an ideal day's food in three' meals is suggested. Through calling attention of the children to the teeth of the dog or cat, they are given a little lesson serving to show them that with their own different kinds of teeth, they are entitled to make use of both meat and grain foods. The value of good teeth, the necessity for cleansing them, and matters of like importance are emphasized by a little story of the "Battle of the Brushes," in which at a meeting one after another sets forth his rights to be chairman, the broom claiming that he bears the brunt of the day's work in the house, and the clothes brush and hair brush bringing forth their various merits, but the tooth brush finally being selected on account of its fundamental necessity.

Microbes, the mouth as a gateway to the body, the necessity for fighting the fly and mosquito, and the spread of germ diseases are topics considered in successive chapters, the spread of the germs being brought home to the children through a reference to the game of "Button, button, who's got the button." If the first boy put the button into his pocket, there would not be any game. In the same way, if the first child coming down with a disease were prevented from passing the germs to some one else, this would be practical prevention.

The second volume is of higher grade than the first, speaking from the school teacher's point of view. It considers more closely and intimately the living machine,

the bony system, the circulatory system, the relation of air to health, the value of cleanliness, the necessity for pure water and good food, the fighting of insect pests, and the control of communicable diseases. How germs pass from mouth to mouth is discussed, and the illustrations show two little school girls doing their sums with the same pencil and each moistening the pencil in her mouth. Questions for discussion and review follow all of the chapters.

The volumes are well illustrated with pictures that appeal to the little student, and useful tables are a part of the second volume. For both of the volumes, Walter Camp has written a chapter on the relations of physical exercise to health, and other important additions have been made since the publication of the earlier volumes.

✤

Handbook on Health and How to Keep It. *Walter Camp. D. Appleton & Co. 1920. Pp. 210 and XIV. Price $1.50.*

Mr. Camp's book is written in an extremely interesting style. Far from being a prosaic list of rules for health, it abounds with interesting personal items illustrating the principles he presents. The five chapters are upon the following subjects: Problems of Youth and Age, Daily Dozen Set-Up, Reviewing Follies, Children, Schoolboy and Collegian and Industrial Workers.

The Daily Dozen Exercises were devised by Camp primarily for use in army and navy drills. Camp emphasizes that the important thing in exercise is to give the abdomen and thorax the most attention. The arms and legs, he says, get a fair amount of exercise anyway, even under sedentary conditions, whereas the vital organs ordinarily do not receive their fair share of exercise. Accordingly the daily dozen are devoted very largely to bending exercises of one kind or another.

Camp claims that 10 minutes per day with the daily dozen combined with 20 or 30 minutes of walking or other light exercise in the air, even the brain worker can maintain the best health, and cites the records of cabinet officers and other government officials who during the war labored at Washington, D. C., under the most strenuous conditions, but remained fit through the moderate exercise recommended.

A. W. H.

ASSOCIATION NEWS

HEALTH EMPLOYMENT BUREAU
HELP WANTED

Help-wanted announcements will be carried free in this column until further notice. Copy goes to the printer on the first of each month. In answering keyed advertisements, please mail replies separately and to editorial office in Boston, Mass.

The Health Employment Bureau also sends lists of applicants to prospective employers without charge.

A Progressive Superintendent of Health for a city of 70,000 population. Salary $3,500. Experience necessary. Address Z. F. 388, care of this *Journal*.

Assistant Bacteriologist. Salary $1,800. Applicant must have college degree, graduate in medicine preferred. Apply to Commissioner of Health, Baltimore, Maryland, stating educational training, experience and references.

Medical Assistant for 75-bed Tuberculosis Sanatorium. Must be single, with experience in diagnosis of Tuberculosis. Salary $2,000, with increase in reasonable time to good man. Send credentials to Dr. James A. Price, Irene Byron Hospital. Fort Wayne, Ind.

POSITIONS WANTED

Position - wanted announcements will henceforth be carried in this column. The charge is $2 per insertion. Copy should be received at this office by the first of the month.

Will be at liberty to accept location as health officer or to do general sanitary and publicity work about October 1. Now have the rank of Major in Reserve Corp and commission in Public Health Service as P. A. Surgeon. Further details by correspondence. Address 128, W. W. E., care of this *Journal*.

Wanted: Position as Medical Inspector of Schools by a Woman Physician experienced in this work. California preferred. References. Address H. C. M., 126, care of this *Journal*.

A young woman, college graduate with one year of post-graduate work, wants a position as head of a laboratory. Experience in bacteriology, serology, and chemistry acquired in both hospital and Public Health work. Prefers location in Ohio, but all good offers considered. Address P. H., 130, care of this *Journal*, Boston address.

□

LIST OF NEW MEMBERS
Proposed for Election to the
A. P. H. A.
August 3 to September 7, 1920, inclusive.
Names of Sponsors are set in Bold Face Type.
Names of New Members are in Light Face Type.

ALABAMA
J. D. Dowling, M. D., Birmingham.
A. D. Brown, Chief Sanitary Officer, Birmingham.
W. H. Godwin, M. D., Birmingham.
B. C. Howse, Sanitary Inspector, Fairfield.
H. T. McGhee, M. D., Pratt City.
H. G. Tuggle, Sanitary Inspector, Wylam.
CALIFORNIA
W. H. Kellogg, M. D., Berkeley.
Stanley B. Freeborn, State Board of Health, Berkeley.
Walter T. Harrison, M. D., Asst. Surgeon, U. S. P. H. Service, San Francisco.
Louis L. Williams, M. D., Asst. Surgeon General, U. S. P. H. S., San Francisco.
L. M. Powers, M. D., Los Angeles.
Elmer R. Pascoe, M. D., Assistant Health Commissioner, Los Angeles.
I. R. Bancroft, M. D., Los Angeles.
Marie Potts, R. N., Fresno.
Pauline J. Pitney, Supervisor of Nursing, Los Angeles.
Adelaide C. Brown, R. N., Oakland.
R. A. Archibald, Oakland.
Walter J. Stewart, D. V. S., M. D., Oakland.

S. P. S. Edwards, M. D., Ontario.
F. F. Abbott, M. D., Ontario.
W. M. Dickie, M. D., Sacramento.
F. O. Pryor, M. D., Health Officer, Santa Rosa.
Molly H. Orr, R. N., San Bernardino.
Mrs. F. C. Brunette, Salinas.
Mary L. Cole, R. N. San Francisco.
Lillien J. Martin, M. D., San Francisco.
William C. Hassler, M. D., San Francisco.
Lawrence Arnstein, Jr., San Francisco.
Helen C. Welch, R. N., San Francisco.
Agnes Walker, M. D., San Francisco.
Millicent Cosgave, M. D., San Francisco.
CONNECTICUT
Ettore Ciampolina, M. D., New Haven.
Mudr LadislaV Prochazka, Prague, Czechoslovakia.
Philip S. Platt, New Haven.
Frank E. Platt, Scranton, Pa.
A. W. Hedrich, Boston, Mass.
John H. Hoover, M. D., Health Officer, Voluntown.

806

FLORIDA

Ralph N. Greene, M. D., Jacksonville.
John M. Whitfield, M. D., Panama City.
A. C. Hamblin, M. D., Tampa.
Eddie E. Morress, Perry, Taylor County.
A. W. Hedrich, Boston, Mass.
A. C. Hamblin. M. D., Tampa.

GEORGIA

H. N. Old, Thomasville.
John Schreiber, M. D., County Health Officer, Thomasville.
A. W. Hedrich, Boston, Mass.
American Red Cross, Dept. of Civilian Relief Library, Atlanta.

IDAHO

A. W. Hedrich, Boston, Mass.
Emery M. Roller, Moscow.

ILLINOIS

W. A. Evans, M. D., Chicago.
James M. Dinnen, M. D., Ft. Wayne, Ind.
John Dill Robertson, M. D., Chicago.
E. A. Schlageter, M. D., Health Department, Chicago.
John C. Alford, Supervisor, Department of Health, Chicago.
Herman B. Meyers, Publisher, American Food Journal, Evanston.
Martin M. Ritter, M. D., Chicago.
Moor Mud Baths, Atten. John Weber, Jr., Mgr., Waukesha, Wis.
Edmond A. Holberg, M. D., Supervising Health Officer, Chicago.
Paul Hansen, Chicago.
W. C. Clarke, M. D., Cain.
C. M. Roos, Water Works Superintendent, Cairo.
M. Kern, M. D., Chicago.
Henry M. Hollester, Chicago.
S. S. Winner, M. D., Chicago.
John C. Foley, M. D., Health Officer, Waukegan.
A. W. Hedrich, Boston, Mass.
Fred Wendell, Chicago.
W. J. Harding, Decatur.
Hugh S. Baker, City Milk and Dairy Inspector, Decatur.
Clyde S. Jones, M. D., East St. Louis.
Hampton W. Edwards, R. N., PoplarVille, Ky.
W. J. Garard, M. D., Galesburg.
B. A. Harrison, M. D., Colchester.
A. W. Bouseman, M. D., Health Officer, Fountain Green.
Edith Y. Holstrom, Geneseo.
American Red Cross, Moline.
H. M. Bascom, Peoria.
George W. Burton, Peoria.
C. St. Clair Drake, M. D., Springfield.
J. J. Lahey, Madison.
Harold R. Roberts, M. D., Maywood.
Frank S. Needham, Commissioner of Health, Oak Park.
Department of Public Health, Springfield.

IOWA

Edyth Howerton, R. N., Esterville.
Hannah Sandquist, School Nurse, Marshfield, Ore.

MARYLAND AND DISTRICT OF COLUMBIA

Mrs. Francis K. Carey, Baltimore.
Emily B. Baily, Baltimore.
Charles J. Bonaparte, Baltimore.
Helen H. Carey, Associate Director Children's Playground Ass'n, Baltimore.
Mrs. Franklin P. Cator, Baltimore.
Mrs Benjamin W. Corkrane, Baltimore.
B. Howell Griswold, Jr., Baltimore.
Mrs. Francis M. Jencks, V. P. Women's Civic League, Baltimore.
W. H. Maltbie, Baltimore.
James H. Preston, Baltimore.
Provident Hospital, Baltimore.
L. Wardlew Miles, Head Master, Gilman County School, Baltimore.
Mary Gordon Thom, Baltimore.
Miles White, Jr., Baltimore.
Richard J. White, Trustee, Johns Hopkins Hospital, Baltimore.
Louisa McE. Fowler, Head of St. Timothy's School, CatonsVille.
Mrs. James Findlay, Hagerstown.
Civic League, Sugar City, Colo.
Mrs. William A. Perry, New York City.
Roscoe G. Brown, M. D., Washington.
Aldrich R. Burton, M. D., U. S. P. H. S. Lecturer, Washington.
Major Wm. H. Lloyd, M. C., Camp Meade.
Arthur G. Coumbs, M. D., Washington.

Sol Pincus, Washington.
Joel I. Connolly, Lincoln, Neb.
Lieut. Alan Sutton, Washington.
Major P. F. McGuire, M. C., U. S. A., Army Medical School, Washington.
Major Samuel A. White, M. C., U. S. A., Army Medical School, Washington.
A. W. Hedrich, Boston, Mass.
National Canners' Association, Attention, Frank E. Gorrell, Secretary, Washington.

MASSACHUSETTS

A. W. Hedrich, Boston, Mass.
O. L. Boye, Sykehus, Bergen, Norway.

MICHIGAN

W. J. Deacon, M. D., Lansing.
S. R. Hill, M. D., State Department of Health, Lansing.
W. C. Hirn, Lansing.
Edmund H. Eitel, Highland Park, Ill.
J. Ritchie, Jr., Boston.
Michigan State Normal College, Atten. of E. McCrickett, Ypsilanti, Mich.

MINNESOTA

C. E. Smith, Jr., M. D., St. Paul.
G. W. Moore, M. D., Health Officer, Hopkins.
George A. LoVe, M. D., County Health Officer, Preston.

MISSISSIPPI

W. S. Leathers, M. D., University.
Dr. Petritch, New York City.

MISSOURI

C. W. Schery, M. D., St. Louis.
Charles M. Denison, M. D., Pathologist and Bacteriologist, St. Louis.
Dora J. Silverman, M. D., St. Louis.
A. W. Hedrich, Boston, Mass.
Laura E. Mann, R. N., Director of Nursing, Independence.

MONTANA

Clara A. Link, R. N., Red Lodge.
Bess E. Lawler, R. N., Kelso, Washington.

NEW JERSEY

E. M. Reilly, M. D., Montclair.
Bayard T. Garrabrant, Sanitary Inspector, Montclair.
Louis Schneider, M. D., Newark.
Francis E. Knowles, M. D., So. Orange.

NEW MEXICO

C. E. Waller, M. D., Santa Fe.
Gladys L. Harris, P. H. N., Albuquerque.
Harriet C. Moreno, R. N., Magdalena.
Hon. J. H. Wagner, State Supt. of Public Instruction, Santa Fe.

NEW YORK

Edward S. Godfrey, M. D., Albany.
John L. Rice, M. D., State Board of Health, Albany.
B. R. Rickards, Albany.
G. B. Clark, M. D., Health Officer, Armonk.
Jacob Gutman, M. D., Brooklyn.
Charles Norris, M. D., Chief Medical Examiner, New York City.
Louis C. Wood, M. D., Poughkeepsie.
Howard P. Carpenter, Director, Hudson River State Hospital Laboratory, Poughkeepsie.
Albert M. Bell, M. D., Health Officer, Sea Cliff.
George E. Hannett, Syracuse.
Clarence Goldsmith, Chicago, Ill.
Edward Clark, M. D., Buffalo.
W. H. Baker, M. D., State Health Officer, Williamsville.
J. A. Conway, M. D., Hornell.
J. H. Van Marter, Groton.
Halsey J. Ball, M. D., Glens Falls.
Walter A. Leonard, M. D., Health Officer, Cambridge.
John J. Mahoney, M. D., Jamestown.
Edwards J. Loughlen, M. D., Health Officer, AndoVer.
Jasper W. Coller, M. D., Health Officer, WellsVille.
George W. Roos, M. D., Health Officer, WellsVille.
Walter L. Dodd, New York City.
Mr. Harry P. Hammond, Sanitary Engineer, Brooklyn.
Mrs. Ethel M. Hendriksen, Rochester.
Isaac Adler, Rochester.
Willis W. Bradstreet, M. D., Health Officer, Rochester.
John F. Forbes, M. D., Rochester.
Mrs. Rose E. Stuber, Rochester.
A. W. Hedrich, Boston, Mass.
Herbert N. Shenton, Columbia University, New York City.
Eva F. MacDougall, New York City.

OHIO
Louise Sitzenstock and
G. E. Harmon, M. D., Cleveland.
   Annie E. Irving, Superintendent of Nurses, Huron Road Hospital, Cleveland.
A. W. Hedrich, Boston, Mass.
   H. C. Schoepfle, M. D., Department of Health, Sandusky.

OKLAHOMA
Ruth Frances Horel, Oklahoma City.
   F. R. Horel, M. D., County Health Officer, Arcata, Cal.

PENNSYLVANIA
Lawrence M. Rosenfeld, Ph. D., Philadelphia.
   Mr. K. Hobart Roatch, Clinical Chemist, Philadelphia.

RHODE ISLAND
B. U. Richards, M. D., Providence.
   L. C. Clark, Providence.
   Howard Edwards, LL. D, President, State College, Kingston.
Lester A. Round, Ph. D., and
Prof. F. P. Gorham, Providence.
   Minot J. Crowell, Central Falls.

TENNESSEE
A. W. Hedrich, Boston, Mass.
   J. J. Durrett, M. D., Superintendent of Health, Memphis.

UTAH
T. P. Beatty, M. D., Salt Lake City.
   American Smelting & Refining Co., Atten: of Roy A. White, Salt Lake City.

VERMONT
Charles F. Dalton, M. D., Burlington.
   C. B. Crowell, Brattleboro.

VIRGINIA
Robert A. Martin, M. D., Petersburg.
   H. A. Burke, M. D., Venereal Clinic, Petersburg.
   Claiborne Powell, City Physician, Petersburg.

WEST VIRGINIA
S. L. Jepson, M. D., Charleston.
   C. A. Cabell, Carbon.
   C. A. Pearse, Jochim.
   G. K. Cabell, Wevaco.

WISCONSIN
W. W. Johnston, M. D., Racine.
   Central Association, Atten. of Miss Kate Mender, Racine.
   Edith C. Chandler, Exec. Secretary, Racine Chapter, A. R. C., Racine.
H. L. Wilson, M. D., Racine.
   Catherine Pfister, Public Health Nurse, Racine.

CANADA
J. W. S. McCullough, M. D., Toronto Ont.
   Institute of Public Health, Atten. H. W. Hill, M. D., London, Ontario.

PHILIPPINE ISLANDS
A. W. Hedrich, Boston, Mass.
   Rafael Villafranca, M. D., District Inspector, Lucena, Tayabas, P. I.

CONVENTIONS, CONFERENCES AND MEETINGS

October 4-7, Pittsburgh, Pa.—Medical Society of the State of Pennsylvania.

October 4-7, Waterloo, Ia.—Tri-State District Medical Society.

October 4-8, Montreal, Can.—American Hospital Association.

October 4-10, Montreal, Can.—American Association of Occupational Therapy.

October 6-7, Providence, R. I.—New England Surgical Society.

October 6-8, Chicago, Ill.—American Association of Railway Surgeons.

October 7-8, Augusta, Me.—Maine Public Health Association.

October 7-8, Richmond, Va.—North Atlantic Tuberculosis Conference.

October 7-8, Rutland, Vt.—Vermont State Medical Society.

October 9, Ottawa, Can.—Canadian Association for the Prevention of Tuberculosis.

October 11-12, Wilmington, Del.—Delaware State Medical Society.

October 11-13, St. Louis, Mo.—American Child Hygiene Association.

October 12-13, Oklahoma City, Okla.—Oklahoma State Public Health Conference.

October 12-14, Chicago, Ill.—Mississippi Valley Medical Association.

October 15-16, Roswell, N. Mex.—New Mexico State Medical Society.

October 19-20, Omaha, Neb.—Nebraska State Nurses' Association.

October 20, Lakewood, N. J.—New Jersey Anti-tuberculosis League.

October 21, Montreal, Can.—Royal Edward Institute.

October 22-26, New York City—American Dietetic Association.

October 27, Albany, N. Y.—New York State Association of Public Health Laboratories.

October 28, Boston, Mass.—Massachusetts Association of Boards of Health.

October, Milwaukee, Wis. — Wisconsin Anti-tuberculosis Association.

November 8-11, Louisville, Ky.—Southern Medical Association.

November 13, Boston, Mass.—Massachusetts Society for Social Hygiene, Inc.

November 15, Louisville, Ky.—American Association of Medical Milk Commissioners.

November 20-23, San Antonio, Tex.—Texas State Conference Social Welfare.

November 22, Washington, D. C.—Association for the Prevention of Tuberculosis of the District of Columbia.

December 2, Providence, R. I.—Rhode Island Medical Society.

December 6, Petersburg, Va.—Medical Society of Virginia.

December 6-30, Washington, D. C.—Regional Health Conference.

December 12-20, Montevideo, Uruguay—Sixth International Sanitary Conference of the American Republics.

·PUBLIC HEALTH NOTES

Abstracts by D. GREENBERG, M. P. HORWOOD, JAMES A. TOBEY and HOMER N. CALVER.

Public Health Surveys.—Dr. Harold. B. Wood defines a public health survey as an accounting of the health conditions and needs of a community. The purpose of a health survey is to detect the presence and correlation of all conditions and factors affecting health, and to formulate practical and economical measures to decrease disease and increase comfort. 'A survey serves as a guide for city planning, municipal development, health activities, and charitable services. The scope of a health survey is outlined as follows:

Introduction—
Brief historical outline.
Geographical location.
Geological formations.
Racial settlements and distribution.
General review of public health and physical efficiency.
Industrial developments.

Vital Statistics—
Population, growth and influencing factors.
Birth and death rates, giving trend and reasons.
Influencing factors and how to control them.
Racial characteristics of birth and death rates.
Reportable diseases, prevalence and rates.
Methods of control and their effects.

Child Welfare—
Prenatal influences, effects, 'solution.
Infant mortality, factors, causes, and solution.
Preschool problems.

School Children—
Statistics, distribution, effect of location upon schools.
Prevalence of diseases among school children, control.
Medical inspection.
School buildings and grounds.

Communicable Diseases—
Statistics of outbreaks; sources and methods of control.
Public protection ·against disease.
Educational work done and needed.

Tuberculosis—
Prevalence, factors, distribution, ·causes.

Local modes of transmission, house influences.
Dispensary effects and community needs.

Typhoid Fever—
Prevalence, transmission, protection.

Venereal Disease—
Dangers, prevalence, prevention.

Food Supplies—
Conditions of production and storage.
Adulteration and wholesomeness.
Degree of inspection and results.
Disposal of spoiled or poor foods.
Prevalence of diseases among handlers.

Milk Supply—
Amount, source, distribution, availability.
safety and cleanliness, city standard bacterial counts, causes, variations, trend.

Water Supply—
Source, safety, quality, distribution, protection, control, results.

Sewage Disposal—
Methods, proportion, distribution, safety.
local effects, treatments of sewage.

Garbage Disposal—
Methods, desirability, nuisances, control.

Street Cleaning—
Methods of collection and disposal of rubbish.

Personal Hygiene—
Standards of living and effects.
Overcrowding, housing conditions, tenementation.
Condition and use of yards and lots.
Parks and playgrounds.

Industrial Hygiene—
Kinds, distribution and sanitation of factories.
Occupational diseases: prevalence and control.
Industrial accidents: prevalence and control.
Sanitary improvements and social welfare.

Health Department:
Development, methods of appointment.
Divisions, efficiency and needs.
Activities, methods, results obtained.
Budget; distribution. and needed changes.
Recommendations. .
Modern Medicine, May, 1920—(*M. P. H.*)

809

Meningococcus Carriers. — The writers give the results of an investigation of 905 carriers who were examined and treated at the Army cerebrospinal fever center at Netley, between September, 1916, and April, 1919. Of the 905 examined, 86 (9.5 percent.) were case carriers after cerebrospinal fever, and 819 (90.5 percent.) were apparently healthy accidental carriers, who had not showed any signs of the disease. The case carriers remained infected for an average period of 5½ months, the longest period in any one case during which meningococci were observed being 634 days. Accidental, or healthy, carriers remained infected for an average period of 24 days, discharge from isolation being effected as follows:

9.3 percent of the healthy carriers were discharged during the first week, and for the second, third and fourth weeks the figures run 14.8, 17.2, and 15.3. Two succeeding fortnights give percentages of 12.0 and 11.3 respectively, the total for the eight weeks being 79.9 per cent.

Carriers were treated in various ways—in "inhalation chambers" with chloramine T and zinc sulphate, by hand-spraying with flavine and adrenalin, with chloramine in paraffin, and with "electrosal," and by the direct application of perchloride of iron and of mercuric ointment. It did not appear that any of the methods employed had any effect on the meningococci in the nasopharynx. It appeared, rather, that some of the forms of period. Seventeen of the carriers who were treated with either chloramine or zinc sulphate for a period of 102 days remained carriers at the end of the treatment; and cultures taken from the nasopharynx within half an hour of exposure to the "Levick Spray," with either drug, frequently yielded a pure growth of meningococci. The cocci, found in the nasopharynx of a carrier, did not tend to alter in type throughout the carrying period; amongst the 905 carriers a change of type was observed in only a single case.—D. Embleton and G. H. Stevens, *Jour. Roy. Army Med. Corps*, 1919, XXXIII, 312.—(*D. G.*)

✦

Standardization of Municipal Health Organization.—It is very doubtful whether it is desirable to standardize the organization and detailed activities of health departments. Very often there are variations in traditions, customs and other circumstances which make standardization not only impossible but undesirable. The fundamentals in public health work are the same for all cities and should be standardized. The best solution of a particular community's problem is a careful study of that problem, leading to a special plan to meet the particular conditions that prevail. As far as possible, however, health departments should attempt to divorce themselves from street cleaning, collection and disposal of refuse, housing inspection and plumbing inspection. They should, however, maintain supervision and control of these functions insofar as they affect the health and welfare of the people. In order to accomplish its aim to prevent disease, protect the public health, and eliminate corrigible physical and mental defects, a health department should have the following divisions: administration, vital statistics, child hygiene, communicable diseases, public health education, sanitary engineering, food inspection and hospitals and sick relief. The health officer should attempt as far as possible to coöperate with and utilize the voluntary and unofficial agencies in a community that are interested and active in promoting the public health. Very often these volunteer organizations are pioneers in health problems and can be used as experimental stations in public health work. It is important, however, that the health officer should be able to supervise all the health activities which go on in a community—Allan J. McLaughlin, M. D., *Public Health Reports, April* 30, 1920.—(*M. P. H.*)

✦

How to Tell Bad Canned Food.—A can, the contents of which is suitable for consumption, when opened should be free from swell or escaping gas. The contents should have the proper color, texture, odor for the product canned, and should be absolutely free from any form of offensive odor. All these things should be noted before the product is tasted.

On the other hand, if the vegetable, fish, meat, or fruit in the can smells and looks wholesome, as far as is now known there is no danger from its consumption. The home canner, therefore, can go ahead with her canning operations, feeling sure that her family will be safe from food poisoning if she observes the simple precautions.—*Weekly News Letter*, June 23, 1920, U. S. Dept. Agric.—(*J. A. T.*)

SERBIAN HEALTH POSTERS

This spirited poster, prepared for the Red Cross work in Serbia by the artist who designed the very attractive posters for the tuberculosis campaign in France under the coöperation of the International Health Board and the French Government, illustrates one of the means of attacking this disease in a stronghold. The idea of warfare is admirably carried on by the soldier rushing to attack the foes, while the method of dissemination from the sick man to the well soldier is shown above. The legend of the poster is the following:

TYPHUS
IS CARRIED FROM THE SICK
TO THE WELL
BY THE LOUSE
HE BITES THE SICK MAN AND THEN
INFECTS THE WELL

Then in the lighter letters to the left is the warning, "The trenches of the louse are the seams of the clothing," and below, again in large letters, "It is necessary to fight the louse."

The second poster is a lesson in cleanliness. The man bathing in the primitive tub of the Continent, with the kettle of hot water at hand with which to keep his bath hot, is surrounded by the legend, "To avoid typhus, get rid of lice." Then in lighter letters is the query, "How?" and underneath is the answer, "By plenty of bathing and washing of the clothing," illustrated by the woman at work with her laundry.

The question of typhus is not one that has disturbed the United States very much thus far, save on its tropical borders, but in the central European countries it is a very serious problem and one which the authorities since the beginning of the war have been endeavoring to solve.

These posters come to the Journal through the courtesy of Mr. Edward Stuart, till very recently in charge of the work in France.

STATE HEALTH NOTES—
LEGISLATION

Canada, Opium and Narcotic Drug Act and Amendments.—Through the courtesy of J. A. Amyot, M. D., Deputy Minister, Canadian Department of Health, the Journal is able to present a summary of the legislation in the province with reference to opium and narcotics.

Under the Act of 1911 provision is made for confining the use of opium and narcotic drugs to medicinal or scientific purposes and the sale of these drugs is confined to physicians, veterinary surgeons, dentists, bona fide wholesale druggists or retail druggists, or on prescriptions issued by physicians, veterinary surgeons or dentists for medicinal purposes, or when prescribed for the medical treatment of a person under professional care by such physician.

All druggists, wholesale and retail, are required to record the sale of these drugs in a suitable book.

Under this Act it is an offense for any person to smoke opium or to have in his possession opium prepared or being prepared for smoking. It is also an offense to export or attempt to export any. narcotic drugs from Canada to a foreign country which prohibits their entry.

The drugs mentioned in the schedule to this Act are as follows: cocaine or any salts or compounds thereof, morphine or any salts or compounds thereof, opium, eucaine or any salts or compounds thereof.

In May, 1918, an Order-in-Council was passed under the War Measures Act restricting the importation or exportation of these drugs under license. This Order-in-Council was superseded on December 31, 1919, by an Act of Parliament perpetuating the licensing system. These licenses are issued for each individual shipment imported or exported and in the case of an import license is conditional on the importer taking an affidavit that he will report his sales of the drugs so imported under license, to the Department of Health at the end of each month.

When these reports are received in the Department they are carefully tabulated and show the quantity of drugs received by all druggists, physicians, dentists and veterinary surgeons. Where it is noticed that any of the persons mentioned receive what are considered abnormal supplies, the matter is further followed up and detailed statements are required showing the disposition of the drugs so received. In this way the Department is in a position to trace these drugs from the time of importation into Canada through the wholesaler, retailer and physician and find out exactly how the drugs were actually used or consumed.

It might be here mentioned that this system has been found to be very effective and the Department has been successful in reducing, by an enormous quantity, the amount of drugs imported into Canada as compared with the quantities imported during a similar period before the restrictions became effective. We have also been very successful in stamping out to a very large extent the practice of physicians prescribing these drugs to addicts simply to supply their appetite in this regard and not in an attempted cure of the habit. This system has also been the means of searching out those druggists who have been dealing illicitly in these drugs in the past.

At the recent session of Parliament a further Amendment to the Opium & Narcotic Drug Act was passed, which is to be proclaimed and become effective on September the 1st next. This Act goes much further than the previous legislation in dealing with the handling and control of these drugs in Canada.

Under the existing Act various penalties are provided for different offenses, as for instance persons dealing in these drugs other than those permitted by law: druggists furnishing drugs to persons other than on prescription: physicians prescribing drugs for other than medicinal purposes: persons found guilty of conducting opium dens: These offenses are all enumerated under different sections and the penalties vary from a maximum fine of fifty dollars to five hundred dollars or from three months imprisonment to a year according to the offense committed under the Act.

Under the new Act the offense is made the same and the penalties provided are a fine not exceeding one thousand dollars and costs and not less than two hundred dollars and costs, or to a term of imprisonment for one year, or to both fine and imprisonment.

In addition to requiring a license for each individual importation or exportation, all wholesale druggists and manufacturers and all retail druggists who manufacture narcotic drugs or preparations containing the same are required to obtain an annual license to deal in these drugs, and all druggists who do not manufacture and all physicians, veterinary surgeons and dentists are required to furnish the Department with a declaration stating that they are engaged in the sale or distribution of these drugs.

Provision is also made under the Act whereby all physicians, veterinary surgeons and dentists are required to furnish on request, any information under any regulation made under the Act with respect to the drugs received, dispensed, prescribed, given away or distributed. Refusal to furnish such information incurs a penalty of not more than one thousand dollars and costs or not less than two hundred dollars and costs or to a year of imprisonment, or to both fine and imprisonment.

In addition to requiring all druggists, wholesale or retail, and all manufacturers to keep a record of their sales of these drugs they will be required under the New Act to keep a record of their receipts showing from whom received and the quantity, etc., and the date. They are also required to keep a record of the quantity of narcotics used in manufacturing together with a record of the quantity of such preparations manufactured.

Under the new Act provision is made for the marking and packing of opium and narcotic drugs, which are intended for export, in such a manner as to denote clearly the contents of the packages.

The number of ports or places in Canada where these drugs may be imported or exported is limited.

Provision is made in this Act for the sale of preparations (without prescription) containing a limited quantity of narcotic drugs to the liquid ounce similar to the quantities permitted under the Harrison Narcotic Law of the United States, but such preparations are required to contain active medicinal drugs other than the narcotic in sufficient proportion to confer upon the preparation or remedy valuable medicinal qualities other than those possessed by the narcotic drugs alone, and further such preparations must have printed in a conspicuous place on the main panel or label on the wrapper of the bottle, box or container, the following warning,

"IT IS UNLAWFUL TO ADMINISTER THIS PREPARATION TO A CHILD UNDER TWO YEARS OF AGE AS IT CONTAINS (INSERT NAME OF DRUG) AND IS DANGEROUS TO ITS LIFE."

The schedule to the Act of 1911 has been amended by adding after the word "opium" —"Or its preparations, or any opium alkaloids or their derivatives, or salts or preparations of opium alkaloids or their derivatives."

◆

California.—Pasadena has just passed an ordinance which requires the physical inspection and medical examination of all food handlers, and provides for the exclusion of persons having active cases of tuberculosis, venereal disease and other communicable diseases from all occupations related to food production and handling. This is the first city in the state to follow the example of New York and other Eastern cities.

◆

Delaware.—The State Board of Health adopted in July a resolution requiring the tuberculin testing of dairy herds unless the milk be pasteurized. On and after August 1, 1920, no milk or cream shall be sold within the state unless it is pasteurized according to the regulations of the Board, or unless it is obtained from cows that have successfully passed the tuberculin testing within one year, the cows being numbered with non-removable ear tags and the records properly kept. A penalty is attached to violation of this regulation.

A further regulation provides that no person other than a duly licensed physician shall practice midwifery in the state unless such person shall be duly licensed as a midwife by the State Board of Health. The regulation demands a license every year and any person may make complaint of the incompetency of a midwife or the failure to report births. Persons desiring to obtain license are required to furnish suitable references as to cleanliness, education, character, and experience. A penalty is provided for failure to fulfill the requirements of the regulation.

New York.—Under the provisions of a law passed at the last session of the legislature, the Health Bureau, Albany, N. Y., became a separate department, on July 1. Dr. Clarence W. Buckmaster will be the Commissioner, with a salary of $5,000, and Dr. C. Umsted has been selected for Deputy, at a salary of $3,300.

There will be a number of changes in the new department, the most important of which will be the taking over by the Health Bureau of the Tuberculosis Commission.

The State Department of Health adopted in April a number of amendments to the sanitary code. The first of these adds encephalitis lethargica to the diseases requiring notification and divides the latter into two groups for convenience of administration: One the ordinary diseases, and the other the venereal diseases. Another amendment adds encephalitis lethargica to the diseases that are to be reported by physicians if they are found in dairy farms, and this disease has been added to the list of those in which persons who may not be removed without the authority of the board of health, for which placards must be posted, and for which opportunities for contact infection are forbidden. Children from the household are excluded from the schools, and the patient is subject to removal to a hospital, isolation, or restriction of movement. The disease is among those that will debar the person from the handling of foods, and carriers of the disease germs shall be subject to the special rules and regulations of the State Department.

A further amendment forbids firms, corporations, or authorities owning, in charge of, or in control of a lavatory or washroom in any hotel, lodging house, restaurant, factory, school, store, office building, railway or trolley station, or public conveyance by land or water, providing any towel for common use. The term 'common use" here means for use by more than one person without cleansing.

✦

New York City.—The Board of Health of the city of New York has amended the Sanitary Code to include the forbidding of the use of any animal hair that has not

been sterilized in the manufacture of brushes or cloth. The manufacturer of shaving brushes, tooth brushes, or other toilet brushes intended for human use shall cause his name or trademark, place of manufacture, and the word "Sterilized" to be permanently, clearly, and legibly painted or stamped on every such brush before offering it for sale in the city of New York. Provision is made that the word "sterilized" shall be safeguarded by the actual sterilization according to a process prescribed or approved by the Board of Health. No person in the city of New York shall sell or have in his possession with the intent to sell any brush which does not conform to this regulation. The Board of Health prescribes two processes of sterilization: Boiling the hair in water at a temperature of 212° F. for at least three hours; or placing the hair in an autoclave in which a ten-inch vacuum has been produced. Live steam at 15 pounds shall be kept up in the autoclave for three hours.

✦

North Dakota.—A recent pamphlet issued by the State Board of Health contains the public health laws of the state together with the rules and regulations of the State Board.

✦

Pennsylvania.—In the May issue of the *Pennsylvania Health Bulletin* the State Department of Health presents a *Synopsis of the Health Laws* of the Commonwealth. Three previous publications have dealt with the same laws, a *Digest of Health Laws* published in 1916 and two *Bulletins*, 97 and 103, issued in 1917 and 1919 respectively. The Digest and the Bulletins give the phraseology of the laws, while this Synopsis presents abstracts, noting the purpose of the law, referring to its place in the Acts, and outlining the penalties and naming the persons responsible and the courts before which any action should be brought. A second part of the *Synopsis* contains the regulations of the Advisory Board which have the force of law, while a third section includes the orders, rulings and instructions issued from the central office of the State Department of Health.

Legislation on Physical Education

In 1920 the General Assembly of Virginia, after passing a law requiring health examination, health instruction and the conduct of wholesome physical activities, has set aside $25,000 for the State Board of Education, to be used for physical education in the public elementary and high schools, and an equal sum for the State Board of Health, to be applied to child welfare and school medical inspection. County boards of supervisors and city councils are authorized to make appropriations for health examinations and physical education and the employment of school nurses, physicians and physical directors.

The General Assembly of Kentucky has enacted a law requiring the State Board of Education to draw up a course of study in physical education for all common schools, occupying periods of not less than thirty minutes each school day devoted to instruction in health and safety, physical exercises, and recess play. A manual for the use of all teachers in common schools will be prepared by the Superintendent of Public Instruction in coöperation with the State Board of Health. Normal schools supported wholly or in part by public funds shall contain one or more courses in physical education.

In Mississippi the legislature has passed a law which becomes operative as soon as Federal assistance is available. This law provides that all pupils in elementary and secondary schools, whether public, private or parochial, shall receive instruction in physical education as prescribed by the State Board of Education, which is given considerable latitude in drawing up regulations.

The National Physical Education Service of Washington has been active in the different states aiding the local organizations in their movements towards physical efficiency as a national asset.

✛

The JOURNAL requests State and Municipal Health Officers to send forward notes for this Section that can be helpful to other officials in similar positions. Exchange of experiences is a great educator.

STATE HEALTH NOTES—GENERAL

National and International.—The sixth International Sanitary Conference of the American Republics will be held in Montevideo, Uruguay, December 12-20, 1920, under the presidency of Dr. E. Fernández Espiro and the auspices of the Government of Uruguay. One of the features of the conference is to be a round-up of sanitary procedure and conditions in the republics represented. Each delegation is requested so send in a written memoir, accompanied by its abstract, to the Secretary of the Conference, 15 days before its opening. This memoir, which is for the information of other delegations, is to include the following items:

1. Sanitary laws, ordinances, and regulations imposed since the 5th Conference.

2. Adoption of the resolutions passed by the preceding conferences.

3. Enumeration of the contagious diseases which may have prevailed since the 5th Conference (in particular influenza), measures adopted to avoid its propagation, number of cases and deaths.

4. Considerations relative to the outbreak and development of bubonic plague; methods employed to combat it; their results.

5. Frequency of epidemic cerebrospinal meningitis, transmissible anterior poliomyelitis, and lethargic encephalitis.

6. Actual status of the combat against tuberculosis, yellow fever, malaria, trachoma, and ankylostomiasis.

7. Data relative to leprosy and the measures put in practice to prevent its diffusion.

8. Actual status of the combat against avariosis (venereal diseases).

9. Organization and operation of the service of disinfection. Work carried out.

10. Movement of population and rate of mortality during the last five-year period.

11. Water supply and sewerage service. Their extent.

12. Application of different systems of paving.

13. Organization and operation of the service of maritime sanitation.

14. Work of the Health Commissions of each one of the American Republics.

In response to a generally expressed desire for help in carrying on child welfare programs, the Children's Bureau of the U. S. Department of Labor has issued a set of outlines for the use of clubs and classes. These programs are comprised under five heads, the Community and the Child; Child Welfare in Rural and Village Communities; Care of the Mother, the Baby and the Young Child; Detailed Outlines on Infant Mortality, Children in Industry, Recreation, and Children in Need of Special Care; and Development and Present Status of Infant Welfare Work in Other Countries.

"What next?" is the question that thousands of bewildered children asked when the school doors closed behind them for the last time. An army of over 1,000,000 children between 14 and 16 years old, says the Children's Bureau, marches out of the schools each year to become wage earners. In a pamphlet entitled "Advising Children in Their Choice of Occupation and Supervising the Working Child" the Bureau tells what happens to these children and offers suggestions for helping them get the proper start in life.

The legal right to remain ignorant is annually granted to thousands of children in states where child labor and education laws are backward. According to an account of the administration of the Federal Child Labor Law soon to be published by the Children's Bureau, only 783 children out of 19,696 to whom certificates were issued, or less than 4 per cent, had attended or completed the eighth grade, though completion of the eighth grade is generally regarded as necessary to secure even the rudiments of an education.

✦

Venezuela.—This South American republic is quite up to date in its methods of informing the public with reference to pests that carry disease. One of the circulars recently published warns against the fly, using illustrations that follow the fly from the outhouse past the garbage can and the spittoon to the baby and the dinner table, while another is directed to the ratproofing of granaries and storage places for fruits and other foods.

Canada.—The Canadian Red Cross Society has awarded to Miss Jean E. Browne of Saskatchewan a scholarship of $1500 in public health nursing to be held for one year at the University of London, England. This and similar scholarships in other lands are one of the first fruits of the League of Nations. Miss Browne who goes as the representative of Canada, is an honor graduate of the Toronto Normal School and the General Hospital Training School for Nurses in the same city. In 1911 she organized the health work of the Regina public schools in Saskatchewan and since 1917 has been Director of School Hygiene for the Department of Education of that province.

✦

California.—California's highways are now marked by a new feature, the brilliant symbol of the American Red Cross showing plainly above first aid kits for those injured in accidents. Chapters in the foothill cities of Southern California have chosen intersections and dangerous stretches of roadway where accidents have been most frequent as the best locations for the first aid equipment.

✦

Colorado.—The University of Colorado in coöperation with the Colorado Fuel and Iron Co. during the school year of 1919-20 conducted two courses of four months each in public health nursing at the hospital of the Minnequa steel works with field experience in Pueblo and the near-by mining camps. The third course is under way, having begun September 20, and applicants were required to have come from accredited schools of nursing with the certificate of graduation, with limited numbers from senior classes of such schools. The courses are given by members of the University faculty and by other well known physicians and surgeons.

✦

Georgia.—Dr. M. A. Fort of Grand Bay, Ala., has been elected Commissioner of Health of Brooks County at Quitman, Ga.

Dr. J. D. Applewhite has resigned as Commissioner of Health of Lowndes County and has been elected Commissioner of Health of Clark County at Athens.

Dr. Eugene O. Chimene has been elected

temporary Commissioner of Health of Floyd County at Rome.

Dr. ·C. C. Applewhite, P. A. Surgeon U. S. Public Health Service, has been detailed to the University of Georgia for the purpose of establishing the School of Public Health and Hygiene with the medical department at Augusta.

Twenty-five counties have adopted the Ellis Health Law.

·

Illinois.—A school of Diagnosis of Tuberculosis for acting assistant surgeons and local examiners engaged in the care of sick and wounded soldiers, has been established by the U. S. Public Health Service at Springfield. The school is conducted through the coöperation of the State Department of Public Health, the Illinois Tuberculosis Association, the Springfield Tuberculosis Dispensary and the Palmer Tuberculosis Sanatoria. Dr. George Thos. Palmer, Chief of the Division of Tuberculosis of the State Department of Public Health, is Director of the school. Courses covering a period of seven days of three sessions each, with classes limited to· ten Service men will be given every other week till the end of autumn.

Through the ·coöperation of the State Department of Public Health, the State Department of Public Welfare, and the Illinois Society for the Prevention of Blindness, clinics for the diagnosis and treatment of trachoma have been established at Mount Vernon, Harrisburg, and Benton. These clinics are under the general supervision of Dr. E. V. L. Brown, representing the Illinois Society for the Prevention of Blindness.

The Better Babies Conference conducted by the State Department of Health has become one of the important features of the annual Illinois State Fair. This Conference has grown from a small beginning to the place where it now occupies practically the entire second floor of the Exposition Building. Last year 650 infants were entered for examination. It serves as a rallying ground for persons from all parts of the state interested in child welfare, and is responsible for the inspiration and development of scores of local child welfare movements.

Mr. Harry F. Ferguson has been ap-

pointed Acting Chief of the Division of Sanitary Engineering of the State Department of Public Health' to ·succeed Paul Hansen, resigned. Mr. Hansen will engage in professional sanitary engineering in Chicago.

Mr. Baxter K. Richardson has been appointed Acting Chief of the Division of Surveys and Rural Hygiene of the State Department of Public Health to fill the place of Paul L. Skoog, who has been granted a year's leave of absence.

Dr. Thomas G. Hull has been appointed Acting Chief of the Division of Diagnostic Laboratories of the State Department of Public Health to succeed Martin DuPray, who retired from public service to conduct a private diagnostic laboratory.

✦

Maine.—Dr. George Holden Coombs of Waldoboro, has been appointed Director of the Division of Venereal Disease in place of Dr. H. E. Hitchcock, resigned. The division is maintained jointly by the State Department of Health and the U. S. Public Health Service and has been in existence about two years.

The courts in Maine have held the fly to be a nuisance. An opinion given by Justice Spear of the Maine Supreme Court affirms this. A guest at a hotel left with his family on account of the flies which infested the dining room near his table, thereby breaking a two weeks' contract. The hotel proprietor sued him and recovered, but on an appeal to the higher court, Justice Spear rendered an opinion and granted a new trial. The keynote of the opinion is contained in this quotation from it:

"The real issue involves but a single question of fact; was the defendant justified in leaving the hotel on account of the fault of the plaintiff in allowing flies to collect at the defendant's table in such numbers as to become insanitary and repulsive? We think he was. It is a matter of common knowledge that the house fly has come to be regarded by enlightened understanding, not only as one of the most annoying and repulsive of insects, but as one of the most dangerous in its capacity to gather, carry and disseminate the germs of disease. He is the meanest· of all scavengers. He delights in reveling in all kinds of filth. Of every vermin; he is above all others the least able to prove an alibi when charged with having been in touch with every kind of corruption and with having been contaminated with the germs thereof. The danger with which his presence is fraught is a matter of common knowledge and hence of judicial notice."

✠

Michigan. — The ranking of Michigan counties and cities as to safety for babies has brought to the State Health Department many questions about the relative healthfulness of rural and urban districts. Health Commissioner R. M. Olin has issued some comparisons which show that last year many rural districts had a higher infant death rate than some large cities. In six counties babies born in larger cities had a better chance to live than in rural and semi-urban parts of the counties. The rates here given are deaths per thousand births in 1919:

Wayne County—Detroit, 98; rural, 121.
Jackson County—Jackson, 102; rural, 102.
Alpena County—Alpena, 125; rural, 172.
Gogebic County—Ironwood, 105; rural, 113.
Manistee County—Manistee, 60; rural, 94.
Grand Traverse County—Traverse City, 65; rural, 109.

In some other counties the cities had unenviable records compared with surrounding rural districts:

Ingham County—Lansing, 130; rural, 64.
Kent County—Grand Rapids, 84; rural, 68.

Bay County—Bay City, 101; rural, 45.
Genesee County—Flint, 110; rural, 88.
Delta County—Escanaba, 97; rural, 76.
Ishpeming County — Marquette, 114; rural, 85.
Menominee County — Menominee, 99; rural, 81.
St. Clair County—Port Huron, 132; rural, 98.
Chippewa County—Sault Ste. Marie, 96; rural, 76.

"Our purpose in issuing these facts," said Commissioner Olin, "is to remind parents and health officers throughout all sections of Michigan that babies can be saved in these most dangerous weeks by steps easily within reach."

Minnesota.—Dr. Hibbert W. Hill has resigned from his position as Executive Secretary of the Minnesota Public Health Association to become Director of the Institute of Public Health of the Western University, London, Ont. He began his health work in Minnesota as Director of the Division of Epidemiology for the Minnesota State Board of Health, and in 1914 was made Secretary of the Public Health Association where he has been till now with the exception of two years during the war in which he was Health Officer of the first (Canadian) Military District, with the rank of captain. His work in Minnesota included the organization of the 87 county health associations, a health crusade and the issue of publications reaching 13,500 persons every week.

✠

New Jersey.—A conference of the physicians conducting the 15 free venereal disease clinics in the state was called by the N. J. Bureau of Venereal Disease Control at the Newark City Dispensary on July 19th. The eleven clinicians, who were able to attend spent half an hour inspecting the gonorrhea clinic for men which was under way at the time. The number of patients who attend this clinic was so great that it was necessary to work out a plan for simultaneous treatments in order that all could be taken care of within the time limits adopted for the clinic. Dr. C. R. O'Crowley, in charge, explained the method of keeping records and pointed out the duty of each physician. Four physicians attend every clinic; the first takes the history and diagnoses new cases; the second examines and treats the acute cases; the third treats the chronic cases; and the fourth treats post-operative and special conditions. The physicians change positions every third month, so that during the course of the year, each physician gains experience in all phases of the treatment.

After completing the examination and record each physician takes his patient to an adjoining room, which is unusually well equipped for the administration of the approved treatments for gonorrhea, and here the indicated treatment is administered with the aid of orderlies and nurses. Cystoscopic examinations are made at another hour, each physician attending in turn. The syphilis clinics are conducted on other days and in other rooms; and in both clinics the sexes are separated. At the close of this inspection, the clinicians met in the conference rooms of the Dispensary, where Dr. O'Crowley gave a synopsis of the treatment of gonorrhea, advocating the use of freshly made Argyrol solution rather than permanganate or silver salts; he stressed the danger of instrumentation in the early stages of acute gonorrhea. This synopsis was followed by a paper, "Experience in the Treatment of Syphilis at the Camden Clinic," by Dr. A. H. Lippincott, who dwelt upon the necessity for social workers in inducing proper attendance at the clinic.

The New Jersey Child Hygiene Bureau has opened two new stations, one at Lambertville and the other at Frenchtown, the latter to be the center of work to include two adjoining towns. The program will include school hygiene.

Child Hygiene nurses in the New Jersey State Department of Health are now receiving a minimum salary of $1,200 annually with a maximum for higher positions up to $2400 a year, which places New Jersey above or at least on an equal plane with other state departments of health.

The State Child Hygiene Bureau under the direction of Dr. Julius Levy, conducts 61 Baby Keep-Well Stations throughout the entire state and as soon as additional nurses are obtained, the work will be extended to the several additional communities from whom requests have been received to have nurses carry on this work.

✦

New Mexico.—Dr. R. L. Bradley has been appointed Health Officer of Roswell.

An outbreak of typhoid fever in Roswell was traced, by Dr. G. S. Luckett, Chief of the Division of Preventable Diseases, State Health Department, to a contaminated milk supply. A carrier of two years' standing was found to be milking at the dairy from which 21 cases received milk or ice cream.

San Marcial owes important sanitary improvements to an inundation of the town by the Rio Grande. Under the charge of Mr. H. F. Gray, sanitary engineer of the State Board of Health, extensive drainage operations were undertaken and a system

for the sanitary disposal of excreta installed. The State Board provided for the drainage from an emergency fund, while the citizens of the town furnished the money for the other improvements.

✦

New York.—By recent action of the Public Health Council botulism, as well as lethargica encephalitis, is added to the list of reportable diseases. A complete record of the amended regulations is to be found in the Health Officers' Bulletin for June. The Council has added to the qualifications required of midwives who apply for licenses that there be given evidence of cleanliness in their homes.

One of the very serious difficulties arising from the delays in transportation has been the fact that the chemicals necessary for the purification of water have been unobtainable. The situation affects at least 115 municipalities in the state, which are entirely dependent on chemicals for the purity of their water. The State Board of Health has taken up the matter both by treating with the railways and the U. S. Interstate Commission and also by informing the municipalities how best to proceed in the emergency, and what to do in order to secure more prompt delivery of the merchandise.

Among the results of health week recently conducted at Granville, no less than five persons with tuberculosis were discovered and cared for. One of the lectures bore upon the subject of pasteurization of milk, and in consequence pasteurized milk is now being delivered for the first time in the town.

✦

North Carolina.—The campaign against malaria in this state has evolved most interesting features. One of the most popular of these was the contest in which a prize of $50 was awarded for the best essay on the disease by a school child. The idea was suggested by the North Carolina Landowners' Association, which offered $25, and this was supplemented by an equal sum given by Dr. Clarence Poe, editor of the *Progressive Farmer*. The State Board of Health assisted by making the contest a part of the general educational plan, and the success in this is evidenced by the fact that the school children of 36 counties were represented in the essays. The prize was awarded to Miss Rachel Grimsley of Jacksonville, Onslow county. A young man, Bernard McDuffie, was in the second place.

The State Board regards the contest as one of the most valuable pieces of educational work that it has accomplished. It extended over several months, maintaining interest and attention during this time, and incidentally about 100,000 pieces of literature were distributed. The counties offered prizes as well as the state one. The requirements made it necessary for the children to make a study of the conditions that induce and affect malaria, and the parents were, of course, drawn into the study. The contest touched those parts of the state that are most affected by malaria, and cannot fail to have important beneficial results.

Anti-malaria work is conducted in North Carolina by the State Board of Health in coöperation with the U. S. Public Health Service in a number of districts, among them, Goldsboro, Tarboro, Farmington and Wilmington.

The present season has been characterized in North Carolina by a number of sharp outbreaks of typhoid fever. Examples of three, five and even six cases in the same family are used to impress on the people the infectiousness of the disease, illustrating how whole families may contract the malady. The general situation in the state is very much improved, the mortality being in 1919 only about one-half that of 1914. Vaccination campaigns are now under way in eight or ten counties.

North Carolina is conducting a very active campaign against venereal disease under the direction of Dr. Millard Knowlton, Regional Consultant, U. S. P. H. S. The physicians are given no opportunity to remain ignorant of the laws and regulations. Copious literature is circulated among them with very definite instructions, and the responsibilities of the doctor are clearly set forth. In this state the decision as to whether a case shall be reported by name and address rests with the physician. He is the one who can best determine whether the case is one which should be cared for by the health authorities. By this procedure the authorities are relieved of the necessity of investigating every case, a duty that would follow if all cases were reported by name.

✦

Ohio.—The Ohio Society for the Prevention of Tuberculosis at its meeting in May assumed a broader field, changed its name to Ohio Public Health Association, and amended its charter and elected officers, among whom are: President, Dr. C. B. Bliss of Sandusky; Treasurer, Mr. Theo. S. Huntington of Columbus, and Secretary, Dr. Robert G. Paterson of Columbus. One of the objects of the organized association is to foster the establishment of local public health leagues in each county in the state and local anti-tuberculosis societies upon which to build these leagues. Summit County Red Cross Chapter was the first to affiliate and it will be the agent of the state association in its county. The Dayton society met in July to discuss the formation of a Montgomery County Public Health League, the subject being still under consideration to be acted upon in September.

The Association has issued a hand book giving the details of its organization, has secured a professional publicity and educational director of experience, Mr. E. W. Baird of Columbus, and has under way a modern health crusade and the Christmas stamp campaign.

As a part of a Peace Time Program the Cincinnati Chapter, American Red Cross, is establishing a permanent Bureau of Information. This Bureau is to be a collection of material on social work, health information, psychiatric service, disaster relief, community service and reference files of Red Cross activities.

✦

Tennessee.—A course in Public Health Nursing has been established at George Peabody College, Nashville. Three months will be devoted to work on the campus, which includes economic subjects, community and individual problems, rural institutions, home management and practical English for public workers. Theoretical work will be followed by three months' field work in the city of Nashville and rural communities in various parts of the state.

Virginia.—Dental work for children is now being prosecuted in various parts of the state. No less than five counties have men equipped for the work, some with portable outfits so as to reach the more isolated districts, while in others central clinics have been established to which the children come in large numbers. Arlington and Fairfax counties have whole-time dentists who will continue the work throughout the year, the former making a charge of $1.50 for each child. These clinics have penetrated even into the country of the mountain people, to the intense delight of the health workers who have hitherto been without such aid. Meanwhile a dental survey is in progress under Dr. E. J. Applewhite of Newport News, and by the time the schools open in the fall the program will be pretty well determined. This in the end is intended to include every school child in the state. For the benefit of teachers, lectures in oral hygiene have been given throughout the state at the summer schools by a unit of the U. S. Public Health Service, headed by Lieutenant-Colonel Harry B. Butler, D. R. C.

Forty-four cases of tuberculosis in a clinic that examined 275 persons, 154 of whom were declared to be healthy, is the record for Augusta county recently. Of the tuberculates, 23 were active cases, two of these advanced, with 21 arrested cases and six suspicious.

✛

Wisconsin.—That Racine, Wis., realizes the importance and value of public health work is evidenced by the coöperation of the City Council in granting appropriations to carry on this work and in otherwise strengthening and upholding the Health Department. The Council has just authorized the issuance of $130,000 in bonds for the erection of a hospital for the care of communicable diseases.

As a result of a vaccination campaign instituted last fall in Racine, when 8,500 school children were successfully vaccinated, there has not been a case of smallpox among school children for the past nine months. In every instance written consent of the parents of the children was first received.

✛

Philippines.—Acting Director of Health, Dr. Vincente de Jesus, has appointed a Leprosy Investigation Committee to meet at Manila from time to time on call of the Chairman thereof, for the purpose of undertaking investigations in connection with the treatment of leprosy, according to the latest developments of scientific research. The personnel of the committee is the following: Dr. José P. Bantug, Philippine Health Service, Chairman; Dr. H. W. Wade, University of the Philippines, Pathologist and Bureau of Science; Dr. Liborio Gomez, Bureau of Science, Bacteriologist; Dr. Daniel de la Paz, University of the Philippines, Pharmacologist; Dr. Granville A. Perkins, Bureau of Science, Chemist, and Dr. Proceso Gabriel, Philippine Health Service, and Dr. Luis Guerrero, University of the Philippines, Clinicians.

□

RELIEF FOR AUSTRIAN PHYSICIANS

In an appeal for relief funds, the American Relief Committee for Sufferers in Austria (261 Madison Ave., New York City) makes a special plea in favor of Austrian physicians. Vienna, whose great schools of medicine and surgery have for three centuries attracted the students of all nations, is today battling for its very existence. Physicians are among those who suffer acutely from the great scarcity of food. Their incomes have been reduced to almost nothing by the depreciation of money, they can not do manual labor and the scanty government ration is wholly inadequate. They are obliged to sink their pride and appeal for help. At the same time they need strength to combat the ills of the people, an undernourished population. The committee guarantees that every dollar contributed will be given to the physicians, administration costs being defrayed from other funds.

PUBLIC HEALTH
LABORATORY NOTES

Abstracted by Francis H. Slack, M. D., and Mr. James M. Strang.

Method for fixing films of Human Blood Cells during the ameboid movement of Leucocytes and Thrombocytes.— A watch glass covered by a second watch glass, on the inside of which is laid a filter paper moistened with water, is placed in an incubator at a temperature of 38° C. On a well-cleaned cover slip is placed a drop of Deetjen's solution (0.75 percent sodium chloride, 0.5 percent magnesium sulphate, 0.01 percent sodium bicarbonate), previously heated to body temperature, to which is added a very small drop of blood from the finger. This cover slip is placed in the space between the watch glasses which is kept moist by the wet filter paper. After about 20 minutes in the incubator, the covering watch glass is quickly replaced by another one, on the inside of which a filter paper is placed moistened with a solution of 40 percent formaldehyde. In this manner the leucocytes and thrombocytes which have continued their ameboid movement while in the damp space are quickly fixed at body temperature. After about half an hour the cover slip is taken out of the incubator and the mixture of Deetjen's solution and blood is carefully run off so that part of the red blood corpuscles, leucocytes, and thrombocytes are left adhering to the cover slip. The film can now be stained and treated further in the usual way. The best results are obtained if the film is stained while still wet. —M. A. Van Henverden, M. D., Jour. Expt. Med., Aug. 1, 1920.

✚

Importance of Blood Groups in Complement Fixation Reactions.— Erythrocytes should always be obtained from a Group IV individual (Moss' classification) when preparing cell suspensions for complement fixation reactions in which an anti-human hemolytic system is used, since Group IV erythrocytes are never acted upon by the isohemolysins present in human serum nor by the natural anti-human hemolysin present. Human serums may contain hemolysins for Groups I, II or III erythrocytes. An additional source of error, when human cell suspensions are made up at random, is introduced by the presence of anti-human hemolysin in guinea-pig serum selective for Group I and Group II human cells.—William C. Williams, Jour. Expt. Med., Aug. 1, 1920.

✚

Use of Tissue in Broth in the Production of Diphtheria toxin.— The authors draw the following conclusions: Diphtheria toxin can be produced regularly in broth to which pieces of sterile guinea-pig liver have been added. The medium must be inoculated immediately after the addition of the tissue. Broth prepared with certain American peptones gives satisfactory results when enriched with liver tissue. The most favorable reaction of the broth ranges from plus 0.3% to neutral to phenolphthalein. The broth at the time of testing should have a reaction ranging from P_H 8.0 to P_H 8.3, although a favorable reaction is not the only essential for toxin production. The addition of liver tissue reduces the necessary period of incubation. Strains of *B. diphtheriæ* other than Park-Williams No. 8 have produced a toxin of high potency by this method.—G. H. Robinson and P. D. Meader, Jour. Inf. Dis., Aug., 1920.

✚

Investigations and Experiences with the Sachs-Georgi Reaction for the Serum Diagnosis of Syphilis.— The great majority of cases examined by the Sachs-Georgi test give results concordant with those of the Wassermann. In 154 examinations, the author had divergent results only 15 times. In another set of 99 serums which were negative by the Wassermann, five were positive by flocculation. Three of these five were from patients having high fever from causes other than syphilis, in the other two syphilis was not excluded. The reaction is therefore held to be non-specific in certain cases of fever.—Munster. Munchen. Med. Woch. 1919, May 19, 505. Abst. Bull. Inst. Past. 1920, 18, 260.

INDUSTRIAL HYGIENE AND OCCUPATIONAL DISEASE

Abstracted by Drs. E. R. Hayhurst and E. B. Starr.

Physiological Cost of Muscular Work.— Waller demonstrated a method and apparatus for measuring the physiological cost of the various forms of mechanical work as done by a dock laborer, a painter, a carpenter and a tailor. The method consisted in measuring the CO_2 expired by the workers. The apparatus consists of three parts: (1) A collecting bag, with valve mouthpiece and tape to receive the expired air of the subject for, say, a minute or half a minute; (2) an analyser, to measure directly the percentage of CO_2 present in the expired air; and (3) a spirometer, to measure its volume in litres. The calorific value per cc. CO_2 is taken as equal to 5.55 calories. Waller demonstrated that at rest a man expires 60 calories per hour, while at work (walking at $3\frac{1}{2}$ miles an hour) he expires 320 calories. The small value (60 calories per hour) represents the cost of bare life without work —that is, the basal cost. The procedure for tradesmen was to collect the expired air for a period of one minute every hour from each man during the six days of work. The amount of CO_2 and its calorific value were then computed. The physiological cost of work per hour in four workmen varied from 84 to 127 calories per hour; that for 4 compositors on the *British Medical Journal* being 101 to 105 calories per hour.—A. D. Waller, *Brit. Med. Jour.*, No. 3094, April 17, 1920, 537-538.

＋

Eyesight of Miners.—The (British) Illuminating and Engineering Society arranged a meeting on February 24th on the subject of eyesight of miners. Dr. T. Lister Llewellyn stated that lighting values in mines are extremely low owing to two factors: (1) The insufficiency of the light generated, and (2) the very feeble illumination that enters the eye of the miner owing to the high proportion of the light absorbed by the blackness of the coal face. In the safety lamp mines only one-fiftieth of the value of the illuminant reaches the coal face, and only one-five-hundredth

part, the eye of the miner. The electric-battery head-lamp proved to be the best in such mines. The economic loss to the country from miner's nystagmus is at least £1,000,000 per annum. Dr. H. S. Elworthy believed that much eye fatigue is due to the absence of color relief in the coal mine. Whitewashing the posts and roofs of the workings would give much relief. A rich yellow light with a tinge of red is the most comfortable light. Blue light which occurs in bad air and in certain mines where the coal face has a bluish tint is irritating and more nystagmus is found in such mines. Dr. J. S. Haldane doubted that the quality of the air of such mines had much to do with nystagmus. He considered the disease to be local neurasthenia induced by the fatigue of trying to see in darkness.

Mr. Armitage representing a Yorkshire colliery, stated that his company had installed 10,000 electric lamps of special type which has been followed by (1) reduction of nystagmus, (2) fewer accidents, and (3) quicker movement of the men. The whole cost of their use worked out at 1.29d. ($2\frac{1}{2}$ cents) per shift. Dr. F. Shufflebotham considered the affliction a general nervous disorder and not an eye disease. Mr. Elwood commented on the fact that there had been a great increase in the disease since the war. A number of other speakers thought that some other factor than light alone was the cause. Mr. Butler pointed out that it took some 10 to 25 years for the disease to develop and Dr. Hartford stated that miners who were free from the disease on enlistment had subsequently, under the stress of war, developed the symptoms, so that there was evidence of latency. Others substantiated this statement. At the conclusion Dr. Llewellyn called attention to an experiment which had been carried out before their eyes: during the meeting their oil lamps had burned out but the electric lamps were going as well as ever.—*Brit. Med. Jour.*, No. 3088, March 6, 1920, 327-328.

Does It Pay to Employ an Industrial Nurse and What Should Be Her Qualifications?—"Yes, because:

1. She gives first aid in case of injury, thereby preventing infection and shortening the period of disability.

2. She cares for minor ailments, thereby enabling the employees to continue work.

3. She is on the alert to prevent the introduction and spread of contagious diseases through the plant.

4. She prevents illness by giving instruction in ways of keeping well.

5. She advises regarding correction of physical defects.

6. She visits and arranges for the care of those absent because of illness, thereby enabling an earlier return to work. She helps in case of family illness or trouble, thereby relieving the mind of the worried employee and enabling him to give his undivided attention to his work.

7. She teaches the rules of hygiene and sanitation. She advocates suitable precautions in the dangerous trades.

8. She is at all times a friend in need and interprets to the employee the plans of the employer for the establishment of various forms of industrial betterment."

"She should have a personality which gains and holds confidence, quick and sound judgment, tact and optimism. In addition to being a registered nurse, she should, if possible, have had a post-graduate course in Public Health Nursing. Such a course insures knowledge of the preventive side of her work, which counts so largely in keeping employees well and on their jobs."—*Modern Hospital*, February, 1920, p. 160.

✦

Conditions Affecting Health in the Millinery Industry.—This report is a fairly complete discussion covering the materials and activities entering into millinery manufacture including a list of poisonous substances, kinds of machinery, kinds of goods and the reports of industrial inspectors made in connection with a sanitary overhauling of millinery establishments in New York City. Among poisons used are to be noted wood alcohol, arsenic and white lead, as well as benzine, benzol, turpentine, anilin dyes and anilin. The great irregularity of hours of employment, the surreptitious employment of children, and the large number of foreigners are special features for health consideration.—Hubbard and Kefauver, *Bulletin of New York City Dept. of Health*, April, 1920, Vol. 10, No. 4, 82-97.

✦

Tuberculosis From an Industrial Viewpoint.—Dr. Brownlee divides cases of tuberculosis into three classes: The young adult (Y. A.), the middle-aged (M. A.), and the old-aged (O. A.). The Y. A. and O. A. cases are acute while the M. A.'s are chronic and this group is subject to environmental conditions and is eminently curable. Y. A. and O. A. types are far more difficult propositions. Y. A. phthisis is principally a racial and family disability and is affected by movements of population whereas M. A. phthisis being a hygienic and physical strain disease is principally affected by hygienic conditions of work and feeding. The M. A. group is essentially one of individual resistance to environmental conditions and hence can be controlled by controlling those conditions.—Henry A. Ellis, *Lancet*, No. 5053, July 3, 1920, 44-45.

✦

Chronic Zinc Poisoning; Does It Exist?—Seiffert, who studied zinc smelting, concludes that lead is not so important among zinc smelterers as a poison as is commonly supposed. The damage due to zinc is underestimated. Zinc dust is swallowed, passes into the gastro-intestinal tract and gradually produces illness. The worst forms are the dusts of zinc blende (ZnS) and calamine ($ZnCO_3$) which contain large amounts of $ZnSO_4$ and $ZnCO_3$. The symptoms are attacks of colic, vomiting and diarrhea. Chronic zinc poisoning in these workmen cannot be denied, in fact is the chief cause of occupational disease in that industry. Lead is only of secondary interest. (The abstractor who has studied this question of zinc poisoning rather extensively believes that such symptoms are hardly to be construed as chronic constitutional zinc poisoning but that they are probably due to the local and irritative effects of continual ingestion of zinc salts perhaps changed to zinc chloride in the stomach, with the usual irritative or semi-caustic local action.)—Seiffert, *Off. Gsdhtsplge*, III, 44-67, 85-98, 116-143.

PUBLIC HEALTH NOTES

Heat-Stroke. Under the title of "Heat Hyperpyrexia" two important papers have been published,—the clinical aspect by Dr. W. H. Willcox, lately consulting physician to the Mesopotamian Expeditionary Force, and the physiological aspect by Leonard Hill, Director of the Department of Applied Physiology, Medical Research Committee, with some valuable comments later by K. G. Hearne and Maj.-Gen. (Ret.) Wm. Pike. When temperature reached 110° F. in the shade heat-stroke made its appearance and the number of cases increased with increase in temperature. A temperature of 120° F., in spite of all precaution induced a large number of heat-stroke cases. The effect of heat was undoubtedly cumulative in action since it was the succession of several hot days which was dangerous and a man who had been exposed might develop the attack in the night or early morning after the atmospheric temperature had fallen. High humidity produced more cases. Heat-stroke occurred especially in men past 40 years of age in whom it was also more severe. Stagnation of air, the degrees of which were estimated by Dr. Hill's kata-thermometer, was directly responsible as a factor. Failing to drink enough water, imbibing of alcohol, exertion during the heat of the day, absence of a protective helmet or of umbrellas, as well as predisposing diseases with fevers such as malaria, were also direct factors. There are four types of disease from exposure to heat: (1) Heat exhaustion (mild type) with weakness, fainting rapid pulse, slight fever or subnormal temperature and small mortality, (2) gastric type with suffused face, restlessness, marked nausea and occasional vomiting and absent mouth temperature. The pulse will be normal for several days, but the rectal temperature often shows a rise of about two degrees; the knee-jerks were absent. This is a dangerous type and after several days suddenly develops fatal heat hyperpyrexia. (3) Choleraic or gastro-intestinal type. Here the onset is sudden with collapse, slight fever, vomiting, diarrhea, cramps in abdomen and extremeties; mortality is high. (4) Heat hyperpyrexia. This is the common type (72½ of the severe cases). The onset is often sudden with temperature reaching 110° F. and with rapid loss of consciousness; the onset may, however, be more gradual with frequent urination, a characteristic early symptom after which the temperature mounts rapidly. The treatment for the first type requires rest, keeping cool and aperient medicine. The gastric type requires free purgation, great care in protection from heat, large doses of sodium bicarbonate cold rectal enemas of the same salt. The choleraic type requires normal saline subcutaneously the cardiac stimulants in addition to the protection from heat. The fourth type demands immediate stripping of the patient and constant application of a spray of cold water or constant rubbing of ice until the rectal temperature comes down to 102° F., the patient being under a fan during the process. Convulsions were treated by venesection, 10 to 20 ounces of blood being withdrawn. Respiratory failure was treated by artificial respiration and oxygen. Morphine and chloroform (inhalations) were inferior to venesection. Leonard Hill declares that so long as the body is exposed to cooling breeze, the exposure to sun cannot produce sun-stroke. The heating effect of protein-rich food must be avoided. A wet-bulb temperature of 80° F. may be the limit for muscular work. Breathing hot air may produce exhaustion even when the skin is exposed to a cool atmosphere. So long as sweating remains active and there is a breeze there is no danger of heat-stroke. Heavy clothing on soldiers marching in close column on a calm day are prime factors. One treatment to apply immediately when sweating ceases in a man, is to start artificial sweating by means of a water spray and fan. Persons about to suffer heat-stroke can be picked out by their dry skins. Those who cease to sweat complain of any breeze present. Maj.-Gen. Miles says that two points always precede an attack of heat hyperpyrexia, namely, frequency of urination and absence of sweating. These facts were pointed out in his lecture 40 years ago by Prof. McLean at Netley.—*Brit. Med. Jr.*, No. 3090, March 20, 1920, 392-397, and No. 3093, April 10, 1920, 521.

American Journal of Public Health

Official Monthly Publication of the American Public Health Association

Publication office: 124 W. Polk Street, Chicago, Ill.

Editorial office: 169 Massachusetts Ave., Boston, Mass.

Subscription price $4 per year. American Public Health Association membership, including subscription, $5 per year.
Subscriptions and memberships may be sent to the A. P. H. A., 169 Massachusetts Ave., Boston, Mass.

| Vol. X | NOVEMBER, 1920 | No. 11 |

PRESIDENTIAL ADDRESS OF W. S. RANKIN, M. D.

PRESENTED TO THE ANNUAL MEETING OF THE AMERICAN PUBLIC HEALTH
ASSOCIATION, SAN FRANCISCO, CALIFORNIA, SEPTEMBER 13, 1920.

INTRODUCTORY

Ladies and Gentlemen:

If I understand the sentiments and the traditions of this Association, I know that your selection of a presiding officer is determined by considerations that lie above and beyond mere personal relations and ends. Nevertheless, anyone called to serve as your President would have to be totally unmindful of that distinguished group of leaders in the public health movement who have occupied this office not to feel the humility that comes from walking in their steps and the honor of sitting in their places. I deeply appreciate the personal distinction that you have conferred upon me.

On my election to the Presidency of the Association, nearly a year ago, I at once began to consider what were our major interests—what matters were of such large and common concern as should appeal to the different administrative and scientific groups represented in this organization. There seemed to be three such matters of outstanding importance: the first was the maintenance of the health and vigor of the Association, keeping up the momentum of the growth developed under the preceding administration; the second was the acceptance by the Association of both its

opportunity and its obligation to assist other national agencies in the coördination and enlargements of federal health activities; the third was the recognition by the Association of the still greater need and the larger opportunity of assisting in the coördination and development of the extra-governmental public health agencies. In this address I will confine myself to a discussion of what has been accomplished during the past year with respect to each of these three major interests of our Association.

GROWTH AND PRESENT CONDITION OF
THE ASSOCIATION

Self-preservation is the first law of nature for every individual and agency. The development of self is a primary duty for it is only out of a strong self that efficient service comes. So with this Association, if it is to occupy the place of service which is open to it, if it fears God and takes its part, it must look first to the condition of its own life, must increase its power and influence, must maintain a healthy growth. Enlargement of our membership, of our funds, of our power to work, is our primary duty.

Less than a year ago, at our last meeting in New Orleans, President Frankel stated that the Association should have a minimum income of $50,000 per annum and a membership of not less than 6,000. His ideal of yesterday has become the achievement of today. The income of the Association in 1918 was $22,000; in 1919, $33,000; and in 1920, $49,015.04. Members and subscribers for the same years were, for September, 1918, 2,345; for September, 1919, 4,044; and for September, 1920, 6,000. The growth of the Association in membership, subscribers and funds during the past five years is shown in Chart A.

CHART A

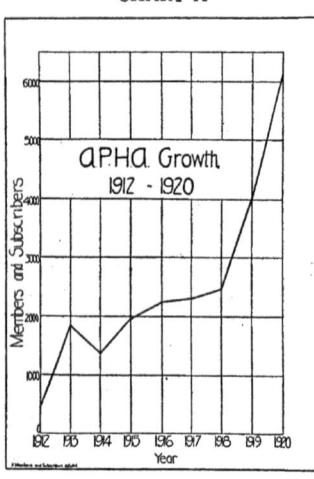

The membership campaign that has been carried on during the past six months was on a basis of state and provincial quotas, the quota for each state and province being fixed largely in proportion to its population. The six leaders in the campaign in the percentage of the quota reached are: Utah, 472; New Mexico, 364; North Carolina, 290; California, 195; Colorado, 142; and Saskatchewan, 142. The six leaders in the campaign in the total number of new members added to the Association are:

New York, 208; North Carolina, 172; California, 168; Maryland and the District of Columbia, 146; Ohio, 109; and Illinois, 107. There were 16 states and provinces that secured the quota of new members assigned them; two other states and provinces exceeded 75 per cent of their quotas, making a total of 18 states and provinces that exceeded 75 per cent of their quotas. Chart B indicates the present standing of the states and provinces according to the number of members in proportion to their population.

The membership campaign should be continued during the coming year until the Association has not less than 7,500 members and the campaign for corporate and sustaining memberships should be vigorously pushed until there is a total of 500 sustaining members— about eight or ten $50 memberships for each membership district—state and province. These objectives are neither impracticable nor ambitious, and are easily obtainable with a normal interest on the part of the members of the Association. Sixteen states and provinces in reaching their quota of a 7,500 membership have demonstrated that such a regular membership is possible and that without any great difficulty. The possibilities of a successful appeal in behalf of sustaining and corporate members was demonstrated in one state where a single letter soliciting corporate and sustaining memberships was addressed to a list of 85 public-spirited and financially-able individuals and corporations, and which brought in 15 sustaining and corporate members, a total in funds of $750 for the support of the Association. In many states and provinces the chairman of the membership committee, in most cases the chief executive health officer, assumed direction of the campaign with the complete understanding that his activities would be limited on account of special duties that could not be set aside. Many of these officials will wish to have their states and provinces represented as strongly in the Association in proportion to population as any other state or province, and will be glad to coöperate with the officers of the Association during the coming year in arranging for a special membership drive to complete their quotas.

In connection with the growth of the

CHART B

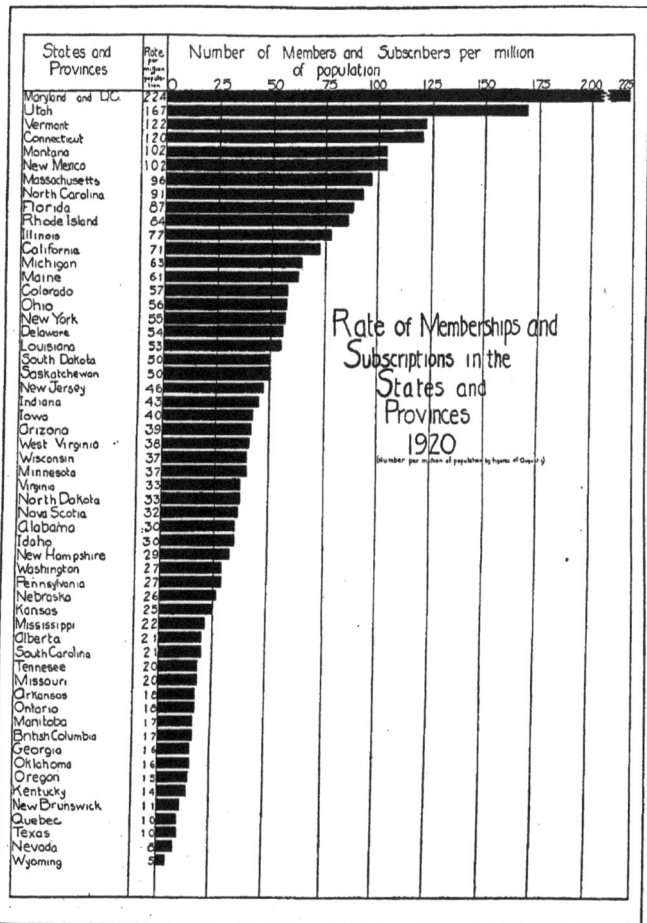

States and Provinces	Rate per million popula- tion	Number of Members and Subscribers per million of population
Maryland and D.C.	224	
Utah	167	
Vermont	122	
Connecticut	120	
Montana	102	
New Mexico	102	
Massachusetts	96	
North Carolina	91	
Florida	87	
Rhode Island	84	
Illinois	77	
California	71	
Michigan	63	
Maine	61	
Colorado	57	
Ohio	56	
New York	55	
Delaware	54	
Louisiana	53	
South Dakota	50	
Saskatchewan	50	
New Jersey	46	
Indiana	43	
Iowa	40	
Arizona	39	
West Virginia	38	
Wisconsin	37	
Minnesota	37	
Virginia	33	
North Dakota	33	
Nova Scotia	32	
Alabama	30	
Idaho	30	
New Hampshire	29	
Washington	27	
Pennsylvania	27	
Nebraska	26	
Kansas	25	
Mississippi	22	
Alberta	21	
South Carolina	21	
Tennesee	20	
Missouri	20	
Arkansas	18	
Ontario	18	
Manitoba	17	
British Columbia	17	
Georgia	16	
Oklahoma	16	
Oregon	15	
Kentucky	14	
New Brunswick	11	
Quebec	10	
Texas	10	
Nevada	6	
Wyoming	5	

Rate of Memberships and Subscriptions in the States and Provinces 1920

(Number per million of population by figures of Census)

Association during the past year and as an important new activity it is a pleasure to announce the creation of a committee for a careful and rather complete survey of municipal health procedure, made possible through a generous appropriation of $5,000 by the Metropolitan Life Insurance Company. A committee for this survey, consisting of Prof. C.-E. A. Winslow, Dr. Chas. V. Chapin, Dr. Louis I. Dublin and Dr. W. H. Frost, has been appointed.

COORDINATION OF FEDERAL HEALTH ACTIVITIES

The members of the Association will recall that it was pointed out at the New Orleans meeting last year that Federal health activities were now being conducted by 33 bureaus, scattered about under five Cabinet Departments; that there was not only a lack of coördination between these bureaus and departments, but that there existed considerable overlapping of work, some conflict of interests, and, as was demonstrated at that meeting, actual opposition; that the need for replacing our present patchwork of Federal health activities with a consolidated program of carefully considered and properly related public health functions was apparent to all; that the Association placed itself on record as recognizing the aforestated defects and needs in unanimously adopting, by a rising vote, the following resolution:

"WHEREAS, it is believed that the development, maintenance and protection of health in its citizens is one of the fundamental functions of civil government; and

"WHEREAS, lack of coördination in National Program and administration and lack of orderly proportionate expansion of the functions of the Federal health service in the United States has resulted from the present distribution of functions among various departments of the Government; therefore, be it

"RESOLVED, by the American Public Health Association, that measures should be taken to assure for the future a National Health Program and a coordinated Federal health administration; and further be it

"RESOLVED, that to accomplish these ends a standing committee of members of the American Public Health Association be appointed by the President of the Association to study the needs of the National Health situation, confer with other agencies and to do whatever lies in its power to secure the appointment of a special Congressional Commission on the coördination of the Federal health activities along the general line of the so-called France Bill."

In adopting this Resolution the American Public Health Association brought itself into concert of action with the Council on Health and Public Instruction, representing the American Medical Association, and the Conference of State and Provincial Health Authorities, both of which organizations had previously taken identical positions. The President of the Association, in accordance with the above Resolution, appointed as your Committee on the Coördination of Federal Health Activities, Dr. Haven Emerson, Dr. Lee K. Frankel and Dr. Chas. V. Chapin. This Committee is now working in harmony with a Committee representing the American Medical Association and composed of Dr. Victor C. Vaughan, Dr. Frederick R. Green and Dr. W. S. Rankin, and a Committee representing the Conference of State and Provincial Health Authorities and composed of Dr. S. J. Crumbine, Dr. C. St. Clair Drake and Dr. A. W. Freeman.

These three committees, working together as one, and in line with the Resolution of the Association, prepared and brought to the attention of Congress Concurrent Resolutions 14 and 33, the first being the Senate Resolution and the second the House Resolution. This Concurrent Resolution provides: (1) for a Congressional Commission to make a survey of present Federal health departments, divisions, bureaus, offices, and agencies, the laws creating them and defining their functions, any overlapping of work and conflict of interest, their coördination and the appropriations provided for them; (2) that the Commission is authorized to summons persons, to have them produce records, to administer oaths,—in short, is fully empowered to secure such information as it may need in arriving at sound conclusions; (3) that the Commission shall make such recommendations as to coördinating and improving the public health work of the Federal Government as the survey suggests; and (4) that such funds as the Commission may need in employing experts for assisting in the actual work of the survey shall be paid out of the contingent funds of the Senate and the House. This Concurrent Resolution was introduced in the Senate by Senator France and has passed the Senate. The Resolution was introduced in the House by Mr. Dennison, of Illinois, and was referred to the Committee on Rules but not reported out during the last session. The Resolution having passed the Senate, will go over on the calendar and will not need to be reintroduced in the Senate at the next session of Congress. Mr. Dennison has stated that he will call up the Resolution in the House early in the next session. A number of the leaders of both parties in the Senate and in the House have been conferred with and there seems to be not only no opposition to the Concurrent Resolution, but a very general sentiment in favor of it.

The American Medical Association, meeting in New Orleans in April, of this year, approved and endorsed the Concurrent Resolution 14 (the Resolution that has passed the Senate), and urged its passage by the House. The Association took the further position that the survey called for "will furnish the fundamental information needed and will mark a long step forward in the se-

curing of such a national health organization as our country requires." It will be noted that the American Medical Association in the aforestated action seems to take the position that the survey of federal health activities should be preliminary to taking steps for securing a national health department with a cabinet officer, to which form of federal health administration the Association in a subsequent resolution committed itself. The important point, not to be lost sight of, is that the Congressional survey is regarded by the three agencies working together, the American Medical Association, the American Public Health Association and the Conference of State and Provincial Health Authorities, as the first step in the reorganization of federal health activities.

The present outlook for real improvement in the public health functions of the Federal Government is most encouraging for the following reasons: (1) there seems to be a general and rather thorough understanding of the existing defects and the remedies needed; (2) leaders in Congress seem favorable to a study and reorganizing of federal health activities; (3) the political outlook, as it bears upon federal health work, is encouraging. The National Platform of the Republican Party says: "The public health activities of the Federal Government are scattered through numerous departments and bureaus, resulting in inefficiency, duplication and extravagance. We advocate a greater centralization of the work of the federal, state and local health agencies." While it is to be regretted that the National Platform of the Democratic Party is silent on so important a question as national health, the great interest taken by Governor Cox of Ohio in the development of one of the most advanced state health programs lends every encouragement to believe that if the next administration is Democratic national health work will be well cared for.

COORDINATION OF EXTRA-GOVERNMENTAL
HEALTH AGENCIES

Dr. Geo. E. Vincent, President of the
Rockefeller Foundation, a little more
than a year ago referred to the large
number of extra-governmental national
health agencies as the "57 varieties."
Recently the American Red Cross has
listed 139 voluntary organizations that
have some sort of a national health program. It seems safe to say that there
are in this country about as many voluntary national organizations for the
prevention of unnecessary deaths as
there are causes of deaths—189—given
in the international classification. This
highly divided state of national public
health influences results in wastefulness,
weakness and confusion:

In *wastefulness* of both money and
energy: of money from the diversion of
funds collected from the people to maintain so large a number of organizations;
of energy on account of overlapping
functions. Like the proud-flesh, that
grows but does not serve, this excessive
organization of civic interest in health
uses too large a proportion of the funds
drawn from the public to maintain office
forces and far too little of these funds
in useful service.

In *weakness*, from the division of
public interest in health conservation
into small and, relatively speaking, ineffective fractions. Like the individual
fibers of a rope, almost useless in themselves, these many fibers, bound into one
strong cord, would be capable of lifting
great burdens of suffering and expense
from the shoulders of our people.

In *confusion*, because the majority of
these voluntary health organizations, in
addition to their smaller and internal
objective, the improvement of their individual members and the standardization of methods, have as their larger,
common, ultimate objective the average
citizen and home. In reaching this
larger objective the average citizen
and home, these organizations have two

possible routes: one a direct appeal
by letter, prepared literature, press,
and public meeting, to the individual and family; the other an indirect route, the quicker and more
economical, through that agency that
represents the average citizen and home,
namely, his government, national, state
or local. In electing this second route
to its objective the extra-governmental
agency undertakes to persuade the government to reach through its channels
the citizen and home and either to influence or compel the citizen to adopt a
certain line of conduct. If successful in
persuading the governmental agency to
assume such a task the extra-governmental agency releases its resources and
forces for new endeavors in the extra-
governmental field. Consider now, if
you please, the confusion resulting from
so many extra-governmental agencies
attempting to persuade the government,
either national, state or local, to patch its
general program with the special interest
of the voluntary agency. Obviously, a
government's health program must be a
balanced ration, must consider not special diseases and special groups, but the
general public health needs. An extra-
governmental agency's health program,
nine times in ten, is a special health program dealing, in one case, solely with
tuberculosis, in another with venereal
diseases, in another with mental hygiene,
or with child hygiene, or with recreation, or with public health nursing, or
with malaria, or cancer, et cetera. There
is inevitable conflict and confusion between the general program of the government, representing the majority, and
the special program of the extra-
governmental agency, representing a
minority. In the case of the direct appeal from the voluntary agency to the
citizen, the confusion resulting is even
greater because the citizen, requested by
multiple agencies to do so many and
various things, is less able than his government to respond.

The cure for this wastefulness,

weakness and confusion in the public health field is coördination. Coördination removes the wastefulness of overlapping effort and unnecessary overhead charges; it replaces the weakness of excessive and unrelated division with the strength of unity, twisting the many weak, relatively useless, fibers into one strong rope; it does away with confusion in objectives by properly relating the many special programs into one general program, and thereby permits the voluntary and the governmental agency to pursue parallel courses and without conflict.

Coördination not only cures wastefulness with economy, weakness with strength, confusion with understanding, and conflict with coöperation, but it enables public health leadership to go beyond the interests of the professional and scientific groups with an effective appeal for enlistment of the support of the people themselves in the public health movement. United leadership permits a united and tremendously multiplied following, as I shall now attempt to indicate.

United leadership, through a coördination of the voluntary public health agencies would provide a balanced program of essentials that could be carried to the ultimate objective, the American citizen, either by the direct or the indirect route, largely through the means of a popular health magazine. I have such assurance that I am practically certain that sufficient funds for the publication of a first class popular health magazine, attractive in appearance, entertaining and informing in composition, in every respect a high-class periodical, are available whenever a coördination of existing voluntary agencies is brought about. With a magazine of the type described the opportunity and the means for reaching and organizing the people in support of public health would be at hand. Without such a magazine, without something to give the average citizen what in itself is worth his member-

ship dues of three, four or five dollars, and something that retains and augments his interest in the public health movement, it is impossible to enlist general support. Consider in this connection what the Journal of the American Medical Association means to that organization of something more than 75,000 members. Without the Journal it would never have been possible to have developed the Association to its present strength, and if the Journal were discontinued tomorrow the Association would undergo almost a fatal shrinkage. The National Geographic Society is a still more remarkable organization, an organization of 630,000 members, developed through the means of an attractive publication. The point has been made, however, on good authority, that the success of a popular health magazine cannot be predicated upon the large circulation of the *National Geographic* for the reason that the subject treated in the latter lends itself so well to beautiful illustrations. While flora, fauna and art are most entertaining, through the photographs, it is a fact that the subject of health holds a more extensive and intensive interest than the subject of geography. It is conservative to say that from ten to one hundred persons are interested in health where one person is interested in the subject of geography. And again, and most important, where the publication devoted to geography has had to make its own way without assistance, a popular health magazine would, from the outset, have as its friends and promoters health departments, federal, state and local, rural and urban, Red Cross Chapters, civic and philanthropic organizations, and tens of thousands of the more progressive, public-spirited physicians and nurses of the country. This point should not be lost sight of: the magazine is all-important; it is an essential means, but not the objective. The objective is to reach the people, to make them participants in the public health movement.

Coördinated leadership makes possible the magazine; the magazine makes possible the organization of county and district health societies with memberships ranging from 100 to 1,000. These county and district societies make possible, through federation, the state and provincial societies with memberships ranging from 5,000 to 25,000; these state and provincial health societies make possible, through federation, a great American health association, with a membership of from a half million to several million. The plan of this organization would be democratic, each local society represented in a state or provincial house of delegates in proportion to the number of its members, and each state and provincial society in turn represented in the central or American association would provide a whole-time digeneral, the plan followed by the American Medical Association would be easily possible. The financial strength of both state and provincial and American association in proportion to its members. In general, the plan followed by the Ameri-ciation would provide a whole-time directing personnel. This directing personnel of the extra-governmental agency should be in close touch with the official health agencies, but not dominated by them. The governmental and the extra-governmental fields should be kept separate, the one to carry out the expressed will of the majority and the other to convert minority ideas into majority convictions and law.

POSSIBILITIES FOR COÖRDINATION

During the last six months Dr. Livingstone Farrand, Dr. Chares J. Hatfield and the speaker have held several informal conferences regarding the possibilities of bringing about coördination of extra-governmental health agencies. As an outcome of these informal conferences it was found possible to secure practically the full time service of Dr. Donald B. Armstrong for visiting many leaders in the public health movement,

conspicuously identified with the more important extra-governmental agencies, and for collecting opinions and impressions on the possibilities of coördination of these agencies. Dr. Armstrong in this time has conferred with more than 100 leaders who are identified with more than 20 of the larger national health agencies. He has also collected and examined the constitutions and by-laws, statements of policies, and reports of extra-governmental health agencies and has gone through much literature that relates directly or indirectly to the principles of affiliations and coördinations of social groups. The impressions gained by Dr. Armstrong through these conferences and studies may be stated as follows: (1) there is a general recognition on the part of all leaders that a coördination of extra-governmental health agencies is necessary in the interest of efficiency; (2) these leaders believe that coördination is possible; (3) they seem to be willing to go more than half-way to bring it about; and (4) they feel that the initial steps should be taken at an early date.

Three possible plans for coördinating these voluntary agencies have been suggested:

The first plan is the organization of state and provincial health societies with constituent county and district societies, respectively, each county and district society to be represented in the state or provincial society by delegates in proportion to membership. The organization would be effected through the leadership of state and local health officials, officers in state and county medical societies, and in some states through now existing voluntary health agencies. The state and provincial health societies would be organized into an American health association, each state and province being represented in the general association by delegates in proportion to membership. This organization in the several branches at first would be restricted, perhaps, largely to a nucleus of professional groups, but with the publication of a popular health magazine, made possible through federation, the more intelligent people, the leaders in the community, would be enlisted. This plan, if followed, would ignore existing national associations, which would either satisfy themselves with a limited sphere of action or become a part of the general organization.

The second plan proposed is: (1) that the important national associations come together in an affiliation or a conference or a merger; (2) that through a central committee, a plan for state and provincial and local societies be developed and urged for adoption upon states and provinces. While the first plan represents an organization effected from the bottom up, the second plan represents an organization brought about from the top down. The second plan has the advantage over the first in conserving and utilizing national leadership and resources. The two are not incompatible. The organization may start from both ends.

The third plan proposed, and the one which Dr. Armstrong found by far the most popular with the leaders whom he consulted, consists of bringing together the leaders of the larger national health agencies, at first informally, and subsequently, after these leaders have conferred with the officers of their organizations, bringing together formally the representatives of the more important agencies for the purpose of effecting a conference, with the maintenance, perhaps, of a simple but full-time staff to be associated and housed with and probably financed by the Red Cross. The idea here, to quote Dr. Armstrong, "is a marriage between the Red Cross resources of influence and funds and the specialized channels of service of the voluntary health agencies." Under this Red Cross Conference plan each organization represented in the conference would preserve its sovereignty, but would come into working relations

with other health organizations and under a steady, growing influence would find common ground for unity of purpose and concert of action.

There is a general impression among the leaders with whom Dr. Armstrong has conferred that the initial step in the development of coördinated activities, that is, the calling together informally for the first conference of representatives of different organizations, should be left to Dr. Livingstone Farrand. It is perhaps best for such a movement to start, not with some particular health agency, but through some one who is equally interested in the objectives of all of them and whose relation with the entire group is cordial. Such a course will prove more satisfactory than if one public health agency appeared to assume the role of leader and called the others to order. My understanding is that Dr. Farrand will call the initial and informal conference in October.

The three plans of organization are thoroughly democratic in principle. Each makes possible a popular health magazine and, through it, an extension of the organization of the public health interests to the masses of the people, or, to quote Dr. Frederick R. Green, "to treat the intelligent people of this country not as beneficiaries in the public health movement, but as participants."

Popular, active participation, not passive interest, in the public health movement, is essential to any large and real success. The greatest weakness in the appeal of the true prophets of public health is that they have been satisfied to reach, and, relatively speaking, have not reached beyond, the scientifically and officially interested groups. They have fallen short of their real objective, the American citizen and home. On the other hand, the greatest strength of the false prophets, those who teach erroneous doctrines of the functions and impairments of the body and the prevention and cure of disease, is that they, not having a scientific and official group to which to appeal, have gone directly to Caesar, the American citizen. Just at this time, I am reliably informed, there is widespread propaganda on the Pacific Slope for an amendment to state constitutions forbidding compulsory vaccination under any circumstances. These anti-vaccinationists realize that to get a legislative reaction favorable to their ideas they must bring it about as a reflex response to popular demand—they must reach not the few, the leaders, but the multitude, the voters. We shall do well not to lose sight of their strategy.

Until this larger objective of the As-sociation, the enlistment of the masses in its work, is attained, its thought and energies should not be diverted into other and smaller channels of service. An affiliation, a coördination of machinery and functions, may call for some sacrifice of identity, that trademark of selfishness, but if the Association is as big as its real friends believe it to be, it will not protest against sacrifices of identity for larger service, but will be guided by that eternal principle, namely, For whosoever will save his life shall lose it; and whosoever will lose his life for a righteous cause shall find it.

☐

RETURN OF THE NOVA SCOTIA PUBLIC HEALTH CARAVANS

In the October issue, page 779, the readers of the JOURNAL had the story and saw the picture of the start of the Nova Scotia health caravans. After a triumphal tour of 49 days among the fishing villages of the Province they returned to Halifax and a tremendous public health pageant greeted them in a natural amphitheatre of Citadel Hill. There were 5,000 persons gathered below the old fort, where a choir of 200 sang "Onward, Christian Soldiers," and other appropriate hymns and patriotic songs. The Lieutenant-Governor of the Province presided at this great home-coming event, and there were addresses by local notables.

PRESENT STATUS OF PLAGUE, WITH HISTORICAL REVIEW

W. H. KELLOGG, M. D.

Director Bureau of Communicable Diseases, State Board of Health, Sacramento, Cal.

Read before General Sessions, American Public Health Association, at San Francisco, Cal., September 15, 1920.

Health officers have known something of the early plague situation in California, but never before has the story been related in such stirring fashion as in this paper. It is an experience that, fortunately, seldom goes to such lengths. The necessity for strenuous extermination activities now against plague carriers is patent.

THE first appearance of plague on the North American Continent was in 1900 at San Francisco, when the body of a Chinese, dead of this disease, was discovered in the Chinese quarter. I was then bacteriologist for the City Board of Health, and the case was referred to me by the city physician, who was required to sign the death certificates of Chinese dying unattended by white physicians. We had been on the lookout for plague, as, it was present in Honolulu, which port it had reached on its westward march in December, 1899. This case was proven bacteriologically to be plague, and the Board of Health of San Francisco, on receipt of the preliminary findings, placed the entire district known as Chinatown, comprising about twelve square blocks, in quarantine, the quarter being roped off and police placed on guard.

The events which followed will be referred to later. For the present, suffice it to say that the disease continued to manifest its presence by the discovery of cases now and then until a total of 121 cases and 113 deaths had been reached by February, 1904, when the last case of this series was found.

In May, 1907, a year after the great fire and earthquake, plague was again discovered in San Francisco. A sailor taken to the Marine Hospital from a tug in the bay was found to be suffering from plague, but he died without being able to give any account of himself, and the tug was lost off the Mendocino coast, thus effectually blocking any further investigation. On August 12 the second case of the second epidemic appeared, followed by 13 others before the end of the month.

The citizens of San Francisco, including the politicians, the press, and the doctors, had learned their lesson in the first epidemic, and, as a consequence, we have a history of events in 1907 and 1908 that is in marked contrast to that of 1900 and 1901. Doctor Blue was again called and early placed in charge and, with his previous experience and the unanimous support of all interests, carried on the work under the most favorable conditions, the details of which and results attained being too well known to need description here. The epidemic lasted six months, and the total number of cases was 160, with 77 deaths; this time not in the Chinese quarter alone, but scattered all through the city. The last case of the series occurred on June 30, 1908. During the year 1907 seven cases were found in Seattle, Wash. In the years intervening between February 1, 1908, and the end of the year 1915, inclusive, sporadic cases of human plague of squirrel origin occurred in California to the total number of 13 in the counties of Los Angeles, Alameda, Santa

Clara, San Benito, Contra Costa, San Joaquin and Monterey. During the years 1916, 1917 and 1918 no cases of human plague are known to have occurred anywhere in the United States. Extension of the infection to the ground squirrel population of the rural territory adjacent to San Francisco was first demonstrated in August, 1908, although it is probable that the infection was carried from rats to squirrels in the vicinity of the Port Costa warehouses during the first epidemic in 1900-1904. This probability is indicated by the occurrence of two deaths from plague in widely separated locations in Contra Costa County in August, 1903. The ground squirrels of this state have, therefore, harbored the infection for nearly twenty years, and if it is not eliminated from among them by a very wide and expensive campaign of extermination there seems little room for doubt that a permanent endemic focus has been established. The extent of plague prevalence among the ground squirrels is shown by the following figures from the Public Health Reports of recent date. For the period of the report, which varies with different counties from a few days to three months, ending July 10, 1920, infected squirrels were found as shown below:

Alameda County 28, Contra Costa County 46, Merced 1, Monterey 3, San Benito 16, San Mateo 3, San Joaquin 4, Santa Clara 12, Santa Cruz 26, and Stanislaus 2.

The figures for the total number of infected rodents found since the beginning of the work in 1907 are startling. In San Francisco the number of rats found was 398, the last one having been discovered in October, 1908, and in Oakland 126 rats, the last one in December, 1908. Alameda County has a record of 431 squirrels, the last being found in September, 1919. Contra Costa County holds the record, the total number of infected squirrels found being 1,698.

Following the decade ending with 1918, plague showed a tendency toward

recrudescence. In Oakland a series of 13 pneumonic cases occurred,* in August, 1919, the first of the series having its origin in exposure to plague-infected ground squirrels.

This appearance of pneumonic plague in epidemic form, small as was the outbreak, is very disquieting. Plague of squirrel origin seems particularly prone to attack the lungs when transmitted to man, and the danger is that in another such series of cases a sufficient degree of specific organ virulence may be developed to insure the rapid spread of

RUMOR has it that Dr. Kinyoun may soon receive a strong hint from Washington that the quarantine service in San Francisco would be better without him.—*Morning Newspaper.* *Wasp, Oct. 15, 1900.*

this type. If the conclusions of Teague and Barber† are correct, and they appear most plausible, there is much to be feared from this contingency under circumstances permitting extension to some of our eastern states in winter. It is easily possible for a person, after inoculation by a squirrel flea, to travel to some eastern point, reaching his destination before the onset of symptoms. If now he develops a bubo with a secondary pneu-

*Kellogg, W. H.; Am. Jour. Pub. Health, July, 1920, pp. 599-605.
†Oscar Teague and M. A. Barber; Philippine Jour. of Science, 1912, pp. 157-172.

monia, as did the first case of the Oakland series, in the proper climatic surroundings·for transmission of the infection, the role of plague as a.national problem would be immediately recognized. In October of this same year plague reappeared in New Orleans, following an interval of nearly four years since its first appearance in that city. This was followed by three more in October, three in November and five in December.

So far during the present year plague has occurred in California (one sporadic case of squirrel origin), in New Orleans (three cases in May and June), in Galveston, Texas, (two cases), in Pensacola, Florida, (four cases in June and three cases in July), in Beaumont, Texas, (seven cases between June 26 and July 18), and in Port Arthur, Texas, (one case in July). Rat examination by the

Public Health Service in the above-named cities discloses a rat epizoötic in Pensacola, Beaumont, Galveston and New Orleans.

The disease is present in so many countries now that a list of those harboring it would include most of the nations of the world. In Europe it has been reported recently in Greece, England, Italy, Malta, Russia and France. In July, 1919, a dock laborer in Liverpool died of plague, and there is little doubt that the infection prevails among the rats of that city. Human cases have recently been reported from Hawaii, and a sharp outbreak is in progress in Vera Cruz, Mexico, where it was first discovered in May of this year. Several cases have occurred recently in Newfoundland.

The events previously referred to as having followed the finding of the first case in 1900, and which served to insure

CAN ANY ONE TELL WHO INSPIRED THE RAID?

intelligent handling of the second epidemic were most remarkable, and as they relate to the difficulties of the Board of Health, they will, I am sure, be of interest to all health officers.

This unparalleled series of medico-political events was initiated by the action of the San Francisco Board of Health in quarantining Chinatown. While in the light of our present day knowledge of plague control methods the quarantine of the quarter in this manner was not a necessary procedure, it must be remembered that this was the first appearance in history of plague in North America and the first on the Western Hemisphere, excepting at Santos, Brazil, where it had appeared two months before.

It had been absent from western Europe for two hundred years until the Oporto appearance in August, 1899. Having in mind the historical epidemics of the middle ages and the more recent mortality in India, it is not to be wondered at that the Board of Health expected a rapid spread of the disease, and that it attempted to keep it within the confines of the quarter in which it was discovered.

No further cases being found during the next few days, the newspapers, on the qui vive for an opportunity to attack the mayor, who had just been elected under the new charter, took heart and gambled on the chance that there would be no epidemic. They launched a campaign of vilification against the Health Board and the Federal quarantine officer, Doctor Kinyoun, that for unexampled bitterness, unfair and dishonest methods, probably never had been and never again will be equalled. (See reproductions of newspaper cartoons accompanying).

The campaign of denial of the presence of plague and of resistance to the Board of Health became a political issue of the most violent character. It involved health officers and boards, both city and state, and the U. S. Marine Hospital Service; local politicians, members of the State Central Committee of the political party then in power in the state, but not in the city; State Senators, the Governor of the state, the Secretary of State of the United States, the Secretary of the Treasury and the President himself.

Every local paper except one was aligned with the opposition, but it is only fair to state that this one backed the political party of the mayor who had appointed the Board of Health.

The line-up of the medical profession was interesting. A number of men possessing no claim to special knowledge of the subject, never having seen cases of plague, with no training as pathologists, and without seeing either cases or specimens of local origin, broke into print with interviews, stating positively that no plague existed in the city. Most of the physicians taking part in the controversy against the Board of Health were attached in various capacities to a certain private medical school, now defunct, whose president was appointed by the Governor as a member of his reorganized State Board of Health, he having found it necessary to change the complexion of the original board, which was in sympathy with the local board.

The following is an official statement of the San Francisco Clinical Society, an organization of the faculty and graduates of this school, and it serves as an example of the character of the "scientific" opinion used against the board:

"Resolutions of the San Francisco Clinical Society:

"That no infected vessel could reach the port of San Francisco without cases having developed.

"Of the eleven suspected cases reported by the local Board of Health, no two deaths have occurred in the same house, and no focus of infection has ever been discovered. This is positively contrary to the world's history of plague.

"No clinical history of any suspected case of plague has been secured and no diagnosis of a living case has ever been made.

"Only bacteriological tests have been relied upon for the purpose of diagnosis, and such tests are known to be confirmatory evidence only, and alone are never conclusive.

"The health of the supposed infected district has been better and the death rate lower during the past three months of this year, when plague is claimed to have existed, than during any previous months in any previous year in San Francisco;

"Therefore, be it resolved that it is our firm conviction, based upon the strongest and most conclusive evidence, that no case of plague exists, or has ever existed, in the city of San Francisco."

The Chinese colony numbered about 20,000, and included many wealthy societies, as well as wealthy men. The Chinese are great litigants and employ the best of legal talent. Being citizens of a foreign nation, they have entrée to our federal courts.

The first action was an application for an injunction against the requirement of a certificate of Haffkinization which was being required by the Public Health Service, then the Marine Hospital Service, of all Orientals desiring to leave the

The Bubonic Brigade Picked the Lock With a Jimmy.

city. This was granted on the ground that the requirement was discriminatory. Following this action of the Federal Court, the State Board of Health urged the local board to re-establish the rope cordon around Chinatown, which was done by ordinance of the Board of Supervisors. After this quarantine had been in effect about two weeks, the Chinese, with their staff of highly-paid attorneys, sought to enjoin the Board of Health against interfering in any way with the free movements of these people.

In deciding this case and issuing the injunction, the judge took some pains to express his personal opinion as follows: "If it were within the province of this court to decide the point, I should hold that there is not, and never has been, a case of plague in this city."

In the hearing of this case the attorney for the Board was not permitted to introduce any evidence bearing on the existence of plague in answer to the unsupported statements of council for the Chinese and in answer to their quotation of spurious "authorities."

The Governor of the state early formed an opinion that coincided with that held by the opponents of the Board and he became particularly vigorous, not only in his statements in the press, but in his acts calculated to harass any who held contrary opinions.

In reply to a telegram from Secretary of State Hay, he sent a long summary of alleged facts supporting his denial of the existence of plague, after having made, as he said, an exhaustive investigation, in the course of which he did not consult any member of the local Department of Health or of the Marine Hospital Service, or any of their records. This telegram was concurred in and carried the signatures of the presidents of two private schools of medicine and several prominent merchants and bankers.

This telegram was the last straw for Doctor Bazet, member of the State Board of Health, and he resigned. The Governor appointed in his place the President of one of the colleges, as before mentioned. After arbitrarily removing Doctor Henderson of Sacramento, he had a Board of Health, the personnel of which in the majority, coincided with him in his opinions. About the same time, Doctor Ryfkogel, bacteriologist for the State Board, was removed following a plague report by him.

Two men rated as bacteriologists and who were unable to find evidence of plague, were found and one was employed by the State Board of Health and the other by the attorneys for the Chinese.

The Governor's message in January, 1901, devoted a great deal of space to the plague question. He reviewed in a vitriolic manner the course of events relating to the plague controversy, referring to "the recklessness of certain city officials of San Francisco, assisted by a federal officer, one Doctor Kinyoun," as being responsible for the "fearful shadow cast upon the state." The following choice quotation is extracted: "Could it have been possible that some dead body of a Chinaman had innocently, or otherwise, received a post mortem inoculation in a lymphatic region by someone possessing the imported plague bacilli, and that honest people were thereby deluded?" and further—"assuming that we are justified in believing that the false reports of the plague which were temporarily credited at Washington, in other states and in foreign countries, were innocently circulated, may we not have cause to think that in certain instances, when prosecuting scientific investigations within this State, with all sorts of slides, cultures, etc., for the purpose of discovery and comparison, some investigator innocently caused slides and cultures containing genuine imported bacilli to be accidentally mixed with or substituted for harmless slides and cultures, prepared from human suspects, and in that way the medical departments in Washington as well as in this State were deceived and induced to foster the false reports?"

The Governor recommended that it be made a felony, punishable by life imprisonment, to import plague bacilli, plague cultures or plague slides, without written authority from the State Board of Health, and the same penalty was to attach to any person within the state who should develop plague cultures or make slides from any plague case within the state. Another suggestion was that it should be made a felony for any person, board or corporation to write or publish the existence of plague within the state unless the State Board of Health had first determined such to be the fact and had duly entered the record at length on its minutes. It is to the credit of the Legislature that none of these bills were

CITIZEN: "Oh, for a St. Patrick!"

passed. As an example of newspaper animosity, an evening paper of June 16, 1900, contained an editorial in large type headed "These men are marked," in which the names of the Board, Dr. J. M. Williamson, President, and Doctors Baum, Bazet, McCarthy, and Vincent Buckley were emblazoned across the page in heavy faced 18 point Gothic. I quote one paragraph:

"The Board will be known in municipal political history as the Bubonic Board. There will never be any difficulty in distinguishing or designating it from any of the former or subsequent sanitary commissions of this municipality, but the individuals who compose it should be made to stand forth as the perpetrators of the greatest crime that has ever been committed against the city."

These men are indeed marked; marked as men of sterling integrity, as men who had the courage of their convictions and who stood steadfast against the most virulent combination of falsehood and personal attack that probably ever was endured by any Board of Health before or since. They were attacked by editors, supervisors, mayors, governors, judges of the Federal Courts and by their fellow citizens. They served without pay and suffered loss of practice and prestige. They were overwhelmed temporarily with a cloud of suspicion, distrust and positive hate that was almost universal in the community, but they withstood both threats and bribes. Their names should be indelible in the annals of public health and to them should be added that of Dr. Kinyoun, the Federal Quarantine Officer of the time.

Under weight of the powerful political attack upon Dr. Kinyoun, the Surgeon General engaged the services of a special commission composed of Doctors F. G. Novy, L. F. Barker and Simon Flexner. Upon their arrival in the state late in June, 1901, the Governor wired a message of protest to the President of the United States in which he stated that the commission was about to commence investigations "ignoring the state authorities in the matter and proceeding in line with reports heretofore made by Dr. J. J. Kinyoun to the Surgeon General of the Marine Hospital Service." The Governor hoped that there had been "no intentional discourtesy on the part of the officer directed by the Treasury Department to supervise this investigation." The Secretary of the Treasury replied to this message assuring the Governor that no discourtesy was intended and expressed the desire of the department that the commission should make its investigations in its own way "unhampered by detailed instructions from the Public Health and Marine Hospital Service or *any other influence.*"

Immediately upon receipt of this reply from the Secretary of the Treasury the bills intended to throttle the Commission in its work and also to hamper local health departments were introduced into the legislature. It is an ill wind that blows nobody good and one of the bills that happened to have merit was passed and is now in the Political Code of this state. This is Paragraph 2979a, which gives valuable and far-reaching powers to the State Board of Health.

The special commission sent by the Surgeon General was fortunate in observing six cases of plague within a few days and their report was submitted on February 28, 1901. This report, of course, settled the matter even in the minds of those doctors who had heretofore been sceptical of the findings of local bacteriologists and the campaign of abuse in the newspapers ceased rapidly, but no acknowledgment of error was ever made by any of these newspapers and all news concerning plague was suppressed. This attitude on the part of the San Francisco papers is still maintained.

The Governor, doubtless, feeling obliged to recognize in some manner the turn in affairs and desiring to present the appearance of coöperation with the Federal Government in eradicative measures that were plainly inevitable, sent to Washington a "special health commission" of five members composed of three newspaper editors, an attorney for the Southern Pacific Railroad and a prominent shipbuilder. This committee on its return published a report. As President Williamson of the local Board said in his annual report for 1902: "The purpose of the report is palpably one of deception. Its contents add nothing whatever to scientific information and contribute still less to veracity." This document, although supposed to be the report of a commission sent to Washington to assure the President and the Surgeon General that California would coöperate in the eradication of plague, was mostly taken up with matter intended to justify the Governor in his previous course. It reproduces many telegrams that passed between the Executive and the Departments of State and of the Treasury in Washington, eulogies of the Governor by the Commission and a "report" of the State Board of.Health. It is interesting to note that in the account of coöperative cleaning up measures in Chinatown that were carried on under Surgeon J. H. White, the boast is made that Dr. White's advice was disregarded and 30,000,000 cubic feet of space fumigated with three hundred pounds of sulphur! instead of with thirty tons, thereby effecting a great saving to the State.

The Secretary of the State Board of Health, in a letter to the Governor, which is reproduced in this report of the Commission, says: "At the conclusion of the work, as thorough and as searching as it could possibly be made, no case of bubonic plague was found nor was any indication of its having been there discovered. If plague had existed in San Francisco just prior to this sanitary investigation it would have been there during the months of April, May and June because no efforts had been made to suppress it and no precautions taken to prevent its spread. It is safe, therefore, to say that the evil reports of the presence of that disease in San Francisco were based upon error in diagnosis upon the part of incompetent investigators. We take great pleasure in assuring you that plague does not exist in San Francisco and that it never has had lodgment there nor elsewhere in California."

Bear in mind that this was written six months after the work of Doctors Flexner, Barker and Novy. The State Board of Health which had been engaged in cleaning up Chinatown in coöperation with the City Board, ceased work in June, 1902. Doctor White left for Washington soon after and the situation settled down to a struggle of the local board with insufficient funds, the State Board denying the existence of plague and the newspapers suppressing all facts.

Recollection of these experiences with the press prompts the query in one's mind, Are these things possible today? Let me quote from the Los Angeles *Times* of June 20, 1920, a paragraph from an article by one Harry Ellington Brook, N. D. (whatever that stands for): "A few cases of bubonic plague appeared recently at Vera Cruz. Such cases still appear occasionally in tropical countries, where filthy conditions prevail. Bubonic plague, typhus and smallpox are filth diseases. Under improved sanitary conditions smallpox would be as rare as bubonic plague, had it not been kept alive by vaccination. There is no more danger of bubonic plague becoming epidemic in a climate like that of California, where people are cleanly, than there is of seeing cactus sprouting on cement sidewalks." There are few diseases concerning which we have such exact knowledge of the cause, mode of spread and method of control as we have of plague, and none that are easier of control given the necessary financial support. The message I would carry to the ears of government, national, state and municipal authorities, were it possible to do so, would be: Wage a relentless warfare against the rat in all the seaports of this country regardless of whether or not plague has yet appeared. Accompany this with laboratory examinations of rats so as to know the exact moment plague appears and to have information of the progress of the epizoötic among them when it does appear; and finally, enforce rat-proof construction, particularly of wharves and warehouses. Plague usually travels in ships. It enters new territory by way of the seaports. The outposts of defence must be here located.

The problem of plague among the squirrels of California is enormous. It can be eradicated from among them, but it never will be at the present rate of work by the state and federal authorities. With plague present in five seaports and in four states at the present moment, the sooner the situation is realized and met by Congress and the Legislature of the State with an appropriation of a million dollars at the very least, the sooner will the spectre of bubonic plague vanish from our midst.

報 日 西 中

CHUNG SAI YAT PO

A CHINESE DAILY.
PUBLISHED AT 804 SACRAMENTO STREET,
SAN FRANCISCO, CALIFORNIA.

VOL. 1 NO. 109   FRIDAY, JUNE 22, 1900   PER YEAR $ 6.00
PUBLISHED BY THE CHUNG SAI YAT PO PUB. CO.
Entered at the Post Office at San Francisco, Cal. as Second Class Matter, April 1, 1900.

日 七 廿 月 五 年 六 十 二 緒 光

五 拜 禮 號 九 零 百 一 第 紙 聞 新

擬 捉 狼 醫 圖

METHODS OF PLAGUE CONTROL

FRINECH SIMPSON,

Surgeon, United States Public Health Service, San Francisco Quarantine Station, Angel Island, Cal.

Read before General Sessions, American Public Health Association, September 15, 1920, at San Francisco, Cal.

> If we are economically and efficiently to ward off plague we must rid ourselves of the rat. This demands coördination of effort, management, organization and funds. Rat destruction and rat-proofing are preventive measures that fortunately do not involve financial loss, while they will eliminate the dangerous rodent from the homes and environment of men.

MEDICAL knowledge of plague contained no rational measures of control until the year 1903, when the relationship between the rat and the disease was officially recognized and generally accepted. Here began the real advance in our knowledge of control, and when later, in 1908, the Indian Plague Commisison found the rat flea to be the infective agent, this Commission was able to establish the following important facts: that bubonic plague is primarily a disease of rodents, transported by the rat and transmitted by the flea; that the disease is rarely transmitted in any other manner; that there is a seasonal increase in fleas, and that this increase is followed by an increase in rodent plague; that at a temperature above 85° F. fleas cease to multiply and that the infective micro-organism disappears from their bodies. Hence, epidemics, are seasonal in occurrence, are confined to warm latitudes and decline when the temperature rises above 85° F.

These statements are now generally accepted as facts and form the foundation of modern methods of control; but before describing the manner of application, it seems essential that brief mention be made of the rodents and fleas encountered in plague control work in this country. In California, plague is confined to a small endemic focus among the ground-squirrels. The flea found infesting these animals and their burrows is usually present in great numbers, and the ground-squirrel appears to be its selective host. It readily bites man.

The three plague rats of the United States with which we are concerned, are the Norway, or *Mus Norvegicus;* the Alexandrian rat, or *Mus Alexandrinus,* and the Indian black rat, or *Mus rattus.* All are flea-ridden, all are semidomesticated, and all litter continuously throughout the year. All are homed in our seaports and under normal conditions all will be found occupying the same premises—the Norway in the ground under floors, rattus and Alexandrinus in the walls and on upper floors.

The Norway determines this division of quarters. He is a burrowing rat, and demands the ground for harborage and purposes of propagation, and, being the largest and strongest, he drives the associated species to upper floors. The Norway rat is but rarely found on shipboard, and then only as an accidental traveler. The absence of ground prevents burrowing and propagation, and he suffers extermination. On shore he is a migrant, capable of traveling many blocks in a single night; many miles in a few days. Unrestrained in his normal habitat, the ground, he flourishes and exceeds in numbers the associated species. Both Alexandrian and black rats are world travelers; they are common both on ships

845

and on shore, finding in either case a satisfactory home between walls, in enclosed spaces, in cargo and in merchandise, where, if allowed to remain undisturbed, they will breed and multiply. On ships the Alexandrinus generally predominates over the rattus. Both are trap-shy, cunning and remarkable climbers.

These rats are the selective hosts of two varieties of fleas, X. *Cheopis* and *C. fasciatus*. The former, *Cheopis*, is the common flea of India. Both transmit plague, are subject to seasonal increase, and apparently prefer to confine their activities to the rodent host. When the rat is no longer available, they seek and readily bite man. They require mammalian blood for propagation, but eggs are laid away from the host preferably in rat-nests.

This brief reference to the bionomics of rats and fleas as related to bubonic plague indicates clearly that man is a negligible factor; that control of the disease demands fundamentally the elimination of rats and fleas in ships and on shore.

In modern practice, plague control measures on vessels are applied continuously for the prevention of the introduction of disease; whereas, on shore, control measures constitute a brief, costly and intensive process, applied systematically only after the appearance of the disease at the point of invasion, and abandoned as soon after its disappearance as circumstances will permit.

PLAGUE CONTROL ON VESSELS

In 1908, Eager collected all available statistics covering the occurrence of cases of human plague reported on ships, from the incidence of the present pandemic in 1894, up to and including the year 1907. He found that in 13 years a total of 140 vessels had reported human plague aboard, with a total of 229 cases and 122 deaths. One hundred and twenty-six of these vessels were steam-propelled.

Intermittent statistics through the years following indicate that ship infection continues to be reported in about the same yearly proportion. In 1919, 13 vessels reported plague aboard; in 1912, 15 vessels; in 1916, four vessels; in 1917, three vessels. From April, 1919, to the present year and month, August, 1920, 11 vessels, all steam-propelled, have reported plague, with a total of 46 cases and 12 deaths.

The cases above reported were all human cases, but in the light of present knowledge and experience, it can be reasonably assumed that contact with rat-plague was the source of origin, and that infection probably occurred aboard ship.

With plague now abroad in some port or place in practically every important maritime country, and with vessels from these ports in daily contact with the wharves of innumerable American cities, it is remarkable that the invasion of our ports has not occurred with greater frequency. Freedom is due, no doubt, to the control imposed through National Quarantine operations. National Quarantine is a federal measure of plague control, under the direction of the Public Health Service. It is enforced under national statutes and regulations, and is applied and in daily operation in every port of entry to the United States.

In connection with plague control, its effects are brought to bear on vessels at three distinct points: first, before the vessel departs; second, while en route, and, third, on arrival in the United States.

Before departure from any foreign port, the master of any vessel destined for the United States must first obtain from the American consul in that port a bill of health. This document becomes a part of the ship's papers, and over the signature of the consul sets forth the sanitary conditions of the port relative to plague or other quarantinable disease. If plague is present, the vessel is required to fumigate before departure, breast-off from the wharf and maintain rat-guards on all mooring lines; cargo, if capable of harboring rats and fleas, must be certified as rat-free. In addition, the bill contains other sanitary information relating to the vesssl, personnel and cargo, and the document is of great importance in establishing the sanitary status of the vessel on arrival. In addition to these protective measures, whenever epidemic disease of a quarantinable nature is present in a foreign port with which we have commercial relations, it is the general practice to detail a medical officer of the Service to such port to observe and report the status bf such disease in its relation to shipping, and this information is furnished quarantine officers in home ports.

During the voyage, all cases of illness and death are required to be recorded, and, accompanied by the clinical records, constitute a part of the ship's papers. Such records are of great importance in determining the health status of the vessel on arrival.

On arrival in the United States, vessels from any foreign port or place, before entry, must first submit to medical inspection. Medical officers are continuously on duty in every port of entry the purpose of conducting this inspection, which includes examination of the ship's papers, the medical inspection of passengers and crew, and, if required, a sanitary inspection of the compartments of the vessel. After a consideration of these sources of information, decision is made as to fumigation, which is required under the following circumstances:

Vessels from ports plague-infected or suspected of plague infection, are required to fumigate at the end of each voyage to the United States, such fumigation to be applied before entry, if there is plague or suspicion of plague aboard, and after entry and discharge of cargo, if the vessel presents a clean bill of health. All other vessels are required to fumigate periodically, at the end of each six-month period.

Quarantine then is that measure of control used to prevent plague entrance, and chief reliance is placed upon the fumigation of the vessel for the destruction of rats and fleas.

The gaseous agents now employed for this purpose are sulphur dioxide and hydrocyanic acid. Sulphur dioxide is the more commonly and widely used of the two, and has been employed as a gaseous disinfectant since the eighteenth century. It is fatal to animal and insect life, but possesses inherent disadvantages which will not permit its routine use as a fumigant. It corrodes metal, bleaches dyestuffs, injures certain foods, endangers the vessel from fire and requires an exposure of from six to twelve hours to produce its maximum effects. In plague control work it is gradually being replaced by hydrocyanic acid gas. As a salt, hydrocyanic acid is widely used industrially, and, as a gas, has long been employed as an insecticide in the fruit industry. At New Orleans, in 1915, Creel and his assistants experimentally determined its practical value as a rat and flea destructant, standardized the quantities required, and initiated its employment as a routine ship fumigant. It is ideal for this purpose. It is rapidly fatal to animal and insect life; it is readily prepared aboard ship; is not injurious to metals, fabrics or food, and produces its effects within two hours' time. Because of the saving of ship's time, it is less costly than sulphur. After an experience of five years, it can be declared safe for ship and house fumigation, provided essential precautionary measures are rigidly observed.

After exposure of the vessel to one or the other of the above fumigants, all compartments are ventilated and the vessel searched for rats. Rats found dead are noted as to number, species and location in the vessel, and when laboratory facilities are available for the detection of rodent plague, they are sent to such laboratory for examination.

When the measures here outlined are consistently and periodically employed, few rats will be found infesting the vessel. These may be considered an irreducible minimum, and as infective material, so much diluted that the vessel may be declared safe as a plague risk.

PLAGUE CONTROL ON SHORE

Plague generally appears first in some seaport, and usually announces its presence through the death of some human victim. Then we find that, stealthily, it has already invaded the rat population. Should this invasion prove of limited extent, prompt, energetic measures may quickly stamp it out. But usually it is found that rodent disease has already extended over wide areas. Control then becomes an immense sanitary problem, requiring for its solution money, laws and men—men to operate an effective campaign of eradication; laws to enforce their requirements, and money to pay the cost. A sanitary campaign established upon these fundamental requirements must provide and include the following:

1. *Sanitary Director.* The services of a sanitarian, trained in plague eradicative work, must be at once obtained; a conference held with state and municipal authorities, a plan of campaign agreed upon, and such director authorized to obtain medical personnel and proceed with the organization.

2. *Funds.* An appropriation must be made, immediately available, as credit against which may be charged salaries of employees and emergency purchases.

3. *Headquarters.* A suitable business establishment, preferably on the ground floor, must be selected, furnished, and a clerical force at once employed for the care of correspondence, reports and records which will rapidly accumulate.

4. *Laboratory.* A fully-equipped laboratory must be made immediately available, and placed under the direction of an accomplished bacteriologist, experienced in plague work.

5. *Laws.* An ordinance must be enacted and made immediately effective, defining specifically its purpose and directing in detail the methods of repair, construction and reconstruction of all buildings according to modern rat-proofing requirements. The garbage ordinance, if required, must be revised and strengthened.

6. *Courts.* The full coöperation of all city officials concerned in the administration of municipal or magistrate courts should be early obtained, and the need for full and immediate public compliance with all sanitary laws made clear.

7. *Press and Public.* Full and complete information relative to the occurrence of cases and the progress of the campaign should be officially reported to the press for daily publication. The public, through business organizations, civic and religious societies and like organizations, should receive the benefit of a general education campaign relating to the character of the disease, and the methods of control.

The above measures are all susceptible of rapid inauguration, and their effects may be made operative at the very incidence of the work. When completely effective, they will permit the rapid, systematic and intelligent handling of a campaign for plague eradication.

The measures requiring immediate application are those essential to the prevention of further human cases. They include, 1, notification of the occurrence of human cases; 2, inspection of the dead; 3, immediate destruction of recognized foci of rat plague.

The notification of the cases of plague, and the inspection of the dead, provide information as to residence and place of employment, and generally supply the earliest information as to location of plague foci. This permits the immediate and complete destruction of rats at that focus, and prevents further cases. For this purpose there should be employed two organizations, known as flying squads—a fumigation squad and a wrecking squad. Both should be provided truck transportation facilities and should be composed of trained, dependable men. The fumigation squad should be supplied with all materials necessary to prepare and fumigate a building with hydrocyanic acid gas. The wrecking squad should be furnished pulicides, spray-pumps and utensils, for the spraying of yards, lots and other open areas, for the destruction of fleas; and tools and implements for use in removing floors, rubbish and debris, in the destruction of rat harbors. These measures, employed at known or suspected foci of plague, are of great importance in preventing the spread of rat plague and the further occurrence of human plague.

In addition, and as rapidly as the facilities incident to organization will permit, these measures must be followed by trapping operations for the detection of unrecognized rat-plague, and by rat-proofing, for the elimination of rats and the prevention of the return of the disease.

Trapping. Following close upon the employment of the flying squads, there should be placed in the field an extensive trapping organization, composed of carefully selected, steady, reliable men. They should be supplied with 20-inch wire cage-traps, for the capture of live rodents, but chief reliance should be placed upon the "official" snap-trap, baited with bread or bacon. These men should receive, in addition to salary, a bounty on rats trapped, and to encourage and insure the accurate and careful tagging of rats as to location where caught, they should be paid a "bonus" of $5.00 for every correctly tagged plague rat captured.

This trapping force should be systematically spread out over and beyond the area suspected of rodent infection, and all rats trapped should be forwarded daily to the laboratory for examination. The value of systematic trapping must not be underestimated. It reduces the rat population and furnishes information as to its extent. It permits the collection

of fleas, and it is the only reliable means we possess for the early detection and delimitation of rodent plague-foci, and through this information it permits the application of intensive destructive measures at the point of infection, and this materially aids in the control of the disease.

Rat-proofing. To sustain life, rats require two things, food and harborage. It therefore follows that the protection of foodstuffs and the removal of harborage will eliminate rats.

This can be effected through the application of the following measures:

1. By the construction or reconstruction of all buildings in a rat-proof manner.

2. By removal of all materials covering yards, sidewalks and passageways which will permit rat refuge.

3. By the protection or removal of all garbage and waste food.

While simple as to direction, the complete and thorough application of these measures, when necessary in an extensive community, will require the unremitting and painstaking efforts of a corps of trained sanitary inspectors, many months of work, and vast expenditures of funds.

Happily, these measures are all economic—the costly reconstruction required improves and adds value to the structure, and when effectively applied will eliminate the rat from the home and environment of man, and prevent any possible return of bubonic plague.

AUTHORITIES CONSULTED

Reports on Plague Investigations in India, 1908, *Journal of Hygiene.*

Report of International Plague Conference, Mukden, 1912.

Early History of Quarantine, Eager, 1903.

The Present Pandemic of Plague, Eager, 1908.

Bionomics of Rodent and Human Fleas, Mitzmain, 1910.

Maritime Quarantine, Cofer, 1910.

Bubonic Plague, Creel, 1914.

Extension of Plague of the Bubonic Type, Creel, 1916.

Outbreak and Suppression of Plague in Porto Rico, Creel, 1913.

Hydrocyanic Acid Gas, Creel, Faget & Wrightson, 1915.

Cyanide Gas for the Destruction of Insects, Creel and Faget, 1916.

□

PUBLIC HEALTH NURSING

Some illustrations of the different fields of public health nursing are here presented through the courtesy of the National Organization* which illustrate to some extent how widely the efforts of such associations are distributed. The red man and the negro represent distant sections of the country and the nurse is active in both. She is giving attention to the baby in the tent of the Shoshone In-

medical inspector in his enormously important work among the young people over whom the municipality exercises close watch, and who thereby are safeguarded to an extent not generally appreciated.

dians or establishing bettered oral conditions among the negroes in Louisiana. These efforts assure for the future far more healthful conditions for both these races, sadly neglected till the new lights in health administration were established. The ubiquitous nurse she should be termed. Here she is in the home during the raging of the influenza taking suggestions from the doctor as he hurries away on his route of many calls and there she is at work in her school duties, aiding the school

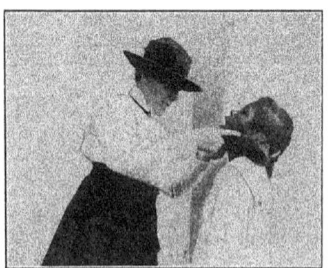

One of the striking means whereby this organization has sought to impress on the people the value of its work and of nursing in general, has been by means of a film, "An Equal Chance." The moral of the "movie pictures" of course does not need to be expressed in words, for its mission in emphasizing the need of more nurses is self-evident. Such carefully prepared evidence is its own proof, and the community should be brought to realize as quickly as possibly the potentialities of public health nursing.

*National Organization for Public Health Nursing, No. 156 Fifth Avenue, New York City.

DIAGNOSIS AND DETECTION OF RODENT PLAGUE

C. L. WILLIAMS,

Passed Assistant Surgeon, U. S. Public Health Service,
New Orleans, La.

Read before General Session, American Public Health Association, at San Francisco, Cal., September 15, 1920.

Stories of his own observations by one who has had experience are the most valuable kind of lessons. This authority places before his readers details of the diagnosis of plague and practical laboratory methods. He outlines the essential features of technique and determination clearly and accurately and has here really a preparatory course in plague detection that it is not easy to get from books.

THE paper here presented deals principally with the signs of plague as they occur in rats and guinea pigs and the laboratory procedure employed in their detection and confirmation.

IMPORTANCE OF THE LABORATORY

In an eradicative campaign, a laboratory probably is not an essential, but it aids so materially in the successful operation of such a campaign that it has come to be regarded as a necessity. While the laboratory has no direct hand in the actual destruction of rats, it has a very marked influence upon the destruction of plague-infected rats and is the only factor that sheds any trustworthy and sustained light upon the course of the epizoötic. While an expensive feature, the information supplied is probably worth many times the cost, particularly the demonstration of the presence or absence of infection and the location of foci.

Briefly the laboratory gives information on the following points, the relationship of which to eradicate measures must be fairly clear:

Demonstration of presence of plague.
Intensity of the infection.
Delineation of infected area.
Location of foci.
Efficacy of eradicative measures both general and at specific foci.

Amount and variations in flea infestation.

Absence of infection.

Upon the demonstration of the presence of plague depends the institution of eradicative measures. If the infection is severe, intensive eradicative measures must be applied as rapidly and completely as possible; if light, time may be safely taken for the organization of a smaller but more efficient and less expensive force, a contrast of conditions recently illustrated in Beaumont and Galveston, Texas. Delineation of the infected area enables the concentration of eradicative efforts within it, though trapping must to some extent be maintained in all parts of the community in order to detect at once any spread. Location of foci concentrates intensive measures such as fumigation at these points, the efficacy of which measures are determined in the laboratory by examination of rats captured at these foci subsequent to treatment. General efficiency of the campaign may be shown in the rapid decline in the percentage of infected animals. Amount and variations of flea infestation indicate what may be expected as to the severity of an epizoötic; increases in the flea count give advance warning of increase in the percentage of infected rats.

Probably the most important function

of the laboratory is to set a place in time for the last infected rat discovered. From this point is computed the end of the campaign as successfully completed. It is information that can be gained from no other source and is the only information of this nature even approaching accuracy. Human cases are poor guides for in New Orleans during the first epizoötic infected rats were diagnosed in the laboratory for more than one year after the last human case. Past experience in other eradicative campaigns is no better guide than human cases for in San Francisco the last infected rat was found eleven months after the inception of the campaign, while in San Juan, Porto Rico, this period was only three months, and in New Orleans very nearly three years.

ROUTINE LABORATORY PROCEDURE

All rats should be immersed in kerosene oil by the trapper, for the purpose of killing fleas, before being brought to the laboratory. Each rat should have a tag attached giving the address where secured, the date and a statement as to whether the rodent was trapped, found dead or killed by fumigation.

Where less than 300 rats a day are brought in there should be no difficulty in examining them at once upon arrival. Where the numbers are large, or they are brought in at a late hour, it becomes necessary to place them on ice over night.

The laboratory should be equipped with at least one long narrow table covered with sheet metal. At one end of this the rats are dumped out of the cans and an attendant sorts them and calls off the address and species to another attendant who records these in a book giving each rat a serial number. The rats are passed along the table to the tackers who tack each to a shingle, belly up, using magnetic hammers and putting the tacks through the paws. They are then passed on to dissectors who reflect the skin over the entire ventral surface,

exposing neck, axillæ and groins, and thoroughly open the abdomen without, however, disturbing the chest. Six to eight-inch mouse-tooth forceps and six to eight-inch scissors with short blades are the most convenient instruments for dissecting.

Finally the rats reach the examiners at the far end of the table, who carefully inspect each rat and open the chest to determine the presence of pleural effusion. For this inspection a bright light is essential. Where daylight is relied upon it is best obtained through a skylight. The writer prefers electric drop lights properly shaded and placed on the table directly above the rats as being more reliable and supplying a light of constant intensity.

The great majority of rats are so evidently negative that they can be discarded after careful scrutiny. Those without injection in which the liver and spleen appear normal are very rarely infected. About ten per cent, however, as a rule, will suggest plague and must be more minutely examined. About half of these will be seen to be negative on more careful inspection and can be thrown out. The remainder are placed on a separate table, smears made from each and examined. These rats are finally divided into "plague infected," "suspicious" and "negative." Tissues from suspicious ones are inoculated into guinea pigs for confirmation, the negative are thrown out, the positive and suspicious are finally recorded and burned. Negative rats are knocked off the shingles and disposed of by incineration or burial. The shingles are continued in use. Special form cards should be used for records of the infected and suspicious rats and inoculated guinea pigs.

Guinea pigs may be inoculated cutaneously, subcutaneously, or intraperitoneally. The first is the most used but is likely to be ineffective when only a few plague bacilli are present so that suspected resolving cases and cases where only a few *B. pestis* are believed to be present should be reserved for the subcutaneous method. Intraperitoneal injection should be confined to material from human cases which is seldom contaminated. In such cases it gives results in two days, but it cannot be relied upon when the inoculated material is highly contaminated, as is generally the case with rat tissues.

For a cutaneous inoculation the animal is shaved without soap or water over an area about ¾ inch square, shaving being maintained until the surface is moderately abraded. Over this area the material for inoculation is smeared and rubbed in with some blunt instrument. Very few organisms besides plague will produce systemic infection through such a surface so that this method seems to filter out contaminating bacteria.

Subcutaneous inoculation may be performed either with a syringe or by the "pocket" method. For inoculation with a syringe the suspected tissues must first be ground in a small mortar, and emulsified in salt solution. The pocket inoculation is accomplished by cutting a slit through the skin, separating the subcutaneous tissues with the handle of a scalpel and tucking a piece of tissue into the pocket so formed. Either method is satisfactory. Intraperitoneal inoculations must of course be done with a syringe.

Inoculated guinea pigs are placed in small-sized garbage cans with a layer of vaseline smeared inside near the top to prevent exit of fleas. They are kept thus ten days, when if alive and healthy they are marked negative and may be returned to stock and used again. If found sick or with buboes at the expiration of ten days, they are killed and examined. Plague-infected guinea pigs usually die in five or six days. When dead they are tacked to shingles and examined in the same manner as are rats.

Smears are made from the liver and spleen in all suspicious cases and from buboes, abscesses or other special lesions when present. They are best tained with carbol thionin, a good formula being:

Stock A.

Carbol thionin (Gruebler) 2 grams
95% Alcohol .... 100 cc.

Stock B.

Liquid carbolic acid .... 2 cc.
Distilled water .... 100 cc.

For use mix 25 cc. of stock A with 100 cc. of B.

This stains in ten seconds or less, and does not appreciably overstain. It is regretted that all American thionin so far used by the writer has been very unsatisfactory. Ten grammes of the American stain must be used in stock A solution. Lacking good thionin, methylene blue is probably the next best stain in general use.

PROTECTION OF WORKERS

For protection reasonable care in handling is safer than any mechanical means. Laboratory infections are rare, but have occurred in a few instances. Rubber gloves may be worn though they are soon ruined by the oil on the rats. Jars of disinfectant should be always at hand as well as strong carbolic acid and iodine for treatment of cuts and scratches. Vaccination probably gives some protection for a few months, although reports on its use are conflicting. In New Orleans it is very little used.

LABORATORY ERROR

When large numbers of rats must be dissected daily, it is impossible to use separate instruments on each rat. Of necessity occasionally infection will be carried over into negative rats, which rats in some instances may show lesions rousing sufficient suspicion to cause inoculation of guinea pigs. The error may be minimized by training the dissectors to recognize the signs of plague, and requiring them to change to sterile instruments after dissecting a suspicious animal. In practice, the error is a small one as is shown by the close checking of inoculation results in guinea pigs with the signs of plague in rats.

DIAGNOSIS

The diagnosis of infected rats are in the last analysis based upon a demonstration of the presence of *Bacillus pestis*, although in actual practice many cases are declared positive after a review of the gross lesions only. There is always a slight margin of error in basing conclusions on gross lesions so that the first case in a community must be completely confirmed by the isolation of the causative organism and the study of its characteristics, including practically the carrying out of Koch's postulates. Having confirmed the presence of *B. pestis* in the first rodent case many of the subsequent ones may be safely diagnosed from gross lesions, the percentage of error being too small to be of practical importance, particularly in these instances when borne out as is nearly always the case, by the appearance in smears of organisms with the characteristic morphology of the plague bacillus. When infected rats become few in numbers, and the prospect of seeing the last one appears, it becomes important that full confirmation be secured in each case so that the continued presence of the infection may be indisputably proven.

It must not be supposed from the above that all rats during the height of an epizoötic are diagnosed only on gross lesions. Far from it. About fifty per cent of plague rats will show indefinite lesions, which must be confirmed, while a very large number of rats not infected show signs that raise suspicion of plague which can only be set at rest by the negative results of animal tests.

GROSS LESIONS OF ACUTE PLAGUE IN RATS

The cardinal or major signs of acute plague are five in number: injection, bubo, granular liver, large dark spleen and pleural effusion. It is rare that all occur in any one rat, and equally rare that any of them appears alone. Usually, two, three, or four are found in combination. These signs are characteristic of plague, and occur in other conditions with such exceeding rarity that most workers in this field are inclined to agree with the Indian Plague Commission that a well-marked case may be safely diagnosed even when culture and animal test are negative. The writer is inclined to include the appearance of organisms of the typical plague morphology in smears as the sixth cardinal sign of plague, although towards the end of a campaign it assumes considerably more importance than this, as will be discussed.

Injection: This is the most constant of all the plague signs, occurring as moderate, marked, or intense in about 75% of all acute plague-infected rats. It is the most readily noted and when marked and of the proper color is an almost certain index of plague. Characteristically, the injection is evidently acute and of the entire body, skin, muscles, and viscera, though it is best seen against the back ground of the skin, where it assumes a distinctly purplish hue. It is usually associated with an increased amount of fluid in all the tissues so that the reflected skin surface is wet and glistening, the muscles develop a peculiar pink, waxy translucency, and on the inner chest wall beneath the sternun usually appears an area of gelatinous edema. The injection appears in all sizes of vessels but is particularly marked in the long vessels lying in the subcutaneous tissue from the axilla almost to the groin on either side. As a rule it is fairly evenly distributed, in a few cases only being confined to particular regions, as the shoulders, groin or to one side only. It is usual for it to be more pronounced about a bubo.

Bright red infections, old-appearing congestions often associated with thickening of the tissues, and injections confined to the smaller vessels are seldom due to plague. The experienced eye differentiates these at once, though one untrained is apt to regard many of them as suspicious.

Buboes: These unique plague lesions occur among rats in no other known naturally-contracted disease. Among guinea pigs *B. pseudo tuberculosis rodentum,* and among guinea pigs and ground squirrels *B. tularense* cause buboes, but these organisms have never been found in naturally-infected rats. Occasionally, necrotic lymph glands, usually with tough capsules and more or less liquid contents, occur which are not due to plague, but the writer after examining over half a million rats cannot recall ever having seen a typical bubo in one that was not plague-infected.

The characteristic bubo consists of one or two, rarely more, enlarged caseous or partly caseous lymph glands buried in inflammatory connective tissue, or else surrounded by acutely congested gelatinous edema. The mass is usually firm, may be hemorrhagic, and is nearly always the center of an area of marked injection. It is seldom larger than 1 cm. by .5 cm.. The caseous material is not liquid but soft, rather dry, and easily broken up. Early or beginning buboes may not be distinctly caseous and may lack the surrounding tissue coat but are generally in the center of marked injection, are of a cream white opaque appearance, and, on section, exude a semi-purulent fluid as a rule rich in plague bacilli. They cannot be classed as "typical," though frequently unmistakable to the trained eye.

Enlarged congested glands frequently occur in plague rats, but also frequently occur in negative ones. They are not classed as buboes. Large lymph glands are frequently seen in rats, particularly the older ones; they seldom show any injection, are tough, and dull gray in color. Usually in such cases the glands are large in all the regions where lymph

nodes are found. Occasionally in rat leprosy one finds large, very soft, seminecrotic, hemorrhagic glands. They are apt to be associated with ulcers, lack the firmness of the plague bubo and appear in a mass of soft, evenly hemorrhagic tissue, probably best described as messy. The hemorrhage about a plague bubo is splotchy.

Buboes should be looked for at the sites of the various lymph nodes. These are principally the ventral aspect of the neck, the axillæ, the groins, and the lumbar region. In the neck they are arranged as a deep crescent arching over the two large submaxillary glands; in the axillæ they are covered by the pectoral muscles, which must be cut to expose them; in the groins they appear as a string of glands and are generally reflected with the skin; in the lumbar region they are found as two long narrow row glands with a few smaller ones lying along either side of the aorta, just opposite its bifurcation.

The distribution of buboes in these various locations has varied very considerably in different parts of the world. Mesenteric buboes, however, have occurred with extreme scarcity in naturally-infected rats, according to all published reports. In India, 75% of all rats with single buboes had them in the neck, while in San Francisco 75% of such rats had buboes in the groins. The New Orleans figures for the present epizoötic stand half way between these, cervical buboes occurring in 28%, axillary in 23%, inguinal in 43%, and pelvic in 6%. These contrasts are brought out in Table I.

TABLE I

Showing rats with single buboes and contrasting the locations of these in India, San Francisco and New Orleans

	Neck Percent	Axilla Percent	Groin Percent	Pelvis Percent
Indian Plague Commission, 2,923 rats	75	15	6	4
*San Francisco, 40 rats	2	20	73	5
New Orleans, 111 rats	28	23	43	6

*Combined figures of Wherry, Walker and Howell and the Federal Laboratory.

In India, of rats with multiple buboes, 54.5% had one in the neck. In San Francisco neck buboes were rarely seen in such cases; in New Orleans of 34 rats with multiple buboes every one had an inguinal; 20 had an axillary and 7 a cervical bubo.

Again the proportion of infected rats showing buboes has varied. In India 85% had them, in San Francisco 40%, in New Orleans 33%.

These variations are difficult to explain. Possibly they are connected with variations of. climate, but more likely with a difference in fleas. In India the prevailing flea is the *Lœmopsylla cheopis*, in San Francisco the *Ceratpohalus fasciatus;* in New Orleans the *Cheopis* markedly predominates, but was rarely found in such numbers as occur in India. Further, in New Orleans a relatively considerable percentage of *Ctenopsylla musculi* are found on rats.

It might be thought that the difference in species of rats might account for it, but this is not the case, judging from the rather limited New Orleans figures. Here the percentage of *rattus* and *Alexandrinus* with buboes was less than the total for all acutely-infected rats, being only 25% of 220 rats, while of the Norway species 42% had buboes. Among 50 *rattus* and *Alexandrinus* with single buboes the distribution was neck 38%, axilla 22%, groin 38%, pelvis 2%, these figures being only slightly higher for the neck than those in all rats with single buboes. (Table I.)

Granular liver: This important but elusive sign is apt to present more difficulty in its detection than any other, so that were it not for the fact that usually other conditions of the liver first draw attention, and that it is in the great majority of cases associated with other plague signs, many times it would be missed. The difficulty is in seeing the granules, for while they are often quite plain, they are oftener obscure and. being small in size can frequently only definitely be made out in the brightest light. Fortunately, in a plague rat the liver whether granular or not is almost uniformly enlarged and presents a plump and rounded appearance which arrests attention at once, if attention has not already been centered by observation of injection, bubo, or other signs. In well-marked cases, the liver is frequently injected, pink in color, and shows, though in less degree, the waxy translucency seen in the muscles. It is firm and springy instead of flabby and tends to hold its shape. Granules occur more or less marked in about 60% to 70% of all acute cases.

The granules are of two varieties. Most often they are diffuse, yellowish, irregular in shape and size, approximately pinhead size granules varying in clearness from the obvious to so faint as to be almost indistinguishable. They give the organ frequently a finely-mottled rather than a granular appearance. The word diffuse is used in describing them in contradistinction to discrete, since close inspection shows that they are not sharply outlined but fade off into the surrounding tissue, not infrequently merging into one another. They may vary in numbers from a few to so many as to render the liver almost completely necrotic. Less often is seen a "peppered" sprinkling of very fine "pin point" white or gray granules requiring a bright light to distinguish them with certainty. When seen at all they are usually profusely scattered over the surface though in some cases they are recorded as few in number.

Typical granules are only occasionally · simulated by other conditions. Sharply-marked granules and spotty markings of the liver generally few in number are not unusual in conditions other than plague, but one familiar with the granular liver of plague would find no difficulty in differentiating. It is well to bear in mind that plague granules almost never occur without acute enlargement of the liver and are usually associated with other signs of plague.

Large dark spleen: As has been reported by several writers the size of the spleen in rats varies within wide limits so that it is difficult to say when one is enlarged. Probably, therefore, a better description would be to say "plump" dark spleen. The condition presented is a spleen which has rapidly swollen so that the capsule is too small, consequently the organ appears bulging with the edges rounded. Usually it is dark in color, differing distinctly from the red of normal spleens, is firm, friable, and may occasionally show granules, necrotic areas, hemorrhagic spots or other lesions. It appears in from 60 to 70% of acutely-infected rats according to different reports.

In rats killed in the early stages of plague the spleen is more apt to be moderately enlarged and bright pink or red in color, due to injection, the extravasation of blood in its tissue which produces the dark color not yet having occurred.

Pleural effusion: A clear, copious, serous, pleural effusion in a rat showing any other well-marked sign of plague practically clinches the diagnosis. When it occurs it is usually copious or moderate in amount. In the recent New Orleans series, it was found to be slight in only 47 of a total of 222 cases in which this sign was present. It is nearly always associated with other well-marked signs of plague; for example, in the above mentioned 222 cases 200 were associated with distinct injection and 154 with granular liver while only 13 were in rats recorded with only slight signs of plague.

Association of lesions: As mentioned previously, two or more of the lesions of plague usually occur in association. This is well shown in Table II where the occurrence of various lesions with injection is shown. This table also brings out the distinct increase in the intensity and multiplication of lesions as the injection is found more intense.

TABLE II

Association of injection of various degrees with other lesions, among 441 acutely-infected rats, New Orleans, 1919-1920

	No. of rats in group	Well-marked Plague	Buboes	Gran. Liver	Pleural Effusion	Large dark spleen	Pos. Smears
					Percent showing		
No injection	49	30	8	40	10	27	53
Slight injection...	60	58	5	55	30	58	47
Moderate injection	67	67	24	58	43	55	64
Marked injection.	225	84	38	59	61	71	79
Intense injection..	40	100	75	72	70	60	100

The writer can recall only one case where a bubo was the only sign of plague and not more than three or four where a typical granular liver was alone.

Relative occurrence of lesions: Table III shows the relative occurrence of different lesions as reported from Bombay, San Francisco and New Orleans.

TABLE III

Relative occurrence of acute lesions in Bombay, San Francisco and New Orleans

	Injection	Bubo	Granular Liver	Large, dark spleen	Pleural Effusion
			Percent Showing		
Indian Plague Commission, Bombay, 4,000 rats.....	69	85	58	..	72
San Francisco, Wherry, Walker & Howell, 88 rats.	59	14	14	68	71
Federal Laboratory, 62 rate.	85	57	87	74	59
New Orleans, 441 rats.....	*75	33	58	61	50

*Slight injections omitted.

In this table the New Orleans figures would be higher throughout were the rats showing very slight or no signs of plague, some 50 or 60 in number, left out of consideration. These rats would have been missed had not guinea pigs been very extensively employed to weed out from the large number of similarly-marked but not infected rats.

Unusual signs in acute plague: The signs listed in Table IV are of infrequent occurrence. Many of these when not accompanied by evidence of an acute process are regarded as indicative of resolving plague. All in this table have been recently seen in well-marked acute cases in New Orleans.

TABLE IV

Unusual lesions in acute plague, New Orleans, 1919-1920

Spleen:

Profusely granular	5
Hemorrhagic granules	1
Large granules, 2 millimeter diam	1
Hemorrhagic spots	3
Caseous spots with homorrhagic areole	1
Areas and zones of caseation	10
Almost entire spleen caseous	1
Recent adhesions	3
Ruptured	1
Recent scars	2
Very large spleen 2½ in. x ¾ in.	1

Liver:

Areas of caseation	4
Single lobe entirely caseous	1
Abscess in axilla (apparently bubo)	1
Caseous spots in lungs	1

PLAGUE WITH SLIGHT SIGNS AND NO SIGNS

The discovery of plague-infected rats with slight or no signs of the disease depends principally on how accurate it is desired that the laboratory diagnosis should be. It is in most cases a weeding-out process through inoculation of guinea pigs from all slightly suspicious rats. Rats with no signs are usually regarded as suspicious on account of being captured at known highly-infected locations. In a few cases in New Orleans it was believed justifiable to record a positive diagnosis upon the appearance of typical *B. pestis* in smears from rats presenting no gross lesions, but killed by fumigation in company with numerous well-marked plague rats.

On account of the importance of the last few infected rats, the writer believes that toward the end of an eradicative campaign smears should be made and examined, so far as practicable, from all rats brought to the laboratory. We have records of 17 plague-infected rats in the first New Orleans epizoötic that were discovered by this means, none of which presented any of the gross lesions of plague and had all been passed as negative on naked eye examination by men highly trained in plague diagnosis.

Advanced putrefaction frequently obscures signs of plague. Such rats however are usually found dead and are given careful inspection, especially smear examination, in consequence of being regarded with more suspicion than are trapped rats. They should not be considered as true "cases without signs" and are listed separately in Tables V and VI.

The writer believes that use of the large number of guinea pigs necessary to weed out many of these poorly marked rats is, during the period of relatively high infection, too great a price for their discovery, but that the search should be made more and more intensive as the proportion of infected rats decreases.

TABLE V

Infected rats with slight gross lesions of plague, showing various signs on which suspicion was principally based, New Orleans, 1919-1920

	No. of Susp.	
Most prominent sign—	rats	Smears
Injection	5	5
Injection only sign	1	0
Large congested liver	22	18
Waxy liver only sign	1	0
Pleural effusion	1	0
Putrid, some evidence of injection, etc.	6	6
Total	36	29

TABLE VI

Infected rats with no gross lesions of plague, New Orleans, 1919-1920

	No. of
Basis of suspicion or diagnosis—	rats
Putrid, inoculated account suspicious smears	5
Putrid, from highly infected buildings, diagnosis based on smears	6
Good condition, from suspected locations, inoculated account suspicious smears	5
Good condition, from highly infected buildings, diagnosis based on smears	9
Total	23

RESOLVING PLAGUE

The role of resolving plague is as yet a matter of conjecture. Some writers express the possibility of it being a factor in the prolongation or recrudescence of an epizoötic, though this is based at present mostly on negative evidence. It is interesting to note that no cases were found in San Francisco and only one in Porto Rico in both of which places the epizoötic was relatively short, while on the other hand they have been rather numerous in New Orleans where the epizoötic has exhibited extreme tenacity, both in general and at specific foci. On the other hand it has been observed in New Orleans that resolving cases in which living plague bacilli could be demonstrated, were definitely grouped near acute plague foci, while cases with similar lesions but negative on guinea tests did not show any such marked grouping, suggesting that the bacilli are not long-lived in these rats, the positive ones still being near the point of infection while the negative, with a longer time interval, had largely migrated to other quarters.

The signs of resolving plague as described by the Indian Plague Commission are principally various lesions of the spleen, caseous nodules, irregular caseous areas, zones of caseation through the entire substance of the organ, granules, abscesses, scars and adhesions; and abscesses at the site of old buboes. To these the writer would add from his own observations: transverse linear rupture of the spleen and the resultant transverse linear scar; discrete granules of the liver, few in number, without any acute sign, and moderate or slight pleural effusion without any other evidence of acute plague, as, in all probability evidence of resolution. The Indian Plague Commission makes the statement, with which the writer agrees, that similar lesions are caused by other diseases than plague, but it showed that among rats from plague-free locations these signs occurred in markedly fewer numbers than in infected communities.

The great majority of resolving cases cannot be confirmed by guinea pig or cultural test since in most instances the causative bacilli are gone. Hence the correctness of the diagnosis cannot usually be proven. In New Orleans 8.7% of all suspected resolving cases were shown to harbor virulent plague bacilli. Guinea pigs were always inoculated subcutaneously so that it is believed that very few positive cases were missed through failure to infect the test animal as frequently happens where the cutaneous inoculation method is used to confirm resolving cases. Table VII lists the New Orleans series both negative and positive (guinea pig test), with principal lesions observed.

TABLE VII

Rats suspected of resolving plague. Results of guinea pig inoculations and tabulation of principal lesions, New Orleans, November 1, 1919, to February 29, 1920

Description of lesions	No. of rats in each group	No. of con- firmed cases	Percent confirmed
Total number of suspicious cases	1,019	89	8.7
Spleen lesions	770	72	11.2
Caseous areas and zones.	123	17	13.8
Granules	41	6	14.6
Broad or heavy scars, bisecting bands of fibrous tissue, etc.	109	10	9.2
Fresh transverse linear rupture	10	4	40
*Transverse linear scars..	400	29	7.3
Adhesions	161	17	10.5
Abscesses	13	2	15.4
Liver lesions	218	13	5.9
Discrete granules	173	12	6.9
Caseous areas	31	1	3.2
Scars, adhesions or abscesses	22	0	0.0
Pleural effusion	101	9	8.9
Peripheral abscesses at sites of lymph nodes	23	3	13
Multiple lesions (included above)	152	17	11.2

*Linear scars are also due to other conditions more often than most lesions listed. However, 7.3% positive is a high figure for a lesion that frequently must be months old.

PROPORTION OF RATS FOUND INFECTED

In this country where eradication immediately begins upon the discovery of plague in a community, most of the rats brought into the laboratory have been trapped. Among these the proportion of infected ones has seldom risen over 2 or 3 per cent and is usually lower. As eradication proceeds the proportion of infected rats declines, rapidly at first, then more gradually and may go as low as .01% or less before becoming zero. The highest proportion recorded in this country was recently seen in Beaumont, Texas, where 75 or 15% of the first 500 rats were found infected. Most of these however were picked up dead in various parts of the city. When trapping operations were well under way the percentage of infected rats fell to a low figure.

EXAMINATION OF SMEARS

As indicated above the writer is inclined to regard positive or suspicious smears as the sixth cardinal sign of plague, and to give it equal weight, but no more, with the other signs in arriving at a conclusion. In making this statement, however, it is necessary to caution the reader that bacilli more or less resembling plague are frequently seen in smears from negative rats so that the avoidance of confusion requires long experience. Indeed occasionally one sees, though nearly always in small numbers, organisms in smears from rats which are not *B. pestis* but morphologically indistinguishable from it. Despite this when in a smear from rat tissues appear considerable numbers of organisms of typical morphology the picture presented is at least as characteristic as is any of the gross lesions. *B. pestis* grown on artificial media (except salt agar) show variable appearance and their morphology is not to be relied upon. One not thoroughly familiar with plague should be very guarded in diagnosis of smears and should not declare one positive unless it shows all of the following characteristics: lightly-staining, rounded-end bacilli in considerable numbers scattered about the field without any particular arrangement; a portion of these showing distinctly heavier staining at the poles shading to almost or quite clear in the central part; variations in size of individuals from short cocco-bacillary or ring-like coccoid forms through all intervening sizes to individuals 2 or 2½ times as long as broad.

Smears from acutely-infected rats usually show *B. pestis*, while in those from resolving cases it is rarely found. It is rare indeed for smears from a typical bubo to be negative, though occasionally it is necessary to make several smears from different parts before finding the bacilli. Table VIII lists acute cases in New Orleans with results of smear examination.

TABLE VIII

Acute cases of plague in rats with numbers showing positive, suspicious and negative smears, New Orleans, 1919-1920

Number of Acute Cases	Number Positive Smears	Number Suspicious Smears	Number Negative Smears
441	315	87	39

PLAGUE IN MICE

Mice are known to be more resistant to plague than are rats so that it is only natural to find that infected mice are much more seldom encountered. As a matter of fact they are very seldom found except in heavily infected buildings, and then as a rule only after the epizoötic has practically passed through the rat population. Since November, 1919, a total of 30 plague-infected mice have been discovered in New Orleans among well over 100,000 examined.

While the signs of plague in mice are essentially the same as in rats their detection is a much more difficult matter on account of the small size of the animals on the poor condition in which they are usually received. The trap usually employed in rat catching in this country is the so-called "snap" trap in which a stiff wire actuated by a heavy spring snaps over and crushes the rat to the base of the trap. One can readily appreciate what happens to a mouse struck a blow sufficient to kill a full grown rat. About the best you can do with that mouse in the laboratory is to guess at whether it has plague. Sometimes infected mice are recovered after fumigation, however, and in these, injection, bubo, granular liver, large dark spleen, and very occasionally pleural effusion can be demonstrated. We have seen two proven infected mice believed to be resolving cases. Several of this series represent a number from one address inoculated in combination. In such instances they are recorded as one mouse. Table IX lists the lesions as seen in this group:

TABLE IX

Plague-infected mice. Occurrence of various lesions, New Orleans, 1919-1920

Description of Lesions	No. of Mice
Total infected mice	30
No. discernible lesions	9
Composite inoculation	4
Inoculated because caught at infected location	5
Injection	14
Slight	1
Moderate	6
Marked	6
Intense	1
Buboes, 2 ing., 1 ing. and ax.	3
Large injected liver	11
Granular liver	6
Pleural effusion	1
Large dark spleen	10
Resolving plague	2
Spleen scar	1
Caseous area in spleen	1

PLAGUE IN GUINEA PIGS

Since these animals are relied upon for confirmation of plague infection in so large a proportion of cases, it is essential that the signs of plague in guinea pigs be well understood. As in rats, plague is here an acute disease, inoculated animals rarely living longer than ten days, and usually dying in five or six days. In general the evidences of infection are similar to those in rats with some important variations. A clearer impression can therefore probably be conveyed by contrasting the various lesions with analagous ones in rats.

Site of inoculation: This does not appear in naturally-infected rats but is a constant sign in all artificially inoculated animals. It varies from a small patch of hemorrhagic infiltration to a wide area of thickened hemorrhagic edematous tissue surrounded by gelatinous edema. Ulcers may form beneath a cutaneous inoculation, but necrosis or pus at the site of a subcutaneous inoculation is generally the result of the presence of other organisms in the injected material. Very widespread, intensely hemorrhagic reactions are usually due to a small bacillus belonging to the hemorrhagic septicemia group.

Injection: As a rule less marked in the guinea pig and confined more to the larger vessels. Slight injections are common and intense ones rare. Rather widespread subcutaneous gelatinous edema is common.

Bubo: Very large in size compared to that in the rat. After cutaneous or subcutaneous inoculations it is a very constant sign usually appearing in the groin, where it commonly involves a whole string of glands which become the caseous central portion in a common thick mass of highly-congested connective tissue frequently markedly hemorrhagic. Section of this mass reveals the caseous material that is all that is left of the glands. Early buboes may show the separate, large, partly-caseous

glands surrounded by injected gelatinous edema.

Liver: As in the rat nearly always distinctly enlarged and injected. Granules are of frequent occurrence but larger than in the rat and few in number.

Spleen: The most characteristic sign in guinea pigs occurs in the spleen. This organ normally about 2 cm. by 1.5 cm. and a few millimeters thick becomes enormously enlarged frequently more than doubling all of its dimensions. It is dark, friable, and profusely studded with white granules characteristically varying in size from a pinhead to two or three millimeters in diameter. Not infrequently where the spleen has rested against the abdominal wall there appear in the latter small areas of congestion and hemorrhage.

Lungs: Pleural effusion is quite rare in plague-infected guinea pigs. Substituted for it we frequently find in the lungs small round dull red spots with white or gray caseous centers. In some cases these caseous foci are quite large.

Smears: In typical cases of plague in guinea pigs plague bacilli can practically always be demonstrated in smears. If the animal has died within one or two days from rough handling, pneumonia or other cause other than plague, signs may be poorly developed and smears negative.

As in rats, the signs in guinea pigs may differ considerably in degree, so that close observation and not unusually the inoculation of additional animals may become necessary to make a diagnosis, particularly if death has occurred within the first three days after inoculation.

Guinea pigs that have been inoculated intraperitoneally with a relatively pure culture of plague, such as aspirated material from a human bubo, generally die in two days, presenting a different but no less characteristic picture. Buboes are absent. Gelatinous edema and small hemorrhages often appear where the needle has been withdrawn through the muscles and subcutaneous tissues. The viscera are intensely injected, the liver and spleen enlarged and may show small beginning granules. Most characteristically there appears within the abdomen a thick, ropy, milky, mucoid fluid containing enormous numbers of *B. pestis*. When the injected material is contaminated a confusing picture usually appears.

Plague-like diseases: As stated above, two organisms produce plague-like diseases in guinea pigs. The signs presented so closely resemble plague as frequently to be indistinguishable from it. Neither of these organisms occurs naturally in rats so that one would hardly ever meet them in guinea pigs inoculated from rats. They should be borne in mind, however, as possible causes of deaths among stock animals. One of these, which occurs naturally in ground squirrels (*B. tularense*) does not resemble *B. pestis* morphologically and has been artificially cultivated directly from tissues only on a special egg media. *B. pseudotuberculosis* rodentium is morphologically and culturally identical with *B. pestis*. It differs from it only in that it is avirulent to rats and requires as a rule a longer time to kill guinea pigs. Several workers have shown that rats may be immunized against *B. pestis* by subcutaneous inoculation with *B. pseudotuberculosis*, and S. Rowland has succeeded in growing from virulent *B. pestis* a culture in every way identical with this first-named organism.

BACTERIOLOGY OF PLAGUE

The sum of the experience of many workers on plague leads to the conclusion that the *B. pestis* is an easily identified organism, in the bacteriologic differentiation of which only four media are necessary. Discussion will therefore be confined to these. They are, plain agar with slightly alkaline reaction, broth, litmus milk and agar plus 2.5% to 3% sodium chloride.

Differentiation starts with isolation of a pure culture. This is usually readily done on agar plates. In cold weather, portions of liver, spleen and heart's blood from the suspected rat may be streaked over a plate with good chances of securing a growth from which a pure culture can be easily picked. In hot weather tissues of the rats, usually when received, are contaminated with too many rapidly multiplying putrefactive organisms for plague to be isolated. In such cases a pure culture is obtained from the inoculated guinea pig by killing it on the fourth or fifth day, or sooner if well-marked bubo appears, and making cultures at once from the liver, spleen and bubo.

Bacillus pestis grows slowly on the media mentioned, appearing on agar as small translucent whitish colonies which are usually, though not always, sticky when touched with a platinum needle. In broth frequently a thin pellicle appears on the surface, which is easily broken up and settles in small flocks and granules some of which adhere to the side of the tube. The "stalactite" formation spoken of in some reports requires entire freedom from vibration for its production and is rarely seen.

On agar it grows as a short rod, in broth frequently in short chains, while on salt agar literally astounding involution forms occur; tremendous rods, enormous cocci, balloon shapes, club and dumbbell forms. The appearance of these involution forms on salt agar is almost pathognomonic, no other organism (except *B. pseudotuberculosis rodentium*) that is at all likely to be confused with plague giving rise to any such growth.

In litmus milk it produces no change or slight acidity, shown as a rule more by a lighter blue color than by any distinct red.

Having secured an organism with the above cultural charactertistics it becomes necessary, for complete confirmation, to carry out Koch's postulates by infecting one or more rats (white or wild) with the culture, observing the signs of plague and isolating the original organisms from its tissues. Control, serum-protected rats are hardly necessary since no other known disease with gross lesions of plague is produced in *rats* by any organism with the cultural characteristics given above.

One often hears of organisms closely resembling the plague bacillus. It is a bugbear, however, that in practice is rarely encountered. The two organisms, *B. pseudotuberculosis rodentium* and *Bacterium tularense*, which cause plague-like diseases in guinea pigs are both either nonpathogenic to rats, or if they do in a few instances infect, they fail to produce plague-like signs. In the case of the former there is good reason to believe that it may be a strain of plague that has lost its virulence for rats and become of diminished virulence for guinea pigs.

It is not always easy to isolate *B. pestis* from a given case. Some strains when taken from animal tissue grow very poorly at first on agar or fail entirely to grow. In such instances the use of serum agar or blood agar will overcome the difficulty. Once growing on this they will generally readily transfer to plain agar. In some cases it is difficult to develop involution forms on salt agar. Repeated subculture will usually bring them forth or variation in the amount of salt may have this result.

PLAGUE IN GROUND SQUIRRELS

To be complete for the United States a description of plague as it appears in ground squirrels should be included, but this would greatly prolong this paper. Those interested are referred to the excellent description by McCoy.

PLAGUE IN OTHER RODENTS

While practically all rodents are susceptible to plague, few naturally infected ones, besides those already mentioned, have been discovered in this country. In San Francisco McCoy found one naturally infected field rat *(Neotoma)* and in New Orleans there was trapped recently a field rat *(Hesperomys pulustris)* which proved infected.

COLLATERAL LABORATORY OBSERVATIONS

It is usually desired to determine the species and sex of rats brought to the laboratory. Briefly the *rattus* can be easily separated from the *Norvegicus* by the relatively slenderer lines, longer legs, more membranous ears, dark black hair, and the tail longer than the head and body together. *Alexandrianus* differs from *rattus* only in having black, gray or brownish hair with a white belly. Crosses between *rattus* and *Alexandrinus* are occasionally seen. Determination of sex should be done after dissection by locating the testicles or uterus for in the young males frequently the testicles are undescended making it difficult to distinguish them externally from the females.

CONCLUSION

In concluding the writer regrets to inform his readers that despite all this necessarily long description that some have just waded through and that others will miss by reading the conclusion first, they will not have an altogether accurate picture of a plague rat in their minds until they have seen one. To this end it is suggested that those who may have to conduct the examination of rats secure preserved specimens, which while not quite the same as fresh tissue, give a better conception of the various lesions than any written description can possibly present. Such specimens can be secured in limited numbers from the Hygienic Laboratory of the U. S. Public Health Service, Washington, D. C.

REFERENCE

Plague has been rather completely dealt with by the Indian Plague Commission, whose reports appeared in the Journal of Hygiene, Cambridge, England, and by various officers of the United States Public Health Service, principally Creel, McCoy and Simpson, most of whose reports are in the Public Health Bulletins and Public Health Reports. Persons interested are referred to these publications where also will be found extensive bibliographies. McCoy's description of plague in ground squirrels and of a plague like disease will be found in the following:

Public Health Bulletin No. 43. I. Studies Upon Plague in Ground Squirrels. II. A Plague Like Disease of Rodents. By George W. McCoy, U. S. P. H. Service, Washington, D. C.

☐

NOVA SCOTIA NOTABLES

This group of citizens, assembled in the rain before the City Hall in Halifax, is there on account of interest in the Nova Scotia Red Cross Public Health Caravan, and in public health generally, and preventive methods. The figure in the center with the tall hat is His Honor, the Lieutenant-Governor, with Mrs. Grant on his right and on his left a Government House guest, Miss TenBroeck of London, England. The tall man over the Governor's right shoulder is the Provincial Health Officer, Dr. W. H. Hattie. The clergyman in the rear is Dean Llwyd of the Anglican Church. In white shoes in the front row is Miss Helen Creighton of Dartmouth, driving one of the ambulances. To the left of the boy scouts is Dr. D. A. Craig, tuberculosis examiner for the Massachusetts-Halifax Health Commission, while behind the man who is showing in full his Red Cross arm band is His Worship, John S. Parker, Mayor of Halifax. Starting at the flagpole are Mr. H. E. Mahon, Treasurer of the Red Cross; Col. Woodbury, in charge of the organization; Dr. Edgar Douglas, in charge of Caravan No. 1, and Dr. J. A. Doull, in charge of No. 2.

BOTULISM

Ernest C. Dickson, B.A., M.D.

*Associate Professor of Medicine, Stanford University Medical School,
San Francisco, Cal.*

Read before joint session of Laboratory, Public Health Administration and Food and Drugs Sections,
American Public Health Association, at San Francisco, Cal., September 14, 1920.

Much that has been written about botulism is not true and
truths have been so distorted as to convey false impressions.
This paper presents truths plainly and without bias. Two things
are important—canned foods that show any signs of spoilage
must be destroyed, so that neither animals nor man can eat
them, and boiling "ready to serve" canned foods will always
make them safe.

THE term Botulism has become particularly well known in the United States during the past few months because of the sensational manner in which a portion of the daily press gave prominence to a few outbreaks of food poisoning of this type. As a result of this publicity the impression has been widely disseminated that we are face to face with a new and terrible disease and that California food products, particularly ripe olives, are especially liable to be contaminated with its poison. Much that has been written in the press about botulism is not true, and many of the facts have been so distorted that a false impression has been established. It is the object of this paper to attempt to present the problem in its true light and to urge that it be approached in an unbiased manner. It is only by facing the facts that we can hope to establish methods by which all danger of food poisoning of this type can be removed.

Botulism is not a new disease. The first recorded outbreak was described in 1735 and by 1802 the number had become so great in Würtemberg that an official bulletin was issued in which the people were warned against the use of spoiled sausages and were instructed as to the best methods for preparing and curing sausages. Since that time there have been many outbreaks of botulism in Europe, particularly in southern Germany, and in Würtemberg the incidence was so great that about 1820 a law was passed which required that all outbreaks should be reported to the authorities.

The word botulismus or botulism was derived from the Latin, botulus, meaning sausage, and in the earlier medical literature was used synonymously with Wurstvergiftung, or sausage poisoning. As time elapsed, however, it became evident that the peculiar symptom-complex which had been observed in these cases of sausage poisoning was also produced in poisoning from preserved meat and fish and the term was gradually extended to include certain types of meat poisoning and fish poisoning as well as sausage poisoning. Within recent years an outbreak of food poisoning which was undoubtedly of the same type occurred at Darmstadt in Germany, in which the cause of the poisoning was canned white beans which were served as salad, but, although a strain of *Bacillus botulinus* was isolated from the beans, the full significance of this outbreak was to a large extent overlooked.

The cause of botulism was discovered by Van Ermengem in 1894, when he investigated an outbreak of food poisoning at Ellezelles in Belgium, in which 23 persons were ill and 3 died after eating ham which had been preserved in brine. Van Ermengem found that the poisoning was caused by a toxin which is produced by the growth of a spore-bearing, anaërobic bacillus which he called *Bacillus botulinus*. The organism grows actively at ordinary room temperature and elaborates its toxin which is extremely poisonous for various animals and fowl as well as for man, and which is not destroyed by the action of the digestive ferments.

Van Ermengem's observations were repeatedly confirmed in Europe, but in spite of the results of the investigations of the Darmstadt outbreak the impression became general that the organism could not produce its toxin except in the presence of protein of animal origin. A few years ago I was able to prove that protein of animal origin is not essential for the development of the toxin, and investigations of numerous outbreaks of food poisoning in this country have shown that many have been caused by the ingestion of canned vegetables or fruits in which the organism had grown and produced its toxin.

In connection with our investigation of outbreaks of botulinus intoxication it became evident that the toxin is a frequent cause of so-called limber-neck in chickens and other domestic fowl. Buckley and Shippen have shown that it may produce symptoms of forage poisoning in horses and mules, while Graham and his associates have repeatedly demonstrated that *B. botulinus* could be recovered from silage and other fodder which was responsible for the poisoning of various domestic animals.

The term botulismus, therefore, has now a much wider significance than when it was coined to include only cases of sausage poisoning. It now is used to indicate poisoning with the toxin of *B. botulinus* and includes all cases of poisoning of human beings, animals or fowl, in which the symptoms were caused by the botulinus toxin whether in meats, fish, fruits, vegetables, or fodder.

The number of recorded outbreaks of botulism affecting human beings in the United States has not been large, but it is probable that many cases have escaped notice because of the mildness of the symptoms, or because they have been grouped under the general diagnosis of ptomaine poisoning. We have record of 54 outbreaks affecting human beings, of which all but 3 have occurred within the past 11 years, and in which 228 persons were poisoned.* In 9 the food which caused the poisoning was not known, but of the remaining 45, 38 were caused by the ingestion of preserved food, of fruit, or vegetable origin.

In addition to the outbreaks in which human beings were poisoned there is record of 22 more in which domestic animals or fowl were poisoned by eating food which had been prepared for human consumption, but which had been recognized as spoiled and had been discarded. In all, therefore, there have been at least 76 outbreaks of poisoning of this type from foods prepared for human consumption, and of these 76, 62 were caused by foods of fruit or vegetable origin.

This fact is of considerable interest when viewed in comparison with the recorded causes of the poisoning in Europe. According to Bitter's recent report there has only been one outbreak in Germany in which the cause was shown to be food of other than animal origin, although he states that in approximately 25 percent of the cases the cause of the poisoning was not determined. In the United States, on the other hand, over 80 percent of all the outbreaks which were caused by foods prepared for human consumption, were due to the presence of the toxin in foods of fruit or vegetable origin. This does not include all those outbreaks of forage poisoning

*The figures quoted in this paper include all recorded outbreaks to June 30, 1920.

in animals in which the toxin was contained in fodder which was also of vegetable origin.

The mortality of the recorded outbreaks of botulism in the United States has been very high, 67.98 percent, but it is probable that this is considerably in excess of the true mortality since only the more severe outbreaks have been recorded in most parts of the country. A comparison with the mortality in Germany is extremely interesting, since in that country botulism has been a reportable disease. According to Mayer's report in 1913 from data obtained from official records the mortality was 44.9 percent, but in 1919 Bitter's report of the outbreaks in Prussia since 1897 showed an average mortality of only 16.2 percent. Bitter pointed out that of the cases taken from official records between 1897 and 1913, in which all cases were recorded, the mortality was only 8.6 per cent, but that of the cases recorded in the medical literature since 1913, it had been 32.6 percent, indicating that only the more severe cases had been recorded in the literature. This author also stated that the mortality varied greatly in different outbreaks depending upon the type of food which was responsible for the poisoning and tending to be lower in proportion to the probability of the food being sufficiently cooked before it is eaten. It is interesting in this respect that the outbreaks in the United States have been almost exclusively caused by preserved foods which were served as salad or dessert without being cooked after they were removed from the container, and it is possible that the high mortality in this country may be so explained.

It has frequently been stated that botulism is a problem which especially affects the Pacific Coast States, but in my opinion this is not the case. It is true that there have been more recorded outbreaks in California than in any other state in the Union, but that is probably largely due to the fact that careful search has been made for them in California. Independent investigations of various observers have resulted in the isolation of *B. botulinus* from foods which were grown within the states and preserved for human consumption or for the use of domestic animals in New York, New Jersey, Indiana, Illinois, Kentucky, South Dakota, Idaho, Washington, Oregon and California, and that food which epidemiological investigations indicated as the probable cause of outbreaks of botulism were grown and preserved in Ohio and Kansas. With such a wide distribution of the *B. botulinus* one can scarcely believe that the problem is of importance only in the Pacific Coast States.

The active investigation of botulism in California covers a period of nearly seven years during which time some data have been accumulated which may be of assistance in indicating the line of investigation which should be undertaken in other States where *B. botulinus* is known to occur. The work was done in the laboratories of the Stanford University Medical School until the past few months, and during the war was aided by the California State Council of Defense, but recently it has been possible to enlarge the scope of the investigation because of a grant of money which was made by the National Canners' Association and the California Olive Association for a study of botulism in California. At the present time the University of California, the United States Public Health Service and Stanford University are coöperating in the work, the laboratory investigations being divided between the laboratories of the George William Hooper Foundation for Medical Research and of the Stanford University Medical School, while the epidemiological investigation is being made by an officer of the U. S. P. H. S., who has been detailed to California for that purpose.

In our investigations we have studied the outbreaks of poisoning of human beings as they occurred, have noted the coincidence of poisoning of domestic animals or fowl which have eaten portions of the discarded food, have compared the distribution of outbreaks of poisoning of human beings with outbreaks of forage poisoning in domestic animals and are making an exhaustive study of the distribution of B. botulinus in nature. The greater part of the results of the recent investigations are not yet ready for publication, but certain data are available which are of interest.

In California, as in the country as a whole, by far the greatest number of outbreaks of botulism have been caused by the ingestion of canned vegetables and fruits, the majority of which were home-canned products. Prior to June 30th of this year we had record of 54 such outbreaks within the state, all of them caused by foods prepared for human consumption, and many of them including domestic animals or fowl as well as human beings among the victims. In a number of instances the animals and fowl were poisoned by remnants of food which were discarded from the table after the meal which had caused the poisoning of the human beings, and in these instances the chickens were usually ill in from 12 to 24 hours before the human beings showed signs of poisoning, a fact which may be of some importance in serum therapy.

It has been found that outbreaks occur in all parts of the state, but that they seem to be more frequent in certain sections. An extremely interesting observation is the evident relationship which exists between the distribution of forage poisoning of animals in California and of outbreaks of botulism affecting human beings. It must not be understood that all the recorded cases of forage poisoning in California are presumed to have been due to the botulinus toxin, but judging from the results of the experiments of Buckley and Shippen and the observations of Graham and his associates in Kentucky and Illinois, as well as from a limited number of observations in California, there is every reason to believe that at least a portion of the outbreaks of forage poisoning in this state are botulinus intoxications. The reasons for the concentration in certain areas have not yet been determined.

The isolation of B. botulinus from foods which have been the cause of poisoning or from the crops or gizzards of chickens which have died after eating the poisonous food has become so frequent as to be almost a matter of routine. There is little difficulty in establishing the presence of the toxin, although it is exceedingly difficult to get the organism out in pure culture. The method which we have adopted is to make a suspension of the suspected material in broth or normal salt solution, heat it in a water bath at 60° C. for an hour, and inoculate into flasks of glucose infusion broth prepared according to the formula of Van Ermengem, but adjusted to a PH of from 8 to 8.4. In these flasks the medium is covered with liquid paraffin and incubated for about one month. Tests are then made for the presence of toxin by inoculating guinea pigs or white mice, and if the animals succumb to the injections of the material, which has been passed through a diatomaceous filter, tests are made with antitoxin for definite diagnosis. When botulinus toxin has been demonstrated the organism is isolated in pure culture by fishing the characteristic colonies from shake cultures made in deep glucose agar or liver agar. The method has proved successful in many instances and is recommended because of its simplicity.

An interesting fact which is now generally recognized is that there are at least two distinct strains of B. botulinus in this country which we have called Types A and B. A specific antitoxin can be prepared for each of these types, but each is specific for its homologous toxin only, and neither has any appreciable effect in protecting against the toxin of the other type. This is of prime importance in connection with the serum therapy of botulism, as it is essential that either the type of the toxin which caused the poisoning be known in every instance or that a polyvalent serum or quantities of both types of serum be administered to the patients. It is a curious fact that the greater number of strains of *B. botulinus* which have been isolated in the eastern states have been Type B, whereas the majority of those found in the West, and also those recovered in the East from foods which had been preserved in California, have been Type A. It is also of interest that two toxin producing strains which were obtained from Germany, and botulinus antitoxin prepared from the Van Ermengem strain which was obtained through the courtesy of the director of the Koch Hygienic Institute at Berlin, are all apparently homologous with our Type B.

The use of botulinus antitoxin as a therapeutic measure is deserving of mention. In so far as the published records can be interpreted they seem to coincide with our experience with botulinus antitoxin in that no appreciable benefit has been derived from its use. However, it is my opinion that the antitoxin has not been given a fair trial. We have shown in laboratory experiments that if the homologous antitoxin is given in sufficient quantities at the same time as, or shortly after the toxin is administered to guinea pigs, it protects in 100 percent of cases, whereas, if the antitoxin is not given until from 24 to 30 hours after the administration of an amount of toxin which will kill the animal in 48 hours none of the animals survive. In all the instances of which I have knowledge the administration of antitoxin to human beings has been delayed until several days after the ingestion of the poison, and in several instances a Type B serum was administered in cases in which the toxin was later proved to be Type A. Under these circumstances one is not justified in concluding that the serum has no therapeutic value. It must be used early and in sufficient quantities, and either a polyvalent serum or a mixture of both types of serum must be administered if one is to hope to obtain any satisfactory results.

If the serum can be administered early enough, there is no reason why it should not prove as satisfactory as in laboratory experiments. It is possible that in some instances the early development of limber-neck in chickens which have eaten discarded human food may afford indication for the administration of the antitoxin to the human victims in time to be of value.

In our treatment of cases we are insisting that the usual tests for hypersensitiveness to horse serum be made and that, if hypersensitive, the patient be desensitized by giving subcutaneous, intramuscular and intravenous injections of 1 cc. of serum at intervals of one hour. The administration of the serum is by intravenous injection, one hour after the last desensitizing injection, and large quantities of serum of both types are given slowly, not more than 1 cc. of serum being injected per minute.

The relationship of *B. botulinus* to the preservation of foods, whether at home or commercially, is of the utmost importance. The facts that the organism is a spore bearer, and that the spores are unusually resistant to heat, that is a toxin producer, that its toxin is not destroyed by the digestive juices, and that it grows readily and produces its toxin in fruits, vegetables and meats at room temperatures, are all reasons why it is essential that in preserving foods the utmost care should be taken to prevent as much as possible its access to the food and to employ sufficiently thorough processes to ensure the destruction of any spores which may be present. This is not a simple procedure. It has been shown repeatedly that various vegetables and fruits which were grown in the owner's garden under hygienic conditions which were at least as favorable as in the majority of kitchen gardens, and where the vegetables and fruits have been canned at home with the most careful precautions, have later been responsible for the poisoning of persons or of domestic fowl, because of the presence of the botulinus toxin. Moreover, it has been shown that fruits and vegetables purchased in the open market and canned at home have also been responsible for subsequent outbreaks of botulism. It is therefore clear that under existing conditions we cannot depend upon the exclusion of *B. botulinus* from the raw foods which are to be preserved, but that we must depend upon the sterilizing process to kill what spores may happen to be present.

The temperature of boiling water is not sufficiently high to ensure the destruction of the spores. It has been found that all the strains of *B. botulinus* are not equally resistant to heat, but that some of them are extremely resistant. Mrs. Burke, in our laboratories, has shown that one strain which she tested withstood 15 pounds pressure in the autoclave, that is a temperature of 250° F., for ten minutes, and that two withstood immersion in live steam in an Arnold sterilizer for four hours, while Miss Edmondson, at the Bureau of Chemistry in the U. S. Department of Agriculture, recorded another strain which resisted ten pounds pressure in the autoclave, 240° F., for 15 minutes. It is obvious that many of the methods employed in preserving food, particularly the home-canning methods, are inefficient if spores of the more resistant strains of *B. botulinus* happen to be contained within the can.

In so far as the commercial canning industry is concerned, the chief difficulty to the present time has been from ripe olives. The number of persons poisoned by the ripe olives was unfortunately rather large, but it must, in fairness, be emphasized that only four lots of olives of all the olives packed have been shown to be contaminated with toxin of *B. botulinus*. The number of outbreaks was not large, and the mortality was no higher than has occurred in many outbreaks from home-canned products, but

the latter have not been so widely featured in the daily press. The olive canning industry of California has taken steps to ensure as much as possible that there will be no recurrence of this type of poisoning, and are heartily coöperating with the State Board of Health in the attempt to standardize their processes. Under a recent ruling of the State Board of Health it is required that all ripe olives canned in brine must be processed at 240° F. (ten pounds pressure in the retort) for at least 40 minutes, and that the brine in the shipping and holding tanks must be of such concentration as will prevent excessive fermentation.

There has been some difference of opinion as to whether food which contains the botulinus toxin is always so spoiled as to readily attract the attention of the one who opens the container. It is probable that there is always more or less marked evidence of spoilage in food contaminated with *B. botulinus* toxin, but it is wrong to believe that it is always very evident. In the laboratory I have seen a few cans of vegetables which had been experimentally inoculated in which there was no macroscopic evidence of spoilage and in which but little odor could be detected, although they contained a virulent toxin, but in the majority of instances the signs of spoilage were very marked and the odor was offensive. However, there are numbers of instances on record in which the housewife who opened the jars of vegetables could not determine that the food was spoiled, even after she had smelled and tasted it, although her subsequent illness and death were evidence that the toxin had been present in considerable amounts. In some cases the offensive odor was not noted until the food became heated during the process of cooking, and there are several instances in which persons who ate the food as salad with salad dressing did not notice anything unusual in its taste or odor. It cannot therefore be stated that only food which is obviously unfit for consumption is liable to contain the botulinus toxin, but it should be emphasized that any preserved food which shows the slightest sign of spoilage should be discarded without being tasted, and should not be left where human beings or domestic animals or fowl may have access to it. The toxin of *B. botulinus* is destroyed by heat, and if canned food is thoroughly heated through after it is removed from the container all danger of botulinus poisoning will be removed. It may be added that there are few, if any, "ready to serve" canned foods which are in any way damaged by being boiled and, if necessary, cooled before they are eaten.

In our investigation from the beginning we have had the cordial coöperation of the State Boards of Health in California and in the adjoining states which we have visited from time to time when outbreaks of botulism were reported. Three of the Western states, California, Oregon and Arizona, and New York State have made botulism a reportable disease, and we hope that other states will soon follow the example. We greatly appreciate the coöperation of the U. S. P. H. S. in detailing a trained epidemiologist to assist in the work in California and we believe that only by coöperation on the part of the State and Federal authorities in all parts of the country will it be possible to gain a true perspective of the economic importance of botulism in the United States and to standardize methods for its prevention and control.

□

COMPARISON OF THE BACTERIAL COUNTS FROM MACHINE AND HAND WASHED DISHES AND THEIR SIGNIFICANCE

Roy S. Dearstyne
*City Health Department,
Charlotte, N. C.*

More and more it becomes evident that carelessly washed dishes and utensils in eating places and at soda fountains are potential disseminators of infections. Principles like this, however, need to be confirmed by observation. This paper furnishes practical facts that point to the health value of machine dish washing.

ONE of the most potent sources of danger from the standpoint of sanitation in restaurant inspection is the matter of cleaning and handling dishes and utensils in public eating places. Many cities have stringent regulations regarding the handling of restaurant utensils, but the fact remains that despite the most elaborate system of inspection, such places are for the greater part of the time "running under their own head," and are placing before the public utensils of questionable cleanliness and sterility. That such a condition is a factor in the spread of infectious diseases can hardly be questioned.

The following work was done during the early spring and summer of 1919 while the writer was connected with the Health Department of the City of Alexandria, Va., and was the outcome of a question of the relative safety of various methods of dish cleaning used in eating places in that city. Unfortunately, only one eating house was available which had a thoroughly modern mechanical dishwasher, and whose proprietor utilized proper precautions in using it. The rest of the places represented every phase of the old system of washing in hot water, and drying with a towel, from the worst to the best, and included various degrees of temperature, soapiness, and cleanliness which the respective proprietors considered adequate and necessary.

In this work, the technique employed was as follows: For coffee mugs and water glasses, 100 cc. sterile water dilution blanks were carried to the eating houses and poured, with aseptic precautions into the cups and glasses as ready for public use. A sterile, moistened cotton swab was then taken, and that section of the cup or glass which could reach the lips of any person using it, was thoroughly swabbed. It was then emulsed in the dilution. This was then poured back into the blank which was taken to the laboratory where agar plates were poured, and counts read at the end of 48 hours incubation at $37\frac{1}{2}°$ C. For knives, forks, and spoons, sterile moistened swabs were rubbed over that portion of the utensil which might come in contact with the user's mouth or food to be eaten, and the same procedure in enumerating organisms followed from this point as in the cases of coffee mugs and water glasses.

In the following tabulations, restaurants 1 and 2 were Greek lunches, kept in a fairly clean condition. Number 3 was a negro lunch room, in which the dishes were washed in a dish pan, probably representing as bad a condition as could be found. Number 4 was a new, up-to-date lunch room, lacking only the electric dish washer. Number 5 was an ordinary lunch with the usual conditions prevailing. Number 6 was, as noted,

equipped with a thoroughly modern electric dish washer, and the proprietor took pride in the condition of his glassware and utensils. All of the places, with the exception of Number 3, had an adequate supply of boiling water, but it is questionable whether it was used at all times.

Table 1 represents an average of 9 of the lowest of 10 counts taken on each utensil at each place.

TABLE 1

Restaurant Numbers, Hand washed

Utensil—	1	2	3
Coffee Mugs	26,000	100,000	290,000
Water Glasses	23,000	130,000	120,000
Spoons	3,400	8,200	70,000
Knives	1,500	20,000	No test
Forks	1,500	11,000	3,200
	4	5	*6
Coffee Mugs	160,000	130,000	3,700
Water Glasses	33,000	No test	1,700
Spoons	13,000	17,000	2,000
Knives	6,400	2,700	1,400
Forks	2,600	7,600	1,600

*Machine washed.

Table 2 shows the highest and lowest individual bacterial counts obtained on each utensil at each place.

TABLE 2

Restaurant Numbers

Utensils— 1	Highest	Lowest
Coffee Mugs	63,000	1,000
Water Glasses	50,000	2,000
Spoons	7,700	1,000
Knives	4,000	600
Forks	6,200	500

Utensils— 2	Highest	Lowest
Coffee Mugs	760,000	12,000
Water Glasses	630,000	24,000
Spoons	32,000	1,700
Knives	63,000	3,200
Forks	31,000	4,000

Utensils— 3	Highest	Lowest
Coffee Mugs	890,000	46,000
Water Glasses	380,000	10,000
Spoons	300,000	5,000
Knives	No test	4,800
Forks	50,000	4,800

Utensils— 4	Highest	Lowest
Coffee Mugs	890,000	23,000
Water Glasses	1,200,000	2,500
Spoons	600,000	1,800
Knives	26,000	1,400
Forks	220,000	700

Utensils— 5	Highest	Lowest
Coffee Mugs	570,000	8,000
Water Glasses	No test	No test
Spoons	620,000	1,000
Knives	4,800	1,100
Forks	82,000	1,200

Utensils— 6	Highest	Lowest
Coffee Mugs	13,000	1,000
Water Glasses	2,700	1,200
Spoons	17,000	400
Knives	8,500	500
Forks	3,200	900

Chart 1 is a graphic representation of the average relative difference in bacterial count between machine and hand washed dishes, from a numerical standpoint.

Little work has actually been done on the question as to whether or not there is danger of disease transmission through restaurant utensils. Many opinions have been expressed, however, and the concensus of these opinions seems to indicate that there is a real danger, especially in the transmission of certain respiratory throat and skin diseases. Actual proof of this, however, is hard to obtain. The comprehensive and valuable work by Col. Cumming in the July issue of the AMERICAN JOURNAL OF PUBLIC HEALTH, entitled *Influenza and Pneumonia as Influenced by Dish Washing in 370 Public Institutions*, presents probably the most tangible connection of disease transmission through restaurant utensils recorded, and undoubtedly will be the basis of more investigational work on this subject.

CHART I

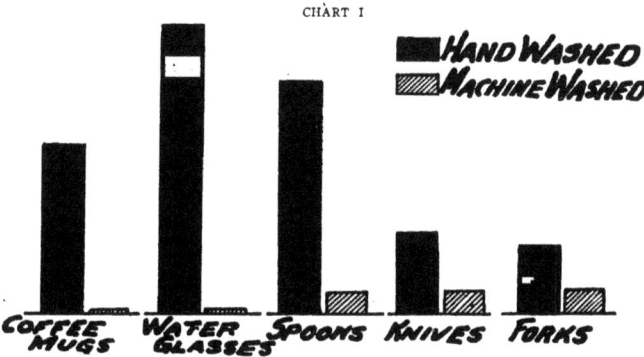

HAND WASHED
MACHINE WASHED

COFFEE MUGS   WATER GLASSES   SPOONS   KNIVES   FORKS

CONCLUSIONS

1. It is certain that in most restaurants and other public eating places, too little attention is paid to washing, drying and handling dishes and utensils.

2. The value of the machine dish washer over the old system of hand washing as determined by the numerical bacteria growth on utensils can be seen from the above tabulations.

Protection of Sand-Blasters Against the Dust Hazard. — Helmets provided with positive air pressure and the simpler forms of respirators afford substantially complete protection. The introduction of 2½ to 3 cu. ft. of air per minute through a ¼ in. hole at the top of the helmet, beneath which a deflector plate is placed (or the cap worn), will suffice. In cold weather the air should be taken from a room or chamber equipped with a small heating coil. About 2 ft. of tubing, which should be light, should be permanently connected with the helmet. There should be no air valve in reach of the worker, but the air control should be under the supervision of a foreman. The cost of maintaining this continuous air supply is a minor item.—Winslow, et al, *Public Health Reports*, March 5, 1920, 518-531, abstracted by Monthly Labor Review, U. S. B. of L. S., May, 1920, 154-156.

VALUE OF BRILLIANT-GREEN IN ELIMINATING ERRORS DUE TO THE ANAEROBES IN THE PRESUMPTIVE TEST FOR B. COLI

THEODORE C. MUER and ROBERT L. HARRIS,
Mount Prospect Laboratory,
Brooklyn, N. Y.

Read before Laboratory Section, American Public Health Association, at New Orleans, La.
October 28, 1919

A well tested method will always be especially a help to health officers for the reason that so many presentations are of matters still in the experimental stage. This brief article is based on a considerable use in practical work and the method may take its place among the pretty well established ones.

BRILLIANT-GREEN (commercial salt of Tetraethyldiamino-Triphenyl-Carbinol) has been used extensively for some time for "restraining" *B. coli* in broth and agar, and it may seem anomalous to recommend it for "favoring" its growth in bile, nevertheless, experiments conducted at Mt. Prospect Laboratory, by the authors, have proven it a valuable aid for the detection of the colon bacillus in water.

In fact it would seem as though the production of more than 10% of gas in brilliant-green lactose bile no longer is a "presumptive," but a "positive" test for *B. coli.* Using various dilutions of the dye it was found that a dilution of 1-10,000 not only prevented the growth of *B. welchii, B. sporogenes* and several other anaërobes which interfere with the growth of *B. coli*, but also had no restraining action on *B. coli.*

A study of table No. 1 will show *B. welchii* eliminated by a dilution of 1-30,000, *B. coli* requiring a dilution of 1-100 to show similar effect.

Comparisons were made with several other media using 129 samples of water of various degrees of pollution, as shown in tables Nos. II, III and IV:

TABLE NO II

Comparison of results obtained, using five different samples of water, in Standard Lactose Beef Broth and Brilliant-Green Lactose Bile.

Sample No.	Standard Broth			Brilliant-Green Lactose-Bile		
	0.1	1.0	10 cc.	0.1	1.0	10 cc.
1	0	0	0	0	0	0
2	0	0	+	0	0	0
3	0	0	0	+	+	+
4	+	+	+	+	+	+
5	+	+	+	0	+	+

TABLE NO. III

Relative isolation from nine samples of water examined for B. coli, in the following four media:

Medium	Number of dilutions from which B. coli was isolated
Plain Lactose Peptone Bile..	19
Brilliant-Green Lactose Bile..	22
Lactose Beef Broth..........	14
Gentian-Violet (1-20,000) Lactose Broth	10

TABLE NO. IV

Comparison of 115 samples of water planted in both Plain Lactose Peptone Bile and Brilliant-Green Lactose Bile.

Medium	Number of dilutions from which B. coli was isolated	Number of dilutions from which B. welchii was isolated
Plain Lactose-Peptone Bile	34	18
Brilliant-Green Lactose Bile	51	0

NOTE: This table demonstrates the interference with the growth and test for *B. coli* in ordinary media by *B. welchii*, since *B. coli* must have been present as shown by the brilliant-green lactose bile.

TABLE NO. 1

Comparative growth of B. coli and B. welchii in Brilliant Green Lactose Bile using Various dilutions of the dye.

Amount of Brilliant-Green	1-100	1-200	1-350	1-500	1-700	1-1,000	1-2,000	1-3,500	1-5,000	Per cent gas after 7 days
B. coli	0	6	38	43	50	48	55	55	55	

Amount of Brilliant-Green	1-1,000	1-2,000	1-3,000	1-5,000	1-10,000	1-20,000	1-30,000	1-50,000	1-100,000	Per cent gas after 7 days
B. welchii.......	0	0	0	0	0	0	0	80	85	

In the foregoing comparisons all tubes showing 10% of gas, or more, were plated on litmus lactose agar and examined for typical red colonies. Those tubes showing gas and no red colonies were examined microscopically for typical large non-motile bacilli of the *B. welchii* type.

As a rule the colonies from the brilliant-green bile tubes were practically pure cultures of *B. coli*, and showed stronger acid production in that confirmatory litmus lactose agar plates were a mass of red colonies.

The composition of the medium used is as follows:

Distilled water ..... 1,000 grams.
Oxgall (dried) .... 50 "
Peptone .... 10 "
Lactose .... 10 "
Brilliant-green ..... 0.1 "

DIRECTIONS FOR PREPARATION

1. Heat 1 liter of distilled water in double boiler until water in outer vessel boils.
2. Add 50 grams of dried oxgall and 10 grams of peptone, stirring until all ingredients are dissolved.
3. Continue boiling for one hour.

4. Remove from flame and add 10 grams of powdered lactose.
5. Filter through cotton flannel until clear.
6. To each liter of the filtrate add 10 cc. of a 1% solution of brilliant-green.
7. Tube and sterilize in autoclave for 15 minutes at 15 lbs. pressure.

We have had satisfactory results with different brands and samples of dye obtained from Bayer & Co., Leitz & Co., and Merck & Co., all of New York City.

This medium has been used at Mt. Prospect Laboratory, the Mt. Kisco Laboratory and the Catskill Laboratory for the past nine months for all routine work and thus far we have failed to find any of the various strains of *B. welchii* to develop in it. It has proven itself particularly valuable in the examination of chlorinated waters.

Attempt by the authors to use brilliant-green, in suitable dilution in lactose beef broth, similarly to its use in bile, have thus far been unsuccessful, as there is not as great a range of selective inhibition in this medium.

□

TUBERCULOSIS CHRISTMAS SEAL CAMPAIGN

HEALTHY NEW YEAR

Here is the Tuberculosis Christmas Seal for 1920. No, it is not a Red Cross Seal.

For the first time in the history of "Sealdom," the Red Cross is entirely left off the seal and the National Tuberculosis Association and its 1920 affiliated agencies are appealing to the American public for the support of the nation-wide anti-tuberculosis campaign on the strength of a Tuberculosis Christmas Seal, featuring the Double-Barred Cross, the international emblem of the fight against tuberculosis.

It will require every dollar that can be raised to support the growing tuberculosis movement in every state in the Union. The Christmas Seals and the Health Bonds, a new and unique feature of the Seal Sale, not only tell the story of tuberculosis and its prevention, but provide the sinews of war for the 1921 fight against this disease.

URGENT NEED FOR THE STANDARDIZATION OF LABORATORY WORK

Arthur Lederer, M. D., C. P. H.

*P. A. Surgeon (Reserve), U. S. Public Health Service,
Chicago, Ill.*

Read before Laboratory Section, American Public Health Association, at San Francisco, Cal.,
September 13, 1920.

As a practical man familiar with the technique of the laboratory
this author urges the need of establishing standards in laboratory
practice. "This task will have to be faced in the near future,"
he writes, "And I believe that the A. P. H. A. is the proper organization to assume this important duty."

THE call for standardization of laboratory work has been voiced in the past by many who have become impressed with its necessity. The American Public Health Association deserves a great deal of credit for having made a successful beginning several years ago with the standardization of laboratory procedures pertaining to water, sewage and milk. At that time these called for the important consideration from the public health standpoint as the most potent mediums of infection. Our conception of what constitutes public health has in late years become much broadened. It is not so long ago that a public health laboratory doing sputums, Widals, diphtheria cultures, urethral smears and water and milk analyses was considered as rendering maximum service to the community. Today the work of such a laboratory serving a large community includes all phases of sanitary bacteriology, clinical bacteriology, serology, pathological histology, sanitary chemistry, biological chemistry, food chemistry and toxicology. It is a fact that such a laboratory today is doing much work which formerly was done only in large hospitals and in commercial institutions. We accept a sound doctrine today that any disease in which communicability has not been definitely ruled out should

be a source of public concern. A good many sanitarians go still further advising free laboratory service to sick, indigent individuals even in cases which clearly do not endanger the public health. It is not the object of this paper to discuss the merits or demerits of this conception, but merely to emphasize that the signs of the times point in that direction. In spite of the fact that public health work and institutional hospital work have grown to be more and more alike in scope, it is a fact that on the whole the hospital pathologist is not interested in the American Public Health Association. The reason for this is apparent. There are comparatively few water and milk examinations to be made in hospitals and beyond that the pathologist receives no technical assistance and inspiration from the Association except it be in an occasional publication and from the "Laboratory Notes" of the Journal. This attitude of indifference could be changed if the Association would agitate the standardization of the procedures with which he is more closely concerned and which beyond doubt come within the province of public health in the most conservative sense of the meaning. No one will doubt for a moment for instance that the standardization of the Wassermann test in this country is a crying need.

The question arises as to how far we shall go in our attempts to standardize laboratory procedures. There is as much objection to going too far as there is to not going far enough. For instance, there is surely no need for standardizing tests such as the ones for albumin in urine or for free hydrochloric acid in gastric juice. While it is difficult to draw a distinct line it should be recognized that the bacteriological and serological procedures of a public health aspect should be standardized first. This includes the Wassermann and allied complement tests, also the identification of the meningococcus, pneumococcus, and the miscellaneous streptococci and the isolation of the intestinal pathogenic organisms from the excreta. Other tests may be added as the work of standardization proceeds and as necessity may indicate. For the present the procedures mentioned would constitute a good nucleus to start out from. No one should under-estimate the difficulty of attempting to standardize the Wassermann test. First of all it will be necessary to decide on the method to be employed. The second big question is the one of reagents and this pertains not only to the complement fixation tests, but to all serologic laboratory procedures as well. Definite instructions should be given for the preparation of antigens and amboceptor. In order to insure uniformity of products, it is important that they should be put out by one reliable, preferably non-commercial institution on a sufficiently large scale to supply the demand of the entire country, Providing that the appropriation permits, I would like to see the Hygienic Laboratory of the U. S. Public Health Service take charge of the production of the amboceptor and antigens for the miscellaneous complement fixation tests. The importance of uniformity of the antigens is so great as to out-weigh consideration of a commercial nature. The question of the supply of uniformly agglutinating

and precipitating sera is not quite so pressing.

Attention should be directed to the excellent reports which appear from time to time of the special committee of the British Medical Research Committee functioning under the National Health Insurance Act upon the standardization of pathological methods. This special committee has published, within the last few years, several bulletins on the laboratory diagnosis of venereal diseases which are admirable for their thoroughness of detail. The preparation of these reports is in the hands of medical laboratory men for it is recognized that the veracity of the results of the tests can only be gauged by corresponding clinical observations. It is very important not to lose sight of the fact that the standardization of such tests as the Wassermann is not purely a laboratory matter where a few technically trained men can get together and arbitrarily decide on the details. The closest clinical coöperation is necessary for after all while it is important to have one uniform method, it is still more important to employ a method which furnishes the clinician with the most accurate information. The Special English Research Committee was not empowered to standardize laboratory procedures, but to "consider how far it may be practicable and desirable to obtain the standardization of routine pathological methods." The Wassermann test was the first to be considered. The results of this inquiry were two reports; one on the technical features and another on the diagnostic value of the test. The committee received coöperation from the Canadian Army Medical Corps and, to some extent, from the U. S. Army Medical Corps. The committee expressed the opinion that obvious advantages are to be obtained by the standardization of approved methods. At present the value of the diagnosis provided by any given laboratory cannot be estimated. Two committees considered two alternative courses. One was to recommend a demand that every report upon Wassermann tests made officially for military or public purposes, should include a statement of the method employed. The second was to define precisely the procedure of a standard method, setting limits upon minor variations of technique and to recommend that all official tests should be made by this method only. It was emphasized that direct scientific advantage would be gained if one standardized method would obtain sole recognition, but that in the present state of knowledge it was impossible to lay down with confidence the lines of optimum procedure for the performance of the test. However, it was recommended that for official use only these methods should be accepted which conform with the original Wassermann test. In the absence of a standardized method, the importance of a standardized antigen and hemolytic amboceptor was pointed out. The opinion was expressed that the laboratories in which the Wassermann test is performed for public service should be few rather than many. On the whole one is impressed with the fact that the committee is very strongly in favor of adopting the original Wassermann as the official method.

Another publication of the British Research Committee discusses in detail the various methods of diagnosis of gonococcal infections and the detection of spirochetes of syphilis. We may well look forward with pleasure to the publication of other bulletins from this special committee. No laboratory man in this country can afford to overlook them. A large number of other excellent publications of the Medical Research Committee deal with miscellaneous bacteriological and epidemiological subjects.

It must not be forgotten that laboratory work in England is more centralized than it is in this country. We have here public health laboratories which are far removed from each other; we have laboratories in small communities conducted by workers qualified in technique, but not competent in the refinements of the test nor in interpretations. Conditions here are such as to call for standardization more strongly than is the case in England.

Some commendable work on the standardization of laboratory procedures was done in this country by the army laboratories during the great war. We are also indebted to Dr. Kolmer and others for much valuable research on the standardization of the Wassermann test, all of which will be found to be of great assistance at the time when the tasks of standardization will be faced.

One word as to the possible argument that standardization of the test, such as the Wassermann test, may discourage research. I do not believe that this constitutes a valid objection. Standardization does not imply that the test as officially recommended will be adhered to rigidly from year to year. Scientific truth seekers will always contribute their bit and it will be up to the governing body to investigate each piece of research with the view to incorporation or substitution. The body having standardization in charge can of necessity never make a final report. This deducts in no way from the great importance of the work.

No standardization would be complete without a standard report card which will embody directions as to collection of material and mailing, precise data on the history and an appropriate column for the insertion of the results of the test. A great deal of judgment is required to obtain a form which will be satisfactory for all purposes. There is no reason why such a blank should not be made to prove equally satisfactory to public health laboratories as well as to purely clinical laboratories. As a general rule the blank calling for the minimum amount of pertinent information and the minimum number of insertions is the most·satisfactory. The busy physician prefers the insertion of crosses or the underscoring of printed answers to information required in longhand.

The organization to accomplish standardization of the most important serologic and bacteriologic procedures which have a bearing on public health is no small matter and must be approached with caution. However, the task will have to be faced sometime in the near future and may as well be faced now. I believe that the American Health Association is the proper organization to assume this important duty; on the other hand the Association should not hesitate to call on anyone else outside of its membership for coöperation. There are many men, particularly in the medical profession, who are not members of the Association, but whose work and counsel along these lines would prove valuable. It would first be necessary to establish in a broad sense the policy to

be followed. Any committee appointed for this purpose must be allowed the widest latitude in order to be able to accomplish something worth while. Once the policy is established the details can be taken care of by sub-committees appointed by the chairman of the main committee, which might perhaps be named the "Committee on the Standardization of Pathological Methods" similar to the designation of the British organization. It has been experienced in the past that men called upon by the American Public Health Association on similar previous occasions have given freely of their time and talents and they will do so again. The function of this committee which may change in its composition will not cease since proper cognizance must be taken of the continuous research particularly in serology. I believe that early action by this Association will be indorsed and heartily appreciated by everyone concerned, particularly by the laboratory workers and public health officials.

☐

Unified Medical Service in Wales.—Two points are brought out in the Report of the Welsh Consultative Council: (1) there is an entire lack of organization in medical service; (2) the personnel and institutions already in existence, if properly organized, would go far to meet the needs of an efficient service. A plan is proposed whereby this organization might be effected. The country is divided into medical areas, each area being subdivided into districts. In each district would be established an institute acting as a headquarters for six types of service: (1) general hospital; (2) maternity and infant welfare center with tuberculosis and other clinics; (3) medical institute with laboratory, library and facil-

ities for meetings; (4) center from which nursing service and health visiting would be directed; (5) base for ambulance service, and (6) center for public health administration. Smaller secondary institutes would be required in certain localities. These institutes would depend on the main institute of the, district which in turn would be based on the medical center for the area. The Report indicates that the plan is essentially practical inasmuch as very little modification of existing services would be necessary. The plan should be a valuable one for it makes use of all available medical service, coördinates it into a workable organization and indicates where addition would be needed.—*Lancet*, May 29, 1920. (*H. N. C.*)

EDITORIAL SECTION

AMERICAN JOURNAL OF PUBLIC HEALTH
Publication Office: 124 W. Polk Street, Chicago, Ill.
EDITORIAL OFFICE: 169 MASSACHUSETTS AVE., BOSTON, MASS.

A. W. HEDRICH, C. P. H., Editor　　　　　　　　　　J. RITCHIE, Jr., Associate Editor

Editorial Assistants

E. R. HAYHURST, M.D.　　　　P. M. HOLMES, M.D.　　　　FRANCIS H. SLACK, M.D.
DAVID GREENBERG　　　　　　JAMES A. TOBEY　　　　　　JAMES M. STRANG
M. P. HORWOOD, M.S.　　　　　　　　　　　　　　　　HOMER N. CALVER

Board of Advisory Editors

PETER H. BRYCE, M.D., Ottawa, Canada　　　　PROF. M. J. ROSENAU, Boston, Mass.
CHARLES V. CHAPIN, M.D., Providence, R. I.　　PROF. W. T. SEDGWICK, Cambridge, Mass.
EUGENE R. KELLEY, M.D., Boston, Mass.　　　　PROF. GEORGE C. WHIPPLE, Cambridge, Mass.
W. A. EVANS, M.D., Chicago, Ill.　　　　　　　PROF. S. M. GUNN, Paris, France.

All expressions of opinion and all statements of supposed facts are published on authority of the writer under whose name they appear, and are not to be regarded as expressing the views of the American Public Health Association, unless such statements or opinions have been adopted by vote of the Association.

NOTICE TO SUBSCRIBERS: Subscription Price, payable in advance, $4.00 per year for United States and possessions; $4.50 for Canada and other foreign countries. Single copies, 50 cents postpaid. Membership in the American Public Health Association, including subscription to Journal, $5.00 per year. In Change of Address please give both old and new address, and mail before the 25th of the month to take effect with the current issue. Mailing Date, 20th of each month. Advertisements accepted only when commendable, and worth while both to reader and advertiser. News Items, interesting clippings and illustrations are gladly received, together with name of sender. Copyright, 1919, by A. W. Hedrich.

PROBLEM OF THE RAT

Communications of importance presented at the meeting in San Francisco and published in this issue of the JOURNAL bring to attention that most imperative health procedure, the extermination of the rat. This should be taken up by our states, municipalities and communities as a serious undertaking, because this common rodent is an animal that harbors the flea that communicates bubonic plague to man. It should be taken up betimes, because the plague is truly knocking at our doors. While the Quarantine Service of the country will watch the human immigrants, the disease may enter unheralded through undesirable rodent visitors and become widely disseminated among native rats before its presence is announced by human cases. At the time when the first human case is announced it may be taken for granted that the native rat population is largely infected, with potentialities for widespread further infection and the certainty of large expenditures in warfare on the flea, the rat and the disease. This has been well attested by experience.

The fight against the rat is no children's pastime to be accompanied by rhyming slogans to make it interesting; it is truly work for men to be undertaken betimes in our ports and to be carried on in sober, serious earnest.

Plague is not an imaginary danger, for while there is the suggestion of a tropical Orient in its rapid course, it has shown that it has power for evil in temperate climates. There is no need of panic or excitement, for proper measures calmly undertaken can discount all its possible ills.

How troublesome the plague can be has already been demonstrated in this country. In California a decade ago it gained a foothold, there were some human victims, and animal hosts became infected. The experience of the West Coast is testimony of the tenacity with which it clings.

Those who are familiar with the West Coast story—those who are not may learn of its serious aspects by reading the Plague Symposium a few pages before this one in the JOURNAL—will realize how the flea may change its host, and how with a native wild animal will have opportunities for travel. The recent "flare-up" in California shows how the disease may be quiescent between active outbursts. It is fortunate that in the Far West it has been the stay-at-home ground squirrel that has been the selected host of the flea. On other coasts more rapid travelers may readily lend themselves to the distribution of the disease to our discomfiture, pecuniary loss and potential danger.

It is unfortunate that so many American citizens, keen-sighted as they are in business operations, do not become awakened to the need of prevention till circumstances enforce the vastly greater undertaking of the cure. We apparently prefer the dramatic motor engine whizzing through the streets towards the fire and the excitement of the conflagration to the dull prevention of fireproof or fire-resisting construction. We are alive in an instant with a wealth of invention when disease is really in our midst, and pour out money like water when the mischief has been started, but we are largely uninterested in the montonous routine processes that will ward off disease. The value of prophylaxis against typhoid fever was shown indisputably in the recent war, but the application of it and of good sanitation in preventing this disease at home is very much neglected. It is the same with the rat, we are seemingly indifferent to its dangers.

Those who will read the stirring conclusions of Dr. Kellogg in these pages will realize how pressing is the situation. It is one that calls for preparedness in our ports. The means for this are simple, to exterminate the rats in our homes, warehouses and wharves and to keep them away in the future by better building construction. The process of extermination is simple, but it is not so easy, for rats, having lived by their wits for untold centuries have developed remarkable intelligence. Having lived in the homes of men they are to a large extent trap-shy, and keen-scented as they are it will require every artifice against them. In California poison is employed against the ground squirrels as a practicable means of destroying these hosts of the plague flea.

Rat-proofing houses and storage places will deprive rodents of their hiding places. This is costly, but it is a measure of economy in preventing the waste of the hundred millions of dollars each year that these animals are said to eat or destroy. Proper care of family foods and household wastes would starve them so that they could no longer live in the homes of men. This, however, demands an advanced state of public health education. In the meantime it lies with the health authorities to take such public measures as may be within their power towards improving the situation, measures which will have for their aim the extermination of the rat.

VARIETIES OF CITY HEALTH OFFICERS

A recently issued reprint of the U. S. Public Health Service presents a list of the health officers for 1920 in cities of more than 10,000 population in this country. From the point of view of standardization, an analysis of this list brings out some interesting facts. It is evident that much is still to be accomplished in this direction, if indeed a real start has yet been made.

According to the 1917 estimates of the Census Bureau there are 708 communities to be listed with greater population than 10,000, and of these 685, or about 96 percent have health officials. There are about 60 different titles employed, which may suggest the desirability of having some standard one. Of these health officials, 536 or about 78 percent have the degree, M. D., and 266 or about 38 percent are on a full-time basis. It is worth a thought that today only a little more than one-third of our American cities of 10,000 inhabitants have a full-time health officer.

Of the officers with the degree, M. D., three have also a D. P. H., one a C. P. H. and one an LL. B. Of the 149 laymen who are health officials three have the D. P. H., one the P. H. D., one has C. E., one is a pharmacist, one a nurse and five are veterinary doctors. Degrees are not specified for any of the others. The question as to what extent a college degree shall be required for health officers is one to which there are two sides, but it is evident from these facts that there exist in the country no well defined requirements in the matter.

A consideration of health officers with reference to whether they are full-time or part-time leads to the showing that there is quite as little system here as in the other particulars noted.

Alabama and South Carolina are the only states having nothing but full-time city health officials. Arizona, Delaware, Idaho, Nevada, Oklahoma, Oregon, and Wyoming have no full-time city health officials. In West Virginia and Indiana only 10 percent of the health officials are on a full-time basis and in Mississippi only 12 percent. New Jersey leads in full-time health officials with 71 percent, Pennsylvania has 64 percent and Massachusetts 54 percent. Then come Michigan with 42 percent, Ohio with 32 percent, Connecticut with 30 percent and California with 27 percent. The Empire State of New York has only 19 percent full-time city health officials, Texas only 16 percent and Illinois only 20 percent. In New York every health official is an M. D., as is also the case in Connecticut. In California, Illinois, Indiana, Michigan and Texas more than 95 percent of the health officials are M. Ds. In Pennsylvania only 26 percent have this degree, in Massachusetts only 32 percent and in New Jersey only 40 percent. Of the physicians only about 26 percent are on a full-time basis; of the laymen about 80 percent are full-time officials.

It is true, of course, that there are differences of situation, temperament and education of populations that make the local problems of health officers different in different places, but vagaries in local legislation that lead to such divergences as these need not be. The health of the people is America's strongest asset, and it behooves us to formulate the requirements of the officers to whom this health is confided in some fairly systematic and logical manner.

J. A. T.

REQUEST FOR BACK NUMBERS OF THE TRANSACTIONS

The American Public Health Association desires to secure copies of volumes lacking in its sales series of TRANSACTIONS to fill orders for sets that have been received. It needs copies of Volumes III, V, VI, and XXVIII. Any member wishing to dispose of any of these volumes will please address the Secretary, A. P. H. A., 169 Massachusetts Avenue, Boston 17, Mass.

BOOKS AND REPORTS
REVIEWED

Applied Anatomy and Kinesiology—The Mechanism of Muscular Movement. *Wilbur Pardon Bowen, M. S. Second edition. Philadelphia: Lea & Febiger. Pp. 334. Price, $3.50.*

In view of the interest of the world of today in physical education, examination and training the work of Dr. Bowen is timely. The book comes from a well-known publisher and is one of *The Physical Education Series,* of which R. Tait McKenzie, M. D., of Philadelphia is editor.

This book will find a useful field in a number of ways. It has a good deal of anatomy; some discussion of mechanics, especially with reference to the movements of the bones by the muscles; it enters somewhat into the field of hygiene and devotes much attention to gymnastics. For the full performance of his duty the physician may readily need a better understanding of muscular action that is given in his preparatory studies or his experience in the hospitals, and here he will find presented in convenient form studies of the seventy-five pairs of muscles that are involved in general posture in the usual—and even the unusual—movements of the body.

The various topics are taken up intelligently, the language is not too technical for the general reader and there are desirable incidentals, such as a table of sines, for those who wish to go a little more deeply into the details, mathematical and scientific, of the various problems. There is much in the volume on muscular control, voluntary and automatic, quite a bit about the nervous system and detailed considerations of the offices and action of the more important muscles, which are taken in groups and are accompanied by discussions of the related gymnastic exercises. There is a chapter on breathing and another on the upright position of man with its advantages and disadvantages. In this matter there is the explanation of that reversion to an ancestral type in the athlete's crouching start for the race.

Quizzes at the ends of the chapters fit the volume for text-book purposes, and a bibliography is another step in the same direction. The book is well illustrated.

✦

Diagnostic Methods. *Ralph W. Webster, M.D., Ph.D. 6th edition. Philadelphia: P. Blakiston's Son & Co. 1920. Pp. 844. Price, $9.00.*

It is now four years since the last edition of this popular laboratory book appeared. Nearly one hundred pages of new text have been added in the sixth edition. The illustrations remain unchanged. The new material inserted pertains mostly to the recent advances in the science of blood and urine chemistry. The important work of Folin and his associates has been incorporated. The section dealing with the reaction of the blood has been entirely rewritten to bring it up to the present day conception of hydrogen—Ion concentration. The functional renal diagnosis and Mosenthal's test meal for renal function are exhaustively treated. In the discussion of parasitology of the blood a full account of the *Leptospira ictero-hemorrhagica* is given. The coagulo reaction of Hirschfeld and Klinger is incorporated among the serum reactions for syphilis. The discussion also includes the gas bacillus of Welch which plays such an important part in the study of wound infections.

It may have been well to include a full description of routine laboratory procedures such as the typing of pneumococci and the detection of lead in excretions. The late methods for the determination of basal metabolism are not touched upon. A few additional appropriate illustrations, particularly in the chapter dealing with the Wassermann reaction, would add interest to the text.

A very desirable feature of the book is the exhaustive list of references which is to be found at the foot of each page. In this respect Webster's book appeals to the research worker more strongly than do most other books covering the same ground. The new edition can be heartily recommended to the laboratory profession.

ARTHUR LEDERER, M. D.

Hygiene: Dental and General. *Clair Elsmere Turner. St. Louis: C. V. Mosby Co., 1920. Pp. 400. Price, $4.00.*

A beneficiently contagious interest in public health has spread in a great many directions from Professor Sedgwick's laboratory at the Massachusetts Institute of Technology. One of the secondary foci of infection was established some time ago in the Tufts College Dental School and has spread, through the interest of prominent dentists, to the whole profession. The leading schools of dentistry have at present a standardized course in Hygiene which is equal, so far as emphasis on social prevention goes, to the instruction given on the same line in many schools of medicine. This development has been made possible largely through the interest and coöperation of the staff of the Department of Biology and Public Health at Technology; and the author of this new book on "Hygiene: Dental and General" holds assistant professorship in both the Institute of Technology and the Tufts College Medical and Dental School.

The course in hygiene here presented is designed to give to the dentist a knowledge of the laws of personal hygiene which he can apply in the instruction of his patients and a knowledge of the general principles of public health which will assist him to assume a position of intelligent leadership as a citizen. After a very brief chapter on Dental Hygiene as such, in which the limitations of orthodontia are alluded to and the importance of breast feeding in developing the teeth is discussed, Professor Turner passes to the four main fields of physiology, assimilation, action, sensation and reproduction, and discusses each from the hygienic standpoint. The treatment of dietary hygiene might to advantage be amplified and made more practical; but the chapters on exercise (of which Posture is properly held to be the primary element) and on the Central Nervous System are original in conception and clear and effective in presentation. The chapter on Heredity may prove a little deep for the average student and the table of diseases subject to Mendelian heredity on p. 89 contains some rather doubtful items, including diabetes, which is classified as a kidney disease.

Professor Turner then passes to the communicable diseases, with a good historical chapter, a somewhat technical discussion of immunity, a chapter on oral prophylaxis (in which focal infections are discussed with sanity and balance), and a chapter on communicable diseases, wisely devoted chiefly to tuberculosis, venereal disease and the common cold, the rarer acute contagia being covered by the American Public Health Association Committee Report, reproduced as an appendix. The book closes with a series of chapters on the broader sanitary and administrative problems of public health, food control, water supply, sewage disposal, ventilation, school hygiene, industrial hygiene and health department organization.

It is a little hard on the pioneer figure in Dental Hygiene, Dr. A. C. Fones of Bridgeport, to call him A. L. Fownes on p. 153 and A. E. Fones on p. 286. In general, however, the book is well edited. Professor Turner presents a clear and well-balanced view of the fields of personal hygiene and public health as they bear upon the work of the dentist; and his book, the first of its kind in this field, should prove of the greatest value in mobilizing the dental profession of the country in the wider campaign for the prevention of preventable disease.

C.-E. A. WINSLOW.

✦

Mother and Child.—This is a magazine devoted to the health of these important members of the family and the community, published by the American Child Hygiene Association. It is issued every other month, from the office of the Association, 1211 Cathedral street, Baltimore, Md. The October issue, Vol. I, No. 3, contains articles on "Children in Central Europe," by Julia C. Lathrop; "The New-born Infant," by J. W. Ballantyne, M. D., of the Edinburgh Royal Maternity Hospital; "Salvaging Crippled Children," by Mary Perkins Ivey, R. N.; "Preventing Decay in Children's Teeth," by Henry Larned Keith Shaw, M. D., and "High School Nutrition Classes," by Mrs. Ira Couch Wood, together with editorials, reviews, news notes and items of popular interest. The little magazine is well printed, well illustrated and admirably adapted to the purpose of interesting the public in child hygiene.

The Newer Methods of Blood and Urine Chemistry. *R. B. H. Gradwohl, M.D., and A. J. Blaivas, St. Louis, Mo. C. V. Mosby Company. 1920. Pp. 418. Illustrated. Price $5.00.*

The second edition of this well known book covers nearly two hundred pages more than are found in the first edition. It is divided into three parts. Part I, entitled "Technique of Blood Chemistry," is essentially the same as that in the early edition excepting that a brief chapter on "Lipoids" has been added. The determination of the acetone bodies is more fully discussed. Part II deals with the "Chemical Analysis of Urine." In addition to the Hellige colorimeter, the author furnishes a description of the Duboscq and Bock-Benedict colorimeters. The greatest number of changes and additions are found in Part III, which deals with "Blood Findings and Their Interpretation."

The chapter on "Blood Sugar," covering 71 pages (25 in the first edition), contains the latest data on the sugar contents in tissues, sugar tolerance and metabolism. The relation of blood chemistry to nephritis and to surgical procedures is also thoroughly discussed.

An entirely new chapter on "Basal Metabolism" has been incorporated. This chapter is of particular interest to the clinician, since it opens up a remarkably interesting field in diagnosis. It is fortunate that the author succeeded in incorporating in an "Appendix" Folin's and Wu's new methods of blood examination which require much smaller amounts of blood for complete analyses. The value of the book is greatly enhanced by the insertion of this recent piece of literature.

A number of illustrations have been added and the text is remarkably free from typographical errors. The authors have succeeded in maintaining a high standard. The publication will assuredly hold its place among the indispensable laboratory reference books.

ARTHUR LEDERER, M.D.

✦

Palestine's first medical Journal, *Harefooah (Medicine)*, has made its appearance, published by the Jewish Medical Association of Palestine. It is a quarterly and dedicated to the memory of Jewish physicians and nurses who laid down their lives in the years of upheaval in the Holy Land. The purposes of the journal and the medical association that is publishing it are to strengthen and coödinate the medical forces of the country, to collaborate with doctors outside of Palestine, to prepare a soil for Jewish scientific work and to help in the establishment of a Jewish university.

✦

Digest of Programs of National Organizations Carrying on Some Phase of Child Welfare. *Compiled by The American Child Hygiene Association. Mss. 69 pp.*

In connection with its convention at St. Louis, October 11-13, 1920, the American Child Hygiene Association has prepared a digest of programs of national organizations that carry on some phase of child welfare. This is a work of correlation much needed in almost every branch of public service, and excellently well accomplished in this instance. A manifolded pamphlet of 69 pages is the result.

From this it appears that no less than 66 different country-wide organizations have one or more departments devoted to the benefit of children, including patriotic, home economics and health associations, boy scouts and camp fire girls, women's club federations, suffrage associations, societies undertaking public health nursing or the study of special diseases, playground associations, nutritional clinics, and not forgetting such organizations as the Knights of Columbus, the Council of Jewish Women and the Y. W. H. A. Kindergarten associations, day nurseries, settlement associations, the Russell Sage Foundation, Salvation Army and a number of government departments all have more or less interest in this work.

The pamphlet outlines for each of these interested associations its official name, its home address and its program. Anyone who is interested in the welfare of children will find in this pamphlet a mine of information. So far as the associations themselves are concerned, this plain statement of the lines along which they are working, or intending to work, should be of the greatest benefit towards coöperation, coördination and the avoidance of overlapping.

Report of the Health and Sanitary Survey of the City of New Orleans, 1918-1919. Conducted jointly by the Board of Health for the Parish of Orleans and the City of New Orleans and the Metropolitan Life Insurance Company of New York. Inspections and compilations by Walter L. Dodd.

To those who have visited the picturesque city of New Orleans, or to those who are familiar with the previous association of New Orleans with yellow fever and bubonic plague, this report will be of interest. It will also be interesting to public health and social workers in general, since it represents a thorough study of the health conditions and health organization of a large and important American community.

The report considers first the early sanitary history of New Orleans, describing the prevalence of yellow fever, cholera, smallpox and bubonic plague and the steps that were taken to eradicate these diseases. The development of the present system of health organization is also carefully traced.

New Orleans has not grown very rapidly. In 1910 its population was 339,075. The population of the city has increased in recent decades primarily through interstate migration, so that the native-born element is very large. The principal foreign elements are Germans, Italians, Irish and French in the order named.

The other vital statistics of the city are considered separately. There are separate chapters for measles, whooping cough, scarlet fever, diphtheria, typhoid fever and tuberculosis. In each case the specific death rate for each disease is given from 1880-1917. Comparisons of these rates are made with those that prevailed in other cities in various sections of the country. Studies in race, sex, age and color distribution are also made. It is shown that communicable diseases are not completely reported. It is estimated that at least 15% of measles cases are not reported; that the reporting of cases of whooping cough is very poor; that the number of cases of typhoid fever reported is incomplete, and that the same is true for tuberculosis. The number of deaths from diphtheria is considered too high. From 1911 to 1916 there were 458 deaths from diphtheria as compared with 302 deaths from measles, whooping cough and scarlet fever combined. The reasons

given are that an early diagnosis is not made, and that physicians do not employ the laboratory facilities which are available to aid them. It is recommended that all diphtheria contacts should be examined bacteriologically and that the Shick test and the toxin-antitoxin mixture should be employed on children of the pre-school age. The death rate from scarlet fever is exceedingly low, being in the six years from 1911 to 1916 only 21.

Although the specific death rate from typhoid fever has been above 21.6 since 1914, the actual death rate from this cause is probably only one-half as great. The higher rate is due to the large number of non-residents who die of typhoid fever in the city hospitals after they have been brought to the city for treatment. Thus in 1917, of 87 deaths from typhoid fever, 40 were those of non-residents.

The tuberculosis death rate is very high. Since 1910 the specific death rate from this disease has varied between 236.0 and 290.2. The latter rate prevailed in 1917. The rate for the whites in that year was 191.8 and for the negroes 570.0. In 1910 the negro element of the population comprised 26.3%. There are many reasons for the great prevalence of tuberculosis. In the first place very little is done to combat the disease. There is only one tuberculosis dispensary, one which is operated by the Louisiana Anti-Tuberculosis League. The cases that appear for examination are usually advanced. Only one nurse is employed to visit patients in the home. There is a small camp at which incipient cases of tuberculosis are cared for. There is, however, no physician in attendance. Children under eight years of age and negroes are not accommodated. There are no day camps for children of tuberculous families, nor are there any open-air schools or classes. Public health education is entirely neglected. Hospital facilities for the tuberculous are inadequate. Sputum cups are not provided, and the number of sputum samples examined is small. The housing problem in the city is also serious.

Approximately 15,000 gallons of milk are consumed daily in New Orleans. This milk comes from farms within a radius of 100 miles from the city. On account of the lack of cooling at the point of production or in trains, 100,000 gallons of milk soured in 1917 before arriving in the city. Only one-third of the milk is pasteurized by the holding method. Sixty percent of the milk is not pasteurized at all, and 10% is pasteurized by the flash method. Pasteurization is not supervised or checked. Milk handlers are not medically examined. None of the milk is graded.

The water supply of the city is excellent. The old cisterns and other mosquito-breeding places have in the main been abandoned. The raw water is obtained from the Mississippi River, then is passed through grit chambers, then coagulated with lime and sulphate of iron, and finally treated on mechanical filters. The filtered water is disinfected with liquid chlorine as it is pumped into the mains. The daily water consumption is 33,000,000 gallons. The water supply is under constant expert control and supervision. New Orleans has learned the value of a safe and adequate water supply.

Similarly the sewerage and drainage systems are excellent. There are 497 miles of sewers in use, serving nearly all of the built-up sections of the city. Privies which abounded in the city only 15 years ago have materially decreased. The present method of disposal consists in discharging the coarsely screened sewage by means of high lift pumps into the plentiful waters of the Mississippi.

The refuse from the city, after collection, is used for filling in low places. Although the rubbish is supposed to be separated from the garbage, this is unsatisfactorily done. In only about one-half of the cases is the garbage stored in covered, water-tight cans. Garbage from large hotels is collected by private scavengers and fed to hogs. The collecting wagons are frequently uncovered, so that nuisances from this source are common. All forms of refuse in the district known as Algiers are collected in a special wagon, hauled to the incinerator and burned. Large dead animals are removed by a private rendering company and treated for economic gain.

The health department is organized very

unsatisfactorily. The department has no public health nurses and only three physicians who serve on a part time basis. The medical inspection of school children is not well administered. The reporting of births is incomplete, so that no accurate idea of the infant mortality rate is available. Infant and child welfare work are almost entirely neglected. Tuberculosis, the sanitary control of the milk supply, the control of health conditions in industry, are also seriously neglected. Public health education is not conducted. The laboratories of the health department have an inadequate personnel and the number of specimens examined is entirely too small. The bulk of the laboratory work consists of tests for diphtheria, tuberculosis, typhoid and malaria. The records of the department are kept unsatisfactorily. There are 57 sanitary inspectors, only 15 of whom are engaged in the control of communicable disease. No epidemiologist is employed. The per capita expenditure for health work in 1917 was 36 cents.

From the foregoing summary it is evident that the study has been very complete and that New Orleans desires to know the truth as a foundation towards establishing a better condition of affairs. The report has been so closely considered that one is a bit surprised to find in it no statement of the general mortality rate, no report on food handling establishments and no table of contents.

MURRAY P. HORWOOD, M. S.

M. P. H. A. NEWS

Maine now has a health journal of its own. In September the M. P. H. A. News, the magazine of the Maine Public Health Association, made its initial appearance and will be issued each month hereafter. The paper contains news articles on health work all over the state; appointments of health workers; reports of conference and plans for growth of the Association; editorials; pictures and cartoons. The M. P. H. A. News is circulated among the members of the Association.

ASSOCIATION NEWS

Experienced woman laboratory technician who can handle Malaria, Hookworm, Intestinal parasites, Diphtheria, Widal, smear test for Gonorrhea, Rabies, and Milk, both bacteriological and chemical. Salary about $150 per month. Address 398, W. F. W., care of this Journal, Boston address.

$2,500 a year for recent M. D. who can teach Hygiene and carry on private research in bacteriology or serology. Address 399, G. M. D., care of this Journal, Boston address.

Chief Bacteriologist, Diagnostic Laboratory, Illinois State Department of Public Health. Salary, $2,400 to start, with good prospect of increase the coming year. The degree of M. D. desired but not required. Applicant should have working knowledge of Public Health problems in serology, bacteriology, and microscopical pathology. Position is under Civil Service, temporary appointment to be made immediately, and permanent appointment to depend upon ability to pass Civil Service examination. For further information, address Dr. C. St. Clair Drake, Director, State Department Public Health, Springfield, Illinois.

Wanted: Two assistant sanitary engineers for the Sanitary Engineering Division of the State Department of Health. Salaries ranging from $1,800 to $2,500 to start. Recent graduates with sanitary engineering training can qualify. For additional information, address E. S. Tisdale, Director and Chief Engineer, West Virginia State Department of Health, Charleston, W. Va.

School of Public Health desires woman bacteriologist to take charge of Public Health Laboratory and assist in teaching, full time position. Salary $1,800 as minimum, depending on qualifications. State fully age and experience. Address 406,

H. A. R., care of this Journal, Boston address.

Wanted: Public Health Nurses for American Red Cross Chapter in Michigan. Address 140 North Saginaw Street, Pontiac, Michigan.

Supervising nurse, Protestant faith, who has had course in public health nursing, and is capable of handling some phases of pioneer work. Must be qualified to handle staff of five nurses. Organization comparatively new. Salary $150 per month. Address 377, J. G., care of this Journal, Boston address.

Woman laboratory worker for health department of town of 30,000 near New York. Usual culture work and milk and water analysis. Address 408, L. B. H., care of this Journal, Boston address, stating experience, salary expected, etc.

Wanted: An experienced laboratory technician. Applicants should give in first letter a detailed account of their experience in laboratory work and state salary expected. Address 410, V. H. C., care of this Journal, Boston address.

Full time county health officer in West Virginia; population approximately 45,000; salary, $3,000 and travel expenses. Address Director, Rural Sanitation, State Department of Health, Charleston, W. Va.

✦

Am at liberty to accept position as health officer or to do general sanitary and publicity work about October 1. Now have the rank of Major in Reserve Corp and commission in public health service as P. A. Surgeon. Further details by correspondence. Address 128, W. W. E., care of this Journal, Boston address.

Sanitary adviser for a food products company desires a change. Can show experience in municipal and industrial sanitation; licensed health officer. Further details by correspondence. Salary $2,700. Address 133, G. J., care of this Journal, Boston, address.

Young woman graduate of a teachers' college, B. S. degree, with five years' experience in public health laboratory work (two as director of a city laboratory), would like a position in public health education, or an executive position in a health department. Has had some experience in public speaking. Present salary $2,800. Further details on request. Address 131, S. P. M., care of this Journal, Boston address.

Captain, Construction Division, U. S. Army, about to be discharged, desires position in Public Health work, or as Supt. of Water Works or Sewage Plant. Have B. S. in chemistry and D. V. M., with 13 years experience in laboratory work; Milk and Meat Inspection work; Supt. of Water and Sewage Plants. Address 130 P. R. C., care of this Journal, Boston address.

Licensed Health Officer and Camp Sanitary Inspector of the U. S. Army about to sever connections with the army is anxious to make connections with large industrial corporation, Health Commission of city, progressive town or Sanitary Officer of steamship line. Is graduate physician and surgeon of fifteen years' experience; licensed to practice in New York, New Jersey and Massachusetts. Would be willing to travel in the United States or foreign countries. Address Dundas R. Campbell Major, Medical Corps, Camp Devens, Mass.

Wanted: Administrative and medical work in public health or municipal hospital in locality desiring progressive development of municipal health facilities. Qualifications: 2½ years' experience in municipal hospital and health administration; licensed under Pennsylvania State Board, and National Board of Medical Examiners; good references. Address: 134, B. L. H., care of this Journal, Boston address.

Woman of maturity, now assistant bacteriologist in a large health laboratory, desires a change. Would like serology and microscopic diagnosis for a venereal clinic, hospital, or group of physicians. Reliable Wassermann routine. Address 135, H. B., care of this Journal, Boston address.

□

NEWLY ELECTED OFFICERS

At the San Francisco meeting of the Association, on September 15, 1920, the following officers of the A. P. H. A., to serve during the ensuing year, were elected:

President, Dr. M. P. Ravenel, Columbia, Mo.

First vice-president, Dr. T. B. Beatty, Salt Lake City, Utah.

Second vice-president, Dr. L. I. Dublin, New York City.

Third vice-president, Dr. W. C. Hassler, San Francisco, Cal.

Secretary, Mr. A. W. Hedrich, Boston, Mass.

Treasurer, Dr. Roger I. Lee, Cambridge, Mass.

The Executive Committee remains unchanged, the elected members whose terms expire this year being reelected; Dr. Bryce to fill the unexpired term of Dr. Ravenel, who becomes a member *ex officio*, and the others with terms expiring in 1923. The Committee now stands: Dr. M. P. Ravenel (1921), Dr. Roger I. Lee (1921), A. W. Hedrich (1921), Dr. W. A. Evans (1921),

Dr. A. J. McLaughlin (1921), Dr. Peter H. Bryce (1922), Lee K. Frankel, Ph. D., (1922), Dr. W. S. Rankin (1923), Dr. Charles J. Hastings (1923).

The Section officers are the following:

1. **Health Administration Section —** Chairman: Dr. Francis G. Curtis, West Newton, Mass.; Vice-Chairman: Dr. H. F. Vaughan, Detroit, Mich.; Secretary: Dr. W. H. Kellogg, Berkeley, Cal.; Rep. to B. D.: Dr. E. C. Levy, Richmond, Va.; Executive Committee: Dr. G. A. Jordan, St. Louis, Mo.; Dr. M. S. Fraser, Winnipeg, Man.

2. **Industrial Hygiene Section**—Chairman: Dr. A. J. Lanza, Cleveland, O.; Vice-Chairman: Dr. Philip King Brown, San Francisco, Cal.; Secretary: Dr. W. A. Sawyer, Rochester, N. Y.; Rep. to B. D.: Dr. J. W. Schreschewsky, Washington, D. C.

3. **Sociological Section**—Chairman: Dr. W. H. Brown, Washington, D. C.; Vice-Chairman: P. S. Platt, C. P. H., New Haven, Conn.; Secretary: R. Justin Miller, San Francisco, Cal.; Rep. to B. D.: Dr. Ira S Wile, New York City.

4. Food and Drugs Section—Chairman: John P. Street, Indianapolis, Ind.; Vice-Chairman: R. E. Doolittle, Chicago, Ill.; Secretary: Prof. James O. Jordan, Boston, Mass.; Rep. to B. D.: Prof. James O. Jordan, Boston, Mass.; Cor. Secy.: C. H. Lawall, Philadelphia, Pa.

5. Laboratory Section—Chairman: Dr. R. G. Perkins, Cleveland, O.; Vice-Chairman: Dr. B. L. Arms, Jacksonville, Fla.; Secretary: A. P. Hitchens, Washington, D. C.; Rep. to B. D.: Dr. W. H. Kellogg, Berkeley, Cal.

6. Vital Statistics Section—Chairman: Dr. Henry B. Hemenway, Springfield, Ill.; Vice-Chairman: Dr. R. W. Hall, Jackson, Miss.; Secretary: Wm. F. Petrie, Lansing, Mich.; Rep. to B. D.: Dr. L. I. Dublin, New York City.

7. Sanitary Engineering Section—Chairman: S. A. Greeley, Chicago, Ill.; Vice-Chairman: Theodore Horton, Albany, N. Y.; Secretary: E. D. Rich, Lansing, Mich.; Rep. to B. D.: Robert Spurr Weston, Boston, Mass.

□

LIST OF NEW MEMBERS
Proposed for Election to the

A. P. H. A.
September 8 to October 9, 1920, inclusive.

Names of Sponsors are set in **Bold Face Type.**
Names of New Members are in Light Face Type.

ALABAMA
C. H. Kibbey, M. D., Fairfield.
　James A. Grimes, Divisional Sanitary Inspector, Ensley.

CALIFORNIA
Margaret Beattie, Berkeley.
　Adriana Jongeneel, San Rafael.
M. Dorothy Beck, Berkeley.
　Alice Potter, Berkeley.
Prof. Edith S. Bryan, Berkeley.
　Helen J. Dahl, R. N., Sebastopol.
　Agnes Bryant, Public Health Nurse, Berkeley.
　Mollie E. Johnson, R. N., San Francisco.
　Alma B. Shaffer, R. N., Berkeley.
John N. Force, M. D., Berkeley.
　Kathryn LeHane, Berkeley.
W. H. Kellogg, M. D., Berkeley.
　John N. Force, M. D., Berkeley.
F. L. Rogers, M. D., Long Beach.
　Albert de Ruiz, Long Beach.
R. L. Taylor, M. D., Long Beach.
　Alice Kimball, City Bacteriologist, Long Beach.
L. M. Powers, M. D., Los Angeles.
　J. F. Bushong, V. M. D., City Veterinarian, Los Angeles.
　Arthur M. Rogers, M. D., Los Angeles.
Kirby Smith, M. D., Oakland.
　E. E. Curtis, Navy Yard, Mare Island.
W. M. Dickie, M. D., Sacramento.
　George A. Broughton, M. D., City Health Officer, Oxnard.
Milton J. Ferguson, Sacramento.
　Sarah S. Oddie, Librarian A. L. A., San Francisco.
Allen F. Gillihan, M. D., Sacramento.
　Pearl Chase, Social Service, Santa Barbara.
　Ada May Jessen, R. N., P. H. Nurse, Cherry Way.
　Alice J. Liles, R. N., P. H. Nurse, Watsonville.
　William J. Norris, M. D., Prescott, Ariz.
F. F. Gundrum, M. D., Sacramento.
　Gustave Wilson, M. D., Sacramento.
Gus F. Jones, Sacramento.
　Olga Bridgman, M. D., San Francisco.
　Frederick Wm. Browning, M. D., Health Officer, Hayward.
　C. F. Metcalf, M. D., So. Pasadena.
Ida M. Thiele, R. N., Sacramento.
　R. W. Wilcox, M. D., Long Beach.
State Board of Health, Sacramento.
　George Parrish, M. D., Health Commissioner, Portland, Ore.

Philip K. Brown, M. D., San Francisco.
　Mary J. Mentzer, M. D., San Francisco.
Mary L. Cole, San Francisco.
　Edna J. Shirpser, Children's Hospital, San Francisco.
Wm. C. Hassler, M. D., San Francisco.
　W. T. Cummins, M. D., San Francisco.
　Celestine J. Sullivan, San Francisco.
　W. T. McArthur, M. D., Los Angeles.
Johanna E. Tow, M. D., San Francisco.
　Caroline EVers, San Francisco.
A. W. Hedrich, Boston, Mass.
　Reba L. Dobson, R. N., Livermore.
　Allen H. Williams, M. D., Santa Barbara.
　Bertha Wright, Berkeley.

CONNECTICUT
David Greenberg, New Haven.
　Florence M. Redfield, R. N., New Haven.
E. Louise Smellie, New Haven.
　James D. McGaughey, M. D., U. S. P. H. S., Wallingford.
Irving L. Hamant, M. D.
　Helen H. Jenkins, Exec. Comm. N. O. P. H. Nursing, Norfolk.

FLORIDA
Ralph N. Greene, M. D., Jacksonville.
　John A. Graham, Bradentown.

IDAHO
E. R. Dooley, Twin Falls.
　Bert T. Barr, Deputy State Food Inspector, St. Anthony.
　C. W. Dill, M. D., Shoshone.

ILLINOIS
H. Bundesen, M. D., Chicago.
　Clara Jacobson, M. D., Chicago.
Sarah M. Hobson, Chicago.
　Rhoda P. Barstow, M. D., Chicago.
H. C. Merker, M. D., Chicago.
　Samuel J. McNeill, M. D., Chicago.
Langdon Pearse, Chicago.
　Floyd W. Mohlman, Ph. D., Chemist, Sanitary District of Chicago.
C. F. Shronts, M. D., Momence.
　O. N. Carr, M. D., Grant Park.
C. St. Clair Drake, M. D., Springfield.
　R. Edman Greenfield, Bacteriologist, State Water Survey, Urbana.
J. Howard Beard, M. D., Urbana.
　Gertrude E. Moulton, Urbana.
Lethe E. Morrison, Urbana.
　Acelia M. Leach, U. of Ill., Urbana.

A. W. Hedrich, Boston, Mass.
   W.·O. Manion, M. D., Chicago.
INDIANA
J. N. Hurty, M. D., Indianapolis.
   John H. Hewitt, M. D., V.-P., State Board of Health, Terre Haute.
Claude Dallene, M. D., Oölitic.
   John A. Rowe, Chairman, Lawrence Co., A. R. C., Bedford.
IOWA
A. W. Hedrich, Boston, Mass.
   J. B. Heefner, M. D., State Board of Health, Des Moines.
   Iowa State College Library, Ames.
   Edwin H. Sands, Housing Commissioner, Des Moines.
KANSAS
S. J. Crumbine, M. D., Topeka.
   Kenneth F. Maxey, M. D., Director, State Public Health Laboratory, Topeka.
A. W. Hedrich, Boston, Mass.
   F. L. Loveland, M. D., Topeka.
MAINE
C. F. Kendall, M. D., Biddeford.
   Henry W. Owen, Saco.
MARYLAND AND DISTRICT OF COLUMBIA
Roscoe C. Brown, M. D., Washington.
   Aldrich R. Burton, M. D., U. S. P. H. S., Washington.
Mrs. Francis K. Carey, Baltimore.
   Mrs. George H. Cook, Baltimore.
   J. Harris McDowell, Baltimore.
   Mrs. Donald Symington, Garrison.
H. C. Cumming, Surgeon General, Washington.
   Reynolds Hayden, Commander, M. C., U. S. N., Washington.
Col. J. F. Siler, Washington.
   Major James E. Baylis, M. D., Cambridge, Mass.
James A. Tobey, Washington.
   Harry Wilkinson, A., R. C., San Francisco, Cal.
MASSACHUSETTS
Mildred Ashley, Boston.
   Eva M. Lord, R. N., Forge Village.
A. W. Hedrich, Boston.
   Elinor Reilly, Farmingham.
   H. R. Anders, Lowell.
   Eva B. Southwick, Waban.
W. G. Ward, Brookline.
   Albert F. Noble, Somerville.
MICHIGAN
W. C. Hirn, Lansing.
   Donald M. Hatch, Wyandotte.
MINNESOTA
A. W. Hedrich, Boston, Mass.
   Abraham H. Kaplan, St. Paul.
MONTANA
J. X. Newman, Missoula.
   F. D. Pease, M. D., City Health Officer, Missoula.
NEBRASKA
Benjamin Bailey, M. D., Lincoln.
   Katharine H. K. Wolfe, M. D., Hygiene Dir., Public Schools, Lincoln.
NEW MEXICO
C. E. Waller, M. D., Santa Fe.
   Margaret Tupper, R. N., Dir. P. H. Nurses, State Board of Health, Santa Fe.
NEW YORK
B. R. Rickards, Albany.
   Oswald T. Avery, M. D., New York City.
   Mrs. Mary C. Carey, R. N., Supt., Hospital for Communicable Diseases, Yonkers.
   L. W. F. Carstein, Long Beach.
   Robert A. Cooke, M. D., New York City.
   Alphonse R. Douchez, M. D., Baltimore, Md.
   R. Henderson, New York City.
   Ward J. MacNeal, M. D., Dir. Labs., N. Y. Post-Graduate Med. School, Forest Hills.
   Onondaga County Tuberculosis Assn., Atten.
   Minnie E. Freeman, Exec. Sec'y, Syracuse.
   Arthur W. Thomas, Ph. D.
   Asst. Prof. of Food Chemistry, Columbia University, New York City.
   Francis C. Wood, M. D., Dir. Cancer Research, Columbia University, New York City.
   Hans Zinsser, M. D., Prof. Bacteriology, Columbia University, New York City.
J. R. Bolton, M. D., Beacon.
   Mrs. Josephine Williams, R. N., Beacon.
John J. Mahoney, M. D., Jamestown.
   G. L. Meads, Dir. Alleghany County Hygienic Lab., Belmont.
LeRoy W. Hubbard, M. D., Mt. Vernon.
   Harriet Thompson, R. N., Patchogue.
Haven Emerson, M. D., New York City.
   Prof. Barbara H. Bartlett, R. N., U. of Washington, Seattle, Wash.

Walter W. R. May, New York City.
   Willard C. Smith, U. S. P. H. S., Washington, D. C.
Lawson Purdy, M. D., New York City.
   Jno. I. D. Bristol, New York City.
A. V. Salomon, M. D., New York City.
   Alta E. Dines, R. N., New York City.
A. W. Hedrich, Boston, Mass.
   Charles F. Powlison, Sec. Nat'l Child Welfare Assn., New York City.
NORTH CAROLINA
E. F. Long, M. D., Raleigh.
   R. V. Yokeley, M. D., County Health Officer, Lexington.
W. S. Rankin, M. D., Raleigh.
   Frederick D. Hopkins, Supervisor of Field Service, N. T. A., New York City.
R. B. Wilson, Raleigh.
   W. B. Otey, Industrial Nurse, Gastonia.
OHIO
Wm. H. Peters, M. D., Cincinnati.
   Wm. N. Lipscomb, M. D., Georgetown, Ky.
Ernest H. Strong, Cleveland.
   Margaret Trevor, Cleveland.
R. E. Miles, Columbus.
   Gardner Lattimer, Columbus.
A. W. Hedrich, Boston, Mass.
   Jane L. Tuttle, Supt., Visiting Nurses' Assn., Columbus.
OKLAHOMA
Ruth Frances Horel, Oklahoma City.
   Mrs. Mary P. Hindman, P. H. N., Berkeley, Cal.
   Miss Louise E. McRoberts, San Francisco, Cal.
   Dorothy Smith, P. H. N., Pomona, Cal.
PENNSYLVANIA
Perkins Boynton, Chester.
   Roy B. Champion, Chester.
D. F. Owen, McKeesport.
   David P. McCune, M. D., McKeesport.
Charles A. Hunter, State College.
   Alton C. Simpson, Penn. State College, State College.
A. B. Farquhar, York.
   Austin M. Grove, M. D., Supt. Public Safety, York.
SOUTH CAROLINA
J. A. Hayne, M. D., Columbia.
   Philip B. Warner, Exec. Sec'y, S. C. Tuberculosis Assn., Columbia.
A. W. Hedrich, Boston, Mass.
   Helen B. Fenton, Columbia.
VERMONT
C. W. Many, M. D., Burlington.
   Nepolian J. Caron, M. D., South Hero.
VIRGINIA
Wm. P. Caton, M. D., Fairfax.
   F. M. Brooks, M. D., Swetnam.
R. A. Martin, M. D., Petersburg.
   J. M. Burke, M. D., Chief Surgeon, S. A. L., Petersburg.
   C. T. Jones, M. D., City Physician, Petersburg.
WASHINGTON
A. W. Hedrich, Boston, Mass.
   Thurston County Anti-Tuberculosis League, Olympia.
WISCONSIN
A. M. Murphy, La Crosse.
   W. A. Henke, M. D., La Crosse.
A. W. Hedrich, Boston, Mass.
   Central Association, Atten. Kate L. Mehlder, Genl. Supt., Racine.
CANADA
Charles J. Hastings, M. D., Toronto, Ont.
   Hamilton C. Cruikshank, M. B., Dir. of Labs., Dept. of Public Health, Toronto, Ont.
   A. Grant Fleming, M. D., Deputy Medical Officer of Health, Toronto, Ont.
   Henry A. Rowland, PhM. B., Sec'y, Dept. of Public Health, Toronto, Ont.
MEXICO
A. Pruneda, M. D., and J. E. Monjaras, Mexico City.
   Gabriel Malda, Pres. Superior Board of Health, Mexico City.
PHILIPPINE ISLANDS
Acting Director of Health, Manila.
   Tirso Coronel, M. D., P. I. Health Service, Indang, Cavite.
Director of Health, Manila.
   Francisco Xavier, L. M., District Health Officer, Cebu.
A. W. Hedrich, Boston, Mass.
   Alfonso Raquel, M. D., District Health Officer, Cagayan, Misamis.
   Bonifacio Mencias, M. D., Medical Officer, P. H. S., Intramuros, Manila.

STORIES FROM THE DAY'S WORK

Brief stories of helpful experience are solicited—EDITOR

Sugar Catches More Flies Than Vinegar.
—This works out well in public health work also.

I find that expressed appreciation of efforts put forth by local health officers gives me bigger and more lasting results by far than the use of authority or the show of power. To illustrate: In the town of X recently, I found that the health officer, though willing, was not getting the results he wanted. The local officials of the town were very slow to give him the proper co-operation, the physicians were negligent in reporting their cases of communicable diseases, and the sanitary conditions of that town were far below the average. By the use of authority and the show of power matters could easily have been made worse. Appreciation expressed of the efforts put forth by the health officer, even though they were unsuccessful, put new life where it was needed. With him I called upon the mayor and several other officials of the town and the physicians, and pointed out the value of up-to-date birth and death records to their citizens, showed them the value of accurate records of communicable diseases in their community, and pointed out the flagrant insanitary conditions which could be easily corrected while appealing to their civic pride—all done in a spirit of co-operation and an appreciation of their local handicaps—with a result that new life has been instilled there and the health officer is beginning to get the good results he wanted.

JOHN A. KAPPELMAN, M.D.,
Health Officer,
Canton, Ohio.

✚

Health Controversy with a College.—A few years ago a young lady came from a Southern state to complete her education in a well known university. She had no friends in the North so she took a room in the ladies' dormitory at the university. The young woman had never been vaccinated and the authorities at the university asked no questions about a little thing like that, although smallpox was somewhat prevalent in various places in the surrounding country.

The young lady student came down with smallpox. A very competent and diplomatic health officer who has since served as surgeon in the English army in France, was detailed to handle the case. He met and overcame some opposition in securing the vaccination of the inmates of the dormitory. The victim was placed in the isolation hospital. All went well until the matron of the dormitory heard that the young lady had recovered and would soon be released from the hospital. She informed me that the Department of Health could not return the lady student to her home at the dormitory, and that we should be obliged to find some other place for her, even although she had paid her tuition, had secured a room at the dormitory and this was her only home. While in Chicago attending school she had placed herself under the care of the university and was going to be thrown on to the street by this philanthropic educational institution.

I explained to the matron that it was an unfortunate attitude to assume towards a homeless and friendless girl who had placed herself in their care. I explained further that she was no possible menace to health when discharged from the hospital. The faculty, however, supported the matron, insisted that some other home be provided, and after some discussion complaint was made to the Health Department demanding my discharge. The commissioner, however, declined to do this, suggesting to the university that it might publish the correspondence if it wished. Finally after a long controversy the university authorities did furnish a room for the student, but outside the college grounds.

If the university authorities had exercised as much zeal in securing the vaccination of students on entrance as they did afterwards in their mistaken policy, this story would not have been written. It is an illustration of the misunderstanding of conditions of disease dissemination not uncommon even among those in high official position.

HEMAN SPALDING, M. D.,
Chief of Bureau of Medical Inspection, Department of Health, Chicago, Ill.

FROM DISTANT COUNTRIES

IMPROVED HANDLING OF FOODS IN BRAZIL

The JOURNAL is indebted to Dr. Alvaro Sanches, Director of Health of Sao Carlos, a suburb of Sao Paulo, Brazil, for a group of photographs showing some of the types of good sanitary work in this populous section of Brazil. The district of which Sao Paulo is the center has a total population

Under the shade of tropical trees the street vendor of sweets and pastry has his wares exposed to all the dust incident to this out-of-door location, together with the handling with perhaps unwashed fingers of the various comestibles. In the second picture there are notable improvements. A glass acse protects the cakes and candy from dirt and other contamination, while the vendor of the wares has been instructed in the use of the fork in place of his fingers. It is rather interesting to see that he apparently has already attracted a better class of customers.

of about 700,000 inhabitants, with two-thirds of them in the principal city itself, and in all of the sections modern health work has been accomplished along most excellent lines. The illustrations might be labeled "Before and after taking," after the style of the old remedies, and certainly indicate remedies that are up to date and valuable.

The boy with his belt of pockets and a narrow-necked bottle in each, closed by an ordinary cork which probably sees service many times, is a type of the old diurnal delivery of milk in this town. It is not so primitive as driving the cow from door to door, but this and a similar method in which the man on horseback had his saddle bags filled with milk bottles, should not find a place in modern milk delivery. Dr. Sanches has effected here a really great improvement. The negro driver of the milk wagon, improved at least to the extent of a coat, and shoes to his feet, now delivers his load of wide-mouthed milk bottles, regularly sealed with the paper disk. Pasteurization is but a step further in the right direction.

The third pair of pictures is one that has its lesson for grocery and provision stores even in the United States. The helter-skelter arrangement of the first, its disorder, its 'exposure of foods, its jumbling of strange and incongruous companions, one does not need to travel to South America to see, but the second picture illustrates the work of the health department in reforming this kind of store. Glass cases now takes the place of the open counters; the goods are snugly packed away in regular order. A cleanly person would feel much more at home in such a store as this than in the one represented in the other picture.

These will serve to illustrate to Northern health officers the excellent work that is being done by their brethren south of the equator.

It should be further said that these improvements are of a type carried out along other lines of sanitation in Brazil, where street improvements, bettered water supplies, and care of sewage go hand in hand with the advances suggested by commerce in the public utilities.

BUILDING REGULATIONS FOR VENEZUELA

Inhabitants of the northern temperate zone are inclined to look askance at sanitary administration lying within the tropics. It is interesting in this connection, therefore, to present some of the tenement house regulations of the Republic of Venezuela. These compare so favorably with those of sections of the United States that it seems well to present them quite in detail. They have been furnished through the courtesy of Dr. L. G. Chacin, Itriago, Director of National Health of Venezuela.

The tenement house is defined as a house or part of a house which is let for apartments or is inhabited by two or more families who live independently, with a common right to the passageways, stairways, courts, baths, etc., and who cook separately in the same house.

The land where a tenement house is built must be firm and dry, and sites that were damp or marshy shall be dried. Land which has been filled in by means of materials subject to decomposition shall be sufficiently disinfected in the judgment of the health officer of the place.

Every building constructed for tenement purposes shall have its principal facade on the street or public way. The rooms intended for sleeping rooms shall be of a size in ratio to the number of persons for whom they are destined, at the rate of 20 cubic metres as a minimum for each person over ten years, and 12 cubic metres for each person under ten years. Under no conditions shall there be admitted a greater number of persons than the house or part of the house can contain according to the present provision. Each house shall have a door with exit to the street or to the court, yard or alley, with an opening of not less than 2.5 metres by 1.2 metres. As a means of ventilation there shall be over each door an opening of equal breadth and at least 30 centimetres in height. This opening may be protected by metal wire or netting which shall not reduce the space for ventilation by more than one-third. Papers and rubbish shall not be permitted to collect in the holes, cracks, or windows of the rooms so as to interfere with the entrance of the light or air.

Article 4 of this sanitary code establishes the following regulations to which tenement houses must conform:

a. There shall be reserved for a court or courts on the lot where the house is built a space of not less in area than 15% of the land built upon. The pavement of the court must be impermeable and inclined sufficiently for drainage. . . . The only cultivation permitted is that of flowers.

b. Where there is a pipe water supply, all the tenement houses must have a provision of water sufficient for the needs of the tenants and for the fulfillment of the provisions of this or other regulations. Where rain water is collected in wells or cisterns, such wells or cisterns must be kept entirely clean and in accordance with all the rules in force or which may be formulated with reference to the extinction of mosquitoes.

c. Where there is a pipe water supply and sewers, every tenement house must have a water-closet for each 15 adults or children over four years. Where they are absent, there shall be built fly-proof and rat-proof latrines arranged according to the provisions in force or passed in the future. In tenement houses of more than one story, there must be a water-closet or latrine for each floor, unless the number of inhabitants of the floor does not reach a specified number. The side occupied by the water-closet or latrine must have one of its sides at least not bounded by any other room; it must have a capacity of at least 25 cu. metres, a height of at least 3 metres, impermeable floors and walls, sufficient light and ventilation, with a window of prescribed size. This room must not communicate directly with the kitchen.

d. All tenement houses must have a shower bath for each 25 persons, on an independent side, with a capacity of not less than 25 cu. metres, a height of not less than 3 metres, impermeable floors and walls, the latter waterproofed to a height of not less than 1.5 metres and in no case communicating directly with the kitchen. In the cases of tenement houses of more than one story there must be a bath on each floor unless the number of inhabitants does not reach the prescribed figure.

895

e. All newly-constructed tenement houses must have an independent space for the kitchen for each apartment. This space must be of a prescribed size, and each kitchen must be provided with a sanitary refrigerator. Cooking outside of the kitchen is forbidden.

Tenement houses of more than one story must be provided with open stairways constructed of fire-proof materials, protected against the weather, and built in such a way as not to obstruct or impede the ventilation of the rooms. Those of three or more floors shall have in addition for each 100 tenants a fire-proof fire escape of a breadth of at least 1.25 metres.

It is forbidden to build in free spaces of the tenement houses or to deposit materials there excepting those which are being used in repairing the houses.

The courts and places of common use such as porches, passageways, stairways, baths, etc., must be kept completely clean.

With reference to the use of rooms in tenement houses it is forbidden to carry on any industry or occupation dangerous or harmful to neighbors; to establish stables or barns; to raise or care for poultry or any kind of animals except cats and birds in cages. Only clothes of the people of the houses can be washed, in a place with impermeable floors and walls, with a sufficient incline of the floors to permit drainage. Where there is no sewer system and the conditions of the land permit, the drainage shall be by means of drains. These must cease being used and be replaced by sewer connections when a sewer system is established where none exists at the present time.

Cases of contagious or reportable diseases must be reported immediately in writing by the owner or the head of the family to the health officer of the municipality. Strict compliance is enjoined to the orders of the health officer with respect to the sick person, his associates, utensils, clothes, etc.

The room or rooms of a tenement house in which persons have resided who were attacked by contagious diseases cannot be inhabited without having been previously disinfected by the health service, and whitewashed or painted by the proprietor, if necessary in the judgment of the health officers. The disinfection shall be within 48 hours following the death or removal of the sick person.

It is not permitted to build, remodel, or rebuild a tenement house unless the plan has been approved by the board of health, which must arrive at a decision within eight days of notification.

Converting some other building into a tenement house must conform to the rules established for tenement houses of new construction. Alterations of this kind cannot be made without the approval of the health officer. Existing tenement houses must be modified as far as possible to conform to the newer regulations, and the health officer has authority to vacate tenement houses that in his opinion would be injurious to the health of the occupants.

Owners of tenements are required to appoint superintendents or janitors satisfactory to the health officer, who shall be responsible for keeping clean the courts, passageways, cisterns, etc., and in good repair the sanitary equipment of these buildings. The tenants are obliged to deposit in a container furnished by the owner of the building all sweepings, fruit skins, household wastes, etc. These cannot be thrown into the courts, yards, passageways, halls, stairways, or other places in common use. Tenants infringing upon this provision either by carelessness or intention, or who cause harm to the sanitary equipment are responsible before the law.

Articles in the sanitary code provide punishment by fines or imprisonment for failure to observe the regulations. Repetition of the offense subjects the offender to double fine.

OHIO PUBLIC HEALTH ASSOCIATION

The Ohio Public Health Association is the new name of the voluntary state-wide health organization in Ohio, which represents the organized efforts of thousands of citizens of the Buckeye commonwealth to promote proper health administration. It was formerly known as the Ohio Society for the Prevention of Tuberculosis and continues to function as the state agency in the national movement for the prevention of the dread white plague.

Objects of the state association are:

1. The promotion of the organization and work of local public health leagues.

2. The dissemination of knowledge concerning the prevention of disease with particular reference to the prevention of tuberculosis.

3. The encouragement and support of organized official work for the prevention of disease.

4. Securing proper legislation for the prevention of disease.

· 5. Encouragement of adequate provision for the prevention of disease by the establishment of hospitals, dispensaries, nursing service of every description and otherwise to do all things and act having as their object the prevention of disease.

6. The study of conditions regarding the prevalence of preventable disease, especially tuberculosis, in the state of Ohio.

The work of the association is educational. It does not undertake to do actual health work and in no way trespasses upon the functions of the official health organization. Its policy is to initiate and demonstrate methods and means for meeting the various public health problems and then pass them over to the official organization for adoption. Under Ohio's new health code it is optional with each community whether it will employ a full time health officer and public health nurses. It is the purpose of the voluntary agency to demonstrate to each community which does not already have adequate health protection, the benefits to be derived, and, to supplement temporarily, where necessary, the work of either the state or local official health machinery. It is recognized that taxation is the fairest way of paying for health protection, but in many localities taxpayers are slow to accept the fact that health is purchasable and that their community is in need of that degree of health protection which all authorities agree can come only through the employment of trained health officers and public health nurses.

State legislatures and county officials who have the appropriation of funds and levying of taxes for health administration are guided by the sentiment of the public in their respective districts. That sentiment must be crystallized and guided by proper organization and education. State and local officials who have the administration of funds for public health are not always in position to secure legislation needed. It is here that the voluntary health agency can step in and help to carry out the program desired.

The past year or two has witnessed the development in Ohio and other agricultural states of strong organizations of farmers and live stock men, prepared to go before the state legislatures and Congress in the interest of crops, swine, cattle and horses. The secret of the success of the Anti-Saloon League of America in its long war against the liquor traffic was in voluntary organization of the "folks back home."

Ohio is building a militant state-wide health organization which will be ready at all times to uphold the hands of state and local health officials and go before the public in the cause of a healthier and happier state.

The State Department of Health welcomes the activities of the voluntary organizations—in fact, is depending upon this co-operation in extending the benefits of the new state health law recently adopted.

The Ohio Public Health Journal, commenting on the phase of the voluntary health organization, says:

"Voluntary health organizations which have rendered such valuable service to many Ohio communities in past years should not consider their work ended with the entrance of the new district health boards into the field. There is still a wide field for the voluntary organization—especially this year, when the new official organization is in its infancy.

"Associations which have been maintaining public health nurses would do well to continue that policy for the present, at least. In this beginning year, with many of the district boards handicapped by shortage of funds, assistance of this kind will fill a great need.

"Each association maintaining a nurse should place her under the full supervision of the official health authority, unless the district board has failed to install an efficient health organization. This union will promote the efficiency of both the official and the unofficial nursing staffs by preventing duplications of effort. The Red Cross has recognized the need of such coöperation by agreeing to place all its public health nurses under the direction of officially constituted health authorities.

"In the work of educating the public both by precept and by demonstration, to a greater appreciation of the benefits to be derived from adequate health protective machinery, the volunteer health organization must continue to play an important part. By encouraging, aiding and supplementing their local health departments and by keeping the cause of health constantly in the public eye, they can help to dispel the lack of interest and lack of information which still exists in many localities. Now that an immediate means of providing adequate health protection is at hand, these educational duties assume an importance greater than ever before.

"Voluntary organizations have done much to raise health standards in Ohio. The still wider field that is opening offers them an opportunity to increase their service to the public."

The Ohio State Medical Association, at its last convention, endorsed the purposes of the association and became affiliated with the Ohio Public Health Association, electing two members of the board trustees to represent the medical profession. The Ohio Hospital Association is likewise represented on the board of the Ohio Public Health Association.

A brief history of the voluntary health organization in Ohio is here given.

In 1901' nearly 20 years ago, those in charge of the State Board of Health recognized the absolute necessity of some form of voluntary organization through which the general public might be aroused to the menace of tuberculosis. Men and women in the state, of recognized influence and willing to take up the crusade against tuberculosis were called in by the State Board of Health and there was formed the Ohio Society for the Prevention of Tuberculosis.

First efforts were directed toward the securing of legislation which would permit the erection of state and county sanatoria for the care of those afflicted with tuberculosis. Through the efforts of this organization these laws were secured and a state sanatorium for the treatment of incipient cases was established in 1914.

Local societies affiliated with the state organization at the same time were busy at home promoting the establishment of county and district hospitals for the treatment and care of tuberculosis, establishment of dispensaries and open-air schools. A number of the county and district hospitals are now prepared to care for advanced cases as well as incipient cases.

The Ohio Society for the Prevention of Tuberculosis also blazed the trail in this state for the establishment of public health nursing service. Today there is hardly a community in the state that does not have a public health nurse, employed either directly under the local official health organization or by some welfare organization.

Since 1911 the voluntary state-wide health activities as well as the work of local societies has been financed wholly from the proceeds of the Red Cross Christmas seals, sold annually under the direction of the National Tuberculosis Association.

Beginning in 1920 the Ohio Public Health Association will carry on the usual campaign for the sale of these seals, but entirely separate from the Red Cross. It is planned to sell in the state more than $200,000 worth of seals. In most instances 80% of this money will remain in the community where it was raised for local public health work.

Local societies are planning their work for the coming year and will go before the public at Christmas time seeking support through the sale of the little seals.

While the fight against tuberculosis is to be continued by the state and local voluntary organizations, the new program of the voluntary agencies in Ohio will be much broader. It is recognized that tuberculosis is a general health problem and, taking a lesson from the strategy of Marshal Foch, which gained him the supreme victory, we shall rearrange our plan of attack and strike all along the line, using all our forces.

Local anti-tuberculosis societies in a number of counties are uniting with other organizations, including child welfare bodies and similar organizations, and forming local public health leagues, affiliated with the state health association.

Demonstrating to the schools of the state the value of teaching school hygiene and health instruction to the school youth is an important branch of the work of the Ohio Public Health Association for the ensuing year. The Modern Health Crusade system, founded by the National Tuberculosis Association, is being introduced in the rural schools of a half dozen counties in the state under the supervision of the Ohio Public Health Association, which employs a state crusade director. The State Department of Public Instruction is coöperating in the movement and, while more or less of an experiment this year, it is expected that this work will ultimately be adopted as a part of the school curriculum.

H. E. ROULFS.

☐

PUBLIC HEALTH NOTES

Abstracts by D. GREENBERG, M. P. HORWOOD, JAMES A. TOBEY and HOMER N. CALVER.

Shall General Hospitals Care for the Tuberculous?—In 1916 the National Tuberculosis Association recommended that general hospitals should admit tuberculosis patients and should provide separate wards for them. Recently this recommendation has received the endorsement of Surgeon General Cumming of the U. S. Public Health Service. The following reasons are given: The provision of such beds would "insure earlier diagnosis, would make possible the training of interns, would popularize treatment in the home climate, would provide convenient facilities for the observation and prompt treatment of patients and would eventually increase the ability of the family physician in making an early diagnosis." It is believed that the next great step in the anti-tuberculosis movement must be to provide adequate hospital facilities with every tuberculosis clinic. This does not mean that a new hospital must be erected with every existing clinic, but that a working relationship will be established between the clinics and existing hospitals.—Modern Hospital, July, 1920. (M. P. H.)

✛

Value of Municipal Dairy Inspection.—Improvement in a milk supply cannot be made by establishing model milk ordinances and conducting laboratory examinations on the milk supply. The important factor is thorough and intelligent farm inspection, at which time the defects in methods or equipment may be demonstrated to the farmer, and means for introducing the necessary improvements clearly shown. It is also important to maintain constant supervision over milk stations and pasteurizing plants through frequent inspections. Bacterial counts may be very important, but they can only supplement farm inspections as a means of improving the milk supply.—C. V. Craster, M. D., American City, August, 1920. (M. P. H.)

✛

Overcoming Growths of Fungi in Tidal Waters.—It is stated that the best method of overcoming growths of fungi resulting from the discharge of sewage farm effluent, drainage water, etc., is to store the discharges in a sufficiently large lagoon to accomplish biological self-purification, which is accomplished ultimately by fish life. Waters so treated will not support growths of fungi. Nothing is stated regarding the possibility of such lagoons becoming nuisances through the accumulation of sludge.—Kolkiwtz & Zahn, Zeit. f. Wasser. u. Abwasser 7, 40. (R. S. W.)

Rôle of the Hospital in the Public Health Campaign.—Hospitals are very different to-day from what they were only a generation ago. The modern hospital may be defined as an institution whose objects are the care and treatment of the physically and mentally ill and injured, the education of patients in hygiene, both personal and public, the clinical training of doctors, nurses and hospital social workers, the advancement of medical science, and the prevention of disease. In the modern public health campaign hospitals are necessary for the care and treatment of contagious diseases, of tuberculosis and venereal diseases; for the education of public health nurses, and also for the education of the patients in the principles of personal hygiene. From 1904, the year when the National Tuberculosis Association was organized, to 1919, the number of tuberculosis hospitals, sanatoria and day camps increased from 111 to 600. Although the number of contagious disease hospitals has increased, there is still a woful shortage. That the hospital can play an important part in the venereal disease campaign is evidenced by the work of Horner of the Boston City Hospital. Of 500 patients examined, 16% had syphilis, although only 2% had been identified by other means than the Wassermann. It is estimated that at least 10% of the population suffer from syphilis, and that 20% to 50% of all males below 40 suffer from gonorrhea. It is evident, therefore, that the hospital can be of invaluable assistance in detecting and treating cases of venereal disease. That the hospitals are beginning to realize their responsibility and duty towards this important phase of the public health campaign is made evident by the report of the U. S. Public Health Service, that 499 venereal disease clinics were in operation at the end of 1919. The great value of the hospital in teaching patients the principles of hygiene is also evident, for the patients are then in an unusually receptive mood. Information concerning food and diet, ventilation, clothing, the need of a proper mental attitude and other phases of personal hygiene can be disseminated with great profit.—Joseph J. Weber, *Modern Hospital*, July, 1920. *(M. P. H.)*

Tuberculosis in Cleveland—A Survey of Immediate Needs.—As part of the health and hospital survey of Cleveland being conducted under the direction of Dr. Haven Emerson, a study of the tuberculosis situation and its needs has been made by Dr. D. B. Armstrong. The study has been quite thorough and it is found that Cleveland has already done much to control tuberculosis. For instance, there is a Bureau of Tuberculosis in the Cleveland Health Department. There are also seven tuberculosis clinics maintained by the same department. The Health Department has a staff of 80 or more general public health nurses, who devote considerable time in finding and treating cases of tuberculosis. About 500 beds are provided in municipal and private institutions for the care of early and advanced cases of tuberculosis among all ages. There is also a very active anti-tuberculosis league that conducts a splendid educational campaign. There is also an excellent organization to control the milk supply and general sanitary conditions, the infant welfare and school health work and the dispensing of relief. Cleveland has been a pioneer in the development of the health center idea. The attendance at the tuberculosis clinics between 1914 and 1918 has been over 61,000. For every death from tuberculosis in 1918, 4.7 active cases of the disease were registered, a ratio which is higher than that in other communities. The death rate from tuberculosis has diminished from 225 per 100,000 population from 1865 to 1869, to 145 per 100,000 population from 1913 to 1917.

In spite of all this excellent work, between 1,000 and 1,200 people die of tuberculosis in Cleveland every year, and there are almost 6,000 known cases of the disease. Dr. Armstrong makes the following recommendations for a more energetic campaign against tuberculosis. It is important that more cases of early tuberculosis should be discovered. Cases of tuberculosis should be reported as soon as the diagnosis is made. Expert medical advisory consultation service on diagnosis and treatment should be established in connection with the health centers. Post-graduate medical training in tuberculosis should be provided in the medical schools. About 450 additional beds for the care of tuberculosis cases should be provided. Patients should be encouraged to remain at the sanatorium until they are either cured or the disease is arrested. About 150 additional public health nurses should be provided to find suspicious cases. There should be a more intensive educational campaign on the dangers of infection, personal hygiene, food hygiene and measures to increase resistance. The anti-spitting ordinance should be enforced and dangerous consumptives should be segregated. There should also be immediate relief to the serious housing problem. A full-time chief in the Bureau of Tuberculosis should be appointed. The work of the Tuberculosis League should be adequately financed, and finally a campaign of industrial hygiene, sanitation and welfare work should be inaugurated as an important measure in the fight against tuberculosis. —*Modern Medicine,* July, 1920. *(M. P. H.)*

✛

Work of the Rockefeller Foundation In 1919.—The following list indicates the extent and splendid quality of the public health work conducted by the Rockefeller Foundation in 39 different governmental areas. Yellow fever control was successfully extended in Ecuador, Nicaragua, Honduras and Salvador. Much progress has been made through coöperative campaigns in the cure and prevention of hookworm in 13 Southern states of the American Union, in seven of the states in Brazil, in five islands of the West Indies, in five countries of Central America, in Ceylon, the Seychelles Islands, China and Queensland. Demonstrations in the control of malaria were continued in Arkansas and Mississippi, and arrangements were made for extending the program to eight other Southern states. The anti-tuberculosis work in France was widened to include 21 departments. A modern medical school was established in Peking. Pre-medical schools were aided in Changsha, Shanghai and Nanking. Medical courses were supported in Tsinanfu. Seventeen hospitals in various parts of China were aided. Help was given towards the support of the Institute of Hygiene in Sao Paulo University in Brazil. The School of Hygiene and Public Health at Johns Hopkins University was entirely supported. Fellowships in Ameri-

can universities were granted to 72 students of medicine and public health from China, Brazil, Salvador, Czecho-Slovakia and the United States.

The work of Dr. Hideyo Noguchi in discovering the apparent cause of yellow fever and the eradication of yellow fever from Guayaquil deserve special mention. Dr. Noguchi showed that the blood from patients in the early stages of yellow fever was infectious for guinea pigs; that the disease could be transferred from one group of guinea pigs to another; that dogs and monkeys could also be infected both by inoculation and by the bite of infected *Stegomyia* mosquitoes. Finally the cause of the disease was isolated from the blood and was found to be a minute, delicate, thread-like spiral organism which was called *Leptospira icteroides.* Noguchi was also able to develop a serum against yellow fever which gives great promise for the future. By means of a well-organized and thorough campaign against the mosquito, consisting of drainage, filling, oiling, screening and the use of minnows to devour *Stegomyia* larvæ, Guayaquil has been freed of yellow fever for the first time since 1842. Not a single new case has developed in Guayaquil since May, 1919. The report abounds in many splendid examples of public health work in many fields and in many countries.—*(M. P. H.)*

✛

Sewage Utilization at Munich.—According to published plans, subsiding basins for sewage have been provided for Munich sewage, and the settled sewage is disposed of on the sandy district to the north of the city. Gradually the barren tract is accumulating valuable arable land. For the reclamation of the tract, the basin sludge mixed with loam is used. Already seventy carloads (German) of this kind of fertilizer are availed of daily. The disposal method can be practiced for a hundred years hence and the Isar be kept clean meanwhile. The editor recommends the method for the consideration of other cities, and remarks upon the happy conditions at Munich.— *Zeit, f. Wasser. u. Abwasser,* 7, 50. *(R. S. W.)*

Council of Child Health Activities.—As a step toward preventing duplication of effort and increasing the effectiveness of health work among children there has just been created the Council of Coördinating Child Health Activities. The founder members are the American Child Hygiene Association, the American Red Cross, the Child Health Association of America, the National Child Labor Committee, and the National Organization for Public Health Nursing. The formal announcement says:

"Organizations for doing health work among children are more and more appreciating the pressing need of correlating their activities. It is felt that not only is there much duplication and, therefore, much waste of effort, but also that many opportunities for developing well-rounded programs for the health of children are thus lost."

The federated organizations have held a number of conferences and have formed the Council, the principal objects of which are:

"1. To define and develop so clearly their own work that each organization will be working in harmony and coöperation with all the others.

"2. To develop new methods which will lead to meeting more effectively some of the special problems still unsolved.

"3. To afford an opportunity for any organization dealing with the health of children to submit its plan and program for suggestions.

"The council will act as an advisory and coördinating agency."—(J. A. T.)

✠

Prevention of Goiter.—The results of a study carried on for a period of 30 months show that simple goiter can be prevented very simply and cheaply. Of 2,190 school children taking 2 grams of sodium iodid twice yearly, only 5 have shown enlargement of the thyroid gland, while of 2,305 children not taking this prophylactic, 495 have shown enlargement of the thyroid. Furthermore, of 1,182 pupils with thyroid gland enlargement at the first examination and who took the prophylactic, 773 thyroids have decreased in size, while of 1,048 pupils with thyroid enlargement who did not take the prophylactic, 145 thyroids have decreased in size.

In the practical application of the preventive treatment, one must keep in mind the three periods when simple thyroid enlargement most commonly occurs: (1) fetal, (2) adolescence, (3) pregnancy. The prevention of goiter in mother and fetus would seem to be a responsibility of the medical profession, supplemented with public education. The prevention of goiter in adolescence should be a public health measure and could be handled in the public schools. Education of the pupils could be combined with the actual administration so that after leaving school they could continue the treatment if necessary. Physicians in industrial medicine could render an important service in this field. The manner and form of administration of the iodin is described in detail.—D. Marine and O. P. Kimball, *Arch. Int. Med.,* June 15, 1920, 661. *(D. G.)*

✠

Organizing for Public Health Emergencies.—The gist of this article is that no community is immune to disaster and that preparations should be considered for such emergencies which might or would present public health problems, as epidemics, floods, fires, explosions, tornadoes, earthquakes and wrecks. The necessity for central authority in time of disaster is cited and an executive having the qualifications of energy, tact, ability and common sense is needed. A survey of local resources should be made and checked up at intervals. Time often means a question of life and death. Experience may be a good teacher, but it would not be gained at the expense of some person or group of persons. Health officials should look ahead and be prepared for any possible contingency.—J. A. Tobey, *Health News,* N. Y. State Department of Health, June, 1920.

✠

Influenza and Pulmonary Tuberculosis.—Further evidence of the part played by epidemic influenza as an exciting cause of clinical tuberculosis is presented by the author in a summary of the replies to a questionnaire sent to the largest sanatoriums in the country. Of 7,871 patients admitted to these institutions from October 1, 1918, to October 1, 1919, 1,170, or 15 percent, were perfectly free, according to their history, from any known clinical tuberculosis prior to the epidemic.—M. F. Sloan, *Amer. Rev. of Tuberculosis,* June, 1920, 262. *(D. G.)*

GRADUATING EXERCISES OF MOTHERCRAFT SUMMER CLASSES

Wherever mothercraft is given a carefully prepared course is followed, and at the close of this essays are written, some of which are read at the graduating exercises. In this picture that is reproduced herewith a little girl may be seen reading her essay, "The Care of Baby." About 350 girls received their diplomas at these exercises in Newton, Mass., at the playgrounds under the supervision of Ernst Hermann.

Similar instruction has been given at several other centers. Typical of the essays that are prepared for these graduations is the following written by Lillian E. Licopola:

The Care of the Baby

What is to be more desired than a healthy, happy baby? What more as we hear it gurgle happily as it clutches some little toy in its chubby fingers. Surely we will help in the noble task of keeping more babies well and happy, for there are really too few babies who have the proper care.

A little baby is like the tender shoot of a plant. To make it blossom well we will have to nourish it well, guard it against its enemy, disease, and let it thrive in a good atmosphere. A good system of home sanitation is very necessary if we want the forces of nature to do their best for us.

The eyes of a baby must be protected because carelessness has blinded many. Bathing should happen often and his dresses must be simple, neat and comfortable. They should not in any way hamper his movements, as a baby should have exercise. Crying is good for the baby because it expands his lungs, but it is not to be indulged in to excess.

A mother should nurse her baby for several important reasons. Breast milk is nature's food for the baby and is fresh, sterile and is always ready at hand. It is the least expensive food that can be given. If a bottle must be used for the baby the best substitute for breast milk is properly modified cow's milk. A physician should direct how it is to be prepared. Such milk should be cared for well and should be delivered in sealed jars, never in open cans.

There are countless other rules for the care of babies and though seemingly trifling and unimportant, they mean very much. If they are followed to the best of our ability we will get our heart's desire—a well and happy baby.

903

Significance of Exposure to Tuberculosis in Infancy.—The author has compared the family histories of 100 patients suffering from pulmonary tuberculosis with the family histories of 100 healthy persons, his object being to find out how many in each class had been exposed to infection from tuberculosis in infancy. Both the tuberculous and the healthy were under the age of 40, but while about 50 of the healthy persons belonged to the same social strata as the tuberculous, the remaining 50 belonged to the professional classes, and consisted of students and nurses. In 51 percent of the patients suffering from pulmonary tuberculosis it was found that there had been exposure to infection within the first fifteen years of life. Only 13 percent of the healthy persons had been thus exposed within the same period. Within the first five years of life 15 percent of the tuberculous had been exposed to infection, whereas only 1 percent of the healthy persons had been thus exposed within the same period. The term "exposure to infection" was confined to cases in which the person concerned had lived in close touch with a coughing consumptive. In the tuberculous class there were 27 cases in which one or other parent had been consumptive, in six cases a brother or sister, in 11 cases some other relation, and in seven cases the child had been in close touch with a consumptive who was no relation. In the healthy class there were three cases in which the parents had been tuberculous, four cases in which a brother, sister or other relative had been tuberculous, and six cases in which the tuberculous "contact" had been no relation. The author concludes that these figures show some relation between exposure to infection in infancy and pulmonary tuberculosis in adult life. But he admits his investigations do not directly show what the nature of this relationship is.—A. Wallgren, *Upsala Läkareforenings Förhandlingar*, 1915, 20, 359, *Tubercle*, April 1920, 327.—(*D. G.*)

✛

Attacking Malnutrition.—The method of attacking malnutrition as carried on by the Association for Improving the Condition of the Poor in New York City, begins with a careful examination of the child by a physician skilled in dealing with children. After any physical defects disclosed by the examination are attended to, the next problem consists in a readjustment of the child's food habits. The latter work is conducted by a group of trained dietitians.

Two groups of children are cared for, children of preschool age and school children. With the latter group nutrition classes are conducted; with the former, intensive work is carried on in the home. In this home work the dietitian carries a small weight chart, and records the losses or gains of the child on each visit. The weighing is done in the home by means of a scale, which combines the qualities of weighing accurately and yet is sufficiently light to be carried readily by the visiting dietitian. In addition to the weighing a record is made of the actual food habits of the child, and these are checked up on each visit.

Revisits to the home are made once a week. This intensive work is continued for a period of sixteen weeks and longer if conditions warrant and if the physician decides that it will be helpful. After the intensive work is discontinued, the home is revisited once a month, the child reweighed and again checked up on its food habits. In this way the child is kept under observation for a period of at least twelve months from the time that it first became a case receiving active attention.

Preliminary results of the work are available. In one group of 62 children 24% gained less than the average expected gain of children of this height and age; and 62% gained more than the average expected gain. The median of actual gain for the entire group was 175% (the average expected gain of normal children of that height and age being 100%). In a second group of 54 children, 13% gained less than the normal expected gain and 87% gained more than the average expected gain. The median for this group was 220%. In a third group of 61 children, 31% gained less than the normal weight, whereas 67% gained more than the normal expected gain.

As a result of the work carried on thus far the author feels that a nutrition class or clinic while very useful in the attack on malnutrition, is only an incidental feature and that the campaign if it is really to be preventive in character must be made on a group of children who are too young for the class method of treatment, and that the chief emphasis must be placed on the home.—B. B. Burritt, *Survey*, June 19, 1920, 405 (*D. G.*)

The School Lunch.—Many school children are required for one reason or another to take their luncheons in school. It is therefore important that the school lunch problem should be handled with as much intelligence as other problems affecting the health and welfare of children. A hot lunch is always preferable to the cold variety, but where the hot lunch is not available the cold should be made as attractive as possible. The container should preferably be of the collapsible kind and made of tin. This is well ventilated and can be readily cleaned. Sometimes tin cracker boxes, paper boxes, or baskets are used. The food should be wrapped in wax paper to prevent drying. Everything should be done to enhance the appearance of the materials in the lunch box so as to make the food attractive. The lunch box should contain, besides the food, paper napkins, paper cups and other paper containers necessary for cooked foods, and a small knife, fork and spoon. Wherever possible a thermos bottle should be used to carry the liquid. The lunch should be well regulated from the dietary standpoint and should be varied from day to day. Most menus must necessarily be restricted to sandwiches, fruit and a dessert. The filling for the sandwiches can, however, be varied considerably. Even the bread itself can be varied from the ordinary white bread to raisin bread, nut bread, brown bread, rolls, biscuits, muffins, and corn bread. The article also suggests numerous foods as possibilities for school luncheons. A. W. Sandwall, *The Commonhealth*, January-February, 1920.—(*M. P. H.*)

✦

Medical Officer vs. the Alphabet.—Although Englishmen are proverbially slow in catching glints of humor, Lord Sands of Edinburgh seems a notable exception. A recent little address in a case of an architect against the War Office shows that the learned judge is quite aware of the absurdities of official red tape and the official custom of designating by letters, which are enigmas to the layman, the different officials and officers. The following from the *Medical Officer* is credited to Lord Sands, and will be appreciated by all who have occasion to wait till the intricacies of regular procedure are straightened out before proceeding to some necessary task. "Even in the throes of a great war," said the judge, "when a medical officer, holding a local command, required the advice of an architect in connection with some suggestion which he desired to submit for sanction, were it only the introduction of a stove, the proper course was that the medical officer in question should communicate his request to the D. D. M. S., who, if he approved, would transmit it to the Q. M. C., who would lay it before the B. G. A., who might instruct the S. O. R. E., who would communicate with the C. R. E., who would detail an engineer officer, if available, to advise the C. M. O. Apparently, if such officer were not available, either the matter must wait or else it must find its way back around the alphabet in order that the D. D. M. S. might be able to transmit to the C. M. O. the B. G. A.'s authority to consult an architect as to whether a stovepipe should be carried through the wall or up the chimney. But we won the war."

✦

Do Calories Measure the Value of Food?—This question is asked by Dr. Henry Dwight Chapin, who arrives at the conclusion that heat measurement alone is not a safe guide for the calculation of food values. Foods that build rather than those that readily undergo oxidation must be properly gauged if we are to have healthy development. Some form of biologic testing of foods must be elaborated if an always reliable gauge of nutrition is to be established.—*Sc. Am.*, March 28, 1920. (*H. N. C.*)

✦

The Cost of Sickness.—According to a computation made after careful investigation by the United States government, the working people of the United States lose every year 270,000,000 working days through sickness. This is equivalent to more than 900,000 years, and in a century to 90,000,000 years.

Consider for a moment the enormous economic waste involved in this loss of time. Basing our estimate upon the present prices of labor, the amount of time lost through sickness reaches an aggregate of more than $1,000,000,000 annually; and nearly all this sickness is due to ignorance and is easily preventable.—*Good Health.*

Health Work of North Carolina Landowners' Association.—Land owners are notable for the skill with which they set forth commercial advantages of their communities, but it has remained for the North Carolina Landowners' Association to add to such activities an educational campaign in hygiene and sanitation. This is to be conducted in eastern North Carolina and will be in the form of free illustrated lectures by Dr. Charles E. Low, formerly Superintendent of Health for Wilmington and New Hanover counties. This is done in coöperation with the State Board of Health.

The need of work is evident from the high typhoid rate in North Carolina. In 1918 there were 568 deaths from that disease in the state. In 1919, through education and law enforcement by the State Board of Health and local health organizations, the number was reduced to 427—approximately 25%. With this encouragement the Landowners' Association is adding its influence to those already at work. The principle upon which this business association undertakes the expenditure of its own funds is that the deaths and sickness due to typhoid in 1918 and 1919 represent an economic loss of $5,000,000 from a preventable disease.

There are only two states in the registration area which have a higher malaria death rate than North Carolina. The immense amount of chronic malaria and consequent physical incapacity is one of the greatest factors in retarding the material development of eastern North Carolina. Hookworm is another debilitating disease common in these warm latitudes.

The free illustrated health lectures will include discussions of the diseases mentioned, and the relation of insects to their transmission, together with the consideration of soil and water pollution, and the necessity of privy sanitation. Undernourishment, faulty diet and the need of a larger and well-cared for milk supply will also be considered.

The State Board of Health acting independently will follow this campaign by one of vaccination against typhoid wherever the coöperation of county commissioners can be obtained.

Problem of the Birth Rate.—The second report of the National Birthrate Commission of England has just appeared. In speaking of the low birth rate of the middle classes it is pointed out that: "The classes which have demonstrated superior capacity for the struggle of life in the past by rising in the social scale have, during the recent past, ceased to contribute anything like their fair share to the nation's capital of men and women." The chief cause of declining birth rates is declared to be voluntary restriction: "Race-suicide has begun. While the practice of restricting the family began with the educated and professional classes, it is gradually spreading through the whole community for reasons which are not far to seek. Child-bearing, nursing, and rearing of children are tedious and full of anxieties, especially if sufficient domestic assistance is not forthcoming. For the middle and upper classes the costs of education are very large and threaten to increase."

The moral question, whether it is permissible in any conditions to restrict the family, is discussed and a somewhat hesitating conclusion in the affirmative reached. But it is pointed out that the refusal to accept the burden of parenthood on unworthy grounds is not only often an evidence of selfishness, but, if it becomes general, will also have as its consequence a slackening of the moral fibre of the nation. To stimulate the birth-rate various suggestions are examined. One is the endowment of motherhood, but it is pointed out in the report that to do this the present yield of income tax would have to be doubled. Another proposal is to take greater care of the unmarried mother and eliminate the enormous mortality of illegitimate children. The compulsory notification of venereal diseases is considered. The report also favors a certificate of health as a legal obligation for persons contemplating marriage, and to prevent irregular unions it declares that State assistance to start young couples on the land in this country, or after emigration, together with State help during pregnancy and the puerperium, would be of great assistance in carefully selected cases.—*Medical Officer*, June 5, 1920, 220, (*D. G.*).

Encephalitis Lethargica.—So much has recently been published in the newspapers about the appearance of sleeping sickness in various parts of Europe, and even of the United States, that the League of Red Cross Societies has deemed it advisable to call attention, through its *Bulletin*, to a few of the striking features of the disease, and to some of the popular misconceptions concerning it.

The name "sleeping sickness" should be applied only to the African sleeping sickness, and because of the difference in origin of the European disease it should be called encephalitis lethargica, the name given to it by Von Economo when he first described it in Vienna in 1917, before which time, although it is probable that the disease had been present in sporadic form, it was not recognized. There have been several outbreaks observed in various European countries and in America.

The disease has been regarded at times as due to food poisoning; as representing an unusual form of poliomyelitis; as related to influenza because it is frequently present in localities wherein influenza is epidemic; or as consequent upon the war because of abnormal physical and mental conditions. Studies seem to show that the disease represents an inflammation of certain portions of the brain and nervous apparatus, and a filterable virus has been obtained from the mucous membrane of the nose and throat of patients dying of the disease, which reproduces in monkeys and rabbits symptoms and lesions similar to those found in human beings. The general belief at the present time is that encephalitis lethargica is an independent disease of infectious origin.

"At the present state of our knowledge," says the *Bulletin*, "it would seem that encephalitis lethargica is met with over a widespread area, but that it is only mildly epidemic, and that it is slightly if at all contagious in the usual acceptance of this word; that individual susceptibility seems to play a distinct role in its incidence and possibly many persons harbor the causative virus or micro-organism, probably in the nose and throat, without showing any symptoms whatsoever; that no causal relationship between it and epidemic influenza has yet been demonstrated; and that its main symptoms are fever, paralysis of certain muscles of the eye, and sleepiness."

Although encephalitis lethargica has been occupying such a prominent position in the press, there is no recognized, specific treatment offering any real hope of cure. This is only to be expected, however, in the case of a disease of which the exact nature and its method of propagation and dissemination is unknown, except that the infection is first localized in the nose and throat. Recent work, however, gives the hope of increased knowledge and a possible and rational cure in the comparatively near future.—*Bulletin*, League of Red Cross Societies.

✛

Sanitary Survey of Rockford, Ill.—In a special bulletin, the Illinois Department of Health publishes the results of a sanitary survey of Rockport, Ill., as conducted by Paul L. Skoog. The estimated population of the city for July 1, 1917, was 56,609. Of the inhabitants about 40 percent were of Scandinavian origin. Twenty-one percent of the entire population was foreign born. The foreign population was made up of Scandinavians, Italians, Poles and Lithuanians. An analysis of the vital statistics showed that births and communicable diseases were not entirely reported. It is estimated that 90 percent of the births are reported. While all the deaths are reported, the death certificates are frequently either inaccurately made out or have certain facts omitted. During 1917 the infant mortality rate was 110 per 1,000 births. The crude death rate during the five years from 1913 to 1917 has varied from a minimum of 10.5 in 1914 to a maximum of 12.9 in 1917.

One of the most commendable forms of health protection in the community is the medical inspection of school children. The Board of Education controls this work and employs a school physician, four nurses and a dentist. The latter is employed on a half-time basis. Approximately 9,000 grade school children get the benefit of the medical service.

Among the recommendations made, the following are important: That the city employ a full-time, well-trained health officer; that the personnel of the health department include an epidemiologist and public health nurses; that a modern contagious disease hospital conveniently located be erected; that the work of the public health laboratory be increased; that an active and extensive campaign for infant welfare be inaugurated; that the health department wage a more vigorous campaign of health education and publicity; that the appropriation for health work be increased to equal that of the police department; that the health department undertake to control several diseases; that other communicable diseases be more adequately controlled; that the use of open privies which is prohibited by-law be abandoned; that fly breeding places be supervised; that all dairies should be required to sterilize effectively all milk bottles and other milk utensils; that all connections between the public supply mains and the factory fire protection systems be abandoned; and that the sewerage system be greatly extended.—(M. P. H.)

✛

Experimental Pellagra.—The authors describe an experiment carried out in a penitentiary to test the possibility of producing pellagra in previously healthy men by feeding a monotonous diet, principally of cereals. The subjects of the experiment were eleven white adult male convicts who volunteered for the purpose. All persons other than the volunteers resident on the farm were under observation as controls—a total of 108. The general sanitary environment was the same for subjects and controls. No direct communication with the outside was permitted the volunteers. There was no special restriction imposed on the controls.

The average food intake by the convict controls varied between 3,500 and 4,500 calories, between 90 and 110 grams of protein, 95 and 135 grams of fat, and between 540 and 580 grams of carbohydrate. Approximately from 20 to 35 percent of the protein was from animal food. The ingredients of the experimental diet were highly milled wheat flour, maize meal and grits, cornstarch, white rice, cane sugar, cane syrup, sweet potatoes, pork fat, cabbage, collards, turnips, turnip greens, coffee, Royal baking powder, salt and pepper. In its essential make-up the experimental diet was probably not entirely typical of the average pellagra producing diet. The average intake by the volunteers varied between 2,500 and 3,500 calories, between 41 and 54 grams of protein, between 91 and 134 grams

of fat, and between 387 and 513 grams of carbohydrate.

After six months of observation none of the controls developed any evidence of pellagra. On the other hand six of the eleven volunteers developed typical evidence of pellagra.—J. Goldberger and G. A. Wheeler, *Arch. Int. Med.*, May, 1920, 451. *(D. G.)*

✛

National Institute of Hygiene.—At the last session of the council of the University of Paris approval was given to an arrangement between M. J. L. Breton, Minister of Hygiene, and Professor Roger, Dean of the medical faculty, acting on behalf of the Minister of Public Instruction. The agreement promises creation by the Minister of Hygiene of a national institute designed for the instruction of students in all matters pertaining to hygiene, for the training of specialists in hygiene and of non-medical technicians, and finally for the development by every possible means of scientific research as applied to hygiene.—*Jour. A. M. A.*, June 5, 1920, p. 1587.

✛

War on Tuberculosis in Europe.—Relentless warfare on tuberculosis which is reaping almost unhindered toll among the undernourished populations of Europe, is advocated by the Medical Advisory Board of the League of Red Cross Societies, whose first annual meeting at Geneva has just ended. Increase in dispensary facilities, establishment of open-air schools for children and special education of the medical profession and the general public regarding tuberculosis are urged. Anti-tuberculosis demonstrations in countries where the disease is prevalent will be made.

In formulating the policy of the league regarding international health improvement and disease prevention, intensive study has been given essential phases of the work by the world's leading medical scientists assembled at Geneva. Besides recommending definite action in the war on tuberculosis, the Medical Board studied plans to combat epidemics, venereal diseases and malaria and suggested measures for the improvement of child health. Immediate organization of a child welfare unit and special training for doctors and nurses by means of scholarships by the league are favored as a beginning for improved health among children.

NOTES FROM FOREIGN LANDS
Translated by Mr. Homer N. Calver

Delivering the Dominician.—One of the benefits of living in a country occupied by the United States is having the advantage of intelligent health regulation that cannot always be laid down for any part of the United States itself. The state Secretary for Health of Santo Domingo is an American Naval Officer. In a letter to the District Sanitary officials of the island he calls attention to the fact that a patent medicine company in New York has started a campaign in Santo Domingo for the sale of its "malaria specific." Instead of merely warning the public against its use he invokes the law and its sale is prohibited. Thus America does for others what she cannot do for herself.—*Bol. Oficial, Rep. Dominicana,* May 30, 1920. *(H. N. C.)*

✛

World-Wide Sanitation.—This is an appropriate subject for a leading article in the first issue of a journal that deals with the International Problems of Public Health. Furthermore, it is a distinct compliment to the sanitary achievement of Americans and at the same time it is eminently fitting that this subject should be set forth by Professor Whipple.

Scientists already can see that world sanitation is not an impossibility. Statesmen and men of business are coming to regard it as a necessity. The new "Age of Power" has brought with it conditions fundamentally affecting the lives and health of people the world over. Modern industry has brought indoor life, monotonous work, low wages, congestion of population, faulty sanitation and bad housing. With improved means of communication has come speedier transmission of disease. World sanitation needs, therefore, to be directed in three main channels: (1) the safeguarding of home life; (2) the safeguarding of industrial life; (3) the prevention of the transmission of disease.

The science of health is one common to the physician and the engineer, applied by the former directly to man through the art of hygiene and by the latter to environment through the art of sanitation. Housing, industrial sanitation, excreta disposal, water purification and world pestilences are fields of endeavor for sanitarians. The attack on the world-wide problems in these fields, however, must be made on a world-wide basis.

The Office International d'Hygiene Publique created at Paris by International agreement in 1907, has creditably fulfilled its function of spreading information. The League of Nations also has established a medical section. There is needed, however, an active central health service. This may be obtained by the coöperation or amalgamation of existing bodies, or if necessary by the organization of some new body.

World-wide sanitation is possible, but it will not come until there are sanitarians in every land and clime. New schools of sanitation must be established in strategic places and there must be a great spreading of the gospel of cleanliness throughout the world.—George C. Whipple, *Int. Jour. Pub. Health,* July, 1920. *(H. N. C.)*

✛

Capillary Differentiation of Bacilli.—An interesting modification of the technique of separating *B. typhosus* from *B. coli* by means of capillary attraction is possible by the use of filter paper. A strip of this is dipped into a solution containing a mixture of these organisms. The paper is then cut into pieces and the pieces seeded in culture media. In the media sown with pieces from the lower end of the strip, *B. coli* will grow. Pieces from the upper end of the strip will contain *B. typhosus* in pure culture.—*Bull. Offi. Int. d'Hygiene Pub.,* February, 1920. *(H. N. C.)*

✛

A Worm Enemy of the Mosquito.—In *La Semana Medica* of Buenos Aires, Lischetti notes some curious observations on a worm of the genus *Planaire.* Six of these worms in four hours were able to destroy 106 Culex mosquito larvæ. After 10 minutes. they renewed the chase against 200 more.

The author describes the method of attack whereby the worm attaches itself to one of the breathing tubes of the larva. The victim is then carried to the bottom of the water and the worm devours the interior of the larva leaving only its chitinous envelope remaining. Adult larvae and pupæ are almost always able to escape the worm.—*Bull. Off. Int. d'Hyg. Pub.,* March, 1920. *(H. N. C.)*

Further Observations on Botanical Mosquito Control.—Public health lays all sciences under tribute. In the May issue of the JOURNAL there was noted the observation made in Corsica that duckweed growing on the surface of pools prevented the growth of the larvæ of the Anopheles. In the *Bulletin of the Royal Spanish Society of Natural History* for October, 1919, Caballero makes an interesting report on the same subject.

In the botanical laboratory of the University of Barcelona there were being grown for purposes of instruction, various acquatic plants in three large aquariums. One day the laboratory was found to be infested by a swarm of Stegomyia and at the same time there were noted in aquariums B and C large numbers of the larvæ of this species. The third aquarium, A, contained no larvæ. Here were growths of *Lemn minor* (duckweed) and *Chara fœtida*. An examination of the outdoor reservoir from which the Chara had been transplanted into aquarium A showed it to be also free from mosquito larvæ though Culex abounded in the vicinity. The author undertook a series of experiments to determine if there really was a relation between the growth of Chara and the development of mosquitoes. He placed an aquarium containing this plant in a place swarming with mosquitoes. In a similar aquarium he placed eggs, larvæ and pupæ of the Stegomyia, Culex and Anopheles. In every case these died more or less rapidly.

It was noted by the Caballero that on the surface of the water in the aquarium in which the Chara was sown there began to form at the end of 24 hours iridescent whitish patches resembling those of a drop of oil. These patches little by little covered the entire surface with a fine continuous light gray film. A similar substance was observed on the surface of the reservoir. It appears without doubt that it is this film, which, preventing the mosquito larvæ from reaching the surface, caused their extinction.

It is not stated just what quantity of Chara is the minimum amount necessary to prevent the development of mosquitoes. It is possible that other varieties of the Characeæ will produce the same result. In any case the hardiness, rapidity of growth and world-wide prevalence of *Chara fœtida* should encourage its introduction into those places that are favorable to mosquito breeding.—*Bull. Off. Int. d'Hyg. Pub.*, March, 1920. (*H. N. C.*)

✦

Serbian Health Centers.—Since the arrival of the American Commission to Serbia at its field headquarters in that country, last October, child welfare and health centers have been established at five strategic points; a preventorium has been opened; another preventorium and a general hospital will be opened in the immediate future, with the assistance of the Ministry of Health and largely at its expense; public health education through the department of extension is contemplated; if funds permit, a campaign against tuberculosis in the districts reached by the centers; and a traveling health center was ready to begin work early in April. If the present campaign for funds in the United States continues successfully, the program of the Commission will be extended to other parts of Jugo-Slavia.—*News Summary*, Children's Bureau, Washington, D. C., June 1, 1920. (*H. N. C.*)

✦

Boundaries of Health.—"We have a very good health officer, we pay him a very good salary, he gives us very good advice, and we take very good care not to follow it." This remark must surely have been made by a town councillor of Nottingham, England, for this town now finds itself in an awkward position for not following the advice of its health officer. Thirty-one years ago when he took office he recommended the abolishment of the dry system of sewerage and advocated the extensive adoption of water carriage. Each year he preached the same sermon, adducing statistics to show the dangers of the prevalent system. This growing city now wants to extend its borders to take in several other districts. The British Ministry of Health however notes that (1) sewage disposal arrangements are totally inadequate (2) no satisfactory explanation is given of why approximately 30,000 pail closets still exist in the city, and (3) 10,000 dwellings in the city are unfit for human habitation, members of the town council themselves being owners of some of these houses. In view of these conditions the Minister of Health does not consider that he would be justified in granting any extension of the present city boundaries.—Editorial, *Medicine Officer*, June 12, 1920. (*H. N. C.*)

✦

Sanitary Science in China.—Several years have elapsed since China first rubbed her drowsy eyes and awoke from several centuries of lethargic sleep. It is not surprising therefore to find that the Chinese Republic has accepted along with other western standards, the modern methods of teaching medicine and the principles of sanitary science and public health. In the calendar of preventive medicine, nine years is not reckoned a very long time in which to put into effect new series of measures that will eradicate disease-producing conditions that have existed for hundreds of years. Great credit is therefore due the new government for the progressive way in which it has, with outside aid, notably that of the Rockefeller Foundation, instituted modern methods of disease prevention and control. Numerous hospitals and medical schools have been established and the Tsinanfu Institute is a unique school for the propagation of hygienic ideas among the masses. A committee on terminology has been appointed to determine the terms to be used throughout China.

Dr. Peter's work as a secretary of the Joint Council of Public Health Education has already been described in this country. By means of traveling exhibits, movies, lantern slides, etc., the vast ignorant mass of Chinese are being taught the modern principles of hygiene and sanitation.—W. L. Teh, *Lancet*, May 29, 1920. (*H. N. C.*)

◻

CONVENTIONS, CONFERENCES, MEETINGS

November 4-5, Carbondale, Ill.—Southern Illinois Medical Association.

November 8-11, Louisville, Ky.—Southern Medical Association.

November 10-12, Atlanta, Ga. — National Drainage Congress.

November 13, Boston, Mass.—Massachusetts Society for Social Hygiene, Inc.

November 15, Louisville, Ky.—American Association of Medical Milk Commissioners.

November 18, Twin Cities, Minn.—Minnesota Public Health Association.

November 20-23, San Antonio, Tex.—Texas State Conference Social Welfare.

November 22, Washington, D. C.—Association for the Prevention of Tuberculosis of the District of Columbia.

November 24-29, Chicago, Ill.—Health and Sanitation Exposition.

December 2, Providence, R. I.— Rhode Island Medical Society.

December 6, Petersburg, Va.—Medical Society of Virginia.

December 6-11, Washington, D. C.—All-American Conference on Venereal Diseases. First Regional Health Conference. See advertisement, page xx.

December 6-30, Washington, D. C.—Regional Health Conference.

December 12-20, Montevideo, Uruguay—Sixth International Sanitary Conference of the American Republics.

December 14-16—Hot Springs, Va.—Southern Surgical Association.

December 22-26, New York City—American Dietetic Association.

December 27, Richmond, Va.—Virginia Health Officers' Association.

December 27, Richmond Va.—Virginia Conference of Health Workers.

December 27-January 1, Chicago, Ill.—American Association for the Advancement of Science.

December 29, San Francisco, Cal.—League for Conservation of Public Health.

December 30, Chicago, Ill.—Physiological Society.

January —, 1921, Boston, Mass.—Massachusetts Society for Mental Hygiene.

January 11, ——, Neb.—Nebraska State Nurses Association.

January 17-21, Atlantic City, N. J.—National Canners' Association.

January 27, Boston, Mass.—Massachusetts Association of Boards of Health.

STATE HEALTH NOTES—GENERAL

Alabama.—In his special message to the extra session of the Legislature the Governor of Alabama took occasion to report on the activities of the State Board of Health in the interests of an appropriation for its use. He noted that there had been a complete reorganization and that the Board had been able to handle its appropriation in such a way as to more than double the amount expended under its supervision. These are some of Governor Kilby's statements:

The Bureau of Statistics promises to place Alabama in the registration area within the coming year. Great progress has, been made in the control of communicable diseases. Practically every public water supply furnishing water to centers of population has been inspected and such improvements made as were necessary for the protection of the public health. A number of insanitary eating houses and lunch stands have been closed and others have been required to be made sanitary. Several thousand school children have been examined and the defects in several hundred have been remedied. Successful operations for mosquito control and anti-malarial work have been conducted in a number of communities.

There have been a number of free antityphoid treatments administered for the prevention of typhoid fever, and 1,000 free treatments are now distributed weekly to the several health officers. Midwives in every county in the state except 12 have been examined and furnished with sanitary kits containing sterile dressings for the baby and mother and a solution of nitrate of silver to be dropped into the eyes of infants immediately after birth for the prevention of blindness. The organizing of counties into health units goes on apace. The greatest obstacle is found in the scarcity of trained men to fill the office of county health officer. The public health nursing activities of the Red Cross and the Anti-tuberculosis League of Alabama have been coördinated with the State Bureau of Infant Hygiene and Public Health Nursing. The work of this bureau has found expression in infant welfare clinics, the weighing and measuring of babies and giving advice to mothers. The 15 child-caring institutions of the state have been visited and a report of the findings has been sent to the superintendents of the institutions, with proper recommendations.

"Your especial attention is directed to the work of the Bureau of Venereal Disease Control," said Governor Kilby, in taking up what is a most important portion of the work of the State Board. "These diseases are striking at the very foundation of our social system and their control is the imperative call of the hour. The Board of Health has had to fight every step of the way in the administration of this law. It has met resistance in unexpected quarters and recently has had a fight in the courts." It appears that 55 of the counties, or 85% of the population, have either free or coöperative clinics. A computation in dollars and cents of the work of this bureau alone will demonstrate the magnitude of the dividends paid on money invested in public health work.

The laboratory has continued its work and maintained its position of usefulness despite inadequate facilities. Nearly 3,500 persons have received antirabic treatment, with only four deaths, while in the same time 23 persons who were untreated died from the disease, and this is testimony to the value of the department, which, in addition, has discovered and treated numerous cases suffering with other communicable diseases. "With the expansion of the work of the Health Department," said the Governor, the Laboratory becomes more and more a necessity. A modern building with modern equipment would seem to be an imperative need." In conclusion Governor Kilby congratulated the state that while bubonic plague has made its appearance in every other important port along the Gulf of Mexico, the port of Mobile has been protected.

One of the results of the spirited presentation of conditions by the executive was the introduction of a bill, passed by the Senate and now before the House, appropriating $35,000 for the erection of a new laboratory building for the State Board.

A round table meeting of all the heads of departments in the Alabama State Board of Health was convened on September 4 to formulate coördinated plans for the department as a whole.

Colorado.—Three of the four first place winners in the International Mine Rescue and Safety First meet at Denver, Colo., September 9-11, were of Eastern teams. First place in the first aid contests was won by the New River Company, Captain Louis Roncaglione, of Scarbro, W. Va. First place in the mine rescue contests was won by the H. C. Frick Coke Company of Leisenring, Pa., Captain S. Cominsky. First place in resuscitation work was won by the team from the Knox County Operators' Association, Captain John Moore, Bicknell, Ind. The fourth team to win first place was from the Wadge Mine of the Victor American Coal Company, Denver, Colo., Captain Robert Halbert, and its victory was on a combination of mine rescue and first aid work.

There were 85 teams in competition and on Saturday evening, September 11, all of the contestants assembled to listen to addresses and to witness the bestowal of gold medals and diplomas.

✛

Georgia.—Dr. Gordon T. Crozier has been elected Commissioner of Health of Lowndes County, Valdosta, Georgia, to succeed Dr. J. D. Applewhite, resigned. Dr. D. H. Allen, Jr., has been elected Commissioner of Health of Baldwin County, Milledgeville, Georgia. The School of Public Health and Hygiene of the Medical Department of the University of Georgia opened for its first session on September 15.

✛

Maine.—Six centenarians died in Maine last year, this being somewhat larger than the average number, three women, one of them, Mary Goddard, having an age of 108 and three men, two of them having touched the mark of 102 years. The largest number of persons of more than one hundred years of age to die in a single year was 12 in 1916, while in 1911 there were 9 and in 1903 and 1912 the number was 8; 110 to 113 is occasionally touched by these very old people.

Maine had in 1919 fewer births and fewer deaths than at any time before within the past 15 years. There were 1,085 fewer births recorded than in 1918 and 3,268 deaths less, so that on the whole there has been a gain in population. Marriages and divorces were in 1919 at a maximum, there being one divorce for every six marriages.

In 12 out of the 20 cities of Maine the infant mortality was lowered last year, Waterville showing a figure of 62 per thousand births against 129 the preceding year; Bangor reduced the figure from 117 to 67 and Portland from 83 to 67.

Maine has established a rating for summer resort hotels, giving a state certificate to those with satisfactory sanitation. These certificates indicate a clean bill of health, and the display of them is an assurance to the guests of healthfulness and care. "The work of the Health Department in hotel inspection is attracting favorable comment in such prominent magazines as the Literary Digest and the publicity thus obtained is proclaiming Maine a safe vacation land," says Dr. L. D. Bristol, Commissioner of Health.

✛

Massachusetts.—Mothercraft, the regular teaching of school children the elements of home-making and of the care of babies, flourishes in the state of its origin into many other places into which it has been introduced. Forty-one Massachusetts cities have had regular classes during the past year and 12 others have plans settled to begin the work. About 1,500 girls have been in these classes which have had the aid and support of prominent women's organizations in the state.

During the past twelve months inquiries have come from 32 states concerning the plan for the education of school girls in health and the care of babies. That the Massachusetts plan for establishing this kind of instruction is extending beyond the confines of our own country is shown by the inquiries that have been received from England, Norway, Sicily, France and Australia. The Victorian Order of Nurses in Canada became interested in the work and have established this instruction throughout the Dominion with the enthusiastic approval of the government authorities and the school officials.

✛

Michigan.—A search for all probable cases of tuberculosis among Michigan's ex-soldiers is now being made by the 4,500 physicians within the state.

Under the direction of Dr. R. M. Olin,

Commissioner of the Michigan Department of Health, letters were mailed to every physician in the state asking that each report to the department any case where an ex-service man is known to be suffering from tuberculosis, organic disease, or mental derangement.

The present combing of Michigan for known, or suspected, sufferers with tuberculosis, is one of the many steps to be made by the department, in an effort to control the disease, since taking over the clinics of the Anti-Tuberculosis organization July 1. It is said to mark the inauguration of the department's active fight against tuberculosis in Michigan.

The answer to the question whether gas cases are certain to develop tuberculosis is now being sought by Dr. George H. Ramsey, who is in charge of the tuberculosis clinics of the Department of Health. The present opinion is, however, that while gas may have made the lungs of the soldiers more susceptible to tubercule bacilli, development of the disease is not inevitable. From his experience over-seas Dr. Ramsey is thoroughly familiar with the immediate effects of gas upon its victims.

A municipal Infant Welfare clinic has recently been organized in Pontiac, Mich., under the direction of Dr. C. A. Neafie, health officer.

Deaths attributable to alcoholism amounted to 15 in 1919, according to the annual report of the Detroit Department of Health. This is the lowest since 1914. In 1917 there were 136 deaths charged to this cause.

Detroit reports that the Health Department nurses, during October, November and December, 1919, discovered in the homes of children absent from school 21 cases of scarlet fever, 13 of diphtheria, 26 of whooping cough, 133 of measles, 45 of chicken-pox, and 2 of mumps. The majority of these cases would never have come to the attention of the Health Department had not the school nurses been on duty.

Eighty-eight per cent of school children are in need of corrective dental treatment according to the report of the Detroit authorities.

There are 12 baby clinics scattered over Detroit. Eight are maintained wholly by the Health Department. With four the department joins hands with other organizations in a coöperative effort. The department, through its field nurses and its clinics, sees about 5,000 of the annual baby crop of 25,000.

✦

New Jersey.—This state is suffering for the need of nurses. Public health work everywhere is being retarded by the shortage of nurses; public sentiment and public money in many places are ready, but workers are needed. In New Jersey, particularly, the chief need for the progress of child hygiene teaching under the State Department of Health is the need for nurses; nurses who are willing to go into rural communities; nurses who love babies enough and see into the future where they can visualize healthier and better boys and girls, because of the work done by them, when those boys and girls were babies and their mothers were ignorant of the value of mother-craft as it is taught by the Bureau of Child Hygiene.

✦

New Mexico.—H. F. Gray, chief of the Division of Sanitary Engineering and Sanitation, has made inspections of public water supplies at Orogrande, Alamogordo, Carrizozo, Socorro and Estancia. He has been appointed Collaborating Sanitary Engineer by the surgeon general of the U. S. Public Health Service, for the coöperative certification of water supplies used by interstate carriers.

✦

New York.—At the request of the Public Health Council the Engineering Division of the State Health Department is making a sanitary survey of the Palisades Interstate Park. This park, which is some 36,000 acres in extent, lies between the Palisades and the Ramapo Mountains, extending over into New Jersey. It is controlled by a joint commission and supported by funds from the two states. There are about sixty public camps within the reservations, with boats and camp equipment, and these are rented to responsible organizations. In addition permits are issued for individual camps. Each of the permanent camps is supplied with water and with sewerage facilities. The survey will include detailed studies of sanitary conditions at all the camps.

The Engineering Division is also looking into the sanitary conditions of county fairs, with reference to water supplies, sewage disposal and garbage and refuse disposal and toilet facilities. The authorities in charge of the fairs will be advised with reference to proper methods of procedure and it is intended to remove many of the sources of dissatisfaction at the grounds of the fairs.

The incidence of anterior poliomyelitis in New York state, exclusive of New York City, has been the following:

	Cases
January to July	10
July	4
August	6
September (1-22)	9
	—
	29

While this number of cases is not abnormal and should cause no apprehension, the sharp rise in the number of cases reported in the eastern part of Massachusetts during the summer months makes it advisable for every health officer to be on the alert. The New York City Department of Health states that there has been no unusual incidence of poliomyelitis, 43 cases and three deaths being the toll of this disease since January 1.

Seventy-nine cases of typhoid developing at Seneca Falls have apparently been due to the contamination of the village water supply from an infected private water supply through a leaky automatic check valve. How many typhoid epidemics must occur before managers of industrial concerns will learn that single automatic check valves can not be depended upon?

Health officers are urged by the New York authorities to investigate all private industrial water supplies in their district where the water is of questionable quality. Where single automatic check valves are discovered the manufacturer in question should be urged to completely sever all connection between the public and private supplies or to install a double check valve in accordance with the recommendations of the Engineering Division of the State Department of Health, which may be obtained on application. The *Journal* has discussed this subject. See *Public Water Supply Contaminated by an Interconnected Private Water Supply*, September, 1920, issue.

The following health district consolidations have recently been ordered: Montgomery County: town of Palatine, Palatine Bridge and village of Nelliston; Jefferson County: town of Housfield and village of Sacket Harbor.

✛

Correction.—On page 814 of the October *Journal* it is stated that the Health Bureau of Albany, N. Y., has been made a separate department under Dr. Clarence W. Buckmaster. This should refer to Yonkers and not to Albany.

✛

New York City.—Fifty-one dental clinics in Manhattan are giving their services to the public free or at nominal charges, according to a directory of dental clinics which is being published by the Health Service Department of New York County Chapter American Red Cross. Eleven of these clinics specialize in work for children.

The directory is the result of a canvass recently made by the Health Service Department, and gives location and office hours of each clinic; the type of work done, whether general, surgical or X-ray; the character of the charge, if nominal; and the agency conducting the clinic.

It is to be distributed generally among day nurseries, settlement houses and other public health and social agencies where dental information will reach the largest number of people.

More than 275 inquiries on health subjects were received during July alone by the Health Information Bureau of New York Chapter American Red Cross, according to a report of the bureau just issued.

This is an increase of over 100% on the total of inquiries for June, which in turn doubled the totals for May. Inquiries as to clinics and dispensaries lead in number, with requests for advice on tuberculosis sanatoriums, and the proper feeding of tuberculosis patients, a close second. Inquiries come as much from individuals as from institutions, according to the report, so that it is not only the public health agencies of the city which are finding this clearing-house for health information valuable, but the average citizen.

North Carolina.—Compared with last year North Carolina at the close of August was the richer by more than half a million dollars saved by the reduction of typhoid fever. During the three summer months, when the toll of typhoid is heaviest, there were 692 less cases this year than last, and about 70 less deaths from this cause.

The figures by months of cases of typhoid reported to the State Board of Health for 1919 were: June, 432; July, 741; August, 503; for 1920, June, 152; July, 396; August, 436. Total for 1919 was 1,676, as against 984 for the present season.

Five years ago the number of typhoid cases in the state was running in excess of 7,000 a year. The remarkable reduction, with its consequent saving of life, has been accomplished by an intensive and extensive campaign against this disease, which has reached virtually every corner of the state.

✚

Texas.—Dr. C. W. Goddard, state health officer for Texas, having resigned September 1st to accept the chairmanship of the medical staff of the University of Texas, Dr. Oscar Davis was appointed by Gov. W. P. Hobby to succeed him. Dr. Goddard served as health officer since February, 1919, and during that period rendered excellent service in raising the health standard of Texas. Dr. Davis served with the department prior to Dr. Goddard's administration and has been with it ever since as director of the Bureau of Venereal Diseases.

The winner of the state prize of $25 in the health essay contest conducted in the state normal colleges during the summer sessions was S. M. Calloway of San Marcos, a student in the Southwest Texas State Normal College in that city. This announcement is made by the Texas Public Health Association, which conducted the contest and awarded the prizes.

✚

Virginia.—"Banish the common drinking cup and you will have gone a long way toward getting rid of diphtheria and scarlet fever." This is the message that the State Board of Health is sending broadcast throughout Virginia now when the schools are reopening and the season for those diseases is approaching.

Among the means of disease transfer, the common drinking cup ranks as the chief; and that is why the board is urging its abolishment. It is perfectly simple to fasten a drinking socket where there is running water and it is not so difficult to attach these to pumps.

The big health event of the year in Richmond is scheduled for October 7-8, when the North Atlantic Tuberculosis Conference, to be held under the auspices of the National Tuberculosis Association, will convene at the Jefferson Hotel auditorium. Between 200 and 300 persons actively interested in the war on tuberculosis will attend the conference and will hear discussions of methods in every-day use in the fight against the great white plague.

A joint campaign directed by the State Board of Health, the U. S. Public Health Service and the International Health Board was recently concluded at West Point, and people are now sitting at night on unscreened porches, something they had never done before. This undertaking on the part of West Point involved the expenditure of a considerable sum of local money for drainage and oiling; but the results have been satisfactory far beyond expectation; and already the work here has influenced other places in the vicinity to inaugurate similar efforts.

An interesting demonstration of the value of sanitation in reducing the incidence of and deaths from infantile diarrhea comes from Dr. William S. Keister, Field Director for Albemarle for the State Board of Health.

Dr. Keister reports that physicians of the town of Crozet, Albemarle County, declare that no cases of infantile diarrhea have occurred this summer since the sanitation of the community. Health workers believe that this disease, which brings death to so many little ones, can be abolished along with typhoid fever by proper sanitation and the consequent disarming, to a great degree, of the fly menace.

At the call of the State Health Commissioner a conference of city health officers was recently held at the State Capitol. At that meeting it transpired that Richmond and Norfolk were conducting a general campaign for the destruction of rats, which are the chief carriers of the plague. The State Health Department, in conjunction with the United States Public Health Service, was requested at the meeting to coöperate in a rat survey of the Hampton Roads cities, Norfolk, Portsmouth and Newport News, for the purpose of determining whether any of the rats in those cities are affected. Virginia realizes that there is no occasion for hysteria, but it is not going to neglect obvious means of precaution.

✢

West Virginia.—F. F. Farnsworth, P. A. Surgeon, U. S. P. H. Service; Director of the Bureau of Venereal Diseases, has reported on the second year of the coöperative work. The need of the work is sufficiently established in the percentage of arrested individuals examined who were found infected, namely, 71. The activities of the year are briefly these:

Number of cases venereal disease reported 11,650
Number of physicians making these reports 685
Number of free clinics controlled by this bureau 9
Number of cases treated in clinics controlled by bureau 1,126
Number of cases treated in hospitals not controlled by bureau.......... 2,564
Number of doses of Arsphenamine furnished free by this bureau...... 2,671
Number of cases arrested and examined 540
Per cent of those examined found infected 71%
Number of cases detained or quarantined 187
Number of pamphlets distributed.....57,422
Number of moving picture showings. 105
Number of stereopticon slide showings 186
Total attendance at these showings.. 3,500
Number of public addresses made.... 156

Total attendance at these meetings...22,150
Number of legal prosecutions (some still pending) 47
Number of convictions (this does not take into consideration ordinary police court prosecutions)......... 11

Free clinics were established and maintained to the number of nine, in Wheeling two, Parkersburg, Bluefield, Charleston, Glendale, Huntington and Elkins, two. In addition to these a large number of physicians are coöperating with the state in giving free treatments both in private practice and in public hospitals. The laboratory has made 2,700 Wassermann tests and other examinations. Some 20,000 doses of Arsphenimine were administered. One of the important features of the work is that every dollar of federal or state money used in the work has set in motion at least ten other dollars in the hands of interested citizens.

✢

Wisconsin.—To acquaint medical men of the state more fully with their obligations as guardians of the public health, representatives of the Wisconsin State Board of Health recently visited a number of county medical societies and addressed them on public health movements whose success is largely dependent upon the practicing physicians. These speakers were Dr. Robert Olesen, acting Epidemiologist; Dr. W. D. Stovall, Director of the State Laboratory; and Dr. I. F. Thompson and Dr. G. W. Henika, of the Bureau of Social Hygiene.

Citizens of Appleton, Wis., and adjoining communities have subscribed $500,000 to build a new St. Elizabeth's hospital to enlarge the city's hospital facilities which are now totally inadequate for the demand.

Dr. A. J. Dana has been elected health officer of Fond du Lac, Wis., to succeed Dr. N. J. Malloy, resigned.

The JOURNAL is always pleased to publish items of interest with reference to health procedure in the different states. Every month a blank form of request for such items together with a sheet outlining the kind of news desired is sent to every State Department of Health in the country. If no items appear in this section of Public Health Notes, it is because no response has been made to these requests.

PUBLIC HEALTH
LABORATORY NOTES

Abstracted by Francis H. Slack, M. D., and Mr. James M. Strang.

Once a Typhoid Carrier, Always a Typhoid Carrier.—The following description of the routine followed in the laboratories of the Massachusetts State Department of Health for the detection of typhoid carriers is of interest. "The bacteriologic laboratory distributes a double mailing case enclosing a rubber-stoppered test-tube containing 30% glycerol in 0.6% sodium chloride solution. This outfit is used for sending specimens of feces and urine to the laboratory. The amount of feces sent is, as a rule, about one-fifth of the total volume of the emulsion and the amount of urine about one-half. As soon as the specimen arrives at the laboratory it is streaked with a platinum loop on large (13 cm.) plates of Endo's medium prepared fresh each day. The eosin-methylene blue agar of Holt, Harris and Teague is also used. For specimens of feces two plates of each medium are used and two or three loopfuls of the feces suspension are used to a plate. For urine, approximately 20 loopfuls to a plate are used. After 18-24 hours, incubation at body temperature, six or more colonies resembling *B. typhosus* are fished and each inoculated into 2 cc. nutrient broth. Should no suspicious colonies be seen but many colonies of the colon group, fresh plates are streaked with the specimen, then 24 hours older. It has been found that glycerol inhibits colon bacilli more than typhoid and that an older specimen showing fewer colon colonies on a plate occasionally gives positive results because there is less overgrowth of the typhoid bacilli with other organisms.

After 4-6 hours' incubation at 37° C., the broth cultures are examined in hanging drop for motile bacilli resembling typhoid. If any are found they are mixed with a typhoid agglutinating serum, in appropriate dilution, and examined within an hour for agglutination.

If one of the cultures is completely agglutinated it is inoculated into dextrose and lactose broths in fermentation tubes. A culture-forming acid in dextrose broth and no gas in either sugar broth within 48 hours in reported as *B. typhosus*"—Stanley H. Osborn and Edith A. Beckler, *Jour. Inf., Dis.*, Aug., 1920.

✦

Elective Staining of Influenza Bacilli.—The material containing the bacilli is spread out in a thin film, dried in air and fixed in alcohol. After treating with 5% mercuric chloride for 15 minutes, a warm 10% solution of sodium hyposulphite is added for 1 minute, the preparation is stained and washed with carbolic fuchsin for 10 minutes. The slide is again washed, decolorized with 5% anilin chlorhydrate for 15 to 30 minutes and, after washing again, counter-stained with methylene blue for 1 minute. The Pfeiffer bacilli are colored red with black central bodies, while other organisms stain blue. By this method of staining the author found these bacilli in the blood, especially in all cases of grippe.—*Palina, Centralbl. f. Bakt.* 1919, 83, 507.

✦

Can the Sachs-Georgi and Meinicke Reactions Replace the Wassermann in Every Case?—In more than 700 cases examined, 86% gave concordant results by the Sachs-Georgi and Wassermann tests. Several cases of fevers which were not syphilitic and a few of soft chancre gave a negative reaction. As a rule there are about 5% more positive cases by the S-G than by the Wassermann test. The age of the specimen for the S-G test is very important, the results from a serum 5 days old cannot safely be trusted. In about 3% of the cases, the S-G test cannot be carried out on account of spontaneous flocculation of the serum. The Meinicke reaction was tried on 366 serums and in 12% of the cases, was found to be positive for subjects who were non-syphilitic.—Merzweiler, *Deutsch. Med. Woch.* 1919, Nov. 13, *Abst. in Bull. Inst. Past.* 1920, 18, 262.

INDUSTRIAL HYGIENE AND OCCUPATIONAL DISEASE

Abstracted by Drs. E. R. Hayhurst and E. B. Starr.

Strength Tests in Industry.—Different jobs have different standard strengths. Some individuals also have fluctuations in physical condition daily. Tests of daily variations in strength are fundamental in fatigue. A special method of testing strength is described for most of the readily available muscles in the body and several illustrations are presented. The data upon which the conclusions are based represent 5,518 tests among 305 factory workers in two establishments, the first, a brass factory, engaged at the time in making shell fuses, and the second, a large automobile factory. Strength as affected by external factors, as a criterion of physical condition, as a criterion of fatigue and as a test of the effects of work upon night-workers was experimentially determined. There is a distinct tendency for the strength of all male workers in a single environment to fluctuate similarly from day to day. External factors act on all the workers alike. Psychical influences, such as the arrival of pay day may be operative. Strong male workers show less fatigue than do weaker workers regardless of· the nature of the work. External factors, such as temperature and relative humidity, affect strength. The impairment of physique due to exhaustion may be so severe as to require considerable time for recovery to normal strength. There is evidence that the effects of fatigue are persistent, in that they tend to appear on the day following a day of fatigue. Days of poor physical condition are most likely to be followed by days of fatigue than are days of good condition. There is no evidence that the strain of night work in an eight-hour shift, changing every two weeks, impairs physique. However, a permanent night shift, working 12 hours nightly 5 nights in a week, averaged 15% lower in strength than the day shift doing precisely the same work; but the evidence is insufficient to decide whether or not this poorer showing was actually due to night work. The most pronounced indications of fatigue are presented in an operation requiring close concentration and carried on in a disagreeable environment.—E. G. Martin,` U. S. Public Health Reports, August 13, 1920, Form 35, No. 33, 1895-1926.

✦

Safe Practices in Cleaning and Finishing Rooms in Foundries.—The first part of this bulletin discusses accident prevention in particular, after which special sections are given to correct methods for removal or control of dust and of sand-blasting with a citation of the desirability for the physical examination of workers since some apparently strong men may have a predisposition to diseases of the lungs. Protection to the eyes in welding, precaution in dipping and pickling rooms, safe types of clothing, precautions against the dangers of painting are discussed in other sections. The illumination sections are devoted to daylight, washing the windows, white-washing the walls, artificial light, and portable lamps. The bulletin is well illustrated.—National Safety Council, 168 North Michigan Avenue, Chicago, No. M. E. 1 (revised 1920).

✦

Finding Employment for Disabled Civilians.—The Institute for Crippled and Disabled Men, 101 East Twenty-third Street, New York City, has recently compiled tables to show what jobs men with certain disabilities have secured through its bureau. The institute now has records of 2,200 cases of men and boys suffering from orthopedic difficulties. The Institute has placed 1,800 handicapped men. The list of occupations which men with different deformities have secured covers six pages of the citation. One result of this survey is the discovery of how few men with arm amputations (only 165) have been placed. A one-armed man cannot place himself without almost superhuman efforts. Many of the placements for these have not been constructive. The bureau is always on the search for jobs for which men with arm disabilities can be trained.—Gertrude R. Stein, Monthly Labor Review, Bureau of Labor Statistics, Washington, D. C., April, 1920, 147-154.

919

Chronic Copper Poisoning, Does It Exist?
—Peigney had the opportunity of studying the effects of work in a French factory engaged in the manufacture of fuses during the war. The plant employed on the average 2000 women and 700 men. The work was with copper. While various ailments were observed, those peculiar to the industry were reduced to gastro-intestinal troubles which affected particularly the younger women workers. Peigney describes the 36 operations carried on and the exposure to copper sometimes associated with oil, sometimes as dust, etc. He next describes a number of typical cases of poisoning alleged to be due to copper. In brief, about one-third of the women employees suffered from acute gastro-intestinal attacks consisting of colic, nausea, vomiting, and profuse diarrhea. The colicy feature was not pronounced. There was pallor, prostration and considerable sweating. There was no fever. The pharynx was reddened. The attacks lasted from one to several days, sometimes accompanied with bladder pain and frequent urination. After a year or so an immunity seemed to be established. Peigney considers these attacks due to the salt action of ingested copper and that it is not a true constitutional copper poisoning in the sense of a destructive affair like lead with its grave anemia but that it is an irritation of the organism extending even to the blood forming tissues and resulting in some cases in an increase in the blood elements, including the leucocytes. These blood changes were noticeable during the first two years' employment; thereafter the blood finding became normal.—Peigney, *Revue D' Hygiene*, Jan.-Feb., 1918, Vol. XL, No. 1, 66-85.

✦

Poisoning by Heavy Metals.—Salant and his associates have been engaged in research on the toxicity of heavy metals for some years and he presents a summary of various papers published elsewhere. The presence of these heavy metals in the canning industry has been of chief concern. The action of zinc when taken by mouth is not very injurious but when introduced directly into the circulation it produces

marked heart depression and slowed action of smooth muscles. It is a general protoplasmic poisoning. On elimination, it damages the kidneys and produces albuminuria and sugar in the urine. When taken by the mouth some of the ingested zinc is absorbed from the intestinal canal and this is also the main channel of elimination, the kidneys playing a very subordinate role in ridding the body of zinc. It is stored in considerable amounts in the liver. Experiments with tin showed that moderately large amounts given daily with food for fairly long periods may prove harmful to health. It resembles zinc in being eliminated principally by the intestinal canal although the kidneys will excrete more tin than they will zinc. Tin is very slowly absorbed from the intestines, probably because of the insolubility of its salts. It was found that copper sulphate in the circulation produces a prompt depression of the heart action. A more detailed study of the influence of nickel, copper, cadmium, and zinc on the isolated heart will appear shortly in the *Journal of Pharmacology and Experimental Therapeutics*. While some of the heavy metals are very poisonous, it is necessary to recognize the very important fact that they are apparently well borne for a considerable length of time when taken with food. Disturbances of function, or diseases, of the intestinal canal may permit these metals to become absorbed and exert their poisonous effects. The public is entitled to the benefit of the doubt in these cases and caution should be exercised in permitting the manufacture and sale of foods containing even small amounts of such metals.—Wm. Salant, *Jour. of Industrial Hygiene*, June, 1920, 72-77.

✦

Manufacture and Use of Wood Alcohol.—The National Committee for the Prevention of Blindness coöperating with the Safety Institute of America and the National Safety Council has prepared recommendations covering the manufacture and use of wood alcohol which are regarded as fair to the manufacturer, while at the same time aiming to protect the people from misuse of the poison.—Gordon L. Berry, *Safety*, Sept. Oct., 1919.

American Journal of Public Health

Official Monthly Publication of the American Public Health Association
Publication office: 124 W. Polk Street, Chicago, Ill.
Editorial office: 169 Massachusetts Ave., Boston, Mass.

Subscription price $4 per year. American Public Health Association membership, including subscription, $5 per year. Subscriptions and memberships may be sent to the A. P. H. A., 169 Massachusetts Ave., Boston, Mass.

| Vol. X | DECEMBER, 1920 | No. 12 |

SOCIAL USES OF MEDICINE

D. B. ARMSTRONG, M. D., M. A., M. S.,
Framingham, Mass.

Read before Sociological Section, American Public Health Association, at San Francisco, Cal.,
September 16, 1920

Seventy percent of our people need medical or dental treatment, but go without because of lack of proper medical organization. Dr. Armstrong is not merely critical, but is constructive. He shows the absurdity of making physicians dependent on sickness for support, and outlines a plan of community procedure on a rational basis.

IN the practice of medicine today is found much that is admirable from the point of view of personal service and community welfare. Ingrained in the system of private medical practice is also much that is chaotic and wasteful, much that is destructive of the best interests of society. Side by side with the glorious spirit of individual self-sacrifice, characteristic of medicine throughout the ages, students of social organization are increasingly conscious today of elements tending toward the perpetuation of inadequacies in disease control, serious qualitative and quantitative deficiencies in diagnosis and treatment, resulting in an inevitable loss to society in preventive and therapeutic potentialities unutilized, and retarding the development of scientific medical knowledge, as well as the elevation and standardization of practical medical service.

ACCOMPLISHMENTS OF MEDICINE

Yet marvelous has been the progress of medicine in the last few decades. Great have been the benefits to mankind resulting from unselfish effort and untiring struggle against the captains of disease and death. Many are the trophies of victory won in this fight to lay a firmer physical foundation for economic, social and spiritual evolution. The sanitation of whole countries has made possible the exploitation of the resources of nature. Smallpox robbed of its terrors, yellow fever conquered, typhoid fever reduced to a disease of minor importance in most self-respecting communities— these are a few of the conquests of *preventive* medicine.

Still, the necessary characterization of these accomplishments as preventive, is not wholly encouraging. This is progress in disease prevention, but it is not essentially a reflection of growth in the routine practice of medicine, the diagnosis, treatment and cure of the everyday minor or serious affections. Unfortunately, the same methods responsible for the advances in epidemiology are not applicable to the control of many of the remaining scourges affecting society. Dependent upon still undeveloped methods is the ultimate control of such major factors in our present mortality as tuberculosis, cancer, kidney and heart disease, probably the less specific respiratory affections, venereal disease, etc.

These advances in disease prevention are in fact a direct measure of organization in medicine. They are the result of organized research, of the social organization of medicine through health departments, sanitary commissions, or similar social devices. The type of medical social organization devised to meet these problems has accomplished part of its task admirably. It still has other fields to conquer. Yet without further and different development in the organized social group use of other existing resources and methods for disease control, we cannot hope for substantial progress in many vital fields. As Sir James Mackenzie has put it, in his recent volume on *The Future of Medicine:* "The next step is to recognize, that if progress cannot be carried further with our present conceptions and methods, we must look out for a new concept, as well as new methods."

INADEQUACIES OF MEDICAL PRACTICE

What is the situation in many fields of medicine today? Investigation shows that 70% or more of any typical population group is in need of medical or dental advice or treatment, for minor or serious ills. How many are ever brought into contact with corrective medical advice? How many are advised or treated while the affection is in its incipiency? How many, even when brought under medical surveillance, receive competent and thorough-going advice or treatment?

In what percentage are the laboratory and other technical "instruments of precision" for diagnosis and treatment, although theoretically available for all, actually applied? Why do many physicians everywhere, in spite of state provision, still make or fail to make diagnoses of diphtheria without throat cultures, or syphilis without a Wassermann?

Recent surveys have shown that there exists in normal communities three times as much active tuberculosis as is usually under observation. Why is it that in most communities 20% of the tuberculosis cases first come to the knowledge of the health authorities when reported at death? How infinitesimal is the percentage of surgically curable cancer that is detected in time? What health officer is bold enough to claim that even a substantial proportion of the venereal disease in his community is receiving adequate medical treatment? How many adults or children in the typical urban population ever receive an annual medical inspection—admittedly essential to the detection of early disease and the promotion of hygienic living?

The present method of unorganized private medical practice, devoted and conscientious as are the rank and file of the profession striving *individually* to meet these problems, has been tried and found wanting. Real progress in all allied fields has been concomitant with some degree at least of social organization. Can private practice, through socialization, be converted into a far more effective social instrument?

We all know that the individual in the system is not responsible for this seemingly hopeless and chaotic condition. He is a victim, with those he is seeking to serve, rather than a promoter of the system. The status of medicine today is one of the many symptoms of the semi-anarchistic, individualistic organization of social life. It shares with other phases of the unsocialized state the glaring imperfections of society. Synthetic-minded leaders in all walks are seeking an adequate program. Indeed, this is conspicuously true in medicine. Unfortunately, here as elsewhere, progress or even the experimentation essentially prerequisite to progress, must be made against the lethargic opposition of many who lack the spacious-mindedness necessary to grasp the significance of the present acute problems of this war-altered world. The problem of utilizing social forces for the physical betterment of man presents many inherent difficulties. Change. there must be. Shall that change be radically disruptive or conservatively constructive?

NEED FOR SOCIALIZATION

As some one has put it, "the whole world is yeasty." Changes are inevitable, changes involving new relations, new social adjustments, new usages for social organization. Now, is it not true that past history shows a tendency toward the development of new social instruments? Certainly this is true of medical history in particular. The great modern advances in disease control, barring a few unpremeditated, unplanned, accidental discoveries by isolated individuals, have been the result of organization, either for laboratory research, field study, or other experimentation. Shall we not therefore find, that in order to solve the major difficulties of medical practice today, we shall have to have a further socialized organization of the forces now wasted or imperfectly used? Certainly no doubt can remain as to the inadequacy of the present day arrangement, particularly on the side of case treatment. Speaking with international authority Sir Arthur Newsholme says:

"That the work done on behalf of the community, *plus* the work accomplished by private medical practitioners, is not equal to national needs, is obvious to anyone considering the vast amount of avoidable disease in our midst. Why is this and what is the remedy? . . .

The medical provision made in a large proportion of cases is belated and inadequate; it commonly does not include the full resources of medicine; and in perhaps a still larger proportion of cases medical advice is not obtained, or being obtained is not followed. This applies even more to hygienic than to clinical medical advice."

In the face of these difficulties there are those in the medical ranks who would urge that the physician be concerned only with clinical medicine, only with the treatment of individual cases, leaving disease prevention, and the promotion of hygiene and allied problems, entirely to the sanitarian and the social worker. The weakness of this must, however, be apparent to anyone seeing the problem as a whole. It is one problem, a problem of social medicine—a movement that must push forward in a united advance on the bulwarks of disease. We cannot separate the treatment from the prevention of disease without jeopardizing the success of both.

SOCIALIZATION TO DATE

At what preliminary conclusions have we therefore arrived? Is not the answer the "socialization of medicine"? Why is this phrase to the average medical man "like a red flag to the Attorney General"? Is the socialization of medicine something new and unheard of? Have we none of it to date? Is it something terrible that is going to befall us over night? Are we being led astray by fools captured by catch-words?

On the contrary, the socialization of medicine began with the earliest clinic, hospital or health department; and has slowly and inevitably broadened in scope and increased in momentum, to the inestimable benefit of the public and of the medical profession itself.

Indeed, the social tendencies in medicine today are following many sound precedents. There was a time, for instance, when most communities got their water supply from individual wells.

Then there came a time when a common (social) water supply was found to be safer, cheaper, and in every way better. Medical service is now passing from this individualistic stage to the stage of social conservation and social control.

Those who object to the theory of "socialization" do not usually oppose its practice. Consider such universally accepted examples as the following:

1. The development of a medical coöperative group method of treating disease—namely the hospital public ward.

2. The establishment of diagnostic and treatment facilities for large social groups, medical equipment and personnel being employed in common—namely, the clinic or dispensary, and all out-patient service.

3. Community health organization, official and private health bodies—representing the interests of the whole community as to disease prevention and control.

4. The employment of medical service for large population groups in society, as for the school children, the industrial workers, etc.

5. The development of group practice and specialty clinics, rendering available diagnostic and treatment facilities otherwise beyond the reach of the average physician and patient as well.

6. The fostering of routine medical examination and advisory work for large unorganized groups of individuals by the employment of organized medical forces, such as through the Life Extension Institute, and other agencies.

7. The preparation of vaccines, sera, etc., by the state, for social use.

8. Finally, and perhaps most significant thus far, the employment of *organized medical* forces, in the development of general *social machinery* for the prevention and treatment of disease and disability, as in accident and sickness insurance, imperfect as is our social organization in these fields at present, inadequate and unsatisfactory as has been the practical provision on the medical side.

Are not these measures more than "a tendency toward the socialization of medicine"? What, in fact, is the "socialization of medicine"?

Before reaching a definition of this term, let us say once and for all that this is not an attempt at the analysis of detailed method in the present medical system. It is more an effort to interpret the existing spirit and doctrine of medical service and disease control. Neither is it the plan to outline and discuss specific recommendations, such as health insurance, for instance. Rather, it is hoped to indicate certain broad lines delimiting the range and direction of future progress. Our interests are not in the theories but in the practical program. Our argument is not for "the type of mind that would rather play with a perfect theory than improve an imperfect world."

WHAT IS SOCIALIZATION?

What does the socialization of medicine mean? Does it not mean the use of medical knowledge and facilities for constructive social ends? This implies the social attitude, namely, the attitude of service.

Now, from this point of view, there are few who will not agree that the practice of medicine, in spirit and motive, is the most socialized instrument for physical betterment at work in the world today. The physician has the spirit of service. He succeeds to the extent to which, through his unorganized individual efforts, he is bettering the lives of others. He possesses the social attitude; his social defects are therefore largely those of method and organization. All that is implied by the term is admirably expressed by Sir Arthur Newsholme:

"The definition of the sense in which I employ the term socialization in medicine—would include the rendering available for every member of the community, irrespective of any necessary relation to the ordinary conditions of individual payment, of all the potentialities of preventive and curative medicine." ⁻

IMPENDING SOCIAL DEVELOPMENTS

We need not be concerned over the spirit of service essential to this object. It is there and always has been. How can medical facilities be organized practically, for the attainment of this end? That is the great problem, upon the solution of which real progress in further disease elimination depends. Still, do not all the current manifestations of socialization previously discussed bring us several steps further in the direction of the goal? Are we not on the verge of fresh developments in this same direction? What, in fact, are the impending developments in the social life of medicine through which we may hope to see the methods of medical practice more nearly approximate the admirable social spirit which inspires the medical world? Perhaps a few of these "next steps" may be indicated as follows:

1. The further development of public and private health organizations, using their machinery for disease control, for the elimination of non-communicable and degenerative causes of disease and premature death, such as cardiac, nephritic, and other affections, as through dietary education, cardiac classes, etc.

2. The further development of adequate training for medical men in medical schools in the science of disease prevention and early detection, the principles of hygienic living, as well as the treatment and cure of specific cases of disease.

3. Adequate post-graduate instruction, providing a means for continuous, up-to-date contact with the more recent medical discoveries, possibly involving periodic re-examinations on the essentials of diagnosis and treatment—thus strengthening the relation between the

State and the physician, with the object of better medical service.

4. The extension of clinic and dispensary medical facilities on a pay basis for wider groups in the population—a further socialized use of the clinic method.

5. A great extension of organized, age-group diagnostic and advisory work, bound to come in the near future, including full-time medical, dental, nursing and clinical personnel and equipment for school children, industrial workers, etc., and providing facilities for routine medical examinations.

6. Organized efforts to provide annual medical examinations for the population at large, through such agencies as the Life Extension Institute, medical examination clubs, national medical examination campaigns, etc.

7. The development under government auspices of expert itinerant advisory and consultant service for the general practitioners on diagnosis and treatment, covering difficult and doubtful cases in many of the specialties such as tuberculosis, infant welfare, internal medicine, etc.

8. Possibly the districting of medical service, at least to meet epidemic emergencies, leading perhaps to the setting up of competitive standards of excellence, graded on a basis of disease prevented and health maintained.

9. The reincarnation of the "old family physician," as the guardian of the family's health and the teacher of family hygiene—the treatment of the family to be carried out on the "keep well" basis, a practice erroneously said to be common in China, but one which shows definite signs of development in this country.

10. The further and more equitable development, as an experiment at least, of accident and sickness insurance, merely an item in the whole program of socialization, but one around which centers most of the storms of discussion at the present time.

HANDICAPS OF PRESENT-DAY PRACTICE

"The physicians are opposed to the socialization of medicine." Any one will tell us that, but is it true? Certainly they do not like the term. Certainly they do not favor health insurance. But that is only one aspect of the tendency so manifest today. Any one who has had any experience with the initiation of practically any of the phases of socialization enumerated above, with one or two exceptions, will testify that the physicians not only are in favor of the measures, but give them full coöperation and hearty support.

In fact, it would be difficult to imagine why the physicians should be opposed, why they should approve the *status quo*. Surely they are not in love with present conditions. The doctor accepts his lot with superior good-will, but he works in the face of almost intolerable obstacles. A few of the disagreeable elements which, to a great degree unnecessarily, burden the life of the general practitioner are:

1. More than any other occupational group the physicians are called upon to meet the demands of long hours, excessive over time, night work, etc.—all, with relatively few exceptions, for a "white wing's" pay.

2. Not only is he under-paid for the services he performs, but the doctor's collections are frequently poor. It is considered poor etiquette to be too "business-like" in insisting upon payment and he faces the subtle public sentiment that rather discredits the man in medicine who "makes money"—a condition that prevails in no other calling.

3. He is required to maintain the morale of the soldier—takes the risks of the soldier—yet there is for him no remuneration while in training, no promotion, no pension, no discharge—a life with the severest duties and with few rights.

4. From him is demanded more volunteer service, without compensation, or recognition, than is the case in any other profession.

5. While he may have been an excellent student in school, an enthusiast for research, a man who had genuine scientific interests, the economic pressure to which he is subjected in practice will not only give him no chance for continued study, but will often dull his sense of scientific values and his enthusiasm for worthy endeavor.

6. If a general practitioner striving to develop a specialty, he has to fight for every minute of time to study. Then, he must face that part of the public that sneers at specialists, and at the same time expects to find for a dollar office call all the specialties combined in one man—a surgeon, an ophthalmologist, a pediatrician, a tuberculosis expert, and what not, never realizing, in the words of the old adage, that "a jack of all trades is master of none."

7. Economic pressure, again, will probably prevent the devotion of his time and interest to the work for which he is best fitted. How many potentially excellent neurologists or research men are wasting their time on routine life insurance examinations, to eke out a living?

8. If he has devoted years to thorough training, he is still likely in some communities to find himself in competition with a graduate of a correspondence school or a night diploma mill.

9. He may start out with high ideals of service, with the desire to keep accurate records, anxious to meet his full obligations to his patients. How often does one see these early ideals recede with the hard earned knowledge into the dim past, in the face of competitive economic pressure for a living? How many men would like to keep accurate case records if time allowed? How many would like to act according to their conscience and perhaps call more frequently upon patients, if this did not have the appearance of selling them-

selves and forcing their services? How many would like to follow up their cases, preventing possible serious sequallæ, if time and custom permitted?

GLORIES OF THE PROFESSION

This is the practice of medicine, except for the favored few. Does it mean an easy existence for the physician? Does it mean the best service for the public? Yet in spite of these handicaps, we find in every community many medical men performing a noble service under a tremendous burden. There is scarcely an American community without its old family physician, interested in all good movements, trusted with leadership in all vital matters, struggling along in poverty, concerned only with his obligations and opportunities for service and self-sacrifice. His example brings to us a realization that these limitations upon practical medical service, while they represent just grievances, are equally significant in reflecting the glories of the profession.

THEORY OF MEDICINE

If this is the practice of medicine, what is its theory? Does the theory more nearly coincide with our ideals of what medicine should be?

The theory of medicine has developed in three stages: First, the physician existed as an individual in the community with the sole object of *making sick people well;* second, there was added the conception that he might also *keep people well*—a social conception, requiring organization, and hence our health departments and allied social devices; third, and finally, there is being added a new idea, namely, that the physician should not only cure sickness and prevent sickness, but he should also *create health.*

As the theory has developed, socialization has proceeded to attempt to put it into practice. How well it has succeeded must be more or less evident from what has gone before. In theory

the physician exists to prevent sickness and to create health. In theory he is free to act as the noblest servant of mankind. In practice he is earning a precarious and meagre living in a competitive business. Is there needed a new coat for his wife? He must pray for an epidemic. In other words, his income depends on sickness and not on health. A community educated to the social use of medical machinery would reward its physicians for an increase in health and a decrease in sickness. The doctor is now penalized for this very combination.

Yet, in the face of these mal-adjustments worthy of Alice in Wonderland, the physician continues a glorious, if somewhat blind service to duty and humanity. Strangest of all, in spite of these discouragements, the majority of physicians seem willing to fight for the privilege of economic serfdom. Can this be anything more than a gross misconception of the objects and purposes of socialization, a tremendous ignorance of the benefits that lie along the path of social organization in medicine?

OBJECTIONS TO SOCIAL MEDICINE

What indeed are the practical objections offered by physicians and others to these progressive developments in medicine? Consider only a few of the arguments presented against the social movement, arguments directed generally against the extension of social insurance, this being the line of social development most conspicuously and energetically promoted at the present time.

1. The injection of the State into the affairs of medicine will interfere with the normal relations between the physician and the patient.

Yet we have seen that this relation is largely an economic one, very unsatisfactory for both the physician and patient. The physician comes into contact with the patient only when called. He does not follow the case to a complete cure unless the patient bids him so to do. To force his services when he alone may know how absolutely essential they are is out of the question. There is, in fact, in the existing relation very little to insure the proper care of the case, the protection of society, or the proper remuneration of the physician. There is a tremendous opportunity for improvement in this relationship. Indeed, if the present relation must be accepted as the "normal relation," then something decidedly abnormal would seem greatly to be preferred.

2. So-called "State Medicine" would seriously interfere with the physician's income.

Yet everyone knows how meagre and uncertain is the income of the average physician today. Besides, it is a reward for the amount of illness in the community, and not compensation for the amount of health preserved or created. Further, at present the physicians are performing only a fraction of the amount of work that needs to be done, and that will never get done under present conditions. For the additional preventive and creative work that should be undertaken under a reasonable arrangement, there would be supplementary remuneration for the medical profession. Socialization would quadruple the "business" of the profession.

3. Socialization would level downward.

A wise plan of State medicine, placing reward for service on an emulative basis, with a system of promotion from less important occupations (or possible districts) to more important ones, the standards being disease prevented, sickness cured and health created, would eliminate the unfit, elevate and standardize practice, increase compensation, and level upward rather than downward.

4. Socialization would eliminate "personality" from the Service.

It is true that certain steps toward socialization thus far developed do depreciate somewhat the value of personality. In hospital service this is undoubtedly a factor, the public wards being less attractive because of a relative lack of choice of physicians on the part of the patients.

Certainly, any wise system of public medicine gradually and cautiously developed along lines previously indicated, must recognize the "art" as well as the science of medicine, and must take every precaution to preserve the value of the personal elements. Of course this "personality" factor has disadvantages as well as advantages. The poorly trained quack frequently has more "personality" than the scientifically trained physician. On the other hand, higher and more uniform standards of training and practice would minimize the importance of the personal choice factor. There would be a leveling upward as to medical proficiency. Further, after all of the physicians, with the incompetents eliminated, were properly related to the community and the community's treatment facilities, such as hospitals, clinics, etc., there would be no question of inadequate hospital and medical relations, physicians without hospital connections, etc.

5. State control over the practice of medicine tends to make patients a litigation problem (particularly in health insurance) rather than a scientific problem.

In the first place, such a result could not fairly be called "socialization," for the primary aim of current social tendencies is to increase the scientific treatment of illness, to render more available the existing instruments for diagnosis and treatment, and to decrease the percentage of cases that go untreated altogether, scientifically or otherwise. As a matter of fact, the ordinary every-day practice of medicine as carried out at the present time could scarcely be made less scientific.

6. State control would make "the case" purely a scientific problem, ignoring the human factor.

This delightfully contradictory objection is often stated in the same breath with ·the one preceding, and answers itself.

7. Socialization tends to break down individual self-reliance, self-respect, and the willingness on the part of the patient to meet his own obligations.

It is claimed that of all the people needing or not needing treatment in a community, if treatment facilities are made too readily available and attractive, there will be a certain percentage who will take unfair advantage of the opportunity. These people, either not in need of treatment or quite able to pay adequately for private care, will fall back on the State, exaggerating trivialities, adopting malingering tactics, etc. According to the argument this is a load the State cannot afford to carry.

On the other hand under present conditions 70% or more of our population is in need of treatment, and largely fails to get it. This represents a much greater State liability and one which the State can much less afford to carry. '

8. There will result a tremendously expensive and unwieldy political machine into the unsympathetic arms of which medicine will fall.

As a matter of fact, the largest element in such organization as may be necessary to administer the program of social medicine, would be the medical profession itself. Errors in the plan, defects in the provision for medical work, vicious manipulation of the system as a whole, can all be eliminated by the medical profession itself if it gets into the. game in the beginning, shapes the development of the program, and contributes its constructive genius to the further growth of the whole system.

Undoubtedly it is up to the physicians to take the lead and initiative in the development of the social control of medicine. The movement should be governed from the inside and not from the outside. In this way only can the adequacy of the plan from the medical point of view be assured. Very significant is the statement of an English authority on this point (Sir Arthur Newsholme).

"It is, I think, clear that the State will year by year take an increasing hand in medical matters. It is useless, even if it were desired, to attempt to oppose the inevitable and desirable trend towards a vastly increased utilization by the State of medical science in the interests of humanity. It is for physicians to guide the course of events, and to insure that no plant is sown which will afterwards need to be uprooted; that no development is permitted which will hinder the fulfillment of our ideal."

BENEFITS OF SOCIALIZATION TO THE PHYSICIAN

A few of the many advantages of a further social control of medicine to the private physician may be summarized briefly here. A social system properly planned should insure more regularity of service as to hours, a tremendous increase in the amount of worth-while work accomplished, an enhanced income, a reward on a rational basis of accomplishment, better opportunities to study and specialize, opportunity for expert consultation and coöperation, and the elimination of the necessity for frequently putting economic consideration ahead of the patient's welfare.

The individual trained to treat the ills of his fellow-man should be assured of an adequate income, not dependent on a chance excess of illness in his community. In medicine the relative cost factor should be eliminated both for the patient and the physician. Society cannot afford preventable illness. Society cannot afford to leave its elimination to a haphazard system in which the patient and the doctor make their decisions under the pressure of economic necessity. This ideal is approximated even now in one form of socialized medical service, namely, the hospital. Here there are, for instance, laboratory and research facilities for all, rich and poor alike, and the cost factor is partially at least eliminated, the basis being service. The socialization of medicine should eventually 'eliminate from the physician's life this hampering element of economic pressure. The man who is teaching medicine as well as the man who is practicing it, should be free from worry and undue stress on the side of self and family maintenance.

BENEFITS TO SOCIETY

Equally obvious must be the advantage to society. Through socialization in its many phases, every individual should receive the advantages of special facilities and expert service, regardless of his paying ability. From the social point of view, preventable sickness always is too expensive. We could afford to obtain medical service at any cost for the 70% in need of it, and not only for the few who can now afford it. If it is cheaper "to prevent than to cure," and if "a stitch in time saves nine," then the prevention, early detection, and adequate treatment of disease will materially lower the charges upon the community for illness costs. Finally, society would be operating on a rational, economically sound basis, utilizing its medical resources to the full.

THE MAIN FACTORS IN THE PROBLEM

To summarize the outstanding factors in the socialization problem:

1. The problem is an extremely difficult one, dealing as it does so extensively with the human factor. It would be a stupendous error to leave out of the reckoning the element of human psychology in such an enterprise. Because of the difficulties, there are bound to be errors, false starts and partial failures.

2. The program needs the coöperation and guidance of the medical profession. To succeed, it must have their study, sympathetic criticism and constructive aid. For all of the medical work of the world, the medical examination work, hygienic education, the work among infants, in schools, in factories, etc., there will be necessary a most efficient system of medical service. Plans must be made to provide wisely for the increase in numbers of medically trained individuals needed under social control.

3. The medical profession is social in spirit, though in need of socialization as to method. Not so much can be said for the spirit and attitude of the general public toward the service which it expects from the medical profession. There is greatly needed an infusion of the spirit of service and community responsibility for disease control into the great mass of people everywhere. At present each individual thinks of his private health as a private matter. He calls the doctor only when he is sick— and frequently waits until 2 A. M. to do that. He wishes to maintain his earning capacity and avoid pain, but has very little sense of duty to keep well as an obligation to society. He does, however, think it is the duty of the doctor to make him well after he becomes sick— once more the duty being altogether on the side of the physician.

The physician has never had a real chance in social organization. He is only given the sick and relatively discouraging individuals to look after. He has never had an opportunity to keep the community well, to do a genuinely fundamental job.

In one of our largest cities, there are 10,000 physicians treating individual cases of illness and 300 or so (in the Department of Health, mostly on part-time) enjoying the privilege of keeping the whole people well. All should participate in this privilege.

The physician has been given a disagreeable, if not impossible task—that of putting together the pieces. It is to be hoped that before long he will demand of the public the opportunity to share in the operation of community life as a whole. This apparently is dependent on the development of a spirit of service, a social attitude on the part of the public he seeks to serve. Little by little this *will to be healthy*, this essential counterpart to the spirit of service in the medical profession, is becoming a reality. The object of medicine is a healthy community life. Up to the present time, however, the doctor has been expected to do all the work, either individually or through the gradually developing medico-social organizations. It is essential that we all do our part. The results of this inter-play and community of spirit will be an increased scope for the medical service, better training, greater uniformity of methods and higher standards of practice.

THE SPIRIT OF SERVICE

In conclusion, what must be demanded are a maximum service for the sick regardless of their ability to pay, and a chance for the physician to give maximum service in disease prevention, treatment, and cure. The medical profession must be aroused to its opportunity and obligations. State and county medical societies, as well as the American Medical Association, could with advantage appoint commissions to study the whole problem of social tendencies in medicine, not only the health insurance piece-meal aspect of it. The problem should be approached with a sympathetic spirit of digested idealism. Certainly it would be a more valuable contribution for a medical society to study current needs and practices, to formulate a program, to help work it out in coöperation with social and health organizations, than, ostrich like, to stick its head in the ground and protest with

its heels by the passage of a futile anti-health insurance resolution.

Let us remember that social medicine means the organized effective use of medical facilities, the rendering available of these facilities for all people in need —a service basis. This does not mean "state medicine," so-called. Any group in the community mày employ medical devices socially. The school committee that employs a school doctor, the factory group engaging an industrial physician, the town or county civic or health committee or tuberculosis society that offers expert consultation services to the physicians and the people, the state department of health that districts the community for treatment purposes in influenza epidemic times, the state university, or state medical society, that attempts the post-graduate education and standardization of the medical profession—all of these movements, any collective movements that tend to improve and stabilize medical service, that render more nearly all of the resources of medicine available, for the masses of people, particularly for disease prevention and elimination, are social medicine. Social medicine is therefore simply community medicine. It may be under official or private auspices, local, state, or national control! Above all, it is not only health insurance. Indeed, experimentation might prove this particular device to be anti-social in character. The final test of any program is service rendered.

Social medicine will never spring full grown from the lap of the existing chaos. A practical working program must be conceived—a program through the gradual execution of which all may learn to "breathe the ampler air of service."

In the January issue of the JOURNAL will appear the Symposium on Narcotic Drug Control as presented at the San Francisco meeting of the A. P. H. A.

STANDARDIZATION OF LABORATORY METHODS

AUGUSTUS B. WADSWORTH, M.D.,

Division of Laboratories and Research, New York State Department of Health, Albany, N. Y.

Address of Chairman before Laboratory Section, American Public Health Association, at San Francisco, Cal., September 13, 1920·

I WISH to make a few general remarks in regard to the standardization of laboratory work, a subject which is to be discussed by various speakers at this first session. The subject is appropriate for us to consider. The urgent need for the standardization of laboratory procedures has for a number of years engaged the thought of some of our best workers, and the Laboratory Section of the American Public Health Association has rendered notable service in formulating standard methods for routine work in laboratories.

I wish to emphasize the need for formulating definitely all the regular technical procedures to be used in routine work, and for strictly and faithfully seeing to it that these procedures are followed if satisfactory and uniform results are to be obtained from different laboratories. In short, the methods should be formulated and all work thoroughly supervised and controlled.

The technical procedures used in the laboratory for examination and analysis, for diagnosis or the treatment of disease, are the outcome of much research and investigation, and almost invariably have been due to the experienced work of eminent scientists. There is an early stage during which standardization is not desirable, in fact quite impossible; and the later stage during which it becomes more and more.possible, desirable, and, ultimately, necessary.

Work and study must be expanded in every direction during the early period of experimentation and it must be carried on by qualified workers capable of interpreting the significance of their results, but in the practical application of these results, the field of investigation is narrowed and limited to the task of determining the precise technique which shall best accomplish the end in view.

At this point less experienced workers may carry on the work and, finally, the routine performances of the tests may be accomplished by technicians, trained perhaps in only one branch of work. In the development of laboratory methods there is a natural process of standardization continuously in operation, year by year. The development of laboratory work in medicine is characterized in its present stage by great variation in methods, due to the spirit of research and investigation which tests, compares, and ultimately improves existing processes. All of this work is of the utmost importance, and of course should not be discouraged, but this variation should not creep into the performance of practical tests, the results of which are to be used in the routine care of the sick. The results of laboratory tests must be uniform to inspire confidence, and uniform results can only be obtained by uniform methods. The need for standard methods in laboratory work is easily apparent, and especially where the development of a great volume of work is concerned which may include many thousands of cases of disease, situated at remote distances, instead of being limited to the study of isolated cases in hospital beds near by.

One of the chief reasons for the organization of the laboratory section of the American Public Health Association was to give laboratory workers an opportunity to meet and to discuss their methods of work. This original purpose of the Section has always been and still is of great practical value. The work

932

has gradually expanded through the activities of the committees that have been appointed from time to time to study and report on various laboratory methods. The standard methods for water and sewage analysis and the bacterial examination of milk, which have been formulated and several times revised, are notable examples of this pioneer work.

Successful standardization by the Section of the methods of different branches of the work is entirely due to the personal efforts of the members of the committees assigned to the task. Similarly, the failure in some cases to arrive at a satisfactory conclusion may possibly be attributed to lack of facilities or of experience on the part of the committee. The tasks have been arduous and thankless.

All of these difficulties of the committees of the Laboratory Section have been clearly recognized, and last year Professor Gorham recommended the appointment of a committee on standard methods whose duties would supplant those of all other committees on standard methods. This action would, I am sure, be a marked step in advancement, and would help to eliminate some of the difficulties which have beset the path of former committees. In my opinion, however, there should be a paid secretary whose duty it would be to bring together and to correlate in a business-like manner all the various activities of the section.

The character of its membership places the Laboratory Section of the American Public Health Association in a peculiarly favorable position to render a great public health service. The Association has no power to enforce its regulations, but must rely upon the accuracy and precision of its recommendations and the pressure of public opinion in order to have them adopted.

It is possibly largely due to the work of the Laboratory Section of the American Public Health Association that the United States government, through the Hygienic Laboratory at Washington, has developed a satisfactory control of the manufacture and sale of various biologic products in so far as they enter into interstate commerce. In this action our government followed the example of Germany, where these products had been for several years under government control.

In Germany many phases of laboratory work have been controlled by the government, but standardization is incomplete. In Great Britain and France control of standardization was not developed until the war. During the war the British Medical Research Committee undertook the standardization of laboratory procedures. An admirable series of reports is now being issued by this committee on the standardization of pathological methods. The committee also assumes the responsibility of directing the biological tests, and plans to issue licenses for the manufacture and sale of certain therapeutic products. Recently an international congress was held in Brussels to consider the practicability of obtaining standardization of laboratory methods through an international commission.

Excellent in many ways as has been Federal control through the liberal interpretation of the Interstate Commerce Act, it is becoming more and more apparent with the enormous increase in laboratory activities that the public welfare requires further safeguards. While the physician and the patient can be assured by government regulation of properly standardized antitoxin or arsphenamine, the laboratory where the diagnosis of diphtheria or syphilis has been made may be without control or regulation of any kind. The practicing physician and the patient are, in most instances, as unable through training to form a competent opinion of the technical procedures of the laboratory as of the standardization of antitoxin or of the toxicity estimations of an arsenical product. Federal control as now limited to interstate commerce regulations, must necessarily be inadequate control.

Under these circumstances, the responsibility for supervision and standardization of laboratory procedures must become one of more local and sectional or of state concern. Since this problem is one which must be met in every state, the means taken by the State of New York to meet its obligations in this direction may be of special interest and value, although the work is still far from complete.

In 1914, in New York State, apart from the Federal supervision and control in interstate commerce of biologic products, there was no attempt at control or standardization of laboratory procedures. The public health laboratories of the state, of the cities and counties, all operated independently of one another. With the revision of the Public Health law and the enactment of the Sanitary Code, together with subsequent amendments, the necessary power was placed with the Department of Health to make possible the development of a broad policy of state control, and the standardization of all laboratory work outside of the City of Greater New York. This law, therefore, made possible the actual supervision of laboratory service to between five and six million population, since in New York State the regulations of the Sanitary Code have the force of law. Physicians and health officers were required to have laboratory examinations made for the diagnosis of certain classes of diseases and for the release of cases from quarantine. It was specified that these examinations should be made in laboratories which had received the approval of the Commissioner of Health, and that examinations made in laboratories not so approved were without legal standing and that health

officers have no authority to accept them. Provision was also made for the inspection of laboratories by the Commissioner of Health or his representative.

It was recognized from the start that the carrying out of the policy of state supervision would be a matter of years, and that to be successful, the central laboratory must with painstaking care develop methods of standardization of the highest order, and tactfully help the smaller laboratories to recognize the value to themselves of state control. Growth would have to be gradual. The supervision of laboratories engaged in public health work, and the standardization of the technical procedures used in them, has been one of the functions of the Division of Laboratories and Research of the State Department of Health. The task has been doubly difficult on account of the war.

At first the inspection of all the public health laboratories of the state outside of the Greater City of New York was made to determine the character of the equipment and the personnel of the staff engaged in the work in each laboratory. Then minimum requirements for approval were formulated, and, to secure approval, the laboratories were obliged to sign an agreement to maintain these minimum requirements. These inspections and the agreements brought the central laboratory and the local laboratories into closer touch than had hitherto been possible. The central laboratory in Albany was then able to supplement and aid the local laboratories in their work, and to become a substantial support upon which they could lean in times of stress and emergency. Since many difficulties were encountered because of differences of opinion, conferences were held at intervals in order to provide opportunity for free discussion, and an association of public health laboratory workers of the state was formed which holds one meeting in conjunction with the State Medical Society and a mid-year meeting at the central laboratory at Albany.

Furthermore, the different workers are brought into close, personal contact with the staff of the central laboratory. Demonstrations of new methods are made possible, and the standard methods of the central laboratory are available for inspection. The workers from different local laboratories are from time to time assigned to the central laboratory at Albany to be trained in the technical procedures of their work. Frequently the staff of some local laboratory is depleted for one reason or another, and an assignment of members of the central laboratory staff to this local laboratory enables it to carry on its work. Complete coöperation has been developed by such ways and means.

. Meanwhile, the work of standardization has progressed, and minimum standards have been developed, increased and enlarged in scope to include not only the procedures that are required by law to be carried out in laboratories approved by the Commissioner, but other procedures not affected by these laws and regulations. These have been added to complete the standardization of laboratory methods, and to enable the local laboratories to standardize all of their work.

Recently an important improvement has been added, that of keeping records. At first the laboratories were only required to keep the records for a specified time, six months. The way in which the records should be kept is now definitely specified, and the forms for reporting have been standardized. It is apparently a small matter now to determine the practical efficiency of a laboratory in making examinations of permanent preparations, such as the examinations of diphtheria cultures. Comparison of the practical efficiency of distant laboratories in other diagnostic procedures was much more difficult, but it was accomplished by requiring the laboratories to forward duplicate specimens to the central laboratory at Albany, and by comparing the two series of results obtained. In other instances, specimens were prepared or selected in the central laboratory and sent to the local laboratories together with the clinical information necessary for examination and reporting.

Great stress has been placed upon periodic inspection, and now no laboratory is approved that has not been inspected as to equipment and staff, and also put to the practical test of securing uniform results by its standard methods.

As a result of all this experience with the standardization of laboratory procedure in New York State it is evident that for control to be effective there must be some authority to enforce standard methods and to supervise the laboratories that are using them. This authority may be legal as in the federal, state or municipal control of laboratory work or it may be simply that of public opinion as in the case of the standard methods of water analysis promulgated by the Laboratory Section of the A. P. H. A. But even these methods of water analysis have been recognized by the courts so that they now have become vested with some degree of legal authority.

Standardization, however, will fail, despite the fact that the necessary legal authority has been obtained and the necessary requirements prescribed, if constant supervision is not exercised by inspection and practical testing of the work of the laboratory. This is necessary for the maintenance of the equipment, character of the work of the staff, and the condition of the records.

A CLASSIFICATION OF DIPHTHERIA BACILLI BASED ON THE TOLUIDIN BLUE-IODINE METHOD OF STAINING

Henry Albert, M.D.,

*Professor of Pathology and Bacteriology, University of Iowa,
Director, Laboratories for the Iowa State Board of Health,
Iowa City, Iowa.*

Read before Laboratory Section, American Public Health Association, at San Francisco, Cal.,
September 14, 1920.

Differential diagnosis of diphtheria bacilli has always been puzzling. This author discusses a special staining process which develops granules or bars, not visible with other stains. The new morphology affords criteria for determining non-virulent forms of bacilli. The author suggests and illustrates a convenient classification.

VARIATIONS in the size, shape and structure of diphtheria bacilli were noticed soon after the discovery of the organism. It was also observed that these features had some relationship to the virulence of diphtheria bacilli, the more granular ones being, as a rule, more virulent than the more solid staining types. Neisser[1] believed that by the method of staining which he devised, it was possible to distinguish definitely virulent from non-virulent forms. Subsequent experience has, however, shown that not much dependence can be placed on the Neisser method nor any of its numerous modifications, such as those recommended by Beck[2] and more recently by Debrè and Letulle[3], in distinguishing those bacilli which are capable of producing disease from those which are non-virulent.

The most elaborate morphological classification of diphtheria bacilli suggested to date is that of Wesbrook[4]. This classification was made more with the idea of recognizing the frequency of occurrence of various morphological types of diphtheria or diphtheria-like bacilli than in distinguishing between virulent and non-virulent forms of the microorganism.

The chief criticisms of this classification are:

1. It is based on the staining of the bacilli by Loeffler's methylene blue, a method which does not have as great selective or differential value as have certain staining methods more recently described[5]. It does not differentiate the several types with sufficient distinctness.

2. Several of the types are apparently misplaced in the classification, as revealed by other methods of staining.

3. It is unnecessarily elaborate, there being no good reason for separating many of the types into such a large number of subdivisions.

The method of staining with toluidin-blue and iodine devised by the author[5]

1. M. Neisser: *Zur Differentialdiagnose des Diphtheriebacillus*, Zeitschr. f. Hyg., xxiv, p. 443, 1897. The formula for this stain may be found in any textbook on bacteriology.
2. F. A. Beck: *Method for Staining the Diphtheria Bacillus.* Jour. A. M. A., July 13, 1918, p. 109.
3. Debrè and Letulle. Presse Medicale, 27, 1919, p. 515.
4. *Transactions of the Association of American Physicians*, 1900.

5. H. Albert: *A New Stain for Diphtheria Bacilli.* Jour. A. M. A., Jan. 3, 1920, Vol. 74, p. 29, also H. Albert: *Diphtheria Bacillus Stains with a Description of a "New" One.* A. J. P. H., April, 1920, p. 334.

PLATE I

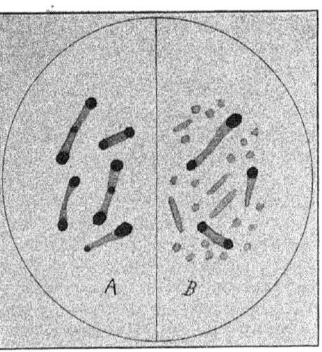

Diphtheria bacilli stained by the Toluidin blue—Iodine method.
A—Typical diphtheria bacilli—pure culture.
B—Diphtheria bacilli and other bacteria, chiefly Staphylococci—culture from a clinical case.

indicates very clearly that the chromatic substance of diphtheria bacilli tends to collect at certain places which accordingly take a more intense stain, producing a barred and granular appearance.

The development of bars often precedes granule formation. In such cases the chromatic substance of the bars becomes concentrated in the form of granules and, at the same time, so changed

PLATE II

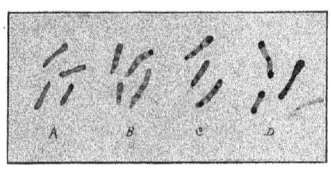

Variations in internal structure of diphtheria bacilli revealed by the Toluidin blue—Iodine method.
A—Solid forms.
B—Barred forms.
C—Barred granular forms.
D—Granular forms.

that they will become metachromatic, that is, they will take a different stain from that of the remainder of the bacillus.

Although the rapidity with which granules develop depends somewhat on certain environmental factors, we have found that when the toluidin blue-iodine stain is applied to cultures of virulent diphtheria bacilli grown on blood serum media, many granular or granular and barred forms will always be present.

Three significant features regarding diphtheria bacilli, brought out by our stain as compared with the usual Loeffier's methylene blue, are:

.1. Many bacteria of cultures which show only solid forms, by Loeffier's methylene blue, are barred or granular by the toluidin blue-iodine stain.

PLATE III

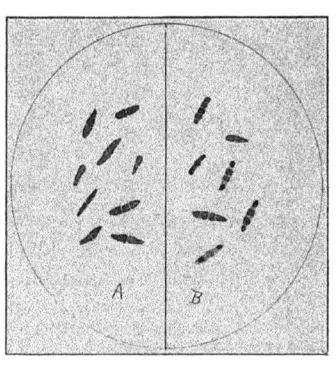

Short diphtheria bacilli stained by two different methods.
A—Loeffler's methylene blue (so-called solid form).
B—Toluidin blue—Iodine (barred and granular form).

2. Many cultures showing barred but no granular forms by Loeffler's methylene blue, have many bacilli with granules, as revealed by our stain.

3. Although certain cultures showing only solid or barred types of the bacilli

as revealed by the Loeffler methylene blue stain, are virulent, no cultures that did not show some granular forms when stained by the toluidin blue-iodine method were found to be virulent. This conclusion is based on 126 virulence tests.

This is a point of great significance. By every other method of staining which we have tried we have been able to find some cultures, the bacilli of which were virulent but which did not contain gran-

PLATE IV

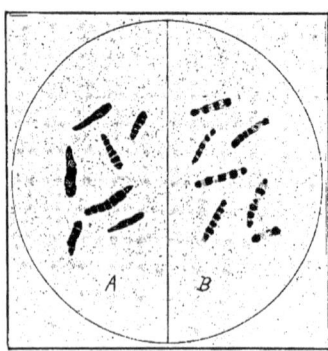

Difference in certain diphtheria bacilli as revealed by two different staining methods.
A—Loeffler's methylene blue (forms solid and barred, no granular).
B—Toluidin blue—Iodine (forms barred and granular).

ules. This does not mean that only virulent diphtheria bacilli contain granules but so far as we have been able to determine, all diphtheria or diphtheria-like bacilli which fail to produce some granular forms as revealed by our stain, are non-virulent.

In spite of the many objections that have been urged against a morphological classification of diphtheria bacilli, we believe that the following reasons will justify such a classification:

1. The advisability of recognizing different types of the diphtheria bacilli for purposes of comparison.

2. The relative permanence of type of certain cultures of diphtheria bacilli in spite of the fact that the morphology of many may be made to vary considerably.

Our classification of diphtheria bacilli based on the toluidin blue-iodine method of staining contains only barred and granular forms, since we were unable to find any virulent cultures which contained only the solid types. Aside from the club-shaped forms, the size is indicated by their length—as short, medium and long. Intermediate forms containing both bars and granules are common. The rather solid forms which are also seen may be regarded as immature or atypical forms. The classification includes the following eight types:

Granular G 1—short (1-2 μ long and with 1 or 2 granules).

G 2—medium (2-5 μ long and with 2 or 3 granules).

G 3—long (5-7 μ long and with 2-5 or more granules).

G 4—club-shaped (2-6 μ long and with 1 to 5 or more granules).

Barred B 1—short (1-2 μ long and with 1 or 3 bars. When 2, they are usually at the ends giving the bacillus or diplococcus or diplobacillus appearance).

B 2—medium (2-5 μ long and with 3 to 4 or more bars).

B 3—long (5-7 μ long and with 3 to 6 or more bars).

B 4—club-shaped (2-6 μ long and with 1 to 5 or more bars).

The following plate, V, represents the classification in graphic form.

The following table presents the types of the classification just given with the corresponding types of Wesbrook's classification:

Author's types (Stain-Toluidin blue-iodine)	Wesbrook's types (Stain-Loeffler's methylene blue)
G¹	....E. F. G. (also some D², E¹, E², F², G²).
G²	......C. D. (also some C¹, C², D¹).
G³	.... B. (also some B¹, B²).
G⁴	.... A. (also some A¹, A²).
B¹	.... C¹, C², D¹.
B²	.... D², E¹, E², F², G².
B³	.... B¹, B².
B⁴	.... A¹, A².

Of special significance is the fact that Wesbrook's solid forms fall, for the most part, in the group of barred bacilli when stained by the author's method. Many bacilli of the Wesbrook type fall into two of the groups of the author's classification. Thus many of Wesbrook's solid forms contain granules or bars or both when stained with the toluidin blue-iodine method. (See plates III and IV.)

SUMMARY AND CONCLUSIONS

1. Present classifications of diphtheria bacilli from morphological and staining reaction points of view are of comparatively little value since they do not enable virulent diphtheria bacilli to be distinguished from non-virulent forms. The best known of these classifications, Wesbrook's, is also needlessly elaborate and unwieldly.

2. The toluidin blue-iodine (author's) method of staining by virtue of its selective staining effects on diphtheria bacilli has the following distinctive advantages over the usual (Loeffler's methylene blue) method of staining:

a—Many bacilli of cultures which show only solid forms by Loeffler's methylene blue, are barred or granular.

b—Many bacilli of cultures which show only barred forms by Loeffler's methylene blue, are granular.

c—No cultures which did not contain some granular forms, when stained by the toluidin blue-iodine method, were found to be virulent, whereas certain cultures showing only solid or barred types as revealed by Loeffler's methylene blue are virulent.

3. Although certain non-virulent diphtheria bacilli contain granules when stained by the author's method, all diphtheria or diphtheria-like bacilli which fail to produce some granular forms by this method were found to be non-virulent. This is not true of any other method of staining.

PLATE V

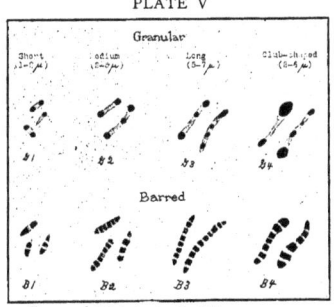

Types of Diphtheria Bacilli.
Based on the Toluidin blue—Iodine method of staining.
G2 = Granular medium.
B4 = Barred club-shaped.

4. A classification of diphtheria bacilli based on morphology and staining properties is desirable not only for purposes of comparison but also because of the relative permanence of type of certain cultures.

5. The author's classification of diphtheria bacilli based on the toluidin blue-iodine method of staining, contains eight classes—four granular and four barred. Intermediate forms containing both bars and granules are common. The rather solid forms may be regarded as either immature or atypical.

6. The author's classification includes the following types: G1 (granular short); G2 (granular medium); G3 (granular long); G4 (granular club-shaped); B1 (barred short); B2 (barred medium); B3 (barred long); B4 (barred club-shaped).

RELATIVE FUNCTIONS OF OFFICIAL AND NON-OFFICIAL HEALTH AGENCIES:
A SYMPOSIUM

INTRODUCTION

The immediate interest in this question was excited by an article contributed to the JOURNAL for November, 1919, page 827 *et seq.*, by H. W. Hill, entitled, "What is the Matter with Public Health?" In this Dr. Hill suggests that the official health officer has police powers which are oftentimes neglected to take up voluntary work not really within his province.

He states that the conscientious health officer who does his whole duty against disease will have his hands full, while the non-compulsory fields have staunch and willing workers waiting. As to the program of public health he considers it no longer a matter for individual communities to face and believes in "a nation-wide coördination, a building of individuals into compact organizations, coöperation of these with each other, and a close coöperation, but not union, with the official police powers."

In the JOURNAL for December, 1919, page 951 *et seq.*, is a reply to Dr. Hill by Dr. Carl E. McCombs, entitled, "Public Health Departments and Private Health Agencies." Dr. McCombs holds that health officers should undertake all kinds of health work, that divided responsibility will result in lowering standards, that compulsory health work is dependent upon the educational preparation of the people and this to be effective should be brought to the public by the one who has official authority, namely, the health officer.

In the August, 1919, JOURNAL, page 673 *et seq.*, Dr. Hill reiterates his earlier convictions. His statement is, in brief, that the health officer should assume no more duties until he is able to accomplish his existing ones, and should leave to voluntary associations the largely experimental, wholly voluntary activities which include oftentimes therapeutics and general hygiene. Health officers should first accomplish what he terms, "their notoriously neglected first duty, the control of infection," and then if they wish, ask for popular support and sympathy. He does not believe that health officers as a class should undertake the education of the public, he thinks that they are not authorized to undertake education, therapeutics and hygiene, not able at present to do it and that it would be unwise for them to enter just now into this field.

In view of the importance of the matter and the evident interest aroused it was decided to present the subject with discussions at the meeting in San Francisco. Dr. Emerson and Dr. Hatfield, whose papers follow immediately, agreed to present arguments from the point of view of the official agency and the non-official one, respectively. At the meeting there was much discussion, the occasion being the General Session of Monday evening, September 13. These discussions may be found in the report of that meeting, in this issue of the JOURNAL, page 957 *et seq*. Just before the meeting the view presented by Dr. Nesbitt was received, and although it could not be included in the program, it is here given as part of the symposium, while the paper presented before the Massachusetts Association of Boards of Health at its October meeting in Boston, presents the view point of an experienced Eastern health officer. Before the annual meeting of the Canadian Public Health Association in June last, Dr. W. H. Hattie read a paper entitled, "The Coördination of State and Private Enterprises in Public Health Work," which gives the view point of an official outside of the limits of the United States. It is also presented here.

RELATIVE FUNCTIONS OF HEALTH AGENCIES
I. VIEWPOINT OF THE OFFICIAL AGENCY

HAVEN EMERSON, M. D.,

New York City

Read before General Sessions. American Public Health Association, at San Francisco, Cal., September 13, 1920

DEFINITIONS should precede discussions, and agreements upon premises is the best insurance for good reasoning, so in the presence of the officers of all varieties of health agencies, little or big, official and non-official, I may be permitted as a representative of that health organization of longest standing, the medical profession, to introduce for the consideration of those who will follow, those more experienced in health administration, the topic of the meeting.

As we find in the practice of medicine among individuals, errors of physical structure and of function which must be prevented or relieved, so we find in communities very similar disturbances of social structure leading to those disorders of functions of which the results are expressed in high morbidity and mortality rates. We face today a complexity of the methods and personnel required for a group or clinic diagnosis of individual human ills almost as great as the organization of the human body itself. Parallel to this development in the machinery for diagnosis and treatment of disease in the individual, there has grown up in a similar orderly fashion and with an entirely comparable object the structure of so-called public health agencies whose functions are, first to arrive at a diagnosis and then to apply the appropriate remedy.

We are to consider today the functions, not of the patient but of the physician, not the technic of diagnosis or the theory of therapeutics, but the manner of work of the guardians of the public health, not the organization of the machine, the morphology of the organ, but the uses the agencies are put to.

We are not at the moment engaged upon a study of the equipment of the community's composite family physician, the official and non-official health agency, nor yet his educational qualifications, but the primary objects of his life.

From the moment that mind of man conceived the two facts of communicability and preventability of disease health organizations became inevitable. When the group, the *demos*, decided that no unit, no *homo*, was of so much value that he and his possessions should be permitted to jeopardize the safety of the race, the nation, the village, the household, laws erecting the machinery of health administration were passed.

When the limitations of exact science and human skill in detecting disease were recognized and the role of the person rather than of the premises, or of the material thing or object, in causing disease was made plain, personal hygiene became an objective to supplement sanitation, or in other words education grew in importance as compared with the enforcement of laws.

As long as man progresses he will search for new facts to explain old ones, he will test theory with facts, he will compare old methods with new. Wherever the laws of supply and demand fail to meet the needs of a community for the diagnosis, the preventive and curative medical and associated services for the sick, the community looks to its health agencies, private and public, to supply what the individual physician or voluntary associations of physicians have not given it.

There have been developed in public

941

health agencies the six great functions which may be called control, diagnosis, education, research, treatment, contact. There is a distinction implied in the title "official and non-official," which would perhaps be better indicated by using the terms obligatory and voluntary, suggesting that the former are created under the laws of the nation or one of its political subdivisions to fullfill recognized government functions and are supported by each and every tax payer, while the latter spring from the imagination and altruism of the few, derive their authority from the broad tolerance of the community or from its needs, and live on the self-imposed contributions of a small minority of the population.

With a few important exceptions the objectives of the government and of the citizen agencies are the same and I believe there is no function served by any voluntary agency that is not authorized and in some way served by one or more, of the tax payers' health agencies. It would be difficult to point to any useful field of activity, or function contributing to public health, that is not made possible by enabling laws for the United States Public Health Service, for the Ministry of Health of Canada or for the Departments of Health of many of our states and municipalities. In fact, it is probably correct to say that even an unwilling legal interpreter of the statutes could not deny the rights of the Surgeon General of the United States Public Health Service or the Commissioner of Health of the City of New York to carry on any or all of the activities which even the teachers and theorists in public health have proposed as desirable or the sociologists and statisticians have proved to have a bearing upon the duration of life and the development of vigorous health.

The functions of official, compulsory tax-supported health agencies are comprised within six main groups and those of the non-official, voluntary subscription or donation-supported health agencies, are largely limited to four of these:

Inspection and Control.
Diagnosis or Epidemiology.
Education or Interpretation.
Research and Demonstration.
Treatment, preventive and curative.
Contact and Coöperation.

Of these, the last four occupy the energies of and offer an almost unlimited field for legitimate and useful service of the non-official health agencies.

Inspection and Control:—By inspection and control are meant those specified functions for which health officers are held responsible under the law, those functions depending on right of entry and the privilege of examining suspected persons, premises or possessions for causes or cases of preventable disease. In this group fall the control of food and drugs, the general functions of abatement and control of sanitary nuisances, the control of all manner of preventable diseases whether communicable, occupational or due to habits, where exposure to the cause of disease and disability is not wholly under the control of the individual exposed. Whether we deal with international quarantine, with interstate traffic in drugs and food, or with hazardous trades in industrial communities as health problems, the principle is the same, is accepted in law and is supported in the courts when enforced; namely, that the health of the individual is a public asset in which the civil government has an interest and for the protection of which broad police powers may be exercised. It must be obvious that this not a function which can properly be delegated to any agency other than one specifically authorized by law to employ that very jealously guarded right to invade the home and approach the person of those not accused of crime. Even in small ways where this function is found to be served by delegation to a private agency, because of inadequacy of public service personnel, the impropriety is evident, the success of such delegation doubtful and the damage to good administrative policy is considerable. I have in mind a city where the enforcement of a local ordinance requiring the inspection of day nurseries is delegated by the Commissioner of Health to the local Day Nursery Association. The secretary of the association has served as the inspector but she is responsible for her position to the directors of the very institutions she is expected to criticise and if necessary to close, and not to the Commissioner of Health, who has no authority over her. The result has been lax and inadequate compliance with the law. Such functions, i.e., inspection for and control of standards required by law should not be attempted by non-official or private agencies nor should they be permitted to enter this field.

Diagnosis or Epidemiology:—By diagnosis or epidemiology is meant the series of closely coördinated processes including the collection and tabulation of vital statistics, the analysis of reports of field work as of diagnosticians, school medical inspectors, visiting nurses, sanitary and factory inspectors which are required, to permit of the formation of an opinion by the health officer or his epidemiologist upon any variation from sound community health. This is the function which can be compared with the obtaining of the past history, the chief complaint, the physical examination, the laboratory evidence, all elements contributing to diagnosis of disease or estimate of approximate health in a private patient. Epidemiology is the science or study of disease as it occurs in groups and, as I conceive it, this is the most important professional function of the director or chief technical officer in any organization devoted to health development and protection, and to serve this function we find records kept, of births, deaths, morbidity and the wide range of population phenomena by which we de-

tect the signs of early disorder, the degree of the injury while it is in progress and from which we calculate loss in numbers, strength and quality in the community. This function is in its strict professional sense served only by the official public health agency because only here is to be found all the information upon which all aspects of a community's health can be judged. There are, however, in the fields of tuberculosis, venereal disease, child hygiene, mental disease, cancer, cardiac disease, blindness, etc., national, state and local health agencies which have made and are now making studies which in some localities are more complete and useful than can be found in the offices of the respective departments of health. Non-official health agencies are rarely so organized as to provide the quality of overhead staff officers, the expert field agents, or are old enough to have that long continuity of records, observation and experience, necessary to permit of scientific epidemiological work. They must in any event if they would escape the fate of the private specialist who never acquired a broad foundation in general medicine, refer to the official agency for much of the comparative data and supporting facts.

Real epidemiological work is being done by the International Health Board, by the Metropolitan Life Insurance Company, by the New York Tuberculosis Association, and much valuable contributory information has been developed and used effectively by other non-official health agencies in various specialties of preventive medicine. There is a feature of this work by non-official agencies which is worth noting because of the similarity of it to non-official diagnosis in private practice of medicine. The licensed practitioner as well as the official public health agency must bear the responsibility for opinions expressed, and there is no escape for him from errors of judgment and opinion. The voluntary diagnostician is often free with his opinions because he cannot be held responsible for the results. So we see occasionally communities suffering from too much self-medication, in the form of hysterical educational propaganda arising from irresponsible diagnosis of the public's ills. There is nothing so stabilizing or so conducive to humility as to attempt to arrive at a diagnosis and prescribe treatment for the results of which you will be held personally and officially responsible. It is this permanent enduring responsibility which tends to make the health officer offer more conservative advice than his prototype, the director of the volunteer agency, sometimes proposes, whose courage, initiative and originality are often more of an asset to him than a sound knowledge of the pathology of communities.

So, if one must select among the functions which are more appropriate to the official than to the non-official health agency, we are forced to assume that inspection and control together with diagnosis or epidemiology are chiefly and more appropriately, if not at all times exclusively, functions of the tax-payers' agency than they are of the volunteer or non-official health agency.

Education and Interpretation:— Under education and treatment, synonymous terms in great part, we include the functions which deal with application of preventive medicine to the mass, the details of instruction to mothers, to lead workers, to people with colds, to janitors, householders, users of privies and wells, to farmers, legislators, to school children, and to communities in the midst of epidemic disease. This is the direct advice of the community's physician to his clientele, his one and yet multiple patient. Here we find the greatest field for the non-official as well as for the official agency. Has not every non-official health agency owed its birth to the determination of a group of men and women, usually a majority of them physicians, to do something to bring

knowledge into use? Enough facts have been known for decades which if applied would have salvaged not less than half of our annual wastage from disease, but the facts were not distributed, or if so were not accepted, or if accepted were misapplied. Here is common ground. Common in objective, identical from the basis of facts, but varied as the minds of men in application. Here we need the tempting approach of the teacher, the lure of the lecturer, and all the ingenuity of the fanatic who believes that ultimate salvation depends on knowing how to boil a diaper, or sterilize milk, when and what to eat, why air must be clean, cool and circulating, and the necessity of coming clean to table, the value of continence, of recreation, of annual medical examinations, etc. Here is a free-for-all, a career calling for the best which the Health Officer and the Executive Secretary or Director of a national volunteer agency can develop. And yet nothing in all the field of public health work is so full of confusion, or has been so wasteful, so inefficient, so inaccurate, so baffling to the consumer, the public to be taught. A chief diagnostician is of no use if the treatment is given helter skelter by all the neighbors, if advice is the product of imagination rather than of a knowledge of facts.

Direction in this function of education should come from the community's physician, for in education there will always be the elements of inquiry and response, and give and take of class room, and it is my opinion that the health officer if he is in any way alive to his opportunities and is a responsive member of his own community learns and knows more of the reaction, the response to educational propaganda than the private or special agent can know. The health officer is hampered by limitations of appropriation, by an overwhelming detail of duties calling for incessant labor and there is usually lacking the opportunity to stand apart and with academic peace

of mind construct a campaign or prepare appealing statements. No field of
endeavor, no function, no accomplishment offers more rewards to the non-
official health agency than does this of
education, and the great popularization
of interest in national health is largely
due to the work of such as are here
represented. The interest is aroused, but
it remains to establish knowledge in the
minds of the people of the few simple
facts which the individual must himself
apply in his personal conduct and habits
of life before it can be said that permanent results have been obtained. To my
mind the plan and text of all educational
material issued by non-official health
agencies should be submitted, as to a
censor, a friendly and eager consultant,
to the head of the official health agency
responsible for the population to be approached. And on the other side I believe the public health officer is not honestly serving his community patient unless he includes and amalgamates in any
educational effort, initiated in his office
all of the other resources, non-official,
volunteer, or tax-supported which can be
persuaded to take part and contribute to
the distribution of fact and argument.
Interpretation and explanation of science
are as much the duty of health agencies
as they are of schools and colleges.

   Research and Demonstration:—Research is merely another name for study,
and without study, dry rot soon de-
vitalizes any agency. Atrophy, gangrene,
senility are the penalties paid by any
organization that is without provision
for self analysis, for experiment, for advance into the borderline, where general
principles must be made to give way to
the gentle but insistent pressure of the
new small fact, the little disconcerting
bit of proof which throws into the discard our older habits of thought and
action. Routine is constantly fighting
innovation. Openmindedness struggles
against complacency. A single unit, if
nothing more, must be provided in every

agency, even if it be no more than a
compartment in the director's mind
which is always asking questions. Is
isolation necessary? Do smells cause disease? Have we taught any one by a
"movie" picture? Is worry or work the
cause of fatigue? Is it lack of sense or
lack of justice, that gives the poor a high
death rate? Have we learned something
new or merely rediscovered old facts?

   Here, as in Education, there is no let
or hindrance to the human mind. There
can be no preemption of the field of research. Direction and a joint endeavor
are of the essence of modern study, but
it is better to allow free rein to the
spirit of search, to the sleuth hound of
science than to attempt any handicap or
restraint. No personal or official reputation is so precious that it has a right
to protection against truth. No official
may long evade the embarrassment
which comes from the disclosure that his
executive acts have been based on misconceptions or misinterpretation of facts.
It is particularly in the field of that
corollary of research, the proof of the
fact by demonstration that the non-
official health agency makes a most valuable contribution. Quick to act, free
from precedent, single minded, clear in
objective, the non-official agency can devote itself in the spirit of the crusader
to make the little flame of fact illuminate
a nation and salvage a race. It is to
the everlasting glory of our brotherhood
that what can help mankind to conquer
disease is a matter of international gift.
The demonstrations of the means and
results of life saving come as near to
the miracles of religious history as we
can conceive and still retain our critical
judgment.

   Treatment, Preventive and Curative:—The function of treatment of
disease has so long been presumed to be
exclusively that of the medical profession engaged in the practice of medicine
that the inclusion of this function among
those of official and non-official health
agencies requires a brief explanation.

Now that we recognize that prevention requires diagnosis as well as the treatment of already existing disease, we must provide at least as skilful and well coördinated diagnostic service for the well as in the past have been provided for the sick. It takes, if anything, more skill and more delicate appreciation of symptoms and finer qualitative analysis in the laboratory to catch the early evidence of approaching deterioration or onset of disease than it does to make a diagnosis in a well established case of sickness. So, it falls properly within the province of the public health agencies, both official and non-official, to see that opportunities and facilities for examination for the detection of health are provided. Up to the present time the medical practitioner has been so involved and his time so fully occupied in the diagnosis and treatment of disease that he has not carved out a career for himself, individually or collectively, in this new realm of medical practice.

Furthermore, in many parts of this country and now of other countries, sadly stripped of their physicians by war and pestilence, the natural distribution of physicians fairly, adequately and uniformly through the population has been disturbed and we find in the larger cities and in the centers of prosperity more physicians than are needed, if their services were well organized, and a dearth of physicians, nurses, hospitals and dispensaries in large rural areas where the most helpless and on the whole most needy of our population are found.

Sickness breeds sickness and since early detection of disease is the key to disease control, community organization for health protection, whether official or non-official, cannot escape the responsibility nor should they decline the privilege of organizing services, both personal and institutional, for the diagnosis and the preventive and curative treatment of disease. The expression of this need has already appeared in the assumption by public health departments of a great variety of diagnostic clinics for tuberculosis, venereal disease, infant welfare, pre-natal care and so forth, and now we see in the health center, adjacent if not incorporated activities of actual group diagonsis and dispensary care alongside of the prophylactic facilities previously considered the limit of health department dispensary work.

What appears to be the most important single move in this direction is the proposed legislation authorizing communities of the state of New York to support by taxation, under the auspices of the State Department of Health, diagnostic and medical and nursing treatment services with all the benefits of a consultation group. In this field it is to be hoped that the non-official agency will, as in the tuberculosis and child hygiene movements, serve to demonstrate the need until such time as the tax-payers can be convinced that this is as legitimate a function of government as are public education, police protection or fire protection services.

Contact and Coöperation:—By the words contact and coöperation are meant those functions through which both official and non-official health agencies maintain affiliation not only among themselves but with the community as a whole. Neither the health officer nor the executive secretary of the private agency can feel that his office is adequately served if he has omitted to provide for liaison of the most intimate and enduring quality with the widest possible range of organized groups, whether these are departments of government or represent the spirit of private initiative. Jealousy and suspicion have no part in the make-up of public health work and competition should be in the direction of excelling in good services rather than in exclusiveness of action or objective. In this function, as in most of the others above described, it should be upon the health officer that the responsibility for initiative falls and such coördination as is required should be at his request and with his full knowledge. In theory this may be accepted, but as a matter of experience no such exclusive leadership, dominance or control can be accepted while public health administration is blighted by party politics, and personal ambitions block community volunteer efforts.

Why are all the possible good deeds for health's sake not performed adequately by the official health agencies? Not, I believe, in the main because of lack of imagination, lack of courage or lack of knowledge on the part of directors of public health service, but chiefly because of lack of appropriation and insufficient support from public opinion. It is to develop willingness to make appropriation after education of the public in the needs of public service for health that the non-official health agencies can serve, in standing shoulder to shoulder with the health officer when he appears before the public—either in mass meetings or before appropriating bodies of the government.

Until our crude and incomplete machinery of civil government, our very haphazard and discontinuous service of the people through elected and civil service employees is perfected to meet in its entirety the natural ambition and legitimate desire of people in cities and on the farm for education and protection which will permit "growth to be more perfect, decay less rapid, death more remote and life more vigorous and successful," there will continue to develop from the hearts and with the ready hands of the community those supplementary agencies which have become so numerous and active as almost to embarrass us with their prodigality.

There can be but one master of a ship, and in organization leadership cannot be divided nor responsibility evaded. Leadership and responsibility must be carried by the official public health agency. It is my belief that the most rapid progress towards economical and efficient public service for health protection, perhaps the most democratic service which can be rendered by a government, should be accomplished through the acceptance of direction and leadership from the officers of the official health agencies. The time has not yet arrived when the permanence, the disinterestedness, the capacity for intellectual leadership can be found widespread among health officers to justify our sacrificing the precious spirit of individual non-official initiative, for the sake of the entirely logical relationship just suggested. As an association, we have, ourselves, recommended the policy of centralization within one department or bureau of the Federal Government of all Federal health agencies. Perhaps the most important guarantee of our sincerity in this matter would be to provide, at the earliest opportunity, for a merger of organization and interests of private health agencies under some central body, comparable to the Federal bureau which we picture as desirable in the official field.

I trust that in defining my own conception of the functions of official and non-official health agencies I have in some measure clarified rather than confused the subject of the session, and that those who follow may etch out more clearly the details of the picture I have sketched.

The Symposium on Smallpox from the San Francisco meeting will be an attraction of one of the issues of the JOURNAL early next year.

RELATIVE FUNCTIONS OF HEALTH AGENCIES
II. VIEWPOINT OF THE NON-OFFICIAL AGENCY

CHARLES J. HATFIELD, M. D.,

Managing Director, National Tuberculosis Association,
New York City

Read before General Sessions, American Public Health Association, at San Francisco, Cal., September 13, 1920

As a prelude to a discussion of the proper functions of a non-official health agency, it is of interest to know something of the history of such organizations in the United States. A brief and incomplete chronological list of some of these agencies will answer our present purpose. It is as follows:

1844 American Medico-Psychological Association.

Purpose: Discussion of medical topics, chiefly relating to the care of the insane.

1847 American Medical Association.

Purpose: To promote the science and art of medicine and to endeavor to unite in one compact organization the medical profession of the United States for the purpose of fostering the growth and diffusion of medical knowledge.

1872 American Public Health Association.

Purpose: Development and advancement of public hygiene; correlation of principles and practices; and the promotion of public hygiene as a distinct profession.

1874 American Purity Alliance.

Purpose: Moral education, social hygiene.

1876 American Association for the Study of the Feeble-Minded.

Purpose: To discuss all questions relating to the causes of feeble-mindedness and the condition of the feeble-minded; to consider their management, training and education, and lend influence toward the establishment of institutions for their care.

1876 American Academy of Medicine.

Purpose: Study of social medicine or the sociological problems having medical factors.

1901 National Association for the Study of Epilepsy and Care and Treatment of Epileptics.

Purpose: To stimulate interest in epilepsy and epileptics along social and medical lines, especially to advocate public care in separate institutions where research may be carried out.

1904 National Association for the Study and Prevention of Tuberculosis.

1905 American Society of Sanitary and Moral Prophylaxis.

Purpose: To limit the spread of diseases which have their origin in the social evil; to study every means, sanitary, moral and administrative, which promises to be effective for this purpose.

1906 National Vigilance Committee.

Purpose: Protection of women and girls and the suppression of the white slave traffic.

1907 Committee of One Hundred (of the American Association for advancement of Science) on National Health.

Purpose: To establish in Washington a National Department of Health; to educate public opinion in health matters; and to further health legislation.

1908 Committee on the Prevention of Blindness of the Russell Sage Foundation.

Purpose: To conduct a national campaign for the prevention of blindness and to take such measures in coöperation with the medical profession and others as shall lead to the elimination of such causes.

1909 American Association for Study and Prevention of Infant Mortality.

Purpose: Study of infant mortality

.n all its relations; dissemination of knowledge concerning its causes and prevention; and the encouragement of methods for its prevention.

1909 Rockefeller Sanitary Commission.

Purpose: Eradication of Hookworm disease.

1912 The American Social Hygiene Association.

Purpose: For the conservation of the family, the repression of prostitution, the reduction of venereal diseases, and the promotion of sound sex education.

1912 National Child Welfare Association, Inc.

Purpose: Originates and publishes exhibit material which visualizes the principles and conditions affecting .the health, well being and education of children; coöperates with educators, public health agencies, and all child welfare groups in community, city or state-wide service through exhibits, child welfare campaigns, etc.

1912 National Organization for Public Health Nursing.

Purpose: To stimulate the extension of public health nursing; to develop standards of technjque; to maintain a central bureau of information.

1913 American Society for the Control of Cancer.

Purpose: To disseminate knowledge concerning symptoms, diagnosis, treatment and prevention.

1917 Child Health Organization of America.

Purpose: To arouse public interest in the health of school children; to encourage the systematic teaching of health in the schools; to develop new methods of interesting children in the forming of health habits; to publish and distribute pamphlets for teachers and public health .workers and health literature for children; to advise in organization of local child health programmes.

. We may believe that the reason for the formation of these associations was in every case the need of investigation, education and official action in connec-

tion with the phase of public welfare towards which attention was directed. Recognition of this need at the time it is recorded may be explained perhaps as a manifestation of some movement in community or individual psychology, through which a group of individuals was brought to see what was needed and was induced to attempt to meet the need. The underlying. purpose was without doubt to supplement and to develop existing health agencies. It would seem that this is a fair statement of the proper purpose arfd general function of any non-official health agency.

In discussing the correlation of health activities from the view-point of the non-official agency, we must start with complete acceptance of the fact that the duly appointed health officer is the sole agent responsible for the health of the territory he represents. His functions are obligatory, and no part of the obligation can be handed over to others. When the organization of our communities has reached the point of universal completeness; when all our officials are all wise, and are striving only for perfection; and when the public is educated to a point where it can recognize its needs and will provide money in sufficient quantity to enable the officials to meet the needs, then it may be useless to consider the functions of non-official health agencies. But that time is not yet come. In most places officials and official action are not yet perfect; the public is not yet thoroughly aroused and educated; and we must admit that any aid toward the desired end is welcome, provided it is properly worked into the general plan.

The reason for existence of the non-official health agency is the imperfect provision of facilities for our official health agencies. Its primary function therefore is to supplement and assist the official health agency in whatever way it can.

There are, of course, certain functions of the official agency that a voluntary agency cannot touch. These are the right of control or quarantine, and the determination of disease—epidemiology. As the official agent has the ultimate and legal responsibility, he only has the right to exercise these functions.

In other directions, however, there are definite lines of activity on which the voluntary body may properly help. They are all educational, but may be differentiated under the heads of Legislation, Education, Research, Demonstration, Standardization, and Coöperation. Under each of them, the non-official agency may have a useful part to play.

Legislation:—The first may be dismissed in a few words. Certainly we do not wish or need a constantly increasing set of laws. But in a state that has inadequate or badly drawn laws governing public health, and when a campaign for the revision and perfection of such laws is necessary, the non-official body has a duty to perform. Health legislation must always be watched and legislatures must be educated. Attacks on existing health regulations by Christian Scientists, anti-vaccinationists, and anti-vivisectionists are never ceasing. To assist in warding off such attacks is properly a function of the voluntary agency.

Education:—Education of the public as to the facts of community health, and the stimulation of the body of citizens to demand their dues, and to demand also that their health official be supplied with proper facilities for doing his work, this, perhaps, is the most important function of a voluntary agency. There are, moreover, reasons why such forms of popular education may be carried on with peculiar fitness and effectiveness by a non-official agency. In our country official pronouncements do not always fall on attentive ears, but we are interested when a friend or someone whom we know by reputation makes a statement that concerns us. Thus the individuals grouped together voluntarily can each be a center from which authentic information radiates. Theoretically at least, the effect of educational propaganda is multiplied by the number of active members in the voluntary agency.

Research:—Recognition of the need of research or investigation of the basis for proper health preservation is growing every day. We must examine the methods in use in preventing disease in the light of the best and latest scientific knowledge. We must keep our minds always open to possible improvements in method. Our health officials, however interested they may be in advancing knowledge, cannot rightly be expected to carry on investigations, if they at the same time attend conscientiously to the myriad details of administrative work. It is true that some of our officials arrange their laboratories so that investigative processes are carried on in addition to routine work. It is true, also, that research is by no means limited to the laboratory, and that no active-minded officer can administer his office to his own satisfaction without constant inquiry and investigation as to the efficacy of the methods he is using. Nevertheless the primary duty of the paid official is to protect the health of his people. Research proper may well be included in the functions of the non-official agency.

Demonstration:—When a new conception as to method of work or treatment is announced and approved by competent authorities in any part of the world, it is often necessary to make a test or demonstration before it can be incorporated into an official health program. Moreover, a new procedure may be successful in one part of the country, and a failure in another. The over-worked health officer usually cannot make the test; he has neither the time nor the money for it; if he fails, he may be accused of wasting public funds. Here, again, the non-official agency finds its field. If the demonstration is a success, the new method can be included in the official program and the purpose has been accomplished.

Standardization: — By standardization is meant the testing of men and methods in public health work by accepted and authoritative standards. It should be recognized that standards are constantly changing. It is, of course, the routine duty of the health official to enforce existing standards; but to advance the standards or to create new ones, he may properly call on the voluntary agency for assistance.

Cooperation:—At the present time and at this meeting the last function that has been named in this paper—cooperation—is of paramount interest. We all feel the strain of possible duplication of expenditure of money and effort. It is reported that in certain states, three or four non-official health organizations are planning to develop their work, using the same people on their various boards of directors, appealing to the same public for funds, and sometimes putting out programs that are in many respects the same. If this is true, it is an absurd and intolerable situation. The coordination of various public bodies interested in public health work is also a vital service that the non-official agency can best render. So long as there exist competitive scrambles for appropriations of various public departments from one general treasury, so long will it be impracticable to consider one public body as fundamentally a coordinating agency of all of the others. This function can best be performed by the outside non-official agencies, and in many states and cities it is a very necessary function to perform.

What can be done? In the first place the non-official agencies should come together on whatever common basis can be found. The beginning may be slight and tentative; but if a program of common activities and money to finance the program can be found, there is strong hope that the bond will strengthen and develop into a real union. It can be accomplished

if we do not kill the tender plant by forcing its growth, and if it is not blighted by jealousy, suspicion and seeking for place!

Next, there must be the closest cooperation between the non-official and the official health agencies,—national, state and local. As has been said above, the official is from every point of view the responsible head of the work; he has been chosen by constituted authorities, and is supported by taxes contributed by the citizens of the community, state or nation to bear the burden of public health. He has no choice as to the kind or degree of responsibility he will assume. It is all his. If we accept this as truth, it must be plain that the voluntary agency that does not coordinate its work closely with the program of the health authorities, provided of course the program is a good one, and by reason of the lack of coordination hampers or lessens the efficiency of the health officials—is worse than useless.

It is plain, therefore, that our ideal picture of the position of the non-official agency is as standing back of and supporting the health official in every move he makes that is for the public benefit. The official is the apex of the wedge; massed behind him are the citizens representing enlightened public opinion; the coordinated strength of the combination is directed toward some advance for the common good.

This is a pretty picture, and true so long as we assume that the health official will always be wise, conscientious and free from political or selfish interests. But sometimes, enlightened public opinion can enthusiastically endorse and fight for the program of the health official of this year; next January he may be displaced, however wise, efficient and highly regarded he may be, and a man of an altogether different type and equipment may be put in his place, a purely political appointee, such as we have seen in more than one of our great cities in recent years. Is it the function of the non-official agency to stand behind such an official in order to help him to enforce measures that may not be wise, that may not be honest, or that may be taken for the direct or indirect purpose of building up the political power of himself or the mayor or governor who appointed him?

Public health has been said to be the most democratic of all community interests. No member of a community, rich or poor, young or old, is independent of or separated from the health problem of the community. It is fair to assume that the non-official health agency should be the embodiment of the democratic interest, the group consisting of few or many individuals who in themselves typify the various units in the community.

The enforcement of public health measures is, on the other hand, one of the most autocratic functions provided for under our form of government. Like a police mandate, a public health order should mean instant obedience or prompt punishment. From an academic viewpoint the close coördination of the democratic non-official agency and the autocratic health official presents points of difficulty.

American psychology has some bearing on the coöperation of the official and the non-official health agencies. An independent group of individuals each with his or her own circle of influence can be of great value in many ways. As has been indicated, each independent individual represents a teaching force that may spread and multiply with geo-

metrical progression. No factor designed to influence public opinion can be more valuable.

An ideal combination, therefore, in all forms of health work would seem to be the health officer and the non-official body working in close coöperation, but with a clear distinction between them. If the non-official body is too closely incorporated in the official agency, it loses its identity in the public view, becomes a mere adjunct to the office; and the effect is a lessening of the force of the combination. Instead of many pronouncements in favor of some progressive step in community health, there is but one, and that stamped as official.

Moreover, groups of citizens, each of weight and influence in his own field, cannot be continuously interested in helping an official to get over his program. Why should they pay taxes to employ and support the work of an official and then devote their time to doing his work under his direction?

Are non-official health organizations worth while? The writer believes emphatically that they are.

Can they exist if tied up too closely with official agencies? No. It seems too close affiliation will stifle independence and initiative; thus will be lost the valuable assistance that health officials need and appreciate.

Can the non-official agencies be coördinated so that there will be no duplication of work either between each other or between the non-official and the official agencies? Such coördination is not only possible; it must surely come.

RELATIVE FUNCTIONS OF HEALTH AGENCIES
III. WHAT IS THE MATTER WITH PUBLIC HEALTH?

CHARLES T. NESBITT, M. D.,
Director of Health,
Akron, O.

To one who has been trying to visualize and build public health service as a function of municipal government for ten long and difficult years the discussion as to what is the matter with public health now is extremely interesting. Dr. Hill and Dr. McCombs have opened a big subject the discussion of which is of vital importance at this stage of the evolution of public health work. We must decide soon just what we are going to do, whether we are going to take our rightful place among governmental agencies, organized on the sound basis of constitutional and governmental precedent, or as in the past wander off into the seductive field of propaganda stunts and social service. The Health Officer of today finds himself and his work so variously distributed and his value to the community estimated on such varied counts and activities, that he is continuously between two fires. On one hand he has the administrative organization of his own city or other political unit. His administration expects him to be a smoothly functioning part of the governmental machine, exercising his official authority in strict accordance with the letter of the law. The legal department of the organization and the judiciary under whose guidance he exercises his police power hold him strictly to their standards and opinions as is right and proper. The Health Officer is a sworn officer of the law, he must proceed in strict accordance with orderly government. On the other hand the philanthropic agencies of a voluntary nature which are in every community, and the groups that are interested in specific things, the things not being always philanthropic, expect him to serve their ends in every cause even remotely affecting human welfare. If there happens to be no law which will serve their ends they frequently call upon the board of health or the commission to enact such a law without any regard for the basic principles of government or statutory and constitutional limitations. If for any reason there is not immediate compliance these groups are apt to become peeved and critical. If the board of health complies and passes the desired regulation its executive is more than apt to find his prosecutions laughed out of court, if they ever get that far, and his board and himself discredited. The wise health officer is not apt to become enthused over any law in support of which he cannot find precedent and opinion, nor will he enter upon activities that encroach upon ·the functions of other governmental departments, that operate exclusively for the benefit of any special group, or that occasion such a degree of discomfort and sacrifice on the part of the public that the desired result is overshadowed by the hardships imposed in its accomplishment.

The laws that have been enacted by boards of health in response to group demands present a curiously interesting treat to the student of public health administration who has given some attention to the study of our form of government and to the fundamentals of the law. The violation of every human right seems to have been attempted and the idea that seems to have been dominant with the proponents of these laws is, that the enactment carried with it both acceptance and enforcement. In fact in 99 cases out of 100 the enacting body has no adequate means of enforcing its mandates. The origin of these laws almost without exception can be found in the enthusiasm of some health officer or board who in responding to group pressure did not take the time to examine into the merits and values of the proposed procedures.

The plan now in operation in Akron may present some features that will interest those who, like ourselves, are earnestly trying to dig municipal public health service from beneath the avalanche of questionable duties and responsibilities that has descended upon it from the lofty heights of altruistic urge.

On January first of the present year the city of Akron reörganized its municipal government under the provisions of a carefully built charter which provided for the commission form of government. Seven major departments were established, Administration, Safety, Law, Public Service, Public Health, Social Service and Finance. All departments save Public Health are under the direct control of the Council and the Chief Administrator. A Public Health Commission is provided which consists of "five citizens," who are appointed by the chief administrator to serve for a term of five years. The initial appointments to be made for one, two, three, four, and five years, respectively, so that there will be but one change in personnel each year. The Health Commission is the legislative body on all health matters and selects and appoints the Director of Health and his subordinates. The seven departmental directors constitute the cabinet of the Chief Administrator. Under the guidance of the Chief Administrator there has been built up a most remarkable system of coöperation in the various departments. Duties have been distributed in such a way that overlapping services leave no gaps and the spirit of sympathetic helpfulness dominates the whole organization.

Social service and public health are administered under separate departments equal in standing with each other and all the other departments. This was done by the Charter Commission for the direct purpose of attempting the separation of matters of general welfare such as poor relief, medical and nursing service to the indigent and other purely charitable activities from the field of public health. The Department of Social Service is as yet incompletely organized. The Department of Public Health is organized as follows: Divisions of Administration, Laboratories, Public Health Nursing, Sanitation, Communicable Disease, Vital Statistics, Dairy and Food Control and Education. Recognizing that disease prevention depends primarily upon the conduct and understanding of the individual, our organization is taught that its highest duty is to urge by demonstration and advice in its every contact with the public the benefits of hygienic living. It is taught that its function under the law must provide at all times text and example and the opportunity to teach individuals the methods of disease prevention. Our medical school inspection, infant welfare, preschool age and pre-natal work admits us to families in all classes of society and our nurses are taught that by being of real service to these families they can establish the respect and confidence that will make their advice acceptable and usable and will gain for the Department the kind of influence it must have in order to achieve its purposes. The sanitary inspectors, the dairy and food inspectors and the other attachés are instructed in the same way. We try to serve the public in every possible way at all times and make each service the means of educating someone or some group in the business of healthful living. We use our police powers, which are specifically conferred by Charter, only in such cases as are not amenable to instruction and advice. We bring no indefinite cases into court. Each case is prepared and the evidence is ready and we prosecute under sound laws only. There are plenty of such laws. Our physicians are not permitted to engage in private practice. They can undertake only such remedial work outside of contagion as is clearly emergent. When the Social Service Department is fully organized we shall turn over to it the medical and surgical correction of all cases, excepting the contagious, and it will determine indigency and secure the service necessary from our hospitals and general clinics. We shall continue to treat venereals and contagious cases only. We shall keep our divisional activities because each is absolutely essential to proper control of infection and to our fundamental function which is to serve the whole people by teaching them the methods of living that preserve health and the detail of disease prevention.

The outside agencies in Akron participated actively in the construction of this plan. They saw without much argument the growing diffusiveness of public health effort and the necessity for drawing a sharp line of demarcation between social service and public health. They saw the wisdom of limiting the medical service of public health strictly to the preventive field and the necessity for firmly establishing public health in a field of its own on a permanent plane of equality with the other governmental departments. They are right behind the city government in this experiment and are not demanding spectacular and picturesque demonstrations of efficiency. They want, as we do, a public health service that is built solidly on public approbation and appreciation that has been honestly won. When they wish to know how efficient the service is they ask the man in the street. The medical and welfare services of the industries are closely linked with the general scheme. Matters of public health policy are settled in conference with representatives of all agencies interested. There is no conflict because the principals in each organization have an active part in the selection of methods and agencies. The Health Commission is widely representative and the general good is the dominating thought.

The description of our situation may sound utopian but for the present, at least, it is a fair statement.

When public health workers get down to brass tacks in a definite field, the limits of which are fixed in accordance with sound governmental function, most of what is now the matter with public health will have disappeared.

☐

FOOD VALUE OF MILK

Another example of the value of milk in feeding animals, more striking even than those shown in the August issue of the JOURNAL, is here presented. These animals, 18 months old, in neither instance give any evidence to lead one to imagine any sickness to have interfered with growth, but they show a great difference in size. One had milk regularly, the other was supplied with other forms of nourishment. They were in the group recently exhibited at the Grand Central Palace, New York City, and are reproduced through the courtesy of the New York State Department of Farms and Markets.

RELATIVE FUNCTIONS OF HEALTH AGENCIES

IV. RELATION BETWEEN OFFICIAL AND NON-OFFICIAL HEALTH AGENCIES

FRANCIS GEORGE CURTIS, M.D.

Chairman, Board of Health,
Newton, Mass.

Read before the Massachusetts Association of Boards of Health, at Boston, Mass., October 28, 1920.

AMONG the fads which are so popular at the present day, "Public Health" holds a very prominent position, as is shown by the large and increasing number of associations which are in existence everywhere, each with the avowed object of instructing the public in health matters.

It is a very insignificant community which has not in its midst one or more of these non-official agencies, each of which is perfectly willing to do public health work, often with very little regard for the officially recognized agencies.

The methods by which the non-official agencies get their start are very simple, but at the same time very effective.

One method is to hold a meeting, or several meetings, on public health and show how the citizens are lacking in modern health protection: they show how very necessary such protection is in order that the citizens may be kept healthy; that the infant mortality rate may be reduced or that tuberculosis may be controlled, etc.

After they have done all this they announce, in the proper way, that they will supply a public health nurse, for example, without any expense to the town and will undertake the work of supervising the health of the citizens.

This is a very subtle method of attack, because we all know the lure of getting something for nothing, and the chances are that a small town will gladly accept the offer.

Another method is for a number of persons to get together and decide that it would redound to the glory of the town, and perhaps incidentally of themselves, to establish a clinic or a dispensary for the treatment of any one of the list of human ailments which have been popularized lately. No sooner said than done and the work is started as a "demonstration" and carried on until it dies of inanition or is unloaded upon the community to be carried on successfully by the official agency.

These are not imaginary pictures: they are statements of what is actually occurring around us, every day.

The writer believes that the time has come for the boards of health to face this condition frankly and to take action to put these non-official agencies in the positon in which they belong, namely, that of adjuncts to the health department, taking their orders from it and supplementing its work, and he further believes that if boards of health do not do this, and do it now, they will wake up too late, only to find themselves in a subordinate position.

Consider for a moment how difficult it will be for a board of health to persuade the tax payers to appropriate money for school inspection or care of tuberculosis or any other necessary function, when a non-official association says that it will do the work, without any expense. Consider also the value of the vital statistics of a community in which such work has been done by an irresponsible association which has no connection with the board of health and has no responsibility to it.

We all know that a quarter of a century ago, the board of health was looked upon as more or less of a joke; its chief duties consisted of placarding houses for communicable disease, fumigating rooms after such diseases, abating nuisances, removing garbage and frightening people about the condition of their plumbing. Almost anyone knew enough to go on the board of health, but no one wanted to, while its medical member had to be coaxed to accept the appointment and sometimes felt that he was losing caste among his fellows by so doing.

Contrast this with the board of health of the present day with its corps of trained men; men who have devoted years to the study of their profession, many of them holding the degree of D. P. H., or its equivalent won by hard work in the field; men, trained in laboratory work, preventive medicine and in all branches of public health work, who devote their lives to the protection of the communities whose health is in their care.

The work done by the pioneers in public health has brought about a change in the attitude of the public towards boards of health and instead of being ridiculed they are respected and looked up to.

It has brought about another change also and one which I believe is responsible, in part, for the present situation. It has made public health popular and has caused shrewd persons to seize upon it as a means of justifying the existence of certain non-official agencies, by doing work which can and should be done by the board of health.

They apparently wish to appropriate all of the successes which the pioneers of public health have achieved, use them for their own advantage and leave for the board of health only such parts of the work as they themselves cannot do because of lack of legal authority.

That this controversy between official and non-official agencies is not imaginary was clearly shown at the recent meeting of the American Public Health Association at San Francisco. Part of one session of the general association was devoted to a symposium on this very question and in some of the section meetings the question was touched upon.

There is no doubt but that both the official and non-official agencies have their place in the community; the latter are in existence and will undoubtedly continue to exist for some time, but the important question to be decided is which shall lead and direct the work.

In the opinion of the writer there is and can be but one answer to this question. The leader and director must be the official agency; in other words, the board of health. When one considers the many functions of a modern board of health and how they reach out and touch almost every phase of community life it is evident that any non-official agency which attempts to do public health work independently is simply trying to usurp one or other of the functions of the board of health or else to reduplicate its work for some reason.

The chief reason why the board of health should lead and direct this work is because it is established by law; it is the servant of the people, responsible to the people for what it does and for the manner in which it does it. It has been entrusted with great powers. In this state, the board of health acting under the law is practically omnipotent; there is hardly anything that one can think of that the board of health cannot do, and to use a slang phrase, "get away with," provided it acts within the law and it is not difficult to do that. But the very powers given to the health officer, as the representative of the official agency, carry with them a sense of responsibility which makes him more careful in the exercise of those powers than the representative of the irresponsible non-official agency.

The health officer is the tax payer's man and consequently is more conservative; more prone to count the cost, in all senses of the word, than is the non-official man.

The law, which is after all only crystallized public opinion, has given great powers and also great responsibilities to the legally-constituted official agency and its legally-appointed agents and I know of no legal authority which allows it to delegate these functions to non-official agencies. It is, however, true that these non-official agencies or some of them do not agree with this view.

Some of the non-official agencies argue that the chief reason for their existence is to be found in the poor organization of the official agencies; they claim that if they, the non-official agencies, did not carry on the work which they do, the public would be deprived of the care and instruction to which it has a right; and they say that it is only in those communities in which the boards of health do not function properly that the non-official ones are active. The objection to that idea is that the right of deciding what constitutes the proper thing under the law, is claimed by one of the parties to the controversy, and one which has no standing before the law. The agency whose sole excuse for existence depends upon the failure of another to do the proper thing, would very soon decide that its rival had failed, if it had the power to decide and was not responsible to the community for the correctness of its decision.

If the non-official agencies confined their independent activities to those communities in which the official ones do not function properly, they would have a better case, but it is a known fact that they do not so limit themselves.

There is hardly a function of public health work which the board of health cannot and does not perform better than the non-official agency.

In questions pertaining to administration the health department must necessarily work them out better; its overhead is less and its view point is wider. In the matter of control of disease and the disposal of the individual patient, the tax payer's doctor, the health officer, must be in charge and decide what must be done. Often in the end it is the tax payer's money which must pay the bills and his representative should be in control and decide how it shall be used.

The *education of the public* in matters pertaining to health is a very important function of a modern board of health and should always be under its control. This is a function which appeals very strongly to the volunteer agency and it is here that it can do much real harm and hamper the board of health to the greatest degree.

It seems a peculiar dispensation of Providence that the public is always more ready to accept the statements of the non-official agency than it is to believe those published by its own board of health. Perhaps this is because the former has no legal responsibility and its main idea is to get its information before the public in a striking, catchy manner, and sometimes, I regret to say, without strict regard for fact. The most difficult statement to confute is "the lie that apes the truth," and the statements of the volunteer agencies usually have a modicum of truth.

But no matter how reckless the statements of the volunteer agency may be nor how much they may be misunderstood by the public when they are correct, it is never the unofficial agency which is held responsible but the board of health which is criticized, and criticized severely, if its action does not agree with what the critic believes the unofficial statement meant to say.

Often the fact contained in an educational leaflet or catch word issued by a non-official agency may be perfectly correct but utterly impossible to carry out because of undue expense or because it is impracticable. This makes no difference to the critic; he immediately comes to the conclusion that his health officer is behind the age or is not doing his duty and he is not at all bashful about saying so. If, however, the health officer should attempt to carry out one of the expensive suggestions of the volunteer agency and then call upon the taxpayer to pay the bills, it needs no clairvoyant to tell what would happen.

The volunteer agency is never troubled by any apprehensions in regard to cost, and its suggestions, while good, are often impossible of adoption because the result is not commensurate with the expense involved in accomplishing it.

In this very important function of public health work, there is no question but that the health officer should be in absolute control, and, if for any reason, he cannot publish educational matter himself, he should at least have the opportunity to pass upon all such matter before it is issued by the volunteer agency.

The health officer of the present day is a practical man, interested, not in any particular branch of public health work but in all, and he is much better able to judge of the effect upon his own community, and his own work, of any particular leaflet or catch word, than is a non-official agency, interested usually in only one particular function of the work, which employs a publicity man to turn out catchy stuff without any particular regard to its effect.

Research work or the study of disease is another function which should be under the control of the board of health; it is under no obligation to justify its existence by showing that it is doing something, no matter what, and it can therefore proceed more slowly, test out its results at leisure and be sure that its conclusions are justified before announcing them.

One marked feature of the unofficial agency is that it must always keep itself before the public and it is therefore very prone to explode prematurely. Furthermore, it may jump at conclusions and announce as fact something which is at best only a working hypothesis.

Even that increasingly popular institution, the health centre, belongs properly to the board of health. A health center, after all, is simply a place where the benefits of preventive medicine and good advice on matters pertaining to public health are offered to the community at large and who should more properly oversee and direct this than the taxpayer's own doctors and nurses?

It is very gratifying to be able to record that Massachusetts has recognized the truth of this fact and that, under the provisions of Chap 100 of the General Acts of 1920, cities and towns may establish dental, medical and *health* clinics and, in connection therewith, may conduct campaigns of general education relative to matters of public health and furthermore that all these shall be under the control of the board of health and that any money appropriated for their support shall be expended by the board of health.

The question as to how the board of health shall keep control of these functions or resume control, if it has lost it, is not an easy one to answer. The non-official agencies have a very strong foothold in many places and appeal very strongly to the public and it must, in all fairness, be admitted that their claim that they are doing work which the board of health ought to do but isn't, is very often true. It seems, therefore, that the first thing for boards of health to do is to become really active and do something more than placard a few houses for diphtheria or scarlet fever.

In many communities it is true that the local board of health lacks the trained personnel to do much active work, but it can always ask the District Health Officer for advice and assistance. It is not meant that the local board should ask the state to do its work, but only that it should consult with the representatives of the state as to the best methods of procedure.

Too often the local board of health acquiesces in the usurpation of some of its functions or, which is much worse, turns them over voluntarily to some non-official agency. The writer has often called the office of a board of health and asked for information· only ·to be told that some local association was doing that work and that the required information was not on file. In the humble opinion of the writer such a reply at once stamps a board of health as failing in its duty. The information asked for was in regard to a legitimate function of a board of health and the public should be able to obtain it from the main office, provided it was in existence. If the work is being done at all, the board of health should do it, or if temporarily unable to, should see that it is done, under its direction; and proper reports filed.

The writer believes that in this state, at least, the local board of health has ample power to control all matters pertaining to public health and should do so. Its obligation to do this is increased if it has voluntarily turned over the work to some other agency, and has failed to require proper reports of the work.

In those communities where the non-official agencies are powerful and have a strong hold upon the public, the health officer, as the representative of the legal authorities, should keep in close touch with the non-official · agencies either personally or through his public health nurses; he should attend their meetings and do all in his power to direct their energies in the right direction.

A little diplomacy will go a long way and often a quiet suggestion in regard to a method of procedure or a simple question, may be the means of putting the health officer in a position to control the matter under consideration, but he should never forget the fact that he is the representative of the board of health which has control of such matters by law. He should be very careful to explain the law governing such cases as may come up for discussion. The trouble with many non-official agencies seems to be that they are ignorant of the law and do not understand that a local board of health, powerful as it appears to be, is bound by the law and must be able to justify its acts by the law.

The writer has often found that a short explanation of how a board of health must act and that its apparent slowness in acting, in cases where rapid action was not necessary, was due, not to carelessness, but really to careful consideration, has resulted in his getting control of the situation.

On the other hand he has been able to show that the unauthorized interference of the volunteer agency has resulted in unnecessary delay in settling the case, often to the detriment of the physical welfare of the individual it was trying to help.

If the health officer can once persuade the non-official agencies to work with him, instead of acting independently, he will find that he has acquired an addition to his working force—whose usefulness will depend in great measure upon himself—and he will have gone far towards realizing the picture presented at the San Francisco meeting by a speaker who showed "the unofficial agencies standing back of and helping the official agencies" and also that he will have eliminated the proviso "as long as we feel that the latter is doing the proper thing," because, as they are helping in the work, they will feel that it is the proper thing.

□

Three important Symposiums from the San Francisco meeting are scheduled for early numbers of the JOURNAL in 1921,— Narcotic Drug Control, Smallpox and Health Centers.

RELATIVE FUNCTIONS OF HEALTH AGENCIES
V. COÖRDINATION OF STATE AND PRIVATE ENTERPRISES IN PUBLIC HEALTH WORK

W. H. HATTIE, M. D.,
Provincial Health Officer,
Halifax, N. S.

[At the annual meeting of the Canadian Public Health Association, June 21-22, 1920, Dr. Hattie presented his address. By way of introduction he spoke of the war and its lessons and then referred to the vastly more important war, that of public health on disease. With this preamble he entered upon his main subject, his words being here presented through the courtesy of the Public Health Journal, official organ of the Canadian association.]

Nothing has been more heartening to public health workers than the growth and spread of interest in public health possibilities which recent years have witnessed. The stimulus has been felt in many ways, and has aided greatly in furthering advance. While zeal may at times have outstripped prudence, leading to multiplicity of organizations with resultant overlapping and perhaps clashing of interests, the tendency towards co-ördination of effort had been steadily becoming more evident. And now that the League of Red Cross Societies has been formed with so magnificent a purpose in view, "the improvement of health, the prevention of disease, and the mitigation of suffering throughout the world," we have an ally, the strength of which can scarcely be overestimated, and which has the unquestioned confidence of the people of every nation. If then, we take advantage of this alliance and determine upon effectively correlating the activities of all agencies with similar aims, whether they be state or private organizations, in a united endeavor to improve the general health, we should make tremendous strides towards our common goal. And because of Red Cross connection, there should develop a feeling of mutual interest and sympathy among nations which should become a most important factor in securing and preserving peace throughout the world.

It is particularly gratifying to those in the service of the state that the League of Red Cross Societies has definitely recognized that the protection of the health of the people is a responsibility and a function of government, and has decided that public health work under Red Cross auspices will be supplementary or complementary to that undertaken by other voluntary and state agencies. The readiness of so powerful an organization to enter the public health field in what might almost appear to be a subordinate position is indicative of the splendid spirit which actuates Red Cross activities generally. It, moreover, shows the consistency of an organization which has won a reputation for such efficiency as can be attained only through centralization of authority. So fine an example will doubtless overcome any hesitation which other agencies might have in agreeing to carry on their undertakings under greater or less control by a Central Authority. It is very human to desire independence of action, and to crave public applause, but in the great work of saving life and of increasing the comfort and happiness of mankind the attitude of all good workers will be one of complete unselfishness.

When, therefore, it is said that the general direction of all health work should be in the hands of the health administrator of the state, it is not because of any wish that such official should receive anything more than merited kudos for the results achieved. It is because such an official is the logical person to whom this great responsibility should be assigned. Much public health work can be carried on only under statutory enactments, for the formulation and enforcement of which the state is responsible. Practically all the progress which has been made in this work has been either initiated by or made possible by state health organizations. Much the larger part of the expenditure which has thus far been made on behalf of the public health has been from state funds. Officials of the state have opportunities for acquiring information as to both general and local needs and for determining the most promising lines of action which are in exceptional instances available to private persons. And the people generally have come to look to the state for leadership in such matters. If, therefore, we are to agree upon the principle of unity of action, it would appear that the coördinating and harmonizing force should be the state organization. It certainly could not be hoped that any private enterprise could be assigned such a place without arousing the antagonism of other agencies which are doing most useful work along similar lines.

The amount of control which the state organization might exert over private enterprises should, however, not be more than is necessary to prevent wastage of funds and effort. As far as possible there should be no interference with autonomy. Every possible assistance should be rendered, every encouragement should be offered, and every credit should be given by the state organization to the coöperating agencies. And while all private activity in respect to health work should perhaps be conditional to the sanction and oversight of the state organization, the pressing need for such private activity and the unquestioned value of a great deal of the opinion which evolves from such sources, should prevent any unreasonable interference with the work they are carrying on. There should, of course, be frequent conferences in order that there may be definite and complete understanding in respect to policy and the relationship between the various organizations.

While not suggesting that there should be any diminution of state activity or lessening of state responsibility in matters which are definitely functions of the state, it would appear that unofficial organizations could materially aid in the furtherance of our aims by encouraging investigation along promising new lines, especially through financial assistance to laboratories; by assistance through endowment or otherwise in the teaching of public health to medical students and others—as to graduate nurses who desire to enter our fields, and to those who wish to engage in welfare work; and by assistance to national organizations now engaged in propaganda which has a bearing on public health. The proposal of the Red Cross Society to provide in whole or in part for the support of public health nurses in communities in which local funds are insufficient for such a purpose is a most practical method of coöperation. Further assistance might be rendered by furnishing paid and voluntary workers to help at health centers, health clinics, etc., in rendering clerical aid, stimulating interest, distributing relief, and carrying on such other work as does not require technical training, so as to conserve the time and energy of those who have such training. In such ways immense impetus would be given to the work of the official agencies.

The inspiring program which the League of Red Cross Societies has laid down, and the splendid work on behalf of the public health which has been carried on by the Victorian Order of Nurses, anti-tuberculosis leagues, child welfare organizations, local nursing associations, women's institutes and kindred enterprises, merit our heartiest commendation. The self sacrifice shown by so many of our people, who have given freely of their time, energy and substance in the effort to ameliorate the conditions of their less fortunate fellows cannot ·be too highly extolled. Those holding positions in the service of the state owe to these noble people a really burdensome debt of gratitude. We need the stimulus and the encouragement as well as the help they give. It is with no desire that their activities should be curtailed, or that any irritating restraint should be put upon them, that it is suggested that they should work under state direction, but rather to increase their efficiency and to obtain through harmonious coöperation the best possible results in "the improvement of health, the prevention of disease and the mitigation of suffering."

☐

RELATIVE FUNCTIONS OF HEALTH AGENCIES
VI. DISCUSSION

At the San Francisco meeting of the A. P. H. A., following the papers on this subject by Dr. Haven Emerson and Dr. Charles J. Hatfield at the general session of Monday evening, September 13, 1920, there was a general discussion. The speakers were Surgeon General Hugh S. Cumming, Dr. John A. Ferrell, Dr. William F. Snow, Dr. E. A. Peterson, Dr. Frederick R. Green, Dr. Donald B. Armstrong, Professor Edith S. Bryan, Dr. L. A. Powers and Dr. Frankwood E. Williams. From the stenographer's notes of the session the following minutes of the meeting have been prepared, which in general follow quite closely the language of the speakers in their main arguments.

The first speaker in this discussion was HUGH S. CUMMING, Surgeon General, U. S. Public Health Service. Dr. Cumming spoke of the interest felt by the officers of the Service in the movement of the American Medical Association for the unification of Federal governmental activities. His arguments were to the effect that, as both speakers had said, public health is a governmental function. At first sight then the necessity for the non-official health agency would seem to involve the confession that the governmental agency was inefficient, lacked adequate legislation or adequate appropriations. On behalf of the official side we prefer to think that it is lack of such legislation and appropriations in some form ·of government. We cannot use this as a defense. In our form of government, however large the appropriation might be, however adequate the legislation might be, there would still exist the absolute necessity for voluntary agencies.

There are two ways of carrying out the health legislation: One is by attempting to enforce a law which may have been enacted against the will of the people and the other is to get the people in the proper frame of mind to obey the law voluntarily.

Under our form of government at least and with the American people, the enforcement of the law against public sentiment is, I think, absolutely impossible. We have had demonstrations of that along other lines.

Now the main difficulty as I see it with the federal and, I am sure, the state agencies, is to get in such contact with the individual man, and particularly with the man who needs instruction, that he will understand why the law has been passed and the necessity for obeying it.

I think that our unofficial bodies are doing and can do more work along that line in educating the individual, in getting the official body in contact with the individual, than in any other way as regards routine of improvement of public health.

It goes without saying that no governmental agency is fully equipped suddenly to assume responsibility for and to handle great calamities and epidemics. That is exactly, of course, where the Red Cross has done such a noble work, not only in war but in times of peace.

I am glad to see that the Public Health Association is taking up this work of inducing the people to take an interest in the necessity for more adequate public health legislation than exists. In every country I think that will be one of the most important features of non-official bodies.

DR. JOHN A. FERRELL, Director for the United States of the International Health Board, was the second speaker, whose remarks were the following:

The consideration given at this meeting to a discussion of this topic is really a continuation of discussions which have been under way during the past three or four years. The situation is gradually clearing, and the public and private health agencies are finding common ground. The outlook for real team play is encouraging. I was requested to present the point of view of the non-official health agency, I presume, because of my connection with the International Health Board.

This board as a non-official agency is peculiarly situated in that its annual resources are derived as income from an endowment fund; its organization is limited to board members and staff members; and there is no occasion for seeking special donations or for conducting membership drives. Its point of view, accordingly, could not be expected to represent that held by non-official health agencies differently situated. I shall, therefore, limit my remarks to the point of view of the International Health Board.

The board is a working agency of the Rockefeller Foundation in the field of public health. It has operated in no state or country except upon invitation from the government. A working relationship has been established with government departments of health in more than thirty states and countries throughout the world. The field activities in which it coöperates without exception have been conducted in coöperation with government, and, in so far as practicable, through and in the name of government. Although its financial aid in a number of countries has been limited to the control of special diseases which lend themselves to concrete demonstrations, its broader and deeper interest has been to aid, as opportunities arise, in the development of strong, well-rounded, efficient public health agencies, adequately financed with public funds.

Public health authorities generally have encountered difficulty in securing appropriations for new projects. Legislative bodies will provide funds for continuing work the usefulness of which has been demonstrated. The private agency can coöperate with the public agency financially and otherwise in conducting demonstrations of more effective methods for conducting the work to which the government is already committed, and in demonstrating the value and economic practicability of new undertakings. Once the demonstration is made, and the taxpayer and legislator satisfied as to its value, the legally constituted agency can, with comparative ease, obtain the funds for its extension as a part of the government program. Coöperation of this character is welcomed by the public agency, and offers to the private agency an exceptional opportunity for service. It results in broadening the public health program and in increased legislative support on a permanent basis for the public agency.

The International Health Board, in addition to lending aid in demonstration measures for the control of hookworm disease, malaria, yellow fever, and other diseases, on the basis outlined, has contributed toward increasing the number of trained health officers. The development of public health work in many states and countries is already far in advance of the supply of qualified health officers. The situation has led to the granting of a limited number of fellowships to promising health officers who are sincerely desirous of better qualifying themselves for their duties by studying in institutions which offer creditable courses in public health. Moreover, assistance has been given toward the establishment of training facilities at strategic points. Scholarships have likewise been provided for training scientists desiring better to qualify themselves for teaching the fundamental branches of public health.

The governmental agencies have welcomed coöperation along the lines described and have expressed the opinion that as a result their efficiency has increased and the scope of their work broadened. The relationship at every point has been harmonious. The public and private agency has had the same objective. There has been mutual understanding and an absence of conflict of interest. Where public and private health agencies can share in a common task, there would seem to be for each a definite field of usefulness where real service can be performed which will inspire the confidence and support of the public.

DR. W. F. SNOW, of New York City, began his discussion by stating that in the company present he could see the representatives of at least twenty or thirty private volunteer agencies of which when Health Officer of California he had asked for assistance in various ways.

Sometimes it was the development of some experiment which we believed would lead to some demonstrated measure of efficiency for effecting work in the state. Sometimes it was to carry out in some limited area a demonstration of measures that we knew were practical but measures which we could not stand behind and say of them to the legislature or to a given board of trustees of a town that they had ever been tried, practiced and proved to be feasible within the normal taxation of the community.

There are many times when all of us who have been health officers have faced a situation in which we wanted, in the language of President Wilbur's and President Barrows' students, to "Let George do the job." We have always turned to the volunteer agency to do the job and usually they have carried it through.

I think the discussions which have gone on this evening in presenting the viewpoints of the two agencies might well be summed up in a re-statement of what Dr. Ferrell has just said, that it is the function of a volunteer agency, and will be for years to come perhaps, first to experiment with incomplete evidence as to administrative measures.

Our universities will always be looked to, I think, to find the academic facts, to work out our field of scientific facts which we may apply to the preservation of health and to the combating of disease.

Beyond that there is still a field of further experimentation in which we want to take a set of scientific phenomena and see if we may apply them through any of our social and administrative machinery.

When we have proved that case then comes the necessity of proving it from the taxpayer's standpoint; prove it from the mayor's or governor's point of view, as to whether we can fit it into our administrative machinery.

I think we must look to private agencies to test out just such preliminary steps. Once we have those things proved, they can be applied through the administrative machinery.

Then again we probably will have to look to these agencies to develop public opinion to get behind the health officer in applying these measures.

It is the function of volunteer agencies to shape public opinion toward such legislative action.

Again it is necessary, as Dr. Ferrell has pointed out, for them to aid financially in the beginning and the extension work at least of pioneer efforts in public administration with every new attack we make for the preservation of health.

One last thing: Speaking from the point of view of the volunteer association, I think it is important to have in mind that the volunteer association can watch progress of its public health officials. After a measure has been proved practical, is in operation, it still remains of importance that we have some individual volunteer agency that is watching that measure to see that it is effectively enforced. If it is, well and good; if it is not, that volunteer agency is depended upon to see that the officials who have been charged with the duty of enforcing it do their work effectively.

If it is lack of funds, as Dr. Cumming suggested, we must see that the taxpayer provides the funds. If it is lack of initiative on the part of the health officer we must see that we have one that can do the work.

To my mind the program of study and the development of correlation, coöperation and the merger of the volunteer agencies suggested in the closing remarks of our President Rankin, are entirely sound and I believe much may be expected to come from the series of conferences this coming year which he has mentioned.

DR. E. A. PETERSON of the Red Cross, Washington, D. C., in outlining the situation stated that both the official and the non-official agencies will do "what the folks will allow it to do."

Now why the official agency cannot do all of the good things in the field of health need not be discussed here. We know that it cannot. We know that there are so many good men in health work today that if it were possible to do all the good things they would be done.

But we also face these facts, that on the one hand here is a mass of knowledge, but as Dr. Emerson says, there has not been a transference of that knowledge, so that there seems to be a tremendous amount of work which some other phase of our expression must take care of.

I am one who believes that there is just as firm a foundation for the unofficial agency as there is for the official agency; that is, a law is not the final thing, the final rock upon which we can place any kind of a building.

With the relative functions as I have just stated, each agency can do what its supporters will allow it to do. If there is a gap between them, if there is a body of knowledge here that our experts have gathered and it is not made available over there, we ought to bridge the gap. The unofficial agency can be very important in such a field.

Dr. Peterson recognized the equally firm foundation in the sociology of the country of the two agencies, and assured his hearers that it is not a question of making the non-official agency the tail to a kite, for it is a kite by itself. The relative functions of the two have nothing to do with their regard for one another, but with the regard of the people towards them. The official agency should do as much as it can considering the limitations that surround it. What it cannot do the non-official agency may accomplish.

"I do not believe," he said in closing, "that the non-official agency can do its best work by tieing up absolutely to the health officer. That non-official agency must have a little kite of its own and to help the health officer most we must seem to help him little, because of a psychology which I think you all understand."

DR. FREDERICK R. GREEN of Chicago, Ill., was the next speaker and referred to the history of this discussion, which at every recent meeting "has bobbed up to the surface and has been discussed a little while and apparently gone out of existence again until the next meeting."

To the superficial observer there has been little if any progress made as far as actual accomplishment goes. At the same time

those who have been entering the discussions know and it is apparent to us, that we have been gradually, slowly if you will, necessarily on account of the magnitude of the interests involved, gradually getting to an understanding and working out some general principles.

I think that those of you who recall the first program when this question was up for discussion—I think at the meeting in Jacksonville in 1914—and the various papers and discussions on the question held then, and compare it with the one held tonight, you will agree that there has been decided progress. There has been a very apparent acceptance of a number of different general propositions governing this question, on the part of all the speakers taking part in the discussion.

In the first place everyone has agreed, I think, that the ultimate object toward which we all of us were working and the ultimate goal toward which all of us want to attain, was the organization of adequate and official governmental machinery in the public health field, from the top down to the bottom; such organization for the public health as may be necessary to handle the problems of the federal government, whatever their limitations may be; the organization in each state of an effective state organization that will handle the problems of the state public health, and in each city of any size, or whatever the unit agreed upon, one which will handle the local problem.

That is the ultimate object toward which we are all striving and I think that has now come to be generally accepted and admitted.

If that is true and that is the goal toward which we are working, then it necessarily follows that the voluntary organizations must necessarily be temporary organizations, whatever that may mean. They are for the working out of certain definite problems and for the carrying on of certain functions until the federal machinery may be constituted to such a point where it can properly take them over.

If that is the case, then it also follows that there are certain definite functions which those temporary organizations should perform. First, that they should be regarded as stop-gaps to fill in the time until the governmental organizations can be mobilized and properly organized to take over those functions; second, for educating the public; third, for arousing interest in the public which will lead to the proper machinery.

Then it follows that the task is too large, that of educating the public for instance, for any one class. I want to include the class which I represent, the medical profession. While I think it is perfectly true, as Dr. Hatfield says, that the educated, scientific medical profession must be of necessity one of the largest, and while it is of the highest importance, I have repeatedly urged in the meetings of the American Medical Association that the medical profession, both as individuals and as an organization, should take a leading part in public health leadership; yet it should never be forgotten that it is necessarily a function of the government and not of any one profession or class.

It is in accordance with these general principles that the Council on Health and Public Instruction has endeavored to carry on its own activities, rather than the development of any single function or the monopolizing of the field, recognizing the fact that we should merely form a hub around which other organizations could group and with which others could affiliate and coördinate.

That I take to be the function of the Council of Public Instruction in the medical profession and is its contribution in working out this problem.

DR. DONALD B. ARMSTRONG of Framingham, Mass., expressed the opinion that Dr. Emerson had struck the keynote when he said that "the leadership and responsibility for this thing must be carried by the official public health agencies."

Is it not true that toward this question of the relation of public to private functions we have at least three types of minds? We have, in the first place, what you might call the engulfing mind, which would like to see the public service take over every function as soon as possible.

In the second place, we have the discouraged mind that does not believe in any public service, that is discouraged about

public service and wants to see the public officers and officials keep their hands off things as long as possible.

In the third place, you have a type of mind, I think, which represents most of us, which I might call in contrast to the engulfing mind and the discouraged mind, the courageous mind that recognizes the failures of public service but has faith in democracy; is not content only with getting the best service possible out of bad men but is desirous of getting the best possible men into public service.

Now if the functions of the private agency are as Dr. Hatfield has outlined, namely, that of research and demonstration and also of the encouragement of public officials in upholding their hands in the carrying out of their functions, then is it not true that the heart of the public health program does at the present time and always will belong to the public official and will be concerned primarily with practical service?

In the second place is it not true that the fringe of public health activities, the less tangible activities such as research and demonstration and education perhaps, will in part and perhaps always, belong to the private agencies; and that finally on this basis of public interest in public health it will, at least for as long a time as we can foresee, be the privilege and the obligation of private agencies through the creation of lay organizations and official organizations and through the building up of public service ideals, to create a sentiment and a background which will uphold and support adequately and will demand satisfactory public service from the officials concerned with public health?

PROFESSOR EDITH S. BRYAN of Berkeley, Cal., spoke from the viewpoint of teacher and trainer of a group that holds an important place in modern public health work, the public health nurse, and expressed herself most eager to seek in both agencies that which is good. "I am also bound," she said, "to note in both agencies that which is weak because it is impossible to know when you are training the public health nurse where she will go, whether to the official or the non-official agency. Therefore she must go out with a conception of that which is best in each and with a knowledge of that which is weak in either, if she is going to be able to do a just and fair and honest work for the people for whom she is laboring.

"As I have said, it is training that we are doing at the university, and we are most eager to encourage (together with a real knowledge of the work, either official or non-official) an enthusiasm and optimism and idealism, recognizing that the woman's part of the public health work as done in nursing can not be done without these three factors.

"To give them these three things in relationship to both official and non-official agencies is our task. It is a great one, a worthy one, and their work in these agencies will show whether it has been well done or not.

"Before united leadership can be gained there is one other thing that must come; united sympathy must be born and the birth cannot come without months of preparation and that preparation must come in the hearts of the leaders of these two representing agencies—not only in the hearts of the great leaders but also the hearts of the leaders of the little local organizations. Petty jealousies must vanish; fear of one another must be gone if this real sympathy can be allowed to be born—and it must come.

"I think we all recognize that the amount of work to be done by the public health nurses under these two agencies never was greater than now, and we have to teach these girls, we must make them see the value of Martha's work and Mary's, the one who is 'busy about many things' and the one who is thinking deeply about those which count most. I leave it to you to determine which is the Martha agency and which is the Mary agency. It will probably depend upon which you are working with, which one you will call by either name. As we have said, it is impossible for either agency to do all the work.

"Since the opening of the Conference on Friday, I have heard two comments from officials in public health which better express some of the difficulties for the nurse in working with these agencies than anything I can give you.

"One of the officials said, 'It is impossible for me to make a recommendation for the elimination of a certain evil because of the political influence which would be brought to bear on those who are doing the work.' There is a handicap which we cannot but recognize.

"Another was that an official speaking of his coördinate said, 'That man is too thoroughly under the thumb of the anti bodies to ever use his full influence to do the work that should be done by his agency,' showing that there are sometimes limitations which the best of people cannot overcome.

"Yet we do recognize that the other agency lacks the power to do by compulsion some things that must be done to us American people in order that we live in the most unselfish way, for we not all of us are inherently unselfish.

"And so to both agencies my plea is this: the public health nurse, trained to go out and do the great work, knows not during her training whether she is to work under the official or the non-official agency. We are sending her out with an idealism that she can do a great work with either.

"As she comes to either let us hope that that idealism need not be destroyed by any adverse feeling."

DR. L. A. POWERS of Los Angeles, Cal., spoke very briefly, voicing the opinion that the discussion of the evening had outlined the whole matter more clearly than had been done before, and noting that he saw in the suggestions a fair road to success, because it is by means of education and not by law or anything of that kind, that coöperation between the two kinds of agencies is to be attained.

DR. FRANKWOOD E. WILLIAMS of New York was the last speaker in the discussion and took for his theme the value of the minority.

All progress, of course, when you come to think about it, comes through the activities of minorities. The greatest official organizations we have in the country, the

United States Public Health Service, represented at one time the minority view. This organization itself, the American Public Health Association, represented at one time in the American Medical Association a minority point of view.

To speak then with disparity of minorities is to ignore their power. An official health organization represents the crystallized majority opinion. It represents the minority views from time to time that have become the majority view and have been congealed into law.

It would be most unfortunate if after that were accomplished there should be no more minority opinion upon the subject. An official health organization can never represent the first thought or the best thought or the most progressive or advanced thought in public health.

I do not mean by that that individuals in an official health organization cannot be the leaders in public health thought, that there cannot be individuals in the organization who will be the most progressive or most advanced in their thought of any public health workers in the country. There can be and frequently are; but as officials they cannot be because they can represent officially only a part, that part which has been provided for them by law. Beyond that they cannot go.

Now if by some magic the program of every non-official organization that exists today could in this second be realized and every part of this organization and those programs put over in the non-official organizations of whatever type you choose, there would still be need for non-official health organizations because nobody believes surely that the program of the American Tuberculosis Association as it consists today, or the American Hygiene Association or Mental Hygiene or any other, represents the ultimate program of any one of those organizations.

And were those programs as they exist tonight to be adopted there would still be further programs and further minority views that would still call for the existence of these organizations.

Some sort of arrangement is desirable; there should be coöperation. Better not that which is more superficial and may be artificial and may be dangerous. I like better what Dr. Armstrong has voiced in his preliminary report, in which he speaks not of coöperation but of integration. If we can have an integration then we will have a very useful organization. If it is merely a superficial and artificial coöperation then it is very questionable. But always there must be minority views.

□

MEANING AND PURPOSE OF SOCIALIZING MEDICINE

IRA S. WILE, M. D.,
New York City

Address of the Chairman before Sociological Section, American Public Health Association, at San Francisco, Cal., September 13, 1920

ONE of the functions of a Section Chairman of the American Public Health Association should be the presentation of an annual message. The aim is not the utterance itself, but the exposition of such views as may serve to stimulate thought, guide the development of the section, or suggest possibilities for more effective public service.

The Sociological Section is comparatively young, and the reasons for its creation are more marked today than at the time of its formation. One might well pause to inquire, what is meant by socializing medicine? What is its meaning and purpose?

Medicine may be defined as the healing art. This includes the science of the preservation of health, as well as the science of treating disease for the purpose of cure. The science and art of medicine require no more extended definition.

Sociology, as a science, treats of the origin and history of society and social phenomena, the progress of civilization, and the laws controlling human intercourse.

It is patent, that there is an overlapping of territory in which are to be found phases of preventive and curative medicine interwoven with social phenomena and laws controlling human intercourse. , Experience has demonstrated that social medicine is more than the medical interpretation of social data, and, similarly, is not limited to the social interpretation of medical facts. Personal hygiene relates to individual living, but even this is partially determined by a variety of social phenomena, as for example, the nature of the water supply, housing facilities, interior toilets, low wages, large families, and a vast assortment of conditions wholly or partially beyond personal control. Many of the problems of individual hygiene are determined by social organization and social practice. The social viewpoint considers the public as an aggregate of units functioning as a developing organism, and possessing as many problems in the aggregate life of the community as are to be found in the fulfillment of the destiny of any individual unit that helps constitute it.

Primitive medicine, as viewed from the standpoint of the anthropologist, was essentially individual, but the beginnings of a social point of view were manifest in the religious endeavors to combat disease, and to account for epidemic diseases. In the medieval period of history, the foundations of socialized medicine were implanted as institutions including hospitals, nursing and education. The development of the family practitioner led to a focussing of attention upon the family as a larger unit for professional care. His interests contemplated the welfare of the family group, with a consideration of the relation of individual affliction to familial welfare. The finest flower of medical practice, in its transitional phase flourished in the domain of family practice.

As in industry, an analytical process, born of scientific experimentation, influenced the growth of medicine so as to increase its complexity, making obvious the need for differentiation of function. In many instances this division of labor resulted in a condition analogous to process serving in industry. The individual and the family shared in the analytical process so that they both became congeries of systems to be studied, probed and treated by specialists, if a maximum efficiency were to be secured. The recognition of the continuous subdivision of medical practice gave rise to types of investigation which proved that neither the individual nor the family were completely masters of their physical well-being, nor could they, unaided, make the adjustments requisite for their own protection. Hence, during the 19th Century syntheses of medicine became effective through attempts at organization in the interest of the race. The fruition of these efforts to serve humanity as a whole, has been manifest in the accentuation of the social aspects of medicine during this first fifth of the 20th Century.

We have become accustomed to distinguish between private practice and public medicine; and in public medicine as well as in private practice we have differentiated between curative and preventive methods. It is true that health officers, in their descent from the priestly class, have always been charged with a certain measure of responsibility for serving public health. There was not, however, such a frenzy of organization of constructive character until there occurred the recognition of the limitations of individual and familial action, and the need for the coöperation of the integrated mass. It is not necessary to stress the historical development through the emphasis upon sanitation, the institution of machinery for detecting diseases and handicaps, the growth of organized methods of research, health surveys, and the introduction of plans for communal efforts through various types of social groups. Medical service has grown along social lines so as to affect large groups of the population through medical inspection of schools, baby welfare stations, clinics, hospitals, industrial hygiene, working men's compensation, and such more remote factors as zoning laws, abatement acts, minimum wage laws, and attempts at the reduction of specific diseases such as typhoid, malaria, yellow fever, smallpox, syphilis, ophthalmia neonatorum, and kindred diseases, for the relief and prevention of which the coöperation of large groups or communities is requisite.

In the campaigns against infant mortality and tuberculosis, it was early recognized that medicine in its narrowest concept had been unavailing. The two main factors responsible for these deadly conditions were ignorance and poverty. In consequence, our efforts were directed against these two unfortunate phenomena of social failure, with a result that is well known. In both of these instances, social medicine was essential for the accomplishment of the desired results.

The aim at the reduction of mortality had been inaccurate, while stress was placed upon advising new methods of individual treatment. The attempts at modifying therapeutic measures so as to accomplish greater results were not barren. Only, however, when there had grown ideas for the protection and conserving of communal health, did social medicine function adequately as a prophylactic force. Social medicine then came to mean the conservation of human resources as evidenced in the development of a higher standard of effective healthful citizenship. This meaning of socializing medicine is being transformed into a more positive idea of creating health. It purposes to serve the race through enriching it, promoting a useful longevity through securing conditions favorable to the development of personal and communal health, along physical, mental, and moral lines.

Social medicine is antithetic to individual medicine in its basal concepts. It aims to function through the social group for the benefit of the social group. It recognizes health as a right rather than as a privilege. It refuses to acknowledge the propriety of a stratification of the population in so far as health is concerned, and aims to afford equal opportunities for all groups of the population, regardless of color, creed or social and economic distinction. Socializing medicine, in a word, is democratizing medicine. In the equalizing of health opportunities, prophylactic and therapeutic, it aims to unite rather than separate peoples. Health is a universal factor, and its utility is not to be denied to any one because of circumstances largely determined and controlled by a federation or union of human beings, constituting a group accidentally or purposely united by ties of blood, language, occupation, government, or predilection.

It is manifest, that in its wider meaning social medicine must weigh and interpret social problems in the light of national and international health. On the other hand, it is bound to evaluate disease in terms of defects of the social organism. By both of these processes it reaches out in administration to wholesale practice rather than retail methods.

I may be pardoned for calling your attention to present day tendencies to translate problems of dependency and delinquency into terms of medical causation. It is equally trite to point out the efforts that are being made to reveal the etiological factors of disease in organic maladjustments. It may not be equally obvious that social medicine is seeking to harmonize right living with right government, so that right living and right government may be achieved. A review of the programs of the Sociological Section indicates a constant endeavor to emphasize and support health as a factor in human progress, enabling the individual and the race to function efficiently. To this end our programs have been dynamic, though our point of view has been relatively static. This is not an evidence of conservatism in program making but rather an evidence of the fact that we have been trying to catch up with our ideals and have not attempted to rush forward until certain of our grounds. Basically, we have recognized that, "the strength of the pack is the wolf, and the strength of the wolf is the pack."

At present, we are in a transitional stage in the socialization of medicine because of the difficulty of recognizing the distinction between individual practice and group organization. To many, the term socialization of medicine is fraught with sinister significance. Our unsatisfactory medical organization has given rise to unwarranted fears on the part of many, who in their own private practice give evidence of a broad social viewpoint. The opposition to the socialization of medicine rises mainly from the failure to grasp its meaning and purpose. The private practice of medicine will not be interdicted, but its sphere of influence and application will be altered. The technics of medical diagnosis, laboratory research, and private practice possess particular interest only in relation to their practical influence upon social betterment and the improvement of human stamina. Now and in the immediate future we shall require many types of agencies, machinery, and institutions to meet adequately the problem of today that will not be necessary at a later age when there will be a better adjustment of social vision to social accomplishments, and medical ideals will have been tinctured with the necessities of social practice.

The socialization of medicine arises from a transference of viewpoint from the individual to the mass. Thus there arises a re-interpretation of existent problems in the light of social causation, social pathology, social diagnosis, and social treatment. Particularization of methods to be employed is determined by an appreciation of the social nexus between specific individuals and their communities. Private practice is certainly impotent to prevent or control typhoid fever, bubonic plague, syphilis, or uncinariasis. The medical social treatment involved for these conditions must be differentiated because of the varying elements in the social causation and social pathology. Social rather than individual peculiarities determine the character of the social prognoses.

The social treatment is similarly dependent upon an understanding of the multitudinous factors entering into the group or community involved. Social practice absorbs individualistic phenomena without annihilating them, if such be desirable for the community. This fact obtains whether one deals with traits of character development, methods of industry, or with medical procedures.

In the future there will be a greater coördination of organization so as to reach throughout the land to raise standards of living, to teach the mode and methods of living, and to make possible the attainment of a complete, healthful life. Then all persons will be enabled to live safely and completely in harmony with the ideas of good citizenship, and with a better understanding of the nature and significance of organized brotherly love. Organized preventive medicine, with curative medicine supplementary, will function through social institutions in the interests of the human race. The welfare of the individual man is not to be sacrificed, but man and the race are to progress together through a richer understanding of the interweaving of their destinies. Herein lies the significance, the meaning, and the purpose of socializing medicine.

PRACTICAL DISINFECTION OF TUBERCULOUS SPUTUM

WILLIAM ROYAL STOKES, M. D., SC. D., AND C. H. DOUTHIRT, M. D.,
*Bureau of Bacteriology, City Department of Health,
Baltimore, Md.*

Read before Laboratory Section, American Public Health Association, at New Orleans, La., October 30, 1919

Here experts have disagreed and the investigation seeks to settle one point definitely, what dilution of what chemical is practicable to disinfect tuberculous sputum. It is an initial bit of research suggestive of a series of similar ones whereby efficient dilutions of various disinfectants can be determined for use with different infectious materials.

THE practical disinfection of tuberculous sputum is a subject which does not seem to have received special attention and the directions in most of the text books differ considerably. Kendall[1] states that tubercle bacilli in sputum are killed in 24 hours by mixing the sputum with an equal volume of 5% carbolic acid, and Hiss and Zinsser[2] state that 5% carbolic acid will only produce complete disinfection of tubercular sputum in from 5 to 6 hours. Kolle and Wassermann[3] say that bichloride of mercury is not suited for the destruction of tubercle bacilli in sputum since it coagulates the albumen and prevents penetration of the disinfectant. They also state that 5% carbolic acid in equal amounts and 3% carbolic acid in from 8 to 12 times the amount of sputum will destroy the tubercle bacillus in 24 hours if it is once stirred around in this material. Two and one-half per cent carbolic acid will not destroy the tubercle bacillus in 24 hours. Absolute alcohol in 10 times the quantity will disinfect the sputum in 10 hours.

Owing to these facts Stokes and Schmitz[4] performed some experiments with antiformin and carbolic acid in order to effect a penetration of the disinfectant to the tubercle bacillus. The antiformin by dissolving the mucus al-

lowed the germicide to come into direct contact with the organism. Our experiments showed that a 6% solution of carbolic acid in antiformin in an equal quantity of the sputum would destroy the tubercle bacillus in half an hour, and this would represent an actual 3% solution of carbolic acid in the mixture of antiformin and sputum. The sputum contained large numbers of tubercle bacilli and their virulence was tested upon guinea pigs. The disinfected sputum was also centrifugalized, the antiformin washed out of the sediment, and the sediment from 15 cc. was then injected into guinea pigs.

A second disinfectant which was a saponified kresol dissolving easily in water was used as a 6% solution and this mixed with an equal quantity of sputum killed the tubercle bacillus in 2 hours. Weaker solutions of both carbolic acid and this saponified kresol ranging from 2 to 5% failed to kill the tubercle bacillus in the sputum.

The second experiments which we wish to record were performed by combining various strengths of two other disinfectants with various strengths of sodium hydroxide. Disinfectant No. 1

1. Bacteriology, General, Pathological and Intestinal, 1916, p. 484.
2. Text Book of Bacteriology, 1918, p. 486.
3. Hand Book of Pathogenic Microorganisms, 1903, p. 109.
4. Amer. Jour. Pub. Heal., Vol. 2, No. 5, May, 1912, p. 359.

consists of hydroxyl substitution products of the aromatic series, having the group formula Cn H_2n-3—OH and contains 40% of oxidized hydrocarbons from tar, 30% of neutral hydrocarbons from tar and 30% of a saponifier. Disinfectant No. 2 consists of phenols, kresols and others of the series occurring in coal tar in solution with soap. These crude disinfectants were used for the purpose of destroying the tubercle bacillus in the sputum and the sodium hydroxide was used for dissolving the mucus and pus so that the disinfectant could get into direct contact with the bacilli. The solutions were added in equal quantity to the sputum and were not stirred up in any way after they were poured in on top of the sputum. The experiments were conducted in the usual sputum bottle used for the collection of this material in most health department laboratories. This will hold 35 cc. of fluid but only 10 cc. of sputum were used, and 10 cc. of the disinfecting fluid were added slowly without stirring. The mixture was then allowed to stand at the room temperature for the various lengths of time indicated in Table No. 1.

At the end of this time interval about 2 cc. of the mixture were placed in a centrifugal tube and enough 10% antiformin was added to fill up the 15 cc. centrifugal tube. This was done in order to destroy any pyogenic bacteria which might kill the experimental animals, but the antiformin has no effect upon the tubercle bacillus itself. This was centrifugalized for 5 minutes and the supernatant fluid was pipetted off. The sediment was then thoroughly mixed in 15 cc. of salt solution and centrifugalized a second time. This was for the purpose of washing out any antiformin which is quite irritating when injected into guinea pigs. The supernatant fluid was then pipetted off and the sediment mixed in 2 cc. of salt solution. This was then injected subcutaneously into the thigh of a guinea pig. This is a convenient method for

the early detection of tuberculosis since the inguinal gland will enlarge in from one to two weeks if live tubercle bacilli are present, and these organisms can be easily demonstrated in stained specimens from the enlarged gland. This method of determining the destruction of the tubercle bacillus was always carried out.

The inoculated guinea pig was kept for one month and at the end of that time 1 cc. of pure, old tuberculin was injected subcutaneously into the abdominal wall. If there is no tuberculosis present the guinea pigs will survive this injection but if they are tuberculous the pigs will die within 24 hours. All pigs, however, showing negative results were chloroformed and autopsied and the glands and viscera were carefully examined for any signs of tuberculosis.

As a control the sputum was examined and it was only used if it contained large numbers of tubercle bacilli: Two cc. of such sputum was then mixed with 4 cc. of a 10% solution of antiformin and allowed to stand for 15 minutes in order to destroy any pyogenic bacteria. The mixture was then centrifugalized, the antiformin removed and the sediment washed again with salt solution. The sediment with about 2 cc. remaining supernatant fluid was then injected into the thigh of a guinea pig. At the end of 2 weeks the inguinal gland was always enlarged and the guinea pig died in 24 hours after the injection of 1 cc. of tuberculin. Tubercle bacilli were always recovered from the gland and frequently from the tubercles present in the spleen and liver of the animal. These controls, therefore, confirmed the presence of virulent bacilli in the sputum before it was mixed with the disinfectant.

The sputum selected for experimentation was the most tenacious and thick material which could be obtained, as we wished to subject the disinfection process to the most extreme conditions possible to find.

TABLE No. 1

Showing Various Dilutions of Disinfectant and Caustic Soda Solution Before Mixture with Sputum and Result of Inoculation in Guinea Pigs of the Mixture of Sputum and Disinfectant

Disinfectant—	Percentage of Dilution	Percentage of Dilution— Caustic Soda	Duration of Exposure to Disinfectant	Result of Inoculation
No. 1	0.3	0.5	½ hour	Extensive tuberculosis
No. 1	0.3	0.5	1 hour	Extensive tuberculosis
No. 1	0.3	0.5	2 hours	Extensive tuberculosis
None (Control Pig)	.0	.0	0 hour	Extensive tuberculosis
No. 1	0.6	1.0	½ hour	Extensive tuberculosis
No. 1	0.6	1.0	1 hour	Inguinal gland tuberculous
No. 1	0.6	1.0	2 hours	Extensive tuberculosis
None (Control Pig)	.0	.0	0 hour	Extensive tuberculosis
No. 1	1.0	1.0	½ hour	No tuberculosis
No. 1	1.0	1.0	1 hour	No tuberculosis
No. 1	1.0	1.0	2 hours	No tuberculosis
None (Control Pig)	.0	.0	0 hour	Extensive tuberculosis
No. 1	1.0	1.0	½ hour	No tuberculosis
No. 1	1.0	1.0	1 hour	No tuberculosis
No. 1	1.0	1.0	2 hours	No tuberculosis
None (Control Pig)	.0	.0	0 hour	Inguinal gland tuberculous
No. 2	1.0	1.0	½ hour	No tuberculosis
No. 2	1.0	1.0	1 hour	No tuberculosis
No. 2	1.0	1.0	2 hours	No tuberculosis
None (Control Pig)	.0	.0	0 hour	Extensive tuberculosis

An examination of Table No. 1 will show that a solution consisting of 1% of disinfectant No. 1 or 2, containing also 1% of caustic soda in distilled water, will destroy the tubercle bacillus in tuberculous sputum if added to this material in equal amounts. This destruction will take place in half an hour. The caustic soda causes the sputum gradually to dissolve and the disinfectant then penetrates to the bacilli and destroys them. The actual percentage of the disinfectant and alkali in the mixture of sputum and disinfectant is 0.5%.

CONCLUSIONS

The custom of simply placing sputum in a 5% solution of carbolic acid and expecting it to be disinfected in a short time is probably a dangerous procedure since it gives a sense of false security and the tuberculous sputum is not disinfected. The use of a 1% solution of disinfectant No. 1 or 2, and perhaps other such disinfectants will destroy the tubercle bacillus in sputum if the disinfectant also contains 1% of caustic soda. This is important in the practical disinfection of sputum and the solution might also be used in the sputum bottles which are sent through the mail to hygienic laboratories for the diagnosis of suspected tuberculosis. The Rideal-Walker or the Hygienic Laboratory carbolic acid co-efficient used for testing the strength of a disinfectant has no direct bearing upon its destructive action upon the tubercle bacillus in sputum since the high co-efficients of these kresols would suggest that a very high dilution of the disinfectant should be used in sputum, and yet we find that it takes a 1% solution of a kresol to cause the destruction of the tubercle bacillus in sputum.

Further work should be done in order to hit upon a standard which might measure the real practical efficiency of the disinfectant when used upon various materials. It would seem that a 1% solution, as mentioned above, is efficient for tubercular sputum and probably therefore for the sputum of influenza, pneumonia and other respiratory disease. Similar experiments should be performed in order to test the destructive action of various disinfectants upon feces and other excreta, as it might be that the addition of the caustic alkali to the disinfectant might render the kresols much more efficient. Dilutions of practical efficiency, therefore, for the various disinfectants when used upon different infectious materials could thus be established.

The above work would suggest that the official liquor *cresolis compositus* which contains a large percentage of alkali and kresol might prove an efficient disinfectant for sputum, and a few experiments such as those described in the article might easily determine this point.

CHILD HYGIENE

JULIUS LEVY, M. D.,

*Director, Division of Child Hygiene, Newark Department of Health,
Newark, N. J.*
Consultant, Bureau Child Hygiene, New Jersey Dept. of Health.

Chairman's Address before Child Hygiene Sessions, American Public Health Association, at San Francisco, Cal., September 14, 1920.

IT SEEMS that the public has at last awakened to its responsibility for the life, health, and happiness of its children. This has followed a little slowly, perhaps, upon the long recognized principle that the public is responsible for the educational and moral welfare of the child, but this handicap in the element of time will soon be overcome by the momentum that the movement for the physical welfare of the child has developed.

This general interest in the life and health of the child is variously designated, depending somewhat upon the particular contact that a person has had with the child problem or, perhaps, by his or her special experience with, or outlook on life.

The publicist, the legislator, or the business man, having acquired through the great war, a better realization of the value of food, coal, forests, and manpower, and the seriousness of wastage in these important elements for the world's preservation, is ready to adopt the idea of preventing human wastage, securing of human efficiency, and is apt to apply the words "Child Conservation" to the modern movement to safe-guard the health and happiness of children.

The social worker, the philanthropist, the teacher, the criminologist, many physicians and psychologists, who have become aware of the large number of men who are physically unfit for military service, the large number of school children who are hampered in mental and moral development by physical defects, the great number of men, women, and children who lead unsuccessful lives and are unable to adjust themselves to society on account of defects and deformities,

physical or mental, are apt to apply the words "Child Welfare" to the work that is being undertaken for the protection of the life of the child, influenced undoubtedly in their designation, by the pressing need for institutions for the feeble-minded, dispensaries and hospitals for the sick, clinics for the defective and deformed, physical training for the weak, organized charity for the dependent.

Pediatricians and public health workers, who have learned that many disorders of later life, most defects and deformities of early youth, a great deal of the mental retardation and moral distortions of early childhood and adolescence are the result of improper nurture and nutrition in early infancy, of unfortunate heredity and poor prenatal environment, feel that the only proper designation of the modern movement for the protection and well being of children is "Child Hygiene." They are influenced, perhaps, by the derivation of the word, "Hygiene," from the Greek, "to be healthy," and which has for its function the task of rendering "Growth more perfect, decay less rapid, life more vigorous, death more remote."

Preventive Child Hygiene work must begin at the beginning. It may be of interest to indicate to what an extent many of the defects and deformities that were discovered in the young men who applied for military service, or even the defects and deformities that are found in school children, begin in early infancy and in the pre-school period.

It is estimated that 2% of school children in the State of New Jersey have heart disease, this means 12,000 children. This is partly the result of contagious diseases in early life which leave the heart muscles anemic and flabby, with little reserve force to meet the requirements of vigorous childhood.

Spinal curvature and poor posture, which have given considerable impetus to the movement for physical training, have a basis in anemia and malnutrition which are the result of improper care and feeding in the first years of life. While these conditions are frequently discovered in school children, they develop as the result of improper nutrition of the first two years of life and improper guidance in the pre-school period. Deformities of the bones, such as pigeon breast, bow-legs, knock-knee, weak feet or flat foot, so frequently found in school children of the poorer neighborhoods, are particularly the result of rickets, a disease of poor nutrition and faulty hygiene that occurs usually between six months and two years. In various schools it has been estimated that from 3 to 30% of the children are suffering from the results of rickets. It has been very gratifying in Newark to discover after several years of supervision of the Italian babies that rickets has been almost eliminated from this group. The relation of rickets to defects and deformities is well illustrated by the reports from the British army where defects of extremities, flat feet, malformations of chest and spine and stunted growth were responsible for 41.78 rejections per thousand applications. In a series of 717 cripples under 16 years of age 10% of the conditions were found to be due to rickets.

Of 22,000 school children in London 2% showed some eye disease, of which three-fourths was said to be due to unwashed faces and dirty hands. Fifteen per cent of all eye troubles of school children are said to be due to a form of disease of the eyelids and cornea, which is the cause of a great deal of blindness and begins between the fourth and sixth years of life and is found among children suffering from malnutrition during early infancy. Of 408 cases of hypermetropia (far sightedness) 103 were noted before six years of age and of 378 cases of hypermetropia with astigmatism 186 cases were noted before six years of age. Blindness is probably the most serious and saddest blight that can befall any child and when we remember that 84% of this blindness is the result of neglected ophthalmia neonatorum and that effectively organized child hygiene work can absolutely eliminate ophthalmia neonatorum as the cause of blindness, we have an excellent illustration of the value of preventive work during the pre-school period over the methods now employed and approved by certain men and women who are unable to visualize the great task of preventive medicine and hygiene.

Departments of health in the development of their Child Hygiene plans should be influenced by these considerations and seek the active coöperation of all who are willing to devote themselves to the program of prevention. Among the many activities that come under this head special emphasis is to be placed upon the perfection of birth registration, the supervision of expectant mothers, the improvement of obstetrical service, the extension of maternal nursing, the instruction of mothers in child nurture, the supervision of the child from conception to adolescence, in the home, the school, playground or shop, and the removal of economic, social, and sanitary conditions that interfere with the integrity of the family and the well-being of the mothers and children. Child Hygiene includes, therefore, all the activities that are necessary for the protection of the life and the happiness of the child and embraces in platonic coöperation all the agencies that affect the physical and mental well-being of the coming generation. Nothing, therefore, that is essential to the well-being of the family is foreign to the interest of preventive child hygiene work. While it is devoted to the science of making "growth more perfect, life more vigorous," one of the direct results of its activities is to make "decay less rapid and death more remote." *We would emphasize that it is not desired to permit conditions to develop that would require doctors, clinics and medicine, crutches and braces, when right living and health environment can prevent their need.* It cannot permit itself to spend for the treatment of a few the money that will maintain in health the many; to spend for the discovery of defects in school children the money that will prevent these defects from developing when applied to the instruction of the mother in child nurture and to the supervision of children of pre-school age; to spend in the treatment of marasmus, atrophy, summer complaint, the money that can prevent marasmus, atrophy and summer complaint and make healthy romping children if the money is spent in teaching and helping mothers to nurse their babies. It is to be remembered that there is only a limited amount of money and energy available. Shall a public health department spend it "to make growth more perfect, life more vigorous," or merely "to make decay a little less rapid and death a little more remote?"

□

JUDGING THE KEEPING QUALITY OF MILK BY A Ph METHOD

L. H. COOLEDGE, A. M., and R. W. WYANT, M.S.,
*Michigan Agricultural College,
East Lansing, Mich.*

Read before Laboratory Section, American Public Health Association, at San Francisco, Cal.
September 16, 1920.

With constantly increasing milk supply areas for large cities knowledge of how long the milk will keep is important. Bacterial counts, while important for other information, do not give definite answers about this. A hydrogen-ion test may be applied which will afford a reasonable judgment on this point.

THE method usually applied in a study of the sanitary condition of dairy products is the bacteriological count. This is determined by the plating method, which gives an approximation of the number of groups of live bacteria present in the sample, or by the microscopic method, which gives an approximation of the total number of bacteria, both dead and living, which are present. Either of these methods is a valuable aid in judging the care which has been exercised in producing the milk, and the precautions observed to prevent the growth of any bacteria which may have gained entrance.

The bacteriological count tells little or nothing about the actual ability of the bacteria present to produce the changes which would make the dairy product unfit for the purpose intended, and it is often the case that the sample of milk with so high a bacteriological count that it would be condemned under most of our city ordinances is actually a good grade of milk when judged as to keeping quality and type of fermentation which develops when held at the temperatures common to the home.

To find a method for examining market milk which would give readings more nearly representing the actual ability of the bacteria and enzymes present to produce· the changes of interest to the producer and consumer, the writers have made a study of the ability of bacteria and enzymes present in milk to cause a change in hydrogen-ion concentration of a broth solution to which the milk was added, and the whole incubated for not more than eight hours.

Ordinary bouillon cube broth was prepared and the indicator, Di bromo thymol sulphon phthalein (Brom thymol blue), added. The broth was then adjusted to PH 7.0 and 10 cc., portions placed in large test tubes and sterilized.

One-tenth cc. of each sample of milk to be tested was added to a tube of the broth-indicator solution prepared above and the whole incubated at 37° C. At the end of one hour periods the samples were examined and the PH of any tubes showing marked change accurately determined by comparing with standard tubes containing indicator and solutions of known hydrogen-ion concentration. A comparator has been designed in this laboratory which greatly facilitates this colorimetric hydrogen-ion determination.

The samples of milk containing many very active bacteria will show a change in PH at the end of one or two hours while the better samples will show little change at the end of eight hours.

A score has been given to samples with a final reading of PH 5.8 at the end of one to eight hours and to the samples having different readings at the end of eight hours.

Under this system certified milk will score 95 or 100. The other grades will score from 20 to 95.

This system of scoring milk checks up only in a general way with the bacterial count but checks very closely with the actual keeping quality of the milk. A sample of milk for instance having a PH reading of 6.2 at the end of eight hours would score. 75 and be on the verge of souring at the end of 24 hours if kept at room temperature. Samples scoring more than 75 would be sweet at the end of 24 hours, while samples scoring under 75 would be sour at that time. Likewise, samples scoring 55 would be on the verge of souring at the end of 20 hours, while those scoring 60 or better would be sweet and those scoring under 55 would be sour. A very few exceptions to these rules are found. One can tell from the score how long a sample of milk may be expected to remain sweet if kept at a certain temperature.

SUMMARY

It seems to the writers that this method gives results which tell what the producer, dealer and consumer desire to know, viz., the length of time that a sample of milk may be expected to remain sweet under certain conditions. This cannot be judged by the bacterial count using either the plate or microscopic method.

The technique of making the test is so simple that anyone who can match colors may be taught in a few hours' time to grade milk.

The cost of the test is one tube of broth for each sample examined.

The time required to pick out the poorest samples of milk is from one to four hours, while the best samples may be given their proper grade at the end of eight hours.

There is no expensive equipment necessary.

EDITORIAL SECTION

AMERICAN JOURNAL OF PUBLIC HEALTH
Publication Office: 124 W. Polk Street, Chicago, Ill.
EDITORIAL OFFICE: 169 MASSACHUSETTS AVE., BOSTON, MASS.

A. W. HEDRICH, C. P. H., Editor   J. RITCHIE, Jr., Associate Editor

Editorial Assistants

E. R. HAYHURST, M.D.   P. M. HOLMES, M.D.   FRANCIS H. SLACK, M.D.
DAVID GREENBERG   JAMES A. TOBEY   JAMES M. STRANG
M. P. HORWOOD, M.S.   HOMER N. CALVER

Board of Advisory Editors

PETER H. BRYCE, M.D., Ottawa, Canada   PROF. M. J. ROSENAU, Boston, Mass.
CHARLES V. CHAPIN, M.D., Providence, R. I. PROF. W. T. SEDGWICK, Cambridge, Mass.
EUGENE R. KELLEY, M.D., Boston, Mass.   PROF. GEORGE C. WHIPPLE, Cambridge, Mass.
W. A. EVANS, M.D., Chicago, Ill.   PROF. S. M. GUNN, Paris, France.

All expressions of opinion and all statements of supposed facts are published on authority of the writer under whose name they appear, and are not to be regarded as expressing the views of the American Public Health Association, unless such statements or opinions have been adopted by vote of the Association.

NOTICE TO SUBSCRIBERS: Subscription Price, payable in advance, $4.00 per year for United States and possessions; $4.50 for Canada and other foreign countries. Single copies, 50 cents postpaid. Membership in the American Public Health Association, including subscription to Journal, $5.00 per year. In Change of Address please give both old and new address, and mail before the 25th of the month to take effect with the current issue. Mailing Date, 20th of each month. Advertisements accepted only when commendable, and worth while both to reader and advertiser. News Items, interesting clippings and illustrations are gladly received, together with name of sender. Copyright, 1919, by A. W. Hedrich.

THE OFFICIAL AND THE NON-OFFICIAL HEALTH AGENCY

Probably no group of opinions ever brought together at once has till now reflected so many phases of opinion in the question of how official and unofficial health agencies are to work together as does the symposium in this issue of the Journal. The articles set forth the conservative point of view of the trained physician on the one hand and the energy and scope of vision of the keen business man on the other, and between the two lie various suggestions as to lines of coöperation. On the one hand there is the professional health administrator, responsible to the last penny to his auditor for compliance with the strict letter of the law as it may locally be interpreted, and on the other the flexibility that a comparatively free agent may have in the trying out of promising experiments. The second course is not legally open to the usual professional health officer, yet it is a most important factor to the betterment of the health of the people.

A couple of examples from other fields of work will serve perhaps to illustrate possibilities of accomplishment by the hand that is free. Twenty-five years ago or more Mr. A. L. Rotch established on Great Blue Hill near Boston a private meteorological observatory. It was his property, his own venture and there was no one to question his acts. He chose for one of his departments here to undertake the development of promising suggestions as yet untried. At considerable cost he ventured on experiments in determining the height of clouds. He was wonderfully successful and following his entering wedge measurements of the kind became a part of the regular duties of many observatories here and abroad.

At a fortunate moment a tailless kite was brought to the Blue Hill Observatory and on Mr. Rotch's experiments with this new device an international system of synchronous kite flights was established. Practically all that was known of air conditions at great heights (until the Great War gave impetus to research) was thus due to the initiative of a "non-official" meteorological agency.

980

A second illustration may be drawn from the famous Lowell Institute of Boston, the trustee of which is the President of Harvard University, A. Lawrence Lowell. Although to a majority of those who know its name the Institute suggests a superb series of lecture courses, this is only one of its functions.

Long ago it seemed clear to the father of President Lowell, then trustee of the Institute, that a school to teach drawing especially, was a desideratum. He established and maintained such a school for a number of years. It proved so successful that the State saw the value of the experiment and proceeded to establish the Massachusetts Normal Art School. President Lowell felt that there was opportunity to give the laboring man a better opportunity for learning at a special school, and established one. This was speedily taken over by a local industrial organization that was convinced of its importance. At the present moment the Lowell Institute is maintaining a school for industrial foremen. This has been carried beyond the experimental stage and it is very plain that there must presently be added to the public school system a school adapted in its times and conditions to the needs of ambitious wage earners in employment, who seek to become better workmen and leaders in their vocations. It required the quiet, flexible control of a private agency to establish these needs and to set them forth in terms of such success that the public was made to feel the necessity of undertaking itself to fill the needs.

The conditions in education parallel those in public health, with the difference that education has now acquired so flexible a public management that municipalities and their populations do not stand aghast when experimental departures are suggested from the regular routine. In public health there is quite as much need for freedom to try out seemingly favorable leads, but neither public sentiment of today nor the legal environment of administration will permit this. Here most certainly there is a field for the private agency.

There is, however, one factor to the limitations of professional health officers that no one of the writers in the Symposium has emphasized, but which nevertheless is of greatest practical importance, the question of what it is possible for the health officer to undertake.

There is perhaps no better outline of the situation of the professional health administrator than that expressed a while ago in an address before the students of a local school. The speaker said, "In his community as it is and with the condition of the public mind as he finds it, the health officer must select the few most important things that his appropriations will permit him to undertake." Such a health officer is not in the class of political appointees, against the existence of which it is futile to shut the eyes, but is a sincere man who seeks honestly to do his duty. Cities exist in which the routine work required by law makes most serious inroads into appropriations, much of it of the "decency" order rather than true health work. Again, the health officer's carefully figured appropriation is cut down a third or a half by the Council or governing body. He had every penny of his estimate accounted for in needed work for the health of his community, and must omit a fairly large part of this work. What chance has an officer under such conditions, and the conditions are not overdrawn,—what chance has he to undertake other than what he can of old, stereotyped and even antiquated routine, and how can he be expected to keep abreast of the progress in his profession?

It may be well to theorize about doing your work so excellently that your community will rise to a man to your support, but it needs more than the average of knowledge, skill and understanding of the psychology of a population to get such results easily in the complex of modern city or community life.

Here comes in one of the functions of the non-official agency. Working in coöperation with the official agency it is able to fill gaps, to back the health officer in his requests and to prove itself a force in the health education of the people. The essential of this help is coöperation but coöperation is what is unfortunately sometimes forgotten. In the excitement of the movement the non-official agency may forget the fact that health work does not admit of competition. The requirements in caring for public health are that all agencies join forces and under the advice of a competent official, public health administrator the non-official agencies will find plenty of opportunity for accomplishment.

PROGRESS OF GOVERNMENT ACQUISITION OF THE QUARANTINE

In the JOURNAL for October, page 802, in speaking of the acquisition of the quarantine service by the U. S. Government, the statement was made that, "One by one the ports of the Atlantic and Gulf states came under Government quarantine supervision, with Boston and New York alone outstanding." This statement made from the memory of discussions at the time of the transfer of the Boston station proves to have been somewhat in error. The port of Baltimore should have been included for it retained local control until 1917, about a year longer than Boston.

In the course of the correspondence with the U. S. Public Health Service with reference to the matter, Assistant Surgeon General R. H. Creel, in charge of the quarantine, has furnished information concerning the dates of the transfer of different ports to Government control. This has historical interest and is here given in abstract. It has value certainly in this respect, that it shows the way in which the U. S. Government acquired its control of the quarantine, not by exercise of authority or by seizure, but through the realization on the part of local authorities that the National Government is best fitted to maintain a uniform and standardized system. In guarding the gates of a great country against the entry of disease uniformity and standardization are important fundamental factors.

The sequence of acquisition by the U. S. Public Health Service of the quarantine of the principal ports follows and the list exhibits some examples of neighboring ports putting themselves under Government control at the same time, while some other dates show a goodly measure of independence and difference of opinion within the same state.

Government control of the quarantine seems to have been appreciated first on the West Coast, for in 1888 San Francisco and San Diego, Cal., and Port Townsend, Wash., were acquired by the Federal Government followed in 1889 by the station at Cape Charles, Va. In 1892 Delaware Breakwater, Del., became a Government station followed in 1893 by Reedy Island, Del., and in 1894 by Cape Fear, N. C. In 1889 the Columbia River, Ore., station was acquired and the next year, 1900, three important ports on the South Atlantic coast, Savannah, Ga., and Tampa and Key West, Fla., were taken over from the local authorities. In 1900 quarantines were established at Honolulu and Hawaiian ports, in the Philippines and in Porto Rico, while that for the Virgin Islands dates from 1917. In 1903 Portland, Me., became a Government station and the same year twelve small ports in Florida and Georgia were given up to the U. S. P. H. S. In 1905 Perth Amboy, N. J., became a Government station followed in 1907 by Alexandria, Va., and Mobile, Ala. The year 1918 was one of considerable activity in acquiring control of the quarantine of Southern ports, and Charleston, Beaufort and Port Royal in South Carolina and Newbern and Washington in North Carolina were ceded to the National Government. In 1909 the Government took charge in New Orleans, La., and Pascagoula, Miss., in 1911, Galveston, Texas, and in 1912 Eastport, Me., and Providence, R. I., were added to the growing list of ports in which the Government had been given complete quarantine control. Then followed Boston, Mass., and Darien, Ga., in 1916, Baltimore in 1917 and Marcus Hook in 1919.

The control in Baltimore has been under a lease, pending an appropriation from Congress for the purchase of the plant. This has been secured and the physical transfer will be completed before the close of the present year.

At Philadelphia the situation has been unusual. Reedy Island, Del., about eighty miles below the city, has been a station of the U. S. P. H. Service for more than twenty-five years, operating for the entire Delaware River section, For a number of years past the State of Pennsylvania has had its own quarantine station at Marcus Hook about five miles below the city of Philadelphia. There resulted a duplication of quarantine formalities in the inspection of vessels from foreign ports. Pennsylvania discontinued its quarantine, the station at Marcus Hook was taken over by the Government last year and is now the station for the Delaware, Reedy Island being used for detention and disinfection purposes.

At the present moment the port of New York is operated by the State, but an appropriation is available for the purchase of the plant and the New York State Legislature has passed an Act enabling its transfer to the United States. This will probably be effective by the first of the incoming year, and from that moment the administration of the whole country so far as its quarantine regula- tions are concerned will be on the same model. It is a victory of peace of more value than are most victories of war.

The attention of state health societies of general or of special character is directed to two matters in recent issues of the JOURNAL, which will be of interest to them. In the issue for September, page 742, there is the report of the A. P. H. A. Committee on State Health Societies. One fact evident at the first glance is the great number and variety of such associations. With so many there should be considered the possibilities of coördination and coöperation.

The Ohio Public Health Association is the result of a carefully considered plan in a state where public health administration has received much attention the past year or two. The great voluntary health organization of the state has at the same time established itself on a new basis. It is evident that there is involved much thought and consideration. Because of this, the JOURNAL requested the Secretary, Mr. H. E. Roulfs, to outline the new form of the association and present the reasons for the change. His article is to be found in the November JOURNAL, page 897. State associations will do well to read the report of Mr. Roulfs.

With this issue of the JOURNAL Dr. Arthur Lederer again assumes charge of the Public Health Laboratory Notes. While Dr. Lederer has been fitting himself to his new sphere of activities in Chicago, the notes have been prepared by Dr. F. H. Slack and Mr. J. M. Strang. The departure of Mr. Strang to a distant position and an increase of the normal duties of Dr. Slack have been reasons for their discontinuance of the work. The thanks of JOURNAL readers is due to these two young men for a considerable period of excellent presentation of the Laboratory Notes.

BOOKS AND REPORTS
REVIEWED

A Manual of Physical Diagnosis. *Austin Flint, M. D., 8th Edition, Revised by Henry C. Thacher, M. S., M. D., Philadelphia: Lea and Febiger, 1920. P. 326. Price, $3.00.*

The eighth edition of Flint's Physical Diagnosis has been somewhat amplified by a discussion of the irritable heart, and of normal cardiac variations, by a fuller account of pericarditis and of pulmonary tuberculosis and by attention to the bronchopneumonia of the recent epidemic of influenza.

As in the early editions, much emphasis is laid on percussion and auscultation, methods of examination which as Thacher says are in danger of neglect now that so much reliance is placed on laboratory methods. An instructive discussion of the physics of sound introduces the reader to the detailed account of the physical examination of lungs and heart. There are some very good descriptions in these chapters, especially those of the causes of flatness, dullness and abnormal resonance; of rales, of phthisis, of sounds and murmurs, and of the pulse. At times, however, there are repetitions in the first half of the book, and there are some omissions and errors. There is no discussion of arrhythmic respiration, such as Cheyne-Stokes breathing. In the account of auricular flutter the following sentence appears (p. 269): "The change from normal rhythm to auricular flutter is not abrupt, as in paroxysmal tachycardia, but is separated by a period of auricular fibrillation." This should read: "The change from auricular flutter back to normal rhythm is not abrupt, etc." On the next page the paragraph, "Inspiration may cause decrease in the size, even to obliteration, and frequency of the pulse, in cases of inflammations and tumors of the mediastinum, pericardial effusions and adhesions (*pulsus paradoxus*)." As a matter of fact, the frequency is not decreased with inspiration in the paradoxical pulse and moreover the paradoxical pulse is dependent on the type of respiration (thoracic) of the subject (who may be perfectly normal) and not on the pathological lesions.

Again, on page 280, the mitral direct murmur (*mitral stenosis*) is said to begin sometimes with the second sound and to continue to the following first sound. It never begins with the second sound—there is always a short but definite interval between the second sound and the beginning of the murmur, as the authors show correctly in their diagram of the murmurs on page 279. This point is very important, for it helps to differentiate the diastolic murmurs of aortic regurgitation and mitral stenosis. In the discussion of patency of the *ductus arteriosus* on page 331, the aid sometimes obtained in establishing the diagnosis by the finding of a high pulse pressure and Corrigan pulse should be added.

In the last chapter there is an excellent scheme of physical examination but in the text very little is written except concerning the lungs and heart. Practically no mention is made of head, neck, extremities and reflexes and very little of the abdominal organs. It would seem wiser to limit the book strictly to the chest and to entitle it as such, for example, "Physical Examination of Heart and Lungs."

The book can be recommended to the medical profession because of its unusually good discussion of auscultation and percussion.

PAUL D. WHITE, M. D.

✦

Nursing Mental Diseases. *Harriet Bailey, R. N., New York: Macmillan Company, 1920. P. 175. Price, $1.60.*

There is no dearth of literature either scientific or popular on the subject of mental disease, but little has been put into a form that is at once scientific and popular and also compact. For that reason "Nursing Mental Diseases" by Harriet Bailey, R. N., has a special value. Within the compass of 175 pages she has put together what constitute the minimum essentials of the knowledge which those should have who have any contact with mental cases.

Her method of presentation of her material has been to give first, a brief history of the care of the mentally sick, and then after touching on some legal aspects of mental disorders, she treats briefly the cause of, and preventive measures for, mental disease. All this is by way of introduction to the real subject matter of the book: the nursing of the different types of mental cases. This part of the text is divided into six chapters, each of which deals with one phase of the subject, such as "Nursing in the Toxic Cases."

The author has a happy way of subdividing each subject, using centered sideheadings—devices which makes the book easily readable either as text book or as a guide to the family in dealing with a troublesome case. Especially valuable is the space given to children with neuropathic tendencies and to the subject of those born mentally deficient, which includes a summary of the Binet-Simon tests for intelligence age as arranged for the Johns Hopkins Dispensary.

Perhaps no greater praise of the clear logical style of the book can be given than to say that in these brief paragraphs Miss Bailey has expressed clearly and simply the whole theory of the psycho-analysts who belong to the school of Freud.

This is a book which it would be well for every normal person to read. It would be helpful in many ways, especially in making it possible to guard against some of the easily prevented mental breakdowns. It is a cheerful, optimistic book not of the Pollyanna type but of the wholesome kind that broad-minded, scientifically trained persons are peculiarly fitted to make.

MAY BLISS DICKINSON, R. N.

✛

Pasteurization of Milk. *Report of Committee on Milk Supply of the Sanitary Engineering Section, A. P. H A., Boston: A. P. H. A., 'August, 1920. P. 32, Paper. Price, 35 cents.*

This report has recently been published in pamphlet form, and contains up-to-date information on milk pasteurization which should be in the hands of everyone interested in the improvement of milk supplies. The phases of milk pasteurization covered by this report include the present status of milk pasteurization, the effect of pasteurization on the composition of milk, the process of milk pasteurization, the analytical control of pasteurization plants and state and

municipal supervision of the pasteurization of milk.

The first section of the report is devoted to the present status of milk pasteurization in the United States and the Dominion of Canada, giving the number of plants in operation, the state, territorial and provincial control exercised over these plants, the control exercised over the production of market milk in our largest cities, and a review of the official definitions of pasteurization established by the various departments of our Federal Government interested in milk supplies, and by the various state boards and departments of health. This review calls attention to the lack of control and uniformity of methods and the absence of public appreciation of pasteurization as a means of safeguarding public health.

The effect of pasteurization on the composition of milk is covered by a review of the results of experiments on the effect of heat on milk and experiments on infant feeding.

The process of milk pasteurization is limited to a discussion of the "holding" process, and a definition of "pasteurization."

The material included under the heading of mechanical features and the operation of pasteurizing plants is discussed from the viewpoint of methods used. The methods considered are the pasteurization of milk in bottles, and the pasteurization of milk with intermittent and continuous flow apparatus. A list of mechanical defects in pasteurization apparatus which affect the process of pasteurization is also discussed under this subject.

The phase of the report covering the analytical control of pasteurization plants includes a discussion of the physical, chemical or physico-chemical and biological methods and procedure used to determine the effectiveness of the pasteurization process.

The last section of the report deals with state and municipal supervision of the pasteurization of milk, containing a discussion of the time and temperature requirements, the department of a state or municipality to control pasteurization, requirements regarding apparatus, qualifications of plant operators, bacterial results, and penalties for violations of regulations.

Standard Methods for the Sanitary Analysis of Milk. *Third Edition.* Boston: *American Public Health Association, 1920.* *Price, 30 cents.*

A summary of the more important changes from the second edition follows:

1. The scope of the report has been broadened to cover the sediment test and the examination of milk for the presence of long chain streptococci.

2. A summary of required procedures is given at the end of the report.

3. Encouragement is given for further investigation of promising new laboratory methods.

4. Official recognition is given to microscopic counts made directly from unpasteurized milk.

5. Methods for determining the H-ion concentration of agar media are given.

6. It is recommended that the practice of speaking of agar plate counts as showing the "number of bacteria per cc.," be discontinued and the words "number of colonies" used.

7. It is insisted that punitive actions should be based upon the average results from a series of samples, and that, where possible, the routine counts should be verified by suitable procedures when actions based on their use are likely to be questioned.

The first edition of the Standard Methods for Milk Examination was prepared and issued in 1910. A second edition of this report was prepared in 1916 by a committee which worked in coöperation with committees from the Society of American Bacteriologists and the American Dairy Science Association.

The present third edition report has been prepared by a committee consisting of W. H. Park, chairman; M. P. Ravenel, R. S. Breed, J. A. Anderson and H. A. Harding, with B. H. Stone and W. R. Stokes as adjunct members. This committee has sought and obtained the coöperation of still other associations interested in the sanitary control of milk in an effort to make the report truly representative of American laboratory workers.

✛

The American Red Cross Health Center. *American Red Cross, Washington, D. C. P. 64.*

In September, 1919, the American Red Cross issued a pamphlet entitled "Health Centers. A Field for Red Cross Activity." This pamphlet announced what was to be the peace time program of the Red Cross in the field of public health, but was written in general and somewhat vague terms. This new pamphlet, which is dated September 1, 1920, presents a definite and practical project. There are nine chapters and an appendix, which discuss what the American Red Cross Health Center is, how to select and equip a place, how to put people in touch with existing agencies, how to distribute health literature, how to carry on an active campaign of health education, how to prepare and conduct health exhibits and demonstrations, how to give health instructions through class and club work, how to conduct growth and nutrition clinics, how to begin organizing a Red Cross Health Center, and construction and cost. Much valuable information as to sources of public health literature, suggested topics for health lectures, lantern slides and motion pictures on health, exhibits, health playlets and health stories is given. It is to be noted that this Red Cross conception of a health center is an institution for health education and information, which is adaptable to any type of community. It is stated that a subsequent pamphlet will consider lines of development, such as clinics and other medical activities. The booklet is illustrated with 28 pictures, besides many diagrams and drawings. The cover displays an attractive picture in colors entitled, "The Spirit of the American Red Cross." The whole pamphlet is most attractively gotten up and is an important and valuable addition to public health literature. With this pamphlet for inspiration, Red Cross Chapters should be able to contribute in a logical and practical manner to public health.

The Symposium on Health Centers from the meeting of the Association in San Francisco will be presented in an early issue of the JOURNAL.

ASSOCIATION NEWS

PROCEEDINGS AND DISCUSSIONS OF THE AMERICAN PUBLIC HEALTH ASSOCIATION AT SAN FRANCISCO, CAL., SEPTEMBER 13-17, 1920

MEETINGS OF THE BOARD OF DIRECTORS

Twenty-one members of the Board of Directors of the A. P. H. A. were present at San Francisco and participated in two meetings, September 13 and 15, respectively. In addition to routine business the following matters were acted upon:

Officers were elected for the ensuing year, the list of them being given in the November issue of the JOURNAL, page 889, and on the first white advertising page in the current issue.

Dr. Lee, the treasurer, reported from the auditor's report as follows: Total income for the fiscal year, $49,015.04; total expense, $49,235.33; cash on hand September 1, 1920, $2,763.10.

Through a resolution disapproval was expressed of the proposed amendments to the California constitution aiming to prohibit compulsory vaccination, to prohibit vivisection, to create a separate licensing board for chiropractors, and to extend the use of drugs to chiropractors.

The Committee on Federal Health Coördination advised against activities calling at this time for a ministry of public health. Instead, it was felt best to support the joint resolution already introduced into Congress, calling for an investigation of present federal health activities with a view to coördinating the latter.

It was voted to appoint a committee to meet with a committee of the National Association of the Motion Picture Industry for the purpose of discussing a plan of utilizing motion picture theaters in the promotion of public health and in the combating of epidemics.

The Maine Public Health Association was elected as an affiliated society.

Designs for association insignia were considered but none were adopted. The committee was instructed to continue its efforts in obtaining new designs.

Appreciation was expressed of the importance of committee reports on public health standards, and the Executive Committee was instructed to promote this work.

It was voted to appoint a committee to undertake activities in opposition to the anti-vaccinationists.

The meeting place for the 50th annual meeting was not definitely selected, but the Executive Committee was instructed to make the selection after careful investigation of facilities and coöperation available.

The Executive Committee voted to take especial pains for the 50th annual meeting to insure programs of the greatest value. To this end the Executive Committee will confer with section program officers and formulate rules governing the preparation of all programs. Since the next annual meeting will be of international importance, the programs will include representatives of foreign countries and will in general be of international significance.

RESOLUTIONS ADOPTED BY THE AMERICAN PUBLIC HEALTH ASSOCIATION, SAN FRANCISCO, CAL., SEPTEMBER 16, 1920.

The report of the committee on Resolutions was a portion of the business of the General Sessions at the San Francisco meeting of the association on Thursday afternoon, September 16, 1920. Dr. Haven Emerson, chairman of the committee, read the successive resolutions, which were adopted one at a time by the meeting.

1. **Report of the Committee on Necrology.** This report was voted to be a resolution by the members present at the session and was adopted.

Your committee begs to report the deaths of several members of the association during the past year who had played a prominent part in its work.

In October, 1919, died Dr. D. Orvananos, for many years the first and efficient secretary of the Federal Board of Health of Mexico. Like his coadjutor, Dr. Liceaga, Dr. Orvananos possessed all the qualities of a great secretary. Learned, diligent and courteous, he performed the great task of developing health work in Mexico at a time when little exact knowledge was possessed of the origin of the endemic diseases of the tropics.

His affability was constant and his sympathies as wide as the continent. The association sends to his family and many friends these words of appreciation and the assurance that his memory will long remain green with those who had learned to know and appreciate him.

A yet greater loss occurred to the association in the death of Major General Wm. Crawford Gorgas, an honorary member of the association since 1915. His work in Cuba, in Panama and in South Africa are known to all, and his death, while on another international mission, especially illustrates not more the fact that science knows no country than that the great Anglo-Saxon mother nation recognizes in her offspring, wherever born, those qualities of head and heart which reach around the world in their search for advancing human betterment. With other brothers across the seas we lay our wreath of amaranth on the grave of him, loved, respected and admired, and extend to his desolate family words of sympathy for one who has lent signal honor to this association by his long membership in it and distinguished credit to public health throughout the whole known world.

———

Dr. Louis Caballero died in July, 1920, and while not known to many, owing to the absence which war conditions demanded, is recalled as one who always played a prominent part in public health in his own country of Mexico.

———

Dr. Henry B. Baker of Michigan, ex-president of the association, died a few days ago. One of the earliest public health workers, his work did much to popularize public health in Michigan and throughout the United States.

Of a retiring disposition he was not known to new members beyond his own state, but the older members will long recall his annual reports as among the most

extended and best work of the early nineties. We extend to his family our sympathy and express the satisfaction of knowing that he died full of years and meritorious achievements.

———

Dr. H. W. Kimball of Providence died in March, 1920, and was but a short time a member, but was known to his friends as an enthusiastic worker on health, as was Dr. R. Makibbin of Baltimore, also but two years a member; like Dr. Louis M. Palmer of Framingham, Mass., and Dr. Stafford Baker Smith of New York City.

To the friends of all of these more recent members the association extends its sympathy and expresses its regrets that in the strange mysteries of the Fates the thread of life so slender should have been cut when the powers of these workers for human betterment were at their highest. But we may well recall the words of Horace "Non Omnis Moriar," and remember that the waves of human action flow on, bearing their influence for good to the farthest confines of space.

2. Resolution Concerning Public Health Conditions in Porto Rico.

WHEREAS, the island of Porto Rico has been an American dependency since 1898, and

WHEREAS, the health conditions of the island remain to this day in a most deplorable condition of neglect, the death rate being twice as high as now prevails in continental United States, and

WHEREAS, this condition is largely due to the prevalence of such diseases as hookworm, malaria, diarrhea and enteritis, dysentery, infantile tetanus and others which are all amenable to enlightened public health control, and

WHEREAS, the continuance of the present state of public health in Porto Rico is a matter for which the government of the United States is primarily responsible,

Be It Resolved, First, that the American Public Health Association appoint a committee of five, of which the General Secretary shall be a member, which shall assist in the organization of a branch of the American Public Health Association in the island and the coördination of the activities of such non-official health organizations of the United States as the American Red

Cross, the International Health Board, the National Tuberculosis Association, National Child Welfare Association, etc., for the carrying out of a comprehensive health program.

Second: That this committee direct the attention of Congress, at its next session, to the need for a well coördinated and supported official health program for the island under federal direction and at federal expense, to be continued for a number of years, until such health administration can be transferred to the authorities of Porto Rica, and

Third: That the American Public Health Association send a copy of this resolution to the Secretary of War and to the Congress when it convenes in December, 1920.

3. Resolution Concerning Rat Extermination.

WHEREAS, the sea coast cities of many nations have been subjected to numerous attacks of Bubonic Plague, and

WHEREAS, many of the cities along the sea coasts are making heroic efforts to prevent the plague by rat-proofing buildings and exterminating rats, and

WHEREAS, the agricultural regions of the American Continent, some of which are situated far inland, are badly infested with rats, and

WHEREAS, very little effort to exterminate rats is being made in agricultural sections, therefore

Be It Resolved, that the federal, state and municipal governments of the countries included within the American Public Health Association put forth every effort to exterminate rats or other animals that may carry plague-infecting fleas, the same effort to be put forth inland as has been put forth along the sea coast;

Be It Resolved, that a committee be appointed by the president of this association, whose duty shall be to assist the federal, state, and municipal authorities in the extermination of plague-carrying animals;

Be It Further Resolved, that the federal agricultural departments, the state agricultural departments, the county farm bureaus, and agricultural, horticultural, livestock, poultry or other farm organizations be requested to put forth an earnest and continued effort to exterminate animals known to be capable of transmitting plague.

4. Narcotic Drug Resolution.

WHEREAS, there seems to be, among medical men and health administrators, a wide variance of opinion as to the nature of narcotic drug addiction, and

WHEREAS, narcotic drug addiction constitutes a public health problem of great importance, and

WHEREAS, under these conditions it is well nigh impossible for health officials to formulate a uniform working program for the alleviation or control of this condition; therefore,

Be It Resolved, First, that Dr. W. S. Rankin of this association be empowered to appoint a committee for the purpose of making a thorough investigation of the subject of narcotic drug addiction, and that this committee report their findings to the association at its next annual meeting.

5. Resolution Concerning the Fess-Capper Bill.

RESOLVED, that the American Public Health Association endorses the object of the Fess-Capper Bill for Physical Education, which proposes federal financial and technical assistance to the states in the establishment of physical education; and

Resolved Further, that in so far as the administration of the proposed bill relates to sanitation of school buildings and school grounds and the detection and treatment of physical and mental defects, this particular responsibility should be discharged by the United States Public Health Service; and

Resolved Further, that Section 13 of the bill should be amended so as to leave to the legislative bodies of the state the designation of state machinery through which the provisions of the bill shall be carried into effect within the state and that subsequent sections of said bill be amended to accord with the change in Section 13; and

Resolved Further, that this resolution be laid before the Committee on Education and Labor of the Senate and Committee on Labor in the House by a special committee representing this association.

6. Resolution on Venereal Disease Program.

RESOLVED, that it is the sense of this association that the war-time program of official and non-official health agencies for combating the venereal diseases should be carried on as a civilian program with such modifications as civilian administration and community conditions may require.

7. Resolution on a Section of Public Health Nursing.

WHEREAS, the services of the Public Health Nurse constitute essential professional activities of all modern official and non-official health agencies, and

WHEREAS, their contribution to the methods and principles of public health development and protection have been important and valuable,

Be It Resolved, that this meeting recommend to the Board of Directors that a section on Public Health Nursing be provided for and established in the American Public Health Association.

8. Resolution on the Amendments to the California State Constitution.

The American Public Health Association views with concern the effort being made in California amending the constitution of the state, to nullify the vaccination laws and to forbid animal experimentation. The development of public health and the reduction in mortality in all civilized countries have been so clearly the result of vaccination, inoculation and medical research that any attempt to retard the progress of these preventive measures, must be deprecated by all individuals, laymen and health officials alike, who are interested in eradicating preventable disease and maintaining the highest standards of the public health;

RESOLVED, that the American Public Health Association emphatically disapproves of measures to be voted upon by the people of the state of California on November 2, next, which in any way, limit the freedom of medical research or interfere with the scientific prevention of communicable disease.

9. Resolution of Thanks.

RESOLVED, that the gratitude of the association be extended to all who have coöperated in making the San Francisco meetings an occasion ever to be remembered by our members and guests. The association wishes particularly to acknowledge the invaluable services of the League for the Conservation of Public Health and its executive manager, Mr. Celestine J. Sullivan. We also owe a debt of gratitude to the local

arrangements committee: Dr. Wm. C. Hassler, Mr. Guy P. Jones, Dr. G. G. Moseley, Dr. W. H. Kellogg, Dr. Joseph H. Catton, Mr. Robert L. Webb, Dr. Morton R. Gibbons, Mrs. Katherine I. Barnett, Mrs. H. C. Eldridge, Miss Eleanor Stockton, Miss A. M. Tridel, Miss Anita Eldridge, Mrs. E. F. Galbraith, the Governor of the state of California, the Mayor of San Francisco, the officials of the state and local health departments, the presidents and coöperating members of the faculties of the University of California and Leland Stanford Junior University, the auditorium committee of the San Francisco Board of Supervisors, the Hotels Palace and Whitcomb, the San Francisco Convention and Tourist League, the newspapers of San Francisco, the State Board of Charities and Correction, and all others who gave so generously of their time and energies that this annual meeting might be successful.

Resolved Further, that the Secretary be instructed to communicate the deep appreciation of the association to all of the foregoing.

10. Resolution Concerning Representation of American Public Health Association at Congress on International Classification of Causes of Death, to Be Held in Paris in October, 1920.

Adopted by Vital Statistics, Sept. 15, 1920.

WHEREAS, the section on Vital Statistics approves the report of the committee on the International Congress for the revision of the International Classification of Causes of Death and endorses all of its findings;

Be It Resolved, that a similar action be taken by the General Session of the association, and

Be It Further Resolved, that the general association appoint a representative or representatives who shall attend the International Congress in Paris this October, and who shall present to the Congress the findings of the above mentioned committee as the contribution of the American Public Health Association.

11. Resolution Concerning Work of U. S. Public Health Service in Collecting Industrial Morbidity Statistics.

Adopted by Vital Statistics Section, Sept. 15, 1920.

WHEREAS, the U. S. Public Health Service has accepted the recommendations of the Committee on Industrial Morbidity Statistics of the Vital Statistics Section, and

WHEREAS, the U. S. Public Health Service has put into operation a plan by which sixty-four industrial establishments, with a total of 247,000 employees, are now regularly reporting or are prepared to report regularly, their industrial morbidity experience, and

WHEREAS, this work of the U. S. Public Health Service is seriously curtailed by lack of financial support,

Be It Resolved, that the American Public Health Association approves the efforts of the U. S. Public Health Service along this line, and

Be It Resolved, that there be urged upon Congress the desirability of making ample provision for the adequate support and continuance of this work.

12. Resolution concerning the desirability of all interested agencies, public and private, being represented at the annual meeting of the American Public Health Association.

Adopted by the Vital Statistics Section, Sept. 15, 1920.

WHEREAS, the meetings of the American Public Health Association are for the purpose of improving and harmonizing the various agencies engaged in the protection of human life and health, and

WHEREAS, participation in the deliberations, by representatives of all governmental organizations dealing with these problems is necessary in order to attain the best results, and

WHEREAS, these meetings promote governmental efficiency, rather than give private advantage to participants,

Be It Resolved, That it is the opinion of this association that in attending the meetings of this association, the members are performing a public duty, and

Be It Resolved, That every national and state department, bureau or board, dealing with the subjects discussed should be officially represented at every annual session of the American Public Health Association, and

Be It Resolved, That the Secretary of the Association be instructed to send a copy of these resolutions to the President of the

United States and the governor of each state, to the governor general of the Dominion of Canada, and each province of the Dominion, to the president of Mexico and to the president of Cuba, and also to the official head of each national or state office dealing with the protection of human life and health and allied subjects.

13. Resolution concerning the desirability of the Congress of the United States enacting a general law requiring registration of births and deaths.

Resolved, That it is desirable that the Congress of the United States enact a general law requiring the registration of every birth and death occurring within the United States and its territories and dependencies; but such enactment should not serve to displace efficient registration under state laws.

Secondly, That this law should make state and local registrars special agents of the Bureau of Census, and entitle them to the use of the postal frank in the discharge of all their official business.

Thirdly, Such enactment should provide that all original certificates of birth or death should be left on file in the office of the state in which such births or deaths occurred; and that in all states having laws for birth and death registration in harmony with the provisions of the model bill, the collection of birth and death certificates should be entrusted to state officers; but in territories and states not operating under laws in compliance with the provisions of the model bill the Bureau of the Census should be empowered to establish such registration, and organize the necessary field force therefor, but that the original certificates should be preserved in the state or territorial office, to be turned over to the state whenever it shall be prepared to enforce efficient registration.

Fourthly, The federal act should provide for the making of transcripts in the state offices, at federal expense, for transmission to the Bureau of Census within a reasonable time after the certificates have been received.

14. Resolution recommending bureaus of publicity for state and city health departments.

Resolved, That the American Public Health Association advises the establishment of a bureau of publicity and education as an integral part of every state and important city board of health in order to place and keep fundamental health facts before the people.

✛

PROCEEDINGS—GENERAL SESSIONS

GENERAL SESSIONS, SEPT. 13, 1920, 7:45 P. M.

The first full session of the forty-ninth annual meeting of the American Public Health Association was called to order by David P. Barrows, Ph. D., LL. D., President of the University of California, chairman of the General Committee in charge of the meeting, who in a few well chosen words welcomed the gathering in the name of the committee and of the university. After reading a telegram of regrets from Governor Stephens, who was absent from the state, President Barrows introduced Dr. R. L. Wilbur, President of Leland Stanford, Jr. University, who referred to the public health situation in California, and welcomed the visitors in the name of California as well as that of his university. The welcome was extended so as to include the city of San Francisco by Mr. Rainey, who spoke for the Mayor in his unavoidable absence. Dr. Barrows then gave over the conducting of the meeting to Dr. W. S. Rankin, President of the Association, who delivered his presidential address. (See *Journal* for November, 1920, pages 825-834.)

After some matters of business Dr. Rankin introduced Dr. Haven Emerson and Dr. Charles J. Hatfield, who presented papers on the relative functions of official and of non-official health agencies, Dr. Emerson taking the point of view of the official agency. These papers are to be found in this issue of the *Journal*, pages 941 and 948 respectively. Following the papers came the general discussion of the subject by a number of speakers. The Discussion may be found in this issue of the JOURNAL, pages 963 *et seq.*, following the Symposium on the duties of official and non-official health agencies.

✛

GENERAL SESSIONS, SEPTEMBER 15, 1920

The first paper of the session was that of Louis I. Dublin, Ph. D. of New York City entitled, "The Serious Situation of Porto Rico," with discussion by Dr. Donald

B. Armstrong, followed by the paper entitled, "Publicity and Public Health," by Celestine J. Sullivan, which was discussed by Dr. C. J. Hastings of Toronto, Ont., and Wr. William Simpson of San José. Then followed the symposium on plague in which Dr. W. H. Kellogg, Dr. C. L. Williams and Dr. Friench Simpson had each a paper. For these papers see the November *Journal*, pp. 835-863. In the discussion Surgeon General H. W. Cumming, Dr. Alphonso Pruneda of Mexico City, Dr. Mark F. Boyd of Galveston, Tex., and Dr. E. H. Bullock of Kansas City took part. There was incidentally some discussion concerning resolutions on Porto Rico and rat extermination, which were among those accepted at the third of the General Sessions.

Dr. Robert T. Legge read the report of the committee on the Standardization of Public Health Degrees, action on which was taken at the third General Session. The business was closed for the session by the election of five directors with terms to expire in 1923, Dr. S. J. Crumbine, Dr. J. A. Ferrell, Dr. Charles J. Hatfield, Dr. M. M. Seymour and Dr. R. L. Wilbur.

GENERAL SESSIONS, SEPTEMBER 16, 1920

The first business of the third of the General Sessions of the association was with reference to the committee on Standardization of Public Health Degrees, which had previously reported. It was voted to refer the report to the same committee for action during the course of the year. The report of the committee on Resolutions was presented and accepted, the resolutions being adopted one at a time by the meeting. They are given in this issue of the JOURNAL, page 987.

The paper by Dr. George Hoyt Whipple on "The Value of Animal Experimentation to Mankind" was then presented, followed by the report by Dr. Charles J. Hastings of the Committee on Smallpox.

The list of officers to serve during the ensuing year was announced and President-elect Ravenel made a brief address of appreciation of the honor. Two papers served to close the session and the meeting as well, one by President Ray Lyman Wilbur of Leland Stanford University, on "Vaccination and the Student," and the other an outline of the legislation dealing with vaccination by Chester Rowell, editor of the Fresno *Republican*, "a staunch supporter of preventive medicine," according to the words of Chairman W. S. Hassler, M. D., in intro-ducing him. These papers, together with the report of Dr. Hastings, will be presented together in a later issue of the JOURNAL, in a Symposium on Smallpox.

☐

LIST OF NEW MEMBERS
Proposed for Election to the

A. P. H. A.

October 10 to November 8, 1920, inclusive.
Names of Sponsors are set in **Bold Face Type.**
Names of New Members are in Light Face Type.

CALIFORNIA
S. C. Long, M. D., Bakersfield.
Peter J. Cuneo, M. D., Health Officer, East Bakersfield.
W. M. Dickie, M. D., Los Angeles.
A. M. Besemer, Eureka.
Anna H. DeVinne, San Francisco.
Alice L. Goetz, M. D., Santa Barbara.
F. L. Rogers, Long Beach.
John C. Yates, M. D., San Diego.
Mrs. E. S. Edson, R. N., Sacramento.
J. C. Havely, Sacramento.
George B. Worthington, M. D., San Diego.
Felix E. Ashcroft, M. D., City Health Officer, Chula Vista.
Margaret M. Johnson, San José.
Laura W. Barry, R. N., San José.
Guy S. Millbery, San Francisco.
Louis Graham, D. D. S., President, California State Dental Association, San Francisco.
Agnes Walker, M. D., San Francisco.
H. E. Torgersen, M. D. C., San Francisco.
A. W. Hedrich, Boston, Mass.
Ada May Jessen, R. N., Public Health Nurse, Niles.

CONNECTICUT
Stanley H. Osborn, M. D., Hartford.
J. R. Harris, M. D., Superintendent of Health, New Britain.

FLORIDA
A. C. Hamblin, M. D., Jacksonville.
A. B. Cannon, M. D., Sumner.

ILLINOIS
Paul Hansen, Chicago.
Carl E. Black, Sr., M. D., Jacksonville.
S. R. Klein, M. D., Chicago.
Alfred E. Staps, M. D., Chicago.
C. St. Clair Drake, M. D., Springfield.
Verna Tucker, Wilmette.

INDIANA
O. E. Current, M. D., Farmland.
Charles L. Botkin, M. D., Deputy County Health Commissioner, Farmland.
Miles F. Porter, M. D., Ft. Wayne.
H. A. Duemling, M. D., Ft. Wayne.

KANSAS
C. M. Siever, Manhattan.
Milton S. McGrew, M. D., Holton.

LOUISIANA
A. W. Hedrich, Boston, Mass.
C. L. Williams, M. D., New Orleans.

MAINE
A. W. Hedrich, Boston, Mass.
W. J. Young, M. D., Health Officer, Waterville.

MARYLAND AND DISTRICT OF COLUMBIA
James A. Tobey, Washington.
William H. Slaughter, M. D., P. A. Surgeon, U.S.P.H.S., New York City.

MASSACHUSETTS
Mildred F. Ashley, Boston.
Mrs. Helen B. Berry, Public Health Nurse, Somerville.
C. R. Davis, Boston.
Hope Fagan, Bacteriologist, Gorton-Pew Fisheries Company, Gloucester.

May Bliss Dickinson, Boston.
Amelia A. Meagher, R. N., State Board of Health, Los Angeles.
Cecelia A. Lemner, Boston.
Josephine E. Thurlow, R. N., Supt., Training School for Nurses, Cambridge.
A. W. Hedrich, Boston.
Department of Animal Industry, Atten. of Lester H. Howard, Director, Boston.
Charles L. Foster, M. D., Lieut.-Colonel, Medical Corps, U. S. A., Brookline.
Prof. Milton Rosenau, Boston.
William R. Redden, M. D., Boston.
Mrs. E. G. Harvey, Brookline.
Harold W. Dana, M. D., Boston.
Mary K. Lakeman, M. D., Brookline.
Louise McLean, M. D., Industrial School for Girls, Lancaster.
Willard E. Ward, Brookline.
Arthur A. Cushing, M. D., Medical Director. Brookline Health Centre, Brookline.
Elizabeth S. Campbell, R. N., Dorchester.
Mrs. Irene A. Garden, R. N., Public Health Nurse, Melrose.
R. B. Sprague, M. D., Foxboro.
Bennet B. Bristol, Board of Health, Foxboro.
Russ W. Harding, Franklin.
Ethel L. Perkins, District Nurse, Franklin.

MICHIGAN
A. W. Hedrich, Boston, Mass.
William De Lano, Grand Rapids.
W. J. Deacon, M. D., Lansing.
George H. Ramsey, M. D., Medical Inspector, Department of Health, Lansing.

MONTANA
J. N. Newman, Missoula.
Russel K. Lewis, Missoula.

NEBRASKA
Marion A. Jensen, Nebraska City.
M. M. MacVean, M. D., City Health Officer, Nebraska City.

NEW YORK
B. R. Rickards, Albany.
Edward S. Cole, Upper Montclair, N. J.
John N. Fleischer, Assoc. Secretary, Nassau County Assn., Mineola.
O. J. Hallenbeck, M. D., Canadaigua.
Harry M. Smith, M. D., Medical Inspector of Schools, Canadaigua.
A. O. Hahl, M. D., Clarence.
Clarence H. Mackey, M. D., Health Officer, Lancaster.
L. M. Rohr, M. D., Jamaica.
Laura M. Riegelman, M. D., Chief, Child Hygiene, N. Y. C., Brooklyn.
Michael M. Schultz, M. D., Dept. of Health, N. Y. C., Hollis.
George R. Bedinger, New York City.
Anne A. Stevens, General Director, Maternity Center Assn., New York City.
G. T. Buckell, New York City.
L. Bradley Conklin, Dept. of Hygiene, Cornell Univ. Medical College, New York City.
Lee K. Frankel, M. D., New York City.
Thaddeus P. Hyatt, D. D. S., Dental Director, Metropolitan Life Ins. Co., New York City.

Gertrude Seymour, New York City.
    Daisy M. O. Robinson, M. D., Regional Con-
    sultant, U.S.P.H.S., New York City.
Pearl E. Parker, R. N., Rhinebeck.
    Harriett E. Wooley, Rhinecliff.
E. M. Bogardus, Yonkers.
    Elton G. Littell, M. D., Medical Director, Dept.
    of Education, Yonkers.
A. W. Hedrich, Boston, Mass.
    Board of Education, Ithaca.

OHIO

R. C. Engle, M. D., Cleveland.
    H. J. Burdick, M. D., Cleveland Heights.
R. E. Miles, Columbus.
    F. E. Burleson, Exec. Sec'y, Better Akron Fed-
    eration, Akron.
K. R. Teachnor, M. D., Hamilton.
    Hugh M. Moore. M. D., Deputy Health Com-
    missioner, Oxford.

PENNSYLVANIA

Charles O. Struse, Harrisburg.
    William V. Becker, Supervisor of Sanitation,
    Dept. of Public Health, Philadelphia.
A. W. Hedrich, Boston, Mass.
    P. M. Williams, Philadelphia.

TEXAS

V. M. Ehlers, Austin.
    Clyde C. Hays, City Sanitarian, Waco.

UTAH

H. J. Sears, M. D., Salt Lake City.
    W. M. Stookey, M. D., Salt Lake City.

VERMONT

C. H. Burr, M. D., Montpelier.
    Mrs. George P. Barber, Exec. Sec'y, Washing-
    ton County Chap., A. R. C., Montpelier.

WISCONSIN

George P. Barth, M. D., Milwaukee.
    William F. Reich, M. D., Medical Inspector of
    Schools, Health Dept., Milwaukee.

PORTO RICO

H. W. Green, Central Aguirre.
    Etienu Totti, Sanitary Engineer, Dept. of
    Health, San Juan.

FOREIGN

A. W. Hedrich, Boston, Mass.
    Sociedade de Medicina Cirurgia, Sao Paulo,
    Brazil, South America.

□

MEMBERS OF THE A. P. H. A. ELECTED TO THE VARIOUS SECTIONS AT THE ANNUAL MEETING IN SAN FRANCISCO, CAL., SEPTEMBER 13-17, 1920.

VITAL STATISTICS SECTION

Chauncey Blackburn................Columbia, S. C.
Fred M. Brougher, M. D..............Belen, Miss.
S. J. Byrne, M. D..................Brooklyn, N. Y.
Chicago Tuberculin Institute............Chicago, Ill.
Teofilo Corpons, M. D.........Cabanatuan, P. I.
J. H. Dunkley, M. D ....Roanoke, Va.
George B. Gascoigne................Cleveland, O.
Rollig L. P. Hall, M. D ....Chicago, Ill.
Augenio Hernando, M. D...........Manila, P. I.
Kathryn E. Huenenk..................Kohler, Wis.
Enfemio Jara....................Sunna, P. I.
Francis H. Lally, M. D..............Milford, Mass.
Philip Leiboff...................New York City
J. H. Morrison, M. D..........Hope, Ind.
L. E. Ross.......................Sacramento, Cal.
John O. Spain...................Washington, D. C.
Roxana H. Vivian..............Wellesley, Mass.
C. E. Waller, M. D..............Santa Fe, N. M.
Hazel Wedgwood ....Boston, Mass.
P. B. Williamson, M. D..........Poplarville, Miss.

PUBLIC HEALTH ADMINISTRATION SECTION

Attendance and registration at the annual meeting of the Section is the only requirement for membership in the Section. Forty-five Association members so registered at San Francisco.

SANITARY ENGINEERING SECTION

J. E. Acker........................Atlanta, Ga.
Walter W. Burdette....................Rosslyn, Va.
George B. Gascoigne................Cleveland, O.
Ralph Hilscher ....Berkeley, Cal.
I. Russell Riker.................Caldwell, N. J.
Edward G. Sheilby................Riverside, Cal.
Perry Thompson..................Yonkers, N. Y.

INDUSTRIAL HYGIENE SECTION

Miss Mary Anne Abel...........Birmingham, Ala.
Murray A. Auerbach..................Atlanta, Ga.
E. D. Baker, M. D...............Twin Bridges, Mont.
Philip D. Bourland, M. D........Lake Linden, Mich.
Fred M. Brougher, M. D..........Belen, Miss.
Philip King Brown, M. D.......San Francisco, Cal
Robert McG. Carruth................New Roads, La.
Harriet E. Chalmers, M. D..........Pennhurst, Pa.

Ettore Ciampolini, M. D............Cambridge, Mass.
Philip Colquhoun, M. D..........Waterville, Quebec
Rufus Baker Crain, M. D...........Brookline, Mass.
A. Girard Cranch, M. D..............Cleveland, O
Douglas Treat Davidson, M. D......Mendham, N. J.
Director, Employees' Medical and Service Bureau
....................................Philadelphia, Pa.
R. C. Eaton, M. D......................Chicago, Ill.
Frederick Edminster, M. D...........Detroit, Mich.
Edwin Fauver.....................Rochester, N. Y.
Alan Gregg.....................Rio Janeiro, Brazil
K. E. Huenenk........................Kohler, Wis.
Bernice Jenkins..................New York City
Everett Judson....................Chicago, Ill.
Charles A. Kofoid..................Berkeley, Cal.
Mary Laird, R. N...............Rochester, N. Y.
Frederick S. Lee, M. D..............New York City
Henry M. Loomis...............Washington, D. C.
Frank I. Mayer....................Newark, O.
Charles S. Prest, M. D...........New York City
Laurie Jean Reid, R. N............Helena, Mont.
Bernard C. Roloff....................Chicago, Ill.
R. R. Sayers, P. A. Surgeon, U. S. P. H. S......
...................................Washington, D. C.
E. Scarlett.........................Hamilton, Ont.
Laura M. Smith, R. N...........Valmora, N. Mex.
H. DeWitt Valentine...............Milwaukee, Wis.
Hazel Wedgwood, R. N..............Boston, Mass.
Florence A. Welch..................Fulton, N. Y.

FOOD AND DRUGS SECTION

Walter W. Burdette....................Rosslyn, Va.
Mrs. Francis King Carey............Baltimore, Md.
Walter L. Dodd....................New York City
R. C. Eaton, M. D....................Chicago, Ill.
Rena S. Eckman....................Jackson, Mich.
Carl R. Fellers.................San Francisco, Cal.
Ruth S. Funk....................Urbana, Ill.
Frank G. Gephart, Ph. D............New York City
Meyer Edward Jaffa..............Berkeley, Cal.
Stewart A. Koser..............Washington, D. C.
H. A. Knapp, M. D................Cleveland, O.
Henry M. Loomis................Washington, D. C.
Professor William Herbert Lowe......Paterson, N. J.

J. Lawrence McCormick..............Boston, Mass.
Percy Davol Meader.................Baltimore, Md.
Lethe Eleanora Morrison..............Urbana, Ill.
Arthur F. Noble..................Somerville, Mass.

Roger G. Perkins......................Cleveland, O.
Olin S. Pettingill..............Greenwood Mt, Mc.
Clarence R. Potteiger, D. V. M....Camp Meade, Md.
Charles S. Wagner...................Tottenville, N. Y.

☐

EMPLOYMENT BUREAU

HELP WANTED

Help-wanted announcements will be carried free in this column until further notice. Copy goes to the printer on the 10th of each month for publication on the 20th. Mail to Boston office as early as possible.

In answering keyed advertisements, please mail replies separately to editorial office in Boston, Mass. In replying give age, professional training, salary requirements, previous positions held and three or more references.

Wanted: Assistant chemist for state board of health laboratory in New England. Analysis of water and food. Address, stating age, references and experience, 413, H. D. C., care of this Journal, Boston address.

The Illinois State Department of Public Health is in need of an assistant analyst in the Water and Sewage Laboratory at Springfield. The services of a man are preferred. The position is under Civil Service, temporary appointment at first, followed later by examination which recent graduates or other persons properly qualified should be able to pass. According to State law, preference is given to persons who have served in military or naval service. The present salary available is $1,500 per year, but good opportunity for advancement if additional appropriations are granted by legislature convening within a few months is offered. For additional information, address Dr. C. St. Clair Drake, Director, State Health Department, Springfield, Ill.

Wanted: Whole-time health officer for head health department for city and county; population 30,000; four nurses and stenographer. State experience, reference and minimum salary. Address 416, M. E. C., care of this Journal, Boston address.

Wanted: Bacteriologist as second assistant, state health laboratory in Middle West. Address 415, M. O., care of this Journal, Boston address.

POSITIONS WANTED

Position-wanted announcements will henceforth be carried in this column. The charge is $2 per insertion. Copy should be received at this office by the 10th of the month.

Graduate of Massachusetts Institute of Technology desires location in medical laboratory or health department of industrial concern. At present has charge of bacteriological, chemical and X-ray laboratories of medical department of a corporation. References from past and present employers. Address 137, B. J. C., care of this Journal, Boston address.

A graduate in physical education, medicine and public health, with a valuable experience in each line of work, would like a position in educational work with college, public schools or industrial organization. Address 136, R. F. J., care of this Journal, Boston address.

Young woman graduate of a teachers' college, B.S. degree, with five years' experience in public health laboratory work (two as director of a city laboratory), would like a position in public health education, or an executive position in a health department. Has had some experience in public speaking. Present salary $2,800. Further details on request. Address 131, S. P. M., care of this Journal, Boston address.

Wanted: Position as bacteriologist by woman with training in bacteriology and serology. Especially interested in research work in bacteriology of foods. Experience in public health work. M.A. degree. References. Address 139, B. M., care of this Journal, Boston address.

State health officer with four years' experience desires to make a change. Experience and references furnished. Address 139, H. C. E., care of this Journal, Boston address.

PUBLIC HEALTH NOTES

Abstracts by D. Greenberg, M. P. Horwood, James A. Tobey and Homer N. Calver.

First Aid in Infant Feeding.—The two most important safeguards in the prevention of infant deaths, according to Dr. Jacob Sobel, are proper prenatal instruction and supervision of the mother, and the feeding of the infant with breast milk. According to the author Dr. Jacobi believed that 100% of the women, including even the flower and fashion of the land, could be made to nurse their infants. He maintained that by breast feeding it would be possible to save 100,000 babies that die or become invalids through no other cause than unnatural feeding. That the infant needs the best care and attention which the mother can give, and requires breast milk in order to battle for its life is indicated by the following comparisons. The most dangerous occupation in the world is that of being a baby. It has less chance to live a week than a man of ninety, and to live a year, than a man of eighty. It is less likely to survive its first year than an aviator who makes ascensions daily has of being alive at the end of the first year. Being an infant is six times more dangerous than life in the trenches. The need for breast feeding is therefore quite obvious, as it is the best way to aid the infant through this dangerous period. It must be remembered, however, that although good breast milk is better than good artificial feeding, that good artificial feeding is better than poor breast milk.—*N. Y. Med. Jour.*, September 25, 1920. (*M. P. H.*)

Use of Fresh Vaccines in Whooping Cough.—The author reports the results of a series of cases of whooping cough treated with freshly prepared vaccines at various periods of the disease. In five no results were obtained, and of these three were early in the disease and the other two very late. Of the eleven remaining cases, in nine a very material improvement took place and in four of these a practical cure was obtained. Such results have convinced the author that these vaccines should have an extended use, particularly in institutions where controls might be used to demonstrate whether we might not have in such vaccines a valuable method for reducing the large mortality from whooping cough. R. G. Freeman, *Archives of Pediatrics*, July, 1920, 410. (*D. G.*)

Health Instruction in the Schools of the U. S.—Fifty-eight per cent of the teachers of the United States are trying to teach their pupils to care for their health, according to statistics recently prepared by the Bureau of Education. Thirty-two per cent of the schools use textbooks or some sort of classroom instruction in health matters; 15% use the Modern Health Crusade of the Anti-Tuberculosis Association, and 19% weigh and measure the children according to the plans suggested by the Bureau of Education and the Child Health Organization of America. In other words, 15.6% of the 760,563 children in the schools reporting were weighed and measured at some time or times during the year. One and nine-tenths per cent of these same schools have medical inspection, and only 29 schools, less than 1% have nutritional clinics and feeding.

Utah stands at the head of the list of states in this respect with 72% of her schools using scales; 81% of the children are weighed. Iowa is second with 54% of the schools weighing 51% of the children. Minneosta is third with 31% of her schools weighing 46% of the children. Other states in their order are Indiana, California, Pennsylvania, Illinois and New York.

At the foot of the list is Oklahoma, with only 4% of the schools weighing 0.4% of the children, and Texas with 5% of the schools weighing 1.2% of the children. Ohio is third from the foot with 2%, while Nebraska, West Virginia, Virginia, Mississippi, Michigan and Alabama are not much better.—(*School Life*, U. S. Bureau of Education, September 1, 1920.) (*J. A. T.*)

World Sanitation: A Twentieth Century Possibility.—The first issue of the International Journal of Public Health, published by the League of Red Cross Societies, made its appearance in July, 1920. The journal abounds in excellent articles by such well known scientific men as Dr. A. Calmette, Dr. Richard P. Strong and Prof. G. C. Whipple. Professor Whipple, in his article on World Sanitation, shows the need of public health protection on an international scale. The world is too intimately knit together today, by rapid means of transportation, to enable any part of the world to be indifferent to the plagues which afflict other countries. The need for modern systems of water supply and sewerage is urgent in some parts of the world to diminish typhoid fever and cholera. Buildings must be protected from rats to aid in the campaign against plague. Factories and mines must be adequately lighted and ventilated. Food supplies must be protected and properly stored. Adequate housing facilities must be provided. Cities must be properly planned. Malaria and yellow fever centers must be abolished, and the numerous other activities of a complete public health program must be included. The proposed scope of work to be attempted by the League of Red Cross Societies is indicated by the organization of the General Medical Department of the League. This department includes divisions on vital statistics, communicable diseases, tuberculosis, malaria, sanitation, industrial hygiene, child welfare, nursing, social hygiene and medical information. It will be necessary to determine at first hand the exact sanitary conditions in many countries before intelligent remedial measures can be taken. In order to do this, detailed sanitary surveys of these countries will be necessary. Professor Whipple gives the most complete and comprehensive outline for a sanitary survey that has yet been published.—*International Journal of Public Health*, July, 1920. (*M. P. H.*)

✛

Factors in a Low Venereal Record.—On the basis of 14,444 replies from a questionnaire sent to 37 of the largest camps in the United States, the author analyzes the factors making for a low venereal disease record in the army of the United States. This inquiry supports the belief that chastity is largely influenced by public opinion and, in the Army by the official attitude in regard to it. Section ii of General Order 135, War Department, December 23, 1919, expresses a department attitude as definitely opposed to illicit intercourse, to all recogni-

tion, encouragement or regulation of prostitution; it directs all officers to support the sound policy outlined, and it calls for such frequent and explicit reports as to keep all surgeons and commanders informed at all times as to conditions obtaining in their organizations. Current weekly reports of venereal disease incidence indicate that it is having an excellent effect.

Unchaste men are no more continent in the United States than they were in France. In fact they seem to be less so, as the reported contact rate is much higher. Presumably this is due to lack of the barrier of a different language and to the constant presence of women, *i. e.*, the absence of devastated or army areas, as in France, in which women did not live. It is possible that the distracting interests, campaign, seeing strange country, visiting points of interest, very active welfare work after the armistice, were more potent in France.—P. M. Ashburn, *Military Surgeon*, August, 1920. (*D. G.*)

✛

Ministry of Motherhood.—New South Wales has created the first Ministry of Motherhood. The new cabinet officer is charged with the duty of making provision for mothers and children forced to enter industry for a livelihood. The plans of the ministry have not been worked out but the administration of an endowment fund for mothers will come within its province. The fund, obtained from a graduated income tax, is expected to yield $25,000,000 annually.—*Ch. Bur. News Summary*, August 30, 1920. (*H. N. C.*)

✛

Remote Results from Delayed Antitoxin Administration.—There are several important adverse consequences of delay in giving diphtheria antitoxin which may be summarized as follows: (1) Increased case mortality. (2) Increased number of cases requiring tracheotomy. (3) Causation of paralytic and other complications resulting in unnecessary constitutional damage. (4) The production of carriers. (5) Increased number of cases requiring a prolonged course of hospital treatment, leading to difficulties of administration, due to both overcrowding in hospital and inability to remove cases to hospital owing to lack of accommodation.—G. H. Dart, *Medical Officer*, July 10, 1920. (*D. G.*)

New Grades for Army Medical Corps.— Those who have served in the Medical Department of the Army will be interested in the new system of grades which has been established for the enlisted men of the Medical Corps. By a system of specialists' ratings which carry an extra monthly pay of $3 to $25 there have been provided technicians of various kinds such as clinical, laboratory, dispensary, X-ray and sanitary. These are all men of the grade of private or privates first class. In addition, the former designation of the first three grades of sergeants has been changed. Master hospital sergeants become master sergeants, hospital sergeants are now either technical sergeants or sergeants first class and the former sergeant first class is now a staff sergeant.—*Med. Mil. Rev.*, September 15, 1920. (*H. N. C.*)

✦

Typhoid Carriers.—The Massachusetts State Department of Health now has a list of 51 known typhoid bacillus carriers, who were apparently responsible for 493 cases of typhoid fever. Of these carriers, 21 transmitted to infection to others through milk; and 18 through their occupation as food handlers. It is believed that the remaining 12 disseminated the infection either through food or by direct contact. The intermittent nature of the carrier danger was manifested in the case of four carriers. One carrier did not cause any known cases in 1909, 1910 or 1914 to 1918 inclusive. Yet, in 1919, 29 cases of typhoid fever occurred on his milk route, and for the first time typhoid bacilli were isolated from his feces. *Weekly Bulletin*, N. Y. C. Health Department, September 25, 1920. (*M. P. H.*)

✦

Virulence of Diphtheria from Patients and Carriers.—Tests were made during a period of two years with 250 strains of the diphtheria bacillus. Ninety per cent of the strains that were isolated from cases of clinical diphtheria from the day of onset to and including one year after onset, were virulent for guinea pigs. Eighty per cent of the strains isolated from a smaller series of healthy contact carriers who acquired the bacilli during epidemics were virulent, while only 10% of the strains isolated from noncontact carriers were virulent. The noncontact carriers of this series were persons

in state institutions or schools where there were no cases of diphtheria, who, nevertheless carried diphtheria bacilli in their secretions. Ninety per cent of the cultures that were obtained from convalescent patients during the first three months after the onset of the disease and from contact carriers were virulent. When the results obtained with cultures from convalescent carriers in whom the duration of infection is less than three months are examined, it is found that of 147 strains of *B. diphtheriae*, 136 or 92.5% are virulent.—A. B. Wadsworth, *Jour. Amer. Med. As.*, June 12, 1920. (*D. G.*)

✦

Medical Council of Red Cross League.—The first meeting of the Medical Council of the League of Red Cross Societies was held in Geneva, July 5 to 8. Dr. Simon Flexner presided. In general the Council considered a plan of coöperation between the League and other health organizations. It was decided that the League should first centralize medical information and distribute it. This will be accomplished by various pamphlets and periodicals, including the new International Journal of Public Health. The immediate creation of a commission for infant welfare was approved. This will be sent to work in some country that will engage gradually to take over the work. Experimental tuberculosis demonstrations were recommended for certain places in Europe and an anti-malarial campaign for Spain was approved. There were particularly recommended schools for public health nurses and the adoption of a common international system of vital statistics. Regional venereal disease conferences were encouraged. The first of these will be held in Washington, December 6-11.—*Rev. Inst. de la Croix Rouge*, August, 1920. (*H. N. C.*)

✦

Righteous Indignation.—The following story comes from the city of New York education department:

Micky came home from school sniffling. "You've been licked?" questioned his mother. "I ain't ," said Micky. "There was a doctor at school this mornin', and he said I had ad'noids." "Phwat's thim?" asked the mother. "They're things in your head as has to be took out," answered Micky. "It's a dom lie!" exploded his mother. "I've finecombed y're head ivry Saturday night and niver a one did I find."

Soaps in Relation to Hand Washing.—Sterile hands are not obtained in the ordinary process of hand washing. More bacteria were found to be removed by the ordinary toilet soaps than by the special soaps. In other words the cleansing properties of a soap are more important than its "germicidal" or "antiseptic" constituents. The soap solutions obtained in hand washing are of no practical germicidal or antiseptic value. In the whole process of hand washing done in the usual manner, the special so-called "germicidal" or "antiseptic" soaps exhibit none of these properties. Therefore these terms are not proper to use in connection with soaps. Finally, since the hands may serve as a medium for the conveyance of bacteria in infectious diseases, it is important to remove these bacteria, and this may be done by the ordinary toilet soaps as effectively, if not more so, as by the special brands of so-called "germicidal" and "antiseptic" soaps.—J. F. Norton, *Jour. A. M. A.,* July 31, 1920. (*D. G.*)

✦

Minimum Standards of Organization for Municipal Health Departments.—The work of any health department is to prevent disease, promote good health, and increase the years of life. The diseases which afflict man, and which interfere with the efforts of the health officer to prolong life, may be divided into six groups. (1) Those due to animal and vegetable parasites. (2) Those due to the conditions in the environment. (3) Those due to occupational influences. (4) Those due to faulty diet. (5) Those due to faulty habits. (6) Those due to heredity. One or more of these causes of disease may act during the life of an individual. These may occur during the period previous to conception; during the intra-uterine period; during the period of birth; during the preschool period; during the school period; during the productive and reproductive period; and finally during the period of old age.

The work of a health department may be divided under eight heads, namely, executive and administrative, vital statistics, communicable diseases, child hygiene, food inspection, sanitation, industrial hygiene, and education. The amount of money necessary to maintain a minimum health organization should vary from 50 cents to $1 per capita per annum. A city of 10,000 should have an annual appropriation for health work of 75 cents per capita. The following is an outline of the organization and expenses of a minimum health organization for a city of 10,000:

1 Health Officer	$3,000
1 Public Health Nurse	1,200
1 Clerk	1,000

Total salaries	$5,200
Maintenance	2,300

Total	$7,500

For a city of 25,000 the proposed minimum organization and expenses are as follows:

1 Health Officer	$3,500
1 Epidemiologist	2,500
3 Public Health Nurses	3,600
1 Milk Inspector	1,500
1 Sanitary Inspector	1,200
1 Statistical Clerk	1,200
1 Stenographer	1,000

Total salaries	$14,500
Maintenance	4,250

Total	$18,750

In both cases all the employees are on a full-time basis.—*Jour. A. M. A.,* September 18, 1920. (*M. P. H.*)

✦

Defects of the Heart.—In discussing the heavier incidence of defects of the heart, functional and organic, upon older girls as compared with boys, Dr. W. H. Hamer in a report to the London County Council Education Committee, says: "This difference, repeated year after year, calls for insistent warning that the conditions under which the girls are brought up, lack something that is enjoyed by the boys. It is the more striking when it is considered that difference in the incidence of heart defect between boys and girls does not exist in the eight-year old group, and is therefore developed during four years of school life. There can be no doubt that the effect is due to the denial of opportunities to the girls which are open for boys for participating in outdoor games and sports." Dr. Hamer closes with the quotation: "She grows as a flower does—she will wither without sun; she will decay in her sheath, as a narcissus will, if you do not give her air enough."—*Medical Officer,* June 19, 1920, 246. (*D. G.*)

Orange Juice Considered in a New Light.—It has been shown by Osborne and Mendel that orange juice possess something more than an attractive flavor and antiscorbutic virtues in the feeding of infants. They have demonstrated the presence of water-soluble *B*, the antineuritic vitamine, in both the juice and the inner peel of the orange. Evidently when orange juice or tomato juice (which is also rich in vitamine content) is added to the diet of an infant something more than an antiscorbutic is furnished. It has been noted that in every case when the antiscorbutic dose of orange juice is 15 cc. was increased to 45 cc. a day to infants whose weight had remained stationary for a number of days there was a marked stimulation of growth. A mere increase in food intake (calories) of itself had no such influence on the rate of gain. In feeding orange juice provided the quantity is not too small one is administering at least two highly beneficial adjuvants to the diet. This fact and the growing practice of enlarging the diet of milk fed infants by the use of fruit juices etc. is significant further in view of the recent demonstration by Osborne and Mendel that cow's milk from a comparative standpoint is not rich in·water-soluble vitamin. These authors have pointed out how recent studies of the antiscorbutic value of cow's milk have indicated that on this score it must be classed as less valuable than many of the raw fruits and vegetables. Whereas quantities of the latter—less than 10 grams daily—will prevent scurvy in guinea pigs on a diet otherwise devoid of antiscorbutic material, from 100 to 150 cc. daily of raw cow's milk are required for this species, while monkeys require larger quantities. Similarly relatively large quantities of milk are required to produce the increased intake of food and improved rate of growth which are readily secured by very small quantities of many green vegetables.—Editorial *Jour. A. M. A.* June 19, 1920, *(D. G.)*

✚

Syphilis As a Factor in Fœtal Mortality. —The author reports a critical study of 302 fœtal deaths occurring in 4,000 consecutive deliveries at the Johns Hopkins Hospital. Of the 4,000 cases there were 1,439 white and 2,161 black women, in whom a positive Wasserman reaction was present in 2.5 and 16.3 percent respectively. Upon analyzing the causes of death he obtained the following figures:

	Cases	Pct.
Syphilis	104	34.44
Dystocia	46	15.20
Toxemia	35	11.55
Prematurity	32	10.59
Placenta previa and premature separation	16	5.28
Deformity	11	3.64
Eleven other causes	32	10.69
Cause unknown	26	8.61

As large as these figures seem, they do not entirely represent the ravages of syphilis since a more careful search might have revealed the presence of spirochetes in the tissues of a considerable fraction of the autopsies in which the cause of death was attributed to prematurity, as well as in a certain number included in the unknown group. Moreover, these figures do not include the cases of congenital syphilis which appeared in babies which were discharged alive, or in whom the disease developed later. The author notes that this unusually large incidence of syphilis can only apply to hospital services with a large black clientele, and will not be found in private practice or in hospitals in communities in which the majority of inhabitants are white, or in which the colored people are more intelligent than in the vicinity of Baltimore. In this series of cases there were 99 white and 203 black infant deaths and in them syphilis was the etiological factor in 12.12 and 45.23 percent, respectively.

Considering the question of the reduction of fœtal mortality the author notes how difficult it is with our present state of knowledge to combat any of the causes except syphilis. At the present time a program directed against syphilis appears to offer the most promising field for immediate results. In such a program all obstetrical patients should be encouraged to register not later than the third or fourth month of·pregnancy, and a routine Wasserman should be made at the first visit and in case the result is positive, intensive treatment should be started immediately. In the case of the ignorant patient, mere advice to return at stated dates for treatment will not suffice, and it will. be necessary for the social worker to follow her into the home and insist upon the necessity of following all directions implicitly.—J. W. Williams, *Bull. of Johns Hopkins Hosp.*, May, 1920, 141. *(D. G.)*

Association of Laboratories.—The New York Association of Public Health Laboratories, recently organized, is an evidence of the realization by the laboratories themselves of the needs of coördination in the interests of uniform methods and higher standards.

The purposes of the Association, as outlined in the constitution, are "to increase the efficiency of the laboratories engaged in public health work in the State; to unify the interests of their workers by stimulating among them the spirit of common understanding and coöperation; and to encourage the constant effort toward the improvement and standardization of technical methods to the end of securing increasingly high standards of scientific achievement in the work performed by the several laboratories."

Laboratories approved by the State Commissioner of Health are alone represented in the Association. To receive approval by the Commissioner of Health, they must maintain at least the minimum standard of efficiency considered essential before their regular reports can be accepted by the Health Department.

The membership of the Association, which includes both active and associate members, is made up of representatives of laboratories engaged in public health work, qualified workers in these laboratories, and other persons actively interested in the public health work in the State. Thirty-three laboratories in the State are represented in the Association. Warren B. Stone, M. D., Director of the City and County Laboratory, Schenectady, was elected President of the Association; William A. Bing, M. D., Director Ontario County Laboratory, Canandaigua, Vice-President; and Mary B. Kirkbride, Bacteriologist, State Department of Health, Albany, Secretary-Treasurer.

✛

National Plan for Recruiting Student Nurses.—There is in every community an acute shortage of competent nurses.

In order to help correct this condition, the three National Nursing Associations— American Nurses' Association, the National League of Nurse Education and the National Organization of Public Health Nursing—together with the American Red Cross, have arranged a national movement which will continue indefinitely for the purpose of recruiting students to fill the Hospital Training Schools, and distributing information relative to nursing education and the opportunities open to graduates of the profession.

It is suggested that if in each community a committee were formed, a recruiting committee, results might be obtained. Such a committee should be formed by representatives of groups like Red Cross chapters, governing and auxiliary boards of hospitals, hospital and training school superintendents, local medical and nursing organizations, physicians, board of education, press, chamber of commerce and women's clubs.

These committees could secure information about nurses' schools, demands for nurses, secure speakers, present the plans before training schools, get local publicity, place posters, and arrange public meetings, plays, pageants, etc. They could also bring into coöperation the city officials, and associations of physicians, alumni, farmers and the Church, and prove a clearing house for information concerning nurses and the needs. The American Red Cross offers its services in order that such a plan may be put into operation with the minimum of delay.

✛

Diphtheria and Bad Drains.—Old superstitions regarding the causation of disease have for the most part given way before the scientific demonstration of the true relation between disease and its cause. One of the most popular of these old superstitions, one that perhaps some of the younger generation have not even heard of, is that diphtheria was caused by bad air or sewer gas emanating from broken drains or leaky plumbing. This superstition is still met with more or less frequently among the laity but a public health worker or even a physician who suggested such a relation would, to say the least, not be considered "up-to-date." It is with some astonishment therefore that one reads in the columns of one of the most progressive of all public health journals the following note, *without comment*, "In recent years typhoid fever has been less prevalent in

Workington, but diphtheria has been on the increase. In 1919 there were as many as 110 cases, and Dr. Thompson is justified in referring its persistence to the existence of insanitary conditions. In this connection he urges the need for examining and where found necessary, the relaying of school drains. It is suggestive, he says, that there were very few cases of diphtheria among the children attending the north side school, where the conservancy system prevails."

The note from which this is quoted justly praises the health officer in question for his persistence in attacking year after year and month after month, insanitary conditions in the face of a discouraging lethargy of local authorities. Many health officers might well take heart from such an example of perseverence. It is unfortunate, however, that this tenacity should extend to the retention of outworn theories.— *Medical Officer*, Aug. 7, 1920.

✛

Few Prisoners with Tuberculosis in Massachusetts Prisons.—During the summer the Department of Corrections of the state in coöperation with the Division of Tuberculosis of the Department of Public Health made an examination of the inmates of all the correctional institutions in the state with reference to the prevalence of tuberculosis. There were 1,571 inmates of the fourteen state and county prisons examined by tuberculosis experts from the four state sanatoria. The remarkable showing of the examination is that only seven prisoners were found to have active tuberculosis. These men were referred to the prison hospital for treatment. No one of them was found in the state institutions, all of them being inmates of county prisons. Two of the institutions, the Reformatory for Women and the Bridgewater State Farm were not examined, since they have their own consumptive colonies.

✛

Train Wrecks Due to Paresis.—At the recent meeting in Atlantic City of the American Association of Railroad Chief Surgeons one of their number made the startling assertion: "That four recent wrecks had been traced to engineers suffering from paresis."

Biologic Products in Public Health Works.—The importance of biologic products not only to cure disease but to prevent disease is a fact which health officers generally recognize today. The first biologic product to be used in public health work was smallpox vaccine. Its use has saved millions of lives. Prior to the employment of vaccination in Sweden, the deaths from smallpox were about 20 per 1,000,000 population. After vaccination was made compulsory the deaths were less than 20 per 100,000,000 population. The first biologic product used to prevent disease was diphtheria antitoxin. The average reduction of mortality from diphtheria due to the use of diphtheria antitoxin has been not less than 50 percent. Not less than 10,000 units should be given as an initial dose in a case of diphtheria. In a case of laryngeal diphtheria, the dose should be larger and should be repeated, according to the needs of the patient. Where quick results are necessary, antitoxin should be given intravenously. For prophylactic purposes, the dose of antitoxin is 1,000 units. The immunity, however, lasts but three weeks.

No vaccine has yet been prepared against influenza, but a definite vaccine has been prepared against pneumonia, which is apparently efficient. The success of the typhoid vaccine is well known. Its value has been demonstrated during the mobilization on the Mexican border and in the great war. It is customary now to inoculate against typhoid fever, paratyphoid A and paratyphoid B simultaneously and better results are thus obtained. The Schick test is being used more extensively to detect the susceptibles to diphtheria, and a toxin-antitoxin mixture is being used to establish an active immunity against diphtheria. Park has immunized 4,000 susceptibles, including 1,000 infants under one week old, by the use of toxin-antitoxin, during the past three years. Other biologic products in general use are tetanus antitoxin, rabies vaccine, cholera vaccine and plague vaccine. Biologic products in order to be efficient must be manufactured under the best conditions and must be kept in an ice box until ready for use.—John F. Anderson, M. D. *New Jersey Public Health News*, April, 1920. (*M. P. H.*)

Municipal Health in Albania.—The medieval city of Elbassan, Albania, which has until recently been one of the most unprogressive communities in the world, has adopted an extensive public health program. The city authorities have enthusiastically taken up health work which has been introduced by the American Red Cross and are energetically seconding the efforts of the American Relief Corps. Already a general dispensary, an infant welfare station, a milk organization, a woman's clinic, and a food inspection unit have been established. It is hoped that a reduction in infant mortality may be accomplished; at present five out of every eight children die at birth or at an early age, according to the medical officer in charge of the newly instituted public health work.—(*J. A. T.*)

✛

The Carrier in Food Poisoning.—An interesting outbreak of paratyphoid fever traced to a carrier is described. The outbreak was confined to one house in which ten persons were living, all of whom were affected. It was ascertained that a stew of steak and liver had been prepared and consumed, the gravy being saved until the following day and warmed up with a Yorkshire pudding. Two days previous the woman who undertook the preparation of the food was taken ill, and the climax of her illness was reached two days later, although she continued to attend to her household duties. In consequence the liver gravy was infected. Subsequent bacteriological study revealed the presence of the paratyphoid bacillus in the blood of those affected.—*Lancet,* August 14, 1920. (*D. G.*)

✛

Water Supply of the Republic of Austria.—Chief Engineer Alexander Swetz in *Zeitschrift für Wasser und Abwasser,* 1920, 7, page 59-61, gives a general description of the water supply conditions in Austrian municipalities, particularly Vienna, as they are affected by the economic distress, the shortage of labor, etc., resulting from the war. At the present time many of the works are inadequate to give proper service.—(*R. S. W.*)

✛

Control of Summer Diarrhea.—Our efforts to control the infantile diarrheas should be directed towards the regulation of the environment of the infant population. This can be accomplished only through education of those who are concerned with the care and management of infants. The mother, the nurse, as well as the other attendants must be brought to realize the possibility of transmission of diarrheal disease through different channels. The control becomes largely a problem of personal hygiene for those who are responsible for the care of the infant. There must be due regard to feeding, cleanliness and clothing of infants and to the exclusion of flies.—D. H. Bergey, *Archives of Pediatrics,* August, 1920, 462. (*D. G.*)

✛

Record for Preventive Medicine.—There were gathered in New York early in June 304 Boy Scouts. These boys, from 101 cities, were on their way to Europe to represent the Boy Scouts of America. In spite of the fact that measles and scarlet fever and chickenpox were introduced into the group not a single secondary case occurred during their whole journey to Europe and back. The secret of this success was in careful and thorough physical inspection carried out daily or twice daily. All boys showing inflammatory condition of the nose or throat were promptly segregated and treated.—*Med.-Mil. Rev.,* September 15, 1920. (*H. N. C.*)

✛

An Airplane Ambulance.—The United States military aviation authorities have just completed a new design for airplane ambulances. One of these machines was recently flown from the Air Service Experiment Station, McCook Field, Dayton, O., to Bolling Field, Washington, D. C. Although previous models of airplane ambulance were in use at flying fields in this country during the war, they were all simple modifications of the Curtis training planes. The new ambulance has a fuselage designed primarily to carry the sick or wounded and provides space for two litter patients, a medical attendant and the pilot. A D. H. 4 type of air plane is used. with certain modifications in design to increase its safety and stability. Several ambulances of this type are now being built for use on the Mexican border.—*Medico-Military Review,* U. S. A., July 15, 1920. (*J. A. T.*)

School Medical Inspection In New York City During 1919.—The work conducted in New York City for the protection of the health of school children is extensive and varied. Not only does it consist of routine medical examinations by physicians and nurses, and of home visits by the nurses, and numerous examinations and much corrective work by the dentists, but also of special studies on particular phases of the work. As a result of a special nutrition survey conducted in 43 schools, the following amounts of malnutrition were discovered:

Kindergarten ....40% Malnutrition
First year ....43% Malnutrition
Second year ....40% Malnutrition
Third year ....37% Malnutrition
Fourth year ....37% Malnutrition
Fifth year ....35% Malnutrition
Sixth year ....32% Malnutrition
Seventh year ....26% Malnutrition
Eighth year ....22% Malnutrition
Ninth year ....21% Malnutrition

The following table gives the summary of regular examinations for physical defects:

	1919.	1918.
Number of children examined	248,978	247,735
Having defective vision..	7.2%	9.4%
Having defective hearing.	0.5%	0.4%
Having defective nasal breathing .	11.6%	10.0%
Having hypertrophied tonsils	15.3%	17.5%
Having cardiac disease....	1.5%	1.2%
Having pulmonary disease	0.3%	0.2%
Having orthopedic defects	0.9%	0.7%
Having nervous affections	0.6%	0.6%
Having defective teeth....	62.3%	65.2%

Summary of cases terminated:

Defects of vision corrected by glasses	49.1%	51.5%
Defective nasal breathing corrected by surgical means..	20.9%	22.0%
Hypertrophied tonsils corrected by surgical means..	19.0%	20.3%
Orthopedic defects corrected by surgery	0.8%	2.5%

During 1919 there were increases in the number of cases of measles, diphtheria and chickenpox. There was also a large increase in the number of cases of pediculosis. The number of cases of trachoma declined from 2,052 in 1918 to 1,675 in 1919. During 1919, 19,828 individuals were vaccinated against smallpox.

Not only were the children under close supervision of the medical inspectors and the school nurses, but the coöperation of the teachers was enlisted in helping to find cases of communicable disease, and in teaching the children the essentials of healthy living. Dr. Jacob Sobel, *Monthly Bulletin of New York City Department of Health*, September, 1920. (M. P. H.)

□

SUMMER PLAYGROUND INSTRUCTION

During the past summer instruction in mothercraft has been given on several playgrounds where little girls ten to fourteen years are taught the principles of caring for their own health and for the babies in the home. This valuable instruction which is carried on under the auspices of the Massachusetts State Federation of Women's Clubs, Mrs. George Minot Baker, President, reaches young girls of the districts where infant mortality is generally highest. This instruction is not confined to playgrounds, of course, for in the regular school year it is presented to classes in public and private schools and before groups of Girl Scouts and Camp Fire Girls. Here is a group of children on one of the playgrounds in Newton, Mass.

STATE HEALTH NOTES—GENERAL

National.—The United States Public Health Service needs hundreds of graduate nurses for its general hospital work, but also and particularly for the care of former soldiers suffering from nervous and mental disorders. So great is its need for the latter class that it is probable that at present enough trained nurses are not available in the country. The Public Health Service accordingly purposes to establish a training school for nursing in neuropsychiatric diseases in its special hospital (No. 9) on Gray's Ferry Road, near Philadelphia, where nurses with general training may take a special course in this class of work. This hospital has a capacity of 240 patients and will afford exceptional opportunities for instruction in the most modern treatment.

An appeal is made to nurses to come forward for this work, for if they do not do so there seems to be no one to take their place. The hospitals now operated by the United States Public Health Service are already 150 nurses short, and the service faces the necessity of opening several new ones with an inadequate force. Applications should be made to the Surgeon General, United States Public Health Service, Washington, D. C.

The new Government hospital, where the United States Public Health Service will provide special care and treatment for shell-shocked soldiers has been opened and the transfer effected of over 100 patients from the temporary hospital at Cape May, N. J. The new institution is in charge of Surgeon E. H. Mullan, an experienced regular officer of the Service, who has been the commanding officer at Cape May.

According to information furnished by the Children's Bureau, Washington, D. C., most of the work in which children are employed is temporary or seasonal. In the first month after starting to work 10% of the boys and 8% of the girls were out of jobs for at least one week. The proportion of unemployment became less as the children became used to industry. Throughout their work histories the boys showed a greater tendency to unemployment than the girls.

The Pullman Car Service is giving the American Red Cross First Aid training to the entire force of colored maids employed on the transcontinental trains. Several of the women have already finished the course and now carry as part of their equipment the regulations first aid kit. The Pullman Company has arranged with the New York County Chapter of the Red Cross to give the course of training in First Aid and Home Hygiene to some hundreds of maids reporting to its New York terminal.

More than 13,000 American communities were touched by the activities of the American Red Cross during the year ending June 30, 1920, according to the annual report of the organization covering that period.

During the year a Red Cross Department of Health Service has been organized; its Nursing Service has been extended to meet a growing demand for public health nursing until over 36,000 nurses are on its rolls; its First Aid to Injured courses have been widely taught, 6,000 persons having been awarded First Aid certificates during the year, and the A. R. C. has been the chief factor in the formation of the League of Red Cross Societies, with headquarters in Geneva.

The Department of Health service was established December 1, 1919. On June 30, 1920, there were in active operation 128 health centers, from which radiate innumerable activities designed to improve the health of the community, while 435 Red Cross Chapters were actively engaged in disease-prevention work.

It has maintained many different departments, a Bureau of First Aid to the Injured, a Water First Aid Service, a Bureau of Medical Social Service and a Department of Nursing.

Of the 604 nurses attached to the various A. R. C. commissions in Europe when the armistice was signed, all but 116 had returned to the United States by June 30, 1920. Of these 66 were in Poland, 46 in the Balkans, 2 in France and two in Bohemia. Six scholarships to prepare nurses for foreign service have been established at King's College. Enrollment in the Red Cross nursing service increased during the year from 35,426 to 36,705. On June 30 there were in active service 504 in the Army,

321 in the Navy and 943 in the Public Health corps.

In order to increase the number of qualified public health nurses, for which there is urgent demand, 288 scholarships have been established and 67 loans have been made from National Fund to public health nursing. In addition approximately 250 scholarships have been awarded by the various chapters.

Development in class instruction in Home Hygiene and Care of the Sick has increased three-fold during the fiscal year, the number having increased from 34,033 to 93,093. During June, 1920, 2,090 nurse instructors were conducting classes in this branch of work.

One of the important results of the work done by the Red Cross Health and Nursing Departments has been that 35 states have practically adopted a uniform method of working in connection with the Red Cross whereby a bureau of public health nursing has been instituted under the direction of the state public health officer.

The Red Cross medical report for July, 1920, showed 96 physicians, 9 dentists, 10 pharmacists and one laboratory man, making a total of 116 medical personnel in Europe. This number, however, has been cut rapidly by the expiration of contracts so that there are now only about 50 medical men still in Red Cross service in Europe.

✦

Connecticut.—An Institute for Industrial Nurses, the first of its kind, was held this fall at the New Haven School for Public Health Nursing. Fifty-four registered public health nurses from eight states attended. The varied industries represented and the discussions of the nurses brought out very clearly the fact that, while no fixed rules can be worked out to fit all places, it is possible to state definitely the fundamental principles of industrial nursing.

The program lasted ten days and included lectures and round tables on public health nursing, industrial nursing, industrial hygiene, industrial diseases, records, ethics of industrial nursing and medicine, industrial relations, social problems, industrial psychology, nutrition, health education, as well as excursions to manufacturing plants. Four periods were given over to lectures on recreation and other methods of counteracting the industrial monotony. Play demonstrations were given and everyone jonied in folk dancing and simple games.

The nurses were asked to express their opinions as to the most valuable features of the Institute. Some quotations follow:

"It is difficult to say which feature of the Institute has been of the most value, but possibly the discussion of our problems made us feel that we were giving as well as receiving help, although we derived a great deal of good from all lectures."

"The Institute showed me some ways of handling these problems and the opportunity of meeting so many other nurses in the same line of work was a pleasure indeed."

"I think the most helpful feature of the Institute has been the broadened vision of the possibilities and responsibilities of industrial nursing."

Most of the nurses wished for a larger Institute, with more round tables and excursions. Others suggested a shorter period because it would be easier to be relieved of their duties for one week. The desire for an Institute next year was unanimous.

The interest of employers was shown by the fact that many nurses attended at the expense of their firms.

✦

Georgia.—An intensive educational campaign is being conducted throughout the larger cities of the state among the negroes by Dr. J. P. Bowdoin, Venereal Disease Control Officer. Drs. A. R. Barton and R. B. Stewart, colored physicians, are putting on moving pictures and giving lectures. Over 7,000 men were reached during the month of September.

Among other matters of interest to the entire state, and to health officers in particular, is the new school for feeble minded. The state has just been given possession of this property and as soon as the preliminary organization can be perfected and the necessary changes made, the school will be opened. This can only be done in a small way, as no provision was made for maintaining the school.

The State Board of Health has had exhibits at several of the fairs, especially the

Southeastern Fair, Atlanta, and the Georgia State Fair at Macon. Free moving pictures, besides the stereomatograph, were used. The child welfare department booth was a feature.

A conference of county health officers was held at Atlanta, October 7 and 8, with excellent attendance. Child welfare was a prominent subject, with the exhibition of a modern baby health center by Drs. De-Vilbiss and Bocker. Soil pollution and malaria were other subjects of great local importance under discussion. The conference was under the charge of Dr. C. C. Applewhite.

Dr. H. D. Allen, Jr., has been elected commissioner of health of Baldwin county.

Marion county has recently adopted the Ellis Health Law. This makes the twenty-sixth county in the state to adopt this measure, which gives them a full time commissioner of health.

The city of Griffin and Spaulding county have recently adopted a $10,000 budget with which to begin their city and county health work.

✦

Maine.—Twelve cases of poliomyelitis, or infantile paralysis, have been reported from ten Maine towns since Sept. 1, eight of them during September and four new cases since the beginning of October. These are practically the first reports of the disease in Maine in 1920, and while far from indicating an epidemic, have put the health authorities on their guard, especially in view of the fact that in several sister states infantile paralysis is now prevalent in alarming proportions.

Maine's famous "fly case," which has been in the courts off and on for the past six months, has again resulted in defeat for the fly, at the hands of the jury in the York County Supreme Court.

At this last trial of the case, the landlord of the Colonial Inn at Ogunquit, who had brought suit against a former guest at his hostelry for leaving the Inn before the expiration of his contract, was defeated. Frederick A. Sweet of Worcester, the defendant, who left the Inn on account of the many flies which he alleged infested the dining room, was the victor.

The landlord first brought suit last May and was awarded a verdict of $128.78, but the defendant took the case to the law court, where Justice Spear, in recognition of the opinions of health authorities that the fly is a filthy and disease-spreading insect, ordered a new trial.

A quota of $60,000 has been named for Maine which means the sale of four million Christmas seals and approximately $20,000 in health bonds, which are in denominations of $5 to $1,000. Ninety-five per cent of the money from the sale stays in Maine, to be devoted to the cause of better health in the Pine Tree State.

The Maine Public Health Association having had at its disposal in 1920 a budget of about $25,000, is seeking to double this figure during 1921. There will be a corresponding extension of the functions of the association, which will include modern health crusade, nursing service, and coöperation with local associations.

✦

Maryland.—Johns Hopkins University has under way a six weeks' intensive course in training health officers. On each week day laboratory demonstrations and practical exercises occupy the morning hours. The other work is to be done in the afternoons. Lectures are given on five of the week days. An idea of the character of the course may be obtained from the following program of lectures: public health law, selected topics in hygiene, principles of nutrition, immunity, principles of public health administration.

✦

Massachusetts.—Dr. Eugene R. Kelley, Commissioner of Public Health, has requested $25,000 from the Governor and Council that plague prevention measures may be inaugurated in the seaport cities and towns of Massachusetts. This work will be done in conjunction with other New England states having seaport communities.

At a recent conference held at the State House of the Commissioners of Health of Connecticut, Rhode Island, New Hampshire, Maine and Massachusetts, a request was made that an officer of the U. S. Public Health Service might be detailed as an adviser in this work in each of the states represented. P. A. Surgeon L. L. Williams, Jr., has been detailed for this work.

It is planned to conduct a rodent survey in each seaport community. The Harvard Medical School, through Dr. Milton J. Rosenau, Professor of Preventive Medicine, has offered space for the laboratory examination of the rats. The personnel for this survey consists of a consulting director, bacteriologists, an expert rat trapper with six assistants, dieners and laboratory and clerical assistants. Strenuous efforts are being made to interest local authorities in enacting building regulations which will secure rat-proofing of new and old constructions. In the event that plague-infected rats are found, intensive trapping and rat-proofing will be undertaken.

As the infection is found in the rat some months before it appears in the human family, the wisdom of this survey is apparent.

+

Michigan.—Through the autumn examinations have been conducted by local authorities in many districts in coöperation with the Michigan Department of Health for the purpose of detecting diphtheria carriers. The largest survey yet attempted began September 20, when the department's "laboratory on wheels," manned by five technicians, started examination of 6,000 school children in St. Clair county. Surveys have been made, or are now being conducted, at Manistee, Marion, Ithaca, Northland, New Baltimore, Fowlerville, Bellville, Barryton, Hopkins, Vicksburg, Mancellona and Greenville.

These carriers are not clinically sick, but they would, if not discovered, make other children sick, cost the community hundreds of dollars to care for an epidemic, and possibly death and desolation to several homes by the loss of loved ones, asserted Dr. William J. V. Deacon, Director of the Bureau of Communicable Diseases. "If the work has saved the life of only one child in the state of Michigan, it is well worth the money cost and effort."

Deaths from whooping cough and from automobile accidents, numbering 398 and 238 respectively, for the first 9 months this year in Michigan, are both due to the same cause, according to Dr. Deacon. That cause, he asserts, is carelessness.

One-half of the cases of whooping cough occur among children under three years of age, the same officer declares, and the sole exciting cause is contagion. By far the greater number of children exposed to whooping cough take it. Momentary exposure is enough to transmit the infection to another person. It is here that carelessness enters in. There should be no epidemics of whooping cough if parents regarded the health of other people's children half as much as their own. Under no circumstances should the child suffering from whooping cough be permitted to come in contact with other children.

Subdued gradually by white men from the time when Jean Nicolet first invaded their territory in 1634, the question now arises as to whether Michigan Indians will be exterminated by the great white plague of their white conquerors. Officials of the Michigan Department of Health believe the Indians will be exterminated in time unless the state makes strenuous efforts to save them. A survey of part of the Indians in the Upper Peninsula made during the past summer under the direction of Dr. R. M. Olin, State Health Commissioner, reveals that 63% are either positive or suspected sufferers of tuberculosis.

With 7,234 cases of diphtheria reported in Michigan from January 1, to November 5, this disease, which was more prevalent in Michigan during 1918 than in any other state in the union or country in the world, now shows an increase of 30% over last year and two and one-half times the average for the past 12 years.

In the testing of more than 15,000 cultures from the throats of school children in the past few weeks, 155 carriers of virulent diphtheria organisms were found by the State Department of Health. These carriers have been isolated and treated by family physicians, successive tests being made of cultures by the state laboratories to determine when the patients are safe for release.

That Michigan is no longer "outostriching the ostrich" in the national fight against venereal disease, and that the new policy is one of frank recognition of the diseases and a comprehensive and determined effort to eliminate them in contrast to the old method of the public shutting its eyes, is shown by the annual report of the venereal disease division of the Michigan Department of Health. In a recent survey of 444 cities in the United States, conducted by the U. S. Public Health, Michigan ranks among the first states in the Union, if not at the top of the list, in measures taken toward eradication of these so-called social diseases. Of ten cities with 500,000 or more population, Detroit ranks first; among the 57 with 100,000 to 500,000 population, Grand Rapids is third; among 59 with 50,000 to 100,000, Flint is sixth, Saginaw is thirteenth; of 123 with 25,000 to 50,000, Lansing is third, Jackson fourth, Battle Creek sixth, Kalamazoo eleventh, Bay City twenty-third; and of 193 cities with 25,000 population or less, Ann Arbor is fortieth, Pontiac forty-ninth, and Port Huron fifty-fifth.

Comparative freedom in Michigan this season from epidemics of bronchial pneumonia, mastoiditis, and ear and nose infections, following attacks of minor ailments, such as measles, whooping-cough, scarlet fever and common colds, is predicted by the Michigan Department of Health. This belief is based upon reports from the state laboratory, which is making a systematic study of the seasonal variation of certain strains of the hemolytic streptococci group of bacteria.

Appreciating the benefits accruing to physically subnormal children by attendance during the winter in open air classes, the Detroit Board of Education decided to continue one school throughout the summer.

The following half-day schedule was in force:

8:30- 9:15—Class work.
9:15- 9:45—Shower baths (3 times weekly).
9:45-10:00—Lunch.
10:00-11:15—Class work.
11:15-11:30—Recess.
11:30-11:35—Preparation for dinner.
11:35-12:10—Dinner.
12:10-12:20—Tooth brush drill.
12:20- 1:10—Rest period.
1:10   —Dismissed for the day.

The school was in session from June 28 to August 21, a period of eight weeks. The total enrollment was thirty-eight. Attendance was purely voluntary and amounted to 88%, as computed from the enrollment days and the days present. From June 16, the close of the regular school session, to June 28, the opening of the summer school, 20 children lost an average of 0.4 pounds (14 lost, 4 were unchanged, 2 gained).

Twenty-five children were present in the summer school more than 20 days, the average being 29 days. Their weight at entrance was 60.1 pounds. Their normal weight was 67.1 pounds. They were thus 7 pounds under weight, or about 10%. In 29 days under the half-day open air school regime they gained 1.9 pounds. Not one child lost weight. Four failed to gain, but did not lose. Twenty-one gained from half a pound to four pounds.

To sum up, these children started to lose weight on being turned out of school in the middle of June. The summer session rescued them from this downward course and again put them on their feet, causing a gain twice that of the normal child.

Dr. George T. Palmer, Epidemiologist of the Detroit Department of Health, presents some striking figures with reference to diphtheria. He calls attention to the fact that although it is known that antitoxin if properly administered in sufficient dosage will prevent fatalities from the disease, it is still true that deaths have not fallen off the way they should in Detroit. The figures for that city are these:

Annual Death Rate
per 100,000.

1914	26.7
1915	17.1
1916	35.8
1917	49.6
1918	30.0
1919	33.1

It seems most difficult to secure more effective use of antitoxin.

The number of cases of diphtheria, except for variations from year to year, has not decreased since 1914.

Annual Case Rate
per 1,000.

1914	3.42
1915	2.93
1916	4.98
1917	5.43
1918	3.08
1919	3.80

In order to see whether intensive work

may not be effective here, the plan has been inaugurated of a wide application of the Schick test to discover school children susceptible to diphtheria. To these susceptibles will be given toxin-antitoxin to stimulate the natural production of antitoxin, which in turn will render the person immune to diphtheria, in all probability immune for life.

✛

New Jersey.—New Jersey's Child Hygiene Bureau work for 1919 has resulted in the lowest infant mortality rate in the history of the State, 2,359 fewer babies having died than in the preceding year. In 1919 the infant mortality rate was 84.7. If the same rate had obtained during that decade, 19,955 fewer babies would have died.

The prevention of the unnecessary separation of mothers and children, and the elimination of baby farms, has been made possible by an addition to the Sanitary Code, which now requires anyone who boards one or more children to obtain a license from the State Department of Health and to conform to its regulations.

A survey of the physical conditions of certain day nurseries by the N. J. Child Hygiene Bureau has indicated the need of control and supervision. Regulations have been prepared to be incorporated in the Sanitary Code, which will require all day nurseries to obtain a license from the Department of Health and to conform to its regulations for the proper care and protection of children.

The bureau is particularly interested in the perfection of birth registration. A survey has been made, and while the study was not sufficiently extensive to permit positive statements, it appears that there is considerable variation in different parts of the State. In some localities the study indicated only 66% of the births reported, while in many communities the study showed 97% to 98%.

In New Jersey, the midwives attend one-third of the births in the State, and, in certain cities and counties, more than one-half of the births. The Child Hygiene Bureau has devoted itself to improve the obstetrical services rendered by the midwives.

The Montclair, New Jersey, Board of Health has undergone a reorganization following the appointment of a new board, consisting of Dr. James Spencer Brown, president, and Herbert B. Larner, formerly of the U. S. Public Health Service, health officer. Another infant hygiene clinic has been added to the department and a new laboratory completely equipped. The laboratory will be in charge of Miss Helen G. Jacobs, Simmons College, 1918, who for the past two years has been connected with the laboratory staff of the New Hampshire State Board of Health.

✛

New York.—On the first of July the Department of Health of Niagara Falls modified its system of educational nursing in child welfare by dividing the entire city into three districts and placing a nurse in each district. The nurse is furnished weekly with the list of births in her district. Each new baby is visited by the nurse; if a physician is in charge the nurse makes no further visit except at his request; if no physician is in attendance, but the mother does not wish further visits, the nurse does not call again except in certain special cases where later tentative visits seem advisable. Where the babies are not doing well the nurse seeks to get them under medical care and whenever the mother can be so induced, well babies and those artificially fed according to home ideas are taken to the child welfare station for registration and supervision.

Clinics for the venereal diseases were established in Plattsburgh early in the fall, two sessions being held weekly. These clinics are held at the Board of Health rooms at the City Hall.

One hundred and seventy babies were entered at the second annual baby show at Gouverneur Fair in St. Lawrence county. The mother of one of the babies, who has captured a prize both years, said the instruction and literature received at the contest last year had enabled her to maintain the proper growth for her child.

Dr. Edward S. Godfrey, Acting Director of the Division of Communicable Diseases, N. Y. State Health Department, has recently been appointed Director, *vice* Dr. F. M. Meader, resigned. Dr. Geo. S. Shaw of Camillus, N. Y., has been appointed a Sanitary Supervisor and assigned to Albany, Greene, Schoharie, Rensselaer and Columbia counties. Dr. Shaw is a graduate of Syracuse Medical College and served in various capacities during the war, retiring with the rank of major. Dr. H. J. Ball, until recently in charge of the above district, has been transferred to Oneida, Herkimer, Madison, Otsego and Lewis counties.

Dr. E. R. Ritchie, formerly Health Officer of the village of Brewster, Putnam county, has been appointed Sanitary Supervisor and assigned to Westchester, Dutchess and Putnam counties. Dr. Edward S. Marsh, Consultant in Venereal Diseases, State Department of Health, has recently been appointed Assistant Professor of Hygiene and Preventive Medicine at Long Island Medical College.

Through the appointment of Mrs. A. D. Roberts as Health Secretary in Livingston county, a new combination of forces for public health has been effected. The Board of Supervisors of the county has appropriated the necessary amount for the salary of the health secretary; the Livingston County Tuberculosis Committee has assumed responsibility for the office equipment, transportation and the cost of attending conferences, public meetings, etc.; while the work will be under the supervision of a committee consisting of the Chairman of the Public Health Committee of the Board of Supervisors, the Chairman of the Livingston County Tuberculosis Association, and the District Sanitary Supervisor of the State Department of Health.

✛

North Carolina.—In the October issue of the State Board of Health's bulletin a successful warfare against diphtheria is indicated in statistics beginning with 1915. Then there were 525 deaths in each 100,000 population. In 1916 the number was 418, in 1917 it was 308, in 1918 the drop was to 252 and in 1919 to 242. Available statistics for 1918 show that there were 252 deaths in 1,306 cases and in 1919 there were 242 deaths in 3,519 cases, the fatality in the first being 18.47% and in the second 6.88%. Thus there is a marked, a radical reduction in deaths. To antitoxin belongs the credit for this assault on the citadels of disease. This antitoxin is furnished by the State Board of Health at 25c, which is below cost. Appropriations from the legislature makes up the difference.

The North Carolina authorities realize that there is no specific for measles and whooping cough, but it knows that it is possible to lessen the toll from these diseases. The first precaution is to avoid having them. If measles is abroad in the community the order is to keep the child away from it. If the child gets it the thing to do is to send the victim to bed and keep him there. By careful treatment there will be no dangerous aftermath which really makes measles highly fatal. Whooping cough does its worst in youth. The baby under one year stands one chance in eight of dying; from one to two, 1 in every 10; from two to three the rate is 1 in every 30; from three to four, it is 1 in every 50, and from four to five, 1 in 200 die. The application is obvious.

✛

Nova Scotia. — Dalhousie University, Halifax, has under way its second course in public health nursing. The students are graduates of schools in nursing, the standing of which is satisfactory to the University. The length of the course is six months and the special studies include social hygiene, federal quarantine, immigration problems, home nursing, first-aid teaching, soldiers' civil reëstablishment, together with mental and industrial hygiene. Practical field work may be taken up to six mornings a week. The courses are made possible through the coöperation of the University, the Victorian Order of Nurses and the official health organizations of the province and private organizations in Halifax and Dartmouth.

✛

Oregon.—For the first time in American history the citizens of a state, directed by a representative of the U. S. Public Health Service, are by voluntary service, with almost no money, carrying out a successful state-wide investigation into the numbers and condition of the misfits and down-and-outers of the community. The state is Oregon and the classes investigated are the dependent, delinquent and mentally deficient. The work is not yet complete, but, according to Surgeon-General Cumming, of the Public Health Service, enough has been done to show that the results will vie with that of similar work done in other states by a trained official force. Dr. Cumming, in fact, thinks that it is amazing that the public could be brought to take such interest in such abstruse work and considers that Oregon's example might well be followed by other States where similar work is hanging fire because of lack of money.

✛

Texas.—Most children of today do not get enough variety of food, do not take enough time to eat their meals, and do not get enough sleep. This is the statement made by Miss Pearl N. Hyer, R. N. public health nurse of the Texas Public Health Association. In her physical examinations in the public schools Miss Hyer has discovered that these three things are responsible for 50% of Texas children being underweight. To help remedy this defect among the children the Association is undertaking a campaign of public education.

✛

Philippines.—A committee has been appointed for the purpose of drafting a bill for submission to the incoming Legislature by the coöperating health and scientific agencies of Manila. The purpose of the bill will be the regulating of the operation of private chemical, pathological and bacteriological laboratories in the islands. The committee is to make definite recommendations relative to the professional qualifications of the proprietors and technical assistants of these establishments by providing for an adequate theoretical and practical examination of the usual laboratory procedures and requiring a minimum standard of equipment in apparatus, glassware, reagents, chemicals, test animals, etc.

The committee comprises Dr. H. W. Wade, U. of P., Chairman; Dr. Luis Guerrero, U. of P.; Dr. Liborio Gomez, B. S.; Dr. Proceso Gabriel, P. H. S.

The officials from the Bureau of Science and the University of the Philippines are detailed under authority of their respective bureau chiefs. The member from the Philippine Health Service will act as recorder. The committee is to meet from time to time at the headquarters of the Philippine Health Service at the call of the chairman thereof.

Pending the drafting of the necessary legislation outlined above, the committee will act in an advisory capacity to the Acting Director of Health on such questions as may come up with regard to existing private chemical, pathological and bacteriological laboratories.

✛

Utah.—The Department of Public Instruction of this state is calling attention to the danger and the cost of the mentally defective. They reproduce very rapidly and not less than two-thirds of the defectives are children of defectives. They contribute largely to the population of prisons, asylums and institutions. The 1 per cent of the defective children in public schools will contribute to these institutions if proper care is not taken of them. In a campaign of public education the authorities make note of the fact that an adequate state program is necessary. Such program should include identification, registration, proper education, supervision and segregation.

The Department furnishes regularly to teachers a syllabus of instruction in safety, health habits and hygiene. There are issued leaflets for review of the text books, the whole procedure having the elements of a very useful course of study undertaken in the public schools.

✛

Virginia.—A cageful of rats was one of the spectacular exhibits at the Greensville fair. The rats were not intended to serve as attractive but rather as horrible examples to illustrate the warnings that lined the booth where they were shown.

The State Board of Health and the U. S. Public Health Service are jointly staging this unusual spectacle. The rats are to be shown as nuisances, as destroyers of food and as menaces to life and health. As a matter of fact, there is not a single good word said for the rats, and the live ones in the cage are not picked with the idea that they will inspire good wishes.

Henry County has recently closed its first dental clinic for children. Hundreds of the little ones were attended to; their teeth received the care necessary to prevent later troubles. The cost of the work was trifling and the results have made a lasting impression. Henry County appropriated $300 for the clinic and the State Board of Health contributed a like sum. This $600 fund paid the salary of a dentist who gave three months to the work. Each child who had his teeth cleaned paid twenty-five cents for that service, and each filling cost the same sum. These trifling collections paid all costs of the clinic except the salary, which was settled by the County and State Health Board appropriations.

Pictures illustrating the details of work in malaria prevention are being made at West Point, Va., where a very successful campaign for mosquito extermination was recently concluded.

The movies will give a very fair idea of the simplicity of the operations, such as ordinary ditching for draining, the use of dynamite in ditching, oiling of pools, etc.

During the coming months, the joint work of the Public Health Service, the Virginia Board of Health and the International Health Board will consist principally of malaria surveys; and it is the intention of these agencies to finish at least one complete county survey which it is believed will furnish not merely statistics for future operations, but will yield information that should enable coming campaigns to be conducted with less loss motion and experimentation.

Inspired by the example of modern war offices, Virginia Polytechnic Institute has inaugurated for its cadet corps a system of medical and physical examinations very similar to those adopted for testing army recruits.

Arlington County is asking that some other Virginia county will challenge it for supremacy in health activities. In support of its claims it offers the September record of its health unit, just compiled by Dr. J. W. Cox, U. S. P. H. S., its health officer.

Among the items of interest, and showing what a health unit may accomplish, the Arlington report shows that 1,365 pupils were examined during the month, that 33 children were treated outside clinics and 286 pupils were treated at clinics, a large majority of the latter for dental troubles to which so many later difficulties are now being attributed.

□

CONVENTIONS, CONFERENCES, MEETINGS

December 2, Providence, R. I., Rhode Island Medical Society.

December 6, Petersburg, Va., Medical Society of Virginia.

December 6-11, Washington, D. C., All-American Conference on Venereal Diseases. First Regional Health Conference.

December 9-11, Bridgeport, Conn., National Housing Conference.

December 12-20, Montevideo, Uruguay, Sixth International Sanitary Conference of the American Republics.

December 14-16, Hot Springs, Va., Southern Surgical Association.

December 22-26, New York City, American Dietetic Association.

December 27, Richmond, Va., Virginia Health Officers' Association.

December 27, Richmond, Va., Virginia Conference of Health Workers.

December 27-January 1, Chicago, Ill., American Association for the Advancement of Science.

December 28-30, Chicago, Ill., Society of American Bacteriologists.

December 29, San Francisco, Cal., League for Conservation of Public Health.

December 30, Chicago, Ill., American Physiological Society.

January —, 1921, Boston, Mass., Massachusetts Society for Mental Hygiene.

January 11, ——, Nebraska, Nebraska State Nurses Association.

January 17-21, Atlantic City, N. J., National Canners' Association.

January 26-27, Lewiston, Me., Maine State Nurses Association.

January 27, ——, Iowa Tuberculosis Association.

January 27, Boston, Mass., Massachusetts Association of Boards of Health.

February —, Austin, Tex., Texas Public Health Association.

February 1, New York City, New York Tuberculosis Association.

February 1-3, Montreal, Can., Engineering Institute of Canada.

June 6-10, Boston Mass., American Medical Association.

INDUSTRIAL HYGIENE AND
OCCUPATIONAL DISEASE

Abstracted by Drs. E. R. Hayhurst and E. B. Starr.

Case Report Showing the Relation Between Occupation and Bronchial Asthma.—Bronchial asthma may be of two types: sensitive to proteins, and non-sensitive to proteins. The case cited was that of a man aged 44 years, a baker for 26 years, who had suffered continually from chronic bronchial asthma of the sensitive type for a period of 14 years. About every second or fourth week he developed an acute attack. General examination was negative except that his lungs showed some emphysema. The patient was tested with proteins from about 100 vegetable and meat sources and to most of the common pus-producing organisms. It was discovered that he was sensitive only to rye and wheat and wheat globulin. Naturally his trade compelled him to spend a great deal of his time exposed to these proteins. The author cites a similar case report from literature. Three methods of treatment are possible: (1) eliminate the offending protein and change the occupation; (2) heat or boil the offending protein, which explains why some persons can eat baked or boiled substances which cause anaplylactic symptoms when raw, and (3) desensitizing the patient with the same offending proteins by careful subcutaneous injections or feeding. The latter appears to be the preferred method.—Jacob Rosenbloom, *A. J. Med. Scs.*, September, 1920, pp. 414-417.

✦

Sickness and Absenteeism in Industrial Establishments.—What proportion of absenteeism is caused by sickness? An Eastern manufacturing company with 6,700 employes permitted an investigation of this subject. With the opportunities offered by visiting nurses and the services of a physician, reliable information was secured. Absences of less than three days were not investigated, and of all absenteeism, disabling illness probably did not constitute more than 33% of the total lost time during the year 1919, the balance of lost time being due to purely personal reasons. The peak of absenteeism was reached in May, but March, April and December were the months when disabling illness was the highest. There appears to be hardly any relationship at all between the illness rate and the rate of absences, although there was an apparent high correlation between seasonal variations for sickness and absenteeism. There was a marked increase of sickness in persons of 40 or more years of age. Few deductions could safely be drawn, but the information indicated that fruitful fields are open for further exploration in this matter. There were marked differences in rates between different departments, but the question of other possible factors such as age, sex, nationality, housing conditions, etc., was not investigated.—Dean K. Brundage, *Public Health Reports*, Sept. 10, 1920

✦

Indicators for Carbon Dioxide and Oxygen in the Air.—The authors claim to have solved the problem of supplying a simple and reasonably accurate instrument for indicating the ratio of carbon dioxide and oxygen in the air that people who work in confined places breathe. Many similar devices are on the market; some are good, some absolutely worthless. The instrument in question is simple, portable, and uses the process of absorbing the gases in a solution of caustic soda. The oxygen determinator is likewise simple, portable, and uses the process of absorbing the oxygen in an alkaline pyrogallate solution. Minute descriptions, details, diagrams and illustrations are given and tables showing the accuracy of the instruments. The carbon dioxide instrument is accurate to within $\pm 0.2\%$ of the total carbon dioxide present in the air; the oxygen apparatus to within $\pm 0.5\%$. The instruments were used to test the air in a submerged submarine on Aug. 1, 1918. They were checked by an Orsat analytical apparatus which proved their efficiency. In a space of about four hours oxygen gradually decreased from 20% to 18.6%, and carbon dioxide gradually increased from 0.5% to 1.8%.—Milligan, Crites and Wilson, *Technical Paper 228. U. S. Bureau of Mines.* 1920.

Eye Strain in Relation to Industry.— Eye strain should not be understood as the overuse of a pair of optically perfect eyes, but the use of imperfect eyes. Practically no human eyes are optically perfect; that is perfectly adapted to the purposes which under present conditions they are expected to serve. In the past the visual apparatus was used almost solely for distant vision, while civilization now demands constant and accurate vision at near range. The mechanism for this does not exist, and the attempt to compel the function brings diseases. Headaches and migraines lead the list of symptoms, but a long list of other afflictions involving even the stomach and digestive tract, spinal curvature, etc., are included. All of these morbid diseases are preventable by the use of two simple devices: (1) scientific spectacles, and (2) a proper position of the head and body when occupied at work. The author arranges occupations in five groups, in the order of their eye-strain characteristics. To the first group belongs the so-called "natural occupations" (agriculture, hunting, fishing, etc.), which have the lowest eye-strain effects, while in group 5, requiring close eye work, from 80% to 100% of persons are believed to suffer. The following rules obtain: (1) The nearer the object the greater the eye strain. (2) The more constant the focalization the more severe the eye strain. (3) Decreasing illumination results in a geometrical increase of eye strain. 4) Exposure of eyes during labor to wind, cold, heat, dust, etc., causes inflammatory troubles and eye strain. (5) Abnormal positions of the head and body may add enormously to the ocular injuries and eye strain. (6) Age is a factor; everyone needs spectacles, especially for close work, after 43. (7) The coöperation of the two eyes must be synchronous. (8) Probably 6% of children are naturally left-handed caused by left-eyedness. (9) Astigmatism or incorrect posture may so tilt the head and body as to set up a curvature of the spine. The article concludes with a consideration of the light in factory work rooms, schools, etc., about which surprisingly little is actually understood.—George M. Gould, *Amer. Jour. of Physiological Optics*, January, 1920, abstracted by *Monthly Labor Review*, July, 1920.

$20,000 a Year for Paper Cuspidors.— In this paper, entitled "How Henry Ford Saves Men and Money," it is stated that each department has a constant supply of paper cuspidors and sawdust which are supplied each morning to every man who is accustomed to spitting while at work. At the end of the shift he throws his used cuspidor into the refuse can. The sawdust and cuspidors cost the company $60 a day, $20,000 a year. It further states that $6,000 a day, or close to $2,000,000 a year, are spent to keep the windows washed, the floors swept and scrubbed, and the plant generally clean. Heat prostrations, which used to occur in the cyanide furnace rooms and the annealing furnace rooms, have been done away with and the labor turnover reduced 25%, the output increased and the working force reduced 50% by placing canopies over these furnaces and exhausting the hot air. These brought the working temperature from 133°-135° F. down to 80° F. The cost of installation was $11,400, and it paid for itself the first month in the saving of labor alone.—Lewis Resnick, *National Safety News*, Sept. 13, 1920.

✦

Lead Poisoning and Its Prevention.— The author, who is chairman of the Manufacturing Committee of the National Lead Company, goes into details of the mechanical features connected with the safe handling of white lead and lead in dusty forms and several illustrations are included. The prime object behind all is to keep the lead dust out of the nose and mouth of the worker and the writer takes the position that most dust hazards can either be eliminated or substantially reduced by special machinery including dust systems. Where lead is used in paints, the dust hazards would seem to disappear, but when painters sandpaper the painted surfaces, there is an exception. The remedy is to moisten sandpaper in a light mineral oil. This practice is not only safe but saves time and does a better job. Mr. E. J. Cornish, president of the National Lead Company, offers to confer with the representatives of any users of lead products at all times for the purpose of bettering conditions.—C. P. Tolman, Eighth Annual Proceedings, *National Safety Council*, (1919), 448-458.

Blacksmithing and Plumbing in Relation to Disease in Their Vicinity.—Blacksmiths and plumbers do not conserve the heat and gases escaping from their forges which necessarily escape to the surrounding atmosphere. A lead melting furnace was found to emit, in the city of Glasgow, lead, manganese and iron. An analysis made of fine deposits in a vicinity where death is declared to have occurred in a young girl from inherited and acquired poisoning (lead and manganese), showed manganese 0.102% and iron 3.40% with presence of lead and arsenic. He recommends that in blacksmithing the chimney of the forge be provided with a cap or hood. The author contends that the forges of blacksmiths, tinsmiths and plumbers all emit manganese which is deposited in the vicinity and is a hazard to the health of the community.—James Gairdner, *Lancet* (London), Oct. 2, 1920, pp. 726-727.

✛

A Study of Factory Sanitation in Foreign Dye Works.—The writer describes personal impressions received in visiting dye works in France, Switzerland, England and Germany. The dangers from well-known poisons such as nitro-benzine and aniline are recognized everywhere. There is a controversy as to the relative dangers with these poisons when absorbed through the skin or inhaled as fumes. Dinitro-benzine is dreaded in British factories both because of the dermatitis and because of systemic poisonings. The methods of protection for workers in these substances are described by the author and the original article should be consulted. Avoidance of work in warm weather is a feature with some of the poisons and food and medical care are given special attention. Alice Hamilton, 8th Annual Proceedings, *National Safety Council* (1919), 436-448.

✛

A Simple and Inexpensive Respirator for Dust Protection.—For those who must contend with dust in a breathing atmosphere and have to put up with a respirator, this short bulletin is very material. The respirators are made of one-half ounce of clean absorbent cotton pinned or fastened to a piece of cheese-cloth which is long enough to tie about the head and wide enough to cover thoroughly the nose and mouth. This simple device keeps out dust for a period of four hours or more. Careful tests show no lead dust drawn through the gauzy material. The respirators are cheap, light in weight, do not obstruct vision, can be changed daily at little expense, may be washed when necessary, are not apt to be interchanged by workmen, do not break, rust or wear out, or cause excessive perspiration while they absorb what sweat is produced. They cause no irritation to the skin and are easily changed to fit the face. They are recommended to comply with the Industrial Code of the State of New York. The Bulletin is amply illustrated.—Special Bulletin No. 90, *New York Industrial Committee*, Department of Labor, 10 pages.

✛

Where Courses in Industrial Medicine May be Taken.—Briefly, Harvard University, The University of Cincinnati, Rush Medical College (The University of Chicago), and the Ohio State University give courses in Industrial Medicine, while courses in Public Health including Industrial Hygiene are given at Johns Hopkins, the University of Pennsylvania, Yale University, and a number of other institutions. A Clinic for Functional Reëducation, established by Dr. W. Gilman Thompson in Feb., 1918, in New York City, is meeting with good success. A number of hospitals as well as some departments of health have clinics on occupational diseases. Medical students are not awake to the possibilities of industrial medicine and according to Hayhurst the course of medical training blocked out by the Council on Education of the American Medical Association does not provide for enough appropriate training in medical sociology, medical economics, "mass" medicine, etc., to suit the demands of the times. (Those interested should read this article in full.)—Shuford, *Monthly Labor Review*, May, 1920, U. S. B. of L. S., Washington, D. C.

✛

Hours of Work as Related to Output and Accident Rate.—The outstanding feature of the 8-hour system is steady maintenance of output, while the outstanding feature of the 10-hour system is the decline of the output.—*Public Health Bull.* No. 106, Feb., 1920, abstracted, Monthly Labor Review,

PUBLIC HEALTH
LABORATORY NOTES

Abstracted by Arthur Lederer, M. D.

Standard Microscopic Equipment. — A standard microscopic equipment has been selected for use in the Army Medical Department, according to information given out by Surgeon-General Ireland. The models are the Bausch and Lomb FFS8 and Spencer 44H, including the Spencer folding microscope for portable laboratories in the field. A recent survey of the Medical Corps equipment disclosed that there are many different makes and models in use in the service, and all of these are to be replaced by the new models. The reason for the selection of these types lies in the fact that oculars, objectives, condensers, mechanical stages and dark field illuminators of these models are interchangeable.—Anon., *Jour. A. M. A.*, 75, 885. (1920.)

✛

Types of Streptococci in Sputum of Bronchial Asthmatics.—The authors studied the types of streptococci in the sputum of bronchial asthmatics during two seasons. The types present are not numerous. Practically all of the hemolytic streptococci were of four types; of the non-hemolytic streptococci three types were met with particularly. The organisms in the nasal secretion may vary radically from those occurring in the sputum. Autogenous vaccines should be employed in the treatment of these cases rather than stock vaccines.—J. Adkinson and I. C. Walker, *Jour. Med. Research* (Boston), 41, 457. (1920.)

✛

Estimating the Number of Organisms in a Vaccine.—The number of organisms is estimated by means of the nephelometer. The results are very satisfactory and as accurate as those obtained with the microscope. The method requires very little time.—G. C. Dunham, *Jour. Immun.*, 5, 337. (1920.)

✛

Paraffin Seals for Anaërobic Fluid Cultures.—Tubes sealed with solid paraffin with the technique employed by the author give a greater percentage of positive growths with stock anaërobic cultures than parallel groups sealed with liquid paraffin. This advantage is due to the prevention of the downward defusion of oxygen by convection currents in the tubes sealed by the solid paraffin method.—Leonard R. Thompson, *Jour. Infect. Dis.*, 27, 240. (1920.)

✛

Studies in Epidemic (Lethargic) Encephalitis.—Berkefeld filtrates of brain material, nasopharyngeal mucous membrane and nasal washings from cases of epidemic encephalitis have produced in rabbits and monkeys lesions typical of this disease. Spinal fluid and blood have also produced the disease experimentally in these animals. Many of the animals have succumbed with the typical picture of epidemic encephalitis. The virus has been passed through many series of animals. It can be preserved for many months in 50% glycerol. By means of the ascitic-tissue culture methods perfected by Noguchi it has been possible to cultivate a minute, filtrable organism from cases of epidemic encephalitis from brain, nasopharyngeal mucous membrane, nasopharyngeal washings, spinal fluid and blood. The same organism has been recovered from the brain and nasopharyngeal mucous membrane of animals that have been inoculated with virus and cultures and which have succumbed to the experimental disease. The cultures thus recovered have produced the disease when injected into other animals and organism has again been recovered. Positive animal inoculations have been obtained with the 11th generation of this organism. Epidemic encephalitis can be differentiated from epidemic poliomyelitis for these reasons: rabbits are susceptible to infectious material from epidemic encephalitis and not from poliomyelitis. Monkeys are very susceptible to poliomyelitis and relatively refractory to material from epidemic encephalitis. Spinal fluid from poliomyelitis is innocuous when injected into rabbits and monkeys, whereas spinal fluid from cases of epidemic encephalitis produces in both of these animals lesions typical of the disease.—Leo Loewe and Israel Strauss, *Jour. Infect. Dis.*, 27, 250. (1920.)

✦

Body Temperature Taken in Freshly Voided Urine.—The simple method of determining the body temperature by observation of the temperature of the freshly passed urine is of practical value. This will apply principally to cases in which measurement by rectum is impossible or obnoxious as, for instance, in timid patients (children and hysterics) or in hypochondriacs, who should not be acquainted with the existence of high temperature. It may also be of value as a new diagnostic method in diseases of the urinary tract. This will depend upon a larger number of observations and will be reported in due time. The author has devised a simple apparatus which he calls a "urothermometer" for the purpose of collecting urinary specimens without loss of body heat.—Theodore Kasparek, *Jour. Lab. Clin. Med.*, 5, 791. (1920.)

✦

Acetone in the Cerebro-Spinal Fluid in Tuberculosis Meningitis. — The cerebrospinal fluid of 23 cases of tuberculous meningitis in children gave with four exceptions an intense acetone reaction with Ricci and Frommer's tests. The urine in each of the 23 cases showed a large quantity of acetone except in three cases, in which only a small amount was present. The cerebrospinal fluid in these cases showed an absence of acetone.—G. Genoese, *La Pediatria,* May 15, 1920; *British Med. Jour.,* September 11, 1920.

✦

Alcohol in Cerebro-Spinal Fluid.—The occurrence of alcohol in cerebro-spinal fluid was first described in 1913. The authors find that the meninges are permeable to alcohol, which appears in the cerebro-spinal fluid an hour and a half after injection of large quantities, diminishes after 48 hours, but persists for as long as eight days. The presence of alcohol in the fluid does not denote any active meningeal reaction. Estimation of alcohol may possess diagnostic significance with regard to nervous diseases, and from medico-legal points of view.— Marinesco and Paulian, *Bul. et Mém. de la Soc. Méd. des Hôp. de Bucarest,* May 26, 1920; *British Med. Jour.,* September 11, 1920.

Diagnosis of Anthrax from Purifying Animal Tissues.—Many anthrax like organisms are encountered in the examination of partially putrified animal tissues for *B. anthracis.* Guinea pig inoculations frequently fail because of the death of the animals from a malignant œdema-like infection before any anthrax organisms which may be present have time to develop. The author describes a cultural method well suited for the differentiation between true anthrax and anthrax like organisms.—W. A. Hagan, *Jour. Bact.,* 5, 343. (1920.)

✦

Viability of Meningococci in Yeast Agar Medium.—Meningococcus cultures in semisolid yeast agar when stored either at room temperature or in the incubator at 37° C. were still fully viable after five months. In all likelihood the antigenic nature of the organisms remains unaltered as it may be indicated by comparative agglutination tests.—F. Eberson, *Jour Bact..* 5, 431. (1920.)

✦

Cutaneous Vaccination Against Anthrax. —If the first vaccine of anthrax is rubbed into the shaven skin of the guinea pig a local inflammatory reaction appears which persists usually for four to six days. If, however, the second vaccine or the virus itself be used, the reaction is always fatal, death from septicemia resulting about the fourth day. A guinea pig into which the first vaccine has been rubbed successfully withstands friction with the second vaccine, and later with the virus; further, it resists subcutaneous inoculation with the second vaccine and the virus. The rabbit is as easily, if not more easily, vaccinated by these means. The degree of protection given is very great.—Besredka, *Compt. Rend. Soc. Biol.,* May 29, 1920; *British Med. Jour.,* September 11, 1920.

✦

Alkali Reserve in Pellagra.—Of the 56 patients tested for alkali reserve by the alveolar method and by the determination of the carbon dioxide bound by the blood plasma, none showed a marked depletion of the alkali reserve, about one-third showing a slightly subnormal level, while the great number were within normal limits. There would seem to be little uncompensated acidosis in pellagra.—M. X. Sullivan and R. E. Stanton, *Arch. Int. Med.,* 26 ,41. (1920.)

Narcotic Drug Addiction.—There is no substance formed in the blood serum of a human being who has acquired a high tolerance to morphine, which is capable of conferring any degree of immunity to the toxic action of morphine on an animal into which it is injected.—Emil J. Pellini and Arthur D. Greenfield, *Arch. Int. Med.*, 26, 279. (1920.)

✦

Bactericidal Power of Whole Blood and Antibodies in Serum.—The bactericidal power of blood as determined by the method of Heist and Solis-Cohen (Jour. Immun. 4, 147) is the most dependable criterion of the actual immunity of the animal. The development of the bactericidal power of the blood against typhoid and Shiga bacilli is practically identical with that of the serum. The route of inoculation makes no material difference in the rapidity or height of the development of bactericidal power. The agglutinins and complement fixing bodies are only roughly comparable to the bactericidal power. The leukocyte and phagocytic index are of no value in determining the degree of immunity. In the rabbit immunized to typhoid and dysentery bacilli, lysis occurs with great rapidity, and a short incubation period is sufficient. No evidence could be secured as to the mechanism of lysis. Phagocytosis, in all probability, is not a factor. Citrating and defibrinating blood of rabbits immunized to typhoid and dysentery bacilli does not effect the bactericidal activity save to slow the reaction. In the blood of typhoid and dysentery-immune animals, contaminating organisms may grow luxuriantly. A short incubation period removes most of the difficulty due to contaminants. The refractory state of Teague and McWilliams is shown to depend probably on the rapid rise in bactericidal power, and the rapidity of mobilization of this power varies with the route of injection. Inactivation of serum of immunized rabbits does not materially reduce the bactericidal action.—J. H. Black, Kenneth Fowler and Paul Pierce, *Jour. A. M. A.*, 75, 915. (1920.)

✦

Complement Fixation Reaction in Tuberculosis.—The article is the result of the author's experience with 6,500 reactions. The Miller antigen is serviceable, practical

and efficient for the complement fixation test in tuberculosis. The reaction is specific for tuberculosis and, when positive, should be interpreted as indicating tuberculosis of some degree of activity. When the Wassermann and tuberculosis fixation reactions are both positive, they should be interpreted without relation to one another. The positive fixation reaction can be interpreted as indicating tuberculosis, either active at the time, or recently active. The focus may or may not be of clinical significance, which fact must be determined by other means. The negative fixation reaction indicates either absence of infection, excessive activity of the disease, exhausting the antibody, or arrest of the disease with spontaneous disappearance of antibody no longer required. —W. Warner Watkins and Clarence N. Boynton, *Jour. A. M. A.*, 75, 933. (1920.)

✦

Determination of Ammonia in Culture Media in the Presence of Urea.—In order to determine the presence of small amounts of ammonia in culture media in the presence of urea and other nitrogenous bodies it is necessary to displace the ammonia without decomposing these other bodies. Magnesium may be used to distil in vacuo if a low temperature; about 35° C., is maintained. To prevent a loss of ammonia by the formation of relatively undecomposable magnesium-ammonium phosphate, the phosphoric acid usually present in culture media must be removed before distillation.— P. Thomas. *Abst. in Bull. de l'Inst. Past.* 1920, 18, 290.

✦

Significance of the Sachs-Georgi Reaction for Lues Diagnosis in Children.—In two series of examinations of 178 and 200 serums, results concordant with the Wassermann test were found in 94% and 93% of the cases. Febrile conditions in non-syphilitic patients did not interfere with the reaction. Scheer emphasizes the advantage of the small amount of serum required for this reaction. He mixes 1 part of serum (.002cc.) with 9 parts of saline and five parts of cholesterine extract, incubates at 37° C. for two hours and leaves at room temperature for 18-20 hours. — Scheer. *Munch. Med. Woch.* 1919, Aug. 8: *Abst. in Bull. Inst. Past.* 1920, 18, 261.

AMERICAN
JOURNAL OF
PUBLIC HEALTH

THE JOURNAL of the AMERICAN
PUBLIC HEALTH ASSOCIATION

Just a Few of the Good
Things Here are:

Dr. Bishop's Paper on Addiction Disease
And the Committee's Report on the same
Subject,
What Dr. Kellogg has found out about Masks,
Dr. Ravenel's Preventive Medicine and War,
Drs. Lumsden and Stiles on Privy Problems
And a View of Macedonia, Cradle of Typhus
and Malaria

The INDEX for 1919 Accompanies this Number.

PUBLISHED MONTHLY AT
10 DEPOT STREET, CONCORD, N. H.

ADDRESS CORRESPONDENCE TO
EDITORIAL OFFICE, 169 MASSACHUSETTS AVE.
BOSTON, MASS.

Subscription Price, $4.00 per Year. Single Copies, 50 cents.
A. P. H. A. Membership, Including Subscription, $5.00 per Year.
Entered as second-class matter at the post-office at Concord, N. H.

An Inexpensive
High Quality

ELECTRIC DRYING OVEN

Pittsburgh Model

2204. DRYING OVEN (*Sterilizer*), **ELECTRIC**
PITTSBURGH MODEL

Three heats, approximately 100°, 200° and 300° C. Has no automatic regulator, yet will hold a very even temperature.

Recommended as a sterilizer for glassware and soil bacteria, a drying oven for flour testing and domestic science, and for many other scientific and technical laboratory purposes.

Inside measurement, 10x11x6 inches, with one shelf. Mineral wool between the inner and outer steel walls; nickeled trimmings; glass door; shutter controlled ventilators.

COMPLETE WITH 300° C THERMOMETER, PLUG, AND 6 FEET OF CORD **$25.00**

IN STOCK FOR IMMEDIATE DELIVERY

SCIENTIFIC MATERIALS COMPANY
Everything for the Laboratory
PITTSBURGH, PA.

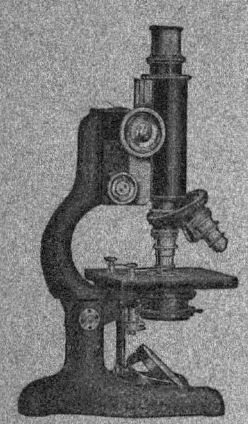

AMERICAN
JOURNAL OF
PUBLIC HEALTH

THE JOURNAL of the AMERICAN
PUBLIC HEALTH ASSOCIATION

READ in THIS ISSUE:

Winslow's Editorial on
            Salaries of Health Officers

Hemenway on Economics of
            Health Administration

Van Dine and LePrince on
            Anti-Malarial Measures,
And Pierce on Venereal Disease Control

REMEMBER THE SAN FRANCISCO MEETING, A. P. H. A.
AUGUST 30, SEPTEMBER 3, 1920.

PUBLISHED MONTHLY AT
124 W. Polk STREET, Chicago, Ill.
ADDRESS MATTER FOR PUBLICATION TO
EDITORIAL OFFICE, 169 MASSACHUSETTS AVE.
BOSTON, MASS.

Subscription Price, $4.00 per Year. Single Copies, 50 cents.
A. P. H. A. Membership, Including Subscription, $5.00 per year.

Application for Entry as second-class matter at the post-office at Chicago, Ill., pending.

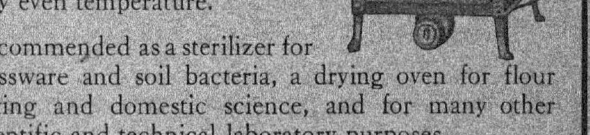

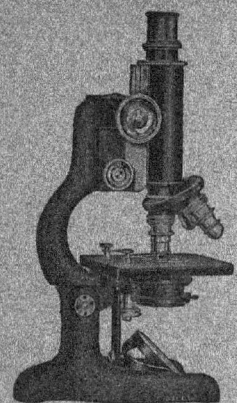

JOURNAL OF
PUBLIC HEALTH

THE JOURNAL of the AMERICAN
PUBLIC HEALTH ASSOCIATION

THIS MONTH YOU HAVE
The Fundamental Subject of Child Hygiene,
by A. J. McLaughlin, M.D., F. S. Crum, Ph. D.,
H. O. Jones, M. D., C. W. East, M. D., and
Grace Whitford, M. D.
With Suggestions from Atlantic Shore, Gulf
and Great Lakes
Help for Health Officers in Budgets, by E. C.
Meyer, Ph. D. and Haven Emerson, M. D.
Aboriginal Health Practices in Africa, by
P. A. E. Sheppard, M. D.
SAN FRANCISCO MEETING, A. P. H. A.
AUGUST 30—SEPTEMBER 3, 1920.

PUBLISHED MONTHLY AT
124 W. Polk STREET, Chicago, Ill.
ADDRESS MATTER FOR PUBLICATION TO
EDITORIAL OFFICE, 169 MASSACHUSETTS AVE.
BOSTON, MASS.

Subscription Price, $4.00 per Year. Single Copies, 50 cents.
A. P. H. A. Membership, Including Subscription, $5.00 per year.

Application for Entry as second-class matter at the post-office at Chicago, Ill.; pending

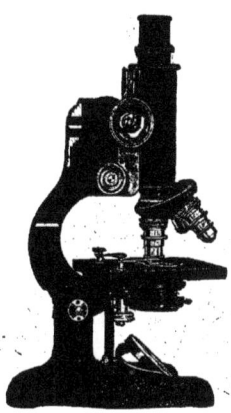

Microscope FFS8
Includes Two Eyepieces and Three
Objectives in Revolving Nosepiece.
$110.00

Bausch and Lomb
Microscopes

WHEN you buy a Bausch & Lomb Microscope, you buy the cumulative results of 66 years of optical endeavor and manufacturing experience.

During that period we have developed every optical refinement and mechanical improvement demanded by the practices of modern microscopy.

Our optics—designed, tested and controlled in manufacture by our own Scientific Bureau—have withstood the most exacting, long-time tests of research laboratories.

Our side fine adjustment is of the most approved lever type —highly sensitive and durable.

There is a Bausch & Lomb model for every microscopical requirement. Write for our new complete catalog.

Bausch & Lomb Optical Co.

MAKERS OF

Photographic Lenses, Microscopes, Projection Apparatus (Balopticons), Ophthalmic Lenses and Instruments, Photomicrographic Apparatus, Range Finders and Gun Sights for Army and Navy, Searchlight Reflectors, Stereo-Prism Binoculars, Magnifiers and other High-Grade Optical Products.

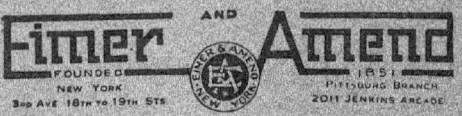

JOURNAL OF
PUBLIC HEALTH

THE JOURNAL of the AMERICAN
PUBLIC HEALTH ASSOCIATION

TAKE NOTICE THAT THE

1920 Campaign for a Total of 7500 Members
Is Underway!
It Is a Campaign by States.
For Plan of It See Page 369 of this Issue.
Give Your State Membership Chairman Your Support.
President Rankin's Article Will Tell You Why.
It Is the First One In This Number of the JOURNAL.

SAN FRANCISCO MEETING, A. P. H. A.
AUGUST 30—SEPTEMBER 3, 1920.

Published monthly on the 20th by the American Public
Health Association at
124 W. Polk Street, Chicago, Ill.

ADDRESS EDITORIAL MATTER TO

**169 MASSACHUSETTS AVE.
BOSTON, MASS.**

Subscription Price, $4.00 per Year. Single Copies, 50 cents.
A. P. H. A. Membership, Including Subscription, $5.00 per year.

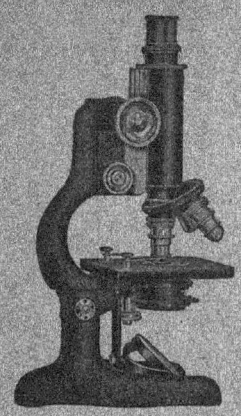

WHY *the* DUBOSCQ COLORIMETER?

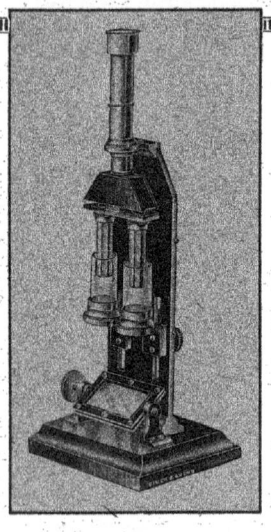

The Duboscq Colorimeter, made by Eimer & Amend, has distinctive mechanical improvements over the original French make.

It is equipped with adjustable cylinders, and the monocular telescope gives a circular divided field which eliminates the errors incident to the comparison of two separate fields.

The Duboscq is the standard instrument for the determination of total nitrogen in urine, urea in urine, etc.

Immediate delivery can be made from stock.

Eimer AND Amend

FOUNDED 1851

NEW YORK
3RD AVE 18TH TO 19TH STS

PITTSBURG BRANCH
2011 JENKINS ARCADE

MAY 1 4 192?

AMERICAN
JOURNAL OF
PUBLIC HEALTH

THE JOURNAL of the AMERICAN
PUBLIC HEALTH ASSOCIATION

TWO THINGS FOR YOUR ATTENTION
IN THIS JOURNAL

Besides the Array of Good Articles and Useful Public
Health Notes:

1.—Story of the Campaign and Lists of New Members.

2.—Suggestions About Special Trains to the California
Meeting.

NOTICE REVISED DATE!

A. P. H. A. Meeting, San Francisco, Cal.,
September 13-17, 1920

Published monthly on the 20th by the American Public
Health Association at
124 W. Polk Street, Chicago, Ill.

ADDRESS EDITORIAL MATTER TO
169 MASSACHUSETTS AVE.
BOSTON, MASS.

Subscription Price, $4.00 per Year. Single Copies, 50 cents.
A. P. H. A. Membership, Including Subscription, $5.00 per year.

Entered as second class matter January 20, 1920, at the postoffice at Chicago, Illinois, under
the Act of March 3, 1879. Acceptance for mailing at special rate of postage provided for in
Section 1103, Act of October 3, 1917, authorized February 28, 1920.

An Inexpensive High Quality

ELECTRIC DRYING OVEN

Pittsburgh Model

2204. DRYING OVEN (*Sterilizer*), **ELECTRIC**
PITTSBURGH MODEL

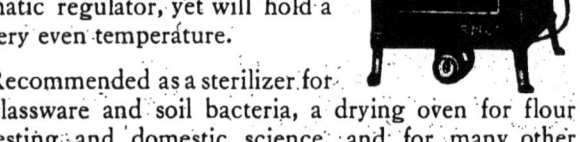

Three heats, approximately 100°, 200° and 300° C. Has no automatic regulator, yet will hold a very even temperature.

Recommended as a sterilizer for glassware and soil bacteria, a drying oven for flour testing and domestic science, and for many other scientific and technical laboratory purposes.

Inside measurement, 10x11x6 inches, with one shelf. Mineral wool between the inner and outer steel walls; nickeled trimmings; glass door; shutter controlled ventilators.

COMPLETE WITH 300° C THERMOMETER,
PLUG AND 6 FEET OF CORD *$25.00*

IN STOCK FOR IMMEDIATE DELIVERY

SCIENTIFIC MATERIALS COMPANY

Everything for the Laboratory.
PITTSBURGH, PA.

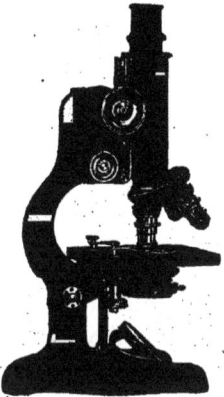

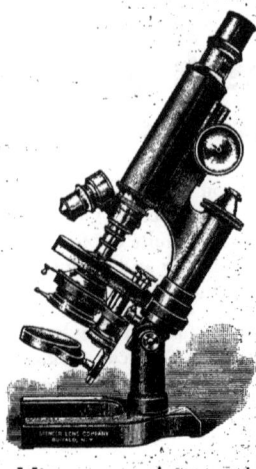

JOURNAL OF
PUBLIC HEALTH

THE JOURNAL *of the* AMERICAN
PUBLIC HEALTH ASSOCIATION

IN THE JUNE JOURNAL

Dr. Meyer tells about Community Medicine

Mr. Loomis outlines Plans of Canners to Improve their
Products

Dr. Carter and Mr. Stromquist discuss Malaria Control

Mr. Fair suggests Standards for Bathing Pools

See other valuable Articles and the Notes Section.

ARE YOU REPRESENTED ON Pages 559 to 565?

A. P. H. A. Meeting, San Francisco, Cal.,
September 13-17, 1920

For Railway Rates, See Page 544

Published monthly on the 20th by the American Public
Health Association at

124 W. Polk Street, Chicago, Ill.

ADDRESS EDITORIAL MATTER TO

169 MASSACHUSETTS AVE.
BOSTON, MASS.

Subscription Price, $4.00 per Year. Single Copies, 50 cents.
A. P. H. A. Membership, Including Subscription, $5.00 per year.

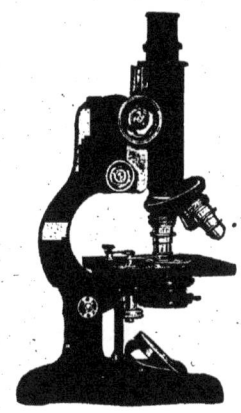

MICROSCOPE FFS8
Includes Two Eyepieces and Three
Objectives in Revolving Nosepiece

Price, $132.00

Bausch and Lomb
Microscopes

WHEN you buy a Bausch & Lomb Microscope, you buy the cumulative results of 66 years of optical endeavor and manufacturing experience.

During that period we have developed every optical refinement and mechanical improvement demanded by the practices of modern microscopy.

Our optics—designed, tested and controlled in manufacture by our own Scientific Bureau—have withstood the most exacting, long-time tests of research laboratories.

Our side fine adjustment is of the most approved lever type —highly sensitive and durable.

There is a Bausch & Lomb model for every microscopical requirement. Write for our new complete catalog.

Bausch & Lomb Optical Co.

419 St. Paul St., Rochester, N. Y.

New York   Washington   Chicago   San Francisco

MAKERS OF

Photographic Lenses, Microscopes, Projection Apparatus (Balopticons), Ophthalmic Lenses and Instruments, Photomicrographic Apparatus, Microtomes, Centrifugal Apparatus, Range Finders and Gun Sights for Army and Navy, Searchlight Reflectors, Stereo-Prism Binoculars, Magnifiers and other High-Grade Optical Products and Accessories.

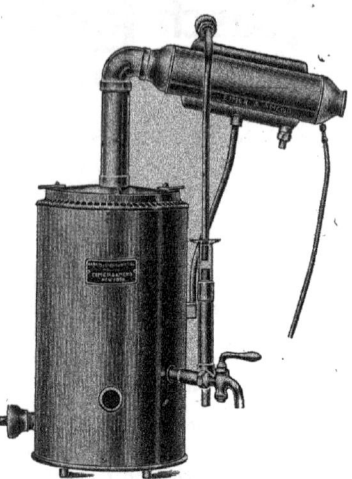

JOURNAL OF
PUBLIC HEALTH

THE JOURNAL of the AMERICAN
PUBLIC HEALTH ASSOCIATION

IN THIS JOURNAL

Dr. Ferrell studies Salaries of Health Officers •
Lt. Col. Cumming discusses Dishwashing
Dr. Kellogg tells about Plague in California.
Dr. Dowling writes about Hookworm Disease
And the customary Editorials and Notes

List beginning page 612 raises number of New Members to 1500.

Have You sent in your Member?

A. P. H. A. Meeting, San Francisco, Cal.,
September 13-17, 1920

Association Headquarters at the Palace Hotel
Meetings at the Auditorium, Civic Center

Published monthly on the 20th by the American Public
Health Association at
124 W. Polk Street, Chicago, Ill.

ADDRESS EDITORIAL MATTER TO
169 MASSACHUSETTS AVE.
BOSTON, MASS.

Subscription Price, $4.00 per Year. Single Copies, 50 cents.
A. P. H. A. Membership, Including Subscription, $5.00 per year.

Entered as second class matter January 20, 1920, at the postoffice at Chicago, Illinois, under
the Act of March 3, 1879.. Acceptance for mailing at special rate of postage provided for in
Section 1103, Act of October 3, 1917, authorized February 28, 1920.

LEITZ MICROSCOPES ARE THE STANDARD OF THE WORLD

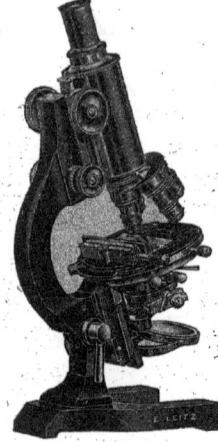

Research and Micro Photographic Microscope "AA."

Leitz Microscopes
And Other Leitz Apparatus

It is with grateful appreciation that we acknowledge the many inquiries we have received during a period when we could give negative advice only relative to the supply of Leitz Apparatus.

The interest which has been manifested is proof of how highly the quality of Leitz products has been appreciated. The confidence issued by our valued patrons will be rewarded in knowing that *the present "Leitz-Quality" of optical and mechanical workmanship is not only equal to the high standard which has been recognized prior to the war but that important scientific developments have advanced this standard to a still further degree.*

We are now able to accept orders for Leitz Microscopes and other Leitz Instruments. Our present stock is still restricted, while we will soon have available a complete assortment of Leitz products. Orders for importation can be executed within approximately ninety days; orders placed for delivery from stock will be filled promptly for those items on hand. Consignments will reach us at frequent intervals and serious delay is therefore not anticipated.

NOTE: Upon request we will forward a list of Leitz Publications for your selection.

Kindly specify the article you are interested in and we will submit literature and estimate.

E. LEITZ
INC.
NEW YORK
60 EAST 10TH ST.

For Superior Dark Ground Work

we recommend the equipment shown-above, which consists of the following:.

FFS Side Fine-Adjustment Microscope, with 16mm, 4mm and 1.9mm objectives on revolvable nosepiece, 10X eyepiece, dark-ground illuminator in screw substage, funnel stop for oil immersion objective and carrying case $140.00

No. 1745 Auxiliary Condenser, with blue glass filter.......$5.75

No. 1782 Microscope Lamp, with high grade condenser on adjustable support, 6-volt, gas-filled Mazda bulb and transformer for use on house circuit, 110 volts, alternating current...........$23.50

The various parts of this equipment will, of course, be supplied separately or as a group. Write for descriptive circular.

Bausch & Lomb Optical Co.

419 St. Paul St., Rochester, N. Y.

New York   Washington   Chicago   San Francisco

MAKERS OF

Photographic Lenses, Microscopes, Projection Apparatus (Balopticons), Ophthalmic Lenses and Instruments, Photomicrographic Apparatus, Microtomes, Centrifugal Apparatus, Range Finders and Gun Sights for Army and Navy, Searchlight Reflectors, Stereo-Prism Binoculars, Magnifiers and other High-Grade Optical Products and Accessories.

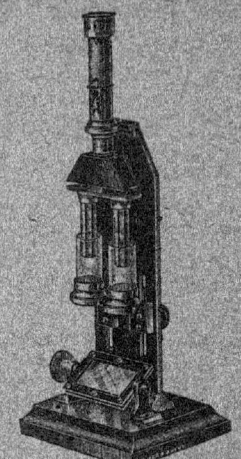
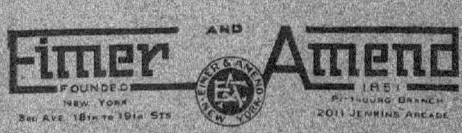

R,Vrrrrr,

AMERICAN
JOURNAL OF
PUBLIC HEALTH

THE JOURNAL of the AMERICAN
PUBLIC HEALTH ASSOCIATION

Industrial Clinics—National Department of Public
Health—Health Slogans—Types of Fatigue—Anthrax
in Massachusetts—Vaccines in Public Health—School
Meals and Malnutrition—and more discussion, "What
is the matter with Public Health." Also the Editorials
and customary Notes Section

If you have not done so already why not send in
the name of your New Member before Annual
meeting time—San Francisco, September 13-17.

Published monthly on the 20th by the American Public
Health Association at
124 W. Polk Street, Chicago, Ill.

ADDRESS EDITORIAL MATTER TO
169 MASSACHUSETTS AVE.
BOSTON, MASS.

Subscription Price, $4.00 per Year. Single Copies, 50 cents.
A. P. H. A. Membership, including Subscription, $5.00 per year.

Entered as second class matter January 20, 1920, at the postoffice at Chicago, Illinois, under
the Act of March 3, 1879. Acceptance for mailing at special rate of postage provided for in
Section 1103, Act of October 3, 1917, authorized February 28, 1920.

For Superior Dark Ground Work

we recommend the equipment shown above, which consists of the following:

FFS Side Fine-Adjustment Microscope, with 16mm, 4mm and 1.9mm objectives on revolvable nosepiece, 10X eyepiece, dark-ground illuminator in screw substage, funnel stop for oil immersion objective and carrying case $140.00

No. 1745 Auxiliary Condenser, with blue glass filter.......$5.75

No. 1782 Microscope Lamp, with high grade condenser on adjustable support, 6-volt, gas-filled Mazda bulb and transformer for use on house circuit, 110 volts, alternating current...........$23.50

The various parts of this equipment will, of course, be supplied separately or as a group. Write for descriptive circular.

Bausch & Lomb Optical Co.

419 St. Paul St., Rochester, N. Y.

New York   Washington   Chicago   San Francisco

MAKERS OF

Photographic Lenses, Microscopes, Projection Apparatus (Balopticons), Ophthalmic Lenses and Instruments, Photomicrographic Apparatus, Microtomes, Centrifugal Apparatus, Range Finders and Gun Sights for Army and Navy, Searchlight Reflectors, Stereo-Prism Binoculars, Magnifiers and other High-Grade Optical Products and Accessories.

 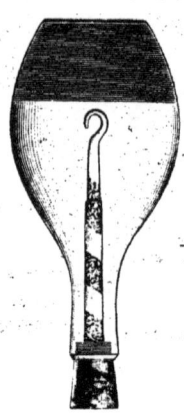

Earp Thomas Culture Flask

(Patented)

A Permanent Container for Micro-Organisms of Every Kind

Laboratory workers have experienced great difficulty in handling bacterial specimens. The especial dangers are contamination, on the one hand, and moisture evaporation, on the other. Both of these dangers, general-ly exist, and in the end, singly or together, they usually cause the loss of the specimen. By the use of the Earp Thomas Culture flask, contam-ination and evaporation are both effectually prevented.

The stopper preserves the contents of the flask sterile. It may be used with any media—liquid solutions, broths, viscous substances, gelatin, or volatile chemicals.

Write for Bulletin No. 271.

JOURNAL OF
PUBLIC HEALTH

THE JOURNAL *of the* AMERICAN
PUBLIC HEALTH ASSOCIATION

PRESENTING THIS MONTH

Dr. Tonney's outline of Control of Pasteurization

Discussion by Roberts and Parks of different Phases of the Meat Supply

Saville's story about risks of Check Valves and the Story of the Malaria Campaign in Cuba by Dr. Villuendas

A. P. H. A. Meeting, San Francisco, Cal.,
September 13-17, 1920

Meetings at the Auditorium, Civic Center
Headquarters Hotel: The Palace

Published monthly on the 20th by the American Public Health Association at

124 W. Polk Street, Chicago, Ill.

ADDRESS EDITORIAL MATTER TO

169 MASSACHUSETTS AVE.
BOSTON, MASS.

Subscription Price, $4.00 per Year. Single Copies, 50 cents.
A. P. H. A. Membership, Including Subscription, $5.00 per year.

Entered as second class matter January 20, 1920, at the postoffice at Chicago, Illinois, under the Act of March 3, 1879. Acceptance for mailing at special rate of postage provided for in Section 1103, Act of October 3, 1917, authorized February 28, 1920.

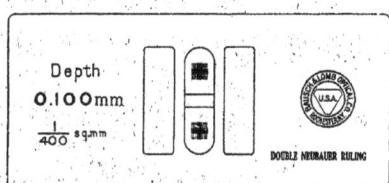

AMERICAN

JOURNAL OF

PUBLIC HEALTH

THE JOURNAL of the AMERICAN PUBLIC HEALTH ASSOCIATION

IN THIS ISSUE

IMPORTANT PAPERS FROM SAN FRANCISCO MEETING

BY

Rude, Ravenel, Schevitz, Cramp and Crum

Published monthly on the 20th by the American Public
Health Association at
124 W. Polk Street, Chicago, Ill.

ADDRESS EDITORIAL MATTER TO

169 MASSACHUSETTS AVE.
BOSTON, MASS.

Subscription Price, $4.00 per Year. Single Copies, 50 cents.
A. P. H. A. Membership, Including Subscription, $5.00 per year.

Entered as second class matter January 20, 1920, at the postoffice at Chicago, Illinois, under
the Act of March 3, 1879. Acceptance for mailing at special rate of postage provided for in
Section 1103, Act of October 3, 1917, authorized February 28, 1920.

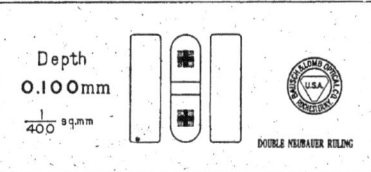

AMERICAN
JOURNAL OF
PUBLIC HEALTH

THE JOURNAL *of the* AMERICAN
PUBLIC HEALTH ASSOCIATION

THE CENTRAL FEATURE THIS MONTH

IS THE

PLAGUE SYMPOSIUM FROM THE
SAN FRANCISCO MEETING

By Dr. Kellogg — Dr. Williams — Dr. Simpson

Historical — Diagnostic — Remedial

Published monthly on the 20th by the American Public
Health Association at
124 W. Polk Street, Chicago, Ill.

ADDRESS EDITORIAL MATTER TO

169 MASSACHUSETTS AVE.
BOSTON, MASS.

Subscription Price, $4.00 per Year. Single Copies, 50 cents.
A. P. H. A. Membership, Including Subscription, $5.00 per year.

Entered as second class matter January 20, 1920, at the postoffice at Chicago, Illinois, under
the Act of March 3, 1879. Acceptance for mailing at special rate of postage provided for in
Section 1103, Act of October 3, 1917, authorized February 28, 1920.

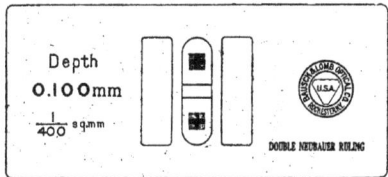

JOURNAL OF
PUBLIC HEALTH

THE JOURNAL *of the* AMERICAN
PUBLIC HEALTH ASSOCIATION

IT IS WORTH YOUR WHILE TO READ

THE UNIQUE SYMPOSIUM ON

OFFICIAL AND NON-OFFICIAL HEALTH
AGENCIES

IN THIS ISSUE OF THE JOURNAL

But There are Other Things You Should Not Miss
In Articles, Proceedings and the Notes Section

Published monthly on the 20th by the American Public
Health Association at
124 W. Polk Street, Chicago, Ill.
ADDRESS EDITORIAL MATTER TO
169 MASSACHUSETTS AVE.
BOSTON, MASS.

Subscription Price, $4.00 per Year. Single Copies, 50 cents.
A. P. H. A. Membership, Including Subscription, $5.00 per year.

Entered as second class matter January 20, 1926, at the postoffice at Chicago, Illinois, under
the Act of March 3, 1879. Acceptance for mailing at special rate of postage provided for in
Section 1103, Act of October 3, 1917, authorized February 28, 1920.

American Journal of Public Health

Official Monthly Publication of the American Public Health Association

Publication office: 124 West Polk Street, Chicago, Ill.

Editorial office: 169 Massachusetts Avenue, Boston, Mass.

Subscription price, $4 per year.   American Public Health Association membership, including subscription, $5 per year.

DECEMBER, 1920   CONTENTS   Vol. X, No. 12

	Page
Social Uses of Medicine	921
By D. B. Armstrong, M.D., M.A., M.S.	
Standardization of Laboratory Methods	932
By Augustus B. Wadsworth, M.D.	
A Classification of Diphtheria Bacilli Based on the Toluidin Blue-Iodine Method of Staining	936
By Henry Albert, M.D.	
Relative Functions of Official and Non-official Health Agencies: A Symposium	940
I. Viewpoint of the Official Agency	941
By Haven Emerson, M.D.	
II. Viewpoint of the Non-official Agency	948
By Charles J. Hatfield, M.D.	

Continued on Page VII

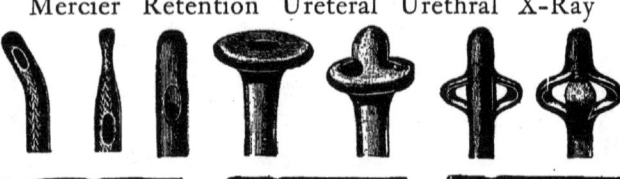

CONTENTS

Continued from Page V

III. What Is the Matter with Public Health?............................... 953
    By Charles T. Nesbitt, M.D.
IV. Relation Between Official and Non-official Health Agencies.............. 956
    By Francis George Curtis, M.D.
V. Coördination of State and Private Enterprises in Public Health Work..... 961
    By W. H. Hattie, M.D.
VI. Discussion 963
    By Ira S. Wile, M.D.
Meaning and Purpose of Socializing Medicine................................. 909
    By Ira S. Wile, M.D.
Practical Disinfection of Tuberculous Sputum.............................. 973
    By William Royal Stokes, M.D., Sc.D., and C. H. Douthirt, M.D.
Child Hygiene 976
    By Julius Levy, M.D.
Judging the Keeping Quality of Milk by a PH Method......................... 978
    By L. H. Cooledge, A.M., and R. W. Wyant, M.S.
Editorials:
    Official and Non-official Health Agency............................... 980
    Progress of Government Acquisition of the Quarantine.................. 982
Book Reviews 984
Association News:
    Proceedings and Discussions of the American Public Health Association
      at San Francisco, Cal., September 13-17, 1920...................... 987
    Meeting of the Board of Directors.................................... 987
    Resolutions 987
    General Sessions 992
    List of New Members.. 993
    Members Elected to the Various Sections............................... 994
    Health Employment Bureau... 995
Public Health Notes.. 996
State Health Notes... 1,005
Conventions, Conferences, Meetings....................................... 1,013
Industrial Hygiene and Occupational Disease.............................. 1,014
Public Health Laboratory Notes.. 1,017

INDEX TO ADVERTISERS

BIOLOGICAL PRODUCTS   Page

Bethlehem Laboratories IX
Harmer Laboratories XIV
Illinois Research Laboratories.... XXXI
Lederle Antitoxin Laboratories.... XXXIV
Mulford Co., H. K................ XXII
Squibb & Sons, E. R.............. XV

FOOD PRODUCTS

Borden's Farm Products Company,
  Inc. XXX
Horlick's Malted Milk Co......... V
Mellin's Food Company........... XXX
Quaker Oats Company............ XXIII

HELP WANTED .... 995, XXXIII

**INSURANCE CO. SERVICE
TO HEALTH OFFICERS**

Metropolitan Life Insurance Co... XXIX
Prudential Insurance Company of
  America XXVIII

LABORATORIES

Abbott Laboratories XI
Bendiner & Schlesinger.......... XXXIII
Boston Bio-chemical Laboratory... XXXIII
Pease Laboratories, Inc.......... XXXIII

LABORATORY APPARATUS AND SUPPLIES

Bausch & Lomb Optical Co....... XXXV
Central Scientific Company........ XVIII
Daigger & Co., A................ VIII
Digestive Ferments Company...... IV
Elmer & Amend.................. Back Cover
Greiner Company, Emil........... XXVI
International Equipment Company XXVI
E. Leitz, Inc.................... VIII
Machlett & Son, E............... XXXII
Mahady Company, E. F........... II

LIQUID CHLORINE AND APPARATUS   Page

Mueller, V., & Co................ VI
Parke, Davis & Co............... XIII
Sargent & Co., E. H............. XVIII
Spencer Lens Company............ XVI
Thomas Company, Arthur H....... XII
Thomas Company, F. H........... XXIV
Will Corporation VI

LIQUID CHLORINE AND APPARATUS

Wallace & Tiernan Co., Inc....... X

POSITIONS WANTED 995

PUBLIC HEALTH COURSES

Harvard Medical School........... XXIV
University of Pennsylvania........ XXIV

SANITARY ENGINEERS

Fuller & McClintock.............. XXXIII
Hill and Ferguson................ XXXIII
Hoad & Decker.................... XXXIII
Keerl & Conklin.................. XXXIII
Metcalf & Eddy.................... XXXIII
Weston & Sampson................ XXXIII

STANDARD HEALTH LITERATURE

A. P. H. A. Publications........XXVII, XXXII

STEREOPTICONS AND MOTION PICTURES

Educational Exhibition Co. XXXI
National Motion Pictures Co. XXXI
Victor Animatograph Co. XXXI

DON'T OVERLOOK THESE

Associated Series Bureau.......... XXXIII
Boston Drinking Cup Co. XXX
Burnitol Manufacturing Co. XXV
Railway Utility Company.......... XVI
Stearns' Electric Paste........... XXXII

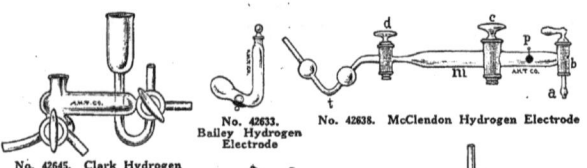
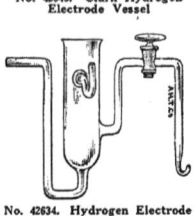
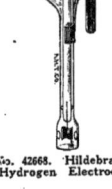
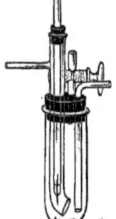

Laboratory Diagnostic Agents

ANTIGENS

Acetone Insoluble Antigen (Beef Heart), in 5-cc vials.
Cholesterinized Beef Heart Antigen, in 5-cc vials.
Cholesterinized Human Heart Antigen, in 5-cc vials.
Gonococcus Antigen, in 1-cc bulbs and packages of six 1-cc bulbs.
Tubercle Antigen, in 5-cc vials.

AMBOCEPTORS

Anti-Human Amboceptor, in 1-cc bulbs.
Anti-Sheep Amboceptor, in 1-cc bulbs.

SERA

Anti-Human Precipitin Serum, in 1-cc bulbs.
Human Blood Typing Serum, Type 2, package of five capillary tubes (clear glass).
Human Blood Typing Serum, Type 3, package of five capillary tubes (amber glass).
Antipneumococcic Serum (Diagnostic) Types 1, 2 and 3, each in 10-cc vials.
Antityphoid Serum, in 10-cc vials.
Antiparatyphoid Serum, "A," in 10-cc vials.
Antiparatyphoid Serum, "B," in 10-cc vials.
Antimeningococcic Serum, Groups 1, 2, 3 and 4, each in 10-cc vials.

Parke, Davis & Company

SQUIBB

Research & Biological Laboratories

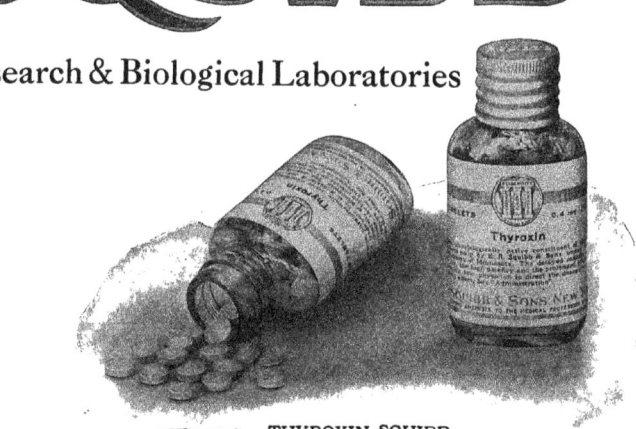

THYROXIN SQUIBB

The chemically pure, physiologically active constituent of the thyroid gland, introduced by Kendall and made by E. R. SQUIBB & SONS under license of the University of Minnesota. Possesses all the activity of desiccated thyroid and offers the advantage of accuracy in dosage and therapeutic effect. Marketed in tablets of 1/320, 1/160, 1/80, and 1/32 grain each for administration by mouth. Crystalline Thyroxin for intravenous use is supplied in vials of 10 milligrammes to 100 milligrammes.

NOW READY FOR DISTRIBUTION.

SEASONABLE BIOLOGICALS

ANTIPNEUMOCOCCIC SERUM SQUIBB
Type I

DIPHTHERIA ANTITOXIN SQUIBB
(Small in Bulk—Low in Solids)

LEUCOCYTE EXTRACT SQUIBB
(An adjunct to Serum and Vaccine Therapy)

SMALLPOX VACCINE SQUIBB
(In Capillary Tubes)

THROMBOPLASTIN SQUIBB
(Physiologic Hemostatic)
(Local and Hypodermic)

For almost three-quarters of a century this seal has been justly accepted as a guaranty of trustworthiness.

E·R·SQUIBB & SONS, NEW YORK
MANUFACTURING CHEMISTS TO THE MEDICAL PROFESSION SINCE 1858

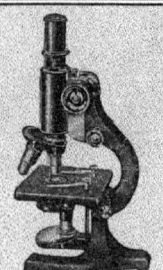

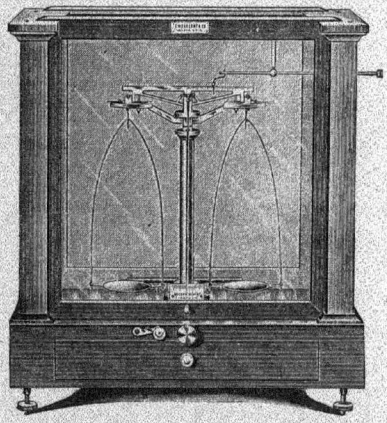

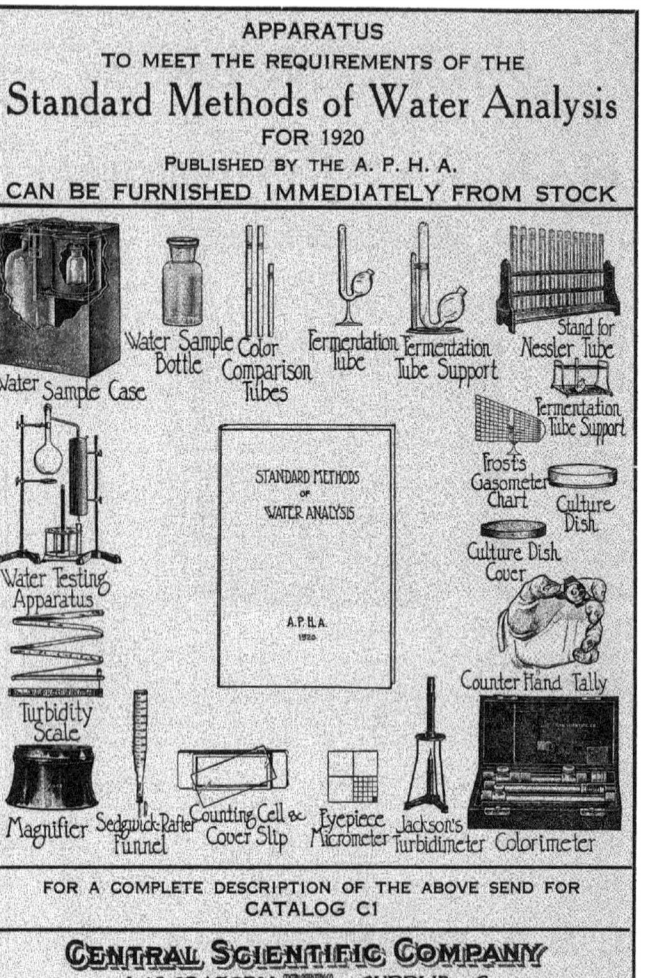

STANDARD METHODS

and other Publications of the A. P. H. A.

Standard Methods for the Examination of Water and Sewage. Chemical and bacteriological. (Committee Report to the Laboratory Section). Third edition, 1920. Pp. 115. Paper cover, 60c; cloth, $1.25.

Standard Methods for the Bacteriological Examination of Milk. (Committee Report to the Laboratory Section). Third edition, 1920. Pp. 24. Paper cover, 30c.

Standard Methods for the Examination· of Air. (Committee Report to the Laboratory Section. 1916.) Pp. 19. Paper cover, 25c.

Pasteurization of Milk. (Committee Report to the Sanitary Engineering Section. 1920.) Pp. 32. Paper cover, 35c.

REPRINTS

An Index for Public Health Literature. 1918. R. R. Harkness and C. E. Turner. Pp. 2. 10c.

Health Quotations. 1920. James A. Tobey. Pp. 4. 10c.

Order from

American Public Health Association

169 Massachusetts Avenue
Boston 17, Mass.

American Public Health Association
169 Massachusetts Avenue
Boston 17, Mass.

Send me:

Standard Methods for the Examination of Water and Sewage.

........paper cover, 60c

........cloth, $1.25

........Standard Methods for the Bacteriological Examination of Milk, 30c

........Standard Methods for the Examination of Air, 25c

.... Pasteurization of Milk. 35c

........An Index for Public Health Literature, 10c

.......Health Quotations, 10c

·I enclose $......................
(Your check or postage stamps will do. We pay postage when payment is in advance)

Name ....

Address ....

Envious and foul disease, could there not be
One beauty in an age and free from thee!

> *Ben Johnson (1563-1637)*

It seems hard to believe that in the Seventeenth Century, Small Pox was so prevalent that practically no one escaped the disease.

Small Pox could again become a scourge to the world if our children were not vaccinated.

One duty of the social worker is to see that all children are vaccinated in infancy and again at about the age of twelve.

"Small Pox and Its Prevention" tells of the history of the disease, its ravages, the discovery of vaccination and the benefits of vaccination to mankind. If it will help you write to the

Welfare Division

THE METROPOLITAN LIFE INSURANCE COMPANY

Number 1, Madison Avenue
New York, N. Y.

BACTERIOLOGICAL STAINS

Dry Stains   **Chemicals**
Staining Solutions
Culture Media   **Reagents**
Embedding Material

For the purpose of diagnosing clinical cases where accuracy is of PARAMOUNT importance, laboratory technicians find our products indispensable on account of their UNIFORM QUALITY, SOLUBILITY, PURITY and SHARP STAINING EFFECTS.

Our complete price list will be mailed free on request

Illinois Research Laboratories
now located in new quarters at
127 No. Dearborn Street, Chicago, Ill.

Teach the Necessary Laws of Health
by the VISUAL METHOD

Progress will quickly be made toward the eradication of all diseases by visualizing the causes. Proclaim warfare against the baffling germs of disease and

VISUALIZE Health Lectures
by use of the
VICTOR Portable Stereopticon

and VICTOR Patented Featherweight Slides

Special slide lecture set on Tuberculosis. Slides made from any copy.

Catalogs Mailed Upon Request

Victor Animatograph Company
(Incorporated)
225 Victor Bldg.   **Davenport, Iowa**

ROUT THE RAT
AND
PREVENT PLAGUE

"THE RAT MENACE"

A MOTION PICTURE showing the great harm done by the rat. Also shows practical means of exterminating this pest.

One of the best means of educating the public to a realization of the rat menace.

Every Health Officer Should Have This Picture

Write for Bulletin

National Motion Pictures Company
Manufacturers and Distributors
Motion Picture Films, Slides and Machines
EDUCATIONAL FILMS A SPECIALTY
Indianapolis, Indiana

Live Lantern Slides
for Health Lectures

A picture tells more at a glance than a hundred words of narrative, and its message is remembered far longer.

EDEXCO LANTERN SLIDES

will add force and entertainment to your Health Talks.

Our new list comprises over a thousand slides on School, Child, Baby and Mouth Hygiene; Flies, Mosquitoes, Milk and Tuberculosis.

Send a Postal Today

for our new list of slides—it is FREE for the asking.

EDUCATIONAL EXHIBITION CO.

331 Custom House St., Providence, R. I.

PUBLIC HEALTH CLIPPINGS

The knowledge acquired by education must, ultimately and alone, be trusted to bring home to a nation that the acquisition of health means the acquisition of wealth.
—*Sykes.*

Of Beauty and Glands

"Shakespeare's most famous poem,' wrote a schoolboy, "was 'Venus and Adenoids.' "
—*Boston Transcript.*

His Day Off

"Don't you want to see a remarkable cataract?" said the guide to him. "Nope," was the reply, "I'm an eye doctor and on my vacation."—*Louisville Courier-Journal.*

Realizing It Now

"Nursing is an art which concerns every family in the world."—*Florence Nightingale.*

Health Is Wealth

Health first—low taxes afterward.
Can all garbage in a garbage can. You can.
The hope of the nation lies in its HEALTHY citizens.
The only good fly is a dead fly.
Your body is a delicate machine. Take care of it.
You need fresh air—day and night.
Disease prevention is even more important than fire prevention.—*Illinois Health News.*

Up to Date

The fashionable physician walked in, in his breezy way, and nodding smilingly to his patient:
"Well, here I am, Mrs. Adams," he announced. "What do you think is the matter with you, this morning?"
"Doctor, I hardly know," murmured the fashionable patient, languidly. "What is new?"—*Ex.*

Health and Exercise

Good health requires exercise; exercise stimulates circulation, respiration and the activity of the digestive system—the great trinity for life and health.
The brain worker and people of sedentary habits are especially in need of daily physical exercise.

Grains

Puffed to Bubbles
Food Cells Exploded

We seal whole wheat in guns and roll it for an hour in 550 degrees of heat. The trifle of moisture in each food cell is thus changed to steam.

When the guns are shot, over 100 million steam explosions occur in very kernel.

The food cells are blasted for easy digestion. The grains are puffed to bubbles, thin, flimsy and crisp, eight times normal size.

Puffed Rice is whole rice puffed in like way. Corn Puffs are corn hearts puffed.

Puffed Grains, we believe, are generally considered the ideal form of grain food. No other process so fits cereals for digestion.

Puffed Wheat
Puffed Rice
Corn Puffs

PUBLIC HEALTH CLIPPINGS—Continued

Bathing

Bathe daily, if possible; don't be a faddist, but use common sense as to the temperature of the water.—*Buffalo Sanitary Bulletin.*

✛

Get on to High Gear

Things move along so rapidly nowadays that the one who said "it can't be done" is interrupted by someone doing it.—*Abbograms.*

✛

Severe But Short

Epidemics come and go; dementia pro-Cox was as short-lived as the recent attack of Ponzilitis.—*Boston Transcript.*

✛

See that the new baby is registered in the Bureau of Vital Statistics, and when he grows up he will have no trouble in proving his rights.—*Cumberland, Md., Health Bulletin.*

✛

Coughs and sneezes spread diseases. Preventable disease is not merely accidental. It is due to criminal carelessness. Wealth without health is a mockery.—*Illinois Health News.*

✛

Only a Beginning

"Anyhow," said the optimist, "we have made the Fourth of July safe and sane." "Yes," replied the pessimist; "but there are 364 days in the year still to be looked after."—*The Mixer,* Illinois Steel Co.

✛

The person who sneaks out of a diphtheria house and slays little children with the germs he scatters is not one whit better than the murderer who sneaks into your home and slays your sleeping babe. When will the community awake to this fact and demand fitting punishment? — *Wisconsin Health Bulletin.*

✛

And Then—What?

Teacher—"Arthur, compare the adjective sick."
Bright Boy—"Sick, sicker, dead."—*W. J. R. C. News.*

The
Safe
Way
Is The
Easy
Way

No. 5. COVERED SPUTUM CUP.
'An all-paper "Burnitol" Cup.

"To be Certain —
Burn-it-All"

There is only one safe and satisfactory method of collecting and disposing of SPUTUM, and that is by using paper receptacles, made for the purpose, which can be burned entire with their contents, making it unnecessary to take any chance of infection.

BURNITOL SPUTUM CUPS
Are the Recognized Standard.

Two Popular Models.

Made of the finest grade of heavyweight pliable paper, thoroughly treated and highly finished. Will not crack or break when FOLDING. Burnitol cups have turned-in flaps with interlocking corners to prevent spilling of contents—a very practical feature, as experienced nurses know. Although pliable, they possess remarkable stiffness and rigidity.

FREE SAMPLES
AND CATALOG CONTAINING FULL PARTICULARS OF BURNITOL PRODUCTS MAILED UPON REQUEST.

Burnitol Manufacturing Co.

Chicago Office: San Francisco Office:
37 N. Market St.   635 Howard St.

General Office and Factory:
Everett Station, Boston, Mass.

SEE
THAT
THUMB
HOLD?

An added convenience for the easy withdrawal of the fillers.

This COVERED HOLDER model made in polished nickel or lacquer finish.

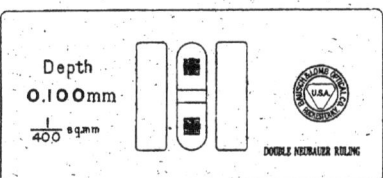

Lightning Source UK Ltd.
Milton Keynes UK
UKHW021324170119
335636UK00009B/974/P